KU-603-323

VRIO

"VALUE. RARITY. IMITABILITY. ORGANIZATION."

What Is It?

This book is not just a list of concepts, models and theories. It is the first undergraduate textbook to introduce a **theory-based, multi-chapter organizing framework** to add additional structure to the field of strategic management.

"VRIO" is a mechanism that integrates two existing theoretical frameworks: the positioning perspective and the resource-based view. It is the primary tool for accomplishing internal analysis. It stands for four questions one must ask about a resource or capability to determine its competitive potential:

1. **The Question of Value:** Does a resource enable a firm to exploit an environmental opportunity, and/or neutralize an environmental threat?

2. **The Question of Rarity:** Is a resource currently controlled by only a small number of competing firms?

3. **The Question of Imitability:** Do firms without a resource face a cost disadvantage in obtaining or developing it?

4. **The Question of Organization:** Are a firm's other policies and procedures organized to support the exploitation of its valuable, rare, and costly-to-imitate resources?

What's the Benefit of the VRIO Framework?

The VRIO framework is the organizational foundation of the text. **It creates a decision-making framework for students** to use in analyzing case and business situations.

Students tend to view concepts, models, and theories (in all of their coursework) as fragmented and disconnected. Strategy is no exception. This view encourages rote memorization, not real understanding. VRIO, by serving as a consistent framework, connects ideas together. This encourages real understanding, not memorization.

This understanding enables students to better analyze business cases and situations—the goal of the course.

The VRIO framework makes it possible to discuss the formulation and implementation of a strategy simultaneously, within each chapter.

Because the VRIO framework provides a simple integrative structure, we are actually able to address issues in this book that are largely ignored elsewhere— including discussions of vertical integration, outsourcing, real options logic, and mergers and acquisitions, to name just a few.

Other Benefits

Element	Description	Benefit	Example
Chapter Opening Cases	We have chosen firms that are familiar to most students. Opening cases focus on iTunes' success in the music download industry, the challenges associated with the growth of the organic food industry, whether or not Harley Davidson should abandon its traditional brand strength in the face of changes in demand, how Ryanair has become the lowest cost airline in the world, how Victoria's Secret differentiated its products, how ESPN has diversified its operations, how Tony Hawk has used alliances to build his personal brand, and so forth.	By having cases tightly linked to the material, students can develop strategic analysis skills by studying firms familiar to them.	114-116
Full Length Cases	This book contains selective, part-ending cases that underscore the concepts in each part. This provides a tight link to the chapter concepts to reinforce understanding of recent research. These are 1) decision oriented, 2) recent, 3) student-recognized companies, and 4) cases where the data are only partly analyzed.	Provides a tight link to chapter concepts, facilitating students' ability to apply text ideas to case analysis.	1-6-1-14 *(Concepts and Cases only)*
Strategy in Depth	For professors and students interested in understanding the full intellectual underpinnings of the field, we have included an optional *Strategy in Depth* feature in every chapter. Knowledge in strategic management continues to evolve rapidly, in ways that are well beyond what is normally included in introductory texts.	Customize your course as desired to provide enrichment material for advanced students.	248
Research Made Relevant	The *Research Made Relevant* feature highlights very current research findings related to some of the strategic topics discussed in that chapter.	Shows students the evolving nature of strategy.	150
Challenge Questions	These might be of an ethical or moral nature, forcing students to apply concepts across chapters, apply concepts to themselves, or extend chapter ideas in creative ways.	Requires students to think critically.	109
Problem Set	*Problem Set* asks students to apply theories and tools from the chapter. These often require calculations. They can be thought of as homework assignments. If students struggle with these problems they might have trouble with the more complex cases. These problem sets are largely diagnostic in character.	Sharpens quantitative skills, and provides a bridge between chapter material and case analysis.	68-69
Ethics and Strategy	Highlights some of the most important dilemmas faced by firms when creating and implementing strategies.	Helps students make better ethical decisions as managers.	293
Global Perspectives	Most firms, most of the time, need to be concerned about global issues. Thus, we have integrated a global perspective into each chapter in two ways: 1) Each chapter has a section that discusses the issues raised in that chapter in a global context; 2) Each chapter includes a *Global Perspectives* feature that provides an extended example of a strategic issue in a global context.	Gets students to think about the global implications of strategic decision making.	236
Strategy in the Emerging Enterprise	Growing number of graduates work for small and medium-sized firms. This feature presents an extended example, in each chapter, of the unique strategic problems facing those employed in small and medium-sized firms.	This feature highlights the unique challenges of doing strategic analysis in emerging enterprises, and small and medium-sized firms.	58
Tools for the Professors	We have provided a suite of tools to help support you, the professor. They include: ■ Instructor's Manual ■ Case Teaching Notes ■ Computerized Test Bank ■ Test Bank ■ Companion Web site		

Strategic Management and Competitive Advantage

Concepts and Cases

Second Edition

Jay B. Barney
The Ohio State University

William S. Hesterly
The University of Utah

PEARSON
Prentice Hall

Upper Saddle River, New Jersey 07458

Library of Congress Cataloging-in-Publication Data

Barney, Jay B.
  Strategic management and competitive advantage: concepts and cases/Jay B. Barney, William S.
Hesterly–2nd ed.
      p. cm.
  Includes bibliographical references and index.
  ISBN 0-13-233823-8 (alk. paper)
  1. Strategic planning—Case studies. 2. Business planning—Case studies. 3. Industrial
management—Case studies. 4. Competition—Case studies. I. Hesterly, William S. II. Title.
  HD30.28.B36834 2008b
  658.4'012--dc22   2007014609

Editor-in-Chief: David Parker
Senior Acquisitions Editor: Mike Ablassmeir
Manager, Product Development: Ashley Santora
Assistant Editor: Keri Molinari
Editorial Assistant: Kristen Varina
Marketing Manager: Anne Howard
Marketing Assistant: Susan Osterlitz
Senior Managing Editor: Judy Leale
Associate Managing Editor: Renata Butera
Project Manager, Production: Kelly Warsak
Permissions Project Manager: Charles Morris
Senior Operations Supervisor: Arnold Vila
Operations Specialist: Michelle Klein
Creative Director: Christy Mahon
Senior Art Director: Janet Slowik

Interior Design: Raven Design
Cover Design: Anthony Gemmellaro
Cover Illustration: Gary Hovland
Illustrator (Interior): P.J. Loughran, Gary Hovland
Illustrator (Figure Art): ElectraGraphics, Inc.
Director, Image Resource Center: Melinda Patelli
Manager, Rights and Permissions: Zina Arabia
Manager, Visual Research: Beth Brenzel
Manager, Cover Visual Research & Permissions: Karen Sanatar
Image Permission Coordinator: Ang'john Ferreri
Composition: Prepare, Inc.
Full-Service Project Management: Prepare, Inc.
Printer/Binder: Courier/Kendallville
Cover Printer: Phoenix Color Corp.
Typeface: 10/12 Palatino

Credits and acknowledgments borrowed from other sources and reproduced, with permission, in this textbook appear
on appropriate page within text.

Copyright © 2008, 2006 by Pearson Education, Inc., Upper Saddle River, New Jersey 07458.
Pearson Prentice Hall. All rights reserved. Printed in the United States of America. This publication is protected by
Copyright and permission should be obtained from the publisher prior to any prohibited reproduction, storage in a
retrieval system, or transmission in any form or by any means, electronic, mechanical, photocopying, recording, or
likewise. For information regarding permission(s), write to: Rights and Permissions Department.

Pearson Prentice Hall™ is a trademark of Pearson Education, Inc.
Pearson® is a registered trademark of Pearson plc
Prentice Hall® is a registered trademark of Pearson Education, Inc.

Pearson Education LTD.
Pearson Education Singapore, Pte. Ltd
Pearson Education, Canada, Ltd
Pearson Education–Japan

Pearson Education Australia PTY, Limited
Pearson Education North Asia Ltd
Pearson Educación de Mexico, S.A. de C.V.
Pearson Education Malaysia, Pte. Ltd.

10 9 8 7 6 5 4 3 2 1
ISBN-13: 978-0-13-233823-3
ISBN-10: 0-13-233823-8

This book is dedicated to my expanding family: my wife, Kim; our children, Lindsay, Kristian, and Erin; their spouses, Ryan, Amy, and Dave; and most of all, our five grandchildren, Isaac, Dylanie, Audrey, Chloe, and Lucas. They all help me remember that no success could compensate for failure in the home.

Jay B. Barney
Columbus, Ohio

This book is for my family who has taught me life's greatest lessons about what matters most. To my wife, Denise; my sons, Drew, Ian, Austin, and Alex; my daughters, Lindsay and Jessica (and their husbands, Matt and John); and grandchildren, Ellie, Owen, and Emerson.

William Hesterly
Salt Lake City, Utah

Brief Contents

Part 1: THE TOOLS OF STRATEGIC ANALYSIS

Part 2: BUSINESS-LEVEL STRATEGIES

Part 3: CORPORATE STRATEGIES

Contents

Part 1: THE TOOLS OF STRATEGIC ANALYSIS

Chapter 3: Evaluating a Firm's Internal Capabilities   72

End-of-Part 1 Cases

Part 2: BUSINESS-LEVEL STRATEGIES

Chapter 4: Cost Leadership   114

Chapter 5: Product Differentiation   144

End-of-Part 2 Cases

Part 3: CORPORATE STRATEGIES

Chapter 6: Vertical Integration   178

Chapter 7: Corporate Diversification   206

End-of-Part 3 Cases

Appendix: Analyzing Cases and Preparing for Class Discussions   343

Preface

The first thing you will notice as you look through this book is that it is much shorter than most textbooks on strategic management. There is not the usual second edition increase in number of pages and bulk. We're strong proponents of the philosophy that often less is more. The general tendency is for textbooks to get longer and longer as authors make sure that their books leave out nothing that is in other books. We take a different approach. Our guiding principle in deciding what to include is: "Does this concept help students analyze cases and real business situations?" For many concepts we considered, the answer is no. But, where the answer is yes, the concept is in the book.

The second thing you will notice in a quick browse through the book is that we have a point of view. We recalled our own educational experience and the textbooks that did and didn't work for us then. Those few that stood out as the best did not merely cover all of the different topics in a field of study. They provided a framework that we could carry around in our heads, and they helped us to see what we were studying as an integrated whole rather than a disjointed sequence of loosely related subjects. This text is integrated around the VRIO framework. As those of you familiar with the resource-based theory of strategy recognize, the VRIO framework addresses the central questions around gaining and sustaining competitive advantage. The VRIO logic of competitive advantage is applied in every chapter. It is simple enough to understand and teach yet broad enough to apply to a wide variety of cases and business settings.

Our consistent use of the VRIO framework does not mean that any of the concepts fundamental to a strategy course are missing. We still have all of the core ideas and theories that are essential to a strategy course. Ideas such as the five forces framework, value chain analysis, generic strategies, and corporate strategy are all in the book. Because the VRIO framework provides a single integrative structure, we are able to address issues in this book that are largely ignored elsewhere—including discussions of vertical integration, outsourcing, real options logic, and mergers and acquisitions, to name a few.

We also have designed flexibility into the book. Each chapter has five short sections that present specific issues in more depth. These sections allow instructors to adapt the book to the particular needs of their students. "Strategy in Depth" examines the intellectual foundations that are behind the way managers think about and practice strategy today. "Global Perspectives" discusses an extended example that highlights the global challenges associated with that chapter's topic. "Strategy in the Emerging Enterprise" presents examples of strategic challenges faced by new and emerging enterprises. "Ethics and Strategy" delves into some of the dilemmas that managers face as they confront strategic decisions. "Research Made Relevant" includes recent research related to the topics in that chapter.

We have also included cases—including many new cases in this edition—that provide students an opportunity to apply the ideas they learn to business situations. The cases include a variety of contexts, such as entrepreneurial, service, manufacturing, and international settings. The power of the VRIO framework is that it applies across all of these settings. Applying the VRIO framework to many topics and cases throughout the book leads to real understanding instead of rote memorization. The end result is that students will find that they have the tools they need to do strategic analysis. Nothing more. Nothing less.

Acknowledgments

Obviously, a book like this is not written in isolation. We owe a debt of gratitude to all those at Prentice Hall who have supported its development. In particular, we want to thank David Parker, Editor-in-Chief; Mike Ablassmeir, Senior Acquisitions Editor; Keri Molinari, Assistant Editor; Kathleen McLellan, Market Development Manager; Anne Howard, Marketing Manager; Judy Leale, Senior Managing Editor; Renata Butera, Associate Managing Editor; Kelly Warsak, Project Manager; Janet Slowik, Senior Art Director; and Kristen Varina, Editorial Assistant.

Many people were involved in reviewing early drafts of this manuscript. Their efforts undoubtedly improved the manuscript dramatically. Their efforts are largely unsung, but very much appreciated.

Thank you to these professors who participated in early manuscript reviews:

Yusaf Akbar—*Southern New Hampshire University*

Pam Braden—*West Virginia University at Parkersburg*

Mustafa Colak—*Temple University*

Ron Eggers—*Barton College*

Michael Frandsen—*Albion College*

Michele Gee—*University of Wisconsin, Parkside*

Peter Goulet—*University of Northern Iowa*

Rebecca Guidice—*University of Nevada Las Vegas*

Laura Hart—*Lynn University, College of Business & Management*

Tom Hewett—*Kaplan University*

Phyllis Holland—*Valdosta State University*

Paul Howard—*Penn State University*

Richard Insinga—*St. John Fisher College*

Homer Johnson—*Loyola University Chicago*

Marilyn Kaplan—*University of Texas at Dallas*

Joseph Leonard—*Miami University*

Paul Maxwell—*St. Thomas University, Miami*

Stephen Mayer—*Niagara University*

Richard Nemanick—*Saint Louis University*

Hossein Noorian—*Wentworth Institute of Technology*

Ralph Parrish—*University of Central OKlahoma*

Raman Patel—*Robert Morris College*

Jiten Ruparel—*Otterbein College*

Roy Simerly—*East Carolina University*

Sally Sledge—*Christopher Newport University*

David Stahl—*Montclair State University*

David Stephens—*Utah State University*

Philip Stoeberl—*Saint Louis University*

Ram Subramanian—*Grand Valley State University*

Thomas Turk—*Chapman University*

Henry Ulrich—*Central Connecticut State soon to be UCONN*

Floyd Willoughby—*Oakland University*

Author Biographies

JAY B. BARNEY

Jay Barney is Chase Chair for Excellence in Corporate Strategy at the Max M. Fisher College of Business, The Ohio State University. He received his Ph.D. from Yale and has held faculty appointments at UCLA and Texas A&M. Jay has published over 80 articles, journals, and books; has served on the editorial boards of *Academy of Management Review, Strategic Management Journal*, and *Organization Science;* and has served as an associate editor of *The Journal of Management*, senior editor at *Organization Science*, special issue editor of *Strategic Management Journal*, and associate editor at the *Strategic Entrepreneurship Journal*. He received the College of Business Distinguished Research Award at Texas A&M in 1992, and in 1997 was awarded an honorary doctorate by the University of Lund (Sweden). He currently holds honorary visiting professor positions at Waikato University (Hamilton, New Zealand), Sun Yat-Sen University (Guangzhou, China), Brunel University (Uxbridge, United Kingdom), and Peking University (Beijing, China). Jay teaches business policy and strategy and has taught in executive programs at UCLA, Texas A&M, Ohio State, Michigan, Southern Methodist University, Texas Christian University, Bocconi University (Milan, Italy), and for McKinsey and Company. He has consulted for a wide variety of public and private organizations, including Hewlett-Packard, Texas Instruments, Arco, Koch Industries Inc., and Nationwide Insurance, focusing on implementing large-scale organizational change and strategic analysis. He received teaching awards at UCLA, Texas A&M, and Ohio State. Jay was elected to the executive committee of the Business Policy and Strategy Division of the Academy of Management in 1989 and subsequently served as assistant program chair and program chair, chair elect, and chair of the BPS Division. In 2001 Jay was elected a Fellow of the Academy of Management, and in 2005, he received the Irwin Outstanding Educator Award for the Business Policy and Strategy Division of the Academy of Management.

WILLIAM S. HESTERLY

William Hesterly is the Associate Dean for Academic Affairs and the Zeke Dumke Professor of Management in the David Eccles School of Business, University of Utah. After studying at Louisiana State University, he received bachelors, and masters, degrees from Brigham Young University and a Ph.D. from the University of California, Los Angelels.

He has taught in a variety of executive programs in both universities and for both large and small companies. Professor Hesterly has been recognized multiple times as the outstanding teacher in the MBA Program at the David Eccles School of Business and he has also been the recipient of the Student's Choice Award.

Professor Hesterly's research on organizational economics, vertical integration, organizational forms, and entrepreneurial  networks has appeared in top journals including the *Academy of Management Review, Organization Science, Strategic Management Journal, Journal of Management*, and the *Journal of Economic Behavior and Organization.* Currently, he is studying the sources of value creation in firms and also the determinants of who captures the value from a firm's competitive advantage. Recent papers in this area have appeared in the *Academy of Management Review* and *Managerial and Decision Economics.* His research on the history of innovation in Major League Baseball recently appeared in the journal *Business History.*

Professor Hesterly's research was recognized with the Western Academy of Management's Ascendant Scholar Award in 1999. Dr. Hesterly has also received best paper awards from the Western Academy of Management and the Academy of Management.

Dr. Hesterly serves on the editorial board of *Strategic Organization* and has previously served on the boards of *Organization Science* and the *Journal of Management.* He has served as Department Chair and also as Vice-President and President of the faculty at the David Eccles School of Business at the University of Utah. Professor Hesterly has served as a consultant to *Fortune* 500 firms in the electronic, office equipment, paper, telecommunications, energy, aerospace, and medical equipment industries. He has also consulted with smaller firms in several other industries.

PART 1 THE TOOLS OF STRATEGIC ANALYSIS

What Is Strategy and the Strategic Management Process?

LEARNING OBJECTIVES

After reading this chapter, you should be able to:

1. Define strategy.

2. Describe the strategic management process.

3. Define competitive advantage and explain its relationship to economic value creation.

4. Describe two different measures of competitive advantage.

5. Explain the difference between emergent and intended strategies.

6. Discuss the importance of understanding a firm's strategy even if you are not a senior manager in a firm.

7. Describe how the strategic management process can be extended to include international business activities.

Catching iTunes

It all began with Napster—uploading digital music files and then sharing them with others on the Web. Nothing could be easier. Hard drives around the world began to fill with vast music libraries, all for free. There was only one little problem: It turned out that such downloading was illegal.

Not that this stopped illegal downloads. Indeed, even today there are 40 illegal music downloads for every legal one. Not surprisingly, the music industry continues to sue those engaging in this practice; over 12,000 such lawsuits have been filed around the world so far.

But declaring some music downloads illegal only created a new market, with new competitive opportunities: the legal download market. After just a few years, iTunes has emerged as a clear winner in this legal download market. In 2006, iTunes had 72 percent of the online music business. Its sales were large enough to make it the number four music retailer of any kind in the world. The second-most successful firm in the online music market, -eMusic, has only 10 percent market share. Other contenders include Yahoo! Music, Napster, Rhapsody, and Zune, all with less than 5 percent of the market for legal music downloads.

So, why has iTunes been so successful? iTunes is a division of Apple and understanding iTunes' success begins by recognizing the link between the iTunes Web site and iPod, Apple's incredibly successful MP3 portable music player. The iPod is generally recognized as one of the simplest, most elegant music listening devices ever created. Efforts to imitate iPod's simple interface and software have, according to most reviewers, simply failed. So Apple began with a great music-playing product, the iPod.

Apple made it easy to link the iPod to its iTunes Web site. Even technological neophytes can download songs from iTunes to their iPods in just a few minutes. Of course, to make the transfer as seamless as possible, Apple developed proprietary software that makes it impossible to play music downloaded from iTunes on anything except an iPod. That means once you start downloading music from iTunes to your iPod, you are unlikely to change to another music Web site because you would have to download and pay for the music a second time.

Pretty clever. Build a great player—the iPod—develop proprietary download software—iTunes—and you have built-in customer loyalty. It is also pretty profitable. As the number of iPod/iTunes users continued to grow, more and more music producers were willing to sign agreements to let Apple distribute their music through iTunes. The result was Apple's dominance of the legal music download industry.

So, can anyone catch iTunes? Several firms are trying.

Downloads from eMusic can be played on iPods. That's the good news. The bad news is that eMusic downloads are not copy protected, which is why they can be played on an iPod or on any other MP3 player. Without copy protections, eMusic has been unable to convince major record labels to use its Web site to distribute music.

Yahoo! Music and Napster (a reorganized version of the original download firm) do copy protect their downloads, but they use software provided by Microsoft that is incompatible with the iPod. Both sites let users "rent" music for a flat monthly fee. As long as you pay the fee, you get to listen to the music; forget to pay the fee, and you don't get to listen.

Real Network's Rhapsody is trying to re-create the synergy between player and Web site that iPod/iTunes enjoys, but with Microsoft software and two alliance partners, ScanDisc (the number-two MP3 manufacturer in the world) and BestBuy (the number-two music retailer in the world).

Of all Apple's competitors, Microsoft is trying to re-create the iPod/iTunes strategy most closely. Indeed, Microsoft has developed a hardware/software "ecosystem" called Zune. Ironically, music downloaded in the Zune system can only be played on Zune hardware and not on MP3 players that use Microsoft software to download music from other Web sites. Early evaluations of Zune are mixed, and 2006 Christmas sales of Zune players were disappointing.

Of course, it is hard to know if any of these strategies, or other strategies, will be able to overcome iTunes' dominance of the legal download market. Moreover, even as these other firms fight for a position in this market, Apple continues to introduce new MP3 players, including the iPod Nano and iPod Shuffle, that reinforce iTunes' dominant position in the industry.

Sources: E. Smith (2006). "Can anybody catch iTunes?" *The Wall Street Journal,* November 27, pp. R1 +; J. Chaffin and A. van Duyn (2006). "Universal backs free music rival to iTunes." August 29, www.ft.com/cms/s; I. Fried (2006). "Microsoft: Zune sales to top 1 million by June." December 6, www.news.com; P. Thurrott and K. Furman (2004). "Illegal music downloads jump despite RIAA legal action." January 22, www.connectedhomemag.com.

F iguring out how iTunes has come to dominate the music download industry and what competitors can do about it will go a long way in determining a firm's performance in this industry. The process by which these kinds of questions are answered is the strategic management process; the answer a firm develops for these questions is a firm's strategy.

Strategy and the Strategic Management Process

Although most can agree that a firm's ability to survive and prosper depends on choosing and implementing a good strategy, there is less agreement about what a strategy is, and even less agreement about what constitutes a good strategy. Indeed, there are almost as many different definitions of these concepts as there are books written about them.

Defining Strategy

In this book, a firm's **strategy** is defined as its theory about how to gain competitive advantages.[1] A good strategy is a strategy that actually generates such advantages. Apple's and Microsoft's *theory* of how to gain a competitive advantage in the music download-for-a-fee business is to link the music download business with particular MP3 players. Yahoo! Music and Napster's theory is that users will only want to rent their music, while Rhapsody is trying to emulate the iPod/iTunes synergy through strategic alliances.

Each of these theories of how to gain competitive advantages in the music download-for-a-fee business—like all theories—is based on a set of assumptions and hypotheses about the way competition in this industry is likely to evolve, and how that evolution can be exploited to earn a profit. The greater the extent to which these assumptions and hypotheses accurately reflect how competition in this industry actually evolves, the more likely it is that a firm will gain a competitive advantage from implementing its strategies. If these assumptions and hypotheses turn out not to be accurate, then a firm's strategies are not likely to be a source of competitive advantage.

But here is the challenge. It is usually very difficult to predict how competition in an industry will evolve, and so it is rarely possible to know for sure that a

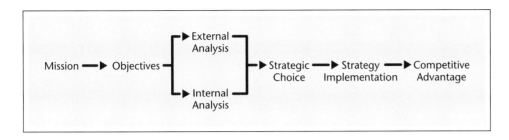

Figure 1.1   The Strategic Management Process

firm is choosing the right strategy. This is why a firm's strategy is almost always a theory: It's a firm's best bet about how competition is going to evolve, and how that evolution can be exploited for competitive advantage.

The Strategic Management Process

Although it is usually difficult to know for sure that a firm is pursuing the best strategy, it is possible to reduce the likelihood that mistakes are being made. The best way to do this is for a firm to choose its strategy carefully and systematically and to follow the strategic management process. The **strategic management process** is a sequential set of analyses and choices that can increase the likelihood that a firm will choose a good strategy; that is, a strategy that generates competitive advantages. An example of the strategic management process is presented in Figure 1.1. Not surprisingly, this book is organized around this strategic management process.

A Firm's Mission

The strategic management process begins when a firm defines its mission. A firm's **mission** is its long-term purpose. Missions define both what a firm aspires to be in the long run and what it wants to avoid in the meantime. Missions are often written down in the form of **mission statements**. Table 1.1 contains examples of several mission statements taken from well-known firms.

Some Missions May Not Affect Firm Performance. As shown in Table 1.1, most mission statements incorporate common elements. For example, many define the businesses within which a firm will operate—automobiles for Ford; computer hardware, software, and services for IBM. Some define how a firm will compete in those businesses—doing everything direct at Dell, and just winning at the Oakland Raiders. Many even define the core values that a firm espouses—the "soul of Dell" and Anheuser-Busch's values, for examples.

Indeed, mission statements often contain so many common elements that some have questioned whether having a mission statement even creates value for a firm.[2] Moreover, even if a mission statement does say something unique about a company, if that mission statement does not influence behavior throughout an organization, it is unlikely to have much impact on a firm's actions. After all, Enron's 1999 annual report includes the following statement of values:

> *Integrity: We work with customers and prospects openly, honestly, and sincerely. When we say we will do something, we will do it; when we say we cannot or will not do something, then we won't do it.*[3]

This statement was published at exactly the same time that senior management at Enron was engaging in activities that ultimately defrauded investors, partners, and Enron's own employees, and that landed some Enron executives in jail.[4]

Table 1.1   **Examples of Mission Statements Taken from Several Well-Known Firms**

Johnson & Johnson

Our Credo

We believe our first responsibility is to the doctors, nurses and patients, to mothers and fathers and all others who use our products and services. In meeting their needs everything we do must be of high quality. We must constantly strive to reduce our costs in order to maintain reasonable prices. Customers' orders must be serviced promptly and accurately. Our suppliers and distributors must have an opportunity to make a fair profit.

We are responsible to our employees, the men and women who work with us throughout the world. Everyone must be considered as an individual. We must respect their dignity and recognize their merit. They must have a sense of security in their jobs. Compensation must be fair and adequate, and working conditions clean, orderly and safe. We must be mindful of ways to help our employees fulfill their family responsibilities. Employees must feel free to make suggestions and complaints. There must be equal opportunity for employment, development and advancement for those qualified. We must provide competent management, and their actions must be just and ethical.

We are responsible to the communities in which we live and work and to the world community as well. We must be good citizens—support good works and charities and bear our fair share of taxes. We must encourage civic improvements and better health and education. We must maintain in good order the property we are privileged to use, protecting the environment and natural resources.

Our final responsibility is to our stockholders. Business must make a sound profit. We must experiment with new ideas. Research must be carried on, innovative programs developed and mistakes paid for. New equipment must be purchased, new facilities provided and new products launched. Reserves must be created to provide for adverse times. When we operate according to these principles, the stockholders should realize a fair return.

Dell

Dell is building its technology, its business, and its communities through direct relationships with our customers, our employees, and our neighbors. Through this process, we are committed to bringing value to customers and adding value to our company, our neighborhoods, our communities, and our world through diversity, environmental and global citizenship initiatives.

The core elements of the "soul of Dell":

Customers: We believe in creating loyal customers by providing a superior experience at a great value.

The Dell Team: We believe our continued success lies in teamwork and in the opportunity each team member has to learn, develop, and grow.

Direct Relationships: We believe in being direct in all we do.

Global Citizenship: We believe in participating responsibly in the global marketplace.

Winning: We have a passion for winning in everything we do.

IBM

At IBM, we strive to lead in the invention, development, and manufacture of the industry's most advanced information technologies, including computer systems, software, storage systems, and microelectronics. We translate these advanced technologies into value for our customers through our professional solutions, services, and consulting businesses worldwide.

The Oakland Raiders

Just Win–Baby!

Sources: © Johnson & Johnson; Used with permission of Dell Computer Corporation; Used with permission of IBM.

Some Missions Can Improve Firm Performance. Despite these caveats, research has identified some firms whose sense of purpose and mission permeates all that they do. Some of these **visionary firms**, or firms whose mission is central to all they do, have been compiled by Jim Collins and Jerry I. Porras in their book *Built to Last*, and are presented in Table 1.2.[5] One interesting thing to note about visionary firms is their long-term profitability. From 1926 through 1995, an investment of $1 in one of these firms would have increased in value to $6,536. That same dollar invested in an average firm over this same time period would have been worth $415 in 1995.

These visionary firms earned substantially higher returns than average firms even though many of their mission statements suggest that profit maximizing, although an important corporate objective, is not their primary reason for existence. Consider what Jim Burke, a former CEO at Johnson & Johnson (one of the visionary firms identified in Table 1.2), says about the relationship between profits and his firm's mission and mission statement:

> *All our management is geared to profit on a day-to-day basis. That's part of the business of being in business. But too often, in this and other businesses, people are inclined to think, "We'd better do this because if we don't, it's going to show up on the figures over the short-term." [Our mission] allows them to say, "Wait a minute. I don't have to do that." The management has told me that they're . . . interested in me operating under this set of principles.*[6]

Table 1.2 **A Sample of Visionary Firms**

3M	Hewlett-Packard	Nordstrom
American Express	IBM	Philip Morris
Boeing	Johnson & Johnson	Procter & Gamble
Citicorp	Marriott	Sony
Ford	Merck	Wal-Mart
General Electric	Motorola	Walt Disney

Source: J. C. Collins and J. I. Porras. *Built to last: successful habits of visionary companies.* New York: Harper Collins Publishers, Inc. ©1994 James C. Collins and Jerry I. Porras. Reprinted with permission by Jim Collins.

Some Missions Can Hurt Firm Performance.   Although some firms have used their missions to develop strategies that create significant competitive advantages, missions can hurt a firm's performance as well. For example, sometimes a firm's mission will be very inwardly focused and defined only with reference to the personal values and priorities of its founders or top managers, independent of whether those values and priorities are consistent with the economic realities facing a firm. Strategies derived from such missions or visions are not likely to be a source of competitive advantage.

For example, Ben & Jerry's Ice Cream was founded in 1977 by Ben Cohen and Jerry Greenfield, both as a way to produce super-premium ice cream and as a way to create an organization based on the values of the 1960s counterculture. This strong sense of mission led Ben & Jerry's to adopt some very unusual human resource and other policies. Among these policies, the company adopted a compensation system whereby the highest paid firm employee could earn no more than five times the income of the lowest paid firm employee. Later this ratio was adjusted to seven to one. However, even at this level, such a compensation policy made it very difficult to acquire the senior management talent needed to ensure the growth and profitability of the firm without grossly overpaying the lowest paid employees in the firm. When a new CEO was appointed to the firm in 1995, his $250,000 salary violated this compensation policy.

Indeed, though the frozen dessert market rapidly consolidated through the late 1990s, Ben & Jerry's Ice Cream remained an independent firm, partly because of Cohen's and Greenfield's commitment to maintaining the social values that their firm embodied. Lacking access to the broad distribution network and managerial talent that would have been available if Ben & Jerry's had merged with another firm, the company's growth and profitability lagged. Finally, in April 2000, Ben & Jerry's Ice Cream was acquired by Unilever. The 66 percent premium finally earned by Ben & Jerry's stockholders in April 2000 had been delayed for several years. In this sense, Cohen's and Greenfield's commitment to a set of personal values and priorities was at least partly inconsistent with the economic realities of the frozen dessert market in the United States.[7]

Obviously, because a firm's mission can help, hurt, or have no impact on its performance, missions by themselves do not necessarily lead a firm to choose and implement strategies that generate competitive advantages. Indeed, as suggested in Figure 1.1, while defining a firm's mission is an important step in the strategic management process, it is only the first step in that process.

Objectives

Whereas a firm's mission is a broad statement of its purpose and values, its **objectives** are specific measurable targets a firm can use to evaluate the extent to which it is realizing its mission. Consider, for example, 3M's mission statement in Table 1.3. This statement emphasizes the importance of finding innovative products and producing high returns for shareholders. However, it is also possible to link specific objectives to each of the elements of this mission statement. This is also done in Table 1.3. For example, for the Investor Mission, possible objectives might include: growth in earnings per share averaging 10 percent or better per year, a return on employed capital of 27 percent or better, at least 30 percent of sales from products that are no more than four years old, and so forth.

High-quality objectives are tightly connected to elements of a firm's mission and are relatively easy to measure and track over time. Low-quality objectives

Table 1.3   **3M's Value Statement**

Our Values:
Satisfy our customers with superior quality, value and service.
Provide investors an attractive return through sustained, quality growth.
Respect our social and physical environment.
Be a company employees are proud to be part of.

Source: Courtesy of 3M Company.

As suggested in Abrahams (1995), these values could be expanded to include specific objectives:

Satisfy our customers with superior quality, value, and service:
Possible objectives

- Provide the highest quality products and services consistent with our customers' requirements and preferences.
- Make every aspect of every transaction a satisfying experience for our customers.
- Find innovative ways to make life easier and better for our customers.

Provide investors with an attractive return through sustained quality growth:
Possible objectives

- Growth in earnings per share averaging 10 percent a year or better.
- A return on capital employed of 27 percent or better.
- A return on stockholders' equity of between 20 and 25 percent.
- At least 30 percent of our sales each year from products new in the last four years.

Respect our social and physical environment:
Possible objectives

- Comply with all laws and meeting or exceeding regulations.
- Keep customers, employees, investors, and the public informed about our operations.
- Develop products and processes that have a minimal impact on the environment.
- Stay attuned to the changing needs and preferences of our customers, employees, and society.
- Maintain uncompromising honesty and integrity in every aspect of our operations.

Be a company that employees are proud to be part of:
Possible objectives

- Respect the dignity and worth of individuals.
- Encourage individual initiative and innovation in an atmosphere characterized by flexibility, cooperation, and trust.
- Challenge individual capabilities.
- Value human diversity and providing equal opportunity for development.

Source: J. Abrahams (1995). *The mission statement book.* Berkeley, CA: TenSpeedPress, pp. 400–402.

either do not exist or are not connected to elements of a firm's mission, are not quantitative, or are difficult to measure or difficult to track over time. Obviously, low-quality objectives cannot be used by management to evaluate how well a mission is being realized. Indeed, one indication that a firm is not that serious about realizing part of its mission statement is when there are no objectives, or only low-quality objectives, associated with that part of the mission.

External and Internal Analysis

The next two phases of the strategic management process—external analysis and internal analysis—occur more or less simultaneously. By conducting an **external analysis**, a firm identifies the critical threats and opportunities in its competitive environment. It also examines how competition in this environment is likely to evolve and what implications that evolution has for the threats and opportunities a firm is facing. A considerable literature on techniques for and approaches to conducting external analysis has evolved over the last several years. This literature is the primary subject matter of Chapter 2 of this book.

Whereas external analysis focuses on the environmental threats and opportunities facing a firm, **internal analysis** helps a firm identify its organizational strengths and weaknesses. It also helps a firm understand which of its resources and capabilities are likely to be sources of competitive advantage and which are less likely to be sources of such advantages. Finally, internal analysis can be used by firms to identify those areas of its organization that require improvement and change. As with external analysis, a considerable literature on techniques for and approaches to conducting internal analysis has evolved over the past several years. This literature is the primary subject matter of Chapter 3 of this book.

Strategic Choice

Armed with a mission, objectives, and completed external and internal analyses, a firm is ready to make its strategic choices. That is, a firm is ready to choose its "theory of how to gain competitive advantage."

The strategic choices available to firms fall into two large categories: business-level strategies and corporate-level strategies. **Business-level strategies** are actions firms take to gain competitive advantages in a single market or industry. These strategies are the topic of Part Two of this book. The two most common business-level strategies are cost leadership (Chapter 4) and product differentiation (Chapter 5).

Corporate-level strategies are actions firms take to gain competitive advantages by operating in multiple markets or industries simultaneously. These strategies are the topic of Part 3 of this book. Common corporate-level strategies include vertical integration strategies (Chapter 6), diversification strategies (Chapters 7 and 8), strategic alliance strategies (Chapter 9), and merger and acquisition strategies (Chapter 10).

Obviously, the details of choosing specific strategies can be quite complex, and a discussion of these details will be delayed until later in the book. However, the underlying logic of strategic choice is not complex. Based on the strategic management process, the objective when making a strategic choice is to choose a strategy that (1) supports the firm's mission, (2) is consistent with a firm's objectives, (3) exploits opportunities in a firm's environment with a firm's strengths, and (4) neutralizes threats in a firm's environment while avoiding a firm's weaknesses. Assuming that this strategy is implemented—the last step of the strategic management process—a strategy that meets these four criteria is very likely to be a source of competitive advantage for a firm.

Strategy Implementation

Of course, simply choosing a strategy means nothing if that strategy is not implemented. **Strategy implementation** occurs when a firm adopts organizational policies and practices that are consistent with its strategy. Three specific organizational policies and practices are particularly important in implementing a strategy: a firm's formal organizational structure, its formal and informal management control systems, and its employee compensation policies. A firm that adopts an organizational structure, management controls, and compensation policy that are consistent with and reinforce its strategies is more likely to be able to implement those strategies than a firm that adopts an organizational structure, management controls, and compensation policy that are inconsistent with its strategies. Specific organizational structures, management controls, and compensation policies used to implement the business-level strategies of cost leadership and product differentiation are discussed in Chapters 4 and 5. How organizational structure, management controls, and compensation can be used to implement corporate-level strategies, including vertical integration, strategic alliance, and merger and acquisition strategies, is discussed in Chapters 6, 9, and 10, respectively. However, there is so much information about implementing diversification strategies that an entire chapter, Chapter 8, is dedicated to the discussion of how this corporate-level strategy is implemented.

What Is Competitive Advantage?

Of course, the ultimate objective of the strategic management process is to enable a firm to choose and implement a strategy that generates a competitive advantage. But what is a competitive advantage? In general, a firm has a **competitive advantage** when it is able to create more economic value than rival firms. **Economic value** is simply the difference between the perceived benefits gained by a customer that purchases a firm's products or services and the full economic cost of these products or services. Thus, the size of a firm's competitive advantage is the difference between the economic value a firm is able to create and the economic value its rivals are able to create.[8]

Consider the two firms presented in Figure 1.2. Both these firms compete in the same market for the same customers. However, Firm I generates $180 of economic value each time it sells a product or service, whereas Firm II generates $150 of economic value each time it sells a product or service. Because Firm I generates more economic value each time it sells a product or service, it has a competitive advantage over Firm II. The size of this competitive advantage is equal to the difference in the economic value these two firms create, in this case, $30 ($180 − $150 = $30).

However, as shown in the figure, Firm I's advantage may come from different sources. For example, it might be the case that Firm I creates greater perceived benefits for its customers than Firm II. In panel A of the figure, Firm I creates perceived customer benefits worth $230, whereas Firm II creates perceived customer benefits worth only $200. Thus, even though both firms' costs are the same (equal to $50 per unit sold), Firm I creates more economic value ($230 − $50 = $180) than Firm II ($200 − $50 = $150). Indeed, it is possible for Firm I, in this situation, to have higher costs than Firm II and still create more economic value than Firm II if these higher costs are offset by Firm I's ability to create greater perceived benefits for its customers.

Alternatively, as shown in panel B of the figure, these two firms may create the same level of perceived customer benefit (equal to $210 in this example) but have different costs. If Firm I's costs per unit are only $30, it will generate

Figure 1.2 The Sources of a
Firm's Competitive
Advantage

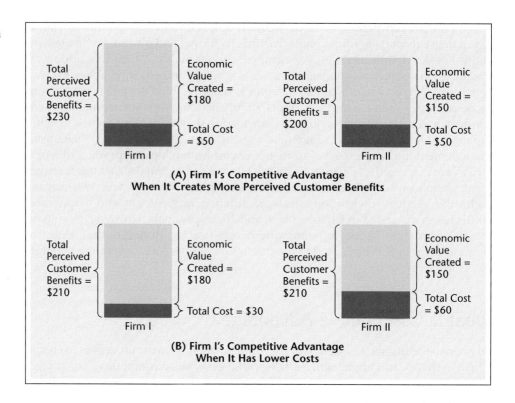

**(A) Firm I's Competitive Advantage
When It Creates More Perceived Customer Benefits**

**(B) Firm I's Competitive Advantage
When It Has Lower Costs**

$180 worth of economic value ($210 − $30 = $180). If Firm II's costs are $60, it will generate only $150 of economic value ($210 − $60 = $150). Indeed, it might be possible for Firm I to create a lower level of perceived benefits for its customers than Firm II and still create more economic value than Firm II, as long as its disadvantage in perceived customer benefits is more than offset by its cost advantage.

A firm's competitive advantage can be temporary or sustained. As summarized in Figure 1.3, a **temporary competitive advantage** is a competitive advantage that lasts for a very short period of time. A **sustained competitive advantage**, in contrast, can last much longer. How long sustained competitive advantages can

Figure 1.3 Types of
Competitive Advantage

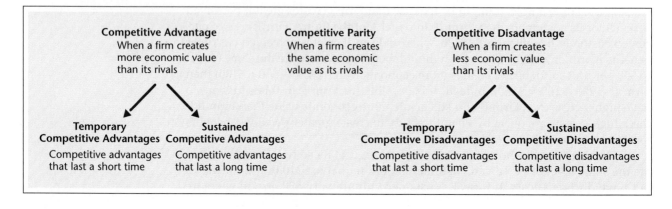

Research Made Relevant

For some time, economists have been interested in how long firms are able to sustain competitive advantages. Traditional economic theory predicts that such advantages should be short-lived in highly competitive markets. This theory suggests that any competitive advantages gained by a particular firm will quickly be identified and imitated by other firms, ensuring competitive parity in the long run. However, in real life competitive advantages often last longer than what traditional economic theory predicts.

One of the first scholars to examine this issue was Dennis Mueller. Mueller divided a sample of 472 firms into eight categories, depending on their level of performance in 1949. He then examined the impact of a firm's initial performance on its subsequent performance. The traditional economic hypothesis was that all firms in the sample would converge on an average level of performance. This did not occur. Indeed, firms that were performing well in an earlier time period tended to perform well in later time periods, and firms that performed poorly in an earlier time period tended to perform poorly in later time periods as well.

Geoffrey Waring followed up on Mueller's work by explaining why competitive advantages seem to persist longer in some industries than in others. Waring found that, among

How Sustainable Are Competitive Advantages?

other factors, firms that operate in industries that (1) are informationally complex; (2) require customers to know a great deal in order to use an industry's products; (3) require a great deal of research and development; and (4) have significant economies of scale are more likely to have sustained competitive advantages compared to firms that operate in industries without these attributes.

Peter Roberts studied the persistence of profitability in one particular industry—the U.S. pharmaceutical industry. Roberts found that not only can firms sustain competitive advantages in this industry, but that the ability to do so is almost entirely attribut-

able to the firms' capacity to innovate by bringing out new and powerful drugs.

The most recent work in this tradition was published by Anita McGahan and Michael Porter. They showed that both high and low performance can persist for some time. Persistent high performance is related to attributes of the industry within which a firm operates and the corporation within which a business unit functions. In contrast, persistent low performance was caused by attributes of a business unit itself.

In many ways, the difference between traditional economics research and strategic management research is that the former attempts to explain why competitive advantages should not persist, whereas the latter attempts to explain when they can. Thus far, most empirical research suggests that firms, in at least some settings, can sustain competitive advantages.

Sources: D. C. Mueller (1977). "The persistence of profits above the norm." *Economica*, 44, pp. 369–380; P. W. Roberts (1999). "Product innovation, product-market competition, and persistent profitability in the U.S. pharmaceutical industry." *Strategic Management Journal*, 20, pp. 655–670; G. F. Waring (1996). "Industry differences in the persistence of firm-specific returns." *The American Economic Review, 86*, pp. 1253–1265; A. McGahan and M. Porter (2003). "The emergence and sustainability of abnormal profits." *Strategic Organization, 1*(1), pp. 79–108.

last is discussed in the Research Made Relevant feature. Firms that create the same economic value as their rivals experience **competitive parity**. Finally, firms that generate less economic value than their rivals have a **competitive disadvantage**. Not surprisingly, competitive disadvantages can be either temporary or sustained, depending on the duration of the disadvantage.

The Strategic Management Process, Revisited

With this description of the strategic management process now complete, it is possible to redraw the process, as depicted in Figure 1.1, to incorporate the various options a firm faces as it chooses and implements its strategy. This is done in Figure 1.4. Figure 1.4 is the organizing framework that will be used throughout this book.

Measuring Competitive Advantage

A firm has a *competitive advantage* when it creates more economic value than its rivals. *Economic value* is the difference between the perceived customer benefits associated with buying a firm's products or services and the cost of producing and selling these products or services. These are deceptively simple definitions. However, these concepts are not always easy to measure directly. For example, the benefits of a firm's products or services are always a matter of customer perception, and perceptions are not easy to measure. Also, the total costs associated with producing a particular product or service may not always be easy to identify or associate with a particular product or service. Despite the very real challenges associated with measuring a firm's competitive advantage, two approaches have emerged. The first estimates a firm's competitive advantage by examining its accounting performance; the second examines the firm's economic performance. These approaches are discussed in the following sections.

Accounting Measures of Competitive Advantage

A firm's **accounting performance** is a measure of its competitive advantage calculated by using information from a firm's published profit and loss and balance sheet statements. A firm's profit and loss and balance sheet statements, in turn, are typically created using widely accepted accounting standards and principles. The application of these standards and principles makes it possible to compare the accounting performance of one firm to the accounting performance of other firms, even if those firms are not in the same industry. However, to the extent that these

Figure 1.4 Organizing Framework

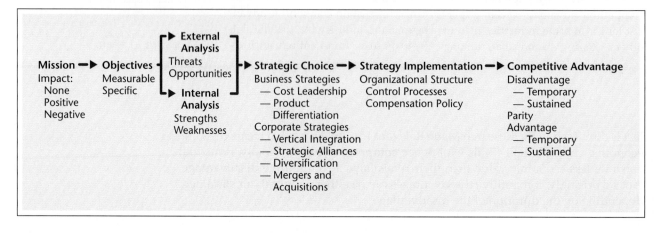

Global Perspectives

Historically, there have been important differences in accounting standards in different countries around the world. These differences can have a significant effect on the profits, losses, and capital stock a firm reports, and thus a significant effect on a firm's performance as measured by its accounting ratios. This suggests that those interested in determining whether, say, Matsushita (a Japanese consumer electronics firm) is outperforming Philips (a Dutch consumer electronics firm) must take into consideration the accounting standards and practices of these two firms.

One of the most important of these accounting differences has to do with how a firm values its current assets. Many countries, including the United States and Japan, require firms to carry assets on their books according to their historical cost, minus depreciation. However, this approach sometimes understates the true market value of these assets. For example, it may have cost a firm $100 million to construct a building on a particular piece of land. Using the historical cost approach, this building will be valued at $100 million, minus depreciation, on a firm's books. However, the value of the land may have skyrocketed since it was purchased and used to erect a building. It could now be worth $1 billion, not just $100 million. Some countries—including the United Kingdom, the Netherlands, and Australia—let firms restate the value of their assets on their books to reflect current market values. This can have a significant impact on a firm's balance sheet, which, in turn, can affect a firm's accounting ratios.

Another way accounting practices vary around the world is how firms are allowed to value their inven-

Accounting Around the World

tories. Two general approaches to valuing inventories exist: LIFO (last in, first out) and FIFO (first in, first out). When inflation is high, LIFO approaches to valuing inventories tend to raise a firm's reported cost of goods sold and reduce its reported profits (and tax liability) compared to FIFO. U.S., Canadian, and Japanese firms can use either LIFO or FIFO methods of accounting for inventory. In the United Kingdom, Brazil, and New Zealand, both methods are legal, but most firms use FIFO; in Australia, LIFO is illegal.

Countries also vary in the extent to which they allow firms to operate multiple sets of books, one for financial reporting and one for tax reporting. For example, in the United States most firms have two sets of books. The first presents the financial status of the firm to the financial community. The second reports the financial status of the firm to the government for tax purposes. Not surprisingly, it is usually the case that the performance of a firm as reported to the financial community is more positive than the performance of a firm as

reported to the government. After all, firms—just like most people—do not like to pay taxes. However, in Germany, firms are not allowed to keep two sets of books. The accounting numbers they report to the financial community are also used to establish their tax liability. In an effort to reduce this liability, it is not uncommon for German firms to engage in accounting practices that have the effect of reducing their reported performance. Thus, when comparing U.S. and German firms in the same industry it is important to recognize that legal differences between these countries have the effect of biasing the reported performance of the German firms downward, when compared to U.S. firms. This means, for example, that just because Daimler-Chrysler's reported accounting performance is, say, lower than Ford's in a given year, the difference between the actual performance of these firms may not be as large as implied by a simple accounting ratio analysis.

All of this greatly complicates the application of accounting measures of competitive advantage for firms that are headquartered in different countries, especially when those countries have important differences in their accounting rules and regulations. However, over time, as markets have become more global, differences in accounting standards have tended to shrink. Although we certainly are not in a world where the standard accounting practices of Japan are the same as the standard accounting practices in Germany, these differences have become smaller over time.

Sources: F. Choi (1997). *International accounting and finance handbook,* 2nd ed. New York: Wiley; F. Choi and R. Levich (1990). The capital market effects of international accounting diversity. Homewood, IL: Dow-Jones Irwin; R. Griffin and M. Pustay (1999). *International business,* 2nd ed. Reading, MA: Addison-Wesley.

standards and principles are not applied in generating a firm's accounting statements, or to the extent that different firms use different accounting standards and principles in generating their statements, it can be difficult to compare the accounting performance of firms. As described in the Global Perspectives feature, these issues can be particularly challenging when comparing the performance of firms in different countries around the world.

One way to use a firm's accounting statements to measure its competitive advantage is through the use of accounting ratios. **Accounting ratios** are simply numbers taken from a firm's financial statements that are manipulated in ways that describe various aspects of a firm's performance. Some of the most common accounting ratios that can be used to characterize a firm's performance are presented in Table 1.4. These measures of firm accounting performance can be grouped into four categories: (1) **profitability ratios**, or ratios with some measure of profit in the numerator and some measure of firm size or assets in the denominator; (2) **liquidity ratios**, or ratios that focus on the ability of a firm to meet its short-term financial obligations; (3) **leverage ratios**, or ratios that focus on the level of a firm's financial flexibility, including its ability to obtain more debt; and (4) **activity ratios**, or ratios that focus on the level of activity in a firm's business.

Of course, these ratios, by themselves, say very little about a firm. To determine how a firm is performing, its accounting ratios must be compared with some standard. In general, that standard is the average of accounting ratios of other firms in the same industry. Using ratio analysis, a firm earns **above average accounting performance** when its performance is greater than the industry average. Such firms typically have competitive advantages, sustained or otherwise. A firm earns **average accounting performance** when its performance is equal to the industry average. These firms generally enjoy only competitive parity. A firm earns **below average accounting performance** when its performance is less than the industry average. These firms generally experience competitive disadvantages.

Consider, for example, the performance of Apple Computer. Apple's financial statements for 2005 and 2004 are presented in Table 1.5. Losses in this table would be presented in parentheses. Several ratio measures of accounting performance are calculated for Apple in these two years in Table 1.6.

Clearly, Apple's accounting performance improved from 2004 to 2005. It made $1.3 billion in profits in 2005, while it made only $276 million in profits in 2004. This is reflected in the ROA and ROE percentages in Table 1.6. Its relatively high gross margin suggests that Apple sells highly differentiated products at a relatively high price. Not surprisingly, the other financial ratios suggest that Apple is a very liquid firm, with plenty of cash on hand, and that it might have some additional debt capacity if important growth opportunities present themselves.

Economic Measures of Competitive Advantage

The great advantage of accounting measures of competitive advantage is that they are relatively easy to compute. All publicly traded firms must make their accounting statements available to the public. Even privately owned firms will typically release some information about their accounting performance. From these statements, it is quite easy to calculate various accounting ratios. One can learn a lot about a firm's competitive position by comparing these ratios to industry averages.

Table 1.4 **Common Ratios to Measure a Firm's Accounting Performance**

Ratio	Calculation	Interpretation
Profitability Ratios		
1. Return on total assets (ROA)	$\dfrac{\text{profit after taxes}}{\text{total assets}}$	A measure of return on total investment in a firm. Larger is usually better.
2. Return on equity (ROE)	$\dfrac{\text{profit after taxes}}{\text{total stockholder's equity}}$	A measure of return on total equity investment in a firm. Larger is usually better.
3. Gross profit margin	$\dfrac{\text{sales} - \text{cost of goods sold}}{\text{sales}}$	A measure of sales available to cover operating expenses and still generate a profit. Larger is usually better.
4. Earnings per share (EPS)	$\dfrac{\text{profits (after taxes)} - \text{preferred stock dividends}}{\text{number of shares of commor stock outstanding}}$	A measure of profit available to owners of common stock. Larger is usually better.
5. Price earnings ratio (p/e)	$\dfrac{\text{current market price/share}}{\text{after-tax earnings/share}}$	A measure of anticipated firm performance—a high p/e ratio tends to indicate that the stock market—anticipates strong future performance. Larger is usually better.
6. Cash flow per share	$\dfrac{\text{after-tax profit} + \text{depreciation}}{\text{number of common shares stock outstanding}}$	A measure of funds available to fund activities above current level of costs. Larger is usually better.
Liquidity Ratios		
1. Current ratio	$\dfrac{\text{current assets}}{\text{current liabilities}}$	A measure of the ability of a firm to cover its current liabilities with assets that can be converted into cash in the short term. Recommended in the range of 2 to 3.
2. Quick ratio	$\dfrac{\text{current assets} - \text{inventory}}{\text{current liabilities}}$	A measure of the ability of a firm to meet its short-term obligations without selling off its current inventory. A ratio of 1 is thought to be acceptable in many industries.
Leverage Ratios		
1. Debt to assets	$\dfrac{\text{total debt}}{\text{total assets}}$	A measure of the extent to which debt has been finance a firm's business activities. The higher, the greater the risk of bankruptcy.
2. Debt to equity	$\dfrac{\text{total debt}}{\text{total equity}}$	A measure of the use of debt versus equity to finance a firm's business activities. Generally recommended less than 1.
3. Times interest earned	$\dfrac{\text{profits before interest and taxes}}{\text{total interest charges}}$	A measure of how much a firm's profits can decline and still meet its interest obligations. Should be well above 1.
Activity Ratios		
1. Inventory turnover	$\dfrac{\text{sales}}{\text{inventory}}$	A measure of the speed with which a firm's inventory is turning over.
2. Accounts receivable turnover	$\dfrac{\text{annual credit sales}}{\text{accounts receivable}}$	A measure of the average time it takes a firm to collect on credit sales.
3. Average collection period	$\dfrac{\text{accounts receivable}}{\text{average daily sales}}$	A measure of the time it takes a firm to receive payment after a sale has been made.

Table 1.5   **Apple Computer's Financial Statements for 2005 and 2004 (numbers in millions)**

	2005	2004
Net sales	13,931	8,279
Cost of goods sold	9,888	6,020
Gross margin	4,043	2,259
Selling, general and administrative expenses	1,859	1,421
Other operating expenses	534	512
Total operating expenses	2,393	1,933
Operating income (loss)	1,650	326
Other income, net	165	57
Total income (loss), before taxes	1,815	383
Provision for (benefit from) income taxes	480	107
Net income, after taxes	1,335	276
Inventories	165	101
Total current assets	10,300	7,055
Total assets	11,551	8,050
Total current liabilities	3,484	2,651
Total liabilities	4,085	2,974
Total shareholders' equity	7,466	5,076

Table 1.6   **Some Accounting Ratios for Apple Computer in 2005 and 2004**

	2005	2004
Return on assets (ROA)	11.56%	3.43%
Return on equity (ROE)	17.89%	5.44%
Gross profit margin	29.02%	27.29%
Current ratio	2.96	2.66
Quick ratio	2.90	2.62
Debt to assets	.35	.37
Debt to equity	.55	.59

However, accounting measures of competitive advantage have at least one significant limitation. Earlier, economic profit was defined as the difference between the perceived benefit associated with purchasing a firm's products or services and the cost of producing and selling that product or service. However, one important component of cost typically is not included in most accounting measures of competitive advantage—the cost of the capital a firm employs to produce and sell its products. The **cost of capital** is the rate of return that a firm promises to pay its suppliers of capital to induce them to invest in the firm. Once these investments are made, a firm can use this capital to produce and sell products and services. However, a firm must provide the promised return to its sources of capital if it expects to obtain more investment capital in the future. **Economic mea-**

sures of competitive advantage compare a firm's level of return to its cost of capital instead of to the average level of return in the industry.

Generally, there are two broad categories of sources of capital: **debt** (capital from banks and bondholders) and **equity** (capital from individuals and institutions that purchase a firm's stock). The **cost of debt** is equal to the interest that a firm must pay its debt holders (adjusted for taxes) in order to induce those debt holders to lend money to a firm. The **cost of equity** is equal to the rate of return a firm must promise its equity holders in order to induce these individuals and institutions to invest in a firm. A firm's **weighted average cost of capital**, or **WACC**, is simply the percentage of a firm's total capital which is debt times the cost of debt, plus the percentage of a firm's total capital; that is, equity times the cost of equity. A simple approach to measuring a firm's WACC is described in the Strategy in Depth feature.

Conceptually, a firm's cost of capital is the level of performance a firm must attain if it is to satisfy the economic objectives of two of its critical stakeholders: debt holders and equity holders. A firm that earns above its cost of capital is likely to be able to attract additional capital, because debt holders and equity holders will scramble to make additional funds available for this firm. Such a firm is said to be earning **above normal economic performance** and will be able to use its access to cheap capital to grow and expand its business. A firm that earns its cost of capital is said to have **normal economic performance**. This level of performance is said to be "normal" because this is the level of performance that most of a firm's equity and debt holders expect. Firms that have normal economic performance are able to gain access to the capital they need to survive, although they are not prospering. Growth opportunities may be somewhat limited for these firms. In general, firms with competitive parity usually have normal economic performance. A firm that earns less than its cost of capital is in the process of liquidating. **Below normal economic performance** implies that a firm's debt and equity holders will be looking for alternative ways to invest their money, someplace where they can earn at least what they expect to earn; that is, normal economic performance. Unless a firm with below normal performance changes, its long-term viability will come into question. Obviously, firms that have a competitive disadvantage generally have below normal economic performance.

Measuring a firm's performance relative to its cost of capital has several advantages for strategic analysis. Foremost among these is the notion that a firm that earns at least its cost of capital is satisfying two of its most important stakeholders—debt holders and equity holders. Despite the advantages of comparing a firm's performance to its cost of capital, this approach has some important limitations as well.

For example, it can sometimes be difficult to calculate a firm's cost of capital. This is especially true if a firm is **privately held**—that is, if it has stock that is not traded on public stock markets or if it is a division of a larger company. In these situations, it may be necessary to use accounting ratios to measure a firm's performance.

Moreover, some have suggested that although accounting measures of competitive advantage understate the importance of a firm's equity and debt holders in evaluating a firm's performance, economic measures of competitive advantage exaggerate the importance of these two particular stakeholders, often to the disadvantage of other stakeholders in a firm. These issues are discussed in more detail in the Ethics and Strategy feature.

Strategy in Depth

A firm's weighted average cost of capital (WACC) can be an important benchmark against which to compare a firm's performance. However, calculating this number can sometimes be tricky. Fortunately, it is possible to obtain all the information needed to calculate a firm's WACC—at least for publicly traded firms—from information published in outlets such as Moody's, Standard and Poor's, Dun and Bradstreet, and Value Line. These publications are in every major business school library in the world and are also available online.

To calculate a firm's WACC, five pieces of information are required: (1) a firm's debt rating, (2) its marginal tax rate, (3) its Beta, (4) the risk-free and market rates of return in the years is being calculated a firm's WACC and (5) information about a firm's capital structure.

Typically, a firm's debt rating will be presented in the form of a series of letters—for example, AA or BBB–. Think of these ratings as grades for a firm's riskiness: an "A" is less risky than an "AA," which is less risky than a "BBB+," and so forth. At any given point in time, a firm with a given debt rating has a market-determined interest. Suppose that the market-determined interest rate for a firm with a BBB debt rating is 7.5 percent. This is a firm's before-tax cost of debt. However, because interest payments are tax deductible in the United States, this before-tax cost of debt has to be adjusted for the tax savings a firm has from using debt. If a firm is reasonably large, then it will almost certainly have to pay the

Estimating a Firm's Weighted Average Cost of Capital

largest marginal tax rate, which in the United States has been 39 percent. So, the after-tax cost of debt in this example is (1 – .39) (7.5), or 4.58 percent.

A firm's *Beta* is a measure of how highly correlated the price of a firm's equity is to the overall stock market. Betas are published for most publicly traded firms. The *risk-free rate of return* is the rate the U.S. federal government has to pay on its long-term bonds to get investors to buy these bonds, and the market rate of return is the return investors would obtain if they purchased one share of each of the stocks traded on public exchanges. Historically, this risk-free rate of return has been low—around 3 percent. The *market rate of return* has averaged around 8.5 percent in the United States. Using these numbers, and assuming that a firm's Beta is equal to 1.2, the cost of a firm's equity

capital can be estimated using the Capital Asset Pricing Model, or CAPM, as follows:

Cost of Equity = Risk Free Rate of Return + (Market Rate of Return – Risk Free Rate of Return) Beta

For our example, this equation is:

$$9.6 = 3.0 + (8.5 - 3.0)1.2$$

Because firms do not gain tax advantages from using equity capital, the before- and after-tax cost of equity is the same.

To calculate a firm's WACC, simply multiple the percentage of a firm's total capital; that is, debt times the after-tax cost of debt, and add it to the percentage of a firm's total capital; that is, equity times the cost of equity. If a firm has total assets of $5 million and stockholders' equity of $4 million, then it must have debt with a market value of $1 million. The WACC for this hypothetical firm thus becomes:

WACC = (Stockholders' Equity/Total Assets) Cost of Equity + (Debt/Total Assets) After-Tax Cost of Debt
$$= 4/5 (9.6) + 1/5 (4.58)$$
$$= 7.68 + .916$$
$$= 8.59$$

Obviously, firms can have a much more complicated capital structure than this hypothetical example. Moreover, the taxes a firm pays can be quite complicated to calculate. There are also some problems in using the CAPM to calculate a firm's cost of equity. However, even with these caveats, this approach usually gives a reasonable approximation to a firm's weighted average cost of capital.

The Relationship Between Economic and Accounting Performance Measures

The correlation between economic and accounting measures of competitive advantage is high. That is, firms that perform well using one of these measures usually perform well using the other. Conversely, firms that do poorly using one of these measures normally do poorly using the other. Thus, the relationships among competitive advantage, accounting performance, and economic performance depicted in Figure 1.5 generally hold.

However, it is possible for a firm to have above average accounting performance and simultaneously have below normal economic performance. This could happen, for example, when a firm is not earning its cost of capital but has above industry average accounting performance. Also, it is possible for a firm to have below average accounting performance and above normal economic performance. This could happen when a firm has a very low cost of capital and is earning at a rate in excess of this cost, but still below the industry average.

Emergent Versus Intended Strategies

The simplest way of thinking about a firm's strategy is to assume that firms choose and implement their strategies exactly as described by the strategic management process in Figure 1.1. That is, they begin with a well-defined mission and objectives, they engage in external and internal analyses, they make their strategic choices, and then they implement their strategies. And there is no doubt that this describes the process for choosing and implementing a strategy in many firms.

For example, FedEx, the world leader in the overnight delivery business, entered this industry with a very well-developed theory about how to gain competitive advantages in this business. Indeed, Fred Smith, the founder of FedEx (originally known as Federal Express), first articulated this theory as a student in a term paper for an undergraduate business class at Yale University. Legend has it that he received only a "C" on the paper, but the company that was founded on the theory of competitive advantage in the overnight delivery business developed in that paper has done extremely well. Founded in 1971, FedEx had 2006 sales in excess of $32 billion and profits of over $3 billion.[9]

Other firms have also begun operations with a well-defined, well-formed strategy, but have found it necessary to modify this strategy so much once it is actually implemented in the marketplace that it bears little resemblance to the theory with which the firm started. **Emergent strategies** are theories of how to gain competitive advantage in an industry that emerge over time or that have been

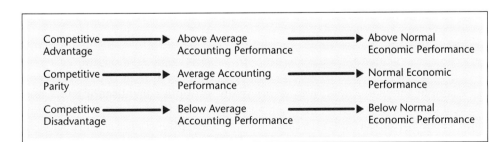

Figure 1.5 Competitive Advantage and Firm Performance

Ethics and Strategy

Considerable debate exists about the role of a firm's equity and debt holders versus its other stakeholders in defining and measuring a firm's performance. These other stakeholders include a firm's suppliers, its customers, its employees, and the communities within which it does business. Like equity and debt holders, these other stakeholders make investments in a firm. They, too, expect some compensation for making these investments.

On the one hand, some argue that if a firm maximizes the wealth of its equity holders, it will automatically satisfy all of its other stakeholders. This view of the firm depends on what is called the *residual claimants* view of equity holders. This view is that equity holders only receive payment on their investment in a firm after all legitimate claims by a firm's other stakeholders are satisfied. Thus, a firm's equity holders, in this view, only receive payment on their investments after the firm's employees are compensated, its suppliers are paid, its customers are satisfied, and its obligations to the communities within which it does business have been met. By maximizing returns to its equity holders, a firm is ensuring that its other stakeholders are fully compensated for investing in a firm.

On the other hand, some argue that the interests of equity holders

Stockholders Versus Stakeholders

and a firm's other stakeholders often collide, and that a firm that maximizes the wealth of its equity holders does not necessarily satisfy its other stakeholders. For example, whereas a firm's customers may want it to sell higher-quality products at lower prices, a firm's equity holders may want it to sell low-quality products at higher prices; this obviously would increase the amount of money left over to pay off a firm's equity holders. Also, whereas a firm's employees may want it to adopt policies that lead to steady performance over long periods of time—because this will lead to stable employment—a firm's

equity holders may be more interested in its maximizing its short—term profitability, even if this hurts employment stability. The interests of equity holders and the broader community may also clash, especially when it is very costly for a firm to engage in environment-friendly behaviors that could reduce its short-term performance.

This debate manifests itself in a variety of ways. For example, many groups that oppose the globalization of the U.S. economy do so on the basis that firms make production, marketing, and other strategic choices in ways that maximize profits for equity holders, often to the detriment of a firm's other stakeholders. These people are concerned about the effects of globalization on workers, on the environment, and on the cultures in the developing economies where global firms sometimes locate their manufacturing and other operations. Managers in global firms respond by saying that they have a responsibility to maximize the wealth of their equity holders. Given the passions that surround this debate, it is unlikely that these issues will be resolved soon.

Sources: T. Copeland, T. Koller, and J. Murrin (1995). *Valuation: Measuring and managing the value of companies.* New York: Wiley; L. Donaldson (1990). "The ethereal hand: Organizational economics and management theory." *Academy of Review,* 15, pp. 369–381.

radically reshaped once they are initially implemented.[10] The relationship between a firm's intended and emergent strategies is depicted in Figure 1.6.

Several well-known firms have strategies that are at least partly emergent. For example, Johnson & Johnson was originally a supplier of antiseptic gauze and medical plasters. It had no consumer business at all. Then, in response to complaints about irritation caused by some of its medical plasters, J&J began enclosing a small packet of talcum powder with each of the medical plasters it sold. Soon customers were asking to purchase the talcum powder by itself, and the company

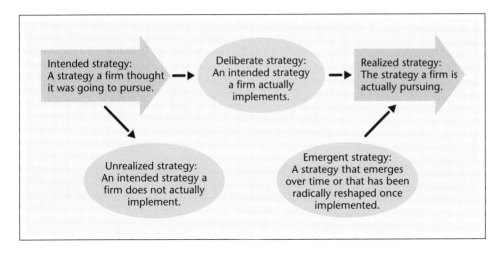

Figure 1.6 Mintzberg's Analysis of the Relationship Between Intended and Realized Strategies

Sources: Reprinted from "Strategy formation in an adhocracy," by H. Mintzberg and A. McHugh, published in *Administrative Science Quarterly, 30*, No. 2, June 1985, by permission of Administrative Science Quarterly. Copyright © 1985 by Administrative Science Quarterly.

introduced "Johnson's Toilet and Baby Powder." Later, an employee invented a ready-to-use bandage for his wife. It seems she often cut herself while using knives in the kitchen. When J&J marketing managers learned of this invention, they decided to introduce it into the marketplace. J&J's Band-Aid products have since become the largest selling brand category at J&J. Overall, J&J's intended strategy was to compete in the medical products market, but its emergent consumer products strategies now generate over 40 percent of total corporate sales.

Another firm with what turns out to be an emergent strategy is the Marriott Corporation. Marriott was originally in the restaurant business. In the late 1930s, Marriott owned and operated eight restaurants. However, one of these restaurants was close to a Washington, D.C., airport. Managers at this restaurant noticed that airline passengers would come into the restaurant to purchase food to eat on their trip. J. Willard Marriott, the founder of the Marriott Corporation, noticed this trend and negotiated a deal with Eastern Airlines whereby Marriott's restaurant would deliver prepackaged lunches directly to Eastern's planes. This arrangement was later extended to include American Airlines. Over time, providing food service to airlines became a major business segment for Marriott. Although Marriott's initial intended strategy was to operate in the restaurant business, it became engaged in the emergent food service business at over 100 airports throughout the world.[11]

Some firms have almost entirely emergent strategies. PEZ Candy, Inc., for example, manufactures and sells small plastic candy dispensers with cartoon and movie character heads, along with candy refills. This privately held firm has made few efforts to speed its growth, yet demand for current and older PEZ products continues to grow. In the 1990s, PEZ doubled the size of its manufacturing operation to keep up with demand. Old PEZ dispensers have become something of a collector's item. Several national conferences on PEZ collecting have been held, and some rare PEZ dispensers were once auctioned at Christie's. This demand has enabled PEZ to raise its prices without increases in advertising, sales personnel, and movie tie-ins so typical in the candy industry.[12]

Of course, one might argue that emergent strategies are only important when a firm fails to implement the strategic management process effectively. After all, if this process is implemented effectively, then would it ever be necessary to fundamentally alter the strategies that a firm has chosen?

In reality, it will often be the case that at the time a firm chooses its strategies, some of the information needed to complete the strategic management process may simply not be available. As suggested earlier, in this setting a firm simply has to make its "best bet" about how competition in an industry is likely to emerge. In such a situation, a firm's ability to change its strategies quickly to respond to emergent trends in an industry may be as important a source of competitive advantage as the ability to complete the strategic management process. For all these reasons, emergent strategies may be particularly important for entrepreneurial firms, as described in the Strategy in the Emerging Enterprise feature.

Strategy in the Emerging Enterprise

*E*very entrepreneur—and would-be entrepreneur—is familiar with the drill: If you want to receive financial support for your idea, you need to write a business plan. Business plans are typically 25 to 30 pages long. Most begin with an Executive Summary; then move quickly to describing an entrepreneur's business idea, why customers will be interested in this idea, how much it will cost to realize this idea; and usually end with a series of charts that project a firm's cash flows over the next five years.

Of course, because these business ideas are often new and untried, no one—including the entrepreneur—really knows if customers will like the idea well enough to buy from this firm. No one really knows how much it will cost to build these products or produce these services—they've never been built or produced before. And, certainly, no one really knows what a firm's cash flows will look like over the next five years or so. Indeed, it is not unusual for entrepreneurs to constantly revise their business plan to reflect new information they have obtained about their business idea and its viability. It is not even unusual for entrepreneurs to fundamentally revise their central business idea as they begin to pursue it in earnest.

The truth is, most decisions about whether to create an entrepreneurial firm take place under condi-

**Emergent Strategies and
Entrepreneurship**

tions of high uncertainty and high unpredictability. In this setting, the ability to adjust on the fly, to be flexible, and to recast a business idea in ways that are more consistent with customer interests may be a central determinant of a firm's ultimate success. This, of course, suggests that emergent strategies are likely to be very important for entrepreneurial firms.

This view of entrepreneurship is different from the popular stereotype. In the popular view, entrepreneurs are assumed to be hit by a "blinding rush of insight" about a previously unexploited market opportunity. In reality, entrepreneurs are more likely to expe-

rience a series of smaller insights about market opportunities. But typically, these periods of insight will be preceded by periods of disappointment, as an entrepreneur discovers that what he or she thought was a new and complete business model is, in fact, either not new or not complete or both. In the popular view, entrepreneurship is all about creativity, about being able to see opportunities others cannot see. In reality, entrepreneurship may be more about tenacity than creativity, because entrepreneurs build their firms step-by-step out of the uncertainty and unpredictability that plague their decision making. In the popular view, entrepreneurs can envision their success well before it occurs. In reality, although entrepreneurs may dream about financial and other forms of success, they usually do not know the exact path they will take, nor what success will actually look like, until after they have arrived.

Sources: S. Alvarez and J. Barney (2005). "How do entrepreneurs organize firms under conditions of uncertainty?" *Journal of Management, 31* (5), pp. 776–793; S. Alvarez and J. Barney (2004). "Organizing rent generation and appropriation: Toward a theory of the entrepreneurial firm," *Journal of Business Venturing, 19*, pp. 621–636; W. Gartner (1988). "Who is the entrepreneur? is the wrong question." *American Journal of Small Business, 12*, pp. 11–32; S. Sarasvathy (2001). "Causation and effectuation: Toward a theoretical shift from economic inevitability to entrepreneurial contingency." *Academy of Management Review, 26*, pp. 243–264.

Why You Need to Know About Strategy

At first glance, it may not be obvious why students would need to know about strategy and the strategic management process. After all, the process of choosing and implementing a strategy is normally the responsibility of senior managers in a firm, and most students are unlikely to be senior managers in large corporations until many years after graduation. Why study strategy and the strategic management process now?

In fact, there are at least three very compelling reasons why it is important to study strategy and the strategic management process now. First, it can give you the tools you need to evaluate the strategies of firms that may employ you. We have already seen how a firm's strategy can have a huge impact on its competitive advantage. Your career opportunities in a firm are largely determined by that firm's competitive advantage. Thus, in choosing a place to begin or continue your career, understanding a firm's theory of how it is going to gain a competitive advantage can be essential in evaluating the career opportunities in a firm. Firms with strategies that are unlikely to be a source of competitive advantage will rarely provide the same career opportunities as firms with strategies that do generate such advantages. Being able to distinguish between these types of strategies can be very important in your career choices.

Second, once you are working for a firm, understanding that firm's strategies, and your role in implementing those strategies, can be very important for your personal success. It will often be the case that expectations of how you perform your function in a firm will change, depending on the strategies a firm is pursuing. For example, as we will see in Part Two of this book, the accounting function plays a very different role in a firm pursuing a cost leadership strategy versus a product differentiation strategy. Marketing and manufacturing also play very different roles in these two types of strategies. Your effectiveness in a firm can be reduced by doing accounting, marketing, and manufacturing as if your firm were pursuing a cost leadership strategy when it is actually pursuing a product differentiation strategy.

Finally, although it is true that strategic choices are generally limited to very experienced senior managers in large organizations, in smaller and entrepreneurial firms many employees end up being involved in the strategic management process. If you choose to work for one of these smaller or entrepreneurial firms—even if it is not right after graduation—you could very easily find yourself to be part of the strategic management team, implementing the strategic management process and choosing which strategies this firm should implement. In this setting, a familiarity with the essential concepts that underlie the choice and implementation of a strategy may turn out to be very helpful.

The Strategic Management Process in an International Context

Thus far, the description of the strategic management process has ignored the fact that most firms make strategic choices within a global competitive context. Indeed, there are currently relatively few firms that do not have to consider some aspects of global competition when they make their strategic choices. How are these global considerations incorporated into the strategic management process?

This can happen in one of two ways. First, some have suggested that global strategies are a unique category of strategy, separate from the business and corporate strategies listed under the strategic choice section of the strategic management process in Figure 1.4. The logic behind this conclusion is straightforward: Conceiving and implementing international strategies require a set of skills that are qualitatively different from the skills required to conceive and implement either business or corporate strategies. For example, those who pursue international opportunities for competitive advantage must know about legal systems in different countries; understand differences in consumer tastes and culture; and be able to operate simultaneously in different time zones, different languages, and different currencies—all while trying to identify and exploit opportunities for competitive advantage around the world.

A second perspective on international strategies acknowledges that these strategies do often place special demands on the managers and firms that pursue them, but that international strategies are just one way—albeit a very important way—that firms can pursue their business or corporate strategies. That is, rather than being a separate type of strategy, this perspective suggests that international strategies may be a means by which a firm realizes competitive advantages from implementing its business or corporate strategies.

Take, for example, a cost leadership business strategy. As will be described in detail in Chapter 4, one very common feature of firms that pursue a low-cost strategy is low-cost manufacturing. Many low-cost firms develop their own low-cost manufacturing capability. However, more firms are beginning to outsource their manufacturing to firms that have significant manufacturing cost advantages. In many cases, these firms are outsourcing to firms located in China, Malaysia, the Philippines, or other countries in Asia. In this setting, the decision to outsource manufacturing to an Asian company is driven by the desire to have the low-cost manufacturing needed to implement a cost leadership strategy. That is, the decision to "go international" is a means to an end—the implementation of a cost leadership strategy—rather than an end in and of itself.

A similar conclusion can be made about a firm's decision to begin selling in countries outside its home market. If a firm has decided it needs to diversify its operations—a classic corporate strategy that will be discussed in detail in Chapter 7—it may begin to sell into multiple geographic markets. If those geographic markets happen to span country borders, then this firm is pursuing an international strategy. However, as before, the decision to go international in this setting is a means to an end—diversifying a firm's operations—rather than an end in and of itself.

The perspective adopted in this book is that international strategies are typically used by firms to help them realize a particular business or corporate strategy. That said, it is also acknowledged that pursuing a particular business or corporate strategy through international means can create unique challenges, and opportunities, for firms. Thus, each chapter in this book will include a section that examines the challenges and opportunities associated with completing a particular stage of the strategic management process in an international context.

SUMMARY

A firm's strategy is its theory of how to gain competitive advantages. These theories, like all theories, are based on assumptions and hypotheses about how competition in an industry is likely to evolve. When those assumptions and hypotheses are consistent with the actual evolution of competition in an industry, a firm's strategy is more likely to be able to generate a competitive advantage.

One way that a firm can choose its strategies is through the strategic management process. This process is a set of analyses and decisions that increase the likelihood that a firm will be able to choose a "good" strategy, that is, a strategy that will lead to a competitive advantage.

The strategic management process begins when a firm identifies its mission, or its long-term purpose. This mission is often written down in the form of a mission statement. Mission statements, by themselves, can have no impact on performance, enhance a firm's performance, or hurt a firm's performance. Objectives are measurable milestones firms use to evaluate whether they are accomplishing their mission. External and internal analyses are the processes through which a firm identifies its environmental threats and opportunities and organizational strengths and weaknesses. Armed with these analyses, it is possible for a firm to engage in strategic choice. Strategies can be classified into two categories: business-level strategies (including cost leadership and product differentiation) and corporate-level strategies (including vertical integration, strategic alliances, diversification, and mergers and acquisitions). Strategy implementation follows strategic choice and involves choosing organizational structures, management control policies, and compensation schemes that support a firm's strategies.

The ultimate objective of the strategic management process is the realization of competitive advantage. A firm has a competitive advantage if it is creating more economic value than its rivals. Economic value is defined as the difference between the perceived customer benefits from purchasing a product or service from a firm and the total economic cost of developing and selling that product or service. Competitive advantages can be temporary or sustained. Competitive parity exists when a firm creates the same economic value as its rivals. A competitive disadvantage exists when a firm creates less economic value than its rivals, and it can be either temporary or sustained.

Two popular measures of a firm's competitive advantage are accounting performance and economic performance. Accounting performance measures competitive advantage using various ratios calculated from a firm's profit and loss and balance sheet statements. A firm's accounting performance is compared with the average level of accounting performance in a firm's industry. Economic performance compares a firm's level of return to its cost of capital. A firm's cost of capital is the rate of return it had to promise to pay to its debt and equity investors to induce them to invest in the firm.

Although many firms use the strategic management process to choose and implement strategies, not all strategies are chosen this way. Some strategies emerge over time, as firms respond to unanticipated changes in the structure of competition in an industry.

Students need to understand strategy and the strategic management process for at least three reasons. First, it can help in deciding where to work. Second, once you have a job it can help you to be successful in that job. Finally, if you have a job in a small or entrepreneurial firm you may become involved in strategy and the strategic management process from the very beginning.

Although pursuing international opportunities for competitive advantage can create unique challenges and opportunities for firms, in this book such international strategies are analyzed as different ways that firms can realize the competitive advantages associated with the business and corporate strategies identified in the strategic management process. That said, the unique challenges and opportunities associated with using international operations to realize these business and corporate strategies will be examined in each chapter of the book.

CHALLENGE QUESTIONS

1. Some firms publicize their corporate mission statements by including them in annual reports, on company letterheads, and in corporate advertising. What, if anything, does this practice say about the ability of these mission statements to be sources of sustained competitive advantage for a firm? Why?

2. Little empirical evidence indicates that having a formal, written mission statement improves a firm's performance. Yet many firms spend a great deal of time and money developing mission statements. Why?

3. Is it possible to distinguish between an emergent strategy and an ad hoc rationalization of a firm's past decisions? Explain.

4. Both external and internal analyses are important in the strategic management process. Is the order in which these analyses are conducted important? If yes, which should come first: external analysis or internal analysis? If the order is not important, why not?

5. Will a firm that has a sustained competitive disadvantage necessarily go out of business? a firm with below average accounting performance over a long period of time? a firm with below normal economic performance over a long period of time?

6. Can more than one firm have a competitive advantage in an industry at the same time? Is it possible for a firm to simultaneously have a competitive advantage and a competitive disadvantage?

PROBLEM SET

1. Write objectives for each of the following mission statements.

(a) We will be a leader in pharmaceutical innovation.
(b) Customer satisfaction is our primary goal.
(c) We promise on-time delivery.
(d) Product quality is our first priority.

2. Rewrite each of the following objectives to make them more helpful in guiding a firm's strategic management process.

(a) We will introduce five new drugs.
(b) We will understand our customers' needs.
(c) Almost all of our products will be delivered on time.
(d) The number of defects in our products will fall.

3. Do firms with the following financial results have below normal, normal, or above normal economic performance?

(a) ROA = 14.3%, WACC = 12.8%
(b) ROA = 4.3%, WACC = 6.7%
(c) ROA = 6.5%, WACC = 9.2%
(d) ROA = 8.3%, WACC = 8.3%

4. Do these same firms have below average, average, or above average accounting performance?

(a) ROA = 14.3%, Industry Avg. ROA = 15.2%
(b) ROA = 4.3%, Industry Avg. ROA = 4.1%
(c) ROA = 6.5%, Industry Avg. ROA = 6.1%
(d) ROA = 8.3%, Industry Avg. ROA = 9.4%

5. Is it possible for a firm to simultaneously earn above normal economic returns and below average accounting returns? What about below normal economic returns and above average accounting returns? Why or why not? If this can occur, which measure of performance is more reliable: economic performance or accounting performance? Explain.

6. Examine the following corporate Web sites and determine if the strategies pursued by these firms were emergent, deliberate, or both emergent and deliberate. Justify your answer with facts from the Web sites.

(a) www.walmart.com
(b) www.ibm.com
(c) www.homedepot.com
(d) www.cardinal.com

7. Using the information provided, calculate this firm's ROA, ROE, gross profit margin, and quick ratio. If this firm's WACC is 6.6 percent and the average firm in its industry has an ROA of 8 percent, is this firm earning above or below normal economic performance and above or below average accounting performance?

Net sales	6,134	Operating cash	3,226	Total assets	5,161
Cost of goods sold	(4,438)	Accounts receivable	681	Net current liabilities	1,549
Selling, general administrative expenses	(996)	Inventories	20	Long-term debt	300
		Other current assets	0	Deferred income taxes	208
Other expenses	(341)	Total current assets	3,927	Preferred stock	0
Interest income	72	Gross properties, plant, equipment	729	Retained earnings	0
Interest expense	(47)	Accumulated depreciation	(411)	Common stock	3,104
Provision for taxes	(75)	Book value of fixed assets	318	Other liabilities	0
Other income	245	Goodwill	0	Total liabilities and equity	5,161
Net income	554	Net other operating assets	916		

END NOTES

1. This approach to defining strategy was first suggested in Drucker, P. (1994). "The theory of business." *Harvard Business Review, 75,* September-October, pp. 95–105.
2. Bart, C. K., and M. C. Baetz (1998). "The relationship between mission statements and firm performance: An exploratory study." *Journal of Management Studies, 35* (6), pp. 823–854.
3. See www.enron.com.
4. See Emshwiller, J., D. Solomon, and R. Smith (2004). "Lay is indicted for his role in Enron collapse." *Wall Street Journal,* July 8, pp. A1 +; Gilmartin, R. (2005). "They fought the law." *BusinessWeek,* January 10, pp. 82–83.
5. These performance results were presented originally in Collins, J. C., and J. I. Porras (1997). *Built to last: successful habits of visionary companies.* New York: HarperCollins.
6. Quoted in Collins, J. C., and J. I. Porras (1997). *Built to last: successful habits of visionary companies,* New York: HarperCollins.
7. See Theroux, J., and J. Hurstak (1993). "Ben & Jerry's Homemade Ice Cream Inc.: keeping the mission(s) alive." Harvard Business School Case No. 9-392-025; Applebaum, A. (2000). "Smartmoney.com: Unilever feels hungry, buys Ben & Jerry's." *Wall Street Journal,* April 13, pp. B1 +.

8. This definition of competitive advantage has a long history in the field of strategic management. For example, it is closely related to the definitions provided in Barney (1986, 1991) and Porter (1985). It is also consistent with the value-based approach described in Peteraf (2001), Brandenburger, and Stuart (1999), and Besanko, Dranove, and Shanley (2000). For more discussion on this definition, see Peteraf and Barney (2004).
9. FedEx's history is described in Trimble, V. (1993). *Overnight success: Federal Express and Frederick Smith, its renegade creator.* New York: Crown.
10. Mintzberg, H. (1978). "Patterns in strategy formulation." *Management Science,* 24(9), pp. 934–948, and Mintzberg, H. (1985). "Of strategies, deliberate and emergent." *Strategic Management Journal,* 6(3), pp. 257–272. Mintzberg has been most influential in expanding the study of strategy to include emergent strategies.
11. The J&J and Marriott emergent strategy stories can be found in Collins, J. C., and J. I. Porras (1997). *Built to last: successful habits of visionary companies.* New York: HarperCollins.
12. See McCarthy, M. J. (1993). "The PEZ fancy is hard to explain, let alone justify." *Wall Street Journal,* March 10, p. A1, for a discussion of PEZ's surprising emergent strategy.

Evaluating a Firm's External Environment

LEARNING OBJECTIVES

After reading this chapter, you should be able to:

1. Describe the dimensions of the general environment facing a firm and how this environment can affect a firm's opportunities and threats.

2. Describe how the structure-conduct-performance (S-C-P) model suggests that industry structure can influence a firm's competitive choices.

3. Describe the "five forces model of industry attractiveness" and indicators of when each of these forces will improve or reduce the attractiveness of an industry.

4. Describe how rivals and substitutes differ.

5. Discuss the role of complements in analyzing competition within an industry.

6. Describe four generic industry structures and specific strategic opportunities in those industries.

7. Describe the impact of tariffs, quotas, and other nontariff barriers to entry on the cost of entry into new geographic markets.

8. Describe the differences between multinational, global, and transnational opportunities.

Organic Opportunities

The organic food market is exploding—growing by up to 20 percent per year over the last several years. Retail companies, including Wild Oats and Whole Foods, have teamed with organic food producers, including Hain Celestial and Dean Foods, to respond to growing consumer demand for organic foods. In 2006, organic foods accounted for 2.5 percent of all grocery spending. If additive-free "all natural" foods are included, the market share of organic foods goes up to almost 10 percent. All this despite the fact that organic foods often sell for as much as a 50 percent premium compared to non-organic foods.

This growth and higher profits have led a number of firms to explore opportunities in the organic food market. Many of these new entrants are not known for their "organic" approaches to the food business. On the retail side, firms such as Wal-Mart and Costco have increased their organic food offerings. Indeed, in 2006 Wal-Mart announced that it wanted to become the center for affordable organic foods in the United States, doubling the number of organic products it offered in 375 of its stores. Large food producers, including General Mills (maker of the decidedly nonorganic breakfast cereal, Trix), Kraft Foods (Kraft's boxed macaroni and cheese is many things, but it is not organic), and Kellogg (producer of Cocoa Krispies and Frosted Flakes), have all entered this industry.

The growth of the organic food market has created some interesting problems. For example, what is "organic food"? The U.S. Department of Agriculture states that for a food to be called "organic," food producers must not use most pesticides, hormones, antibiotics, synthetic fertilizers, bioengineering, or radiation. But in many consumers minds, "organic" implies an entire approach to producing food—everything from how animals are treated (letting cows graze naturally) to where the food is sold (sell only locally to avoid burning fossil fuels). Is a producer that meets the USDA standard but not these other unofficial standards really an "organic producer"? The government thinks so. Wal-Mart and Costco think so. General Mills, Kraft Foods, and Kellogg all think so. But many consumers and organic food activists don't think so and are trying to set additional standards for defining an "organic" product.

Even if these new standards were put in place, the industry faces another challenge. Consumers want truly organic products and are willing to pay relatively high prices for them, but, in return, they want the same quality of product—or better—than they can get from nonorganic sources. However, much of that perceived quality—the shiny red apple, the crisp leaf lettuce, the stable and smooth peanut butter—only exists because of nonorganic production methods. Organic production methods inconsistently generate this same perceived level of quality. This inconsistency has created challenges for food manufacturers who are trying to deliver a consistent high-quality product with raw materials that are inconsistent in their quality.

But it's not just the quality of these organic raw materials; it is their simple availability. In 2007, demand for organic milk (i.e., milk from cows that eat only organic feed) was twice the supply. To meet this demand, the number of organic cows producing milk in the United States would have to double to 280,000. Yet the number of dairy farms in the United States has dropped from 334,000 in 1980 to 60,000 in 2006. Most of these remaining dairy farms are very large, with over 500 cows that are rarely given the opportunity to just graze. And the land available to support a more organic approach to managing dairy herds continues to shrink. This has led to shortages in the availability of organic milk—both to sell directly to consumers and to sell to food producers for the manufacture of organic yogurt, ice cream, and other dairy products.

Shortages in organic products have not been limited to milk. Demand for organic apples, blueberries, spices, bananas, strawberries, and many other products has simply outstripped supply. This has led some organic food producers to begin to import supposedly organic foods from China, Turkey, New Zealand, Madagascar, and so forth. Although some of these countries—such as New Zealand—have strict controls on what constitutes "organic food," others have neither strict definitions nor strict controls.

All this leads to a very broad question: Is it really possible to scale up the organic food industry to become a large part of our diet? The answer to this question will go a long way to determining the profitability of food producers and retailers in the United States as well as the kinds of food we are likely to consume over the next decades.

Sources: D. Brady (2006). "The organic myth." *BusinessWeek*, October 16, pp. 51 +; C. Dimitri and C. Greene (2002). *Recent Growth Patterns in the U.S. Organic Foods Market*. Agricultural Information Bulletin No. 777, U.S. Department of Agriculture, September (available at www.ers.usda.gov/ publications).

The strategic management process described in Chapter 1 suggested that one of the critical determinants of a firm's strategies is the threats and opportunities in its competitive environment. If a firm understands these threats and opportunities, it is one step closer to being able to choose and implement a "good strategy"; that is, a strategy that leads to competitive advantage.

While there are obvious opportunities in the organic food market—including increased demand and high margins—there are threats as well–including inconsistent definitions of what constitutes "organic" food and variability in supply quality.

However, it is not enough to recognize that it is important to understand the threats and opportunities in a firm's competitive environment. A set of tools that managers can apply to systematically complete this external analysis as part of the strategic management process is also required. These tools must be rooted in a strong theoretical base, so that managers know that they have not been developed in an arbitrary way. Fortunately, such tools exist and will be described in this chapter.

Understanding a Firm's General Environment

Any analysis of the threats and opportunities facing a firm must begin with an understanding of the general environment within which a firm operates. This **general environment** consists of broad trends in the context within which a firm operates that can have an impact on a firm's strategic choices. As depicted in Figure 2.1, the general environment consists of six interrelated elements: technological change, demographic trends, cultural trends, the economic climate, legal and political conditions, and specific international events. Each of these elements of the general environment is discussed in this section.

In 1899, Charles H. Duell, commissioner of the United States patent office, said, "Everything that can be invented has been invented."[1] He was wrong. Technological changes over the last few years have had significant impacts on the ways firms do business and on the products and services they sell. These impacts have been most obvious for technologies that build on digital information—computers, the Internet, cell phones, and so forth. Many of us routinely use digital products or services that did not exist just five years ago—including TiVo. However, rapid technological innovation has not been restricted to digital technologies. Biotechnology has also made rapid progress over the last 10 years. New

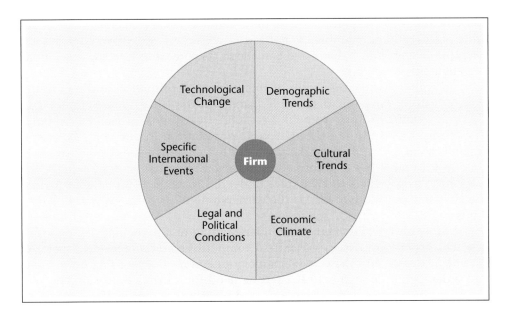

Figure 2.1   The General
Environment Facing Firms

kinds of medicines are now being created. As important, biotechnology holds the promise of developing entirely new ways of both preventing and treating disease.[2]

Technological change creates both opportunity, as firms begin to explore how to use technology to create new products and services, and threats, as technological change forces firms to rethink their technological strategies. Indeed, in Chapter 1 we saw how one technological innovation—downloading digital music from the Internet—has changed competition in the music industry.[3]

A second element of the general environment facing firms is demographic trends. **Demographics** is the distribution of individuals in a society in terms of age, sex, marital status, income, ethnicity, and other personal attributes that may determine buying patterns. Understanding this basic information about a population can help a firm determine whether its products or services will appeal to customers and how many potential customers for these products or services it might have.

Some demographic trends are very well known. For example, everyone has heard of the "baby boomers"—those who were born shortly after World War II. This large population has had an impact on the strategies of many firms, especially as the boomers have grown older and have had more disposable income. However, other demographic groups have also had an impact on firm strategies. This is especially true in the automobile industry. For example, minivans were invented to meet the demands of "soccer moms"—women who live in the suburbs and have young children. The 3-series BMW seems to have been designed for "Yuppies"—the young, urban, and upwardly mobile adults of the 1970s and 1980s, whereas the Jeep Liberty and Nissan Exterra seem to have been designed for the so-called Generation Y—young men and women currently in their twenties and either just out of college or anticipating graduation shortly.

In the United States, an important demographic trend over the last 20 years has been the growth of the Hispanic population. In 1990, the percentage of the U.S. population that was African American was greater than the percentage that was Hispanic. However, by 2000, people of Latin descent outnumbered African Americans. By 2010, it is expected that Hispanics will constitute almost 15 percent of the U.S. population, whereas the percentage of African Americans will remain constant at less than 8 percent. These trends are particularly notable in the South and Southwest. For example, 36 percent of children under 18 in Houston are Hispanic, 39 percent in Miami and San Diego, 53 percent in Los Angeles, and 61 percent in San Antonio.[4]

Of course, firms are aware of this growing population and its buying power. Indeed, Hispanic disposable income in the United States jumped 29 percent, to $652 billion, from 2001 to 2003. In response, firms have begun marketing directly to the U.S. Hispanic population. In one year, Procter & Gamble spent $90 million marketing directly to Spanish-speaking customers. Procter & Gamble has also formed a 65-person bilingual team to manage the marketing of products to Hispanics. Indeed, Procter & Gamble expects that the Hispanic population will be the cornerstone of its sales growth in North America.[5]

Firms can try to exploit their understanding of a particular demographic segment of the population to create a competitive advantage—as Procter & Gamble is doing with the U.S. Hispanic population—but focusing on too narrow a demographic segment can limit demand for a firm's products. The WB, the alternative television network created by Time Warner in 1995, has faced this dilemma. Initially, the WB found success in producing shows for teens— classics such as *Dawson's Creek* and *Buffy the Vampire Slayer*. However, in 2003 the WB saw an 11 percent drop in viewership and a $25 million drop in advertising revenues. Although it did not leave its traditional demographic behind, the WB began producing some programs intended to appeal to older viewers. Ultimately, the WB merged with UPN to form a new network, the CW network. CW is a joint venture between CBS (owner of UPN) and Time Warner (owner of the WB)."[6]

A third element of a firm's general environment is cultural trends. **Culture** is the values, beliefs, and norms that guide behavior in a society. These values, beliefs, and norms define what is "right and wrong" in a society, what is acceptable and unacceptable, what is fashionable and unfashionable. Failure to understand changes in culture, or differences between cultures, can have a very large impact on the ability of a firm to gain a competitive advantage.

This becomes most obvious when firms operate in multiple countries simultaneously. Even seemingly small differences in culture can have an impact. For example, advertisements in the United States that end with a person putting their index finger and thumb together mean that a product is "okay"; in Brazil, the same symbol is vulgar and offensive. Ads in the United States that have a bride dressed in white may be very confusing to the Chinese, because in China white is the traditional color worn at funerals. In Germany, women typically purchase their own engagement rings, whereas in the United States men purchase engagement rings for their fiancées. And what might be appropriate ways to treat women colleagues in Japan or France would land most men in U.S. firms in serious trouble. Understanding the cultural context within which a firm operates is important in evaluating the ability of a firm to generate competitive advantages.[7]

However, cultural differences can also be a source of opportunity for firms. This is especially the case if a firm in one culture is able to identify and popularize elements taken from a different culture. As described in the Global Perspectives feature, elements of Japanese culture have been transferred to the U.S. marketplace.

Global Perspectives

**Pokémon Invades
Louis Vuitton**

*I*t may have begun with Pokémon, Hello Kitty, and the Mighty Morphin Power Rangers, but Japanese style is rapidly becoming an important design feature in many products sold around the world and in the United States. Although it is difficult to describe a single simple element of this Japanese style, much of the new Japanese look is derived from a particular form of Japanese cartoon animation called *anime*. Whether in films or in 2-inch-thick comic books called *manga*, anime is characterized by highly stylized arts-based movements of characters with white, round, oversized eyes; dark black pupils; and a shock of unruly hair. Colors in anime are bold, the action furious. Characters clash in mythic adventures that pit good against evil in the science fiction of the future.

But this look—stylized, colorful, futuristic—has moved way beyond cartoons, comic books, and action figures. Elements of this Japanese look appear in many products sold around the world. These include the stylized action sequences in movies such as *The Last Samurai* and *Lost in Translation*; in cell phones

built by Sony Ericsson that are imported from Japan into the United States; in cars with futuristic designs, such as Nissan's full-size truck, the Titan; and even in Louis Vuitton's line of Murakami handbags—designed by Japanese artist Takashi Murakami—that now generates $300 million in sales worldwide.

Even cultural icons in the United States are being replaced by Japanese-influenced products. For example, in

the 1980s and 1990s street racers in the United States used to modify their American-made V8 Camaros and Firebirds to race on city streets. But, with the popularity of the movie *Fast and Furious* movies, American cars are being replaced, more and more often, with modified Japanese cars—Toyotas, Hondas, and Nissans are replacing Camaros and Firebirds as the preferred hot rod of today's street racers. The smaller and lighter Japanese cars are particularly well-suited for yet another Japanese import—drifting. *Drifting* is a form of car racing in which drivers purposely slide their cars around corners in what is known as a "four-wheel drift."

And although it is a long way from Pokémon and Hello Kitty to Murakami handbags and drifting cars racing down winding roads, all of these products are connected by a common Japanese look traceable to a uniquely Japanese art form—anime.

Sources: C. Palmeri and N. Byrnes (2004). "Is Japanese style taking over the world?" *BusinessWeek,* July 26, pp. 56 +; G. Parker (2004). "Students used to take Japanese for jobs; now it's for fun." *Wall Street Journal,* August 5, pp. A1 +; C. Matlack, R. Tiplady, D. Brady, R. Berner, and H. Tashiro (2004). "The Vuitton machine." *BusinessWeek,* March 22, pp. 98 +; http://streetracing.tiora.net/japan/drift.

A fourth element of a firm's general environment is the current economic climate. The **economic climate** is the overall health of the economic systems within which a firm operates. The health of the economy varies over time in a distinct pattern: Periods of relative prosperity, when demand for goods and services is high and unemployment is low, are followed by periods of relatively low prosperity, when demand for goods and services is low and unemployment is high. When activity in an economy is relatively low, the economy is said to be in **recession.** A severe recession that lasts for several years is known as a **depression.** This alternating pattern of prosperity followed by recession, followed by prosperity, is called the **business cycle.**

Throughout the 1990s, the world, and especially the United States, enjoyed a period of sustained economic growth. Some observers even speculated that the government had become so skilled at managing demand in the economy through adjusting interest rates that a period of recession did not necessarily have to follow a period of sustained economic growth. Of course, the business cycle reared its ugly head again in 1999 with a sudden downturn in stock markets around the world, beginning with the technology sector in the United States and spreading to the entire world economy by 2000. Over a period of just a few months, much of the economic value that had been created through the 1990s disappeared. CEOs of Internet companies that had once been valued at billions of dollars now found themselves managing Web sites that were treated as virtually worthless in the market.

However, for every downturn in the economic climate there is an upturn. For example, at one point in 1999 Amazon.com's stock was valued at $100 per share, for a market value of almost $50 billion. At $50 billion, Amazon's market value was greater than the market value of Ford and General Electric. By 2000, Amazon's stock had fallen to $6 per share; but just three years later, in 2003, Amazon's stock had rebounded to $50 per share and its market value to $21 billion. In 2005, it had annual sales of almost $8.5 billion and $359 million in earnings.[8] The ability to survive the technology bust of 1999 has positioned Amazon.com—along with other Internet firms, including eBay, Google, and Yahoo!—to be a dominant player in the Internet for the foreseeable future.

A fifth element of a firm's general environment is **legal and political conditions.** The legal and political dimensions of an organization's general environment are the laws and the legal system's impact on business, together with the general nature of the relationship between government and business. These laws and the relationship between business and government can vary significantly around the world. For example, in Japan, business and the government are generally seen as having a consistently close and cooperative relationship. Indeed, some have observed that one reason that the Japanese economy has been growing so slowly over the last decade has been the government's reluctance to impose economic restructuring that would hurt the performance of some Japanese firms—especially the largest Japanese banks. In the United States, however, the quality of the relationship between business and the government tends to vary over time. In some administrations, rigorous antitrust regulation and tough environmental standards—both seen as inconsistent with the interests of business—dominate. In other administrations, antitrust regulation is less rigorous and the imposition of environmental standards is delayed, suggesting a more business-friendly perspective.

A final attribute of a firm's general environment is **specific international events.** These include events such as civil wars, political coups, terrorism, wars between countries, famines, and country or regional economic recessions. All of these specific events can have an enormous impact on the ability of a firm's strategies to generate competitive advantage.

Of course, one of the most important of these specific events to have occurred over the last several decades was the terrorist attacks on New York City and Washington, D.C. on September 11, 2001. Beyond the tragic loss of life, these attacks had important business implications as well. For example, it took over five years for airline demand to return to pre–September 11 levels. Insurance companies had to pay out billions of dollars in unanticipated claims as a result of the attacks. Defense contractors saw demand for their products soar as the United States and some of its allies began waging war in Afghanistan and then Iraq.

A firm's general environment defines the broad contextual background within which it operates. Understanding this general environment can help a firm identify some of the threats and opportunities it faces. However, this general environment often has an impact on a firm's threats and opportunities through its impact on a firm's more local environment. Thus, while analyzing a firm's general environment is an important step in any application of the strategic management process, this general analysis must be accompanied by an analysis of a firm's more local environment if the threats and opportunities facing a firm are to be fully understood. The next section discusses specific tools for analyzing a firm's local environment and the theoretical perspectives from which these tools have been derived.

The Structure-Conduct-Performance Model of Firm Performance

In the 1930s, a group of economists began developing an approach for understanding the relationship among a firm's environment, behavior, and performance. The original objective of this work was to describe conditions under which competition in an industry would *not* develop. Understanding when competition was not developing in an industry assisted government regulators in identifying industries where competition-enhancing regulations should be implemented.[9]

The theoretical framework that developed out of this effort became known as the **structure-conduct-performance (S-C-P) model;** it is summarized in Figure 2.2. The term **structure** in this model refers to industry structure, measured by such factors as the number of competitors in an industry, the heterogeneity of products in an industry, the cost of entry and exit in an industry, and so forth.

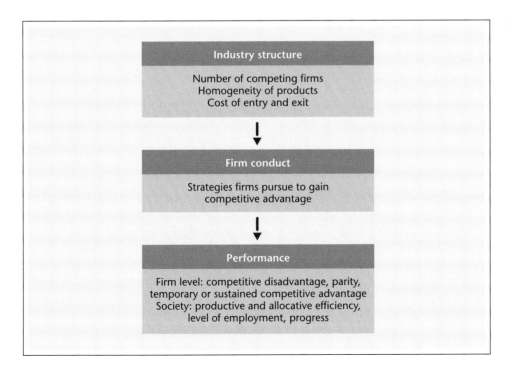

Figure 2.2 The Structure-Conduct-Performance Model

Ethics and Strategy

One of the basic tenets of economic theory is that society is better off when industries are very competitive. Industries are very competitive when there are large numbers of firms operating in an industry, when the products and services that these firms sell are similar to each other, and when it is not very costly for firms to enter into or exit these industries. Indeed, as is described in more detail in the Strategy in Depth feature, these industries are said to be *perfectly competitive.*

The reasons that society is better off when industries are perfectly competitive are well known. In such industries, firms must constantly strive to keep their costs low, their quality high, and, when appropriate, innovate if they are to even survive. Low costs, high quality, and appropriate innovation are generally consistent with the interests of a firm's customers, and thus consistent with society's overall welfare.

Indeed, concern for **social welfare,** or the overall good of society, is the primary reason the S-C-P model was developed. This model was to be used to identify industries where perfect competition was not occurring, and thus where social welfare was not being maximized. With these industries identified, the government could then engage in activities to increase

Is a Firm Gaining a Competitive Advantage Good for Society?

the competitiveness of these industries, thereby increasing social welfare.

Strategic management scholars turned the S-C-P model upside down by using it to describe industries where firms could gain competitive advantages and attain above-average performance. However, some have asked that if strategic management is all about creating and exploiting competitive imperfections in industries, is strategic management also all about reducing the overall good of society for advantages to be gained by a few firms? It is not surprising that individ-

uals who are more interested in improving society than improving the performance of a few firms question the moral legitimacy of the field of strategic management.

However, there is another view about strategic management and social welfare. The S-C-P model assumes that any competitive advantages a firm has in an industry must hurt society. The alternative view is that at least some of the competitive advantages exist because a firm addresses customer needs more effectively than its competitors. From this perspective, competitive advantages are not bad for social welfare; they are actually good for social welfare.

Of course, both perspectives can be true. For example, a firm such as Microsoft has engaged in activities that at least some courts have concluded are inconsistent with social welfare. However, Microsoft also sells applications software that is routinely ranked among the best in the industry, an action that is consistent with meeting customer needs in ways that maximize social welfare.

Sources: J. B. Barney (1986). "Types of competition and the theory of strategy." *Academy of Management Review,* 11, pp. 791–800; H. Demsetz (1973). "Industry structure, market rivalry, and public policy." *Journal of Law and Economics,* 16, pp. 1–9; M. Porter (1981). "The contribution of industrial organization to strategic management." *Academy of Management Review,* 6, pp. 609–620.

Conduct refers to the strategies that firms in an industry implement. **Performance** in the S-C-P model has two meanings: (1) the performance of individual firms and (2) the performance of the economy as a whole. Although both definitions of performance in the S-C-P model are important, as suggested in Chapter 1, the strategic management process is much more focused on the performance of individual firms than on the performance of the economy as a whole. That said, the relationship between these two types of performance can sometimes be complex, as described in the Ethics and Strategy feature.

The logic that links industry structure to conduct and performance is well known. Attributes of the industry structure within which a firm operates define the range of options and constraints facing a firm. In some industries, firms have very few options and face many constraints. In general, firms in these industries can only gain competitive parity. In this setting, industry structure completely determines both firm conduct and long-run firm performance.

However, in other, less competitive industries, firms face fewer constraints and a greater range of conduct options. Some of these options may enable them to obtain competitive advantages. However, even when firms have more conduct options, industry structure still constrains the range of options. Moreover, as will be shown in more detail later in this chapter, industry structure also has an impact on how long firms can expect to maintain their competitive advantages in the face of increased competition.

The Five Forces Model of Environmental Threats

As a theoretical framework, the S-C-P model has proven to be very useful in informing both research and government policy. However, the model can sometimes be awkward to use to identify threats in a firm's local environment. Fortunately, several scholars have developed models of environmental threats based on the S-C-P model that are highly applicable in identifying threats facing a particular firm. The most influential of these models was developed by Professor Michael Porter and is known as the "five forces framework."[10] The **five forces framework** identifies the five most common threats faced by firms in their local competitive environments and the conditions under which these threats are more or less likely to be present. The relationship between the S-C-P model and the five forces framework is discussed in the Strategy in Depth feature.

To a firm seeking competitive advantages, an **environmental threat** is any individual, group, or organization outside a firm that seeks to reduce the level of that firm's performance. Threats increase a firm's costs, decrease a firm's revenues, or in other ways reduce a firm's performance. In S-C-P terms, environmental threats are forces that tend to increase the competitiveness of an industry and force firm performance to competitive parity level. The five common environmental threats identified in the five forces framework are: (1) the threat of entry, (2) the threat of rivalry, (3) the threat of substitutes, (4) the threat of suppliers, and (5) the threat of buyers. The five forces framework is summarized in Figure 2.3.

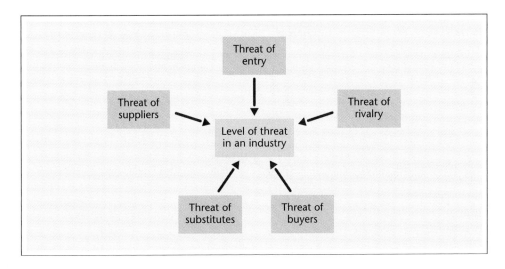

Figure 2.3 Five Forces Model of Environmental Threats

Source: Adapted with the permission of The Free Press, a division of Simon & Schuster Adult Publishing Group from *Competitive Strategy:* Techniques for Analyzing Industries and Competitors by Michael E. Porter. Copyright © 1980, 1998 by The Free Press. All rights reserved.

Strategy in Depth

*T*he relationship between the five forces framework and the S-C-P model turns on the relationship between the threats identified in the framework and the nature of competition in an industry. When all five threats are very high, competition in an industry begins to approach what economists call *perfect competition*. When all five threats are very low, competition in an industry begins to approach what economists call a *monopoly*. Between perfect competition and monopoly, economists have identified two other types of competition in an industry—*monopolistic competition* and *oligopoly*—where the five threats identified in the framework are moderately high. These four types of competition, and the expected performance of firms in these different industries, are summarized in the table below.

Industries are **perfectly competitive** when there are large numbers of competing firms, the products being sold are homogeneous with respect to cost and product attributes, and entry and exit costs are very low. An example of a perfectly competitive industry is the spot market for crude oil. Firms in perfectly competitive industries can expect to earn only competitive parity.

The S-C-P Model and the Five Forces Framework

In **monopolistically competitive industries,** there are large numbers of competing firms and low-cost entry into and exit from the industry. However, unlike the case of perfect competition, products in these industries are not homogeneous with respect to costs or product attributes. Examples of monopolistically competitive industries include toothpaste, shampoo, golf balls, and automobiles. Firms in such industries can earn competitive advantages.

Oligopolies are characterized by a small number of competing firms, by homogeneous products, and by high entry and exit costs. Examples of oligopolistic industries include the U.S. automobile and steel industries in the 1950s and the U.S. breakfast cereal market today. Currently, the top four producers of breakfast cereal account for about 90 percent of the breakfast cereal sold in the United States. Firms in such industries can earn competitive advantages.

Finally, **monopolistic industries** consist of only a single firm. Entry into this type of industry is very costly. There are few examples of purely monopolistic industries. Historically, for example, the U.S. Post Office had a monopoly on home mail delivery. However, this monopoly has been challenged in small-package delivery by FedEx, larger-package delivery by UPS, and in mail delivery by e-mail. Monopolists can generate competitive advantages—although they are sometimes managed very inefficiently.

Source: J. Barney (2007). *Gaining and sustaining competitive advantage,* 3rd ed. Upper Saddle River, NJ: Pearson Higher Education.

Types of Competition and Expected Firm Performance

Type of Competition	Attributes	Examples	Expected Firm Performance
Perfect competition	Large number of firms Homogeneous products Low-cost entry and exit	Stock market Crude oil	Competitive parity
Monopolistic competition	Large number of firms Heterogeneous products Low-cost entry and exit	Toothpaste Shampoo Golf balls Automobiles	Competitive advantage
Oligopoly	Small number of firms Homogenous products Costly entry and exit	U.S. steel and autos in the 1950s U.S. breakfast cereal	Competitive advantage
Monopoly	One firm Costly entry	Home mail delivery	Competitive advantage

The Threat of Entry

The first environmental threat identified in the five forces framework is the threat of new entry. **New entrants** are firms that have either recently started operating in an industry or that threaten to begin operations in an industry soon. For Amazon.com, Barnes & Noble.com and Borders.com are new entrants to the online book-ordering business. Amazon largely invented this way of selling books, and both Barnes & Noble and Borders later followed with their entry into this market, even though both these firms already operated in the traditional book sales industry. For ESPN in the television sports industry, both the Fox Sports Regional Network and the College Sports Television (CSTV) network are new entrants. The Fox Regional Sports Network consists of several regional sports channels that broadcast both national and regional sporting events, sports news shows, and sports entertainment shows—including *The Best Damn Sports Show Period*. CSTV is a new (founded in spring of 2003) sports cable and satellite channel that specializes in college sports.[11]

According to the S-C-P model, new entrants are motivated to enter into an industry by the superior profits that some incumbent firms in that industry may be earning. Firms seeking these high profits enter the industry, thereby increasing the level of industry competition and reducing the performance of incumbent firms. With the absence of any barriers, entry will continue as long as any firms in the industry are earning competitive advantages, and entry will cease when all incumbent firms are earning competitive parity.

The extent to which new entry acts as a threat to an incumbent firm's performance depends on the cost of entry. If the cost of entry into an industry is greater than the potential profits a new entrant could obtain by entering, then entry will not be forthcoming, and new entrants are not a threat to incumbent firms. However, if the cost of entry is lower than the return from entry, entry will occur until the profits derived from entry are less than the costs of entry.

The threat of entry depends on the cost of entry, and the cost of entry, in turn, depends on the existence and "height" of barriers to entry. **Barriers to entry** are attributes of an industry's structure that increase the cost of entry. The greater the cost of entry, the greater the height of these barriers. When there are significant barriers to entry, potential entrants will not enter into an industry even if incumbent firms are earning competitive advantages.

Four important barriers to entry have been identified in the S-C-P and strategy literatures. These four barriers, listed in Table 2.1, are (1) economies of scale, (2) product differentiation, (3) cost advantages independent of scale, and (4) government regulation of entry.[12]

Economies of Scale as a Barrier to Entry

Economies of scale exist in an industry when a firm's costs fall as a function of its volume of production. **Diseconomies of scale** exist when a firm's costs rise as a function of its volume of production. The relationship among economies of scale, diseconomies

Table 2.1 **Barriers to Entry into an Industry**

1. Economies of scale
2. Product differentiation
3. Cost advantages independent of scale
4. Government regulation of entry

Figure 2.4   Economies
of Scale and the Cost of
Production

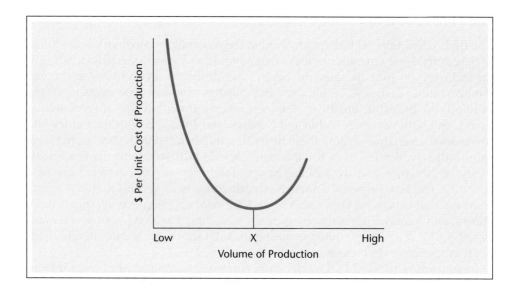

of scale, and a firm's volume of production is summarized in Figure 2.4. As a firm's volume of production increases, its costs begin to fall. This is a manifestation of economies of scale. However, at some point a firm's volume of production becomes too large and its costs begin to rise. This is a manifestation of diseconomies of scale. For economies of scale to act as a barrier to entry, the relationship between the volume of production and firm costs must have the shape of the line in Figure 2.4. This curve suggests that any deviation, positive or negative, from an optimal level of production (point X in Figure 2.4) will lead a firm to experience much higher costs of production.

To see how economies of scale can act as a barrier to entry, consider the following scenario. Imagine an industry with the following attributes: The industry has five incumbent firms (each firm has only one plant); the optimal level of production in each of these plants is 4,000 units (X = 4,000 units); total demand for the output of this industry is fixed at 22,000 units; the economies-of-scale curve is as depicted in Figure 2.4; and products in this industry are very homogeneous. Total demand in this industry (22,000 units) is greater than total supply (5 × 4,000 units = 20,000). Everyone knows that when demand is greater than supply prices go up. This means that the five incumbent firms in this industry will have high levels of profit. The S-C-P model suggests that, absent barriers, these superior profits should motivate entry.

However, look at the entry decision from the point of view of potential entrants. Certainly, incumbent firms are earning superior profits, but potential entrants face an unsavory choice. On the one hand, new entrants could enter the industry with an optimally efficient plant and produce 4,000 units. However, this form of entry will lead industry supply to rise to 24,000 units (20,000 + 4,000). Suddenly, supply will be greater than demand (24,000 > 22,000), and all the firms in the industry, including the new entrant, will earn negative profits. On the other hand, the new entrant might enter the industry with a plant of smaller-than-optimal size (e.g., 1,000 units). This kind of entry leaves total industry demand larger than industry supply (22,000 > 21,000). However, the new entrant faces a serious cost disadvantage in this case because it does not produce at the low-cost position on the economies-of-scale curve. Faced with these bleak alternatives, the potential entrant simply does not enter even though incumbent firms are earning positive profits.

Of course, potential entrants have other options besides entering at the efficient scale and losing money or entering at an inefficient scale and losing money.

For example, potential entrants can attempt to expand the total size of the market (i.e., increase total demand from 22,000 to 24,000 units or more) and enter at the optimal size. Potential entrants can also attempt to develop new production technology, shift the economies-of-scale curve to the left (thereby reducing the optimal plant size), and enter. Or, potential entrants may try to make their products seem very special to their customers, enabling them to charge higher prices to offset higher production costs associated with a smaller-than-optimal plant.[13]

Any of these actions may enable a firm to enter an industry. However, these actions are costly. If the cost of engaging in these "barrier-busting" activities is greater than the return from entry, entry will not occur, even if incumbent firms are earning positive profits.

Historically, economies of scale acted as a barrier to entry into the worldwide steel market. To fully exploit economies of scale, traditional steel plants had to be very large. If new entrants into the steel market had built these efficient and large steel-manufacturing plants, they would have had the effect of increasing the steel supply over the demand for steel, and the outcome would have been reduced profits for both new entrants and incumbent firms. This discouraged new entry. However, in the 1970s the development of alternative mini-mill technology shifted the economies-of-scale curve to the left by making smaller plants very efficient in addressing some segments of the steel market. This shift had the effect of decreasing barriers to entry into the steel industry. Recent entrants, including Nucor Steel and Chaparral Steel, now have significant cost advantages over firms still using outdated, less efficient production technology.[14]

Product Differentiation as a Barrier to Entry

Product differentiation means that incumbent firms possess brand identification and customer loyalty that potential entrants do not. Brand identification and customer loyalty serve as entry barriers because new entrants not only have to absorb the standard costs associated with starting production in a new industry; they also have to absorb the costs associated with overcoming incumbent firms' differentiation advantages. If the cost of overcoming these advantages is greater than the potential return from entering an industry, entry will not occur, even if incumbent firms are earning positive profits.

Numerous examples exist of industries in which product differentiation tends to act as a barrier to entry. In the brewing industry, for example, substantial investments by Budweiser, Miller, and Coors (among other incumbent firms) in advertising (will we ever forget the Budweiser frogs?) and brand recognition have made large-scale entry into the U.S. brewing industry very costly.[15] E. & J. Gallo Winery, a U.S. winemaker, faces product differentiation barriers to entry in its efforts to sell Gallo wine in the French market. The market for wine in France is huge—the French consume 16.1 gallons of wine per person per year, for a total consumption of over 400 million cases of wine, whereas U.S. consumers drink only 1.8 gallons of wine per person per year, for a total consumption of less than 200 million cases. Despite this difference, intense loyalties to local French vineyards have made it very difficult for Gallo to break into the huge French market— a market where American wines are still given as "gag gifts" and only American theme restaurants carry U.S. wines on their menus. Gallo is attempting to overcome this product differentiation advantage of French wineries by emphasizing its California roots—roots that many French consider to be exotic—and downplaying the fact that it is a U.S. company, corporate origins that are less attractive to many French consumers.[16]

Cost Advantages Independent of Scale as Barriers to Entry

In addition to the barriers that have been cited, incumbent firms may have a whole range of cost advantages, independent of economies of scale, compared to new entrants. These cost advantages can act to deter entry, because new entrants will find themselves at a cost disadvantage vis-à-vis incumbent firms with these cost advantages. New entrants can engage in activities to overcome the cost advantages of incumbent firms, but as the cost of overcoming them increases the economic profit potential from entry is reduced. In some settings, incumbent firms enjoying cost advantages, independent of scale, can earn superior profits and still not be threatened by new entry because the cost of overcoming those advantages can be prohibitive. Examples of these cost advantages, independent of scale, are presented in Table 2.2; they include (1) proprietary technology, (2) managerial know-how, (3) favorable access to raw materials, and (4) learning-curve cost advantages.

Proprietary Technology.   In some industries, **proprietary** (i.e., secret or patented) **technology** gives incumbent firms important cost advantages over potential entrants. To enter these industries, potential entrants must develop their own substitute technologies or run the risks of copying another firm's patented technologies. Both of these activities can be costly. Numerous firms in a wide variety of industries have discovered the sometimes substantial economic costs associated with violating another firm's patented proprietary technology. For example, in the 1990s Eastman Kodak had to pay Polaroid $910 million and Intel had to pay Digital $700 million for violating patents. More recently, Roche Holding had to pay Igen International $505 million and Genentech had to pay City of Hope National Medical Center $500 million for violating patents. Eolas had to pay $521 million for infringing a Microsoft patent, and Gateway had to pay $250 million for violating an Intergraph patent.

Indeed, in the United States at least 20 firms have had to pay some other firm over $100 million for violating the other firm's patents. And this does not include the numerous patent infringement suits that are settled out of court, suits that involve literally billions of dollars exchanging hands. Obviously, if an industry has several firms with proprietary technologies, these technologies can substantially increase the cost of entry into that industry.[17]

Table 2.2   **Sources of Cost Advantage, Independent of Scale, That Can Act as Barriers to Entry**

Proprietary technology. When incumbent firms have secret or patented technology that reduces their costs below the costs of potential entrants, potential entrants must develop substitute technologies to compete. The cost of developing this technology can act as a barrier to entry.

Managerial know-how. When incumbent firms have taken-for-granted knowledge, skills, and information that take years to develop and that is not possessed by potential entrants. The cost of developing this know-how can act as a barrier to entry.

Favorable access to raw materials. When incumbent firms have low-cost access to critical raw materials not enjoyed by potential entrants. The cost of gaining similar access can act as a barrier to entry.

Learning-curve cost advantages. When the cumulative volume of production of incumbent firms gives them cost advantages not enjoyed by potential entrants. These cost disadvantages of potential entrants can act as a barrier to entry.

The number of patent infringement suits filed in the United States has increased every year for the past 15 years. The number of such suits in 1991 was 1,171; the number in 2004 (the last year for which complete data are available) was 3,075. Since 1994, the median damage award in a patent infringement suit has been $8. million. Currently, 60 percent of the patent infringement suits filed lead to financial compensation. Patent suits are distributed across numerous industries, including electronic equipment (14.6 percent), chemicals (14 percent), measuring instruments (13.4 percent), computer equipment (12.2 percent), and business services (9.8 percent).[18]

Managerial Know-How.   Even more important than technology per se as a barrier to entry is the managerial know-how built up by incumbent firms over their history.[19] **Managerial know-how** is the often-taken-for-granted knowledge and information that are needed to compete in an industry on a day-to-day basis.[20] Know-how includes information that it has taken years, sometimes decades, for a firm to accumulate that enables it to interact with customers and suppliers, to be innovative and creative, to manufacture quality products, and so forth. Typically, new entrants will not have access to this know-now, and it will often be costly for them to build it quickly.

One industry where this kind of know-how is a very important barrier to entry is the pharmaceutical industry. Success in this industry depends on having high-quality research and development skills. The development of world-class research and development skills—the know-how—takes decades to accumulate. New entrants face enormous cost disadvantages for decades as they attempt to develop these abilities, and thus entry into the pharmaceutical industry has been quite limited.[21]

Favorable Access to Raw Materials.   Incumbent firms may also have cost advantages, compared to new entrants, based on favorable access to raw materials. If, for example, only a few sources of high-quality iron ore are available in a specific geographic region, steel firms that have access to these sources may have a cost advantage over those that must ship their ore in from distant sources.[22]

Learning-Curve Cost Advantages.   It has been shown that in certain industries (such as airplane manufacturing) the cost of production falls with the cumulative volume of production. Over time, as incumbent firms gain experience in manufacturing their costs fall below those of potential entrants. Potential entrants, in this context, must endure substantially higher costs while they gain experience, and thus they may not enter the industry despite the superior profits being earned by incumbent firms. These learning-curve economies are discussed in more detail in Chapter 4.

Government Policy as a Barrier to Entry

Governments, for their own reasons, may decide to increase the cost of entry into an industry. This occurs most frequently when a firm operates as a government-regulated monopoly. In this setting, the government has concluded that it is in a better position to ensure that specific products or services are made available to the population at reasonable prices than competitive market forces. Industries such as electric power generation and elementary and secondary education have been (and to some extent, continue to be) protected from competitive entry by government restrictions on entry.

Although the government has acted to restrict competitive entry in many industries in the past, the number of such industries and the level of this entry restriction have both fallen dramatically over the last several years. Indeed, in the United States deregulation in the electric power generation industry has been occurring at a rapid pace. And although the bankruptcy of Enron may delay the relaxing of government-imposed barriers to entry into this industry, most observers agree that these restrictions will continue to be less important in the future. Entry is even occurring in the primary and secondary school industry with the creation of "charter schools"—schools that provide educational alternatives to traditional public school systems.

The Threat of Rivalry

New entrants are an important threat to the ability of firms to maintain or improve their level of performance, but they are not the only threat in a firm's environment. A second environmental threat in the five forces framework is **rivalry**—the intensity of competition among a firm's direct competitors. Both Barnes & Noble.com and Borders.com have become rivals of Amazon.com. CBS, NBC, Fox, USA Networks, and TNN—to name a few—are all rivals to ESPN.

Rivalry threatens firms by reducing their economic profits. High levels of rivalry are indicated by such actions as frequent price cutting by firms in an industry (e.g., price discounts in the airline industry), frequent introduction of new products by firms in an industry (e.g., continuous product introductions in consumer electronics), intense advertising campaigns (e.g., Pepsi versus Coke advertising), and rapid competitive actions and reactions in an industry (e.g., competing airlines quickly matching the discounts of other airlines).

Some of the attributes of an industry that are likely to generate high levels of rivalry are listed in Table 2.3. First, rivalry tends to be high when there are numerous firms in an industry and these firms tend to be roughly the same size. Such is the case in the laptop personal computer industry. Worldwide, over 120 firms have entered the laptop computer market, and no one firm dominates in market share. Since the early 1990s, prices in the laptop market have been declining 25 to 30 percent a year. Profit margins for laptop personal computer firms that used to be in the 10 to 13 percent range have rapidly fallen to 3 and 4 percent.[23]

Second, rivalry tends to be high when industry growth is slow. When industry growth is slow, firms seeking to increase their sales must acquire market share from established competitors. This tends to increase rivalry. Intense price rivalry emerged in the U.S. fast-food industry—with 99-cent Whoppers at Burger King and "dollar menus" at Wendy's and McDonald's—when the growth in this industry declined.[24]

Third, rivalry tends to be high when firms are unable to differentiate their products in an industry. When product differentiation is not a viable strategic option, firms are often forced to compete only on the basis of price. Intense price competition is typical of high-rivalry industries. In the airline industry, for example, intense competition on longer routes—such as between Los Angeles and New York and Los Angeles and Chicago—has kept prices on these routes down. These routes have relatively few product differentiation options. However, by creating hub-and-spoke systems, certain airlines (American, United, Delta) have been able to develop regions of the United States where they are the dominant carrier. These

Table 2.3   **Attributes of an Industry That Increase the Threat of Rivalry**

1. Large number of competing firms that are roughly the same size
2. Slow industry growth
3. Lack of product differentiation
4. Capacity added in large increments

hub-and-spoke systems enable airlines to partially differentiate their products geographically, thus reducing the level of rivalry in segments of this industry.[25]

Finally, rivalry tends to be high when production capacity is added in large increments. If, in order to obtain economies of scale, production capacity must be added in large increments, an industry is likely to experience periods of oversupply after new capacity comes on line. This overcapacity often leads to price cuts. Much of the growing rivalry in the commercial jet industry between Boeing and AirBus can be traced to the large manufacturing capacity additions made by AirBus when it entered the industry.[26]

The Threat of Substitutes

A third environmental threat in the five forces framework is substitutes. The products or services provided by a firm's rivals meet approximately the same customer needs in the same ways as the products or services provided by the firm itself. **Substitutes** meet approximately the same customer needs, but do so in different ways. Close substitutes for Amazon.com include Barnes & Noble and Borders bookstores. Television is a somewhat more distant substitute for Amazon, because the popularity of television comedies, dramas, and documentaries dampens demand for books. Substitutes for ESPN include sports magazines, sports pages in the newspapers, and actually attending sporting events.

Substitutes place a ceiling on the prices firms in an industry can charge and on the profits firms in an industry can earn. In the extreme, substitutes can ultimately replace an industry's products and services. This happens when a substitute is clearly superior to previous products. Examples include electronic calculators as substitutes for slide rules and mechanical calculators, electronic watch movements as substitutes for pin–lever mechanical watch movements, and compact discs as substitutes for long-playing (LP) records (although some audiophiles continue to argue for the sonic superiority of LPs). An open question remains about the extent to which online downloading of music will replace compact discs.

Substitutes are playing an increasingly important role in reducing the profit potential in a variety of industries. For example, in the legal profession private mediation and arbitration services are becoming viable substitutes for lawyers. Computerized texts are becoming viable substitutes for printed books in the publishing industry. Television news programs, especially services such as CNN, are very threatening substitutes for weekly newsmagazines, including *Time* and *Newsweek.* In Europe, so-called superstores are threatening smaller food shops. Minor league baseball teams are partial substitutes for major league teams. Cable television is a substitute for broadcast television. Groups of "Big Box" retailers are substitutes for traditional shopping centers. Private mail delivery systems (such as those in the Netherlands and Australia) are substitutes for government postal services. Home financial planning software is a partial substitute for professional financial planners.[27]

The Threat of Suppliers

A fourth environmental threat in the five forces framework is suppliers. **Suppliers** make a wide variety of raw materials, labor, and other critical assets available to firms. Suppliers can threaten the performance of firms in an industry by increasing the price of their supplies or by reducing the quality of those supplies. Any profits that were being earned in an industry can be transferred to suppliers in this way. For Amazon, book publishers and, more recently, book authors are critical suppliers, along with the employees that provide programming and logistics capabilities to

Table 2.4   **Indicators of the Threat of Suppliers in an Industry**

1. Suppliers' industry dominated by small number of firms.
2. Suppliers sell unique or highly differentiated products.
3. Suppliers are *not* threatened by substitutes.
4. Suppliers threaten forward vertical integration.
5. Firms are *not* important customers for suppliers.

Amazon. Critical suppliers for ESPN include sports leagues—such as the NFL and the NHL—as well as the TV personalities that staff ESPN television shows.

Some supplier attributes that can lead to high levels of threat are listed in Table 2.4. First, a firm's suppliers are a greater threat if the *suppliers'* industry is dominated by a small number of firms. In this setting, a firm has little choice but to purchase supplies from these firms. These few firms thus have enormous flexibility to charge high prices, to reduce quality, or in other ways to squeeze the profits of the firms to which they sell. Much of Microsoft's power in the software industry reflects its dominance in the operating system market, where Windows remains the de facto standard for most personal computers. For now, at least, if a company wants to sell personal computers, it is going to need to interact with Microsoft. It will be interesting to see if Linux-based PCs become more powerful, thereby limiting some of Microsoft's power as a supplier.

Conversely, when a firm has the option of purchasing from a large number of suppliers, suppliers have less power to threaten a firm's profits. For example, as the number of lawyers in the United States has increased over the years (up 40 percent since 1981, currently over 1 million), lawyers and law firms have been forced to begin competing for work. Some corporate clients have forced law firms to reduce their hourly fees and to handle repetitive simple legal tasks for low flat fees.[28]

Second, suppliers are a greater threat when what they supply is unique or highly differentiated. There was only one Michael Jordan, as a basketball player, as a spokesperson, and as a celebrity (but *not* as a baseball player). Jordan's unique status gave him enormous bargaining power as a supplier and enabled him to extract much of the economic profit that would otherwise have been earned by the Chicago Bulls and Nike. Currently, there is only one Le Bron James. In the same way, Intel's unique ability to develop, manufacture, and sell microprocessors gives it significant bargaining power as a supplier in the personal computer industry.

The uniqueness of suppliers can operate in almost any industry. For example, in the highly competitive world of television talk shows, some guests, as suppliers, can gain surprising fame for their unique characteristics. For example, one woman was a guest on eight talk shows. Her claim to fame: She was the tenth wife of a gay, con-man bigamist. Talk show hosts can also exercise significant power as suppliers. King World, the distributor of the *Oprah* talk show, has depended on *Oprah* for as much as 40 percent of its revenues. This, of course, has given the show's host, Oprah Winfrey, significant leverage in negotiating with King World.[29]

Third, suppliers are a greater threat to firms in an industry when suppliers are *not* threatened by substitutes. When there are no effective substitutes, suppliers can take advantage of their position to extract economic profits from firms they supply. Both Intel (in microprocessors) and Microsoft (in PC operating systems) have been accused of exploiting their unique product positions to extract profits from customers.

When there are substitutes for supplies, supplier power is checked. In the metal can industry, for example, steel cans are threatened by aluminum and plastic containers as substitutes. In order to continue to sell to can manufacturers, steel companies have had to keep their prices lower than what would otherwise have been the case. In this way, the potential power of the steel companies is checked by the existence of substitute products.[30]

Fourth, suppliers are a greater threat to firms when they can credibly threaten to enter into and begin competing in a firm's industry. This is called **forward vertical integration;** in this situation, suppliers cease to be suppliers only and become suppliers *and* rivals. The threat of forward vertical integration is partially a function of barriers to entry into an industry. When an industry has high barriers to entry, suppliers face significant costs of forward vertical integration, and thus forward integration is not as serious a threat to the profits of incumbent firms. (Vertical integration is discussed in detail in Chapter 6.)

Finally, suppliers are a threat to firms when firms are *not* an important part of suppliers' business. Steel companies, for example, are not too concerned with losing the business of a sculptor or of a small construction company. However, they are very concerned about losing the business of the major can manufacturers, major white-goods manufacturers (i.e., manufacturers of refrigerators, washing machines, dryers, and so forth), and automobile companies. Steel companies, as suppliers, are likely to be very accommodating and willing to reduce prices and increase quality for can manufacturers, white-goods manufacturers, and auto companies. Smaller, "less important" customers, however, are likely to be subject to greater price increases, lower-quality service, and lower-quality products.

The Threat of Buyers

The final environmental threat in the five forces framework is buyers. **Buyers** purchase a firm's products or services. Whereas sellers act to increase a firm's costs, buyers act to decrease a firm's revenues. Amazon.com's buyers include all those who purchase books online as well as those who purchase advertising space on Amazon's Web site. ESPN's buyers include all those who watch sports on television as well as those who purchase advertising space on the network. Some of the important indicators of the threat of buyers are listed in Table 2.5.

First, if a firm has only one buyer, or a small number of buyers, these buyers can be very threatening. Firms that sell a significant amount of their output to the U.S. Department of Defense recognize the influence of this buyer on their operations. Reductions in defense spending have forced defense companies to try even harder to reduce costs and increase quality to satisfy government demands. All these actions reduce the economic profits of these defense-oriented companies.[31] Firms that sell to large retail chains have also found it difficult to maintain high levels of profitability. Powerful retail firms—such as Wal-Mart and Home Depot— can make significant and complex logistical and other demands on their suppliers and, if suppliers fail to meet these demands, buyers can "fire" their suppliers. These demands can have the effect of reducing the profits of suppliers.

Table 2.5   **Indicators of the Threat of Buyers in an Industry**

1. Number of buyers is small.
2. Products sold to buyers are undifferentiated and standard.
3. Products sold to buyers are a significant percentage of a buyer's final costs.
4. Buyers are *not* earning significant economic profits.
5. Buyers threaten backward vertical integration.

Second, if the products or services that are being sold to buyers are standard and not differentiated, then the threat of buyers can be greater. For example, farmers sell a very standard product. It is very difficult to differentiate products such as wheat, corn, or tomatoes (although this can be done to some extent through the development of new strains of crops, the timing of harvests, pesticide-free crops, and so forth). In general, wholesale grocers and food brokers can always find alternative suppliers of basic food products. These numerous alternative suppliers increase the threat of buyers and force farmers to keep their prices and profits low. If any one farmer attempts to raise prices, wholesale grocers and food brokers simply purchase their supplies from some other farmer.

Third, buyers are likely to be more of a threat when the supplies they purchase are a significant portion of the costs of their final products. In this context, buyers are likely to be very concerned about the costs of their supplies and constantly on the lookout for cheaper alternatives. For example, in the canned food industry, the cost of the can itself can constitute up to 40 percent of a product's final price. Not surprisingly, firms such as Campbell Soup Company are very concerned about keeping the price of the cans they purchase as low as possible.[32]

Fourth, buyers are likely to be more of a threat when they are *not* earning significant economic profits. In these circumstances, buyers are likely to be very sensitive to costs and insist on the lowest possible cost and the highest possible quality from suppliers. This effect can be exacerbated when the profits suppliers earn are greater than the profits buyers earn. In this setting, a buyer would have a strong incentive to enter into its supplier's business to capture some of the economic profits being earned by the supplier. This strategy of **backward vertical integration** is discussed in more detail in Chapter 6.

Finally, buyers are more of a threat to firms in an industry when they have the ability to vertically integrate backward. In this case, buyers become both buyers and rivals and lock in a certain percentage of an industry's sales. The extent to which buyers represent a threat to vertically integrate, in turn, depends on the barriers to entry that are not in place in an industry. If there are significant barriers to entry, buyers may not be able to engage in backward vertical integration, and their threat to firms is reduced.

The Five Forces Model and Average Industry Performance

The five forces model has three important implications for managers seeking to choose and implement strategies. First, this model describes the most common sources of local environmental threat in industries. These are the threat of entry, the threat of rivalry, the threat of substitutes, the threat of suppliers, and the threat of buyers. Second, this model can be used to characterize the overall level of threat in an industry. Finally, because the overall level of threat in an industry is, according to S-C-P logic, related to the average level of performance of a firm in an industry, the five forces model can also be used to anticipate the average level of performance of firms in an industry.

Of course, it will rarely be the case that all five forces in an industry will be equally threatening at the same time. This can sometimes complicate the anticipation of the average level of firm performance in an industry. Consider, for example, the four industries in Table 2.6. It is easy to anticipate the average level of performance of firms in the first two industries: In Industry I, this performance will be high; in Industry II, this performance will be low; however, in Industries III and IV it is somewhat more complicated. In these mixed situations, the real question to ask in anticipating the average performance of firms in an industry is, "Are one or

Table 2.6   **Estimating the Level of Average Performance in an Industry**

	Industry I	**Industry II**	**Industry III**	**Industry IV**
Threat of entry	High	Low	High	Low
Threat of rivalry	High	Low	Low	High
Threat of substitutes	High	Low	High	Low
Threat of suppliers	High	Low	Low	High
Threat of buyers	High	Low	High	Low
Expected average firm performance	High	Low	?	?

more threats in this industry powerful enough to appropriate most of the profits that firms in this industry might generate?" If the answer to this question is yes, then the anticipated average level of performance will be low. If the answer is no, then this anticipated performance will be high.

Even more fundamentally, the five forces framework can be used only to anticipate the average level of firm performance in an industry. This is acceptable if a firm's industry is the primary determinant of its overall performance. However, as described in the Research Made Relevant feature, research suggests that the industry a firm operates in is far from the only determinant of its performance.

Another Environmental Force: Complementors

Recently, Professors Adam Brandenburger and Barry Nalebuff have suggested that another force needs to be added to Porter's five forces framework.[33] These authors distinguish between competitors and what they call a firm's *complementors.* If you were the CEO of a firm, the following is how you could tell the difference between your competitors and your complementors: Another firm is a **competitor** if your customers value your product less when they have the other firm's product than when they have your product alone. Rivals, new entrants, and substitutes are all examples of competitors. In contrast, another firm is a **complementor** if your customers value your product more when they have this other firm's product than when they have your product alone.

Consider, for example, the relationship between producers of television programming and cable television companies. The value of these firms' products partially depends on the existence of each other. Television producers need outlets for their programming. The growth in the number of channels on cable television provides more of these outlets and thus increases the value of these production firms. Cable television companies can continue to add channels, but those channels need content. So, the value of cable television companies depends partly on the existence of television production firms. Because the value of program-producing companies is greater when cable television firms exist, and because the value of cable television companies is greater when program-producing companies exist, these types of firms are complements.

Brandenburger and Nalebuff go on to argue that an important difference between complementors and competitors is that a firm's complementors help to increase the size of a firm's market, whereas a firm's competitors divide this market among a set of firms. Based on this logic, these authors suggest that although it is usually the case that a firm will want to discourage the entry of competitors into its market, it will usually want to encourage the entry of complementors.

Research Made Relevant

**The Impact of Industry
and Firm Characteristics
on Firm Performance**

For some time now, scholars have been interested in the relative impact of the attributes of the industry within which a firm operates and the attributes of the firm itself on its performance. The first work in this area was published by Richard Schmalansee. Using a single year's worth of data, Schmalansee estimated the variance in the performance of firms that was attributable to the industries within which firms operated versus other sources of performance variance. Schmalansee's conclusion was that approximately 20 percent of the variance in firm performance was explained by the industry within which a firm operated—a conclusion consistent with the S-C-P model and its emphasis on industry as a primary determinant of a firm's performance.

Richard Rumelt identified some weaknesses in Schmalansee's research. Most important of these was that Schmalansee had only one year's worth of data with which to examine the effects of industry and firm attributes on firm performance. Rumelt was able to use four years' worth of data, which allowed him to distinguish between stable and transient industry and firm effects on firm performance. Rumelt's results were consistent with Schmalansee's in one sense: Rumelt also found that about 16 percent of the variance in firm performance was due to industry effects, versus Schmalansee's 20 percent. However, only about half of this industry effect was stable. The rest represented year-to-year fluctuations in the business conditions in an industry. This result is broadly inconsistent with the S-C-P model.

Rumelt also examined the impact of firm attributes on firm performance and found that over 80 percent of the variance in firm performance was due to these firm attributes, but that over half of this 80 percent (46.38 percent) was due to stable firm effects. The importance of stable firm differences in explaining differences in firm performance is also inconsistent with the S-C-P framework. These results are consistent with another model of firm performance called the *Resource-Based View,* which will be described in Chapter 3.

Since Rumelt's research, efforts to identify the factors that explain variance in firm performance have accelerated. At least nine articles addressing this issue have been published in the literature. One of the most recent of these suggests that while the impact of the industry, the corporation, and the business on business unit performance can vary across industries and across corporations, that overall, business unit effects are larger than either corporate or industry effects.

Sources: R. P. Rumelt (1991). "How much does industry matter?" *Strategic Management Journal,* 12, pp. 167–185; R. Schmalansee (1985). "Do markets differ much?" *American Economic Review,* 75, pp. 341–351; V. F. Misangyi, H. Elms, T. Greckhamer, and J. A. Lepine (2006). "A new perspective on a fundamental debate: A multilevel approach to industry, corporate, and business unit effects." *Strategic Management Journal,* 27(6), pp. 571–590.

Returning to the television producers/cable television example, television producers will actually want cable television companies to grow and prosper and constantly add new channels, and cable television firms will want television show producers to grow and constantly create new and innovative programming. If the growth of either of these businesses slows, it hurts the growth of the other.

Of course, the same firm can be a complementor for one firm and a competitor for another. For example, the invention of satellite television and increased popularity of DirecTV and the Dish Network represent a competitive challenge to cable television companies. That is, DirecTV and, say, Time Warner Cable, are competitors. However, DirecTV and television production companies are complementors to each other. In deciding whether to encourage the entry of new complementors, a firm has to weigh the extra value these new complementors will create against the competitive impact of this entry on a firm's current complementors.

It is also the case that a single firm can be both a competitor and a complementor to the same firm. This is very common in industries where it is important to create technological standards. Without standards for, say, the size of a CD, how information on a CD will be stored, how this information will be read, and so forth, consumers will often be unwilling to purchase a CD player. With standards in place, however, sales of a particular technology can soar. To develop technology standards, firms must be willing to cooperate. This cooperation means that, with respect to the technology standard, these firms are complementors. And indeed, when these firms act as complementors, their actions have the effect of increasing the total size of the market. However, once these firms cooperate to establish standards, they begin to compete to try to obtain as much of the market they jointly created as possible. In this sense, these firms are also competitors.

Understanding when firms in an industry should behave as complementors and when they should behave as competitors is sometimes very difficult. It is even more difficult for a firm that has interacted with other firms in its industry as a competitor to change its organizational structure, formal and informal control systems, and compensation policy and start interacting with these firms as a complementor, at least for some purposes. Learning to manage what Brandenburger and Nalebuff call the "Jekyll and Hyde" dilemma associated with competitors and complementors can distinguish excellent from average firms.

Industry Structure and Environmental Opportunities

Identifying environmental threats is only half the task in accomplishing an external analysis. Such an analysis must also identify opportunities. Fortunately, the same S-C-P logic that made it possible to develop tools for the analysis of environmental threats can also be used to develop tools for the analysis of environmental opportunities. However, instead of identifying the threats that are common in most industries, opportunity analysis begins by identifying several generic industry structures and then describing the strategic opportunities that are available in each of these different kinds of industries.[34]

Of course, there are many different generic industry structures. However, four are very common and will be the focus of opportunity analysis in this book: (1) fragmented industries, (2) emerging industries, (3) mature industries, and (4) declining industries. A fifth industry structure—international industries—will be discussed later in the chapter. The kinds of opportunities typically associated with these industry structures are presented in Table 2.7.

Table 2.7 **Industry Structure and Environmental Opportunities**

Industry Structure	Opportunities
Fragmented industry	Consolidation
Emerging industry	First-mover advantages
Mature industry	Product refinement
	Investment in service quality
	Process innovation
Declining industry	Leadership
	Niche
	Harvest
	Divestment

Opportunities in Fragmented Industries: Consolidation

Fragmented industries are industries in which a large number of small or medium-sized firms operate and no small set of firms has dominant market share or creates dominant technologies. Most service industries, including retailing, fabrics, and commercial printing, to name just a few, are fragmented industries.

Industries can be fragmented for a wide variety of reasons. For example, the fragmented industry may have few barriers to entry, thereby encouraging numerous small firms to enter. The industry may have few, if any, economies of scale, and even some important diseconomies of scale, thus encouraging firms to remain small. Also, close local control over enterprises in an industry may be necessary— for example, local movie houses and local restaurants—to ensure quality and to minimize losses from theft.

The major opportunity facing firms in fragmented industries is the implementation of strategies that begin to consolidate the industry into a smaller number of firms. Firms that are successful in implementing this **consolidation strategy** can become industry leaders and obtain benefits from this kind of effort, if they exist.

Consolidation can occur in several ways. For example, an incumbent firm may discover new economies of scale in an industry. In the highly fragmented funeral home industry, Service Corporation International (SCI) found that the development of a chain of funeral homes gave it advantages in acquiring key supplies (coffins) and in the allocation of scarce resources (morticians and hearses). By acquiring numerous previously independent funeral homes, SCI was able to substantially reduce its costs and gain higher levels of economic performance.[35]

Incumbent firms sometimes adopt new ownership structures to help consolidate an industry. Kampgrounds of America (KOA) uses franchise agreements with local operators to provide camping facilities to travelers in the fragmented private campgrounds industry. KOA provides local operators with professional training, technical skills, and access to its brand name reputation. Local operators, in return, provide KOA with local managers who are intensely interested in the financial and operational success of their campgrounds. Similar franchise agreements have been instrumental in the consolidation of other fragmented industries, including fast food (McDonald's), muffler repair (Midas), and motels (La Quinta, Holiday Inn, Howard Johnson's).[36]

The benefits of implementing a consolidation strategy in a fragmented industry turn on the advantages larger firms in such industries gain from their larger market share. As will be discussed in Chapter 4, firms with large market share can have important cost advantages. Large market share can also help a firm differentiate its products.

Opportunities in Emerging Industries: First-Mover Advantages

Emerging industries are newly created or newly re-created industries formed by technological innovations, changes in demand, the emergence of new customer needs, and so forth. Over the last 30 years, the world economy has been flooded by emerging industries, including the microprocessor industry, the personal computer industry, the medical imaging industry, and the biotechnology industry, to name a few. Firms in emerging industries face a unique set of opportunities, the exploitation of which can be a source of superior performance for some time for some firms.

The opportunities that face firms in emerging industries fall into the general category of first-mover advantages. **First-mover advantages** are advantages that come to firms that make important strategic and technological decisions early in the development of an industry. In emerging industries, many of the rules of the game and standard operating procedures for competing and succeeding have yet to be established. First-moving firms can sometimes help establish the rules of the game and create an industry's structure in ways that are uniquely beneficial to them. In general, first-mover advantages can arise from three primary sources: (1) technological leadership, (2) preemption of strategically valuable assets, and (3) the creation of customer-switching costs.[37]

First-Mover Advantages and Technological Leadership

Firms that make early investments in particular technologies in an industry are implementing a **technological leadership strategy.** Such strategies can generate two advantages in emerging industries. First, firms that have implemented these strategies may obtain a low-cost position based on their greater cumulative volume of production with a particular technology. These cost advantages have had important competitive implications in such diverse industries as the manufacture of titanium dioxide by DuPont and Procter & Gamble's competitive advantage in disposable diapers.[38]

Second, firms that make early investments in a technology may obtain patent protections that enhance their performance.[39] Xerox's patents on the xerography process and General Electric's patent on Edison's original light bulb design were important for these firms' success when these two industries were emerging.[40] However, although there are some exceptions (e.g., the pharmaceutical industry and specialty chemicals), patents, per se, seem to provide relatively small profit opportunities for first-moving firms in most emerging industries. One group of researchers found that imitators can duplicate first movers' patent-based advantages for about 65 percent of the first mover's costs.[41] These researchers also found that 60 percent of all patents are imitated within four years of being granted—without legally violating patent rights obtained by first movers. As we will discuss in detail in Chapter 3, patents are rarely a source of sustained competitive advantage for firms, even in emerging industries.

First-Mover Advantages and Preemption of Strategically Valuable Assets

First movers that invest only in technology usually do not obtain sustained competitive advantages. However, first movers that move to tie up strategically valuable resources in an industry before their full value is widely understood can gain sustained competitive advantages. **Strategically valuable assets** are resources required to successfully compete in an industry. Firms that are able to acquire these resources have, in effect, erected formidable barriers to imitation in an industry. Some strategically valuable assets that can be acquired in this way include access to raw materials, particularly favorable geographic locations, and particularly valuable product market positions.

When an oil company such as Royal Dutch Shell (because of its superior exploration skills) acquires leases with greater development potential than was expected by its competition, the company is gaining access to raw materials in a way that is likely to generate sustained competitive advantages. When Wal-Mart opens stores in medium-sized cities before the arrival of its competition, Wal-Mart is making it difficult for the competition to enter into this market. And, when breakfast cereal companies expand their product lines to include all possible combinations of wheat, oats, bran, corn, and sugar, they, too, are using a first-mover advantage to deter entry.[42]

First-Mover Advantages and Creating Customer-Switching Costs

Firms can also gain first-mover advantages in an emerging industry by creating customer-switching costs. **Customer-switching costs** exist when customers make investments in order to use a firm's particular products or services. These investments tie customers to a particular firm and make it more difficult for customers to begin purchasing from other firms. These investments tie customers to a particular firm and make it more difficult for customers to begin purchasing from different firms.[43] Such switching costs are important factors in industries as diverse as applications software for personal computers, prescription pharmaceuticals, and groceries.[44]

In applications software for personal computers, users make significant investments to learn how to use a particular software package. Once computer users have learned how to operate particular software, they are unlikely to switch to new software, even if that new software system is superior to what they currently use. Such a switch would require learning the new software and determining how it is similar to and different from the old software. For these reasons, some computer users will continue to use outdated software, even though new software performs much better.

Similar switching costs can exist in some segments of the prescription pharmaceutical industry. Once medical doctors become familiar with a particular drug, its applications, and side effects, they are sometimes reluctant to change to a new drug, even if that new drug promises to be more effective than the older, more familiar one. Trying the new drug requires learning about its properties and side effects. Even if the new drug has received government approvals, its use requires doctors to be willing to "experiment" with the health of their patients. Given these issues, many physicians are unwilling to rapidly adopt new drug therapies. This is one reason that pharmaceutical firms spend so much time and money using their sales forces to educate their physician customers. This kind of education is necessary if a doctor is going to be willing to switch from an old drug to a new one.

Customer-switching costs can even play a role in the grocery store industry. Each grocery store has a particular layout of products. Once customers learn where different products in a particular store are located, they are not likely to change stores, because they would then have to relearn the location of products. Many customers want to avoid the time and frustration associated with wandering around a new store looking for some obscure product. Indeed, the cost of switching stores may be large enough to enable some grocery stores to charge higher prices than what would be the case without customer-switching costs.

First-Mover Disadvantages

Of course, the advantages of first moving in emerging industries must be balanced against the risks associated with exploiting this opportunity. Emerging industries are characterized by a great deal of uncertainty. When first-moving firms are making critical strategic decisions, it may not be at all clear what the right decisions are. In such highly uncertain settings, a reasonable strategic alternative to first moving may be retaining flexibility. Where first-moving firms attempt to resolve the uncertainty they face by making decisions early and then trying to influence the evolution of an emerging industry, they use flexibility to resolve this uncertainty by delaying decisions until the economically correct path is clear and then moving quickly to take advantage of that path.

Opportunities in Mature Industries: Product Refinement, Service, and Process Innovation

Emerging industries are often formed by the creation of new products or technologies that radically alter the rules of the game in an industry. However, over time, as these new ways of doing business become widely understood, as technologies diffuse through competitors, and as the rate of innovation in new products and technologies drops, an industry begins to enter the mature phase of its development. As described in the Strategy in the Emerging Enterprise feature, this change in the nature of a firm's industry can be difficult to recognize and can create both strategic and operational problems for a firm.

Common characteristics of **mature industries** include (1) slowing growth in total industry demand, (2) the development of experienced repeat customers, (3) a slowdown in increases in production capacity, (4) a slowdown in the introduction of new products or services, (5) an increase in the amount of international competition, and (6) an overall reduction in the profitability of firms in the industry.[45]

The fast-food industry in the United States has matured over the last 10 to 15 years. In the 1960s, the United States had only three large national fast-food chains: McDonald's, Burger King, and Dairy Queen. Through the 1980s, all three of these chains grew rapidly, although the rate of growth at McDonald's outstripped the growth rate of the other two firms. During this time period, however, other fast-food chains also entered the market. These included some national chains, such as Kentucky Fried Chicken, Wendy's, and Taco Bell, and some strong regional chains, such as Jack in the Box and In and Out Burger. By the early 1990s, growth in this industry had slowed considerably. McDonald's announced that it was having difficulty finding locations for new McDonald's that did not impinge on the sales of already existing McDonald's. Except for non–U.S. operations, where competition in the fast-food industry is not as mature, the profitability of most U.S. fast-food companies did not grow as much in the 1990s as it did in the 1960s through the 1980s. Indeed, by 2002 all the major fast-food chains were either not making very much money, or, like McDonald's, actually losing money.[46]

Opportunities for firms in mature industries typically shift from the development of new technologies and products in an emerging industry to a greater emphasis on refining a firm's current products, an emphasis on increasing the quality of service, and a focus on reducing manufacturing costs and increased quality through process innovations.

Refining Current Products

In mature industries, such as home detergents, motor oil, and kitchen appliances, few, if any, major technological breakthroughs are likely. However, this does not mean that innovation is not occurring in these industries. Innovation in these industries focuses on extending and improving current products and technologies. In home detergents, innovation recently has focused on changes in packaging and on selling more highly concentrated detergents. In motor oil, packaging changes (from fiber foil cans to plastic containers), additives that keep oil cleaner longer, and oil formulated to operate in four-cylinder engines are recent examples of this kind of innovation. In kitchen appliances, recent improvements include the availability of refrigerators with crushed ice and water through the door, commercial-grade stoves for home use, and dishwashers that automatically adjust the cleaning cycle depending on how dirty the dishes are.[47]

Strategy in the Emerging Enterprise

*I*t began with a 5,000-word e-mail sent by Steve Balmer, CEO of Microsoft, to all 57,000 employees. Whereas previous e-mails from Microsoft founder Bill Gates—including one in 1995 calling on the firm to learn how to "ride the wave of the Internet"—inspired the firm to move on to conquer more technological challenges, Balmer's e-mail focused on Microsoft's current state and called on the firm to become more focused and efficient. Balmer also announced that Microsoft would cut its costs by $1 billion during the next fiscal year. One observer described it as the kind of e-mail you would expect to read at Procter & Gamble, not at Microsoft.

Then the other shoe dropped. In a surprise move, Balmer announced that Microsoft would distribute a large portion of its $56 billion cash reserve in the form of a special dividend to stockholders. In what is believed to be the largest such cash dispersion ever, Microsoft distributed $32 billion to its stockholders and used an additional $30 billion to buy back stock. Bill Gates received a $3.2 billion cash dividend. These changes meant that Microsoft's capital structure was more similar to, say, Procter & Gamble's, than to an entrepreneurial, high-flying software company.

What happened at Microsoft? Did Microsoft's management conclude that the PC software industry was no longer emerging, but had matured to the point that Microsoft would have to alter some of its traditional strategies? Most observers believe that Balmer's e-mail, and the decision to reduce its cash reserves, signaled that Microsoft had come to

Microsoft Grows Up

this conclusion. In fact, although most of Microsoft's core businesses—its Windows operating systems, its PC applications software, and its server software—are still growing at the rate of about $3 billion a year, if they were growing at historical rates these businesses would be generating $7 billion in new revenues each year. Moreover, Microsoft's new businesses—video games, Internet services, business software, and software for phones and handheld computers—are adding less than $1 billion in new revenues each year. That is, growth in Microsoft's new businesses is not offsetting slower growth in its traditional businesses.

Other indicators of the growing maturity of the PC software industry, and Microsoft's strategic changes, also exist. For example, during 2003 and 2004 Microsoft resolved most of the outstanding antitrust litigation it was facing, abandoned its employee stock option plan in favor of a stock-based

compensation scheme popular with slower-growth firms, improved its systems for receiving and acting on feedback from customers, and improved the quality of its relationships with some of its major rivals, including Sun Microsystems, Inc. These are all the actions of a firm that recognizes that the rapid growth opportunities that existed in the software industry when Microsoft was a new company do not exist any more.

What Microsoft has to do now is to get its entire organization—all its employees, suppliers, and even its customers—used to the idea that high growth has been abandoned as a goal and replaced by maximizing returns for Microsoft's shareholders. Whether Microsoft will be able to retain all of its high-flying technical and managerial talent in this new world has yet to be seen. Indeed, Microsoft recently announced that Bill Gates will withdraw from his day-to-day responsibilities at the firm by 2008.

Microsoft may also have to get used to not being able to easily attract all the best technical and managerial talent it wants. But, if the PC software industry has really evolved from being an emerging industry to a mature one, these are the kinds of strategic changes that a firm such as Microsoft will have to make if it wants to retain its place in the industry.

Sources: J. Greene (2004). "Microsoft's midlife crisis." *BusinessWeek,* April 19, 2004, pp. 88 +; R. Guth and S. Thurm (2004). "Microsoft to dole out its cash hoard." *Wall Street Journal,* Wednesday, July 21, 2004, pp. A1 +, S. Hamm (2004). "Microsoft's worst enemy: Success." *BusinessWeek,* July 19, 2004, p. 33; www.microsoft.com/billgates/speeches/2006/00-15transition.asp.

Emphasis on Service

When firms in an industry have only limited ability to invest in radical new technologies and products, efforts to differentiate products often turn toward the quality of customer service. A firm that is able to develop a reputation for high-quality customer service may be able to obtain superior performance even though its products are not highly differentiated.

This emphasis on service has become very important in a wide variety of industries. For example, in the convenience food industry, one of the major reasons for slower growth in the fast-food segment has been growth in the so-called "casual dining" segment. This segment includes restaurants such as Chili's and Applebee's. The food sold at fast-food restaurants and casual dining restaurants overlaps—they both sell burgers, soft drinks, salads, chicken, desserts, and so forth—although many consumers believe that the quality of food is superior in the casual dining restaurants. In addition to any perceived differences in the food, however, the level of service in the two kinds of establishments varies significantly. At fast-food restaurants, food is handed to consumers on a tray; in casual dining restaurants, wait staff actually bring food to consumers on a plate. This level of service is one reason that casual dining is growing in popularity.[48]

Process Innovation

A firm's **processes** are the activities it engages in to design, produce, and sell its products or services. **Process innovation,** then, is a firm's effort to refine and improve its current processes. Several authors have studied the relationship between process innovation, product innovation, and the maturity of an industry.[49] This work, summarized in Figure 2.5, suggests that in the early stages of industry development, product innovation is very important. However, over time product innovation becomes less important, and process innovations designed to reduce manufacturing costs, increase product quality, and streamline management become more important. In mature industries, firms can often gain an advantage by manufacturing the same product as competitors, but at a lower cost. Alternatively, firms can manufacture a product that is perceived to be of higher quality and do so at a competitive cost. Process innovations facilitate both the reduction of costs and the increase in quality.

The role of process innovation in more mature industries is perhaps best exemplified by the improvement in quality in U.S. automobiles. In the 1980s,

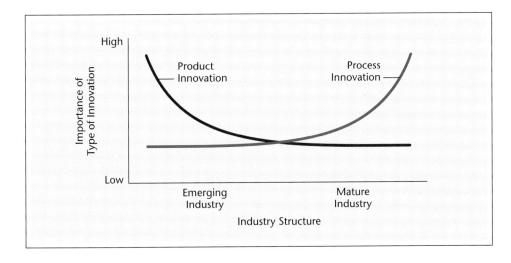

Figure 2.5 Process and Product Innovation and Industry Structure

Source: Taken from Hayes and Wheelwright, "The dynamics of process-product life cycles." *Harvard Business Review,* March–April, pp. 127–136.

Japanese firms such as Nissan, Toyota, and Honda sold cars that were of significantly higher quality than those produced by U.S. firms General Motors, Ford, and Chrysler. In the face of that competitive disadvantage, the U.S. firms engaged in numerous process reforms to improve the quality of their cars. In the 1980s, U.S. manufacturers were cited for car body panels that did not fit well, bumpers that were hung crookedly on cars, and the wrong engines being placed in cars. Today, the differences in quality between newly manufactured U.S. and Japanese automobiles are very small. Indeed, one well-known judge of initial manufacturing quality—J. D. Powers—now focuses on items such as the quality of a car's cup holders and the maximum distance at which a car's keyless entry system still works to establish quality rankings. The really significant quality issues of the 1980s are virtually gone.[50]

Opportunities in Declining Industries: Leadership, Niche, Harvest, and Divestment

A **declining industry** is an industry that has experienced an absolute decline in unit sales over a sustained period of time.[51] Obviously, firms in a declining industry face more threats than opportunities. Rivalry in a declining industry is likely to be very high, as is the threat of buyers, suppliers, and substitutes. However, even though threats are significant, firms do have opportunities they can exploit. The major strategic opportunities that firms in this kind of industry face are leadership, niche, harvest, and divestment.

Market Leadership

An industry in decline is often characterized by overcapacity in manufacturing, distribution, and so forth. Reduced demand often means that firms in a declining industry will have to endure a significant shakeout period until overcapacity is reduced and capacity is brought in line with demand. After the shakeout, a smaller number of lean and focused firms may enjoy a relatively benign environment with few threats and several opportunities. If the industry structure that is likely to exist after a shakeout is quite attractive, firms in an industry before the shakeout may have an incentive to weather the storm of decline—to survive until the situation improves to the point that they can begin to earn higher profits.

If a firm has decided to wait out the storm of decline in hopes of better environmental conditions in the future, it should consider various steps to increase its chances of survival. Most important of these is that a firm must establish itself as a **market leader** in the preshakeout industry, most typically by becoming the firm with the largest market share in that industry. The purpose of becoming a market leader is *not* to facilitate tacit collusion (see Chapter 9) or to obtain lower costs from economies of scale (see Chapter 6). Rather, in a declining industry the leader's objective should be to try to facilitate the exit of firms that are not likely to survive a shakeout, thereby obtaining a more favorable competitive environment as quickly as possible.

Market leaders in declining industries can facilitate exit in a variety of ways, including purchasing and then deemphasizing competitors' product lines, purchasing and retiring competitors' manufacturing capacity, manufacturing spare parts for competitors' product lines, and sending unambiguous signals of their intention to stay in an industry and remain a dominant firm. For example, overcapacity problems in the European petrochemical industry were partially resolved when Imperial Chemical Industries (ICI) traded its polyethylene plants to British Petroleum for BP's polyvinylchloride (PVC) plants. In this case, both firms were able to close some excess capacity in specific markets (polyethylene and PVC), while sending clear signals of their intention to remain in these markets.[52]

Market Niche

A firm in a declining industry following a leadership strategy attempts to facilitate exit by other firms, but a firm following a **niche strategy** in a declining industry reduces its scope of operations and focuses on narrow segments of the declining industry. If only a few firms choose a particular niche, then these firms may have a favorable competitive setting, even though the industry as a whole is facing shrinking demand.

Two firms that used the niche approach in a declining market are GTE Sylvania and General Electric (GE) in the vacuum tube industry. The invention of the transistor and followed by the semiconductor just about destroyed demand for vacuum tubes in new products. GTE Sylvania and GE rapidly recognized that new product sales in vacuum tubes were drying up. In response, these firms began specializing in supplying *replacement* vacuum tubes to the consumer and military markets. To earn high profits, these firms had to refocus their sales efforts and scale down their sales and manufacturing staffs. Over time, as fewer and fewer firms manufactured vacuum tubes, GTE Sylvania and GE were able to charge very high prices for replacement parts.[53]

Harvest

Leadership and niche strategies, though differing along several dimensions, have one attribute in common: Firms that implement these strategies intend to remain in the industry despite its decline. Firms pursuing a **harvest strategy** in a declining industry do not expect to remain in the industry over the long term. Instead, they engage in a long, systematic, phased withdrawal, extracting as much value as possible during the withdrawal period.

The extraction of value during the implementation of a harvest strategy presumes that there is some value to harvest. Thus, firms that implement this strategy must ordinarily have enjoyed at least some profits at some time in their history, before the industry began declining. Firms can implement a harvest strategy by reducing the range of products they sell, reducing their distribution network, eliminating less profitable customers, reducing product quality, reducing service quality, deferring maintenance and equipment repair, and so forth. In the end, after a period of harvesting in a declining industry, firms can either sell their operations (to a market leader) or simply cease operations.

In principle, the harvest opportunity sounds simple, but in practice it presents some significant management challenges. The movement toward a harvest strategy often means that some of the characteristics of a business that have long been a source of pride to managers may have to be abandoned. Thus, where prior to harvest a firm may have specialized in high-quality service, quality products, and excellent customer value, during the harvest period service quality may fall, product quality may deteriorate, and prices may rise. These changes may be difficult for managers to accept, and higher turnover may be the result. It is also difficult to hire quality managers into a harvesting business, because such individuals are likely to seek greater opportunities elsewhere.

For these reasons, few firms explicitly announce a harvest strategy. However, examples can be found. GE seems to be following a harvest strategy in the electric turbine business. Also, United States Steel and the International Steel Group seem to be following this strategy in certain segments of the steel market.[54]

Divestment

The final opportunity facing firms in a declining industry is divestment. Like a harvest strategy, the objective of **divestment** is to extract a firm from a declining industry. However, unlike harvest, divestment occurs quickly, often soon after a pattern of decline has been established. Firms without established competitive advantages may find divestment a superior option to harvest, because they have few competitive advantages they can exploit through harvesting.

In the 1980s, GE used this rapid divestment approach to virtually abandon the consumer electronics business. Total demand in this business was more or less stable during the 1980s, but competition (mainly from Asian manufacturers) increased substantially. Rather than remain in this business, GE sold most of its consumer electronics operations and used the capital to enter into the medical imaging industry, where this firm has found an environment more conducive to superior performance.[55]

In the defense business, divestment is the stated strategy of General Dynamics, at least in some of its business segments. General Dynamics' managers recognized early on that the changing defense industry could not support all the incumbent firms. When General Dynamics concluded that it could not remain a leader in some of its businesses, it decided to divest those and concentrate on a few remaining businesses. Since 1991, General Dynamics has sold businesses worth over $2.83 billion, including its missile systems business, its Cessna aircraft division, and its tactical aircraft division (maker of the very successful F-16 aircraft and partner in the development of the next generation of fighter aircraft, the F-22). These divestitures have left General Dynamics in just three businesses: armored tanks, nuclear submarines, and space launch vehicles. During this time, the market price of General Dynamics stock has returned almost $4.5 billion to its investors, has seen its stock go from $25 per share to a high of $110 per share, and has provided a total return to stockholders of 555 percent.[56]

Of course, not all divestments are caused by industry decline. Sometimes firms divest certain operations to focus their efforts on remaining operations, sometimes they divest to raise capital, and sometimes they divest to simplify operations. These types of divestments reflect a firm's diversification strategy and are explored in detail in Chapter 11.

Threat and Opportunity Analysis in an International Context

Obviously, the analysis of threats and opportunities in a firm's environment is not complete until the international dimensions of that environment are considered. Both threat analysis—using the five forces framework and the concept of complementors—and opportunity analysis—focusing on international opportunities—can be applied in this international context. Each of these international extensions will be considered in turn.

Analysis of Environmental Threats in an International Context

All of the threats identified in the five forces framework apply to the analysis of international competitive threats. It is certainly the case that rivals, new entrants, substitutes, suppliers, and buyers can all be international firms. Indeed, there is nothing in the five forces framework that cannot be applied in understanding international firms as a source of competitive threat.

However, of the five forces identified by Porter it is usually the case that one of these—the threat of entry—is particularly salient in the analysis of international threats. This is because important barriers to entry still exist in international business. These barriers to entry typically fall into one of three categories: tariffs, quotas, or nontariff trade barriers.

Tariffs as a Barrier to Entry

Tariffs are taxes levied on goods or services imported into a country. Tariffs have the effect of increasing the price of an imported good or service, sometimes well above the price of the same good or service produced by a domestic firm. There are three types of tariffs: **ad valorem tariffs,** where the tariff is calculated as a percentage of the market value of an import, regardless of its weight or volume; **specific tariffs,** where the tariff is calculated as a percentage of the weight or volume of the goods being imported, regardless of its market value; and **compound tariffs,** where both the market value and the weight or volume are used in calculating a tariff.

Calculating the tariffs on specific imported items can be quite complex, because different products can have different tariffs, and determining which product category a particular import falls into can be very ambiguous. For example, leather ski gloves imported into the United States are subject to a 5.5 percent ad valorem tariff. But if those ski gloves are designed for cross country skiing, they are subject to only a 3.5 percent ad valorem tariff. In one case, a firm was looking to import "Reindeer Caps" from China. These were hats to be worn primarily at Christmas parties, with fabric reindeer antlers that would play various Christmas carols and shout "Merry Christmas." For tariff purposes, was the item a toy, a hat, or a festive article? These three product categories carry different tariffs in the United States.[57]

Quotas as a Barrier to Entry

Quotas are a numerical limit on the number of particular items that are allowed to be imported into a country. Quotas have been used in many countries to protect politically powerful domestic industries, including textiles, automobiles, and agriculture. Although quotas do not raise the price of imported goods directly, they have the effect of reducing the supply of those goods in a particular country. This reduced supply, in turn, typically raises the price of those products or services that are sold within a country.

Nontariff Trade Barriers

Besides quotas, countries can use a variety of other nontariff mechanisms to increase the cost of entry into a geographic market. The other **nontariff trade barriers** include establishing product performance standards that cannot be met by imports, restricting access to domestic distribution channels, imposing local purchasing requirements for government purchases, and a variety of environmental and labor regulations that foreign firms must meet if they are to do business in a country. Often, domestic firms do not have to meet the same standards as firms looking to import into a country. When this is the case, these other nontariff activities clearly act as a barrier to entry.

For example, entry into Japanese markets has historically been very difficult because of other nontariff trade barriers.[58] In the early 1990s, International Game Technology (IGT), a leading U.S. manufacturer of slot machines, sought entry into the large Japanese gambling market (Japan has over two-thirds of the world's slot machines, approximately 800,000 in total). IGT's entry was deterred, however, because its slot machines did not meet government slot machine standards. Unfortunately, knowledge about what these standards were was available only to members of the Japanese industry's trade association, and to become a member of this trade association a firm needed to have been manufacturing slot machines in Japan for at least three years. It took several years for IGT to overcome this "Catch-22" barrier to entry.[59]

Similar barriers exist to entry into the Japanese beer industry. Four firms—Kirin, Asahi, Sapporo, and Suntory—dominate this industry with over 78 percent of the Japanese beer market. In order for foreign firms to begin producing beer in Japan, they must obtain a license from the ministry of finance. However, to obtain such a license, a firm must already be producing 2 million liters of beer in Japan. This barrier to entry has effectively limited non–Japanese beers to the expensive import market in Japan.[60]

Why Do Governments Impose Tariff and Nontariff Barriers to Entry?

Given that the effect of tariff and nontariff barriers to entry is almost always to raise the price of goods or services in a country, an important question becomes: Why would governments choose to erect such barriers? First, like any other tax, tariffs raise revenue for the government. Indeed, tariffs are often more politically palatable than other forms of taxation because they are hidden in the final price of the goods or services. A tariff is not added to the base price of a product or service, as with a sales tax. Nor do tax payers receive a bill from the government every six months, as with property taxes. Indeed, consumers pay this tax, and they do not even have to file an income tax return to do so.

Second, tariff and nontariff barriers have the effect of strengthening demand for products and services produced by domestic firms. This can give domestic firms time to build their capabilities before engaging in full-fledged global competition. It can also secure higher levels of employment in an industry. Both tariff and nontariff barriers to entry can be politically very beneficial to a government.

Analysis of Opportunities in an International Context

Not only can threat analysis be extended to an international context, but opportunity analysis can as well. Indeed, it is an assumption of business in the twenty-first century that competitive opportunities are becoming more international in scope. Even industries that appear likely to be national or regional in focus (Broadway plays, for example, are by definition produced only in New York City) have, over the last several years, become more international in character (many major Broadway hits are transfers from the West End in London, and regional traveling companies exhibit these plays throughout the world). International competition has some very obvious effects on the level and kinds of opportunities in an industry.[61] Opportunities in international industries generally fall into three large categories: multinational opportunities, global opportunities, and transnational opportunities.

Multinational Opportunities

Firms pursuing **multinational opportunities** in international industries operate simultaneously in several national or regional markets, but these operations are independent of each other and are free to choose how to respond to the specific needs of each national or regional marketplace. Some well-known firms that have pursued multinational international opportunities include Nestlé and General

Motors. Only a small percentage of Nestlé's products are sold throughout the entire world. Rather, managers within each country where Nestlé operates have the responsibility to discern local tastes, design products to be consistent with those tastes, and to market these specially designed products locally. In a similar way, GM encourages very little interaction between its U.S. and European operations. Cars designed for the European market and sold under GM's Opal brand name have infrequently been sold in the United States and relatively few Chevrolets and Oldsmobiles designed for the U.S. market are sold in Europe.

Pursuing multinational opportunities in international industries has at least two advantages. First, this strategy enables firms to respond rapidly to changing conditions in a country or region. If threats or opportunities appear in one part of the world but not in others, a multinational firm can quickly move to neutralize threats or exploit opportunities in those geographic regions where it is needed. For example, by operating at least partially as a multinational, McDonald's enables many of its European franchises to sell beer and wine alongside Big Macs and fries. Such sales do not represent an opportunity in McDonald's home market of the United States.

Second, although there are relatively few operational interactions between divisions and headquarters in a multinational company, impressive organizational resources can be quickly marshaled should they be required to exploit an opportunity or neutralize a threat in a particular country or region. McDonald's, for example, has been able to use all of its technological and management skills to open franchises in Moscow and other eastern European cities.[62]

Global Opportunities

Where as firms pursuing multinational opportunities operate in countries or regions in an independent manner, those pursuing **global opportunities** seek to optimize production, distribution, and other business functions throughout the world by addressing all the markets in which they operate. If manufacturing costs are very low and quality is very high in plants located in Singapore, global organizations will locate manufacturing facilities there. If particular research and development skills and technology are widely available in Great Britain, global organizations will locate their R&D operations there. If capital is less costly in New York, global organizations will locate their financial functions there. In this manner, the cost and quality of each organizational function can be optimized. Examples of global organizations include IBM and Ford Motor Company. Global strategies have the obvious advantage of locating operations in geographic positions that reduce costs and maximize quality in all business functions.

However, global strategies also have associated costs and risks. First, because the delivery of products or services in a global organization requires inputs from numerous operations all over the world, a global strategy puts a great deal of emphasis on coordination. Coordination can be difficult across divisions within a single country; it can be even more difficult across divisions in different countries or regions. Differences in language, culture, legal systems, and traditional business practices may complicate coordination efforts.

Second, locating interdependent units in geographically disparate areas can create significant transportation costs. The very low cost of manufacturing automobile transmissions in Mexico may be effectively increased by the need to transport those transmissions to Japan to be installed in automobiles. This is less of a problem for a firm that ships products that are relatively light, small, and have very high profit margins.

Finally, exploiting global strategies may limit a firm's ability to respond to local needs, opportunities, and threats. Firms pursuing global opportunities in international industries are well designed to respond to global markets and less well designed to respond to a series of local markets. If the structure of the markets in which a firm operates does not significantly vary by country or region, a global approach may be a particularly attractive opportunity.

Transnational Opportunities

Recently, another opportunity has been described in international industries—operating as a transnational firm. Some have argued that the traditional tradeoff between global integration and local responsiveness can be replaced by a transnational approach that exploits the advantages of both global integration and local responsiveness. Firms exploiting a **transnational opportunity** in an international industry treat their global operations as an integrated network of distributed and interdependent resources and capabilities.[63] In this context, a firm's operations in each country are not simply independent activities attempting to respond to local market needs; they are also repositories of ideas, technologies, and management approaches that the firm may be able to use and apply in its other global operations. Put differently, operations in different countries can be thought of as "experiments" in the creation of capabilities. Some of these experiments will work and generate important new capabilities for an entire firm; others will fail to generate benefits for a firm.

When an operation in a particular country develops a capability in manufacturing a particular product, providing a particular service, or engaging in a particular activity that can be used by other countries, the country operating with this capability can achieve global economies of scale by becoming the firm's primary supplier of this product, service, or activity. In this way, local responsiveness is retained as managers in that country constantly search for new capabilities that will enable them to maximize profits in their particular markets, and global integration and economies of scale are realized as country operations that have developed unique capabilities become suppliers for all other country operations. Firms that pursue transnational strategies include HP and Honda.

SUMMARY

The strategic management process requires that a firm engage in an analysis of threats and opportunities in its competitive environment before a strategic choice can be made. This analysis begins with an understanding of the firm's general environment. This general environment has six components: technological change, demographic trends, cultural trends, economic climate, legal and political conditions, and specific international events. Although some of these components of the general environment can affect a firm directly, more frequently they affect a firm through their impact on its local environment.

The structure-conduct-performance (or S-C-P) model is a theoretical framework that enables the analysis of a firm's local environment and that links the structure of the industry within which a firm operates, its strategic alternatives, and firm performance. In this model, *structure* is defined as industry structure and includes those attributes of a firm's industry that constrain a firm's strategic alternatives and performance. *Conduct* is defined as a firm's strategies. *Performance* refers either to the performance of a firm in an industry or the performance of the entire economy—although the former definition of performance is more important for most strategic management purposes.

The S-C-P model can be used to develop tools for analyzing threats in a firm's competitive environment. The most influential of these tools is called the "five forces framework." The five forces are: the threat of entry, the threat of rivalry, the threat of substitutes, the threat of suppliers, and the threat of buyers. The threat of entry depends on the existence and "height" of barriers to entry. Common barriers to entry include economies of scale, product differentiation, cost advantages independent of scale, and government regulation. The threat of rivalry depends on the number and competitiveness of firms in an industry. The threat of rivalry is high in an industry when there are large numbers of competing firms, competing firms are roughly the same size and have the same influence, growth in an industry is slow, there is no product differentiation, and productive capacity is added in large increments. The threat of substitutes depends on how close substitute products and services are—in performance and cost—to products and services in an industry. Whereas rivals all meet the same customer needs in approximately the same way, substitutes meet the same customer needs, but do so in very different ways. The threat of suppliers in an industry depends on the number and distinctiveness of the products suppliers provide to an industry. The threat of suppliers increases when a supplier's industry is dominated by a few firms, when suppliers sell unique or highly differentiated products, when suppliers are not threatened by substitutes, when suppliers threaten forward vertical integration, and when firms are not important customers for suppliers. Finally, the threat of buyers depends on the number and size of an industry's customers. The threat of buyers is greater when the number of buyers is small, products sold to buyers are undifferentiated and standard, products sold to buyers are a significant percentage of a buyer's final costs, buyers are not earning significant profits, and when buyers threaten backward vertical integration. Taken together, the level of these threats in an industry can be used to determine the expected average performance of firms in an industry.

One force in a firm's environment not included within the five forces framework is complementors. Where competitors (including rivals, new entrants, and substitutes) compete with a firm to divide profits in a market, complementors increase the total size of the market. If you are a CEO of a firm, you know that another firm is a complementor when the value of your products to your customers is higher in combination with this other firm's products than when customers use your products alone. Where firms have strong incentives to reduce the entry of competitors, they can sometimes have strong incentives to increase the entry of complementors.

The S-C-P model can also be used to develop tools for analyzing strategic opportunities in an industry. This is done by identifying generic industry structures and the strategic opportunities available in these different kinds of industries. Four common industry structures are fragmented industries, emerging industries, mature industries, and declining industries. The primary opportunity in fragmented industries is consolidation. In emerging industries, the most important opportunity is first-mover advantages from technological leadership, preemption of strategically valuable assets, or creation of customer-switching costs. In mature industries, the primary opportunities are product refinement, service, and process innovation. In declining industries, opportunities include market leadership, niche, harvest, and divestment.

Threat and opportunity analysis can be applied in an international context as well. In this context, all the five forces may be operating. However, barriers to entry are a particularly important consideration for firms contemplating international operations. In this context, barriers to entry can take one of three forms: tariffs, quotas, and other nontariff barriers. All these barriers typically have the effect of increasing the price of goods or services in a country. Finally, in international industries, opportunities include multinational, global, and transnational strategies.

CHALLENGE QUESTIONS

1. Your former college roommate calls you and asks to borrow $10,000 so that he can open a pizza restaurant in his hometown. In justifying this request, he argues that there must be significant demand for pizza and other fast food in his hometown because there are lots of such restaurants already there and three or four new ones are opening each month. He also argues that demand for convenience food will continue to increase, and he points to the large number of firms that now sell frozen dinners in grocery stores. Will you lend him the money? Why or why not?

2. According to the five forces model, one potential threat in an industry is buyers. Yet unless buyers are satisfied, they are likely to look for satisfaction elsewhere. Can the fact that buyers can be threats be reconciled with the need to satisfy buyers?

3. Government policies can have a significant impact on the average profitability of firms in an industry. Government, however, is not included as a potential threat in the five forces model. Should the model be expanded to include government (to make a "six forces" model)? Why or why not?

4. How would you add complementors to the five forces model? In particular, if an industry has large numbers of complementors, does that make it more attractive, less attractive, or does it have no impact on the industry's attractiveness? Justify your answer.

5. Opportunities analysis seems to suggest that strategic opportunities are available in almost any industry, including declining ones. If that is true, is it fair to say that there is really no such thing as an unattractive industry? If yes, what implications does this have for the five forces model? If no, describe an industry that has no opportunities.

6. Is the evolution of industry structure from an emerging industry to a mature industry to a declining industry inevitable? Why or why not?

PROBLEM SET

1. Perform a five forces analysis on the following two industries:

The Pharmaceutical Industry

The pharmaceutical industry consists of firms that develop, patent, and distribute drugs. Although this industry does not have significant production economies, it does have important economies in research and development. Product differentiation exists as well, because firms often sell branded products. Firms compete in research and development. However, once a product is developed and patented, competition is significantly reduced. Recently, the increased availability of generic, nonbranded drugs has threatened the profitability of some drug lines. Once an effective drug is developed, few, if any, alternatives to that drug usually are available. Drugs are manufactured from commodity chemicals that are available from numerous suppliers. Major customers include doctors and patients. Recently, increased costs have led the federal government and insurance companies to pressure drug companies to reduce their prices.

The Textile Industry

The textile industry consists of firms that manufacture and distribute fabrics for use in clothing, furniture, carpeting, and so forth. Several firms have invested heavily in sophisticated manufacturing technology, and many lower-cost firms located in Asia have begun fabric production. Textiles are not branded products. Recently, tariffs on some imported textiles have been implemented. The industry has numerous firms; the largest have less than 10 percent market share. Traditional fabric materials (such as cotton and wool) have recently been threatened by the development of alternative chemical-based materials (such as nylon and rayon), although many textile companies have begun manufacturing with these new materials as well. Most raw materials are widely available, although some synthetic products periodically may be in short supply. There are numerous textile customers, but textile costs are usually a large percentage of their final product's total costs. Many users shop around the world for the lowest textile prices.

2.   Perform an opportunities analysis on the following industries:

(a) Since the tragedies of 9/11, the U.S. airline industry has seen a consistent drop-off in sales. This has forced many U.S. airline companies to cut back their employment, and several—including USAir and United—have had to declare bankruptcy.

(b) The U.S. beer industry is dominated by three companies: Anheuser-Busch, the Miller Brewing Company, and Adolf Coors. In addition, the industry has several regional brewers and a large number of very small microbrewers that manufacture and sell beer in small quantities.

(c) The United States has over 3,000 property and automobile insurance companies. The largest companies, including GEICO, Progressive, Allstate, and Safeco, control less than 20 percent of the property and automobile market.

(d) Portable memory chips—sometimes worn around the neck like a necklace—may be an important substitute for floppy discs. These memory chips come in various sizes (from 64K to 256K) and range in price from $6 to $150. They plug into a computer's USB port, self-load, and act like an extra computer hard drive.

(e) In 2003, the German firm DHL acquired the U.S. firm Airborne Express to become the third largest player in the small-package delivery business—behind UPS and FedEx. Overseas shipments continue to be a growing part of this industry.

3.   For each of the following firms identify at least two competitors (rivals, new entrants, or substitutes) and two complementors.

(a) Yahoo!
(b) Microsoft
(c) Dell
(d) Boeing
(e) McDonald's

END NOTES

1. See (2003). *The big book of business quotations.* New York: Basic Books, p. 209.
2. See Weintraub, A. (2004). "Repairing the engines of life." *BusinessWeek,* May 24, 2004, pp. 99 + for a discussion of recent developments in biotechnology research and the business challenges they have created.
3. See the opening case in Chapter 1.
4. See Grow, B. (2004). "Hispanic nation." *BusinessWeek,* March 15, 2004, pp. 59 +.
5. Ibid.
6. Barnes, B. (2004). "The WB grows up." *Wall Street Journal,* July 19, 2004, pp. B1 +; money.cnn.com/2006/01/24/news/companies/cbs_warner, accessed February 2007.
7. These and other cultural differences are described in Rugman, A., and R. Hodgetts (1995). *International business.* New York: McGraw-Hill. A discussion of the dimensions along which country cultures can vary is presented in a later chapter.
8. See Deutschman, A. (2004). "Inside the mind of Jeff Bezos." *Fast Company,* August 2004, pp. 53 +; and Amazon's 2005 10-K report at www.sec.gov/Archives/edgar.
9. Early contributors to the structure-conduct-performance model include Mason, E. S. (1939). "Price and production policies of large scale enterprises." *American Economic Review,* 29, pp. 61–74; and Bain, J. S. (1956). *Barriers to new competition.* Cambridge, MA: Harvard University Press. The major developments in this framework are summarized in Bain, J. S. (1968). *Industrial organization.* New York: John Wiley & Sons, Inc.; and Scherer, F. M. (1980). *Industrial market structure and economic performance.* Boston: Houghton Mifflin. The links between this framework and work in strategic management are discussed by Porter, M. E. (1981a). "The contribution of industrial organization to strategic management." *Academy of Management Review,* 6, pp. 609–620; and Barney, J. B. (1986c). "Types of competition and the theory of strategy: Toward an integrative framework." *Academy of Management Review,* 1, pp. 791–800.
10. The five forces framework is described in detail in Porter, M. E. (1979). "How competitive forces shape strategy." *Harvard Business Review,* March–April, pp. 137–156; and Porter, M. E. (1980). *Competitive strategy.* New York: Free Press.
11. Recently, ESPN also entered the college sports cable business with the introduction of the ESPN-U channel. See http://sports.espn.go.com/espntv.
12. These barriers were originally proposed by Bain, J. S. (1968). *Industrial organization.* New York: John Wiley & Sons, Inc.; and Porter, M. E. (1980). *Competitive strategy.* New York: Free Press. It is actually possible to estimate the "height" of barriers to entry in an industry by comparing the cost of entry into an industry with barriers and the cost of entry into that industry if barriers did not exist. The difference between these costs is the "height" of the barriers to entry.
13. Another alternative would be for a firm to own and operate more than one plant. If there are economies of scope in this industry, a firm might be able to enter and earn above-normal profits. An economy of scope exists when the value of operating in two businesses simultaneously is greater than the value of operating in these two businesses separately. The concept of economy of scope is explored in more detail in Part Three of this book.

14. See Ghemawat, P., and H. J. Stander III (1992). "Nucor at a cross-roads." Harvard Business School Case No. 9-793-039.

15. See Montgomery, C. A., and B. Wernerfelt (1991). "Sources of superior performance: Market share versus industry effects in the U.S. brewing industry." *Management Science*, 37, pp. 954–959.

16. Stecklow, S. (1999). "Gallo woos French, but don't expect Bordeaux by the jug." *Wall Street Journal*, March 26, pp. A1 +.

17. See www.bustpatents.com/awards.html.

18. See www.pwc.com/images/us/eng/about/svcs/advisor for a very informative report written by PWC about patents and patent violators.

19. See Kogut, B., and U. Zander (1992). "Knowledge of the firm, combinative capabilities, and the replication of technology." *Organization Science*, 3, pp. 383–397; and Dierickx, I., and K. Cool (1989). "Asset stock accumulation and sustainability of competitive advantage." *Management Science*, 35, pp. 1504–1511. Both emphasize the importance of know-how as a barrier to entry into an industry. More generally, intangible resources are seen as particularly important sources of sustained competitive advantage. This will be discussed in more detail in Chapter 5.

20. See Polanyi, M. (1962). *Personal knowledge: Towards a post-critical philosophy*. London: Routledge & Kegan Paul; and Itami, H. (1987). *Mobilizing invisible assets*. Cambridge, MA: Harvard University Press.

21. See Henderson, R., and I. Cockburn (1994). "Measuring competence: Exploring firm effects in pharmaceutical research." *Strategic Management Journal*, 15, pp. 361–374.

22. See Scherer, F. M. (1980). *Industrial market structure and economic performance*. Boston: Houghton Mifflin.

23. See Saporito, B. (1992). "Why the price wars never end." *Fortune*, March 23, pp. 68–78; and Allen, M., and M. Siconolfi (1993). "Dell Computer drops planned share offering." *Wall Street Journal*, February 25, p. A3.

24. Chartier, John (2002). "Burger battles." CNN/Money, http://money.cnn.com, December 11.

25. See Ghemawat, P., and A. McGahan (1995). "The U.S. airline industry in 1995." Harvard Business School Case No. 9-795-113.

26. Labich, K. (1992). "Airbus takes off." *Fortune*, June 1, pp. 102–108.

27. See Pollock, E. J. (1993). "Mediation firms alter the legal landscape." *Wall Street Journal*, March 22, p. B1; Cox, M. (1993). "Electronic campus: Technology threatens to shatter the world of college textbooks." *Wall Street Journal*, June 1, p. A1; Reilly, P. M. (1993). "At a crossroads: The instant-new age leaves *Time* magazine searching for a mission." *Wall Street Journal*, May 12, p. A1; Rohwedder, C. (1993). "Europe's smaller food shops face finis." *Wall Street Journal*, May 12, p. B1; Fatsis, S. (1995). "Major leagues keep minors at a distance." *Wall Street Journal*, November 8, pp. B1 +; Norton, E., and G. Stern (1995). "Steel and aluminum vie over every ounce in a car's construction." *Wall Street Journal*, May 9, pp. A1 + Paré, T. P. (1995). "Why the banks lined up against Gates." *Fortune*, May 29, p. 18; "Hitting the mail on the head." *The Economist*, April 30, 1994, pp. 69–70; Pacelle, M. (1996). "'Big Boxes' by discounters are booming." *Wall Street Journal*, January 17, p. A2; and Pope, K., and L. Cauley (1998). "In battle for TV ads, cable is now the enemy." *Wall Street Journal*, May 6, pp. B1 +.

28. Tully, S. (1992). "How to cut those #$%* legal costs." *Fortune*, September 21, pp. 119–124.

29. Jensen, E. (1993). "Tales are oft told as TV talk shows fill up airtime." *Wall Street Journal*, May 25, p. A1; (1995). Jensen, E. "King World ponders life without Oprah." *Wall Street Journal*, September 26, p. B1.

30. See DeWitt, W. (1997). "Crown Cork & Seal/Carnaud Metalbox." Harvard Business School Case No. 9-296-019.

31. Perry, N. J. (1993). "What's next for the defense industry." *Fortune*, February 22, pp. 94–100.

32. See "Crown Cork and Seal in 1989." Harvard Business School Case No. 5-395-224.

33. See Brandenburger, A., and B. Nalebuff (1996). *Co-opetition*. New York: Doubleday.

34. This approach to studying opportunities was also first suggested in Porter, M. E. (1980). *Competitive strategy*. New York: Free Press.

35. Jacob, R. (1992). "Service Corp. International: Acquisitions done the right way." *Fortune*, November 16, p. 96.

36. Porter, M. E. (1980). *Competitive strategy*. New York: Free Press.

37. For the definitive discussion of first-mover advantages, see Lieberman, M., and C. Montgomery (1988). "First-mover advantages." *Strategic Management Journal*, 9, pp. 41–58.

38. See Ghemawat, P. (1991). *Commitment*. New York: Free Press.

39. See Gilbert, R. J., and D. M. Newbery (1982). "Preemptive patenting and the persistence of monopoly." *American Economic Review*, 72(3), pp. 514–526.

40. See Bresnahan, T. F. (1985). "Post-entry competition in the plain paper copier market." *American Economic Review*, 85, pp. 15–19, for a discussion of Xerox's patents; and Bright, A. A. (1949). *The electric lamp industry*. New York: Macmillan, for a discussion of General Electric's patents.

41. See Mansfield, E., M. Schwartz, and S. Wagner (1981). "Imitation costs and patents: An empirical study." *Economic Journal*, 91, pp. 907–918.

42. See Main, O. W. (1955). *The Canadian nickel industry*. Toronto: University of Toronto Press, for a discussion of asset preemption in the oil and gas industry; Ghemawat, P. (1986). "Wal-Mart store's discount operations." Harvard Business School Case No. 9-387-018, for Wal-Mart's preemption strategy; Schmalansee, R. (1978). "Entry deterrence in the ready-to-eat breakfast cereal industry." *Bell Journal of Economics*, 9(2), pp. 305–327; and Robinson, W. T., and C. Fornell (1985). "Sources of market pioneer advantages in consumer goods industries." *Journal of Marketing Research*, 22(3), pp. 305–307, for a discussion of preemption in the breakfast cereal industry. In this latter case, the preempted valuable asset is shelf space in grocery stores.

43. Klemperer, P. (1986). "Markets with consumer switching costs." Doctoral thesis, Graduate School of Business, Stanford University; and Wernerfelt, B. (1986). "A special case of dynamic pricing policy." *Management Science*, 32, pp. 1562–1566.

44. See Gross, N. (1995). "The technology paradox." *BusinessWeek*, March 6, pp. 691–719; Bond, R. S., and D. F. Lean (1977). *Sales, promotion, and product differentiation in two prescription drug markets*. Washington, D.C.: U.S. Federal Trade Commission; Montgomery, D. B. (1975). "New product distribution: An analysis of supermarket buyer decision." *Journal of Marketing Research*, 12, pp. 255–264; Ries, A., and J. Trout (1986). *Marketing warfare*. New York: McGraw-Hill; and Davidson, J. H. (1976). "Why most new consumer brands fail." *Harvard Business Review*, 54, March–April, pp. 117–122, for a discussion of switching costs in these industries.

45. Porter, M. E. (1980). *Competitive strategy*. New York: Free Press.

46. Gibson, R. (1991). "McDonald's insiders increase their sales of company's stock." *Wall Street Journal*, June 14, p. A1; and Chartier, John (2002). "Burger Battles." CNN/Money, http://money.cnn.com, December 11. McDonald's lost money for only one quarter. It has since repositioned itself with nice upscale fast foods and has returned to profitability.

47. Descriptions of these product refinements can be found in Demetrakakes, P. (1994). "Household-chemical makers concentrate on downsizing." *Packaging*, 39(1), p. 44; Reda, S. (1995). "Motor oil: Hands-on approach." *Stores*, 77(5), pp. 48–49; and Quinn, J. (1995). "KitchenAid." *Incentive*, 169(5), pp. 46–47.

48. Chartier, John (2002). "Burger Battles." CNN/Money, http://money.cnn.com, December 11.

49. See Hayes, R. H., and S. G. Wheelwright (1979). "The Dynamics of process-product life cycles." *Harvard Business Review*, March–April, p. 127.

50. See www.jdpowers.com.

51. See Porter, M. E. (1980). *Competitive strategy*. New York: Free Press; and Harrigan, K. R. (1980). *Strategies for declining businesses*. Lexington, MA: Lexington Books.

52. See Aguilar, F. J., J. L. Bower, and B. Gomes-Casseres (1985). "Restructuring European petrochemicals: Imperial Chemical Industries, P.L.C." Harvard Business School Case No. 9-385-203.

53. See Harrigan, K. R. (1980). *Strategies for declining businesses*. Lexington, MA: Lexington Books.

54. See Klebnikov, P. (1991). "The powerhouse." *Forbes*, September 2, pp. 46–52; and Rosenbloom, R. S., and C. Christensen (1990). "Continuous casting investments at USX corporation." Harvard Business School Case No. 9-391-121.

55. Finn, E. A. (1987). "General Eclectic." *Forbes*, March 23, pp. 74–80.

56. See Smith, L. (1993). "Can defense pain be turned to gain?" *Fortune*, February 8, pp. 84–96; Perry, N. J. (1993). "What's next for the defense industry?" *Fortune*, February 22, pp. 94–100; and Dial, J., and K. J. Murphy (1995). "Incentive, downsizing, and value creation at General Dynamics." *Journal of Financial Economics*, 37, pp. 261–314.

57. U.S. customs decided that this item should be treated as a hat and charged a compound tariff of 37.7 cents per kilogram plus 13.4 percent of the market value of these items. See Griffin, R., and M. Pustay (1999). *International business*. Reading, MA: Addison-Wesley, pp. 215–216.

58. See Tuller, L. W. (1991). *Going global: New opportunities for growing companies to compete in world markets.* Homewood, IL: Irwin. Given Japan's recent economic troubles, some of these difficulties in entering the Japanese markets seem to be going away.

59. Schlesinger, J. M. (1993). "Tough gamble: A slot-machine maker trying to sell in Japan hits countless barriers." *Wall Street Journal,* May 11, p. A1.

60. (1994). "Only here for the Biru." *The Economist,* May 14, pp. 69–70.

61. See Bartlett, C. A., and S. Ghoshal (1989). *Managing across borders: The transnational solution.* Boston: Harvard Business School Press; and

Bartlett, C., and S. Ghoshal (1993). "Beyond the M-form: Toward a managerial theory of the firm." *Strategic Management Journal,* 14, pp. 23–46

62. Blackman, A. (1990). "Moscow's Big Mac attack." *Time,* February 5, p. 51; and Bartlett, C. A., and S. Ghoshal (1989). *Managing across borders: The transnational solution.* Boston, MA: Harvard Business School Press.

63. Bartlett, C. A., and S. Ghoshal (1989). *Managing across borders: The transnational solution.* Boston, MA: Harvard Business School Press.

Evaluating a Firm's Internal Capabilities

LEARNING OBJECTIVES

After reading this chapter, you should be able to:

1. Describe the critical assumptions of the resource-based view.

2. Describe four types of resources and capabilities.

3. Apply the VRIO framework to identify the competitive implications of a firm's resources and capabilities.

4. Apply value chain analysis to identify a firm's valuable resources and capabilities.

5. Describe the kinds of resources and capabilities that are likely to be costly to imitate.

6. Describe how a firm uses its structure, formal and informal control processes, and compensation policy to exploit its resources.

7. Discuss how the decision of whether to imitate a firm with a competitive advantage affects the competitive dynamics in an industry.

8. Discuss how firms can exploit their current resources or develop new resources through their international operations.

Your Grandpa's Harley

Harley Davidson has one of the best known brands in the world. To most consumers, Harley Davidson stands for independence, freedom, rebelliousness, and toughness. Its motorcycles are big and loud, its owners fiercely loyal. This image began in the 1950s with the Marlon Brando movie *The Wild Bunch* and was reinforced in the 1960s with the movie *Easy Rider*. Even in its worst days, during the 1980s, when Harley

Davidson almost went out of business, the image of its motorcycles, built up over a period of 50 years, remained unchanged. Even today, the Harley brand still promises the biggest, baddest, loudest ride on the street.

Unfortunately, the median age of a Harley buyer in 2006 was 47. Hardly the young, rebellious youth image normally associated with Harley.

Part of Harley's challenge in addressing the youth market is the price of its motorcycles. A top-end new Harley is likely to cost over $36,000. At that price, only financially secure—that is, older—riders may be able to afford a Harley.

However, some observers think that Harley's problems are more fundamental than just price. Younger riders seem to prefer Japanese and Italian high-performance motorcycles manufactured by Honda, Suzuki, Yamaha, Kawasaki, and Ducati. These motorcycles are just the opposite of Harleys—low to the ground, lightweight, and covered by fairings that reduce wind resistance. These sports bikes have low centers of gravity, which enable their riders to scream at high speed around even the tightest corners. Riding a big, heavy, and loud Harley may feel great on long road trips on freeways, but the sports bikes will outperform the bigger bikes every time on a winding road.

So, is it time for Harley Davidson to abandon its traditional brand or at least to augment its brand by introducing its own sports motorcycles? It turns out that Harley Davidson has introduced such a motorcycle, under the brand name Buell. It hasn't sold very well. Does this mean that Harley should abandon its effort to build a sports motorcycle, or should the low sales of the Buell product line lead Harley to refocus its efforts on building new and better sports bikes?

Answering this question depends on just how powerful Harley's brand really is. As Harley contemplates its future, it will need to consider several issues. For example, although younger riders prefer to purchase sports motorcycles, by about age 35 most committed riders abandon relatively uncomfortable sports motorcycles in favor of larger, more comfortable bikes. Also, the Harley brand has international appeal. In 2006, 22.5 percent of all Harleys were sold in China and Japan. Indeed, Harley claims 26 percent of the market for heavyweight motorcycles in Japan. The Harley image is also attractive in England and Germany, as well as other European countries. Finally, the loyalty of Harley's customers is legendary. One Harley owner said it best: "You're not going to change the bike you ride when you've got its name tattooed on your shoulder." And most of those tattoos say "Harley Davidson."

Can such a powerful brand, built up over so many years, help Harley Davidson overcome its growing image as your grandfather's motorcycle company?

Source: J. Weber (2006). "Harley just keeps on cruisin'." *BusinessWeek,* November 6, pp. 71 +.

Harley Davidson has a unique resource—its brand name. The value of this resource going forward and whether or not it should try to change its position are both uncertain.

The Resource-Based View of the Firm

In Chapter 2, we saw that it was possible to take some theoretical models developed in economics—specifically the S-C-P model—and apply them to develop tools for analyzing a firm's external threats and opportunities. The same is true for analyzing a firm's internal strengths and weaknesses. However, whereas the tools described in Chapter 2 were based on the S-C-P model, the tools described in this chapter are based on the **resource-based view** of the firm, or the **RBV.** The RBV is a model of firm performance that focuses on the resources and capabilities controlled by a firm as sources of competitive advantage.[1]

What Are Resources and Capabilities?

Resources in the RBV are defined as the tangible and intangible assets that a firm controls that it can use to conceive of and implement its strategies. Examples of resources include a firm's factories (a tangible asset), its products (a tangible asset), its reputation among customers (an intangible asset), and teamwork among its managers (an intangible asset). Harley's tangible assets include its factories and distribution system. Harley's intangible assets include its brand.

Capabilities are a subset of a firm's resources and are defined as the tangible and intangible assets that enable a firm to take full advantage of the other resources it controls. That is, capabilities alone do not enable a firm to conceive of and implement its strategies, but they enable a firm to use other resources to conceive of and implement such strategies. Examples of capabilities might include a firm's marketing skills and teamwork and cooperation among its managers. At Harley, the cooperation among marketing and manufacturing to produce the "biggest, baddest, loudest" ride on the road is an example of a capability.

A firm's resources and capabilities can be classified into four broad categories: financial resources, physical resources, individual resources, and organizational resources. **Financial resources** include all the money, from whatever source, that firms use to conceive of and implement strategies. These financial resources include cash from entrepreneurs, equity holders, bondholders, and banks. **Retained earnings,** or the profit that a firm made earlier in its history and invests in itself, are also an important type of financial resource.

Physical resources include all the physical technology used in a firm. This includes a firm's plant and equipment, its geographic location, and its access to raw materials. Specific examples of plant and equipment that are part of a firm's physical resources are a firm's computer hardware and software technology, robots used in manufacturing, and automated warehouses. Geographic location, as a type of physical resource, is important for firms as diverse as Wal-Mart (with its operations in rural markets generating, on average, higher returns than its operations in more competitive urban markets) and L. L. Bean (a catalogue retail firm that believes that its rural Maine location helps its employees identify with the outdoor lifestyle of many of its customers).[2]

Human resources include the training, experience, judgment, intelligence, relationships, and insight of *individual* managers and workers in a firm.[3] The importance of the human resources of well-known entrepreneurs such as Bill Gates (Microsoft) and Steve Jobs (currently at Apple) is broadly understood.

However, valuable human resources are not limited to just entrepreneurs or senior managers. Each employee at a firm like Southwest Airlines is seen as essential for the overall success of the firm. Whether it is the willingness of the gate agent to joke with the harried traveler, or a baggage handler hustling to get a passenger's bag into a plane, or even a pilot's decision to fly in a way that saves fuel—all of these human resources are part of the resource base that has enabled Southwest to gain competitive advantages in the very competitive U.S. airline industry.[4]

Whereas human resources are an attribute of single individuals, **organizational resources** are an attribute of groups of individuals. Organizational resources include a firm's formal reporting structure; its formal and informal planning, controlling, and coordinating systems; its culture and reputation; as well as informal relations among groups within a firm and between a firm and those in its environment. At Southwest Airlines, relationships among individual resources are an important organizational resource. For example, it is not unusual to see the pilots at Southwest helping to load the bags on an airplane to ensure that the plane leaves on time. This kind of cooperation and dedication shows up in an intense loyalty between Southwest employees and the firm—a loyalty that manifests itself in low employee turnover and high employee productivity, even though over 80 percent of Southwest's employees are unionized.

Critical Assumptions of the Resource-Based View

The RBV rests on two fundamental assumptions about the resources and capabilities that firms may control. First, different firms may possess different bundles of resources and capabilities, even if they are competing in the same industry. This is the assumption of firm **resource heterogeneity**. Resource heterogeneity implies that for a given business activity, some firms may be more skilled in accomplishing this activity than other firms. In manufacturing, for example, Toyota continues to be more skilled than, say, General Motors. In product design, Apple continues to be more skilled than, say, IBM. In motorcycles, Harley Davidson's reputation for big, bad, and loud rides separates it from its competitors.

Second, some of these resource and capability differences among firms may be long lasting, because it may be very costly for firms without certain resources and capabilities to develop or acquire them. This is the assumption of **resource immobility**. For example, Toyota has had its advantage in manufacturing for at least 30 years. Apple has had product design advantages over IBM since Apple was founded in the 1980s. And Harley has been able to retain its brand reputation for at least 50 years! It is not that GM, IBM, and Harley's competitors are unaware of their disadvantages. Indeed, some of these firms—notably GM and IBM—have made progress in addressing their disadvantages. However, despite these efforts, Toyota, Apple, and Harley continue to enjoy advantages over their competition.

Taken together, these two assumptions make it possible to explain why some firms outperform other firms, even if these firms are all competing in the same industry. If a firm possesses valuable resources and capabilities that few other firms possess, and if these other firms find it too costly to imitate these resources and capabilities, the firm that possesses these tangible and intangible assets can gain a sustained competitive advantage. The economic logic that underlies the RBV is described in more detail in the Strategy in Depth feature.

Strategy in Depth

The theoretical roots of the resource-based view can be traced to research done by David Ricardo in 1817. Interestingly, Ricardo was not even studying the profitability of firms; he was interested in the economic consequences of owning more or less fertile farm land.

Unlike many other inputs into the production process, the total supply of land is relatively fixed and cannot be significantly increased in response to higher demand and prices. Such inputs are said to be **inelastic in supply**, because their quantity of supply is fixed and does not respond to price increases. In these settings, it is possible for those who own higher-quality inputs to gain competitive advantages.

Ricardo's argument concerning land as a productive input is summarized in Figure 3.1. Imagine that there are many parcels of land suitable for growing wheat. Also, suppose that the fertility of these different parcels varies from high fertility (low costs of production) to low fertility (high costs of production). It seems obvious that when the market price for wheat is low, it will only pay farmers with the most fertile land to grow wheat. Only these farmers will have costs low enough to make money when the market price for wheat is low. As the mar-

Ricardian Economics and the Resource-Based View

ket price for wheat increases, then farmers with progressively less fertile land will be able to use it to grow wheat. These observations lead to the market supply curve in panel A of Figure 3.1: As prices (P) go up, supply (S) also goes up. At some point on this supply curve, supply will equal demand (D). This point determines the market price for wheat, given supply and demand. This price is called P^* in the figure.

Now consider the situation facing two different kinds of farmers. Ricardo assumed that both these farmers follow traditional economic

logic by producing a quantity (q) such that their marginal cost (MC) equals their marginal revenue (MR); that is, they produce enough wheat so that the cost of producing the last bushel of wheat equals the revenue they will get from selling that last bushel. However, this decision for the farm with less fertile land (in panel B of the figure) generates revenues that exactly equal the average total cost (ATC) of the only capital this farmer is assumed to employ, the cost of his land. In contrast, the farmer with more fertile land (in panel C of the figure) has an average total cost (ATC) less than the market-determined price, and thus is able to earn an above-normal economic profit. This is because at the market-determined price, P^*, MC equals ATC for the farmer with less fertile land, whereas MC is greater than ATC for the farmer with more fertile land.

In traditional economic analysis, the profit earned by the farmer with more fertile land should lead other farmers to enter into this market; that is, to obtain some land and produce wheat. However, all the land that can be used to produce wheat in a way that generates at least a normal return given the market price P^* is already in production. In particular, no more very fertile land is available, and fertile

The VRIO Framework

Armed with the RBV, it is possible to develop a set of tools for analyzing all the different resources and capabilities a firm might possess and the potential of each of these to generate competitive advantages. In this way, it will be possible to identify a firm's internal strengths and its internal weaknesses. The primary tool for accomplishing this internal analysis is called the VRIO framework.[5] The acronym, *VRIO* in **VRIO framework** stands for four questions one must ask about a resource or capability to determine its competitive potential: the question of

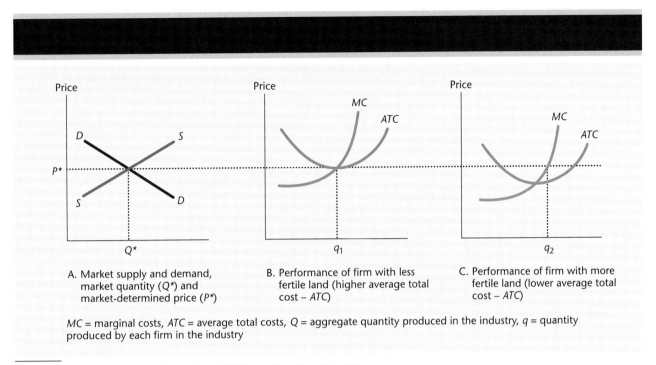

A. Market supply and demand, market quantity (Q*) and market-determined price (P*)

B. Performance of firm with less fertile land (higher average total cost – ATC)

C. Performance of firm with more fertile land (lower average total cost – ATC)

MC = marginal costs, ATC = average total costs, Q = aggregate quantity produced in the industry, q = quantity produced by each firm in the industry

Figure 3.1   The Economics of Land with Different Levels of Fertility

land (by assumption) cannot be created. This is what is meant by land being inelastic in supply. Thus, the farmer with more fertile land and lower production costs has a sustained competitive advantage over those farmers with less fertile land and higher production costs. Therefore, the farmer with the more fertile land is able to earn an above-normal economic profit.

Of course, at least two events can threaten this sustained competitive advantage. First, market demand may shift down and to the left. This would force farmers with less fertile land to cease production and would also reduce the profit of those with more fertile land. If demand shifted far enough, this profit might disappear altogether.

Second, farmers with less fertile land may discover low-cost ways of increasing their land's fertility, thereby reducing the competitive advantage of farmers with more fertile land. For example, farmers with less fertile land may be able to use inexpensive fertilizers to increase their land's fertility. The existence of such low-cost fertilizers suggests that although *land* may be in fixed supply, *fertility* may not be. If enough farmers can increase the fertility of their land, then the profits originally earned by the farmers with the more fertile land will disappear.

Of course, what the RBV does is recognize that land is not the only productive input that is inelastic in supply, and that farmers are not the only firms that benefit from having such resources at their disposal.

Source: D. Ricardo (1817). *Principles of political economy and taxation.* London: J. Murray.

Value, the question of **R**arity, the question of **I**mitability, and the question of **O**rganization. These four questions are summarized in Table 3.1.

The Question of Value

The **question of value** is: "Do resources and capabilities enable a firm to exploit an external opportunity or neutralize an external threat?" If a firm answers this question with a "yes," then its resources and capabilities are valuable and can be considered *strengths*. If a firm answers this question with a "no," its resources and

Table 3.1   **Questions Needed to Conduct a Resource-Based Analysis of a Firm's Internal Strengths and Weaknesses**

1. *The Question of Value.* Does a resource enable a firm to exploit an environmental opportunity and/or neutralize an environmental threat?
2. *The Question of Rarity.* Is a resource currently controlled by only a small number of competing firms?
3. *The Question of Imitability.* Do firms without a resource face a cost disadvantage in obtaining or developing it?
4. *The Question of Organization.* Are a firm's other policies and procedures organized to support the exploitation of its valuable, rare, and costly-to-imitate resources?

capabilities are *weaknesses*. There is nothing inherently valuable about a firm's resources and capabilities. Rather, they are only valuable to the extent that they enable a firm to enhance its competitive position. Sometimes, the same resources and capabilities can be strengths in one market and weaknesses in another. The Global Perspectives feature discusses this issue in more detail.

Valuable Resources and Firm Performance

Sometimes it is difficult to know for sure whether a firm's resources and capabilities really enable it to exploit its external opportunities or neutralize its external threats. Sometimes this requires detailed operational information that may not be readily available. Other times, the full impact of a firm's resources and capabilities on its external opportunities and threats may not be known for some time.

One way to track the impact of a firm's resources and capabilities on its opportunities and threats is to examine the impact of using these resources and capabilities on a firm's revenues and costs. In general, firms that use their resources and capabilities to exploit opportunities or neutralize threats will see an increase in their net revenues, or a decrease in their net costs, or both, compared to the situation in which they were not using these resources and capabilities to exploit opportunities or neutralize threats. That is, the value of these resources and capabilities will generally manifest itself in either higher revenues or lower costs or both, once a firm starts using them to exploit opportunities or neutralize threats.

Applying the Question of Value

For many firms, the answer to the question of value has been "yes." That is, many firms have resources and capabilities that are used to exploit opportunities and neutralize threats, and the use of these resources and capabilities enables these firms to increase their net revenues or decrease their net costs. For example, Sony has a great deal of experience in designing, manufacturing, and selling miniaturized electronic technology. Sony has used these resources and capabilities to exploit opportunities, including video games, digital cameras, computers and peripherals, handheld computers, home video and audio, portable audio, and car audio. 3M has used its resources and capabilities in substrates, coatings, and adhesives, along with an organizational culture that rewards risk-taking and creativity, to exploit opportunities in office products, including invisible tape and Post-It notes. Sony's and 3M's resources and capabilities—including their specific technological skills and their creative organizational cultures—have made it possible for these firms to respond to, and even create, new opportunities.[6]

Global Perspectives

Despite the best efforts of American college students, beer consumption in the United States is no longer increasing. In an effort to expand their sales, both Anheuser-Busch and Miller Brewing are trying to enter the European market. Unfortunately, many Europeans do not like American beer. They consider it to be "watered-down" and "tasteless." None of this was helped when these two powerhouse U.S. firms first introduced their "light" beers to Europe. Unfortunately, "light beer" in Europe means "low-alcohol-content beer," and sales of Bud Light and Miller Light never met expectations. Indeed, Miller changed the name of its light beer in Europe to Miller Pilsner. Pilsner beer is a category of lighter-bodied beer.

In an effort to grow their sales and overcome the perception that American beers are "lightweight," Anheuser-Busch and Miller are adopting very different strategies. Anheuser-Busch is actually playing up its American roots. It uses the same commercials in Europe as it does in the United States. The American eagle remains prominently displayed on the Budweiser can, and the Clydesdales still pull the old-fashioned beer wagon in some Budweiser ads. In 2006, Anheuser-Busch finally received permission to use the "Bud" name on its products throughout Europe after a several-year struggle with Czech brewery Budějovický Budvar, which also claimed this brand name.

Does It Pay to Be an American Beer in Europe?

Anheuser-Busch is also signing up European sports stars as spokespersons for Budweiser. Budweiser was the official beer of the 2006 Olympics in Torino, Italy, and at the 2006 FIFA World Cup, and Anheuser-Busch recently locked up sponsorship of the 2010 and 2014 FIFA World Cups.

Anheuser-Busch hopes that the European fascination with U.S. brands—including McDonald's Big Mac—will ultimately transfer to its products and offset current tensions between the United States and Europe regarding the Iraq War.

In Europe, Budweiser is priced as an expensive import beer. Its market share in the United Kingdom—a critical, but very mature beer-drinking market—increased from 2.7 percent in 2000 to only 3 percent in 2005.

In contrast, Miller downplays its American roots. Indeed, Miller is trying to be viewed as just another European beer company with an upscale product. For example, to serve the Russian market, Miller opened a Russian brewery just 84 miles from Moscow. Also, rather than using U.S.–based ads, Miller has developed a European ad campaign that markets its beer as part of a new, hipper lifestyle that is distinctly European, not made-over American. Miller's sales in Russia increased by 70 percent from 2002 to 2003, at a time when the overall market for upscale beers in that country increased by only 30 percent. In 2006, Miller had only 5 percent of the Russian market, but 15 percent of the profits in that market. Miller is looking to repeat that success in other European countries, especially in Eastern Europe.

So, is being an American beer a valuable resource or not? As suggested in the text, a resource is not inherently valuable or not valuable. It depends on the specific market demand for that resource. In the United States, being an American beer can be a valuable resource, but it may turn out to be less valuable in Europe.

Sources: J. Barney (2001). "Is the resource-based 'view' a useful perspective for strategic management research? Yes." *Academy of Management Review*, 26, pp. 41–56; D. Bilefsky and C. Lawton (2004). "In Europe, marketing beer as 'American' may not be a plus." *Wall Street Journal*, July 21, pp. B1+; http://news.moneycontrol.msn.com; [accessed] February 2007 www.cee-foodindustry.com; Anheuser-Busch Annual Report, 2005.

Unfortunately, for other firms the answer to the question of value appears to be "no." The merger of AOL and Time Warner was supposed create a new kind of entertainment and media company; it is now widely recognized that Time Warner has been unable to marshal the resources necessary to create economic value. Time Warner wrote-off $90 billion in value in 2002; its stock price has been at

Strategy in the Emerging Enterprise

*E*ntrepreneurial firms, like all other firms, must be able to answer "yes" to the question of value. That is, decisions by entrepreneurs to organize a firm to exploit an opportunity must increase revenues or reduce costs beyond what would be the case if they did not choose to organize a firm to exploit an opportunity.

However, entrepreneurs often find it difficult to answer the question of value before they actually organize a firm and try to exploit an opportunity. This is because the impact of exploiting an opportunity on a firm's revenues and costs often cannot be known, with certainty, before that opportunity is exploited.

Despite these challenges, entrepreneurs often are required to not only estimate the value of any opportunities they are thinking about exploiting, but to do so in some detail and in a written form. Projections about how organizing a firm to exploit an opportunity will affect a firm's revenues and costs are often the centerpiece of an entrepreneur's **business plan**—a document that summarizes how an entrepreneur will organize a firm to exploit an opportunity, along with the economic implications of exploiting that opportunity.

Two schools of thought exist as to the value of entrepreneurs writing business plans. On the one hand, some authors argue that writing a business plan is likely to be helpful for entrepreneurs, because it forces them to be explicit about their assumptions, exposes those assumptions to others

Are Business Plans Good for Entrepreneurs?

for critique and analysis, and helps entrepreneurs focus their efforts on building a new organization and exploiting an opportunity. On the other hand, other authors argue that writing a business plan may actually hurt an entrepreneur's performance, because writing such a plan may divert an entrepreneur's attention from more important activities, may give entrepreneurs the illusion that they have more control of their business than they actually do, and may lead to decision-making errors.

Research supports both points of view. Scott Shane and Frederic Delmar have shown that writing a business plan significantly enhances the probability that an entrepreneurial firm will survive. In contrast, Amar Bhide shows that most entrepreneurs go through

many different business plans before they land on one that describes a business opportunity that they actually support. For Bhide, writing the business plan is, at best, a means of helping to create a new opportunity. Because most business plans are abandoned soon after they are written, writing business plans has limited value.

One way to resolve the conflicts among these scholars is to accept that writing a business plan may be very useful in some settings and not so useful in others. In particular, when it is possible for entrepreneurs to collect sufficient information about a potential market opportunity so as to be able to describe the probability of different outcomes associated with exploiting that opportunity—a setting described as *risky* in the entrepreneurship literature—business planning can be very helpful. However, when such information cannot be collected—a setting described as *uncertain* in the entrepreneurship literature—then writing a business plan would be of only limited value, and its disadvantages might outweigh any advantages it might create.

Sources: S. Shane and F. Delmar (2004). "Planning for the market: Business planning before marketing and the continuation of organizing efforts." *Journal of Business Venturing*, 19, pp. 767–785; A. Bhide (2000). *The origin and evolution of new businesses.* New York: Oxford; R. H. Knight. (1921). *Risk, uncertainty, and profit.* Chicago: University of Chicago Press; S. Alvarez and J. Barney. (2006). "Discovery and creation: Alternative theories in the field of entrepreneurship." Unpublished paper, Entrepreneurship Center, Fisher College of Business, The Ohio State University.

record lows, and there have been rumors that it will be broken up. Ironically, many of the segments of this diverse media conglomerate continue to create value. However, the company as a whole has not realized the synergies that it was expected to generate when it was created. Put differently, these synergies—as resources and capabilities—are apparently not valuable.[7]

Using Value-Chain Analysis to Identify Potentially Valuable Resources and Capabilities

One way to identify potentially valuable resources and capabilities controlled by a firm is to study that firm's value chain. A firm's **value chain** is the set of business activities in which it engages to develop, produce, and market its products or services. Each step in a firm's value chain requires the application and integration of different resources and capabilities. Because different firms may make different choices about which value-chain activities they will engage in, they can end up developing different sets of resources and capabilities. This can be the case even if these firms are all operating in the same industry. These choices can have implications for a firm's strategies, and, as described in the Ethics and Strategy feature, they can also have implications for society more generally.

Consider, for example, the oil industry. Figure 3.2 provides a simplified list of all the business activities that must be completed if crude oil is to be turned into consumer products, such as gasoline. These activities include exploring for crude oil, drilling for crude oil, pumping crude oil, shipping crude oil, buying crude oil, refining crude oil, selling refined products to distributors, shipping refined products, and selling refined products to final customers.

Different firms may make different choices about which of these stages in the oil industry they want to operate. Thus, the firms in the oil industry may have very different resources and capabilities. For example, exploring for crude oil is very expensive and requires substantial financial resources. It also requires access to land (a physical resource), the application of substantial scientific and technical knowledge (individual resources), and an organizational commitment to risk-taking and exploration (organizational resources). Firms that operate in this stage of the oil business are likely to have very different resources and capabilities than those that, for example, sell refined oil products to final customers. To be successful in the retail stage of this industry, a firm needs retail outlets (such as stores and gas stations), which are costly to build and require both financial and physical resources. These outlets, in turn, need to be staffed by

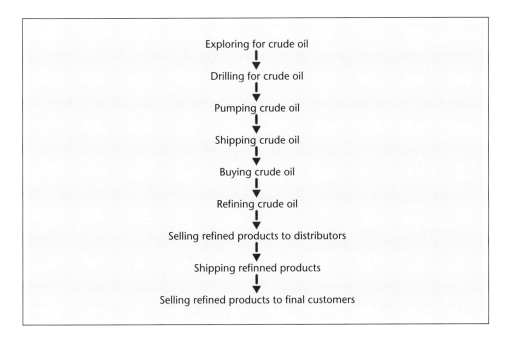

Figure 3.2 A Simplified Value Chain of Activities of Oil-Based Refined Products such as Gasoline and Motor Oil

Ethics and Strategy

Strategic management adopts the perspective of a firm's owners in discussing how to gain and sustain competitive advantages. Even when adopting a stakeholder perspective (see the Ethics and Strategy feature in Chapter 1), how a firm can improve its performance and increase the wealth of its owners still takes center stage.

However, an exclusive focus on the performance of a firm and the wealth of its owners can sometimes have broader effects—on society and on the environment—that are not fully recognized. Economists call these broader effects "externalities," because they are external to the core issue in economics and strategic management of how firms can maximize their performance. They are external to this issue because firms generally do not bear the full costs of the externalities their profit-maximizing behavior creates.

Externalities can take many forms. The most obvious of these has to do with pollution and the environment. If, for example, in the process of maximizing its performance a firm engages in activities that pollute the environment, the impact of that pollution is an externality. Such pollution reduces our quality of life and hurts the environment, but the firm creating this pollution often does not bear the full costs of doing so.

Other externalities have to do with a firm's impact on the public's health. For example, when tobacco companies maximize their profits by selling tobacco to children, they are also creating a public health externality. Getting children hooked on tobacco early on might be good for the bottom line of a tobacco com-

Externalities and the Broader Consequences of Profit Maximization

pany, but it increases the chances of these children developing lung cancer, emphysema, heart disease, and the other ailments associated with tobacco. Obviously, these individuals absorb most of the adverse consequences of these diseases, but society suffers as well from the high health care costs that are engendered.

Put differently, while adopting a simple profit-maximizing perspective in choosing and implementing strategies can have positive impacts for a firm, its owners, and its stakeholders, it can also have negative consequences for society as a whole. Two broad solutions to this problem of externalities have been proposed. First, governments can take on the responsibility of directly monitoring and regulating the behavior of firms in areas where these kinds of externalities are likely to develop. Second, governments can use lawsuits and regulations to ensure that firms directly bear more of the

costs of any externalities their behavior might generate. Once these externalities are "internalized," it is then a matter of self-interest for firms not to engage in activities that generate negative externalities.

Consumers can sometimes also help internalize the externalities generated by a firm's behavior by adjusting their consumption patterns to buy products or services only from companies that do not generate negative externalities. Consumers can even be more proactive and let firms know which of the their strategies are particularly troubling. For example, many consumers united to boycott firms with operations in South Africa when South Africa was still implementing a policy of apartheid. Ultimately, this pressure not only changed the strategies of many firms; it also helped change South Africa's domestic policies. More recently, consumer pressures on pharmaceutical companies forced these firms to make their AIDS drugs more accessible in less developed countries in Africa; similar pressures forced Nike to adjust the wages and working conditions of the individuals who manufacture Nike's shoes. To the extent that sufficient demand for "socially responsible firms" exists in the marketplace, it may make profit-maximizing sense for a firm to engage in socially responsible behavior by reducing the extent to which its actions generate negative externalities.

Sources: "AIDS in Africa." *British Medical Journal,* June 1, p. 456; J. S. Friedman (2003). "Paying for apartheid." *Nation,* June 6, pp. 7 +; L. Lee (2000). "Can Nike still do it?" *BusinessWeek,* February 21, pp. 121 +.

salespeople—individual resources—and marketing these products to customers through advertisements and other means can require a commitment to creativity—an organizational resource.

However, even firms that operate in the same set of value-chain activities in an industry may approach these activities very differently, and therefore may develop very different resources and capabilities associated with these activities. For example, two firms may sell refined oil products to final customers. However, one of these firms may sell only through retail outlets it owns whereas the second may sell only through retail outlets it does not own. The first firm's financial and physical resources are likely to be very different from the second firm's, although these two firms may have similar individual and organizational resources.

Studying a firm's value chain forces us to think about firm resources and capabilities in a disaggregated way. Although it is possible to characterize a firm's resources and capabilities more broadly, it is usually more helpful to think about how each of the activities a firm engages in affects its financial, physical, individual, and organizational resources. With this understanding, it is possible to begin to recognize potential sources of competitive advantage for a firm in a much more detailed way.

Because this type of analysis can be so helpful in identifying the financial, physical, individual, and organizational resources and capabilities controlled by a firm, several generic value chains for identifying them have been developed. The first, proposed by the management-consulting firm McKinsey and Company, is presented in Figure 3.3.[8] This relatively simple model suggests that the creation of value almost always involves six distinct activities: technology development, product design, manufacturing, marketing, distribution, and service. Firms can develop distinctive capabilities in any one or any combination of these activities.

Michael E. Porter has developed a second generic value chain.[9] This value chain, presented in Figure 3.4, divides value-creating activities into two large categories: primary activities and support activities. Primary activities include inbound logistics (purchasing, inventory, and so forth), production, outbound logistics (warehousing and distribution), sales and marketing, and service (dealer support and customer service). Support activities include infrastructure (planning, finance, information services, legal), technology development (research and development, product design), and human resource management and development. Primary activities are directly associated with the manufacture and distribution of a product. Support activities assist a firm in accomplishing its primary activities. As with the McKinsey value chain, a firm can develop strengths or

Figure 3.3 The Generic Value Chain Developed by McKinsey and Company

Technology development	Product design	Manufacturing	Marketing	Distribution	Service
Source Sophistication Patents Product/process choices	Function Physical characteristics Aesthetics Quality	Integration Raw materials Capacity Location Procurement Parts production Assembly	Prices Advertising/ promotion Sales force Package Brand	Channels Integration Inventory Warehousing Transport	Warranty Speed Captive/independent Prices

Figure 3.4 The Generic
Value Chain Developed
by Porter

Sources: Reprinted with permis-
sion of The Free Press, a Division
of Simon and Schuster Adult
Publishing Group, from
Competitive Advantage: *Creating and
Sustaining Superior Performance*
by Michael E. Porter.
Copyright ©1985, 1998 by Michael
E. Porter. All rights reserved.

weaknesses in any one or in any combination of the activities listed in Porter's value chain. These activities, and how they are linked to one another, point to the kinds of resources and capabilities a firm is likely to have developed.

The Question of Rarity

Understanding the value of a firm's resources and capabilities is an important first consideration in understanding a firm's internal strengths and weaknesses. However, if a particular resource or capability is controlled by numerous competing firms, then that resource is unlikely to be a source of competitive advantage for any one of them. Instead, valuable but common (i.e., not rare) resources and capabilities are sources of competitive parity. Only when a resource is not controlled by numerous other firms is it likely to be a source of competitive advantage. These observations lead to the **question of rarity**: "How many competing firms already possess particular valuable resources and capabilities?"

Consider, for example, competition among television sports channels. All the major networks broadcast sports. In addition, several sports-only cable channels are available, including the best-known all-sports channel, ESPN. Several years ago, ESPN began televising what were then called alternative sports—skateboarding, snowboarding, mountain biking, and so forth. The surprising popularity of these programs led ESPN to package them into an annual competition called the "X-Games." "X" stands for "extreme," and ESPN has definitely gone to the extreme in including sports in the X-Games. The X-Games now include sports such as sky-surfing, competitive high diving, competitive bungee cord jumping, and so forth. ESPN broadcasts both a summer X-Games and a winter X-Games. No other sports outlet has yet made such a commitment to so-called extreme sports, and it has paid handsome dividends for ESPN—extreme sports have very low-cost broadcast rights and draw a fairly large audience. This commitment to extreme sports has been a source of at least a temporary competitive advantage for ESPN.

Of course, not all of a firm's resources and capabilities have to be valuable and rare. Indeed, most firms have a resource base that is composed primarily of valuable but common resources and capabilities. These resources cannot be sources of even temporary competitive advantage, but are essential if a firm is to gain competitive parity. Under conditions of competitive parity, although no one firm gains a competitive advantage, firms do increase their probability of survival.

Consider, for example, a telephone system as a resource or capability. Because telephone systems are widely available, and because virtually all organizations have access to telephone systems, these systems are not rare, and thus are not a source of competitive advantage. However, firms that do not possess a telephone system are likely to give their competitors an important advantage and place themselves at a competitive disadvantage.

How rare a valuable resource or capability must be in order to have the potential for generating a competitive advantage varies from situation to situation. It is not difficult to see that if a firm's valuable resources and capabilities are absolutely unique among a set of current and potential competitors, they can generate a competitive advantage. However, it may be possible for a small number of firms in an industry to possess a particular valuable resource or capability and still obtain a competitive advantage. In general, as long as the number of firms that possess a particular valuable resource or capability is less than the number of firms needed to generate perfect competition dynamics in an industry, that resource or capability can be considered rare and a potential source of competitive advantage.

The Question of Imitability

Firms with valuable and rare resources are often strategic innovators, because they are able to conceive of and engage in strategies that other firms cannot because they lack the relevant resources and capabilities. These firms may gain the first-mover advantages discussed in Chapter 2.

Valuable and rare organizational resources, however, can be sources of sustained competitive advantage only if firms that do not possess them face a cost disadvantage in obtaining or developing them, compared to firms that already possess them. These kinds of resources are **imperfectly imitable**.[10] These observations lead to the **question of imitability**: "Do firms without a resource or capability face a cost disadvantage in obtaining or developing it compared to firms that already possess it?"

Imagine an industry with five essentially identical firms. Each of these firms manufactures the same products, uses the same raw materials, and sells the products to the same customers through the same distribution channels. It is not hard to see that firms in this kind of industry will have normal economic performance. Now, suppose that one of these firms, for whatever reason, discovers or develops a heretofore unrecognized valuable resource and uses that resource either to exploit an external opportunity or to neutralize an external threat. Obviously, this firm will gain a competitive advantage over the others.

This firm's competitors can respond to this competitive advantage in at least two ways. First, they can ignore the success of this one firm and continue as before. This action, of course, will put them at a competitive disadvantage. Second, these firms can attempt to understand why this one firm is able to be successful and then duplicate its resources to implement a similar strategy. If competitors have no cost disadvantages in acquiring or developing the needed resources, then this imitative approach will generate competitive parity in the industry.

Sometimes, however, for reasons that will be discussed later, competing firms may face an important cost disadvantage in duplicating a successful firm's valuable resources. If this is the case, this one innovative firm may gain a **sustained competitive advantage**—an advantage that is not competed away through strategic imitation. Firms that possess and exploit costly-to-imitate, rare, and valuable resources in choosing and implementing their strategies may enjoy a period of sustained competitive advantage.[11]

For example, other sports networks have observed the success of ESPN's X-Games and are beginning to broadcast similar competitions. NBC, for example, has developed its own version of the X-Games, called the "Gravity Games," and even the Olympics now includes sports that were previously perceived as being "too extreme" for this mainline sports competition. Several Fox sports channels broadcast programs that feature extreme sports, and at least one new cable channel (Fuel) broadcasts only extreme sports. Whether these efforts will be able to attract the competitors that the X-Games attract, whether winners at these other competitions will gain as much status in their sports as do winners of the X-Games, and whether these other competitions and programs will gain the reputation among viewers enjoyed by ESPN will go a long way to determining whether ESPN's competitive advantage in extreme sports is temporary or sustained.[12]

Forms of Imitation: Direct Duplication and Substitution

In general, imitation occurs in one of two ways: **direct duplication** or **substitution**. Imitating firms can attempt to directly duplicate the resources possessed by the firm with a competitive advantage. Thus, NBC sponsoring an alternative extreme games competition can be thought of as an effort to directly duplicate the resources that enabled ESPN's X-Games to be successful. If the cost of this direct duplication is too high, then a firm with these resources and capabilities may obtain a sustained competitive advantage. If this cost is not too high, then any competitive advantages in this setting will be temporary.

Imitating firms can also attempt to substitute other resources for a costly to imitate resource possessed by a firm with a competitive advantage. Extreme sports shows and an extreme sports cable channel are potential substitutes for ESPN's X-Games strategy. These shows appeal to much the same audience as the X-Games, but they do not require the same resources as an X-Games strategy requires (i.e., because they are not competitions, they do not require the network to bring together a large number of athletes all at once). If substitute resources exist, and if imitating firms do not face a cost disadvantage in obtaining them, then the competitive advantage of other firms will be temporary. However, if these resources have no substitutes, or if the cost of acquiring these substitutes is greater than the cost of obtaining the original resources, then competitive advantages can be sustained.

Why Might It Be Costly to Imitate Another Firm's Resources or Capabilities?

A number of authors have studied why it might be costly for one firm to imitate the resources and capabilities of another. Four sources of costly imitation have been noted.[13] They are summarized in Table 3.2 and discussed below.

Unique Historical Conditions.   It may be the case that a firm was able to acquire or develop its resources and capabilities in a low-cost manner because of its unique historical conditions. The ability of firms to acquire, develop, and use resources often depends on their place in time and space. Once time and history pass, firms that do not have space-and-time-dependent resources face a significant cost disadvantage in obtaining and developing them, because doing so would require them to re-create history.[14]

ESPN's early commitment to extreme sports is an example of these unique historical conditions. The status and reputation of the X-Games was created

Table 3.2   **Sources of Costly Imitation**

Unique Historical Conditions. When a firm gains low-cost access to resources because of its place in time and space, other firms may find these resources to be costly to imitate. Both first-mover advantages and path dependence can create unique historical conditions.

Causal Ambiguity. When competitors cannot tell, for sure, what enables a firm to gain an advantage, that advantage may be costly to imitate. Sources of causal ambiguity include when competitive advantages are based on "taken-for-granted" resources and capabilities, when multiple nontestable hypotheses exist about why a firm has a competitive advantage, and when a firm's advantages are based on complex sets of interrelated capabilities.

Social Complexity. When the resources and capabilities a firm uses to gain a competitive advantage involve interpersonal relationships, trust, culture, and other social resources that are costly to imitate in the short term.

Patents. Only a source of sustained competitive advantage in a few industries, including pharmaceuticals and specialty chemicals.

because ESPN happened to be the first major sports outlet that took these competitions seriously. The X-Games became the most important competition in many of these extreme sports. Indeed, for snowboarders, winning a gold medal in the X-Games is almost as important—if not more important—as winning a gold medal in the Winter Olympics. Other sports outlets that hope to be able to compete with the X-Games will have to overcome both the status of ESPN as "the worldwide leader in sports" and its historical advantage in extreme sports. Overcoming these advantages is likely to be very costly, making competitive threats from direct duplication, at least, less significant.

Of course, firms can also act to increase the costliness of imitating the resources and capabilities they control. ESPN is doing this by expanding its coverage of extreme sports and by engaging in a "grassroots" marketing campaign that engages young "extreme athletes" in local competitions. The purpose of these efforts is clear: to keep ESPN's status as the most important source of extreme sports competitions intact.[15]

Unique historical circumstances can give a firm a sustained competitive advantage in at least two ways. First, it may be that a particular firm was the first in an industry to recognize and exploit an opportunity, and being first gave the firm one or more of the first-mover advantages discussed in Chapter 2. Thus, although in principle other firms in an industry could have exploited an opportunity, that only one firm did so makes it more costly for other firms to imitate the original firm.

A second way that history can have an impact on a firm builds on the concept of **path dependence**.[16] A process is said to be path dependent when events early in the evolution of a process have significant effects on subsequent events. In the evolution of competitive advantage, path dependence suggests that a firm may gain a competitive advantage in the current period based on the acquisition and development of resources in earlier periods. In these earlier periods, it is often not clear what the full future value of particular resources will be. Because of this uncertainty, firms are able to acquire or develop these resources for less than what will turn out to be their full value. However, once the full value of these resources is revealed, other firms seeking to acquire or develop these resources will need to pay their full known value, which (in general) will be greater than the costs incurred by the firm that acquired or developed these resources in some earlier period. The cost of acquiring both duplicate and substitute resources would rise once their full value became known.

Consider, for example, a firm that purchased land for ranching some time ago and discovered a rich supply of oil on this land in the current period. The difference between the value of this land as a supplier of oil (high) and the value of this land for ranching (low) is a source of competitive advantage for this firm. Moreover, other firms attempting to acquire this or adjacent land will now have to pay for the full value of the land in its use as a supply of oil (high), and thus will be at a cost disadvantage compared to the firm that acquired it some time ago for ranching.

Causal Ambiguity.   A second reason why a firm's resources and capabilities may be costly to imitate is that imitating firms may not understand the relationship between the resources and capabilities controlled by a firm and that firm's competitive advantage. In other words, the relationship between firm resources and capabilities and competitive advantage may be **causally ambiguous**.

At first, it seems unlikely that causal ambiguity about the sources of competitive advantage for a firm would ever exist. Managers in a firm seem likely to understand the sources of their own competitive advantage. If managers in one firm understand the relationship between resources and competitive advantage, then it seems likely that managers in other firms would also be able to discover these relationships and thus would have a clear understanding of which resources and capabilities they should duplicate or seek substitutes for. If there are no other sources of cost disadvantage for imitating firms, imitation should lead to competitive parity and normal economic performance.[17]

However, it is not always the case that managers in a particular firm will fully understand the relationship between the resources and capabilities they control and competitive advantage. This lack of understanding could occur for at least three reasons. First, it may be that the resources and capabilities that generate competitive advantage are so taken for granted, so much a part of the day-to-day experience of managers in a firm, that these managers are unaware of them.[18] Organizational resources and capabilities such as teamwork among top managers, organizational culture, relationships among other employees, and relationships with customers and suppliers may be almost "invisible" to managers in a firm.[19] If managers in firms that have such capabilities do not understand their relationship to competitive advantage, managers in other firms face significant challenges in understanding which resources they should imitate.

Second, managers may have multiple hypotheses about which resources and capabilities enable their firm to gain a competitive advantage, but they may be unable to evaluate which of these resources and capabilities, alone or in combination, actually create the competitive advantage. For example, if one asks successful entrepreneurs what enabled them to be successful, they are likely to reply with several hypotheses, such as "hard work, willingness to take risks, and a high-quality top management team." However, if one asks what happened to unsuccessful entrepreneurs, they, too, are likely to suggest that their firms were characterized by "hard work, willingness to take risks, and a high-quality top management team." It may be the case that "hard work, willingness to take risks, and a high-quality top management team" are important resources and capabilities for entrepreneurial firm success, but other factors may also play a role. Without rigorous experiments, it is difficult to establish which of these resources have a causal relationship with competitive advantage and which do not.

Finally, it may be that not just a few resources and capabilities enable a firm to gain a competitive advantage, but that literally thousands of these organizational attributes, bundled together, generate these advantages. When the resources and capabilities that generate competitive advantage are complex networks of relationships between individuals, groups, and technology, imitation can be costly.

Whenever the sources of competitive advantage are widely diffused across people, locations, and processes in a firm, those sources will be costly to imitate. Perhaps the best example of such a resource is knowledge itself. To the extent that valuable knowledge about a firm's products, processes, customers, and so on, is widely diffused throughout an organization, competitors will have difficulty imitating that knowledge, and it can be a source of sustained competitive advantage.[20]

Social Complexity.   A third reason that a firm's resources and capabilities may be costly to imitate is that they may be socially complex phenomena, beyond the ability of firms to systematically manage and influence. When competitive advantages are based in such complex social phenomena, the ability of other firms to imitate these resources and capabilities, either through direct duplication or substitution, is significantly constrained. Efforts to influence these kinds of phenomena are likely to be much more costly than they would be if these phenomena developed in a natural way over time in a firm.[21]

A wide variety of firm resources and capabilities may be **socially complex**. Examples include the interpersonal relations among managers in a firm, a firm's culture, and a firm's reputation among suppliers and customers.[22] Notice that in most of these cases it is possible to specify how these socially complex resources add value to a firm. Thus, there is little or no causal ambiguity surrounding the link between these firm resources and capabilities and competitive advantage. However, understanding that an organizational culture with certain attributes or quality relations among managers can improve a firm's efficiency and effectiveness does not necessarily imply that firms lacking these attributes can engage in systematic effort to create them, or that low-cost substitutes for them exist. For the time being, such social engineering may be beyond the abilities of most firms. At the very least, such social engineering is likely to be much more costly than it would be if socially complex resources evolved naturally within a firm.[23]

It is interesting to note that firms seeking to imitate complex physical technology often do not face the cost disadvantages of imitating complex social phenomena. A great deal of physical technology (machine tools, robots, and so forth) can be purchased in supply markets. Even when a firm develops its own unique physical technology, reverse engineering tends to diffuse this technology among competing firms in a low-cost manner. Indeed, the costs of imitating a successful physical technology are often lower than the costs of developing a new technology.[24]

Although physical technology is usually not costly to imitate, the application of this technology in a firm is likely to call for a wide variety of socially complex organizational resources and capabilities. These organizational resources may be costly to imitate, and, if they are valuable and rare, the combination of physical and socially complex resources may be a source of sustained competitive advantage. The importance of socially complex resources and capabilities for firm performance has been studied in detail in the field of strategic human resource management, as described in the Research Made Relevant feature.

Patents.   At first glance, it might appear that a firm's patents would make it very costly for competitors to imitate its products.[25] Patents do have this effect in some industries. For example, patents in the pharmaceutical and specialty chemical industry effectively foreclose other firms from marketing the same products until a firm's patents expire. As suggested in Chapter 2, patents can raise the cost of imitation in a variety of other industries as well.

However, from another point of view a firm's patents may decrease, rather than increase, the costs of imitation. When a firm files for patent protection, it is forced to reveal a significant amount of information about its product. Governments require this information to ensure that the technology in question is patentable. By obtaining a patent, a firm may provide important information to competitors about how to imitate its technology.

Moreover, most technological developments in an industry are diffused throughout firms in that industry in a relatively brief period of time, even if the technology in question is patented, because patented technology is not immune from low-cost imitation. Patents may restrict direct duplication for a time, but they may actually increase the chances of substitution by functionally equivalent technologies.[26]

The Question of Organization

A firm's potential for competitive advantage depends on the value, rarity, and imitability of its resources and capabilities. However, to fully realize this potential, a firm must be organized to exploit its resources and capabilities. These observations lead to the **question of organization**: "Is a firm organized to exploit the full competitive potential of its resources and capabilities?"

Numerous components of a firm's organization are relevant to the question of organization, including its formal reporting structure, its formal and informal management control systems, and its compensation policies. A firm's **formal reporting structure** is a description of who in the organization reports to whom; it is often embodied in a firm's **organizational chart**. **Management control systems** include a range of formal and informal mechanisms to ensure that managers are behaving in ways consistent with a firm's strategies. **Formal management controls** include a firm's budgeting and reporting activities that keep people higher up in a firm's organizational chart informed about the actions taken by people lower down in a firm's organizational chart. **Informal management controls** might include a firm's culture and the willingness of employees to monitor each others' behavior. **Compensation policies** are the ways that firms pay employees. Such policies create incentives for employees to behave in certain ways.

These components of a firm's organization are often called **complementary resources and capabilities**, because they have limited ability to generate competitive advantage in isolation. However, in combination with other resources and capabilities they can enable a firm to realize its full potential for competitive advantage.[27]

For example, it has already been suggested that ESPN may have a sustained competitive advantage in the extreme sports segment of the sports broadcasting industry. However, if ESPN's management had not taken advantage of its opportunities in extreme sports by expanding coverage, ensuring that the best competitors come to ESPN competitions, adding additional competitions,

Research Made Relevant

Strategic Human Resource Management Research

Most empirical tests of the RBV have focused on the extent to which history, causal ambiguity, and social complexity have an impact on the ability of firms to gain and sustain competitive advantages. Among the most important of these tests has been research that examines the extent to which human resource practices that are likely to generate socially complex resources and capabilities are related to firm performance. This area of research is known as *strategic human resources management.*

The first of these tests was conducted as part of a larger study of efficient low-cost manufacturing in the worldwide automobile industry. A group of researchers from Massachusetts Institute of Technology developed rigorous measures of the cost and quality of over 70 manufacturing plants that assembled mid-size sedans around the world. They discovered that at the time of their study only six of these plants had simultaneous low costs and high-quality manufacturing—a position that obviously would give these plants a competitive advantage in the marketplace.

In trying to understand what distinguished these six plants from the oth-

ers in the sample, the researchers found that, not surprisingly, these six plants had the most modern and up-to-date manufacturing technology. However, so did many of the less effective plants. What distinguished these effective plants was not their manufacturing technology, per se, but their human resource (HR) practices. These six plants all implemented a bundle of such practices that included participative decision making, quality circles, and an

emphasis on team production. One of the results of these efforts—and another distinguishing feature of these six plants—was a high level of employee loyalty and commitment to a plant, as well as the belief that plant managers would treat employees fairly. These socially complex resources and capabilities are the types of resources that the RBV suggests should be sources of sustained competitive advantage.

Later work has followed up on this approach and has examined the impact of HR practices on firm performance outside the manufacturing arena. Using a variety of measures of firm performance and several different measures of HR practices, the results of this research continue to be very consistent with RBV logic. That is, firms that are able to use HR practices to develop socially complex human and organizational resources are able to gain competitive advantages over firms that do not engage in such practices.

Sources: J. P. Womack, D. I. Jones, and D. Roos (1990). *The machine that changed the world.* New York: Rawson; M. Huselid (1995). "The impact of human resource management practices on turnover, productivity, and corporate financial performance." *Academy of Management Journal,* 38, pp. 635–672; J. B. Barney and P. Wright (1998). "On becoming a strategic partner." *Human Resource Management,* 37, pp. 31–46.

and changing up older competitions, then its potential for competitive advantage would not have been fully realized. Of course, the reason that ESPN has done all these things is because it has an appropriate organizational structure, management controls, and employee compensation policies. By themselves, these attributes of ESPN's organization could not be a source of competitive advantage; however, they were essential for ESPN to realize its full competitive advantage potential.

Having an appropriate organization in place has enabled ESPN to realize the full competitive advantage potential of its other resources and capabilities. Having an inappropriate organization in place prevented Xerox from taking full advantage of some of its most critical valuable, rare, and costly-to-imitate resources and capabilities.

Through the 1960s and early 1970s, Xerox invested in a series of very innovative technology development research efforts. It managed these efforts by creating a stand-alone research center in Palo Alto, California (Palo Alto Research Center—PARC), and staffing it with a large group of highly creative and innovative scientists and engineers. Left to their own devices, these scientists and engineers at Xerox PARC developed an amazing array of technological innovations: the personal computer, the "mouse," Windows-type software, the laser printer, the "paperless office," Ethernet, and so forth. In retrospect, it is clear that the market potential of these technologies was enormous. Moreover, because they were developed at Xerox PARC, they were rare. Xerox might have been able to gain some important first-mover advantages if the organization had been able to translate these technologies into products, thereby increasing the cost to other firms of imitating these technologies.

Xerox possessed the resources and capabilities, but it did not have an organization in place to take advantage of them. No structure existed whereby Xerox PARC innovations could become known to managers at Xerox. Indeed, most Xerox managers—even many senior managers—were unaware of these technological developments through the mid-1970s. Once they finally became aware of them, very few of the technologies survived Xerox's highly bureaucratic product development process, a process whereby product development projects were divided into hundreds of minute tasks and progress in each task was reviewed by dozens of large committees. Even innovations that survived the product development process were not exploited by Xerox managers, because management compensation at Xerox depended almost exclusively on maximizing current revenue. Short-term profitability was relatively less important in compensation calculations, and the development of markets for future sales and profitability was essentially irrelevant. Xerox's formal reporting structure, its explicit management control systems, and its compensation policies were all inconsistent with exploiting the valuable, rare, and costly-to-imitate resources it had developed. Not surprisingly, the company failed to exploit any of its potential sources of sustained competitive advantage.[28]

Applying the VRIO Framework

The questions of value, rarity, imitability, and organization can be brought together into a single framework to understand the return potential associated with exploiting any of a firm's resources or capabilities. This is done in Table 3.3.

Table 3.3 **The VRIO Framework**

Is a resource or capability:				
Valuable?	**Rare?**	**Costly to imitate?**	**Exploited by organization?**	**Competitive implications**
No	—	—	No	Competitive disadvantage
Yes	No	—	↑	Competitive parity
Yes	Yes	No	⇅	Temporary competitive advantage
Yes	Yes	Yes	Yes	Sustained competitive advantage

The relationship of the VRIO framework to strengths and weaknesses is presented in Table 3.4.

If a resource or capability controlled by a firm is not valuable, it will not enable a firm to choose or implement strategies that exploit environmental opportunities or neutralize environmental threats. Organizing to exploit this resource will increase a firm's costs or decrease its revenues. These types of resources are weaknesses. Firms will either have to fix these weaknesses or avoid using them when choosing and implementing strategies. If firms do exploit these kinds of resources and capabilities, they can expect to put themselves at a competitive disadvantage compared to those that either do not possess these nonvaluable resources or do not use them in conceiving and implementing strategies.

If a resource or capability is valuable but not rare, exploitation of this resource in conceiving and implementing strategies will generate competitive parity. Exploiting these types of resources will generally not create competitive advantages, but failure to exploit them can put a firm at a competitive disadvantage. In this sense, valuable-but-not-rare resources can be thought of as organizational strengths.

If a resource or capability is valuable and rare but not costly to imitate, exploiting this resource will generate a temporary competitive advantage for a firm. A firm that exploits this kind of resource is, in an important sense, gaining a first-mover advantage, because it is the first firm that is able to exploit a particular resource. However, once competing firms observe this competitive advantage, they will be able to acquire or develop the resources needed to implement this strategy through direct duplication or substitution at no cost disadvantage, compared to the first-moving firm. Over time, any competitive advantage that the first mover obtained would be competed away as other firms imitate the resources needed to compete. Consequently, this type of resource or capability can be thought of as an organizational strength and as a **distinctive competence**.

If a resource or capability is valuable, rare, and costly to imitate, exploiting it will generate a sustained competitive advantage. In this case, competing firms face a significant cost disadvantage in imitating a successful firm's resources and capabilities. As suggested earlier, this competitive advantage may reflect the unique history of the successful firm, causal ambiguity about which resources to imitate, the socially complex nature of these resources and capabilities, or any

Table 3.4   **The Relationship Between the VRIO Framework and Organizational Strengths and Weaknesses**

Is a resource or capability:				
Valuable?	**Rare?**	**Costly to imitate?**	**Exploited by organization?**	**Strength or weakness**
No	—	—	No	Weakness
Yes	No	—	↑	Strength
Yes	Yes	No	↕	Strength and distinctive competence
Yes	Yes	Yes	Yes	Strength and sustainable distinctive competence

patent advantages a firm might possess. In any case, attempts to compete away the advantages of firms that exploit these resources will not generate competitive advantage, or even competitive parity, for imitating firms. Even if these firms are able to acquire or develop the resources or capabilities in question, the very high costs of doing so would put them at a competitive disadvantage. These kinds of resources and capabilities are organizational strengths and **sustainable distinctive competencies**.

The question of organization operates as an adjustment factor in the VRIO framework. For example, if a firm has a valuable, rare, and costly-to-imitate resource and capability but fails to organize itself to take full advantage of this resource, some of its potential competitive advantage could be lost (this is the Xerox example). Extremely poor organization, in this case, could actually lead a firm that has the potential for competitive advantage to gain only competitive parity or competitive disadvantages.

Applying the VRIO Framework to Southwest Airlines

To examine how the VRIO framework can be applied in analyzing real strategic situations, consider the competitive position of Southwest Airlines. Southwest Airlines has been the only consistently profitable airline in the United States over the last 30 years. While many U.S. airlines have gone in and out of bankruptcy, Southwest has remained profitable. How has it been able to gain this competitive advantage?

Potential sources of this competitive advantage fall into the two big categories: Operational choices Southwest has made and Southwest's approach to managing its people. On the operational side, Southwest has chosen to fly only a single type of aircraft (Boeing 737), only flies into smaller airports, has avoided complicated hub-and-spoke route systems, and, instead, flies a point-to-point system. On the people-management side, despite being highly unionized, Southwest has been able to develop a sense of commitment and loyalty among its employees. It is not unusual to see Southwest employees go well beyond their narrowly defined job responsibilities, helping out in whatever way is necessary to get a plane off the ground safely and on time. Which of these—operational choices or Southwest's approach to managing its people—are more likely to be a source of sustained competitive advantage?

Southwest's Operational Choices and Competitive Advantage

Consider first Southwest's operational choices. First, do these operational choices reduce Southwest's costs or increase the willingness of its customers to pay—that is, are these operational choises valuable? It can be shown that most of Southwest's operational choices have the effect of reducing its costs. For example, by flying only one type of airline, Southwest is able to reduce the cost of training its maintenance staff, reduce its spare parts inventory, and reduce the time its planes are being repaired. By flying into smaller airports, Southwest reduces the fees it would otherwise have to pay to land at larger airports. Its point-to-point system of routes avoids the costs associated with establishing large hub and spoke systems. Overall, these operational choices are valuable.

Second, are these operational choices rare? For most of its history, Southwest's operational choices have been rare. Only recently have large incumbent airlines and smaller new entrants begun to implement similar operational choices.

Third, are these operational choices costly to imitate? Several incumbent airline firms have set up subsidiaries designed to emulate most of Southwest's operational choices. For example, Continental created the Continental Lite division, United created the Ted division, and Delta created the Song division. All these division chose a single type of airplane to fly, flew into smaller airports, adopted a point to point route structure, and so forth.

In addition to these incumbent airlines, many new entrants into the airline industry—both in the United States and elsewhere—have adopted similar operational choices as Southwest. In the United States, these new entrants include AirTran Airlines, Allegiant Airlines, Jet Blue, Skybus Airlines, Spirit Airlines, and Virgin American Airlines.

Thus, while Southwest's operational choices are valuable and have been rare, they are apparently not costly to imitate. This is not surprising since these operational choices have few of the attributes of resources or capabilities that are costly to imitate. They do not derive from a firm's unique history, they are not path dependent, they are not causally ambiguous, nor are they socially complex.

Finally, is Southwest organized to fully exploit its operational choices? Most observers agree that Southwest's structure, management controls, and compensation policies are consistent with its operational choices.

Taken together, this analysis of Southwest's operational choices suggests that they are valuable, have been rare, but are not costly to imitate. While Southwest is organized to exploit these opportunities, they are likely to be only a source of temporary competitive advantage for Southwest.

Southwest's People Management and Competitive Advantage

A similar VRIO analysis can be conducted for Southwest's approach to people management. First, is this approach valuable, that is, does it reduce Southwest's costs or increase the willingness of its customers to pay?

Employee commitment and loyalty at Southwest is one explanation of why Southwest is able to get higher levels of employee productivity than most other U.S. airlines. This increased productivity shows up in numerous ways. For example, the average turnaround time for Southwest flights is around 18 minutes. The average turn around time for the average U.S. airline is 45 minutes. Southwest Airline employees are simply more effective in unloading and loading luggage, fueling, and catering their airplanes than employees in other airlines. This means that Southwest Airlines airplanes are on the ground for less time and in the air more time than its competitors. Of course, an airplane is only making money if it is in the air. This seemingly simple idea is worth hundreds of millions of dollars in lower costs to Southwest.

Has such loyalty and teamwork been rare in the U.S. airline industry? Over the last 15 years, the U.S. airline industry has been wracked by employment strife. Many airlines have had to cut employment, reduce wages, and in other ways strain their relationship with their employees. Overall, in comparison to incumbent airlines, the relationship that Southwest enjoys with its employees has been rare.

Is this relationship costly to imitate? Certainly, relationships between an airline and its employees have many of the attributes that should make them costly to imitate. They emerge over time, they are path dependent, causally ambiguous, and socially complex. It is reasonable to expect that incumbent airlines, airlines that already have strained relationships with their employees, would have difficulty imitating the relationship Southwest enjoys with its employees. Thus, in comparison to incumbent airlines, Southwest's approach to managing its people is probably valuable, rare, and costly to imitate. Assuming it is organized appropriately (and this seems to be the case), this would mean that—relative to incumbent airlines—Southwest has a sustained competitive advantage.

The situation may be somewhat different for new entrants into the U.S. airline industry. These airlines may not have a history of strained employee relationships. As new firms, they may be able to develop more valuable employee relationship from the very beginning. This suggests that, relative to new entrants, Southwest's approach to people management may be valuable and rare, but not costly to imitate. Again, assuming Southwest is organized appropriately, relative to new entrants into the U.S. airline industry, Southwest's people management capabilities may be a source of only a temporary competitive advantage.

Imitation and Competitive Dynamics in an Industry

Suppose a firm in an industry has conducted an analysis of its resources and capabilities, concludes that it possesses some valuable, rare, and costly-to-imitate resources and capabilities, and uses these to choose a strategy that it implements with the appropriate organizational structure, formal and informal management controls, and compensation policies. The RBV suggests that this firm will gain a competitive advantage even if it is operating in what a five forces analysis (see Chapter 2) would suggest is a very unattractive industry. Examples of firms that have competitive advantages in unattractive industries include Southwest Airlines, Nucor Steel, Wal-Mart, and Dell, to name a few.

Given that a particular firm in an industry has a competitive advantage, how should other firms respond? Decisions made by other firms given the strategic choices of a particular firm define the nature of the **competitive dynamics** that exist in an industry. In general, other firms in an industry can respond to the advantages of a competitor in one of three ways. First, they can choose to limit their response. For example, when Airbus decided to build a super-jumbo airliner designed to dominate international travel for the next 30 years, Boeing limited its responses to redesigning some aspects of two of its existing planes, the 777 and the 747. Second, they can choose to alter some of their business tactics. For example, when Southwest Airlines began operating out of Philadelphia's airport and charged very low airfares, US Airways—the airline that used to dominate the Philadelphia market—lowered its fares as well. Finally, they can choose to alter their strategy—their theory of how to gain competitive advantage (see Chapter 1). For example, when Dell's direct and Internet-based approach to selling personal computers became dominant, Gateway decided to abandon its retail stores in favor of a direct and Internet-based approach.[29] A firm's responses determines the structure of the competitive dynamics in an industry.

Not Responding to Another Firm's Competitive Advantage

A firm might not respond to another firm's competitive advantage for at least three reasons. First, this firm might have its own competitive advantage. By responding to another firm's competitive advantage, it might destroy, or at least compromise, its own sources of competitive advantage. For example, digital timekeeping has made accurate watches available to most consumers at reasonable prices. Firms such as Casio have a competitive advantage in this market because of its miniaturization and electronic capabilities. Indeed, Casio's market share and performance in the watch business continue to climb. How should Rolex—a manufacturer of very expensive, nonelectronic watches—respond to Casio? Rolex's decision has been: *Not at all.* Rolex appeals to a very different market segment than Casio. Should Rolex change its strategies—even if it replaced its mechanical self-winding design with the technologically superior digital design—it could easily compromise its competitive advantage in its own niche market.[30] In general, when a firm already possesses its own sources of competitive advantage, it will not respond to different sources of competitive advantage controlled by another firm.

Second, a firm may not respond to another firm's competitive advantage because it does not have the resources and capabilities to do so. A firm with insufficient or inappropriate resources and capabilities—be they physical, financial, human, or organizational— typically will not be able to imitate a successful firm's resources either through direct duplication or substitution. This may very well be the case with US Airways and Southwest Airlines. It may simply be beyond the ability of US Airways to imitate Southwest's managerial resources and capabilities. In this setting, US Airways is likely to find itself at a sustained competitive disadvantage.[31]

Finally, a firm may not respond to the advantages of a competitor because it is trying to reduce the level of rivalry in an industry. Any actions a firm takes that have the effect of reducing the level of rivalry in an industry and that also do not require firms in an industry to directly communicate or negotiate with each other can be thought of as **tacit cooperation**. Explicit cooperation, where firms do directly communicate and negotiate with each other, is discussed in detail in Chapter 9's analysis of strategic alliances.

Reducing the level of rivalry in an industry can benefit all firms operating in that industry. This decision can have the effect of reducing the quantity of goods and services provided in an industry to below the competitive level, actions that will have the effect of increasing the prices of these goods or services. When tacit cooperation has the effect of reducing supply and increasing prices, it is known as **tacit collusion**. Tacit collusion can be illegal in some settings. However, firms can also tacitly cooperate along other dimensions besides quantity and price. These actions can also benefit all the firms in an industry and typically are not illegal.[32]

For example, it may be that firms can tacitly agree not to invest in certain kinds of research and development. Some forms of R&D are very expensive, and although these investments might end up generating products or services that could benefit customers, firms might still prefer to avoid the expense and risk. Firms can also tacitly agree not to market their products in certain ways. For example, before regulations compelled them to do so, most tobacco companies had already decided not to put cigarette vending machines in locations usually frequented by children, even though these machines could have generated significant revenues. Also, firms can tacitly cooperate by agreeing not to engage in

Table 3.5   **Attributes of Industry Structure That Facilitate the Development of Tacit Cooperation**

1. Small Number of Competing Firms
2. Homogeneous Products and Costs
3. Market Share Leader
4. High Barriers to Entry

certain manufacturing practices, such as outsourcing to developing countries and engaging in environmentally unsound practices.

All of these actions can have the effect of reducing the level of rivalry in an industry. And reducing the level of rivalry can have the effect of increasing the average level of performance for a firm in an industry. However, tacit cooperative relationships among firms are sometimes difficult to maintain. Typically, in order for tacit cooperation to work an industry must have the structural attributes described in Table 3.5. First, the industry must have relatively few firms. Informally communicating and coordinating strategies among a few firms is difficult enough; it is even more difficult when the industry has a large number of firms. For this reason, tacit cooperation is a viable strategy only when an industry is an oligopoly (see Chapter 2).

Second, firms in this industry must be homogeneous with respect to the products they sell and their cost structure. Having heterogeneous products makes it too easy for a firm to "cheat" on its tacitly cooperative agreements by modifying its products, and heterogeneous cost means that the optimal level of output for a particular firm may be very different from the level agreed to through tacit cooperation. In this setting, a firm might have a strong incentive to increase its output and upset cooperative agreements.

Third, an industry typically has to have at least one strong market-share leader if firms are going to tacitly cooperate. This would be a relatively large firm that has established an example of the kind of behavior that will be mutually beneficial in the industry, and other firms in the industry sometimes fall into line with this example. Indeed, it is often the market-share leader that will choose not to respond to the competitive actions of another firm in the industry in order to maintain cooperative relations.

Finally, the maintenance of tacit cooperation in an industry almost always requires the existence of high barriers to entry. If tacit cooperation is successful, the average performance of firms in an industry will improve. However, this higher level of performance can induce other firms to enter into this industry (see Chapter 2). Such entry will increase the number of firms in an industry and make it very difficult to maintain tacitly cooperative relationships. Thus, it must be very costly for new firms to enter into an industry for those in that industry to maintain their tacit cooperation. The higher these costs, the higher the barriers to entry.

Changing Tactics in Response to Another Firm's Competitive Advantage

Tactics are the specific actions a firm takes to implement its strategies. Examples of tactics include decisions firms make about various attributes of their products—including size, shape, color, and price—specific advertising approaches adopted by a firm, and specific sales and marketing efforts. Generally, firms change their tactics much more frequently than they change their strategies.[33]

When competing firms are pursuing approximately the same strategies, the competitive advantages that any one firm might enjoy at a given point in time are most likely due to the tactics that that firm is pursuing. In this setting, it is not unusual for competing firms to change their tactics by imitating the tactics of the firm with an advantage in order to reduce that firm's advantage. Although changing one's tactics in this manner will only generate competitive parity, this is usually better than the competitive disadvantage these firms were experiencing.

Several industries provide excellent examples of these kinds of tactical interactions. In consumer goods, for example, if one company increases its sales by adding a "lemon scent" to laundry detergent, then lemon scents start showing up in everyone's laundry detergent. If Coke starts selling significant amounts of C2—a soft drink with half the sugar and half the carbs of regular Coke—can Pepsi's low-sugar/low-carb product be far behind? And when Delta Airlines cuts it airfares, can American and United be far behind? Not surprisingly, these kinds of tactical changes, because they initially may be valuable and rare, are seldom costly to imitate, and thus are typically only sources of temporary competitive advantage.

Sometimes, rather than simply imitating the tactics of a firm with a competitive advantage, a firm at a disadvantage may "leap frog" its competitors by developing an entirely new set of tactics. Procter & Gamble engaged in this strategy when it introduced its laundry detergent, Tide, in a new, concentrated formula. This new formulation required new manufacturing and packaging equipment—the smaller box could not be filled in the current manufacturing lines in the industry—which meant that Tide's competitors had to take more time in imitating the concentrated laundry detergent tactic than other tactics pursued in this industry. Nevertheless, within just a few weeks other firms in this market were introducing their own versions of concentrated laundry detergent.

Indeed, some firms can become so skilled at innovating new products and other tactics that this innovative capability can be a source of sustained competitive advantage. Consider, for example, the performance of Sony. Most observers agree that Sony possesses some special management and coordination skills that enable it to conceive, design, and manufacture high-quality miniaturized consumer electronics. However, virtually every time Sony brings out a new miniaturized product several of its competitors quickly duplicate that product through reverse engineering, thereby reducing Sony's technological advantage. In what way can Sony's socially complex miniaturization resources and capabilities be a source of sustained competitive advantage when most of Sony's products are quickly imitated through direct duplication?

After Sony introduces each new product, it experiences a rapid increase in profits attributable to the new product's unique features. This increase, however, leads other firms to reverse-engineer the Sony product and introduce their own versions. Increased competition results in a reduction in the profits associated with a new product. Thus, at the level of individual products, Sony apparently enjoys only temporary competitive advantages. However, looking at the total returns earned by Sony across all of its new products over time makes clear the source of Sony's sustained competitive advantage: By exploiting its resources and capabilities in miniaturization, Sony is able to constantly introduce new and exciting personal electronics products. No single product generates a sustained competitive advantage, but, over time, across several such product introductions, Sony's resource and capability advantages lead to sustained competitive advantages.[34]

Changing Strategies in Response to Another Firm's Competitive Advantage

Finally, firms sometimes respond to another firm's competitive advantage by changing their strategies. Obviously, this does not occur very often, and it typically only occurs when another firm's strategies usurp a firm's competitive advantage. In this setting, a firm will not be able to gain even competitive parity if it maintains its strategy, even if it implements that strategy very effectively.

Changes in consumer tastes, in population demographics, and in the laws that govern a business can all have the effect of rendering what once was a valuable strategy as valueless. However, the most frequent impact is changes in technology. For example, no matter how well made a mechanical calculator is, it is simply inferior to an electronic calculator. No matter how efficient the telegraph was in its day, it is an inferior technology to the telephone. And no matter how quickly one's fingers can move the beads on an abacus, an electronic cash register is a better way of keeping track of sales and making change in a store.

When firms change their strategies, they must proceed through the entire strategic management process, as described in Chapter 1. However, these firms will often have difficulty abandoning their traditional strategies. For most firms, their strategy helps define what they do and who they are. Changing its strategy often requires a firm to change its identity and its purposes. These are difficult changes to make, and many firms wait to change their strategy until absolutely forced to do so by disastrous financial results. By then these firms not only have to change their strategy—with all that implies—they have to do so in the face of significant financial pressures.

The ability of virtually all strategies to generate competitive advantages typically expires, sooner or later. In general, it is much better for a firm to change its strategy before that strategy is no longer viable. In this way, a firm can make a planned move to a new strategy that maintains whatever resources and capabilities it still possesses while it develops the new resources and capabilities it will need to compete in the future.

Implications of the Resource-Based View

The RBV and the VRIO framework can be applied to individual firms to understand whether these firms will gain competitive advantages, how sustainable these competitive advantages are likely to be, and what the sources of these competitive advantages are. In this way, the RBV and the VRIO framework can be understood as important complements to the threats and opportunities analyses described in Chapter 2.

Table 3.6   **Broader Implications of the Resource-Based View**

1. The responsibility for competitive advantage in a firm:
   Competitive advantage is every employee's responsibility.
2. Competitive parity and competitive advantage:
   If all a firm does is what its competition does, it can gain only competitive parity. In gaining competitive advantage, it is better for a firm to exploit its own valuable, rare, and costly-to-imitate resources than to imitate the valuable and rare resources of a competitor.
3. Difficult to implement strategies:
   As long as the cost of strategy implementation is less than the value of strategy implementation, the relative cost of implementing a strategy is more important for competitive advantage than the absolute cost of implementing a strategy.
   Firms can systematically overestimate and underestimate their uniqueness.
4. Socially complex resources:
   Not only can employee empowerment, organizational culture, and teamwork be valuable; they can also be sources of sustained competitive advantage.
5. The role of the organization:
   Organization should support the use of valuable, rare, and costly-to-imitate resources. If conflicts between these attributes of a firm arise, change the organization.

However, beyond what these frameworks can say about the competitive performance of a particular firm, the RBV has some broader implications for managers seeking to gain competitive advantages. Some of these broader implications are listed in Table 3.6 and discussed in the following section.

Where Does the Responsibility for Competitive Advantage in a Firm Reside?

First, the RBV suggests that competitive advantages can be found in several of the different resources and capabilities controlled by the firm. These resources and capabilities are not limited to those that are controlled directly by a firm's senior managers. Thus, the responsibility for creating, nurturing, and exploiting valuable, rare, and costly-to-imitate resources and capabilities for competitive advantage is not restricted to senior managers, but falls on every employee in a firm. Therefore, employees should go beyond defining their jobs in functional terms and instead define their jobs in competitive and economic terms.

Consider a simple example. In a recent visit to a very successful automobile manufacturing plant, the plant manager was asked to describe his job responsibilities. He said, "My job is to manage this plant in order to help the firm make and sell the best cars in the world." In response to a similar question, the person in charge of the manufacturing line said, "My job is to manage this manufacturing line in order to help the firm make and sell the best cars in the world." A janitor was also asked to describe his job responsibilities. Although he had not been present in the two earlier interviews, the janitor responded, "My job is to keep this facility clean in order to help the firm make and sell the best cars in the world."

Which of these three employees is most likely to be a source of sustained competitive advantage for this firm? Certainly, the plant manager and the manufacturing line manager *should* define their jobs in terms of helping the firm make and sell the best cars in the world. However, it is unlikely that their responses to this question would be any different than the responses of other senior managers at other manufacturing plants around the world. Put differently, although the definition of these two managers' jobs in terms of enabling the firm to make and sell the best cars in the world is valuable, it is unlikely to be rare, and thus it is likely to be a source of competitive parity, not competitive advantage. However, a janitor who defines her job as helping the firm make and sell the best cars in the world instead of simply to clean the facility is, most would agree, quite unusual. Because it is rare, it might be a source of at least a temporary competitive advantage.[35]

The value created by one janitor defining her job in competitive terms rather than functional terms is not huge, but suppose that all the employees in this plant defined their jobs in these terms. Suddenly, the value that might be created could be substantial. Moreover, the organizational culture and tradition in a firm that would lead employees to define their jobs in this way is likely to be costly for other firms to imitate. Thus, if this approach to defining job responsibilities is broadly diffused in a particular plant, it seems likely to be valuable, rare, and costly to imitate, and thus a source of sustained competitive advantage, assuming the firm is organized to take advantage of this unusual resource.

In the end, it is clear that competitive advantage is too important to remain the sole property of senior management. To the extent that employees throughout an organization are empowered to develop and exploit valuable, rare, and costly-to-imitate resources and capabilities in the accomplishment of their job responsibilities, a firm may actually be able to gain sustained competitive advantages.

Competitive Parity and Competitive Advantage

Second, the RBV suggests that if all a firm does is create value in the same way as its competitors, the best performance it can ever expect to gain is competitive parity. To do better than competitive parity, firms must engage in valuable and rare activities. They must do things to create economic value that other firms have not even thought of, let alone implemented.

This is especially critical for firms that find themselves at a competitive disadvantage. Such a firm certainly should examine its more successful competition, understand what has made this competition so successful, and, where imitation is very low cost, imitate the successful actions of its competitors. In this sense, benchmarking a firm's performance against the performance of its competitors can be extremely important.

However, if this is all that a firm does, it can only expect to gain competitive parity. Gaining competitive advantage depends on a firm discovering its own unique resources and capabilities and how they can be used in choosing and implementing strategies. For a firm seeking competitive advantage, it is better to be excellent in how it develops and exploits its own unique resources and capabilities than it is to be excellent in how it imitates the resources and capabilities of other firms.

This does not imply that firms must always be first movers to gain competitive advantages. Some firms develop valuable, rare, and costly-to-imitate resources and capabilities in being efficient second movers—that is, in rapidly imitating and improving on the product and technological innovations of other firms. Rather than suggesting that firms must always be first movers, the RBV suggests that, in order to gain competitive advantages, firms must implement strategies that rely on valuable, rare, and costly-to-imitate resources and capabilities, whatever those strategies or resources might be.

Difficult-to-Implement Strategies

Third, as firms contemplate different strategic options, they often ask how difficult and costly it will be to implement different strategies. As long as the cost of implementing a strategy is less than the value that a strategy creates, the RBV suggests that the critical question facing firms is not "Is a strategy easy to implement or not?" but rather "Is this strategy easier for us to implement than it is for our competitors to implement?" Firms that already possess the valuable, rare, and costly-to-imitate resources needed to implement a strategy will, in general, find it easier (i.e., less costly) to implement a strategy than firms that first have to develop the required resources and then implement the proposed strategy. For firms that already possess a resource, strategy implementation can be natural and swift.

In understanding the relative costs of implementing a strategy, firms can make two errors. First, they can overestimate the uniqueness of the resources they control. Although every firm's history is unique and no two management teams are exactly the same, this does not always mean that a firm's resources and capabilities will be rare. Firms with similar histories operating in similar industries will often develop similar capabilities. If a firm overestimates the rarity of its resources and capabilities, it can overestimate its ability to generate competitive advantages.

For example, when asked what their most critical sources of competitive advantage are, many firms will cite the quality of their top management team, the quality of their technology, and their commitment to excellence in all that they do. When pushed about their competitors, these same firms will admit that they too have high-quality top management teams, high-quality technology, and a commitment to excellence in all that they do. Although these three attributes can be sources of competitive parity, they cannot be sources of competitive advantage.

Second, firms can sometimes underestimate their uniqueness and thus underestimate the extent to which the strategies they pursue can be sources of sustained competitive advantage. When firms possess valuable, rare, and costly-to-imitate resources, strategy implementation can be relatively easy. In this context, it seems reasonable to expect that other firms will be able to quickly imitate this "easy-to-implement" strategy. Of course, this is not the case if these resources controlled by a firm are, in fact, rare and costly to imitate.

In general, firms must take great care not to overestimate or underestimate their uniqueness. An accurate assessment of the value, rarity, and imitability of a firm's resources is necessary to develop an accurate understanding of the relative costs of implementing a firm's strategies, and thus the ability of those strategies to generate competitive advantages. Often, firms must employ outside assistance in helping them describe the rarity and imitability of their resources, even though managers in firms will generally be much more familiar with the resources controlled by a firm than outsiders. However, outsiders can provide a measure of objectivity in evaluating the uniqueness of a firm.

Socially Complex Resources

Over the last several decades, much has been written about the importance of employee empowerment, organizational culture, and teamwork for firm performance. Most of this work suggests that firms that empower employees, that have an enabling culture, and that encourage teamwork will, on average, make better strategic choices and implement them more efficiently than firms without these organizational attributes. Using the language of the RBV, most of this work has suggested that employee empowerment, organizational culture, and teamwork, at least in some settings, are economically valuable.[36]

Resource-based logic acknowledges the importance of the value of these organizational attributes. However, it also suggests that these socially complex resources and capabilities can be rare and costly to imitate—and it is these attributes that make it possible for socially complex resources and capabilities to be sources of sustained competitive advantage. Put differently, the RBV actually extends and broadens traditional analyses of the socially complex attributes of firms. Not only can these attributes be valuable, but they can also be rare and costly to imitate, and thus sources of sustained competitive advantage.

The Role of Organization

Finally, resource-based logic suggests that an organization's structure, control systems, and compensation policies should support and enable a firm's efforts to fully exploit the valuable, rare, and costly-to-imitate resources and capabilities it controls. These attributes of organization, by themselves, are usually not sources of sustained competitive advantage.

These observations suggest that if there is a conflict between the resources a firm controls and that firm's organization, the organization should be changed. However, it is often the case that once a firm's structure, control systems, and compensation policies are put in place they tend to remain, regardless of whether they are consistent with a firm's underlying resources and capabilities. In such settings, a firm will not be able to realize the full competitive potential of its underlying resource base. To the extent that a firm's resources and capabilities are continuously evolving, its organizational structure, control systems, and compensation policies must also evolve. For these attributes of organization to evolve, managers must be aware of their link with a firm's resources and capabilities and of organizational alternatives.

Internal Analysis in an International Context

The RBV and the VRIO framework can also be applied in the analysis of firm decisions to enter into international markets. This logic suggests two broad reasons why firms may begin operating in multiple businesses: (1) to take advantage of current resource and capability advantages in new geographic markets and (2) to develop new resource and capability advantages by beginning to operate in new geographic markets. Organizing to implement these international strategies is also important. However, because exploitation of international markets is almost always a specific example of a corporate diversification strategy, the discussion of how to organize such international ventures will be delayed until Chapter 8 analysis of implementing corporate diversification strategies.

Exploiting Current Resource Advantages in New Markets

Suppose a firm already has a sustained competitive advantage in its domestic market. One logical way for a firm with such an advantage to increase its growth and profitability is to exploit those same capabilities in new geographic markets by beginning international operations. However, that a firm's resources are valuable, rare, and costly to imitate in one country does not necessarily mean they will be in a different country.

Several firms have been successful in using their competitive advantage in one country to gain competitive advantages in another country. Coca-Cola, for example, has used its strong brand name—Coke—as a way of entering markets around the world. Currently, Coca-Cola actually sells more Coke products outside of the United States than it sells domestically. Sony used its technical and innovative capabilities to become a dominant player in the U.S. consumer electronics market. BMW used its engineering skills developed by building cars to run at 120 mph on the German autobahn to become an important part of the luxury sports sedan market in the United States. In all these cases, what were valuable, rare, and costly-to-imitate resources or capabilities in a firm's home market also turned out to be valuable, rare, and costly-to-imitate resources in nondomestic markets as well.

However, that a resource or capability is a source of sustained competitive advantage in one country does not guarantee that it will also be valuable, or valuable and rare, or valuable, rare, and costly to imitate in another country. For example, Disney has tried to leverage its brand name and its ability to create and manage theme parks internationally. Its theme park in Asia, Tokyo Disneyland, has been a significant financial success. However, the Disney Company has only a small financial stake in Tokyo Disneyland, so this theme park's financial success has not benefited Disney that much. In contrast, Disney's theme park in Europe, EuroDisney, located just outside of Paris, France, has been a financial drag on the Disney Company. After several financial restructuring efforts, EuroDisney is finally beginning to have a positive impact on the financial position of the Disney Company. But it has taken many years and many millions of dollars to get EuroDisney on a financially secure footing. Apparently, the "Disney experience" at EuroDisney is simply not as valuable as the "Disney experience" in Florida, California, or Tokyo.[37] It is too early to tell if Disney's Hong Kong theme park will follow in the footsteps of Tokyo Disneyland or EuroDisney.

When contemplating the exploitation of a firm's valuable, rare, and costly-to-imitate resources and capabilities in a new geographic market, all four of the VRIO questions are important. Certainly, the value of a firm's resources in a new market may differ from the value of those same resources in its home market. EuroDisney is an example of this problem. Also, if a firm is contemplating entry into a more competitive market than its home market, it is likely that what were rare and costly-to-imitate resources in the home market will be less rare and less costly to imitate in a new, more competitive, geographic market. As some authors have observed, firms looking to take advantage of their resources in new geographic markets are more likely to be successful if their home markets are highly competitive in the first place.[38] If a firm's valuable resources are a source of sustained competitive advantage in a highly competitive home market, they are more likely to be sources of sustained competitive advantage in other, less competitive, geographic markets—assuming, of course, they are still valuable.

Developing New Resources and Capabilities in New Markets

One of the most compelling reasons for firms to begin operations outside their domestic markets is to develop new resources and capabilities. By beginning such operations, firms can gain a greater understanding of their strengths and weakness. By exposing these resources and capabilities to new competitive contexts, traditional resources can be modified and new resources can be developed.

Of course, for international operations to affect a firm's resources and capabilities, firms must learn from their experiences in nondomestic markets. Learning in this context is anything but automatic. Many firms that begin operations in a nondomestic market encounter challenges and difficulties and then immediately withdraw from their international efforts. Other firms continue to try to operate internationally but are unable to learn how to modify and change the core resources. One study identified three critical determinants of the ability of a firm to develop new resources and capabilities through its international operations: the intent to learn, the transparency of learning partners, and the receptivity to learning.[39]

A firm that has a strong intent to learn from its international operations is more likely to learn than a firm without this intent. Moreover, this intent must be communicated to all those who work in a firm's international activities. Compare, for example, a quote from a manager whose firm failed to learn from its international operations with a quote from a manager whose firm was able to learn from these operations:[40]

> *Our engineers were just as good as [our partner's]. In fact, theirs were narrower technically, but they had a much better understanding of what the company was trying to accomplish. They knew they were there to learn, our people didn't.*

> *We wanted to make learning an automatic discipline. We asked the staff every day, "What did you learn from [our partner] today?" Learning was carefully monitored and recorded.*

Obviously, the second firm was in a much better position than the first to learn from its international operations and to develop new resources and capabilities.

The transparency of learning partners is also an important determinant of the ability to develop new resources and capabilities from international operations. Some international business partners are more open and accessible than others. These differences can reflect different organizational philosophies, practices, and procedures, as well as differences in the culture of a firm's home country. For example, knowledge in Japanese and many other Asian cultures tends to be context specific and deeply embedded in the broader social system. This makes it difficult for many Western managers to understand and appreciate the subtlety of Japanese business practices and Japanese culture. This, in turn, limits the ability of Western managers to learn from their operations in the Japanese market or from their Japanese partners.[41]

In contrast, knowledge in most Western cultures tends to be less context specific, less deeply embedded in the broader social system. Such knowledge can be written down, taught in classes, and be transmitted, all at a relatively low cost. Japanese managers working in Western economies are more likely to be able to appreciate and understand Western business practices, and thus more able to learn from their operations in the West and from their Western partners.

Finally, firms vary in their receptiveness to learning about new resources and capabilities. A firm's receptiveness to such learning is affected by its culture, its operations, and its history. Research suggests that, before firms can learn from their international operations, they must be prepared to *unlearn*. Unlearning requires a firm to modify or abandon traditional ways of engaging in business. Unlearning can be difficult, especially if a firm has a long history of success using old patterns of behavior and if those old patterns of behavior are reflected in its organizational structure, formal and informal management controls, and compensation policies.

SUMMARY

The resource-based view (RBV) is an economic theory that suggests that firm performance is a function of the types of resources and capabilities controlled by firms. Resources are the tangible and intangible assets a firm uses to conceive of and implement its strategies. Capabilities are a subset of resources that enable a firm to take advantage of its other resources. Resources and capabilities can be categorized into financial, physical, human, and organizational resources categories.

The RBV makes two assumptions about resources and capabilities: the assumption of resource heterogeneity (that some resources and capabilities may be heterogeneously distributed across competing firms) and the assumption of resource immobility (that this heterogeneity may be long lasting). These two assumptions can be used to describe conditions under which firms will gain competitive advantages by exploiting their resources.

A tool for analyzing a firm's internal strengths and weaknesses can be derived from the RBV. Called the VRIO framework, this tool asks four questions about a firm's resources and capabilities in order to evaluate their competitive potential. These questions are the question of value, the question of rarity, the question of imitability, and the question of organization.

A firm's resources and capabilities are valuable when they enable it to exploit external opportunities or neutralize external threats. Such valuable resources and capabilities are a firm's strengths. Resources and capabilities that are not valuable are a firm's weaknesses. Using valuable resources to exploit external opportunities or neutralize external threats will have the effect of increasing a firm's net revenues or decreasing its net costs.

One way to identify a firm's valuable resources and capabilities is by examining its value chain. A firm's value chain is the list of business activities it engages in to develop, produce, and sell its products or services. Different stages in this value chain require different resources and capabilities, and differences in value-chain choices across firms can lead to important differences among the resources and capabilities controlled by different companies. Two generic value chains have been developed, one by McKinsey and Company and another by Michael Porter.

Valuable and common (i.e., not rare) resources and capabilities can be a source of competitive parity. Failure to invest in such resources can create a competitive disadvantage for a firm. Valuable and rare resources can be a source of at least a temporary competitive advantage. There are fewer firms able to control such a resource and still exploit it as a source of at least temporary competitive advantage than there are firms that will generate perfect competition dynamics in an industry.

Valuable, rare, and costly-to-imitate resources and capabilities can be a source of sustained competitive advantage. Imitation can occur through direct duplication or through substitution. A firm's resources and capabilities may be costly to imitate for at least four reasons: unique historical circumstances, causal ambiguity, socially complex resources and capabilities, and patents.

To take full advantage of the potential of its resources and capabilities, a firm must be appropriately organized. A firm's organization consists of its formal reporting structure, its formal and informal control processes, and its compensation policy. These are complementary resources in that they are rarely sources of competitive advantage on their own.

The VRIO framework can be used to identify the competitive implications of a firm's resources and capabilities—whether they are a source of competitive disadvantage, competitive parity, temporary competitive advantage, or sustained competitive advantage— and the extent to which these resources and capabilities are strengths or weaknesses.

When a firm faces a competitor that has a sustained competitive advantage, the firm's options are not to respond, to change its tactics, or to change its strategies. A firm may choose not to respond in this setting for at least three reasons. First, a response might weaken its own sources of sustained competitive advantage. Second, a firm may not have the resources required to respond. Third, a firm may be trying to create or maintain tacit cooperation within an industry.

The RBV has a series of broader managerial implications as well. For example, resource-based logic suggests that competitive advantage is every employee's responsibility. It also suggests that if all a firm does is what its competition does, it can gain only competitive parity, and that in gaining competitive advantage it is better for a firm to exploit its own valuable, rare, and costly-to-imitate resources than to imitate the valuable and rare resources of a competitor. Also, resource-based logic implies that as long as the cost of strategy implementation is less than the value of strategy implementation, the relative cost of implementing a strategy is more important for competitive advantage than the absolute cost of implementing a strategy. It also implies that firms can systematically overestimate and underestimate their uniqueness. With regard to a firm's resources and capabilities, resource-based logic suggests that not only can employee empowerment, organizational culture, and teamwork be valuable; they can also be sources of sustained competitive advantage. Also, if conflicts arise between a firm's valuable, rare, and costly-to-imitate resources and its organization, the organization should be changed.

Finally, the RBV and the VRIO framework can also be applied in an international context. In general, firms pursue international opportunities to either exploit their currently valuable, rare, and costly-to-imitate resources and capabilities in new markets or to develop new resources and capabilities. The ability to develop new resources and capabilities through international operations depends on a firm's intent to learn, the transparency of its international business partners, and its receptiveness to learning.

CHALLENGE QUESTIONS

1. Which of the following approaches to strategy formulation is more likely to generate economic profits: (a) evaluating external opportunities and threats and then developing resources and capabilities to exploit these opportunities and neutralize these threats or (b) evaluating internal resources and capabilities and then searching for industries where they can be exploited? Explain your answer.

2. Which firm will have a higher level of economic performance: (a) a firm with valuable, rare, and costly-to-imitate resources and capabilities operating in a very attractive industry or (b) a firm with valuable, rare, and costly-to-imitate resources and capabilities operating in a very unattractive industry? Assume both these firms are appropriately organized. Explain your answer.

3. Which is more critical to sustaining human life—water or diamonds? Why do firms that provide water to customers generally earn lower economic performance than firms that provide diamonds?

4. Will a firm currently experiencing competitive parity be able to gain sustained competitive advantages by studying another firm that is currently experiencing sustained competitive advantages? Why or why not?

5. Your former college roommate calls you and asks to borrow $10,000 so that he can open a pizza restaurant in his hometown. He acknowledges that there is a high degree of rivalry in this market, that the cost of entry is low, and that there are numerous substitutes for pizza, but he believes that his pizza restaurant will have some sustained competitive advantages. For example, he is going to have sawdust on his floor, a variety of imported beers, and a late-night delivery service. Will you lend him the money? Why or why not?

6. In the text, it is suggested that Boeing did not respond to Airbus's announcement of the development of a super-jumbo aircraft. Assuming this aircraft will give Airbus a competitive advantage in the segment of the airliner business that supplies airplanes for long international flights, why did Boeing not respond?

(a) Does it have its own competitive advantage that it does not want to abandon?
(b) Does it not have the resources and capabilities needed to respond?
(c) Is it trying to reduce the level of rivalry in this industry?

7. Which firm is more likely to be successful in exploiting its sources of sustained competitive advantage in its home market than in a highly competitive, nondomestic market: (a) a firm from a less competitive home country or (b) a firm from a more competitive home country? Why?

8. What are some indicators that a firm is engaging in an international strategy to develop new resources and capabilities?

PROBLEM SET

1. Apply the VRIO framework in the following settings. Will the actions described be a source of competitive disadvantage, parity, temporary advantage, or sustained competitive advantage? Explain your answers.

(a) Procter & Gamble introduces new, smaller packaging for its Tide laundry detergent.
(b) American Airlines announces a 5-percent across-the-board reduction in airfares.
(c) The Korean automobile firm Hyundai announces a 10-year, 100,000 mile warranty on its cars.
(d) Microsoft makes it easier to transfer data and information from Microsoft Word to Microsoft Excel.
(e) Merck is able to coordinate the work of its chemists and biologists in the development of new drugs.
(f) Ford patents a new kind of brake pad for its cars.
(g) Ashland Chemical, a specialty chemical company, patents a new chemical.
(h) The New York Yankees sign All-Star pitcher Randy Johnson to a long-term contract.
(i) Michael Dell uses the money he has made from Dell to purchase the Dallas Cowboys football team.
(j) Ted Turner uses the money he has made from his broadcasting empire to purchase the Atlanta Braves baseball team.

2. Identify three firms you might want to work for. Using the VRIO framework, evaluate the extent to which the resources and capabilities of these firms gives them the potential to realize competitive disadvantages, parity, temporary advantages, or sustained advantages. What implications, if any, does this analysis have for the company you might want to work for?

3. You have been assigned to estimate the present value of a potential construction project for your company. How would you use the VRIO framework to construct the cash-flow analysis that is a part of any present-value calculation?

END NOTES

1. The term *"the resource-based view"* was coined by Wernerfelt, B. (1984). "A resource-based view of the firm." *Strategic Management Journal*, 5, pp. 171–180. Some important early contributors to this theory include Rumelt, R. P. (1984). "Toward a strategic theory of the firm." In R. Lamb (ed.), *Competitive strategic Management* (pp. 556–570). Upper Saddle River, NJ: Prentice Hall; and Barney, J. B. (1986). "Strategic factor markets: Expectations, luck and business strategy." *Management Science*, 32, pp. 1512–1514. A second wave of important early resource-based theoretical work includes Barney, J. B. (1991). "Firm resources and sustained competitive advantage." *Journal of Management*, 7, pp. 49–64; Dierickx, I., and K. Cool (1989). "Asset stock accumulation and sustainability of competitive advantage." *Management Science*, 35, pp. 1504–1511; Conner, K. R. (1991). "A historical comparison of resource-based theory and five schools of thought within industrial organization economics: Do we have a new theory of the firm?" *Journal of Management*, 17(1), pp. 121–154; and Peteraf, M. A. (1993). "The cornerstones of competitive advantage: A resource-based view." *Strategic Management Journal*, 14, pp. 179–191. A review of much of this early theoretical literature can be found in Mahoney, J. T., and J. R. Pandian (1992). "The resource-based view within the conversation of strategic management." *Strategic Management Journal*, 13, pp. 363–380. The theoretical perspective has also spawned a growing body of empirical work, including Brush, T. H., and K. W. Artz (1999). "Toward a contingent resource-based theory." *Strategic Management Journal*, 20, pp. 223–250; Marcus, A., and D. Geffen (1998). "The dialectics of competency acquisition." *Strategic Management Journal*, 19, pp. 1145–1168; Brush, T. H., P. Bromiley, and M. Hendrickx (1999). "The relative influence of industry and corporation on business segment performance." *Strategic Management Journal*, 20, pp. 519–547; Yeoh, P.-L., and K. Roth (1999). "An empirical analysis of sustained advantage in the U.S. pharmaceutical industry." *Strategic Management Journal*, 20, pp. 637–653; Roberts, P. (1999). "Product innovation, product-market competition and persistent profitability in the U.S. pharmaceutical industry." *Strategic Management Journal*, 20, pp. 655–670; Gulati, R. (1999). "Network location and learning." *Strategic Management Journal*, 20, pp. 397–420; Lorenzoni, G., and A. Lipparini (1999). "The leveraging of interfirm relationships as a distinctive organizational capability." *Strategic Management Journal*, 20, pp. 317–338; Majumdar, S. (1998). "On the utilization of resources." *Strategic Management Journal*, 19(9) pp. 809–831; Makadok, R. (1997). "Do inter-firm differences in capabilities affect strategic pricing dynamics?" *Academy of Management Proceedings '97*, pp. 30–34; Silverman, B. S., J. A. Nickerson, and J. Freeman (1997). "Profitability, transactional alignment, and organizational mortality in the U.S. trucking industry." *Strategic Management Journal*, 18 (Summer special issue), pp. 31–52; Powell, T. C., and A. Dent-Micallef (1997). "Information technology as competitive advantage." *Strategic Management Journal*, 18(5), pp. 375–405; Miller, D., and J. Shamsie (1996). "The Resource-Based View of the firm in two environments." *Academy of Management Journal*, 39(3), pp. 519–543; and Maijoor, S., and A. Van Witteloostuijn (1996). "An empirical test of the resource-based theory." *Strategic Management Journal*, 17, pp. 549–569; Barnett, W. P., H. R. Greve, and D. Y. Park (1994). "An evolutionary model of organizational performance." *Strategic Management Journal*, 15 (Winter special issue), pp. 11–28; Levinthal, D., and J. Myatt (1994). "Co-evolution of capabilities and industry: The evolution of mutual fund processing." *Strategic Management Journal*, 17, pp. 45–62; Henderson, R., and I. Cockburn (1994). "Measuring competence? Exploring firm effects in pharmaceutical research." *Strategic Management Journal*, 15, pp. 63–84; Pisano, G. P. (1994). "Knowledge, integration, and the locus of learning: An empirical analysis of process development." *Strategic Management*

Journal, 15, pp. 85–100; and Zajac, E. J., and J. D. Westphal (1994). "The costs and benefits of managerial incentives and monitoring in large U.S. corporations: When is more not better?" *Strategic Management Journal*, 15, pp. 121–142.

2. Ghemawat, P. (1986). "Wal-Mart stores' discount operations." Harvard Business School Case No. 9-387-018, on Wal-Mart; Kupfer, A. (1991). "The champion of cheap clones." *Fortune*, September 23, pp. 115–120; and Holder, D. (1989). "L. L. Bean, Inc.—1974." Harvard Business School Case No. 9-676-014, on L. L. Bean. Some of Wal-Mart's more recent moves, especially its international acquisitions, are described in Laing, J. R. (1999). "Blimey! Wal-Mart." *Barron's*, 79, p. 14. L. L. Bean's lethargic performance in the 1990s, together with its turnaround plan, is described in Symonds, W. (1998). "Paddling harder at L. L. Bean." *BusinessWeek*, December 7, p. 72.

3. For an early discussion of the importance of human capital in firms, see Becker, G. S. (1964). *Human capital.* New York: Columbia University Press.

4. Heskett, J. L., and R. H. Hallowell (1993). "Southwest Airlines: 1993 (A)." Harvard Business School Case No. 9-695-023.

5. See Barney, J. (1991). "Firm resources and sustained competitive advantage." *Journal of Management*, 17, pp. 99–120.

6. See Schlender, B. R. (1992). "How Sony keeps the magic going." *Fortune*, February 24, pp. 75–84; and (1999). "The weakling kicks back." *The Economist*, July 3, p. 46, for a discussion at Sony. See Krogh, L., J. Praeger, D. Sorenson, and J. Tomlinson (1988). "How 3M evaluates its R&D programs." *Research Technology Management*, 31, pp. 10–14.

7. Anders, G. (2002). "AOL's true believers." *Fast Company*, July pp. 96 +. In a recent *Wall Street Journal* article, managers of AOL Time Warner admitted they are no longer seeking synergies across their businesses. See Karnitschnig, M. (2006). "That's All, Folks: After years of pushing synergy, Time Warner, Inc. says enough." *Wall Street Journal*, June 2, A1+.

8. See Grant, R. M. (1991). *Contemporary strategy analysis.* Cambridge, MA: Basil Blackwell.

9. Porter, M. E. (1987). *Competitive advantage.* New York: Free Press.

10. Lipman, S., and R. Rumelt (1982). "Uncertain imitability: An analysis of interfirm differences in efficiency under competition." *Bell Journal of Economics*, 13, pp. 418–438; Barney, J. B. (1986). "Strategic factor markets: Expectations, luck and business strategy." *Management Science*, 32, pp. 1512–1514; and Barney, J. B. (1986). "Organizational culture: Can it be a source of sustained competitive advantage?" *Academy of Management Review*, 11, pp. 656–665.

11. Note that the definition of sustained competitive advantage presented here, though different, is consistent with the definition given in Chapter 1. In particular, a firm that enjoys a competitive advantage for a long period of time (the Chapter 1 definition) does not have its advantage competed away through imitation (the Chapter 3 definition).

12. See Breen, B. (2003). "What's selling in America." *Fast Company*, January, pp. 80 +.

13. These explanations of costly imitation were first developed by Dierickx, I., and K. Cool (1989). "Asset stock accumulation and sustainability of competitive advantage." *Management Science*, 35, pp. 1504–1511; Barney, J. B. (1991). "Firm resources and sustained competitive advantage." *Journal of Management*, 7, pp. 49–64; Mahoney, J. T., and J. R. Pandian (1992). "The resource-based view within the conversation of strategic management." *Strategic Management Journal*, 13, pp. 363–380; and Peteraf, M. A. (1993). "The cornerstones of competitive advantage: A resource-based view." *Strategic Management Journal*, 14, pp. 179–191.

14. Dierickx, I., and K. Cool (1989). "Asset stock accumulation and sustainability of competitive advantage." *Management Science*, 35,

pp. 1504–1511. In economics, the role of history in determining competitive outcomes was first examined by Arthur, W. B. (1989). "Competing technologies, increasing returns, and lock-in by historical events." *Economic Journal*, 99, pp. 116–131.

15. See Breen, B. (2003). "What's selling in America." *Fast Company*, January, pp. 80 +.

16. This term was first suggested by Arthur, W. B. (1989). "Competing technologies, increasing returns, and lock-in by historical events." *Economic Journal*, 99, pp. 116–131. A good example of path dependence is the development of Silicon Valley and the important role that Stanford University and a few early firms played in creating the network of organizations that has since become the center of much of the electronics business. See Alley, J. (1997). "The heart of Silicon Valley." *Fortune*, July 7, pp. 86 +.

17. Reed, R., and R. J. DeFillippi (1990). "Causal ambiguity, barriers to imitation, and sustainable competitive advantage." *Academy of Management Review*, 15(1), pp. 88–102, suggest that causal ambiguity about the sources of a firm's competitive advantage need only exist among a firm's competitors for it to be a source of sustained competitive advantage. Managers in a firm, they argue, may fully understand the sources of their advantage. However, in a world where employees freely and frequently move from firm to firm, such special insights into the sources of a firm's competitive advantage would not remain proprietary for very long. For this reason, for causal ambiguity to be a source of sustained competitive advantage, both the firm trying to gain such an advantage and those trying to imitate it must face similar levels of causal ambiguity. Indeed, Wal-Mart recently sued Amazon for trying to steal some of its secrets by hiring employees away from Wal-Mart. See Nelson, E. (1998). "Wal-Mart accuses Amazon.com of stealing its secrets in lawsuit." *Wall Street Journal*, October 19, p. B10. For a discussion of how difficult it is to maintain secrets, especially in a world of the World Wide Web, see Farnham, A. (1997). "How safe are your secrets?" *Fortune*, September 8, pp. 114 +. The international dimensions of the challenges associated with maintaining secrets are discussed in Robinson, E. (1998). "China spies target corporate America." *Fortune*, March 30, pp. 118 +.

18. Itami, H. (1987). *Mobilizing invisible assets*, Cambridge, MA: Harvard University Press.

19. See Barney, J. B., and B. Tyler (1990). "The attributes of top management teams and sustained competitive advantage." In M. Lawless and L. Gomez-Mejia (eds.), *Managing the High Technology Firm* (pp. 33–48). Greenwich, CT: JAI Press, on teamwork in top management teams; Barney, J. B. (1986). "Organizational culture: Can it be a source of sustained competitive advantage?" *Academy of Management Review*, 11, pp. 656–665, on organizational culture; Henderson, R. M., and I. Cockburn, (1994). "Measuring competence? Exploring firm effects in pharmaceutical research." *Strategic Management Journal*, 15, pp. 63–84, on relationships among employees; and Dyer, J. H., and H. Singh (1998). "The relational view: Cooperative strategy and sources of interorganizational competitive advantage." *Academy of Management Review*, 23(4), pp. 660–679, on relationships with suppliers and customers.

20. For a discussion of knowledge as a source of competitive advantage in the popular business press, see Stewart, T. (1995). "Getting real about brain power." *Fortune*, November 27, pp. 201 +; Stewart, T. (1995). "Mapping corporate knowledge." *Fortune*, October 30, pp. 209 +. For the academic version of this same issue, see Simonin, B. L. (1999). "Ambiguity and the process of knowledge transfer in strategic alliances." *Strategic Management Journal*, 20(7), pp. 595–623; Spender, J. C. (1996). "Making knowledge the basis of a dynamic theory of the firm." *Strategic Management Journal*, 17 (Winter special issue), pp. 109–122; Hatfield, D. D., J. P. Liebeskind, and T. C. Opler (1996). "The effects of corporate restructuring on aggregate industry specialization." *Strategic Management Journal*, 17, pp. 55–72; and Grant, R. M. (1996). "Toward a knowledge-based theory of the firm." *Strategic Management Journal*, 17 (Winter special issue), pp. 109–122.

21. Porras, J., and P. O. Berg (1978). "The impact of organizational development." *Academy of Management Review*, 3, pp. 249–266, have done one of the few empirical studies on whether or not systematic efforts to change socially complex resources are effective. They found that such efforts are usually not effective. Although this study is getting older, it is unlikely that current change methods will be any more effective than the methods examined by these authors.

22. See Hambrick, D. (1987). "Top management teams: Key to strategic success." *California Management Review*, 30, pp. 88–108, on top management teams; Barney, J. B. (1986). "Organizational culture: Can it be a source of sustained competitive advantage?" *Academy of Management Review*, 11, pp. 656–665, on culture; Porter, M. E. (1980). *Competitive strategy*. New York: Free Press; and Klein, B., and K. Leffler (1981). "The role of market forces in assuring contractual performance." *Journal of Political Economy*, 89, pp. 615–641, on relations with customers.

23. See Harris, L. C., and E. Ogbonna (1999). "Developing a market oriented culture: A critical evaluation." *Journal of Management Studies*, 36(2), pp. 177–196.

24. Lieberman, M. B. (1987). "The learning curve, diffusion, and competitive strategy." *Strategic Management Journal*, 8, pp. 441–452, has a very good analysis of the cost of imitation in the chemical industry. See also Lieberman, M. B., and D. B. Montgomery (1988). "First-mover advantages." *Strategic Management Journal*, 9, pp. 41–58.

25. Rumelt, R. P. (1984). "Toward a strategic theory of the firm." In R. Lamb (ed.), *Competitive strategic management* (pp. 556–570). Upper Saddle River, NJ: Prentice Hall, among others, cites patents as a source of costly imitation.

26. Significant debate surrounds the patentability of different kinds of products. For example, although typefaces are not patentable (and cannot be copyrighted), the process for displaying typefaces may be. See Thurm, S. (1998). "Copy this typeface? Court ruling counsels caution." *Wall Street Journal*, July 15, pp. B1 +.

27. For an insightful discussion of these complementary resources, see Amit, R., and P. J. H. Schoemaker (1993). "Strategic assets and organizational rent." *Strategic Management Journal*, 14(1), pp. 33–45.

28. See Kearns, D. T., and D. A. Nadler (1992). *Prophets in the dark*. New York: HarperCollins; and Smith, D. K., and R. C. Alexander (1988). *Fumbling the future*. New York: William Morrow.

29. (2004). "Gateway will close remaining retail stores." *Wall Street Journal*, April 2, p. B2; Michaels, D. (2004). "AA Airbus, picturing huge jet was easy; building it was hard." *Wall Street Journal*, May 27, pp. A1 +; Zeller, W., A. Michael, and L. Woellert (2004). "The airline debate over cheap seats." *Wall Street Journal*, May 24, pp. A1 +.

30. (2004). "Casio." *Marketing*, May 6, p. 95; Weisul, K. (2003). "When time is money—and art." *BusinessWeek*, July 21, p. 86.

31. That said, there have been some "cracks" in Southwest's capabilities armor lately. Its CEO suddenly resigned, and its level of profitability dropped precipitously in 2004. Whether these are indicators that Southwest's core strengths are being dissipated or there are short-term problems is not yet known. However, Southwest's stumbling would give US Airways some hope. Trottman, M., S. McCartney, and J. Lublin (2004). "Southwest's CEO abruptly quits 'draining job.'" *Wall Street Journal*, July 16, pp. A1 +.

32. One should consult a lawyer before getting involved in these forms of tacit cooperation.

33. This aspect of the competitive dynamics in an industry is discussed in Smith, K. G., C. M. Grimm, and M. J. Gannon (1992). *Dynamics of competitive strategy*. Newberry Park, CA: Sage.

34. Schlender, B. R. (1992). "How Sony keeps the magic going." *Fortune*, February 24, pp. 75–84.

35. Personal communication.

36. See, for example, T. Peters and R. Waterman (1982), *In Search of Excellence*, New York: Harper Collins; J. Collins and J. Porras (1994), *Built to last*, New York: Harper Business; J. Collins (2001), *Good to great*, New York: Harper Collins; and W. G. Bennis and R. Townsend (2006), *Reinventing leadership*, New York: Harper Collins.

37. Collis, D. (1988). "The Walt Disney Company (A): Corporate strategy." Harvard Business School Case No. 1-388-147; Rukstad, N. M., and D. Collis (2001). "The Walt Disney Company: The entertainment king." Harvard Business School Case No. 9-701-035.

38. Porter, M. E. (1990). *The competitive advantage of nations*. New York: Free Press.

39. See Hamel, G. (1991). "Competition for competence and inter-partner learning within international strategic alliances." *Strategic Management Journal*, 12, pp. 83–103.

40. Quoted in Hamel, G. (1991). "Competition for competence and inter-partner learning within international strategic alliances." *Strategic Management Journal*, 12, p. 86.

41. See, for example, Peterson, R. B., and J. Y. Shimada (1978). "Sources of management problems in Japanese–American joint ventures." *Academy of Management Review*, 3, pp. 796–804.

Case 1-1: Bill Drayton's "Ashoka"*

The Social Entrepreneur's "Social Enterprise"

"While a business entrepreneur may thrive on competition and profit, a social entrepreneur has a different motivation: a commitment to leading through inclusiveness of all actors in society and a dedication to changing the systems and patterns of society."[1]

— **Ashoka Fellows in India**

"At a time when socialism has proven a dismal failure, and government programs have created as many problems as they solve, Ashoka may well be showing us the path to a better world."[2]

— *Forbes Magazine*

Social entrepreneurship was an unknown concept to people before 1980. The Industrial Revolution in the UK had led to the division of society into two halves; namely, the business and social sectors. While the business sector grew rapidly, the other half of the society lagged behind. However, after the establishment of Ashoka in 1980 the social sector began to develop. Bill Drayton, the founder of Ashoka, focused on innovation for the development of the social sector. The enterprise that he founded is responsible for bringing in major social reforms in various countries. Social entrepreneurs, who are called "fellows" in Ashoka, are the people behind this development. These entrepreneurs are financially and professionally supported by the enterprise.

About Social Entrepreneurship

Social entrepreneurship is a term used to describe the application of business principles to the social sector or citizen sector as termed by Drayton, President and CEO of Ashoka. As Ashoka defines it, social entrepreneurship is solving social problems entrepreneurially. It was Peter Drucker who first introduced the term "social sector" in his book *Post-Capitalist Society*, where he described the need for another sector, in addition to the public and private sector, to satisfy the social needs of the people. After the Industrial Revolution of 1700 in the United Kingdom, the society was divided into two unequal sectors; namely, business and social. Over the years, the business sector became enterprising and competitive, growing at a rapid rate. But the other half of the society, supported by taxes and protected from competition, lagged behind the business sector. Governments financially supported the people involved in this field so that there would be less competition among them for obtaining funds. Though the social entrepreneurial movement had started way earlier with individual social entrepreneurs like Florence Nightingale, Maria Montessori, and others, the social sector was slow to develop. As compared to the business sector, the social sector remained backward and unproductive.

After the establishment of Ashoka in 1980 social entrepreneurship gained increased attention. This was a time when more and more people came forward to respond to the increasing gap between the rich and poor. The imbalance between the business and social sector, and ineffectiveness of the traditional non-profit organizations and government bureaucracies were the reasons analysts cited for the upsurge in the social sector. Social entrepreneurs, who with their creativity, knowledge, and innovation, were determined to solve social problems, brought about major changes. The world witnessed many individuals who with their determination brought changes in different fields across various countries (Annexure l). David Bornstein,

* This case was written by Sushma, under the direction of Souvik Dhar, ICFAI Business School Case Development Centre. It is intended to be used as the basis for class discussion rather than to illustrate either effective or ineffective handling of a management situation. The case was compiled from published sources. © 2006, ICFAI Business School Case Development Centre. Reference no 806–029–1.

author of the book *How to Change the World: Social Entrepreneurs and the Power of New Ideas*, said, "What business entrepreneurs are to the economy, social entrepreneurs are to social change. They are the driven, creative individuals who question the status quo, exploit new opportunities, refuse to give up, and remake the world for the better."[3] More individuals entered into this sector and the social sector began to become entrepreneurial and competitive. According to the Department of Trade and Industry in the United Kingdom, there are more than 1,500 social enterprises across the world. They employ half a million people and also contribute £18 billion[4] every year to the global economy. Analysts anticipate that the number of social enterprises as well as that of social entrepreneurs would increase further in the coming years. Increases in the number of social entrepreneurs and their improved access to capital has contributed to the enhancement of the social sector. The sector combined the advantages of both businesses and non-

profit organizations. Prominent business schools have also begun to offer courses and projects on social entrepreneurship, which were earlier not included in the curriculum. Drayton anticipates that there will be a re-integration of business and the social sector in the future. The revolution in the social sector has changed the way society organizes itself and the way social problems are solved.

Inception of Ashoka

In 1980, Ashoka, one of the leading social enterprises in the world, was founded by Drayton. He named the enterprise after the Indian emperor Ashoka of the third century B.C. Speaking in an interview, Drayton said the idea for establishing an organization for social entrepreneurs came to his mind when he was studying at Harvard in 1963. During those days, Drayton actively participated in the Civil

---

Annexure 1 List of Social Entrepreneurs

Historical Examples of Leading Social Entrepreneurs

Susan B. Anthony (U.S.) - Fought for women's rights in the United States, including the right to control property, and helped spearhead adoption of the 19th amendment.

David Brower (U.S.) - An environmentalist and conservationist, he served as the Sierra Club's first executive director and built it into a worldwide network for environmental issues. He also founded Friends of the Earth, the League of Conservation Veters and The Earth Island Institute.

Vinoba Bhave (India) - Founder and leader of the Land Gift Movement, he caused the redistribution of more than 7,000,000 acres of land to aid India's untouchables and landless. Mahatma Gandhi described him as his mentor.

Frederick Law Olmstead (U.S.) - Creator of major urban parks, including Rock Creek Park in Washington, D.C., and Central Park in New York City, he is generally considered to have developed the profession of landscape architecture in America.

Mary Montessori (Italy) - Developed the Montessori approach to early childhood education.

Gifford Pinchot (U.S.) - Champion of the forest as a multiple-use environment, he helped found the Yale School of Forestry and created the U.S. Forest Service, serving as its first chief.

Florence Nightingale (U.K.) - Founder of modern nursing, she established the first school for nurses and fought to improve hospital conditions.

Margaret Sanger (U.S.) - Founder of the Planned Parenthood Federation of America, she led the movement for family planning efforts around the world.

John Muir (U.S.) - Naturalist and conservationist, he established the National Park System and helped found the Sierra Club.

Jean Monnet (France) - Responsible for the reconstruction and modernization of the French economy following World War II, including the establishment of the European Coal and Steel Community (ECSC). The ECSC and the European Common Market were Monnet's mechanisms to integrate Europe and were direct precursers of the European Union, which have shaped the course of European history and global international affairs.

John Woolman (U.S.) - Led U.S. Quakers to voluntarily emancipate all their slaves between 1758 and 1800, his work also influenced the British Society of Friends, a major force behind the British decision to ban slaveholding. Quakers, of course, became a major force in the U.S. abolitionist movement as well as a key part of the infrastructure of the Underground Railroad.

Some Present Day Social Entrepreneurs

Dr. Verghese Kurien (India) - Founder of the AMUL Daily Project, which has revolutionized the dairy industry through the production chain of milk, small producers, consumer products, and health benefits for workers.

Bill Drayton (U.S.) - Founded Ashoka, Youth Venture, and Get America Working!

Muhammad Yunus (Bangladesh) - Founder of microcredit and the Grameen Bank.

Marian Wright Edelman (U.S.) - Founder and president of the Children's Defense Fund (C.D.F.) and advocate for disadvantaged Americans and children.

Source: "What Is a Social Entrepreneur?," www.ashoka.org.

Rights Movement in the U.S., which was based on Mahatma Gandhi's ideas. He founded a number of organizations ranging from Harvard's Ashoka Table, a discussion group based on social sciences, to Yale Legislative Services. In 1963, he went to India to join Vinoba Bhave's Bhoodan (land gift) movement.[5] This movement had a great influence on Drayton. Even Drayton admitted that it was Bhave from whom he learned about changing society and also the process of change. In 1980, Drayton established Ashoka in India, with a budget of $50,000.[6] Initially, Drayton faced financial problems in running the enterprise. He called on various corporations and foundations to support the enterprise, but his efforts failed.

His search ended in 1984 when the John D. and Catherine T. MacArthur Foundation[7] awarded him $200,000.[8] After 1984, he went on to successfully raise millions of dollars for the enterprise. The enterprise led by Drayton is responsible for bringing about major social reforms in various countries. According to some experts, the whole credit goes to Drayton for bringing these reforms in society. Drayton's work has not been just confined only to the expansion of Ashoka, but also contributed much to the development of the social sector. Speaking on this, J. Gregory Dees, professor at Duke University's Fuqua School of Business said, "Bill was the pioneer; he really laid the foundation for the rest of us."[9]

Ashoka: Bill Drayton's Social Enterprise

Since the founding of Ashoka, Drayton has not only been instrumental in expanding the enterprise's network of entrepreneurs, but also in developing the social sector. The network of Ashoka's social entrepreneurs is spreading across the world at a very fast rate. To increase its network further, Ashoka plans to select more fellows in the near future. Every year it elects nearly 150 leading social entrepreneurs from various countries to its global fellowship. Ashoka elected its first social entrepreneurs in India in 1981. Since then, Ashoka appointed more than 1,700 fellows in 60 countries across the world. These fellows work in six broad fields, such as learning/youth development, environment, health, human rights, economic development and civic participation, across Asia, Africa, Latin America, Central Europe, and the United States. These social entrepreneurs, who have the same creativity and determination of any leading business entrepreneur, are provided grants by Ashoka. The social entrepreneurs apply these qualities for solving social problems on a large scale. Grants are offered to the fellows in the form of stipends so

as to enable them to concentrate fully on their ideas that have the ability to bring about changes. Ashoka gets these grants from various sources such, as corporations, business entrepreneurs and individuals. However, it does not accept funds from governments. The ultimate objective of Ashoka behind supporting social entrepreneurs is to make everyone a change maker in the world.

Ashoka fellows have certain achievements to their credit. In 1989, Fabio Rosa, an Ashoka fellow, created Project Light, which brought electricity to thousands of homes and farms for the first time in rural Brazilian communities. There were some fellows who changed the entire pattern of an educational system in some countries. An Ashoka social entrepreneur named Rodrigo Baggio opened more than 100 schools providing computer education in the slums of Brazil. Baggio's project is also being followed by other countries, such as Japan. In Nepal, an Ashoka fellow named Anil Chitrakar successfully stopped deforestation in the country. Another Ashoka fellow named David Green conducted free cataract operations on thousands of patients at Aravind Eye Hospital in India. He also provided expensive medicines to the poorest people of some countries across the world.

Some of the other achievements include providing low-cost electricity to Brazilian farmers, changing the curriculum of India's elementary schools, and financially assisting poor women in Bangladesh to set up their own businesses by providing them micro-credit. A majority of Ashoka's entrepreneurs' work was to find new ideas that were expected to bring changes in their respective fields. From 2000 onwards Ashoka's work, which was earlier limited to only developing countries, began to gain momentum in developed countries like the United States and Canada. Having realized that transferring ideas, skills, and resources between business and social sectors generates benefits, Ashoka developed centers and programs to improve the association between both sectors. For this, it entered into partnership with McKinsey in 1996, Hill & Knowlton, a leading international public relations and public affairs firm, in 2001, and International Senior Lawyers Project, a volunteer legal service provider, in 2002. McKinsey has been providing management consulting, while Hill & Knowlton has been providing public relations expertise and International Senior Lawyers Project has been providing legal support to Ashoka. It also entered into partnership with Skoll Foundation, a foundation of eBay that makes social investments, which granted $1.5 million[10], over three years starting from 2003, for the establishment of the Global Academy for Social Entrepreneurship. The concept of social entrepreneurship coined by Drayton has attracted interest from people from various walks of life, from businessmen to politicians. It has also helped Ashoka in raising funds for the enterprise. With a view to raise funds further, Drayton decided to make social investment attractive to corporations. Drayton said that he aims to find a way to incorporate the social sector in the global financial system.[11] For this he has been visiting financial markets in the United States, and Europe with the aim of convincing corporate individuals to invest in the social sector.

In its efforts to make corporations invest in the social sector, Ashoka has been successful to a large extent. The enterprise states that there has been a change in the thinking of corporations with regard to their role in the social sector. Analysts also agree that the corporate world is awakening to the growth of the social sector. According to Ashoka, many companies have begun to recognize the mission and philosophy of the enterprise. Increases in career opportunities and growing salaries, in the social sector, according to analysts, have been motivating youth to join this sector. Ashoka also strives to attract the next generation with the help of its organization, named Youth Venture. Youth Venture, a sister organization of Ashoka, helps young people in starting businesses that would benefit their communities. To encourage youth, Drayton decided to diversify Youth Venture into other places apart from United States, where it was founded.

Though Ashoka is known for its success in promoting the concept of social entrepreneurship, it has also attracted criticism. Earlier the enterprise was criticized for focussing more on individuals, then it was criticized for the adoption of a business format in the process of designing and managing social projects. Reacting to this, Anamaria Schindler, international director of strategic partnerships of Ashoka in Brazil, said, "Sometimes people criticize us by saying that we impose a business format on the social projects, when our intention is to put the techniques to the service of the ideals and passion of the social entrepreneurs."[12] She further added that it is important to pass on the knowledge to its fellows so as to enable them to have more autonomy, efficiency and influence. In spite of criticisms, Drayton led Ashoka to make the enterprise one of the leading social enterprises in the world.

To improve the association between the business and social sectors, Ashoka continued to enter into partnerships with various ventures. In addition to McKinsey and Hill & Knowlton, Ashoka is also under negotiation with numerous financial institutions to create a new means of financing. Skoll Foundation enhanced its commitment to the cause of Ashoka's social entrepreneurs when in March 2006 it announced partnership with Ashoka by offering $3 million[13] grant to the enterprise. Ashoka is also planning to introduce an online market place where the fund providers and entrepreneurs could directly meet each other. Apart from these ideas the enterprise also plans to introduce a Social Investing Venture (SIV) program. Through this program, the enterprise seeks out leading social entrepreneurs across the world who have brought major structural changes in social finance and provide them the required assistance in their efforts, and enable them to work with other leading entrepreneurs in the social investment field.

Notes

1. "What Is a social entrepreneur?," www.ashoka.org.
2. "Ashoka questions and answers," www.ashoka.org.
3. "What Is social entrepreneurship?," www.fuqua.duke.org.
4. Gilmore, Grainne. "Money is not the only bottom line," http://business.timesonline.co.uk, January 12, 2006.
5. Bhoodan movement was an effort initiated by Vinoba Bhave, in 1951, to eliminate poverty by asking individuals and villages to gift their surplus land, which he redistributed among the untouchables and landless people.
6. "Bill Drayton, CEO, Ashoka," www.stanford.edu, January 26, 2005.
7. The John D. and Catherine T. MacArthur foundation is a private foundation that makes grants to individuals and groups who are engaged in activities to bring about improvement in the human condition.
8. Holmstrom, David. "Change happens, one entrepreneur at a time," http://csmonitor.com, February 10, 1999.

9.   Hus, Caroline. "Entrepreneur for social change. (Bill Drayton, humanitarian worker and founder of non-profit organization Ashoka) (Interview) (Biography)," *US News & World Report*, www.highbeam.com, October 31, 2005.
10. "Skoll Foundation and Ashoka enhance partnership to advance social entrepreneurship around the world." *PR Newswire*, www.highbeam.com, March 21, 2006.
11. Goff, Clare. "Steady rise of the 'citizen sector,'" http://newsft.com, February 28, 2006.
12. Pardini Flavia and Lobo Flavio. "The pioneers of change," www.ashoka.org, March 28, 2001.
13. Ibid.

Case 1–2: Apple Computer, Inc.*

iPods and iTunes[1]

Introduction

A senior vice president at Apple Computer, Inc. happened to glance at the latest news release on CNN.com. It was May 12, 2005, and Microsoft chairman Bill Gates had commented to a German newspaper:

> As good as Apple may be, I don't believe the success of the iPod is sustainable in the long run. You can make parallels with computers: Apple was very strong in this field before, with its Macintosh and its graphics user interface—like the iPod today—and then lost its position. If you were to ask me which mobile device will take top place for listening to music, I'd bet on the mobile phone for sure.[2]

With 70 per cent of the global market for MP3 music players, Apple had sold more than five million iPods in the last quarter alone. Unit sales of iPods accounted for the majority of Apple products sold, an impressive statistic considering iPods had been launched in 2001. As the senior vice president pondered Gates's comments, he wondered whether there were ways to ensure iPod's—and indeed Apple's—success in the future.

The Music Recording Industry

Recorded music, as a form of entertainment, could be encountered anywhere in North America and, indeed, much of the world. Thousands of radio stations broadcast song lists interspersed with commercials; television media make available music videos on popular channels such as MTV; and public venues such as shopping malls, bars, and restaurants play background music. Music tastes among consumers spanned the variety of options from classic rock, heavy metal, rap, country, and other existing and emerging genres. Although only a fraction of the countless recording artists achieved success and fame, the perceived glamour of the music industry continues to draw large numbers of aspiring recording artists, all eager to become the next rock star. Hilary Rosen, chief executive of Recording Industry Association of America (RIAA), a music industry group, stated: "Music isn't some excess luxury people can do without; it's as essential to human existence as water and toilet paper."[3]

Half of all Americans purchased recorded music, in the form of compact discs (CDs) and other media, at least once a year. Sales in the U.S. music industry were estimated at $11.4 billion in 2004 at retail level, down from $13 billion in 1999 (see Exhibit 1). Record label executives believed that a large proportion of this decline was due to online piracy. Rosen believed that global piracy cost the recording industry over US$4 billion a year. Observers countered by saying that, as record labels became more cautious in signing artists, the number of new albums released each year had dropped since its peak in 1999.[4] In addition, the record labels were slow to manage marketing and distribution costs associated with launching a new album, and investors considered the record industry to be a high-cost, high-risk, low-return business.[5] As an article in the *Financial Times* noted:

> The industry knows that record sales will never return to the dizzy heights of the 1980s and 1990s. It will, therefore, combine ruthless cost-cutting with a drive to earn from multiple revenue streams, where different pieces of software by the same artist can be cross-marketed.[6]

The key group that co-ordinated the development and distribution of recorded music was the recording companies, which included four major record labels: Sony BMG, Warner Music, Universal Music, and EMI. Combined, these recording companies produced and distributed 85 percent of all music recorded. Record labels (or recording companies) signed recording artists, developed, produced, marketed, and often distributed the recordings.

* Ken Mark prepared this case study under the supervision of Professor Mary Crossan solely to provide material for class discussion. The authors do not intend to illustrate either effective or ineffective handling of a managerial situation. The authors may have disguised certain names and other identifying information to protect confidentiality.

Ivey Management Services prohibits any form of reproduction, storage, or transmittal without its written permission. This material is not covered under authorization from CanCopy or any reproduction rights organization. To order copies or request permission to reproduce materials, contact Ivey Publishing, Ivey Management Services, c/o Richard Ivey School of Business, The University of Western Ontario, London, Ontario, Canada, N6A 3K7; phone (519) 661-3208; fax (519) 661-3882; e-mail cases@ivey.uwo.ca.

Copyright © 2005, Ivey Management Services Version: (A) 2006-09-22.

Exhibit 1   U.S. Music Industry Shipment and Sales (in millions, net after returns)

	1994	1995	1996	1997	1998	1999	2000	2001	2002	2003	2004
Total Units Shipped	1,123	1,113	1,137	1,063	1,124	1,161	1,079	969	860	798	814
Total Sales at Record Label Level	$12,068	$12,320	$12,534	$12,237	$13,711	$14,585	$14,324	$13,741	$12,614	$11,854	$12,155
Total Retail Units*			818	850	870	789	733	676	658	687	
Total Suggested Retail Value			$10,786	$12,165	$13,048	$12,705	$12,389	$11,549	$11,053	$11,423	

*CDs used in promotional giveaways and other marketing programs account for the difference between record label shipments and retail units.

Source: Recording Industry Association of America, May 2005.

When a consumer purchased a music CD at a retail outlet, he or she was picking up a product that had passed through several steps, shown in Exhibit 2, which contains a chart of the various players in the industry. As only 10 per cent of all artists were "profitable" in the sense that their record shipments, net of returns, generated higher revenues than the costs to produce the records, the four majors were constantly on the lookout for the next chart-topping recording artist. Exhibit 3 lists the various royalty and revenue rates for a typical CD release. In addition, the four majors were constantly on the lookout for fast-growing independent recording labels, acquiring them whenever possible to add to their growth.

Thousands of independent labels accounted for the rest of the music recording industry. Maturing computer technology—advanced music recording software and hardware, high-powered yet low-cost computers, and inexpensive recording media such as CDs—allowed budding recording artists to develop and release independent CDs, often self-marketing them through Internet sites.

Distributors typically sold product from record labels to retail chains, earning an estimated 10 per cent of retail price. In the United States, mass merchandisers such as Wal-Mart and Target accounted for 65 per cent of music retail sales, with the rest being sold in specialty and online stores; in Canada, the equivalent figures were 22 per cent and 78 percent, respectively. Traditional retail was the most dominant sales channel, accounting for 99 percent of sales, with online retail sales accounting for about 1 percent of sales.[7] In the United States, as recorded music was a small proportion of mass merchandisers' total sales, the retailers generally demanded price reductions of between 1 percent and 2 percent per year. These mass merchandisers had limited selections of music, choosing to stock popular releases that appealed to a wide audience. Highly concerned with inventory turns, mass merchandisers generally did not carry deep selection of music in any genre. In the past decade, online retailers began filling this gap, though they accounted for not more than 1 percent of the industry's CD sales.

Exhibit 2   Music Recording Industry Chart

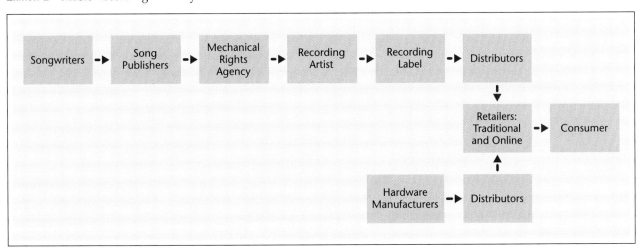

Source: Various articles and industry executives.

Exhibit 3   Various Royalty and Revenue Rates for a Typical CD Release*

Party	As % of Retail Price
Songwriters	0.30%
Song Publishers	0.30%
Mechanical license (for music reproduction)	3.50%
Recording artist-Gross Payments	16.50%
Less packaging costs	4.10%
Less promotional copies	1.20%
Less return reserves	2.90%
Less tours, videos, marketing	*Depends*
Less manager fees	3.30%
Recording artist-Net Payments	*Depends*
Distributors	10.00%
Retail	25.00%
Record label	*Depends*

Average CD retail price = $15.00

*Recording artist-net payments and record label gross profit varied depending on whether record sales could cover an estimated $600,000 in tours, video and marketing costs.

Source: Various articles and industry executives.

Consumers purchased CDs at traditional retailers such as music specialty stores and mass merchandisers, and online retailers. Songs played on the radio were typically available at retail stores—specialty stores, mass merchandisers, online merchants. While production costs had dropped since CDs were first introduced in the 1980s—blank CDs could now be purchased for less than a dollar each—a typical CD continued to cost about $15 at retail. Industry observers believed that the drop in production costs had been offset by growing marketing and promotional costs related to CD launches. At stores, there was a wider variety of music CDs at specialty retailers, compared to mass merchandisers. At retail, consumers had no choice but to purchase the entire CD even if they wanted only a single song from the 10-song playlist.

Hardware advances had enabled the development of segments outside of home entertainment. The launch of Sony's cassette tape-playing Walkman in the late 1970s offered consumers a portable device, and the subsequent proliferation of portable music devices increased choice and reduced prices, which drove demand for both hardware and music records. Until 1998, digital music files could be played only on computers. However, the launch of Diamond Multimedia's Rio 300 MP3 player allowed consumers to carry with them and play 16 digital songs. Within a few months of the Rio's introduction, the number of companies offering MP3 players grew into the hundreds. Within a year, digital storage capacity for MP3 players increased from about one hour to five hours (or about

60 songs). However, there was no set standard for design with regard to placement and sequence of device buttons, nor were there limits to the number of functions a manufacturer could include. The result was that functionality varied significantly from device to device.

Music format technology continued to advance at a rapid pace. Newer formats such as CDs were cross compatible with other systems (for example, music CDs were playable on DVD machines) and could store greater amounts of data versus old formats such as cassette tapes or vinyl LPs (long players). The newest physical format, the DVD, could hold more data than CDs. Digital formats such as MPEG and its later versions such as MP3 increased the ease by which music could be shared. Before the recent arrival of encryption technology, songs could be easily copied or "ripped" from CDs, converted into digital format, then e-mailed as an attachment to many recipients. With older formats such as the cassette tape, it was tedious for consumers to make more than one physical copy of a tape at a single sitting.

The equipment necessary to duplicate CDs ranged from simple home computers with CD burners to high-volume, commercial-grade machines, and both were easily obtainable. CD covers could be easily scanned and printed on high-quality color printers, giving these illegal copies a professional look to them. While pirated copies of CDs were usually sold by street hawkers or through an individual's network, in some countries, large-scale operations dedicated to illegal copying and distribution of CDs existed. In some places, pirated CDs sold for less than 10 per cent of the retail cost of the real thing.

Although piracy was thought to account for a loss of 12 percent of industry revenues annually, piracy itself, according to a music executive, created more "noise" than sales losses. However, music executives noticed that when digital formats became available to consumers, consumers became more interested in downloading music for free versus paying for any CDs, whether authentic or pirated. The RIAA, of which the four major recording labels were members, became increasingly concerned with the ease at which songs could be shared online. While some music was digitally recorded for free distribution, a large amount of digital music in circulation contained pirated music. The RIAA began taking action, suing Web sites such as MP3.com for not paying royalties on the music it made available to consumers. Digital player manufacturers such as Diamond Multimedia were also sued.

In addition to their legal maneuvres, music industry members also attempted to develop standards to combat illegal downloads. In 1998, the Secure Digital Music Initiative (SDMI) was founded by members of the music recording industry to develop secure methods for distributing digital music. Their resulting plan encouraged, in Phase 1, the launch of SDMI-compliant music players that would play SDMI-compliant content only and, in Phase 2, computer applications that would prevent consumers from obtaining or distributing music on illegal sites. The SDMI even ran a "crack SDMI" contest where $10,000 was put up as a prize for hackers who could successfully defeat SDMI's screening technology. Several hacker groups called for a boycott of the contest, saying record labels were trying to limit consumers' "fair use" rights to make copies of music they purchased for their own personal use in a car stereo or laptop computer.[8] To SDMI's dismay, barely a month after the contest was launched, hackers successfully defeated the SDMI systems. Two academics collected the prize but, due to threats of lawsuits from the SDMI, decided not to present their findings in a public forum. (After a few months of legal wrangling, they were allowed to proceed with the publication.)

The RIAA's biggest challenge came in 1999 when a then-unknown university student decided to code and release a peer-to-peer (P2P) file-sharing program named Napster.

Napster and the RIAA

When a roommate complained about the difficulties in finding downloadable music on the Internet, Shawn Fanning, a freshman at Northeastern University, decided to develop a program to change the way people shared music online. His program, Napster, allowed computers to link up with each other and trade files over the Internet. Fanning made Napster available as a free download, and the program acted as a central hub, a P2P network that allowed users to exchange files—music files in particular—with each other, with traffic passing through Napster's centralized servers (though no copies of music files were saved on Napster's computers). When he released Napster, Fanning had no intentions of profiting from it, seeing it as "a cool way to build community."[9]

In 1999, the Internet was rapidly gaining popularity, especially among the teenage population, who swiftly adopted tools such as e-mail. News of Napster spread, especially in college dormitories, as students typically had the high-speed Internet access necessary to download large files quickly.

Even with Napster, downloading music on the Internet was difficult for those who were not technologically inclined. To download a song, a user would have to run a P2P program and search for a song, which would take about 10 seconds to two minutes to process, depending on the popularity of the track. After the program had finished finding other connections on the P2P network to connect to and download music from, users downloaded a particular file from one of the available connections. However, the user ran the risk of the track being corrupt—unable to play after being downloaded—receiving an incomplete version, the wrong version, or being the recipient of a virus-contaminated file.

Users also required a fast Internet connection to download the songs at a reasonable speed; a high-speed connection would be able to download a multimegabyte song within minutes, but a slower dial-up Internet connection could take anywhere from five minutes to half an hour to download the same file. In addition, the other user (from whose computer the user was downloading the song) could unexpectedly shut off the connection by logging off, requiring the user to go back into the system and attempt to find another reliable connection from which to download.

Despite the difficulties involved, by late 1999, millions of users had downloaded from Napster, and the user base was growing at between 5 and 25 percent daily, according to the company.[10] Concerned at the rising amount of Internet bandwidth taken up by students using Napster to trade files, some U.S. colleges moved to block the service altogether. Fanning's uncle, realizing the potential of Fanning's venture, approached venture capitalists and secured seed funding for Napster. Then Fanning dropped out of school and moved west to continue working on his program. According to company executives, in late 1999, Napster aimed to earn revenues through user membership fees, with a portion of the earnings remitted to the recording industry.[11]

Then the RIAA, which represented the major record labels, sued Napster for copyright infringement in December 1999. The RIAA—of which Napster was a member—claimed that Napster facilitated piracy. Knowledge of Napster, already spreading quickly, was given a boost because of the publicity from the lawsuit. Almost immediately, downloads from Napster jumped into the millions per week. During the trial, it was revealed to the court that Napster's goals, as contained in early business plans, were "to bring about the death of the CD" and "make record stores obsolete."[12]

By February 2001, Napster was ordered by the U.S. Court of Appeals to stop the distribution of copyrighted materials. The court ruled that Napster's service was not protected by fair use and that Napster was guilty of two kinds of copyright infringement (contributory and vicarious), had failed to police its system in an attempt to stop the spread of copyrighted works, and had done substantial harm to record companies. "Napster, by its conduct, knowingly encourages and assists the infringement of [record company] copyrights," the court wrote in its decision.[13]

Napster responded by blocking the download of over 250,000 songs by screening for 1.6 million song names. But users simply found a way around this problem by generating new names for songs.

Unfortunately for Napster, the ongoing legal fight was depleting its cash reserves. In early 2000, Napster executives rethought their company's strategy, considering cash-generating ventures like selling advertising, adding e-commerce capabilities to sell concert tickets, or even pursuing co-promotional opportunities with record companies.[14] Then Napster was ordered by the court to stop the exchange of all music on its servers until it could block all music owned by other music companies. This order effectively shut Napster down. Napster's name and assets were eventually sold to Roxio.

Meanwhile, two major alliances in the music industry attempted to launch their own online music distribution sites: MusicNet (Warner Music, BMG, EMI Group, Real Networks), and Pressplay (Universal Music Group and Sony Music Entertainment, partnering with Microsoft for digital media technology and MSN Internet service). The U.S. Department of Justice launched an antitrust investigation to determine whether both alliances were anti-competitive. Music consumers largely dismissed both services.

Napster's notoriety drove other programmers to develop their own version of file-sharing programs: Limewire, Gnutella, Bearshare, Morpheus, Grokster, and Kazaa, to name just a few. The programmers were aided by the fact that the base software code for the mentioned programs had been made available to all by hackers. By 2003, there were at least 14 versions of file-sharing software freely available. Politicians contemplated bills to outlaw P2P programs. The RIAA continued its tactics, suing Napster clones in the courts.

But, unlike Napster, these new file-sharing programs did not require centralized servers to manage traffic. They allowed peers to connect directly with other peers, forming a decentralized network of individual PCs that had no centre. Thus, Kazaa, for example, could not be shut down, as Napster had been forced to, by switching off a set of centralized servers.

The RIAA started relying on a different tactic: using software that sought out pirated music in the file-sharing networks so as to gather evidence against individuals. While it was not illegal for consumers to download music or to make copies for their own personal use, the RIAA argued that making music available for download, en masse, was a violation of the music owners' copyright. In an open letter to music downloaders, Rosen stated:

I think we proved with our lawsuit against Napster that we can stop MP3 trading on the Internet. … All of this litigation is expensive and is just making the prices of CDs higher. Downloaders, you are just making it worse for yourselves. Once the RIAA has stomped out file trading on the Internet and a CD costs $35, it'll be a well-deserved hangover from your free music binge, and you better believe you're going to regret it. … As part of our newly announced War On Consumers, we are … introducing progressive legislation into Congress which would allow us to prosecute individuals for music downloading.[15]

In a well-publicized series of over 500 lawsuits, the RIAA sued and won (small) damages against individuals who were making available to peers more than 1,000 songs on their computer.

In addition, the RIAA hired small independent companies called "spoofers" to dilute file-sharing networks with fake music files. These companies set up accounts on the major file-sharing networks and shared files that were designed to look like actual music. But these dummy files were either totally blank or had only part of the song that the user was looking for. Randy Saaf, the president of the spoofing company MediaDefender, stated that the idea was to frustrate users who were trying to download copyrighted songs.[16]

In addition to the music industry, the film industry was another target of file-sharing consumers. On June 27, 2005, in what was considered a win for both industries, the U.S. Supreme Court ruled, unanimously, in *Metro-Goldwyn-Mayer Studios v. Grokster Ltd.*, that file-sharing companies could be liable for copyright infringement if their products encouraged consumers to illegally swap songs and movies. However, observers noted that even if file-sharing program companies like Grokster collapsed, their software was already installed and being used by millions of consumers. Other companies not named in the case continued to offer new types of file-sharing software with more sophisticated features, such as the capability of handling larger files. Finally, independent programmers were likely to continue to develop file-sharing applications and quietly release them online.[17]

Apple Computer

In 2001, Apple Computer had roughly 3 percent of the worldwide PC computing platform market, trailing Linux (10 percent) and market-leader Microsoft (87 percent). In an industry that had double-digit annual compound growth, Apple's computer hardware sales declined every year. Apple was faced with the challenge of trying to grow its loyal installed user base in a highly saturated and competitive market.

With 25 million Mac users worldwide, Apple had an iconic consumer brand, a loyal customer base, and a reputation for developing innovative products. Apple claimed to produce the entire computing package for a user, which in turn, allowed them to charge higher margins on their products.

The Launch of iPods

In 2001, Apple released the Apple iPod, a hard-drive-based music player with a retail price tag of $399. (Apple's gross margin was 64 percent of the retail price.) It was capable of storing approximately 1,024[18] digital songs, almost 21 times more capacity than the leading MP3 player on the market. Along with the launch of iPod, Apple created an iPod Lounge Web site where users were able to create user profiles, make their own iPod accessories, such as an iPod cover, and submit suggestions and ideas regarding iPod changes. The forum was moderated by Apple employees who sifted through suggestions and presented them to the company.

Apple enlisted a few of the consumers who had been sued by the RIAA to star in television commercials supporting the launch of iPod. Commercials featured dancing silhouettes wearing iPod's distinctive white headphones. As industry observers commented that the iPod was on its way to achieving iconic cult status, many loyal Apple users considered the iPods as Windows users' first introduction to the "Apple way of life." The company also released Apple iPods by Hewlett-Packard and Dell, with the only difference being a small company logo on the back of the Apple iPod underneath the Apple logo.

The Launch of iTunes Software

Concurrently with the launch of iPods, the iTunes software was created in 2001 and bundled with each Apple iPod purchased by users. iTunes was the only program that allowed songs to be played on the Apple iPods, using company's proprietary "FairPlay" Digital Rights Management (DRM) system. DRM referred to the ability of digital content vendors to control how the material could be used on any electronic device with such measures installed. Apple's DRM system worked by encrypting (or "wrapping") each audio file to make it compatible with Apple iPods, and the system prevented songs from being traded on illegal P2P networks. Standard digital formats such as MP3 could not be played on the iPod; a user had to rely on the iTunes software to convert MP3s into Apple's chosen format, Advanced Audio Coding (AAC), before the songs could be played on the iPod.

In addition to encryption, iTunes also managed the songs on the iPods into categories for the user, with features like playlists or random auto filling of iPods from users' personal digital libraries.

The Launch of iTunes Music Store

Before the launch of iTunes Music Store, Steve Jobs, Chief Executive Officer of Apple Computer, Inc., had to convince reluctant record producers and artists to distribute their music online. Jobs personally demonstrated the music service to key recording artists. Jobs emphasized the elegance and simplicity of the iTunes Music Store and indicated that a credit card was all that was required to purchase a song or album. He also emphasized his belief that consumers wanted to "own" the music they downloaded.

The iTunes Music Store was launched in 2003, approximately two years after the iPod was first released. The store began with 200,000 songs available to download, each costing $0.99. Analysts were divided as to the profitability of iTune's digital downloads. While some believed Apple earned one cent per song in gross profit, others believed that the costs of running the iTunes Music Store could well exceed the $0.99 per song that Apple received.[19] Despite Apple's optimistic projections of selling 100 million songs in its first year of operations, only 70 percent of that target was reached. In 2004, iTune's song lineup more than tripled to over 700,000 songs. By March 2005, Apple announced that it had sold 300 million song downloads since the launch of iTunes Music Store.[20]

Throughout his negotiations with the music executives, Jobs touted the inclusion of Apple's digital rights management software. Still, it took 18 months for Jobs and a small team of Apple employees to negotiate deals with the four major labels. As Hilary Rosen, chief executive of the Recording Industry Association of America (RIAA) put it, "If it weren't for Steve Jobs' persistence, I don't think this would have happened."

But Apple's DRM was not infallible: In March 2005, Jon Johansen, a computer programmer, announced that he had developed a new program that stripped the DRM restriction from iTunes, allowing users to download and trade iTunes songs like regular MP3 files.[21] Within a week, Apple announced that it had modified iTunes software to plug the breach in security.[22]

The Launch of Other iPods

Apple widened consumer choice by launching various sizes of iPods and limited edition versions such as a black and red iPod endorsed by the musical group U2. Apple released varying hard-drive iPods that could store up to 4,096 songs, retailing for $499. iPods also continued to be extremely popular. In April 2005, Apple disclosed that it had shipped 5.3 million iPods during its fiscal second quarter ended March 26, up from 807,000 the same period a year ago. In all, Apple revealed that the iPod accounted for $1.01 billion, or 31 percent, of total firm revenue for the quarter. At the end of Apple's second quarter in March 2005, the total number of iPods sold stood at 15 million and counting.[23]

But what caught observers' eyes was the launch of iPod's Shuffle player, a smaller flash memory-based (as opposed to hard drive-based) music device retailing for under $100. Within a few months, the Shuffle was the most popular flash-based memory player on the market, according to Apple's estimates.

Apple Faces Competitors

In terms of digital download competitors, the field was widening. Roxio, which changed its name to Napster, launched an online downloading music service, Napster-To-Go, charging $12.50 a month for unlimited access to songs. Instead of asking users to pay per song, Napster allowed consumers to fill portable digital music players with an unlimited amount of music, for a monthly fee. Users could choose from over 700,000 tracks and had the option of a trial basis, to test out the service for seven days. If the user stopped paying the monthly fee, the songs disappeared from the music player.

Other contenders included Motorola, which announced plans for a mobile cellular phone that offered iTunes-type software. A cell phone customer could pass a song to another person using Bluetooth, a short-distance wireless technology, allowing that friend to listen to a sample before deciding whether to buy it.

RealNetworks released Harmony, a program that would allow music downloads to work on iPods, by allowing RealNetworks' antipiracy software to be compatible with Apple's DRM. Apple responded by suing RealNetworks under the federal Digital Millenium Copyright Act, a law intended to stop illegal hacking of computer systems, and Apple also warned that future software upgrades to iPod could override the RealNetworks software to prevent RealPlayer music files from working. Wal-Mart entered the digital download market with $0.88

cent downloads. Other competitors such as Virgin and Sony were expected to enter the market.

By March 2005, according to analyst estimates, Apple—still the sales leader in online music downloads—was selling approximately 1.35 million iTunes song downloads a day, for a run-rate of around 40 million a month.[24] But music download estimates differed: The NPD Group believed that just 26 million songs were purchased from all legal sites in the month of March 2005. During the same month, NPD estimated that 240 million songs were downloaded for free.[25]

In terms of iPod competitors, Medion, a manufacturing firm, developed and launched what it believed to be a low-cost alternative to the iPod. It was the same size as the iPod and stored approximately 1,000 songs. Medion's key selling point, aside from cost, was that it allowed the user to download a wider variety of music files and formats without having to convert the format to any one standard.

Yet, according to market research firm NPD, Apple, in 2004, continued to command over 90 percent of the digital music hardware market, if one included Hewlett-Packard's version of the iPod (whose sales accounted for 3.6 percent of the market—enough for second place overall). For a chart of Apple's unit sales by product line, see Exhibit 4. In third place was Rio, with 2.8 percent of the market.

What's Next for Apple?

In April 2005, at a technology conference in Los Angeles, a few wireless companies announced that they had developed next-generation cell phones with music-carrying and playing capabilities. Cell phone manufacturers such as Samsung, Sony Ericsson, and Siemens were the most recent competitors to emerge. Because of their unique software systems, the music industry was assured that digital rights could be managed. Samsung released what the company called a 'music smartphone' complete with a three gigabyte hard disk to hold MP3's. But since their entry was fairly recent, industry observers were still unsure about the future of these competitors.

Apple considered creating application programming interfaces for the iPod, such as a To Do List or a Calendar. But Apple's executives initially refused to speculate about the iPod's prospects outside of digital music. A recent development, podcasting, had apparently caused Apple to change its mind. Podcasting, a combination of iPod and broadcasting, allowed users to download station broadcasts (radio or television) and listen to them at their own leisure. The popularity of podcasting had grown to such a level that Steve Jobs announced that the next update of iTunes, due in July 2005, would allow for one-click loading of podcasts. And, with software tools, any podcaster (broadcast provider) would be able to upload content to the iTunes Music Store.

Amidst all the positive news, Apple executives discovered that, in 2005, hackers had written software allowing users to purchase and play songs from the iTunes Store without any FairPlay encryption.

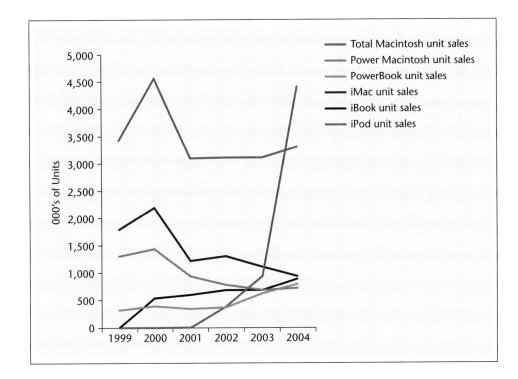

Exhibit 4   Apple Computer Unit Sales by Product Line

Notes

1. This case has been written on the basis of published sources only. Consequently, the interpretation and perspectives presented in this case are not necessarily those of Apple Computer Inc. or any of its employees.
2. "Bill Gates: Cellphone will beat iPod," *CNN/Money*, May 12, 2005.
3. Rosen, Hilary. "An open letter from RIAA president Hilary Rosen to music pirates everywhere," http://www.divisiontwo.com/articles/roseletter.htm, August 26, 2002.
4. Wiser, Mike. "Why do CDs cost so much?" *Frontline*, http://www.pbs.org/wgbh/pages/ forntline/shows/music/inside/faqs.html. May 27, 2004.
5. Horsfall, Robert. "The record industry is in crisis," *Financial Times*, March 25, 2003.
6. Ibid.
7. Interview with music executive, June 2005.
8. Zeidler, Sue. "U.S. hackers insist they beat audio technology," *Reuters News*, October 24, 2000.
9. Levy, Steven. "The man can't stop our music," *Newsweek*, March 27, 2000.
10. "Music industry is caught napping," *The Guardian*, March 16, 2000.
11. Holman, Sean. "Easy listening free software is making it a snap for users to download music…," *Globe and Mail*, December 23, 1999.
12. Conniff, Tamara. "Napster crashed by judge," *Hollywood Reporter*, July 27, 2000.

13. Costello, Sam. "Anti-Napster ruling draws mixed reaction," *IDG News Service and PCWorld.com*, February 12, 2001.
14. "Music industry is caught napping," *The Guardian*, March 16, 2000.
15. Rosen, Hilary. "An open letter from RIAA president Hillary Rosen to music pirates everywhere," http://www.divisiontwo.com/articles/roseletter.htm. August 26, 2002.
16. Wiser, Mike. "Why do CDs cost so much?" *Frontline*. http://www.pbs.org/wgbh/pages/frontline/shows/music/inside/fags.html. May 27, 2004.
17. Schatz Amy, McBride Sarah and Wingfield Nick. "High court to old media: You win," *The Wall Street Journal*, June 28, 2005.
18. Each gigabyte can store approximately 1,024 megabytes. Each digital tune is on average four to five megabytes.
19. Fried, Ina. "Will iTunes make Apple shine?" *CNET News.com*, October 16, 2003.
20. Betteridge, Jan. "iTunes tops 300 million downloads," *PC Magazine*, March 3, 2005.
21. Extreme Tech Staff, "DRM stripped from iTunes downloads," *Extremetech.com*, March 18, 2005.
22. Thompson, Jain. "Apple 'fixes' iTunes hack," *VNUnet Newswire*, March 22, 2005.
23. http://news.ipodworld.co.uk/index.php/weblog/apple_ships_record_quantity_of_ipods, accessed June 28, 2005.
24. Betteridge, Ian. "iTunes tops 300 million downloads," *PC Magazine*, March 3, 2005.
25. Schatz Amy, McBride Sarah and Wingfield Nick. "High Court to old media: You win," *The Wall Street Journal*, June 28, 2005.

Case 1-3: Wal-Mart Stores, Inc.*

As recently as 1979, Wal-Mart had been a regional retailer little known outside the South with only 229 discount stores compared to industry leader Kmart's 1,891 stores. In less than 25 years, Wal-Mart had risen to become the largest U.S. corporation in sales. With over $258 billion (see Exhibits 1 and 2) in revenues, Wal-Mart had far eclipsed Kmart, whose sales had fallen to a fraction of Wal-Mart's. Yet another measure of Wal-Mart's dominance was that it accounted for approximately 17 percent of general merchandise, apparel, and furniture sales in the United States by 1996[1] and as much as 30 percent of goods such as hair products and disposable diapers. *Forbes* put Wal-Mart's success into perspective.

> With 3,550 stores in the U.S. and 1,000 Supercenters to be added in the next five years, all that's left for Wal-Mart is mop-up. It already sells more toys than Toys "R" Us, more clothes than the Gap and Limited combined and more food than Kroger. If it were its own economy, Wal-Mart Stores would rank 30th in the world, right behind Saudi Arabia. Growing at 11 percent a year, Wal-Mart would hit half a trillion dollars in sales by early in the next decade.[2]

The central question facing Wal-Mart, however, was how to continue its remarkable growth (see Exhibit 3). Many observers believed that Wal-Mart was facing a maturing market and would no longer see the growth rates it had enjoyed previously. Domestic growth opportunities in its core business, discount retail centers, were largely limited to the Northeast and West Coast—areas that were notorious for their high costs and mobilization of neighborhood opposition to new Wal-Marts. Supercenters had provided significant growth for Wal-Mart, but it was not clear how long they could deliver the company's customary growth rates. Wal-Mart faced problems in other business areas as well. The Wal-Mart–owned Sam's Club warehouse stores had not measured up to Costco, its leading competitor. International operations were another challenge for Wal-Mart. Faced with slowing growth domestically, it had tried to capitalize on international opportunities. These international efforts, however, had met with only mixed success at best.

Wal-Mart was also a target for critics who attacked its record on social issues.[3] Wal-Mart had been blamed for pushing production from the United States to low-wage overseas producers. Some claimed that Wal-Mart had almost single-handedly depressed wage growth in the U.S. economy. Democratic presidential candidates John Kerry and Howard Dean had both singled out Wal-Mart for criticism in the 2004 U.S. presidential campaign. For many, Wal-Mart had become a symbol of capitalism that had run out of control. Indeed, *Time* magazine asked, "Will Wal-Mart Steal Christmas?"[4] Much of the criticism directed at Wal-Mart did not go beyond angry rhetoric. In many cases, however, Wal-Mart had faced stiff community opposition to building new stores.

With such challenges, some investment analysts questioned whether it was even possible for a company like Wal-Mart, with over $250 billion in sales, to sustain its accustomed high growth rates. To do so, Wal-Mart would have to address a number of challenges, such as maturing markets, competition in discount retailing from both traditional competitors and specialty retailers, aggressive efforts by competitors to imitate Wal-Mart's products and processes, and international expansion. Indeed, some believed that Wal-Mart would need to find new business if it were to continue its historic success.

The Discount Retail Industry

General retailing in the United States evolved dramatically during the twentieth century. Before 1950, general retailing most often took the form of Main Street department stores. These stores typically sold a wide variety of general merchandise. Department stores were also different from other retailers in that they emphasized service and credit. Before World War II, few stores allowed customers to take goods directly from shelves. Instead, sales clerks served customers at store counters. Not until the 1950s did self-help department stores begin to spread. Discount retail stores also began to emerge in the late 1950s. Discount retailers emphasized low prices and generally offered less service, credit, and return privileges. Their growth was spawned by the repeal of fair trade laws in many states. Many states had passed such laws during the Depression to protect local grocers from chains such as the Atlantic & Pacific Company. The laws fixed prices so that local merchants

---

* This case was prepared by William Hesterly for the purpose of classroom discussion.

Exhibit 1   Wal-Mart Stores, Inc., Earnings Statement, 1999–2004

Year Ended	1/31/04	1/31/03	1/31/02	1/31/01	1/31/00
Net Sales	256,329	229,616	204,011	191,329	165,013
Other Income	2,352	1,961	1,812	1,787	1,796
Rental Income	—	—	—	—	—
Total Revenue	**258,681**	**231,577**	**205,823**	**193,116**	**166,809**
Cost of Sales	198,747	178,299	159,097	150,255	129,664
General & Admin.	44,909	39,983	35,147	31,550	27,040
Debt Interest	729	799	1,080	1,104	756
Capital Lease Exp.	267	260	274	279	266
Interest Income	(164)	(132)	(171)	(188)	–
Total Operating Expense	**244,488**	**219,209**	**195,427**	**183,000**	**157,726**
Operating Income	**14,193**	**12,368**	**10,396**	**10,116**	**9,083**
Net Income Before Taxes	**14,193**	**12,368**	**10,396**	**10,116**	**9,083**
Provision for Income Taxes	5,118	4,357	3,765	3,692	3,338
Net Income After Taxes	**9,075**	**8,011**	**6,631**	**6,424**	**5,745**
Minority Interest	(214)	(193)	(183)	(129)	(170)
Net Income Before ExtraOrdinary Items	8,861	7,818	6,448	6,295	5,575
Income from Discount.	193	137	144	—	—
Accounting Change	—	0.00	0.00	0.00	(198)
Net Income	**9,054**	**7,955**	**6,592**	**6,295**	**5,377**
Income Available to Com Excl ExtraOrdinary	**8,861**	**7,818**	**6,448**	**6,295**	**5,575**
Income Available to Com Incl ExtraOrdinary	**9,054**	**7,955**	**6,592**	**6,295**	**5,377**
Basic Weighted Average Shares	4,363	4,430	4,465	4,465	4,451
Basic EPS Excluding ExtraOrdinary Items	**2.03**	**1.76**	**1.44**	**1.41**	**1.25**
Basic EPS Excluding ExtraOrdinary Items	**2.08**	**1.80**	**1.48**	**1.41**	**1.21**
Dilution Adjustment	0.00	0.00	0.00	0.00	0.00
Diluted Net Income	9,054	7,955	6,592	6,295	5,377
Diluted Weighted Average Shares	4,373	4,446	4,481	4,484	4,474
Diluted EPS Excluding ExtraOrdinary Items	**2.03**	**1.76**	**1.44**	**1.40**	**1.25**
Diluted EPS Including ExtraOrdinary Items	**2.07**	**1.79**	**1.47**	**1.40**	**1.20**
DPS-Common Stock	0.36	0.30	0.28	0.24	0.20
Gross Dividends-Common Stock	1,569	1,328	1,249	1,070	890

Exhibit 2   Wal-Mart Stores, Inc., Balance Sheet, 1999–2004

Year Ended	1/31/04	1/31/03	1/31/02	1/31/01	1/31/00
Cash/Equivalents	5,199	2,736	2,161	2,054	1,856
Receivables	1,254	1,569	2,000	1,768	1,341
Inv.-Replac.Cost	—	—	22,749	21,644	20,171
LIFO Reserve	—	—	(135)	(202)	(378)
Prepaid Expenses	1,356	837	1,103	1,291	1,366
Recoverable Cost	—	—	—	—	—
Inventories	26,612	24,401	—	—	—
Assets Discont.	0.00	1,179	—	—	—
Total Current Assets	34,421	30,722	27,878	26,555	24,356
Land	12,699	11,202	10,241	9,433	8,785
Building	38,966	33,345	28,527	24,537	21,169
Fixtures	17,861	15,640	14,135	12,964	10,362
Trans. Equipment	1,269	1,099	1,089	879	747
Depreciation	(15,594)	(13,116)	(11,436)	(10,196)	(8,224)
Net Leases	—	—	—	—	—
Capital Leases	5,092	4,814	4,626	4,620	4,285
Amortization	(1,763)	(1,610)	(1,432)	(1,303)	(1,155)
Goodwill/Intang.	9,882	9,389	8,566	9,059	9,392
Other	2,079	2,594	1,333	1,582	632
Assets Discount.	0.00	729	—	—	—
Total Assets	104,912	94,808	83,527	78,130	70,349
Commercial Paper	3,267	1,079	743	2,286	3,323
Accounts Payable	19,332	16,829	15,617	15,092	13,105
Accrued Liabs.	10,342	8,857	7,174	6,355	6,161
Accrued Taxes	1,377	748	1,343	841	1,129
Cur.Port.LT Debt	2,904	4,536	2,257	4,234	1,964
Cur.Port.Cap.Lse.	196	176	148	141	121
Short Term Debt	—	—	—	—	—
Liabs. Discont.	0.00	294	—	—	—
Total Current Liabilities	37,418	32,519	27,282	28,949	25,803
Long Term Dept	17,102	16,597	15,687	12,501	13,672
Capital Leases	2,997	3,000	3,045	3,154	3,002
Total Long Term Debt	20,099	19,597	18,732	15,655	16,674
Liabs. Discount.	0.00	— 10	—	—	—
Deferred Taxes	2,288	1,859	1,204	1,043	759
Minority Inter.	1,484	1,362	1,207	1,140	1,279
Total Liabilities	61,289	55,347	48,425	46,787	44,515
Common Stock	431	440	445	447	446
Paid In Capital	2,135	1,954	1,484	1,411	714
Retained Earnings	40,206	37,576	34,441	30,169	25,129
Other Comprehen.	851	(509)	(1,268)	—	—
Trans. Adjust.	—	—	—	(684)	(455)
Total Equity	43,623	39,461	35,102	31,343	25,834
Total Liabilities & Shareholders' Equity	104,912	94,808	83,527	78,130	70,349
S/O-Common Stock	4,311	4,395	4,453	4,470	4,457
Total Common Shares Outstanding	4,311	4,395	4,453	4,470	4,457
T/S-Common Stock	—	—	—	—	—
Total Preferred Shares Outstanding	—	—	—	—	—
Employees	1,500,000	1,400,000	1,383,000	1,244,000	1,140,000
Number of Common Shareholders	333,604	330,000	324,000	317,000	307,000

Exhibit 3   Wal-Mart Stores, Inc., Performance by Segment

Wal-Mart Stores Segment Fiscal

Fiscal Year	Segment Net Sales Increase from Prior Fiscal Year	Segment Operating Income (in Billions)	Segment Operating Income Increase from Prior Year	Operating Income as a Percentage of Segment Sales
2003	12.9%	$11.9	16.2%	7.6%
2002	14.1%	$10.2	6.3%	7.3%
2001	12.1%	$9.6	10.5%	7.9%

Sam's Club Segment

Fiscal Year	Segment Net Sales Increase from Prior Fiscal Year	Segment Operating Income (in Billions)	Segment Operating Income Increase from Prior Year	Operating Income as a Percentage of Segment Sales
2003	7.8%	$1.028	0.0%	3.2%
2002	9.7%	$1.028	9.1%	3.5%
2001	8.1%	$0.942	10.8%	3.5%

Net Sales

The company and each of its operating segments had net sales (in millions) for the three fiscal years ended January 31, 2003 as follows:

Fiscal Year	Wal-Mart Stores	Sam's Club	International	Other	Total Company	Total Company Increase From Prior Fiscal Year
2003	$157,121	$31,702	$40,794	$14,907	$244,524	12%
2002	139,131	29,395	35,485	13,788	217,799	14%
2001	121,889	26,798	32,100	10,542	191,329	16%

could not be undercut on price. The repeal of these laws freed discounters to offer prices below the manufacturer's suggested retail price.

Among discount retailers, there were both general and specialty chains. General chains carried a wide assortment of hard and soft goods. Specialty retailers, on the other hand, focused on a fairly narrow range of goods, such as office products or sporting goods. Specialty discount retailers such as Office Depot, Home Depot, Staples, and Circuit City began to enjoy widespread success in the 1980s. One result of the emergence of both general and specialty discount retailers was the decline of some of the best known traditional retailers. Moderate-priced retailers such as Sears and JCPenney had seen their market share decline in response to the rise of discount stores.

A number of factors explained why discount retailers had enjoyed such success at the expense of general old-line retailers. Consumers' greater concern for value, broadly defined, was perhaps most central. Value in the industry was not precisely defined, but involved price, service, quality, and convenience. One example of this value orientation was in apparel. Consumers who once shunned the private label clothing lines found in discount stores as a source of stigma were increasingly buying labels such as Wal-Mart's

Kathie Lee line. According to one estimate, discount stores were enjoying double-digit growth in apparel while clothing sales in department stores had decreased by 3 percent since 1991.[5]

Another aspect of consumers' concern for value involved price. Retail consumers had shown a greater sensitivity to price than in the pre-1990s period. They were less reliant on established brand names in a wide variety of goods and showed a greater willingness to purchase the private label brands of firms such as JCPenney, Sears, Kmart, and Wal-Mart. Convenience had also taken on greater importance for customers. As demographics shifted to include more working mothers and longer workweeks, many American workers placed a greater emphasis on fast, efficient shopping trips. More consumers desired "one-stop shopping" where a broad range of goods were available in one store, to minimize the time they spent shopping. This trend accelerated in the 1990s with the spread of supercenters. Supercenters, which combined traditional discount retail stores with supermarkets under one roof, grew to more than $100 billion in sales by 2001 and blurred some of the traditional lines in retailing.

Larger firms had an advantage in discount retailing. The number of multistore chains had risen dramatically.

Also, the number of retail business failures had risen markedly in the mid-1990s. Most of these failures were individual stores and small chains, but some discount chains such as Venture, Bradlee, and Caldor had filed for bankruptcy. Large size enabled firms to spread their overhead costs over more stores. Larger firms were also able to distribute their advertising costs over a broader base. Perhaps the greatest advantage of size, however, was in relationships with suppliers. Increased size led to savings in negotiating price reductions, but it also helped in other important ways. Suppliers were more likely to engage in arrangements with large store chains such as cooperative advertising and electronic data interchange links.

The Internet posed a greater threat to discount retailers as more people became comfortable with shopping online. By 2004, the number of Internet users had increased dramatically over the nearly 37 million users just eight years earlier. Internet shopping was appealing because of the convenience and selection available, but perhaps the most attractive aspect was the competitive pricing. Some Internet retailers were able to offer steep discounts because of lower overhead costs. Additionally, customers were able to quickly compare prices between different Internet retailers. Despite the great promise of Internet retailing, however, only a few specialty retailers had been profitable. Many traditional retailers had either initiated their own Web sites or had plans to do so.

Large discount retailers such as Wal-Mart derived considerable purchasing clout with suppliers because of their immense size. Even many of the company's largest suppliers gained a high proportion of their sales from Wal-Mart (see Exhibit 4). Suppliers with over $1 billion in sales such as Newell, Fruit of the Loom, Rubbermaid, Sunbeam, and Fieldcrest Cannon received over 15 percent of their sales from Wal-Mart. Many of these large manufacturers also sold a substantial proportion of their output to Kmart, Target, and other discount retailers. Frequently, smaller manufacturers were even more reliant on large discount retailers such as Wal-Mart. For example, Wal-Mart accounted for as much as 50 percent of revenues for many smaller suppliers.

Exhibit 4   Proportion of Sales That Suppliers Receive from Wal-Mart

Revenues	Total 1995	From Wal-Mart	Operating Margin	12-Month Price Change
Newell/housewares, home furnishings	$2,498	15%	20.7%	17%
Fruit of the Loom/apparel	2,478	16%	17.0	300%
Rubbermaid/plastic and rubber products	2,329	15	20.7	−10
Springs Industries/finished fabrics, home furnishings	2,233	12	10.9	10
Westpoint Stevens/linens, home furnishings	1,651	10	1.3	43
Sunbeam/household appliances	1,202	17	10.7	−33
Fieldcrest Cannon/linens, home furnishings	1,095	18	9.4	−13
First Brands/household products	1,053	12	15	38
Coleman/recreational gear	902	10+	14.7	12
Huffy/recreational gear	685	10+	4.6	−31
Roadmaster Industries/recreational gear	675	28	8	−37
Paragon Trade Brands/diapers	519	15	12.7	90
Playtex Products/personal care products	471	15	28.8	10
Ekco Group/housewares	270	10+	17.8	−2
Royal Appliance Manufacturing/vacuum cleaners	270	23	7	−19
Crown Crafts/textiles, home furnishings	214	16	12.3	−39
Armor All Products/auto polishes, protectants	204	20	20.5	−23
Toastmaster/home appliances	187	30	7.3	−38
Windmere/personal care products	185	18	10.6	−4
National Presto Industries/home appliances	123	35	19.8	3
Empire of Carolina/toys	119	17	5.6	−11
General Housewares/household products	117	13	10.6	−32
Safety 1st/child safety products	70	18	16.9	−50
National Picture & Frame/frames, mirrors	61	36	14.2	−3
Ohio Art/toys	43	20	5.9	48

Dollar amounts are in millions.

Source: Forbes, March 11, 1996.

Private label goods offered by discount stores had become much more important in the 1990s and presented new challenges in supplier relationships. Managing private labels required a high level of coordination between designers and manufacturers (who were often foreign). Investment in systems that could track production and inventory were also necessary.

Technology investments in sophisticated inventory management systems, state-of-the-art distribution centers, and other aspects of logistics were seen as critically important for all discount retailers. Discount retailers were spending large sums on computer and telecommunications technology in order to lower their costs in these areas. The widespread use of Universal Product Codes (UPCs) allowed retailers to more accurately track inventories for shop-keeping units (SKUs) and better match inventory to demand. Discount retailers also used electronic data interchange (EDI) to shorten the distribution cycle. EDI involved the electronic transmission of sales and inventory data from the registers and computers of discounters directly to suppliers' computers. Often replenishment of inventories was triggered without human intervention. Thus, EDI removed the need for several intermediate steps in procurement such as data entry by the discounter, ordering by purchasers, data entry by the supplier, and even some production scheduling by supplier managers. Wal-Mart was also pushing the adoption of radio frequency identification (RFID), a new technology for tracking and identifying products. RFID promised to eliminate the need for employees to scan UPC codes and would also dramatically reduce shrinkage, another term for shoplifting and employee pilferage. In November of 2003, Wal-Mart announced that large suppliers would have until January 2005 to implement RFID while smaller suppliers would have until January 2006. Suppliers anticipated that RFID would be costly to implement, but the benefits for Wal-Mart were estimated to be as high as $8 billion in labor savings and $2 billion in reducing shrinkage.

Another important aspect of managing inventory was accurate forecasting. Having the right quantity of products in the correct stores was essential to success. Stories of retailers having an abundance of snow sleds in Florida stores while stores in other areas with heavy snowfall had none were common examples of the challenges in managing inventory. Discounters used variables such as past store sales, the presence of competition, variation in seasonal demand, and year-to-year calendar changes to arrive at their forecasts.

Point-of-sale (POS) scanning enabled retailers to gain information for any purchase on the dollar amount of the purchase, category of merchandise, color, vendor, and SKU number. POS scanning, while valuable in managing inventory, was also seen as a potentially significant marketing tool. Databases of such information offered retailers the potential to "micromarket" to their customers. Upscale department stores had used the POS database marketing more extensively than discounters. Wal-Mart, however, had used such information. For example, POS data showed that customers who purchased children's videos typically bought more than one. Based on this finding, Wal-Mart emphasized placing other children's videos near displays of hot-selling videos.

Competitors

Competition in discount retailing came from both general and specialty discount stores. Among the general discount retailers, Wal-Mart was the largest, followed by Target and Kmart. Kmart had nearly 10 times more sales than the next-largest retailers Dollar General and ShopKo (see Exhibit 5). The most formidable specialty discount retailers included office supply chains such as Office Depot with over $12 billion in sales and Staples with approximately $13 billion, Toys "R" Us with over $11 billion, Circuit City in electronics with nearly $10 billion, and Payless Shoesource with almost $3 billion. In warehouse clubs, Costco and Sam's

Exhibit 5   Discount Department Store Industry Comparisons

	Kmart	Wal-Mart	Target	JCPenney	Sears	Discount Store Average
Sales per Sq. Ft.	$201	$334	$225	$174	$375	$253
Comp. Sales Growth	2.50%	4.90%	6.00%	3.40%	5.80%	3.50%
Total Selling Sq. Ft. (millions)	156	252	79	135	83	NA
Total Stores	2,261	2,558	735	4,084	3,372	NA

Source: Kmart annual report and Wal-Mart 10K.

Club dominated. Costco was the leader with over $42 billion in sales, followed by Sam's Warehouse Club. No other warehouse club chains had sales of even one-sixth of Sam's Club. Wal-Mart was the leader in supercenter chains with more than double the sales of the number-two firm in the category, Grand Rapids, Michigan-based Meijer. Meijer was followed by Fred Meyer, the pioneer in the supercenter format, and by Super Kmart Centers.

Once Wal-Mart's largest competitor, Kmart had experienced a long slide in performance. Kmart operated approximately 1,500 stores at the beginning of 2004 and had sales of $23 billion in 2003, down from $36 billion just four years earlier. Traditionally, Kmart's discount philosophy had differed from Wal-Mart's. Kmart discount centers sought to price close to, but not necessarily lower than, Wal-Mart's everyday low prices. More emphasis was placed on sale items at Kmart. Pricing strategy revolved around several key items that were advertised in Kmart's 73 million advertising circulars distributed in newspapers each Sunday. These items were priced sharply lower than competitors' prices. The effective implementation of this strategy had been impeded by Kmart's difficulty in keeping shelves stocked with sale items and by Wal-Mart's willingness to match Kmart's sale prices. An attempt to imitate Wal-Mart's everyday low pricing strategy failed to deliver sales growth at the same time it squeezed margins, so Kmart returned to its traditional pricing strategy in 2003.

Performance at Kmart had suffered dramatically in the 1990s. It experienced losses of over $300 million from 1993 to 1995 and by 1995 had seen its debt rating fall below investment grade. Various attempts to revitalize the company had fallen short of restoring profitability. A restructuring that closed over 200 stores in the mid-1990s and shuttered another 600 stores in 2002–2003 did not result in profitability in any year from 2001 to 2004. Sales per square foot dropped to $212 in 2002, which was down from $236 a year earlier. By 2004, there was some indication that all the restructuring might have eventually paid off as Kmart reported profitability in the first three quarters of the year. It was still plagued, however, by declining same-store sales. Some suggested that Kmart's primary goal was to serve as a cash cow for ESL Investments, Inc., and its founder Eddie Lampert. Assisted by $3.8 billion in accumulated tax credits, Kmart had generated over $2 billion in positive cash flow in the first three quarters of 2004. The presumption was cash would be used to fund other investments by ESL.[6]

Kmart sought to follow Wal-Mart's pattern in many of its activities. The company expressed a commitment to building a strong culture that emphasized performance, teamwork, and respect for individuals who, borrowing from Wal-Mart, were referred to as associates. Establishing such a culture was particularly challenging in the midst of workforce reductions that had taken Kmart from 373,000 employees in 1990 to 307,000 at the end of 1995, and then an even more precipitous drop to 158,000 in 2004. Kmart had also adopted Wal-Mart departmental structure within stores. Another area in which Kmart emulated Wal-Mart was in offering larger income potential to store managers. Each store manager's bonus was linked to an index of customer satisfaction. Kmart had also sought to close the gap between it and Wal-Mart in technology and distribution. The company made large information technology investments in the mid-1990s.

Although it had been criticized for several years for being slow to adapt, Kmart had shown a new aggressiveness in exploring new store concepts beginning in the mid-1990s. Developing new formats was the company's highest strategic priority. Like Wal-Mart, Kmart had begun to emphasize supercenters (combination supermarkets and discount centers). The first Super Kmart Center was opened in 1992. Kmart had also experimented with another store format in 1995 and subsequently converted a majority of its stores to this format. Dubbed the Big Kmart or high-frequency format, it involved converting traditional stores to a new format which changed the appearance, layout, and product mix of stores. The Big Kmart format emphasized frequently purchased products such as paper goods, dry groceries, soaps, and other consumable items. In both the supercenters and the Big Kmart format, Kmart's goal was to price high-frequency items 1 to 3 percent below leading competitors.

Kmart's strategy in 2004 focused on three major initiatives. First, it defined itself as "the store of the neighborhood." Ethnic groups such as Asians and African Americans were a particular focus of Kmart's neighborhood strategy. Individual store managers were given greater autonomy to customize their merchandise assortments to suit local community needs. A second emphasis in Kmart's strategy was on exclusive branded products. Its most prominent brands included Martha Stewart in home products, Jaclyn Smith and Kathy Ireland in women's apparel, and Route 66 in men's and women's apparel. The "top sellers" program also focused on improving sales and in-stock positions for each of the store's top 300 selling items. Additionally, with further testing of the "store of the future" prototype, significant improvements in the customer shopping experience were expected. The third prong in Kmart's strategy was to further rationalize its operations. Kmart intended to focus more on higher-performing products and to continue to eliminate underperforming stock-keeping units (SKUs) and reallocate shelf space to more profitable items. The company claimed that it had significantly improved the inventory management practices around forecasting and replenishment that had plagued it so often in the past. These practices were particularly critical to a focus on highly advertised products.

Target, Wal-Mart's other large national competitor, was owned by Target Corporation, formerly Dayton Hudson Corporation, based in Minneapolis, Minnesota. Along with Target, the corporation owned Mervyn's, a middle-market promotional department store. It also owned other upscale department stores including Marshall Fields, which operated in several midwestern states. In 2003, Target's 1,225 stores accounted for $41.3 billion of Target Corporation's $48.2 billion in sales and $3.5 billion of its $3.7 billion in profits. Target operated stores in 47 states, including 119 Super Target stores in 19 states. Target was considered an "upscale discounter." The median income of Target shoppers was $57,000 and more than 75 percent had attended or completed college.[7] Target attracted a more affluent clientele through a more trendy and upscale product mix and through a store ambience that differed from most discounters in aspects such as wider aisles and brighter lighting Target had also introduced a proprietary credit card, the Target Guest Card, to differentiate it from other discounters. Pricing at Target was generally not as low as Wal-Mart but was lower than middle-market department stores such as JCPenney and Mervyn's. As with Wal-Mart and Kmart, supercenters were also high on Target's list of strategic priorities. The supercenters, named Super Targets, had opened in many cities and the company planned to aggressively grow in this area. Promotions were an important part of Target's marketing approach. Each week over 100 million Target advertising circulars were distributed in Sunday newspapers. Holiday promotions were also emphasized at Target. Like Kmart, Target had traditionally focused much of its effort on metropolitan areas. In the late 1990s, over half of its stores were in 30 metropolitan markets. Target's philanthropic activities gave it greater visibility. Each year, the company gave 5 percent of its pretax earnings to nonprofit organizations. St. Jude Children's Research Hospital and local schools were perhaps Targest's highest philanthropic priorities.

Wal-Mart's History

Wal-Mart was started in 1962 by Sam Walton. The discount retail industry was then in its infancy. A couple of regional firms had experimented with discount retailing, but that year three major retail firms joined Wal-Mart in entering the discount industry. Kresge Corporation started Kmart, Dayton Hudson began Target, and the venerable F.W. Woolworth initiated Woolco. Sam Walton had been the most successful franchisee in the Ben Franklin variety store chain, but discount stores threatened the success of his 18 stores. Walton was convinced that discount retailing would have a bright future even though most in the industry were highly skeptical of the concept. Indeed, Walton was quickly rebuffed in his efforts to convince Ben Franklin and others to provide financial backing for his proposed venture into discounting. With no major chains willing to back him, Walton risked his home and all his property to secure financing for the first Wal-Mart in Rogers, Arkansas.

Of the four new ventures in discount retailing started that year, Wal-Mart seemed the least likely to succeed. Most Wal-Mart stores were in northwestern Arkansas and adjacent areas of Oklahoma, Missouri, and Kansas. Walton had started his retailing career with Ben Franklin in small towns because his wife Helen did not want to live in any city with a population of over 10,000 people. He had chosen northwestern Arkansas as a base because it allowed him to take advantage of the quail-hunting season in four states. Wal-Mart was, in Sam Walton's words, "underfinanced and undercapitalized"[8] in the beginning. Nevertheless, Walton sought to grow Wal-Mart as fast as he could because he feared new competitors would preempt growth opportunities if Wal-Mart did not open stores in new towns. After five years, Wal-Mart had 19 stores and sales of $9 million. In contrast, Kmart had 250 stores and $800 million in sales.

Walton retained many of the practices regarding customer service and satisfaction that he had learned in the variety stores business. The central focus of Wal-Mart, however, was on price. Walton sought to make Wal-Mart the low-priced provider of any product it sold. As Walton said,

What we were obsessed with was keeping our prices below everybody else's. Our dedication to that idea was total. Everybody worked like crazy to keep the expenses down. We didn't have systems. We didn't have ordering programs. We didn't have a basic merchandise assortment. We certainly didn't have any sort of computers. In fact, when I look at it today, I realize that so much of what we did in the beginning was really poorly done. But we managed to sell our merchandise as low as we possibly could and that kept us right-side up for the first ten years.... The idea was simple: When customers thought of Wal-Mart, they should think of low prices and satisfaction guaranteed. They could be pretty sure they wouldn't find it any cheaper anywhere else, and if they didn't like it, they could bring it back.[9]

By 1970, Wal-Mart had expanded to 30 stores in the small towns of Arkansas, Missouri, and Oklahoma. Sam Walton, however, was personally several million dollars in debt. For Wal-Mart to expand beyond its small region required an infusion of capital beyond what the Walton family could provide. Walton thus decided to offer Wal-Mart stock publicly. The initial public offering yielded nearly $5 million in capital. By the early 1990s, 100 shares of that initial stock offering would increase in value from $1,650 to over $3,000,000.

The other problem that plagued Wal-Mart in its early years was finding a way to keep its costs down. Large vendors were reluctant to call on Wal-Mart and, when they did do business with the company, they would dictate the price and quantity of what they sold. Walton described the situation as, "I don't mind saying that we were the victims of a good bit of arrogance from a lot of vendors in those days. They didn't need us, and they acted that way."[10] Another problem that contributed to high costs was distribution. Distributors did not service Wal-Mart with the same care that they did its larger competitors. Walton saw that "the only alternative was to build our own warehouse so we could buy in volume at attractive prices and store the merchandise."[11]

Wal-Mart increased from 32 stores in 1970 to 859 stores 15 years later. For much of that time Wal-Mart retained its small-town focus. Over half its stores were in towns with populations of under 25,000. Because of its small town operations. Wal-Mart was not highly visible to many others in the retail industry. By 1985, though, that had changed. *Forbes* named Sam Walton the richest man in America. Furthermore, Wal-Mart had begun to expand from its small town base in the south and had established a strong presence in several large cities. By the 1990s, it had spread throughout the United States in both large cities and small towns.

Wal-Mart in 2004

By the beginning of 2004, Wal-Mart's activities had spread beyond its historical roots in domestic discount centers (see Exhibits 6–8). The number of domestic discount centers had declined to 1,568 from a high 1,995 in 1996. Many discount centers had been converted to supercenters, which had almost tripled in the previous five years to 1,251 stores. Wal-Mart Supercenters combined full-line supermarkets and discount centers into one store. Wal-Mart also operated 525 Sam's Clubs, which were warehouse membership clubs. In 1999, Wal-Mart opened its first Neighborhood Markets, which were supermarkets, and it had 49 in operation by 2004.

Operations

From its beginning, Wal-Mart had focused on everyday low prices (EDLP). EDLP saved on advertising costs and on labor costs since employees did not have to rearrange stock before and after sales. In the 1990s, the company changed its traditional slogan, "Always the Lowest Price," to "Always Low Prices. *Always.*" Despite the change in slogan, however, Wal-Mart continued to price goods lower than its competitors. When faced with a decline in profits in the late 1990s, Wal-Mart considered raising margins.[12] Instead of pricing 7 to 8 percent below competitors, some managers believed that pricing only about 6 percent below would raise gross margins without jeopardizing sales. Some investment analysts believed that raising prices would not only boost Wal-Mart's profits but Kmart's also. Other managers and board members, however, were skeptical that price hikes would work at Wal-Mart. They reasoned that Wal-Mart's culture and identity were so closely attached to low prices that broad price increases would clash with the company's bedrock beliefs. It would be difficult to convince managers and associates who had prided themselves on Wal-Mart's low-price philosophy that higher prices were needed. Another concern was that competitors might seize any opportunity to narrow the gap with Wal-Mart.

Wal-Mart had pioneered the use of technology in retail operations for many years and still possessed significant advantages over its competitors. It was the leader in forging EDI links with suppliers. Its Retail Link technology gave over 3,200 vendors POS data and authorization to replace inventory for approximately 2,000 stores.[13] The fine-tuning of its Retail Link system allowed Wal-Mart to reduce inventory by 25 percent of SKUs while still increasing sales in the mid-1990s. Competitors traditionally faced high costs in developing a proprietary EDI system to rival Wal-Mart's. Connecting seamlessly with a large number of suppliers was a daunting task given the complexity and cost of dealing with a large variety of computer and information systems. A recent trend, however, was emergence of intermediaries who provided EDI links between purchasers and suppliers. With the intermediaries, retailers could simply send all their EDI data to one source and various manufacturers could also reduce their difficulties in connecting with a large number of buyers by using one intermediary for transactions with many customers. Such intermediaries also made EDI a more feasible alternative for smaller retailers, who lacked the scale necessary to implement their own EDI systems. In August 2002, Wal-Mart informed suppliers that they would be required to do EDI exchanges over the Internet using AS2, a software package from Isoft Corp. The software package

Exhibit 6   Wal-Mart's Store Count in the United States, end of year, 1996

State	Wal-Mart Stores	Supercenters	Sam's Clubs
Alabama	65	11	8
Alaska	3		3
Arizona	31		6
Arkansas	58	19	4
California	88		26
Colorado	34	2	9
Connecticut	6		3
Delaware	2		1
Florida	116	16	34
Georgia	79	6	15
Hawaii	4		1
Idaho	7		1
Illinois	101	3	24
Indiana	66	6	14
Iowa	45		6
Kansas	43	3	5
Kentucky	60	8	5
Louisiana	62	13	9
Maine	19		3
Maryland	19		10
Massachusetts	23		5
Michigan	39		21
Minnesota	33		9
Mississippi	47	10	4
Missouri	81	27	11
Montana	6		1
Nebraska	13	4	3
Nevada	9		2
New Hampshire	15		4
New Jersey	14		6
New Mexico	19		3
New York	46	4	17
North Carolina	82	1	13
North Dakota	8		2
Ohio	70		22
Oklahoma	61	17	6
Oregon	17		
Pennsylvania	47	5	14
Rhode Island	4		1
South Carolina	49	3	8
South Dakota	8		1
Tennessee	69	19	9
Texas	185	56	51
Utah	13		5
Vermont	1		
Virginia	43	4	10
Washington	13		2
West Virginia	12	2	3
Wisconsin	51		11
Wyoming	9		2
U.S. Totals:	**1,995**	**239**	**433**

Exhibit 6 (continued)   Wal-Mart's Store Count in the United States, end of year, 2003

Fiscal 2003 End-of-Year Store Count

State	Discount Stores	Supercenters	Sam's Clubs	Neighborhood Markets
Alabama	34	49	9	2
Alaska	6	0	3	0
Arizona	24	17	10	0
Arkansas	35	43	4	6
California	133	0	30	0
Colorado	17	29	14	0
Connecticut	27	2	3	0
Delaware	3	3	1	0
Florida	66	87	37	1
Georgia	42	61	20	0
Hawaii	6	0	1	0
Idaho	5	11	1	0
Illinois	81	33	27	0
Indiana	42	42	14	0
Iowa	27	24	7	0
Kansas	29	23	6	0
Kentucky	34	41	5	0
Louisiana	35	47	12	0
Maine	12	9	3	0
Maryland	32	5	13	0
Massachusetts	41	1	3	0
Michigan	48	14	22	0
Minnesota	34	9	12	0
Mississippi	21	41	5	1
Missouri	56	58	14	0
Montana	5	6	1	0
Nebraska	10	11	3	0
Nevada	11	7	5	0
New Hampshire	19	6	4	0
New Jersey	30	0	8	0
New Mexico	6	18	5	0
New York	52	22	18	0
North Carolina	47	52	17	0
North Dakota	8	0	2	0
Ohio	70	28	26	0
Oklahoma	41	40	7	12
Oregon	24	3	0	0
Pennsylvania	50	43	20	0
Rhode Island	8	0	1	0
South Carolina	22	37	9	0
South Dakota	6	4	2	0
Tennessee	33	57	15	2
Texas	117	155	68	24
Utah	6	15	7	1
Vermont	4	0	0	0
Virginia	21	52	13	0
Washington	29	6	2	0
West Virginia	8	20	3	0
Wisconsin	49	20	11	0
Wyoming	2	7	2	0
U.S. Totals:	**1,568**	**1,258**	**525**	**49**

Exhibit 7 International Wal-Mart Stores in 1996

Country	Wal-Mart-Stores	Supercenters	Sam's Clubs	Neighborhood Markets
Argentina	0	1	2	0
Brazil	0	2	3	0
Canada	131	0	0	0
Mexico*	85	1328	0	
Puerto Rico	7	0	4	0

*Mexico includes 3 Superamas, 25 Bodegas, 4 Aurreras, 48 Vips, and 5 Suburbias.

cost as little at $300 for suppliers to connect only with Wal-Mart, though a typical installation could cost much more. Some suppliers were given as little as six weeks to be fully operable on AS2. The transition to Internet-based EDI was nearly complete by November 2003 with 98 percent of Wal-Mart's EDI exchanges taking place over the Internet.[14] Competitors had responded to Wal-Mart's advantage in logistics and EDI by forming cooperative exchanges, but, despite their efforts, a large gap remained between Wal-Mart and its competitors.[15] As a result, Wal-Mart possessed a substantial advantage in information about supply and demand, which reduced both the number of items that were either overstocked or out of stock.

November 2003 was also notable for another Wal-Mart technological initiative. It announced plans to implement radio frequency identification (RFID) to all products by January 2005. Smaller suppliers were given an extra year to comply with this demand. RFID, as its name implies, involves the use of tags that transmit radio signals. It had the potential to track inventory more precisely than traditional methods and to eventually reduce much of the labor involved in activities such as manually scanning bar codes for incoming goods. Some analysts estimated that Wal-Mart's cost savings from RFID could run as high $8 billion.[16]

Technology was only one area where Wal-Mart exploited advantages through its relationships with suppliers. Wal-Mart's clout was clearly evident in the payment terms it had with its suppliers. Suppliers frequently offered 2 percent discounts to customers who paid their bills within 15 days. Wal-Mart typically paid its bills at close to 30 days from the time of purchase but still usually received a 2 percent discount on the gross amount of an invoice rather than the net amount.[17] Several suppliers had attributed performance problems to Wal-Mart's actions. Rubbermaid, for example, had enjoyed rapid growth in revenue and profits before 1995. In 1995, however, it experienced higher raw materials costs. Wal-Mart and other large discount retailers, however, did not allow Rubbermaid to pass its higher costs along in the form of higher prices. At the same time, Wal-Mart gave more shelf space to Rubbermaid's lower-cost competitors. As a result, Rubbermaid's profits dropped by 30 percent and it was forced to cut its workforce by over 1,000 employees.[18] Besides pushing for low prices, the large discounters also required suppliers to pick up an increasing amount of inventory and merchandising costs. Wal-Mart, for example, required large suppliers such as Procter & Gamble to place large contingents of employees at its Bentonville, Arkansas, headquarters in order to service its

Exhibit 8 International Wal-Mart Stores in 2004

Country	Wal-Mart-Stores	Supercenters	Sam's Clubs	Neighborhood Markets
Argentina	0	11	0	0
Brazil	0	13	10	2
Canada	231	0	4	0
China	0	28	4	2
Germany	0	92	0	0
Mexico*	487	83	53	0
Puerto Rico*	9	3	9	32
United Kingdom**	255	12	0	0

*Mexico includes 44 Superamas, 140 Bodegas, 4 Aurreras, 251 Vips, and 52 Suburbias   *Puerto Rico includes 32 Amigos.   **U.K. includes 253 ASDA Stores and 2 George Stores.

account. A *Fast Company* article on Wal-Mart interviewed several former suppliers of the company and concluded that "To a person, all those interviewed credit Wal-Mart with a fundamental integrity in its dealings that's unusual in the world of consumer goods, retailing, and groceries. Wal-Mart does not cheat its suppliers, it keeps its word, it pays its bills briskly. 'They are tough people but very honest; they treat you honestly,' says Peter Campanella, a former Corning manager."[19]

Although several companies such as Rubbermaid and the pickle vendor Vlasic had experienced dramatic downfalls largely through being squeezed by Wal-Mart, other companies suggested that their relationship with Wal-Mart had made them much more efficient.[20] Some critics suggested, however, that these extreme efficiency pressures had driven many suppliers to move production from the United States to nations such as China that had much lower wages. Wal-Mart set standards for all of its suppliers in areas such as child labor and safety. A 2001 audit, however, revealed that as many as one-third of Wal-Mart's international suppliers were in "serious violation" of the standards.[21] Wal-Mart pursued steps to help suppliers address the violations, but it was unclear how successful these efforts were.

At the heart of Wal-Mart's success was its distribution system. To a large extent it had been born out of the necessity of servicing so many stores in small towns while trying to maintain low prices. Wal-Mart used distribution centers to achieve efficiencies in logistics. Initially, distribution centers were large facilities—the first were 72,000 square feet—that served 80 to 100 Wal-Mart stores within a 250-mile radius. Newer distribution centers were considerably larger than the early ones and in some cases served a wider geographical radius. In the early 1990s, over 85 percent of Wal-Mart's products were distributed through distribution centers, in contrast to only 50 percent for Kmart. As a result, Wal-Mart had far more distribution centers than any of its competitors. Cross-docking was a particularly important practice of these centers.[22] In cross-docking, goods were delivered to distribution centers and often simply loaded from one dock to another or even from one truck to another without ever sitting in inventory. Cross-docking reduced Wal-Mart's cost of sales by 2 to 3 percent compared to competitors. Cross-docking was receiving a great deal of attention among retailers with most attempting to implement it for a greater proportion of goods. It was extremely difficult to manage, however, because of the close coordination and timing required between the store, manufacturer, and warehouse. As one supplier noted. "Everyone from the forklift driver on up to me, the CEO, knew we had to deliver on time. Not 10 minutes late. And not 45 minutes early, either.... The message came through

clearly: You have this 30-second delivery window. Either you're there or you're out."[23] Because of the close coordination needed, cross-docking required an information system which effectively linked stores, warehouses, and manufacturers. Most major retailers were finding it difficult to duplicate Wal-Mart's success at cross-docking.

Wal-Mart's logistics system also included a fleet of over 2,000 company-owned trucks. It was able to routinely ship goods from distribution centers to stores within 48 hours of receiving an order. Store shelves were replenished twice a week on average in contrast to the industry average of once every two weeks.[24]

Wal-Mart stores typically included many departments in areas such as soft goods/domestics, hard goods, stationery and candy, pharmaceuticals, records and electronics, sporting goods, toys, shoes, and jewelry. The selection of products varied from one region to another. Department managers and in some cases associates (employees) had the authority to change prices in response to competitors. This was in stark contrast to the traditional practice of many chains where prices were centrally set at a company's headquarters. Wal-Mart's use of technology was particularly useful in determining the mix of goods in each store. The company used historical selling data and complex models that included many variables such as local demographics to decide what items should be placed in each store.

Unlike many of its competitors, Wal-Mart had no regional offices. Instead, regional vice presidents maintained their offices at company headquarters in Bentonville, Arkansas. The absence of regional offices was estimated to save Wal-Mart as much as 1 percent of sales. Regional managers visited stores from Monday to Thursday of each week. Each Saturday at 7:30 A.M., regional vice presidents and a few hundred other managers and employees met with the firm's top managers to discuss the previous week's results and discuss different directions for the next week. Regional managers then conveyed information from the meeting to managers in the field via the videoconferencing links that were present in each store.

Sam's Club

A notable exception to Wal-Mart's dominance in discount retailing was in the warehouse club segment. Despite significant efforts by Wal-Mart's Sam's Club, Costco was the established leader. Sam's Club had far more stores than Costco—532 to 312—yet, Costco still reported 5 percent more sales. Costco stores averaged almost twice the revenue per store as Sam's with $112 million versus $63 million per store for Sam's Club (see Exhibit 9).

Exhibit 9   Costco Versus Sam's Club*

	Costco	Sam's Club
Year founded	1983	1983
U.S. revenues (year ended Aug. 31, 2003)	$34.4 billion	$32.9 billion (est.)
Presidents (or equivalents, since founding)	one	seven
Membership cardholders	42 million	46 million
Members' average salary	$95,333	N.A.
Annual membership fees	$45	$30-35
U.S. warehouses (worldwide)	312 (423 worldwide)	532 (604
Average annual sales (per U.S. location)	$112 million	$63 million
Average transaction	$94	$78
Average sales per square foot	$797	$497
Starting hourly wage	$10	N.A.
Employee turnover per year	23%	45% (WalMart)
Private label (as % of sales)	15%	10%

Source: Heylar, J. "The only company Wal-Mart fears," *Fortune*, November 24, 2003.

To the casual observer, Costco and Sam's Clubs appeared to be very similar. Both charged small membership fees—$45 at Costco and $30 at Sam's—and both were "warehouse" stores that sold goods from pallets. The goods were often packaged or bundled into larger quantities than typical retailers offered. Beneath these similarities, however, were important differences. Costco focused on more upscale small business owners and consumers while Sam's, following Wal-Mart's pattern, had positioned itself more to the mass middle market. Relative to Costco, Sam's was also concentrated more in smaller cities.

Consistent with its more upscale strategy, Costco stocked more luxury and premium branded items than Sam's Club had traditionally done. This changed somewhat when Sam's began to stock more high-end merchandise after the 1990s, but some questioned whether or not its typical customers demanded such items. A Costco executive pointed to the differences between Costco and Sam's customers by describing a scene where a Sam's customer responded to a $39 price on a Ralph Lauren Polo shirt by saying, "Can you imagine? Who in their right mind would buy a T-shirt for $39?" Despite the focus on pricier goods, Costco still focused intensely on managing costs and keeping prices down. Costco set a goal of 10 percent margins and capped markups at 14 percent (compared to the usual 40 percent markup by department stores). Managers were discouraged from exceeding the margin goals.

Some analysts claimed that Sam's Club's lackluster performance was a result of a copycat strategy. Costco was the first of the two competitors to sell fresh meat and produce, gasoline, and introduce a premium private label for many goods. In each case, Sam's followed suit two to four years later.

> "By looking at what Costco did and trying to emulate it, Sam's didn't carve out its own unique strategy," says Michael Clayman, editor of the trade newsletter Warehouse Club Focus. And at least one of the "me too" moves made things worse. Soon after Costco and Price Club merged in 1993, Sam's bulked up by purchasing Pace warehouse clubs from Kmart. Many of the 91 stores were marginal operations in marginal locations. Analysts say that Sam's Club management became distracted as it tried to integrate the Pace stores into its system.[25]

To close the gap against Costco, Wal-Mart started in 2003 to integrate the activities of Sam's Club and Wal-Mart more. Buyers for the two coordinated their efforts to get better prices from suppliers. Like Wal-Mart, Sam's was also promoting the use of RFID to lower costs.

Culture

Perhaps the most distinctive aspect of Wal-Mart was its culture. To a large extent, Wal-Mart's culture was an extension of Sam Walton's philosophy and was rooted in the early experiences and practices of Wal-Mart. The Wal-Mart culture emphasized values such as thriftiness, hard work, innovation, and continuous improvement. As Sam Walton wrote,

> Because wherever we've been, we've always tried to instill in our folks the idea that we at Wal-Mart have our own way of doing things. It may be different and it may take some folks a while to adjust to it at first. But it's straight and honest and basically pretty sim-

ple to figure it out if you want to. And whether or not other folks want to accommodate us, we pretty much stick to what we believe in because it's proven to be very, very successful.[26]

Wal-Mart's thriftiness was consistent with its obsession with controlling costs. One observer joked that "the Wal-Mart folks stay at Mo 3, where they don't even leave the light on for you."[27] This was not, however, far from the truth. Sam Walton told of early buying trips to New York where several Wal-Mart managers shared the same hotel room and walked everywhere they went rather than use taxis. One of the early managers described how these early trips taught managers to work hard and keep costs low:

> *From the very beginning, Sam was always trying to instill in us that you just didn't go to New York and roll with the flow. We always walked everywhere. We never took cabs. And Sam had an equation for the trips: expenses should never exceed 1 percent of our purchases, so we would all crowd in these little hotel rooms somewhere down around Madison Square Garden…. We never finished up until about 12:30 at night, and we'd all go out for a beer except Mr. Walton. He'd say, "I'll meet you at breakfast at six o'clock." And we'd say, "Mr. Walton, there's no reason to meet that early. We can't even get into the buildings that early." And he'd just say, "We'll find something to do."*[28]

The roots of Wal-Mart's emphasis on innovation and continuous improvement could also be seen in Sam Walton's example. Walton's drive for achievement was evident early in life. He achieved the rank of Eagle Scout earlier than anyone previously had in the state of Missouri. Later, in high school, he quarterbacked the undefeated state champion football team and played guard on the undefeated state champion basketball team while serving as student body president. This same drive was evident in Walton's early retailing efforts. He studied other retailers by spending time in their stores, asking endless questions, and taking notes about various store practices. Walton was quick to borrow a new idea if he thought it would increase sales and profits. When, in his early days at Ben Franklin, Walton read about two variety stores in Minnesota that were using self-service, he immediately took an all-night bus ride to visit the stores. Upon his return from Minnesota, he converted one of his stores to self-service, which, at the time, was only the third variety store in the United States to do so. Later, he was one of the first to see the potential of discount retailing.

Walton also emphasized always looking for ways to improve. Wal-Mart managers were encouraged to critique their own operations. Managers met regularly to discuss their store operations. Lessons learned in one store were quickly spread to other stores. Wal-Mart managers also carefully analyzed the activities of their competitors and tried to borrow practices that worked well. Sam Walton stressed the importance of observing what other firms did well rather than what they did wrong. Another way in which Wal-Mart had focused on improvement from its earliest days was in information and measurement. Long before Wal-Mart had any computers, Sam Walton would personally enter measures on several variables for each store into a ledger he carried with him. Information technology enabled Wal-Mart to extend this emphasis on information and measurement.

International Operations

Wal-Mart's entry into the international retail arena had been somewhat recent. As late as 1992, Wal-Mart's entire international operations consisted of only 162,535 square feet of retail space in Mexico. By 1996, however, Wal-Mart operated 276 stores outside of the United States. The company's largest international presence was in Canada and Mexico. Following a 1994 acquisition of Woolco's Canadian stores, Wal-Mart operated 131 discount centers in Canada in 1996. With its Mexican partner Cifra, Wal-Mart had opened 85 discount centers, 13 supercenters, and 28 Sam's Clubs in Mexico. Wal-Mart expanded its international expansion into South America in 1996 by opening three stores in Argentina and five in Brazil. Expansion plans called for more stores in Mexico and South America as well as entry into the Asian market with stores in China, Indonesia, and additional stores in Hong Kong where it had two Sam's Clubs. Wal-Mart had continued its international expansion by entering Europe via major acquisitions in Germany and the United Kingdom.

Although it was the company's fastest-growing division, Wal-Mart's performance in international markets had been mixed, or, as *Forbes* put it, "Overseas, Wal-Mart has won some—and lost a lot."[29] Over 80 percent of Wal-Mart's international revenue came from only three countries: Canada, Mexico, and the United Kingdom (see Exhibit 10).

Wal-Mart had tried a variety of approaches and faced a diverse set of challenges in the different countries they entered. Entry into international markets had ranged from greenfield development to franchising, joint ventures, and acquisitions. Each country that Wal-Mart had entered had presented new and unique challenges. In China, Wal-Mart had to deal with a backward supply chain. It had to negotiate a Japanese environment that was hostile to large chains and protective of its small retailers. Strong foreign competitors were the problem in Brazil and Argentina. Labor

Exhibit 10   Sales Growth by Region

Country	Sales 2003 ($mil)	Annualized Growth 2001-2003
Argentina	$122	2%
Brazil	388	13
Canada	7,165	15
China	673	30
Germany	2,743	-7
Mexico	10,659	17
Puerto Rico	2,413	30
South Korea	836	30
United Kingdom	21,740	14
USA	209,509	11

unions had plagued Wal-Mart's entry into Germany along with unforeseen difficulties in integrating acquisitions. Mistakes in choosing store locations had hampered the company in South Korea and Hong Kong.

Wal-Mart approached it international operations with much the same philosophy they had used in the United States "We're still very young at this, we're still learning,"[30] stated John Menzer, chief executive of Wal-Mart International. Menzer's approach was to have country presidents make decisions. His thinking was that it would facilitate the faster implementation of decisions. Each country president made decisions regarding his own sourcing, merchandising, and real estate. Menzer concluded, "Over time all you really have is speed. I think that's our most important asset."[31]

In most countries, entrenched competitors responded vigorously to Wal-Mart's entry. For example, Tesco, the United Kingdom's biggest grocer, responded by opening supercenters. In China, Lianhua and Huilan, the two largest retailers, merged in 2003 into one state-owned entity named the Bailan Group. Wal-Mart was also not alone among major international retailers in seeking new growth in South America and Asia. One international competitor, the French retailer Carrefour, was already the leading retailer in Brazil and Argentina. Carrefour expanded into China in the late 1990s with a hypermarket in Shanghai. In Asia, Makro, a Dutch wholesale club retailer, was the regional leader. Both of the European firms were viewed as able, experi-

enced competitors. The Japanese retailer Yaohan moved its headquarters from Tokyo to Hong Kong with the aim of becoming the world's largest retailer. Helped by the close relationship between chairman Kazuo Wada and Deng Xiaoping, Yaohan was the first foreign retail firm to receive a license to operate in China and planned to open over a 1,000 stores there. Like Wal-Mart, these international firms were motivated to expand internationally by slowing growth in their own domestic markets. Some analysts feared that the pace of expansion by these major retailers was faster than the rate of growth in the market and could result in a price war. Like Wal-Mart, these competitors had also found difficulty in moving into international markets and adapting to local differences. Both Carrefour and Makro had experienced visible failures in their international efforts. Folkert Schukken, chairman of Makro, noted this challenge: "We have trouble selling the same toilet paper in Belgium and Holland." The chairman of Carrefour, Daniel Bernard, agreed, "If people think that going international is a solution to their problems at home, they will learn by spilling their blood. Global retailing demands a huge investment and gives no guarantee of a return."[32]

It was not known what Wal-Mart's next international moves would be. The *Wall Street Journal* reported that the French hypermarket firm Carrefour might be an acquisition target. There were also rumors that Wal-Mart might acquire the Esselunga chain of Italy or the Daiei or Aeon chains in Japan.

Notes

1. Standard and Poor's Industry Surveys. *Retailing: General*, February 5, 1998.
2. Upbin, Bruce. "Wall-to-Wall Wal-Mart." *Forbes*, April 12, 2004.
3. Nordlinger, Jay. "The new colossous: Wal-Mart is America's store, and the world's, and its enemies are sadly behind." *National Review*, April 19, 2004.
4. Nordlinger, Jay. "The new colossous: Wal-Mart is America's store, and the world's, and its enemies are sadly behind." *National Review*, April 19, 2004.
5. Standard and Poor's Industry Surveys. *Retailing: General*, February 5, 1998.
6. Berner, Robert. "The next Warren Buffett?" *BusinessWeek*, November 22, 2004.
7. Standard and Poor's Industry Surveys. *Retailing: General*, February 5, 1998.
8. Walton, Sam (with John Huey). *Sam Walton: Made in America*. New York: Doubleday, p. 63.
9. Walton, Sam (with John Huey). *Sam Walton: Made in America*. New York: Doubleday, pp. 64–65.
10. Walton, Sam (with John Huey). *Sam Walton: Made in America*. New York: Doubleday, p. 66.
11. *Forbes*, August 16, 1982, p. 43.
12. Pulliam, Susan. "Wal-Mart considers raising prices, drawing praise from analysts, but concern from board." *Wall Street Journal*, March 8, 1996, p. C2.
13. Standard and Poor's Industry Surveys. *Retailing: General*, February 5, 1998.
14. Zimmerman, Ann. "B-2-B—Internet 2.0: To sell goods to Wal-Mart, get on the Net." *Wall Street Journal*, November 21, 2003, p. B1.
15. Useem, Jerry. "America's most admired companies." *Fortune*, February 18, 2003.
16. Boyle, Matthew. *Fortune*, November 10, 2003, p. 46.
17. Schifrin, Matthew. "The big squeeze." *Forbes*, March 11, 1996.
18. Ibid.
19. Fishman, Charles. "The Wal-Mart you don't know." *Fast Company*, December 2003, p. 73.
20. Fishman, Charles. "The Wal-Mart you don't know." *Fast Company*, December 2003.
21. Wal-Mart Web site.
22. Stalk George, Philip Evans and Lawrence E. Schulman. "Competing on capabilities: The new rules of corporate strategy." *Harvard Business Review*, March/April 1992, pp. 57–58.
23. Fishman, Charles. "The Wal-Mart you don't know." *Fast Company*, December 2003, p. 73.
24. Stalk George, Philip Evans and Lawrence E. Schulman. "Competing on Capabilities: The new rules of corporate strategy." *Harvard Business Review*, March/April 1992, pp. 57–58.
25. Helyar, John. "The only company Wal-Mart fears." *Fortune*, November 24, 2003, p. 158.
26. Walton, Sam (with John Huey). *Sam Walton: Made in America*. New York: Doubleday, p. 85.
27. Loeb, Marshall. "Editor's desk: The secret of two successes." *Fortune*, May 2, 1994.
28. Walton, Sam (with John Huey). *Sam Walton: Made in America*. New York: Doubleday, p. 84.
29. Upbin, Bruce. "Wall-to-Wall Wal-Mart." *Forbes*, April 12, 2004.
30. Ibid.
31. Ibid.
32. *Fortune*, "Retailers go global," February 20, 1995.

Case 1-4: Harlequin Enterprises: The Mira Decision*[1]

During June 1993, Harlequin management was deciding whether or not to launch MIRA, a new line of single-title women's fiction novels. With the increased popularity of single-title women's fiction, Harlequin's leading position as the world's largest romance publisher was being threatened. While Harlequin was the dominant and very profitable producer of *series* romance novels, research indicated that many customers were reading as many *single-title* romance and women's fiction books as series romances. Facing a steady loss of share in a growing total women's fiction market, Harlequin convened a task force in December 1992 to study the possibility of relaunching a single-title women's fiction program. Donna Hayes, vice-president of direct marketing, stated:

> *Industry trends reveal that demand for single-title women's fiction continues to grow while demand for series romance remains stable. Our strengths lie in series romance… by any account, launching MIRA (single-title) will still be a challenge for us. How do we successfully launch a single-title women's fiction program?*

Tentatively named "MIRA," Harlequin's proposed single-title program would focus exclusively on women's fiction. Management hoped MIRA's launch would provide the opportunity to continue Harlequin's history of strong revenue growth. Hayes, leader of the MIRA team, knew this was a significant decision for Harlequin. Several years earlier an attempt at single-title publishing—Worldwide Library—had failed. Before going to her executive group for approval, Hayes thought about the decisions the company faced if it wished to enter single-title women's fiction publishing: What were the growth and profitability implications if Harlequin broadened its scope from series romance to single-title women's fiction? What fundamental changes would have to be made to Harlequin's current business model? Did the company have the necessary resources and capabilities to succeed in this new arena? If the company proceeds, how should it go about launching MIRA?

The Publishing Industry[2]

Apart from educational material, traditional single-title book publishing was typically a high-risk venture. Each book was a new product with all the risks attendant on any new product introduction. The risks varied with the author's reputation, the subject matter and thus the predictability of the market's response. Among the numerous decisions facing the publisher were selecting manuscripts out of the thousands submitted each year, deciding how many copies to print and deciding how to promote the book.

Insiders judged one key to success in publishing was the creative genius needed to identify good young authors among the hundreds of would-be writers, and then publish and develop them through their careers. Years ago, Sol Stein of Stein and Day Publishers had commented, "Most successful publishers are creative editors at heart and contribute more than risk capital and marketing expertise to the books they publish. If a publisher does not add value to what he publishes, he's a printer, not a publisher."

Traditional single-title publishers allowed distributors 50 percent margins (from which the retailer's margin would come).[3] Some other typical costs included royalty payments of more than 12 percent, warehouse and handling costs of 4 percent, and selling expenses at 5.5 percent. Advertising generally required 6 percent and printing costs[4] required another 12 percent. The remainder was earnings before indirect overhead. Typically, indirect overhead accounted for 2 percent of the retail price of a book. Because of author advances, pre-publication, promotion, and fixed costs of printing, break-even volumes were significant. And if the publisher failed to sell enough books, the losses could be substantial. Harlequin's core business, series romance fiction was significantly different from traditional single-title publishing.

* Ken Mark prepared this case under the supervision of Professors Rod White and Mary Crossan solely to provide material for class discussion. The authors do not intend to illustrate either effective or ineffective handling of a managerial situation. The authors may have disguised certain names and other identifying information to protect confidentiality.

Ivey Management Services prohibits any form of reproduction, storage or transmittal without its written permission. This material is not covered under authorization from CanCopy or any reproduction rights organization. To order copies or request permission to reproduce materials, contact Ivey Publishing, Ivey Management Services, c/o Richard Ivey School of Business, The University of Western Ontario, London, Ontario, Canada, N6A 3K7; phone (519) 661-3208; fax (519) 661-3882; e-mail cases@ivey.uwo.ca. One-time permission to reproduce granted by Ivey Management Services on February 9, 2007.

Harlequin Enterprises Limited

The word *romance* and the name Harlequin had become synonymous over the last half-century. Founded in 1949, Harlequin began applying its revolutionary approach to publishing—a packaged, consumer-goods strategy—in 1968 shortly after acquiring the publishing business of U.K.-based Mills & Boon. Each book was part of an identifiable product line; consistently delivering the expected benefit to the consumer. With a growth rate of 25 percent per year during the 1970s, Harlequin became the world's largest publisher of women's series romance fiction. It was during this time that Torstar, a newspaper publisher, acquired all of Harlequin Enterprises Ltd.

Over the years, many book publishers had attempted to enter Harlequin's segment of the industry. All had eventually withdrawn. Only once had Harlequin's dominance in series romance fiction been seriously challenged. The "romance wars" began in 1980 when Harlequin took over U.S. distribution of its series products from Simon & Schuster (S&S), a large single-title publisher with established paperback distribution. Subsequently, S&S began publishing series romance fiction under the Silhouette imprint. After several years, a truce was negotiated between Harlequin and S&S. Harlequin acquired Silhouette, S&S's series romance business, and S&S got a 20-year deal as Harlequin's sole U.S. distributor for series fiction.

During the late 1980s and early 1990s, growth in the series market slowed. Harlequin was able to maintain revenues by publishing longer and more expensive series products and generally raising prices. However, as shown in Table 1, global unit volume was no longer growing.

Harlequin's Target Market and Products

Harlequin books were sold in more than 100 international markets in more than 23 languages around the world. Along with romance fiction, Harlequin participated in the series mystery and male action-adventure markets under its Worldwide Library and Gold Eagle imprints. Harlequin

had an estimated 20 million readers in North America and 50 million readers around the world.

With a median age of 41, the Harlequin's romance series reader was likely to be married, well educated, and working outside the home. More than half of Harlequin readers spent at least three hours reading per week. Harlequin series readers were brand loyal; a survey indicated four out of five readers would continue to buy Harlequin books in the next year. Larry Heisey, Harlequin's former chief executive officer and chairman, expanded on the value of Harlequin's products: "I think our books are so popular because they provide relaxation and escape.... We get many letters from people who tell us how much these books mean to them."

While Harlequin had advertised its series product on television, current marketing efforts centred on print media. Harlequin advertised in leading women's magazines such as *Cosmopolitan, Glamour, Redbook,* and *Good Housekeeping*, and general interest magazines such as *People*. The print advertisement usually featured one of Harlequin's series products and also promoted the company's brands.

Romance Series Product: Well Defined and Consistent

Under the Harlequin and Silhouette brands, Harlequin published 13 different series with 64 titles each month. Each series was distinctly positioned, featuring a particular genre (e.g., historical romances) or level of explicitness. Isabel Swift, editorial director of Silhouette, described the different types of series books published by Harlequin:

> Our different lines deliver different promises to our readers. For example, Harlequin Temptation's tagline is sassy, sexy, and seductive, promising that each story will deliver a sexy, fun, contemporary romance between one man and one woman, whereas the Silhouette Romance title, in comparison, is a tender read within a framework of more traditional values.

Overall, the product portfolio offered a wide variety of stories to capture readers' interests. For the positioning

Table 1   **Total Unit Sales (in $000s)**

Year	1988	1989	1990	1991	1992	1993
Operating Revenue	344,574	326,539	348,358	357,013	417,884	443,825
Operating Profit	48,142	56,217	57,769	52,385	61,842	62,589
Total Unit Sales	202	191	196	193	205	199

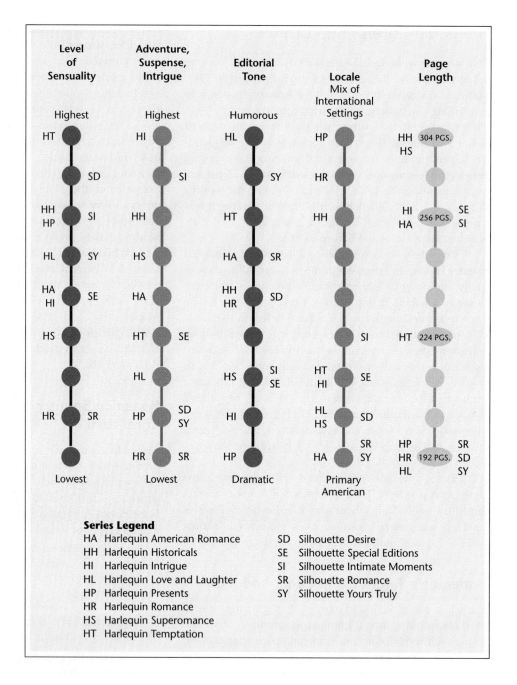

Exhibit 1   Harlequin/Silhouette Series Positioning Scales

Source: Company files.

Series Legend

HA	Harlequin American Romance	SD	Silhouette Desire
HH	Harlequin Historicals	SE	Silhouette Special Editions
HI	Harlequin Intrigue	SI	Silhouette Intimate Moments
HL	Harlequin Love and Laughter	SR	Silhouette Romance
HP	Harlequin Presents	SY	Silhouette Yours Truly
HR	Harlequin Romance		
HS	Harlequin Superomance		
HT	Harlequin Temptation		

of Harlequin's series, see Exhibit 1. Sold in more than a dozen countries. Harlequin had the ability to publish series books worldwide. The average retail price of a Harlequin series novel was $4.40,[5] significantly less than the $7 retail price for the typical single-title paperback novel, and much less than the $15 to $25 for longer, hardcover titles by best-selling authors.

Harlequin's series romance product was fundamentally different from that of traditional single-title publishers: content, length, artwork size, basic formats, and print were all well defined to ensure a consistent product. Each book was not a new product, but rather an addition to a clearly defined product line. Unlike single-title books, Harlequin's series products had a common format. They measured 105 millimetres by 168 millimetres and fit neatly into specially designed racks located primarily in supermarkets and drugstores. Most product lines were 192 to 256 pages in length; some were up to 304 pages in length. Cover designs differed slightly by product line and country, but the look and feel was similar (see Exhibit 2).

Exhibit 2   Typical Harlequin Series Romance Products

Source: Company files.

Harlequin provided prospective series romance authors with plot, style, and book length guidelines. However, crafting the stories still demanded skill and work. As David Galloway, chief executive officer of Torstar, Harlequin's parent company, and the former head of Harlequin observed:

> The books are quite simply good stories. If they weren't, we wouldn't be getting the repeat purchases we do. A lot of writers think they can dash off a Harlequin, but they can't. We've had submissions from Ph.D.'s in English who can certainly write but they can't tell a story.

To ensure a consistent product emerged, Harlequin's editors assessed many elements, including plot, story line, main character(s), setting, percentage of romance in the plot, level of realism, level of fantasy, sensuality, social

and/or individual problems, happy ending, and reading impact. Even though many different authors contributed to series romance, Harlequin's editors ensured a consistent finished product, satisfying the needs of their loyal series romance readers. The consequences of this uniformity were significant. The reader was buying a Harlequin novel, and advertising promoted the Harlequin brands rather than a particular book or author.

Bookstores were not the primary channel for series romance novels. Most retail purchases were made at supermarkets or drugstores and increasingly mass merchandisers like Wal-Mart. But many avid Harlequin readers got the product delivered to their home every month through Harlequin's direct mail service. The standardized size and format made warehousing and distribution more efficient. In addition, the product's consistency enabled standing order distribution to retail. As Pam Laycock, director of new product development, explained:

A major contributor to our success as a series publisher is our standing order distribution. Each series is distributed to a retail location in a predetermined configuration—for example in a series where we publish four titles per month, a retailer may take six copies per title and this level of distribution is generally agreed upon and maintained for the entire year. This approach enables us to more accurately predict monthly print quantities and achieve significant print cost effectiveness.

Orders (and sales) for conventional single-title books were not as predictable. Another significant difference was that series romance books were part of Harlequin's standing order distribution plan. And more like magazines, they were displayed on retail shelves for four weeks. Harlequin's distributors then removed and returned any unsold books, and replaced them with the next month's offerings. By comparison, single-title books were typically displayed at retail from 6 to 12 months or more.

Harlequin's series romance business did not generate or even encourage best-sellers. "Best-sellers (in series romance) would ruin our system," a Harlequin insider stated. "Our objective is consistency in volume. We have no winners and no losers." Unsold books could be returned to the publisher for credit. A consequence of Harlequin's even and predictable sales was that order regulation and returns could be more easily optimized to maximize the contribution to profits.

A comparison of Harlequin's series business model and the operations of traditional "one-off" publishers is presented in Exhibit 3.

With a consistent quality product, standing orders, predictable retail traffic patterns and the ability to produce and deliver books at low costs, Harlequin had achieved great success. Harlequin's series romance business had consistently earned a return on sales of 15 percent. As shown in Exhibit 4, this figure compared favorably with larger traditional publishers.

Loriana Sacilotto, director of retail marketing, explained why Harlequin out-performed other traditional single-title publishers:

There are a variety of reasons why other publishers do not achieve the same margins we enjoy. The main reason is that they are broad in their publishing focus whereas we focus on women's fiction. They don't have the same reader recognition, trust and relationships. We invest in it.

Harlequin Business System

The Global Author–Editor Team. Harlequin had established a strong level of reader trust and brand equity by consistently delivering quality content. Editors in three acquisition centers in Toronto, New York, and London were responsible for working closely with 1,300-plus authors to develop and publish more than 1,000 new titles annually. In addition to the work of its regular writers, Harlequin received approximately 30,000 unsolicited manuscripts per year. Typically, about 100 of these were accepted in any given year.

Exhibit 3   Comparing Harlequin's Series Business Model and a Traditional Publisher's

	Harlequin Series	Single-Title Publisher
Editorial	Emphasizes consistency within established guidelines	Requires separate judgment on potential consumer demand for each manuscript
Rights	Uses standardized contract	Can be a complex process, involving subrights, hard/soft deals, advances, and tying up authors for future books
Author Management	Less dependent on specific authors	Vulnerable to key authors changing publisher
Production	Uses consistent format with focus on efficiency	Emphasizes package, size, and format—cost control secondary
Marketing	Builds the imprint/series	Builds each title/author
Distribution	Supermarkets, drugstores, mass merchandisers, big-box bookstores. Large direct mail	Bookstores (all types) Book clubs and mass merchandisers
Selling	Emphasizes servicing, rack placement, and order regulation	Cover, in-store placement, critical reviews, special promotional tactics (e.g., author signings)
Order Regulation/ Information Systems	Utilizes very sophisticated shipping and returns handling procedures	Historically has not received much attention, and hence, is not as sophisticated

Exhibit 4   Comparison of Harlequin's Performance with Traditional Publisher—1993 (in millions of dollars)

	Harlequin[a]	Simon & Schuster[b]	Harper/Avon[c]
Sales Revenue	417.8	1,929.0	1,210.4
Operating Profit	61.8	218.4	160.8
Identifiable Assets	319.2	2,875.8	2,528.0
R.O.S.	14.8%	11.3%	13.2%
R.O.I.A.	19.4%	7.6%	6.4%

[a] Canadian dollars   [b] U.S. dollars (Cdn$1.20 = US$1)   [c] Australian dollars (Cdn$0.80 = AUD$1)

Series authors received royalties of 13 percent of retail book price. Harlequin's typical series authors had more than 100,000 of each of their books distributed worldwide.

Harlequin's series romance product focused solely on front-list sales. In the publishing world, *front-list* sales refers to the first print runs of a book supporting its initial market launch. *Back-list* refers to books reprinted and reissued years after the book's initial run (often to support an author's subsequent books). Harlequin's series romance novels—unlike a traditional publisher's single-title books—were not available on back-list. However, Harlequin retained these rights.

Printing was a highly competitive business and Harlequin subcontracted its requirements. Costs per series book were typically $0.44 per book compared to the competitors' average costs of $0.88 per single-title soft cover book.

Distribution, Selling, and Promotion.   With its standing orders, Harlequin's distribution costs per book were $0.18, with selling expenses at an average of $0.09 per book. Because it was the dominant player in series romance, Harlequin had relatively low advertising and promotion costs—about $0.22 per book.

In Canada, Harlequin had its own distribution. Elsewhere in the world, independent distributors were employed. In the United States, Pocketbooks, the sales division of Simon & Schuster, a large traditional publisher, handled Harlequin's series romance books. Supermarkets, drugstores, discount department stores, and mass merchandisers accounted for 70 percent of North American retail sales. Specialty big-box bookstores like Barnes and Noble and other chains and independent bookstores accounted for the remainder of retail sales. Globally, Harlequin's products were in over 250,000 retail outlets. Eighty thousand of these outlets were in North America; almost 50,000 of these were supermarkets and drugstores. Harlequin's series products were in 70 percent of supermarkets, but only 55 percent of bookstores. In Europe, kiosks and tobacconists accounted for the largest proportion of retail outlets.

The direct channel handled direct-to-reader book sales. Harlequin's "Reader Service" book club was an important source of sales and profits. Investing in advertising to acquire readers, this direct mail operation offered frequent Harlequin readers the possibility of purchasing every book the company published, delivered right to their doorstep. In the United States, six books were sold through the book club for every 10 sold at retail. Furthermore, a book sold through the book club yielded Harlequin the full cover price, whereas a book sold at retail netted the company approximately half the retail price, and required advertising, distribution costs, and the acceptance of returns from retailers.

Rise of Single-Title Romance

The proliferation of titles and authors during the "Romance Wars" had resulted in the emergence of single-titles as a significant factor in the women's romance fiction market. Exhibit 5 provides the sales breakdown for romance novels.

Exhibit 5   Romance Novel Sales in North America (millions of units)

	1985	1986	1987	1988	1989	1990
Harlequin series romance	77	79	80	82	83	85
Other romance series publishers	12	12	13	13	14	14
Single-title romance books by other publishers	72	79	86	94	102	112
Total romance books	**161**	**170**	**179**	**189**	**199**	**211**

Exhibit 6   Range of Worldwide Titles (1987)

Book Title	Type/Genre	Unit Sales Data	Harlequin Series Author?
Longest Pleasure	Romance	304,000	Yes
Quarantine	Horror	62,000	No
Eve of Regression	Psychological Thriller	55,000	No
War Moon	Suspense	72,000	No
Illusion	Psychological Suspense	35,000	No
Dream Escape	Romance	297,000	Yes
Alien Planet	Science Fiction	71,000	No

In an attempt to capitalize on reader's growing appetite for single-titles, Harlequin launched Worldwide Library in 1986, its first single-title publishing program. This move also gave Harlequin's more accomplished series authors another outlet. Laycock commented:

> Several authors who began their writing careers with Harlequin writing series romance wanted broader opportunities—opportunities that they saw in the single-title women's fiction publishing arena. Prior to the launch of Worldwide Library, Harlequin didn't have publishing opportunities to meet the desires of these authors. As a result, authors would seek out competitive publishers to support their single-title works.

Exhibit 7   Monthly Single-Title Romance Output Analysis North American Market

Single-Title Romance by Category	1985	1989	1991
Contemporary	2	6	12
Historical	22	37	43
Regency	6	8	17
Total	**30**	**51**	**72**
By Publisher			
Zebra (Kensington Publishing)	5	15	21
Bantam/Dell	2	2	8
Diamond	0	0	4
Harper Paperbacks	0	0	3
Avon	4	5	6
Jove	2	2	4
Leisure Books	3	3	5
NAL/Signet	6	7	8
Pocket Books (Simon & Schuster)	1	6	3
Ballantine/Fawcett, Onyx, SMP	4	7	7
Warner Books/Popular Library	3	4	3
Total	**30**	**51**	**72**

Source: Company files.

By 1988, Worldwide was shut down as a result of several problems. "Worldwide could never decide if it was a romance program, a women's fiction program, or a general fiction program," a Harlequin insider commented. Exhibit 6 illustrates a list of typical titles published at Worldwide.

With the shutdown of Worldwide Library, popular authors moved to other publishers. As shown in Exhibit 7, other publishers continued to exploit the popularity of single-title romance novels.

Eager to find ways to grow its publishing business, Harlequin's management reexamined the publishing market. A broader analysis revealed that although Harlequin's series romance had captured well over 80 percent of the North American series romance market by 1990, Harlequin's estimated share of the North American *women's fiction* market was only about 5 percent. Table 2 provides a breakdown of the women's fiction market.

There was substantial overlap in the readership of series romance fiction and other fiction. Mark Mailman, vice-president of market research and analysis added:

> One compelling reason to get into single-title publishing is that when we look at our research on customers, they're reading 20 Harlequin books and 20 single-title books from other publishers. We have an opportunity to take a greater share of that market.

Harlequin's Single-Title Task Force

Faced with slow or no growth in series romance, a Harlequin task force convened in 1992 to study the feasibility of launching a new women's fiction single-title program. To begin, they examined why Worldwide had failed and concluded that overall lack of success was attributable to: editorial parameters that were too broad; less than optimal North American retail distribution; very

Table 2   **North American Women's Fiction Market Size Estimate, 1993 (As a percentage of overall segment sizes in US$ millions)**

	General Fiction	Romance	Mystery	Sci-Fi	Total Fiction
Total Segment Size	2,222	1,220	353	476	4,271
Estimated Women's Fiction Share of Segment	60%	100%	60%	38%	69%

few Worldwide titles distributed through the direct-to-reader channel; global support for the program was not timely and universal; the selection of authors and titles was unsuccessful. The task force report stated:

> In the past few years, sell-through efficiencies in the supermarket channels are not as great as the sell-through efficiencies in both mass merchandisers and bookstores. The more efficient retailer knew that the consumer was spending her discretionary reading dollar to buy a diversity of romantic reads, including those that had previously been thought of as mainstream.
>
> Since a single-title strategy requires a single-title solicitation from the sales force and more expensive single-title packaging, two of Harlequin's strategic lynchpins of our earlier decades have to be rethought (for single-title): standing order program and same format production. However, Harlequin can still capitalize on its global base and its ability to distribute widely to points of purchase that women visit on a regular basis.

MIRA Launch Decision

The task force was preparing its recommendation for MIRA, Harlequin's proposed women's fiction single-title program. The addition of single titles would make a welcome contribution to overhead costs. Currently, indirect overhead costs per series novel were $0.09 per book. Because infrastructure was already in place, it was estimated that MIRA novels would not incur additional indirect overhead costs. Printing costs for single-titles were expected to be $0.71 per book (350 pages on average). Estimated advertising and promotional costs for new single-titles were 6 percent of (the higher) retail price.

Author Management

In the single-title market, authors were categorized into three groups, based on their sales potential: brand new, mid-list, and best-seller (see Exhibit 8). Depending on the author group royalties, sales, and promotional support varied. Best-selling authors were expected to sell more than a million books. Publishers were known to sign established authors for up to a five-book contract with large multimillion dollar advances. It had not been determined whether MIRA should follow suit. In addition to author advances, typical royalties per MIRA-type book were estimated to be 13 percent of the $6.75 retail price.

Exhibit 8   General Industry Contract Terms for Fiction Category by Author Group

	Brand-new Author	Mid-list Author	Best-selling Author
Advance	$10,000 to $30,000	$80,000 to $200,000	$1 million to $5 million
Royalties	5% to 13%	8% to 15%	10% to 17%
Overseas Publishing Schedule	Within 18 months	Within 12 months	Simultaneous
Overseas Publishing Markets	Major markets	All markets	All markets
Minimum Distribution	30,000 to 80,000	100,000 to 400,000	>1 million
Promotional Support per	Possibly some support (up to $50,000)	Support ($100,000)	Very strong support book (more than $300,000)

Sources: Industry sources and casewriter estimates.

A Different Format

Women's fiction books were expected to have many differences from well-defined series romance books. Unlike series romance, topics would cover a broader range of segments including general fiction, science fiction, and mystery. Women's fiction books would be longer in length: 100,000 to 400,000 words compared with a series romance book length of 75,000 words. Naturally, book sizes would be bigger in terms of page length: from 250 to 400 pages versus a norm of 192 to 304 pages for series romance.

Distribution

Harlequin had a strong distribution network for its series romances through supermarkets, drugstores, and discount department stores. Single-title women's fiction novels required more mainstream distribution focusing on retail bookstores. In addition, standing order distribution, a hallmark of Harlequin's series romance business model, would have to be abandoned in favor of relying on orders generated by the distributor's sales force for single-titles.

Success in the United States would be key for MIRA, and in this market, Harlequin relied upon Simon and Schuster's sales force. Since S&S was a major single-title publisher, Harlequin did not know how much support MIRA would be afforded. Harlequin was considering offering better margins to the distributors than those it offered for series romance distribution. Expenses for single-title distribution were expected to be $0.27 per book.

MIRA books would rely more heavily upon distribution through bookstores when distributed through the same channels as the series product. Retailers would be encouraged to shelve MIRA books separately from the series offering. The more intensive selling effort for single titles would require 4 percent of the single title retail price. The new single-title program planned to offer $3.38 in margin to the distribution channel for single-title books (50 percent of the typical retail price of $6.75) versus $2.42 for series books (45 percent of the $4.40 suggested retail price).

Acquiring Single-Title Rights

Harlequin subsidiaries in some countries were already buying rights to publish single titles. By launching MIRA Harlequin could negotiate better global-author deals. The task force report added: "By acquiring mainstream titles through a central acquiring office, the collective clout of Harlequin could create the likelihood of better-selling mainstream titles marketed by all countries in the global enterprise."

Harlequin's author and editor relationships remained strong, so much so that many series authors were enthusiastic about maintaining a long-term relationship with a trusted editor as they pursued their break-out mainstream book. With MIRA, these authors could remain loyal to Harlequin.

How Best to Proceed

There were many issues to be resolved prior to any launch of MIRA. Most pressing was the question of whether Harlequin had the resources and capabilities to succeed in its new women's fiction segment. Certainly there were elements of its series business model that could be transferred to the broader women's fiction market. But what were the gaps? What else did Harlequin need?

Hayes had a several options if MIRA was launched. Several established best-selling authors had begun their writing careers with Harlequin and had moved on to writing single-title books. These authors had established reputations. Harlequin could approach one or more of these authors to sign with MIRA/Harlequin. Such an arrangement would involve a multi-book contract and substantial advances. While risky, this approach would ensure that MIRA's launch attracted attention.

A different, seemingly less risky alternative was to tap into Harlequin's extensive back-list collection and reissue a selection of novels by current best-selling authors currently signed with rival single-title publishers. The physical size of the book and page length could be extended to 250 pages from 192 by adjusting format. In addition, a new, MIRA-branded cover could be produced to repackage the books. Coincident with the launch of this back-list, Harlequin's editors would cultivate and develop existing series authors, encouraging them to write single-title books for MIRA.

Returning to the strategic dilemma that Harlequin faced, Swift commented on the challenge of successfully launching MIRA:

> Our biggest challenge is the requirement to publish on a title-by-title basis. Every new book will have to stand on its own, with its own cover, a new marketing plan and possibly even an author tour. Can we as a company develop the flexibility to remain nimble? How patient should we be in waiting for success? Given Worldwide's poor results, how should we approach this challenge?

Notes

1. To protect confidentiality, all financial information within this case study has been disguised.
2. This section is adapted from the Richard Ivey School of Business case # 9A87M002. Harlequin Enterprises Limited—1979, Peter Killing.
3. All amounts are a percentage of the suggested retail price.
4. Numbers are for the typical paperback. Hardcover books cost more to produce, but as a percentage of its higher retail price, printing costs were roughly the same proportion.
5. All amounts in Canadian dollars unless otherwise specified.

Case 1–5: Nucor in 2005*

Nucor Corp. took first place in the 2005 *BusinessWeek* 50 list of the best performers of the S&P 500 companies. Not bad for a company in an industry often considered unexciting and low tech! In 2004 sales were up 82 percent, from $6 to $12 billion, and earnings went from $.40 to $7.02 per share. In a little over a year the stock price tripled. Longtime employees with $300,000 in their retirement stock saw it rise to over a $1 million. The tons shipped increased 9 percent with the average selling price up 66 percent. However scrap prices were up 74 percent. At the beginning of 2005 prices seemed to be holding up because of the mergers in the United States and the state control of supply in China. And Nucor expected the first quarter of 2005 to double the 2004 results. This was a reasonable expectation since Nucor began the year with 70 percent of its flat-rolled steel output for all of 2005 sold, compared to just 25 percent a year earlier. Furthermore, in 2005 Nucor had two joint ventures with global partners to find alternatives to the use of scrap steel. In Brazil they were working an environmentally friendly way to produce pig iron. With Mitsubishi and the Chinese steelmaker they were building a facility in Western Australia to use the new Hismelt process to produce iron from iron ore finds and cold fines with less energy and pollution.

The previous three years had been among the worst down cycles in the steel industry's history. During those years Nucor acquired failing competitors, increased its steel capacity and achieved a profit in every quarter. The world economy and demand had improved recently as prices went from $300 a ton to $640 a ton. Thus, Nucor expected profits to continue to grow for a while. While bankruptcies had eliminated some excess capacity in the United States and state-controlled China could hold back capacity to maintain prices, global competitors were consolidating, suppliers were raising their prices on iron ore and scrap, and buyers were considering alternatives to steel. Nucor, and its new president Dan DiMicco, faced a challenge in continuing Nucor's reputation for excellence.

* © 2005, Frank C. Barnes *University of North Carolina-Charlotte,* Beverly B. Tyler *North Carolina State University. Used with permission.*

Background

Nucor could be traced back to the company that manufactured the first Oldsmobile in 1897 and became the Reo Truck Company. As the company declined into bankruptcy in the postwar years, a 1955 merger created Nuclear Corp. of America. Following the "conglomerate" trend of the period, Nuclear acquired various "high-tech" businesses, such as radiation sensors, semi-conductors, rare earths, and air-conditioning equipment. However, the company lost money continually and a fourth reorganization in 1966 put forty-year-old Ken Iverson in charge. The building of Nucor had begun.

Ken Iverson had joined the Navy after high school in 1943 and had been transferred from officer training school to Cornell's Aeronautical Engineering Program. On graduation he selected Mechanical Engineering/Metallurgy for a Master's degree to avoid the long drafting apprenticeship in Aeronautical Engineering. His college work with an electron microscope earned him a job with International Harvester. After five years in their lab, his boss, and mentor, prodded him to expand his vision by going with a smaller company.

Over the next 10 years, Iverson worked for four small metals companies, gaining technical knowledge and increasing his exposure to other business functions. He enjoyed working with the presidents of these small companies and admired their ability to achieve outstanding results. Nuclear Corp., after failing to buy the company Iverson worked for, hired him as a consultant to find them another metals business to buy. In 1962, the firm bought a small joist plant in South Carolina that Iverson found, on the condition that he run it.

Over the next four years, Iverson built up the Vulcraft division as Nuclear Corporation struggled. The president, David Thomas, was described as a great promoter and salesman but a weak manager. A partner with Bear Stearns actually made a personal loan to the company to keep it going. In 1966, when the company was on the edge of bankruptcy, Iverson, who headed the only successful division, was named president and moved the headquarters to Charlotte, North Carolina, where he focused the company business first on the joist industry and soon moved into steel production.

He immediately began getting rid of the esoteric, but unprofitable, high-tech divisions and concentrated on the steel joist business he found successful. They built more joist plants and in 1968 began building their first steel mill in South Carolina to "make steel cheaper than they were buying from importers." By 1984, Nucor had six joist plants and four steel mills, using the new "mini-mill" technology.

From the beginning, Iverson had the people running the various plants, called divisions, make all the major decisions about how to build and run Nucor. The original Board was composed of Iverson, Sam Siegel, his financial chief, and Dave Aycock, who had been with the South Carolina joist company before Nuclear acquired it. Siegel had joined Nuclear as an accountant in 1961. He had quit Nuclear but in their crisis agreed to return as treasurer if Iverson were named president. Aycock and Siegel were named vice presidents at the time Iverson was named president.

Dave Aycock had been very impressed with the original owner of Vulcraft, Sanborn Chase. Aycock had started his career as a welder there. He described Chase as "the best person I've ever known" and as "a scientific genius." He said he was a man of great compassion, who understood the atmosphere necessary for people to self motivate. Chase, an engineer by training, invented a number of things in diverse fields. He also established the incentive programs for which Nucor later became known. With only one plant, he was still able to operate with a "decentralized" manner. Before his death in 1960, while still in his 40s, the company was studying the building of a steel mill using newly developed mini mill technology. His widow ran the company until it was sold to Nucor in 1962.

Aycock met Ken Iverson when Nuclear purchased Vulcraft, and they worked together closely for the next year and a half. Located in Phoenix at the corporate headquarters, he was responsible to Iverson for all the joist operations and was given the task of planning and building a new joist plant in Texas. In late 1963 he was transferred to Norfolk, where he lived for the next 13 years and managed a number of Nucor's joist plants. Then in 1977 he was named the manager of the Darlington, South Carolina, steel plant. In 1984, Aycock became Nucor's president and chief operating officer, while Iverson became chairman and chief executive officer.

Aycock had this to say about Iverson: "Ken was a very good leader, with an entrepreneurial spirit. He is easy to work with and has the courage to do things, to take lots of risks. Many things didn't work, but some worked very well." There is the old saying "failure to take risk is failure." This saying epitomizes a cultural value personified by the company's founder and reinforced by Iverson during his time at the helm. Nucor was very innovative in steel and joists. Their plant was years ahead in wire rod welding

at Norfolk. In the late 1960s they had one of the first computer inventory management systems and design/engineering programs. They were very sophisticated in purchasing, sales, and managing and they beat their competition often by the speed of their design efforts.

Between 1964 and 1984 the bankrupt conglomerate became a leading U.S. steel company. It was a fairytale story. Tom Peters used Nucor's management style as an example of "excellence," while the barons of old steel ruled over creeping ghettos. NBC featured Nucor on television and *New Yorker* magazine serialized a book about how a relatively small American steel company built a team, which led the whole world into a new era of steelmaking. As the NBC program asked: "If Japan Can, Why Can't We?," Nucor had! Iverson was rich, owning $10 million in stock, but with a salary which rarely reached $1 million, compared to some U.S. executive's $50 or $100 million. The 40-year-old manager of the South Carolina Vulcraft plant had become a millionaire. Stockholders chuckled and un-unionized hourly workers, who hadn't seen a layoff in the 20 years, earned more than the unionized workers of old steel and more than 85 percent of the people in the states where they worked. Many employees were financially quite secure.

Nucor owed much of its success to its benchmark organizational style and the empowered division managers. There were two basic lines of business, the first being the six steel joist plants which made the steel frames seen in many buildings. The second line included four steel mills that utilized the innovative mini-mill technology to supply the joist plants at first and later outside customers. Nucor was still only the seventh-largest steel company in America. Over its second 20 years, Nucor was to rise to become the second-largest U.S. steel company. A number of significant challenges were to be met and overcome to get there, and once that horizon was reached even greater challenges would arise. Below are described the systems Nucor built and its organization, divisions, management, and incentive system.

Nucor's Organization

In the early 1990s, Nucor's 22 divisions (up to 30 by 2005), one for every plant, had a general manager, who was also a vice-president of the corporation. The divisions were of three basic types, joist plants, steel mills, and miscellaneous plants. The corporate staff consisted of less than 45 people. In the beginning Iverson had chosen Charlotte, North Carolina,"as the new home base for what he had envisioned as a small cadre of executives who would guide a decentralized operation with liberal authority delegated to managers in the field," according to *South* magazine.

Iverson gave his views on keeping a lean organization:

Each division is a profit center and the division manager has control over the day-to-day decisions that make that particular division profitable or not profitable. We expect the division to provide contribution, which is earnings before corporate expenses. We do not allocate our corporate expenses, because we do not think there is any way to do this reasonably and fairly. We do focus on earnings. And we expect a division to earn 25 percent return on total assets employed, before corporate expenses, taxes, interest, or profit sharing. And we have a saying in the company—if a manager doesn't provide that for a number of years, we are either going to get rid of the division or get rid of the general manager, and it's generally the division manager.

A joist division manager commented on being in an organization with only four levels:

I've been a division manager four years now and at times I'm still awed by it: the opportunity I was given to be a Fortune *500 vice-president... I think we are successful because it is our style to pay more attention to our business than our competitors. ... We are kind of a "no nonsense" company.*

The divisions did their own manufacturing, selling, accounting, engineering, and personnel management. A steel division manager, when questioned about Florida Steel, which had a large plant 90 miles away, commented, "I expect they do have more of the hierarchy. I think they have central purchasing, centralized sales, centralized credit collections, centralized engineering, and most of the major functions."

Nucor strengthened its position by developing strong alliances with outside parties. It did no internal research and development. Instead, they monitored other's work worldwide and attracted investors who brought them new technical applications at the earliest possible dates. Though Nucor was known for constructing new facilities at the lowest possible costs, their engineering and construction team consists of only three individuals. They did not attempt to specify exact equipment parameters, but asked the equipment supplier to provide this information and then held the manufacturer accountable. They had alliances with selected construction companies around the country who knew the kind of work Nucor wanted. Nucor bought 95 percent of its scrap steel from an independent broker who followed the market and made recommendations regarding scrap purchases. They did not have a corporate advertising department, corporate public relations department, or a corporate legal or environmental department. They had long-term relationships with outsiders to provide these services.

The steel industry had established a pattern of absorbing the cost of shipment so, regardless of the distance from the mill, all users paid the same delivered price. Nucor broke with this tradition and stopped equalizing freight. It offered all customers the same sales terms. Nucor also gave no volume discounts, feeling that with modern computer systems there was no justification. Customers located next to the plant guaranteed themselves the lowest possible costs for steel purchases. Two tube manufactures, two steel service centers, and a cold rolling facility had located adjacent to the Arkansas plant. These facilities accounted for 60 percent of the shipments from the mill. The plants were linked electronically to each other's production schedules allowing them to functions in a just-in-time inventory mode. All new mills were built on large enough tracks of land to accommodate collaborating businesses.

Iverson didn't feel greater centralization would be good for Nucor. Hamilton Lott, a Vulcraft plant manager, commented in 1997, "We're truly autonomous; we can duplicate efforts made in other parts of Nucor. We might develop the same computer program six times. But the advantages of local autonomy make it worth it." Joe Rutkowski, manager at Darlington steel, agreed. Rutkowski said, "We're not constrained; headquarters doesn't restrict what I spend. I just have to make my profit contribution at the end of year."

South Magazine observed that Iverson had established a characteristic organizational style described as "stripped down" and "no nonsense." "Jack Benny would like this company," observed Roland Underhill, an analyst with Crowell, Weedon and Co. of Los Angeles, "so would Peter Drucker." Underhill pointed out that Nucor's thriftiness doesn't end with its "Spartan" office staff or modest offices. "There are no corporate perquisites," he recited. "No company planes, no country club memberships, no company cars."

Fortune noted, "Iverson takes the subway when he is in New York, a Wall Street analyst reports in a voice that suggests both admiration and amazement." The general managers reflected this style in the operation of their individual divisions. Their offices were more like plant offices or the offices of private companies built around manufacturing rather than for public appeal. They were simple, routine, and businesslike.

Division Managers

The corporate personnel manager described management relations as informal, trusting, and not "bureaucratic." He felt there was a minimum of paperwork, that a phone call was more common than memos and that no confirming memo was thought to be necessary.

A Vulcraft manager commented: "We have what I would call a very friendly spirit of competition from one plant to the next. And of course all of the vice presidents and general managers share the same bonus systems so we are in this together as a team even though we operate our divisions individually." He added, "When I came to this plant four years ago, I saw we had too many people, too much overhead. We had 410 people at the plant and I could see, from my experience at the Nebraska plant, we had many more than we needed. Now with 55 fewer men, we are still capable of producing the same number of tons as four years ago."

The divisions managed their activities with a minimum of contact with the corporate staff. Each day disbursements were reported to corporate office. Payments flowed into regional lock-boxes. On a weekly basis, joist divisions reported total quotes, sales cancellations, backlog, and production. Steel mills reported tons rolled, outside shipments, orders, cancellations, and backlog.

Each month the divisions completed a two-page (11" × 17") "Operations Analysis," which was sent to all the managers. Its three main purposes were (1) financial consolidation, (2) sharing information among the divisions, and (3) corporate management examination. The summarized information and the performance statistics for all the divisions were then returned to the managers.

The general managers met three times a year. In late October they presented preliminary budgets and capital requests. In late February they met to finalize budgets and treat miscellaneous matters. Then, at a meeting in May, they handled personnel matters, such as wage increases and changes of policies or benefits. The general managers as a group considered the raises for the department heads, the next lower level of management for all the plants.

Vulcraft, The Joist Divisions

One of Nucor's major businesses was the manufacture and sale of open web steel joists and joist girders at seven Vulcraft divisions located in Florence, South Carolina; Norfolk, Nebraska; Ft. Payne, Alabama; Grapeland, Texas; St. Joe, Indiana; Brigham City, Utah, and Chemung, New York. Open web joists, in contrast to solid joists, were made of steel angle iron separated by round bars or smaller angle iron. These joists cost less, were of greater strength for many applications, and were used primarily as the roof support systems in larger buildings, such as warehouses and shopping malls.

The joist industry was characterized by high competition among many manufacturers for many small customers. With an estimated 40 percent of the market, Nucor was the largest supplier in the U.S. It utilized national advertising campaigns and prepared competitive bids on 80 percent to 90 percent of the buildings using joists. Competition was based on price and delivery performance. Nucor had developed computer programs to prepare designs for customers and to compute bids based on current prices and labor standards. In addition, each Vulcraft plant maintained its own Engineering Department to help customers with design problems or specifications. The Florence manager commented, "Here on the East Coast we have six or seven major competitors, of course, none of them are as large as we are. The competition for any order will be heavy, and we will see six or seven different prices." He added, "I think we have a strong selling force in the market place. It has been said to us by some of our competitors that in this particular industry we have the finest selling organization in the country."

Nucor aggressively sought to be the lowest-cost producer in the industry. Materials and freight were two important elements of cost. Nucor maintained its own fleet of almost 150 trucks to ensure on-time delivery to all of the states, although most business was regional due to transportation costs. Plants were located in rural areas near the markets they served. Nucor's move into steel production was a move to lower the cost of steel used by the joist business.

Joist Production

On the basic assembly line used at the joist divisions, three or four of which might make up any one plant, about six tons of joists per hour would be assembled. In the first stage eight people cut the angles to the right lengths or bend the round bars to the desired form. These were moved on a roller conveyer to six-man assembly stations, where the component parts would be tacked together for the next stage, welding. Drilling and miscellaneous work were done by three people between the lines. The nine-man welding station completed the welds before passing the joists on roller conveyers to two-man inspection teams. The last step before shipment was the painting.

The workers had control over and responsibility for quality. There was an independent quality control inspector who had the authority to reject the run of joists and cause them to be reworked. The quality control people were not under the incentive system and reported to the engineering department.

Daily production might vary widely, since each joist was made for a specific job. The wide range of joists made control of the workload at each station difficult; bottlenecks might arise anywhere along the line. Each workstation was responsible for identifying such bottlenecks so that the foreman could reassign people promptly to maintain productivity. Since workers knew most of the jobs on the line, including the more skilled welding job, they could be shifted as needed. Work on the line was described by one general manager as "not machine type but mostly physical labor." He said the important thing was to avoid bottlenecks.

There were four lines of about 28 people each on two shifts at the Florence division. The jobs on the line were rated on responsibility and assigned a base wage, from $11 to $13 per hour. In addition, a weekly bonus was paid on the total output of each line. Each worker received the same percent bonus on his base wage. The Texas plant was typical, with the bonus running 225 percent, giving a wage of $27.00 an hour in 1999.

The amount of time required to make a joist had been established as a result of experience; the general manager had seen no time studies in his 15 years with the company. As a job was bid, the cost of each joist was determined through the computer program. The time required depended on the length, number of panels, and depth of the joist. At the time of production, the labor value of production, the standard, was determined in a similar manner. The South Carolina general manager stated, "In the last nine or ten years we have not changed a standard."

The Grapeland plant maintained a time chart, which was used to estimate the labor required on a job. The plant teams were measured against this time for bonus. The chart was based on the historical time required on the jobs. Every few years the time chart was updated. Because some of the changes in performance were due to equipment changes, generally the chart would be increased by half the change and the employee would benefit in pay from the other half. The last change, two years ago, saw some departments pay increased by as much as 10 percent. The production manager at Grapeland considered himself an example for the Nucor policy: "the sky is the limit." He had started in an entry position and risen to the head of this plant of 200 people.

Table 1 **Tons per Man-Hour**

1977	0.163	1982	0.208	1987	0.218
1978	0.179	1983	0.215	1988	0.249
1979	0.192	1984	0.214	1999	0.251
1980	0.195	1985	0.228	2000	0.241
1981	0.194	1986	0.225	2004	0.222

The table below shows the productivity of the South Carolina plant in tons per man-hour for a number of years. The year 1999 set a record for overall tonnage before a downturn, which bottomed in 2002, but had begun to rise again by 2004.

Steel Divisions

Nucor moved into the steel business in 1968 to provide raw material for the Vulcraft plants. Iverson said, "We got into the steel business because we wanted to build a mill that could make steel as cheaply as we were buying it from foreign importers or from offshore mills." Thus, they entered the industry using the new mini-mill technology after they took a task force of four people around the world to investigate new technological advancements. A case writer from Harvard recounted the development of the steel divisions:

By 1967 about 60 percent of each Vulcraft sales dollar was spent on materials, primarily steel. Thus, the goal of keeping costs low made it imperative to obtain steel economically. In addition, in 1967 Vulcraft bought about 60 percent of its steel from foreign sources. As the Vulcraft Division grew, Nucor became concerned about its ability to obtain an adequate economical supply of steel and in 1968 began construction of its first steel mill in Darlington, South Carolina. By 1972 the Florence, South Carolina, joist plant was purchasing over 90 percent of its steel from this mill. The Fort Payne, Alabama plant bought about 50 percent of its steel from Florence. Since the mill had excess capacity, Nucor began to market its steel products to outside customers. In 1972, 75 percent of the shipments of Nucor steel was to Vulcraft and 25 percent was to other customers.

Between 1973 and 1981, Nucor constructed three more bar mills and their accompanying rolling mills to convert the billits into bars, flats, rounds, channels, and other products. Iverson explained in 1984:

In constructing these mills we have experimented with new processes and new manufacturing techniques. We serve as our own general contractor and *design and build much of our own equipment. In one or more of our mills we have built our own continuous casting unit, reheat furnaces, cooling beds, and in Utah even our own mill stands. All of these to date have cost under $125 per ton of annual capacity—compared with projected costs for large integrated mills of $1,200–$1,500 per ton of annual capacity, ten times our cost. Our mills have high productivity. We currently use less than four man hours to produce a ton of steel. Our total employment costs are less than $60 per ton compared with the average employment costs of the seven largest U. S. steel companies of close to $130 per ton. Our total labor costs are less than 20 percent of our sales price.*

In 1987 Nucor was the first steel company in the world to begin to build a mini-mill to manufacture steel sheet, the raw material for the auto industry and other major manufacturers. This project opened up another 50 percent of the total steel market. The first plant in Crawfordsville, Indiana was successful and three additional sheet mills were constructed between 1989 and 1990. Through the years these steel plants were significantly modernized and expanded until the total capacity was three million tons per year at a capital cost of less than $170 dollars per ton by 1999. Nucor's total steel production capacity was 5.9 million tons per year at a cost of 300 dollars per ton of annual capacity. The eight mills sold 80 percent of their output to outside customers and the balance to other Nucor divisions.

By 2005, Nucor had 16 steel facilities producing three times as much as in 1999. The number of bar mills had grown to nine mills with capacity of 6 million tons by the addition of Birmingham's four mills with 2 million tons and Auburn's 400,000 tons. The sheet mills grew to four and increased capacity by one-third with the acquisition of Trico. Nucor–Yamato's structural steel capacity was increased by half a million tons from the South Carolina plant. The new million-ton plate mill opened in North Carolina in 2000. Ninety-three percent of production was sold to outside customers.

All four of the original "bar mills" were actually two mills operating side by side. One mill concentrated on the larger bar products, which had separate production and customer demands, while the other mill concentrated on smaller diameter bar stock. Throughout Nucor each operation was housed in its own separate building with its own staff. Nucor designed its processes to limit work-in-process inventory, to limit space, to utilize a pull approach to material usage and to increase flexibility.

The Steel-Making Process

A steel mill's work is divided into two phases: preparation of steel of the proper "chemistry", and the forming of the steel into the desired products. The typical mini-mill utilized scrap steel, such as junk auto parts, instead of the iron ore, which would be used in larger, integrated steel mills. The typical bar mini-mill had an annual capacity of 200–600 thousand tons, compared with the 7 million tons of Bethlehem Steel's Sparrow's Point, Maryland, integrated plant.

In the bar mills a charging bucket fed loads of scrap steel into electric ore furnaces. The melted load, called a heat, was poured into a ladle to be carried by an overhead crane to the casting machine. In the casting machine the liquid steel was extruded as a continuous red-hot solid bar of steel and cut into lengths weighing some 900 pounds called "billets." In the typical plant, the billet, about four inches in cross section and about 20 feet long, was held temporarily in a pit where it cooled to normal temperatures. Periodically, billets were carried to the rolling mill and placed in a reheat oven to bring them up to 2000°F, at which temperance they would be malleable. In the rolling mill, presses and dies progressively converted the billet into the desired round bars, angles, channels, flats, and other products. After cutting to standard lengths, they were moved to the warehouse.

Nucor's first steel mill, which employed more than 500 people, was located in Darlington, South Carolina. The mill, with its three electric ore furnaces, operated 24 hours per day, 5 1/2 H days per week. Nucor had made a number of improvements in the melting and casting operations. The general manager of the Darlington plant developed a system that involved preheating the ladles, allowing for the faster flow of steel into the caster and resulting in better control of the steel characteristics. Thus, less time, and lower capital investment were required at Darlington than other mini-mills at the time of its construction. The casting machines were "continuous casters," as opposed to the old batch method. The objective in the "front" of the mill was to keep the casters working. At the time the Darlington plant was also perhaps the only mill in the country that regularly avoided the reheating of billets. This saved $10 to $12 per ton in fuel usage and losses due to oxidation of the steel. The cost of developing this process had been $12 million. Not all the research projects had been successful. The company spent approximately $2 million in an unsuccessful effort to utilize resistance-heating. They lost even more on an effort at induction melting. As Iverson told

Metal Producing, "That cost us a lot of money. Time-wise, it was very expensive. But you have got to make mistakes and we've had lots of failures."

The Darlington design became the basis for plants in Nebraska, Texas, and Utah. The Texas plant had cost under $80 per ton of annual capacity. Whereas the typical mini-mill at the time cost approximately $250 per ton, the average cost of Nucor's four mills was under $135. An integrated mill was expected to cost between $1,200 and $1,500 per ton.

The Darlington plant was organized into 12 natural groups for the purpose of incentive pay. Two mills each had two shifts with three groups—melting and casting, rolling mill, and finishing. In melting and casting there were three or four different standards, depending on the material, established by the department manager years ago based on historical performance. The general manager stated, "We don't change the standards." The caster, key to the operation, was used at a 92 percent level—one greater than the claims of the manufacturer. For every good ton of billet above the standard hourly rate for the week, workers in the group received a 4 percent bonus. For example, with a common standard of 10 tons per run hour and an actual rate for the week of 28 tons per hour, the workers would receive a bonus of 72 percent of their base rate in the week's paycheck. In the rolling mill there were more than 100 products, each with a different historical standard. Workers received a 4 percent to 6 percent bonus for every good ton sheared per hour for the week over the computed standard. A manager stated: "Meltshop employees don't ask me how much it costs Chaparral or LTV to make a billet. They want to know what it costs Darlington, Norfolk, Jewitt to put a billet on the ground—Scrap costs, alloy costs, electrical costs, refractory, gas, etc. Everybody from Charlotte to Plymouth watches the nickels and dimes."

Management Philosophy

Aycock, while still the Darlington manager, stated:

The key to making a profit when selling a product with no aesthetic value, or a product that you really can't differentiate from your competitors, is cost. I don't look at us as a fantastic marketing organization, even though I think we are pretty good; but we don't try to overcome unreasonable costs by mass marketing. We maintain low costs by keeping the employee force at the level it should be, not doing things that aren't necessary to achieve our goals, and allowing people to function on their own and by judging them on their results.

To keep a cooperative and productive workforce you need, number one, to be completely honest about everything; number two, to allow each employee as much as possible to make decisions about that employee's work, to find easier and more productive ways to perform duties; and number three, to be as fair as possible to all employees. Most of the changes we make in work procedures and in equipment come from the employees. They really know the problems of their jobs better than anyone else.

To communicate with my employees, I try to spend time in the plant and at intervals have meetings with the employees. Usually if they have a question they just visit me. Recently a small group visited me in my office to discuss our vacation policy. They had some suggestions and, after listening to them, I had to agree that the ideas were good.

In discussing his philosophy for dealing with the workforce, the Florence manager stated:

I believe very strongly in the incentive system we have. We are a non-union shop and we all feel that the way to stay so is to take care of our people and show them we care. I think that's easily done because of our fewer layers of management. … I spend a good part of my time in the plant, maybe an hour or so a day. If a man wants to know anything, for example an insurance question, I'm there and they walk right up to me and ask me questions, which I'll answer the best I know how.

We don't lay our people off and we make a point of telling our people this. In the slowdown of 1994, we scheduled our line for four days, but the men were allowed to come in the fifth day for maintenance work at base pay. The men in the plant on an average running bonus might make $17 to $19 an hour. If their base pay is half that, on Friday they would only get $8 to $9 an hour. Surprisingly, many of the men did not want to come in on Friday. They felt comfortable with just working four days a week. They are happy to have that extra day off.

About 20 percent of the people took the fifth day at base rate, but still no one had been laid off, in an industry with a strong business cycle.

In an earlier business cycle the executive committee decided in view of economic conditions that a pay freeze was necessary. The employees normally received an increase in their base pay the first of June. The decision was made at that time to freeze wages. The officers of the company, as a show of good faith, accepted a 5 percent pay cut. In addition to announcing this to the workers with a stuffer in their pay envelopes, meetings were held. Each production line, or incentive group of workers, met in the plant conference room with all supervision-foreman, plant production manager, and division manager. The economic crisis, the company was facing, was explained to the employees by the production manager and all of their questions were answered.

The Personnel and Incentive Systems

The foremost characteristic of Nucor's personnel system was its incentive plan. Another major personnel policy was providing job security. Also, all employees at Nucor received the same fringe benefits. There was only one group insurance plan. Holidays and vacations did not differ by job. Every child of every Nucor employee received up to $1,200 a year for four years if they chose to go on to higher education, including technical schools. The company had no executive dining rooms or restrooms, no fishing lodges, company cars, or reserved parking places.Jim Coblin, Nucor's vice president of Human Resources, described Nucor's systems for *HRMagazine* in a 1994 article, "No-frills HR at Nucor: a lean, bottom-line approach at this steel company empowers employees." Coblin, as benefits administrator, received part-time help from one of the corporate secretaries in the corporate office. The plants typically used someone from their finance department to handle compensation issues, although two plants had personnel generalists. Nucor plants did not have job descriptions, finding they caused more problems than they solved, given the flexible workforce and non-union status of Nucor employees. Surprisingly, Coblin found performance appraisal a waste of time. If an employee was not performing well, the problem would be dealt with directly. He had observed that when promotional opportunities became available, the performance appraisals were not much help filling the position. So he saw both of these as just more paperwork. The key, he believed, was not to put a maximum on what employee could earn and pay them directly for productivity. Iverson firmly believed that the bonus should be direct and involve no discretion on part of a manager.

Employees were kept informed about the company. Charts showing the division's results in return-on-assets and bonus payoff were posted in prominent places in the plant. The personnel manager commented that as he traveled around to all the plants, he found everyone in the company could tell him the level of profits in their division. The general managers held dinners at least once but usually twice a year with each of their employees. The dinners were held with 50 or 60 employees at a time, resulting in as many as 20 dinners per year. After introductory remarks

the floor was open for discussion of any work-related problems. There was a new-employee orientation program and an employee handbook that contained personnel policies and rules. The corporate office sends all news releases to each division where they were posted on bulletin boards. Each employee in the company also received a copy of the annual report. For the last several years the cover of the annual report had contained the names of all Nucor employees.

Absenteeism and tardiness was not a problem at Nucor. Each employee had four days of absences before pay was reduced. In addition to these, missing work was allowed for jury duty, military leave, or the death of close relatives. After this, a day's absence cost them bonus pay for that week and lateness of more than a half-hour meant the loss of bonus for that day.

Safety was a concern of Nucor's critics. With 10 fatalities in the 1980s, Nucor was committed to doing better. Safety administrators had appointed in each plant and safety had improved in the 1990s. The company also had a formal grievance procedure, although the Darlington manager couldn't recall the last grievance he had processed.

The company had conducted attitude surveys every three years for over two decades. These provided management insight into employee attitudes on 20 issues and allowed comparisons across plants and divisions. There were some concerns and differences but most employees appeared very satisfied with Nucor as an employer. The surveys suggested that pay was not the only thing the workers liked about Nucor. The personnel manager said that an NBC interviewer, working on the documentary "If Japan Can, Why Can't We?" often heard employees say, "I enjoy working for Nucor because Nucor is the best, the most productive, and the most profitable company that I know of."

The average hourly worker's pay was over twice the average earnings paid by other manufacturing companies in the states where Nucor's plants were located. In many rural communities where Nucor had located, they provide better wages than most other manufacturers. The new plant in Hertford County in North Carolina illustrated this point as reported in a June 21, 1998 article in *The Charlotte Observer*, entitled "Hope on the horizon: In Hertford County, poverty reigns and jobs are scarce." Here the author wrote, "In North Carolina's forgotten northeastern corner, where poverty rates run more than twice the state average, Nucor's $300 million steel mill is a dream realized. Upon completion, the plant on the banks of the Chowan River in North Carolina's banks coastal district would have their employees earning a rumored $60,000 a year, three times the local average manufacturing wage. Nucor had recently begun developing its plant sites with the expectation of other companies co-locating to save shipping costs. Four companies have announced plans to locate close to Nucor's property, adding another 100 to 200 jobs. People couldn't believe such wages, but callers to the plant's chief financial officer got "We don't like to promise too much, but $60,000 might be a little low." The average wage for these jobs at Darlington was $70,000. The plant's CFO added that Nucor didn't try to set pay "a buck over Wal-Mart" but went for the best workers. The article noted that steel work is hot and often dangerous, and that turnover at the plant may be high as people adjust to this and Nucor's hard-driving team system. He added, "Slackers don't last." The State of North Carolina had given $155 million in tax credits over 25 years. The local preacher said, "In 15 years, Baron (a local child) will be making $75,000 a year at Nucor, not in jail. I have a place now I can hold in front of him and say 'Look, right here. This is for you.'"

The Incentive System

There were four incentive programs at Nucor, one each for (1) production workers, (2) department heads, (3) staff people, such as accountants, secretaries, or engineers, and (4) senior management, which included the division managers. All of these programs were based on group performance.

Within the production program, groups ranged in size from 25 to 30 people and had definable and measurable operations. The company believed that a program should be simple and that bonuses should be paid promptly. "We don't have any discretionary bonuses. Zero. It is all based on performance. Now we don't want anyone to sit in judgment, because it never is fair...," said Iverson. The personnel manager stated, "Their bonus is based on roughly 90 percent of historical time it takes to make a particular joist. If during a week they make joists at 60 percent less than the standard time, they receive a 60 percent bonus." This was paid with the regular pay the following week. The complete pay check amount, including overtime, was multiplied by the bonus factor. A bonus was not paid when equipment was not operating: "We have the philosophy that when equipment is not operating everybody suffers and the bonus for downtime is zero." The foremen are also part of the group and received the same bonus as the employees they supervised.

The second incentive program was for department heads in the various divisions. The incentive pay here was based on division contribution, defined as the division earnings before corporate expenses and profit sharing are determined. Bonuses were reported to run between 0 and

90 percent (average 35 to 50 percent) of a person's base salary. The base salaries at this level were set at 75 percent of industry norms.

There was a third plan for people who were not production workers, department managers, or senior managers. Their bonus was based on either the division return-on-assets or the corporate return-on-assets depending on the unit they were a part of. Bonuses were typically 30 percent or more of a person's base salary for corporate positions.

The fourth program was for the senior officers. The senior officer had no employment contracts, pension or retirement plans, or other perquisites. Their bases salaries were set at about 75 percent of what an individual doing similar work in other companies would receive. Once return-on-equity 9 percent, slightly below the average for manufacturing firms, 5 percent of net earnings before taxes went into a pool, which was divided among the officers based on their salaries. "Now if return-on-equity for the company reaches, say 20 percent, which it has, then we can wind up with as much as 190 percent of our base salaries and 115 percent on top of that in stock. We get both." Half the bonus was paid in cash and half was deferred. Individual bonuses ranged from zero to several hundred percent, averaging 75 to 150 percent.

However, the opposite was true as well. In 1982 the return was 8 percent and the executives received no bonus. Iverson's pay in 1981 was approximately $300,000 but dropped the next year to $110,000. "I think that ranked by total compensation I was the lowest paid CEO in the *Fortune* 500. I was kind of proud of that, too." In his 1997 book, *Plain Talk: Lessons from a Business Maverick*, Iverson said, "Can management expect employees to be loyal if we lay them all off at every dip of the economy, while we go on padding our own pockets." Even so by 1986, Iverson's stock was worth more than $10 million dollars and the one-time Vulcraft manager was a millionaire.

In lieu of a retirement plan, the company had a profit sharing plan with a deferred trust. Each year, 10 percent of pretax earnings was put into profit sharing for all people below officer level. Twenty percent of this was set aside to be paid to employees in the following March as a cash bonus and the remainder was put into trust for each employee on the basis of percent of their earnings as a percent of total wages paid within the corporation. The employee was vested after the first year. Employees received a quarterly statement of their balance in profit sharing.

The company had an Employer Monthly Stock Investment Plan to which Nucor added 10 percent to the amount the employee contributed on the purchase of any Nucor stock and paid the commission. After each five years of service with the company, the employee received a service award consisting of five shares of Nucor stock. Moreover, if profits were good, extraordinary bonus payments would be made to the employees. For example, in December 1998 each employee received an $800 payment.

According to Iverson:

> *I think the first obligation of the company is to the stockholder and to its employees. I find in this country too many cases where employees are underpaid and corporate management is making huge social donations for self-fulfillment. We regularly give donations, but we have a very interesting corporate policy. First, we give donations where our employees are. Second, we give donations that will benefit our employees, such as to the YMCA. It is a difficult area and it requires a lot of thought. There is certainly a strong social responsibility for a company, but it cannot be at the expense of the employees or the stockholders.*

Having welcomed a parade of visitors over the years, Iverson had become concerned with the pattern apparent at other companies' steel plants: "They only do one or two of the things we do. It's not just incentives or the scholarship program; it's all those things put together that results in a unified philosophy for the company."

Building on Their Success

Throughout the 1980s and 1990s Nucor continued to take the initiative and be the prime mover in steel and the industries vertically related to steel. For example in 1984 Nucor broke with the industry pattern of basing the price of an order of steel on the quantity ordered. Iverson noted, "Some time ago we began to realize that with computer order entry and billing, the extra charge for smaller orders was not cost justified." In a seemingly risky move in 1986 Nucor began construction of a $25 million plant in Indiana to manufacture steel fasteners. Imports had grown to 90 percent of this market as U.S. companies failed to compete. Iverson said, "We're going to bring that business back; we can make bolts as cheaply as foreign producers." A second plant, in 1995, gave Nucor 20 percent of the U.S. market for steel fasteners. Nucor also acquired a steel bearings manufacturer in 1986, which Iverson called "a good fit with our business, our policies and our people."

In early 1986, Iverson announced plans for a revolutionary plant at Crawfordsville, Indiana, which would be the first mini-mill in the world to manufacture flat-rolled or sheet steel, the last bastion of the integrated manufacturers. This market alone was twice the size of the existing market for mini-mill products. It would be a quarter of a billion dollar gamble on a new technology. The plant was expected to halve the integrated manufacturer's three dollars of labor per ton and save $50 to $75 on a $400-a-ton selling price. If it worked the profit from this plant alone would come close to the profit of the whole corporation. *Forbes* commented, "If any mini-mill can meet the challenge, it's Nucor. But expect the going to be tougher this time around." If successful, Nucor had the licensing rights to the next two plants built in the world with this technology.

Nucor had spent millions trying to develop the process when it heard of some promising developments at a German company. In the spring of 1986, Aycock flew to Germany to see the pilot machine at SMS Schloemann-Siemag AG. In December the Germans came to Charlotte for the first of what they thought would be many meetings to hammer out a deal with Nucor. Iverson shocked them when he announced Nucor was ready to proceed to build the first plant of its kind. Keith Busse was given the job of building the Crawfordsville, Indiana, steel sheet plant. The process of bringing this plant online was so exciting it became the basis for a best-selling book by Robert Preston, which was serialized in *New Yorker* magazine. Preston reported on a conversation at dinner during construction between Iverson and Busse. Thinking about the future, Busse worried that Nucor might someday become like Big Steel. He asked, "How do we allow Nucor to grow without expanding the bureaucracy?" He commented on the vice-presidents stacked on vice- presidents, research departments, assistants to assistants and so on. Iverson agreed. Busse seriously suggestsed, "Maybe we're going to need group vice-presidents." Iverson's heated response was, "Do you want to ruin the company? That's the old Harvard Business School thinking. They would only get in the way, slow us down." He said the company could at least double, to $2 billion, before it added a new level of management. "I hope that by the time we have group vice presidents I'll be collecting Social Security."

The gamble on the new plant paid off, and Busse, the general manager of the plant, became a key man within Nucor. The new mill began operations in August of 1989 and reached 15 percent of capacity by the end of the year. In June of 1990 it had its first profitable month and Nucor announced the construction of a second plant in Arkansas.

In December 1992, Nucor signed a letter of intent with Oregon Steel Mills to build a sheet mill on the West Coast to begin in 1994. This project was later canceled. The supply and cost of scrap steel to feed the mini-mills was an important future concern to Iverson. So at the first of 1993 Nucor announced the construction of a plant in Trinidad to supply its mills with iron carbide pellets. The innovative plant would cost $60 million and take a year-and-a-half to complete. In 1994, the two existing sheet mills were expanded and a new $500 million, 1.8-million-ton sheet mill in South Carolina was announced, to begin operation in early 1997.

In what the *New York Times* called their "most ambitious project yet," in 1987 Nucor began a joint venture with Yamato Kogyo, Ltd. to make structural steel products in a mill on the Mississippi River, in direct challenge to the Big Three integrated steel companies. John Correnti was put in charge of the operation. Correnti built and then became the general manager of Nucor-Yamato when it started up in 1988. In 1991 he surprised many people by deciding to double Nucor-Yamato's capacity by 1994. It became Nucor's largest division and the largest wide flange producer in the United States. By 1995, Bethlehem Steel was the only other wide flange producer of structural steel products left and had plans to leave the business.

Nucor started up its first facility to produce metal buildings in 1987. A second metal buildings facility began operations in late 1996 in South Carolina and a new steel deck facility, in Alabama, was announced for 1997. At the end of 1997 the Arkansas sheet mill was undergoing a $120 million expansion to include a galvanizing facility.

In 1995, Nucor became involved in its first international venture, an ambitious project with Brazil's Companhia Siderurgica National to build a $700 million steel mill in the state of Ceara. While other mini-mills were cutting deals to buy and sell abroad, Nucor was planning to ship iron from Brazil and process it in Trinidad.

Nucor set records for sales and net earnings in 1997. In the spring of 1998, as Iverson approached his seventy-third birthday, he was commenting, "People ask me when I'm going to retire. I tell them our mandatory retirement age is 95, but I may change that when I get there." It surprised the world when, in October 1998, Ken Iverson left the board. He retired as chairman at the end the year. Although sales for 1998 decreased 1 percent and net earnings were down 10 percent, the management made a number of long-term investments and closed draining investments. Start-up began at the new South Carolina steam mill and at the Arkansas sheet mill expansion. The plans for a North Carolina steel-plate mill in Hertford were announced. This would bring Nucor's total steel production capacity to 12 million tons per year. Moreover, the plant in Trinidad, which had proven much more expensive than was originally expected, was deemed unsuccessful and closed. Finally, directors approved the repurchase of up to five million shares of Nucor stock.

Still, the downward trends at Nucor continued. Sales and earnings were down 3 percent and 7 percent respectively, for 1999. (See Appendix 1 for financial reports and Appendix 2 for financial ratios.) However, these trends did not seem to affect the company's investments. Expansions were underway in the steel mills and a third building systems facility was under construction in Texas. Nucor was actively searching for a site for a joist plant in the Northeast. A letter of intent was signed with Australian and Japanese companies to form a joint venture to commercialize the strip casting technology. To understand the challenges facing Nucor, industry, technology and environmental trends in the 1980s and 1990s must be considered.

The U.S. Steel Industry in the 1980s

The early 1980s had been the worst years in decades for the steel industry. Data from the American Iron and Steel Institute showed shipments falling from 100 million tons in 1979 to million ton in 1980 and about 85 milion tons in 1981. A slackening in the economy, particularly in auto sales, led the decline. In 1986, when industry capacity was at 130 million tons, the outlook was for a continued decline in per-capita consumption and movement toward capacity in the 90 to 100 million–ton range. The chairman of Armco saw "millions of tons chasing a market that's not there: excess capacity that must be eliminated."

The large, integrated steel firms, such as U.S. Steel and Armco, which made up the major part of the industry, were the hardest hit. *The Wall Street Journal* stated, "The decline has resulted from such problems as high labor and energy costs in mining and processing iron ore, a lack of profits and capital to modernize plants, and conservative management that has hesitated to take risks."

These companies produced a wide range of steels, primarily from ore processed in blast furnaces. They had found it difficult to compete with imports, usually from Japan, and had given market share to imports. They sought the protection of import quotas. Imported steel accounted for 20 percent of the U.S. steel consumption, up from 12 percent in the early 1970s. The U.S. share of world production of raw steel declined from 19 percent to 14 percent over the period. Imports of light bar products accounted for less that 9 percent of the U.S. consumption of those products in 1981, according to the U.S. Commerce Department, while imports of wire rod totaled 23 percent of U.S. consumption.

Iron Age stated that exports, as a percent of shipments in 1985, were 34 percent for Nippon, 26 percent for British Steel, 30 percent for Krupp, 49 percent for USINOR of France, and less than 1 percent for every American producer on the list. The consensus of steel experts was that imports would average 23 percent of the market in the last half of the 1980s.

Iverson was one of the very few in the steel industry to oppose import restrictions. He saw an outdated U.S. steel industry that had to change.

We Americans have been conditioned to believe in our technical superiority. For many generations a continuing stream of new inventions and manufacturing techniques allowed us to far outpace the rest of the world in both volume and efficiency of production. In many areas this is no longer true and particularly in the steel industry. In the last three decades, almost all the major developments in steel making were made outside the U.S. I would be negligent if I did not recognize the significant contribution that the government has made toward the technological deterioration of the steel industry. Unrealistic depreciation schedules, high corporate taxes, excessive regulation and jaw-boning for lower steel prices have make it difficult for the U.S. steel industry to borrow or generate the huge quantities of capital required for modernization.

By the mid 1980s the integrated mills were moving fast to get back into the game: They were restructuring, cutting capacity, dropping unprofitable lines, focusing products, and trying to become responsive to the market. The industry made a pronounced move toward segmentation. Integrated producers focused on mostly flat-rolled and structural grades, reorganized steel companies focused on a limited range of products, mini-mills dominated the bar and light structural product areas, and specialty steel firms sought niches. There was an accelerated shutdown of older plants, elimination of products by some firms, and the installation of new product line with new technologies by others. High-tonnage mills restructured to handle sheets, plates, structural beams, high quality bars, and large pipe and tubular products which allowed resurgence of specialized mills: cold-finished bar manufacturers, independent strip mills and mini-mills.

The road for the integrated mills was not easy. As *Purchasing* pointed out, tax laws and accounting rules slowed the closing of inefficient plants. Shutting down a 10,000-person plant could require a firm to hold a cash reserve of $100 million to fund health, pension, and insurance liabilities. The Chairman of Armco commented, "Liabilities associated with a planned shutdown are so large that they can quickly devastate a company's balance sheet."

Joint ventures had arisen to produce steel for a specific market or region. The Chairman of USX called them "an important new wrinkle in steel's fight for survival" and stated, "If there had been more joint ventures like these two decades ago, the U.S. steel industry might have built

only half of the dozen or so hot-strip mills it put up in that time and avoided today's over-capacity."

The American Iron and Steel Institute reported steel production in 1988 of 99.3 million tons, up from 89.2 in 1987, and the highest in seven years. As a result of modernization programs, 60.9 percent of production was from continuous casters. Exports for steel increased and imports fell. Some steel experts believed the United States was now cost competitive with the Japan. However, 1989 proved to be a year of "waiting for the other shoe to drop," according to *Metal Center News*. U.S. steel production was hampered by a new recession, the expiration of the voluntary import restraints, and labor negotiations in several companies. Declines in car production and consumer goods hit flat-rolled hard. AUJ Consultants told MCN, "The U.S. steel market has peaked. Steel consumption is tending down. By 1990, we expect total domestic demand to dip under 90 million tons."

The U.S. Steel Industry in the 1990s

The economic slowdown of the early 1990s did lead to a decline in the demand for steel through early 1993, but by 1995 America was in its best steel market in 20 years and many companies were building new flat-roll mini-mills. A *BusinessWeek* article at the time described it as "the race of the Nucor look-alikes." Six years after Nucor pioneered the low-cost German technology in Crawfordsville, Indiana, the competition was finally gearing up to compete. Ten new projects were expected to add 20 million tons per year of the flat-rolled steel, raising U.S. capacity by as much as 40 percent by 1998. These mills opened in 1997 just as the industry was expected to move into a cyclical slump. It was no surprise that worldwide competition increased and companies that had previously focused on their home markets began a race to become global powerhouses. The foreign push was new for U.S. firms who had focused on defending their home markets. U.S. mini-mills focused their international expansion primarily in Asia and South America.

Meanwhile, in 1994, U.S. Steel, North America's largest integrated steel producer, began a major business process re-engineering project to improve order fulfillment performance and customer satisfaction on the heels of a decade of restructuring. According to *Steel Times International*, "US Steel had to completely change the way it did business. Cutting labor costs, and increasing reliability and productivity took the company a long way towards improving profitability and competitiveness. However, it became clear that this leaner organization still had to implement new technologies and business processes if it was to maintain a competitive advantage." The goals of the business process re-engineering project included a sharp reduction in cycle time, greatly decreased levels of inventory, shorter order lead times, and the ability to offer real-time promise dates to customers. In 1995, the company successfully installed integrated planning/production/order fulfillment software and results were very positive. U.S. Steel believed that the re-engineering project had positioned it for a future of increased competition, tighter markets, and raised customer expectations.

In late 1997 and again in 1998 the decline in demand prompted Nucor and other U.S. companies to slash prices in order to compete with the unprecedented surge of imports. By the last quarter of 1998 these imports had led to the filing of unfair trade complaints with U.S. trade regulators, causing steel prices in the spot market to drop sharply in August and September before they stabilized. A press release by the U.S. Secretary of Commerce, William Daley, stated, "I will not stand by and allow U.S. workers, communities and companies to bear the brunt of other nations' problematic policies and practices. We are the most open economy of the world. But we are not the world's dumpster." In early 1999, American Iron and Steel Institute reported in its opinion section of its' Web page the following quotes by Andy Sharkey and Hank Barnette. Sharkely said, "With many of the world's economies in recession, and no signs of recovery on the horizon, it should come as no surprise that the United States is now seen as the only reliable market for manufactured good. This can be seen in the dramatic surge of imports." Barnette noted "While there are different ways to gauge the impact of the Asian crisis, believe, me, it has already hit. Just ask the 163,000 employees of the U.S. steel industry."

The Commerce Department concluded in March 1999 that six countries had illegally dumped stainless steel in the United States at prices below production costs or home market prices. The Commerce Department found that Canada, South Korea, and Taiwan were guilty only of dumping, while Belgium, Italy, and South Africa also gave producers unfair subsidies that effectively lowered prices. However, on June 23, 1999, *The Wall Street Journal* reported that the Senate decisively shut off an attempt to restrict U.S. imports of steel despite industry complaints that a flood of cheap imports were driving them out of business. Advisors of President Clinton were reported to have said the President would likely veto the bill if it passed. Administrative officials opposed the bill because it would violate international trade law and leave the United States open to retaliation.

The American Iron and Steel Institute reported that in May 1999, U.S. steel mills shipped 8,330,000 net tons, a decrease of 6.7 percent from the 8,927,000 net tons shipped in May 1998. They also stated that for the first five months of 1999 shipments were 41,205,000 net tons, down 10 percent from the same period in 1998. AISI President and CEO, Andrew Sharkey, III said, "Once again, the May data show clearly that America's steel trade crisis continues. U.S. steel companies and employees continue to be injured by high levels of dumping and subsidized imports. … In addition, steel inventory levels remain excessive, and steel operating rates continue to be very low."

As the 1990s ended, Nucor was the second-largest steel producer in the U.S., behind USX. The company's market capitalization was about two times that of the next smaller competitor. Even in a tight industry, someone can win. Nucor was in the best position because the industry was very fragmented and there are many marginal competitors.

Steel Technology and the Mini-Mill

A new type of mill, the "mini-mill," had emerged in the U.S. during the 1970s to compete with the integrated mill. The mini-mill used electric arc furnaces initially to manufacture a narrow product line from scarp steel. The leading U.S. mini-mills in the 1980s were Nucor, Florida Steel, Georgetown Steel, North Star Steel, and Chaparral. Between the late 1970s and 1980s, the integrated mills' market share fell from about 90 percent to about 60 percent, with the integrated steel companies averaging a 7 percent return on equity, the mini-mills averaging 14 percent, and some, such as Nucor, achieving about 25 percent. In the 1990s mini-mills tripled their output to capture 17 percent of domestic shipments. Moreover, integrated mills market share fell to around 40 percent, while mini-mills share rose to 23 percent, reconstructed mills increased their share from 11 percent to 28 percent, and specialized mills increased their share from 1 percent to 6 percent.

Some experts believed that a relatively new technology, the twin shell electric arc furnace, would help mini-mills increase production and lower costs and take market share. According to the *Pittsburgh Business Times*, "With a twin shell furnace, one shell—the chamber holding the scrap to be melted—is filled and heated. During the heating of the first shell, the second shell is filled. When the heating is finished on the first shell, the electrodes move to the second. The first shell is emptied and refilled before the second gets hot." This increased the production by 60 percent. Twin shell production had been widely adopted in the last few years. For example, Nucor Steel began running a twin shell furnace in November 1996 in Berkeley, South Carolina and installed another in Norfolk, Nebraska, which began operations in 1997. "Everyone accepts twin shells as a good concept because there's a lot of flexibility of operation," said Rodney Mott, vice president and general manager of Nucor-Berkeley. However, this move toward twin-shell furnaces could mean trouble in the area of scrap availability. According to an October 1997 quote in *Pittsburgh Business Times* by Ralph Smaller, vice president of process technology at Kvaerner, "Innovations that feed the electric furnaces' production of flat-rolled (steel) will increase the demand on high quality scrap and alternatives. The technological changes are just beginning and will accelerate over the next few years."

According to a September 1997 *Industry Week* article, steel makers around the world were now closely monitoring the development of continuous "strip casting" technology, which may prove to be the next leap forward for the industry. "The objective of strip casting is to produce thin strips of steel (in the 1-mm to 4-mm range) as liquid steel flows from a tundish—the stationary vessel that receives molten steel from the ladle. It would eliminate the slab-casting stage and all of the rolling that now takes place in a hot mill." Strip casting was reported to have some difficult technological challenges but companies in Germany, France, Japan, Australia, Italy, and Canada had strip-casting projects under-way. In fact, all of the significant development work in strip casting was taking place outside the U.S.

Larry Kavanaph, American Iron and Steel Institute vice president for manufacturing and technology said "Steel is a very high-tech industry, but nobody knows it." Today's most-productive steel making facilities incorporated advanced metallurgical practices, sophisticated process-control sensors, state-of-the art computer controls, and the latest refinements in continuous casting and rolling mill technology. Michael Shot, vice president of manufacturing at Carpenter Technology Corp in Reading, Pennsylvania, a specialty steels and premium-grade alloys, said, "You don't survive in this industry unless you have the technology to make the best products in the world in the most efficient manner."

Environmental and Political Issues

Not all stakeholders were happy with the way Nucor does business. In June, 1998, *Waste News* reported that Nucor's mill in Crawfordsville, Indiana was cited by the United State Environmental Protection Agency for alleged violations of federal and state clean-air rules. The Pamlico-Tar River Foundation, the North Carolina Coastal Federation, and the Environmental Defense Fund had concerns about the state's decision to allow the company to start building the plant before the environmental review were completed.

According to the *News & Observer* Web site, "The environmental groups charge that the mill will discharge 6,720 tons of pollutants into the air each year."

Moreover, there were other concerns about the fast-track approval of the facility being built in Hertford County. First, this plant was located on the banks of one of the most important and sensitive stretches of the Chowan, a principle tributary to the national treasure Albemarle Sound and the last bastion of the state's once vibrant river-herring fishery. North Carolina passed a law in 1997 that required the restoration of this fishery through a combination of measures designed to prevent overfishing, restore spawning and nursery habitats, and improve water quality in the Chowan. "New federal law requires extra care in protecting essential habitat for the herring, which spawn upstream," according to an article in the *Business Journal*. Second were the concerns regarding the excessive incentives the state gave to convince Nucor to build a $300 million steel mill in North Carolina. Some questioned whether the promise of 300 well-paying jobs in Hertford County was worth the $155 million in tax breaks the state was giving Nucor to locate here.

Management Evolution

As Nucor opened new plants each was made a division and given a general manager with complete responsibility for all aspects of the business. The corporate office did not involve itself in the routine functioning of the divisions. There was no centralized purchasing, or hiring and firing or division accounting. The total corporate staff was still less than 25 people, including clerical staff when 1999 began.

In 1984, Dave Aycock moved into the corporate office as President. Ken Iverson was chief executive officer and chairman. Iverson, Aycock, and Sam Siegel operated as an executive board, providing overall direction to the corporation. By 1990, Aycock, who had invested his money wisely, owned over 600,000 shares of Nucor stock, five hotels and farms in three states, and was ready to retire. He was 60, five years younger than Iverson, and was concerned that if he waited, he and Iverson might be leaving the company at the same time. Two people stood out as candidates for the presidency, Keith Busse and John Correnti. In November, Iverson called Correnti to the Charlotte airport and offered him the job. Aycock commented, "Keith Busse was my choice, but I got outvoted." In June 1991 Aycock retired and Keith Busse left Nucor to build an independent sheet mill in Indiana for a group of investors.

Thus, Iverson, Correnti, and Siegel led the company. In 1993, Iverson had heart problems and major surgery.

Correnti was given the CEO role in 1996. The board of directors had always been small, consisting of the executive team and one or two past Nucor vice presidents. Several organizations with large blocks of Nucor stock had been pressing Nucor to diversify its board membership and add outside directors. In 1996, Jim Hlavacek, head of a small consulting firm and friend of Iverson, was added to the board.

Only five, not six, members of the board were in attendance during the board of directors meeting in the fall of 1998, due to the death of Jim Cunningham. Near its end, Aycock read a motion, drafted by Siegel, that Ken Iverson be removed as chairman. It was seconded by Hlavacek and passed. It was announced in October that Iverson would be a chairman emeritus and a director, but after disagreements Iverson left the company completely. It was agreed Iverson would receive $500,000 a year for five years. Aycock left retirement to become chairman.

The details of Iverson's leaving did not become known until June of 1999, when John Correnti resigned after disagreements with the board and Aycock took his place. All of this was a complete surprise to investors and brought the stock price down 10 percent. Siegel commented that "the board felt Correnti was not the right person to lead Nucor into the twenty-first century." Aycock assured everyone he would be happy to move back into retirement as soon as replacements could be found.

In December 1999, Correnti became chairman of rival Birmingham Steel, with an astounding corporate staff of 156 people. With Nucor's organizational changes, he predicted more overhead staff and questioned their ability to move as fast in the future. He noted, "Nucor's trying to centralize and do more mentoring. That's not what grew the company to what it is today."

Aycock moved ahead with adding outside directors to the Board. He appointed Harvey Gantt, principal in his own architectural firm and former mayor of Charlotte; Victoria Haynes, formally BF Goodrich's chief technology officer; and Peter Browning, chief executive of Sonoco. (Biographical sketches of board members and executive management are provided in Appendixes 3 and 4.) Then he moved to increase the corporate office staff by adding a level of executive vice president over four areas of business and adding two specialist jobs in strategic planning and steel technology. When Siegel retired, Aycock promoted Terry Lisenby to CFO and treasurer, and hired a director of IT to report to Lisenby. (See Exhibits 1 and 2 the organization chart in 2000 and 2004.)

Exhibit 1   Nucor Organization Chart 2000

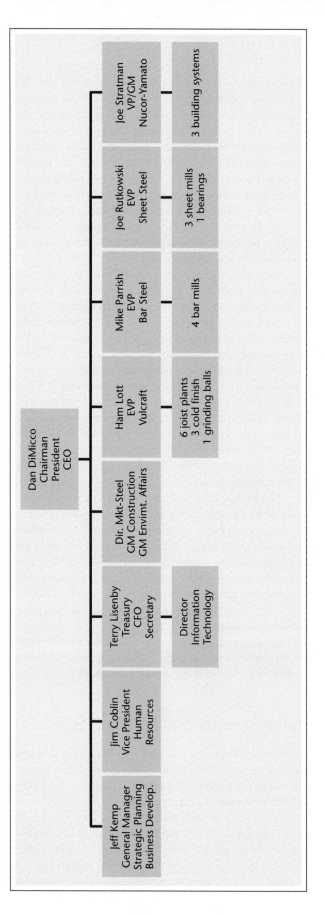

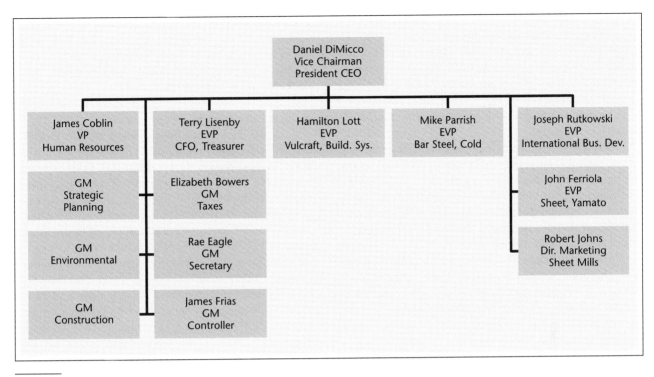

Exhibit 2   Nucor Organization Chart
Executive Management 2004

Jim Coblin, vice president of human resources, believed the additions to management were necessary, saying, "It's not bad to get a little more like other companies." He noted that the various divisions did their business cards and plant signs differently; some did not even want a Nucor sign. Sometimes six different Nucor salesmen would call on the same customer. "There is no manager of human resources in the plants, so at least we needed to give additional training to the person who does most of that work at the plant," he stated. With these new additions there would be a director of information technology and two important committees, one for environmental issues and the second for audit.

He believed the old span of control of 20 might have worked well when there was less competition. Aycock considered it "ridiculous." "It was not possible to properly manage, to know what was going own. The top managers have totally lost contact with the company." Coblin was optimistic that the use of executive vice presidents would improve management. The three meetings of the general managers had slowly increased from about 1 1/2 H days to about 2 1/2 H days and become more focused. The new EVP positions would bring a perspective above the level of the individual plants. Instead of 15 individual detailed presentations, each general manager would give a short, five-

minute briefing and then there would be an in-depth presentation on the group, with team participation. After some training by Lisenby, the divisions had recently done a pretty good job with a SWOT analysis. Coblin thought these changes would make Nucor a stronger global player.

To Jeff Kemp, the new general manager of strategic planning and business development, the big issue was how to sustain earnings growth. In the U.S. steel industry there were too many marginal competitors. The U.S. government had recently added to the problem by giving almost a billion dollars to nine mills, which simply allowed them to limp along and weaken the industry. He was looking for Nucor's opportunities within the steel industry. He asked why Nucor had bought a bearing company. His experience in the chemical industry suggested a need for Nucor to establish a position of superiority and grow globally, driving industry competition rather than reacting. He argued that a company should protect its overall market position, which could mean sacrifices for individual plants. Aycock liked Kemp's background in law and accounting, and had specifically sought someone from outside the steel industry to head up Nucor's strategic planning. By June 2000 Kemp had conducted studies of other industries in the U.S. market and developed a working document that identified opportunities worthy of further analysis.

"Every company hits a plateau," Aycock observed. "You can't just go out and build plants to grow. How do you step up to the next level? I wouldn't say it's a turning point but we have to get our strategic vision and strategic plans." He stated, "We are beginning Nucor's first-ever strategic planning sessions, it was not necessary before." His conclusions were partly the result of an imaging study Nucor had conducted.

In early 2000, Nucor brought in an outside consulting firm to conduct a survey of the company's image as seen by the top 10 to 15 managers, including the corporate office. They also gathered the views of a few analysts and media personnel. In looking at the survey, one saw the managers still agreed that Nucor valued risk taking, innovation, a lean management structure with aggressive, hard-working employees who accepted the responsibility of failure along with the opportunity for success. They seemed to see Nucor as a way of doing business—not just a way of making steel—in terms of values and personality, not just business terms. When asked to associate Nucor's persona with a public figure, John Wayne was the clear choice.

The managers in the field seemed to believe the new layer of management was needed, and were not concerned about a loss of decentralization. They liked the new management team and the changes so far, particularly the improved communications with corporate office. However the corporate managers thought the company was changing much faster than the division managers. They also held a more positive view of the company, on such things as how good the company was in their community or with the environment.

The people from the media had positive views of Nucor as hard-working and committed to its employees, an innovative risk-taking economic powerhouse. Some, most familiar with the company, believed the company needed to do a better job of communicating its vision during a period of transition.

Aycock believed Nucor needed to be quick to recognize developing technology in all production areas. He noted the joint venture to develop a new "strip caster," which would cast the current flat-rolled material in a more finished form. The impact could be "explosive," allowing Nucor to build smaller plants closer to markets. This would be particularly helpful on the West Coast. Nucor would own the U.S. and Brazilian rights, their partners the rest. He was also looking forward to the next generation of steel mills and wanted to own the rights, this time. He praised Iverson's skill at seeing technology and committing to it.

He was very interested in acquisitions, but "they must fit strategically." A bar mill in the upper central Midwest and a flat-rolled plant in the Northeast would be good. A significant opportunity existed in pre-engineered buildings. Aycock intended to concentrate on steel for the next five to six years, achieving an average growth rate of 15 percent per year. In about seven years he would like to see Nucor ready to move into other areas. He said Nucor had already "picked the low hanging grapes" and must be careful in its next moves.

Daniel DiMicco assumed the role of Nucor's president and chief executive officer in September 2000, when David Aycock stepped down as planned. Peter Browning was elected chairman of the board of directors. Aycock retired from the board a year later.

Sales for 2000 increased 14 percent over 1999 to reach a record level. Earnings were also at record levels, 27 percent over 1999. The year had begun on a strong footing but had turned weak by the years' end. While Nucor remained profitable other steel companies faced bankruptcy. A Vulcraft plant was under construction in New York. It was their first northeastern operation and expanded the geographical coverage into a new region. They were also attempting a break-through technological step in strip casting at Crawfordsville, the Castrip process. They sold their grinding ball process and the bearing products operation because they were not a part of their core business.

In the company's annual report DiMicco laid out their plans for 2000 and beyond: "Our targets are to deliver an average annual earnings growth of 10 to 15 percent over the next 10 years, to deliver a return well in excess of our cost of capital, to maintain a minimum average return on equity of 14 percent and to deliver a return on sales of 8–10 percent. Our strategy will focus on Nucor becoming a "market leader" in every product group and business in which we compete. This calls for significant increases in market share for many of our core products and the maintenance of market share where we currently enjoyed a leadership position." While pointing out that it would be impossible to obtain this success through the previous strategy of greenfield construction, he added "there will now be a heavy focus on growth through acquisitions. We will also continue growing through the commercialization of new disruptive and leapfrog technologies."

Steel and Nucor in the Twenty-first Century

In early 2001, *The Wall Street Journal* predicted that all but two of the U.S.'s biggest steel makers would post fourth quarter losses. AK Steel Holding Corp. and Nucor Corp. were expected to have profits for the fourth quarter of 2000, while U.S. Steel Group, a unit of USX Corp., was expected to post a profit for the year but not the fourth quarter. By October 1, more than 20 steel companies in the U.S., including Bethlehem Steel Corp. and LTV Corp., the nations' third- and fourth-largest steel producers, respectively, had filed for bankruptcy protection. Over a dozen producers were operating under Chapter 11 bankruptcy-law protection, which allows them to maintain market share by selling steel cheaper than non–Chapter 11 steel makers. On October 18th, *The Economist* noted that of the 14 steel companies followed by Standard & Poor, only Nucor was indisputably healthy. In the fall of 2001 25 percent of domestic steel companies were in bankruptcy proceedings, although the United States was the largest importer of steel in the world. Experts believed that close to half of the U.S. steel industry might be forced to close before conditions improved.

The world steel industry found itself in the middle of one of its most unprofitable and volatile periods ever, in part due to a glut of steel that had sent prices to 20-year lows. While domestic steel producers found themselves mired in red ink, many foreign steel-makers desperately needed to continue to sell in the relatively open U.S. market to stay profitable. The industry was hovering around 75 percent capacity utilization, a level too low to be profitable for many companies. Three European companies—France's Usinor SA, Luxembourg's Arbed SA, and Spain's Aceralia Corp.—merged to form the world's largest steel company. Two Japanese companies—NKK Corp. and Kawasaki Steel Corp.—merged to form the world's second-biggest steel-maker. These new mega–steel makers could out-muscle U.S. competitors, which were less efficient, smaller and financially weaker than their competitors in Asia and Europe. At this time the largest U.S. steel maker, USX-U.S. Steel Group, was only the 11th largest producer in the world, and continued consolidation in the industry was expected.

In addition to cheap imports, U.S. steel producers faced higher energy prices, weakening demand by customer industries, increasingly tough environmental rules, and a changing cost structure among producers. With the declining economy energy prices began to drop. However, so did demand for construction, automobiles, and farm equipment. Environmental rules led to costly modifications and closings of old plants, which produced coke along with vast clouds of ash and acrid green smoke. In 1990, mini mills accounted for 36 percent of the domestic steel market, but by 2000 the more efficient mini mill had seized 50 percent of the market and the resulting competition had driven prices lower.

Two thousand and one turned out to be one of the worst years ever for steel. There was 9/11, a recession, and a surge of imports. DiMicco broke with Nucor's traditional opposition to government intervention to make a major push for protective tariffs. He stated, "The need to enforce trade rules is similar to the need to enforce any other law. If two merchants have stores side by side, but one sells stolen merchandise at a vast discount, we know that it's time for the police to step in." In March 2002 President Bush, after an investigation and recommendation by the ITC, imposed anti-dumping tariffs under section 201 of the Trade Act of 1974. This restricted some imports of steel and placed quotas of up to 30 percent on others. The move was opposed by many, including steel users. In his March 10, 2002, editorial columnist George Will criticized Bush for abandoning free-trade and pointed out the protection would hamper the necessary actions to restructure the steel industry in America by reducing excess capacity. The European Union immediately threatened reprisals and appealed to the WTO. In December, China imposed its own three-year program of import duties. Steel prices rose 40 percent in 2002 after the tariffs. Within a year, hot-rolled-steel prices increased 50 percent to $260 per ton overs 20 year low of $210. The price had been $361 in 1980. In November 2003, the WTO ruled against the tariffs and, under increasing pressure of retaliation, Bush withdrew the tariffs. While many steel companies floundered, Nucor was able to take advantage of the weakened conditions. In March 2001, Nucor made its first acquisition in 10 years, purchasing a mini-mill in New York from Sumitomo Corp. Nucor had hired about five people to help plan for future acquisitions. DiMicco commented, "It's taken us three years before our team has felt this is the right thing to do and get started making acquisitions." In the challenged industry, he argued it would be cheaper to buy than build plants. They purchased the assets of Auburn Steel, which gave them a merchant bar presence in the Northeast and helped the new Vulcraft facility in New York. They acquired ITEC Steel, a leader in the emerging load bearing light gauge steel framing market and saw an opportunity to aggressively broaden its market. Nucor increased its sheet capacity by roughly one third when it acquired the assets of Trico Steel Co. in Alabama for $120 million. In early 2002, they acquired the assets of Birmingham Steel Corp. The $650 million purchase of four mini-mills was the largest acquisition in Nucor's history. In addition to making acquisitions to efficiently increase their market share and capacity, Nucor was actively working on new production processes that would provide them with technological advantages. They acquired the U.S. and Brazilian rights to the promising Castrip process for strip casting, the process of directly casting thin sheet steel. After development work on the process in Indiana they began full-time production in May 2002 and produced 7,000 tons in the last 10 months of 2002.

Moreover, in April Nucor entered into a joint venture with a Brazilian mining company, CVRD, the world's largest producer of iron-ore pellets, to jointly develop low-cost iron-based products. Success with this effort would give them the ability to make steel from scratch by combining iron ore and coke rather than using scrap steel.

As the year ended they were encouraged by the decrease in total steel capacity and what appeared to be a recovery in prices from record lows and expected slight improvement for 2002. However 2002 proved to be a difficult year for Nucor. Revenue increased 11 percent, earnings improved 43 percent over weak 2001, but the other financial goals were not met. They did increase their steelmaking capacity by more than 25 percent. Looking ahead to 2003 they anticipated a challenging year. However they commented, "Nucor has a long-standing tradition of successfully emerging from industry downturns stronger than ever. It will be no different this time."

During 2003 prices of steel rose in the United States and Asia as global demand outpaced supply in some areas. China, with its booming economy, drove the market. An article in *The Wall Street Journal*, October 15, quoted Guy Dolle, chief executives of Arcelor SA of Luxembourg the world's largest steel maker in terms of steel product shipped, as saying "China is the wild card in the balance between supply and demand." World prices did not soar dangerously because the steel industry continued to be plagued by overcapacity. Still steel-hungry China and other fast-growing nations added to their steel capacity.

Imports of steel commodities into the United States fell in August 2003 by 22 percent. A weakened dollar, the growing demand from China, and tariffs imposed in 2002 by Bush drove away imports. Domestic capacity declined increasing capacity utilization from 77.2 percent to 93.4 percent as producers consolidated, idled plants or went out of business. Prices for iron ore and energy rose, affecting integrated producers. Mini-mills saw their costs rise as world-wide demand for scrap prices rose. Thus, U.S. steel makers boosted their prices. By February 2004, a growing coalition of U.S. steel producers and consumers were considering whether to petition to limit soaring exports of scrap steel from the United States, the world's largest producer of steel scrap. The United States had exported an estimated 12 million metric tons of steel scrap in 2003, a 21 percent increase from 2002. Moreover, the price of scrap steel was up 83 percent from a year earlier to $255 a ton. At the same time the price of hot rolled sheet steel rose 30 percent to $360 a ton. One result was that the International Steel Group (ISG) replaced Nucor as the most profitable

U.S. steel producer. ISG was created when investor Wilbur Ross began acquiring the failing traditional steel producers in America, including LTV, Bethlehem, and Weirton. These mills used iron ore rather than scrap steel.

When 2003 ended Nucor struck a positive note by reminding their investors that they had been profitable every single quarter since beginning operations in 1966. But while Nucor set records for both steel production and steel shipments, net earnings declined 61 percent. While the steel industry struggled through one of its deepest down cycles with weak prices and bankruptcies throughout the industry, Nucor increased its market share and held on to profitability. They worked on expanding their business with the automotive industry, continued their joint venture in Brazil to produce pig iron, and pursued a joint venture with the Japanese and Chinese to make iron without the usual raw materials. In February 2004 they were "optimistic about the prospects for obtaining commercialization" of their promising Castrip process for strip casting in the United States and Brazil. Moreover, Nucor was optimistic because the Administration was using its trade laws to curtail import dumping and Nucor expected higher margins.

Global competition continued. Nucor has good reason to be proactive. According to *The Wall Street Journal* Posco steelworks in Pohang, South Korea, enjoyed the highest profits in the global steel industry as of 2004. Moreover, *BusinessWeek* reported that the company had developed a new technology called Finex, which turns coal and iron ore into iron without coking and sintering and was expected to cut production costs by nearly a fifth and harmful emissions by 90 percent. They had also expanded their 80 Korean plants by investing in 14 Chinese joint ventures. By December 2004 demand in China had slowed and it had become a net steel exporter, sparking concerns of global oversupply.

Global consolidation continued. In October 2004 London's Mittal family announced that they would merge their Ispat International NV with LNM Group and ISG, to create the world's largest steel maker, with estimated annual revenue of $31.5 billion and output of 57 million tons. This would open a new chapter for the industry's consolidation, which had been mostly regional. Although the world's steel industry remains largely fragmented with the world's top 10 steelmakers supplying less than 30 percent of global production, Mittal Steel will have about 40 percent of the U.S. market in flat-rolled steel. Moreover Mittal, which had a history of using its scale to buy lower-cost raw materials and import modern management techniques into previously inefficient state-run mills, was buying ISG, a U.S. company which already owned the lowest-cost, highest profit mills in the United States. In

January 2005 Mittal announced plans to buy 37 percent of China's Hunan Valin Iron & Steel Group Co.

With output of around 20 million metric tons each, U.S. Steel and Nucor face an uncertain environment as the industry consolidates. Some argue if they didn't grow quickly they might be taken over by foreign makers trying to gain entry into the United States According to *Business Week*, Karlis Kirsis, managing partner of World Steel Dynamics Inc. an information service, said "everybody's in play these days" in the wake of the Mittal's planned merger with ISG. Even as they made bids of their own, South Korea's Posco and Belgium's Arcelor might snap them up.

APPENDIX 1a   Balance Sheet 2000–2004

As of	12/31/2004	12/31/2003	12/31/2002	12/31/2001	12/31/2000
Assets					
Cash	779.05	350.33	219	462.35	490.58
Marketable Securities	n/a	n/a	n/a	n/a	n/a
Receivables	962.76	572.48	483.61	330.86	350.18
Total Inventories	1,239.89	560.4	588.99	466.69	461.15
Other Current Assets	193.26	137.35	157.34	133.8	79.53
Total Current Assets	3,174.95	1,620.56	1,448.94	1,393.69	1,381.45
Property, Plant &	2,818.31	2,817.14	2,932.06	2,365.66	2,329.42
Property, Plant &	2,818.31	2,817.14	2,932.06	2,365.66	2,329.42
Deposits & Other Assets	139.95	54.66	n/a	n/a	n/a
Total Assets	6,133.21	4,492.35	4,381.00	3,759.35	3,710.87
Liabilities					
Accounts Payable	471.55	329.86	247.23	189.24	203.33
Curr. Long-Term Debt	n/a	n/a	n/a	n/a	n/a
Accrued Expense	565.28	299.73	319.36	294.92	354.73
Income Taxes	28.96	n/a	8.95	n/a	n/a
Other Current Liabilities	n/a	n/a	n/a	n/a	n/a
Total Current Liabilities	1,065.79	629.6	591.54	484.16	558.07
Deferred Charges/Inc.	514.57	439.85	371.27	329.39	260.05
Long-Term Debt	923.55	903.55	878.55	460.45	460.45
Other Long-Term Liab.	n/a	n/a	n/a	n/a	n/a
Total Liabilities	2,503.91	1,973.00	1,841.36	1,274.00	1,278.57
Shareholder Equity					
Minority Interest	173.31	177.28	216.65	283.89	301.34
Preferred Stock	n/a	n/a	n/a	n/a	n/a
Common Stock	73.75	36.43	36.27	36.13	36.04
Capital Surplus	147.21	117.4	99.4	81.19	71.49
Retained Earnings	3,688.56	2,641.71	2,641.58	2,538.88	2,478.79
Treasury Stock	451.96	453.46	454.26	454.74	455.37
Total Shareholders Equity	3,455.99	2,342.08	2,322.99	2,201.46	2,130.95
Total Liab. & Shareholder Equity	6,133.21	4,492.35	4,381.00	3,759.35	3,710.87

In millions of USD   Data by Thomson Financial   Nucor Web page

APPENDIX 1b   Income Statement 2000–2004

Period Ended	12/31/2004	12/31/2003	12/31/2002	12/31/2001	12/31/2000
Net Sales	11,376.83	6,265.82	4,801.78	4,333.71	4,756.52
Cost of Goods Sold	9,128.87	5,996.55	4,332.28	3,914.28	3,929.18
Gross Profit	2,247.96	269.28	469.5	419.43	827.34
R & D Expenditure	n/a	n/a	n/a	n/a	n/a
Selling, General & Admin Exps	415.03	165.37	175.59	150.67	183.18
Depreciation & Amort.	n/a	n/a	n/a	n/a	n/a
Non-Operating Income	−79.3	−12.4	−49.57	−82.87	−150.65
Interest Expense	22.35	24.63	14.29	6.53	n/a
Income Before Taxes	1,731.28	66.88	230.05	179.37	493.52
Prov. For Inc. Taxes	609.79	4.1	67.97	66.41	182.61
Minority Interest	n/a	n/a	n/a	n/a	n/a
Realized Investment (Gain/Loss)	n/a	n/a	n/a	n/a	n/a
Other Income	n/a	n/a	n/a	n/a	n/a
Net Income Before Extra Items	1,121.49	62.78	162.08	112.96	310.91
Extra Items & Disc. Ops.	n/a	n/a	n/a	n/a	n/a
Net Income	1,121.49	62.78	162.08	112.96	310.91

In millions of USD   Nucor Web page   Data by Thomson Financial

APPENDIX 2   Nucor Valuation Ratios 2004

P/E (TTM)   7.38

Per Share Ratios
Dividend Per Share 0.47
Book Value Per Share   21.54
EPS Fully Diluted   7.02
Revenue Per Share   71.21

Profit Margins
Operating Margin   16.23
Net Profit Margin   9.86
Gross Profit Margin 19.88

Dividends
Dividend Yield   1.13
Dividend Yield—5 Yr. Avg.   1.28
Dividend Per Share (TTM)   0.52
Dividend Payout Ratio   6.66

Growth (%)
5-Year Annual Growth   35.6
Revenue—5-Year Growth   23.19
Div/Share—5-Year Growth   12.57
EPS—5 Year Growth   32.58

Financial Strength
Quick Ratio   1.63
Current Ratio   2.98
LT Debt to Equity   26.72
Total Debt to Equity 26.72
Return on Equity (ROE) Per Share   38.57
Return on Assets (ROA)   25.4
Return on Invested Capital (ROIC)   33.33

Assets
Asset Turnover   1.85
Inventory Turnover 9.7

Data by Thomson Financial   Nucor Web page

APPENDIX 3   Board of Directors and Executive Management

1990
Board: Iverson, Aycock, Cunningham, Siegel, Vandekieft.
Executive Office: Iverson, Aycock, Siegel.

1991 to 1994
Board: Iverson, Aycock, Siegel, Cunningham, Correnti.
Executive Office: Iverson, Siegel, Correnti, Lisenby, Prichard.

1995 to 1996
Board: Iverson, Aycock, Siegel, Cunningham, Correnti, Hlavacek.
Executive Office: Iverson, Siegel, Correnti, Doherty, Prichard.

1997
Board: Iverson, Aycock, Siegel, Cunningham, Correnti, Hlavacek.
Executive Office: Iverson, Siegel, Correnti, Lisenby, Prichard.

1998
Board: Aycock, Siegel, Correnti, Hlavacek, Browning, Gantt, Haynes.
Executive Office: Aycock, Siegel, Correnti, Parrish, Rutowski, Lisenby, Prichard.

1999 to 2000
Board: Aycock, Siegel, Hlavacek, Browning, Gantt, Haynes.
Executive Office: Aycock, Lisenby, DiMicco, Lott, Parrish, Rutowski, Coblin, Prichard.

2002 through 2003
Board: Browning, Daley, DiMicco, Gantt, Haynes, Hlavacek, Milchovich, Waltermire.
Executive Office: DiMicco, Lisenby, Ferriola, Lott, Parrish, Rutkowski, Coblin, Bowers, Frias, Johns, Laxton, Maero, Rowlan, Eagle (new 2003).

APPENDIX 4   Biographies of Selected Board Members and Executive Managers

Peter C. Browning has been the President and Chief Executive Officer of Sonoco Products Company and Senior Officer 1993. He was previously the President, Chairman and Chief Executive Officer of National Gypsum Company. He was elected Chairman of Nucor's Board of Directors in September 2000 and became the Non-Executive Chairman of the Nucor when David Aycock retired from the Board in 2001.

Daniel R. Dimicco was Executive Vice President of Nucor–Yamato Steel, Nucor Steel Hertford (plate division), and Nucor Building Systems before becoming President. He graduated from Brown University in 1972 with a Bachelor of Science in Engineering, Metallurgy, and Materials Science. He received a Masters in Metallurgy from the University of Pennsylvania in 1975. He was with Republic Steel in Cleveland as a Research Metallurgy and Project Leader until he joined Nucor in 1982 as Plant Metallurgist and Manager of Quality Control for Nucor Steel in Utah. In 1988 he became Melting and Castings Manager. In 1991 he became General Manager of Nucor–Yamato and a Vice President in 1992. In September 2000 he was elected President and Chief Executive Officer of Nucor. In 2001 when Aycock retired he became Vice Chairman, President and Chief Executive Officer of Nucor.

Harvey B. Gantt was a partner in Gantt Huberman Architects for more than 25 years. He also served as Mayor of the City of Charlotte, North Carolina, and was active in civic affairs. He was the first African-American graduate of Clemson University. He joined Nucor's Board of Directors in 1998.

Victoria F. Haynes is the President of Research Triangle Institute in Chapel Hill, North Carolina. Until 2000, she was the Chief Technical Officer of the B.F. Goodrich Co. and Vice President of its advanced technology group. She started with Goodrich in 1992 as Vice President of Research and Development. She joined Nucor's Board of Directors in 1998.

James D. Hlavacek is the Managing Director of Market Driven Management. Mr. Hlavacek was a neighbor and long-term friend of Mr. Iverson. He joined Nucor's Board of Directors in 1995.

Terry S. Lisenby is Chief Financial Officer and an Executive Vice President. He graduated from the University of North Carolina at Charlotte in 1976 with a Bachelor of Science in Accounting. Mr. Lisenby held accounting and management positions with Seidman and Seidman, Harper Corporation of America and Concept Development, Inc. He joined Nucor in September 1985 as Manager of Financial Accounting. He became Vice President and Corporate Controller in 1991 and assumed the role of Chief Financial Officer on January 1, 2000.

Hamilton Lott, Jr. is Executive Vice President over the Vulcraft operations, cold-finished operations in Nebraska and the Utah grinding ball plant. He graduated from the University of South Carolina in 1972 with a Bachelor of Science in Engineering and then served in the United States Navy. He joined Nucor in 1975 as a Design Engineer at Florence. He later served as Engineering Manager and as Sales Manager as Nucor's Vulcraft division in Indiana. He was General Manager of the Vulcraft division in Texas from 1987 to 1993 and the General Manager in Florence from 1993 to 1999. He became a Vice President in 1988 and joined the Executive Office in 1999.

D. Michael Parrish is Executive Vice President for the four steel plants and Nucor Fastener. He graduated from the University of Toledo in 1975 with a Bachelors of Science in Civil Engineering. He joined Nucor in September 1975 as a Design Engineer for Vulcraft and became Engineering Manager at Vulcraft in 1981. In 1986 he moved to Alabama as Manufacturing Manager and in 1989 returned to Utah as Vice President and General Manager. In 1991 he took the top job with Nucor Steel Texas and in 1995 at Nucor Steel Arkansas. In January 1999 he moved into corporate office as Executive Vice President.

Joseph A. Rutkowski is Executive Vice Present of Nucor Steel in Indiana, Arkansas; Berkeley, South Carolina; and Nucor Bearing Products. He graduated from John's Hopkins University in 1976 with a Bachelor of Science in Materials Science Engineering. He held metallurgical and management positions with Korf Lurgi Steeltec, North American Refractories, Georgetown Steel and The Bethlehem steel. He joined Nucor in 1989 as Manager of Cold Finish in Nebraska and became Melting and Casting Manager in Utah before becoming Vice President and General Manager of Nucor Steel in Darlington in 1992. In 1998, he moved to Hertford as Vice President, General Manager to oversee the building of the new plate mill.

PART 2

BUSINESS-LEVEL STRATEGIES

Cost Leadership

LEARNING OBJECTIVES

After reading this chapter, you should be able to:

1. Define cost leadership.

2. Identify six reasons firms can differ in their costs.

3. Identify four reasons economies of scale can exist and four reasons diseconomies of scale can exist.

4. Explain the relationship between cost advantages due to learning curve economies and a firm's market share, as well as the limitations of this logic.

5. Identify how cost leadership helps neutralize each of the major threats in an industry.

6. Identify the bases of cost leadership that are more likely to be rare and costly to imitate.

7. Explain how firms use a functional organizational structure to implement business-level strategies, such as cost leadership.

8. Describe the formal and informal management controls and compensation policies firms use to implement cost leadership strategies.

9. Explain how international operations can affect a firm's cost position.

The World's Lowest-Cost Airline

Everyone's heard of low-cost airlines—Southwest, AirTran, and JetBlue, for example. But have you heard of the world's lowest-cost airline? This airline currently gives 25 percent of its seats away for free. Its goal is to double that within a couple of years. And yet, in the first six months of 2006, this airline's profits soared 39 percent, to $422 million on sales of $1.6 billion. And this in spite of a 42-percent increase in jet fuel prices during this same time period!

The name of this airline is Ryanair. Headquartered in Dublin, Ireland, Ryanair flies short flights throughout Western Europe. In 1985, Ryanair's founders started a small airline to fly between Ireland and England. For six years, this airline barely broke even. Then, in 1991, Michael O'Leary—current CEO at Ryanair—was brought on board. O'Leary traveled to the United States and studied the most successful low-cost airline in the world at that time—Southwest Airlines. O'Leary became convinced that once European airspace was deregulated an airline that adopted Southwest's model of quick turnarounds, no frills, no business class, flying into smaller regional airports, and using only a single kind of aircraft could be extremely successful. Prices in the European air market were fully deregulated in 1997.

Since then, Ryanair has become an even lower-cost airline than Southwest. For example, like Southwest, Ryanair only flies a single type of aircraft—a Boeing 737–800. However, to save on the cost of its airplanes, Ryanair orders them without window shades and with seats that do not recline. This saves several hundred thousand dollars per plane and also reduces ongoing maintenance costs. Both Southwest and Ryanair try to make it easy for consumers to order tickets online, thereby avoiding the costs of call centers and travel agents. However, just 59 percent of Southwest's tickets are sold online; 98 percent of Ryanair's tickets are sold online.

This focus on low costs allows Ryanair to have the lowest prices possible for a seat on its airplanes. The average fare on Southwest is $92; the average fare on Ryanair is $53. But, even at those low prices Ryanair is still able to earn comfortable margins—18 percent net margins compared to Southwest's 7 percent net margins.

However, those net margins don't come just from Ryanair's low costs. They also reflect the fact that the fare you pay Ryanair includes only the seat and virtually no other services. If you want any other services, you have to pay extra for them. For example, you want to check bags? It will cost $9.95 per bag. You want a snack on the airplane? It will cost you $5.50. For that you get a not-very-tasty hot dog. You want a bottle of water? It will cost you $3.50. You want a blanket or pillow—they cost $2.50 each.

In addition, flight attendants will sell you all sorts of extras to keep you occupied during your flight. These include scratch-card games, perfume, digital cameras ($137.50), and MP3 players ($165). During 2007, Ryanair will begin offering in-flight mobile telephone service. Not only will this enable passengers to call their friends and family, Ryanair is planning on using this service to introduce mobile gambling on its planes. Now, on your way from London to Paris you will be able to play blackjack, poker, and slot machines. Ryanair has already added online gaming to its Web site.

Finally, to further increase revenues Ryanair sells space on its planes to advertisers. When your seat tray is up, you may see an ad for a cell phone from Vodaphone. When the tray is down, you may see an ad from Hertz.

All of these actions enable Ryanair to keep its profits up while keeping its fares as low as possible. And the results of this strategy have been impressive—from near bankruptcy in 1991, Ryanair now flies 362 routes to 22 countries and is among the largest and most profitable airlines in Europe. In fact, in 2007 Ryanair launched an unfriendly $1.9 billion takeover bid of Aer Lingus, the formerly state-owned airline of Ireland. Unlike Ryanair, Aer Lingus is a long-haul airline, with flights across the Atlantic and Pacific to North America, South America, and Asia. If successful, O'Leary promises to reduce the costs of Aer Lingus dramatically, an act that may begin to revolutionize long-distance travel around the world.

Of course, none of this has happened without some controversy. For example, in October 2006 Ryanair was chosen as the most disliked European airline in a poll of some 4,000 readers of TripAdvisor, a British Web site for frequent travelers. Ryanair's response: These frequent travelers usually have their companies pay for their travel. If they had to pay for their own tickets, they would prefer Ryanair. Also, Ryanair's strong anti-union stance has caused it political problems in many of the union-dominated countries where it flies. (Interestingly, Southwest is highly unionized.) Finally, Ryanair has been criticized for some of its lax security and safety procedures, for how it treats disabled passengers, and for the cleanliness of its planes.

However, if you want to fly from London to Barcelona for $60 round trip, it's hard to beat Ryanair.

Source: K. Capell (2006). "Wal-Mart with wings." *BusinessWeek*, November 27, pp. 44–46; www//en.wikipedia.org/wiki/Ryanair.

R yanair has been profitable in an industry—the airline industry--that has historically been populated by bankrupt firms. It does this by implementing an aggressive low cost strategy.

What Is Business-Level Strategy?

Part One of this book introduced you to the basic tools required to conduct a strategic analysis: tools for analyzing external threats and opportunities (in Chapter 2) and tools for analyzing internal strengths and weaknesses (in Chapter 3). Once you have completed these two analyses, it is possible to begin making strategic choices. As explained in Chapter 1, strategic choices fall into two large categories: business strategies and corporate strategies. **Business-level strategies** are actions firms take to gain competitive advantages in a single market or industry. **Corporate-level strategies** are actions firms take to gain competitive advantages by operating in multiple markets or industries simultaneously.

The two business-level strategies discussed in this book are cost leadership (this chapter) and product differentiation (Chapter 5). The importance of these two business-level strategies is so widely recognized that they are often called **generic business strategies**.

What Is Cost Leadership?

A firm that chooses a **cost leadership business strategy** focuses on gaining advantages by reducing its costs to below those of all its competitors. This does not mean that this firm abandons other business or corporate strategies. Indeed, a single-minded focus on *just* reducing costs can lead a firm to make low-cost products that no one wants to buy. However, a firm pursuing a cost leadership strategy focuses much of its effort on keeping its costs low.

Numerous firms have pursued cost leadership strategies. Ryanair clearly follows this strategy in the retail industry, Timex and Casio in the watch industry, and BIC in the disposable pen and razor market. All these firms advertise their products. However, these advertisements tend to emphasize reliability and low prices—the kinds of product attributes that are usually emphasized by firms pursuing cost leadership strategies.

Table 4.1 **Important Sources of Cost Advantages for Firms**

1. Size differences and economies of scale
2. Size differences and diseconomies of scale
3. Experience differences and learning-curve economies
4. Differential low-cost access to productive inputs
5. Technological advantages independent of scale
6. Policy choices

In automobiles, Hyundai has implemented a cost leadership strategy with its emphasis on low-priced cars for basic transportation. Like Ryanair, Timex, Casio, and BIC, Hyundai spends a significant amount of money advertising its products, but its advertisements tend to emphasize its sporty styling and high gas mileage. Hyundai is positioned as a fun and inexpensive car, not a high-performance sports car or a luxurious status symbol. Hyundai's ability to sell these fun and inexpensive automobiles depends on its design choices (keep it simple) and its low manufacturing costs.[1]

Sources of Cost Advantages

An individual firm may have a cost advantage over its competitors for a number of reasons. Cost advantages are possible even when competing firms produce similar products. Some of the most important of these sources of cost advantage are listed in Table 4.1 and discussed in this section.

Size Differences and Economies of Scale

One of the most widely cited sources of cost advantages for a firm is its size. When there are significant economies of scale in manufacturing, marketing, distribution, service, or other functions of a business, larger firms (up to some point) have a cost advantage over smaller firms. The concept of economies of scale was first defined in Chapter 2. **Economies of scale** are said to exist when the increase in firm size (measured in terms of volume of production) is associated with lower costs (measured in terms of average costs per unit of production), as depicted in Figure 4.1.

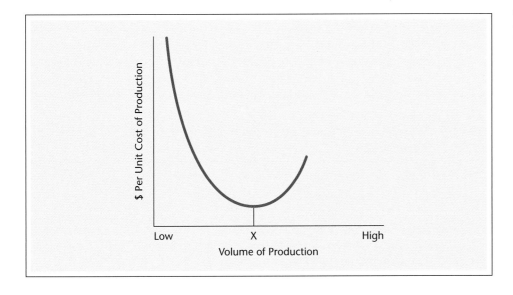

Figure 4.1 Economies of Scale

As the volume of production in a firm increases, the average cost per unit decreases until some optimal volume of production (point X) is reached, after which the average costs per unit of production begin to rise because of **diseconomies of scale** (a concept discussed in more detail later in this chapter).

If the relationship between volume of production and average costs per unit of production depicted in Figure 4.1 holds, and if a firm in an industry has the largest volume of production (but not greater than the optimal level, *X*), then that firm will have a cost advantage in that industry. Increasing the volume of production can reduce a firm's costs for several reasons. Some of the most important of these reasons are summarized in Table 4.2 and discussed below.

Volume of Production and Specialized Machines.   When a firm has high levels of production, it is often able to purchase and use specialized manufacturing tools that cannot be kept in operation in small firms. Manufacturing managers at BIC Corporation, for example, have emphasized this important advantage of high volumes of production. A former director of manufacturing at BIC once observed:

> *We are in the automation business. Because of our large volume, one tenth of 1 cent in savings turns out to be enormous. . . . One advantage of the high–volume business is that you can get the best equipment and amortize it entirely over a short period of time (4 to 5 months). I'm always looking for new equipment. If I see a cost–savings machine, I can buy it. I'm not constrained by money.[2]*

Only firms with BIC's level of production in the pen industry have the ability to reduce their costs in this manner.

Volume of Production and the Cost of Plant and Equipment.   High volumes of production may also enable a firm to build larger manufacturing operations. In some industries, the cost of building these manufacturing operations per unit of production is lower than the cost of building smaller manufacturing operations per unit of production. Thus large-volume firms, other factors being equal, will be able to build lower-per-unit-cost manufacturing operations and will have lower average costs of production.

The link between volume of production and the cost of building manufacturing operations is particularly important in industries characterized by **process manufacturing**—chemical, oil refining, paper and pulp manufacturing, and so forth. Because of the physical geometry of process manufacturing facilities, the costs of constructing a processing plant with increased capacity can be expected to rise as the two-thirds power of a plant's capacity. This is because the area of the surface of some three-dimensional containers (such as spheres and cylinders) increases at a slower rate than the volume of these containers.

Table 4.2   **Why Higher Volumes of Production in a Firm Can Lead to Lower Costs**

With higher production volume . . .
1. firms can use specialized machines . . .
2. firms can build larger plants . . .
3. firms can increase employee specialization . . .
4. firms can spread overhead costs across more units produced . . .
   . . . which can lower per-unit production costs.

Thus, larger containers hold greater volumes and require less material per unit volume for the outside skins of these containers. Up to some point, increases in capacity come at a less-than-proportionate rise in the cost of building this capacity.[3]

For example, it might cost a firm $100 to build a plant with a capacity of 1,000 units, for a per-unit average cost of $.01. But, assuming that the "two-thirds rule" applies, it might cost a firm $465 to build a plant with a capacity of 10,000 units ($465 = 10,000^{2/3}$), for a per-unit average cost of $.0046. The difference between $.01 per unit and $.0046 per unit represents a cost advantage for a large firm.

Volume of Production and Employee Specialization. High volumes of production are also associated with high levels of employee specialization. As workers specialize in accomplishing a narrow task, they can become more and more efficient at this task, thereby reducing their firm's costs. This reasoning applies both in specialized manufacturing tasks (such as the highly specialized manufacturing functions in an assembly line) and in specialized management functions (such as the highly specialized managerial functions of accounting, finance, and sales).

Smaller firms often do not possess the volume of production needed to justify this level of employee specialization. With smaller volumes of production, highly specialized employees may not have enough work to keep them busy an entire workday. This low volume of production is one reason why smaller firms often have employees that perform multiple business functions and often use outside contract employees and part-time workers to accomplish highly specialized functions, such as accounting, taxes, and human resource management.

Volume of Production and Overhead Costs. A firm with high volumes of production has the luxury of spreading its overhead costs over more units and thereby reducing the overhead costs per unit. Suppose, in a particular industry, that the operation of a variety of accounting, control, and research and development functions, regardless of a firm's size, is $100,000. Clearly, a firm that manufactures 1,000 units is imposing a cost of $100 per unit to cover overhead expenses. However, a firm that manufactures 10,000 units is imposing a cost of $10 per unit to cover overhead. Again, the larger-volume firm's average per-unit costs are lower than the small-volume firm's average per-unit cost.

Size Differences and Diseconomies of Scale

Just as economies of scale can generate cost advantages for larger firms, important diseconomies of scale can actually increase costs if firms grow too large. As Figure 4.1 shows, if the volume of production rises beyond some optimal point (point X in the figure), this can actually lead to an increase in per-unit costs. If other firms in an industry have grown beyond the optimal firm size, a smaller firm (with a level of production closer to the optimal) may obtain a cost advantage even when all firms in the industry are producing very similar products. Some important sources of diseconomies of scale for a firm are listed in Table 4.3 and discussed in this section.

Physical Limits to Efficient Size. Applying the two-thirds rule to the construction of manufacturing facilities seems to imply, for some industries at least, that larger is always better. However, there are some important physical limitations to the size of some manufacturing processes. Engineers have found, for example, that cement kilns develop unstable internal aerodynamics at capacities of above

Table 4.3   **Major Sources of Diseconomies of Scale**

When the volume of production gets too large . . .
1. physical limits to efficient size . . .
2. managerial diseconomies . . .
3. worker de-motivation . . .
4. distance to markets and suppliers . . .
   . . . can increase per-unit costs.

7 million barrels per year. Others have suggested that scaling up nuclear reactors from small installations to huge facilities generates forces and physical processes that, though nondetectable in smaller facilities, can become significant in larger operations. These physical limitations on manufacturing processes reflect the underlying physics and engineering in a manufacturing process and suggest when the cost curve in Figure 4.1 will begin to rise.[4]

Managerial Diseconomies.   Although the underlying physics and engineering in a manufacturing process have an important impact on a firm's costs, managerial diseconomies are perhaps an even more important cause of these cost increases. As a firm increases in size, it often increases in complexity, and the ability of managers to control and operate it efficiently becomes limited.

One well-known example of a manufacturing plant that grew too large and thus became inefficient is Crown, Cork and Seal's can-manufacturing plant in Philadelphia. Through the early part of this century, this Philadelphia facility handled as many as 75 different can-manufacturing lines. The most efficient plants in the industry, however, were running from 10 to 15 lines simultaneously. The huge Philadelphia facility was simply too large to operate efficiently and was characterized by large numbers of breakdowns, a high percentage of idle lines, and poor-quality products.[5]

Worker De-Motivation.   A third source of diseconomies of scale depends on the relationship between firm size, employee specialization, and employee motivation. It has already been suggested that one of the advantages of increased volumes of production is that it allows workers to specialize in smaller and more narrowly defined production tasks. With specialization, workers become more and more efficient at the particular task facing them.

However, a significant stream of research suggests that these types of very specialized jobs can be unmotivating for employees. Based on motivational theories taken from social psychology, this work suggests that as workers are removed further from the complete product that is the end result of a manufacturing process, the role that a worker's job plays in the overall manufacturing process becomes more and more obscure. As workers become mere "cogs in a manufacturing machine," worker motivation wanes, and productivity and quality can both suffer.[6]

Distance to Markets and Suppliers.   A final source of diseconomies of scale can be the distance between a large manufacturing facility and where the goods in question are to be sold or where essential raw materials are purchased. Any reductions in cost attributable to the exploitation of economies of scale in manufacturing may be more than offset by large transportation costs associated with moving supplies and products to and from the manufacturing facility. Firms that build highly efficient plants without recognizing these significant transportation costs may put themselves at a competitive disadvantage compared to firms with slightly less efficient plants that are located closer to suppliers and key markets.

Experience Differences and Learning-Curve Economies

A third possible source of cost advantages for firms in a particular business depends on their different cumulative levels of production. In some circumstances, firms with the greatest experience in manufacturing a product or service will have the lowest costs in an industry and thus will have a cost-based advantage. The link between cumulative volumes of production and cost has been formalized in the concept of the **learning curve**. The relationship between cumulative volumes of production and per unit costs is graphically represented in Figure 4.2.

The Learning Curve and Economies of Scale.   As depicted in Figure 4.2, the learning curve is very similar to the concept of economies of scale. However, there are two important differences. First, whereas economies of scale focuses on the relationship between the volume of production at a given point in time and average unit costs, the learning curve focuses on the relationship between the *cumulative* volume of production—that is, how much a firm has produced over time—and average unit costs. Second, where diseconomies of scale are presumed to exist if a firm gets too large, there is no corresponding increase in costs in the learning-curve model as the cumulative volume of production grows. Rather, costs continue to fall until they approach the lowest technologically possible cost.

The Learning Curve and Cost Advantages.   The learning-curve model is based on the empirical observation that the costs of producing a unit of output fall as the cumulative volume of output increases. This relationship was first observed in the construction of aircraft before World War II. Research showed that the labor costs per aircraft fell by 20 percent each time the cumulative volume of production doubled.[7] A similar pattern has been observed in numerous industries, including the manufacture of ships, computers, spacecraft, and semiconductors. In all these cases, increases in cumulative production have been associated with detailed learning about how to make production as efficient as possible.

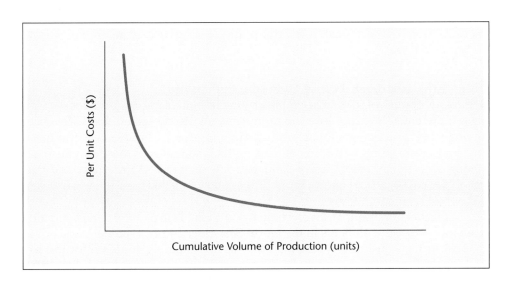

Figure 4.2   The Learning Curve and the Cost of Production

However, learning-curve cost advantages are not restricted to manufacturing. Learning can be associated with any business function, from purchasing raw materials to distribution and service. Service industries can also experience important learning effects. The learning curve applies whenever the cost of accomplishing a business activity falls as a function of the cumulative number of times a firm has engaged in that activity.[8]

The Learning Curve and Competitive Advantage.   The learning-curve model summarized in Figure 4.2 has been used to develop a model of cost-based competitive advantage that links learning with market share and average production costs.[9]

The logic behind this application of the learning-curve model is straightforward: The first firm that successfully moves down the learning curve will obtain a cost advantage over rivals. To move a production process down the learning curve, a firm needs to have higher levels of cumulative volume of production. Of course, firms that are successful at producing high volumes of output need to sell that output to customers. In selling this output, firms are increasing their market share. Thus, to drive down the learning-curve and obtain a cost advantage, firms must aggressively acquire market share.

This application of learning-curve logic has been criticized by a wide variety of authors.[10] Two criticisms are particularly salient. First, although the acquisition of market share is likely to allow a firm to reduce its production costs, the acquisition of share itself is expensive. Indeed, as described in the Research Made Relevant feature, sometimes the cost of acquiring share may rise to equal its value.

The second major criticism of this application of the learning-curve model is that there is, in this logic, no room for any other business or corporate strategies. In other words, this application of the learning-curve implicitly assumes that firms can compete only on the basis of their low costs and that other strategies are not possible. Most industries, however, are characterized by opportunities for at least some of these other strategies, and thus this strict application of the learning-curve model can be misleading.[11]

These criticisms aside, it is still the case that in many industries firms with larger cumulative levels of production, other things being equal, will have lower average production costs. Thus, experience in all the facets of production can be a source of cost advantage even if the single-minded pursuit of market share to obtain these cost reductions may not give a firm above normal economic returns.

Differential Low-Cost Access to Productive Inputs

Besides economies of scale, diseconomies of scale, and learning-curve cost advantages, differential low-cost access to productive inputs may create cost differences among firms producing similar products in an industry. **Productive inputs** are any supplies used by a firm in conducting its business activities; they include, among other things, labor, capital, land, and raw materials. A firm that has differential low-cost access to one or more of these factors is likely to have lower economic costs compared to rivals.

Consider, for example, an oil company with fields in Saudi Arabia compared to an oil company with fields in the North Sea. The cost of obtaining crude oil for the first firm is considerably less than the cost of obtaining crude oil for the second. North Sea drilling involves the construction of giant offshore drilling plat-

Research Made Relevant

Research on the relationship between market share and firm performance has continued over many decades. Early work identified market share as the primary determinant of firm performance. Indeed, one particularly influential article identified market share as being *the key* to firm profitability.

This initial conclusion about the relationship between market share and firm performance was based on the observed positive correlation between these two variables. That is, firms with large market share tend to be highly profitable; firms with low market share tend to be less profitable. The logical conclusion of this empirical finding seems to be that if a firm wants to increase its profitability, it should increase its market share.

Not so fast. It turns out that the relationship between market share and firm profits is not that simple. Consider the following scenario. Suppose that 10 companies all conclude that the key to their profitability is gaining market share. To acquire share from each other, each firm will probably increase its advertising and other marketing expenses as well as reduce its prices. This has the effect of putting a price on the market share that a firm seeks to acquire—that is, these competing firms are creating what might be called a "market for market share." And because there are 10 firms competing for share in this market, this

How Valuable Is Market Share—Really?

market is likely to be highly competitive. Returns to acquiring share in such competitive markets for market share should fall to a normal economic level.

All this analysis suggests that although there may be a cross-sectional positive correlation between market share and firm performance—that is, at a given point in time, market share and firm performance may be positively correlated—this correlation may not be positive over time, as firms seek to increase their market share. Several papers have examined this hypothesis. Two of the most influential of these papers—by Dick Rumelt and Robin Wensley and by Cynthia Montgomery and Birger Wernerfelt—

have shown that markets for market share often do emerge in industries, that these markets are often very competitive, and that acquiring market share in these competitive markets does not improve a firm's economic performance. Indeed, in their study of the consolidation of the beer industry Montgomery and Wernerfelt showed that firms such as Anheuser-Busch and Miller paid so much for the market share they acquired that it actually reduced their profitability.

The general consensus in the literature now seems to be that large market share is an outcome of a competitive process within an industry, not an appropriate objective of firm managers, per se. Thus, firms with particularly valuable strategies will naturally attract more customers, which, in turn, suggests that they will often have higher market share. That is, a firm's valuable strategies generate both high levels of firm performance and large market share. This, in turn, explains the positive correlation between market share and firm performance.

Sources: R. D. Buzzell, B. T. Gale, and R. M. Sultan (1975). "Market share—the key to profitability." *Harvard Business Review*, 53, pp. 97–106; R. Rumelt and R. Wensley (1981). "In search of the market share effect." *Proceedings of the Academy of Management Meetings, 1981*, pp. 2–6; C. Montgomery and B. Wernerfelt (1991). "Sources of superior performance: Market share versus industry effects in the U.S. brewing industry," *Management Science*, 37, pp. 954–959.

---

forms, housing workers on floating cities, and transporting oil across an often-stormy sea. Drilling in Saudi Arabia requires only the simplest drilling technologies, because the oil is found relatively close to the surface.

Of course, in order to create a cost advantage the cost of acquiring low-cost productive inputs must be less than the cost savings generated by these factors. For example, even though it may be much less costly to drill for oil in Saudi Arabia than in the North Sea, if it is very expensive to purchase the rights to drill in Saudi Arabia compared to the costs of the rights to drill in the North Sea, the potential cost advantages of drilling in Saudi Arabia can be lost. As with all sources of cost advantages, firms must be careful to weigh the cost of acquiring that advantage against the value of that advantage for the firm.

Differential access to raw materials such as oil, coal, and copper ore can be important determinants of a cost advantage. However, differential access to other productive inputs can be just as important. For example, it may be easier (i.e., less costly) to recruit highly trained electronics engineers for firms located near where these engineers receive their schooling than for firms located some distance away. This lower cost of recruiting is a partial explanation of the development of geographic technology centers such as Silicon Valley in California, Route 128 in Massachusetts, and the Research Triangle in North Carolina. In all three cases, firms are located physically close to several universities that train the engineers that are the lifeblood of high-technology companies. The search for low-cost labor can create ethical dilemmas, as described in the Ethics and Strategy feature.

Technological Advantages Independent of Scale

Another possible source of cost advantage in an industry may be the different technologies that firms employ to manage their business. It has already been suggested that larger firms may have technology-based cost advantages that reflect their ability to exploit economies of scale (e.g., the two-thirds rule).

Traditionally, discussion of technology-based cost advantages has focused on the machines, computers, and other physical tools that firms use to manage their business. Clearly, in some industries, these physical technology differences between firms can create important cost differences—even when the firms in question are approximately the same size in terms of volume of production. In the steel industry, for example, technological advances can substantially reduce the cost of producing steel. Firms with the latest steel-manufacturing technology will typically enjoy some cost advantage compared to similar-sized firms that do not have the latest technology. The same applies in the manufacturing of semiconductors, automobiles, consumer electronics, and a wide variety of other products.[12]

These physical technology cost advantages apply in service firms as well as in manufacturing firms. For example, early in its history Charles Schwab, a leading discount brokerage, purchased a computer system that enabled it to complete customer transactions more rapidly and at a lower cost than its rivals.[13] Kaiser-Permanente, the largest HMO in the United States, has invested in information technology that doctors can use to avoid incorrect diagnoses and procedures that can adversely affect a patient's health. By avoiding these medical mistakes, Kaiser-Permanente can substantially reduce its costs of providing medical service.[14]

However, the concept of technology can be easily broadened to include not just the physical tools that firms use to manage their business, but any processes within a firm used in this way. This concept of firm technology includes not only the **technological hardware** of companies—the machines and robots—but also the **technological software** of firms—things such as the quality of relations between labor and management, an organization's culture, and the quality of managerial controls. All these characteristics of a firm can have an impact on a firm's economic costs.[15]

Policy Choices

Thus far this discussion has focused on reasons why a firm can gain a cost advantage despite producing products that are similar to competing firms' products. When firms produce essentially the same outputs, differences in economies of scale, learning-curve advantages, differential access to productive inputs, and

Ethics and Strategy

One of the most important productive inputs in almost all companies is labor. Getting differential low-cost access to labor can give a firm a cost advantage.

This search for low labor costs has led some firms to engage in an international "race to the bottom." It is well known that the wage rates of most U.S. and Western European workers are much higher than the wage rates of workers in other, less developed parts of the world. While a firm might have to pay its employees $20 per hour (in wages and benefits) to make sneakers and basketball shoes in the United States, that same firm may only have to pay an employee in the Philippines, or Malaysia, or China $1.00 per day to make the same sneakers and basketball shoes—shoes the firm might be able to sell for $150 a pair in the United States and Europe. Thus, many firms look to overseas manufacturing as a way to keep their labor cost low.

But this search for low labor cost has some important unintended consequences. First, the location of the lowest cost labor rates in the world changes over time. It used to be that Mexico had the lowest labor rates, then Korea and the Philippines, then Malaysia, then China. As the infrastructures of each of these countries evolve to the point that they can support worldwide manufac-

The Race to the Bottom

turing, firms abandon their relationships with firms in prior countries in search of still lower costs in new countries. The only way former "low-cost centers" can compete is to drive their costs even lower.

This sometimes leads to a second unintended consequence of the "race to the bottom": horrendous working conditions and low wages in these low-cost manufacturing settings. Employees earning $1 for working a 10-hour day, six days a week may look good on the corporate bottom line, but many observers are deeply concerned about the moral and ethical issues associated with this strategy. Indeed, several companies—including Nike

and Kmart—have been forced to increase the wages and improve the working conditions of many of their overseas employees.

An even more horrific result of this "race to the bottom" has been the reemergence of what amounts to slavery in some Western European countries and some parts of the United States. In search of the promise of a better life, illegal immigrants are sometimes brought to Western European countries or the United States and forced to work in illegal, underground factories. These illegal immigrants are sometimes forced to work as many as 20 hours a day, for little or no pay—supposedly to "pay off" the price of bringing them out of their less developed countries. And because of their illegal status and language barriers, they often do not feel empowered to go to the local authorities.

Of course, the people who create and manage these facilities are criminals and deserve contempt. But what about the companies that purchase the services of these illegal and immoral manufacturing operations? Aren't they also culpable, both legally and morally?

Sources: R. DeGeorge (2000). "Ethics in international business—A contradiction in terms?" *Business Credit,* 102, pp. 50 +; G. Edmondson, K. Carlisle, I. Resch, K. Nickel Anhalt, and H. Dawley (2000). "Workers in bondage." *BusinessWeek,* November 27, pp. 146 +; D. Winter (2000). "Facing globalization." *Ward's Auto World,* 36, pp. 7 +.

differences in technology can all create cost advantages (and disadvantages) for them. However, firms can also make choices about the kinds of products and services they will sell—choices that have an impact on their relative cost position. These choices are called **policy choices.**

In general, firms that are attempting to implement a cost leadership strategy will choose to produce relatively simple standardized products that sell for relatively low prices compared to the products and prices firms pursuing other business or corporate strategies choose. These kinds of products often tend to have high volumes of sales, which (if significant economies of scale exist) tend to reduce costs even further.

These kinds of choices in product and pricing tend to have a very broad impact on a cost leader's operations. In these firms, the task of reducing costs is not delegated to a single function or a special task force within the firm, but is the responsibility of every manager and employee. Cost reduction sometimes becomes the central objective of the firm. Indeed, in this setting management must be constantly alert to cost-cutting efforts that reduce the ability of the firm to meet customers' needs. This kind of cost-cutting culture is central to Ryanair's ability to implement its cost leadership strategy.

The Value of Cost Leadership

There is little doubt that cost differences can exist among firms, even when those firms are selling very similar products. Policy choices about the kinds of products firms in an industry choose to produce can also create important cost differences. But under what conditions will these kinds of cost advantages actually create value for a firm?

It was suggested in Chapter 3 that one way to tell if a resource or capability—such as the ability of a firm to have a cost advantage—actually creates value for a firm is by whether that resource or capability enables a firm to neutralize its external threats or exploit its external opportunities. The ability of a cost leadership position to neutralize external threats will be examined here. The ability of such a position to enable a firm to exploit opportunities will be left as an exercise. The specific economic consequences of cost leadership are discussed in the Strategy in Depth feature.

Cost Leadership and the Threat of Entry

A cost leadership competitive strategy helps reduce the threat of new entrants by creating cost-based barriers to entry. Recall that many of the barriers to entry cited in Chapter 2, including economies of scale and cost advantages independent of scale, assume that incumbent firms have lower costs than potential entrants. If an incumbent firm is a cost leader, for any of the reasons just listed, then new entrants may have to invest heavily to reduce their costs prior to entry. Often, new entrants will enter using another business strategy (e.g., product differentiation) rather than attempting to compete on costs.

Cost Leadership and the Threat of Rivalry

Firms with a low-cost position also reduce the threat of rivalry. The threat of rivalry is reduced through pricing strategies that low-cost firms can engage in and through their relative impact on the performance of a low-cost firm and its higher-cost rivals.

Cost Leadership and the Threat of Substitutes

As suggested in Chapter 2, substitutes become a threat to a firm when their cost and performance, relative to a firm's current products or services, become more attractive to customers. Thus, when the price of crude oil goes up, substitutes for crude oil become more attractive. When the cost and performance of electronic calculators improve, demand for mechanical adding machines disappears.

In this situation, cost leaders have the ability to keep their products and services attractive relative to substitutes. While high-cost firms may have to charge high prices to cover their costs, thus making substitutes more attractive, cost leaders can keep their prices low and still earn normal or above-normal economic profits.

Strategy in Depth

*A*nother way to demonstrate that cost leadership can be a source of economic value is to directly examine the economic profits generated by a firm with a cost advantage operating in an otherwise very competitive industry. This is done in Figure 4.3.

The firms depicted in this figure are **price takers**—that is, the price of the products or services they sell is determined by market conditions and not by individual decisions of firms. This implies that there is effectively no product differentiation in this market and that no one firm's sales constitute a large percentage of this market.

The price of goods or services in this type of market (P^*) is determined by aggregate industry supply and demand. This industry price determines the demand facing an individual firm in this market. Because these firms are price takers, the demand facing an individual firm is horizontal—that is, firm decisions about levels of output have a negligible impact on overall industry supply and thus a negligible impact on the market-determined price. A firm in this setting maximizes its economic performance by producing a quantity of output (Q) so that marginal revenue equals marginal cost (MC). The ability of firms to earn economic profits in this setting depends upon the relationship between the market-

The Economics of Cost Leadership

determined price (P^*) and the average total cost (ATC) of a firm at the quantity it chooses to produce.

Firms in the market depicted in Figure 4.3 fall into two categories. All but one firm have the average-total-cost curve ATC_2 and marginal-cost curve MC_2. However, one firm in this industry has the average-total-cost curve ATC_1 and marginal-cost curve MC_1. Notice that ATC_1 is less than ATC_2 at the performance-maximizing quantities produced by these two kinds of firms (Q_1 and Q_2, respectively). In this particular example, firms with common average-total-cost curves are earning zero economic profits, while the low-cost firm is earning an economic profit (equal to the shaded area in the figure). A variety of other examples could also be constructed: The cost leader firm could be earning zero economic profits while other firms in the market are incurring economic losses; the cost leader firm could be earning substantial economic profits while other firms are earning smaller economic profits; the cost leader firm could be incurring small economic losses while the other firms are incurring substantial economic losses; and so forth. However, in all these examples the cost leader's economic performance is greater than the economic performance of other firms in the industry. Thus, cost leadership can have an important impact on a firm's economic performance.

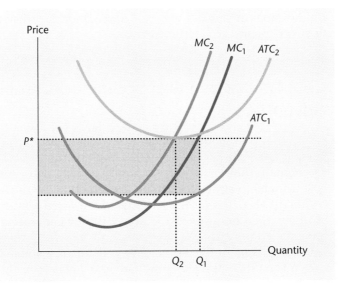

Figure 4.3 Cost Leadership and Economic Performance

Cost Leadership and the Threat of Suppliers

Suppliers can become a threat to a firm by charging higher prices for the goods or services they supply or by reducing the quality of those goods or services. However, when a supplier sells to a cost leader, that firm has greater flexibility in absorbing higher-cost supplies than does a high-cost firm. Higher supply costs may destroy any above-normal profits for high-cost firms but still allow a cost leader firm to earn an above-normal profit.

Cost leadership based on large volumes of production and economies of scale can also reduce the threat of suppliers. Large volumes of production imply large purchases of raw materials and other supplies. Suppliers are not likely to jeopardize these sales by threatening their customers. Indeed, as was suggested earlier, buyers are often able to use their purchasing volume to extract volume discounts from suppliers.

Cost Leadership and the Threat of Buyers

Cost leadership can also reduce the threat of buyers. Powerful buyers are a threat to firms when they insist on low prices or higher quality and service from their suppliers. Lower prices threaten firm revenues; higher quality can increase a firm's costs. Cost leaders can have their revenues reduced by buyer threats and still have normal or above-normal performance. These firms can also absorb the greater costs of increased quality or service and still have a cost advantage over their competition.

Buyers can also be a threat through backward vertical integration. Being a cost leader deters backward vertical integration by buyers, because a buyer that vertically integrates backward will often not have costs as low as an incumbent cost leader. Rather than vertically integrating backward and increasing its cost of supplies, powerful buyers usually prefer to continue purchasing from their low-cost suppliers.

Finally, if cost leadership is based on large volumes of production, then the threat of buyers may be reduced, because buyers may depend on just a few firms for the goods or services they purchase. This dependence reduces the willingness of buyers to threaten a selling firm.

Cost Leadership and Sustained Competitive Advantage

Given that cost leadership can be valuable, an important question becomes, "Under what conditions will firms implementing this business strategy be able to maintain that leadership to obtain a sustained competitive advantage?" If cost leadership strategies can be implemented by numerous firms in an industry, or if no firms face a cost disadvantage in imitating a cost leadership strategy, then being a cost leader will not generate a sustained competitive advantage for a firm. As suggested in Chapter 3, the ability of a valuable cost leadership competitive strategy to generate a sustained competitive advantage depends on that strategy being rare and costly to imitate, either through direct duplication or substitution. As suggested in Tables 4.4 and 4.5, the rarity and imitability of a cost leadership strategy depend, at least in part, on the sources of that cost advantage.

Table 4.4   **The Rarity of Sources of Cost Advantage**

Likely-to-be-rare sources of cost advantage	Less-likely-to-be-rare sources of cost advantage
Leaving-curve economies of scale (especially in emerging businesses)	Economies of scale (except when efficient plant size approximately equals total industry demand)
Differential low-cost access to productive inputs	Diseconomies of scale
Technological "software"	Technological hardware (unless a firm has proprietary hardware development skills)
	Policy choices

The Rarity of Sources of Cost Advantage

Some of the sources of cost advantage listed in Table 4.4 are likely to be rare among a set of competing firms; others are less likely to be rare. Sources of cost advantage that are likely to be rare include learning-curve economies (at least in emerging industries), differential low-cost access to productive inputs, and technological "software." The remaining sources of cost advantage are less likely to be rare.

| V | R | I | O |

Rare Sources of Cost Advantage

Early in the evolution of an industry, substantial differences in the cumulative volume of production of different firms are not unusual. Indeed, this was one of the major benefits associated with first-mover advantages, discussed in Chapter 2. These differences in cumulative volume of production, in combination with substantial learning-curve economies, suggest that in some settings, learning-curve advantages may be rare and thus a source of at least temporary competitive advantage.

Table 4.5   **Direct Duplication of Cost Leadership**

	Source of Cost Advantage	Basis for costly duplication		
		History	Uncertainty	Social Complexity
Low-cost duplication possible	1. Economies of scale	—	—	—
	2. Diseconomies of scale	—	—	—
May be costly to duplicate	3. Learning-curve economies	*	—	—
	4. Technological "hardware"	—	*	*
	5. Policy choices	*	—	—
Usually costly to duplicate	6. Differential low-cost access to productive inputs	***	—	**
	7. Technological "software"	***	**	***

— = not a source of costly imitation   * = somewhat likely to be a source of costly imitation   ** = likely to be a source of costly imitation
*** = very likely to be a source of costly imitation

The definition of differential access to productive inputs implies that this access is often rare. Certainly, if large numbers of competing firms have this same access, then it cannot be a source of competitive advantage.

Technological software is also likely to be rare among a set of competing firms. These software attributes represent each firm's path through history. If these histories are unique, then the technological software they create may also be rare. Of course, if several competing firms experience similar paths through history, the technological software in these firms is less likely to be rare.

Less Rare Sources of Cost Advantage

When the efficient size of a firm or plant is significantly smaller than the total size of an industry, there will usually be numerous efficient firms or plants in that industry, and a cost leadership strategy based on economies of scale will not be rare. For example, if the efficient firm or plant size in an industry is 500 units, and the total size of the industry (measured in units produced) is 500,000 units, then there are likely to be numerous efficient firms or plants in this industry, and economies of scale are not likely to give any one firm a cost-based competitive advantage.

Cost advantages based on diseconomies of scale are also not likely to be rare. It is unusual for numerous firms to adopt levels of production in excess of optimal levels. If only a few firms are too large in this sense, then several competing firms in an industry that are *not* too large will have cost advantages over the firms that are too large. However, because several firms will enjoy these cost advantages, they are not rare.

One important exception to this generalization may be when changes in technology significantly reduce the most efficient scale of an operation. Given such changes in technology, several firms may be inefficiently large. If a small number of firms happen to be sized appropriately, then the cost advantages these firms obtain in this way may be rare. Such changes in technology have made large integrated steel producers "too big" relative to smaller mini-mills. Thus, mini-mills have a cost advantage over larger integrated steel firms.

Technological hardware is also not likely to be rare, especially if it is developed by suppliers and sold on the open market. However, if a firm has proprietary technology development skills, it may possess rare technological hardware that creates cost advantages.

Finally, policy choices by themselves are not likely to be a rare source of cost advantage, particularly if the product or service attributes in question are easy to observe and describe.

The Imitability of Sources of Cost Advantage

Even when a particular source of cost advantage is rare, it must be costly to imitate in order to be a source of sustained competitive advantage. Both direct duplication and substitution, as forms of imitation, are important. Again, the imitability of a cost advantage depends, at least in part, on the source of that advantage.

Easy-to-Duplicate Sources of Cost Advantage

In general, economies of scale and diseconomies of scale are relatively easy-to-duplicate bases of cost leadership. As can be seen in Table 4.5, these sources of cost advantage do not build on history, uncertainty, or socially complex resources and capabilities and thus are not protected from duplication for these reasons.

For example, if a small number of firms obtain a cost advantage based on economies of scale, and if the relationship between production scale and costs is widely understood among competing firms, then firms at a cost disadvantage will rapidly adjust their production to exploit these economies of scale. This can be done by either growing a firm's current operations to the point that the firm exploits economies or by combining previously separate operations to obtain these economies. Both actions enable a firm at a cost disadvantage to begin using specialized machines, reduce the cost of plant and equipment, increase employee specialization, and spread overhead costs more effectively.

Indeed, perhaps the only time economies of scale are not subject to low-cost duplication is when the efficient size of operations is a significant percentage of total demand in an industry. Of course, this is the situation described in Chapter 2's discussion of economies of scale as a barrier to entry. For example, as suggested earlier, BIC Corporation, with its dominant market share in the disposable pen market, has apparently been able to gain and retain an important cost advantage in that market based on economies of scale. BIC's ability to retain this advantage reflects the fact that the optimal plant size in the disposable pen market is a significant percentage of the pen market, and thus economies of scale act as a barrier to entry in that market.

Like economies of scale, in many settings diseconomies of scale will not be a source of sustained competitive advantage for firms that have *not* grown too large. In the short run, firms experiencing significant diseconomies can shrink the size of their operations to become more efficient. In the long run, firms that fail to adjust their size will earn below-normal economic performance and cease operations.

Although in many ways reducing the size of operations to improve efficiency seems like a simple problem for managers in firms or plants, in practice it is often a difficult change to implement. Because of uncertainty, managers in a firm or plant that is too large may not understand that diseconomies of scale have increased their costs. Sometimes, managers conclude that the problem is that employees are not working hard enough, that problems in production can be fixed, and so forth. These firms or plants may continue their inefficient operations for some time, despite costs that are higher than the industry average.[16]

Other psychological processes can also delay the abandonment of operations that are too large. One of these phenomena is known as **escalation of commitment**: Sometimes, managers committed to an incorrect (cost-increasing or revenue-reducing) course of action *increase* their commitment to this action as its limitations become manifest. For example, a manager who believes that the optimal firm size in an industry is larger than the actual optimal size may remain committed to large operations despite costs that are higher than the industry average.[17]

For all these reasons, firms suffering from diseconomies of scale must often turn to outside managers to assist in reducing costs. Outsiders bring a fresh view to the organization's problems and are not committed to the practices that generated the problems in the first place.[18]

Bases of Cost Leadership That May Be Costly to Duplicate

Although cost advantages based on learning-curve economies are rare (especially in emerging industries), they are usually not costly to duplicate. As suggested in Chapter 2, for learning-curve cost advantages to be a source of sustained competitive advantage the learning obtained by a firm must be proprietary. Most recent empirical work suggests that in most industries learning is not proprietary and thus can be rapidly duplicated as competing firms move down the learning curve by increasing their cumulative volume of production.[19]

However, the fact that learning is not costly to duplicate in *most* industries does not mean it is never costly to duplicate. In some industries, the ability of firms to learn from their production experience may vary significantly. For example, some firms treat production errors as failures and systematically punish employees who make those errors. These firms effectively reduce risk-taking among their production employees and thus reduce the chances of learning how to improve their production process. Alternatively, other firms treat production errors as opportunities to learn how to improve their production process. These firms are likely to move rapidly down the learning curve and retain cost advantages, despite the cumulative volume of production of competing firms. These different responses to production errors reflect the organizational cultures of these different firms. Because organizational cultures are socially complex, they can be very costly to duplicate.[20]

Because technological hardware can usually be purchased across supply markets, it is also not likely to be difficult to duplicate. Sometimes, however, technological hardware can be proprietary or closely bundled with other unique, costly to duplicate resources controlled by a firm. In this case, technological hardware *can* be costly to duplicate.

It is unusual, but not impossible, for policy choices, per se, to be a source of sustained competitive cost advantages for a firm. As suggested earlier, if the policies in question focus on easy to observe and easy to describe product characteristics, then duplication is likely, and cost advantages based on policy choices will be temporary. However, if policy choices reflect complex decision processes within a firm, teamwork among different parts of the design and manufacturing process, or any of the software commitments discussed previously, then policy choices can be a source of sustained competitive advantage, as long as only a few firms have the ability to make these choices.

Indeed, most of the successful firms that operate in unattractive industries make policy choices that are costly to imitate because they reflect historical, causally ambiguous, and socially complex firm processes. Thus, for example, Dell's low-product-inventory strategy—a policy with clear low-cost implications—actually reflects the complex linkage between various parts of the value chain within Dell, an unwavering commitment to manufacturing flexibility and efficiency, and an organizational culture that focuses on Web-based sales. Wal-Mart's supply chain management strategy—again, a policy with clear low-cost implications—actually reflects Wal-Mart's unique history, its socially complex relations with suppliers, and its unique organizational culture. And Ryanair's low-price pricing strategy—a strategy that reflects its low-cost position—is possible because of the kind of airplane fleet Ryanair has built over time, the commitment of its employees to Ryanair's success, a charismatic founder and its unique organizational culture. Because these policies reflect costly-to-imitate attributes of these firms, they can be sources of sustained competitive advantage.

However, for these and other firms, it is not these policy choices, per se, that create sustainable cost leadership advantages. Rather, it is how these policies flow from the historical, causally ambiguous, and socially complex processes within a firm that makes them costly to duplicate. This has been the case for the Oakland A's baseball team, as described in the Strategy in the Emerging Enterprise feature.

Costly-to-Duplicate Sources of Cost Advantage

Differential access to low-cost productive inputs and technological software is usually a costly-to-duplicate basis of cost leadership. This is because these inputs often build on historical, uncertain, and socially complex resoues and capabilities. As suggested earlier, differential access to productive inputs often depends on the location of a firm. Moreover, to be a source of economic profits, this valuable location must be obtained before its full value is widely understood. Both these attributes of differential access to productive inputs suggest that if, in fact, it is rare, it will often be costly to duplicate. First, some locations are unique and cannot be duplicated. For example, most private golf clubs would like to own courses with the spectacular beauty of Pebble Beach in Monterey, California, but there is only one Pebble Beach—a course that runs parallel to some of the most beautiful oceanfront scenery in the world. Although "scenery" is an important factor of production in running and managing a golf course, the re-creation of Pebble Beach's scenery at some other location is simply beyond our technology.

Second, even if a location is not unique, once its value is revealed, acquisition of that location is not likely to generate economic profits. Thus, for example, although being located in Silicon Valley provides access to some important low-cost productive inputs for electronics firms, firms that moved to this location after its value was revealed have substantially higher costs than firms that moved there before its full value was revealed. These higher costs effectively reduce the economic profit that otherwise could have been generated. Referring to the discussion in Chapter 3, these arguments suggest that gaining differential access to productive inputs in a way that generates economic profits may reflect a firm's unique path through history.

Technological software is also likely to be difficult to duplicate and often can be a source of sustained competitive advantage. As suggested in Chapter 3, the values, beliefs, culture, and teamwork that constitute this software are socially complex and may be immune from competitive duplication. Firms with cost advantages rooted in these socially complex resources incorporate cost savings in every aspect of their organization; they constantly focus on improving the quality and cost of their operations, and they have employees who are firmly committed to, and understand, what it takes to be a cost leader. Other firms may talk about low costs; these firms live cost leadership. Ryanair, Dell, Wal-Mart, and Southwest are all examples of such firms. If there are few firms in an industry with these kinds of beliefs and commitments, then they can gain a sustained competitive advantage from their cost advantage.

Substitutes for Sources of Cost Advantage

In an important sense, all of the sources of cost advantage listed in this chapter are at least partial substitutes for each other. Thus, for example, one firm may reduce its cost through exploiting economies of scale in large-scale production, and a competing firm may reduce its costs through exploiting learning-curve economies and large cumulative volume of production. If these different activities have similar effects on a firm's cost position, and if they are equally costly to implement, then they are strategic substitutes for each other.

Because of the substitute effects of different sources of cost advantage, it is not unusual for firms pursuing cost leadership to simultaneously pursue *all* the cost-reduction activities discussed in this chapter. Implementation of this *bundle* of cost-reducing activities may have few substitutes. If duplicating this bundle of activities is also rare and difficult, then a firm may be able to gain a sustained competitive advantage from doing so.

Several of the other strategies discussed in later chapters can also have the effect of reducing a firm's costs and thus may be substitutes for the sources of cost reduction discussed in this chapter. For example, one common motivation for firms implementing strategic alliance strategies is to exploit economies of scale in

Strategy in the Emerging Enterprise

*B*aseball in the United States has a problem. Most observers agree that it is better for fans if there is competitive balance in the league—that is, if, at the beginning of the year, the fans of several teams believe that their team has a chance to go to the World Series and win it all. However, the economic reality of competition in baseball is that only a small number of financially successful teams in large cities—the New York Yankees, the Los Angeles Dodgers—have the resources necessary to compete for a spot in the World Series year after year. So-called "small market teams," such as the Pittsburgh Pirates or the Milwaukee Brewers, may be able to compete every once in a while, but these exceptions prove the general rule—teams from large markets usually win the World Series.

And then there is Oakland and the Oakland A's. Oakland (with a population of just over 400,000) is the smallest—and least glamorous—of the three cities in the San Francisco

The Oakland A's: Inventing a New Way to Play Competitive Baseball

Bay Area, the other two being San Francisco and San Jose. The A's play in an outdated stadium—McAfee Coliseum—to an average crowd of 26,038 fans—ranking 19th among the 30 major league baseball teams in the United States. In 2006, the A's player

payroll was $62.2 million, about one-third of the Yankees' player payroll.

Despite these liabilities, from 1999 to 2005 the A's either won their division of eight or placed second. Over this seven-year period, the A's won 58 percent of their games, second only to the Yankees, who won 60 percent of their games over this same period. And, the team made money!

What is the "secret" to the A's success? Their general manager, William Lamar Beane, says that it has to do with three factors: how players are evaluated, making sure that every personnel decision in the organization is consistent with this approach to evaluation, and ensuring that all personnel decisions are thought of as business decisions.

The criteria used by the A's to evaluate players are easy enough to state. For batters, the A's focus on on-base percentage (i.e., how often a batter reaches base) and total bases (a measure of the ability of a batter to hit for power); that is, they focus on the

combination with other firms. Thus, a strategic alliance that reduces a firm's costs may be a substitute for a firm exploiting economies of scale on its own to reduce its costs. As is discussed in more detail in Chapter 8, many of the strategic alliances among aluminum mining and smelting companies are motivated by realizing economies of scale and cost reduction. Also, corporate diversification strategies often enable firms to exploit economies of scale across different businesses within which they operate. In this setting, each of these businesses—treated separately—may have scale disadvantages, but collectively their scale creates the same low-cost position as that of an individual firm that fully exploits economies of scale to reduce costs in a single business (see Chapter 9).

Organizing to Implement Cost Leadership

As with all strategies, firms seeking to implement cost leadership strategies must adopt an organizational structure, management controls, and compensation policies that reinforce this strategy. Some key issues associated with using these organizing tools to implement cost leadership are summarized in Table 4.6.

ability of players to get on base and score. For pitchers, the A's focus on the percentage of first pitches that are strikes and the quality of a pitcher's fast ball. First-pitch strikes and throwing a good fast ball are correlated with keeping runners off base. Thus, not surprisingly, the A's criteria for evaluating pitchers are the reverse of their criteria for evaluating hitters.

Although these evaluation criteria are easy to state, getting the entire organization to apply them consistently in scouting, choosing, developing, and managing players is much more difficult. Almost every baseball player and fan has his or her own favorite way to evaluate players. However, if you want to work in the A's organization, you must be willing to let go of your personal favorite and evaluate players the A's way. The result is that players that come through the A's farm system—the minor leagues where younger players are developed until they are ready to play in the major leagues—learn a sin-

gle way of playing baseball instead of learning a new approach to the game every time they change managers or coaches. One of the implications of this consistency has been that the A's farm system has been among the most productive in baseball.

This consistent farm system enables the A's to treat personnel decisions—including decisions about whether they should re-sign a star player or let him go to another team—as business decisions. The A's simply do not have the resources necessary to play the personnel game the same way as the Los Angeles Dodgers or the New York Yankees. When these teams need a particular kind of player, they go and sign one. Oakland has to rely more on its farm system. But because its farm system performs so well, the A's can let so-called "superstars" go to other teams, knowing that they are likely to have a younger—and cheaper—player in the minor leagues, just waiting for the chance to play in "the show"—the players' nickname

for the major leagues. This allows the A's to keep their payroll costs down and remain profitable, despite relatively small crowds, while still fielding a team that competes virtually every year for the right to play in the World Series.

Of course, an important question becomes: How sustainable is the A's competitive advantage? The evaluation criteria themselves are not a source of sustained competitive advantage. However, the socially complex nature of how these criteria are consistently applied throughout the A's organization may be a source of sustained competitive advantage in enabling the A's to gain the differential access to low-cost productive inputs—in this case, baseball players.

Sources: K. Hammonds (2003). "How to play Beane ball." *Fast Company,* May, pp. 84 +; M. Lewis (2003). *Moneyball.* New York: Norton; A. McGahan, J. F. McGuire, and J. Kou (1997). "The baseball strike." Harvard Business School Case No. 9-796-059.

Table 4.6 **Organizing to Realize the Full Potential of Cost Leadership Strategies**

Organization structure: Functional structure with

1. Few layers in the reporting structure
2. Simple reporting relationships
3. Small corporate staff
4. Focus on narrow range of business functions

Management control systems

1. Tight cost control systems
2. Quantitative cost goals
3. Close supervision of labor, raw material, inventory, and other costs
4. A cost leadership philosophy

Compensation policies

1. Reward for cost reduction
2. Incentives for all employees to be involved in cost reduction

Organizational Structure in Implementing Cost Leadership

As suggested in Table 4.6, firms implementing cost leadership strategies will generally adopt what is known as a **functional organizational structure**.[21] An example of a functional organization structure is presented in Figure 4.4. Indeed, this functional organizational structure is the structure used to implement all business-level strategies a firm might pursue, although this structure is modified when used to implement these different strategies.

In a functional structure, each of the major business functions is managed by a **functional manager**. For example, if manufacturing, marketing, finance, accounting, and sales are all included within a functional organization, then a manufacturing manager leads that function, a marketing manager leads that function, a finance manager leads that function, and so forth. In a functional organizational structure, all these functional managers report to one person. This person has many different titles—including *president, CEO, chair,* or *founder.* However, for purposes of this discussion, this person will be called the **chief executive officer (CEO)**.

The CEO in a functional organization has a unique status. Everyone else in this company is a functional specialist. The manufacturing people manufacture, the marketing people market, the finance people finance, and so forth. Indeed, only one person in the functional organization has to have a multifunctional perspective—the CEO. This role is so important that sometimes the functional organization is called a **U-form structure**, where the "U" stands for "unitary"—because there is only one person in this organization that has a broad, multifunctional corporate perspective.

When used to implement a cost leadership strategy, this U-form structure is kept as simple as possible. As suggested in Table 4.6, firms implementing cost leadership strategies will have relatively few layers in their reporting structure. Complicated reporting structures, including **matrix structures** where one employee reports to two or more people, are usually avoided.[22] Corporate staff in these organizations is kept small. Such firms do not operate in a wide range of business functions, but instead operate only in those few business functions where they have valuable, rare, and costly-to-imitate resources and capabilities.

One excellent example of a firm pursuing a cost leadership strategy is Nucor Steel. A leader in the mini-mill industry, Nucor has only 5 layers in its reporting structure, compared to 12 to 15 in its major higher-cost competitors. Most operating decisions at Nucor are delegated to plant managers, who have full profit-and-loss responsibility for their operations. Corporate staff at Nucor is small and focuses its efforts on accounting for revenues and costs and on exploring new manufacturing processes to further reduce Nucor's operating expenses and expand its business opportunities. Nucor's former president, Ken Iverson, believed that Nucor does

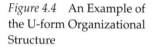

Figure 4.4   An Example of the U-form Organizational Structure

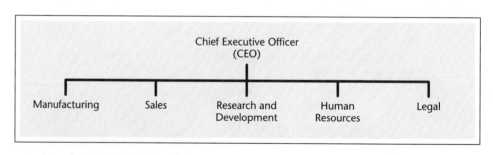

only two things well: build plants efficiently and run them effectively. Thus, Nucor focuses its efforts in these areas and subcontracts many of its other business functions, including the purchase of its raw materials, to outside vendors.[23]

Responsibilities of the CEO in a Functional Organization

The CEO in a U-form organization has two basic responsibilities: (1) to formulate the strategy of the firm and (2) to coordinate the activities of the functional specialists in the firm to facilitate the implementation of this strategy. In the special case of a cost leadership strategy, the CEO must decide on which bases such a strategy should be founded—including any of those listed in Table 4.1—and then coordinate functions within a firm to make sure that the economic potential of this strategy is fully realized.

Strategy Formulation.   The CEO in a U-form organization engages in strategy formulation by applying the strategic management process described in Chapter 1. A CEO establishes the firm's mission and associated objectives, evaluates environmental threats and opportunities, understands the firm's strengths and weaknesses, and then chooses one or more of the business and corporate strategies discussed in this book. In the case of a cost leadership strategy, the application of the strategic management process must lead a CEO to conclude that the best chance for achieving a firm's mission is for that firm to adopt a cost leadership business-level strategy.

Although the responsibility for strategy formulation in a U-form organization ultimately rests with the CEO, this individual needs to draw on the insights, analysis, and involvement of functional managers throughout the firm. CEOs who fail to involve functional managers in strategy formulation run several risks. First, strategic choices made in isolation from functional managers may be made without complete information. Second, limiting the involvement of functional managers in strategy formulation can limit their understanding of, and commitment to, the chosen strategy. This can severely limit their ability, and willingness, to implement any strategy—including cost leadership—that is chosen.[24]

Coordinating Functions for Strategy Implementation.   Even the best formulated strategy is competitively irrelevant if it is not implemented. And the only way that strategies can be effectively implemented is if all the functions within a firm are aligned in a way consistent with this strategy.

For example, compare two firms pursuing a cost leadership strategy. All but one of the first firm's functions—marketing—are aligned with this cost leadership strategy. All of the second firm's functions—including marketing—are aligned with this cost leadership strategy. Because marketing is not aligned with the first firm's cost leadership strategy, this firm is likely to advertise products that it does not sell. That is, this firm might advertise its products on the basis of their style and performance, but sell products that are reliable (but not stylish) and inexpensive (but not high performers). A firm that markets products it does not actually sell is likely to disappoint its customers. In contrast, the second firm that has all of its functions—including marketing—aligned with its chosen strategy is more likely to advertise products it actually sells and thus is less likely to disappoint its customers. In the long run, it seems reasonable to expect this second firm to outperform the first, at least with respect to implementing a cost leadership strategy.

Of course, alignment is required of all of a firm's functional areas, not just marketing. Also, misalignment can emerge in any of a firm's functional areas. Some common misalignments between a firm's cost leadership strategy and its functional activities are listed in Table 4.7.

Table 4.7   **Common Misalignments Between Business Functions and a Cost Leadership Strategy**

	When Function Is *Aligned* with Cost Leadership Strategies	When Function Is *Misaligned* with Cost Leadership Strategies
Manufacturing	Lean, low cost, good quality	Inefficient, high cost, poor quality
Marketing	Emphasize value, reliability, and price	Emphasize style and performance
R&D	Focus on product extensions and process improvements	Focus on radical new technologies and products
Finance	Focus on low cost and stable financial structure	Focus on non-traditional financial instruments
Accounting	Collect cost data and adopt conservative accounting principles	Collect no-cost data and adopt very aggressive accounting principles
Sales	Focus on value, reliability, and low price	Focus on style and performance and high price

Management Controls in Implementing Cost Leadership

As suggested in Table 4.6, cost leadership firms are typically characterized by very tight cost-control systems; frequent and detailed cost-control reports; an emphasis on quantitative cost goals and targets; and close supervision of labor, raw materials, inventory, and other costs. Again, Nucor Steel is an example of a cost leadership firm that has implemented these kinds of control systems. At Nucor, groups of employees are given weekly cost and productivity improvement goals. Groups that meet or exceed these goals receive extra compensation. Plant managers are held responsible for cost and profit performance. A plant manager who does not meet corporate performance expectations cannot expect a long career at Nucor. Similar group-oriented cost-reduction systems are in place at some of Nucor's major competitors, including Chaparral Steel.[25]

Less formal management control systems also drive a cost-reduction philosophy at cost leadership firms. For example, although Wal-Mart is one of the most successful retail operations in the world, its Arkansas headquarters is plain and simple. Indeed, some have suggested that Wal-Mart's headquarters looks like a warehouse. Its style of interior decoration was once described as "early bus station." Wal-Mart even involves its customers in reducing costs by asking them to "help keep your costs low" by returning shopping carts to the designated areas in Wal-Mart's parking lots.[26]

Compensation Policies and Implementing Cost Leadership Strategies

As suggested in Table 4.6, compensation in cost leadership firms is usually tied directly to cost-reducing efforts. Such firms often provide incentives for employees to work together to reduce costs and increase or maintain quality, and they expect *every* employee to take responsibility for both costs and quality. For example, an important expense for retail stores like Wal-Mart is "shrinkage"—a nice way of saying people steal stuff. About half the shrinkage in most stores comes from employees stealing their own companies' products.

Wal-Mart used to have a serious problem with shrinkage. Among other solutions (including hiring "greeters" whose real job is to discourage shoplifters), Wal-Mart developed a compensation scheme that took half the cost savings created by reduced shrinkage and shared it with employees in the form of a bonus. With this incentive in place, Wal-Mart's shrinkage problems dropped significantly.

Cost Leadership in an International Context

As has already been suggested in this chapter, one of the most common reasons that a firm begins international operations is to reduce its cost position. International operations can reduce a firm's costs in at least three ways: (1) by increasing sales to realize economies of scale, (2) by gaining access to low-cost labor, and (3) by gaining access to low-cost raw materials.

Gaining access to new customers for a firm's current products or services can increase a firm's volume of sales. If a firm's production process is sensitive to economies of scale, this increased volume of sales can reduce its costs and enable it to gain cost advantages in both its domestic and nondomestic operations. Many scholars over many years have pointed out the potential of international operations to generate economies of scale.[27] Most recognize that the realization of economies of scale from international operations requires a high degree of integration across firm borders. Integration must focus on those aspects of a firm's operations where economies of scale can be realized. For example, McDonald's attempts to generate training-based economies of scale through the operation of a single management training center for all of its international operations. Firms in the float glass, color television, and chemical industries have all attempted to exploit manufacturing economies of scale through their international operations.[28]

Many firms in the worldwide automobile industry have attempted to realize manufacturing economies of scale through their international operations. According to one estimate, the minimum efficient scale of a single compact-car manufacturing plant is 400,000 units per year.[29] Such a plant would produce approximately 20 percent of all the automobiles sold in Britain, Italy, or France. Obviously, to exploit this 400,000-cars-per-year manufacturing efficiency European automobile firms have had to sell cars in more than just a single-country market. Thus, the implementation of an international strategy has been essential if these firms were to recognize manufacturing economies of scale. Similar economies of scale through international operations can be found through research and development and marketing.

It has already been suggested that firms can engage in international operations to gain access to low-cost labor. As the lowest cost labor in the world shifted from Japan (right after World War II) to South Korea, then to Taiwan, Singapore, and Malaysia, and still later to China, Mexico, and Vietnam, some firms have changed their manufacturing operations accordingly. For example, Mineba, a Japanese ball bearing company, began manufacturing in Japan, shifted its operations to Singapore in the 1970s, and has been operating in Thailand since the 1980s. Hewlett-Packard operates manufacturing and assembly operations in Malaysia and Mexico, Mitsubishi Motors recently opened a manufacturing operation in Vietnam, General Motors operates assembly plants in Mexico, and Motorola has operations in China. All these investments were

Global Perspectives

The Rise of the Maquiladora

One interesting example of firms gaining access to low labor costs through their international strategies is *maquiladoras*. Maquiladoras are manufacturing plants owned by non-Mexican companies that operate in Mexico near the U.S. border. The primary driver behind maquiladora investment is lower labor costs than similar plants located in the United States. In addition, firms exporting from maquiladoras to the United States have to pay duties only on the value added that was created in Mexico; maquiladoras do not have to pay Mexican taxes on the goods processed in Mexico. Also, the cost of the land on which plants are built in Mexico is substantially lower than the cost would be in the United States. However, despite these other advantages, a study by the Banco de Mexico suggests that without the 20 percent cost-of-labor advantage, most maquiladoras would not be profitable.

Given the cost advantages in operating maquiladoras, it is not surprising that investment in this particular international strategy has increased substantially over time. In 1965, there were only 12 maquiladora plants. By 1990, approximately 1,700 were in operation. By 1999, over 3,100 maquiladoras, employing over 1 million people, were in operation. Most of these were U.S. firms operating plants in Mexico. Currently, only oil generates more foreign currency for Mexico than maquiladoras.

Sources: A. DePalma (1994). "Trade pact is spurring Mexican deals in the U.S." *New York Times,* March 17, pp. C1, 3; M. Celestino (1999). "Manufacturing in Mexico." *World Trade,* 12, July, pp. 36–42.

motivated, at least in part, by the availability of low-cost labor in these countries.[30] One interesting approach to gaining access to the low-cost labor market while still remaining close to the boundaries of the United States is described in the Global Perspectives feature.

Finally, firms can engage in international operations to gain access to low-cost raw materials. Indeed, historically, this was the most traditional reason that firms began international operations. For example, in 1600 the British East India Company was formed with an initial investment of £ 70,000 to manage trade between England and the Far East, including India. In 1601, the third British East India Company fleet sailed for the Indies to buy cloves, pepper, silk, coffee, saltpeter, and other products. This fleet generated a 234-percent return on investment. These profits led to the formation of the Dutch East India Company in 1602 and the French East India Company in 1664. Similar firms were organized to manage trade in the New World. The Hudson Bay Company was chartered in 1670 to manage the fur trade, and the rival North West Company was organized in 1784 for the same purpose. All these organizations were created to gain access to low-cost raw materials and products that were available only in nondomestic markets.[31]

Gaining access to low-cost raw materials is still an important reason why some firms engage in international enterprise. In some industries, including the oil and gas industry, virtually the only reason why firms have begun international operations is to gain access to low-cost raw materials.

SUMMARY

Firms producing essentially the same products can have different costs for several reasons. Some of the most important of these are: (1) size differences and economies of scale, (2) size differences and diseconomies of scale, (3) experience differences and learning-curve economies, (4) differential access to productive inputs, and (5) technological advantages independent of scale. In addition, firms competing in the same industry can make policy choices about the kinds of products and services to sell that can have an important impact on their relative cost position. Cost leadership in an industry can be valuable by assisting a firm in reducing the threat of each of the five forces in an industry outlined in Chapter 2.

Each of the sources of cost advantage discussed in this chapter can be a source of sustained competitive advantage if it is rare and costly to imitate. Overall, learning-curve economies, differential access to productive inputs, and technological "software" are more likely to be rare than other sources of cost advantage. Differential access to productive inputs and technological "software" is more likely to be costly to imitate—either through direct duplication or through substitution—than the other sources of cost advantage. Thus, differential access to productive inputs and technological "software" will often be more likely to be a source of sustained competitive advantage than cost advantages based on other sources.

Of course, to realize the full potential of these competitive advantages, a firm must be organized appropriately. Organizing to implement a strategy always involves a firm's organizational structure, its management control systems, and its compensation policies. The organizational structure used to implement cost leadership—and other business strategies—is called a *functional,* or *U-form,* structure. The CEO is the only person in this structure who has a corporate perspective. The CEO has two responsibilities: to formulate a firm's strategy and to implement it by coordinating functions within a firm. Ensuring that a firm's functions are aligned with its strategy is essential to successful strategy implementation.

When used to implement a cost leadership strategy, the U-form structure generally has few layers, simple reporting relationships, and a small corporate staff. It focuses on a narrow range of business functions. The management control systems used to implement these strategies generally include tight cost controls; quantitative cost goals; close supervision of labor, raw materials, inventory, and other costs; and a cost leadership culture and mentality. Finally, compensation policies in these firms typically reward cost reduction and provide incentives for everyone in the organization to be part of the cost-reduction effort.

Firms often pursue a cost leadership strategy by engaging in international operations, and such operations can affect their cost structure in at least three ways: (1) firms can use international sales to exploit economies of scale, (2) firms can operate facilities around the world to gain access to low-cost labor, and (3) firms can operate internationally to gain access to low-cost raw materials.

CHALLENGE QUESTIONS

1. Ryanair, Wal-Mart, Timex, Casio, and Hyundai are all cited as examples of firms pursuing cost leadership strategies, but these firms make substantial investments in advertising, which seems more likely to be associated with a product differentiation strategy. Are these firms really pursuing a cost leadership strategy, or are they pursuing a product differentiation strategy by emphasizing their lower costs?

2. When economies of scale exist, firms with large volumes of production will have lower costs than those with smaller volumes of production. The realization of these economies of scale, however, is far from automatic. What actions can firms take to ensure that they realize whatever economies of sale are created by their volume of production?

3. Firms engage in an activity called "forward pricing" when they estab-lish, during the early stages of the learning-curve, a price for their prod-ucts that is lower than their actual costs, in anticipation of lower costs later on, after significant learning has occurred. Under what conditions, if any, does forward pricing make sense? What risks, if any, do firms engaging in forward pricing face?

4. One way of thinking about orga-nizing to implement cost leadership strategies is that firms that pursue this strategy should be highly centralized, have high levels of direct supervision, and keep employee wages to an absolute minimum. Another approach is to decentralize decision-making authority—to ensure that individuals who know the most about reducing costs make decisions about how to reduce costs. This, in turn, would imply less direct supervision and somewhat higher levels of employee wages. Why is this? Which of these two approaches seems more reasonable? Under what conditions would these different approaches make more or less sense?

5. International operations can reduce a firm's costs by generating economies of scale that it would not otherwise enjoy or by giving a firm access to low-cost labor and/or raw materials. The first of these strategies involves mostly exporting products made in a firm's home country to a nondomestic market, whereas the second involves mostly importing products made outside a firm's home market to its home market. Describe the differences between these two strategies in terms of the types of investments that firms following these two strategies must make in their non-domestic markets and the different management control problems these firms are likely to face.

PROBLEM SET

1. The economies of scale curve in Figure 4.1 can be represented algebraically in the following equation:

$$\text{Average costs} = a + bQ + cQ^2$$

where Q is the quantity produced by a firm and a, b, and c are coefficients that are esti-mated from industry data. For example, it has been shown that the economies of scale curve for U.S. savings and loans is:

$$\text{Average costs} = 2.38 - .615A + .54A^2$$

where A is a savings and loan's total assets. Using this equation, what is the optimal size of a savings and loan? (Hint: Plug in different values of A and calculate average costs. The lowest possible average cost is the optimal size for a savings and loan.)

2. The learning-curve depicted in Figure 4.2 can be represented algebraically by the fol-lowing equation:

$$\text{Average time to produce } x \text{ units} = ax^{-\beta}$$

where x is the total number of units produced by a firm in its history, a is the amount of time it took a firm to produce its first unit, and β is a coefficient that describes the rate of learn-ing in a firm.

Suppose it takes a team of workers 45 hours to assemble its first product ($a = 45$) and 40.5 hours to assemble the second. When a firm doubles its production (in this case, from one to two units) and cuts its production time (in this case, from 45 hours to 40.5 hours), learning is said to have occurred (in this case a 40.5/45, or 90 percent, learning-curve). The β for a 90 percent learning-curve is .3219. Thus, this firm's learning-curve is:

$$\text{Average time to produce } x \text{ units} = 45x^{-.3219}$$

What is the average amount of time it will take this firm to produce six products? (Hint: Simply plug "6" in for x in the equation and solve.) What is the total time it took this firm to produce these six products? (Hint: Simply multiply the number of units produced, 6, by the average time it will take to produce these six products.) What is the average time it will take this firm to produce five products? What is the total time it will take this firm to produce five products? So, what is the total time it will take this firm to produce its sixth product? (Hint: Subtract the total time needed to produce five products from the total time needed to produce six products.)

Suppose a new firm is going to start producing these same products. Assuming this new firm does not learn anything from established firms, what will its cost disadvantage be when it assembles its first product? (Hint: Compare the costs of the experienced firm's sixth product with the cost of the new firm's first product.)

END NOTES

1. Weiner, S. (1987). "The road most traveled." *Forbes*, October 19, pp. 60–64.
2. Christensen, C. R., N. A. Berg, and M. S. Salter (1980). *Policy formulation and administration: A casebook of senior management problems in business*, 8th ed. Homewood, IL: Irwin, p. 163.
3. Scherer, F. M. (1980). *Industrial market structure and economic Performance*. Boston: Houghton Mifflin; Moore, F. T. (1959). "Economies of scale: Some statistical evidence." *Quarterly Journal of Economics*, 73, pp. 232–245; and Lau, L. J., and S. Tamura (1972). "Economies of scale, technical progress, and the nonhomothetic leontief production function." *Journal of Political Economy*, 80, pp. 1167–1187.
4. Scherer, F. M. (1980). *Industrial market structure and economic performance*. Boston: Houghton Mifflin; and Perrow, C. (1984). *Normal accidents: Living with high-risk technologies*. New York: Basic Books.
5. Hamermesh, R. G., and R. S. Rosenbloom (1989). "Crown Cork and Seal Co., Inc." Harvard Business School Case No. 9-388-096.
6. See Hackman, J. R., and G. R. Oldham (1980). *Work redesign*. Reading, MA: Addison-Wesley.
7. This relationship was first noticed in 1925 by the commander of Wright-Patterson Air Force Base in Dayton, Ohio.
8. Learning curves have been estimated for numerous industries. Boston Consulting Group (1970). "Perspectives on experience." Boston: BCG, presents learning curves for over 20 industries while Lieberman, M. (1984). "The learning curve and pricing in the chemical processing industries." *Rand Journal of Economics*, 15, pp. 213–228, estimates learning curves for 37 chemical products.
9. See Henderson, B. (1974). *The experience curve reviewed III—How does it work?* Boston: Boston Consulting Group; and Boston Consulting Group (1970). "Perspectives on experience." Boston: BCG.
10. Hall, G., and S. Howell (1985). "The experience curve from the economist's perspective." *Strategic Management Journal*, 6, pp. 197–212.
11. Hill, C. W. L. (1988). "Differentiation versus low-cost or differentiation and low-cost: A contingency framework." *Academy of Management Review*, 13(3), pp. 401–412.
12. See Ghemawat, P., and H. J. Stander III (1992). "Nucor at a crossroads." Harvard Business School Case No. 9-793-039 on technology in steel manufacturing and cost advantages; Shaffer, R. A. (1995). "Intel as conquistador." *Forbes*, February 27, p. 130 on technology in semiconductor manufacturing and cost advantages; Monteverde, K., and D. Teece (1982). "Supplier switching costs and vertical integration in the automobile industry." *Rand Journal of Economics*, 13(1), pp. 206–213; and McCormick, J., and N. Stone (1990). "From national champion to global competitor: An interview with Thomson's Alain Gomez." *Harvard Business Review*, May/June, pp. 126–135 on technology in consumer electronic manufacturing and cost advantages.
13. Schultz, E. (1989). "Climbing high with discount brokers." *Fortune*, Fall (special issue), pp. 219–223.
14. Schonfeld, Erick (1998). "Can computers cure health care?" *Fortune*, March 30, pp. 111 +.
15. Ibid.
16. See Meyer, M. W., and L. B. Zucker (1989). *Permanently failing organizations*. Newbury Park, CA: Sage.
17. Staw, B. M. (1981). "The escalation of commitment to a course of action." *Academy of Management Review*, 6, pp. 577–587.
18. Hesterly, W. S. (1989). *Top management succession as a determinant of firm performance and de-escalation: An agency problem*, Unpublished doctoral dissertation, University of California, Los Angeles.
19. Barney, J. B. (1986). "Organizational culture: Can it be a source of sustained competitive advantage?" *Academy of Management Review*, 11, pp. 656–665.
20. See Spence, A. M. (1981). "The learning curve and competition." *Bell Journal of Economics*, 12, pp. 49–70, on why learning needs to be proprietary; Mansfield, E. (1985). "How rapidly does new industrial technology leak out?" *Journal of Industrial Economics*, 34(2), pp. 217–223; Lieberman, M. B. (1982). *The learning-curve, pricing and market structure in the chemical processing industries*. Unpublished doctoral dissertation, Harvard University; Lieberman, M. B. (1987). "The learning curve, diffusion, and competitive strategy." *Strategic Management Journal*, 8, pp. 441–452 on why it usually is not proprietary.
21. Williamson, O. (1975). *Markets and hierarchies*. New York: Free Press.
22. Davis, S. M., and P. R. Lawrence (1977). *Matrix*. Reading, MA: Addison-Wesley.
23. See Ghemawat, P., and H. J. Stander III (1992). "Nucor at a crossroads." Harvard Business School Case No. 9-793-039.
24. See Floyd, S. W. and B. Woldridge (1992). "Middle management involvement in strategy and its association with strategic type: A research note." *Strategic Management Journal*, 13, pp. 153–167.
25. Ibid.
26. Walton, S. (1992). *Sam Walton, made in America: My story*. New York: Doubleday.
27. See Fayerweather, J. (1969). *International business management*. New York: McGraw-Hill, and Porter, M. E. (1982). "How global companies win out." *Harvard Business Review*, September–October, pp. 98–108.
28. See Serwer, A. (1994). "McDonald's conquers the world." *Fortune*, October 17, pp. 103–116; Prahalad, C. K., and Y. Doz (1987). *The multinational mission*. New York: Free Press; and Bartlett, C. A., and S. Ghoshal (1989). *Managing across borders: The transnational solution*. Boston: Harvard Business School Press.
29. See Porter, M. E. (1986). "Competition in international industries: A conceptual framework." In M. E. Porter (ed.), *Competition in international industries*. Boston: Harvard Business School Press.
30. See Collis, D. J. (1991). "A resource-based analysis of international competition: The case of the bearing industry." *Strategic Management Journal*, 12 (Summer Special Issue), pp. 49–68; and Engardio, P. (1993). "Motorola in China: A great leap forward." *BusinessWeek*, May 17, pp. 58–59.
31. See Trager, J. (1992). *The people's chronology*. New York: Henry Holt.

Product Differentiation

LEARNING OBJECTIVES

After reading this chapter, you should be able to:

1. Define product differentiation.

2. Describe eleven bases of product differentiation and how they can be grouped into three categories.

3. Describe how product differentiation is ultimately limited only by managerial creativity.

4. Describe how product differentiation can be used to neutralize environmental threats and exploit environmental opportunities.

5. Describe those bases of product differentiation that are not likely to be costly to duplicate, those that may be costly to duplicate, and those that will often be costly to duplicate.

6. Describe the main substitutes for product differentiation strategies.

7. Describe how organizational structure, control processes, and compensation policies can be used to implement product differentiation strategies.

8. Discuss whether it is possible for a firm to implement cost leadership and product differentiation strategies simultaneously.

9. Discuss the trade-off between local responsiveness and international integration as firms pursue product differentiation strategies around the world.

Who Is Victoria, and What Is Her Secret?

Sexy. Glamorous. Mysterious. Victoria's Secret is the world's leading specialty retailer of lingerie and beauty products. With 2002 sales of almost $3.6 billion and operating profits of $614 million, Victoria's Secret sells its mix of sexy lingerie, prestige fragrances, and fashion-inspired collections through over 1,000 retail stores and the almost 400 million catalogues it distributes each year.

But all this glamour and success leaves the two central questions about this firm unanswered: "Who is Victoria?" and "What is her secret?"

It turns out that Victoria is a retired fashion model who lives in an up-and-coming fashionable district in London. She has a committed relationship and is thinking about starting a family. However, these maternal instincts are balanced by Victoria's adventurous and sexy side. She loves good food, classical music, and great wine. She travels frequently and is as much at home in New York, Paris, and Los Angeles as she is in London. Her fashion tastes are edgy enough to never be boring, but practical enough to never be extreme. Her lingerie is an essential part of her wardrobe. Sexy and alluring, but never cheap, trashy, or vulgar, Victoria's lingerie is the perfect complement to her overall lifestyle. Most important, while Victoria knows she is beautiful and sexy, she also knows that it is her brains, not her looks, that have enabled her to succeed in life.

This is who Victoria is. This is the woman that Victoria's Secret's designers design for, the woman Victoria's Secret marketers create advertising for, and the woman to whom all Victoria's Secret sales associates are trained to sell.

And this is her secret—Victoria doesn't really exist. Or, more precisely, the number of real women in the entire world who are like Victoria is very small—no more than a handful. So why would a company like Victoria's Secret organize all of its design, marketing, and sales efforts around meeting the lingerie needs of a woman who, for all practical purposes, doesn't really exist?

Victoria's Secret knows how few of its actual customers are like Victoria. However, it is convinced that many of its customers would like to be treated as if they were Victoria, if only for a few hours, when they come into a Victoria's Secret store. Victoria's Secret is not just selling lingerie; it is selling an opportunity, almost a fantasy, to be like Victoria—to live in an exciting and sexy city, to travel the world, to have refined, yet edgy, tastes. To buy and wear Victoria's Secret lingerie is—if only for a moment or two—an opportunity to experience life as Victoria experiences it.

Practically speaking, building an entire company around meeting the needs of a customer who does not actually exist creates some interesting problems. You can't just call Victoria on the phone and ask her about trends in her lifestyle; you can't form a focus group of people like Victoria and ask them to evaluate new lines of lingerie. In a sense, not only has Victoria's Secret invented Victoria; it also had to invent Victoria's lifestyle—and the lingerie, fragrances, and accessories that go along with that lifestyle. And as long as the lifestyle that it invents for Victoria is desirable to but just beyond the reach of its actual customers, Victoria's Secret will continue to be able to sell a romantic fantasy—along with its bras and panties.

Sources: www.limitedbrands.com; www.victoriassecret.com.

Victoria's Secret uses the fictional character "Victoria" to help implement its product differentiation strategy. As successful as this effort is, however, this is only one of many ways that firms can try to differentiate their products.

What Is Product Differentiation?

Whereas Wal-Mart exemplifies a firm pursuing a cost leadership strategy, Victoria's Secret exemplifies a firm pursuing a product differentiation strategy. **Product differentiation** is a business strategy whereby firms attempt to gain a competitive advantage by increasing the perceived value of their products or services relative to the perceived value of other firms' products or services. These other firms can be rivals or firms that provide substitute products or services. By increasing the perceived value of its products or services, a firm will be able to charge a higher price than it would otherwise. This higher price can increase a firm's revenues and generate competitive advantages.

A firm's attempts to create differences in the relative perceived value of its products or services often are made by altering the objective properties of those products or services. Rolex attempts to differentiate its watches from Timex and Casio watches by manufacturing them with solid gold cases. Mercedes attempts to differentiate its cars from Hyundai's cars through sophisticated engineering and high performance. Victoria's Secret attempts to differentiate its shopping experience from Wal-Mart, and other retailers, through the merchandise it sells and the way it sells it.

Although firms often alter the objective properties of their products or services in order to implement a product differentiation strategy, the existence of product differentiation, in the end, is *always* a matter of customer perception. Products sold by two different firms may be very similar, but if customers believe the first is more valuable than the second, then the first product has a differentiation advantage.

In the world of "craft" or "microbrewery" beers, for example, the consumers' image of how a beer is brewed may be very different from how it is actually brewed. Boston Beer Company, for example, sells Samuel Adams Beer. Customers can tour the Boston Beer Company, where they will see a small row of fermenting tanks and two 10-barrel kettles being tended by a brewmaster wearing rubber boots. However, Samuel Adams Beer is not actually brewed in this small factory. Instead, it is brewed—in 200-barrel steel tanks—in Cincinnati, Ohio, by the Hudepohl-Schoenling Brewing Company, a contract brewing firm that also manufactures Hudy Bold Beer and Little Kings Cream Ale. Maui Beer Company's Aloha Lager brand is brewed in Portland, Oregon, and Pete's Wicked Ale (a craft beer that claims it is brewed "one batch at a time. Carefully.") is brewed in batches of 400 barrels each by Stroh Brewery Company, makers of Old Milwaukee Beer. However, the more consumers believe there are important differences between these "craft" beers and more traditional brews—despite many of their common manufacturing methods—the more willing they will be to pay more for a craft beer. This willingness to pay more suggests that an important "perceptual" basis of product differentiation exists for these craft beers.[1] If products or services are *perceived* as being different in a way that is valued by consumers, then product differentiation exists.

Just as perceptions can create product differentiation between products that are essentially identical, the lack of perceived differences between products with very different characteristics can prevent product differentiation. For example, consumers with an untrained palate may not be able to distinguish between two different wines, even though expert wine tasters would be very much aware of their differences. Those who are not aware of these differences, even if they exist, will not be willing to pay more for one wine over the other. In this sense, for these consumers at least, these two wines, though different, are not differentiated.

Product differentiation is always a matter of customer perceptions, but firms can take a variety of actions to influence these perceptions. These actions can be thought of as different bases of product differentiation.

Bases of Product Differentiation

A large number of authors, drawing on both theory and empirical research, have developed lists of ways firms can differentiate their products or services.[2] Some of these are listed in Table 5.1. Although the purpose of all these bases of product differentiation is to create the perception that a firm's products or services are unusually valuable, different bases of product differentiation attempt to accomplish this objective in different ways. For example, the first four bases of product differentiation listed in Table 5.1 attempt to create this perception by focusing directly on the attributes of the products or services a firm sells. The second three attempt to create this perception by developing a relationship between a firm and its customers. The last five attempt to create this perception through linkages within and between firms. Of course, these bases of product differentiation are not mutually exclusive. Indeed, firms will often attempt to differentiate their products or services along multiple dimensions simultaneously. An empirical method for identifying ways that firms have differentiated their products is discussed in the Research Made Relevant feature.

Focusing on the Attributes of a Firm's Products or Services

The first group of bases of product differentiation identified in Table 5.1 focuses on the attributes of a firm's products or services.

Product Features.   The most obvious way that firms can try to differentiate their products is by altering the features of the products they sell. One industry in which

Table 5.1   **Ways Firms Can Differentiate Their Products**

To differentiate its products, a firm can focus directly on the attributes of its products or services, or

1. Product features
2. Product complexity
3. Timing of product introduction
4. Location

on relationships between itself and its customers, or

5. Product customization
6. Consumer marketing
7. Product reputation

on linkages within or between firms

8. Linkages among functions within a firm
9. Linkages with other firms
10. Product mix
11. Distribution channels
12. Service and support

Sources: M. E. Porter (1980). *Competitive strategy*. New York: Free Press; R. E. Caves and P. Williamson (1985). "What is product differentiation, really?" *Journal of Industrial Economics*, 34, pp. 113–132.

Research Made Relevant

**Discovering the Bases
of Product Differentiation**

Of all the possible bases of product differentiation that might exist in a particular market, how does one pinpoint those that have actually been used? Research in strategic management and marketing has shown that the bases of product differentiation can be identified using multiple regression analysis to estimate what are called **hedonic prices**. A hedonic price is that part of the price of a product or service that is attributable to a particular characteristic of that product or service.

The logic behind hedonic prices is straightforward. If customers are willing to spend more for a product with a particular attribute than they are willing to spend for that same product without that attribute, then that attribute differentiates the first product from the second. That is, this attribute is a basis of product differentiation in this market.

Consider, for example, the price of used cars. The market price of a used car can be determined through the use of a variety of used car buying guides. These guides typically establish the base price of a used car. This base price typically includes product features that are common to almost all cars—a radio, a standard engine, a heater/defroster.

Because these product attributes are common to virtually all cars, they are not a basis for product differentiation.

However, in addition to these common features, the base price of an automobile is adjusted based on some less common features—a high-end stereo system, a larger engine, air conditioning. How much the base price of the car is adjusted when these features are added—$300 for a high-end stereo, $500 for a larger engine, $200 for air conditioning—are the hedonic prices of these product attributes. These product

attributes differentiate well-equipped cars from less-well-equipped cars and, because consumers are willing to pay more for well-equipped cars, can be thought of as bases of product differentiation in this market.

Multiple regression techniques are used to estimate these hedonic prices in the following way. For our simple car example, the following regression equation is estimated:

$$Price = a_1 + b_1(Stereo) + b_2(Engine) + b_3(AC)$$

where *Price* is the retail price of cars, *Stereo* is a variable describing whether a car has a high-end stereo, *Engine* is a variable describing whether a car has a large engine, and *AC* is a variable describing whether or not a car has air conditioning. If the hedonic prices for these features are those suggested earlier, the results of running this regression analysis would be:

$$Price = \$7,800 + \$300(Stereo) + \$500(Engine) + \$200(AC)$$

where $7,800 is the base price of this type of used car.

Source: D. Hay and D. Morris (1979). *Industrial economics: Theory and evidence.* Oxford: Oxford University Press; K. Cowling and J. Cubbin (1971). "Price, quality, and advertising competition." *Economica,* 38, pp. 378–394.

firms are constantly modifying product features to attempt to differentiate their products is the automobile industry. Chrysler, for example, introduced the "cab forward" design to try to give its cars a distinctive look, whereas Audi went with a more radical flowing and curved design to differentiate its cars. For emergency situations, General Motors introduced the "On Star" system, which instantly connects drivers to GM operators 24 hours a day, while Mercedes-Benz continued to develop its "crumple zone" system to ensure passenger safety in a crash. In body construction, General Motors continues to develop its "uni-body" construction system, whereby different parts of a car are welded to each other rather than built on a single frame, while Jaguar introduced a 100-percent aluminum body to help differentiate its top-of-the-line model from other luxury cars. Mazda continues to tinker with the motor and suspension of its sporty Miata, while Nissan introduced the 350 Z—a continuation of the famous 240 Z line—and Porsche changed from air-cooled to water-cooled engines in its 911 series of sports cars. All these—and many more—changes in the attributes of automobiles are examples of firms trying to differentiate their products by altering product features.

Product Complexity.   Product complexity can be thought of as a special case of altering a product's features to create product differentiation. In a given industry, product complexity can vary significantly. The BIC "crystal pen," for example, has only a handful of parts, whereas a Cross or a Mont Blanc pen has many more parts. To the extent that these differences in product complexity convince consumers that the products of some firms are more valuable than the products of other firms, product complexity can be a basis of product differentiation.

Timing of Product Introduction.   Introducing a product at the right time can also help create product differentiation. As suggested in Chapter 2, in some industry settings (i.e., in emerging industries) *the* critical issue is to be a first mover—to introduce a new product before all other firms. Being first in emerging industries can enable a firm to set important technological standards, preempt strategically valuable assets, and develop customer-switching costs. These first-mover advantages can create a perception among customers that the products or services of the first-moving firm are somehow more valuable than the products or services of other firms.[3]

Timing-based product differentiation, however, does not depend only on being a first mover. Sometimes, a firm can be a later mover in an industry but introduce products or services at just the right time and thereby gain a competitive advantage. This can happen when the ultimate success of a product or service depends on the availability of complementary products or technologies. For example, the domination of Microsoft's MS-DOS operating system, and thus ultimately the domination of Windows, was only possible because IBM introduced its version of the personal computer. Without the IBM PC, it would have been difficult for any operating system—including MS-DOS—to have such a large market presence.[4]

Location.   The physical location of a firm can also be a source of product differentiation.[5] Consider, for example, Disney's operations in Orlando, Florida. Beginning with The Magic Kingdom and Epcot Center, Disney built a world-class destination resort in Orlando. Over the years, Disney has added numerous attractions to its core entertainment activities, including MGM Studios, over 11,000 Disney-owned hotel rooms, a $100 million sports center, an automobile racing track, an after-hours entertainment district, and most recently, a $1 billion theme park called "The Animal Kingdom"—all in and around Orlando. Now, families can travel from around the world to Orlando, knowing that in a single location they can enjoy a full range of Disney adventures.[6]

Focusing on the Relationship Between a Firm and Its Customers
The second group of bases of product differentiation identified in Table 5.1 focuses on relationships between a firm and its customers.

Product Customization.   Products can also be differentiated by the extent to which they are customized for particular customer applications. Product customization is an important basis for product differentiation in a wide variety of industries, from enterprise software to bicycles.

Enterprise software is software that is designed to support all of a firm's critical business functions, including human resources, payroll, customer service, sales, quality control, and so forth. Major competitors in this industry include PeopleSoft and Oracle. However, although these firms sell basic software packages, most firms find it necessary to customize these basic packages to meet their specific business needs. The ability to build complex software packages that can also be customized to meet the specific needs of a particular customer is an important basis of product differentiation in this marketplace.

In the bicycle industry, consumers can spend as little as $50 on a bicycle, and as much as—well, almost as much as they want on a bicycle, easily in excess of $10,000. High-end bicycles use, of course, the very best components, such as brakes and gears. But what really distinguishes these bicycles is their customized fit. Once a serious rider becomes accustomed to a particular bicycle, it is very difficult for that rider to switch to alternative suppliers.

Consumer Marketing. Differential emphasis on consumer marketing has been a basis for product differentiation in a wide variety of industries. Through advertising and other consumer marketing efforts, firms attempt to alter the perceptions of current and potential customers, whether or not specific attributes of a firm's products or services are actually altered.

For example, in the soft drink industry, Mountain Dew—a product of PepsiCo—was originally marketed as a fruity, lightly carbonated drink that tasted as light as a "morning dew in the mountains." However, beginning in the late 1990s Mountain Dew's marketing efforts changed dramatically. "As light as a morning dew in the mountains" became "Do the Dew," and Mountain Dew focused its marketing efforts on young, mostly male, extreme-sports–oriented consumers. Young men riding snowboards, roller blades, mountain bikes, and skateboards—mostly upside down—became central to most Mountain Dew commercials. Mountain Dew became a sponsor of a wide variety of extreme sports contests and an important sponsor of the X Games on ESPN. And will we ever forget the confrontation between the young Dew enthusiast and a big horn sheep over a can of Mountain Dew in a meadow? Note that this radical repositioning of Mountain Dew depended entirely on changes in consumer marketing. The features of the underlying product were not changed.

Reputation. Perhaps the most important relationship between a firm and its customers depends on a firm's reputation in its marketplace. Indeed, a firm's **reputation** is really no more than a socially complex relationship between a firm and its customers. Once developed, a firm's reputation can last a long time, even if the basis for that reputation no longer exists.[7]

A firm that has tried to exploit its reputation for cutting-edge entertainment is MTV, a division of Viacom, Inc. Although several well-known video artists—including Madonna—have had their videos banned from MTV, it has still been able to develop a reputation for risk-taking on television. MTV believes that its viewers have come to expect the unexpected in MTV programming. One of the first efforts to exploit, and reinforce, this reputation for risk-taking was *Beavis and Butthead*, an animated series starring two teenage boys with serious social and emotional development problems. More recently, MTV exploited its reputation by inventing an entirely new genre of television—"reality TV"—through its *Real World* and *House Rules* programs. Not only are these shows cheap to produce, they build on the reputation that MTV has for providing entertainment that is a little risky, a little sexy, and a little controversial. Indeed, MTV has been so successful in providing this kind of entertainment that it had to form an entirely new cable station—MTV 2—to actually show music videos.[8]

Focusing on Links Within and Between Firms

The third group of bases of product differentiation identified in Table 5.1 focuses on links within and between firms.

Linkages Between Functions.   A less obvious but still important way in which a firm can attempt to differentiate its products is through linking different functions within the firm. For example, research in the pharmaceutical industry suggests that firms vary in the extent to which they are able to integrate different scientific specialties—such as genetics, biology, chemistry, and pharmacology—to develop new drugs. Firms that are able to form effective multidisciplinary teams to explore new drug categories have what some have called an **architectural competence**, that is, the ability to use organizational structure to facilitate coordination among scientific disciplines to conduct research. Firms that have this competence are able to more effectively pursue product differentiation strategies—by introducing new and powerful drugs—than those that do not have this competence. And in the pharmaceutical industry, where firms that introduce such drugs can experience very large positive returns, the ability to coordinate across functions is an important source of competitive advantage.[9]

Links with Other Firms.   Another basis of product differentiation is linkages with other firms. Here, instead of differentiating products or services on the basis of linkages between functions within a single firm or linkages between different products, differentiation is based on explicit linkages between one firm's products and the products or services of other firms.

This form of product differentiation has increased in popularity over the last several years. For example, with the growth in popularity of stock car racing in the United States, more and more corporations are looking to link their products or services with famous names and cars in NASCAR. Firms such as Kodak, Circuit City, Gatorade, McDonald's, Home Depot, The Cartoon Network, True Value, and Pfizer (manufacturers of Viagra) have all been major sponsors of NASCAR teams. In one year, the Coca-Cola Corporation filled orders for over 200,000 NASCAR–themed vending machines. Visa struggled to keep up with demand for its NASCAR affinity cards, and over 1 million NASCAR Barbies were sold by Mattel—generating revenues of about $50 million. Notice that none of these firms sells products for automobiles. Rather, these firms seek to associate themselves with NASCAR because of the sport's popularity.[10]

In general, linkages between firms that differentiate their products are examples of cooperative strategic alliance strategies. The conditions under which cooperative strategic alliances create value and are sources of sustained competitive advantage are discussed in detail in Chapter 9.

Product Mix.   One of the outcomes of links among functions within a firm and links between firms can be changes in the mix of products a firm brings to the market. This mix of products or services can be a source of product differentiation, especially when (1) those products or services are technologically linked or (2) when a single set of customers purchases several of a firm's products or services.

For example, technological interconnectivity is an extremely important selling point in the information technology business, and thus an important basis of potential product differentiation. However, seamless interconnectivity—where Company A's computers talk to Company B's computers across Company C's data line merging a database created by Company D's software with a database created by Company E's software to be used in a calling center that operates with Company F's technology—has been extremely difficult to realize. For this reason, some information technology firms try to realize the goal of interconnectivity by adjusting their product mix, that is, by selling a bundle of products whose interconnectivity they can control and guarantee to customers. This goal of selling a bundle of interconnected technologies can influence a firm's research and development, strategic alliance, and merger and acquisition strategies, because all these activities can influence the set of products a firm brings to market.

Shopping malls are an example of the second kind of linkage among a mix of products—where products have a common set of customers. Many customers prefer to go to one location, to shop at several stores at once, rather than travel to a series of locations to shop. This one-stop shopping reduces travel time and helps turn shopping into a social experience. Mall development companies have recognized that the value of several stores brought together in a particular location is greater than the value of those stores if they were isolated, and they have invested to help create this mix of retail shopping opportunities.[11]

Distribution Channels.   Linkages within and between firms can also have an impact on how a firm chooses to distribute its products, and distribution channels can be a basis of product differentiation. For example, in the soft drink industry Coca-Cola, PepsiCo, and Seven-Up all distribute their drinks through a network of independent and company-owned bottlers. These firms manufacture key ingredients for their soft drinks and ship these ingredients to local bottlers, who add carbonated water, package the drinks in bottles or cans, and distribute the final product to soft drink outlets in a given geographic area. Each local bottler has exclusive rights to distribute a particular brand in a geographic location.

Canada Dry has adopted a completely different distribution network. Instead of relying on local bottlers, Canada Dry packages its soft drinks in several locations and then ships them directly to wholesale grocers, who distribute the product to local grocery stores, convenience stores, and other retail outlets.

One of the consequences of these alternative distribution strategies is that Canada Dry has a relatively strong presence in grocery stores but a relatively small presence in soft drink vending machines. The vending machine market is dominated by Coca-Cola and PepsiCo. These two firms have local distributors that maintain and stock vending machines. Canada Dry has no local distributors and is able to get its products into vending machines only when they are purchased by local Coca-Cola or Pepsi distributors. These local distributors are likely to purchase and stock Canada Dry products such as Canada Dry ginger ale, but they are contractually prohibited from purchasing Canada Dry's various cola products.[12]

Service and Support.   Finally, products have been differentiated by the level of service and support associated with them. Some firms in the home appliance market, including General Electric, have not developed their own service and support network and instead rely on a network of independent service and support operations throughout the United States. Other firms in the same industry, including Sears, have developed their own service and support networks.[13]

Product Differentiation and Creativity

The bases of product differentiation listed in Table 5.1 indicate a broad range of ways in which firms can differentiate their products and services. In the end, however, any effort to list all possible ways to differentiate products and services is doomed to failure. Product differentiation is ultimately an expression of the creativity of individuals and groups within firms. It is limited only by the opportunities that exist, or that can be created, in a particular industry and by the willingness and ability of firms to creatively explore ways to take advantage of those opportunities. It is not unreasonable to expect that the day some academic researcher claims to have developed the definitive list of bases of product differentiation, some creative engineer, marketing specialist, or manager will think of yet another way to differentiate his or her product.

The Value of Product Differentiation

V R I O

In order to have the potential for generating competitive advantages, the bases of product differentiation upon which a firm competes must be valuable. The market conditions under which product differentiation can be valuable are discussed in the Strategy in Depth feature. More generally, in order to be valuable, bases of product differentiation must enable a firm to neutralize its threats and/or exploit its opportunities.

Product Differentiation and Environmental Threats

Successful product differentiation helps a firm respond to each of the environmental threats identified in the five forces framework. For example, product differentiation helps reduce the threat of new entry by forcing potential entrants to an industry to absorb not only the standard costs of beginning business, but also the additional costs associated with overcoming incumbent firms' product differentiation advantages. The relationship between product differentiation and new entry has already been discussed in Chapter 2.

Product differentiation reduces the threat of rivalry, because each firm in an industry attempts to carve out its own unique product niche. Rivalry is not reduced to zero, because these products still compete with one another for a common set of customers, but it is somewhat attenuated because the customers each firm seeks are different. For example, both a Rolls Royce and a Hyundai satisfy the same basic consumer need—transportation—but it is unlikely that potential customers of Rolls Royce will also be interested in purchasing a Hyundai or vice versa.

Product differentiation also helps firms reduce the threat of substitutes by making a firm's current products appear more attractive than substitute products. For example, fresh food can be thought of as a substitute for frozen processed foods. In order to make its frozen processed foods more attractive than fresh foods, products such as Stouffer's and Swanson are marketed heavily through television advertisements, newspaper ads, point-of-purchase displays, and coupons.

Product differentiation can also reduce the threat of suppliers. Powerful suppliers can raise the prices of the products or services they provide. Often, these increased supply costs must be passed on to a firm's customers in the form of higher prices if a firm's profit margin is not to deteriorate. A firm without a highly differentiated product may find it difficult to pass its increased costs on to customers, because these customers will have numerous other ways to purchase similar products or services from a firm's competitors. However, a firm with a highly differentiated product may have loyal customers or customers who are unable to purchase similar products or services from other firms. These types of customers are more likely to accept increased prices. Thus, a powerful supplier may be able to raise its prices, but, up to some point, these increases will not reduce the profitability of a firm selling a highly differentiated product.

Finally, product differentiation can reduce the threat of buyers. When a firm sells a highly differentiated product, it enjoys a "quasi-monopoly" in that segment

Strategy in Depth

The two classic treatments of the relationship between product differentiation and firm value, developed independently and published at approximately the same time, are by Edward Chamberlin and Joan Robinson.

Both Chamberlin and Robinson examine product differentiation and firm performance relative to perfect competition. As explained in Chapter 2, under perfect competition, it is assumed that there are numerous firms in an industry, each controlling a small proportion of the market, and the products or services sold by these firms are assumed to be identical. Under these conditions, firms face a horizontal demand curve (because they have no control over the price of the products they sell), and they maximize their economic performance by producing and selling output such that marginal revenue equals marginal costs. The maximum economic performance a firm in a perfectly competitive market can obtain, assuming no cost differences across firms, is normal economic performance.

When firms sell differentiated products, they gain some ability to adjust their prices. A firm can sell its output at very high prices and produce relatively smaller amounts of output, or it can sell its output at very low prices and produce relatively greater amounts

The Economics of Product Differentiation

of output. These trade-offs between price and quantity produced suggest that firms selling differentiated products face a downward-sloping demand curve, rather than the horizontal demand curve for firms in a perfectly competitive market. Firms selling differentiated products and facing a downward-sloping demand curve are in an industry structure described by Chamberlin as **monopolistic competition.** It is as if, within the market niche defined by a firm's differentiated product, a firm possesses a monopoly.

Firms in monopolistically competitive markets still maximize their economic profit by producing and selling a quantity of products such that marginal revenue equals marginal cost. The price that firms can charge at this optimal point depends on the demand they face for their differentiated product. If demand is large, then the price that can be charged is greater; if demand is low, then the price that can be charged is lower. However, if a firm's average total cost is below the price it can charge (i.e., if average total cost is less than the demand-determined price), then a firm selling a differentiated product can earn an above-normal economic profit.

Consider the example presented in Figure 5.1. Several curves are relevant in this figure. First, note that a firm in this industry faces downward-sloping demand (*D*). This means that the industry is not perfectly competitive and that a firm has some control over the prices it will charge for its products. Also, the marginal-revenue curve (*MR*) is downward sloping and everywhere lower than the demand curve. Marginal revenue is downward sloping because in order to sell additional levels of output of a single product, a firm must be willing to lower its price. The marginal-revenue curve is lower than the demand curve because this lower price applies to all the products sold by a firm, not just to any additional products the firm sells. The

of the market. Buyers interested in purchasing this particular product must buy it from a particular firm. Any potential buyer power is reduced by the ability of a firm to withhold highly valued products or services from a buyer.

Product Differentiation and Environmental Opportunities

Product differentiation can also help a firm take advantage of environmental opportunities. For example, in fragmented industries firms can use product differentiation strategies to help consolidate a market. In the office-paper industry, marginal-cost curve (MC) is upward sloping, indicating that in order to produce additional outputs a firm must accept additional costs. The average-total-cost curve (ATC) can have a variety of shapes, depending on the economies of scale, the cost of productive inputs, and other cost phenomena described in Chapter 4.

These four curves (demand, marginal revenue, marginal cost, and average total cost) can be used to determine the level of economic profit for a firm under monopolistic competition. To maximize profit, the firm produces an amount (Q_e) such that marginal costs equal marginal revenues. To determine the price of a firm's output at this level of production, a vertical line is drawn from the point where marginal costs equal marginal revenues. This line will intersect with the demand curve. Where this vertical line intersects demand, a horizontal line is drawn to the vertical (price) axis to determine the price a firm can charge. In the figure, this price is P_e. At the point P_e, average total cost is less than the price. The total revenue

obtained by the firm in this situation (price × quantity) is indicated by the shaded area in the figure. The economic profit portion of this total revenue is indicated by the crosshatched section of the shaded portion of the figure. Because this crosshatched section is above average total costs in the figure, it represents a competitive advantage. If this section was below average total costs, it would represent a competitive disadvantage.

Chamberlin and Robinson go on to discuss the impact of entry into the market niche defined by a firm's differentiated product. As discussed in Chapter 2, a basic assumption of S-C-P models is that the existence of above-

normal economic performance motivates entry into an industry or into a market niche within an industry. In monopolistically competitive industries, such entry means that the demand curve facing incumbent firms shifts downward and to the left. This implies that an incumbent firm's customers will buy less of its output if it maintains its prices or (equivalently) that a firm will have to lower its prices to maintain its current volume of sales. In the long run, entry into this market niche can lead to a situation where the price of goods or services sold when a firm produces output such that marginal cost equals marginal revenue is exactly equal to that firm's average total cost. At this point, a firm earns zero economic profits even if it still sells a differentiated product.

Sources: E. H. Chamberlin (1933). *The economics of monopolistic competition.* Cambridge, MA: MIT Press; J. Robinson (1934). "What is perfect competition?" *Quarterly Journal of Economics*, 49, pp. 104–120.

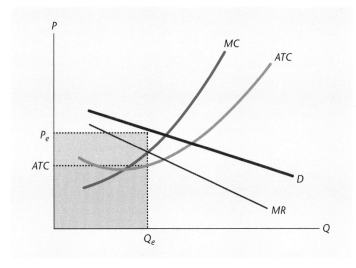

Figure 5.1 Product Differentiation and Firm Performance: The Analysis of Monopolistic Competition

Xerox has used its brand name to become the leading seller of paper for office copy machines and printers. Arguing that its paper is specially manufactured to avoid jamming in its own copy machines, Xerox was able to brand what had been a commodity product and facilitate the consolidation of what had been a very fragmented industry.[14]

The role of product differentiation in emerging industries was discussed in Chapter 2. By being a first mover in these industries, firms can gain product differentiation advantages based on perceived technological leadership, preemption of strategically valuable assets, and buyer loyalty due to high switching costs.

In mature industries, product differentiation efforts often switch from attempts to introduce radically new technologies to product refinement as a basis of product differentiation. For example, in the mature retail gasoline market firms attempt to differentiate their products by selling slightly modified gasoline (cleaner-burning gasoline, gasoline that cleans fuel injectors, and so forth) and by altering the product mix (linking gasoline sales with convenience stores). In mature markets, it is sometimes difficult to find ways to actually refine a product or service. In such settings, firms can sometimes be tempted to exaggerate the extent to which they have refined and improved their products or services. The implications of these exaggerations are discussed in the Ethics and Strategy feature.

Product differentiation can also be an important strategic option in a declining industry. Product-differentiating firms may be able to become leaders in this kind of industry (based on their reputation, unique product attributes, or some other product differentiation basis). Alternatively, highly differentiated firms may be able to discover a viable market niche that will enable them to survive despite the overall decline in the market.

Finally, the decision to implement a product differentiation strategy can have a significant impact on how a firm acts in a global industry. For example, several firms in the retail clothing industry with important product differentiation advantages in their home markets are beginning to enter into the U.S. retail clothing market. These firms include Sweden's H & M Hennes & Mauritz AB, with its emphasis on "cheap chic"; the Dutch firm Mexx (a division of Liz Claiborne); the Spanish company Zara (a division of Inditex SA); and the French sportswear company Lacoste (a division of Devanlay SA).[15]

Product Differentiation and Sustained Competitive Advantage

Product differentiation strategies add value by enabling firms to charge prices for their products or services that are greater than their average total cost. Firms that implement this strategy successfully can reduce a variety of environmental threats and exploit a variety of environmental opportunities. However, as discussed in Chapter 3, the ability of a strategy to add value to a firm must be linked with rare and costly-to-imitate organizational strengths in order to generate a sustained competitive advantage. Each of the bases of product differentiation listed earlier in this chapter varies with respect to how likely it is to be rare and costly to imitate.

Rare Bases for Product Differentiation

The concept of product differentiation generally assumes that the number of firms that have been able to differentiate their products in a particular way is, at some point in time, smaller than the number of firms needed to generate perfect competition dynamics. Indeed, the reason that highly differentiated firms can charge a price for their product that is greater than average total cost is because these firms are using a basis for product differentiation that few competing firms are also using.

Ultimately, the rarity of a product differentiation strategy depends on the ability of individual firms to be creative in finding new ways to differentiate their products. As suggested earlier, highly creative firms will be able to discover or create new ways to do this. These kinds of firms will always be one step ahead of the competition, because rival firms will often be trying to imitate these firms' last product differentiation moves while creative firms are working on their next one.

Ethics and Strategy

*O*ne of the most common ways to try to differentiate a product is to make claims about that product's performance. In general, high-performance products command a price premium over low-performance products. However, the potential price advantages enjoyed by high-performance products can sometimes lead firms to make claims about their products that, at the least, strain credibility, and at the most, simply lie about what their products can do.

Some of these claims are easily dismissed as harmless exaggerations. Few people actually believe that using a particular type of whitening toothpaste is going to make your in-laws like you, or that not wearing a particular type of deodorant is going to cause patrons in a bar to collapse when you lift your arms in victory after a foosball game. These exaggerations are harmless and present few ethical challenges.

However, in the field of health care, exaggerated product performance claims can have serious consequences. This can happen when a patient takes a medication with exaggerated performance claims in lieu of a medication with more modest, although accurate, performance claims. A history of false medical performance claims in the United States led to the formation of the Food and Drug Administration (FDA), a federal regulatory agency charged with evaluating the efficacy of drugs before they are marketed. Historically, the FDA has adopted the "gold standard" of drug approval—not only must a drug

Product Claims and the Ethical Dilemmas in Health Care

demonstrate that it does what it claims, it must also demonstrate that it does not do any significant harm to the patient. Patients can be confident that drugs that pass the FDA approval process meet the highest standards in the world.

However, this "gold standard" of approval creates important ethical dilemmas—mostly stemming from the time it takes a drug to pass FDA inspections. This process can take between five and seven years. During FDA trials, patients who might otherwise benefit from a drug are not allowed to use it because it has not yet received FDA approval. Thus, although the FDA approval process may work very well for people who may need a drug sometime in the future, it works less well for those who need a drug right now.

A growing suspicion among some consumers that the FDA process may prevent effective drugs from being marketed has helped feed the growth of alternative treatments—usually based on some herbal or more natural formula. Such treatments are careful to note that their claims—everything from regrowing hair to losing weight to enhancing athletic performance to quitting smoking—have not been tested by the FDA. And yet, these claims are still made.

Some of these performance claims seem at least reasonable. For example, it is now widely accepted that ephedra does behave as an amphetamine, and thus is likely to enhance strength and athletic performance. Others—including those that claim that a mixture of herbs can actually increase the size of male genitals—seem far-fetched, at best. Indeed, a recent analysis of herbal treatments making this claim found no ingredients that could have this effect, but did find an unacceptably high concentration of bacteria from animal feces that can cause serious stomach disorders. Firms that sell products on the basis of exaggerated and unsubstantiated claims face their own ethical dilemmas. And, without the FDA to ensure product safety and efficacy, the adage *caveat emptor*—let the buyer beware—seems like good advice.

Sources: J. Angwin (2003). "Some 'enlargement pills' pack impurities." *Wall Street Journal*, April 8, p. B1; G. Pisano (1991). "Nucleon, Inc." Harvard Business School Case No. 9-692-041.

The Imitability of Product Differentiation

Valuable and rare bases of product differentiation must be costly to imitate if they are to be sources of sustained competitive advantage. Both direct duplication and substitution, as approaches to imitation, are important in understanding the ability of product differentiation to generate competitive advantages.

Direct Duplication of Product Differentiation

As discussed in Chapter 4, firms that successfully implement a cost leadership strategy can choose whether they want to reveal this strategic choice to their competition by adjusting their prices. If they keep their prices high—despite their cost advantages—the existence of those cost advantages may not be revealed to competitors. Of course, other firms—such as Wal-Mart—that are confident that their cost advantages cannot be duplicated at low cost are willing to reveal their cost advantage through charging lower prices for their products or services.

Firms pursuing product differentiation strategies usually do not have this option. More often than not, the act of selling a highly differentiated product or service reveals the basis upon which a firm is trying to differentiate its products. In fact, most firms go to great lengths to let their customers know how they are differentiating their products, and in the process of informing potential customers they also inform their competitors. Indeed, if competitors are not sure how a firm is differentiating its product, all they need to do is purchase that product themselves. Their own experience with the product—its features and other attributes—will tell them all they need to know about this firm's product differentiation strategy.

Knowing how a firm is differentiating its products, however, does not necessarily mean that competitors will be able to duplicate the strategy at low cost. The ability to duplicate a valuable and rare product differentiation strategy depends on the basis upon which a firm is differentiating its products. As suggested in Table 5.2, some bases of product differentiation—including the use of product features—are almost always easy to duplicate. Others—including product mix, links with other firms, product customization, product complexity, and consumer marketing—can sometimes be costly to duplicate. Finally, still other bases of product differentiation—including links between functions, timing, location, reputation, distribution channels, and service and support—are usually costly to duplicate.

How costly it is to duplicate a particular basis of product differentiation depends on the kinds of resources and capabilities that basis uses. When those

Table 5.2   **Bases of Product Differentiation and the Cost of Duplication**

	History	Uncertainty	Social Complexity
Low-cost duplication usually possible			
1. Product features	—	—	—
May be costly to duplicate			
2. Product mix	*	*	*
3. Links with other firms	*	—	**
4. Product customization	*	—	**
5. Product complexity	*	—	*
6. Consumer marketing	—	**	—
Usually costly to duplicate			
7. Links between functions	*	*	**
8. Timing	***	*	—
9. Location	***	—	—
10. Reputation	***	**	***
11. Distribution channels	**	*	**
12. Service and support	*	*	**

— = Not likely to be a source of costly duplication   * = Somewhat likely to be a source of costly duplication
** = Likely to be a source of costly duplication   *** = Very likely to be a source of costly duplication

resources and capabilities are acquired in unique historical settings, when there is some uncertainty about how to build these resources and capabilities, or when these resources and capabilities are socially complex in nature, then product differentiation strategies that exploit these kinds of resources and capabilities will be costly to imitate. These strategies can be a source of sustained competitive advantage for a firm. However, when a product differentiation strategy exploits resources and capabilities that do not possess these attributes, then those strategies are likely to be less costly to duplicate, and even if they are valuable and rare, will only be sources of temporary competitive advantage.

Bases of Product Differentiation That Are Easy to Duplicate.   The one basis of product differentiation in Table 5.2 that is identified as almost always being easy to duplicate is product features. The irony is that product features are by far the most popular way for firms to try to differentiate their products. Rarely do product features, by themselves, enable a firm to gain sustained competitive advantages from a product differentiation strategy.

For example, virtually every one of the product features used in the automobile industry to differentiate the products of different automobile companies has been duplicated. Chrysler's "cab forward" design has been incorporated into the design of many manufacturers. The curved, sporty styling of the Audi has surfaced in cars manufactured by Lexus and General Motors. GM's "On Star" system has been duplicated by Mercedes. Mercedes' crumple-zone technology has become the industry standard, as has GM's uni-body construction method. Indeed, only the Mazda Miata, Nissan 350 Z, and the Porsche 911 have remained unduplicated—and this has little to do with the product features of these cars and much more to do with their reputation.

The only time product features, per se, can be a source of sustained competitive advantage for a firm is when those features are protected by patents. However, as was discussed in Chapters 2 and 3, even patents provide only limited protection from direct duplication, except in very unusual settings.

Although product features, by themselves, are usually not a source of sustained competitive advantage, they can be a source of a temporary competitive advantage. During the period of time when a firm has a temporary competitive advantage from implementing a product differentiation strategy based on product features, it may be able to attract new customers. Once these customers try the product, they may discover other features of a firm's products that make them attractive. If these other features are costly to duplicate, then they can be a source of sustained competitive advantage, even though the features that originally attracted a customer to a firm's products will often be rapidly duplicated by competitors.

Bases of Product Differentiation That May Be Costly to Duplicate.   Some bases of product differentiation may be costly to duplicate, at least in some circumstances. The first of these, listed in Table 5.2, is product mix.

Duplicating the features of another firm's products is usually not difficult. However, if that firm brings a series of products to market, if each of these products has unique features, and most important, if the products are highly integrated with each other, then this mix of products may be costly to duplicate. Certainly, the technological integration of the mix of information technology products sold by IBM and other firms has been relatively difficult to duplicate for firms that do not manufacture all these products themselves.

However, when this basis of a product mix advantage is a common customer, then duplication is often less difficult. Thus, although having a mall that brings several stores together in a single place is a source of competitive advantage over stand-alone stores, it is not a competitive advantage over other malls that provide the same service. Because there continue to be opportunities to build such malls, the fact that malls make it easier for a common set of customers to shop does not give any one mall a sustained competitive advantage.

Links with other firms may also be costly to duplicate, especially when those links depend on socially complex relationships. The extent to which interfirm links can provide sources of sustained competitive advantage is discussed in more detail in Chapter 9.

In the same way, product customization and product complexity are often easy-to-duplicate bases of product differentiation. However, sometimes the ability of a firm to customize its products for one of its customers depends on the close relationships it has developed with those customers. Product customization of this sort depends on the willingness of a firm to share often-proprietary details about its operations, products, research and development, or other characteristics with a supplying firm. Willingness to share this kind of information, in turn, depends on the ability of each firm to trust and rely on the other. The firm opening its operations to a supplier must trust that that supplier will not make this information broadly available to competing firms. The firm supplying customized products must trust that its customer will not take unfair advantage of it. If two firms have developed these kinds of socially complex relationships, and few other firms have them, then links with other firms will be costly to duplicate and a source of sustained competitive advantage.

The product customization seen in both enterprise software and in high-end customized bicycles has these socially complex features. In a real sense, when these products are purchased, a relationship with a supplier is being established—a relationship that is likely to last a long period of time. Once this relationship is established, partners are likely to be unwilling to abandon it, unless, of course, a party to the exchange tries to take unfair advantage of another party to that exchange. This possibility is discussed in detail in Chapter 9.

Finally, consumer marketing, though a very common form of product differentiation, is often easy to duplicate. Thus, whereas Mountain Dew has established itself as the "extreme games" drink, other drinks, including Gatorade, have also begun to tap into this market segment. Of course, every once in a while an advertising campaign or slogan, a point-of-purchase display, or some other attribute of a consumer marketing campaign will unexpectedly catch on and create greater-than-expected product awareness. In beer, marketing campaigns such as "Tastes great, less filling," "Why ask why?" the "Budweiser Frogs," and "What's Up?" have had these unusual effects. If a firm, in relation with its various consumer marketing agencies, is systematically able to develop these superior consumer marketing campaigns, then it may be able to obtain a sustained competitive advantage. However, if such campaigns are unpredictable and largely a matter of a firm's good luck, they cannot be expected to be a source of sustained competitive advantage.

Bases of Product Differentiation That Are Usually Costly to Duplicate.   The remaining bases of product differentiation listed in Table 5.2 are usually costly to duplicate. Firms that differentiate their products on these bases may be able to obtain sustained competitive advantages.

Linkages across functions within a single firm are usually a costly-to-duplicate basis of product differentiation. Whereas linkages with other firms can be either easy or costly to duplicate, depending on the nature of the relationship that exists between firms, linkages across functions within a single firm usually require socially complex, trusting relations. There are numerous built-in conflicts between functions and divisions within a single firm. Organizations that have a history and culture that support cooperative relations among conflicting divisions may be able to set aside functional and divisional conflicts to cooperate in delivering a differentiated product to the market. However, firms with a history of conflict across functional and divisional boundaries face a significant, and costly, challenge in altering these socially complex, historical patterns.

Indeed, the research on architectural competence in pharmaceutical firms suggests that not only do some firms possess this competence, but that other firms do not. Moreover, despite the significant advantages that accrue to firms with this competence, firms without this competence have, on average, been unable to develop it. All this suggests that such a competence, if it is also rare, is likely to be costly to duplicate and thus a source of sustained competitive advantage.

Timing is also a difficult-to-duplicate basis of product differentiation. As suggested in Chapter 3, it is difficult (if not impossible) to re-create a firm's unique history. If that history endows a firm with special resources and capabilities it can use to differentiate its products, this product differentiation strategy can be a source of sustained competitive advantage. Rivals of a firm with such a timing-based product differentiation advantage may need to seek alternative ways to differentiate their products. Thus, it is not surprising that universities that compete with the oldest universities in the country find alternative ways to differentiate themselves—through their size, the quality of the extramural sports, through their diversity—rather than relying on their age.

Location is often a difficult-to-duplicate basis of product differentiation. This is especially the case when a firm's location is unique. For example, research on the hotel preferences of business travelers suggests that location is a major determinant of the decision to stay in a hotel. Hotels that are convenient to both major transportation and commercial centers in a city are preferred, other things being equal, to hotels in other types of locations. Indeed, location has been shown to be a more important decision criterion for business travelers than price. If only a few hotels in a city have these prime locations, and if no further hotel development is possible, then hotels with these locations can gain sustained competitive advantages.

Of all the bases of product differentiation listed in this chapter, perhaps none is more difficult to duplicate than a firm's reputation. As suggested earlier, a firm's reputation is actually a socially complex relationship between a firm and its customers, based on years of experience, commitment, and trust. Reputations are not built quickly, nor can they be bought and sold. Rather, they can only be developed over time by consistent investment in the relationship between a firm and its customers. A firm with a positive reputation can enjoy a significant competitive advantage, whereas a firm with a negative reputation, or no reputation, may have to invest significant amounts over long periods of time to match the differentiated firm.

Distribution channels can also be a costly-to-duplicate basis of product differentiation, for at least two reasons. First, relations between a firm and its distribution channels are often socially complex and thus costly to duplicate. Second, the supply of distribution channels may be limited. Firms that already have access to these channels may be able to use them, but firms that do not have such access may be forced to create their own or develop new channels. Creating new channels, or developing entirely new means of distribution, can be difficult and costly undertakings.[16] These costs are one of the primary motivations underlying many international joint ventures (see Chapter 9).

Finally, level of service and support can be a costly-to-duplicate basis of product differentiation. In most industries, it is usually not too costly to provide a minimum level of service and support. In home electronics, this minimum level of service can be provided by a network of independent electronic repair shops. In automobiles, this level of service can be provided by service facilities associated with dealerships. In fast foods, this level of service can be provided by a minimum level of employee training.

However, moving beyond this minimum level of service and support can be difficult for at least two reasons. First, increasing the quality of service and support may involve substantial amounts of costly training. McDonald's has created a sophisticated training facility (Hamburger University) to maintain its unusually high level of service in fast foods. General Electric has invested heavily in training for service and support over the last several years. Many Japanese automakers spent millions on training employees to help support auto dealerships, before they opened U.S. manufacturing facilities.[17]

More important than the direct costs of the training needed to provide high-quality service and support, these bases of product differentiation often reflect the attitude of a firm and its employees toward customers. In many firms throughout the world, the customer has become "the bad guy." This is, in many ways, under-standable. Employees tend to interact with their customers less frequently than they interact with other employees. When they do interact with customers, they are often the recipients of complaints directed at the firm. In these settings, hostility toward the customer can develop. Such hostility is, of course, inconsistent with a product differentiation strategy based on customer service and support.

In the end, high levels of customer service and support are based on socially complex relations between firms and customers. Firms that have conflicts with their customers may face some difficulty duplicating the high levels of service and support provided by competing firms.

Substitutes for Product Differentiation

The bases of product differentiation outlined in this chapter vary in how rare they are likely to be and in how difficult they are to duplicate. However, the ability of the bases of product differentiation to generate a sustained competitive advantage also depends on whether low-cost substitutes exist.

Substitutes for bases of product differentiation can take two forms. First, many of the bases of product differentiation listed in Table 5.1 can be partial substitutes for each other. For example, product features, product customization, and product complexity are all very similar bases of product differentiation and thus can act as substitutes for each other. A particular firm may try to develop a competitive advantage by differentiating its products on the basis of product customization only to find that its customization advantages are reduced as another firm alters the features of its products. In a similar way, linkages between functions, linkages between firms, and product mix, as bases of product differentiation, can also be substitutes for each other. IBM links its sales, service, and consulting functions to differentiate itself in the computer market. Other computer firms, however, may develop close relationships with computer service companies and consulting firms to close this product differentiation advantage. Given that different bases of product differentiation are often partial substitutes for each other, it is not surprising that firms pursue these multiple bases of product differentiation simultaneously.

Second, other strategies discussed throughout this book can be substitutes for many of the bases of product differentiation listed in Table 5.1. One firm may try to gain a competitive advantage through adjusting its product mix, and another firm may substitute strategic alliances to create the same type of product differentiation. For example, Southwest Airline's continued emphasis on friendly, on-time, low cost service and United Airlines' emphasis on its links to Lufthansa and other worldwide airlines through the Star Alliance can both be seen as product differentiation efforts that are at least partial substitutes.[18]

In contrast, some of the other bases of product differentiation discussed in this chapter have few obvious close substitutes. These include timing, location, distribution channels, and service and support. To the extent that these bases of product differentiation are also valuable, rare, and difficult to duplicate, they may be sources of sustained competitive advantage.

Organizing to Implement Product Differentiation

V R I O

As was suggested in Chapter 3, the ability to implement a strategy depends on the adjustment of a firm's structure, its management controls, and its compensation policies to be consistent with that strategy. Whereas strategy implementation for firms adopting a cost leadership strategy focuses on reducing a firm's costs and increasing its efficiency, strategy implementation for a firm adopting a product differentiation strategy must focus on innovation, creativity, and product performance. Whereas cost-leading firms are all about customer value, product-differentiating firms are all about style. How the need for style is reflected in a firm's structure, controls, and compensation policies is summarized in Table 5.3.

Organizational Structure and Implementing Product Differentiation

Both cost leadership and product differentiation strategies are implemented through the use of a functional, or U-form, organizational structure. However, whereas the U-form structure used to implement a cost leadership strategy has few layers, simple reporting relationships, a small corporate staff, and a focus on only a few business functions, the U-form structure for a firm implementing a product differentiation strategy can be somewhat more complex. For example, these firms often use temporary cross-divisional *and* cross-functional teams to manage the

Table 5.3 **Organizing to Implement Product Differentiation Strategies**

Organizational Structure:

1. Cross-divisional/cross-functional product development teams
2. Complex matrix structures
3. Isolated pockets of intense creative efforts: Skunk works

Management Control Systems:

1. Broad decision-making guidelines
2. Managerial freedom within guidelines
3. A policy of experimentation

Compensation Policies:

1. Rewards for risk-taking, not punishment for failures
2. Rewards for creative flair
3. Multidimensional performance measurement

development and implementation of new, innovative, and highly differentiated products. These teams bring individuals from different businesses and different functional areas together to cooperate on a particular new product or service.

One firm that has used these cross-divisional and cross-functional teams effectively is the British advertising agency WPP. WPP owns several very large advertising agencies, several public relations firms, several market research companies, and so forth. Each of these businesses operates relatively independently in most areas. However, the corporation has identified a few markets where cross-divisional and cross-functional collaboration is important. One of these is the health care market. To exploit opportunities in the health care market, WPP, the corporation, forms teams of advertising specialists, market research specialists, public relations specialists, and so on, drawn from each of the businesses it owns. The resulting cross-divisional teams are given the responsibility of developing new and highly differentiated approaches to developing marketing strategies for their clients in the health care industry.[19]

The creation of cross-divisional, or cross-functional teams often implies that a firm has implemented some form of matrix structure. As suggested in Chapter 4, a **matrix structure** exists when individuals in a firm have two or more "bosses" simultaneously. Thus, for example, if a person from one of WPP's advertising agencies is assigned temporarily to a cross-divisional team, that person has two bosses: the head of the temporary team and the boss back in the advertising agency. Managing two bosses simultaneously can be very challenging, especially when they have conflicting interests. And as we will see in Chapter 8, the interests of these multiple bosses *will* often conflict.

A particularly important form of the cross-divisional or cross-functional team exists when this team is relieved of all other responsibilities in the firm and focuses all its attention on developing a new innovative product or service. The best-known example of this approach to developing a differentiated product occurred at the Lockheed Corporation during the 1950s and 1960s when small groups of engineers were put on very focused teams to develop sophisticated and top secret military aircraft. These teams would have a section of the Lockheed facility dedicated to their efforts and designated as off-limits to almost all other employees. The joke was that these intensive creative efforts were so engaging that members of these teams actually would forget to shower—hence the name **"skunk works."** Skunk works have been used by numerous firms to focus the creative energy required to develop and introduce highly differentiated products.[20]

Management Controls and Implementing Product Differentiation

The first two management controls helpful for implementing product differentiation listed in Table 5.3—broad decision-making guidelines and managerial freedom within those guidelines—often go together, even though they sound somewhat contradictory. These potential contradictions are discussed in the Strategy in the Emerging Enterprise feature. Managing these contradictions is one of the central challenges of firms looking to implement product differentiation strategies.

Broad decision-making guidelines help bring order to what otherwise might be a chaotic decision-making process. When managers have no constraints in their decision making, they can make decisions that are disconnected from each other and inconsistent with a firm's overall mission and objectives. This results in decisions that are either not implemented or not implemented well.

However, if these decision-making guidelines become too narrow, they can stifle creativity within a firm. As was suggested earlier, a firm's ability to differen-

Strategy in the Emerging Enterprise

*I*n the 1950s, a well-known economist named Joseph Schumpeter suggested that only very large and profitable companies have the resources necessary to invest in creating new and highly innovative products and services. His conclusion suggested that the social evils caused by economic power being concentrated in the hands of a relatively few large and powerful organizations was simply the price society had to pay for innovations that could benefit consumers.

The economic history of the last 30 years or so suggests that one of Schumpeter's key assumptions—that only large firms can afford to be innovative—is wrong. Indeed, over this time period it is clear that a great deal of innovation has occurred through the creation of entrepreneurial firms. Firms such as Dell, Microsoft, Intel, Apple, Home Depot, Cisco, Gateway, Sun, Office Depot, Nike, Oracle, PeopleSoft, Foot Locker, Amazon.com, and Starbucks have all been sources of major innovations in their industries, and all were begun as entrepreneurial ventures in the last 35 years. Indeed, given the impact of these and other entrepreneurial ventures on the worldwide economy during this time period, it is possible to call the last 30 years the "era of the entrepreneur."

What is it about entrepreneurial firms that enables them to develop innovations that sometimes come to dominate a market? Some scholars have suggested that the small size and

Can Only Small Firms Be Innovative?

lack of resources that characterize entrepreneurial start-ups, far from limiting their innovativeness, actually facilitate innovation.

For example, entrepreneurial firms have relatively little to lose when engaging in innovation. If the market accepts their innovation, great; if it doesn't, they can move on to the next innovation. Established firms, however, may have a significant stake in an older technology, an older distribution system, or an older type of customer. Established firms may be unwilling to cannibalize the sales of their current products for new and innovative products.

Moreover, small entrepreneurial firms have relatively few bureaucratic

controls. Information and ideas flow freely in these organizations. Such information flow tends to facilitate innovation. Larger firms, in contrast, have usually installed numerous bureaucratic controls that impede cross-functional communication, and thus slow innovation.

Indeed, some have even argued that the types of people who are attracted to small entrepreneurial firms tend to be more innovative than those who are attracted to larger, more stable companies. People who are comfortable with risk-seeking and creativity may be attracted to an entrepreneurial firm, whereas those who are less comfortable with risk-seeking and creativity may be attracted to larger, more stable firms.

Whatever the reasons, many large firms have come to realize that they cannot afford to be "out innovated" and "outmaneuvered" by entrepreneurial start-ups. In response, larger firms have begun to adopt policies and procedures that try to create the kind of innovativeness and creativity one often sees in entrepreneurial firms. Some firms—such as 3M (see Table 5.4)—have been quite successful in this effort. Others have been less successful.

Sources: C. Christensen (1997). *The innovator's dilemma.* Boston: Harvard Business School Press; J. Schumpeter (1942). *Capitalism, socialism, and democracy.* New York: Harper and Rowe; T. Zenger and E. Rasmusen (1990). "Diseconomies of scale in employment contracts." *Journal of Law, Economics, and Organization,* 6, pp. 65–98.

tiate its products is limited only by its creativity. Thus, decision guidelines must be narrow enough to ensure that the decisions made are consistent with a firm's mission and objectives. Yet, these guidelines also must be broad enough so that managerial creativity is not destroyed. In well-managed firms implementing product differentiation strategies, as long as managerial decisions fall within the broad decision-making guidelines in a firm, managers have the right—in fact, are expected—to make creative decisions.

Table 5.4   **Guiding Innovative Principles at 3M***

1. **Vision.**   Declare the importance of innovation; make it part of the company's self-image.
"Our efforts to encourage and support innovation are proof that we really do intend to achieve our vision of ourselves. . . that we intend to become what we want to be. . . as a business and as creative individuals."

2. **Foresight.**   Find out where technologies and markets are going. Identify articulated and unarticulated needs of customers.
"If you are working on a next-generation medical imaging device, you'll probably talk to radiologists, but you might also sit down with people who enhance images from interplanetary space probes."

3. **Stretch goals.**   Set goals that will make you and the organization stretch to make quantum improvements. Although many projects are pursued, place your biggest bets on those that change the basis of competition and redefine the industry.
"We have a number of stretch goals at 3M. The first states that we will drive 30 percent of all sales from products introduced in the past 4 years. . . . To establish a sense of urgency, we've recently added another goal, which is that we want 10 percent of our sales to come from products that have been in the market for just 1 year. . . . Innovation is time sensitive . . . you need to move quickly."

4. **Empowerment.**   Hire good people and trust them, delegate responsibilities, provide slack resources, and get out of the way. Be tolerant of initiative and the mistakes that occur because of that initiative.
"William McKnight [a former chairman of 3M] came up with one way to institutionalize a tolerance of individual effort. He said that all technical employees could devote 15 percent of their time to a project of their own invention. In other words, they could manage themselves for 15 percent of the time. . . . The number is not so important as the message, which is this: The system has some slack in it. If you have a good idea, and the commitment to squirrel away time to work on it and the raw nerve to skirt your lab manager's expressed desires, then go for it.
"Put another way, we want to institutionalize a bit of rebellion in our labs. We can't have all our people off totally on their own . . . we do believe in discipline . . . but at the same time 3M management encourages a healthy disrespect for 3M management. This is not the sort of thing we publicize in our annual report, but the stories we tell—with relish—are frequently about 3Mers who have circumvented their supervisors and succeeded. We also recognize that when you let people follow their own lead . . . everyone doesn't wind up at the same place. You can't ask people to have unique visions and march in lockstep. Some people are very precise, detail-oriented people . . . and others are fuzzy thinkers and visionaries . . . and this is exactly what we want."

5. **Communications.**   Open, extensive exchanges according to ground rules in forums that are present for sharing ideas and where networking is each individual's responsibility. Multiple methods for sharing information are necessary.
"When innovators communicate with each other, you can leverage their discoveries. This is critically important because it allows companies to get the maximum return on their substantial investments in new technologies. It also acts as a stimulus to further innovation. Indeed, we believe that the ability to combine and transfer technologies is as important as the original discovery of a technology."

6. **Rewards and recognition.**   Emphasize individual recognition more than monetary rewards through peer recognition and by choice of managerial or technical promotion routes. "Innovation is an intensely human activity."
"I've laid out six elements of 3M's corporate culture that contribute to a tradition of innovation: vision, foresight, stretch goals, empowerment, communication, and recognition. . . . The list is . . . too orderly. Innovation at 3M is anything but orderly. It is sensible, in that our efforts are directed at reaching our goals, but the organization . . . and the process . . . and sometimes the people can be chaotic. We are managing in chaos, and this is the right way to manage if you want innovation. It's been said that the competition never knows what we are going to come up with next. The fact is, neither do we."

*As expressed by W. Coyne (1996). *Building a tradition of innovation.* The Fifth U.K. Innovation Lecture, Department of Trade and Industry, London. Cited in Van de Ven et al. (1999), pp. 198–200.

A firm that has worked hard to reach this balance between chaos and control is 3M. In an effort to provide guiding principles that define the range of acceptable decisions at 3M, its senior managers have developed a set of innovating principles. These are presented in Table 5.4 and define the boundaries of innovative chaos at

3M. Within these boundaries, managers and engineers are expected to be creative and innovative in developing highly differentiated products and services.[21]

Another firm that has managed this tension well is British Airways (BA). BA has extensive training programs to teach its flight attendants how to provide world-class service, especially for its business-class customers. This training constitutes standard operating procedures that give purpose and structure to BA's efforts to provide a differentiated service in the highly competitive airline industry. Interestingly, however, BA also trains its flight attendants in when to violate these standard policies and procedures. By recognizing that no set of management controls can ever anticipate all the special situations that can occur when providing service to customers, BA empowers its employees to meet specific customer needs. This enables BA to have both a clearly defined product differentiation strategy and the flexibility to adjust this strategy as the situation dictates.[22]

Firms can also facilitate the implementation of a product differentiation strategy by adopting a **policy of experimentation**. Such a policy exists when firms are committed to engaging in several related product differentiation efforts simultaneously. That these product differentiation efforts are related suggests that a firm has some vision about how a particular market is likely to unfold over time. However, that there are several of these product differentiation efforts occurring simultaneously suggests that a firm is not overly committed to a particular narrow vision about how a market is going to evolve. Rather, several different experiments facilitate the exploration of different futures in a marketplace. Indeed, successful experiments can actually help define the future evolution of a marketplace.

Consider, for example, Charles Schwab, the innovative discount broker. In the face of increased competition from full-service and Internet-based brokerage firms, Schwab engaged in a series of experiments to discover the next generation of products it could offer to its customers and the different ways it could differentiate those products. Schwab investigated software for simplifying online mutual fund selection, online futures trading, and online company research. It also formed an exploratory alliance with Goldman Sachs to evaluate the possibility of enabling Schwab customers to trade in initial public offerings. Not all of Schwab's experiments led to the introduction of highly differentiated products. For example, based on some experimental investments, Schwab decided not to enter the credit card market. However, by experimenting with a range of possible product differentiation moves, it was able to develop a range of new products for the fast-changing financial services industry.[23]

Compensation Policies and Implementing Product Differentiation Strategies

The compensation policies used to implement product differentiation listed in Table 5.3 very much complement the organizational structure and managerial controls listed in that table. For example, a policy of experimentation has little impact on the ability of a firm to implement product differentiation strategies if every time an innovative experiment fails individuals are punished for taking risks. Thus, compensation policies that reward risk-taking and celebrate a creative flair help to enable a firm to implement its product differentiation strategy.

Consider, for example, Nordstrom. Nordstrom is a department store that celebrates the risk-taking and creative flair of its associates as they try to satisfy their customers' needs. The story is often told of a Nordstrom sales associate who allowed a customer to return a set of tires to the store because she wasn't satisfied with them. What makes this story interesting—whether or not it is true—is that

Nordstrom doesn't sell tires. But this sales associate felt empowered to make what was obviously a risky decision, and this decision is celebrated within Nordstrom as an example of the kind of service that Nordstrom's customers should expect.

The last compensation policy listed in Table 5.3 is multidimensional performance measurement. In implementing a cost leadership strategy, compensation should focus on providing appropriate incentives for managers and employees to reduce costs. Various forms of cash payments, stock, and stock options can all be tied to the attainment of specific cost goals, and thus can be used to create incentives for realizing cost advantages. Similar techniques can be used to create incentives for helping a firm implement its product differentiation advantage. However, because the implementation of a product differentiation strategy generally involves the integration of multiple business functions, often through the use of product development teams, compensation schemes designed to help implement this strategy must generally recognize its multifunctional character.

Thus, rather than focusing only on a single dimension of performance, these firms often examine employee performance along multiple dimensions simultaneously. Examples of such dimensions include not only a product's sales and profitability, but customer satisfaction, an employee's willingness to cooperate with other businesses and functions within a firm, an employee's ability to effectively facilitate cross-divisional and cross-functional teams, and an employee's ability to engage in creative decision making.

Can Firms Implement Product Differentiation and Cost Leadership Simultaneously?

The arguments developed in Chapter 4 and in this chapter suggest that cost leadership and product differentiation business strategies, under certain conditions, can both create sustained competitive advantages. Given the beneficial impact of both strategies on a firm's competitive position, an important question becomes: Can a single firm simultaneously implement both strategies? After all, if each separately can improve a firm's performance, wouldn't it be better for a firm to implement both?

No: These Strategies Cannot Be Implemented Simultaneously

A quick comparison of the organizational requirements for the successful implementation of cost leadership strategies and product differentiation strategies presented in Table 5.5 summarizes one perspective on the question of whether these strategies can be implemented simultaneously. In this view, the organizational requirements of these strategies are essentially contradictory. Cost leadership requires simple reporting relationships, whereas product differentiation requires cross-divisional/cross-functional linkages. Cost leadership requires intense labor supervision, whereas product differentiation requires less intense supervision of creative employees. Cost leadership requires rewards for cost reduction, whereas product differentiation requires rewards for creative flair. It is reasonable to ask, "Can a single firm combine these multiple contradictory skills and abilities?"

Some have argued that firms that attempt to implement both strategies will end up doing neither well. This logic leads to the curve pictured in Figure 5.2. This figure suggests that there are often only two ways to earn superior economic performance within a single industry: (1) by selling high-priced products and gaining small market share (product differentiation) or (2) by selling low-priced products

Table 5.5 **The Organizational Requirements for Implementing Cost Leadership and Product Differentiation Strategies**

Cost leadership	Product differentiation
Organizational structure	**Organizational structure**
1. Few layers in the reporting structure	1. Cross-divisional/cross-functional product development teams
2. Simple reporting relationships	2. Willingness to explore new structures to exploit new opportunities
3. Small corporate staff	3. Isolated pockets of intense creative efforts
4. Focus on narrow range of business functions	
Management control systems	**Management control systems**
1. Tight cost-control systems	1. Broad decision-making guidelines
2. Quantitative cost goals	2. Managerial freedom within guidelines
3. Close supervision of labor, raw material, inventory, and other costs	3. Policy of experimentation
4. A cost leadership philosophy	
Compensation policies	**Compensation policies**
1. Reward for cost reduction	1. Rewards for risk-taking, not punishment for failures
2. Incentives for all employees to be involved in cost reduction	2. Rewards for creative flair
	3. Multidimensional performance measurement

and gaining large market share (cost leadership). Firms that do not make this choice of strategies (medium price, medium market share) or that attempt to implement both strategies will fail. These firms are said to be "stuck in the middle."[24]

Yes: These Strategies Can Be Implemented Simultaneously

More recent work contradicts assertions about being "stuck in the middle." This work suggests that firms that are successful in both cost leadership and product differentiation can often expect to gain a sustained competitive advantage. This advantage reflects at least two processes.

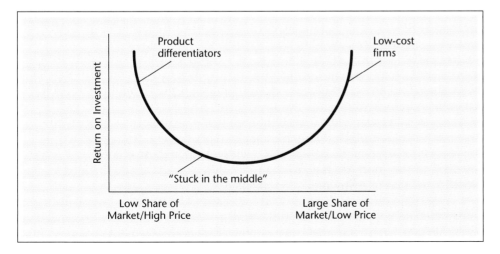

Figure 5.2 Simultaneous Implementation of Cost Leadership and Product Differentiation Competitive Strategies: Being "Stuck in the Middle"

Source: Adapted with the permission of the Free Press, a Division of Simon & Schuster Adult Publishing Group, from *Competitive strategy: Techniques for Analyzing Industries and Competitors* by Michael E. Porter. Copyright © 1980, 1998 by The Free Press. All rights reserved.

Differentiation, Market Share, and Low-Cost Leadership

First, firms that are able to successfully differentiate their products and services are likely to see an increase in their volume of sales. This is especially the case if the basis of product differentiation is attractive to a large number of potential customers. Thus, product differentiation can lead to increased volumes of sales. It has already been established (in Chapter 4) that an increased volume of sales can lead to economies of scale, learning, and other forms of cost reduction. So, successful product differentiation can, in turn, lead to cost reductions and a cost leadership position.[25]

This is the situation that best describes McDonald's. McDonald's has traditionally followed a product differentiation strategy, emphasizing cleanliness, consistency, and fun in its fast-food outlets. Over time, McDonald's has used its differentiated product to become the market share leader in the fast-food industry. This market position has enabled it to reduce its costs, so that it is now the cost leader in fast foods as well. Thus, McDonald's level of profitability depends both on its product differentiation strategy and its low-cost strategy. Either one of these two strategies by itself would be difficult to overcome; together they give McDonald's a very costly-to-imitate competitive advantage.[26]

Managing Organizational Contradictions

Product differentiation can lead to high market share and low costs. It may also be the case that some firms develop special skills in managing the contradictions that are part of simultaneously implementing low-cost and product differentiation strategies. Some recent research on automobile manufacturing helps describe these special skills.[27] Traditional thinking in automotive manufacturing was that plants could either reduce manufacturing costs by speeding up the assembly line or increase the quality of the cars they made by slowing the line, emphasizing team-based production, and so forth. In general, it was thought that plants could not simultaneously build low-cost/high-quality (i.e., low cost *and* highly differentiated) automobiles.

Several researchers at the Massachusetts Institute of Technology examined this traditional wisdom. They began by developing rigorous measures of the cost and quality performance of automobile plants and then applied these measures to over 70 auto plants throughout the world that assembled mid-size sedans. What they discovered was six plants in the entire world that had, at the time this research was done, very low costs *and* very high quality.[28]

In examining what made these six plants different from other auto plants, the researchers focused on a broad range of manufacturing policies, management practices, and cultural variables. Three important findings emerged. First, these six plants had the best manufacturing technology hardware available—robots, laser-guided paint machines, and so forth. However, because many of the plants in the study had these same technologies, manufacturing technology by itself was not enough to make these six plants special. In addition, policies and procedures at these plants implemented a range of highly participative, group-oriented management techniques, including participative management, team production, and total quality management. As important, employees in these plants had a sense of loyalty and commitment toward the plant they worked for—a belief that they would be treated fairly by their plant managers.

What this research shows is that firms *can* simultaneously implement cost leadership and product differentiation strategies if they learn how to manage the contradictions inherent in these two strategies. The management of these contradictions, in turn, depends on socially complex relations among employees, between employees and the technology they use, and between employees and the firm for which they work. These relations are not only valuable (because they enable a firm to implement cost leadership and differentiation strategies) but also socially complex and thus likely to be costly to imitate and a source of sustained competitive advantage.

Recently, many scholars have backed away from the original "stuck in the middle" arguments and now suggest that low-cost firms must have competitive levels of product differentiation to survive, and that product differentiation firms must have competitive levels of cost to survive.[29] For example, the fashion design company Versace—the ultimate product differentiating firm—has recently hired a new CEO and controller to help control its costs.[30]

Product Differentiation in an International Context

The tension that sometimes exists between cost leadership and product differentiation strategies domestically can also exist internationally. Here, this tension is manifest by the need for firms to simultaneously be responsive to local market needs while still integrating operations across multiple countries. On the one hand, local responsiveness enables a firm to implement a product differentiation strategy internationally, and failure to do so can lead to marketing blunders, some of which are described in the Global Perspectives feature. On the other hand, global integration can enable a firm to gain the cost advantages associated with international operations, as described in Chapter 4.

Traditionally, it has been thought that firms had to choose between local responsiveness and international integration. For example, firms such as CIBA-Geigy (a Swiss chemical company), Nestlé (a Swiss food company), and Philips (a Dutch consumer electronics firm) have chosen to emphasize local responsiveness. Nestlé, for example, owns nearly 8,000 brand names worldwide. However, of those 8,000 brands, only 750 are registered in more than 1 country, and only 80 are registered in more than 10 countries. Nestlé adjusts its product attributes to the needs of local consumers, adopts brand names that resonate with those consumers, and builds its brands for long-run profitability by country. For example, in the United States, Nestlé's condensed milk carries the brand name "Carnation" (obtained through the acquisition of the Carnation Company); in Asia, this same product carries the brand name "Bear Brand." Nestlé delegates brand management authority to country managers, who can (and do) adjust traditional marketing and manufacturing strategies in accordance with local tastes and preferences. For example, Nestlé's Thailand management group dropped traditional coffee-marketing efforts that focused on taste, aroma, and stimulation and instead began selling coffee as a drink that promotes relaxation and romance. This marketing strategy resonated with Thais experiencing urban stress, and it prompted Nestlé coffee sales in Thailand to jump dramatically.[31]

Of course, all this local responsiveness comes at a cost. Firms that emphasize local responsiveness are often unable to realize the full economic value possible by integrating their operations across country borders. Numerous firms have focused on appropriating this economic value and have pursued a more integrated international strategy. Examples of such firms include IBM, General Electric, Toyota Motor Corporation, and most major pharmaceutical firms, to name just a few.

Internationally integrated firms locate business functions and activities in countries that have a comparative advantage in these functions or activities. For

Global Perspectives

*L*ack of local responsiveness has led to some well-known—and sometimes quite funny—international product differentiation blunders. For example, General Motors once introduced the Chevrolet Nova to South America, even though "No va" in Spanish means "It won't go." When Coca-Cola was first introduced in China, it was translated into "Ke-kou-ke-la," which turns out to mean either "bite the wax tadpole" or "female horse stuffed with wax," depending on which dialect was being spoken. Coca-Cola reintroduced its product with the name "Ke-kou-ko-le," which roughly translates into "happiness in the mouth."

Coca-Cola is not the only beverage firm to run into problems internationally. Pepsi's slogan "Come alive with the Pepsi generation" was translated into "Pepsi will bring your ancestors back from the dead" in Taiwan. In Italy, a marketing campaign for Schweppes tonic water was translated into Schweppes toilet water—not a terribly appealing drink. Bacardi developed a fruity drink called "Pavian." Unfortunately, "Pavian" means baboon in German. Coors used its "Turn it loose" slogan when selling beer in Spain and Latin America.

International Marketing Blunders

Unfortunately, "Turn it loose" was translated into "Suffer from diarrhea."

Food companies have had similar problems. Kentucky Fried Chicken's slogan "Finger-lickin' good" translates into "eat your fingers off" in Chinese. In Arabic, the "Jolly Green Giant" translates into "Intimidating Green Ogre." Frank Perdue's famous catch phrase—"It takes a tough man to make a tender chicken"—takes on a slightly different meaning when translated into Spanish—: "It takes a sexually stimulated man to make a chicken

affectionate." And Gerber found that it was unable to sell its baby food—with pictures of cute babies on the jar—in Africa, because the tradition in Africa is to put pictures of what is inside the jar on the label. Think about it.

Other product differentiation blunders include Colgate's decision to introduce Cue toothpaste in France, even though Cue is the name of a French pornographic magazine; an American T-shirt manufacturer who wanted to print up T-shirts in Spanish that said "I saw the Pope" (el Papa) but instead printed up T-shirts that said "I saw the potato" (la papa); and Salem cigarettes, whose slogan "Salem—feeling free" translated into Japanese as "When smoking Salem, you feel so refreshed that your mind seems to be free and empty." What were they smoking?

However, of all these marketing blunders, perhaps none tops Electrolux—a Scandinavian vacuum cleaner manufacturer. Although its marketing slogan for the U.S. market does rhyme—"Nothing sucks like an Electrolux"—it doesn't really communicate what the firm had in mind.

Source: Courtesy of Mobility Services International. www.msimobility.com.

example, the production of components for most consumer electronics is research intensive, capital intensive, and subject to significant economies of scale. To manage component manufacturing successfully, most internationally integrated consumer electronics firms have located their component operations in technologically advanced countries such as the United States and Japan. However, because the assembly of these components into consumer products is labor intensive, most internationally integrated consumer electronics firms have located their assembly operations in countries with relatively low labor costs, including Mexico and China.

Of course, one of the costs of locating different business functions and activities in different geographic locations is that these different functions and activities must be coordinated and integrated. Operations in one country might very efficiently manufacture certain components. However, if the wrong components are shipped to the assembly location, or if the right components are shipped at the wrong time, any advantages that could have been obtained from exploiting the comparative advantages of different countries can be lost. Shipping costs can also reduce the returns on international integration.

To ensure that different operations in internationally integrated firms are appropriately coordinated, these firms typically manufacture more standardized products, using more standardized components, than do locally responsive firms. Standardization enables these firms to realize substantial economies of scale and other advantages, but it can limit their ability to respond to the specific needs of individual markets. When international product standards exist, as in the personal computer industry and the semiconductor chip industry, such standard- ization is not problematic. Also, when local responsiveness requires only a few modifications of a standardized product (e.g., changing the shape of the electric plug or changing the color of a product), international integration can be very effective. However, when local responsiveness requires a great deal of local knowledge and product modifications, international integration can create prob- lems for a firm pursuing an international product differentiation strategy.

Recently, it has been suggested that the traditional trade-off between interna- tional integration and local responsiveness can be replaced by a **transnational strategy** that exploits all the advantages of both international integration and local responsiveness.[32] Firms implementing a transnational strategy treat their international operations as an integrated network of distributed and interdependent resources and capabilities. In this context, a firm's operations in each country are not simply indepen- dent activities attempting to respond to local market needs; they are also repositories of ideas, technologies, and management approaches that the firm might be able to use and apply in its other international operations. Put differently, operations in different countries can be thought of as "experiments" in the creation of new resources and capabilities. Some of these experiments will work and generate important new resources and capabilities; others will fail to have such benefits for a firm.

When a particular country operation develops a competence in manufactur- ing a particular product, providing a particular service, or engaging in a particu- lar activity that can be used by other country operations, the country operation with this competence can achieve international economies of scale by becoming the firm's primary supplier of this product, service, or activity. In this way, local responsiveness is retained as country managers constantly search for new com- petencies that enable them to maximize profits in their particular markets, and international integration and economies are realized as country operations that have developed unique competencies become suppliers for all other country operations.

SUMMARY

Product differentiation exists when customers perceive a particular firm's products to be more valuable than other firms' products. Although differentiation can have several bases, it is, in the end, always a matter of customer perception. Bases of product differentiation include: (1) attributes of the products or services a firm sells (including product features, product complexity, the timing of product introduction, and location); (2) relations between a firm and its customers (including product customization, consumer marketing, and repu- tation); and (3) links within and between firms (including links between functions, links with other firms, a firm's product mix, its distribution system, and its level of service and support). However, in the end, product differentiation is limited only by the creativity of a firm's managers.

Product differentiation is valuable to the extent that it enables a firm to set its prices higher than what it would otherwise be able to. Each of the bases of product differentiation identified can be used to neutralize environmental threats and exploit environmental opportunities. The rarity and imitability of bases of product differentiation vary. Highly imitable bases of product differentiation include product features. Somewhat imitable bases include product mix, links with other firms, product customization, and consumer marketing. Costly-to-imitate bases of product differentiation include linking business functions, timing, location, reputation, and service and support.

The implementation of a product differentiation strategy involves management of organizational structure, management controls, and compensation policies. Structurally, it is not unusual for firms implementing product differentiation strategies to use cross-divisional and cross-functional teams, together with teams that are focused exclusively on a particular product differentiation effort, so-called "skunk works." Managerial controls that provide free managerial decision making within broad decision-making guidelines can be helpful in implementing product differentiation strategies, as is a policy of experimentation. Finally, compensation policies that tolerate risk-taking and a creative flair and that measure employee performance along multiple dimensions simultaneously can also be helpful in implementing product differentiation strategies.

A variety of organizational attributes is required to successfully implement a product differentiation strategy. Some have argued that contradictions between these organizational characteristics and those required to implement a cost leadership strategy mean that firms that attempt to do both will perform poorly. More recent research has noted the relationship between product differentiation, market share, and low costs and has observed that some firms have learned to manage the contradictions between cost leadership and product differentiation.

These same tensions can manifest themselves for firms pursuing international strategies. Product differentiation, internationally, requires responsiveness to local markets; cost leadership, internationally, requires a firm to integrate its global operations. Some authors have suggested that a transnational strategy can enable a firm to be both locally responsive and globally integrated.

CHALLENGE QUESTIONS

1. Although cost leadership is perhaps less relevant for firms pursuing product differentiation, costs are not totally irrelevant. What advice about costs would you give a firm pursuing a product differentiation strategy?

2. Product features are often the focus of product differentiation efforts. Yet product features are among the easiest-to-imitate bases of product differentiation and thus among the least likely bases of product differentiation to be a source of sustained competitive advantage. Does this seem paradoxical to you? If no, why not? If yes, how can you resolve this paradox?

3. What are the strengths and weaknesses of using regression analysis and hedonic prices to describe the bases of product differentiation?

4. Chamberlin used the term "monopolistic competition" to describe firms pursuing a product differentiation strategy in a competitive industry. However, it is usually the case that firms that operate in monopolies are less efficient and less competitive than those that operate in more competitive settings (see Chapter 3). Does this same problem exist for firms operating in a "monopolistic competition" context? Why or why not?

5. Implementing a product differentiation strategy seems to require just the right mix of control and creativity. How do you know if a firm has the right mix? Is it possible to evaluate this mix before problems associated with being out of balance manifest themselves? If yes, how? If no, why not?

6. A firm with a highly differentiated product can increase the volume of its sales. Increased sales volumes can enable a firm to reduce its costs. High volumes with low costs can lead a firm to have very high profits, some of which the firm can use to invest in further differentiating its products. What advice would you give a firm whose competition is enjoying this product differentiation and cost leadership advantage?

7. What kinds of organizational and management problems is a firm trying to implement a transnational strategy (as a way to resolve conflicts between product differentiation and cost leadership strategies internationally) likely to face? (Hint: See Table 5.5.)

8. Is a firm implementing a transnational strategy just "stuck in the middle" internationally? If yes, why? If no, why not?

PROBLEM SET

1. For each of the listed products, describe at least two ways they are differentiated.
(a) Ben & Jerry's ice cream
(b) The Hummer H2
(c) The X-Games
(d) The Pussycat Dolls
(e) The movies *Animal House* and *Caddyshack*
(f) Frederick's of Hollywood
(g) Taco Bell

2. Which, if any, of the bases of product differentiation in question #1 are likely to be sources of sustained competitive advantage? Why?

3. Suppose you obtained the following regression results, where the starred (*) coefficients are statistically significant. What could you say about the bases of product differentiation in this market? (Hint: A regression coefficient is statistically significant when it is so large that its effect is very unlikely to have emerged by chance.)

House Price = $125,000* + $15,000* (More than 3 bedrooms)
+ $18,000* (More than 3,500 square feet)
+ $150 (Has plumbing) + $180 (Has lawn)
+ $17,000* (Lot larger than 1/2 acre)

How much would you expect to pay for a 4-bedroom, 3,800-square-foot house on a one-acre lot? How much for a 4-bedroom, 2,700-square-foot house on a quarter-acre lot? Do these results say anything about the sustainability of competitive advantages in this market?

4. Which of the following management controls and compensation policies is consistent with implementing cost leadership? with product differentiation? with both cost leadership and product differentiation? with neither cost leadership nor product differentiation?

(a) Firm-wide stock options

(b) Compensation that rewards each function separately for meeting its own objectives

(c) A detailed financial budget plan

(d) A document that describes, in detail, how the innovation process will unfold in a firm

(e) A policy that reduces the compensation of a manager who introduces a product that fails in the market

(f) A policy that reduces the compensation of a manager who introduces several products that fail in the market

(g) The creation of a purchasing council to discuss how different business units can reduce their costs

5. Identify three industries or markets that have the volume–profit relationship described in Figure 5.2. Which firms in this industry are implementing cost leadership strategies? Which are implementing product differentiation strategies? Are any firms "stuck in the middle"? If yes, which ones? If no, why not? Are any firms implementing both cost leadership and product differentiation strategies? If yes, which ones? If no, why not?

END NOTES

1. See Ono, Y. (1996). "Who really makes that cute little beer? You'd be surprised." *Wall Street Journal*, April 15, pp. A1 +. Since this 1996 article, some of these craft beer companies have changed the way they manufacture the beers to be more consistent with the image they are trying to project.
2. See Porter, M. E. (1980). *Competitive strategy*. New York: Free Press, and Caves R. E., and P. Williamson (1985). "What is product differentiation, really?" *Journal of Industrial Organization Economics*, 34, pp. 113–132.
3. Lieberman, M. B., and D. B. Montgomery (1988). "First-mover advantages." *Strategic Management Journal*, 9, pp. 41–58.
4. Carroll, P. (1993). *Big blues: The unmaking of IBM*. New York: Crown Publishers.
5. These ideas were first developed in Hotelling, H. (1929). "Stability in competition." *Economic Journal*, 39, pp. 41–57; Ricardo, D. (1817). *Principles of political economy and taxation*. London: J. Murray.
6. See Gunther, M. (1998). "Disney's Call of the Wild." *Fortune*, April 13, pp. 120–124.
7. The idea of reputation is explained in Klein, B., and K. Leffler (1981). "The role of market forces in assuring contractual performance." *Journal of Political Economy*, 89, pp. 615–641.
8. See Robichaux M., (1995). "It's a book! A T-shirt! A toy! No, just MTV trying to be Disney." *Wall Street Journal*, February 8, pp. A1 +.
9. See Henderson, R., and I. Cockburn (1994). "Measuring competence? Exploring firm effects in pharmaceutical research." *Strategic Management Journal*, 15, pp. 63–84.
10. See Johnson, R. (1999). "Speed sells." *Fortune*, April 12, pp. 56–70. In fact, NASCAR fans either love or hate Jeff Gordon.
11. Kotler, P. (1986). *Principles of marketing*. Upper Saddle River, NJ: Prentice Hall.
12. Porter, M. E., and R. Wayland (1991). "Coca-Cola vs. Pepsi-Cola and the soft drink industry." Harvard Business School Case No. 9-391-179.
13. Ghemawat, P. (1993). "Sears, Roebuck and Company: The merchandise group." Harvard Business School Case No. 9-794-039.
14. Welsh, J. (1998). "Office-paper firms pursue elusive goal: Brand loyalty." *Wall Street Journal*, September 21, p. B6.
15. See White, E., and K. Palmer (2003). "U.S. retailing 101." *Wall Street Journal*, August 12, pp. B1 +.
16. See Hennart, J. F. (1988). "A transaction cost theory of equity joint ventures." *Strategic Management Journal*, 9, pp. 361–374.
17. Deutsch, C. H. (1991). "How is it done? For a small fee. . ." *New York Times*, October 27, p. 25; Armstrong, L. (1991). "Services: The customer as 'Honored Guest'." *BusinessWeek*, October 25, p. 104.
18. See Yoffie, D. (1994). "Swissair's alliances (A)." Harvard Business School Case No. 9-794-152.
19. "WPP—Integrating icons." Harvard Business School Case No. 9-396-249.
20. Orosz, J. J. (2002). "Big funds need a 'Skunk Works' to stir ideas." *Chronicle of Philanthropy*, June 27, p. 47.
21. Van de Ven, A., D. Polley, R. Garud, and S. Venkatraman (1999). *The innovation journey*. New York: Oxford, pp. 198–200.
22. Prokesch, S. (1995). "Competing on customer service: An interview with British Airways' Sir Colin Marshall." *Harvard Business Review*, November–December, p. 101.
23. Position, L. L. (1999). "David S. Pottruck." *BusinessWeek*, September 27, EB 51.
24. Porter, M. E. (1980). *Competitive strategy*. New York: Free Press.
25. Hill, C. W. L. (1988). "Differentiation versus low cost or differentiation and low cost: A contingency framework." *Academy of Management Review*, 13(3), pp. 401–412.
26. Gibson, R. (1995). "Food: At McDonald's, new recipes for buns, eggs." *Wall Street Journal*, June 13, p. B1.
27. Originally discussed in the Research Made Relevant feature in Chapter 3.
28. Womack, J. P., D. I. Jones, and D. Roos (1990). *The machine that changed the world*. New York: Rawson.
29. Porter, M. E. (1985). *Competitive advantage*. New York: Free Press.
30. Agins, T., and A. Galloni (2003). "Facing a squeeze, Versace struggles to trim the fat." *Wall Street Journal*, September 30, pp. A1 +.
31. Rapoport, C. (1994). "Nestlé's brand building machine." *Fortune*, September 19, pp. 147–156.
32. See Bartlett, C. A., and S. Ghoshal (1989). *Managing across borders: The transnational solution*. Boston: Harvard Business School Press.

Case 2-1: Samsung Electronics*

Introduction

Kun Hee Lee, chairman of the Samsung Group, contemplated his company's strategy while sitting in the basement office of his home. His office had a 100-inch screen on the wall, and in front of the screen there was a short desk, just one foot in height. Lee spent much of his day in this room, studying the strategies of his competitors and overseeing multibillion-dollar investment decisions. Beside his desk were hundreds of DVDs and videos, many examining his competitors' histories and strategies. Every new product made by Samsung and its competitors sat along the walls. Trained as an engineer, Lee eagerly picked apart every product, examining its design and quality of manufacturing.[1]

As he sat next to his low desk and sipped a cup of Korean green tea, Lee wondered whether his legion of Samsung employees was following his stern advice to always demand superiority in product design and process efficiency. He had grave concerns about complacency in his company. He remembered how he mentioned in a senior management meeting: "To an outsider, reprimanding a manager whose division racked up [billions of dollars] in profit might seem bizarre. But I don't see it that way. Our abilities and efforts did play a role in our success, but we must realize that most of it came from the leading companies' negligence, pure luck, and our predecessors' sacrifice."[2]

Under Lee's leadership, Samsung had risen to become the world's leading memory producer for all types of PCs, digital cameras, game players, and other electronics products. As recently as 1987, Samsung was a bit player, years behind its key Japanese rivals. But by 2003, Samsung's memory division towered over its Japanese rivals in both size and profits. Samsung used the earnings from its memory division to invest in other technology products. By 2003, with the help of mobile phones, liquid crystal displays, and memory products, Samsung had generated the second-largest net profit of any electronics company outside of the United States.

In spite of Samsung's current success, Lee now worried about mainland Chinese companies that were beginning to attack Samsung in the same way that Samsung had attacked the Japanese companies 20 years earlier. The memory chip industry was expected to experience a cyclical downturn in 2005, and while Samsung had survived the past two downturns with the best performance in the industry, some outside observers believed that the Chinese entry would fundamentally change industry conditions in the years ahead.

Memory Industry

Over the previous five decades, the semiconductor industry had grown in economic importance. In 2000, the industry enjoyed $200 billion in sales, and the industry grew by an average of 16% per year since 1960.[3] Semiconductor products were classified into two broad categories of chips: memory and logic. Logic chips were used to process information and control processes, and memory chips stored

* This case was prepared by Professor Jordan I. Seigel and Professor James Jinho Chang, Yonsei University. HBS cases are developed solely as the basis for class discussion. Cases are not intended to serve as endorsements, sources of primary data, or illustrations of effective or ineffective management.

Copyright © 2005 President and Fellows of Harvard College. To order copies or request permission to reproduce materials, call 1-800-545-7685, write Harvard Business School Publishing, Boston, MA 02163, or go to http://www.hbsp.harvard.edu. No part of this publication may be reproduced, stored in a retrieval system, used in a spreadsheet, or transmitted in any form or by any means—electronic, mechanical, photocopying, recording, or otherwise—without the permission of Harvard Business School.

information. Memory chips were further classified into DRAM (Dynamic Random Access Memory), SRAM (Static RAM), and Flash. This case focuses on the global memory chip industry, which accounted for $33.7 billion in sales in 2003.

DRAMs accounted for just over half of the memory chip market in 2003. Historically, DRAMs were used mainly in PCs, but the share of DRAMs going to PCs declined from 80% to 67% between 1990 and 2003. Telecommunications and the consumer electronics market were growing consumers of DRAMs in 2003. Communications products such as mobile phones, switches, and hubs were predicted to grow from 3.5% to 7.9% of the DRAM market in 2008; TVs, set-top boxes, and game devices such as Playstation represented 7% of the market in 2003.

Among the other types of memory chips, SRAM and Flash memory accounted for 10% and 32% of industry sales, respectively, in 2003. SRAM was a type of buffer memory that facilitated computer processing and mobile phone functionality. Flash memory, which was the hot-growth area, was used heavily in digital cameras and mobile phones. While DRAMs lost data when power was turned off, Flash memory could continue to store data in the absence of a power source.

The memory industry contained powerful suppliers and price-conscious customers. With each generation of semiconductor equipment, the technology grew more complex and the number of suppliers became more concentrated. Only two or three main players, including Applied Materials, Tokyo Electron, and ASML, dominated key segments of the equipment market. Suppliers of memory raw materials would provide discounts of up to 5% for high-volume buyers. The customers were far more fragmented, with no single OEM controlling more than 20% of the global PC market in 2005. Memory represented 4% to 12% of material costs for an OEM PC producer, and 4% to 7% of material costs for a mobile phone producer. Because rivalry between PC producers was intense, and because the PC producers had to face price-conscious consumers, OEMs negotiated hard on price. It did, however, matter that defective memory could destroy their entire product's value. Because defective memory was hard to detect, OEMs would pay upwards of a 1% average price premium for a reliable supplier.[4]

In 2005, the industry experienced fierce rivalry and large-scale entry by Chinese firms. In late 2004, Samsung had announced a sharp drop in market prices going into 2005. The price drop was due partly to an increase in industry capacity and partly to a normal cyclical downturn. While Samsung succeeded in marketing new types of cutting-edge memory chips, Chinese competitors competing

in the older product lines were willing to sacrifice profits for market share. Whereas the cost of building a new fab had gone up from $200 million in 1985 to $3 billion in 2004, the Chinese firms were having little difficulty raising the money from local and international sources. The Chinese firms did face enormous difficulty in even beginning to produce frontier products because they lacked the necessary organizational experience and tacit knowledge required to master the design and production process. Still, with their easy access to outside finance and talented local engineers, the Chinese had real potential to build these skills over the next decade. In 2005, there were no effective substitutes that could even challenge DRAMs or Flash memory. Still, despite the largely theoretical benefits of new types of memory, memory based on nanotechnology was at least being contemplated. If new types of technology were ever created by industry start-ups, some outside observers believed that the industry incumbents would be locked into established designs and established production methodologies and would be too slow in reacting to the technological shift.

Semiconductor Production Process

A semiconductor was used to perform a desired function in an electronic device (either storing data or processing data). After designers had made a blueprint based on the intended function, the physical shape of the chip was transferred to a mask that could be used to create identical chips. Separately, a cylindrical silicon ingot was shaped to the desired diameter (in 2005, 12 inches), and the silicon ingot was further cut into wafers that were almost unimaginably thin (only 250 to 350 microns thick, thinner than a human hair). Next, companies like Samsung Electronics took the wafers and produced memory chips through a series of thermal, metallurgical, and chemical processing steps. In the course of this production process, billions of electronic circuits were defined within numerous individual chips (also called "dice") on the 12-inch wafer. The result of this production process was the creation of a matrix of rectangular chips on the wafer. Finally, the wafers were sawed into individual chips. Throughout the production process, the chips were tested for reliability.

One of the main tasks of the memory chip producer was to generate as many individual chips in one production step as possible while minimizing defective chips. To accomplish this task, producers made design and process improvements that would allow more electronic circuits to fit on ever-smaller chip sizes as well as ensure more uniformity in the manufacturing process.[5] Roughly once a decade, new technology had allowed memory chip producers to work with larger wafer sizes so that more chips could be cut in one production step. Moreover, memory chip producers invested in process technology so that fewer defective chips would be sent to the OEM purchaser.

Major Memory Competitors in 2005

This section lists Samsung's major competitors in the memory chip industry in 2005. (Companies are listed in alphabetical order.) The financial performance of Samsung and its publicly listed competitors is presented in Exhibit 1.

Elpida Memory, Inc.

Elpida—Japan's only remaining DRAM producer—was established as a joint venture between NEC and Hitachi in December 1999. In the three years after its establishment, Elpida suffered through a period of financial losses due to a DRAM market decline, as well as to a decision not to invest in new products and new product capacity as the market recovered. Subsequently, Elpida decided to focus on developing memory products for mobile devices and consumer electronics products. That way, it could try to sell primarily to Japanese customers who had, until then, bought memory chips from Samsung and Micron. In June 2004, Elpida announced that it would start construction on its second 12-inch wafer fab next to its current manufacturing facility in Hiroshima. The cost of the new facility was $4.5 billion, and Elpida partially financed the new facility through a $100 million investment from Intel, along with a public equity issue.

Hynix Semiconductor, Inc.

South Korea–based Hynix was founded in 1983 as Hyundai Electronics, and it changed its name in 2001 while separating from the financially distressed Hyundai Group. In the early 1990s, Hynix enjoyed some of the same cost advantages as its Korean competitor Samsung, but it lost the technological lead. Moreover, Hynix had trouble timing its capital investments to take advantage of market developments. In 1996, when the DRAM market began experiencing a cyclical decline, Samsung maintained the minimum capital expenditures needed to maintain smooth business operations, while Hynix dramatically increased its capital investments into the downturn. Hynix lost even more ground to Samsung in 1999 when the market began to expand dramatically. Samsung significantly increased its investment in fast response to market growth, while Hynix actually decreased its capital investment.[6] In

1999, Hyundai Electronics acquired LG Semiconductor, the semiconductor unit of LG Group. This acquisition loaded Hyundai Electronics with LG Semiconductor's enormous debt, which together with a cyclical industry downturn forced Hynix almost to the point of collapse in 2001–2002. A multibillion-dollar bailout allowed the company to survive. Still, Hynix was forced to lay off 30% of its workforce and sell all non-core operations. Recently, Hynix entered into a joint venture with ST Microelectronics to build a memory production fab near Shanghai in China.

Also, in April 2005 Hynix paid $185 million to settle charges by the U.S. Department of Justice (DOJ) that it and the other memory manufacturers had conspired to control prices in the United States between April 1999 and June 2002. In exchange for bringing the alleged wrongdoing to the U.S. government's attention, Micron was granted amnesty by the DOJ. In September 2004, Infineon settled its part of the investigation in exchange for a $160 million fine.[7] In December 2004, Samsung set aside $100 million as a contingency to cover any future settlement. All key data analyzed in this case came from the year 2003, by which time the industry's alleged cooperation on price had ceased, according to the DOJ case.

Infineon Technologies AG

Germany-based Infineon was spun off from Siemens in 1999. Siemens had been in the semiconductor business since the beginning of the industry. Throughout the company's history, Siemens' semiconductor unit formed alliances with other industry competitors to reduce investment risk and shorten time-to-market. As a result of its reliance on strategic alliances, the company always managed to stay near the front of the pack in the industry. In recent years, Infineon entered a product purchase and capacity agreement with Taiwan-based DRAM manufacturer Winbond, under which Infineon agreed to license its 0.11um DRAM technology to Winbond in exchange for the output using that technology. Infineon also formed a joint venture with Taiwan-based Nanya Technology to build a new plant in Taiwan. Over the next few years, Infineon planned to invest $1.5 billion (over half its capital budget) in Asia. In 2005 Infineon had more than 25 R&D locations spread all over the globe.

Micron Technology

Micron, based in Boise, Idaho, was founded in 1978. It sold its first DRAM product manufactured at its own facility in 1982 and went public in 1984. Micron was the sole U.S. producer remaining in this industry, and it had expanded its

Exhibit 1   Financial Results (USD, millions)

	1985	1986	1987	1988	1989	1990	1991	1992	
Samsung*									
Net Revenues	1,903	2,271	3,006	4,427	5,896	6,298	6,871	7,741	
Cost of Goods Sold	1,652	1,954	2,586	3,735	4,550	4,836	4,997	5,634	
R&D	11	14	22	38	136	231	371	443	
Net Income	24	37	44	149	233	102	90	92	
Cashflow from Operation	75	116	143	371	1,115	1,074	947	1,177	
Cash & Equivalents (a)	49	45	103	199	80	149	222	355	
Long&Short-term Debt (b)	435	467	598	1,786	2,019	3,086	4,034	4,758	
Net Debt (b – a)	386	422	495	1,587	1,940	2,938	3,812	4,402	
Interest Expense/Debt	48	51	61	89	194	302	414	445	
Total Assets	748	991	1,383	3,370	4,334	5,731	7,568	8,102	
Micron									
Net Revenues	76	49	91	301	446	333	425	506	
Cost of Goods Sold	46	43	69	100	192	178	242	285	
R&D	7	3	5	9	21	36	36	48	
Net Income	0	−34	−23	98	106	5	5	7	
Cashflow from Operation	18	−13	−1	142	165	84	98	121	
Cash & Equivalents (a)	1	5	9	164	161	77	68	73	
Long&Short-term Debt (b)	36	44	45	24	51	99	93	89	
Net Debt (b – a)	34	39	35	−141	−110	22	26	16	
Interest Expense/Debt	2	0	5	1	−15	11	11	9	
Total Assets	133	132	129	388	625	697	706	724	
Infineon									
Net Revenues	0	0	0	0	0	0	0	0	
Cost of Goods Sold	0	0	0	0	0	0	0	0	
R&D	0	0	0	0	0	0	0	0	
Net Income	0	0	0	0	0	0	0	0	
Cashflow from Operation	0	0	0	0	0	0	0	0	
Cash & Equivalents (a)	0	0	0	0	0	0	0	0	
Long&Short-term Debt (b)	0	0	0	0	0	0	0	0	
Net Debt (b – a)	0	0	0	0	0	0	0	0	
Interest Expense/Debt	0	0	0	0	0	0	0	0	
Total Equity	0	0	0	0	0	0	0	0	
Total Assets	0	0	0	0	0	0	0	0	
Hynix									
Net Revenues	0	0	0	0	0	0	0	0	
Cost of Goods Sold	0	0	0	0	0	0	0	0	
R&D	0	0	0	0	0	0	0	0	
Net Income	0	0	0	0	0	0	0	0	
Cashflow from Operation	0	0	0	0	0	0	0	0	
Cash & Equivalents (a)	0	0	0	0	0	0	0	0	
Long&Short-term Debt (b)	0	0	0	0	0	0	0	0	
Net Debt (b – a)	0	0	0	0	0	0	0	0	
Interest Expense/Debt	0	0	0	0	0	0	0	0	
Total Equity	0	0	0	0	0	0	0	0	
Total Assets	0	0	0	0	0	0	0	0	

Source: Thomson Datastream.

Note: Hyundai Semiconductor went public in December 1996. It acquired LG Semiconductor in 1999 and changed its name to Hynix. Micron was incorporated in 1978. Infineon was founded in April 1999, when the semiconductor operations of parent company Siemens AG were spun off to form a separate legal entity. In March 2000, the company went public and is now listed on the Stock Exchanges of Frankfurt and New York. For 1985 to 1998, Siemens AG data were used.

*Parent only.

1993	1994	1995	1996	1997	1998	1999	2000	2001	2002	2003
10,091	14,604	20,898	18,804	13,048	16,629	22,802	27,216	24,418	33,167	36,385
6,874	9,150	12,112	14,123	8,975	11,571	15,419	17,459	18,486	21,910	24,644
678	1,392	1,454	1,512	896	1,378	1,390	1,603	1,824	2,451	2,947
191	1,198	3,234	194	87	259	2,768	4,775	2,222	5,875	4,975
2,050	3,925	6,069	1,978	1,967	4,426	6,179	7,506	4,744	9,325	8,222
539	1,149	1,509	1,141	966	983	1,026	1,534	2,129	4,734	6,667
4,040	4,658	6,054	9,276	9,171	8,461	5,016	3,224	2,040	1,355	968
3,501	3,509	4,546	8,135	8,205	7,477	3,990	1,690	−89	−3,379	−5,699
433	394	482	480	536	924	630	273	155	84	80
8,296	11,314	17,589	19,680	24,251	14,852	20,774	23,788	21,629	27,437	32,892
828	1,629	2,953	3,654	3,516	3,012	3,764	7,336	3,936	2,589	3,091
378	608	1,130	1,835	2,078	2,125	2,107	2,963	1,984	1,146	1,895
57	83	129	192	209	272	322	428	490	561	656
104	401	844	594	332	−234	−69	1,548	−521	−907	−1,280
231	611	1,092	1,055	990	242	827	2,629	1,578	698	447
186	433	556	287	988	649	1,614	2,466	1,678	986	922
80	155	156	480	889	865	1,639	982	531	454	1,086
−106	−279	−400	193	−99	215	26	−1,485	−1,147	−532	164
8	8	7	9	31	65	132	111	27	27	40
966	1,530	2,775	3,752	4,851	4,688	6,965	9,632	8,363	7,431	7,075
0	0	0	0	2,885	3,175	4,208	7,757	6,371	4,966	4,884
0	0	0	0	1,623	2,149	2,421	3,492	4,245	3,085	2,522
0	0	0	0	457	637	733	1,092	1,336	1,011	864
0	0	0	0	−95	−775	60	1,199	−663	−974	−345
0	0	0	0	615	−232	613	2,077	287	73	757
0	0	0	0	340	906	878	1,074	955	1,847	2,185
0	0	0	0	1,139	1,253	996	284	414	1,745	1,978
0	0	0	0	799	347	118	−791	−541	−102	−207
0	0	0	0	22	94	22	0	1	24	41
0	0	0	0	3,205	3,078	3,861	6,368	8,093	7,735	6,539
0	0	0	0	4,402	4,471	6,088	9,254	10,483	9,662	8,018
0	0	0	4,537	6,201	6,288	8,035	9,489	4,097	3,739	4,030
0	0	0	2,721	3,959	4,739	6,584	4,648	3,011	2,015	2,272
0	0	0	0	21	29	68	254	264	338	296
0	0	0	−474	−599	−129	167	−2,280	−3,844	−1,560	−1,770
0	0	0	966	1,192	338	1,607	2,788	−69	933	1,171
0	0	0	346	611	578	811	280	452	255	529
0	0	0	6,045	13,775	8,966	10,379	10,545	4,910	3,414	3,231
0	0	0	5,699	13,165	8,388	9,568	10,265	4,458	3,159	2,702
0	0	0	411	651	941	1,055	1,222	846	434	253
0	0	0	1,449	−1,662	1,096	9,204	7,097	7,892	24,813	4,267
0	0	0	9,910	14,768	11,742	20,911	18,217	11,165	8,891	7,218

memory business primarily through acquisitions. In 1998, Micron purchased the memory chip business of Texas Instruments, including plants in Texas, Italy, Japan, and Singapore. Subsequently, Micron purchased Dominion Semiconductor, a unit of Toshiba located in Virginia. Over its 26-year existence, Micron had encountered numerous periods of severe financial distress. Starting in the late 1990s, Micron exited many of its non-DRAM businesses and reduced its workforce by 10%. As of 2003, Micron was focused almost entirely on DRAM production (accounting for 96% of sales). In September 2003, Micron received a $500 million investment from Intel, and Micron agreed to use the money to invest in next-generation DRAM technology.

Nanya Technology Corporation

Taiwan-based Nanya was the fifth-largest DRAM manufacturer, and it had two manufacturing plants. In 1998, Nanya purchased current-generation DRAM technology from IBM Corporation. In December 2002, Nanya and Infineon launched joint developments for next-generation process technology. The pair of companies formed a joint venture named Inotera, and together they invested a total of $2.2 billion toward a large production facility near Taipei. Inotera began producing 256Mbit DRAM starting in June 2004.

Semiconductor Manufacturing International Corp. (SMIC)

SMIC, established in 2000 and headquartered in Shanghai, was China's largest foundry, manufacturing logic and memory products, including DRAM. Foundries did not design chips as Samsung did, but, rather, took designs from other firms and produced chips based on blueprints. In 2003, SMIC and Infineon signed an agreement that authorized Infineon to license technology to SMIC in exchange for purchasing rights to much of the output. SMIC also made a similar alliance agreement with Japan-based Elpida. To increase its production capacity, SMIC purchased a $1 billion Chinese production facility from Motorola in October 2003. Through this deal, Motorola took a minority stake in SMIC and also agreed to license technology to its Chinese partner in exchange for exclusive purchase of the production capacity. SMIC's revenue had increased from $50.3 million in 2002 to $365.8 million in 2003. In March 2004, the company completed a dual listing on the New York and Hong Kong stock exchanges.

While SMIC was the only Chinese DRAM producer, other Chinese producers had already entered other semiconductor markets for logic chips. As of 2005, few of the Chinese producers had any design capability, and they were producing chips licensed from established incumbents using process technology that was one or two generations old. Still, because of the amount of resources they had attracted from Chinese and foreign investors, these Chinese entrants could afford to sell their products at low prices and grow their market share at the expense of profitability. These Chinese producers of logic chips in 2005 included Advanced Semiconductor Manufacturing Corp. (ASMC) of Shanghai, Grace Semiconductor Manufacturing Corp., HeJian Technology (Suzhou) Co., and Shanghai Hua Hong NEC Electronics Co. Grace Semiconductor, cofounded by the son of former Chinese leader Jiang Zemin in 2000, began production of logic chips in 2003 after raising over $1.6 billion.[8] Combined sales by Chinese producers soared to $771 million in 2003, from just $354 million in 2002.[9] The increase could be attributed mainly to SMIC, the country's most advanced producer, and the other top producers (Shanghai Hua Hong NEC Electronics, and ASMC), which collectively were responsible for 84% of China's 2003 semiconductor production.[10] China had 4% of the world's chip manufacturing capacity as of 2004, but that number was expected to rise to 9% in 2007.[11] While Chinese producers other than SMIC had so far focused on logic chips, there was a possibility that any of them could enter the memory chip market at any time.

Samsung Electronics: Company Overview

In 2005, the Samsung Group, which included Samsung Electronics Company, was the largest conglomerate (termed *chaebol*) in South Korea. The total net sales of the Samsung Group had reached $135 billion in 2004. In that same year, the Group had 337 overseas operations in 58 countries and employed approximately 212,000 people worldwide. The three core business sectors within the Group were electronics, finance, and trade and services.

Samsung Electronics Company, henceforth called "Samsung" in this case, was established in 1969 to manufacture black-and-white TV sets. At the end of 2004, the company had $78.5 billion in net sales, $66 billion in assets, and 113,000 employees. According to Interbrand, the company's brand value increased from $5.2 billion (ranking 43rd in the world) in 2000, to $12.6 billion (ranking 21st in the world) in 2004. In 2004, Samsung stood ahead of many brands such as Philips, Kodak, and Panasonic. Sony ranked 20th by comparison. In 2005 Samsung consisted of five business divisions, including the Semiconductor Business that is the focus of this case. Samsung's other divisions included the

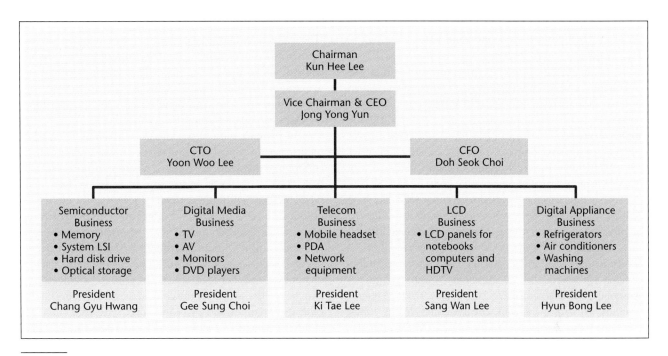

Exhibit 2 Samsung Electronics' Organizational Structure in 2005

Source: Company data.

Digital Media Business, which produced TVs, AV equipment, and computers; the Telecommunications Business, which manufactured mobile phones and network equipment; the LCD Business, which made LCD panels for notebook computers, desktop monitors, and HDTV; and the Digital Appliances Business, which produced and sold refrigerators, air conditioners, and washing machines. The organizational structure is shown in Exhibit 2.

Development of the Memory Business

Korea's semiconductor industry started wafer production in 1974, when a small start-up called Korea Semiconductor Company began manufacturing wafers in October of that year. Without strong financing and proprietary technology, the start-up quickly ran into financial difficulties. Kun Hee Lee, the third son of Samsung Group's founder Byung Chull Lee (who was also chairman at the time), decided to purchase Korea Semiconductor Company using his own personal savings.[12] Kun Hee Lee saw other Korean companies investing in steel and other heavy industries, but he felt that semiconductor investment offered higher growth rates and the chance to move beyond basic industry into the design and marketing of advanced technologies. At that time, Samsung Electronics itself was a producer of low-end consumer electronics. The company relied on labor-intensive assembly lines, importing semiconductors and other advanced products from abroad. Kun Hee Lee merged the two companies and sought to create a global powerhouse for semiconductors and consumer electronics. The first semiconductor developed by the young company was the "watch chip," used in wristwatches. The then-president of South Korea, Jung Hee Park, was so proud of the company's accomplishment that he had his name printed on many of the watches. President Park would personally give the watches as gifts to visiting foreign dignitaries.[13]

During the 1980s, Kun Hee Lee convinced his father that semiconductors represented the future of Samsung Group, and so the Group made Samsung Electronics its star affiliate and gave it most of the Group's resources. The Group wanted to get into DRAMs, the high-growth memory segment in the 1980s and 1990s.[14] So from 1983 to 1985, even as the global semiconductor market went into a recession and Intel exited the DRAM business, Samsung allocated more than $100 million to DRAM development.[15] At the time, it cost $1.30 to produce a single 64K DRAM chip, whereas market prices were at that time below $1.00. Still, Samsung believed that market growth would vindicate its investment strategy, and so losing money for the first several years did not discourage the Group from making further investments. As the capital requirements for a single firm increased during the late 1980s and early 1990s,

Japanese competitors struggled to make the investments necessary to compete in emerging generations of chips.

In the mid-1980s, Samsung was building its first large manufacturing facility. Building semiconductor facilities was difficult and time consuming because the production-related machinery was highly sensitive to dust and electronic shock. At the time, the normal construction period for a new fab lasted 18 months. However, the company wanted to accomplish the same task in just six months. As a result, construction crews worked shifts covering all 168 hours of the week in the midst of a harsh Korean winter. One memorable event during the construction process was the completion of a four-kilometer-long road in just a single day. One day, when the main production equipment was shipped in from abroad, the Samsung installation team could not believe themselves. The same road that had been largely unpaved in the morning had been turned into a two-lane asphalt road by the afternoon.[16] Manual laborers were not the only ones who were reputed to work long hours in voluntary pursuit of the company's mission. In the 1980s, nearly all of the engineers working on DRAM research and development said their weekly schedule consisted of Monday-Tuesday-Wednesday-Thursday-Friday-Friday-Friday.[17]

The company became the prime source of value for Samsung Group, and when Group founder Byung Chull Lee retired, he handed control over to the current chairman, (his son) Kun Hee Lee. It was a reward for what Kun Hee Lee had already accomplished in making Samsung Electronics a viable competitor in the global memory industry. Since 1992, semiconductors had been South Korea's largest export, and as of 2004, Korea's semiconductor exports totaled $25.1 billion, fully 10.4% of the country's export volume. Samsung alone was responsible for 22% of all Korea's exports in 2004, and the company represented 23% of total market value on the Korea Stock Exchange.[18]

Technology Development

To design and produce its first 64K DRAMs in the 1980s, Samsung had required outside technology. Company executives searched around the globe for a company that would license its DRAM technology to Samsung. It found that U.S.-based Micron was willing to accept a cash payment in exchange for teaching Samsung how to produce 64K DRAMs.[19]

To develop frontier technology for the next generation of DRAM, Samsung created what was, at the time, an unusual internal competition across global R&D sites. The company hired one team composed primarily of Korean–Americans with extensive job experience in the semiconductor industry and located that team in California. At the same time, Samsung set up a team in South Korea, also headed by two Korean–Americans with extensive industry experience.[20] The teams were told to be cooperative, but each was to come up with its own solution. The team in California won the competition for designing 256K DRAM, but in the following generation of 1Mbit technology, the team in Korea won.[21] In subsequent years, the company set up competing product development teams throughout its operations.

Beginning with 4Mbit DRAM in the late 1980s, companies faced a critical decision about how to fit four million cells onto a tiny chip. Each cell, a location to store information, consisted of a transistor and a capacitor. Two ideas were debated within the industry for how to fit more cells onto a chip. One idea, called "stacking," involved tearing down what had been a one-level construction on the chip and replacing it with an apartment building-like structure of cells. Each floor of cells would be conveniently stacked on another. Another idea, called "trenching," involved digging below the surface of the chip and creating floors below. Both technologies had pros and cons, with IBM, Toshiba, and NEC using the trench method and Matsushita, Fujitsu, and Hitachi adopting the stack method. Chairman Lee was personally responsible for making the ultimate decision; after analyzing the data, he chose the stacking method. From his perspective, trenching was too complex for its own good.[22] If a problem was discovered in a trench-style chip, one couldn't look inside to see what was wrong because everything was covered and hidden from view. In contrast, the process of stacking was simple and modular, making it far easier to see and fix mistakes.

IBM, Toshiba, and NEC subsequently discovered problems with trenching, but had already made multibillion-dollar commitments to the technology and had created design routines that worked only with the trench design system. When the companies tried to switch technologies to stacking, they lost years of development time. In the meantime, Hitachi became number one in the industry for a time, and Samsung began to catch up with Hitachi.[23]

As of the early 1990s, Samsung had joined the industry's top echelon. Samsung still wanted to be number one, so the company's senior manager devised a plan to increase the size of the wafers used to cut the DRAM chips to eight inches.[24] With a larger wafer, more chips could be cut at the same time. No one else in the industry was willing to take the risk of investing in 8-inch mass production so early. The production technology required was far from being proven viable, but Samsung went ahead and invested $1 billion towards mastering the new technology. The decision paid off. Samsung gained number one market share in the DRAM industry in 1992 and maintained its leadership over the following 13 years.[25] This leadership held up during market peaks and lows. Exhibit 3 shows the evolution of

Exhibit 3   DRAM Average Selling Price (ASP), Operating Cost, and Operating Margin (256Mbit equivalent)

	1Q00	2Q00	3Q00	4Q00	1Q01	2Q01	3Q01	4Q01	1Q02	2Q02	3Q02	4Q02	1Q03	2Q03	3Q03	4Q03	1Q04	Average
Samsung																		
Average Selling Price($)	39.08	38.44	43.79	33.42	20.82	13.24	4.86	5.16	9.31	7.75	6.86	7.58	5.76	5.27	5.79	5.90	6.15	15.25
Operating Cost($)	16.95	13.64	14.41	15.70	12.36	12.02	9.53	7.46	5.72	5.33	4.92	5.33	4.77	4.60	4.00	3.82	3.92	8.50
Operating Margin	57%	65%	67%	53%	41%	9%	-96%	-45%	39%	31%	28%	30%	17%	13%	31%	35%	36%	44%
Micron																		
Average Selling Price($)	32.49	25.13	30.83	25.65	12.59	8.30	3.76	2.85	5.01	7.48	5.25	4.99	5.10	4.33	4.97	5.32	4.51	11.09
Operating Cost($)	34.75	24.00	20.31	19.65	15.81	15.96	12.01	6.67	8.28	8.98	7.97	7.25	7.96	6.65	6.06	5.57	4.75	12.51
Operating Margin	-7%	4%	34%	23%	-26%	-92%	-219%	-134%	-65%	-20%	-52%	-45%	-56%	-53%	-22%	-5%	-5%	-13%
Infineon																		
Average Selling Price($)	26.62	26.50	30.93	16.01	10.58	7.98	4.20	4.38	8.90	7.20	5.50	5.90	4.89	4.69	5.41	5.21	4.95	10.58
Operating Cost($)	18.11	16.69	10.88	14.14	13.46	13.76	12.00	11.00	9.80	8.20	7.50	7.96	5.62	5.10	4.69	4.69	4.75	9.90
Operating Margin	32%	37%	65%	12%	-27%	-73%	-186%	-151%	-10%	-14%	-36%	-15%	-9%	13%	10%	4%	6%	
Hynix																		
Average Selling Price($)	28.72	29.83	37.76	20.95	12.42	7.35	3.86	3.73	8.56	6.30	4.71	4.92	4.57	4.50	5.46	5.36	5.16	11.42
Operating Cost($)	22.21	24.68	23.94	17.40	11.82	8.73	9.33	9.38	6.08	9.15	7.47	6.56	6.16	5.61	4.82	4.37	3.89	10.68
Operating Margin	23%	17%	37%	17%	5%	-19%	-142%	-152%	29%	-45%	-59%	-33%	-35%	-24%	12%	18%	25%	6%
Worldwide																		
Average Selling Price($)	36	33.8	36.5	22.9	14.30	9.02	4.80	3.49	8.58	7.36	6.21	6.14	5.12	4.62	5.47	5.37	5.06	12.63
ASP Quarterly Change		-6%	8%	-37%	-37%	-37%	-47%	-27%	146%	-14%	-16%	-1%	-17%	-10%	19%	-2%	-6%	-5%
Price Premium of Samsung ASP over Competitors' ASP	33%	42%	32%	60%	75%	68%	23%	41%	24%	11%	33%	44%	19%	17%	10%	11%	26%	34%
Operating Margin of (Samsung – Competitors' Average)	41%	45%	22%	36%	57%	70%	86%	101%	54%	57%	77%	68%	53%	42%	30%	27%	28%	53%

Source: Merrill Lynch.

Exhibit 4   DRAM Production Volume by Density in 2003

	Production Volume (million unit, 256Mbit equiv.)									
	Samsung		**Micron**		**Infineon**		**Hynix**		**SMIC**	
4Mbit	—	—	—	—	—	—	—	—	—	—
16Mbit	1.3	0.1%	1.0	0.2%	0.0	0.0%	10.0	1.9%	—	—
64Mbit	16.4	1.8%	29.7	4.4%	0.0	0.0%	33.6	6.4%	—	—
128Mbit	151.6	16.9%	88.1	13.1%	43.7	8.2%	96.8	18.6%	—	—
256Mbit	695.8	77.6%	540.1	80.3%	479.5	89.6%	374.2	71.8%	68.2	100.0%
512Mbit	30.4	3.4%	13.7	2.0%	11.5	2.1%	6.8	1.3%	—	—
1Gbit	1.0	0.1%	0.1	0.0%	0.6	0.1%	0.0	0.0%	—	—
Total	**896.4**	**100.0%**	**672.8**	**100.0%**	**535.3**	**100.0%**	**521.5**	**100.0%**	**68.2**	**100.0%**

Source: "DRAM Supply and Demand Quarterly Statistics: Worldwide, 2003–2005," Gartner, Inc. As the research is over 12 months old, Gartner deems it to be a historical perspective.

Samsung's costs and prices over time relative to its competitors' during the most recent industry cycle (1Q00–1Q04).

Product Mix

As of 2003, Samsung offered over 1,200 different variations of DRAM products. Given that DRAM products were conventionally thought of as commodities, the ability to produce 1,200 different varieties was unprecedented in the memory industry. Product ranged from so-called "frontier products" (e.g., 512Mbit DRAM) at the cutting edge of technology to "legacy products" (e.g., 64Mbit DRAM) that Samsung offered to customers after the industry had moved on to later generations. Within each product generation, there also existed "specialty products" (e.g., DDR2 SDRAM, Rambus DRAM) using customized architectures for niche markets. Exhibits 4 and 5 compare Samsung's product mix with those of its competitors. In the semiconductor industry, prices for new-generation products stayed high for only a few quarters before plunging rapidly (Exhibit 6). After a generation had passed, however, legacy product lines could be transformed into high-value niche products. In 2003, for example, the price of a 16Mbit chip was $19.04, whereas the price of the popular, more advanced 256Mbit chip was only $4.65. Exhibit 7a shows Samsung's overall prices and cost structures compared with its competitors' for 2003. Exhibits 7b to 7e compare prices and cost structures across competitors in 2003 for individual product generations: 64Mbit, 128Mbit, 256Mbit, and 512Mbit. Exhibits 7f to 7i compare prices and cost structures by product line for the then-popular 256Mbit generation in 2003. Exhibits 7j to 7k compare prices and cost structure of specialty products for the 128Mbit generation in 2003.

Exhibit 5   DRAM Production Volume by Product Line in 2003 (million, 256 Mbit equivalent)

	Production Volume (million unit, 256Mbit equiv.)									
	Samsung		**Micron**		**Infineon**		**Hynix**		**Worldwide**	
SDRAM	206.1	23.0%	191.8	28.5%	79.1	14.8%	117.5	22.5%	0.0	0.0%
DDR SDRAM	585.3	65.3%	475.6	70.7%	437.8	81.8%	401.4	77.0%	68.2	100.0%
DDR2 SDRAM	40.4	4.5%	0.0	0.0%	1.7	0.3%	0.0	0.0%	0.0	0.0%
RDRAM	37.9	4.2%	0.0	0.0%	2.4	0.4%	0.0	0.0%	0.0	0.0%
Other DRAM	25.9	2.9%	5.4	0.8%	14.3	2.7%	1.3	0.2%	0.0	0.0%
Total	**896.4**	**100%**	**672.8**	**100%**	**535.3**	**100%**	**521.5**	**100%**	**68.2**	**100%**

Source: "DRAM Supply and Demand Quarterly Statistics: Worldwide, 2003–2005," Gartner, Inc. As the research is over 12 months old, Gartner deems it to be a historical perspective.

Exhibit 6   Worldwide DRAM Average Selling Price History and Forecast; 2000–2010 (Dollars)

	2000	2001	2002	2003	2004	2005(E)	2006(E)	2007(E)	2008(E)	2009(E)	2010(E)
1Mbit	1.51	1.06	1.10	—	—	—	—	—	—	—	—
4Mbit	1.90	1.34	1.28	0.97	0.79	0.51	0.40	—	—	—	—
16Mbit	3.42	1.88	1.61	1.19	0.90	0.62	0.50	0.50	—	—	—
64Mbit	7.18	1.88	1.55	1.88	2.13	1.39	0.74	0.70	0.62	—	—
128Mbit	14.41	2.99	3.30	2.75	3.48	2.41	1.28	1.01	0.90	0.66	—
256Mbit	48.59	6.73	6.22	4.68	4.88	3.67	1.64	1.21	1.10	0.84	0.68
512Mbit	—	150.00	42.11	21.70	12.76	6.75	3.12	2.79	2.53	1.78	1.25
1Gbit	—	—	—	83.57	40.76	18.04	7.29	5.54	4.81	2.22	1.55
2Gbit	—	—	—	—	—	82.93	21.29	11.70	9.68	3.99	3.08
4Gbit	—	—	—	—	—	—	—	125.15	47.00	13.02	7.50
8Gbit	—	—	—	—	—	—	—	—	—	—	93.18
ASP per Megabyte	0.99	0.22	0.21	0.16	0.17	0.11	0.05	0.04	0.04	0.02	0.01
ASP per 256 Mbit Equiv.	31.63	7.08	6.76	5.19	5.49	3.66	1.65	1.42	1.28	0.58	0.42
Annual ASP growth	−17.3%	−77.6%	−4.5%	−23.3%	5.8%	−33.3%	−55.1%	−13.7%	−9.9%	−54.4%	−28.3%

Source: "Forecast: DRAM Market Statistics, Worldwide, 2000–2010 (1Q05 Update)," Gartner, Inc.

Exhibit 7a   Comparison of Operating Profit of DRAM in 2003 (256Mbit equivalent[a])

	Samsung	Micron	Infineon	Hynix	SMIC	Competitors' Weighted Average	Samsung – Competitors' Weighted Average	Competitors' Weighted Average/ Samsung
Average Selling Price	$5.68	$4.93	$5.05	$4.97	$4.43	$4.96	$0.72	87.3%
Fully Loaded Costs	$4.31	$6.61	$5.02	$5.33	$4.84	$5.70	−$1.39	132.2%
Raw materials	1.18	1.93	1.58	1.93	1.84	1.83	−0.65	155.1%
Labor	0.54	0.94	0.76	0.51	0.23	0.74	−0.19	137.0%
Depreciation	1.35	1.88	1.50	1.48	1.63	1.64	−0.29	121.5%
R&D	0.60	0.57	0.71	0.58	0.80	0.62	−0.02	103.3%
SG&A	0.65	1.28	0.46	0.83	0.34	0.87	−0.22	133.8%
Operating Profit (a)	$1.37	−$1.68	$0.02	−$0.36	−$0.41	−$0.74		
Operating Margin	24.1%	−34.1%	0.5%	−7.3%	−9.3%	−15.0%		
Production Volume in 256Mbit equiv. [b]	896.4	672.8	535.3	521.5	68.2			
Operating Profit in $Million (a × b)	$1,224.3	−$1,129.5	$12.9	−$188.1	−$28.1			

[a] Explanation of "256Mbit equivalent" term used above: Each company in the industry uses a slightly different design rule and process technology for each product, along with producing a different mixture of architectures and memory sizes. So that makes it very difficult to do an apples-to-apples comparison for even the same exact product. Therefore, the industry analysts have settled on a common approach for comparing the overall cost competitiveness of a company. The company's total sales and production costs are weighted by memory generation, with the 256Mbit generation given a weight of 1.00, the generations above 256Mbit given a weighting above 1.00 that is proportional to 256Mbit, and the generations below 256Mbit given a weighting below 1.00 that is proportional to 256Mbit.
[b] Total production volume in the sum of DRAM production volumes across all density levels (including 16Mb, 64Mb, 128Mb, 256Mb, 512Mb, and 1Gb).

Exhibit 7b   Cost Breakdown of 64Mbit DRAM in 2003 (256Mbit equivalent)

	Samsung	Micron	Infineon	Hynix	SMIC	Competitors' Weighted Average
Average Selling Price	$8.63	$7.88	—	$8.10	—	$8.00
Fully loaded costs	$2.99	$4.19	—	$3.98	—	$4.07
Raw materials	0.99	0.98	—	1.67	—	1.35
Labor	0.54	0.76	—	0.51	—	0.63
Depreciation	0.35	0.42	—	0.43	—	0.42
R&D	0.15	0.13	—	0.17	—	0.15
SG&A	0.96	1.90	—	1.20	—	1.53
Operating Profit	$5.64	$3.69	—	$4.13	—	$3.92
Operating Margin	65.4%	46.9%	—	50.9%	—	49.0%
Production Volume Units (million)	16.4	29.7	0.0	33.6	0.0	63.3
Production Volume/ Total Production Volume	1.8%	4.4%	0.0%	6.4%	0.0%	3.5%

Exhibit 7c   Cost Breakdown of 128Mbit DRAM in 2003 (256Mbit equivalent)[a]

	Samsung	Micron	Infineon	Hynix	SMIC	Competitors' Weighted Average
Average Selling Price	$6.45	$5.56	$6.34	$5.45	—	$5.66
Fully Loaded Costs	$3.89	$6.22	$4.49	$5.08	—	$5.40
Raw materials	1.09	1.81	1.43	1.83	—	1.75
Labor	0.54	0.94	0.75	0.51	—	0.72
Depreciation	1.09	1.60	1.21	1.33	—	1.41
R&D	0.48	0.48	0.57	0.52	—	0.52
SG&A	0.70	1.39	0.52	0.88	—	1.01
Operating Profit	$2.56	–$0.66	$1.85	$0.37	—	$0.25
Operating Margin	39.6%	–11.9%	29.2%	6.8%	—	3.9%
Production Volume Units (million)	151.6	88.1	43.7	96.8	0.0	228.6
Production Volume/ Total Production Volume	16.9%	13.1%	8.2%	18.6%	0.0%	12.7%

[a] 128Mbit DRAM production volume includes production volumes of various 128Mbit DRAM product lines (such as SDRAM, DDR, DDR2, and Rambus DRAM).

Exhibit 7d   Cost Breakdown of 256Mbit DRAM in 2003 (256Mbit equivalent)[a]

	Samsung	Micron	Infineon	Hynix	SMIC	Competitors' Weighted Average
Average Selling Price	$5.08	$4.48	$4.73	$4.58	$4.43	$4.57
Fully Loaded Costs	$4.15	$6.52	$4.84	$5.42	$4.84	$5.61
Raw materials	1.19	1.98	1.57	2.01	1.84	1.84
Labor	0.54	0.94	0.75	0.51	0.23	0.74
Depreciation	1.27	1.86	1.41	1.56	1.63	1.63
R&D	0.56	0.56	0.67	0.61	0.80	0.62
SG&A	0.59	1.18	0.44	0.74	0.34	0.79
Operating Profit	$0.94	–$2.04	–$0.11	–$0.85	–$0.41	–$1.04
Operating Margin	18.4%	–45.5%	–2.2%	–18.5%	–9.3%	–22.8%
Production Volume Units (million)	695.8	540.1	479.5	374.2	68.2	1462.1
Production Volume/ Total Production Volume	77.6%	80.3%	89.6%	71.8%	100.0%	81.3%

[a] 256Mbit DRAM production volume includes production volumes of various 256Mbit DRAM product lines (such as SDRAM, DDR, DDr2, and Rambus DRAM).

Exhibit 7e   Cost Breakdown of 512Mbit DRAM in 2003 (256Mbit equivalent)

	Samsung	Micron	Infineon	Hynix	SMIC	Competitors' Weighted Average
Average Selling Price	$14.21	$12.11	$13.60	$11.99	—	$12.62
Fully Loaded Costs	$10.52	$17.58	$13.26	$13.81	—	$15.22
Raw materials	1.29	3.17	2.47	2.97	—	2.87
Labor	0.80	1.52	1.20	0.77	—	1.25
Depreciation	4.89	7.78	5.82	6.00	—	6.70
R&D	2.16	2.36	2.74	2.34	—	2.49
SG&A	1.38	2.75	1.02	1.73	—	1.91
Operating Profit	$3.69	–$5.47	$0.34	–$1.82	—	–$2.60
Operating Margin	26.0%	–45.1%	2.5%	–15.2%	—	–21.6%
Production Volume Units (million)	30.4	13.7	11.5	6.8	0.0	32.0
Production Volume/ Total Production Volume	3.4%	2.0%	2.1%	1.3%	0.0%	1.8%

Exhibit 7f   Cost Breakdown of 256Mbit SDRAM in 2003

	Samsung	Micron	Infineon	Hynix	SMIC	Competitors' Weighted Average
Average Selling Price	$4.95	$4.56	$5.00	$4.58	—	$4.67
Fully Loaded Costs	$4.16	$6.62	$4.97	$5.54	—	$5.95
Raw materials	1.20	2.01	1.61	2.05	—	1.92
Labor	0.54	0.95	0.77	0.52	—	0.80
Depreciation	1.28	1.89	1.45	1.59	—	1.71
R&D	0.57	0.57	0.68	0.62	—	0.61
SG&A	0.58	1.21	0.46	0.74	—	0.91
Operating Profit	$0.79	−$2.06	$0.03	−$0.95	—	−$1.28
Operating Margin	15.9%	−45.2%	0.5%	−20.8%	—	−28.0%
Production Volume Units (million)	160.0	162.0	76.7	84.2	0.0	323.0
Production Volume/ Total Production Volume	17.9%	24.1%	14.3%	16.1%	0.0%	18.0%

Exhibit 7g   Cost Breakdown of 256Mbit DDR SDRAM in 2003

	Samsung	Micron	Infineon	Hynix	SMIC	Competitors' Weighted Average
Average Selling Price	$4.72	$4.45	$4.65	$4.57	$4.43	$4.55
Fully Loaded Costs	$4.06	$6.48	$4.81	$5.39	$4.84	$5.51
Raw materials	1.18	1.97	1.56	1.99	1.84	1.82
Labor	0.53	0.93	0.75	0.51	0.23	0.72
Depreciation	1.25	1.85	1.41	1.55	1.63	1.60
R&D	0.55	0.56	0.66	0.60	0.80	0.62
SG&A	0.55	1.17	0.43	0.74	0.34	0.75
Operating Profit	$0.66	−$2.03	−$0.16	−$0.82	−$0.41	−$0.96
Operating Margin	13.9%	−45.6%	−3.4%	−18.0%	−9.3%	−21.2%
Production Volume Units (million)	485.0	378.1	399.7	290.0	68.2	1136.0
Production Volume/ Total Production Volume	54.1%	56.2%	74.7%	55.6%	100.0%	63.2%

Exhibit 7h   Cost Breakdown of 256Mbit DDR2 SDRAM in 2003

	Samsung	Micron	Infineon	Hynix	SMIC	Competitors' Weighted Average
Average Selling Price	$8.83	—	$8.67	—	—	$8.67
Fully Loaded Costs	$4.93	—	$5.72	—	—	$5.72
Raw materials	1.31	—	1.75	—	—	1.75
Labor	0.59	—	0.84	—	—	0.84
Depreciation	1.39	—	1.58	—	—	1.58
R&D	0.62	—	0.74	—	—	0.74
SG&A	1.03	—	0.80	—	—	0.80
Operating Profit	$3.90	—	$2.95	—	—	$2.95
Operating Margin	44.1%	—	34.0%	—	—	34.0%
Production Volume Units (million)	25.7	0.0	1.2	0.0	0.0	1.2
Production Volume/ Total Production Volume	2.9%	0.0%	0.2%	0.0%	0.0%	0.1%

Exhibit 7i   Cost Breakdown of 256Mbit Rambus DRAM in 2003

	Samsung	Micron	Infineon	Hynix	SMIC	Competitors' Weighted Average
Average Selling Price	$9.21	—	$8.45	—	—	$8.45
Fully Loaded Costs	$4.89	—	$5.59	—	—	$5.59
Raw materials	1.28	—	1.71	—	—	1.71
Labor	0.57	—	0.82	—	—	0.82
Depreciation	1.36	—	1.55	—	—	1.55
R&D	0.60	—	0.73	—	—	0.73
SG&A	1.07	—	0.78	—	—	0.78
Operating Profit	$4.32	—	$2.86	—	—	$2.86
Operating Margin	46.9%	—	33.8%	—	—	33.8%
Production Volume Units (million)	25.0	0.0	1.7	0.0	0.0	1.7
Production Volume/ Total Production Volume	2.8%	0.0%	0.3%	0.0%	0.0%	0.3%

Exhibit 7j   Cost Breakdown of 128Mbit DDR2 SDRAM in 2003 (256Mbit equivalent)

	Samsung	Micron	Infineon	Hynix	SMIC	Competitors' Weighted Average
Average Selling Price	$11.30	—	$9.74	—	—	$9.74
Fully Loaded Costs	$4.49	—	$5.27	—	—	$5.27
Raw materials	1.13	—	1.58	—	—	1.58
Labor	0.55	—	0.83	—	—	0.83
Depreciation	1.12	—	1.34	—	—	1.34
R&D	0.50	—	0.63	—	—	0.63
SG&A	1.19	—	0.89	—	—	0.89
Operating Profit	$6.81	—	$4.47	—	—	$4.47
Operating Margin	60.3%	—	45.9%	—	—	45.9%
Production Volume Units (million)	7.1	0.0	0.4	0.0	0.0	0.4
Production Volume/ Total Production Volume	0.79%	0.00%	0.08%	0.00%	0.00%	0.08%

Exhibit 7k   Cost Breakdown of 128Mbit Rambus DRAM in 2003 (256Mbit equivalent)

	Samsung	Micron	Infineon	Hynix	SMIC	Competitors' Weighted Average
Average Selling Price	$11.06	—	$9.64	—	—	$9.64
Fully Loaded Costs	$4.65	—	$5.26	—	—	$5.26
Raw materials	1.19	—	1.58	—	—	1.58
Labor	0.58	—	0.83	—	—	0.83
Depreciation	1.18	—	1.34	—	—	1.34
R&D	0.52	—	0.63	—	—	0.63
SG&A	1.17	—	0.88	—	—	0.88
Operating Profit	$6.41	—	$4.38	—	—	$4.38
Operating Margin	58.0%	—	45.5%	—	—	45.5%
Production Volume Units (million)	5.5	0.0	0.5	0.0	0.0	0.5
Production Volume/ Total Production Volume	0.61%	0.00%	0.10%	0.00%	0.00%	0.10%

Source: Casewriters' estimates based on Merrill Lynch report.

In 2004, Samsung also sought to create the same advantage in Flash memory that it enjoyed in DRAM. As shown in Exhibit 8, Samsung was seeking to move some of its production capacity from DRAMs to Flash memory. Whereas the DRAM market still closely followed growth in PCs, which were becoming a mature, single-digit growth market, Flash memory was tied to growth in digital cameras and camera phones. The Flash memory market was expected to grow at a double-digit rate for at least another five years. That growth was expected to keep Flash prices quite high relative to DRAM prices.[26] Samsung Semiconductor's president proposed a new "Hwang's Law" that was set to eclipse Gordon Moore's theory. In 1965, Moore prophesized that semiconductor density would double every 18 months; his theory turned out to be true for the next 40 years. Chang Gyu Hwang, the head of Samsung's Memory Division, proposed Hwang's Law; namely, that Flash memory density would double every 12 months. And Hwang predicted that Samsung would be the one to accomplish that goal consistently over the coming years.[27] A description of Samsung's performance in Flash memory is presented in Exhibit 9.

Design and Production

Unlike its competitors, Samsung tried to create new uses for DRAMs by putting its manufacturing and R&D in support of design firms such as Rambus. Over time, Samsung had launched new DRAM products with product-specific applications in laptops and personal game players, for example.

Many of these applications shared a common core design. Even two seemingly different architectures, DDR DRAM and Rambus DRAM, shared a common core design.

The difference between them was that Rambus had an enhanced component, a high-speed interface I/O, and so Samsung needed to add additional design work to connect the DRAM core design to the high-speed interface I/O. Samsung actively sought to customize its products around a core design.

Samsung's main R&D facility and all of its fab lines were located at a single site just south of Seoul, South Korea. In contrast, its competitors' facilities were scattered across the globe.[28] With the benefit of collocation and scale of fab investment, Samsung was estimated to have saved an average of 12% on fab construction costs. At Samsung's primary campus, the R&D engineers and production engineers lived together in the same company-provided housing. On a daily basis, they shared meals and their worksites were placed near one another's so that the engineers could quickly solve design and process engineering problems together. The site was located in the mountains on flattened

Exhibit 8   Samsung's Manufacturing Line Sharing (Line A)

	1998	1999	2000	2001	2002
DRAM	78%	45%	28%	40%	27%
Graphic	19%	13%	3%	2%	0%
SRAM	3%	41%	52%	46%	44%
Flash	0%	2%	15%	8%	24%
MROM	0%	0%	2%	5%	5%
Total	100%	100%	100%	100%	100%

Source: Company data.

Exhibit 9   Cost Breakdown of NAND Flash (512Mbit equivalent, 1Q 2004)

	Toshiba (a)	Samsung (b)	(a)/(b)	Toshiba	Samsung
Average Selling Price ($)	9.51	9.48	100.3%		
Fully Loaded Cost	4.55	3.28	138.5%	100.0%	100.0%
Raw materials	1.15	0.79	144.8%	25.2%	24.1%
Labor	0.74	0.45	165.3%	16.3%	13.6%
Utilities	0.13	0.10	138.5%	2.9%	2.9%
SG&A	0.28	0.24	119.3%	6.2%	7.2%
Depreciation	1.10	1.19	92.8%	24.2%	36.1%
R&D	0.51	0.30	170.9%	11.3%	9.1%
Others	0.63	0.22	281.4%	13.9%	6.9%
Operating Profit	4.97	6.20	80.1%		

Source: Merrill Lynch.

land, where the air was remarkably clean and free of dust and other particles. The site extended over several kilometers and was still mostly covered by trees.

In its factories, Samsung produced multiple product architectures on each production line. Process engineers had reputedly figured out how to modify its production equipment for all kinds of contingencies. As with all semiconductor makers, Samsung's production yields depended on the number of good chips that could be cut out of a wafer, which in turn hinged on the size of the wafer and the precision of the design rule used to cut the wafer. Samsung had the ability to learn new design rules and then apply those new design rules towards the production of all product types (including some legacy products). Exhibits 10a **to** 10c compare Samsung's wafer-size mix, design rule, and yield with those of its competitors.

Samsung prided itself on the reliability of its products and its ability to customize products to customer demands. During the 1980s and parts of the 1990s, Lee had seen that his company was producing shoddy products.[29] In a 1994 book delivered to all employees, he explained that the Samsung Group had lost track of quality because its business had begun 55 years earlier selling commodities like sugar and textiles in a growing Korean market. Lee argued that employees must now think of quality first.[30] He also launched mass burnings of shoddy Samsung products: tens of millions of dollars' worth of flawed products would be burned in an open field, and he would speak in the tone of an evangelist and admonish his employees about their quality control. By the late 1990s, the company routinely won key industry competitions for reliability. Prior to 1995, the company had won one major competition. Between 1995 and 2003, the company won awards for reliability and performance from most major customers. Many customers, even rivals of one another, named Samsung their supplier of choice. For instance, the company simultaneously developed a new Flash memory chip for Sony Ericsson and a Flash memory chip customized for Nokia.

Exhibit 10a   Comparison of 8-inch Wafer vs. 12-inch Wafer

	8-inch Wafer	12-inch Wafer	12-inch Wafer/ 8-inch Wafer
Net Die per Wafer[a]	257	616	240%
Assumed Yield Rate	87%	87%	100%
Good Die per Wafer	224	536	240%
Production Cost per Wafer			210%
Depreciation per Wafer	n/a	n/a	200%
Material Cost per Wafer	n/a	n/a	270%
Cost per Chip	n/a	n/a	90%

Source: Company data and casewriters' estimates.

[a] Net Dice per Wafer is based on 0.13μm technology.

Exhibit 10b   Process Technology, Wafer Size, and Net Dice Output

	0.25 μm	0.18 μm	0.15 μm	0.13 μm	0.11 μm
Chip Size (mm)^2	208.9	159.4	120.9	91.3	68.6
Number of Net Die out of 8-inch Wafer	100	137	188	257	352
Number of Net Die out of 12-inch Wafer	240	329	451	616	845

Source: Casewriters' estimates.

Exhibit 10c   Comparison of Production by Wafer Size, Design Rule, and Yield Rate

	Production Volume by Wafer Size			Process Technology		Yield Rate[a]
	8-inch Wafer	12-inch Wafer	Total	Main Design Rule (μm)	% of Usage	
Samsung	88%	12%	100%	0.11	67%	80%
Micron	97%	3%	100%	0.13	80%	60%
Infineon	67%	33%	100%	0.14	80%	67%
Hynix	100%	0%	100%	0.13	72%	50%

Source: Casewriters' estimates based on Gartner, Inc. report (February 2004).

[a] Yield rate is based on 0.11μm technology for 256Mbit.

Human Resource Policies

In the past, Korean companies often hired employees because they came from the right high school or the right region, but Samsung tried to eliminate this practice. It was considered taboo at Samsung to ask a coworker about his or her university or place of origin.[31] Prospective employees were given an aptitude test covering language skills, mathematical knowledge, reasoning, and space perception. Samsung also tried to break the mold of traditional seniority-based promotion, which was still widespread in Asia. Employees were given evaluations on an A, B, C, and D scale every year, and only those who earned two A's within three years were eligible for promotion. As a result of the more meritocratic evaluation system, younger, high-potential, English-speaking managers were quickly promoted up the organizational hierarchy. Among the company's senior-most executives, several had attained their current positions in their early 40s, thus shooting past older employees who might have previously risen to the top based on seniority.

Samsung also put in place programs to invest in employees' global business skills. The Regional Specialist Program, for example, placed high-potential employees in a foreign country to learn the local language and culture for one year. Upon their return, the Regional Specialist produced reports on their experiences that became part of a codified knowledge database. Samsung sponsored hundreds of employees' MBA and Ph.D. studies in foreign countries.

Unlike some other Korean companies, Samsung actively recruited foreign talent, including westerners and members of the Korean diaspora who had long ago left Korea to live and work in the United States and Europe. After hiring one top American executive in the late 1990s, the CEO of Samsung, Jong Yong Yun, sensed that the company might resent the new hire, an outsider who could not speak fluent Korean. Yun declared, "Some of you may want to put [him] on top of a tree and then shake him down. If anybody tries that, they will be severely reprimanded!"[32] The CEO then persuaded his executives to welcome the foreigner. Throughout the top ranks of Samsung Electronics were a number of international recruits who previously worked at top U.S. technology companies. Most prominently, these included Chang Gyu Hwang, current president of Samsung's Semiconductor Business; Oh Hyun Kwon, the head of Samsung's System LSI Division; and Dae Je Chin, recent president of Samsung's Digital Media Business and the current Korean Minister of Information and Communications.

More recently, Chairman Lee created Samsung's Global Strategy Group, which was used to attract talent from around the world to the organization. The Global Strategy Group was a corporate resource that helped to solve business problems at the business-unit level and prepared global managers for important positions. David Steel, the highest-ranking Western manager at Samsung, joined the Global Strategy Group in 1997. Steel had subsequently been promoted to the position of Vice President of Business Development in the Digital Media Business.

Samsung also proudly claimed that it invested more in its employees than almost any other competitor in its industry. When Lee was inaugurated as Group chairman in 1987, he stated in his inauguration speech: "What do our salaried workers worry about as soon as they open the door from their house to work? Probably over 90% will think about their family and their own health, their children's education, and their retirement."

As a result, Lee proposed that the company would take care of 90% of their burden, allowing them to concentrate on innovation and productivity. He also declared that the company would richly reward individuals for their accomplishments, while at the same time not firing people for failure. He declared in the company's guidebook: "Take the example of a horse trainer: The best ones never use a stick or whip, only carrots for reward. At Samsung, we reward outstanding performance; we do not punish failure. This is my personal philosophy and belief. We need punishment only for those who lack ethics, are unfair, tell lies, hold others back or stand in the way of our unified march."[33]

The average salary at Samsung in 2003 was $44,000; the comparable figures for Micron, Infineon, Hynix, and SMIC were estimated to be $54,000, $72,400, $24,600, and $10,800, respectively Beyond base salaries, in 2005 Samsung had three general types of performance-based incentives. First, so-called project incentives rewarded project members from all job functions with cash bonuses at the conclusion of a successful project, such as for the DDR2 rollout. Project incentives ranged from a few thousand dollars to more than $1 million for a project team. Second, productivity incentives rewarded employees for performance at the division level (for example, the Memory Division), but could be modified for each department or team in the division on the basis of its performance and contribution. The productivity Incentives paid up to 300% of annual base salary. Third, a profit sharing program rewarded each member of a division, paying up to 50% of annual base salary, depending on divisional performance as measured by economic value added (EVA).

Samsung established practices that both facilitated debate and encouraged people to agree on a final outcome. For example, before deciding how to design and produce a new product, the company encouraged fierce debates where all levels of experts from junior staff and engineers to senior executives were actively urged to voice their opinions. After considering all views, senior executives made a final decision, and everyone was expected to work toward the common goal.

Strategic Challenges

In 2005, had the competitive environment changed dramatically, and did this change require Samsung to modify its strategy? The company faced new challenges from Chinese entrants who were attacking the DRAM market in much the same way that Samsung did 20 years ago. These companies were using partnerships to learn from industry incumbents like Infineon and Elpida, and they were attracting billions of dollars in outside financing to build state-of-the-art production facilities. Like Samsung in the 1980s, these Chinese producers had the patience to endure years of losses to gain significant market share. Statistics for evaluating the technological capabilities of China's semiconductor industry are presented in Exhibit 11. Although the U.S. government forbade U.S. producers from shipping advanced semiconductor equipment to China, and while the Taiwanese government forbade its companies from shipping cutting-edge production technology to China, these may have been only short-term obstacles in China's path. Instead of purchasing equipment from Taiwan and

the United States, Chinese producers simply went to other countries. China lacked critical infrastructure to support a cutting-edge semiconductor industry, but the government was firmly committed to subsidizing all infrastructure needs around Shanghai and Beijing. The Chinese government was able to provide cheap credit, abundant land, cheap utilities, engineering talent, tax incentives, and other essential resources to anyone who wanted to build a cutting-edge semiconductor facility with a Chinese partner.[34]

One option that Samsung managers had in 2005 was to collaborate actively with a Chinese partner. By 2010, China was expected to become the world's second-largest purchaser of semiconductors, after the United States[35] In spite of the fact that the overall memory chip industry had been growing modestly over the previous year, major producers held back from making major new investments in China. Still, if industry growth picked up sharply, observers from Nikkei Electronics Asia predicted that the major DRAM producers would look to Chinese partners to expand joint investments.[36] The risk in working with the Chinese producers was that intellectual property rights were still not protected fully, and so sharing blueprints and expertise with a Chinese partner could lead to the partner becoming a rival some day. Also, if Samsung's competitive advantage had come from creating a unique culture at the main R&D production site south of Seoul, did moving production to China threaten the survival of that unique company culture?

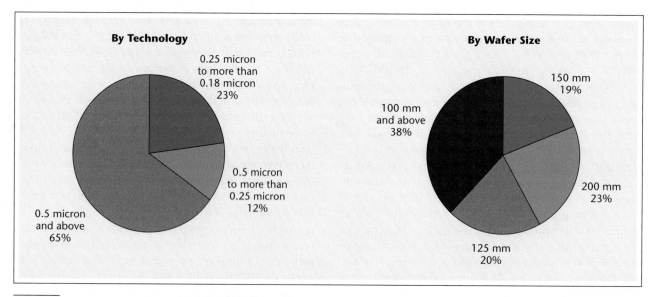

Exhibit 11   China's Chip Production Capacity Breakdown (2001)

Source: Friedrich Wu and Chua Boon Loy, "Rapid Rise of China's Semiconductor Industry: What Are the Implications for Singapore?" *Thunderbird International Business Review* 46 (2004): 109–131.

An alternative option for Samsung was to increase its investment in cutting-edge memory products, particularly for new niche markets. If Samsung was the market leader in terms of low cost and productivity, then many thought that Samsung should not be teaching Chinese competitors how to become more low cost and productive. Instead, Samsung should potentially cede the lower end of the market to the Chinese while trying to develop more high-value niche products.

How should Chairman Lee and the senior management team at Samsung react to the threat of Chinese competition?

Notes

1. Information on Chairman Lee's office comes from Kim Sung-Hong and Woo In-Ho, *Lee Kun Hee's 10-year reform* (Seoul: Kimyoungsa, 2003).
2. "Samsung's second new management vision," *Monthly Chosun*, July 2003.
3. Wojahn, Oliver. "Semiconductors: A silver lining on the horizon," Berenberg Bank, August 27, 2001, p. 5.
4. Casewriters' estimate.
5. "Korean semiconductor industry," Samsung internal document, 2004, p. 7.
6. "Samsung Electronics: To be Better than the best," a report written by J. J. Park and Seung-Hoon Lee, J.P. Morgan Securities (Far East) Ltd., February 2004, p. 13.
7. "Korean Chipmaker Hynix Semiconductor Admits Price Fixing," published by the Associated Press, April 25, 2005.
8. Information for this paragraph comes from James Hines and Kay-Yang Tan, "Foundries in China gearing up for rapid expansion," Gartner Dataquest Research Brief, January 27, 2004.
9. Tan, Kay-Yang. "Market focus: China's foundry industry gaining strength," Gartner Dataquest Focus Report, July 22, 2004, p. 3.
10. Ibid.
11. Wu Friedrich and Chua Boon Loy. "Rapid rise of China's semiconductor industry: What are the implications for Singapore?" *Thunderbird International Business Review* 46 (2004): 109–131.
12. Samsung, Semiconductor Stories Series #42: June 15, 2004, Samsung Electronics [Korea] Web site, http://www.sec.co.kr/index.jsp.
13. "Samsung rising: Why is Samsung strong?" published by Korea Economic Daily newspaper, 2002, p. 35.
14. "Samsung rising: Why is Samsung strong?" p. 67.
15. "Korean semiconductor industry," Samsung internal document, 2004, p. 21.
16. "Korean semiconductor industry," p. 19.
17. Samsung, Semiconductor Stories Series #43: July 20, 2004, http://www.sec.co.kr/index.jsp.
18. "Just being a good company is not enough," *Maeil Business Newspaper*, June 2, 2005, A13., http://www.mk.co.kr.
19. "Korean semiconductor industry," p. 20.
20. Ibid.
21. Linsu, Kim. "The dynamics of Samsung's technological learning in semiconductors," *California Management Review* 39:3 (1997): 86–100.
22. "Samsung rising: Why is Samsung strong?" p. 74.
23. Samsung, Semiconductor Stories Series #7: June 2, 2003, http://www.sec.co.kr/index.jsp.
24. "Korean semiconductor industry," p. 29.
25. Samsung, Semiconductor Stories Series #3: May 5, 2003, http://www.sec.co.kr/index.jsp.
26. Gordon Richard and Norwood Andrew. "Worldwide memory forecast, 1Q04 update," Gartner Dataquest report, February 2004.
27. "Korean semiconductor industry," p. 42.
28. Ibid., p. 50.

29. "Samsung rising: Why is Samsung strong?" p. 69.
30. Lee, Kun Hee. *Samsung's new management* (Seoul: Office of the Executive Staff of the Samsung Group, Second Revised Edition, 1997), p. 69.
31. "Samsung rising: Why is Samsung strong?" p. 182.
32. *Business-Week*, June 16, 2003, p. 64. In the second sentence of the quotation, the wording was clarified by Samsung Electronics in an e-mail to the casewriters on June 22, 2005.
33. Lee, Kun Hee. *Samsung's new management*, p. 57.
34. Wu Friedrich and Loy Chua Boon. "Rapid rise of China's semiconductor industry: What are the implications for Singapore?"
35. Ibid.
36. Lai, Dorothy. "2004: A turning point for China's semiconductor industry," *Nikkei Electronics Asia*, December 2003, http://neasia.nikkeibp.com/nea/200312/srep_278997.html.

Case 2–2: JetBlue

Too Much Turbulence

"If you are a rational person running a big airline, you would stop trying to put people like us out of business, and instead build stone walls around your fortresses and defend those."

– David Neeleman, CEO Jet Blue

"Following its competitive reception in Atlanta, we believe Jet-Blue's willingness to enter competitor hubs has declined, at least for now. Removing these markets from consideration limits new market opportunity at JFK to just 13% of New York City demand,"

– Jamie Baker, JP Morgan' airline analyst

Introduction

JetBlue was a low-cost, low-fare passenger airline with revenues of $102 million in 2003. With a fleet size of 31 aircrafts, and a market capitalization of $1.5 billion, it had grown steadily at a rate of 30%. JetBlue had set a trend in the aviation industry by offering low fares, comfortable, affordable, and convenient point-to-point service. Apart from the highest occupancy rates in the industry, it boasted of record on-time arrivals.

Since 2002, JetBlue had witnessed twelve consecutive quarters of profitability and boasted of the best operating margins in the industry. However, by October 2005, JetBlue's margins and profits were under considerable pressure and it struggled to retain its market share. JetBlue suffered a fourth quarterly net loss of $42.4 million in 2005 as compared to $1.5 million in 2004. Its stock in 2005, was worth half of what it was a year before. CEO David Neeleman had introduced several initiatives to turn JetBlue around. Could JetBlue get through the turbulent times?

Background

The Aviation Industry Scenario

The aftermath of the 9/11 terrorist attacks, the economic slowdown, a decline in business travel, the SARS epidemic, competition by low-cost carriers (LCC's) and rising

* **Case study reference no. 306-349-1**
This case was written by Philip Anil Kumar Xess, under the direction of Kaushik Mukerjee, ICFAI Business School, Pune. It is intended to be used as the basis for class discussion rather than to illustrate either effective or ineffective handling of a management situation. The case was compiled from published sources. ©2006, ICFAI Business School, Pune. No part of this publication may be copied, stored, transmitted, reproduced, or distributed in any form or medium whatsoever without the permission of the copyright owner.

fuel prices had an adverse impact on the bottom line of most major carriers. Nearly half the airline companies, most of which were entrants, had filed for bankruptcies. Airlines like United, US Airways, Delta and Northwest had filed for bankruptcies in 2005. Two airlines, US Airways and American West decided to merge. The larger airlines had been attempting to reduce costs by capacity reductions, but saw no improvement in their earnings.

Meanwhile, LCCs continued to grow with lower total costs, higher labor and asset productivity. The low-cost airline category was dominated by Southwest Airlines, which served sixty cities in the US. It had been growing at the rate of 8 to 10%, which was lower than the growth rate posted by JetBlue. As these carriers grew, their routes overlapped the routes of larger carriers, leading to price competition. During this period, the market share of LCC's grew significantly and they carried more than one-fifth of total passengers in the US. Southwest Airlines, the largest LCC, served 60 cities in the US. Many new entrants were awaiting clearance to enter this lucrative category.

The price of crude oil had risen from $20 per barrel in 2003 to $41.44 in 2004, and to $54.03 in 2005. On August 30, 2005, it was at an all time high of $69.91 per barrel. There was also a huge difference between the prices of crude oil and aviation fuel, and after Hurricane Katrina this difference increased to $30 per barrel. An average fuel price of $70 per barrel in 2005 had increased the airline industry's expenses by about $9.2 billion. The U.S. airline industry reported a collective loss of $40 billion for the final quarter of 2005.

JetBlue

Founded in February 1999, the $130 million startup airline, then called New Air, was a modern, hip, LCC. Neeleman leased a fleet of new Airbus A320s, negotiated gate space at John F. Kennedy airport, and hired the industry's best talents. The New York–based airline's first flight was from

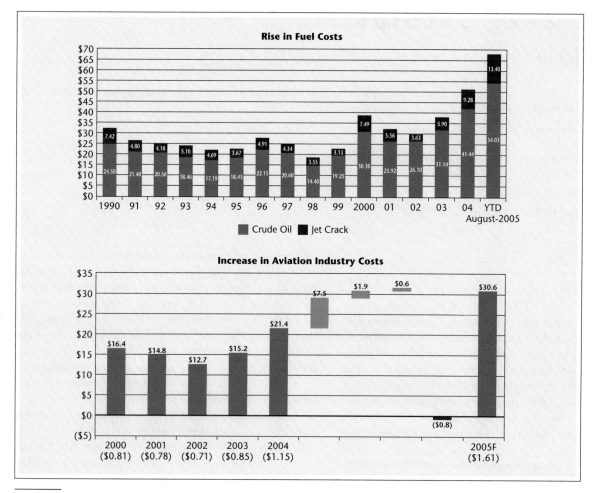

Exhibit 1   **Source:**   http://www.house.gov

New York to Fort Lauderdale on February 11, 2000. A few months later, Neeleman decided that he could cut costs further by purchasing aircraft instead of leasing them. He negotiated an advantageous deal with Airbus whereby New Air purchased 75 planes at a low cost of $4 billion. New Air tried to build its reputation by offering the best amenities. Passengers were offered leather seats and seat-back TVs, an amenity absent in coach class of other airlines. In April 2000, the company changed its name to JetBlue. By the end of 2000, JetBlue was serving 12 cities and had ferried a million passengers. In August 2001, JetBlue decided to expand service out of Long Beach Municipal Airport, near Los Angeles. By then, JetBlue's popularity had grown considerably, especially after a successful IPO and listing on the NASDAQ stock exchange in 2002. The same year, JetBlue acquired Live TV, LLC for $41 million. The diversification plan helped JetBlue broadcast 36 channels of live Direct TV programming for its in-flight entertainment. It also added 100 channels of XM Satellite Radio, Fox TV programs, and 20th Century Fox movies in 2004.

In 2004, JetBlue started offering connections to Boston, Puerto Rico, the Dominican Republic, and the Bahamas. By then, JetBlue had also begun flights from New York's LaGuardia Airport and New Jersey's Newark Liberty International Airport. It was then serving all three New York–area airports. In 2005, it started 10 daily flights between JFK and Logan Airport in Boston, using its newly acquired 100-seat Embraer 190 aircraft. JetBlue was one of the few U.S. airlines making a profit after the 9/11 terrorist attacks.

JetBlue's Business Strategy

JetBlue targeted undereserved markets and large metropolitan areas that commanded high average fares. Instead of flying to major hubs, it decided to provide point-to-point service. It had well planned flight schedules that included short-and long-haul flights covering major cities. It relied on word of mouth publicity to execute its strategy. JetBlue's strategy offered a wide choice of low fares to

Exhibit 2   JetBlue's Annual Profits in Millions

Year	2000	2001	2002	2003	2004	2005
Profits	$21.3	$38.5	$54.9	$102.0	$46.2	($20.3)

Source: www.newsday.com

stimulate demand. It created a single class service with fares averaging 65% less than that of its competitors. All reservations were made ticket-less with the use of Internet reservations. In addition, all seats were assigned, all fares were oneway and there were no discount seats. Jetblue offered fares which were 30 to 40% lower for bookings made 14 days, 7 days and 3 days in advance and its walkup purchase fares were 60 to 70% lower than the fares of its competitors.

JetBlue had developed a low-cost structure. It was a new airline with a fleet of the latest aircrafts. JetBlue planned to use only one type of aircraft with a standard engine. It decided upon the more fuel efficient Airbus A320. The use of standard aircraft helped lower pilot-retraining cost, maintaining better spare, parts inventory, and lower maintenance cost.

JetBlue consistently tried new and innovative ways to cut costs and offer more amenities. It had 1,100 call center operators who worked from their homes around Salt Lake City. In 2004, JetBlue announced that it would add satellite radios with 100 channels to its in-flight entertainment. JetBlue evaluated its proposed routes on factors like existing price levels, current and potential traffic, strength of competitors, and their reaction to intrusion in their markets. As a norm, JetBlue focused on the most attractive and heavily traveled routes, such as the New York–West Coast, and the

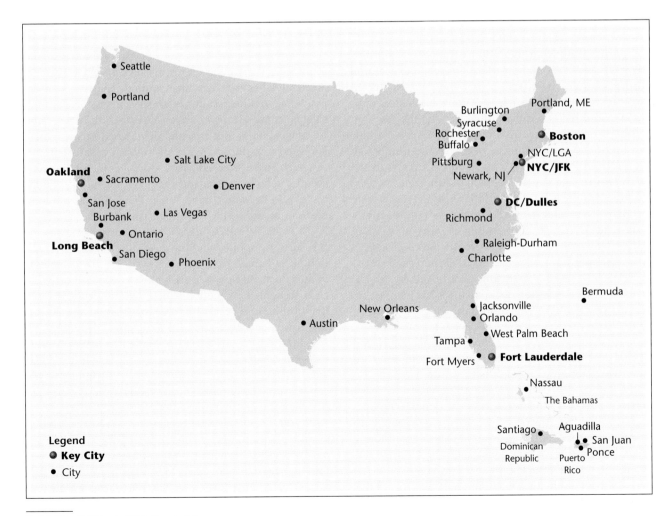

Exhibit 3 JetBlue's 2006 Route Map

Source: www.jetblue.com

New York–Atlanta routes. The success of JetBlue's strategy stemmed from the fact that it offered services in fragmented markets that were not being serviced by existing carriers.

Its aggressive pricing strategy had played a key role in increasing passenger traffic. JetBlue's 30% growth rate was higher than that posted by other low cost carriers. During the same periods LCCs, such as Southwest Airlines grew at the rate of 8 to 10% annually. However, in October 2005, JetBlue's quarterly income dropped from $8.1 million to $2.7 million, even though its market share increased.

JetBlue's Decline

Most of the large carriers who had posted losses or filed for bankruptcy after 9/11, restructured their operations to lower costs. They also tried to compete more on price to attract traffic. Existing LCC's were also expanding their operations even as new players entered the market. The sector grew crowded and routes overlapped, reducing margins. Rising fuel prices hit LCCs like JetBlue hard.

Price wars from the larger competitors affected adversely JetBlue's margins. JetBlue faced competition on the Long Beach–Atlanta route where it had started three flights a day. Delta, a large airline, slashed its fares by 50%, and increased the number of flights. Air Tran leased planes and crew. This reduced JetBlue's margins further and it was forced to decrease the number of flights from three to one and change its focus to the Oakland–Atlanta route. Neeleman admitted that the Atlanta foray was a miscalculation, saying, "We were our own worst enemy by adding too much capacity in certain markets. Instead of adding capacity on existing routes, we had to shift capacity to new markets."[1] JetBlue's operating expenses in 2005 increased 43.3% to $1.65 billion and operating profits fell by 57.1%, to $47.6 million. It had to bear a 99.2% increase in interest payments to $106.5 million, which affected its bottom line.

In January 2005, Delta Airlines started service to eight new destinations. United Airlines and Delta launched their new discount carriers, called Ted and Song, respectively. With Song, Delta targeted JetBlue's east coast customers. In 2005, in a deliberate move to counter JetBlue's aggressive growth, American lowered its fares to $299 each way for coach seats on nonstop flights between JFK and several California destinations, such as Long Beach, Orange County, and San Jose.

With the reduction in leisure and business travel after 9/11, JetBlue's profitable shuttle services on short-haul routes were adversely affected. Unfortunately, the number of business travelers declined further as more

Exhibit 4   JetBlue's Fuel Consumption and Costs

	Year Ended December 31,		
	2005	2004	2003
Gallons consumed (millions)	303	241	173
Total cost (millions)	$488	$255	$147
Average price per gallon	$1.61	$1.06	$0.85
Percent of operating expenses	29.5%	22.1%	17.8%

Source: www.jetblue.com

travelers switched to other modes of transport, such as rental cars and regional rail. In August and September of 2005, JetBlue lost more passengers and revenues after four hurricanes struck Florida, where it offered 40% of its seat miles. The losses amounted to between $8 and $10 million. In the third quarter of 2005, JetBlue cancelled 464 flights.

JetBlue focused on metropolitan passengers and attracted its customers by providing priority check-in, accelerated baggage handling, on-time departure, in-flight amenities that helped in passenger convenience and top safety records. However, adverse weather conditions, traffic congestion at airports, and heightened security measures led to reduced aircraft utilization, unsatisfied passengers, and increased costs. As a result of the new security requirements[2], and changing procedures, airline travel had become cumbersome. This affected JetBlue's on-time record, which dropped from 83.8% in 2004 to 73.5% in 2005. Traffic congestion at airports, especially the JFK airport, spoiled JetBlue's on-time record. Though JetBlue had an all new fuel efficient fleet[3], a 50% increase in auel costs had pushed its fuel costs up. JetBlue's fuel costs accounted for about 23% of the operating expenses in the third quarter of 2004. JetBlue had hedged against fuel price rise. As a result, it paid less than $1.50 per gallon when the market rate was $2.50 in the first half of 2005. In the second half of 2005 and after, only 20% of its fuel costs were hedged, with most of its future hedging having expired. For the remainder of 2005, it had to pay $30 per barrel, putting its margins under pressure.

In July 2005, JetBlue declared that it had purchased "caps" as an insurance against further-price hikes, but the move proved to be too late to start the bargaining process. JetBlue negotiated the price to $65 per barrel for its fuel needs for August 2005, and $66 per barrel for 15% in September, which helped it save some money, though it did not help in the long term. Neeleman admitted that they had not focused on fuel costs, and should have done more

Exhibit 5   Fuel Hedging by Various Airlines

Fuel Hedges: Crude-Equivalent Prices	2005E	2006E	2007E	2008E	2009E
AirTran[1]	74%	23%	16%	0%	0%
	$50	$55	$31		
Alaska[2]	50%	43%	20%	7%	0%
	$30	$40	$45	$49	
America West[2]	57%	12%	0%	0%	0%
	$55	$60			
Frontier[1,2]	17%	0%	0%	0%	0%
	$51				
JetBlue[2]	22%	0%	0%	0%	0%
	$30				
Southwest[2]	85%	65%	45%	30%	25%
	$26	$32	$31	$33	$35
American[2]	6%	0%	0%	0%	0%
	$40				
Continental	0%	0%	0%	0%	0%
Delta	0%	0%	0%	0%	0%
Northwest[2]	6%	0%	0%	0%	0%
	$42				

hedging. In 2005, the carrier had spent about $111.3 million on fuel, up from $57.4 million a year before, thus increasing its per-mile operating costs by 13.4%, to 6.69 cents. By February 2006, JetBlue said that its average fuel costs had increased by 50.3%, to $1.87 per gallon. JetBlue's executives could not predict which way the fuel prices would go. When oil prices rose above $50 per barrel, no one thought that they would break the $70 barrier. The carrier did not have any fuel hedges extending beyond 2006.

JetBlue's Turnaround Strategy

To increase its cost-competitiveness, JetBlue decided to enter smaller markets. This required a shift in strategy. Since its standard Airbus aircraft would not be cost-effective on these routes, JetBlue decided to acquire small aircrafts from Embraer. The carrier faced a two-week delay in the first delivery. A software problem led to a further delay. JetBlue introduced the Embraer aircrafts on the Austin (Texas)–east coast route and planned a service from Boston to Nassau in the Bahamas.

In 2006, JetBlue planned to increase its fares by $10 per ticket. It tried to make a transition from an airline that was used to lower fuel prices to one dealing with higher fuel prices.

JetBlue was building a huge terminal on the area vacated by the bankrupt TWA (Trans World Airlines), at the JFK airport. It had earmarked an investment of $875 million to build a 26-gate terminal that could be expanded to 36 gates. JetBlue, which had been operating 110 flights a day from terminal 6, could operate up to 250 flights a day from the new terminal. The proposed terminal could accommodate 20 million passengers a year. In order to improve its on-time arrival record, JetBlue planned to reduce the turnaround time from 45 and 55 minutes to between 35 and 40 minutes. In some cases the flight schedules would be changed by 5 to 10 minutes to account for persistently late flights.[4]

In January 2006, JetBlue introduced online bag check-in at all locations, where by passengers could drop off their bags at either JetBlue's kiosk[5] or self-service bag drop counters at airports. Customers could check in up to two bags online while the bag tag numbers would automatically get printed on the boarding cards. Passengers traveling from New York's JFK Airport would have an exclusive online bag drop area near the departures roadway[6]. TrueBlue members were offered two bonus points for in online check-in as an incentive.

In July 2005, JetBlue planned to upgrade the size of its seatback TVs. The airline was also increasing the size of overhead bins in all its aircrafts. JetBlue planned to add flights to ten cities with the induction of the Embraer in 2006.

Looking Ahead

David Neeleman wanted JetBlue to become a major carrier with a fleet of 290 planes and 25,000 employees within seven years. By the close of 2006, he intended to hire about 1,800 employees and introduce new flights every three weeks. Neeleman planned to spend around $7 billion to quintuple the fleet by 2011.

JetBlue's decision to acquire Embraer planes had raised some questions. It was the first carrier to use this type of aircraft. Embraer's on-time reliability rate was slightly lower than the Airbus A320, which JetBlue had been using since its inception. The carrier's pilots were not familiar with the aircraft. Moreover, the Embraer aircrafts would be difficult to operate in low visibility conditions. JetBlue was waiting for certification of Rockwell Collins guidance system[7] to address this issue. Analysts[8] said that despite setbacks, JetBlue's outlook was good and it would be around for a long time. They had an efficient management team and there was no need to have doubts about JetBlue's survival. Analysts[9] believed that Logan Airport in Boston could become a focal point for JetBlue from where it could start a number of flights. They expected JetBlue to add flights to Seattle, Sacramento, Phoenix, Syracuse, and Salt Lake City. They believed that JetBlue should also start services to cities like St. Louis and Pittsburgh, where it could target business travelers. Some analysts[10] suggested that the demarcation between LCCs and larger operators had blurred with the latter becoming cost competitive. In 2004, Virgin Group, a low-cost airline operator in Europe and Australia was planning to start a New York–based LCC. Virgin intended to offer services in and around New York, the San Francisco Bay area, and Washington D.C.

JetBlue's cost advantage might suffer when its aircrafts and engines would require multimillion dollar overhauls after operating for several years. JetBlue had indicated that its maintenance costs would increase by 0.2 to 0.3 cents per available seat per mile (ASM) in the next five years. Although JetBlue's employees were not unionized in 2006, a change to a unionized workforce, might result in an increase in operating expenses. Its licensed FAA employee groups if unionized, would require separate bargaining agreements, leading to an increase in labor costs[11].

Analysts[12] were concerned that JetBlue had fore-casted losses for the first quarter and the full year of 2006. JetBlue's stock had been downgraded to "sell" from "neutral," pointing to overvaluation and an increase in competition[13]. Could JetBlue overcome the turbulence?

Annexure 1

David Neeleman was born in October 1959 in Sao Paulo, Brazil. During his childhood he learned entrepreneurship while working at his grandparent's grocery store in Salt Lake City. After dropping out of college, he ventured into the air charter business and joined travel operator June Morris and sold low-cost Hawaii packages. This led to the creation of the low-cost carrier Morris Air, which Neeleman sold to Southwest Airlines for $20 million. Neeleman worked for Southwest for five months, dropping out because he found the work environment full of constraints. Neeleman founded a Canadian discount carrier, WestJet Airlines, and a tickets-less reservation system, "open skies," which he sold to Hewlett-Packard for $22 million in 1999. In January 2000, he launched JetBlue Airways which followed a business strategy similar to Southwest Airlines.

Neeleman's brash style proved useful for JetBlue. He suffers from attention defect disorder (ADD) which includes symptoms such as forgetfulness, distractedness, and restlessness, but Neeleman takes it as an asset. At night he surfs the Internet to get the latest news on the aviation sector. Once a week he flies on his own airline making announcements on the intercom, meeting passengers, and noting suggestions on cocktail napkins. He is the father of nine children, owns 8-percent stake in JetBlue and draws a salary of $286,971.

Annexure 2   Income Statements

	Year Ended December 31,				
	2002	2001	2000	1999	1998
	(in thousands, except per-share data)				
Statements of Operations Data:					
Operating revenues	$ 635,191	$ 320,414	$ 104,618	$ —	$ —
Operating expenses					
Salaries, wages, and benefits	162,191	84,762	32,912	6,000	423
Aircraft fuel	76,271	41,666	17,634	4	—
Sales and marketing	44,345	28,305	16,978	887	—
Landing fees and other rents	43,881	27,342	11,112	447	16
Aircraft rent	40,845	32,927	13,027	324	—
Depreciation and amortization	26,922	10,417	3,995	111	2

Annexure 2   *Continued*

Maintenance materials and repairs	8,926	4,705	1,052	38	—
Other operating expenses	126,823	63,483	29,096	6,405	371
Total operating expenses	530,204	293,607	125,806	14,216	812
Operating income (loss)	104,987	26,807	(21,188)	(14,216)	(812)
Airline Stabilization Act compensation (1)	407	18,706	—	—	—
Other income (expense)	(10,370)	(3,598)	(381)	685	26
Income (loss) before income taxes	95,024	41,915	(21,569)	(13,531)	(786)
Income tax expense (benefit) (2)	40,116	3,378	(239)	233	4
Net income (loss)	$ 54,908	$ 38,537	$ (21,330)	$ (13,764)	$ (790)
Earnings (loss) per common share:					
Basic	$ 1.10	$ 6.59	$ (17.77)	$ (24.54)	$ (1.87)
Diluted	$ 0.84	$ 0.76	$ (17.77)	$ (24.54)	$ (1.87)
Other Financial Data:					
Operating margin	16.50%	8.40%	(20.30)%	—	—
Net cash provided by (used in) operating activities	$ 216,477	$ 111,279	$ 2,824	$ (6,556)	$ (256)
Net cash used in investing activities	(744,461)	(289,855)	(241,130)	(67,452)	(1,147)
Net cash provided by financing activities	657,214	261,695	254,463	80,740	12,917

	Year Ended December 31,				
	2004	**2003**	**2002**	**2001**	**2000**
			(in thousands, except per-share data)		
Statements of Income Data:					
Operating revenues	$ 1,265,972	$ 998,351	$ 635,191	$ 320,414	$ 104,618
Operating expenses					
Salaries, wages and benefits	337,118	267,334	162,191	84,762	32,912
Aircraft fuel	255,366	147,316	76,271	41,666	17,634
Landing fees and other rents	91,181	68,691	43,881	27,342	11,112
Depreciation and amortization	76,540	50,397	26,922	10,417	3,995
Aircraft rent	70,216	59,963	40,845	32,927	13,027
Sales and marketing	63,198	53,587	44,345	28,305	16,978
Maintenance materials and repairs	44,901	23,114	8,926	4,705	1,052
Other operating expenses	214,509	159,116	126,823	63,483	29,096
Total operating expenses	1,153,029	829,518	530,204	293,607	125,806
Operating income (loss)	112,943	168,833	104,987	26,807	(21,188)
Government compensation[(1)]	—	22,761	407	18,706	—
Other income (expense)	(36,121)	(16,155)	(10,370)	(3,598)	(381)
Income (loss) before income taxes	76,822	175,439	95,024	41,915	(21,569)
Income tax expense (benefit)[(2)]	29,355	71,541	40,116	3,378	(239)
Net income (loss)	$ 47,467	$ 103,898	$ 54,908	$ 38,537	$ (21,330)
Earnings (loss) per common share:					
Basic	$ 0.46	$ 1.07	$ 0.73	$ 4.39	$ (11.85)
Diluted[(3)]	$ 0.43	$ 0.96	$ 0.56	$ 0.51	$ (11.85)
Other Financial Data:					
Operating margin	8.9%	16.9%	16.5%	8.4%	(20.3)%
Ratio of earnings to fixed charges[(4)]	1.6×	3.2×	2.7×	1.9×	—
Net cash provided by operating activities	$ 198,420	$ 286,337	$ 216,477	$ 111,279	$ 2,824
Net cash used in investing activities	(719,748)	(987,080)	(879,661)	(365,005)	(263,130)
Net cash provided by financing activities	437,250	789,136	657,214		

Source: www.jetblue.com

Annexure 3 Industry Data

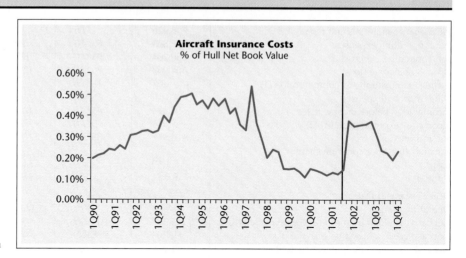

Source: www.spacestation.mit.edu

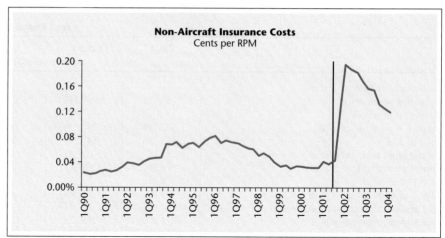

Source: www.spacestation.mit.edu

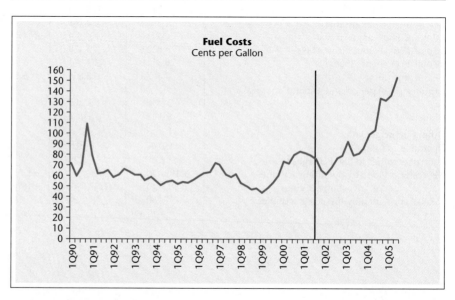

Source: www.spacestation.mit.edu

Annexure 3   *Continued*

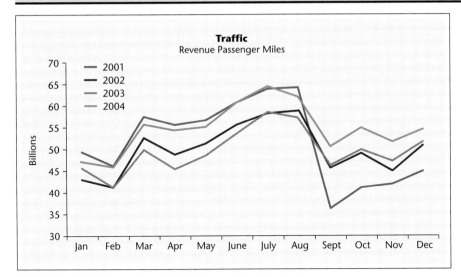

Source: www.spacestation.mit.edu

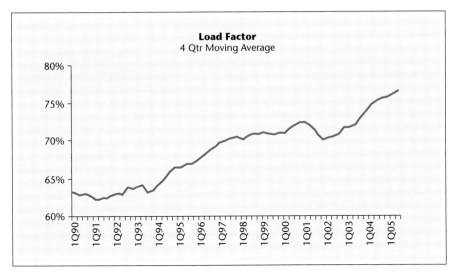

Source: www.spacestation.mit.edu

Annexure 4   Revenues, Profits, and Employment of Leading Airlines

	Revenue		Net income		Return on assets*		Employees	
	2003 $, billion	Change from 2002 (%)	2003 $, million	2002 $, million	2003 (%)	2002 (%)	2003	Change from 2002 (%)
AMR	17.4	0.8	(1.228)	(3.511)	(2.7)	(8.7)	96.400	(12.0)
UAL	13.7	(3.9)	(2.808)	(3.212)	(6.2)	(12.0)	63.000	(12.5)
Delta	13.3	0.0	(773)	(1.272)	(1.1)	(0.7)	75.000	(1.5)
Northwest	9.5	0.2	248	(798)	(1.9)	(6.4)	39.100	(11.8)
Continental	8.9	5.6	38	(451)	2.8	(0.6)	37.680	(14.2)
US Airways	7.0	(15.8)	(1.646)	(2.117)	(2.6)	(20.2)	37.100	(20.4)
Southwest	5.9	7.5	442	241	4.9	4.7	32.847	(2.5)
TOTAL	75.7	(5.6)	(5.727)	(11.114)	n.a	n.a	381.127	n.a

Source: www.people.westminstercollege.edu

Annexure 5   Operating Data of Major Airlines

	Available Seat Miles (billions)		Load Factor (%)		Operating Revenue per Available Seat Mile (cents)		Operating Expense per Available Seat Mile (Cents)	
	2003	2002	2003	2002	2003	2002	2003	2002
United	136.6	148.8	76.5	73.5	9.4	9.4	10.5	11.4
American	185.2	172.2	72.8	70.7	8.7	8.4	10.2	11.1
Delta	134.4	141.7	73.4	72.0	9.9	9.4	10.5	10.3
Northwest	88.6	93.4	77.3	77.1	8.6	8.3	9.9	10.0
Continental	78.4	80.1	75.5	74.1	8.7	8.6	9.4	9.5
Southwest	71.8	68.9	66.8	65.9	8.3	8.0	7.6	7.4
US Airways	58.0	62.3	71.5	69.6	10.6	10.1	11.6	12.7
Air Tran	10.0	8.3	71.1	67.6	8.9	8.6	6.5	6.6
Jet-Blue	13.6	8.2	84.5	83.0	7.3	7.7	6.0	6.1
American West	27.9	27.0	76.4	73.6	9.9	9.7	7.9	8.1
Alaska	2.2	2.3	62.9	62.1	19.0	19.3	17.7	19.5

Source: www.people.westminstercollege.edu

Annexure 6   JetBlue's Operating Statistics

Load factor	85.2%
Number of passengers	14,729,066
Aircraft utilization (hours per day)	13.4
Revenue per available seat mile (cents)	7.18
Cost per seat mile (cents)	6.98
Stage length	1,358 miles
Employees per aircraft	95
Internet %	77.5 %
Revenue (US$)	1.7 billion
Net profit margin (%)	N/A

Source: www.fool.com

Annexure 7   JetBlue's Corporate Culture

JetBlue's corporate culture has helped it maintain a low cost structure and good customer service, which gave it an edge over other airlines. Its management's focus on the welfare of its employees led to the creation of a motivated workforce. JetBlue's corporate culture has five core values: integrity, passion, safety, caring, and fun. This helped it differentiate its product and services. There are four factors contributing to the company's success: providing superior customer service, minimizing costs, retaining employees, and turning a profit. In one of the company's annual reports, David Neeleman acknowledged the contributions of his employees as follows: "At JetBlue, we operate under the belief that great people drive solid operating performance, which yields continued prosperity. Our people are the foundation on which our success is built." JetBlue has 10,000 employees on its roles and its hiring process is stringent. With so many layoffs in the airline industry, JetBlue has a lot of choice. It gives 15% of pre-tax income to a profit-sharing plan and has a stock purchase plan.

Annexure 8   JetBlue's Edge Over Other Airlines in 2002

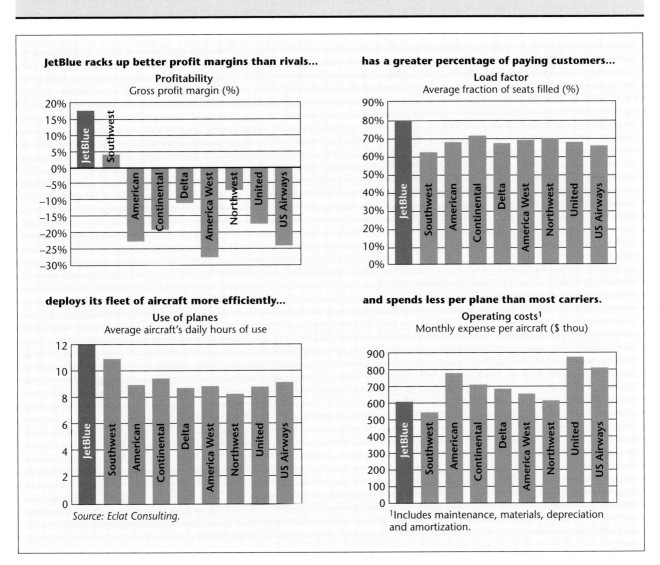

Source: www.forbes.com

Bibliography

1. Hess, Daine. "JetBlue shares fall on concern about prospects," newyorkbusiness.com, January 3, 2006.
2. Munarriz, Rick Aristotle. "JetBlue still under the radar," www.bizjournals.com, January 4, 2006.
3. "Delta joins the mix at Long Beach; will compete directly with JetBlue," www.sltrib.com, January 5, 2006.
4. "Delta's singing a new song October," www.google.co.in, January 23, 2006.
5. Berstein, James. "JetBlue plans flights to 10 more cities," www.airportbusiness.com, January 24, 2006.
6. "Air transport liberalisation: ideal and ordeal," www.flightinternational.com, January 26, 2006.
7. Reuters, "JetBlue CEO cites hiccups in Embraer plane debut," www.usatoday.com, January 27, 2006.
8. Reed, Keith. "JetBlue to gain gates as it beefs up service from Logan," http://en.Wikipedia.org, February 1, 2005.
9. Cameron, Doug. "JetBlue expects full-year loss in 2006," www.msnbc.msn.com, February 1, 2006.
10. Reuters, "JetBlue posts 1st quarterly loss, shares dive," http://today.reuters.com, January 1, 2006.
11. Jackovics, Ted. "JetBlue sees red as fuel prices hit profit, shares," www.redorbit.com, February 2, 2006.
12. Incantalupo, Tom. "JetBlue in the red," www.newsday.com, February 2, 2006.
13. Kirby, Mary. "JetBlue records $20m loss for 2005, calls for $10 per ticket," www.flightinternational.com, February 2, 2006.
14. "JetBlue is failing to run on time," news.cheapflights.com, February 7, 2006.
15. "JetBlue celebrates fifth anniversary by giving away 5 years of free flights," www.primezonemcom, February 28, 2005.
16. Reed, Ted. "JetBlue's growing old fast," www.thestreet.com, March 6, 2006.
17. Lott, Steven. "Delta to replace key JFK mainline transcon flights with Song in summer," www.avitionnow.com, January 26, 2005.
18. Reuters, "JetBlue scrapes profit with fuel hedge," news.airwise.com, January 27, 2005.
19. Reed, Keith. "JetBlue to gain gates as it beefs up service from Logan," www.boston.com, February 1, 2005.
20. "JetBlue tops consumer satisfaction survey," www.consumeraffairs.com, March 24, 2005.
21. Blum, Andrew. "Terminal takes wings," www.businessweek.com, July 21, 2005.
22. Morris, David. "Airline deregulation wasn't cure-all," www.ilsr.org, August 28, 2005.
23. Jonas, David. "Escalating jet fuel prices negate air revenue gains," www.btnonline.com, October 31, 2005.
24. "JetBlue adds online luggage check-in," www.jetblue.com, November 23, 2005.
25. "The steady, strategic ascent of JetBlue Airways," Knowledge@Wharton, www.smarttravel.com, February 2, 2004.
26. Tim-Winship, "JetBlue's hybrid model has potential problems," www.smarttravel.com, February 2, 2004.
27. Zellener, Wendy. "Is JetBlue's flight plan flawed?," www.iirusa.com, February 16, 2004.
28. Reed, Dan. "Long-haul fliers reap benefits of competition," www.usatoday.com, March 15, 2004.
29. Ackman, Dan. "For airlines, it's still 9/11," www.forbes.com, September 13, 2004.
30. Alexander, Keith L. "Airline competition moves to in-flight entertainment," www.washingtonpost.com, November 16, 2004.
31. Gage Deborah and McCormick John. "Delta's last stand," www.baselinemag.com, April 1, 2003.

32. Zellner, Wendy. "JetBlue is strafing the big boys—Again its smaller jets may let it grab more rivals' business," www.businessweek.com, June 23, 2003.
33. Gillin, Eric. "Low-cost carriers steal the show," www.eclipseadvisors.com, July 30, 2003.
34. Tilson, Whitney. "JetBlue's challenges," www.fool.com, September 19, 2003.
35. Whine and cheez/www.airwhiners.net, October 26, 2003.
36. Overby, Stephanie. "Jet blue skies ahead," www.cio.com, July 21, 2002.
37. DiCarlo, Lisa. "JetBlue skies," www.forbes.com, January 21, 2001.
38. "JetBlue- How a discount carrier not only keeps flying but makes money," www.som.yale.edu.
39. "JetBlue Airways Corporation," www.businessfaculty.utoledo.edu.
40. Tayon, Christophe. "Airline Competitive dynamics in the U.S. (1995-2003)m," http://christophe.julbox.net.
41. www.jetblue.com.
42. www.google.com.

Notes

1. "JetBlue's fourth-quarter loss largely 'our own doing,' loss expected for 2006," February 2, 2006, http://atwonline.aero/news/story.html?storyID=3902.
2. Post 9/11, the U.S. government had federalized airport security by hiring about 28,000 workers to tighten security. The incoming baggage's had to follow TSA (Transport security administration) mandated screening through an Explosive detection device. These large machines were placed in the ticketing area and the traveler had to carry the bags to the ticketing counter and then to the nearest machine for which the traveler had to join two lines making check in more time consuming.
3. Fuel expenses were controlled by fuel price and the age of the aircraft and the average length of the flight.
4. Based in Sao Jose dos Campos, Brazil, Embraer was founded in 1969, as a government initiative and then privatised on December 7, 1994. It focused on specific market segments with high growth potential in defence, commercial, and executive aviation.
5. This new online service is a part of JetBlue's online flight check in for customers through its Web site at www.jetblue.com. Customers can select their seat assignments and print their boarding documents from home or office, and proceed directly to the security check point with online check in. Customers may check in online not less than 90 minutes prior to departure, and not more than 24 hours prior to departure.
6. JetBlue started the TrueBlue frequent flyer loyalty program in June 2001. It partnered with American Express Membership rewards loyalty program on December 8, 2004. Card members enrolled in the program will be able to transfer their points directly into JetBlue's TrueBlue frequent flyer program.
7. Rockwell Collins's Head-up Guidance System (HGS) offers energy management and enhanced situational awareness in all flight conditions. All critical primary flight data is displayed in the pilot's forward field of view. The displayed flight path and acceleration information helps the pilot to fly very accurate approaches to a precise landing in all conditions, even in turbulence, crosswinds and on black hole approaches.
8. Stuart Klaskin, aviation consultant, "JetBlue in the red," www.newsday.com.
9. FI Dan Kasper, M.D., and head of aviation practices at LECG LLC, a Cambridge consultancy, "JetBlue to gain gates as it beefs up service from Logan", www.boston.com.
10. Robert Mann, airline consultant, "JetBlue in the red," www.newsday.com.
11. Whitney Tilson, investment manager, "JetBlue's challenges," www.fool.com.
12. Marisa Thompson, analyst for Morningstar, "JetBlue, a former high flyer, loses altitude," biz.yahoo.com.
13. Analysts at Calyon securities and Merrill Lynch.

Case 2–3: Bang & Olufsen and the Electronics Entertainment Industry in 2003*

"Our concept is so strong in every sense, that we don't have to adjust to the market—it is the markets that have to adjust to us. Nothing communicates as strongly as the products themselves. Above all, every one of them communicates Bang & Olufsen—and every one of them has a strong identity. Any form of communication starts by listening to the signals of the products. Only by creating a communication which matches the company's and the products' values do we avoid confusing the identity. Surprising communication which makes the difference—and whose sender everybody would recognise at any time—that's our vision."

— Former Bang & Olufsen CEO, Anders Knutsen[1]

On January 15th 2003, the CEO of Bang & Olufsen, the Danish manufacturer of high-end electronics entertainment products, presented the interim report covering the period June 1-November 30 2002. Despite an overall increase in sales of 3.1% and an increase in margins from 5.0% to 6.6% (see Exhibit 1), analysts responded by lowering the target price of Bang & Olufsen shares. In recent years, B&O had consistently outperformed other manufacturers of luxury goods while its stock price had underperformed the same group (see Exhibits 2, 3, 4). Analysts voiced concern about the 19% decline in sales in Germany. They also seemed to question whether B&O's recent drive into the US market would ever generate profits.

B&O had an impressive track record of stylish audio and video product innovations. At the same time, it continued to be very focused on a small number of products and was running significant losses in the US. Would B&O have to retrench to Europe or could B&O make its magic work around the world? Was its business model sustainable or would it be crowded out by the large electronics companies, which operated globally and leveraged their R&D and marketing capabilities across many product segments? Could it survive as an independent company? These were some of the questions CEO Torben Ballegaard Sorensen, was mulling over in the Spring of 2003.

The Development of the Electronics Entertainment Industry

The foundation for the electronics entertainment industry[2] was laid in 1877, when Thomas Edison succeeded in recovering the song "Mary's Little Lamb" from a strip of tinfoil wrapped around a revolving cylinder. This invention led to the development of the electronic phonograph, which Edison presented in 1888. In 1910, the famous opera singer, Enrico Caruso, was the first to participate in a live broadcast from the Metropolitan Opera in New York. This was followed by the first commercial broadcast in 1921 in Pittsburgh, PA.

Meanwhile, different groups of engineers across Europe were working during the 1920s on the development of the first television concepts. In March 1935, the first television service was inaugurated in Berlin. By November of the same year, television broadcasting had reached the French capital, and throughout the rest of the 1930s, it gained ground across the whole of Europe. In 1939, David Sarnoff, a pioneer in radio and television, introduced broadcasting at the New York World's Fair. NBC and CBS immediately began offering television services.

After World War II, technological innovation gained momentum. New products often featured better quality (e.g., colour television, stereo, Dolby sound), more powerful means of storage (e.g., LP 45 rpm, LP 33 rpm, cassettes, VCR), and improved product features (e.g., lighter and smaller products).

In 1976, the digital era was augured when the American, Dr. Stockham of Soundstream made the first 16-bit digital recording. By 1980, 3M, Mitsubishi, Sony and Studer had all introduced multi-track digital recorders. While the major manufacturers continued to

* This case was written by Karel Cool, BP Professor of European Competitiveness, INSEAD and Hans Ulrik Noergaard, MBA INSEAD 2002, as a basis for class discussion rather than to illustrate either effective or ineffective handling of an administrative situation.

Copyright © 2005 INSEAD

Exhibit 1   Financial Statement for B&O a/s (Consolidated)

(In Mill EUR-(EUR/DKK 7,42))	97/98	98/99	99/00	01/00	01/02	1st half 02/03
Assets						
Cash & S.T. Investments	74.0	17.6	17.5	7.1	22.2	
Receivables (Net)	48.4	51.7	67.0	75.2	81.2	
Total Inventories	63.1	78.5	78.7	92.4	87.9	
Current Assets–Total	185.4	147.8	163.2	174.8	191.3	
Long Term Receivables	4.0	7.7	5.6	3.8	3.7	
Other Investments	2.5	0.0	0.7	0.8	1.1	
Property Plant & Equip–Net	85.4	97.9	114.2	129.0	122.3	
Other Assets	2.2	2.0	5.2	1.9	1.8	
Fixed Assets	94.0	107.6	125.7	135.4	128.9	
Total Assets	279.5	255.4	288.9	310.2	320.2	364.6
Liabilities & Shareholders' Equity						
Accounts Payable	22.7	38.8	38.5	25.1	24.8	
ST Debt & Curr Portion LT Debt	45.6	38.7	35.3	58.6	61.9	
Other Current Liabilities	13.5	9.0	10.8	6.3	6.3	
Current Liabilities–Total	81.8	86.5	84.7	90.1	92.9	
Long Term Debt	26.6	24.8	49.9	52.1	51.7	
Provs For Risks & Charges	7.6	5.1	5.0	6.0	7.0	
Deferred Taxes	6.7	6.8	6.8	7.3	0.9	
Total Liabilities	122.8	123.2	146.4	155.4	152.5	
Minority Interest	0.0	0.0	0.0	0.2	0.0	
Common Equity	156.7	132.2	142.6	154.6	167.7	
Total Liab & Shareholders' Equity	279.5	255.4	288.9	310.2	320.2	
Number of Employees	na	2,668	2,783	2,776	2,908	
Income Statement						
Net Sales or Revenues	420.1	455.6	501.7	513.5	567.7	277.4
Cost of Goods Sold (Excl Dep)	241.0	261.5	281.4	290.9	323.6	
Depreciation, Depletion & Amort	19.6	17.7	21.9	23.1	24.9	
Gross Income	159.5	176.3	198.4	199.5	219.2	
Administration costs	13.5	14.1	15.8	17.5	16.3	
R&D	32.0	34.2	41.5	40.2	44.9	
Distribution & Marketing costs	77.5	84.1	96.0	105.3	123.2	
Operating Expenses–Total	383.7	411.7	456.7	476.9	532.9	
Operating Income	36.4	43.9	45.0	36.5	34.8	18.6
Non-Operating Interest Income	10.7	6.8	12.1	2.3	2.4	
Other Income/Expense Net	16.5	(6.6)	3.5	0.5	0.4	
Earnings Bef Int & Taxes (EBIT)	63.6	44.1	60.6	39.3	37.5	
Interest Expense on Debt	7.6	5.7	15.2	9.1	7.1	
Pretax Income	56.0	38.4	45.4	30.2	30.4	18.3
Income Taxes	14.5	12.7	12.7	10.3	12.0	
Of which Minority share	0.0	0.0	0.1	0.8	1.4	0.3
Net Income Before Pref Div	41.5	25.7	32.8	20.7	19.8	11.3
Dividend	13.5	9.0	10.8	6.3	6.3	
EPS (nominal DKK 10)	17	20	18	12	11	
Quoted share price on 31 May (DKK)	441	462	283	268	235	
P/E	26	23	16	22	21	

Source: Company data.

Exhibit 2 Sector Analysis Household Audio and Video Equipment/Consumer Electronics

1997 to 2001 5-year averages

Ratios:	Company:				
	B&O	**Loewe**	**Philips**	**Sony**	**Thomson**
Profitability Ratios:					
YOY Average Sales Growth	7.28%	3.10%	−5.88%	−1.70%	−0.95%
Return on Total Equity	21.1	16.2	35.1	6.8	15.6
ROA	11.7	4.6	14.1	2.4	5.6
Cost of Goods Sold to Sales	58.2	68.6	64.8	60.5	73.2
Gross Profit Margin	37.5	26.1	29.3	33.5	23.0
Operating Profit Margin	8.9	3.6	3.9	3.1	4.0
Asset Utilisation Ratios:					
Asset Turnover	1.6	1.8	1.1	1.0	1.4
Inventory Turnover	3.7	7.6	4.5	4.8	4.8
Net Sales to Gross Fixed Assets	1.9	2.6	1.8	2.1	2.8
Liquidity Ratios:					
Receivables % of Current Assets	32.8	59.7	43.7	35.1	50.1
Accounts Receivable Days	41.2	78.9	65.8	57.0	87.3
Inventories Days Held	98.0	49.6	79.8	75.7	60.8

Source: Thomson Analytics.

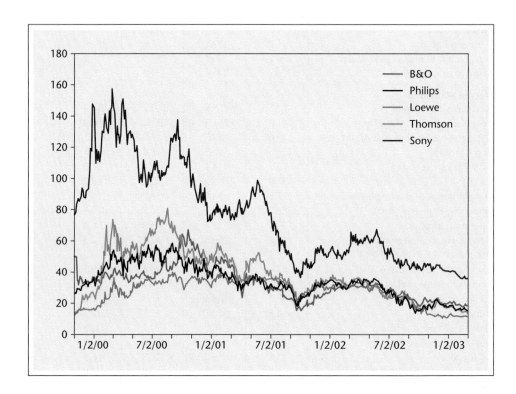

Exhibit 3 Stock Price (EUR) Development 2/11/99–26/02/03

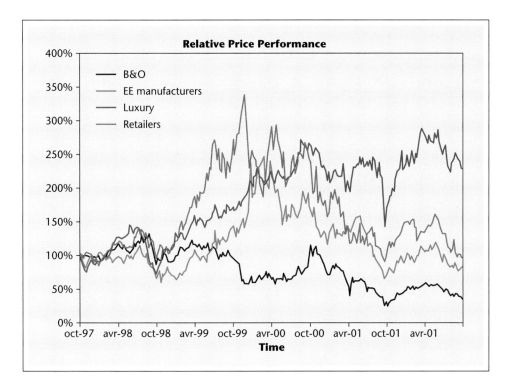

Relative Price Performance

Legend:
- B&O
- EE manufacturers
- Luxury
- Retailers

Y-axis: 0% to 400%
X-axis (Time): oct-97, avr-98, oct-98, avr-99, oct-99, avr-00, oct-00, avr-01, oct-01, avr-01

Exhibit 4 Stock Price (EUR) Development 2/11/99–26/02/03

develop analogue products, research was increasingly directed towards the digital world, with its promise of better quality and greater interactivity. The first tangible result was Sony's launch of the CD player, CDP-101, in 1982. Twenty years later, the industry was promoting High Density-TV (HDTV), Plasma TV, MP3 players with Internet connectivity, etc.

The Market for Electronics Entertainment in Europe and North America

Market Size

In 2002, the market for audio and video products in Europe and North America was about €52.5 billion, split between video product sales of €32 billion and €20.5 billion sales of audio products (see Exhibit 5). The market for electronics entertainment peaked in 2000, when total sales reached €52.9 billion, representing a 0.2% growth over 1999. During the period 2000 to 2002, the industry was stung by the global recession, and sales declined both in Europe and the US.

By 2003, the overall economic outlook remained clouded. Growth of video and audio products up to 2005 was expected to be around 0.5% per year in Europe, and around 2% in the US. These growth projections, however,

masked a substantial variation across product categories. Sales of analogue products were expected to decline, whereas hopes were high for rapid growth of digital and plasma televisions, DVD players and MP3 players.[3]

Mass vs. High-end Segments

The electronics entertainment industry was divided into a high-end segment and a mass-market segment. In 2002, the high-end segment represented about 8% of the total market[4] (€4.2 billion across Europe and the US). This segment was projected to reach €4.4 billion by 2005 (see Exhibit 6 for details). This trend reflected recent wealth increases among consumers in the 1990s. One example of products in this segment was the jumbo television (30+ inch), whose share of all colour TV sets in Germany had increased from 11% in 1998 to 18% in 2000.[5] Products tended to have strong lifestyle brands, high quality, high prices and exclusivity in design and distribution. The German company, Loewe, and Denmark's Bang & Olufsen had been the only major high-end players. Sony, Philips and Thomson had been offering some products in the high-end segment, but remained anchored in the mass market.

By 2002, the mass market was worth €48.3 billion, and was projected to increase to €50.6 billion by 2005. This segment put the emphasis on value for money, product features and low prices. The broad scope of this segment forced manufacturers to carry a wide range of

Exhibit 5   Market Sizes and Growth Rates

(million EUR)	1997	1998	1999	2000	2001	2002	2003[e]	2004[e]	2005[e]
TV, VCR, DVD, Camcorders (1)									
France	2,650	3,000	3,100	3,320	3,380	3,405	3,435	3,470	3,495
Germany	4,175	4,270	4,155	4,040	4,020	4,220	4,185	4,170	4,150
UK	1,197	1,260	1,307	1,323	1,528	1,581	1,594	1,619	1,647
Rest of Europe (2)	4,244	4,513	4,530	4,594	4,723	4,870	4,875	4,898	4,916
US	16,000	16,500	19,300	19,000	17,500	17,950	18,450	19,000	19,700
Total video	28,266	29,543	32,392	32,277	31,151	32,026	32,539	33,157	33,908
Year on Year (YOY) growth		4.5%	9.6%	−0.4%	−3.5%	2.8%	1.6%	1.9%	2.3%
Audio (1)									
France	3,545	3,605	3,660	3,695	3,700	3,700	3,720	3,735	3,760
Germany	3,090	2,995	2,950	3,025	3,025	3,030	3,038	3,052	3,070
UK	844	876	904	929	942	970	1,008	1,017	1,046
Rest of Europe (2)	3,957	3,955	3,975	4,047	4,056	4,074	4,109	4,129	4,167
U.S.	8,360	8,360	8,900	8,905	8,710	8,700	8,715	8,800	9,050
Total audio	19,796	19,791	20,389	20,601	20,433	20,474	20,590	20,733	21,093
YOY growth		0.0%	3.0%	1.0%	−0.8%	0.2%	0.6%	0.7%	1.7%
Total Europe	23,702	24,474	24,581	24,972	25,375	25,850	25,963	26,090	26,251
YOY growth		3.3%	0.4%	1.6%	1.6%	1.9%	0.4%	0.5%	0.6%
Total US	24,360	24,860	28,200	27,905	26,210	26,650	27,165	27,800	28,750
YOY growth		2.1%	13.4%	−1.0%	−6.1%	1.7%	1.9%	2.3%	3.4%
Total Europe + US	48,062	49,334	52,781	52,877	51,585	52,500	53,128	53,890	55,001
YOY growth		2.6%	7.0%	0.2%	−2.4%	1.8%	1.2%	1.4%	2.1%
Total Japan (3)				—	13,000	13260	13,525	13,796	14,072
YOY growth						2.0%	2.0%	2.0%	2.0%
Total Asia Pacific, Middle East (3)					19,800	21,200	22,700	24,300	26,000
YOY growth						7.1%	7.1%	7.0%	7.0%
Total Latin America (3)					6,200	6,620	7,070	7,550	8,060
YOY growth						6.8%	6.8%	6.8%	6.8%
Grand Total					90,585	93,580	96,423	99,536	103,133
YOY growth						3.3%	3.0%	3.2%	3.6%

(1) Source: Euromonitor, Profound Market Briefing June 2002, France, Germany, UK and US TV, VCR and camcorders
(1) Source: Euromonitor, Profound Market Briefing June 2002, France, Germany, UK and US Audio
(2) Case writer's estimate
(3) Includes both audio and video

Source: Customer Market Intelligence, April 2001.

products to meet the demands of the many different consumer types. The product life cycle of mass market products had traditionally ranged between 12 and 18 months.[6] Companies like Sony, Philips, Thomson and Panasonic had traditionally been among the key players in the mass-market segment.

Regional Differences

In 2002, the North American market for audio and video products was €26 billion, of which the high-end segment represented about €2.1 billion (see Exhibit 6). Total sales had fallen by 6.1% in 2001. However, it was expected that

growth would return and range between 1.9% and 3.4% until 2005. The North American market tended to be characterized by intense price competition and a strong focus on marketing. Consumers were often deal-orientated and expected to be able to thoroughly test the product in the store before making a purchase. North American customers also tended to have a higher level of technology literacy than European customers, and were often actively comparing and seeking out product features.

The European market for audio and video products in 2002 stood at €25 billion, of which the high-end segment represented €2 billion (see Exhibit 6). The largest markets were Germany, the UK, France, Italy and Spain, adding up

Exhibit 6   B&O and Loewe's Share of High-End Segment

	2002 Million Eur			High End			Mass Market		
	Total Market	High End	Mass	Total Market	B&O %	Loewe %	Total Market	B&O %	Loewe %
US	26,650	8%	92%	2,132	2.4%	0.8%	24,518	—	—
EU	25,850	8%	92%	2,068	19.8%	13.9%	23,782	0.1%	0.4%
Total	52,500			4,200			48,300		

to more than 85% of the entire European market. The European market had not experienced the same drop in 2001 as the North American market, nor was it expected to realise significant growth until 2005. High-end companies, B&O and Loewe, had their origin in Europe, reflecting the interest of a segment of European customers in style rather than product features.

Digital vs. Analogue Products

Digital products were forecast to play an increasingly important role. In 2002, the digital market was projected to grow at rates of up to 20% per year and reach a total size in North America of €22 billion by 2005. Digital products had historically offered a 25 to 40% higher margin than analogue products.[7] Digital TV was forecast to take almost 25% of total digital sales. Other promising products included DVD players, home satellite systems, digital camcorders, digital cameras, home theatre systems, MP3 players, mobile video, satellite radio, computer software and peripherals, and electronic gaming.

The Video vs. the Audio Market

The video market had been driven by the astounding success of the DVD player. From the introduction in 1998 until 2001, the DVD spread far faster than the CD had done. By 2001, the DVD had reached a market penetration of 25%; the CD had taken nine years to reach the same level of penetration. DVD sales were expected to grow in the near future at 16% annually.[8]

The TV segment witnessed a slower digital migration as sales tended to be limited to a replacement of existing sets. Also, broadcasters appeared unwilling to provide a substantial amount of content in digital format as long as the penetration of digital TVs was limited. In August 2001, the Federal Communications Commission (FCC) ruled that most new TV sets had to be able to read digital signals by 2005. The FCC hoped that this would provide the long awaited incentive for the industry to migrate to digital broadcasting. TV sales were also influenced by the development of flat screen TVs as large as 65-inch, plasma TVs, HDTV, and digital projectors.

Sales of satellite TV equipment were expected to grow by 67% overall, until 2006.[9] The industry had developed "set-top boxes" which allowed analogue TVs to process digital signals. Second-generation set-top boxes would provide the technology required for interactive TV. The market for interactive TV had been estimated to reach a total size of €15–20 billion by 2006.[10] Within interactive TV, personalised content (e.g., no commercials) was expected to be a growth area.

The Personal Video Recorder (PVR) was another promising product. PVRs were positioned as the next generation video players. They could be connected to the Internet, enable Web-TV and select and record shows according to viewing habits. Until 2003, the market for PVRs had remained static at around 1% of the US population. Still, the market had shown strong growth at 16% in 2002.

The total market for audio was estimated to grow from €20.5 billion in 2002 to €21.1 billion in 2005. The main drivers were sales of home theatre systems (28% growth in 2002 to €765 million sales) and MP3 players (14% growth in 2002 to sales of €154 million). Portable audio equipment has been estimated to reach €3.3 billion by 2006.[11]

New Technologies

The transition from the analogue to the digital world continued to change the electronics entertainment market and posed a major challenge to the electronics manufactures. Five concepts were expected to shape the new electronics entertainment world: affordability, portability, interoperability, accessibility and compatibility.[12]

Broadband and wireless (Bluetooth, HomeRF) devices had already significantly changed the way people used the Web. Many predicted that these technologies would become the backbone of tomorrow's home automation. Connectivity with smart sensors and cable and satellite operators would have to be designed. For example, video recorders would have to be able to exchange videos over broadband connections.

Other new products included a Moxi digital entertainment system, which aspired to become the central gateway to all other electronic equipment. This system combined a CD and DVD player, a satellite receiver, a cable box, a PVR and a radio, and could connect to other devices via Bluetooth.[13] Also, portable handheld and hard-drive based products with additional storage capacity were contributing to the convergence of functions. The Panasonic AV-10 contained a camcorder, a camera, an MP3 player, a voice recorder and a viewer. Satellite radio, especially for cars and trucks, was becoming increasingly popular, thanks to its superior quality, service and comfort. Other new trends included new display devices like Mira, a tablet-like screen, or T-Mobile, which combined a PDA, a mobile phone and a digital camera.

The Electronics Entertainment Value Chain

Research and Development

R&D had been one of the key drivers of growth in the electronics entertainment market. It had also led to several

mega battles among corporations to define the standard. Perhaps the most notable battle was the fight in the video cassette recorder (VCR) business in the late 1970s and early 1980s among Sony (Beta), Matsushita/JVC (VHS) and Philips (Video 2000). As only one technology (VHS) became the accepted standard in this market, Sony and Philips had to write off their large investments. For Matsushita/JVC, this victory turned out to be a watershed event in their development. Although standards battles still occurred, the major players had tended to more frequently seek co-development of technologies. To quote Ad Huijser, Philips' Chief Technology Officer, *"We have learned our lessons from the past."*[14] For example, Sony and Philips had co-developed and launched the CD and the DVD. The large consumer electronics companies tended to spend between 4% and 10% of sales on R&D. For Philips, its R&D spending amounted to 9.6% of sales in 2002, 10.2% of sales in 2001, and 7.3% of sales in 2000. For Thomson, this was 3.7% of sales in 2002, 3.5% in 2001, and 3.9% in 2000 (see Exhibit 7 for activity-based expenditures).

Manufacturing

Companies such as Sony and Philips had historically manufactured virtually all their components in-house. During the 1990s, this changed dramatically. Outsourcing of basic

Exhibit 7 Supply Chain Expenditures

Source: Company data–2002 (except 2001 for Thomson) and case writer's estimate figures for Thomson and Philips are consolidated for all their activities.

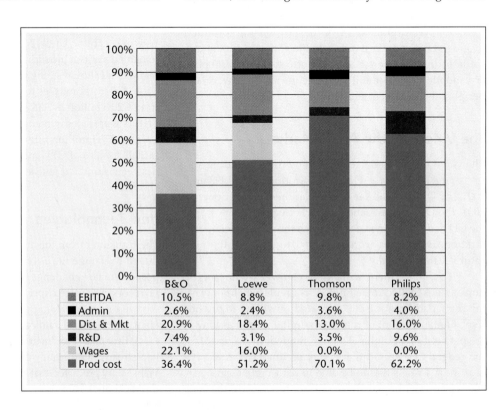

	B&O	Loewe	Thomson	Philips
EBITDA	10.5%	8.8%	9.8%	8.2%
Admin	2.6%	2.4%	3.6%	4.0%
Dist & Mkt	20.9%	18.4%	13.0%	16.0%
R&D	7.4%	3.1%	3.5%	9.6%
Wages	22.1%	16.0%	0.0%	0.0%
Prod cost	36.4%	51.2%	70.1%	62.2%

components became the norm, and even the large manufacturers specialised in a smaller range of key components (e.g., plasma screens), which were often sold to competitors. For example, Bang & Olufsen bought a large range of components from Philips. Because of the increased specialization, both Sony and Philips had significantly reduced the number of production plants worldwide, and shifted production to low-labour cost countries. Since the 1980s, Philips had reduced its number of production facilities from more than 100 to only 14 production sites in 2000.

Marketing and Distribution

Manufacturers used a wide range of marketing approaches to sell their products. The major players relied heavily on TV advertising. In contrast, companies like Bang & Olufsen mainly advertised in high-end lifestyle journals and relied on word-of-mouth publicity and 'one-to-one' marketing (e.g. CRM).

Wholesale distribution of electronics entertainment equipment was typically done in-house through distribution centers dealing directly with large electronic stores and mass merchants. Mass market manufacturers also sold their products through wholesalers that distributed to the fragmented retail market. This retail market had been consolidating, however. High-end manufacturers tended to pay particular attention to distribution as this influenced the buying experience. Bang & Olufsen, for example, had developed a number of stores that exclusively sold their products. Sony had also invested in retail stores, but considered these more a marketing and branding investment than a focus for expansion. Some manufacturers had also implemented the 'store within a store' concept. In particular, the high-end electronics companies, Loewe and B&O, had used this concept extensively to differentiate their products (see Exhibits 8 and 9 for a breakdown of Bang & Olufsen's distribution channels, and see Exhibit 10 for a breakdown of Loewe's distribution channels).

Pricing

Although pricing in the mass market tended to be highly competitive, there remained significant differences in the prices charged by different manufacturers. For example, Bang & Olufsen charged €20,000 for its 42-inch plasma TV, BeoVision 5, whereas Samsung's price for its 61-inch top-of-the-line plasma TV was €14,500. The differences reflected product features, positioning and branding (see Exhibit 11 for price comparisons of TVs from Philips, Grundig, Loewe, B&O, Thomson and Panasonic). Prices gradually declined as new technologies developed.

Key Competitors of Electronics Entertainment Products

Loewe

B&O's most direct competitor was Loewe, the German electronics company, founded in 1923 by Dr. Siegfried Loewe. From its early days, the company focused on technology innovation. It developed the famous Loewe 'triple tube', which many considered to be the first integrated circuit in the world. The Loewe radio, equipped with the triple tube, was the first to reach sales of one million units in Germany, and substantially contributed to the strong growth in the number of listeners between 1926 and 1930.

Scientists at Loewe also focused their R&D on TV technology. This resulted in numerous innovations, including, among others, the first television in the world to be equipped with a square picture tube (1939), the first recorder in the world featuring a cassette tape (1950), and Europe's first stereo colour television (1981). Loewe historically manufactured products with an expected product life cycle of five to six years.[15]

Loewe's products were known for their high quality and elegant design, characteristics which have earned the company no fewer than 132 national and international prizes for 78 of their products since 1981. The company's mission was to offer the best quality products at all price levels. The company's brand campaigns often relied on testimonials with double-page ads featuring personalities from the worlds of design, the arts and entertainment. Although Loewe did not have the luxury lifestyle image of B&O, it had a strong presence in the high-end segment. Its product mix in TV's was also broader that that of B&O, which had led to a better penetration in the mass markets[16] (see Exhibit 12 for a comparison of Loewe and B&O). Loewe sales in 2001 were €372 million (see Exhibit 13 for more financial information on Loewe).

In 2002, Loewe established its distribution in the US. The distribution was set up in cooperation with another high-end manufacturer, Bose, a US sound specialist. Stores were dedicated offering the products of Loewe and Bose, exclusively. Loewe had expected a loss of €0.5 million in the start-up year, but had to revise the number to €2.6 million. It explained that the bigger than expected losses were mainly due to gaps in its product line. Its key product, the 40-inch flat-screen TV, Acordia, had fallen behind the latest standards. It expected that the poor performance would improve once its next generation flat-screen TV was released in the second half of 2003. To stem the losses, Loewe and Bose decided to sell other manufactures' products in their stores.

Exhibit 8 B&O Distribution Channels

Turnover (million Euro)	UK	Germany	Denmark	US/Canada	Switzerland	Holland	SP/Port	Italy
1998/1999	46.9	83.4	77.4	22.4	35.0	28.9	14.9	22.1
1999/2000	57.7	79.2	72.8	27.6	36.8	34.4	18.0	26.8
2000/2001	60.5	75.6	62.9	41.9	37.7	33.4	21.0	26.7
2001/2002	75.3	78.0	64.0	51.2	38.1	39.2	25.6	27.8
2001/2002 growth (3)	25%	3%	8%	20%	n/a	17%	22%	4%
2002/2003 1st half year	40.4	34.5	30.6	22.5	19.0	17.1	16.0	14.6
1st Half growth rate (3)	24%	-19%	13%	-1%	3%	-17%	30%	25%
Number of B1 stores per 31/05/99	33	20	25	n/a	8	10	55	20
Number of B1 stores per 31/05/00	47	47	27	36	14	20	65	28
Number of B1 stores per 31/05/01	61	56	30	55	17	30	68	34
Number of B1 stores per 31/05/02	76	67	32	58	24	35	74	42
Other stores per 31/05/99	n/a	n/a	n/a	24	214	n/a	0	n/a
Other stores per 31/05/00	n/a	n/a	n/a	12	188	150	0	103
Other stores per 31/05/01	80	427	289	0	176	133	0	93
Other stores per 31/05/02	56	387	259	0	161	118	0	85
Number of B1 stores per 30/11/02	80	66	34	60	22	36	78	42
B1 Share of 2000/1999 turnover	n/a	23%	n/a	n/a	n/a	n/a	100%	46%
B1 Share of 2001/2000 turnover	58%	31%	28%	80%	30%	24%	100%	55%
B1 Share of 2002/2001 turnover	67%	35%	35%	100%	32%	27%	100%	58%
B1 Share of 2002/2003 turnover	78%	38%	40%	96%	35%	30%	99%	61%
Growth in B1—mature stores (4)	17%	-10%	22%	-10%	8%	N/A	33%	15%

	France	Asia(1)	Expansion(2)	Sweden	Belgium	Norway	Austria	Japan
1998/1999	20.5	n/a	18.5	13.9	n/a	n/a	n/a	n/a
1999/2000	23.6	n/a	23.1	16.3	n/a	n/a	n/a	n/a
2000/2001	27.0	16.2	13.3	15.1	11.7	8.9	7.8	9.2
2001/2002	29.1	19.0	12.4	14.2	12.4	8.6	7.8	10.2
2001/2002 growth (3)	9%	n/a	7%	2%	6%	2%	n/a	24%
2002/2003 1st half year	12.9	10.8	9.0	7.1	6.3	4.9	4.6	3.4
1st Half growth rate (3)	3%	23%	38%	3%	7%	6%	8%	-18%
Number of B1 stores per 31/05/99	n/a	n/a	n/a	n/a	n/a	n/a	n/a	2
Number of B1 stores per 31/05/00	34	n/a	n/a	17	n/a	n/a	n/a	5
Number of B1 stores per 31/05/01	41	26	42	17	8	14	11	16
Number of B1 stores per 31/05/02	49	35	46	19	13	16	12	18
Other stores per 31/05/99	n/a	0	n/a	n/a	n/a	n/a	n/a	n/a
Other stores per 31/05/00	n/a	0	n/a	n/a	n/a	n/a	n/a	49
Other stores per 31/05/01	86	0	25	41	n/a	29	n/a	33
Other stores per 31/05/02	19	0	19	35	48	20	48	21
Number of B1 stores per 30/11/02	51	40	47	20	12	17	15	16
B1 Share of 2000/1999 turnover	67%	n/a	n/a	n/a	n/a	n/a	n/a	n/a
B1 Share of 2001/2000 turnover	75%	100%	95%	61%	n/a	73%	n/a	n/a
B1 Share of 2002/2001 turnover	84%	100%	95%	63%	n/a	75%	n/a	n/a
B1 Share of 2002/2003 turnover	87%	100%	99%	70%	40%	78%	58%	70%
Growth in B1—mature stores (4)	-6%	n/a	N/a	-1%	11%	-4%	8%	-21%

Source: B&O Interim report 2002/2003 and Annual report 2001/2002.
(1) Singapore, Hong Kong, Malaysia, Korea, Taiwan, Thailand, Indonesia, and Australia   (2) Expansion covers: Russia, Middle East, South America and East Europe.

Exhibit 9   B&O Evolution of Distribution Channels Audio/Visual

	5/31/99	% of turnover	5/31/00	% of turnover	5/31/01	% of turnover	5/31/02	% of turnover	11/30/02	% of turnover
B1 stores	305	32%	410	42%	526	50%	618	61%	638	66%
Stores in stores (1)	2199	40%	1824	37%	669	26%	660	24%	694	23%
Other stores		28%		21%	930	24%	708	15%	582	11%
Total	2504	100%	2234	100%	2125	100%	1986	100%	1914	100%
Turnover growth in mature stores		n/a		16%		4%		6%		7%

Source: B&O Interim report 2002/2003 and various Annual reports.

(1) Split not available prior to 31/05/2000. This 'store in store' numbers are included in Other Stores
Mature store is defined by B&O as a store that has been in operation for more than 2 years

Exhibit 10   Loewe's Distribution Channels

	Description	Allocated Space	No. of Stores 2002	Goal 2002
Forum specialist retailers	The leading retailer in the region–able to conduct thorough consulting	min 25 sq. m	142	180
Studio specialist retailers	One of the leading retailers in its region–able to conduct thorough consulting	12–13 sq. m	577	855
Store specialist retailers	Qualified mass retailer	5–10 sq. m	166	274
Other specialist retailers	Not specifically dedicated	in between other brands	612	214

Source: Company Data.

Exhibit 11   Comparison of Retail Prices of Different Manufactures

	Comparison of colour TV sets		
Manufacturer/model	Tube size in cm	List Price (Euros)	Video Rating
WideScreen 16:9–Europe (1)			
B&O Beo Vision 3	30	3,700	Very Good
Philips 36 PW 9525	34	3,056	Very Good
Loewe Aconda 9381 ZW	30	2,555	Very Good
Grundig MW 82–510/8 DPL	30	1,890	Very Good
Plasma-TVs–US (2)			
Pioneer PDP-5030HD	50	14,091	
Sony PFM50C1	50	10,417	
Philips 50FD9955	50	8,181	
Panasonic TH-50 PHD5U	50	8,699	
Beo Vision 5	42	20,485	
Loewe Spheros 42-S	42	14,600	
Pioneer PDP-4330HD	42	10,455	
Sony PFM-42B1	42	5,909	
Philips 42FD9952	42	5,727	
Panasonic TH-42 PHD5U	42	5,636	
Medion MD 6018	42	5,400	

(1) Source: Deutsche Bank, research report 'Bang & Olufsen and Loewe', 23 April, 2002.   *(2) Source:* http://www.Geodatasys.com/tv.htm, 4 March 2003.

Exhibit 12 Loewe vs B&O—Product Comparison

	B&O	Loewe
Pricing	Top end	Towards high end
Product Line	Focused product mix	Rich product mix
Innovation/NPD cycle	12–36 months	6–24 months
Product life cycle	8 years	5–6 years
Display technologies	Picture tubes, flat screen, plasma	Picture tubes, rear projection, LCD, plasma
Design	Emotional extravagance	Classical elegance
Key competitive strength	Acoustic know-how	Wide range of display technologies
Media	Not a key focus	Strong focus
New products 2002	Beo Vision 5 (plasma), MP3 players	Loewe systems (including Bose) rear projection, LCD 50 cm
Long-term focus	Car audio and acoustic research	Product pipeline underlies innovation and technological advances

Source: Company data, Deutsche Bank "Bang & Olufsen and Loewe," 23 April, 2002.

Sony

Sony was founded in 1945 by Masaru Ibuka, the man who brought transistor technology to Japan. Initially, he established a facility in Tokyo for the repair of radios, and also made short-wave converters, or adaptors, that could easily make medium-wave radios into all-wave receivers. The name Sony was initially just a trademark, but in 1957, it was adopted as the corporate name. Demand for the radios was spectacular. Ibuka's team also found the time to develop an electrical rice cooker! This was the beginning of a long and impressive history of innovation in consumer electronics.

Sony was the leader of the electronics entertainment industry, and offered a wide range of mass market products as well as products aimed at the high-end consumers (see Exhibit 14 for market share data). Sony was known for high quality across its entire product line. It was also known as a leader in the development of new technologies. By 2002, Sony operated 12 Sony outlet stores in the US.

In 2003, Sony was locked in a fierce battle with Microsoft in the game console industry. It had successfully overtaken Sega and Nintendo, and in 2002, depended for 57% of its total profits on this product line. Microsoft, however, had challenged Sony in 2001 for the leadership in this market with the launch of the Xbox. Sony did not want to lose this battle as its other audio/video businesses had come under profit pressure due to intense competition from other consumer electronics manufactures (see Exhibit 13 for aggregate financial information on Sony).

Philips

The foundation for what was to become one of the world's biggest electronics companies was laid in 1891, when Gerard Philips established a company in Eindhoven, the Netherlands, to manufacture incandescent lamps and other electrical products. Philips grew to become Europe's largest electronics group. The company had pioneered many technologies and products, but had, at times, faced difficulties to turn these into commercial successes. The CD-I technology was one example of this. Philips had gone through rounds of restructuring in the 1990s, but had maintained its mass-market focus in consumer electronics. However, similar to Sony, Philips had recently introduced upscale products, and their plasma TVs were selling particularly well. On November 25th 2002, Philips announced that its restructuring in the US was progressing well and that overall sales through upmarket retailers had risen 145% over 2001. Sales of branded TVs were up by 55% compared to the previous year. Entry into high-end retailing had been done through strategic partnerships with premium speciality retailers like Tweeter. In the US, Philips had attempted to sell to the low end of the mass market under the brand Magnavox, while positioning the brand Philips as a premium brand (see Exhibit 13 for aggregate financial information on Philips).

Other Mass Market Players

The French company, Thomson, had been a significant European player, although not of the same standing as Philips. It sold a very wide range of mass-market products.

Exhibit 13   Bang & Olufsen's Competitors

	Thomson Dec 2001 Mil USD	Thomson Dec 2000 Mil USD	Thomson Dec 1999 Mil USD	Sony(1) Mar 2002 Mil USD	Sony(1) Mar 2001 Mil USD	Sony(1) Mar 2000 Mil USD	Philips Dec 2001 Mil USD	Philips Dec 2000 Mil USD	Philips Dec 1999 Mil USD	Loewe Dec 2001 Mil USD	Loewe Dec 2000 Mil USD	Loewe Dec 1999 Mil USD
Assets												
Cash & S.T. Investments	1,365.0	1,507.0	404.0	5,154.0	4,858.0	5,906.0	793.0	1,026.0		8.5	9.7	
Receivables (Net)	2,850.0	2,040.0	1,910.0	9,367.0	10,362.0	9,957.0	5,180.0	6,122.0		85.0	85.1	
Total Inventories	998.0	1,256.0	1,113.0	5,076.0	7,543.0	8,106.0	3,824.0	4,972.0		45.9	41.8	
Other Current Assets	259.0	18.0	52.0	5,556.0	5,057.0	5,603.0	421.0	392.0		0.0	0.0	
Current Assets—Total	5,472.0	4,821.0	3,479.0	25,153.0	27,820.0	29,572.0	10,218.0	12,512.0		139.3	136.7	
Fixed Assets (Net)	1,369.0	954.0	1,096.0	10,640.0	11,474.0	11,845.0	6,879.0	8,515.0		56.3	56.5	
Other Noncurrent Assets	1,884.0	424.0	414.0	25,904.0	23,330.0	22,802.0	17,177.0	15,271.0				
Total Assets	8,725.0	6,199.0	4,989.0	61,697.0	62,624.0	64,219.0	34,274.0	36,298.0		195.5	193.2	
Liabilities & Shareholders' Equity												
Accounts Payable	1,228.0	947.0	881.0	6,552.0	6,460.0	6,429.0	2,890.0	4,007.0		34.4	44.4	
ST Debt & Curr Portion LT Debt	0.0	253.0	336.0	8,455.0	10,251.0	9,679.0	1,133.0	1,642.0		8.9	9.7	
Other Current Liabilities	1,884.0	886.0	970.0	4,276.0	4,463.0	4,273.0	5,709.0	5,210.0		6.7	7.3	
Current Liabilities—Total	3,112.0	2,086.0	2,187.0	19,283.0	21,174.0	20,381.0	9,733.0	10,859.0		51.1	51.7	
Long Term Debt	1,008.0	719.0	27.0	6,321.0	6,749.0	7,678.0	5,878.0	2,151.0		3.8	5.1	
Other Liabilities	63.0	36.0	71.0	1,379.0	1,553.0	2,062.0	2,036.0	442.0		73.5	70.3	
Other Noncurrent Liabilities	1,014.0	926.0	976.0	16,848.0	14,624.0	13,505.0	2,036.0	2,375.0		0.0	0.0	
Total Liabilities	5,197.0	3,767.0	3,261.0	43,831.0	44,100.0	43,626.0	17,826.0	15,827.0		128.4	127.1	
Common Equity	3,528.0	2,432.0	1,728.0	17,866.0	18,524.0	20,593.0	16,447.0	20,471.0		67.1	66.1	
Total Liab & Shareholders' Equity	8,725.0	6,199.0	4,989.0	61,697.0	62,624.0	64,219.0	34,273.0	36,298.0		67.1	66.1	
Shares Outstanding (mil)	265.1	262.5	124.4	922.8	919.6	907.3	1,274.2	1,283.9		7.1	7.2	1,087
Number of Employees	64,328	61,592	55,633	168,000	181,800	189,700	188,643	219,429	226,874	1,170	1,077	
Income Statement												
Net Sales or Revenues	9,353.0	7,734.0	6,723.0	57,117.0	58,518.0	63,082.0	28,824.0	35,658.0	31,459.0	330.1	319.8	311.7
Gross Profit	2,461.0	2,101.0	1,920.0	22,124.0	19,617.0	19,233.0	10,652.0	10,821.0		106.2	100.7	
Selling, Gen & Adm Expenses	1,553.0	1,388.0	1,265.0	16,612.0	13,071.0	14,071.0	8,529.0	5,894.0		63.7	62.5	
Depreciation, Depletion & Amort	386.0	255.0	292.0	4,498.0	4,743.0	2,892.0	2,493.0	2,185.0		19.4	17.2	
Operating Income	522.0	458.0	363.0	1,014.0	1,803.0	2,270.0	(370.0)	2,742.0		23.1	21.0	
Operating Expenses—Total	8,831.0	7,276.0	6,360.0	56,103.0	56,715.0	60,812.0	29,194.0	32,916.0		307.0	298.8	
Other Income/Expense Net	(165.0)	(140.0)	(89.0)	(576.0)	(265.0)	(134.0)	(2,338.0)	7,048.0		(6.8)	(1.7)	
Earnings Bef Int & Taxes (EBIT)	419.7	378.3	296.5	578.7	1,667.8	2,248.8	(2,205.3)	10,082.6		18.3	21.1	
Interest Expense on Debt	(62.7)	(60.3)	(22.5)	(140.7)	(129.8)	(112.8)	(502.7)	(292.6)		(2.0)	(1.8)	
Pretax Income	357.0	318.0	274.0	438.0	1,538.0	2,136.0	(2,708.0)	9,790.0		16.3	19.3	
Income Taxes	124.0	(1.0)	51.0	491.0	924.0	892.0	(375.0)	537.0		7.1	8.1	
Net Income Before Pref Div	233.0	319.0	223.0	(53.0)	614.0	1,244.0	(2,333.0)	9,253.0	1,799.0	9.2	11.2	
Cash Flow												
Net Operating Cash Flow	896.0	349.0	437.0	5,559.0	4,358.0	5,467.0	1,112.0	2,822.0		n/a	n/a	
Net Investing Cash Flow	(1,045.0)	(339.0)	(368.0)	(5,782.0)	(5,753.0)	(4,245.0)	(4,068.0)	(2,264.0)		n/a	n/a	
Net Financing Cash Flow	(30.0)	1,201.0	17.0	641.0	1,076.0	(642.0)	2,816.0	(1,919.0)		n/a	n/a	
Net Change in Cash	(214.0)	1,165.0	135.0	577.0	(151.0)	319.0	(177.0)	(1,170.0)		n/a	n/a	

Source: Company Data and Hoover's, Inc. 1) Consolidated figures for all entities.

Exhibit 14   Regional Market Share Year 2000

(Based on Revenue)	Sony	Philips	Matsushita
Europe	21%	14%	17%
North America	27%	13%	10%
Latin America	24%	10%	19%
Asia Pacific (excl. Japan)	15%	8%	5%
Global (excl. Japan)	22%	11.8%	12.2%
Global (incl. Japan)	22%	13%	10%

In recent years, Thomson had been focusing on the design of its products with the help of several well-known designers (e.g., Philip Starck). The product philosophy was one of creating designs of sufficient quality for the mass market (see Exhibit 13 for aggregate financials). In 1990, Thomson launched Proscan, a high-end brand, but it did not really catch on with consumers. In 1995, Thomson changed its company name to Thomson Multimedia to reflect its increasing focus on this activity. In addition to the above electronics companies, many other competitors were offering products of quality: Toshiba, Samsung, Panasonic, Sharp, Pioneer, Bose, Yamaha, Sanyo, Siemens, JVC and Grundig, whose focus was exclusively the mass market.

Bang & Olufsen A/S

History

B&O was founded on November 17, 1925 by Peter Bang and Svend Olufsen. The first product the two young engineers produced was the world's first radio with a mains plug, "The Eliminator" (1926). This was a technological leap from the traditional battery driven radio. Since this first invention, Bang & Olufsen consistently sought to be an innovator.

In 1938, Bang & Olufsen introduced the first mains radio with push-button operation, the "Master 38CH". The subsequent launch of the "Master deluxe 39" came with 16 permanent stations. This invention, along with the strict use of high quality materials, was instrumental in the creation of B&O's reputation for quality. 1939 also saw the launch of the "BeoLit", the first radio with a Bakelite cabinet. The BeoLit was the first product to carry the famous "Beo" name, which has since labeled all major new products from Bang & Olufsen. In 1940, Bang and Olufsen launched a campaign to sign up authorised Bang & Olufsen dealers to expand its sales in international markets.

In 1954, the famous Danish architect, Poul Hennigsen,[17] expressed his general disgust with the design of the objects that surrounded people in their daily life. As an example, he referred to Bang & Olufsen's top-line radio, "Grand Prix", and quipped, *Is it a fishmonger or a potato merchant who spent his leisure time drawing these things?* Ever since, style and quality became a hallmark of B&O, resulting in numerous international prizes for innovative designs and product quality (especially for acoustics and user-friendliness.[18] Their well-known 1963 slogan, *"B&O, for those who discuss design and quality before price,"* was still being used four decades later.

Throughout the 1970s and 1980s, Bang & Olufsen continued to develop and produce new and innovative products. A highlight of this era was the development of the groundbreaking **BeoLink** system, allowing the user to receive audio and video signals in different rooms through a single operating unit by the use of discreet cabling and infrared remote control units. This was the first remote that was able to simultaneously operate all the different prod-

Exhibit 15   Result for B&O Business Units

	Revenue			Pre tax Profit		
	00/01	01/02	02/03*	00/01	01/02	02/03*
Audio Visual (100% owned)	481.8	530.5	256.6	27.1	30.9	20.1
Telecom (100% owned)	32.9	35.4	20.8	n/a	(1.3)	n/a
Mediocom (100% owned)	31.4	40.0	16.2	4.6	2.2	(0.1)
New Business (100% owned)	0.3	2.3	1.8	(1.5)	(2.6)	(1.1)
Operations (100% owned)	n/a	n/a	n/a	n/a	n/a	n/a

*First Half

Source: Company data.

ucts from the same manufacturer. In 1978, 11 Bang & Olufsen products were accepted into New York's Museum of Modern Art., by 2002, this number had grown to 18.

During the late 1980s and early 1990s, Bang & Olufsen experienced a significant financial crisis. While the company had several products on permanent display at New York's Museum of Modern Art[19] and New York's Metropolitan Museum of Art, they had lost financial control.[20] Finance EVP Peter Thostrup commented on the situation in 1992: "*I can't say that we were a profit-driven company. The products were what the company cared about.*"[21] Many wondered whether B&O would survive. The crises also forced Bang & Olufsen, in the early 1990s, to sell a 25% equity stake to Philips.

The very poor 1990/1991 results led to the replacement of CEO, Vagn Andersen, with Anders Knutsen. Having joined the company in 1973 as Head of the Personnel and Working Environment Department, he worked his way through the company in various positions. In November 1992, the new CEO presented his turnaround plan, "Breakpoint 1993". The plan focused on tight financial control while maintaining the strengths of B&O in design and R&D. More particularly, Knutsen set out to outsource all non-core activities, considering everything from the cafeteria to the production of transistors. A second focus was the reduction of working capital through just-in-time production and improved efficiency in R&D. The third leg of the strategy was a repositioning of the brand from a top-line electronics brand to a true luxury goods brand. The fourth focus was the streamlining of distribution to increase profitability and ensure that the targeted repositioning could be supported.

The turnaround was a success. When Bang & Olufsen released its 1997/1998 results, it also announced that it had bought back the 25% equity stake it had sold to Philips. In 2000, B&O split the company into five separate units in order to support the above strategy (see Exhibit 15 for details). By the end of the decade, B&O was again on firm financial footing and had sharpened its business model. It had also sought out new businesses where it could use its competencies in design (e.g., medical equipment) and had entered the United States market.

Bang & Olufsen's Business Model

Research and Development.   Bang and Olufsen carried out fundamental research in the acoustics area where 30 engineers were actively pursuing new technologies. In addition, another 200 people were carrying out research in video (120), audio (30) and systems integration (40).

However, its primary focus remained design (product design, functionality and systems integration). A remarkable example of this focus was the Beo 1 remote control, which had only 11 buttons, yet could be used to operate all B&O appliances in the house.

Product design had been driven by a small number of highly influential designers (see Exhibit 16). This had resulted in very strong design consistency. Standing out were designers Jakob Jensen and David Lewis who had, more than anybody else, defined the B&O design. The successors to David Lewis were already being groomed by Lewis himself. Bang and Olufsen strongly believed that its designers should not be employees but freelancers. They feared that if designers got too close to Bang & Olufsen, they would start paying too much attention to the problems and limitations in the rest of the organization, and could make them lose their creative edge. While most freelance designers had a dominant part of their activities with B&O, they remained independent.

R&D originated from the "Idealand", which was a central hub around which product design was organised. The R&D was very much team-based. User-interfaces were, for example, developed by an interface designer, a psychologist, a software developer and a narrator.[22] This team design was a conscious decision to ensure that several perspectives were given due consideration. This team structure had also been a cornerstone of B&O's efforts to develop the coherent and integrated home entertainment system, BeoLink (all room, one system, one remote). Considering the high price of the products, B&O customers expected them to last well into the future. In response to this, Bang & Olufsen worked with the rule of thumb that each product had to have an expected product life of eight years. B&O had decided that it was more important that their products were flawless than to be the first to launch a new technology. For example, while other electronics manufacturers had been competing aggressively to get first to market with plasma TV screens, B&O had waited for the arrival of the second-generation plasma screen that offered better picture quality (BeoVision 5, see Exhibit 17). In the meantime, B&O had devoted its efforts to perfecting the design of the TV.

To secure access to new technologies and components at low cost, B&O had or was engaged in strategic partnerships with Ericson and Philips. Philips, in fact, had been a B&O supplier of components for more that 60 years, selling picture tubes, optical discs, DVD and CD players. Other suppliers were Panasonic (plasma screens), Sony, Hitachi and Sanyo.

Exhibit 16 Key Designers

Jacob Jensen (1926-) qualified as a furniture upholsterer and trained at the College of Arts and Crafts. This was supplemented with an early association with Bernadotte & Bjørn's drawing office (1954–1959), the first industrial design drawing office in Denmark. He became a partner in the ID firm Latham, Tyler & Jensen, New York/Chicago (1959–61) and set up his own company in Denmark in 1958. From his drawing office on a hillside sloping down to the Limfjord in North Jutland, he derives inspiration for his severe, horizontal minimalist idiom, in which the characteristic qualities of Danish neo-classicism can be discerned in shape and colour. He has created more than 500 industrial products for Danish and foreign companies (e.g., an astronomical clock for Max René, office chairs for Labofa A/S, Comet telephone for Standard Electric Kirk (1976), toys for LEGO, and kitchen appliances for Gaggenau Hausgeräte GmbH).

Jacob Jensen Design received particular recognition in connection with Bang & Olufsen, where he was chief designer for more than two decades, creating an extensive line of audio products (e.g., BeoLit 600 (1970), BeoGram 4000 (1972) and BeoCenter 9000 (1986)). The working relationship between B&O and Jacob Jensen began in 1965, and went on in various forms until 1991. During the years 1965-1985, the designer developed the exclusive and aesthetic form language which today continues to be the basis of B&O's conceptual and visual platform. From 1985 to 1989, Jensen functioned as advisor to B&O on matters of design and strategy. Altogether, Jacob Jensen has designed more than 100 products for the hi-fi and video company. The majority of these products have been awarded design prizes, both nationally and internationally, and are included in museum collections all over the world.

Up to the late 1990s, Bang & Olufsen had contracts with three designers: David Lewis, Anders Hermansen and Anne Mette Sonnicksen. David Lewis heads his own design studio, and his work for B&O is done partly by himself and partly by his four employees. Lewis used to be employed at Jacob Jensen's design studio. He has thirty years of experience in designing products for B&O, and has been chief designer for them since 1987. His studio spends almost 90% of its time designing for B&O. The rest of the time is spent with other clients including the kitchen appliance producers, Voss and Electrolux.

Anders Hermansen has been working with B&O since the mid-1990s, and designed BeoLab 2000. Until he started working exclusively for B&O from his one-man design studio in northern Zealand, he primarily worked in furniture design. While Hermansen and Lewis work on the same issues, namely overall product design, their style and approach differ. Hermansen is very conscious of functional aspects of the design, while Lewis places greater emphasis on the aesthetic side of designing B&O products. The use of two different design approaches is part of the company's attempt at attaining a more diverse design language, thereby gaining a broader consumer appeal. Anne Mette Sonnicksen is B&O's graphical and interface designer. She is responsible for this part of all B&O products, a job she has performed since the early 1990s from her own design studio in Aarhus, Jutland. Her main task consists of designing interface means for B&O televisions, but her position means that she is involved in all B&O products.

Source: Excerpts from: http://www.beoworld.co.uk/designers.html

---

Production. Bang and Olufsen had outsourced most of its production to suppliers, buying picture tubes from Philips, plasma screens from Panasonic, and peripheral devices from a range of suppliers. In their facilities in Struer, Denmark, B&O produced PCBs (key electronic components) and surface components, and conducted final assembly and quality control. Former CEO Anders Knutsen[23] commented, *"No matter which end of the price range you buy, the Bang & Olufsen special standards of quality are part and parcel of the purchase."*

One product in which analysts and B&O had placed a lot of confidence was the BeoVision 5 plasma television. The BeoVision was the brainchild of the designer, David Lewis, who found his inspiration in the movie, "Fahrenheit 451", which featured a flat wide-screen TV on the wall.[24] The BeoVision had been designed in such a way that it could be attached to the wall, lean against a wall or stand freely in the room. The television was equipped with a brushed aluminium frame, which was intended to serve the same purpose as a *passe-partout* for a painting: to direct the eye and render calmness. To provide interior decoration flexibility to the consumer, B&O decided to offer the frame in several colours: natural, black, red, blue and green.

The frame encapsulated the latest technology, ensuring that the picture quality was optimal. One feature of this technology were sensors that would measure the light intensity of the room and adjust the TV settings accordingly Powerful, built-in speakers were located beneath the screen, with a possibility of Dolby Digital Surround. The BeoVision 5 was only built to order to meet the customer's individual requirements. Because of the precision required to construct the TV, there were 1,000 components assembled by hand before the TV underwent exhaustive testing and quality control.

Exhibit 17   BeoVision 5

Source: © Bang & Olufsen, 2006.

Marketing.   B&O's marketing efforts were closely aligned with the image it aimed to project. Firstly, it did not advertise in mass media or widely distributed publications but only in high-end lifestyle magazines. Secondly, it communicated two messages. One type of advertising showed no product featuring. The objective was to communicate the values B&O wanted to associate with its products. This, for example, could be 'freedom' with reference to the BeoLink system. The other type of advertising usually featured one B&O product (and, exceptionally, several B&O products) in a very sophisticated setting. The overriding theme was picturesque simplicity. The arrival of the Internet brought another marketing medium which B&O tapped to project its core values. Since 1995, B&O has also realised numerous product placements in major Hollywood motion pictures (e.g., The Sum of all Fears; Men in Black II; Minority Report, Vanilla Sky; Unfaithful; Charlie's Angels; Tomorrow Never Dies; Mission Impossible) and some TV series (e.g., Sex in the City).

Distribution.   Facing increasing competition from Japanese manufacturers in the 1970s, B&O started to develop closer ties with selected retailers. These were offered a partnership, referred to as the BeoCenter, the name under which they would sell B&O products exclusively. To further develop this strategy, B&O created a company called "Expo-Competence", which specialized in the design of BeoCenters. The ultimate product was a complete turnkey shop aimed at the exclusive sales of B&O products.

The distribution approach was further developed when B&O experienced the financial crisis of the early 1990s. It had observed that retailers that carried B&O products alongside products of competitors very often focused on price rather than quality. To overcome this, B&O accelerated the implementation of exclusive distribution channels. It also banned non-exclusive retailers that did not agree to play by their rules. As Lars Topholm, B&O CFO, commented, "*We got rid of retailers who were discounting. After all, we don't sell just technology—we sell magic.*"[25] As a direct consequence of this policy, B&O reduced its retailer network from 3,000 to 2,000 outlets between 1994 and 1997.

By 2003, B&O had a retail presence in more than 40 countries. The following retail formats could be distinguished:[26] **B1** shops, selling only B&O products; **B2** shops, with at least 50% of revenues related to B&O products; **B3** shops, with 25–50% of revenues related to B&O products;

C shops, buying at least DKK 500,000 worth of products from B&O per year; **D** shop-in-shops, selling B&O products in shopping centers; **E** shops which were chains buying at least DKK 500,000 from B&O per year. Except for 30 B1 shops in Europe and 20 B1 shops in the US, B&O had no ownership in the distribution channel. The remaining B1 stores were run as franchises. B&O placed very specific demands on training.

The Entry of B&O into the US Market

In 1998, B&O opened its first B1 stores in the US. This signaled its fully-fledged entry into this market, targeting the 1.5% of American consumers (or 4,125,000 people)[27] for whom B&O thought price was of lesser importance. When B&O entered the US, it was faced with a challenge of finding a sufficient number of franchisees because of the limited awareness of the brand. This forced B&O to own the majority of its B1 stores, contrary to their normal strategy. The expansion proved to be very costly, leading to a loss in the US of €3 million in the 2nd half of 2002, compared to a loss of €4 million in the corresponding period of 2001. In addition, provisions of €3.1 million were made to cover the cost of closing stores. This cost had been €0.4 million in 2001 (see Exhibit 18 for details on US). Factors other than costs that were also raised to explain the negative result were bad management, poorly trained sales personnel, choice of the wrong locations that were either too expensive or had suffered from the rapid change in demographics and a lack of a full product portfolio.

In response, Bang and Olufsen abandoned its exclusivity policy and introduced non-B&O branded products, such as a 42-inch Panasonic LCD TV, to fill the gaps. It also changed its objectives for the US from 100 stores by 2004 to profitability. Ole Bek, President Bang & Olufsen America, explained: *"We were looking at a three- to five-year plan, but now we are looking at a six- to seven-, or maybe an eight-year plan."*[28] In December 2002, B&O launched its BeoVision 5 (plasma TV) in the US, and the reviews were very positive.

Because of its relatively limited public relations budget, Bang and Olufsen did not run large campaigns but relied on co-sponsored events in the local area. CEO Torben Ballegaard remained optimistic: *"The market is there. There are plenty of rich people that like our products. We just need to get hold of them. That is our challenge."*[29] With this statement, he referred to the increasing demand for complete home cinema solutions priced in the range of US$50,000 to US$75,000.

Bang & Olufsen New Business Development

By 2003, B&O had five fully owned business units.[30] The corporate unit was responsible for brand building and group staff functions. In addition to *B&O AudioVisual*, B&O had created *B&O Telecom* to develop and market new telephony concepts for dynamic electronic communication in the home, and *B&O New Business* to leverage core competencies. It owned over 75% of B&O ICEpower that developed, produced and marketed products based on powerful amplifier technology. Another business unit was *B&O Medicom*, which targeted the market for medical equipment in collaboration with existing and new partners. The first success had been the development of an insulin injection pen for Novo Nordisk. The pen, which combined design with superior ease of use, was a great success. A fifth unit was *B&O Operations*, which handled purchasing, production and logistics for the B&O Group.

Exhibit 18   B&O Performance in US/Canada

	96/97	97/98	98/99	99/00(1)	00/01	01/02(2)	02/03 1H(3)
Turnover	20.6	20.0	22.4	27.6	41.9	51.2	22.1
Loss	n/a	n/a	n/a	(2.0)	(5.5)	(10.8)	(6.9)
B1 Stores	n/a	n/a	n/a	36	55	58	58

Source: Company data.

(1) 99/00 Loss is case writer's estimate   (2) Loss includes a provision of €0.4 million to bad debt   (3) Loss includes a provision of €3.8 million to discontinuation of stores

The Challenge for Bang & Olufsen

In spite of the confidence expressed by Mr. Torben Ballegaard Sørensen, the stock price of B&O remained depressed (see Exhibit 19 for ownership details). Analysts were impressed with the new products they had seen, but also remained focused on the sales evolution in B&O's key markets and the problems in establishing a beach head in the North American market. Was another financial crisis looming or was B&O well positioned to continue its development as an independent manufacturer?

Exhibit 19   Bang & Olufsen's Ownership Structure

Entity	Capital	Votes
LD (2)	9.99%	15.62%
Nordea (3)	9.58%	15.16%
ATP (2)	7.03%	3.97%
Own Shares	6.67%	7.00%
Others	66.73%	58.25%

(1) Several classes of shares with different voting rights
(2) Government controlled mutual funds
(3) Largest Scandinavian Commercial Bank

Notes

1. Interview with former (1991–2001) Bang & Olufsen CEO, Anders Knutsen, on Danish TV-2, September 1997.
2. For the purpose of this paper, electronics entertainment will cover traditional audio/visual equipment but exclude devices such as gaming consoles and PCs.
3. Bear Stearns, Equity Research, Hard Lines Retailing. Consumer Electronics, March 2002.
4. Estimate based on Loewe and B&O sales compared with overall European market, and also accounting for Sony's, Philips' and Thomson's sales in this segment.
5. Deutsche Bank, Equity Research, Bang & Olufsen and Loewe, April 23, 2002.
6. Philips briefing—*Consumer Electronic Mainstream.*
7. Bear Stearns. "Hard line retailing," March 2002, p. 20.
8. Bear Stearns. "Hard line retailing," March 2002, p. 23.
9. Profound, "US cable and satellite TV equipment market", p. 2.
10. Profound, "US TV, VCR and camcorders market", p. 16.
11. Bear Stearns. "Hard line retailing," March 2002, p. 37.
12. Bear Stearns. "Hard line retailing," March 2002, p. 5.
13. Bear Stearns. "Hard line retailing," March 2002, p. 8.
14. http://www.time.com/time/europe/digital/2002/03/stories/philips.html
15. Crédit Suisse/First Boston Equity Research, October 28, 2002.
16. Deutsche Bank, Equity Research, Bang & Olufsen and Loewe, April 23, 2002.
17. Poul Henningsen was a multitalented architect, but especially his lamp designs have passed the test of time.
18. At the 1967 spring fair In Hannover, B&O received the IF award for the BeoMaster 5000, BeoLab 5000 and BeoVox 2500.
19. http://www.beoworld.co.uk/davidlewis.htm.
20. http://www.cfoeurope.com/199904b.html.
21. Peter Thostrup B&O executive vice president of finance 1995. http:://www.cfoerurope.com/199904b.html.
22. http://www.arts.warterloo.co/acct/couses/acc646/projects2002/bovssony.htm.
23. Interview with former (1991–2001) Bang & Olufsen CEO Anders Knutsen on Danish TV-2, September 1997.
24. B&O Annual report, 2001/2002.
25. Lars Topholm, B&O CFO 1995, http://www.cfoerurope.com/199904b.html.

26. Handelsbanken Research Company report on Bang & Olufsen, April 8, 2002.
27. BNY.dk nr.4 "B&O bliver I cowboy land til den bitre ende."
28. http://twice.com/index.asp?layout=print_page&doc_id=&articleID=CA219245.
29. BNY.dk nr.4 "B&O bliver I cowboy land til den bitre ende."
30. Bang & Olufsen 2001/2002 annual report.

Case 2–4: The Levi's Personal Pair Proposal*

"I'll have my recommendation to you by the end of the week." Heidi Green hung up the phone and surveyed her calendar for appointments that could be pushed into the next week. It was a rainy afternoon in December of 1994 and she had yet to recover from the pre-holiday rush to get product out to retailers.

She had three days to prepare a presentation for the Executive Committee on a new concept called Personal Pair. Custom Clothing Technology Corporation (CCTC) had approached Levi Strauss with the joint venture proposal that would marry Levi's core products with the emerging technologies of mass customization. Jeans could be customized in style and fit to meet each customer's unique needs and taste. If CCTC was correct, this would reach the higher end of the jeans market, yielding stronger profit margins due to both the price premium and the streamlined production process involved.

On the other hand, the technology was new to Levi Strauss and the idea could turn out to be an expensive and time-consuming proposal that would come back later to haunt her, since she would have to manage the venture. The initial market studies seemed supportive, but there was no way to know how customers would respond to the program since there was nothing quite like it out there. She also was unsure whether the program would work as smoothly in practice as the plan suggested.

Company Background and History

Levi Strauss and Co. is a privately held company owned by the family of its founder, Levi Strauss. The Bavarian immigrant was the creator of durable work pants from cloth used for ships' sails, which were reinforced with his patented rivets. The now-famous "waist-overalls," were originally created over 130 years ago for use by California gold rush workers. These were later seen as utilitarian farm- or factory-wear. By the 1950s, Levi's jeans had acquired a Hollywood cachet, as the likes of Marilyn Monroe, James Dean, Marlon Brando, Elvis, and Bob Dylan proudly wore them, giving off an air of rebellious hipness.

The jeans would become a political statement and an American icon, as all jeans soon became known generically as "Levi's." The baby boomer generation next adopted the jeans as a fashion statement, and from 1964–1975, the company's annual sales grew tenfold, from $100 million to $1 billion.[2] By the late 1970s, Levi's had become synonymous with the terms, "authentic," "genuine," "original," and "real," and wearing them allowed the wearer to make a statement. According to some who recognize the brand's recognition even over that of Coke, Marlboro, Nike, or Microsoft, "Levi Strauss has been, and remains, both the largest brand-apparel company in the world and the number one purveyor of blue jeans in the world."

While blue jeans remain the company's mainstay, the San Francisco–based company also sells pants made of corduroy, twill and various other fabrics, as well as shorts, skirts, jackets, and outerwear. The company, with its highly recognizable brand name, holds a top position in many of its markets, and is sold in more than 80 countries. More than half of the company's revenue was from its U.S. sales; nevertheless, Europe and Asia are highly profitable markets. Latin America and Canada are secondary markets, with smaller contributions to overall profits. As the graphic (right) shows, apparel imports were increasing faster than exports during this period.

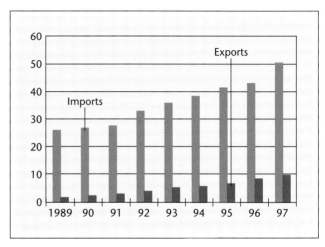

Import and Exports of Apparel (In billions of dollars)

Source: U.S. Department of Commerce.

* The Levi's Personal Pair Proposal. Used with permission of Professor Russell Coff and the Goizueta Business School.

The company's non-denim brand, Dockers, was introduced in 1986, and is sold in the U.S., Canada, Mexico, and Europe. While it is composed of both women's and men's clothing, the men's line of khaki pants occupies the leading position in U.S. sales of khaki trousers and sells well with baby boomers. Sales of Dockers have steadily increased with the rise in casual workplaces, and this line of non-denim products has helped in allowing Levi's to be less reliant on the denim industry.

Competition and the Denim Industry

Denim is "one of the fastest-growing apparel fabrics," and sales have been increasing approximately 10% per year. According to some surveys, an average American consumer owns 17 denim items, which includes 6–7 pairs of jeans.[3] Levi Strauss and Company held the largest market share in 1990, at 31%, followed by VF Corporation's Lee and Wrangler (17.9%), designer labels (6%), The Gap (3%), and department store private labels (3.2%). By 1995, women's jeans had grown to a $2 billion market, of which Levi's held first place.

However, at the same time, many jeans producers were starting to move production to low-cost overseas facilities, which allowed for cost (especially labor) advantages. As the graph (below) shows, this trend was represented throughout the apparel industry and is clearly visible in employment statistics. Indeed, JCPenney, one of Levi's long-time partners, had become a competitor by introducing a cheaper alternative, the Arizona label. They and other rivals had realized that by sourcing all produc-

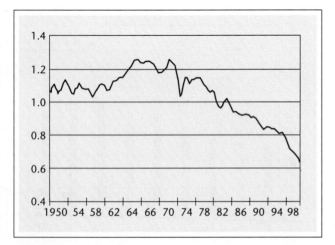

U.S. Apparel Industry Employment (Production workers, in millions)

Source: Bureau of Labor Statistics.

tion in cheap overseas facilities they could enter the business with a cost advantage over Levi Strauss.

Levi's as a private company, which viewed itself as having a strong "social conscience," wanted to avoid being seen as exploiting disadvantaged workers. Accordingly, they preferred to have their jeans "U.S.-made," and Levi Strauss was a leader in providing generous salary and benefits packages to its employees.

Accordingly, it did not relish the notion of entering into price-based competition with rivals committed to overseas production. Their delayed response led to some significant incursions by rivals into Levi's core product arenas.

Levi's also wanted to avoid price-based competition because they had a history of brand recognition and brand loyalty. They were accustomed to the Levi's brand carrying enough clout to justify a reasonable price premium. However, over the years, the brand name carried less cachet, and as hundreds of competitors with similar products dotted the landscape, it became necessary to create valued features that would help to differentiate the product in the eyes of consumers.

Levi Strauss' financial performance is summarized in Exhibit 1 for the period from 1990–1994. While the company was profitable throughout the period, revenue growth had clearly slowed and income growth was quite uneven. This is especially apparent for 1994, the current year, where net income dropped by 35% due to fierce competition for market share and narrowing margins.

Cost Structure

Exhibit 2 provides an estimate of the cost and margins on an average pair of jeans sold through Levi's two outlets. Much of their product was sold through wholesale channels, to be distributed by competing retailers. However, Levi's maintained a chain of Original Levi's Stores (OLS) primarily to help keep them closer to the customer. The profit per pair of jeans was about 30% lower in the wholesale channel ($2 as opposed to $3). This was driven by the 30% margin that accrued to the channel, and which was somewhat balanced by the higher costs of operating the OLS outlets (especially the additional SG&A costs for operating the stores).

Exhibit 2 also indicates the ongoing investment per pair of jeans. Once this is considered, the wholesale outlets are nearly twice as profitable—the pre-tax return on invested capital is 15%, as opposed to 8%. Here, the OLS outlets required additional investment in inventory ($8/pair), which was normally borne by the retailer, and the capital tied up in the retail stores ($20/pair).

Exhibit 1   Levi Strauss Financial Performance

	1994	1993	1992	1991	1990
Income Statement					
Net sales	$6,074,321	$5,892,479	$5,570,290	$4,902,882	$4,247,150
Cost of goods	$3,632,406	$3,638,152	$3,431,469	$3,024,330	$2,651,338
Gross Profit	$2,441,915	$2,254,327	$2,138,821	$1,878,552	$1,595,812
Selling G&A Exp	$1,472,786	$1,394,170	$1,309,352	$1,147,465	$922,785
Non Operating Income	−$18,410	$8,300	−$142,045	$31,650	−$36,403
Interest Exp	$19,824	$37,144	$53,303	$71,384	$82,956
Income Before Taxes	$930,895	$831,313	$634,121	$691,353	$553,668
Taxes	$373,402	$338,902	$271,673	$324,812	$288,753
Net Inc Before Ext Items	$557,493	$492,411	$362,448	$366,541	$264,915
Ext Items	−$236,517	$0	−$1,611	−$9,875	−$13,746
Net Income	$320,976	$492,411	$360,837	$356,666	$251,169
Growth					
Sales Growth	3.1%	5.8%	13.6%	15.4%	
Net Income Growth	−34.8%	36.5%	1.2%	42.0%	
Key Financial Ratios					
Quick ratio	1.57	1.03	0.76	0.87	0.73
SG&A/Sales	24.25	23.66	23.51	23.4	21.73
Receivables Turnover	6.68	6.87	7.67	7.31	6.88
Inventories Turnover	7.76	7.44	7.64	7.5	7.29
Total Debt/Equity	2.57	10.57	34.39	71.82	22.21
Net inc/Sales	5.28	8.36	6.48	7.27	5.91
Net inc/Total assets	8.18	15.84	12.53	13.54	10.51

Mass Customization

Mass customization uses emerging communication and computer technologies to bypass the limitations of traditional mass production methods. From a strategic standpoint, the concept is based on the idea that "the ultimate niche is a market of one."[4] Previously, it was thought that highly-customized products were necessarily expensive to produce; however, with the advent of various information technologies, meeting the customer's needs for flexibility and greater choice in the marketplace is becoming more and more economical.

"A silent revolution is stirring in the way things are made and services are delivered. Companies with millions of customers are starting to build products designed just for you. You can, of course, buy a Dell computer assembled to your exact specifications. . . . But you can also buy pills with the exact blend of vitamins, minerals, and herbs that you like, glasses molded to fit your face precisely, CD's with music tracks that you choose, cosmetics mixed to match your skin tone, textbooks whose chapters are picked out by your professor, a loan structured to meet your financial profile, or a night at a hotel where everyone knows your favorite wine. And if your child does not like any of Mattel's 125 different Barbie dolls, she will soon be able to design her own."[5]

There is, of course, a delicate balance between providing consumers enough flexibility to meet their needs without so much that the decision-making process becomes perplexing and the company's costs spiral out of control trying to meet the customers' phantom needs.

In the early 90s, Levi Strauss found itself facing a dual set of competitors. There were the low-cost, high-volume producers with a distinct advantage over Levi's, and there were also the higher-cost producers of jeans that targeted the affluent end of the denim-buying public. As a high-volume producer with a cost disadvantage, Levi's increasingly found itself at a disadvantage in both the upper and lower ends of the apparel market.

Personal Pair Proposal

Proponents of the Personal Pair project envisioned a niche that would allow Levi's to avoid competing against the low-cost high-volume producers. Market research revealed

Exhibit 2   Profitability Analysis of Women's Jeans

	Wholesale Channel	Original Levi's Store Channel	Personal Pair?	Notes
Operations, per pair				
Gross Revenue	$35	$50		$50 retail price with a 30% channel margin.
Less markdowns	(3)	(5)		Avg. channel markdowns of $5; 60% born by mfg.
Net Revenue	32	45		
Costs				
Cotton	5	5		
Mfg. conversion	7	7		High labor content since all jeans hand-sewn. Wholly owned distribution network for OLS
Distribution	9	11		channel. Add $2 for warehouse to store.
Total	21	23		
COGS				
Gross Margin	11	22		
SG&A	9[1]	19[2]		
Profit Before	$2	$3		
Tax				
Investment, per pair				
Inventory	$4	$12		77 days for Levi's wholesale channel & 240 days for OLS stores to include retail inventory.
Less A/P	(1)	(1)		Reflects 27 days of Accounts Payable.
Accounts	4	0		51-day collection period for wholesale. Retail customers pay immediately.
Receivable				
Net working capital	7	11		
Factory PP&E	5	5		Reflects a sales to fixed asset turnover of 5.33.
Distribution PP&E	1	2		Doubled for OLS channel due to additional retail distribution investment (estimate).
Retail Store	0	20		$2.4M/OLS store for 120,000 pairs sold/yr (est.).
Total Investment	$13	$38		
Pre-tax return on invested capital	15%	8%		

[1]At $9, a little higher than Levi's overall 25% SG&A due to supply chain problems with women's jeans.

[2]The additional $10 reflects an average 22% store expense for retail clothiers (Compact Disclosure database).

Source: Adapted from Carr, 1998.

that only a quarter of women were truly happy with the fit of their jeans, and the company hoped to attract higher-income customers who would be willing to pay a little extra for a perfect fit.

In addition, a mass customization model could lower costs as well as provide the differentiation advantage since the re-engineered process is often more efficient once new technologies are applied. For example, the mass customization model, which operates on the "pull-driven" approach of having the customer drive the production process, would lower distribution costs and inventories of unsold products.

Personal Pair was a jeans customization program made possible through a joint venture with Custom Clothing Technology Corporation (CCTC), in Newton, Massachusetts. CCTC approached Levi Strauss, described the potential of its technology and suggested that, together, the two companies could enter the mass customization arena.

The Personal Pair proposal reflected a form of collaborative customization. This approach helps customers who find the array of choices in the marketplace over-whelming, to narrow down their specific needs. The company enters into a dialogue with customers to help them understand what they need, and is then able to provide specialized products that meet that specific need. Collaborative customizers are able to keep inventories of finished products at a minimum, which brings new products to market faster. That is, they manufacture products in a "just-in-time" fashion to respond to specific customer requests.

How It Would Work. Original Levi's Stores (OLS) would be equipped with networked PC's and Personal Pair kiosks. Trained sales clerks would measure customers' waist, hips, rise, and inseam, resulting in one of 4,224 possible size combinations—a dramatic increase over the 40 combinations normally available to customers. The computer would then generate a code number that corresponded to one of 400 prototype pairs of jeans kept in the kiosk. Within three tries, more measurements would be taken and a perfect fit would be obtained; the customer would then pay for the jeans and opt for Federal Express delivery ($5 extra) or store pickup, with a full money-back guarantee on every pair.

The order was then sent to CCTC in Boston via a Lotus Notes computer program. This program would "translate" the order and match it with a pre-existing pattern at the Tennessee manufacturing facility. The correct pattern would be pulled, "read," and transferred to the cut station, where each pair was cut individually. A sewing line composed of eight flexible team members would process the order, it would be sent to be laundered, and would be inspected and packed for shipping. A bar code would be sewn into each pair to simplify reordering details, and the customer would have a custom-fit pair within three weeks.

Once the program was underway, the proposal suggested that about half of the orders would be from existing customers. Reordering would be simplified and encouraged by the bar code sewn into each pair. In addition, reorders could be handled through a web-based interface.

Pricing. There was some question about how much of a price premium the new product would command. The proposal called for a $15 premium (over the standard $50/pair off the rack) and focus groups suggested that women, in particular, would consider this a fair price to pay for superior fit. However, other's argued that this price point was a bit optimistic, suggesting that $5 or $10 might be more realistic given the lower-priced alternatives.

Planned Scope. The initial proposal was to equip four Original Levi's Stores (OLS) with Personal Pair kiosks and specialized PC's. Once the systems were worked out, this would be expanded to more than 60 kiosks across the U.S. and Canada. In addition, they envisioned opening kiosks in London where they estimated that the product would command a premium of £19 over the original £46 price for standard jeans. The jeans would still be produced in Tennessee and shipped via Federal Express.

Cost Impact. Although the new process would require some investments in technology and process changes, many other costs were projected to drop. These are illustrated by the complex supply chain for the OLS channel (Exhibit 3) and the relatively simple supply chain for the proposed Personal Pair program (Exhibit 4).

- The most obvious ongoing cost savings would be in distribution. Here, the order is transmitted electronically and the final product is shipped directly to the customer at his/her expense. These costs would be nearly eliminated in the proposed program.
- Manufacturing and raw materials would not change much since all jeans are hand sewn and would use the same materials for the traditional and mass-customized processes.
- The portion of SG&A expenses attributable to retail operations would be reduced if 50% of the sales are reorders that do not incur incremental costs in the retail stores ($5/pair savings). However, CCTC would incur its own SG&A costs that would have to be considered (about $3/pair).
- Finally, no price adjustments would be needed in such a tight channel since there would be no inventory of finished product. In the retail channel, about one third of jeans are sold at a discount to clear out aging stock (the discounts average 30%).[6]

Investment Impact. While the factory PP&E was not projected to change much (they would continue to use the same facilities), a number of other factors would impact the invested capital tied up in a pair of jeans (both positively and negatively) under the proposed program:

Increases in invested capital:

- First, there would be an initial $3 million required to integrate the systems of CCTC with Levi's existing systems. This was relatively small since it was a matter of integrating existing systems in the two companies.
- CCTC would also require additional IT investments estimated at $10/pair to maintain the system and upgrade it regularly as scale requirements increased.

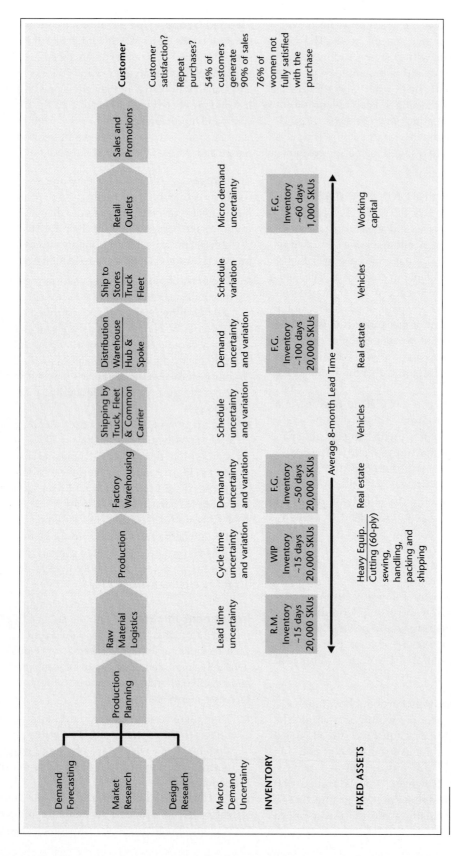

Exhibit 3   Traditional Original Levi's Store Supply Chain

Source: Adapted from Carr, 1998.

Exhibit 4   Personal Pair Value Chain

*Although this approach changes cutting from 60-ply to one, it does not otherwise change manufacturing since jeans were, and are, sewn one pair at a time.

- In addition, the kiosks would take up about one third of the space in the OLS retail stores (about $7/pair for retail space).

Decreases in invested capital:

- The required inventory was significantly lower under the proposed program. Recent estimates calculated Levi's average inventory at about 8 months.[7]   In contrast, the Personal Pair program called for no inventory of finished product and only a small inventory of raw materials (about $1/pair).
- Finally, the proposal suggested that accounts receivable would lead to a net gain of about $2/pair since customers would have paid about 3 weeks prior to receiving the product (similar to the Amazon.com model).

Cost-efficient Mass Customization.   In order for a company to transform an existing product into one that is cost-efficient to mass produce, certain product modifications must be made. The Personal Pair proposal incorporated several of the key elements suggested as helpful for implementing successful mass-customization programs.[8]

First, it is important to introduce the differentiating component of the product (that which must be customized) as late in the production process as possible. For example, paint is not mixed by the manufacturer, but at the point of sale, after being demanded by individual customers. Unfortunately, the making of personalized jeans would not lend itself to a differentiating component late in the production process. Therefore, in this case, the customizing would have to take place at the beginning of the process.

Then, it is helpful if either the product or the process of manufacturing can be easily separated into production modules. Steps in the process can then be reassembled in a different order. For example, a sweater manufacturer might wait until the last possible moment to dye its products in different colors for each season, instead of dying the wool first and knitting the sweaters. This allows for much more flexibility and helps the manufacturer to keep up with fast moving fashion trends. The Personal Pair proposal suggested that the manufacturing process would be modified to allow for better flow—specifically teams would be used to allow for more flexibility and handling of custom products. Unfortunately, since elements in the jean manufacturing process do not always come together in the same way, it would be important that employees accumulate a large range of skills to accommodate idiosyncratic problems that cannot be anticipated.

Finally, it is helpful if either the products or the sub-processes in the manufacturing chain are standardized. This allows for more efficient production and inventory management, whether it be for different types of domestic uses or different markets (for example, international as well as domestic markets were served by a printer manufacturer that allowed all its printers to be adjusted for both 110/220-volt usage). Here, the Personal Pair proposal called for a complex computer program with computerized patterns that were then beamed directly to the cutting floor. This would help them to integrate some technology-enhanced sub-processes with existing standard labor-intensive manufacturing methods.

It also goes without saying that all the parts of the new mass customization process need to come together in an "instantaneous, costless, seamless and frictionless manner."[9]

The Decision.   As Heidi leaned back and gazed outside at the rain-soaked plaza, she considered the pros and cons to the proposal. The proposal carried several risks that she could not fully quantify. First, there was the ability of Levi Strauss to implement new technologies. Second, the cost savings in the proposal were based on CCTC's estimates in their proposal for the program. Would the program still be successful if the costs turned out to be very different? Third, market research indicated that women were not satisfied about fit. How much would they be willing to pay for a better fit?

On another level, she wondered about the competition. If the program were successful, would their low-cost rivals dive into this market as well? Did Levi's have any advantage here? What if they did not move forward with the proposal? Would one of their rivals partner with CCTC?

Bibliography

1. Aron, Laurie Joan. "From push to pull: The supply chain management shifts." *Apparel Industry Magazine*, June 1998, Volume 59, Issue 6, pp. 58–59.
2. "Jeanswear gets squeezed: Plants close at Levi's." *Apparel Industry Magazine*. VF, March 1999, Volume 60, Issue 3, p. 10.
3. Billington, Jim. "How to customize for the real world" *Harvard Management Update*, Reprint #U9704A, 1997.
4. Bounds, Wendy. "Inside Levi's race to restore a tarnished brand." *Wall Street Journal*, August 4, 1998, p. B1.
5. Carr Lawrence, William Lawler and John Shank. "Levi's Personal Pair cases A, B, and Teaching Note." F.W. Olin Graduate School of Business, Babson College, December 1998, #BAB020, BAB021, and BAB520.
6. Chaplin, Heather. "The truth hurts." *American Demographics*, April 1999, Volume 21, Issue 4, pp. 68–69.
7. Charlet Jean-Claude and Erik Brynjolfsson. "Broad vision." *Stanford University Graduate School of Business Case* #OIT-21, March 1998.
8. Church, Elizabeth. "Personal pair didn't fit into Levi Strauss's plans." *The Globe and Mail*, May 27, 1999, p. B13.
9. Collett, Stacy. "Levi shuts plants, misses trends." *Computerworld*, March 1, 1999, p. 16.
10. "Keeping the customer satisfied." *The Economist*. July 14, 2001, pp. 9–10. "Mass customization: A long march." *The Economist*, Special Report. July 14, 2001, pp. 63–65.
11. Ellison, Sarah. "Levi's is ironing some wrinkles out of its sales." *Wall Street Journal*, February 12, 2001, p. B9.
12. Espen, Hal. "Levi's blues." *New York Times Magazine*, March 21, 1999, p. 6.
13. Esquivel Josephine R. and Huong Chu Belpedio. Textile and Apparel Suppliers Industry Overview, Morgan Stanley Dean Witter, March 14, 2001, pp. 1–72.
14. Feitzinger Edward and Hau L. Lee. "Mass customization at Hewlett-Packard: The power of postponement." *Harvard Business Review*, January-February 1997, Reprint #97101, pp. 116–121.
15. FITCH Company Reports, Levi Strauss and Co., February 15, 2001, www.fitchratings.com.
16. FITCH Company Reports, Levi Strauss and Co., October 31, 2000, www.fitchratings.com.
17. FITCH Company Reports, Levi Strauss and Co., March 18, 1999, www.fitchratings.com.
18. Gilbert, Charles. "Did modules fail Levi's or did Levi's fail modules?" *Apparel Industry Magazine*, September 1998, Volume 59, Issue 9, pp. 88–92.
19. Gilmore, James H. "The four faces of mass customization." *Harvard Business Review*, January-February 1997, Reprint #97103, pp. 91–101.
20. Ginsberg, Steve. "Ripped Levi's: Blunders, bad luck take toll." *San Francisco Business Times*, December 11–17, 1998, Vol. 13, Issue 18.
21. Hill, Suzette. "Levi Strauss and Co.: Icon in revolution." *Apparel Industry Magazine*, January 1999, Volume 60, Issue 1, pp. 66–69.
22. Hill, Suzette. "Levi Strauss puts a new spin on brand management." *Apparel Industry Magazine*, November 1998, pp. 46–47.
23. Hofman, Mike. "Searching for the mountain of youth." *Inc.*, December 1999, Volume 21, Issue 18, pp. 33–36.
24. Homer, Eric. "Levi's zips up first ever private deal." *Private Placement Letter*, July 23, 2001.
25. Hunt Bryan C. and Mark O. Doehla. Denim Industry, *FirstUnion Industry Report*, February 23, 1999.
26. Jastrow, David. "Saying no to Web sales." *Computer Reseller News*, November 29, 1999, Issue 871, p. 73.
27. Johnson, Greg. "Jeans war: Survival of the fittest." *Los Angeles Times*, December 3, 1998, p. C1.

28. King, Ralph T., Jr. "Jeans therapy: Levi's factory workers are assigned to teams, and morale takes a hit." *Wall Street Journal*, May 20, 1998, p. A1.
29. Laberis, Bill. "Levi's shows it may not be driver it pretends to be." *Computerworld*, April 12, 1999, Vol. 33, Issue 15, p. 36.
30. Lee, Julian. "Can Levi's ever be cool again?" *Marketing*, April 15, 1999, pp. 28–29.
31. Lee, Louise. "Can Levi's be cool again?" *BusinessWeek*, March 13, 2000, pp. 144–148.
32. Levi Strauss and Company Promotional Materials.
33. Levine, Bettijane. "Fashion fallout from the Levi Strauss layoffs." *Los Angeles Times*, March 1, 1999, p. 1.
34. Magretta, Joan. "The power of virtual integration: An interview with Dell Computer's Michael Dell." *Harvard Business Review*, March-April 1998, Reprint #98208, pp. 73–84.
35. Meadows, Shawn. "Levi shifts on-line strategy." *Bobbin*, January 2000, Vol. 41, Issue 5, p. 8.
36. Merrill Lynch Company Report, Levi Strauss and Co., Global Securities Research and Economics Group, March 23, 2001.
37. Merrill Lynch Company Report, Levi Strauss and Co., Global Securities Research and Economics Group, January 11, 2001.
38. Merrill Lynch Company Report, Levi Strauss and Co., Global Securities Research and Economics Group, September 20, 2000.
39. Munk, Nina. "How Levi's trashed a great American brand." *Fortune*, April 12, 1999, Vol. 139, Issue 7, pp. 82–90.
40. *New York Times*. "The view from outside: Levi's needs more than a patch." February 28, 1999, p.4.
41. Pine, B. Joseph II. "Serve each customer efficiently and uniquely." *Network Transformation*, BCR, January 1996, pp. 2–5.
42. Pine B. Joseph II, Bart Victor and Andrew C. Boynton. "Making mass customization work." *Harvard Business Review*, September-October 1993, Reprint #93509, pp. 108–116.
43. Pressler, Margaret Webb. "Mending time at Levi's: Jeans maker struggles to recapture youth market, reshape its culture." *Washington Post*, April 12, 1998, p. HO1.
44. Reidy, Chris. In marketplace, they're no longer such a great fit." *Boston Globe*, February 23, 1999, p. A1.
45. Reda, Susan. "Internet channel conflicts." *Stores*, December 1999, Vol. 81, Issue 12, pp. 24–28.
46. Robson, Douglas. "Levi showing new signs of fraying in San Francisco." *San Francisco Business Times*, October 15, 1999, Volume 14, Issue 10, p.1.
47. Rosenbush, Steve. "Personalizing service on Web." *USAToday*, November 16, 1998, p. 15E.
48. Schoenberger, Karl. "Tough jeans, a soft heart and frayed earnings." *New York Times*, June 25, 2000, p. 3.
49. Schonfeld, Erick. "The customized, digitized, have-it-your-way economy." *Fortune*, September 28, 1998.
50. Stoughton, Stephanie. "Jeans market now a tight fit for Levi's; Denim leader missed marketing opportunities, failed to spot trends." *Washington Post*, February 23, 1999, p. E1.
51. Trebay, Guy. "What's stonewashed, ripped, mended and $2,222?" *New York Times*, April 17, 2001, p. 10, col. 1.
52. Voight, Joan. "Red, white, and blue: An American icon fades away." *Adweek*, April 26, 1999, Vol. 40, Issue 17, pp. 28–35.
53. Watson Richard T., Sigmund Akselsen and Leyland F. Pitt. "Attractors: Building mountains in the flat landscape of the World Wide Web." *California Management Review*, Volume 40, Number 2, Winter 1998, pp. 36–54.
54. Zito, Kelly. "Levi reveals rare look at inner secrets." *San Francisco Chronicle*, May 6, 2000, p. B1.

Notes

1. This case was prepared by Farah Mihoubi under the supervision of Associate Professor Russell Coff of the Goizueta Business School, as the basis for class discussion, rather than to illustrate either effective or ineffective management. Information assembled from published sources and interviews with company sources. Copyright 2001, by the Goizueta Business School, Case and Video Series, Atlanta, Georgia, 30322, U.S.A. All rights reserved.
2. Espen, 1999.
3. Levine, 1999.
4. Schonfeld, 1998.
5. Schonfeld, 1998.
6. Carr, 1998.
7. Carr, 1998.
8. Billington, 1997.
9. Pine, Victor, and Boynton, 1993, p. 112.

PART 3 CORPORATE STRATEGIES

CHAPTER 6 | Vertical Integration

LEARNING OBJECTIVES

After reading this chapter, you should be able to:

1. Define vertical integration, forward vertical integration, and backward vertical integration.

2. Discuss how vertical integration can create value by reducing the threat of opportunism.

3. Discuss how vertical integration can create value by enabling a firm to exploit its valuable, rare, and costly-to-imitate resources and capabilities.

4. Discuss how vertical integration can create value by enabling a firm to retain its flexibility.

5. Describe conditions under which vertical integration may be rare and costly to imitate.

6. Describe how the functional organization structure, management controls, and compensation policies are used to implement vertical integration.

7. Describe different degrees of vertical integration in an international context.

The Next Generation of Offshoring

If you've ever had to call to get help with your credit card bill, to change an airline ticket, or to solve a software problem, you've probably experienced "offshoring." With offshoring, firms locate some of their key business functions outside of their primary markets. Sometimes these offshore activities are kept within the boundaries of a firm; other times a firm outsources its offshore operations to another firm, typically located in a foreign country.

Offshoring became a popular way to manage routine business activities—including call center management—in the first few years of the twenty-first century. Many of these activities were outsourced to firms in India and the Philippines, where companies could save 40 to 60 percent of the cost of running their own call center operations. If current trends continue, by 2008 offshoring will employ over 4 million people and generate $57 billion in revenue in India alone.

But offshoring has not always gone smoothly. Sometimes it's hard to understand the person on the other end of the line who is trying to help you. Other times, that person doesn't have the local knowledge you need to complete a transaction successfully—like the time a person in India suggested a flight between Los Angeles and San Francisco via Atlanta.

Firms have responded to these service failures in two ways. Some firms have tried to develop more sophisticated and complete software to guide their offshore service providers in the process of helping customers. This software tries to anticipate all the possible problems a customer might have and then provides a call center employee with a series of questions to ask to help identify and then solve these problems. This approach to improving service works well, as long as the problems a call center employee is trying to fix can be anticipated and fixing them does not require a great deal of local knowledge.

When the kinds of problems customers face are too complex to fully anticipate or require a great deal of local knowledge to fix, some firms—including Dell—have abandoned offshoring and brought these services back into their home country or back within the firm's boundaries, or both. The software these firms developed while trying to offshore can still be used to guide local employees, but these local employees can receive the higher levels of training required to fix complex problems. In addition, local employees often already possess the local knowledge required to help resolve customer issues.

Firms are now beginning to explore how to use offshoring to manage much more complex business activities, including software development and other research and development activities. Some of this work is going to traditional offshoring powerhouses such as India and the Philippines. But more and more of this sophisticated research and development work is being offshored to China.

For example, in the last few years firms from a wide variety of countries have opened research and development centers in China, including the French telecommunications firm France Telecom, the Japanese electronics firm NEC, Finland's Nokia, and the U.S. firm Google. Each of these firms has their own R&D operations in China, but they also cooperate with Chinese companies and Chinese universities to do state-of-the-art research.

Cost is an important reason for offshoring research and development to China. However, China has other advantages as well, including a growing population of engineers and scientists—many of whom were trained in Western universities—and fewer restrictions on research activities. For example, Chinese firms have been conducting research on the medical uses of stem cells, research that is very difficult to do in the United States.

Despite some very difficult problems associated with offshoring research and development—including time differences, communication difficulties, and limited protection for intellectual property rights—in many cases the advantages will outweigh the disadvantages. In this sense, research and development may become the "next generation of offshoring."

Sources: M. Kripalani and P. Engardio (2003). "The rise of India." *BusinessWeek,* December 8, pp. 66 +; K. J. Delaney (2003). "Outsourcing jobs—and workers—to India." *Wall Street Journal,* October 13, pp. B1 +; B. Eihhorn (2006). "A dragon in R&D." *BusinessWeek,* November 6, pp. 44 +.

The decision to hire an offshore company to accomplish a specific business function is an example of a decision that determines the level of a firm's vertical integration. This is the case whether the company that is hired to perform these services is located in the United States or India.

What Is Corporate Strategy?

Vertical integration is the first corporate strategy examined in detail in this book. As suggested in Chapter 1, **business strategy** is a firm's theory of how to gain competitive advantage in a single business or industry. The two business strategies discussed in this book are cost leadership and product differentiation. **Corporate strategy** is a firm's theory of how to gain competitive advantage by operating in several businesses simultaneously. Decisions about whether to vertically integrate often determine whether a firm is operating in a single business or industry or in multiple businesses or industries. Other corporate strategies discussed in this book include strategic alliances, diversification, and mergers and acquisitions.

What Is Vertical Integration?

The concept of a firm's value chain was first introduced in Chapter 3. As a reminder, a **value chain** is that set of activities that must be accomplished to bring a product or service from raw materials to the point that it can be sold to a final customer. A simplified value chain of the oil and gas industry, originally presented in Figure 3.1, is reproduced in Figure 6.1.

A firm's level of **vertical integration** is simply the number of steps in this value chain that a firm accomplishes within its boundaries. Firms that are more vertically integrated accomplish more stages of the value chain within their boundaries than firms that are less vertically integrated. A more sophisticated approach to measuring the degree of a firm's vertical integration is presented in the Strategy in Depth feature.

A firm engages in **backward vertical integration** when it incorporates more stages of the value chain within its boundaries and those stages bring it closer to the beginning of the value chain; that is, closer to gaining access to raw materials. When computer companies developed all their own software, they were engaging in backward vertical integration, because these actions are close to the beginning of the value chain. When they began using independent companies operating in India to develop this software, they were less vertically integrated backward.

A firm engages in **forward vertical integration** when it incorporates more stages of the value chain within its boundaries and those stages bring it closer to the end of the value chain; that is, closer to interacting directly with final customers. When companies staffed and operated their own call centers in the United States, they were engaging in forward vertical integration, because these activities brought them closer to the ultimate customer. When they started using independent companies in India to staff and operate these centers, they were less vertically integrated forward.

Of course, in choosing how to organize its value chain, a firm has more choices than whether to vertically integrate or not vertically integrate. Indeed,

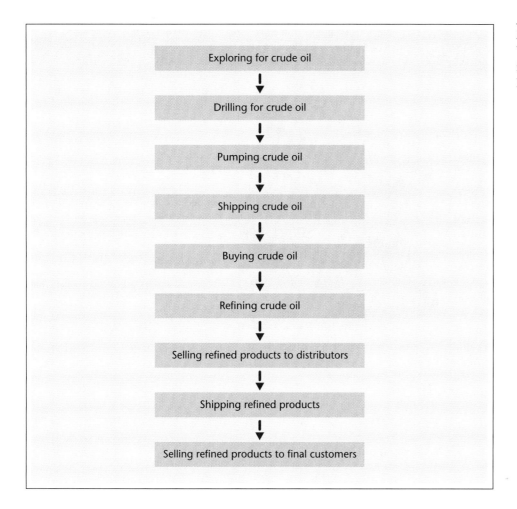

Figure 6.1 A Simplified Value Chain of Activities in the Oil and Gas Industry

between these two extremes a wide range of somewhat vertically integrated options exist. These alternatives include various types of strategic alliances and joint ventures, the primary topic of Chapter 9.

The Value of Vertical Integration

V R I O

The question of vertical integration—which stages of the value chain should be included within a firm's boundaries and why—has been studied by many scholars for almost 100 years. The reason this question has been of such interest was first articulated by Nobel Prize–winning economist Ronald Coase. In a famous article originally published in 1937, Coase asked a simple question: Given how efficiently markets can be used to organize economic exchanges among thousands, even hundreds of thousands, of separate individuals, why would markets, as a method for managing economic exchanges, ever be replaced by firms? In markets, almost as if by magic, Adam Smith's "invisible hand" coordinates the quantity and quality of goods and services produced with the quantity and quality of goods and services demanded through the adjustment of prices—all without a centralized controlling authority. However, in firms, centralized bureaucrats

Strategy in Depth

*I*t is sometimes possible to observe which stages of the value chain a firm is engaging in, and thus the level of that firm's vertical integration. Sometimes, however, it is more difficult to directly observe a firm's level of vertical integration. This is especially true when a firm believes that its level of vertical integration is a potential source of competitive advantage. In this case, the firm would not likely reveal this information freely to competitors.

In this situation, it is possible to get a sense of the degree of a firm's vertical integration—though not a complete list of the steps in the value chain integrated by the firm—from a close examination of the firm's **value added as a percentage of sales**. Valued added as a percentage of sales measures that percentage of a firm's sales that is generated by activities done within the boundaries of a firm. A firm with a high ratio between value added and sales has brought many of the value-creating activities associated with its business inside its boundaries, consistent with a high level of vertical integration. A firm with a low ratio between value added and sales does not have, on average, as high a level of vertical integration.

Value added as a percentage of sales is computed using the following equation in Exhibit 1.

The sum of net income and income taxes is subtracted in both the numerator and the denominator in this equation to control for inflation and

Measuring Vertical Integration

changes in the tax code over time. Net income, income taxes, and sales can all be taken directly from a firm's profit-and-loss statement. Value added can be calculated using the equation in Exhibit 2.

Again, most of the numbers needed to calculate value added can be found either in a firm's profit-and-loss statement or in its balance sheet.

Sources: A. Laffer (1969). "Vertical integration by corporations: 1929–1965." *Review of Economics and Statistics,* 51, pp. 91–93; I. Tucker and R. P. Wilder (1977). "Trends in vertical integration in the U.S. manufacturing sector." *Journal of Industrial Economics,* 26, pp. 81–94; K. Harrigan (1986). "Matching vertical integration strategies to competitive conditions." *Strategic Management Journal,* 7, pp. 535–555.

Exhibit 1

$$\text{vertical integration}_i = \frac{\text{value added}_i - \left(\text{net income}_i + \text{income taxes}_i\right)}{\text{sales}_i - \left(\text{net income}_i + \text{income taxes}_i\right)}$$

where,

$\text{vertical integration}_i$ = the level of vertical integration for firm_i

value added_i = the level of value added for firm_i

net inform_i = the level of net income for firm_i

income taxes_i = firm_i's income taxes

sales_i = firm_i's sales

Exhibit 2

value added = depreciation + amortization + fixed charges + interest expense + labor and related expenses + pension and retirement expenses + income taxes + net income (after taxes) + rental expense

monitor and control subordinates who, in turn, battle each other for "turf" and control of inefficient internal "fiefdoms." Why would the "beauty" of the invisible hand ever be replaced by the clumsy "visible hand" of the modern corporation?[1]

Coase began to answer his own question when he observed that sometimes the cost of using a market to manage an economic exchange must be higher than the cost of using vertical integration and bringing an exchange within the boundary of a firm. Over the years, efforts have focused on identifying the conditions under which this would be the case. The resulting work has described several different situations where vertical integration can either increase a firm's revenues or decrease its costs compared to not vertically integrating; that is, several situations where vertical integration can be valuable. The following sections present three of the most influential of these explanations of when vertical integration can create value for a firm.

Vertical Integration and the Threat of Opportunism

One of the best known explanations of when vertical integration can be valuable focuses on using vertical integration to reduce the threat of opportunism.[2] **Opportunism** exists when a firm is unfairly exploited in an exchange. Examples of opportunism include when a party to an exchange expects a high level of quality in a product it is purchasing, only to discover it has received a lower level of quality than it expected; when a party to an exchange expects to receive a service by a particular point in time and that service is delivered late (or early); and when a party to an exchange expects to pay a price to complete this exchange and its exchange partner demands a higher price than what was previously agreed to.

Obviously, when one of its exchange partners behaves opportunistically, this reduces the economic value of a firm. One way to reduce the threat of opportunism is to bring an exchange within the boundary of a firm, that is, to vertically integrate into this exchange. This way, managers in a firm can monitor and control this exchange instead of relying on the market to manage it. If the exchange that is brought within the boundary of a firm brings a firm closer to its ultimate suppliers, it is an example of backward vertical integration. If the exchange that is brought within the boundary of a firm brings a firm closer to its ultimate customer, it is an example of forward vertical integration.

Of course, firms should only bring market exchanges within their boundaries when the cost of vertical integration is less than the cost of opportunism. If the cost of vertical integration is greater than the cost of opportunism, then firms should not vertically integrate into an exchange. This is the case for both backward and forward vertical integration decisions.

So, when will the threat of opportunism be large enough to warrant vertical integration? Research has shown that the threat of opportunism is greatest when a party to an exchange has made transaction-specific investments. A **transaction-specific investment** is any investment in an exchange that has significantly more value in the current exchange than it does in alternative exchanges. Perhaps the easiest way to understand the concept of a transaction-specific investment is through an example.

Consider the economic exchange between an oil refining company and an oil pipeline building company, which is depicted in Figure 6.2. As can be seen in the figure, this oil refinery is built on the edge of a deep-water bay. Because of this, the refinery has been receiving supplies of crude oil from large tanker ships. However, an oil field exists several miles distant from the refinery, but the only way to transport crude oil from the oil field to the refinery is with trucks—a very expensive way to move crude oil, especially compared to large tankers. But if the oil refining company could find a way to get crude oil from this field cheaply, it would probably make this refinery even more valuable.

Enter the pipeline company. Suppose this pipeline company approaches the refinery and offers to build a pipeline from the oil field to the refinery. In return, all

Figure 6.2   The Exchange
Between an Oil Refinery
and an Oil Pipeline
Company

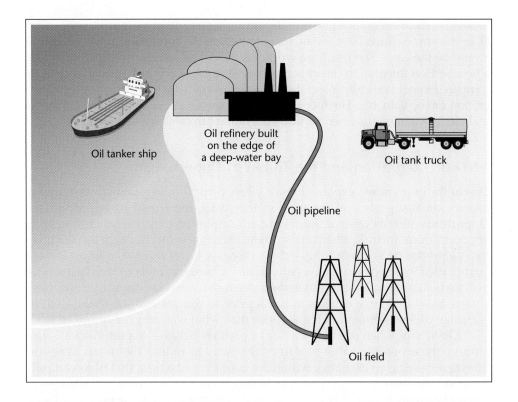

the pipeline company expects is for the refinery to promise to buy a certain number of barrels of crude at an agreed-to price for some period of time, say, five years,
through the pipeline. If reasonable prices can be negotiated, the oil refinery is
likely to find this offer attractive, for the cost of crude oil carried by the pipeline is
likely to be lower than the cost of crude oil delivered by ship or by truck. Based on
this analysis, the refinery and the oil pipeline company are likely to cooperate and
the pipeline is likely to be built.

Now, five years go by, and it is time to renegotiate the contract. Which of
these two firms has made the largest transaction-specific investments? Remember
that a transaction-specific investment is any investment in an exchange that is
more valuable in that particular exchange than in alternative exchanges.

What specific investments has the refinery made? Well, how much is this
refinery worth if this exchange with the pipeline company is not renewed? Its
value would probably drop some, because oil through the pipeline is probably
cheaper than oil through ships or trucks. So, if the refiner doesn't use the pipeline
any longer, it will have to use these alternative supplies. This will reduce its value
some—say, from $1 million to $900,000. This $100,000 difference is the size of the
transaction-specific investment made by the refining company.

However, the transaction-specific investment made by the pipeline firm is
probably much larger. Suppose the pipeline is worth $750,000 as long as it is pump-
ing oil to the refinery. But if it is not pumping oil, how much is it worth? Not very
much. An oil pipeline that is not pumping oil has limited alternative uses. It has
value either as scrap or (perhaps) as the world's largest enclosed water slide. If the
value of the pipeline is only $10,000 if it is not pumping oil to the refinery, then the
level of transaction specific investment made by the pipeline firm is substantially
larger than that made by the firm that owns the refinery: $750,000 – $10,000, or
$740,000 for the pipeline company, versus $100,000 for the refining company.

So, which company is at greater risk of opportunism when the contract is renegotiated—the refinery or the pipeline company? Obviously, the pipeline company has more to lose. If it cannot come to an agreement with the oil refining company, it will lose $740,000. If the refinery cannot come to an agreement with the pipeline company, it will lose $100,000. Knowing this, the refining company can squeeze the pipeline company during the renegotiation by insisting on lower prices or more timely deliveries of higher-quality crude oil, and the pipeline company really cannot do much about it.

Of course, managers in the pipeline firm are not stupid. They know that after the first five years of their exchange with the refining company they will be in a very difficult bargaining position. So, in anticipation, they will insist on much higher prices for building the oil pipeline in the first place than would otherwise be the case. This will drive up the cost of building the pipeline, perhaps to the point that it is no longer cheaper than getting crude oil from ships. If this is the case, then the pipeline will not be built, even though if it could be built and the threat of opportunism eliminated both the refining company and the pipeline company would be better off.

One way to solve this problem is for the oil refining company to buy the oil pipeline company—that is, for the oil refinery to backward vertically integrate.[3] When this happens, the incentive for the oil refinery to exploit the vulnerability of the pipeline company will be reduced. After all, if the refinery business tries to rip-off the pipeline business, it only hurts itself, because it owns the pipeline business.

This, then, is the essence of opportunism-based explanations of when vertical integration creates value: Transaction-specific investments make parties to an exchange vulnerable to opportunism, and vertical integration solves this vulnerability problem. Using language developed in Chapter 3, this approach suggests that vertical integration is valuable when it reduces threats from a firm's suppliers or buyers due to any transaction-specific investments a firm has made.

Vertical Integration and Firm Capabilities

A second approach to vertical integration decisions focuses on a firm's capabilities and its ability to generate sustained competitive advantages.[4] This approach has two broad implications. First, it suggests that firms should vertically integrate into those business activities where they possess valuable, rare, and costly-to-imitate resources and capabilities. This way, firms can appropriate at least some of the profits that using these capabilities to exploit environmental opportunities will create. Second, this approach also suggests that firms should not vertically integrate into business activities where they do not possess the resources necessary to gain competitive advantages. Such vertical integration decisions would not be a source of profits to a firm, because they do not possess any of the valuable, rare, or costly-to-imitate resources needed to gain competitive advantages in these business activities. Indeed, to the extent that some other firms have competitive advantages in these business activities, vertically integrating into them could put a firm at a competitive disadvantage.

This, then, is the essence of the capabilities approach to vertical integration: If a firm possesses valuable, rare, and costly-to-imitate resources in a business activity, it should vertically integrate into that activity; otherwise, no vertical integration. This perspective can sometimes lead to vertical integration decisions that conflict with decisions derived from opportunism-based explanations of vertical integration.

Consider, for example, firms acting as suppliers to Wal-Mart. Wal-Mart has a huge competitive advantage in the discount retail industry. In principle, firms that sell to Wal-Mart could vertically integrate forward into the discount retail market to sell their own products. That is, these firms could begin to compete against Wal-Mart. However, such efforts are not likely to be a source of competitive advantage for these firms. Wal-Mart's resources and capabilities are just too extensive and costly to imitate for most of these suppliers. So, instead of forward vertical integration, most of these firms sell their products through Wal-Mart.

Of course, the problem is that by relying so much on Wal-Mart, these firms are making significant transaction-specific investments. If they stop selling to Wal-Mart, they may go out of business. However, this decision will have a limited impact on Wal-Mart. Wal-Mart can go to any number of suppliers around the world who are willing to replace this failed firm. So, Wal-Mart's suppliers are at risk of opportunism in this exchange, and indeed, it is well known that Wal-Mart can squeeze its suppliers, in terms of the quality of the products it purchases, the price at which it purchases them, and the way in which these products are delivered.

So the tension between these two approaches to vertical integration becomes clear. Concerns about opportunism suggest that Wal-Mart's suppliers should vertically integrate forward. Concerns about having a competitive disadvantage if they do vertically integrate forward suggest that Wal-Mart's suppliers should not vertically integrate. So, should they or shouldn't they vertically integrate?

Not many of Wal-Mart's suppliers have been able to resolve this difficult problem. Most do not vertically integrate into the discount retail industry. However, they try to reduce the level of transaction-specific investment they make with Wal-Mart by supplying other discount retailers, both in the United States and abroad. They also try to use their special capabilities to differentiate their products so much that Wal-Mart's customers insist on Wal-Mart selling these products. And these firms constantly search for cheaper ways to make and distribute higher-quality products.

Vertical Integration and Flexibility

A third perspective on vertical integration focuses on the impact of this decision on a firm's flexibility. **Flexibility** refers to how costly it is for a firm to alter its strategic and organizational decisions. Flexibility is high when the cost of changing strategic choices is low; flexibility is low when the cost of changing strategic choices is high.

So, which is less flexible vertical integration or no vertical integration? Research suggests that, in general, vertically integrating is less flexible than not vertically integrating.[5] This is because once a firm has vertically integrated, it has committed its organizational structure, its management controls, and its compensation policies to a particular vertically integrated way of doing business. Undoing this decision often means changing these aspects of an organization.

Suppose, for example, that a vertically integrated firm decides to get out of a particular business. To do so, the firm will have to sell or close its factories, (actions that can adversely affect both the employees it has to lay off and those that remain), alter its supply relationships, hurt customers that have come to rely on it as a partner, and change its internal reporting structure. In contrast, if a non–vertically integrated firm decides to get out of a business, it simply stops. It cancels whatever contracts it might have had in place and ceases operations in that business. The cost of exiting a non-vertically-integrated business is generally much lower than the cost of exiting a vertically integrated business.

Of course, flexibility is not always valuable. In fact, flexibility is only valuable when the decision-making setting a firm is facing is uncertain. A decision-making setting is **uncertain** when the future value of an exchange cannot be known when investments in that exchange are being made. In such settings, less vertical integration is better than more vertical integration. This is because vertically integrating into an exchange is less flexible than not vertically integrating into an exchange. If an exchange turns out not to be valuable, it is usually more costly for firms that have vertically integrated into an exchange to exit that exchange compared to those that have not vertically integrated.

Consider, for example, a pharmaceutical firm making investments in biotechnology. The outcome of biotechnology research is very uncertain. If a pharmaceutical company vertically integrates into a particular type of biotechnology research by hiring particular types of scientists, building an expensive laboratory, and developing the other skills necessary to do this particular type of biotechnology research, it has made a very large investment. Now suppose that this research turns out not to be profitable. This firm has made huge investments that now have little value. As important, it has failed to make investments in other areas of biotechnology that could turn out to be valuable.

A flexibility-based approach to vertical integration suggests that rather than vertically integrating into a business activity whose value is highly uncertain, firms should not vertically integrate and but should instead form a strategic alliance to manage this exchange. A strategic alliance is more flexible than vertical integration but still gives a firm enough information about an exchange to estimate its value over time.

An alliance has a second advantage in this setting. The downside risks associated with investing in a strategic alliance are known and fixed. They equal the cost of creating and maintaining the alliance. If an uncertain investment turns out not to be valuable, parties to this alliance know the maximum amount they can lose—an amount equal to the cost of creating and maintaining the alliance. On the other hand, if this exchange turns out to be very valuable, then maintaining an alliance can give a firm access to this huge upside potential. These aspects of strategic alliances will be discussed in more detail in Chapter 9.

Each of these explanations of vertical integration has received significant empirical attention in the academic literature. Some of these studies are described in the Research Made Relevant feature.

Applying the Theories to the Management of Call Centers

One of the most common business function to be outsourced, and even offshored, is a firm's call center activities. So, what do these three theories say about how call centers should be managed: When should they be brought within the boundaries of a firm, and when should they be outsourced? Each of these theories will be discussed in turn.

Transaction-Specific Investments and Managing Call Centers

When applying opportunism-based explanations of vertical integration, start by looking for actual or potential transaction-specific investments that would need to be made in order to complete an exchange. High levels of such investments suggest the need for vertical integration; low levels of such investments suggest that vertically integrating this exchange is not necessary.

When the call-center approach to providing customer service was first developed in the 1980s, it required substantial levels of transaction-specific investment.

Research Made Relevant

Of the three explanations of vertical integration discussed here, opportunism-based explanations are the oldest, and thus have received the greatest empirical support. One review of this empirical work, by Professor Joe Mahoney of the University of Illinois, observes that the core assertion of this approach—that high levels of transaction-specific investment lead to higher levels of vertical integration—receives consistent empirical support.

More recent work has begun to examine the trade-offs among these three explanations of vertical integration by examining their effects on vertical integration simultaneously. For example, Professor Tim Folta of Purdue University examined the opportunism and flexibility approaches to vertical integration simultaneously. His results show that the basic assertion of the opportunism approach still holds. However, when he incorporates uncertainty into his empirical analysis, he finds that firms engage in less vertical integration than he finds that firms

Empirical Tests of Theories of Vertical Integration

engage in less vertical integration than predicted by opportunism by itself. In other words, firms apparently worry not only about transaction-specific investments when they make vertical integration choices, they also worry about how costly it is to reverse those investments in the face of high uncertainty.

An even more recent study by Michael Leiblein of The Ohio State University and Doug Miller of the University of Illinois, examines all three of these explanations of vertical integration simultaneously. These authors study vertical integration decisions in the semiconductor manufacturing industry and find that all three explanations hold. That is, firms in this industry worry about transaction-specific investment, the capabilities they possess, the capabilities they would like to possess, and the uncertainty of the markets within which they operate when they make vertical integration choices.

Sources: J. Mahoney (1992). "The choice of organizational form: Vertical financial ownership versus other methods of vertical integration." *Strategic Management Journal,* 13, pp. 559–584; T. Folta (1998). "Governance and uncertainty: The trade-off between administrative control and commitment." *Strategic Management Journal,* 19, pp. 1007–1028; M. Leiblein and D. Miller (2003). "An empirical examination of transaction- and firm-level influences on the vertical boundaries of the firm." *Strategic Management Journal,* 24(9), pp. 839–859.

First, a great deal of special-purpose equipment had to be purchased. And although this equipment could be used for any call center, it had little value except within a call center. Thus, this equipment was an example of a somewhat specific investment.

More important, in order to provide service in call centers, call center employees would have to be fully aware of all the problems likely to emerge with the use of a firm's products. This requires a firm to study its products very closely and then to train call center employees to be able to respond to any problems customers might have. This training was sometimes very complex and very time consuming and represented substantial transaction-specific investments on the part of call center employees. Only employees that worked full-time for a large corporation—where job security was usually high for productive workers—would be willing to make these kinds of specific investments. Thus, vertical integration into call center management made a great deal of sense.

However, as information technology improved, firms found it was possible to train call center employees much faster. Now, all call center employees had to do was follow scripts that were prewritten and preloaded onto their computers. By asking a few scripted questions, call center employees could diagnose most problems. In addition, solutions to those problems were also included on an employee's computer. Only really unusual problems could not be handled by employees working off these computer scripts. Because the level of specific investment required to use these scripts was much lower, employees were willing to work for companies without the job security usually associated with large firms. Indeed, call centers became good part-time and temporary employment opportunities. Because the level of specific investment required to work in these call centers was much lower, not vertically integrating into call center management made a great deal of sense.

Capabilities and Managing Call Centers

In opportunism-based explanations of vertical integration, you start by looking for transaction-specific investments and then make vertical integration decisions based on these investments. In capability-based approaches, you start by looking for valuable, rare, and costly-to-imitate resources and capabilities, and then make vertical integration decisions appropriately.

In the early days of call center management, how well a firm operated its call centers could actually be a source of competitive advantage. During this time period, the technology was new, and the training required to answer a customer's questions was extensive. Firms that developed special capabilities in managing these processes could gain competitive advantages and thus would vertically integrate into call center management.

However, over time, as more and more call center management suppliers were created, and as the technology and training required to staff a call center became more widely available, the ability of a call center to be a source of competitive advantage for a firm dropped. That is, the ability to manage a call center was still valuable, but it was no longer rare or costly to imitate. In this setting, it is not surprising to see firms getting out of the call center management business, outsourcing this business to low-cost specialist firms, and focusing on those business functions where they might be able to gain a sustained competitive advantage.

Flexibility and Managing Call Centers

Opportunism logic suggests starting with a search for transaction-specific investments; capabilities logic suggests starting with a search for valuable, rare, and costly-to-imitate resources and capabilities. Flexibility logic suggests starting by looking for sources of uncertainty in an exchange.

One of the biggest uncertainties in providing customer service through call centers is the question of whether the people staffing the phones actually help a firm's customers. This is a particularly troubling concern for firms that are selling complex products that can have numerous types of problems. A variety of technological solutions have been developed to try to address this uncertainty. But, if a firm vertically integrates into the call center management business, it is committing to a particular technological solution. This solution may not work, or it may not work as well as some other solutions.

In the face of this uncertainty, maintaining relationships with several different call center management companies—each of whom have adopted different technological solutions to the problem of how to use call center employees to assist customers who are using very complex products—gives a firm technological flexibility that it would not otherwise have. Once a superior solution is identified, then a firm no longer needs this flexibility and may choose to vertically integrate into call center management or not, depending on opportunism and capabilities considerations.

Integrating Different Theories of Vertical Integration

At first glance, having three different explanations about how vertical integration can create value seems troubling. After all, won't these explanations sometimes contradict each other?

The answer to this question is yes. We have already seen such a contradiction in the case of opportunism and capabilities explanations of whether Wal-Mart suppliers should forward vertically integrate into the discount retail industry.

However, more often than not, these three explanations are complementary in nature. That is, each approach generally leads to the same conclusion about how a firm should vertically integrate. Moreover, sometimes it is simply easier to apply one of these approaches to evaluate a firm's vertical integration choices than the other two. Having a "tool kit" that includes three explanations of vertical integration enables the analyst to choose the approach that is most likely to be a source of insight in a particular situation.

Even when these explanations make contradictory assertions about vertical integration, having multiple approaches can be helpful. In this context, having multiple explanations can highlight the trade-offs that a firm is making when choosing its vertical integration strategy. Thus, for example, if opportunism-based explanations suggest that vertical integration is necessary because of high transaction-specific investments, capabilities-based explanations caution about the cost of developing the resources and capabilities necessary to vertically integrate and flexibility concerns caution about the risks that committing to vertical integration imply, and the costs and benefits of whatever vertical integration decision is ultimately made can be understood very clearly.

Overall, having three explanations of vertical integration has several advantages for those looking to analyze the vertical integration choices of real firms. Of course, applying these explanations can create important ethical dilemmas for a firm, especially when it becomes clear that a firm needs to become less vertically integrated than it has historically been. Some of these dilemmas are discussed in the Ethics and Strategy feature.

Vertical Integration and Sustained Competitive Advantage

Of course, in order for vertical integration to be a source of sustained competitive advantage, not only must it be valuable (because it responds to threats of opportunism; enables a firm to exploit its own or other firms' valuable, rare, and costly-to-imitate resources; or because it gives a firm flexibility), it must also be rare and costly to imitate, and a firm must be organized to implement it correctly.

The Rarity of Vertical Integration

A firm's vertical integration strategy is rare when few competing firms are able to create value by vertically integrating in the same way. A firm's vertical integration strategy can be rare because it is one of a small number of competing firms that is able to vertically integrate efficiently or because it is one of a small number of firms that is able to adopt a non–vertically integrated approach to managing an exchange.

Ethics and Strategy

*I*magine a firm that has successfully operated in a vertically integrated manner for decades. Employees come to work, they know their jobs, they know how to work together effectively, they know where to park. The job is not just the economic center of their lives; it has become the social center as well. Most of their friends work in the same company, in the same function, as they do. The future appears to be much as the past—stable employment and effective work, all aiming toward a comfortable and well-planned retirement. And then the firm adopts a new outsourcing strategy. It changes its vertical integration strategy by becoming less vertically integrated and purchasing services from outside suppliers that it used to obtain internally.

The economics of outsourcing can be compelling. Outsourcing can help firms reduce costs and focus their efforts on those business functions that are central to their competitive advantage. When done well, outsourcing creates value—value that firms can share with their owners, their stockholders.

Indeed, outsourcing is becoming a trend in business. Some observers

The Ethics of Outsourcing

predict that by 2015 an additional 3.3 million jobs in the United States will be outsourced, many to operations overseas.

But what of the employees whose jobs are taken away? What of their lifetime of commitment, their steady and reliable work? What of their stable and secure retirement? Outsourcing often devastates lives, even as it creates economic value. Of course, some firms go out of their way to soften the impact of outsourcing on

their employees. Those that are near retirement age are often given an opportunity to retire early. Others receive severance payments in recognition of their years of service. Other firms hire "outplacement" companies—firms that specialize in placing suddenly unemployed people in new jobs and new careers.

But all these efforts to soften the blow do not make the blow go away. Many employees assume that they have an implicit contract with the firms they work for. That contract is: "As long as I do my job well, I will have a job." That contract is being replaced with: "As long as a firm wants to employ me, I will have a job." In such a world, it is not surprising that many employees now look first to maintain their employability in their current job—by receiving additional training and experiences that might be valuable at numerous other employers—and are concerned less with what they can do to improve the performance of the firm they work for.

Sources: S. Steele-Carlin (2003). "Outsourcing poised for growth in 2002." *FreelanceJobsNews.com*, October 20; (2003). "Who wins in off-shoring?" *McKinseyQuarterly.com*, October 20.

Rare Vertical Integration

A firm may be able to create value through vertical integration, when most of its competitors are not able to, for at least three reasons. Not surprisingly, these reasons parallel the three explanations of vertical integration presented in this chapter.

Rare Transaction-Specific Investment and Vertical Integration.   First, a firm may have developed a new technology, or a new approach to doing business, that requires its business partners to make substantial transaction-specific investments. Firms that engage in these activities will find it in their self-interest to vertically integrate, whereas firms that have not engaged in these activities will not find it in their self-interest to vertically integrate. If these activities are rare and costly to imitate, they can be a source of competitive advantage for a vertically integrating firm.

For example, the opening case in this chapter suggests that many firms in the computer industry are offshoring some of their key business functions. However, one firm, Dell, recently brought one of these functions—its technical call centers for corporate customers—back from India and re-vertically integrated into this business.[6] The problems faced by corporate customers are typically much more complicated than those faced by individual consumers. Thus, it is much more difficult to provide call center employees the training they need to address corporate problems. Moreover, because corporate technologies change more rapidly than many consumer technologies, keeping call center employees up-to-date on how to service corporate customers is also more complicated than having call center employees provide services to its noncorporate customers. Because Dell needs the people staffing its corporate call centers to make substantial specific investments in its technology and in understanding its customers, it has found it necessary to bring these individuals within the boundaries of the firm and to re–vertically integrate the operation of this particular type of service center.

If Dell, through this vertical integration decision, is able to satisfy its customers more effectively than its competitors, and if the cost of managing this call center is not too high, then this vertical integration decision is both valuable and rare, and thus a source of at least a temporary competitive advantage for Dell.

Rare Capabilities and Vertical Integration.   A firm such as Dell might also conclude that it has unusual skills, either in operating a call center or in providing the training that is needed to staff certain kinds of call centers. If those capabilities are valuable and rare, then vertically integrating into businesses that exploit these capabilities can enable a firm to gain at least a temporary competitive advantage. Indeed, the belief that a firm possesses valuable and rare capabilities is often a justification for rare vertical integration decisions in an industry. Consider, for example, MTV's decision to enter the Indian market, described in the Global Perspectives feature.

Rare Uncertainty and Vertical Integration.   Finally, a firm may be able to gain an advantage from vertically integrating when it resolves some uncertainty it faces sooner than its competition. Suppose, for example, that several firms in an industry all begin investing in a very uncertain technology. Flexibility logic suggests that, to the extent possible, these firms will prefer to not vertically integrate into the manufacturing of this technology until its designs and features stabilize and market demand for this technology is well established.

However, imagine that one of these firms is able to resolve these uncertainties before any other firm. This firm no longer needs to retain the flexibility that is so valuable under conditions of uncertainty. Instead, this firm might be able to, say, design special-purpose machines that can efficiently manufacture this technology. Such machines are not flexible, but they can be very efficient.

Of course, outside vendors would have to make substantial transaction-specific investments to use these machines. Outside vendors may be reluctant to make these investments. In this setting, this firm may find it necessary to vertically integrate to be able to use its machines to produce this technology. Thus, this firm, by resolving uncertainty faster than its competitors, is able to gain some of the advantages of vertical integration sooner than its competitors. Whereas the competition is still focusing on flexibility in the face of uncertainty, this firm gets to focus on production efficiency in meeting customers' product demands. This can obviously be a source of competitive advantage.

Global Perspectives

MTV has a dominant brand in music television in the United States and much of western Europe. Given that this brand is valuable, rare, and costly to imitate in these markets, it is not surprising that MTV has decided to continue its international expansion by moving into Malaysia, Japan, India, and other countries in Asia. However, Viacom—MTV's corporate parent—is finding it necessary to modify much of its content as it tries to introduce MTV in these Asian markets.

For example, when MTV first entered India in 1991 it presented content originally produced for its U.S. station and for the rest of Asia. This included rock-and-roll videos, rap videos, and English-speaking vee-jays. Later, it presented reruns of *The Osbournes.* The only problem with this strategy was that Indian teenagers don't like rock-and-roll videos, rap videos, and English-speaking vee-jays, and were totally mystified by *The Osbournes.* Another successful U.S. MTV product—*MTV Grind*—about spring break, was too risqué for an Indian audience and was cancelled soon after it was first shown.

To respond to this local market, MTV has had to develop more locally

Producing a Hindi Version of
The Osbournes

oriented fare, including *Roadies,* a show based loosely on MTV's popular *Road Rules* program. However, unlike *Road Rules*—where contestants ride across America in a comfortable RV—in *Roadies,* four young men and three young women ride across India on two-wheeled motor scooters. Moreover, all of MTV India's vee-jays now speak Hinglish—a combination of Hindi and English—and present popular Indian music videos.

An even more radical departure for MTV India is its new youth-

oriented soap opera *Kitna Mast Hai Zindagi,* which means *It's a Beautiful Life.* What is most unusual about this production is that, unlike most of the other programming on MTV India, this show is not produced by MTV itself. In an effort to gain a true "Indian" feel to this new soap, MTV India actually outsourced its production to an Indian production company. This company, Balaji Telefilms, already produces a successful prime time soap opera on another Indian cable channel.

These efforts are beginning to pay some dividends in the Indian market. In fact, demand for MTV-like programming was so high that in 2004 MTV introduced VH-1 to the Indian market.

However, MTV India has many challenges left if it is to reach a size and profitability level that will make it an important business for Viacom. For example, currently MTV India is broadcast in Hinglish and reaches the Hindi-speaking population. However, large regions of India speak Tamil, Telegu, and Punjabi, not Hindi. What if someone who speaks Telegu says, "I want my MTV"? How will MTV India respond?

Sources: M. Gunther (2004). "MTV's passage to India." *Fortune,* August 9, pp. 117 +. © 2004 Time Inc. All rights reserved.

Rare Vertical Dis-Integration

Each of the examples of vertical integration and competitive advantage described so far have focused on a firm's ability to vertically integrate to create competitive advantage. However, firms can also gain competitive advantages through their decisions to vertically dis-integrate, that is, through the decision to outsource an activity that used to be within the boundaries of the firm. Whenever a firm is among the first in its industry to conclude that the level of specific investment required to manage an economic exchange is no longer high, or that a particular exchange is no longer rare or costly to imitate, or that the level of uncertainty about the value of an exchange has increased, it may be among the first in its industry to vertically dis-integrate this exchange. Such activities, to the extent they are valuable, will be rare, and thus a source of at least a temporary competitive advantage.

The Imitability of Vertical Integration

The extent to which these rare vertical integration decisions can be sources of sustained competitive advantage depends, as always, on the imitability of the rare resources that gives a firm at least a temporary competitive advantage. Both direct duplication and substitution can be used to imitate another firm's valuable and rare vertical integration choices.

Direct Duplication of Vertical Integration

Direct duplication occurs when competitors develop or obtain the resources and capabilities that enable another firm to implement a valuable and rare vertical integration strategy. To the extent that these resources and capabilities are path dependent, socially complex, or causally ambiguous, they may be immune from direct duplication, and thus a source of sustained competitive advantage.

With respect to offshoring business functions, it seems that the very popularity of this strategy suggests that it is highly imitable. Indeed, this strategy is becoming so common that firms that move in the other direction by vertically integrating a call center and managing it in the United States (like Dell) make news.

But the fact that many firms are implementing this strategy does not mean that they are all equally successful in doing so. These differences in performance may reflect some subtle and complex capabilities that some of these outsourcing firms possess that others do not. These are the kinds of resources and capabilities that may be sources of sustained competitive advantage.

Some of the resources that might enable a firm to implement a valuable and rare vertical integration strategy may not be susceptible to direct duplication. These might include a firm's ability to analyze the attributes of its economic exchanges and its ability to conceive of and implement vertical integration strategies. Both of these capabilities may be socially complex and path dependent—built up over years of experience.

Substitutes for Vertical Integration

The major substitute for vertical integration—strategic alliances—is the major topic of Chapter 9. An analysis of how strategic alliances can substitute for vertical integration will be delayed until then.

Organizing to Implement Vertical Integration

Organizing to implement vertical integration involves the same organizing tools as implementing any business or corporate strategy: organizational structure, management controls, and compensation policies.

Organizational Structure and Implementing Vertical Integration

The organizational structure that is used to implement a cost leadership and product differentiation strategy—the functional, or U-form, structure—is also used to implement a vertical integration strategy. Indeed, each of the exchanges included within the boundaries of a firm as a result of vertical integration decisions are incorporated into one of the functions in a functional organizational structure. Decisions about which manufacturing activities to vertically integrate into determine the range and responsibilities of the manufacturing function within a functionally organized firm; decisions about which marketing activities to vertically integrate into determine the range and responsibilities of the marketing function within a functionally organized firm; and so forth. Thus, in an important sense, vertical integration decisions made by a firm determine the structure of a functionally organized firm.

The CEO in this vertically integrated, functionally organized firm has the same two responsibilities that were first identified in Chapter 4: strategy formulation and strategy implementation. However, these two responsibilities take on added dimensions when implementing vertical integration decisions. In particular, although the CEO must take the lead in making decisions about whether each individual function should be vertically integrated into a firm, this person must also work to resolve conflicts that naturally arise between vertically integrated functions. The approach of one reluctant CEO to this management challenge is described in the Strategy in the Emerging Enterprise feature.

Resolving Functional Conflicts in a Vertically Integrated Firm

From a CEO's perspective, coordinating functional specialists to implement a vertical integration strategy almost always involves conflict resolution. Conflicts among functional managers in a U-form organization are both expected and normal. Indeed, if there is no conflict among certain functional managers in a U-form organization, then some of these managers probably are not doing their jobs. The task facing the CEO is not to pretend this conflict does not exist, or to ignore it, but to manage it in a way that facilitates strategy implementation.

Consider, for example, the relationship between manufacturing and sales managers. Typically, manufacturing managers prefer to manufacture a single product with long production runs. Sales managers, however, generally prefer to sell numerous customized products. Manufacturing managers generally do not like large inventories of finished products; sales managers generally prefer large inventories of finished products that facilitate rapid deliveries to customers. If these various interests of manufacturing and sales managers do not, at least sometimes, come into conflict in a vertically integrated U-form organization, then the manufacturing manager is not focusing enough on cost reduction and quality improvement in manufacturing or the sales manager is not focusing enough on meeting customer needs in a timely way, or both.

Numerous other conflicts arise among functional managers in a vertically integrated U-form organization. Accountants often focus on maximizing managerial accountability and close analysis of costs; R&D managers may fear that such accounting practices will interfere with innovation and creativity. Finance managers often focus on the relationship between a firm and its external capital markets; human resource managers are more concerned with the relationship between a firm and external labor markets.

In this context, the CEO's job is to help resolve conflicts in ways that facilitate the implementation of the firm's strategy. Functional managers do not have to "like" each other. However, if a firm's vertical integration strategy is correct, the reason that a function has been included within the boundaries of a firm is that this decision creates value for the firm. Allowing functional conflicts to get in the

Strategy in the Emerging Enterprise

With a net worth over $1 billion, Oprah Winfrey heads one of the most successful multimedia companies in the United States. One of the businesses she owns—Harpo, Inc.—produces one of the most successful daytime television shows ever (with revenues of over $300 million a year); a magazine with the most successful launch ever and currently 2.5 million paid subscribers (more than *Vogue* and *Fortune*); and a movie production unit. One investment banker estimates that if Harpo, Inc. was a publicly traded firm, it would be valued at $575 million. Other properties Oprah owns—including investments, real estate, a stake in the cable television channel Oxygen, and stock options in Viacom—generate another $468 million in revenues per year.

And Oprah Winfrey does not consider herself to be a CEO.

Certainly, her decision-making style is not typical of most CEOs. She has been quoted as describing her business decision making as "leaps of faith" and "If I called a strategic planning meeting, there would be dead silence, and then people would fall out of their chairs laughing."

Oprah, Inc.

However, she has made other decisions that put her firmly in control of her empire. For example, in 1987 she hired a tough Chicago entertainment attorney—Jeff Jacobs—as president of Harpo, Inc. Whereas Oprah's business decisions are made from her gut and from her heart, Jacobs makes sure that the numbers add up to more revenues and profits for Harpo. She has also been unwilling to license her name to other firms, unlike Martha Stewart who licensed her name to Kmart.

Oprah has made strategic alliances with King World (to distribute her TV show), with ABC (to broadcast her movies), with Hearst (to distribute her magazine), and with Oxygen (to distribute some other television programs). But she has never given up control of her business. And she has not taken her firm public. She currently owns 90 percent of Harpo's stock. She was once quoted as saying, "If I lost control of my business, I'd lose myself—or at least the ability to be myself."

To help control this growing business, Oprah and Jacobs hired a chief operating officer (COO), Tim Bennett, who then created several functional departments, including accounting, legal, and human resources, to help manage the firm. With 221 employees, an office, and a real organization, Harpo is a real company, and Oprah is a real CEO—albeit a CEO with a slightly different approach to making business decisions.

Sources: P. Sellers (2002). "The business of being Oprah." *Fortune,* April 1, pp. 50 +; Oprah.com; Hoovers.com; (2003). "Harpo Inc." October 20.

way of taking advantage of each of the functions within a firm's boundaries can destroy this potential value.

Management Controls and Implementing Vertical Integration

Although having the correct organizational structure is important for firms implementing their vertical integration strategies, that structure must be supported by a variety of management control processes. Among the most important of these processes are the budgeting process and the management committee oversight process, which can also help CEOs resolve the functional conflicts that are common within vertically integrated firms.

The Budgeting Process

Budgeting is one of the most important control mechanisms available to CEOs in vertically integrated U-form organizations. Indeed, in most U-form companies enormous management effort goes into the creation of budgets and the evaluation of performance relative to budgets. Budgets are developed for costs, revenues, and a variety of other activities performed by a firm's functional managers. Often, managerial compensation and promotion opportunities depend on the ability of a manager to meet budget expectations.

Although budgets are an important control tool, they can also have unintended negative consequences. For example, the use of budgets can lead functional managers to overemphasize short-term behavior that is easy to measure and underemphasize longer-term behavior that is more difficult to measure. Thus, for example, the strategically correct thing for a functional manager to do might be to increase expenditures for maintenance and management training, thereby ensuring that the function will have both the technology and the skilled people needed to do the job in the future. An overemphasis on meeting current budget requirements, however, might lead this manager to delay maintenance and training expenditures. By meeting short-term budgetary demands, this manager may be sacrificing the long-term viability of this function, compromising the long-term viability of the firm.

CEOs can do a variety of things to counter the "short-termism" effects of the budgeting process. For example, research suggests that evaluating a functional manager's performance relative to budgets can be an effective control device when (1) the process used in developing budgets is open and participative, (2) the process reflects the economic reality facing functional managers and the firm, and (3) quantitative evaluations of a functional manger's performance are augmented by qualitative evaluations of that performance. Adopting an open and participative process for setting budgets helps ensure that budget targets are realistic and that functional managers understand and accept them. Including qualitative criteria for evaluation reduces the chances that functional managers will engage in behaviors that are very harmful in the long run but enable them to make budget in the short run.[7]

The Management Committee Oversight Process

In addition to budgets, vertically integrated U-form organizations can use various internal management committees as management control devices. Two particularly common internal management committees are the **executive committee** and the **operations committee** (although these committees have many different names in different organizations).

The executive committee in a U-form organization typically consists of the CEO and two or three key functional senior managers. It normally meets weekly and reviews the performance of the firm on a short-term basis. Functions represented on this committee generally include accounting, legal, and other functions (such as manufacturing or sales) that are most central to the firm's short-term business success. The fundamental purpose of the executive committee is to track the short-term performance of the firm, to note and correct any budget variances for functional managers, and to respond to any crises that might emerge. Obviously, the executive committee can help avoid many functional conflicts in a vertically integrated firm before they arise.

In addition to the executive committee, another group of managers meets regularly to help control the operations of the firm. Often called the *operations committee,* this committee typically meets monthly and usually consists of the CEO and each of the heads of the functional areas included in the firm. The executive committee is a subset of the operations committee.

The primary objective of the operations committee is to track firm performance over time intervals slightly longer than the weekly interval of primary interest to the executive committee and to monitor longer-term strategic investments and activities. Such investments might include plant expansions, the introduction of new products, and the implementation of cost-reduction or quality improvement programs. The operations committee provides a forum in which senior functional managers can come together to share concerns and opportunities and to coordinate efforts to implement strategies. Obviously, the operations committee can help resolve functional conflicts in a vertically integrated firm after they arise.

In addition to these two standing committees, various other committees and task forces can be organized within the U-form organization to manage specific projects and tasks. These additional groups are typically chaired by a member of the executive or operations committee and report to one or both of these standing committees, as warranted.

Compensation in Implementing Vertical Integration Strategies

Organizational structure and management control systems can have an important impact on the ability of a firm to implement its vertical integration strategy. However, a firm's compensation policies can be important as well.

We have already seen how compensation can play a role in implementing cost leadership and product differentiation, and how compensation can be tied to budgets to help implement vertical integration. However, the three explanations of vertical integration presented in this chapter have important compensation implications as well. We will first discuss the compensation challenges these three explanations suggest and then discuss ways these challenges can be addressed.

Opportunism-Based Vertical Integration and Compensation Policy

Opportunism-based approaches to vertical integration suggest that employees who make firm-specific investments in their jobs will often be able to create more value for a firm than employees who do not. Firm-specific investments are a type of transaction-specific investment. Whereas transaction-specific investments are investments that have more value in a particular exchange than in alternative exchanges, **firm-specific investments** are investments made by employees that have more value in a particular firm than in alternative firms.[8]

Examples of firm-specific investments include an employee's understanding of a particular firm's culture, his or her personal relationships with others in the firm, and an employee's knowledge about a firm's unique business processes. All this knowledge can be used by an employee to create a great deal of value in a firm. However, this knowledge has almost no value in other firms. The effort to create this knowledge is thus a firm-specific investment.

Despite the value that an employee's firm-specific investments can create, opportunism-based explanations of vertical integration suggest that employees will often be reluctant to make these investments, because, once they do, they become vulnerable in their exchange with this firm. For example, an employee who has made very significant firm-specific investments may not be able to quit and go to work for another company, even if her or she is passed over for promotion, does not receive a raise, or is even actively discriminated against. This is because by quitting this firm, this employee loses all the investment he or she made in this particular firm. Because this employee has few employment options other than his or her current firm, this firm can treat this employee badly and the employee can do little about it. This is why employees are often reluctant to make firm-specific investments.

But the firm needs its employees to make such investments if it is to realize its full economic potential. Thus, one of the tasks of compensation policy is to create incentives for employees whose firm-specific investments could create great value to actually make those investments.

Capabilities and Compensation

Capability explanations of vertical integration also acknowledge the importance of firm-specific investments in creating value for a firm. Indeed, many of the valuable, rare, and costly-to-imitate resources and capabilities that can exist in a firm are a manifestation of firm-specific investments made by a firm's employees. However, whereas opportunism explanations of vertical integration tend to focus on firm-specific investments made by individual employees, capabilities explanations tend to focus on firm-specific investments made by groups of employees.[9]

In Chapter 3, it was suggested that one of the reasons that a firm's valuable and rare resources may be costly to imitate is that these resources are socially complex in nature. Socially complex resources reflect the teamwork, cooperation, and culture that have evolved within a firm—capabilities that can increase the value of a firm significantly, but capabilities that other firms will often find costly to imitate, at least in the short to medium term. Moreover, these are capabilities that exist because several employees—not just a single employee—have made specific investments in a firm.

From the point of view of designing a compensation policy, capabilities analysis suggests that not only should a firm's compensation policy encourage employees whose firm-specific investments could create value to actually make those investments; it also recognizes that these investments will often be collective in nature—that, for example, until all the members of a critical management team make firm-specific commitments to that team, that team's ability to create and sustain competitive advantages will be significantly limited.

Flexibility and Compensation

Flexibility explanations of vertical integration also have some important implications for compensation. In particular, because the creation of flexibility in a firm depends on employees being willing to engage in activities that have fixed and known downside risks and significant upside potential, it follows that compensation that has fixed and known downside risks and significant upside potential would encourage employees to choose and implement flexible vertical integration strategies.

Compensation Alternatives

Table 6.1 lists several compensation alternatives and how they are related to each of the three explanations of vertical integration discussed in this chapter. Not surprisingly, opportunism-based explanations suggest that compensation that focuses on individual employees and how they can make firm-specific investments will be

Table 6.1   **Types of Compensation and Approaches to Making Vertical Integration Decisions**

Opportunism explanations	Salary
	Cash bonuses for individual performance
	Stock grants for individual performance
Capabilities explanations	Cash bonuses for corporate or group performance
	Stock grants for corporate or group performance
Flexibility explanations	Stock options for individual, corporate, or group performance

important for firms implementing their vertical integration strategies. Such individual compensation includes an employee's salary, cash bonuses based on individual performance, and **stock grants**—or payments to employees in a firm's stock—based on individual performance.

Capabilities explanations of vertical integration suggest that compensation that focuses on groups of employees making firm-specific investments in valuable, rare, and costly-to-imitate resources and capabilities will be particularly important for firms implementing vertical integration strategies. Such collective compensation includes cash bonuses based on a firm's overall performance and stock grants based on a firm's overall performance.

Finally, flexibility logic suggests that compensation that has fixed and known downside risk and significant upside potential is important for firms implementing vertical integration strategies. **Stock options**, whereby employees are given the right, but not the obligation, to purchase stock at predetermined prices, are a form of compensation that has these characteristics. Stock options can be granted based on an individual employee's performance or the performance of the firm as a whole.

The task facing CEOs looking to implement a vertical integration strategy through compensation policy is to determine what kinds of employee behavior they need to have for this strategy to create sustained competitive advantages and then to use the appropriate compensation policy. Not surprisingly, most CEOs find that all three explanations of vertical integration are important in their decision making. Thus, not surprisingly, many firms adopt compensation policies that feature a mix of the compensation policies listed in Table 6.1. Most firms use both individual and corporate-wide compensation schemes along with salaries, cash bonuses, stock grants, and stock options for employees who have the greatest impact on a firm's overall performance.

Vertical Integration in an International Context

Examples of vertical integration strategies that lead firms to begin operations beyond their home country borders—in particular, offshoring—have already been featured in this chapter. Currently, the trend in vertical integration decisions in an international context seems to be for firms to reduce their level of vertical integration by outsourcing functions that used to be within their boundaries to independent foreign operations. However, in some settings, firms exploit international

Table 6.2 **Vertical Integration Options When Pursuing International Market Opportunities**

Not Vertically Integrated	Somewhat Vertically Integrated	Vertically Integrated
Importing/exporting	Licensing Strategic alliances Joint ventures	Foreign direct investment

market opportunities not by outsourcing to independent foreign firms, but by entering those international markets in a vertically integrated way.

The vertical integration options available to firms pursuing an international strategy are listed in Table 6.2. These options range from non–vertically integrated (exporting/importing), to somewhat vertically integrated (licensing, strategic alliances, joint ventures), to fully vertically integrated (foreign direct investment). Each of these options is discussed below.

Firms can maintain traditional arm's-length market relationships between themselves and their nondomestic customers and still implement international strategies. They do this by simply importing supplies from nondomestic sources or by exporting their products or services to nondomestic markets. In this way, firms limit any foreign direct investment into nondomestic markets. Of course, firms that adopt this non–vertically integrated approach generally have to work with some partner or partners to receive, market, and distribute their products in a nondomestic market. However, it is possible for exporting firms to use relatively simple contracts to manage their relationships with these foreign partners and thereby maintain arm's-length relationships with them.

The advantages of adopting a non–vertically integrated approach in engaging in an international strategy includes its relatively low cost and the limited risk exposure that firms that pursue international opportunities in this manner face. Firms that are just beginning to consider international strategies can use non–vertically integrated approaches to test international waters—to find out if there is demand for their current products or services, to develop some experience operating in nondomestic markets, or to begin to develop relationships that could be valuable in subsequent international strategy efforts. If firms discover that there is not much demand for their products or services in a nondomestic market, or if they discover that they do not have the resources and capabilities to effectively compete in those markets, they can simply cease their international operations. The direct cost of ceasing these operations can be quite low, especially if a firm's volume of international activity is small and the firm has not invested in plant and equipment internationally. Certainly, if a firm has limited its foreign direct investment it does not risk losing this investment if it ceases international operations.

If a firm decides to move beyond non–vertically integrated approaches in pursuing international strategies, a wide range of somewhat vertically integrated approaches is available. These approaches range from simple **licensing arrangements**, whereby a domestic firm grants a firm in a nondomestic market the right to use its products and brand names to sell products in that nondomestic market, to full-blown joint ventures, whereby a domestic firm and a nondomestic firm create an independent organizational entity to manage international efforts. Again, these options will be discussed in depth in Chapter 9.

Finally, firms may decide to integrate in their international operations by acquiring a firm in a nondomestic market or by forming a new wholly owned subsidiary to manage their operations in a nondomestic market. Obviously, both of these international investments involve substantial direct foreign investment by a firm over long periods of time. These investments are subject to both political and economic risks and should be undertaken only if the value they create is significant.

Although vertical integration in international operations can be expensive and risky, it can have some important advantages for internationalizing firms. First, this approach to internationalization can enable a firm to realize any sources of value that might exist in an international opportunity. Moreover, integration enables managers to use a wider range of organizational controls to limit the threats from any transaction-specific investments that have been made. Finally, unlike strategic alliances, where any profits from international operations must be shared with international partners, integrating into international operations enables firms to capture all the economic profits from their international operations.

SUMMARY

Vertical integration is defined as the number of stages in an industry's value chain that a firm has brought within its boundaries. Forward vertical integration brings a firm closer to its ultimate customer; backward vertical integration brings a firm closer to the sources of its raw materials. In making vertical integration decisions for a particular business activity, firms can choose to be not vertically integrated, somewhat vertically integrated, or vertically integrated.

Vertical integration can create value in three different ways: First, it can reduce opportunistic threats from a firm's buyers and suppliers due to transaction-specific investments the firm may have made. A transaction-specific investment is an investment that has more value in a particular exchange than in any alternative exchanges. Second, vertical integration can create value by enabling a firm to exploit its valuable, rare, and costly-to-imitate resources and capabilities. Firms should vertically integrate into activities in which they enjoy such advantages and should not vertically integrate into other activities. Third, vertical integration typically only creates value under conditions of low uncertainty. Under high uncertainty, vertical integration can commit a firm to a costly to reverse course of action and the flexibility of a non–vertically integrated approach may be preferred.

Often, all three approaches to vertical integration will generate similar conclusions. However, even when they suggest different vertical integration strategies, they can still be helpful to management.

The ability of valuable vertical integration strategies to generate a sustained competitive advantage depends on how rare and costly to imitate the strategies are. Vertical integration strategies can be rare in two ways: (1) when a firm is vertically integrated while most competing firms are not vertically integrated and (2) when a firm is not vertically integrated while most competing firms are. These rare vertical integration strategies are possible when firms vary in the extent to which the strategies they pursue require transaction-specific investments; they vary in the resources and capabilities they control; or they vary in the level of uncertainty they face.

The ability to directly duplicate a firm's vertical integration strategies depends on how costly it is to directly duplicate the resources and capabilities that enable a firm to pursue these strategies. The closest substitute for vertical integration—strategic alliances—is discussed in more detail in Chapter 9.

Organizing to implement vertical integration depends on a firm's organizational structure, its management controls, and its compensation policies. The organizational structure most commonly used to implement vertical integration is the functional, or U-form, organization, which involves cost leadership and product differentiation strategies. In a vertically integrated U-form organization, the CEO must focus not only on deciding which functions to vertically integrate into, but also how to resolve conflicts that inevitably arise in a functionally organized vertically integrated firm. Two management controls that can be used to help implement vertical integration strategies and resolve these functional conflicts are the budgeting process and management oversight committees.

Each of the three explanations of vertical integration suggests different kinds of compensation policies that a firm looking to implement vertical integration should pursue. Opportunism-based explanations suggest individual-based compensation—including salaries and cash bonus and stock grants based on individual performance; capabilities-based explanations suggest group-based compensation—including cash bonuses and stock grants based on corporate or group performance; and flexibility-based explanations suggest flexible compensation—including stock options based on individual, group, or corporate performance. Because all three approaches to vertical integration are often operating in a firm, it is not surprising that many firms employ all these devices in compensating employees whose actions are likely to have a significant impact on firm performance.

Firms in an international context also can choose to not be vertically integrated, somewhat vertically integrated, or vertically integrated. Firms choose to be not vertically integrated when they engage in arm's-length importing or exporting. They choose to be somewhat vertically integrated when they engage in licensing, strategic alliances, or joint ventures; and they choose vertical integration when they engage in foreign direct investment.

CHALLENGE QUESTIONS

1. Some firms have engaged in backward vertical integration strategies in order to appropriate the economic profits that would have been earned by suppliers selling to them. How is this motivation for backward vertical integration related to the opportunism logic for vertical integration described in this chapter? (Hint: Compare the competitive conditions under which firms may earn economic profits to the competitive conditions under which firms will be motivated to avoid opportunism through vertical integration.)

2. You are about to purchase a used car. What kinds of threats do you face in this purchase? What can you do to protect yourself from these threats? How is buying a car like and unlike vertical integration decisions?

3. What are the competitive implications for firms if they assume that all potential exchange partners cannot be trusted?

4. Common conflicts between sales and manufacturing are mentioned in the text. What conflicts might exist between R&D and manufacturing? Between finance and manufacturing? Between marketing and sales? Between accounting and everyone else? What could a CEO do to help resolve these conflicts?

5. Under what conditions would you accept a lower-paying job over a higher-paying one? What implications does your answer have for your potential employer's compensation policy?

6. According to opportunism-based explanations of vertical integration, when should a firm pursue foreign direct investment? According to capabilities-based explanations, when should it pursue these investments? According to flexibility explanations, when should it pursue these investments?

PROBLEM SET

1. Which of the following two firms is more vertically integrated? How can you tell?

(a) Firm A has included manufacturing, sales, finance, and human resources within its boundaries and has outsourced legal and customer service.

(b) Firm B has included manufacturing, sales, legal, and customer service within its boundaries and has outsourced finance and human resources.

2. What is the level of transaction-specific investment for each firm in the following transactions? Who in these transactions is at greater risk of being taken unfair advantage of?

(a) Firm I has built a plant right next door to Firm II. Firm I's plant is worth $5 million if it supplies Firm II. It is worth $200,000 if it does not supply Firm II. Firm II has three alternative suppliers. If it receives supplies from Firm I, it is worth $10 million. If it does not receive supplies from Firm I, it is worth $9.8 million.

(b) Firm A has just purchased a new computer system that is only available from Firm B. Firm A has redesigned its entire production process around this new computer system. The old production process is worth $1 million, the new process is worth $12 million. Firm B has several hundred customers for its new computer system.

(c) Firm Alpha, a fast-food restaurant company, has a contract with Firm Beta, a movie studio. After negotiating with several other potential partners, Firm Alpha agreed to a contract that requires Firm Alpha to pay Firm Beta $5 million per year for the right to use characters from Firm Beta's movies in its packaged meals for children. Demand for children's movies has recently dropped.

(d) Firm I owns and runs a printing press. Firm J uses the services of a printing press. Historically, Firm I has sold its services to many customers. However, it was recently approached by Firm J to become its exclusive supplier of printing-press services. Currently, Firm I is worth $1 million. If it became the sole supplier to Firm J, it would be worth $8 million. To complete this deal, Firm I would have to stop supplying its current customers and modify its machines to meet Firm J's needs. No other firm needs the same services as Firm J. Firm J contacted several other suppliers who said they would be willing to become a sole supplier for Firm J before deciding to propose this arrangement with Firm I.

3.   In each of the following situations, would you recommend vertical integration or no vertical integration? Explain.

(a) Firm A needs a new and unique technology for its product line. No substitute technologies are available. Should Firm A make this technology or buy it?

(b) Firm I has been selling its products through a distributor for some time. It has become the market share leader. Unfortunately, this distributor has not been able to keep up with the evolving technology and customers are complaining. No alternative distributors are available. Should Firm I keep its current distributor or should it begin distribution on its own?

(c) Firm Alpha has manufactured its own products for years. Recently, however, one of these products has become more and more like a commodity. Several firms are now able to manufacture this product at the same price and quality as Firm Alpha. However, they do not have Firm Alpha's brand name in the marketplace. Should Firm Alpha continue to manufacture this product or should it outsource it to one of these other firms?

(d) Firm I is convinced that a certain class of technologies holds real economic potential. However, it does not know, for sure, which particular version of this technology is going to dominate the market. There are eight competing versions of this technology currently, but ultimately, only one will dominate the market. Should Firm I invest in all eight of these technologies itself? Should it invest in just one of these technologies? Should it partner with other firms that are investing in these different technologies?

END NOTES

1. Coase, R. (1937). "The nature of the firm." *Economica*, 4, pp. 386–405.
2. This explanation of vertical integration is known as transactions cost economics in the academic literature. See Williamson, O. (1975). *Markets and hierarchies: Analysis and antitrust implications.* New York: Free Press; Williamson, O. (1985). *The economic institutions of capitalism.* New York: Free Press; and Klein, B., R. Crawford, and A. Alchian (1978). "Vertical integration, appropriable rents, and the competitive contracting process." *Journal of Law and Economics*, 21, pp. 297–326.
3. Another option—forming an alliance between these two firms—is discussed in more detail in Chapter 9.
4. This explanation of vertical integration is known as the capabilities-based theory of the firm in the academic literature. It draws heavily from the resource-based view described in Chapter 3. See Barney, J. B. (1991). "Firm resources and sustained competitive advantage." *Journal of Management*, 17, pp. 99–120; Barney, J. B. (1999). "How a firm's capabilities affect boundary decisions." *Sloan Management Review*, 40(3);

Conner, K. R., and C. K. Prahalad (1996). "A resource-based theory of the firm: Knowledge versus opportunism." *Organization Science*, 7, pp. 477–501.
5. This explanation of vertical integration is known as real-options theory in the academic literature. See Kogut, B. (1991). "Joint ventures and the option to expand and acquire." *Management Science*, 37, pp. 19–33.
6. Kripalani, M., and P. Engardio (2003). "The rise of India." *BusinessWeek*, December 8, pp. 66 +.
7. See Gupta, A. K. (1987). "SBU strategies, corporate-SBU relations and SBU effectiveness in strategy implementation." *Academy of Management Journal*, 30(3), pp. 477–500.
8. Becker, G. S. (1993). *Human capital: A theoretical and empirical analysis, with special reference to education.* Chicago: University of Chicago Press.
9. Barney, J. B. (1991). "Firm resources and sustained competitive advantage." *Journal of Management*, 17, pp. 99–120.

Corporate Diversification

After reading this chapter, you should be able to:

1. Define corporate diversification and describe five types of corporate diversification.

2. Specify the two conditions that a corporate diversification strategy must meet in order to create economic value.

3. Define the concept of "economies of scope" and identify eight potential economies of scope a diversified firm might try to exploit.

4. Identify which of these economies of scope a firm's outside equity investors are able to realize on their own at low cost.

5. Specify the circumstances under which a firm's diversification strategy will be rare.

6. Indicate which of the economies of scope identified in this chapter are more likely to be subject to low-cost imitation and which are less likely to be subject to low-cost imitation.

7. Identify two potential substitutes for corporate diversification.

8. Identify economies of scope that can be realized through international operations.

The Worldwide Leader

The breadth of ESPN's diversification has even caught the attention of Hollywood writers. In the 2004 movie *Dodgeball: A True Underdog Story*, the championship game between the underdog Average Joes and the bad guy Purple Cobras is broadcast on the fictitious cable channel ESPN8. Also known as "the Ocho," ESPN8's theme is "If it's almost a sport, we've got it."

Here's the irony. ESPN has way over eight networks currently in operation.

ESPN was founded in 1979 by Bill and Scott Rasmussen after the father and son duo was fired from positions with the New England Whalers, a National Hockey League team now playing in Raleigh, North Carolina. Their initial idea was to rent satellite space to broadcast sports from Connecticut—the University of Connecticut's basketball games, Whaler's hockey games, and so forth. But they found that it was cheaper to rent satellite space for 24 hours straight than to rent space a few hours during the week, thus a 24-hour sports channel was born.

ESPN went on the air September 7, 1979. The first event broadcast was a slow-pitch softball game. Initially, the network broadcast sports that, at the time, were not widely known to U.S. consumers—Australian rules football, Davis Cup tennis, professional wrestling, minor league bowling. Early on, ESPN also gained the rights to broadcast early rounds of the NCAA basketball tournament. At the time, the major networks did not broadcast these early round games, even though we now know that some of these early games are among the most exciting in the entire tournament.

The longest-running ESPN program is, of course, *Sports Center*. Although the first *Sports Center* contained no highlights and a scheduled interview with the football coach at the University of Colorado was interrupted by technical difficulties, *Sports Center* and its familiar theme have become icons in American popular culture. The 25,000th episode of *Sports Center* was broadcast on August 25, 2002.

ESPN was "admitted" into the world of big-time sports in 1987 when it signed with the National Football League to broadcast Sunday Night Football. Since then, ESPN has broadcast Major League Baseball, the National Basketball Association, and, at various times, the National Hockey League. These professional sports have been augmented by college football, basketball, and baseball games.

ESPN's first expansion was modest—in 1993, it introduced ESPN2. Originally, this station played nothing but rock music and scrolled sports scores. Within a few months, however, ESPN2 was broadcasting a full program of sports.

After this initial slow expansion, ESPN began to diversify its businesses rapidly. In 1996, it added ESPN News (an all-sports news channel), in 1997 it acquired a company and opened ESPN Classics (this channel shows old sporting events), and in 2005 it started ESPNU (a channel dedicated to college athletics).

However, these five ESPN channels represent only a fraction of ESPN's diverse business interests. In 1998, ESPN opened its first restaurant, the ESPN Zone. This chain has continued to expand around the world. Also, in 1998, it started a magazine to compete with the then-dominant *Sports Illustrated.* Called *ESPN The Magazine*, it now has over 2 million subscribers. In 2001, ESPN went into the entertainment production business when it founded ESPN Original Entertainment. In 2005, ESPN started ESPN De Portes, a Spanish-language 24-hour sports channel. And in 2006, it founded ESPN on ABC, a company that manages much of the sports content broadcast on ABC. (In 1984, ABC purchased ESPN. Subsequently, ABC was purchased by Capital Cities Entertainment, and most of Capital Cities Entertainment was then sold to Walt Disney Corporation. Currently, ESPN is a division of Disney.)

And none of this counts ESPN HD, ESPN2 HD, ESPN Pay Per View, ESPN Radio, and

ESPN's retail operations on the Web—ESPN.com.

Of all the expansion and diversification efforts, so far ESPN has only stumbled once. In 2006, it founded Mobile ESPN, a mobile telephone service. Not only would this service provide its customers mobile telephone service, it would also provide them up-to-the minute scoring updates and a variety of other sports information. ESPN spent over $40 million advertising its new service and over $150 million on the technology required to make this service available. Unfortunately, it never signed up more than 30,000 subscribers. The breakeven point was estimated to be 500,000 subscribers.

Despite this setback, ESPN has emerged from being that odd little cable channel that broadcast odd little games to a $5 billion company with operations around the world in cable and broadcast television, radio, restaurants, magazines, books, and movie and television production. Which of those numerous enterprises could be characterized as "the Ocho" is hard to tell.

Sources: T. Lowry (2006). "ESPN's cell-phone fumble." *BusinessWeek,* October 30, pp. 26 +; http://en.wikipedia.org/wiki/ESPN.

ESPN is like most large firms in the United States and the world: It has diversified operations. Indeed, virtually all of the 500 largest firms in the United States and the 500 largest firms in the world are diversified, either by product or geographically. Large single-business firms are very unusual. However, like most of these large diversified firms, ESPN has diversified along some dimensions but not others.

What Is Corporate Diversification?

A firm implements a **corporate diversification strategy** when it operates in multiple industries or markets simultaneously. When a firm operates in multiple industries simultaneously, it is said to be implementing a **product diversification strategy**. When a firm operates in multiple geographic markets simultaneously, it is said to be implementing a **geographic market diversification strategy**. When a firm implements both types of diversification simultaneously, it is said to be implementing a **product-market diversification strategy**. Just how geographically diversified firms really are is examined in the Global Perspectives feature.

We have already seen glimpses of these diversification strategies in the discussion of vertical integration strategies in Chapter 6. Sometimes, when a firm vertically integrates backward or forward it begins operations in a new product or geographic market. This happened to computer software firms when they began manning their own call centers. These firms moved from the "computer software development" business to the "call center management" business when they vertically integrated forward. In this sense, when firms vertically integrate they may also be implementing a diversification strategy. However, the critical difference between the diversification strategies studied here and vertical integration (discussed in Chapter 6) is that in this chapter, product market diversification is the primary objective of these strategies, whereas in Chapter 6 such diversification was often a secondary consequence of pursuing a vertical integration strategy.

Types of Corporate Diversification

Firms vary in the extent to which they have diversified the mix of businesses they pursue. Perhaps the simplest way of characterizing differences in the level of corporate diversification focuses on the relatedness of the businesses pursued by a firm. As shown in Figure 7.1, firms can pursue a strategy of **limited corporate diversification**, of **related corporate diversification**, or of **unrelated corporate diversification**.

Limited Corporate Diversification

A firm has implemented a strategy of **limited corporate diversification** when all or most of its business activities fall within a single industry and geographic market (see Panel A of Figure 7.1). Two kinds of firms are included in this corporate diversification category: **single-business firms** (firms with greater than 95 percent of their total sales in a single product market) and **dominant-business firms** (firms with between 70 and 95 percent of their total sales in a single product market).

Differences between single-business and dominant-business firms are represented in Panel A of Figure 7.1. The firm pursing a single-business corporate diversification strategy engages in only one business, Business A. An example of a single-business firm is the WD-40 Company of San Diego, California. This company manufactures and distributes only one product—the spray cleanser and lubricant WD-40. The dominant-business firm pursues two businesses, Business E and a smaller Business F that is tightly linked to Business E. An example of a dominant business firm is Donato's Pizza. Donato's Pizza does the vast majority of its business in a single product—pizza—in a single market—the United States. However, Donato's also owns a subsidiary that makes a machine that automatically slices and puts pepperoni on pizzas. Not only does Donato's use this machine in its own pizzerias, it also sells this machine to food manufacturers that make frozen pepperoni pizza.

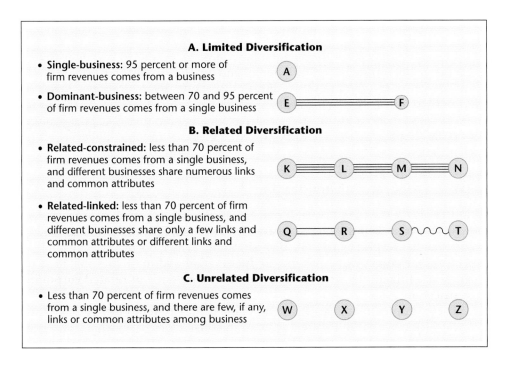

Figure 7.1   Levels and Types of Diversification

Global Perspectives

The same headline seems to appear in every newspaper, in every business book, and in every business class: "Business Is Becoming More Global." The implication is clear: Firms ignore the global nature of their business at their own peril.

In one sense, it is clear that business is becoming more and more global. Large firms, whether headquartered in the United States or abroad, are seeing an ever-larger percentage of their revenues coming from nondomestic sources. Indeed, some firms—such as McDonald's and Coca-Cola—are seen not just as global firms, but as exporters of U.S. culture. However, a careful analysis of where large diversified firms actually sell their products and services tells a somewhat different story. One recent study found that "global diversification" is not really that "global."

In particular, these authors divided the world's economy into

How Global Are Globally Diversified Firms?

three great markets: North America, Europe, and Asia. They then examined the number of firms that have significant sales in just one of these three geographic markets, in two of these markets, and in all three of these mar-

kets. The "globalization of business" hypothesis suggests that large numbers of firms will have significant operations in all three of these markets. This is not the case.

Based on a list of 365 of the largest corporations in the world, this study found that only 9 (2.4 percent) had 20 percent or more of their sales in all three of these global regions, only 25 (5.0 percent) had 20 percent or more of their sales in two of these global regions, while 320 (84.2 percent) had 20 percent or more of their sales in just one of these global regions. This suggests that although it may not be uncommon for firms to sell outside their home country to neighboring countries, it is somewhat more uncommon for firms to have significant sales outside their geographic region.

The list of truly global firms—those that had significant sales in all three regional economies—includes many of the usual suspects, such as

In an important sense, firms pursuing a strategy of limited corporate diversification are not leveraging their resources and capabilities beyond a single product or market. Thus, the analysis of limited corporate diversification is logically equivalent to the analysis of business-level strategies (discussed in Part 2 of this book). Because these kinds of strategies have already been discussed, the remainder of this chapter focuses on corporate strategies that involve higher levels of diversification.

Related Corporate Diversification

As a firm begins to engage in businesses in more than one product or market, it moves away from being a single-business or dominant-business firm and begins to adopt higher levels of corporate diversification. When less than 70 percent of a firm's revenue comes from a single product market and these multiple lines of business are linked, the firm has implemented a strategy of **related corporate diversification**.

The multiple businesses that a diversified firm pursues can be related in two ways (see Panel B in Figure 7.1). If all the businesses in which a firm operates share a significant number of inputs, production technologies, distribution

IBM, Sony, Philips Electronics, Nokia, Intel, Canon, and Coca-Cola. However, several supposedly "global" firms did not show up on this list. For example, Toyota, Unilever, Motorola, Sun Microsystems, 3M, McDonald's, Michelin, and Kodak all have significant sales in two regions of the world, but not all three. For example, only 7.7 percent of Toyota's total sales comes from Europe; only 14 percent of Motorola's total sales comes from Europe; only 14.8 percent of McDonald's total sales comes from Asia; and only 17.2 percent of Kodak's sales comes from Asia.

The list of large firms that have significant sales in only one geographic region is also interesting. This list includes Wal-Mart (94.1 percent of sales in North America), General Motors (81.1 percent in North America), General Electric (59.1 percent in North America), Mitsubishi (86.8 percent in Asia), Volkswagen (68.2 percent in Europe), Ford (66.7 percent in North

America) and Phillip Morris (57.9 percent in North America). Some of these firms—including GM and GE—are thought of as truly international giants. However, this research shows that even these giant international firms are still tied to their historical geographic homes.

These findings have significant implications for the management of international firms. First, they suggest that the products and services of most international firms are not equally accessible across the globe. This is true despite efforts by multinational firms to modify their products to be responsive to local demand. Second, these results suggest that many sources of competitive advantages for firms are valuable only within specific geographic regions and not broadly around the globe. Finally, because firms may have very different market positions in different geographic regions of the world, it may be necessary for

these firms to adopt very different strategies in these regions. For example, Toyota—a firm that has significant sales in Asia and North America—may be able to leverage its reputation for quality by introducing a new brand of luxury automobile—the Lexus. However, because Toyota has such a small market presence in Europe, it has less of a reputation for quality to build on in Europe and thus has been unable to successfully launch the Lexis brand there. Toyota may have to adopt a different approach to the European luxury market or wait to enter that market until its sales in Europe increase dramatically.

Sources: A. Rugman and A. Verbeke (2004). "A perspective on regional and global strategies of multinational enterprises." *Journal of International Business Studies,* 35, pp. 3–18; A. Rugman and A. Verbeke (2002). "A note on the transnational solution and the transaction cost theory of multinational strategic management." *Journal of International Business Studies,* 23, pp. 761–771.

channels, similar customers, and so forth, this corporate diversification strategy is called **related-constrained**. This strategy is *constrained* because corporate managers pursue business opportunities in new markets or industries only if those markets or industries share numerous resource and capability requirements with the businesses the firm is currently pursuing. Commonalities across businesses in a strategy of related-constrained diversification are represented by the linkages among Businesses K, L, M, and N in the related-constrained section of Figure 7.1.

PepsiCo is an example of a related-constrained diversified firm. Although PepsiCo operates in multiple businesses around the world, all of its businesses focus on providing snack-type products, either food or beverages. PepsiCo is not in the business of making or selling more traditional types of food—such as pasta, or cheese, or breakfast cereal. Moreover, PepsiCo attempts to use a single, firmwide capability to gain competitive advantages in each of its businesses—its ability to develop and exploit well-known brand names. Whether it's Pepsi, Doritos, Mountain Dew, or Big Red, PepsiCo is all about building brand names. In fact, PepsiCo has 16 brands that generate $1 billion or more in revenues each year. That is more so-called "power brands" than Nestlé, Procter & Gamble, or Coca-Cola![1]

If the different businesses that a single firm pursues are linked on only a couple of dimensions, or if different sets of businesses are linked along very different dimensions, the corporate diversification strategy is called **related-linked**. For example, Business Q and Business R may share similar production technology, Business R and Business S may share similar customers, Business S and Business T may share similar suppliers, and Business Q and Business T may have no common attributes. This strategy is represented in the related-linked section of Figure 7.1 by businesses with relatively few links between them and with different kinds of links between them (i.e., straight lines and curved lines).

An example of a related-linked diversified firm is Disney. Disney has evolved from a single-business firm (when it did nothing but produce animated motion pictures), to a dominant business firm (when it produced family oriented motion pictures and operated a theme park), to a related-constrained diversified firm (when it produced family oriented motion pictures, operated multiple theme parks, and sold products through its Disney Stores). Recently, it has become so diversified that it has taken on the attributes of related-linked diversification. Although much of the Disney empire still builds on characters developed in its animated motion pictures, it also owns and operates businesses—including a movie studio that produces movies more appropriate for mature audiences, several hotels and resorts that have little or nothing to do with Disney characters, and a television network (ABC) that broadcasts non-Disney-produced content—that are less directly linked to these characters. This is not to suggest that Disney is pursuing an unrelated diversification strategy. After all, most of its businesses are in the entertainment industry, broadly defined. Rather, this is only to suggest that it is no longer possible to find a single thread—like a Mickey Mouse or a Lion King—that connects all of Disney's business enterprises. In this sense, Disney has become a related-linked diversified firm.[2]

Unrelated Corporate Diversification

Firms that pursue a strategy of related corporate diversification have some type of linkages among most, if not all, the different businesses they pursue. However, it is possible for firms to pursue numerous different businesses and for there to be *no* linkages among them (see Panel C of Figure 7.1). When less than 70 percent of a firm's revenues is generated in a single product market, and when a firm's businesses share few, if any, common attributes, then that firm is pursuing a strategy of **unrelated corporate diversification**.

General Electric is an example of a firm pursuing an unrelated diversification strategy. GE's mix of businesses includes aviation products and services (2005 revenues of $15.4 billion), energy products and services (2005 revenues of $17.8 billion), oil and gas products and services (2005 revenues of $3.6 billion), transportation (2005 revenues of $3.6 billion), consumer and industrial products (2005 revenues of $14.1 billion), equipment sales (2005 revenues of $6.6 billion), plastics (2005 revenues of $6.6 billion), health care (2005 revenues of $15.2 billion), NBCUniversal (2005 revenues of $1.8 billion), leasing services (2005 revenues of $11.5 billion), real estate services (2005 revenues of $3.5 billion), and consumer finance and credit cards (2005 revenues of $19.4 billion). It is difficult to see how these businesses are closely related to each other. Indeed, GE tends to manage each of its businesses as if they were stand-alone entities—a management approach consistent with a firm implementing an unrelated diversified corporate strategy.[3]

The Value of Corporate Diversification

V R I O

For corporate diversification to be economically valuable, two conditions must hold. First, there must be some valuable economy of scope among the multiple businesses in which a firm is operating. Second, it must be less costly for managers in a firm to realize these economies of scope than for outside equity holders on their own. If outside investors could realize the value of a particular economy of scope on their own, and at low cost, then they would have few incentives to "hire" managers to realize this economy of scope for them. Each of these requirements for corporate diversification to add value for a firm will be considered below.

What Are Valuable Economies of Scope?

Economies of scope exist in a firm when the value of the products or services it sells increases as a function of the number of businesses that firm operates in. In this definition, the term *scope* refers to the range of businesses in which a diversified firm operates. For this reason, only diversified firms can, by definition, exploit economies of scope. Economies of scope are valuable to the extent that they increase a firm's revenues or decrease its costs, compared to what would be the case if these economies of scope were not exploited.

A wide variety of potentially valuable sources of economies of scope have been identified in the literature. Some of the most important of these are listed in Table 7.1 and discussed below. How valuable economies of scope actually are, on average, has been the subject of a great deal of research, which we summarize in the Research Made Relevant feature.

Diversification to Exploit Operational Economies of Scope

Sometimes, economies of scope may reflect operational links among the businesses a firm engages in. **Operational economies of scope** typically take one of two forms: shared activities and shared core competencies.

Table 7.1 **Different Types of Economies of Scope**

1. Operational economies of scope
   - Shared activities
   - Core competencies
2. Financial economies of scope
   - Internal capital allocation
   - Risk reduction
   - Tax advantages
3. Anticompetitive economies of scope
   - Multipoint competition
   - Exploiting market power
4. Employee and stakeholder incentives for diversification
   - Maximizing management compensation

Research Made Relevant

In 1994, Lang and Stulz published a sensational article that suggested that, on average, when a firm began implementing a corporate diversification strategy, it destroyed about 25 percent of its market value. Lang and Stulz came to this conclusion by comparing the market performance of firms pursuing a corporate diversification strategy with portfolios of firms pursuing a limited diversification strategy. Taken together, the market performance of a portfolio of firms that were pursuing a limited diversification strategy was about 25 percent higher than the market performance of a single diversified firm operating in all of the businesses included in this portfolio. These results suggested that not only were economies of scope not valuable, but, on average, efforts to realize these economies actually destroyed economic value. Similar results were published by Comment and Jarrell using different measures of firm performance.

How Valuable Are Economies of Scope, on Average?

Not surprisingly, these results generated quite a stir. If Lang and Stulz were correct, then diversified firms—no matter what kind of diversification strategy they engaged in—destroyed an enormous amount of economic value. This could lead to a fundamental restructuring of the U.S. economy.

However, several researchers questioned Lang and Stutz's conclusions. Two new findings suggest that, even if there is a 25 percent discount, diversification can still add value. First, Villalonga and others found that firms pursuing diversification strategies were generally performing more poorly before they began diversifying than firms that never pursued diversification strategies. Thus, although it might appear that diversification leads to a significant loss of economic value, in reality that loss of value occurred before these firms began implementing a diversification strategy. Indeed, some more recent research suggests that these relatively poor-performing firms may actually increase their market value over what would have been the case if they did not diversify.

Second, Miller found that firms that find it in their self-interest to diversify do so in a very predictable

Shared Activities. In Chapter 3, it was suggested that value-chain analysis can be used to describe the specific business activities of a firm. This same value-chain analysis can also be used to describe the business activities that may be shared across several different businesses within a diversified firm. These **shared activities** are potential sources of operational economies of scope for diversified firms.

Consider, for example, the hypothetical firm presented in Figure 7.2. This diversified firm engages in three businesses: A, B, and C. However, these three businesses share a variety of activities throughout their value chains. For example, all three draw on the same technology development operation. Product design and manufacturing are shared in businesses A and B and separate for business C. All three businesses share a common marketing and service operation. Business A has its own distribution system.

These kinds of shared activities are quite common among both related-constrained and related-linked diversified firms. At Texas Instruments, for example, a variety of electronics businesses share some research and development activities and many share common manufacturing locations. Procter & Gamble's numerous consumer products businesses often share common manufacturing locations and rely on a common distribution network (through retail grocery pattern. These firms tend to diversify into the most profitable new business first, the second most profitable business second, and so forth. Not surprisingly, the 50th diversification move made by these firms might not generate huge additional profits. However, these profits—it turns out—are still, on average, positive. Because multiple rounds of diversification increase profits at a decreasing rate, the overall average profitability of diversified firms will generally be less than the overall average profitability of firms that do not pursue a diversification strategy—thus, a substantial difference between the market value of nondiversified and diversified firms might exist. However, this discount, per se, does not mean that the diversified firm is destroying economic value. Rather, it may mean only that a diversifying firm is creating value in smaller increments as it continues to diversify.

However, some even more recent research suggests that Lang and

Stulz's original "diversification discount" finding may be reemerging. It turns out that all the papers that show that diversification does not, on average, destroy value, and that it sometimes can add value, fail to consider all the investment options open to firms. In particular, firms that are generating free cash flow but have limited growth opportunities in their current businesses—that is, the kinds of firms that Villalonga and Miller suggest will create value through diversification—have other investment options besides diversification. In particular, these firms can return their free cash to their equity holders, either through a direct cash dividend or through buying back stock.

Mackey and Barney show that firms that do not pay out to shareholders destroy value compared to firms that do payout. In particular, firms that use their free cash flow to pay dividends and buy back stock create value; firms that payout and

diversify destroy some value; and firms that just diversify destroy significant value.

Of course, these results are "on average." It is possible to identify firms that actually create value from diversification—about 17 percent of diversified firms in the United States create value from diversification. What distinguishes firms that destroy and create value from diversification is likely to be the subject of research for some time to come.

Sources: H. P. Lang and R. Stulz (1994). "Tobin's *q*, corporate diversification, and firm performance." *Journal of Political Economy,* 102, pp. 1248–1280; R. Comment and G. Jarrell (1995). "Corporate focus and stock returns." *Journal of Financial Economics,* 37, pp. 67–87; D. Miller (2006). "Technological diversity, related diversification, and firm performance." *Strategic Management Journal,* 27(7), pp. 601–620; B. Villalonga (2004). "Does diversification cause the 'diversification discount'?" *Financial Management,* 33(2), pp. 5–28; T. Mackey and J. Barney (2006). "Is there a diversification discount—really?" Unpublished, Department of Management and Human Resources, The Ohio State University.

stores).[4] Some of the most common shared activities in diversified firms and their location in the value chain are summarized in Table 7.2.

Many of the shared activities listed in Table 7.2 can have the effect of reducing a diversified firm's costs. For example, if a diversified firm has a purchasing function that is common to several of its different businesses it can often obtain volume discounts on its purchases that would otherwise not be possible. Also, by manufacturing products that are used as inputs into several of a diversified firm's businesses, the total costs of producing these products can be reduced. A single sales force representing the products or services of several different businesses within a diversified firm can reduce the cost of selling these products or services. Firms such as IBM, HP, and General Motors have all used shared activities to reduce their costs in these ways.

Failure to exploit shared activities across businesses can lead to out-of-control costs. For example, Kentucky Fried Chicken, when it was a division of PepsiCo, encouraged each of its regional business operations in North America to develop its own quality improvement plan. The result was enormous redundancy and at least three conflicting quality efforts—all leading to higher-than-necessary costs. In a similar way, Levi Strauss's unwillingness to centralize and

Figure 7.2   A Hypothetical
Firm Sharing Activities
Among Three Businesses

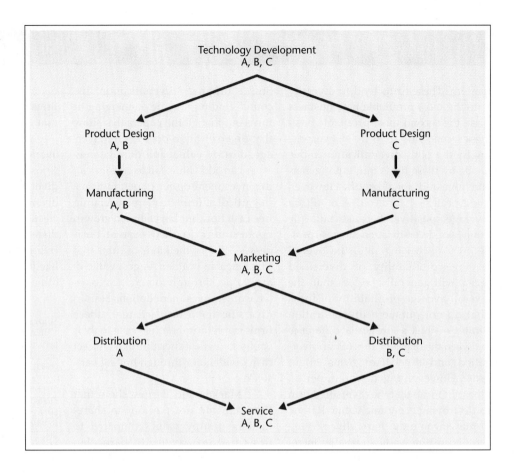

coordinate order processing led to a situation where six separate order-processing computer systems operated simultaneously. This costly redundancy was ultimately replaced by a single, integrated ordering system shared across the entire corporation.[5]

Shared activities can also increase the revenues in diversified firms' businesses. This can happen in at least two ways. First, it may be that shared product development and sales activities may enable two or more businesses in a diversified firm to offer a bundled set of products to customers. Sometimes, the value of these "product bundles" is greater than the value of each product separately. This additional customer value can generate revenues greater than what would have been the case if the businesses were not together and sharing activities in a diversified firm.

In the telecommunications industry, for example, separate firms sell telephones, access to telephone lines, equipment to route calls in an office, mobile telephones, and paging services. A customer that requires all these services could contact five different companies. Each of these five different firms would likely possess its own unique technological standards and software, making the development of an integrated telecommunications system for the customer difficult, at best. Alternatively, a single diversified firm sharing sales activities across these businesses could significantly reduce the search costs of potential customers. This one-stop shopping is likely to be valuable to customers, who might be willing to

Table 7.2 **Possible Shared Activities and Their Place in the Value Chain**

Value Chain Activity	Shared Activities
Input activities	Common purchasing
	Common inventory control system
	Common warehousing facilities
	Common inventory delivery system
	Common quality assurance
	Common input requirements system
	Common suppliers
Production activities	Common product components
	Common product components manufacturing
	Common assembly facilities
	Common quality control system
	Common maintenance operation
	Common inventory control system
Warehousing and distribution	Common product delivery system
	Common warehouse facilities
Sales and marketing	Common advertising efforts
	Common promotional activities
	Cross-selling of products
	Common pricing systems
	Common marketing departments
	Common distribution channels
	Common sales forces
	Common sales offices
	Common order processing services
Dealer support and service	Common service network
	Common guarantees and warranties
	Common accounts receivable management systems
	Common dealer training
	Common dealer support services

Sources: Porter, M. E. (1985). *Competitive advantage*. New York: Free Press; Rumelt, R. P. (1974). *Strategy, structure, and economic performance*. Cambridge, MA: Harvard University Press; Ansoff, H. I. (1965). *Corporate strategy*. New York: McGraw-Hill.

pay a slightly higher price for this convenience than they would pay if they purchased these services from five separate firms. Moreover, if this diversified firm also shares some technology development activities across its businesses, it might be able to offer an integrated telecommunications network to potential customers. The extra value of this integrated network for customers is very likely to be reflected in prices that are higher than would have been possible if each of these businesses were independent or if activities among these businesses were not shared. Most of the regional telephone operating companies in the United States are attempting to gain these economies of scope.[6]

Such product bundles are important in other firms as well. Many grocery stores now sell prepared foods alongside traditional grocery products in the belief that busy customers want access to all kinds of food products—in the same location.[7]

Second, shared activities can enhance business revenues by exploiting the strong, positive reputations of some of a firm's businesses in other of its businesses. For example, if one business has a strong positive reputation for high-quality manufacturing, other businesses sharing this manufacturing activity will gain some of the advantages of this reputation. And, if one business has a strong positive reputation for selling high-performance products, other businesses sharing sales and marketing activities with this business will gain some of the advantages of this reputation. In both cases, businesses that draw on the strong reputation of another business through shared activities with that business will have larger revenues than they would were they operating on their own.

The Limits of Activity Sharing.   Despite the potential of activity sharing to be the basis of a valuable corporate diversification strategy, this approach has three important limits.[8] First, substantial organizational issues are often associated with a diversified firm's learning how to manage cross-business relationships. Managing these relationships effectively can be very difficult, and failure can lead to excess bureaucracy, inefficiency, and organizational gridlock. These issues are discussed in detail in Chapter 8.

Second, sharing activities may limit the ability of a particular business to meet its specific customers' needs. For example, if two businesses share manufacturing activities, they may reduce their manufacturing costs. However, to gain these cost advantages, these businesses may need to build products using somewhat standardized components that do not fully meet their individual customers' needs. Businesses that share distribution activities may have lower overall distribution costs but be unable to distribute their products to all their customers. Businesses that share sales activities may have lower overall sales costs but be unable to provide the specialized selling required in each business.

One diversified firm that has struggled with the ability to meet the specialized needs of customers in its different divisions is General Motors. To exploit economies of scope in the design of new automobiles, GM shared the design process across several automobile divisions. The result through much of the 1990s was "cookie-cutter" cars—the traditional distinctiveness of several GM divisions, including Oldsmobile and Cadillac, was all but lost.[9]

Third, if one business in a diversified firm has a poor reputation, sharing activities with that business can reduce the quality of the reputation of other businesses in the firm.

Taken together, these limits on activity sharing can more than offset any possible gains. Indeed, over the last decade more and more diversified firms have been abandoning efforts at activity sharing in favor of managing each business's activities independently. For example, ABB, Inc. (a Swiss engineering firm) and CIBA-Geigy (a Swiss chemicals firm) have adopted explicit corporate policies that restrict almost all activity sharing across businesses.[10] Other diversified firms, including Nestlé and General Electric, restrict activity sharing to just one or two activities (such as research and development or management training). However, to the extent that a diversified firm can exploit shared activities while avoiding these problems, shared activities can add value to a firm.

Core Competencies.   Recently, a second operational linkage among the businesses of a diversified firm has been described. Unlike shared activities, this linkage is based on different businesses in a diversified firm sharing less tangible resources such as managerial and technical know-how, experience, and wisdom. This source of operational economy of scope has been called a firm's core competence.[11] **Core**

competence has been defined by Prahalad and Hamel as "the collective learning in the organization, especially how to coordinate diverse production skills and integrate multiple streams of technologies." Core competencies are complex sets of resources and capabilities that link different businesses in a diversified firm through managerial and technical know-how, experience, and wisdom.[12]

Two firms that have well-developed core competencies are 3M and Johnson & Johnson. 3M has a core competence in substrates, adhesives, and coatings. Collectively, employees at 3M know more about developing and applying adhesives and coatings on different kinds of substrates than do employees in any other organization. Over the years, 3M has applied these resources and capabilities in a wide variety of products, including Post-it notes, magnetic tape, photographic film, pressure-sensitive tape, and coated abrasives. At first glance, these widely diversified products seem to have little or nothing in common. Yet they all draw on a single core set of resources and capabilities in substrates, adhesives, and coatings.

Johnson & Johnson has a core competence in developing or acquiring pharmaceutical and medical products and then marketing them to the public. Many of Johnson & Johnson's products are dominant in their market segments—Johnson & Johnson's in baby powder, Ethicon in surgical sutures, and Tylenol in pain relievers. And although these products range broadly from those sold directly to consumers (e.g., the BandAid brand of adhesive bandages) to highly sophisticated medical technologies sold only to doctors and hospitals (e.g., Ethicon sutures), all of Johnson & Johnson's products build on the same ability to identify, develop, acquire, and market products in the pharmaceutical and medical products industry.

To understand how core competencies can reduce a firm's costs or increase its revenues, consider how core competencies emerge over time. Most firms begin operations in a single business. Imagine that a firm has carefully evaluated all of its current business opportunities and has fully funded all of those with a positive net present value. Any of the above-normal returns that this firm has left over after fully funding all its current positive net present value opportunities can be thought of as **free cash flow**.[13] Firms can spend this free cash in a variety of ways: They can spend it on benefits for managers; they can give it to shareholders through dividends or by buying back a firm's stock; they can use it to invest in new businesses.

Suppose a firm chooses to use this cash to invest in a new business. In other words, suppose this firm chooses to implement a diversification strategy. If this firm is seeking to maximize the return from implementing this diversification strategy, which of all the possible businesses that it could invest in should it invest in? Obviously, a profit-maximizing firm will choose to begin operations in a business in which it has a competitive advantage. What kind of business is likely to generate this competitive advantage for this firm? The obvious answer is a business in which the same underlying resources and capabilities that gave this firm an advantage in its original business are still valuable, rare, and costly to imitate. Consequently, this first diversification move sees the firm investing in a business that is closely related to its original business, because both businesses will draw on a common set of underlying resources and capabilities that provide the firm with a competitive advantage.

Put another way, a firm that diversifies by exploiting its resource and capability advantages in its original business will have lower costs than those that begin a new business without these resource and capability advantages, or higher revenues than firms lacking these advantages, or both. As long as this firm

Strategy in the Emerging Enterprise

W. L. Gore & Associates is best known for manufacturing a waterproof and windproof, but breathable fabric that is used to insulate winter coats, hiking boots, and a myriad of other outdoor apparel products. This fabric—known as Gore-Tex—has a brand name in its market niche every bit as strong as any of the brand names controlled by PepsiCo or Procter & Gamble. The "Gore-Tex" label attached to any outdoor garment promises waterproof comfort in even the harshest conditions.

But W. L. Gore & Associates did not start out in the outdoor fabric business. Indeed, for the first 10 years of its existence, W. L. Gore sold insulation for wires and similar industrial products using a molecular technology originally developed by DuPont—a technology most of us know as Teflon. Only 10 years after its initial founding did the founder's son, Bob Gore, discover that it was possible to stretch the Teflon molecule to form a strong and porous material that is chemically inert, has a low friction coefficient, functions within a wide temperature range, does not age, and is extremely strong. This is the material called Gore-Tex.

Gore-Tex and Guitar Strings

By extending its basic technology, W. L. Gore and Associates has been able to diversify well beyond its original wire insulation business. With 2005 sales of $1.84 billion, the company currently has operations in medical products (including synthetic blood vessels and patches for soft tissue regeneration), electronics products (including wiring board materials and computer chip components), industrial products (including filter bags for environmental protection and sealants for chemical manufacturing), and fabrics (including Gore-Tex fabric, Wind-Stopper fabric, and CleanStream filters).

And Gore continues to discover new ways to exploit its competence in the Teflon molecule. In 1997, a team of Gore engineers developed a cable made out of the Teflon molecule for use to control puppets at Disney's theme parks. Unfortunately, these cables did not perform up to expectations and were not sold to Disney. However, some guitar players discovered these cables and began using them as strings for their guitars. They found out that these "Gore-Tex" strings sounded great and lasted five times as long as alternative guitar strings. So Gore entered yet another market—the $100 million fretted-stringed-instrument business—with its Elixir brand of guitar strings. Currently, W. L. Gore is the second-largest manufacturer in this market.

The flexibility of the Teflon molecule—and W. L. Gore's ability to explore and exploit that flexibility—has created a diversified company whose original objective was simply to sell insulation for wires.

Sources: www.gore.com; D. Sacks (2003). "The Gore-Tex of guitar strings." *Fast Times*, December, p. 46.

organizes itself to take advantage of these resource and capability advantages in its new business, it should earn high profits in its new business, along with the profits it will still be earning in its original business.[14] This can be true for even relatively small firms, as described in the Strategy in the Emerging Enterprise feature.

Of course, over time this diversified firm is likely to develop new resources and capabilities through its operations in the new business. These new resources and capabilities enhance the entire set of skills that a firm might be able to bring to still another business. Using the profits it has obtained in its previous businesses, this firm is likely to enter another new business. Again, choosing from among all the new businesses it could enter, it is likely to begin operations in a business in which it can exploit its now-expanded resource and capability advantages to obtain a competitive advantage, and so forth.

After a firm has engaged in this diversification strategy several times, the resources and capabilities that enable it to operate successfully in several businesses become its core competencies. A firm develops these core competencies by transferring the technical and management knowledge, experience, and wisdom it developed in earlier businesses to its new businesses. A firm that has just begun this diversification process has implemented a dominant-business strategy. If all of a firm's businesses share the same core competencies, then that firm has implemented a strategy of related-constrained diversification. If different businesses exploit different sets of resources and capabilities, that firm has implemented a strategy of related-linked diversification. In any case, these core competencies enable firms to have lower costs or higher revenues as they include more businesses in their diversified portfolio, compared to firms without these competencies.

Of course, not all firms develop core competencies in this logical and rational manner. That is, sometimes a firm's core competencies are examples of the emergent strategies described in Chapter 1. Indeed, as described in Chapter 1, Johnson & Johnson is an example of a firm that has a core competence that emerged over time. However, no matter how a firm develops core competencies, to the extent that they enable a diversified firm to have lower costs or larger revenues in its business operations, these competencies can be thought of as sources of economies of scope.

Some diversified firms realize the value of these kinds of core competencies through shared activities. For example, as suggested earlier, 3M has a core competence in substrates, adhesives, and coatings. To exploit this, 3M has adopted a multitiered product innovation process. In addition to product innovations within each business unit separately, 3M also supports a corporate research and development lab that seeks to exploit and expand its core competence in substrates, adhesives, and coatings. Because the corporate R&D laboratory is shared by all of 3M's different businesses, it can be thought of as a shared activity.

However, other firms realize the value of their core competencies without shared activities. Although Johnson & Johnson has a core competence in developing, acquiring, and marketing pharmaceutical and medical products, it does not realize this core competence through shared activities. Indeed, each of J&J's businesses is run very independently. For example, although one of its most successful products is Tylenol, the fact that the company that manufactures and distributes Tylenol—McNeil—is actually a division of Johnson & Johnson is not printed on any Tylenol packaging. If you did not know that Tylenol was a J&J product, you could not tell from the bottles of Tylenol you buy.

Although J&J does not use shared activities to realize the value of its core competencies, it does engage in other activities to realize this value. For example, it is not uncommon for members of the senior management team of each of the businesses in J&J's portfolio to have obtained managerial experience in some other J&J business. That is, J&J identifies high-potential managers in one of its businesses and uses this knowledge by giving these managers additional responsibilities in another J&J business. This ability to leverage its management talent across multiple businesses is an example of a firm's core competence, although the realization of the value of that competence does not depend on the existence of a shared activity.

Sometimes, because a firm's core competence is not reflected in specific shared activities, it is easy to conclude that it is not exploiting any economies of scope in its diversification strategy. Diversified firms that are exploiting core competencies as an economy of scope but are not doing so with any shared activities are sometimes called **seemingly unrelated diversified firms**. They may appear to be unrelated diversified firms, but are, in fact, related diversified firms without any shared activities.

One example of a seemingly unrelated diversified firm is the British company Virgin Group. Operating in a wide variety of businesses—everything from record producing, music retailing, air and rail travel, soft drinks, spirits, mobile phones, cosmetics, retail bridal shops, financial services, and providing gas and electricity, to hot air ballooning—the Virgin Group is clearly diversified. The firm has few, if any, shared activities. However, at least two core competencies cut across all the business activities in the group—the brand name "Virgin" and the eccentric marketing and management approach of Virgin's founder, Richard Branson. Branson is the CEO who walked down a "catwalk" in a wedding gown to help publicize the opening of Virgin Brides—the Virgin Group's line of retail bridal shops. Branson is also the CEO who had all of Virgin Air's airplanes repainted with the British "Union Jack" and the slogan "Britain's Real Airline" when British Airways eliminated the British Flag from its airplanes. Whether these two core competencies create sufficient value to justify the Virgin Group's continued existence, and whether they will continue beyond Branson's affiliation with the group, are still open questions.

Limits of Core Competencies.   Just as there are limits to the value of shared activities as sources of economies of scope, so there are limits to core competencies as sources of these economies. The first of these limitations stems from important organizational issues to be discussed in Chapter 8. The way that a diversified firm is organized can either facilitate the exploitation of core competencies or prevent this exploitation from occurring.

A second limitation of core competencies is a result of the intangible nature of these economies of scope. Whereas shared activities are reflected in tangible operations in a diversified firm, core competencies may be reflected only in shared knowledge, experience, and wisdom across businesses. The intangible character of these relationships is emphasized when they are described as a **dominant logic** in a firm, or a common way of thinking about strategy across different businesses.[15]

The intangibility of core competencies can lead diversified firms to make two kinds of errors in managing relatedness. First, intangible core competencies can be illusory inventions by creative managers who link even the most completely unrelated businesses and thereby justify their diversification strategy. A firm that manufactures airplanes and running shoes can rationalize this diversification by claiming to have a core competence in managing transportation businesses. A firm operating in the professional football business and the movie business can rationalize this diversification by claiming to have a core competence in managing entertainment businesses. Such **invented competencies** are not real sources of economies of scope.

Second, a diversified firm's businesses may be linked by a core competence, but this competence may affect these businesses' costs or revenues in a trivial way. Thus, for example, all of a firm's businesses may be affected by government actions, but the impact of these actions on costs and revenues in different businesses may be quite small. A firm may have a core competence in managing relationships with the government, but this core competence will not reduce costs or enhance revenues for these particular businesses very much. Also, each of a diversified firm's businesses may use some advertising. However, if advertising does not have a major impact on revenues for these businesses, core competencies in advertising are not likely to significantly reduce a firm's costs or increase its revenues. In this case, a core competence may be a source of economies of scope, but the value of those economies may be very small.

Diversification to Exploit Financial Economies of Scope

A second class of motivations for diversification shifts attention away from operational linkages among a firm's businesses and toward financial advantages associated with diversification. Three financial implications of diversification have been studied: diversification and capital allocation, diversification and risk reduction, and tax advantages of diversification.

Diversification and Capital Allocation.   Capital can be allocated to businesses in one of two ways. First, businesses operating as independent entities can compete for capital in the external capital market. They do this by providing a sufficiently high return to induce investors to purchase shares of their equity, by having a sufficiently high cash flow to repay principal and interest on debt, and in other ways. Alternatively, a business can be part of a diversified firm. That diversified firm competes in the external capital market and allocates capital among its various businesses. In a sense, diversification creates an **internal capital market** in which businesses in a diversified firm compete for corporate capital.[16]

For an internal capital market to create value for a diversified firm, it must offer some efficiency advantages over an external capital market. It has been suggested that a potential efficiency gain from internal capital markets depends on the greater amount and quality of information that a diversified firm possesses about the businesses it owns, compared with the information that external suppliers of capital possess. Owning a business gives a diversified firm access to detailed and accurate information about the actual performance of the business, its true future prospects, and thus the actual amount and cost of the capital that should be allocated to it. External sources of capital, in contrast, have relatively limited access to information and thus have a limited ability to judge the actual performance and future prospects of a business.

Some have questioned whether a diversified firm, as a source of capital, actually has more and better information about a business it owns, compared to external sources of capital. After all, independent businesses seeking capital have a strong incentive to provide sufficient information to external suppliers of capital to obtain required funds. However, a firm that owns a business may have at least two informational advantages over external sources of capital.

First, although an independent business has an incentive to provide information to external sources of capital, it also has an incentive to downplay or even not report any negative information about its performance and prospects. Such negative information would raise an independent firm's cost of capital. External sources of capital have limited ability to force a business to reveal all information about its performance and prospects and thus may provide capital at a lower cost than they would if they had full information. Ownership gives a firm the right to compel more complete disclosure, although even here full disclosure is not guaranteed. With this more complete information, a diversified firm can allocate just the right amount of capital, at the appropriate cost, to each business.

Second, an independent business may have an incentive not to reveal all the positive information about its performance and prospects. In Chapter 3, the ability of a firm to earn economic profits was shown to depend on the imitability of its resources and capabilities. An independent business that informs external sources of capital about all of its sources of competitive advantage is also informing its potential competitors about these sources of advantage. This information sharing increases the probability that these sources of advantage will be imitated. Because of the competitive implications of sharing this information, firms may choose not to share it, and external sources of capital may underestimate the true performance and prospects of a business.

A diversified firm, however, may gain access to this additional information about its businesses without revealing it to potential competitors. This information enables the diversified firm to make more informed decisions about how much capital to allocate to a business and about the cost of that capital, compared to the external capital market.[17]

Over time, there should be fewer errors in funding businesses through internal capital markets, compared to funding businesses through external capital markets. Fewer funding errors, over time, suggest a slight capital allocation advantage for a diversified firm, compared to an external capital market. This advantage should be reflected in somewhat higher rates of return on invested capital for the diversified firm, compared to the rates of return on invested capital for external sources of capital.

However, the businesses within a diversified firm do not always gain cost-of-capital advantages by being part of a diversified firm's portfolio. Several authors have argued that because a diversified firm has lower overall risk (see the following discussion), it will have a lower cost of capital, which it can pass along to the businesses within its portfolio. Although the lower risks associated with a diversified firm may lower the firm's cost of capital, the appropriate cost of capital to businesses within the firm depends on the performance and prospects of each of those businesses. The firm's advantages in evaluating its businesses' performances and prospects result in more appropriate capital allocation, not just in lower cost of capital for those businesses. Indeed, a business's cost of capital may be lower than what it could have obtained in the external capital market (because the firm is able to more fully evaluate the positive aspects of that business), or it may be higher than what it could have obtained in the external capital market (because the firm is able to more fully evaluate the negative aspects of that business).

Of course, if these businesses also have lower cost or higher revenue expectations because they are part of a diversified firm, then those cost/revenue advantages will be reflected in the appropriate cost of capital for these businesses. In this sense, any operational economies of scope for businesses in a diversified firm may be recognized by a diversified firm exploiting financial economies of scope.

Limits on Internal Capital Markets.   Although internal capital allocation has several potential advantages for a diversified firm, this process also has several limits. First, the level and type of diversification that a firm pursues can affect the efficiency of this allocation process. A firm that implements a strategy of unrelated diversification, whereby managers have to evaluate the performance and prospects of numerous very different businesses, puts a greater strain on the capital allocation skills of its managers than does a firm that implements related diversification. Indeed, in the extreme, the capital allocation efficiency of a firm pursuing broad-based unrelated diversification will probably not be superior to the capital allocation efficiency of the external capital market.

Second, the increased efficiency of internal capital allocation depends on managers in a diversified firm having better information for capital allocation than the information available to external sources. However, this higher-quality information is not guaranteed. The incentives that can lead managers to exaggerate their performance and prospects to external capital sources can also lead to this behavior within a diversified firm. Indeed, several examples of business managers falsifying performance records to gain access to more internal capital have been reported.[18] Research suggests that capital allocation requests by managers are routinely discounted in diversified firms in order to correct for these managers' inflated estimates of the performance and prospects of their businesses.[19]

Finally, not only do business managers have an incentive to inflate the performance and prospects of their business in a diversified firm, but managers in charge of capital allocation in these firms may have an incentive to continue investing in a business despite its poor performance and prospects. The reputation and status of these managers often depend on the success of these business investments, because often they initially approved them. These managers often continue throwing good money at these businesses in hope that they will someday improve, thereby justifying their original decision. Organizational psychologists call this process **escalation of commitment** and have presented numerous examples of managers' becoming irrationally committed to a particular investment.[20]

Indeed, research on the value of internal capital markets in diversified firms suggests that, on average, the limitations of these markets often outweigh their advantages. For example, even controlling for firm size, excessive investment in poorly performing businesses in a diversified firm reduces the market value of the average diversified firm.[21] However, the fact that many firms do not gain the advantages associated with internal capital markets does not necessarily imply that no firms gain these advantages. If only a few firms are able to obtain the advantages of internal capital markets while successfully avoiding their limitations, this financial economy of scope may be a source of at least a temporary competitive advantage.

Diversification and Risk Reduction.   Another possible financial economy of scope for a diversified firm has already been briefly mentioned—the riskiness of the cash flows of diversified firms is lower than the riskiness of the cash flows of undiversified firms. Consider, for example, the riskiness of two businesses operating separately compared to the risk of a diversified firm operating in those same two businesses simultaneously. If both these businesses are very risky on their own, and the cash flows from these businesses are not highly correlated over time, then combining these two businesses into a single firm will generate a lower level of overall risk for the diversified firm than for each of these businesses on their own.

This lower level of risk is due to the low correlation between the cash flows associated with these two businesses. If Business I is having a bad year, Business II might be having a good year, and a firm that operates in both of these businesses simultaneously can have moderate levels of performance. In another year, Business II might be off while Business I is having a good year. Again, the firm operating in both these businesses can have moderate levels of performance. Firms that diversify to reduce risk will have relatively stable returns over time, especially as they diversify into many different businesses with cash flows that are not highly correlated over time.

Tax Advantages of Diversification.   Another financial economy of scope from diversification stems from possible tax advantages of this corporate strategy. These possible tax advantages reflect one or a combination of two effects. First, a diversified firm can use losses in some of its businesses to offset profits in others, thereby reducing its overall tax liability. Of course, substantial losses in some of its businesses may overwhelm profits in other businesses, forcing businesses that would have remained solvent if they were independent to cease operation. However, as long as business losses are not too large, a diversified firm's tax liability can be reduced. Empirical research suggests that diversified firms do, sometimes, offset profits in some businesses with losses in others, although the tax savings of these activities are usually small.[22]

Second, because diversification can reduce the riskiness of a firm's cash flows, it can also reduce the probability that a firm will declare bankruptcy. This can increase a firm's debt capacity. This effect on debt capacity is greatest when the cash flows of a diversified firm's businesses are perfectly and negatively correlated. However, even when these cash flows are perfectly and positively correlated, there can still be a (modest) increase in debt capacity.

Debt capacity is particularly important in tax environments where interest payments on debt are tax deductible. In this context, diversified firms can increase their leverage up to their debt capacity and reduce their tax liability accordingly. Of course, if interest payments are not tax deductible, or if the marginal corporate tax rate is relatively small, then the tax advantages of diversification can be quite small. Recent empirical work suggests that diversified firms do have greater debt capacity than undiversified firms. However, low marginal corporate tax rates, at least in the United States, make the accompanying tax savings on average relatively small.[23]

Diversification to Exploit Anticompetitive Economies of Scope

A third group of motivations for diversification is based on the relationship between diversification strategies and various anticompetitive activities by firms. Two specific examples of these activities are (1) multipoint competition to facilitate mutual forbearance and tacit collusion and (2) exploiting market power.

Multipoint Competition.   Multipoint competition exists when two or more diversified firms simultaneously compete in multiple markets. For example, HP and Dell compete in both the personal computer market and the market for computer printers. Michelin and Goodyear compete in both the U.S. automobile tire market and the European automobile tire market. Disney and AOL/Time Warner compete in both the movie production and book publishing businesses.

Multipoint competition can serve to facilitate a particular type of tacit collusion called **mutual forbearance**. Firms engage in **tacit collusion** when they cooperate to reduce rivalry below the level expected under perfect competition. Consider the situation facing two diversified firms, A and B. These two firms operate in the same businesses, I, II, III, and IV (see Figure 7.3). In this context, any decisions that Firm A might make to compete aggressively in Businesses I and III must take into account the possibility that Firm B will respond by competing aggressively in Businesses II and IV and vice versa. The potential loss that each of these firms may experience in some of its businesses must be compared to the potential gain that each might obtain if it exploits competitive advantages in other of its businesses. If the present value of gains does not outweigh the present value of losses from retaliation, then both firms will avoid competitive activity. Refraining from competition is mutual forbearance.[24]

Mutual forbearance as a result of multipoint competition has occurred in several industries. For example, this form of tacit collusion has been described as existing between Michelin and Goodyear, Maxwell House and Folger's, Caterpillar and John Deere, and BIC and Gillette.[25] Another clear example of such cooperation can be found in the airline industry. For example, America West began service into the Houston Intercontinental Airport with very low introduc-

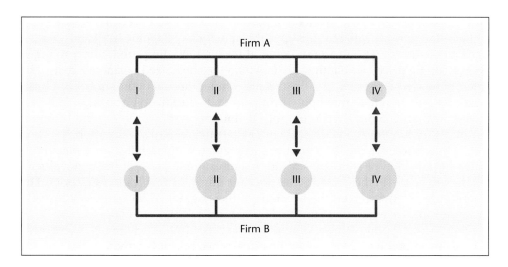

Figure 7.3 Multipoint
Competition Between
Hypothetical Firms A and B

tory fares. Continental Airlines, the dominant firm at Houston Intercontinental, rapidly responded to America West's low Houston fares by reducing the price of its flights from Phoenix, Arizona, to several cities in the United States. Phoenix is the home airport of America West. Within just a few weeks, America West withdrew its low introductory fares in the Houston market, and Continental withdrew its reduced prices in the Phoenix market. The threat of retaliation across markets apparently led America West and Continental to tacitly collude on prices.[26]

However, sometimes multipoint competition does not lead to mutual forbearance. Consider, for example, the conflict between The Walt Disney Company and Time Warner in the early 1990s. As mentioned earlier, Disney operates in the theme park, movie and television production, and television broadcasting industries. Time Warner operates in the theme park and movie and television production industries and also operates a very large magazine business (*Time, People, Sports Illustrated,* among others). From 1988 through 1993, Disney spent over $40 million in advertising its theme parks in Time Warner magazines. Despite this substantial revenue, Time Warner began an aggressive advertising campaign aimed at wooing customers away from Disney theme parks to its own. Disney retaliated by canceling all of its advertising in Time Warner magazines. Time Warner responded to Disney's actions by canceling a corporate meeting to be held in Florida at Disney World. Disney responded to Time Warner's meeting cancellation by refusing to broadcast Time Warner theme park advertisements on its Los Angeles television station.[27]

Some recent research investigates the conditions under which mutual forbearance strategies are pursued, as well as conditions under which multipoint competition does not lead to mutual forbearance.[28] In general, the value of the threat of retaliation must be substantial for multipoint competition to lead to mutual forbearance. However, not only must the payoffs to mutual forbearance be substantial, but the firms pursuing this strategy must have strong strategic linkages among their diversified businesses. This suggests that firms pursuing mutual forbearance strategies based on multipoint competition are usually pursuing a form of related diversification.

Diversification and Market Power. Internal allocations of capital among a diversified firm's businesses may enable it to exploit in some of its businesses the market power advantages it enjoys in other of its businesses. For example, suppose that a firm is earning monopoly profits in a particular business. This firm can use some of these monopoly profits to subsidize the operations of another of its businesses. This cross-subsidization can take several forms, including **predatory pricing**— that is, setting prices so that they are less than the subsidized business's costs. The effect of this cross-subsidy may be to drive competitors out of the subsidized business and then to obtain monopoly profits in that subsidized business. In a sense, diversification enables a firm to apply its monopoly power in several different businesses. Economists call this a **deep pockets model** of diversification.[29]

Diversified firms with operations in regulated monopolies have been criticized for this kind of cross-subsidization. For example, most of the regional telephone companies in the United States are engaging in diversification strategies. The consent decree that forced the breakup of the original AT&T expressly forbade cross-subsidies between these regional companies' telephone monopolies and other business activities, under the assumption that such subsidies would give these firms an unfair competitive advantage in their diversified business activities.[30]

Although these market power economies of scope, in principle, may exist, relatively little empirical work documents their existence. Indeed, research on regulated utilities diversifying into nonregulated businesses in the 1980s suggests not that these firms use monopoly profits in their regulated businesses to unfairly subsidize nonregulated businesses, but that the poor management skills developed in the regulated businesses tend to make diversification less profitable rather than more profitable.[31] Nevertheless, the potential that large diversified large firms have to exercise market power and to behave in socially irresponsible ways has led some observers to call for actions to curtail both the economic and political power of these firms. These issues are discussed in the Ethics and Strategy feature.

Firm Size and Employee Incentives to Diversify

Employees may have incentives to diversify that are independent of any benefits from other sources of economies of scope. This is especially the case for employees in senior management positions and employees with long tenure in a particular firm. These employee incentives reflect the interest of employees to diversify because of the relationship between firm size and management compensation.

Research over the years demonstrates conclusively that the primary determinant of the compensation of top managers in a firm is not the economic performance of the firm but the size of the firm, usually measured in sales.[32] Thus, managers seeking to maximize their income should attempt to grow their firm. One of the easiest ways to grow a firm is through diversification, especially unrelated diversification through mergers and acquisitions. By making large acquisitions, a diversified firm can grow substantially in a short period of time, leading senior managers to earn higher incomes. All of this is independent of any economic profit that diversification may or may not generate. Senior managers need only worry about economic profit if the level of that profit is so low that unfriendly takeovers are a threat or so low that the board of directors may be forced to replace management.

Recently, the traditional relationship between firm size and management compensation has begun to break down. More and more, the compensation of senior managers is being tied to the firm's economic performance. In particular, the use of stock and other forms of deferred compensation makes it in management's best interest to be concerned with a firm's economic performance. These changes in compensation do not necessarily imply that firms will abandon all forms of diversification. However, they do suggest that firms will abandon those forms of diversification that do not generate real economies of scope.

Ethics and Strategy

In 1999, a loose coalition of union members, environmentalists, youth, indigenous peoples, human rights activists, and small farmers took to the streets of Seattle, Washington, to protest a meeting of the World Trade Organization (WTO) and to fight against the growing global power of corporations. Government officials and corporate officers alike were confused by these protests. After all, hadn't world trade increased 19 times from 1950 to 1995 ($0.4 trillion to $7.6 trillion in constant 2003 dollars), and hadn't the total economic output of the entire world gone from $6.4 trillion in 1950 to $60.7 trillion in 2005 (again, in constant 2003 dollars)? Why protest a global economic system—a system that was enhancing the level of free trade and facilitating global economic efficiency—that was so clearly improving the economic well-being of the world's population?

The protestors' message to government and big business was that these aggregate growth numbers masked more truth than they told. Yes, there has been economic growth. But that growth has benefited only a small percentage of the world's population. Most of the population still struggles to survive. The combined net worth of 358 U.S. billionaires in the early 1990s ($760 billion) was equal to the combined net worth of the 2.5 billion poorest people on the earth! Eighty-three percent of the world's total income goes to the richest fifth of the population while the poorest fifth of the world's population receives only 1.4 percent of the world's total income. Currently, 45 to 70 million people worldwide have had to leave their home countries to find work in foreign

Globalization and the Threat of the Multinational Firm

lands, and approximately 1.4 billion people around the world live on less than $1 a day. Even in relatively affluent societies such as the United States, people are finding it increasingly difficult to meet their financial obligations. Falling real wages, economic insecurity, and corporate downsizing have led many people to work longer hours or to hold two or three jobs. While the number of billionaires in the world continues to grow, the number of people facing mind-numbing and strength-robbing poverty grows even faster.

The causes of this apparent contradiction—global economic growth linked with growing global economic decay—are numerous and complex. However, one explanation focuses on the growing economic power of the diversified multinational corporation. The size of these institutions can be immense—many international diversified firms are larger than the entire economies of many nations.

And these huge institutions, with a single-minded focus on maximizing their performance, can make profit-making decisions that adversely affect their suppliers, their customers, their employees, and the environment, all with relative impunity. Armed with the unspoken mantra that "Greed is Good," these corporations can justify almost any action, as long as it increases the wealth of their shareholders.

Of course, even if one accepts this hypothesis—and it is far from being universally accepted—solutions to the growing power of internationally diversified firms are not obvious. The problem is that one way that firms become large and powerful is by being able to meet customer demands effectively. Thus, firm size, per se, is not necessarily an indication that a firm is behaving in ways inconsistent with the public good. Government efforts to restrict the size of firms simply because they are large could easily have the effect of making citizens worse off. However, once firms are large and powerful, they may very well be tempted to exercise that power in ways that benefit themselves at great cost to society.

Whatever the causes and solutions to these problems, the protests in Seattle in 1999 and at every WTO meeting since Seattle have at least one clear message—global growth for growth's sake is no longer universally accepted as the correct objective of international economic policy.

Sources: D. C. Korten (2001). *When corporations rule the world,* 2nd ed. Bloomfield, CT: Kumarian Press; H. Demsetz (1973). "Industry structure, market rivalry, and public policy." *Journal of Law and Economics,* 16, pp. 1–9.

Can Equity Holders Realize These Economies of Scope on Their Own?

Earlier in this chapter, it was suggested that for a firm's diversification strategies to create value, two conditions must hold. First, these strategies must exploit valuable economies of scope. Potentially valuable economies of scope were presented in Table 7.1 and discussed in the previous section. Second, it must be less costly for managers in a firm to realize these economies of scope than for outside equity holders on their own. If outside equity holders could realize a particular economy of scope on their own, without a firm's managers, at low cost, why would they want to hire managers to do this for them by investing in a firm and providing capital to managers to exploit an economy of scope?

Table 7.3 summarizes the discussion on the potential value of the different economies of scope listed in Table 7.1. It also suggests which of these economies of scope will be difficult for outside equity investors to exploit on their own and thus which bases of diversification are most likely to create positive returns for a firm's equity holders.

Most of the economies of scope listed in Table 7.3 cannot be realized by equity holders on their own. This is because most of them require activities that equity holders cannot engage in or information that equity holders do not possess. For example, shared activities, core competencies, multipoint competition, and exploiting market power all require the detailed coordination of business activities across multiple businesses in a firm. Although equity holders may own a portfolio of equities, they are not in a position to coordinate business activities across this portfolio. In a similar way, internal capital allocation requires information about a business's prospects that is simply not available to a firm's outside equity holders.

Table 7.3   **The Competitive Implications of Different Economies of Scope**

Type of Economy of Scope	Are They Valuable?	Can They be Realized by Equity Holders on Their Own?	Positive Returns to Equity Holders?
1. *Operational economies of scope*			
Shared activities	Possible	No	Possible
Core competencies	Possible	No	Possible
2. *Financial economies of scope*			
Internal capital allocation	Possible	No	Possible
Risk reduction	Possible	Yes	No
Tax advantages	Possible—small	No	Possible—small
3. *Anticompetitive economies of scope*			
Multipoint competition	Possible	No	Possible
Exploiting market power	Possible	No	Possible
4. *Employee incentives for diversification*			
Maximizing management compensation	No	No	No

Indeed, the only two economies of scope listed in Table 7.3 that do not have the potential for generating positive returns for a firm's equity holders are diversification in order to maximize the size of a firm—because firm size, per se, is not valuable—and diversification to reduce risk—because equity holders can do this on their own at very low cost by simply investing in a diversified portfolio of stocks. Indeed, although risk reduction is often a published rationale for many diversification moves, this rationale, by itself, is not directly consistent with the interests of a firm's equity holders. However, some scholars have suggested that this strategy may directly benefit other of a firm's stakeholders and thus indirectly benefit its equity holders. This possibility is discussed in detail in the Strategy in Depth feature.

Overall, this analysis of possible bases of diversification suggests that related diversification is more likely to be consistent with the interests of a firm's equity holders than unrelated diversification. This is because the one economy of scope listed in Table 7.3 that is the easiest for outside equity holders to duplicate—risk reduction—is the only economy of scope that an unrelated diversified firm can try to realize. All the other economies of scope listed in Table 7.3 require coordination and information sharing across businesses in a diversified firm that are very difficult to realize in unrelated diversified firms. Indeed, the preponderance of empirical research suggests that related diversified firms outperform unrelated diversified firms.[33]

Corporate Diversification and Sustained Competitive Advantage

VRIO

Table 7.3 describes those economies of scope that are likely to create real economic value for diversifying firms. It also suggests that related diversification can be valuable, and unrelated diversification is usually not valuable. However, as we have seen with all the other strategies discussed in this book, the fact that a strategy is valuable does not necessarily imply that it will be a source of sustained competitive advantage. In order for diversification to be a source of sustained competitive advantage, it must be not only valuable but also rare and costly to imitate, and a firm must be organized to implement this strategy. The rarity and imitability of diversification are discussed in this section; organizational questions are deferred until the next.

The Rarity of Diversification

At first glance, it seems clear that diversification per se is usually not a rare firm strategy. Most large firms have adopted some form of diversification, if only the limited diversification of a dominant-business firm. Even many small and medium-sized firms have adopted different levels of diversification strategy.

However, the rarity of diversification depends not on diversification per se but on how rare the particular economies of scope associated with that diversification are. If only a few competing firms have exploited a particular economy of scope, that economy of scope can be rare. If numerous firms have done so, it will be common and not a source of competitive advantage.

Strategy in Depth

Although diversifying in order to reduce risk generally does not directly benefit outside equity investors in a firm, it can *indirectly* benefit outside equity investors through its impact on the willingness of other stakeholders in a firm to make firm-specific investments. A firm's **stakeholders** include all those groups and individuals who have an interest in how a firm performs. In this sense, a firm's equity investors are one of a firm's stakeholders. Other firm stakeholders include employees, suppliers, and customers.

Firm stakeholders make **firm-specific investments** when the value of the investments they make in a particular firm is much greater than the value of those same investments would be in other firms. Consider, for example, a firm's employees. An employee with a long tenure in a particular firm has generally made substantial **firm-specific human capital investments**. These investments include understanding a particular firm's culture, policies, and procedures; knowing the "right" people to contact to complete a task; and so forth. Such investments have significant value in the firm where they are made. Indeed, such firm-specific knowledge is generally necessary if an employee is to be able to help a firm conceive and implement valuable strategies. However, the

Risk-Reducing Diversification and a Firm's Other Stakeholders

specific investments that an employee makes in a particular firm have almost no value in other firms. If a firm were to cease operations, employees would instantly lose almost all the value of any of the firm-specific investments they had made in that firm.

Suppliers and customers can also make these firm-specific investments. Suppliers make these investments when they customize their products or services to the specific requirements of a particular customer. They also make firm-specific investments when they forgo opportunities to sell to other firms in order to sell to a

particular firm. Customers make firm-specific investments when they customize their operations to fully utilize the products or services of a particular firm. Also, by developing close relationships with a particular firm, customers may forgo the opportunity to develop relationships with other firms. These, too, are firm-specific investments made by customers. If a firm were to cease operations, suppliers and customers would instantly lose almost the entire value of the specific investments they have made in this firm.

Although the firm-specific investments made by employees, suppliers, and customers are risky—in the sense that almost their entire value is lost if the firm in which they are made ceases operations—they are extremely important if a firm is going to be able to generate economic profits. As was suggested in Chapter 3, valuable, rare, and costly-to-imitate resources and capabilities are more likely to be a source of sustained competitive advantage than resources and capabilities without these attributes. Firm-specific investments are more likely to have these attributes than non–firm-specific investments. Non–firm-specific investments are investments that can generate value in numerous different firms.

VRIO The Imitability of Diversification

Both forms of imitation—direct duplication and substitution—are relevant in evaluating the ability of diversification strategies to generate sustained competitive advantages, even if the economies of scope that they create are rare.

Direct Duplication of Diversification

The extent to which a valuable and rare corporate diversification strategy is immune from direct duplication depends on how costly it is for competing firms

Thus, valuable, rare, and costly-to-imitate firm-specific investments made by a firm's employees, suppliers, and customers can be the source of economic profits. And because a firm's outside equity holders are residual claimants on the cash flows generated by a firm, these economic profits benefit equity holders. Thus, a firm's outside equity holders generally will want a firm's employees, suppliers, and customers to make specific investments in a firm because those investments are likely to be sources of economic wealth for outside equity holders.

However, given the riskiness of firm-specific investments, employees, suppliers, and customers will generally only be willing to make these investments if some of the riskiness associated with making them can be reduced. Outside equity holders have little difficulty managing the risks associated with investing in a particular firm, because they can always create a portfolio of stocks that fully diversifies this risk at very low cost. This is why diversification that reduces the riskiness of a firm's cash flows does not generally directly benefit a firm's outside equity holders. However, a firm's employees, suppliers, and customers usually do not have these low-cost diversification opportunities. Employees, for example, are rarely able to make firm-specific human capital investments in a large

enough number of different firms to fully diversify the risks associated with making them. And although suppliers and customers can diversify their firm-specific investments to a greater degree than employees—through selling to multiple customers and through buying from multiple suppliers—the cost of this diversification for suppliers and customers is usually greater than the costs that are born by outside equity holders in diversifying their risk.

Because it is often very costly for a firm's employees, suppliers, and customers to diversify the risks associated with making firm-specific investments on their own, these stakeholders will often prefer that a firm's managers help manage this risk for them. Managers in a firm can do this by diversifying the portfolio of businesses in which a firm operates. If a firm is unwilling to diversify its portfolio of businesses, then that firm's employees, suppliers, and customers will generally be unwilling to make specific investments in that firm. Moreover, because these firm-specific investments can generate economic profits, and because economic profits can directly benefit a firm's outside equity holders, equity holders have an indirect incentive to encourage a firm to pursue a diversification strategy, even though that strategy does not directly benefit them.

Put differently, a firm's diversification strategy can be thought of as compensation for the firm-specific investments that a firm's employees, suppliers, and customers make in a firm. Outside equity holders have an incentive to encourage this compensation in return for access to some of the economic profits that these firm-specific investments can generate. In general, the greater the impact of the firm-specific investment made by a firm's employees, suppliers, and customers on the ability of a firm to generate economic profits, the more likely that pursuing a corporate diversification strategy is indirectly consistent with the interests of a firm's outside equity holders. In addition, the more limited the ability of a firm's employees, suppliers, and customers to diversify the risks associated with making firm-specific investments at low cost, the more that corporate diversification is consistent with the interests of outside equity investors.

Sources: J. B. Barney (1991). "Firm resources and sustained competitive advantage." *Journal of Management,* 17, pp. 99–120; R. M. Stulz (1996). "Rethinking risk management." *Journal of Applied Corporate Finance,* Fall, pp. 8–24; K. Miller (1998). "Economic exposure and integrated risk management." *Strategic Management Journal,* 33, pp. 756–779; R. Amit and B. Wernerfelt (1990). "Why do firms reduce business risk?" *Academy of Management Journal,* 33, pp. 520–533; H. Wang and J. Barney (2006), "Employee incentives to make firm specific investments: Implications for resource-based theories of diversification." *Academy of Management Review,* 31(2), pp. 466–476.

to realize this same economy of scope. As suggested in Table 7.4, some economies of scope are, in general, more costly to duplicate than others.

Shared activities, risk reduction, tax advantages, and employee compensation as bases for corporate diversification are usually relatively easy to duplicate. Because shared activities are based on tangible assets that a firm exploits across multiple businesses, such as common R&D labs, common sales forces, and common manufacturing, they are usually relatively easy to duplicate. The only duplication issues for shared activities concern developing the cooperative cross-business relationships that often facilitate the use of shared activities—issues discussed in the next chapter.

Table 7.4 **Costly Duplication of Economies of Scope**

Less Costly-to-Duplicate Economies of Scope	Costly-to-Duplicate Economies of Scope
Shared activities	Core competencies
Risk reduction	Internal capital allocation
Tax advantages	Multipoint competition
Employee compensation	Exploiting market power

Moreover, because risk reduction, tax advantages, and employee compensation motives for diversifying can be accomplished through both related and unrelated diversification, these motives for diversifying tend to be relatively easy to duplicate.

Other economies of scope are much more difficult to duplicate. These difficult-to-duplicate economies of scope include core competencies, internal capital allocation efficiencies, multipoint competition, and exploitation of market power. Because core competencies are more intangible, their direct duplication is often challenging. The realization of capital allocation economies of scope requires very substantial information-processing capabilities. These capabilities are often very difficult to develop. Multipoint competition requires very close coordination between the different businesses in which a firm operates. This kind of coordination is socially complex and thus often immune from direct duplication. Finally, exploitation of market power may be costly to duplicate because it requires that a firm must possess significant market power in one of its lines of business. A firm that does not have this market power advantage would have to obtain it. The cost of doing so, in most situations, would be prohibitive.

Substitutes for Diversification

Two obvious substitutes for diversification exist. First, instead of obtaining cost or revenue advantages from exploiting economies of scope *across* businesses in a diversified firm, a firm may decide to simply grow and develop each of its businesses separately. In this sense, a firm that successfully implements a cost leadership strategy or a product differentiation strategy in a single business can obtain the same cost or revenue advantages it could have obtained by exploiting economies of scope, but without having to develop cross-business relations. Growing independent businesses within a diversified firm can be a substitute for exploiting economies of scope in a diversification strategy.

One firm that has chosen this strategy is Nestlé. Nestlé exploits few, if any, economies of scope among its different businesses. Rather, it has focused its efforts on growing each of its international operations to the point that they obtain cost or revenue advantages that could have otherwise been obtained in some form of related diversification. Thus, for example, Nestlé's operation in the United States is sufficiently large to exploit economies of scale in production, sales, and marketing, without reliance on economies of scope between U.S. operations and operations in other countries.[34]

A second substitute for exploiting economies of scope in diversification can be found in strategic alliances. By using a strategic alliance, a firm may be able to gain the economies of scope it could have obtained if it had carefully exploited economies of scope across its businesses. Thus, for example, instead of a firm exploiting research and development economies of scope between two businesses it owns, it could form a strategic alliance with a different firm and form a joint research and development lab. Instead of a firm exploiting sales economies of scope by linking its businesses through a common sales force, it might develop a sales agreement with another firm and obtain cost or revenue advantages in this way.

Corporate Diversification in an International Context

Each of the ways that a strategy of corporate diversification can add value, as summarized in Table 7.1, can also be an explanation of why firms pursuing an international strategy can also create value. This is because a firm pursuing an international strategy is pursuing, at least, a strategy of geographic diversification and perhaps a strategy of product-market diversification. In this sense, an international strategy can be thought of as a special case of a corporate diversification strategy. Indeed, some of the economies of scope listed in Table 7.1 are likely to be more valuable in an international context than in a domestic-only context. One of these economies of scope is described in the Global Perspectives feature.

However, pursuing international diversification opportunities can create unique challenges for a firm. Two of these challenges have to do with unique financial risks and the political risks associated with pursuing an international diversification strategy.

Financial Risks and International Diversification

As firms begin to pursue international strategies, they may expose themselves to financial risks that are less obvious within a single domestic market. In particular, currency fluctuations can significantly affect the value of a firm's international investments. Such fluctuations can turn what had been a losing investment into a profitable investment (this is the good news). They can also turn what had been a profitable investment into a losing investment (this is the bad news). In addition to currency fluctuations, different rates of inflation across countries can require very different managerial approaches, business strategies, and accounting practices. Certainly, these financial risks can seem daunting when a firm first begins international operations.

Fortunately, it is now possible for firms to hedge many of these risks through the use of a variety of financial instruments and strategies. The development of money markets, together with growing experience in operating in high-inflation economies, has substantially reduced the threat of these financial risks for firms pursuing international strategies. Of course, the benefits of these financial tools and experience in high-inflation environments do not accrue to firms automatically. Firms seeking to implement international strategies must develop the resources and capabilities they will need to manage these financial risks. Moreover, these hedging strategies can do nothing to reduce the business risks that firms assume when they enter into nondomestic markets. For example, it may be that consumers in a nondomestic market simply do not want to purchase a firm's products or services, in which case this economy of scope cannot be realized. Moreover, these financial strategies cannot manage political risks that can exist.

Political Risks and International Diversification

The political environment is an important consideration in all strategic decisions. Changes in the political rules of the game can have the effect of increasing some environmental threats and reducing others, thereby changing the value of a firm's

Global Perspectives

Using International Strategies to Avoid Taxes

*F*or firms not pursuing an international strategy, diversification can help reduce taxes because of its impact on a firm's debt capacity. The logic that links diversification, debt capacity, and taxes has already been discussed in this chapter: Because diversified firms generally have a low probability of bankruptcy, banks and other sources of debt are more willing to lend to these firms than they would otherwise; because interest payments on debt are tax deductible, a more highly leveraged firm, other factors being equal, will have lower taxes than a less leveraged firm. Thus, corporate diversification can affect a firm's tax liability. However, empirical work on the effect of diversification on tax liability suggests that, on average, this effect is not very large.

However, tax savings can be much more important for firms operating in an international context. Such firms can reduce their tax liability by using internal transfer prices to shift firm profits from high-tax locations to low-tax locations and can locate their operations in what are known as "tax havens."

As will be described in Chapter 8 in detail, a **transfer price** is the price that one part of a diversified firm charges another part of the firm for products or services. These transfer prices can have a substantial impact on the reported profits of a particular unit within a diversified firm. This impact of transfer pricing on a unit's reported profits is what creates the tax-reduction opportu-

nity in an international setting. Suppose one of these units (e.g., the unit selling a product or service) is in a high-tax country, while the second unit (e.g., the unit buying a product or service) is in a low-tax country. By setting the transfer price in this example very high, the corporation is essentially transferring profits that would otherwise be attributed to the first unit to the second unit. It is also shifting those profits from a high-tax country to a low-tax country, thereby reducing its tax liability.

Of course, national tax authorities (such as the IRS) do not approve of such actions and try to prevent firms from using internal transfer prices to avoid paying taxes. They do this by making sure that a firm's internal trans-

fer prices are reasonable and justifiable. However, as we will see in Chapter 8, it is very difficult to calculate the "optimal transfer price" in most settings. Only when it is apparent that the sole purpose of setting a transfer price was to avoid taxes can firms be prevented from engaging in this strategy.

A second way that firms can use their international operations to avoid taxes is by establishing operations in what is known as a **tax haven**. A tax haven is a country that charges little or no corporate tax. In this tax-avoidance strategy, a firm uses transfer prices, licensing fees, dividends, and other activities to book revenues and profits generated in high-tax countries to the operations in the tax haven. Countries that have emerged as tax havens over the last decade or so include Bermuda, the Cayman Islands, Granada, the Netherland Antilles, Liechtenstein, and Luxembourg. Currently, there are more foreign-owned firms registered in the Cayman Islands than there are people who live in the Cayman Islands. Banks on the Caymans have attracted over $300 billion in deposits from foreign investors, or roughly $9.4 million for each person who lives on the Caymans. Obviously, these tax havens are attracting a large number of firms and private investors.

Sources: "Cleaning up by cleaning up." *Euromoney,* April, pp. 73–77; H. French (1991). "Offshore banking gets new scrutiny with BCCI scandal." *New York Times,* September 29, p. 7.

resources and capabilities. However, the political environment can be even more problematic as firms pursue international strategies.

Types of Political Risks

Politics can affect the value of a firm's international strategies at the macro and micro levels. At the macro level, broad changes in the political situation in a country can change the value of an investment. For example, after the Second World

War, nationalist governments came to power in many countries in the Middle East. These governments expropriated, for little or no compensation, many of the assets of oil and gas companies located in their countries. Expropriation of foreign company assets also occurred when the Shah of Iran was overthrown, when a communist government was elected in Chile, and when new governments came to power in Angola, Ethiopia, Peru, and Zambia.[35]

Government upheaval and the attendant risks to international firms are facts of life in some countries. Consider, for example, oil-rich Nigeria. Since its independence in 1960, Nigeria has experienced several successful coups d'état, one civil war, two civil governments, and six military regimes.[36] The prudent course of action for firms engaging in business activities in Nigeria is to expect the current government to change and to plan accordingly.

Of course, government changes are not always bad for international firms. The fall of the Soviet Union and the introduction of capitalism into Eastern Europe created enormous opportunities for firms pursuing international strategies. For example, Volkswagen has invested $6 billion in a Czech automobile firm; Opel (General Motors' European division) has invested $680 million in a car-manufacturing facility in the former East Germany; and General Electric has invested $150 million in a light-bulb manufacturing operation in Hungary since the fall of the Soviet Union.[37]

At the micro level, politics in a country can affect the fortunes of particular firms in particular industries. For example, the success of Japanese automobile companies in the U.S. market has subjected these firms to a variety of political challenges, including local-content legislation and voluntary import quotas. These political risks exist even though there have been no major macro changes in the political system in the United States.[38]

Quantifying Political Risks

Political scientists have attempted to quantify the political risk that firms seeking to implement international strategies are likely to face in different countries. Although different studies vary in detail, the country attributes listed in Table 7.5 summarize most of the important determinants of political risk for firms pursuing international strategies.[39] Firms can apply the criteria listed in the table by evaluating the political and economic conditions in a country and then adding up the scores associated with these conditions. The most recent rankings of the political risks associated with conducting business in different countries are interesting. Not surprisingly, countries in Western Europe and North America are the least risky. The least risky country within which to do business in the entire world is Luxembourg, followed by Switzerland, Norway, Denmark, the United States, and Sweden. In contrast, countries currently experiencing civil unrest and revolution are among the most risky. The most risky country in the world, overall, is North Korea. Other very risky countries include Afghanistan, Iraq, Cuba, the Marshall Islands, and Zaire. Countries in Asia range from very low risk (Singapore and Japan, numbers 17 and 18 overall) to very high risk (North Korea). Countries in Africa and South America tend to be relatively risky.

Managing Political Risk

Unlike financial risks, relatively few tools exist for managing the political risks associated with pursuing an international strategy. Obviously, one option would be to pursue international opportunities only in countries where the political risk is very small. However, it is often the case that significant business opportunities exist in politically risky countries precisely because they are politically risky.

Table 7.5   **Quantifying Political Risks from International Operations**

	Low	High
The political economic environment		
1. Stability of the political system	3	14
2. Imminent internal conflicts	0	14
3. External threats to stability	0	12
4. Degree of control of the economic system	5	9
5. Reliability of country as a trade partner	4	12
6. Constitutional guarantees	2	12
7. Effectiveness of public administration	3	12
8. Labor relations and social peace	3	15
Domestic economic conditions		
1. Size of the population	4	8
2. Per capita income	2	10
3. Economic growth over the last five years	2	7
4. Potential growth over the next three years	3	10
5. Inflation over the last two years	2	10
6. Availability of domestic capital markets to outsiders	3	7
7. Availability of high-quality local labor force	2	8
8. Possibility of employing foreign nationals	2	8
9. Availability of energy resources	2	14
10. Environmental pollution legal requirements	4	8
11. Transportation and communication infrastructure	2	14
External economic relations		
1. Import restrictions	2	10
2. Export restrictions	2	10
3. Restrictions on foreign investments	3	9
4. Freedom to set up or engage in partnerships	3	9
5. Legal protection for brands and products	3	9
6. Restrictions on monetary transfers	2	8
7. Revaluation of currency in the last five years	2	7
8. Balance-of-payments situation	2	9
9. Drain on hard currency through energy imports	3	14
10. Financial standing	3	8
11. Restrictions of the exchange of local and foreign currencies	2	8

Source: Adapted from E. Dichtl and H. G. Koeglmayr (1986). "Country Risk Ratings." *Management International Review*, 26(4), pp. 4–11.

Alternatively, firms can limit their investment in politically risky environments. However, these limited investments may not enable a firm to take full advantage of whatever economies of scope might exist by engaging in business in that country.

One approach to managing political risk is to see each of the determinants of political risk as negotiation points as a firm enters into a new country market. In many circumstances, those in a nondomestic market have just as much interest in a firm doing business in a new market as does the firm contemplating entry. International firms can sometimes use this bargaining power to negotiate entry conditions that reduce, or even neutralize, some of the sources of political risk in a country. Of course, no matter how skilled a firm is in negotiating these entry conditions, a change of government or changes in laws can quickly nullify any agreements.

A final approach to managing political risk is to turn the threat into an opportunity. One firm that has been successful in this way is Schlumberger, an international oil services company. Schlumberger has headquarters in New York, Paris, and the Caribbean; it is a truly international company. Schlumberger management has adopted a policy of strict neutrality in interactions with governments in the developing world. Because of this policy, the company has been able to avoid political entanglements and continues to do business where many firms find the political risks too great. Put differently, Schlumberger has developed valuable, rare, and costly-to-imitate resources and capabilities in managing political risks and is using these resources to generate high levels of economic performance.[40]

SUMMARY

Firms implement corporate diversification strategies that range from limited diversification (single-business, dominant-business) to related diversification (related-constrained, related-linked) to unrelated diversification. In order to be valuable, corporate diversification strategies must reduce costs or increase revenues by exploiting economies of scope that outside equity holders cannot realize on their own at low cost.

Several motivations for implementing diversification strategies exist, including exploiting operational economies of scope (shared activities, core competencies), exploiting financial economies of scope (internal capital allocation, risk reduction, obtaining tax advantages), exploiting anticompetitive economies of scope (multipoint competition, market power advantages), and employee incentives to diversify (maximizing management compensation). All these reasons for diversifying, except diversifying to maximize management compensation, have the potential to create economic value for a firm. Moreover, a firm's outside equity holders will find it costly to realize all of these bases for diversification, except risk reduction. Thus, diversifying to maximize management compensation or diversifying to reduce risk is not consistent with the wealth-maximizing interests of a firm's equity holders. This analysis also suggests that, on average, related diversified firms will outperform unrelated diversified firms.

The ability of a diversification strategy to create sustained competitive advantages depends not only on the value of that strategy, but also on its rarity and imitability. The rarity of a diversification strategy depends on the number of competing firms that are exploiting the same economies of scope through diversification. Imitation can occur either through direct duplication or through substitutes. Costly-to-duplicate economies of scope include core competencies, internal capital allocation, multipoint competition, and exploitation of market power. Other economies of scope are usually less costly to duplicate. Important substitutes for diversification are when relevant economies are obtained through the independent actions of businesses within a firm and when relevant economies are obtained through strategic alliances.

Firms that pursue international business opportunities are implementing a geographic diversification strategy and may be implementing a product-market diversification strategy. All the economies of scope that can exist for firms pursuing a diversification strategy within a country can also exist for firms pursuing a diversification strategy internationally. However, two unique challenges are associated with international diversification: financial risks and political risks.

This discussion set aside important organizational issues in implementing diversification strategies. These issues are examined in detail in the next chapter.

CHALLENGE QUESTIONS

1. One simple way to think about relatedness is to look at the products or services a firm manufactures. The more similar these products or services are, the more related is the firm's diversification strategy. However, will firms that exploit core competencies in their diversification strategies always produce products or services that are similar to each other? Why or why not?

2. A firm implementing a diversification strategy has just acquired what it claims is a strategically related target firm but announces that it is not going to change this recently acquired firm in any way. Will this type of diversifying acquisition enable the firm to realize any valuable economies of scope that could not be duplicated by outside investors on their own? Why or why not?

3. One of the reasons why internal capital markets may be more efficient than external capital markets is that firms may not want to reveal full information about their sources of competitive advantage to external capital markets in order to reduce the threat of competitive imitation. This suggests that external capital markets may systematically undervalue firms with competitive advantages that are subject to imitation. Do you agree with this analysis? If yes, how could you trade on this information in your own investment activities? If no, why not?

4. A particular firm is owned by members of a single family. Most of the wealth of this family is derived from the operations of this firm, and the family does not want to "go public" with the firm by selling its equity position to outside investors. Will this firm pursue a highly related diversification strategy or a somewhat less related diversification strategy? Why?

5. Under what conditions will a related diversification strategy not be a source of competitive advantage for a firm?

6. Suppose a firm has invested heavily in an oil-rich country with an unstable government. If this government was to fall, this firm is likely to lose its investment in this country, and the price of crude oil is likely to go up substantially. Also, suppose this firm has purchased equity positions in a large number of other oil firms that do not have investments in this particular country. In what ways can these equity investments be thought of as a hedge against a firm losing its investment in the unstable country? What, if anything, does your analysis say about the ability of firms to manage political risks indirectly?

PROBLEM SET

1. Visit the corporate Web sites for the following firms. How would you characterize the corporate strategies of these companies? Are they following a strategy of limited diversification, related diversification, or unrelated diversification?

(a) ExxonMobil
(b) Google
(c) General Motors
(d) JetBlue
(e) Citigroup
(f) Entertainment Arts
(g) IBM
(h) Dell
(i) Berkshire Hathaway

2. Consider the following list of strategies. In your view, which are examples of potential economies of scope underlying a corporate diversification strategy? For those strategies that are an economy of scope, which economy of scope are they? For those strategies that are not an economy of scope, why aren't they?

(a) The Coca-Cola Corporation replaces its old diet cola drink (Tab) with a new diet cola drink called Diet Coke.

(b) Apple introduces an iPod MP3 player with a larger memory.

(c) PepsiCo distributes Lay's Potato Chips to the same stores where it sells Pepsi.

(d) Kmart extends is licensing arrangement with Martha Stewart for four years.

(e) Wal-Mart uses the same distribution system to supply its Wal-Mart stores, its Wal-Mart Supercenters (Wal-Mart stores with grocery stores in them), and its Sam's Clubs.

(f) Head Ski Company introduces a line of tennis rackets.

(g) General Electric borrows money from BankAmerica at 3 percent interest and then makes capital available to its jet engine subsidiary at 8 percent interest.

(h) McDonald's acquires Boston Market and Chipotle (two restaurants where many customers sit in the restaurant to eat their meals).

(i) A venture capital firm invests in a firm in the biotechnology industry and a firm in the entertainment industry.

(j) Another venture capital firm invests in two firms in the biotechnology industry.

3. Consider the following facts. The standard deviation of the cash flows associated with Business I is .8. The larger this standard deviation, the riskier a business's future cash flows are likely to be. The standard deviation of the cash flows associated with Business II is 1.3. That is, Business II is riskier than Business I. Finally, the correlation between the cash flows of these two businesses over time is .8. This means that when Business I is up, Business II tends to be down, and vice versa. Suppose one firm owns both of these businesses.

(a) Assuming that Business I constitutes 40 percent of this firm's revenues and Business II constitutes 60 percent of its revenues, calculate the riskiness of this firm's total revenues using the following equation:

$$sd_{I,II} = \sqrt{w^2 sd_I^2 + (1-w)^2 sd_{II}^2 + 2w(1+w)\left(r_{I,II} sd_I sd_{II}\right)}$$

Where $w = .40$; $sd_I = .8$, $sd_{II} = 1.3$, and $r_{I, II} = -.8$

(b) Given this result, does it make sense for this firm to own both Business I and Business II? Why or why not?

END NOTES

1. See Sellers, P. (2004). "The brand king's challenge." *Fortune*, April 5, pp. 192 +.
2. The Walt Disney Company (A). Harvard Business School Case No. 1-388-147.
3. Useem, J. (2004). "Another boss, another revolution." *Fortune*, April 5, pp. 112 +.
4. See Burrows, P. (1995). "Now, TI means 'taking initiative'," *BusinessWeek*, May 15, pp. 120–121; and Rogers, A. (1992). "It's the execution that counts." *Fortune*, November 30, pp. 80–83; Wallas, J., and J. Erickson (1993). *Hard drive: Bill Gates and the making of the Microsoft empire.* New York: Harper Business; and Porter, M. E. (1981). "Disposable diaper industry in 1974." Harvard Business School Case No. 9-380-175. Whether or not Microsoft continues to share activities across operating systems and applications software was one of the key issues at stake in the Microsoft antitrust suit. A more general discussion of the value of shared activities can be found in St. John, C. H., and J. S. Harrison (1999). "Manufacturing-based relatedness, synergy, and coordination." *Strategic Management Journal*, 20, pp. 129–145.
5. See Fuchsberg, G. (1992). "Decentralized management can have its drawbacks." *Wall Street Journal*, December 9, p. B1.
6. See Crockett, R. (2000). "A Baby Bell's growth formula." *BusinessWeek*, March 6, pp. 50–52; and Crockett, R. (1999). "The last monopolist." *BusinessWeek*, April 12, p. 76.
7. de Lisser, E. (1993). "Catering to cooking-phobic customers, supermarkets stress carryout. " *Wall Street Journal*, April 5, p. B1.
8. See, for example, Davis, P., R. Robinson, J. Pearce, and S. Park (1992). "Business unit relatedness and performance: A look at the pulp and paper industry." *Strategic Management Journal*, 13, pp. 349–361.
9. Loomis, C. J. (1993). "Dinosaurs?" *Fortune*, May 3, pp. 36–42.
10. Rapoport, C. (1992). "A tough Swede invades the U.S." *Fortune*, June 29, pp. 776–779.
11. Prahalad, C. K., and G. Hamel (1990). "The core competence of the organization." *Harvard Business Review*, 90, p. 82.
12. See also Grant, R. M. (1988). "On 'dominant logic' relatedness and the link between diversity and performance." *Strategic Management Journal*, 9, pp. 639–642; Chatterjee, S., and B. Wernerfelt (1991). "The link between resources and type at diversification: Theory and evidence." *Strategic Management Journal*, 12, pp. 33–48; Markides, C., and P. J. Williamson (1994). "Related diversification, core competencies, and corporate performance." *Strategic Management Journal*, 15, pp. 149–165; Montgomery, C. A., and B. Wernerfelt (1991). "Sources of superior performance: Market share versus industry effects in the U.S. brewing industry." *Management Science*, 37, pp. 954–959; Liedtka, J. M. (1996). "Collaborating across lines of business for competitive advantage." *Academy of Management Executive*, 10(2), pp. 20–37; and Farjoun, M. (1998). "The independent and joint effects of the skill and physical bases of relatedness in diversification." *Strategic Management Journal*, 19, pp. 611–630.
13. Jensen, M. C. (1986). "Agency costs of free cash flow, corporate finance, and takeovers." *American Economic Review*, 76, pp. 323–329.

14. See Nayyar, P. (1990). "Information asymmetries: A source of competitive advantage for diversified service firms." *Strategic Management Journal,* 11, pp. 513–519; and Robins, J., and M. Wiersema (1995). "A resource-based approach to the multibusiness firm: Empirical analysis of portfolio interrelationships and corporate financial performance." *Strategic Management Journal,* 16, pp. 277–299, for a discussion of the evolution of core competencies.

15. Prahalad, C. K., and R. A. Bettis (1986). "The dominant logic: A new linkage between diversity and performance." *Strategic Management Journal,* 7(6), pp. 485–501.

16. See Williamson, O. E. (1975). *Markets and hierarchies: Analysis and antitrust implications.* New York: Free Press.

17. See Liebeskind, J. P. (1996). "Knowledge, strategy, and the theory of the firm." *Strategic Management Journal,* 17 (Winter Special Edition), pp. 93–107.

18. Perry, L. T., and J. B. Barney (1981). "Performance lies are hazardous to organizational health." *Organizational Dynamics,* 9(3), pp. 68–80.

19. Bethel, J. E. (1990). *The capital allocation process and managerial mobility: A theoretical and empirical investigation.* Unpublished doctoral dissertation, University of California at Los Angles.

20. Staw, B. M. (1981). "The escalation of commitment to a course of action." *Academy of Management Review,* 6, pp. 577–587.

21. See Comment, R., and G. Jarrell (1995). "Corporate focus and stock returns." *Journal of Financial Economics,* 37, pp. 67–87; Berger, P. G., and E. Ofek (1995). "Diversification's effect on firm value." *Journal of Financial Economics,* 37, pp. 39–65; Maksimovic, V., and G. Phillips (1999). "Do conglomerate firms allocate resources inefficiently?" Working paper, University of Maryland; Matsusaka, J. G., and V. Nanda (1998). Internal capital markets and corporate refocusing." Working paper, University of Southern California; Palia, D. (1998). "Division-level overinvestment and agency conflicts in diversified firms." Working paper, Columbia University; Rajan, R., H. Servaes, and L. Zingales (1997). "The cost of diversity: The diversification discount and inefficient investment." Working paper, University of Chicago; Scharfstein, D. S. (1997). "The dark side of internal capital markets II: Evidence from diversified conglomerates." NBER [National Bureau of Economic Research]. Working paper; Shin, H. H., and R. M. Stulz (1998). "Are internal capital markets efficient?" *The Quarterly Journal of Economics,* May, pp. 551–552. But Houston and James (1998) show that internal capital markets can create competitive advantages for firms: Houston, J., and C. James (1998). "Some evidence that banks use internal capital markets to lower capital costs." *Journal of Applied Corporate Finance,* 11(2), pp. 70–78.

22. Scott, J. H. (1977). "On the theory of conglomerate mergers." *Journal of Finance,* 32, pp. 1235–1250.

23. See Brennan, M. (1979). "The pricing of contingent claims in discrete time models." *Journal of Finance,* 34, pp. 53–68; Cox, J., S. Ross, and M. Rubinstein (1979). "Option pricing: A simplified approach." *Journal of Financial Economics,* 7, pp. 229–263; and Stapleton, R. C. (1982). "Mergers, debt capacity, and the valuation of corporate loans." In M. Keenan and L. J. White (eds.), *Mergers and acquisitions.* Lexington, MA: D. C. Heath, Chapter 2; and Galai, D., and R. W. Masulis (1976). "The option pricing model and the risk factor of stock." *Journal of Financial Economics,* 3, pp. 53–82.

24. See Karnani, A., and B. Wernerfelt (1985). "Multiple point competition." *Strategic Management Journal,* 6, pp. 87–96; Bernheim, R. D., and M. D. Whinston (1990). "Multimarket contact and collusive behavior." *Rand Journal of Economics,* 12, pp. 605–617; Tirole, J. (1988). *The theory of industrial organization.* Cambridge, MA: MIT Press; Gimeno, J., and C. Y. Woo (1999). "Multimarket contact, economies of scope, and firm performance." *Academy of Management Journal,* 43(3), pp. 239–259; Korn, H. J., and J. A. C. Baum (1999). "Chance, imitative, and strategic antecedents to multimarket contact." *Academy of Management Journal,* 42(2), pp. 171–193; Baum, J. A. C., and H. J. Korn (1999). "Dynamics of dyadic competitive interaction." *Strategic Management Journal,* 20, pp. 251–278; Gimeno, J. (1999). "Reciprocal threats in multimarket rivalry: Staking our 'spheres of influence' in the U.S. airline industry." *Strategic Management Journal,* 20, pp. 101–128; Gimeno, J., and C. Y. Woo (1996). "Hypercompetition in a multimarket environment: The role of strategic similarity and multimarket contact in competitive de-escalation." *Organization Science,* 7(3), pp. 322–341; Ma, H. (1998). "Mutual forbearance in international business." *Journal of International Management,* 4(2), pp. 129–147; McGrath, R. G., and M.-J. Chen (1998). "Multimarket maneuvering in uncertain spheres of influence: Resource diversion strategies." *Academy of Management Review,* 23(4), pp. 724–740; Chen, M.-J. (1996). "Competitor analysis and interfirm

rivalry: Toward a theoretical integration." *Academy of Management Review,* 21(1), pp. 100–134; Chen, M.-J., and K. Stucker (1997). "Multinational management and multimarket rivalry: Toward a theoretical development of global competition." *Academy of Management Proceedings 1997,* pp. 2–6; and Young, G., K. G. Smith, and C. M. Grimm (1997). "Multimarket contact, resource heterogeneity, and rivalrous firm behavior." *Academy of Management Proceedings 1997,* pp. 55–59. This idea was originally proposed by Edwards, C. D. (1955). "Conglomerate bigness as a source of power." In *Business concentration and price policy.* NBER Conference Report. Princeton, NJ: Princeton University Press.

25. See Karnani, A., and B. Wernerfelt (1985). "Multiple point competition." *Strategic Management Journal,* 6, pp. 87–96.

26. This is documented by Gimeno, J. (1994). "Multipoint competition, market rivalry and firm performance: A test of the mutual forbearance hypothesis in the United States airline industry, 1984–1988." Unpublished doctoral dissertation, Purdue University.

27. See Landro, L., P. M. Reilly, and R. Turner (1993). "Cartoon clash: Disney relationship with Time Warner is a strained one." *Wall Street Journal,* April 14, p. A1; and Reilly, P. M., and R. Turner (1993). "Disney pulls ads in tiff with *Time.*" *Wall Street Journal,* April 2, p. B1. The growth and consolidation of the entertainment industry since the early 1990s has made Disney and Time Warner (especially after its merger with AOL) large entertainment conglomerates. It will be interesting to see if these two larger firms will be able to find ways to tacitly collude or will continue the competition begun in the early 1990s.

28. The best work in this area has been done by Gimeno, J. (1994). "Multipoint competition, market rivalry and firm performance: A test of the mutual forbearance hypothesis in the United States airline industry, 1984–1988." Unpublished doctoral dissertation, Purdue University. See also Smith, F., and R. Wilson (1995). "The predictive validity of the Karnani and Wernerfelt model of multipoint competition." *Strategic Management Journal,* 16, pp. 143–160.

29. See Tirole, J. (1988). *The theory of industrial organization.* Cambridge, MA: MIT Press.

30. Carnevale, M. L. (1993). "Ring in the new: Telephone service seems on the brink of huge innovations." *Wall Street Journal,* February 10, p. A1. SBC recently acquired the remaining assets of the original AT&T and renamed the newly merged company AT&T.

31. See Russo, M. V. (1992). "Power plays: Regulation, diversification, and backward integration in the electric utility industry." *Strategic Management Journal,* 13, pp. 13–27. Recent work by Jandik and Makhija indicates that when a regulated utility diversifies out of a regulated industry, it often earns a more positive return than when an unregulated firm does this [Jandik, T., and A. K. Makhija (1999). "An Empirical Examination of the Atypical Diversification Practices of Electric Utilities: Internal Capital Markets and Regulation." Fisher College of Business, Ohio State University, working paper (September).] This work shows that regulators have the effect of making a regulated firm's internal capital market more efficient. Differences between Russo's (1992) findings and Jandik and Makhija's (1999) findings may have to do with when this work was done. Russo's (1992) research may have focused on a time period before regulatory agencies had learned how to improve a firm's internal capital market. However, even though Jandik and Makhija (1999) report positive returns from regulated firms diversifying, these positive returns do not reflect the market power advantages of these firms.

32. Finkelstein, S., and D. C. Hambrick (1989). "Chief executive compensation: A study of the intersection of markets and political processes." *Strategic Management Journal,* 10, pp. 121–134.

33. See William, J., B. L. Paez, and L. Sanders (1988). "Conglomerates revisited." *Strategic Management Journal,* 9, pp. 403–414; Geringer, J. M., S. Tallman, and D. M. Olsen (2000). "Product and international diversification among Japanese multinational firms." *Strategic Management Journal,* 21, pp. 51–80; Nail, L. A., W. L. Megginson, and C. Maquieira (1998). "How stock-swap mergers affect shareholder (and bondholder) wealth: More evidence of the value of corporate 'focus'." *Journal of Applied Corporate Finance,* 11(2), pp. 95–106; G. R. Carroll; L. S. Bigelow; M.-D. L. Seidel; L. B. Tsai (1966)." "The fates of *De Novo* and *De Alio* producers in the American automobile industry 1885–1981." *Strategic Management Journal,* 17 (Special Summer Issue), pp. 117–138; Nguyen, T. H., A. Seror, and T. M. Devinney (1990). "Diversification strategy and performance in Canadian manufacturing firms." *Strategic Management Journal,* 11, pp. 411–418; and Amit, R., and J. Livnat (1988). "Diversification strategies, business cycles and economic performance." *Strategic Management Journal,* 9, pp. 99–110, for a discussion of corporate diversification in the economy over time.

34. The Nestlé story is summarized in Templeman, J. (1993). "Nestlé: A giant in a hurry." *BusinessWeek,* March 22, pp. 50–54.
35. See Rugman, A., and R. Hodgetts (1995). *Business: A strategic management approach.* New York: McGraw-Hill.
36. Glynn, M. A. (1993). "Strategic planning in Nigeria versus U.S.: A case of anticipating the (next) coup." *Academy of Management Executive* 7(3), pp. 82–83.
37. See Roth, T. (1990). "Bid size showed VW's eagerness to buy Skoda." *Wall Street Journal,* December 11, p. A15; and Tully, S. (1990). "GE in Hungary: Let there be light." *Fortune,* October 22, pp. 137–142.
38. See Ring, P. S., S. A. Lenway, and M. Govekar (1990). "Management of the political imperative in international business." *Strategic Management Journal,* 11, pp. 141–151.
39. Dichtl, E., and H. G. Koeglmayr (1986). "Country risk ratings." *Management Review,* 26(4), pp. 2–10; O'Leary, M. (2002) "Analysts take an optimistic view." *Euromoney,* September, pp. 208–216; Hoti, S. (2004). "Snapshot images of country risk ratings: An international comparison." Unpublished, Department of Economics, University of Western Australia.
40. See Auletta, K. (1983). "A certain poetry—Parts I and II." *The New Yorker,* June 6, pp. 46–109; June 13, pp. 50–91.

Organizing to Implement Corporate Diversification

LEARNING OBJECTIVES

After reading this chapter, you should be able to:

1. Describe the multidivisional, or M-form, structure and how it is used to implement a corporate diversification strategy.

2. Describe the roles of the board of directors, institutional investors, the senior executive, corporate staff, division general managers, and shared activity managers in making the M-form structure work.

3. Describe how three management control processes—measuring divisional performance, allocating corporate capital, and transferring intermediate products—are used to help implement a corporate diversification strategy.

4. Describe the role of management compensation in helping to implement a corporate diversification strategy.

A SOX on All Their Houses

The turn of the twentieth century marked a period of corporate fraud and corruption that rivaled any other in the history of the United States. The list of firms that engaged in fraudulent accounting practices and other illegal activities was long and storied—ImClone, Tyco, WorldCom, and the biggest crook of all, Enron. Scores of senior managers in these firms have faced civil and criminal trials, and some have been sentenced to multidecade prison terms.

In response to this corruption, the U.S. Congress passed the Sarbanes-Oxley Act of 2002. Named after its cosponsors—Senator Paul Sarbanes, D-Maryland, and Congressman Michael Oxley, R-Ohio—the Sarbanes-Oxley Act, also known as SOX, was designed to increase the accountability of U.S. corporations, thereby reducing the likelihood of fraud. Approved by the House of Representatives by a vote of 423–3 and by the Senate by a vote of 99–0, the bill was signed into law by President George Bush on July 30, 2002.

Ever since, the implementation of SOX has been plagued by cost and controversy.

Most business observers recognized the need for some sort of accounting overhaul to, at a minimum, help restore the confidence of shareholders in the U.S. stock market. These same observers have concluded that many of the provisions of the bill are reasonable and prudent. For example, SOX establishes an independent, full-time accounting oversight board (the Public Company Accounting Oversight Board) to monitor and modify certain accounting principles and practices; it outlaws certain "non-audit" services that might create conflicts of interest for accounting firms working with particular clients; and it establishes rules regarding conflicts of interest for stock analysts.

However, other provisions in SOX are more controversial. These include, for example, a requirement that firms establish, and then have audited, certain internal organizational controls; additional responsibilities for boards of directors and audit committees on boards; a requirement that every firm have a statement of ethical practices; and so forth. Some have argued that, at best, these provisions of SOX

will have no impact on the information available to shareholders and, at worst, they will be very costly to implement and may even hurt a firm's shareholders.

Consider, for example, the Ethics Statement requirement. Most firms—before SOX—had ethics statements. Indeed, many of the firms that engaged in the fraud that led to the passage of SOX had such statements—including Enron's statement of ethics presented in Chapter 1. Requiring firms to have such statements, when most already did, did not really have much of an impact on shareholders. It also is not likely to have much impact on corporate fraud.

On the cost side, the total negative economic consequences of implementing SOX have been estimated to be as high as $1.4 trillion. This is the aggregate impact of SOX on the market value of all publicly traded U.S. firms. This includes the direct costs of implementing and auditing internal controls and other provisions mandated by SOX, along with the indirect costs of implementing this legislation as reflected in the price of the stock of firms trading on U.S. stock exchanges. Scholars have shown that SOX has led to an increase in the expense associated with a board of directors, a decline in research and development expenditures, an increase in the value in a firm going private, an increase in the number of firms going public in non–U.S. stock markets, and so forth.

Even this may not reflect the full cost of implementing SOX. As the chief accounting officer at General Motors observed, "The real cost isn't the incremental dollars, it is having people that should be focused on business focused instead on complying with the details of the rules."

However, several observers have argued that SOX has done exactly what it was designed to do—it has restored confidence in U.S. stock markets, it has given stockholders more information than they previously had, and it has forced publicly traded firms to implement organizational controls that reduce the likeli-

hood of the fraud that perpetrated this legislation in the first place.

Sources: I. Zhang (2005). "Economic consequences of the Sarbanes-Oxley Act of 2002."

University of Rochester, Simon Graduate School of Business Administration; D. Solomon and C. Bryan-Low (2004). "Companies complain about the cost of corporate governance rules." *Wall Street Journal*, February 10, 2004, pp. A1 +; "On Trial," *BusinessWeek*, January 12, 2004, pp. 80–81.

This chapter is about how large diversified firms—the kind of firms that Sarbanes-Oxley was designed for—are managed and governed efficiently. The chapter explains how these kinds of firms are managed in a way that is consistent with the interests of their owners—equity holders—as well as the interests of their other stakeholders. The three components of organizing to implement any strategy, which were first identified in Chapter 3—organizational structure, management controls, and compensation policy—are also important in implementing corporate diversification strategies.

V R I O   Organizational Structure and Implementing Corporate Diversification

The most common organizational structure for implementing a corporate diversification strategy is the **M-form**, or **multidivisional**, structure. A typical M-form structure, as it would appear in a firm's annual report, is presented in Figure 8.1. This same structure is redrawn in Figure 8.2 to emphasize the roles and responsibilities of each of the major components of the M-form organization.[1]

Figure 8.1   An Example of M-Form Organizational Structure as Depicted in a Firm's Annual Report

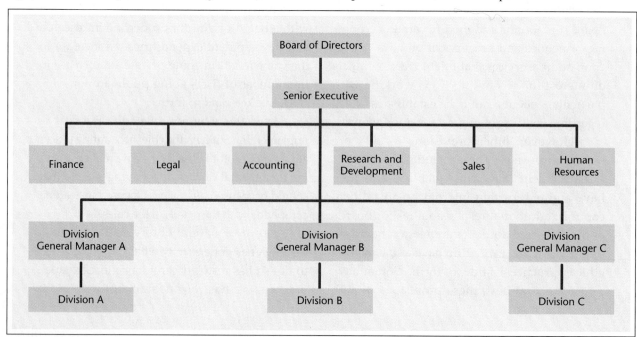

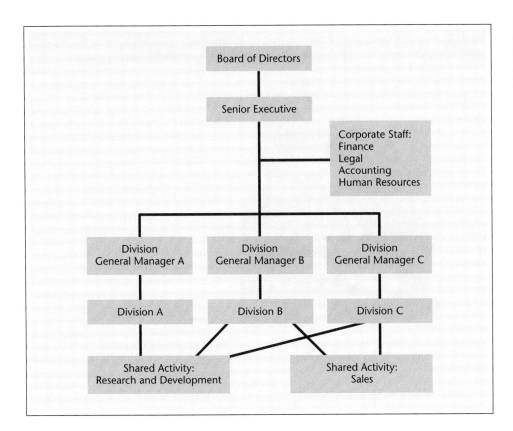

Figure 8.2 An M-Form Structure Redrawn to Emphasize Roles and Responsibilities

In the multidivisional structure, each business that the firm engages in is managed through a **division**. Different firms have different names for these divisions—strategic business units (SBUs), business groups, companies. Whatever their names, the divisions in an M-form organization are true **profit-and-loss centers**: Profits and losses are calculated at the level of the division in these firms.

Different firms use different criteria for defining the boundaries of profit-and-loss centers. For example, General Electric defines its divisions in terms of the types of products each one manufactures and sells (e.g., infrastructure, industrial, NBCUniversal, medical technology, and so forth). Nestlé defines its divisions with reference to the geographic scope of each of its businesses (North America, South America, and so forth). General Motors defines its divisions in terms of the brand names of its products (Cadillac, Chevrolet, Saturn, and so forth). However they are defined, divisions in an M-form organization should be large enough to represent identifiable business entities but small enough so that each one can be managed effectively by a division general manager. Indeed, each division in an M-form organization typically adopts a U-form structure (see the discussion of the U-form structure in Chapters 4, 5, and 6), and the division general manager takes on the role of a U-form senior executive for his or her division.

The M-form structure is designed to create checks and balances for managers that increase the probability that a diversified firm will be managed in ways consistent with the interests of its equity holders. The roles of each of the major elements of the M-form structure in accomplishing this objective are summarized in Table 8.1 and discussed below. Some of the conflicts of interest that might emerge between a firm's equity holders and its managers are described in the Strategy in Depth feature.

Strategy in Depth

In Chapter 7, it was suggested that sometimes it is in the best interest of equity holders to delegate to managers the day-to-day management of their equity investments in a firm. This will be the case when equity investors cannot realize a valuable economy of scope on their own while managers *can* realize that economy of scope.

Several authors have suggested that whenever one party to an exchange delegates decision-making authority to a second party, an **agency relationship** has been created between these parties. The party delegating this decision-making authority is called the **principal**; the party to whom this authority is delegated is called the **agent**. In the context of corporate diversification, an agency relationship exists between a firm's outside equity holders (as principals) and its managers (as agents) to the extent that equity holders delegate the day-to-day management of their investment to those managers.

The agency relationship between equity holders and managers can be very effective as long as managers make investment decisions that are consistent with equity holders' interests. Thus, if equity holders are interested in maximizing the rate of return on their investment in a firm and if managers make their investment decisions with this objective in mind, then equity holders will have few concerns about delegating the day-to-day management of their investments to managers. Unfortunately, in numerous situations the interests of a firm's outside equity holders and its managers do not coincide. When parties in an agency relationship differ in their decision-making objectives, **agency prob-**

Agency Conflicts Between Managers and Equity Holders

lems arise. Two common agency problems have been identified: investment in managerial perquisites and managerial risk aversion.

Managers may decide to take some of a firm's capital and invest it in **managerial perquisites** that do not add economic value to the firm but do directly benefit those managers. Examples of such investments include lavish offices, fleets of corporate jets, and corporate vacation homes. Dennis Kozlowski, former CEO of Tyco International, is accused of "stealing" $600 million in these kinds of managerial perquisites from his firm. The list of goods and services that Kozlowski lavished on himself and those close to him is truly astounding—a multimillion-dollar birthday party for his wife, a $6,000 wastebasket, a $15,000 umbrella stand, a $144,000 loan to a board member, toga-clad waiters at an event, and so on.

As outrageous as some of these managerial perquisites can be, the

second source of agency problems—**managerial risk aversion**—is probably more important in most diversified firms. As discussed in Chapter 7, equity holders can diversify their portfolio of investments at very low cost. Through their diversification efforts, they can eliminate all firm-specific risk in their portfolios. In this setting, equity holders would prefer that managers make more risky rather than less risky investments, because the expected return on risky investments is usually greater than the expected return on less risky investments.

Managers, in contrast, have limited ability to diversify their human capital investments in their firm. Some portion of these investments is specific to a particular firm and has limited value in alternative uses. The value of a manager's human capital investment in a firm depends critically on the continued existence of the firm. Thus, managers are *not* indifferent to the riskiness of investment opportunities in a firm. Very risky investments may jeopardize a firm's survival and thus eliminate the value of a manager's human capital investments. These incentives can make managers more risk averse in their decision making than equity holders would like them to be.

One of the purposes of the M-form structure, and indeed of all aspects of organizing to implement corporate diversification, is to reduce these agency problems.

Sources: M. C. Jensen and W. H. Meckling (1976). "Theory of the firm: Managerial behavior, agency costs, and ownership structure." *Journal of Financial Economics.* 3, pp. 305–360; J. Useem (2003). "The biggest show." *Fortune,* December 8, pp. 157 +; R. Lambert (1986). "Executive effort and selection of risky projects." *Rand Journal of Economics,* 13(2), pp. 369–378.

Table 8.1   **The Roles and Responsibilities of Major Components of the M-Form Structure**

Component	Activity
Board of directors	Monitor decision making in a firm to ensure that it is consistent with the interests of outside equity holders
Institutional investors	Monitor decision making to ensure that it is consistent with the interests of major institutional equity investors
Senior executives	Formulate corporate strategies consistent with equity holders' interests and assure strategy implementation
	Strategy formulation: ■ Decide the businesses in which the firm will operate ■ Decide how the firm should compete in those businesses ■ Specify the economies of scope around which the diversified firm will operate
	Strategy implementation: ■ Encourage cooperation across divisions to exploit economies of scope ■ Evaluate performance of divisions ■ Allocate capital across divisions
Corporate staff	Provides information to the senior executive about internal and external environments for strategy formulation and implementation
Division general managers	Formulate divisional strategies consistent with corporate strategies and assure strategy implementation
	Strategy formulation: ■ Decide how the division will compete in its business, given the corporate strategy
	Strategy implementation: ■ Coordinate the decisions and actions of functional managers reporting to the division general manager to implement divisional strategy ■ Compete for corporate capital allocations ■ Cooperate with other divisions to exploit corporate economies of scope
Shared activity managers	Support the operations of multiple divisions

The Board of Directors

One of the major components of an M-form organization is a firm's **board of directors**. In principle, all of a firm's senior managers report to the board. The board's primary responsibility is to monitor decision making in the firm, ensuring that it is consistent with the interests of outside equity holders.

Research Made Relevant

A great deal of research has tried to determine when boards of directors are more or less effective in ensuring that firms are managed in ways consistent with the interests of equity holders. Three issues have received particular attention: (1) the roles of insiders (i.e., managers) and outsiders on the board; (2) whether the board chair and the senior executive should be the same or different people; and (3) whether the board should be active or passive.

With respect to insiders and outsiders on the board, in one way this seems like a simple problem. Because the primary role of the board of directors is to monitor managerial decisions to ensure that they are consistent with the interests of equity holders, it follows that the board should consist primarily of outsiders because they face no conflict of interest in evaluating managerial performance. Obviously, managers, as inside members of the board, face significant conflicts of interest in evaluating their own performance.

Research on outsider members of boards of directors tends to support this point of view. Outside directors, as compared to insiders, tend to focus more on monitoring a firm's economic

The Effectiveness of Boards of Directors

performance than on other measures of firm performance. Obviously, a firm's economic performance is most relevant to its equity investors. Outside board members are also more likely than inside members to dismiss CEOs for poor performance. Also, outside board members have a stronger incentive than inside members to maintain their reputations as effective monitors. This incentive by itself can lead to more effective monitoring by outside board

members. Moreover, the monitoring effectiveness of outside board members seems to be enhanced when they personally own a substantial amount of a firm's equity.

However, the fact that outside members face fewer conflicts of interest in evaluating managerial performance compared to management insiders on the board does not mean that there is no appropriate role for inside board members. Managers bring something to the board that cannot be easily duplicated by outsiders—detailed information about the decision-making activities inside the firm. This is precisely the information that outsiders need to effectively monitor the activities of a firm, and it is information available to them only if they work closely with insiders (managers). One way to gain access to this information is to include managers as members of the board of directors. Thus, while most research suggests that a board of directors should be composed primarily of outsiders, there is an important role for insiders/managers to play as members of a firm's board.

There is currently some debate about whether the roles of board

A board of directors typically consists of 10 to 15 individuals drawn from a firm's top management group and from individuals outside the firm. A firm's **senior executive** (often identified by the title president or chief executive officer or CEO), its chief financial officer (CFO), and a few other senior managers are usually on the board—although managers on the board are typically outnumbered by outsiders. The firm's senior executive is often, but not always, the **chairman of the board** (a term used here to denote both female and male senior executives). The task of managerial board members—including the board chairman—is to provide other board members information and insights about critical decisions being made in the firm and the effect those decisions are likely to have on a firm's equity holders. The task of outsiders on the board is to evaluate the past, current, and future performance of the firm and of its senior managers to ensure that the actions taken in the firm are consistent with equity holders' interests.[2]

chairman and CEO should be combined or separated and, if separated, what kinds of people should occupy these positions. Some have argued that the roles of CEO and chairman of the board should definitely be separated and that the role of the chairman should be filled by an outside (nonmanagerial) member of the board of directors. These arguments are based on the assumption that only an outside member of the board can ensure the independent monitoring of managerial decision making. Others have argued that effective monitoring often requires more information than what would be available to outsiders, and thus the roles of board chairman and CEO should be combined and filled by a firm's senior manager.

Empirical research on this question suggests that whether these roles of CEO and chairman should be combined or not depends on the complexity of the information analysis and monitoring task facing the CEO and chairman. Brian Boyd has found that combining the roles of CEO and chairman is positively correlated with firm performance when firms operate in slow-growth and simple competitive environments—environments that do not overtax the cognitive capability of a single individual. This finding suggests that combining these roles does not necessarily increase conflicts between a firm and its equity holders. This research also found that separating the roles of CEO and board chairman is positively correlated with firm performance when firms operate in high-growth and very complex environments. In such environments, a single individual cannot fulfill all the responsibilities of both CEO and chairman, and thus the two roles need to be held by separate individuals.

Finally, with respect to active versus passive boards, historically the boards of major firms have been relatively passive and would take dramatic action, such as firing the senior executive, only if a firm's performance was significantly below expectations for long periods of time. However, more recently, boards have become more active proponents of equity holders' interests. This recent surge in board activity reflects a new economic reality: If a board does not become more active in monitoring firm performance, then other monitoring mechanisms will. Consequently, the board of directors has become progressively more influential in representing the interests of a firm's equity holders.

However, board activity can go too far. To the extent that the board begins to operate a business on a day-to-day basis, it goes beyond its capabilities. Boards rarely have sufficient detailed information to manage a firm directly. When it is necessary to change a firm's senior executive, boards will usually not take on the responsibilities of that executive, but rather will rapidly identify a single individual—either an insider or outsider—to take over this position.

Sources: E. Zajac and J. Westphal (1994). "The costs and benefits of managerial incentives and monitoring in large U.S. corporations: When is more not better?" *Strategic Management Journal,* 15, pp. 121–142; P. Rechner and D. Dalton (1991). "CEO duality and organizational performance: A longitudinal analysis." *Strategic Management Journal,* 12, pp. 155–160; S. Finkelstein and R. D'Aveni (1994). "CEO duality as a double-edged sword: How boards of directors balance entrenchment avoidance and unity of command." *Academy of Management Journal,* 37, pp. 1079–1108; B. K. Boyd (1995). "CEO duality and firm performance: A contingency model." *Strategic Management Journal,* 16, pp. 301–312; F. Kesner and R. B. Johnson (1990). "An investigation of the relationship between board composition and stockholder suits." *Strategic Management Journal,* 11, pp. 327–336.

Boards of directors are typically organized into several subcommittees. An **audit committee** is responsible for ensuring the accuracy of accounting and financial statements. A **finance committee** maintains the relationship between the firm and external capital markets. A **nominating committee** nominates new board members. A **personnel and compensation committee** evaluates and compensates the performance of a firm's senior executive and other senior managers. Often, membership on these standing committees is reserved for external board members. Other standing committees reflect specific issues for a particular firm and are typically open to external and internal board members.[3]

Over the years, a great deal of research has been conducted about the effectiveness of boards of directors in ensuring that a firm's managers make decisions in ways consistent with the interests of its equity holders. Some of this work is summarized in the Research Made Relevant feature.

Global Perspectives

How common is it for large diversified firms around the world to be owned or dominated by single families? Most people are surprised to find out just how common family dominated firms are in the United States. Indeed, one-third of the firms in the Standard & Poor's 500 have their founding families still involved in day-to-day management. Such firms include Marriott, Walgreens, Wrigley, Alberto-Culver, Campbell Soup, Dell, and Wal-Mart.

However, as important as these family dominated firms are in the U.S. economy, they are not the dominant force that such firms are in many countries around the world. In fact, one recent study found that they can be a very important force in the economy of many countries. For example, in New Zealand, 9 of the 20 largest firms in the economy are family dominated; in Argentina, 13 of the 20 largest firms in the economy are family dominated; in Mexico, all 20 of the 20 largest firms in the economy are family dominated. By

The Family Firm in the United States and the World

comparison, only 4 of the 20 largest firms in the United States are family dominated, and only 1 of the 20 largest firms in the United Kingdom is family dominated.

These results suggest that the model of corporate governance that is

normally taught in the United States—with large numbers of shareholders owning stock in professionally managed firms—is actually the exception around the world. In many countries—including Argentina, Belgium, Canada, Denmark, Greece, Hong Kong, Israel, Mexico, New Zealand, Portugal, Singapore, South Korea, Sweden, and Switzerland—over one-third of the 20 largest firms are dominated by family owners.

Family ownership of large diversified corporations has advantages and disadvantages. On the positive side, many of the agency problems (see the Strategy in Depth feature) that exist in professionally managed firms are less important in family dominated firms. After all, managers in family dominated firms are not "playing" with other people's money, they are "playing" with their own family's money. Family dominated firms can also make strategic decisions faster than large bureaucratic firms, they

Institutional Owners

Historically, the typical large diversified firm has had its equity owned in small blocks by millions of individual investors. The exception to this general rule was family owned or dominated firms, a phenomenon discussed in more detail in the Global Perspectives feature. When a firm's ownership is spread among millions of small investors, it is difficult for any one of these investors to have a large enough ownership position to influence management decisions directly. The only course of action open to such investors if they disagree with management decisions is to sell their stock.

However, the growth of institutional owners has changed the ownership structure of many large diversified firms over the last several years. **Institutional owners** are usually pension funds, mutual funds, insurance companies, or other groups of individual investors that have joined together to manage their investments. In 1970, institutions owned 32 percent of the equity traded in the United States. By 1990, institutions owned 48 percent of this equity. In 2005, they owned 59 percent of all equity traded in the United States and 69 percent of the equity of the 1,000 largest firms in the United States.[4]

Institutional investors can use their investment clout to insist that a firm's management behaves in ways consistent with the interests of equity holders.

tend to create a sense of loyalty among their employees, and they tend to invest for long-term growth rather than being forced to respond to short-term fluctuations in the stock market. Indeed, in the United States over the last 10 years family dominated firms have outperformed firms not owned by a family—in terms of income growth—21 to 11.5 percent.

On the negative side, family dominated firms have some significant limitations. First, because senior leadership positions in these firms, especially those outside the United States, tend to be reserved for family members, such firms often do not have access to the broader professional management skills available to other firms. Also, because family interests tend to weigh heavily in strategic decision making in these firms, outside investors will often be reluctant to invest in such firms. This suggests that family dominated firms may often face important capital con-

straints. Finally, because much of a particular family's wealth tends to be tied up in the family firm, it is difficult for family members to purchase equities and other investments to diversify their personal investment portfolios. Thus, in order to obtain the benefits of portfolio diversification for their family owners, family dominated firms often engage in a strategy of unrelated diversification. As was suggested in Chapter 7, this is a very expensive way for a firm's owners to diversify their risk.

Overall, although family dominated businesses have advantages and disadvantages, research indicates that the predominance of family dominated businesses in a country's economy is negatively correlated with the overall level of growth in that economy. Countries whose economies are dominated by family owned businesses tend to grow less quickly than countries whose economies are not dominated by

family owned businesses. This negative correlation probably reflects the primary reason that family firms are still important in many economies around the world. When individuals in a country are not confident that the legal and political system will protect their personal property rights, they develop alternative ways to protect those rights. Large and powerful family firms are another way of protecting personal property rights. This suggests that the sanctity of personal property rights in a country explains both the level of economic growth in that country and the extent to which family firms dominate a country's economy.

Sources: R. Morck and B. Yeung (2004). "Family control and the rent-seeking society." *Entrepreneurship: Theory and Practice,* Summer, pp. 391–409; R. LaPorta, F. Lopez-de-Salinas, A. Shleifer, and R. Vishny (1999). "Corporate ownership around the world." *Journal of Finance,* 54, pp. 471–520; J. Weber, L. Lavelle, T. Lowry, W. Zellner, and A. Barrett (2003). "Family, Inc." *BusinessWeek,* November 10, pp. 100 +.

Observers who assume that institutional investors are interested more in maximizing the short-term value of their portfolios than in the long-term performance of firms in those portfolios fear that such power will force firms to make only short-term investments. Recent research in the United States and Japan, however, suggests that institutional investors are not unduly myopic. Rather, as suggested earlier, these investors use approximately the same logic equity investors use when evaluating the performance of a firm. For example, one group of researchers examined the impact of institutional ownership on research and development investments in R&D–intensive industries. R&D investments tend to be longer term in orientation. If institutional investors are myopic, they should influence firms to invest in relatively less R&D in favor of investments that generate shorter-term profits. This research showed that high levels of institutional ownership did not adversely affect the level of R&D in a firm. These findings are consistent with the notion that institutional investors are not inappropriately concerned with the short term in their monitoring activities.[5]

More generally, other researchers have shown that high levels of institutional ownership leads firms to sell strategically unrelated businesses. This effect of institutional investors is enhanced if, in addition, outside directors on a firm's board have substantial equity investments in the firm. Given the discussion of the value of unrelated diversification in Chapter 7, it seems clear that these divestment actions are typically consistent with maximizing the present value of a firm.[6]

The Senior Executive

As suggested in Table 8.1, the senior executive (the president or CEO) in an M-form organization has two responsibilities: strategy formulation and strategy implementation. *Strategy formulation* entails deciding which set of businesses a diversified firm will operate in; *strategy implementation* focuses on encouraging behavior in a firm that is consistent with this strategy. Each of these responsibilities of the senior executive is discussed in turn.

Strategy Formulation

At the broadest level, deciding which businesses a diversified firm should operate in is equivalent to discovering and developing valuable economies of scope among a firm's current and potential businesses. If these economies of scope are also rare and costly to imitate, they can be a source of sustained competitive advantage for a diversified firm.

   The senior executive is uniquely positioned to discover, develop, and nurture valuable economies of scope in a diversified firm. Every other manager in this kind of firm either has a divisional point of view (e.g., division general managers and shared activity managers) or is a functional specialist (e.g., corporate staff and functional managers within divisions). Only the senior executive has a truly corporate perspective. However, the senior executive in an M-form organization should involve numerous other divisional and functional managers in strategy formulation to ensure complete and accurate information as input to the process and a broad understanding of and commitment to that strategy once it has been formulated.

Strategy Implementation

As is the case for senior executives in a U-form structure, strategy implementation in an M-form structure almost always involves resolving conflicts among groups of managers. However, instead of simply resolving conflicts between functional managers (as is the case in a U-form), senior executives in M-form organizations must resolve conflicts within and between each of the major managerial components of the M-form structure: corporate staff, division general managers, and shared activity managers. Various corporate staff managers may disagree about the economic relevance of their staff functions, corporate staff may come into conflict with division general managers over various corporate programs and activities, division general managers may disagree with how capital is allocated across divisions, division general managers may come into conflict with shared activity managers about how shared activities should be managed, shared activity managers may disagree with corporate staff about their mutual roles and responsibilities, and so forth.

   Obviously, the numerous and often conflicting relationships among groups of managers in an M-form organization can place significant strategy implementation burdens on the senior executive.[7] While resolving these numerous conflicts, however, the senior executive needs to keep in mind the reasons why the firm began pursuing a diversification strategy in the first place: to exploit real economies of scope that outside investors cannot realize on their own. Any strategy implementation decisions that jeopardize the realization of these real economies of scope are inconsistent with the underlying strategic objectives of a diversified firm. These issues are analyzed in detail later in this chapter, in the discussion of management control systems in the M-form organization.

The Office of the President: Chairman, CEO, and COO

It is often the case that the roles and responsibilities of the senior executive in an M-form organization are greater than what can be reasonably managed by a single individual. This is especially likely if a firm is broadly diversified across numerous complex products and markets. In this situation, it is not uncommon for the tasks of the senior executive to be divided among two or three people: the **chairman of the board**, the **chief executive officer**, and the **chief operating officer (COO)**. The primary responsibilities of each of these roles in an M-form organization are listed in Table 8.2. Together, these roles are known as the **office of the president**. In general, as the tasks facing the office of the president become more demanding and complex, the more likely it is that the roles and responsibilities of this office will be divided among two or three people.

Corporate Staff

The primary responsibility of **corporate staff** is to provide information about the firm's external and internal environments to the firm's senior executive. This information is vital for both the strategy formulation and the strategy implementation responsibilities of the senior executive. Corporate staff functions that provide information about a firm's external environment include finance, investor relations, legal affairs, regulatory affairs, and corporate advertising. Corporate staff functions that provide information about a firm's internal environment include accounting and corporate human resources. These corporate staff functions report directly to a firm's senior executive and are a conduit of information to that executive.

Corporate and Divisional Staff

Many organizations re-create some corporate staff functions within each division of the organization. This is particularly true for internally oriented corporate staff functions such as accounting and human resources. At the division level, divisional staff managers usually have a direct "solid-line" reporting relationship to their respective corporate staff functional managers and a less formal "dotted-line" reporting relationship to their division general manager. The reporting relationship between the divisional staff manager and the corporate staff manager is the link that enables the corporate staff manager to collect the information that the senior executive requires for strategy formulation and implementation. The senior executive can also use this corporate staff–division staff relationship to communicate corporate policies and procedures to the divisions, although these policies can also be communicated directly by the senior executive to division general managers.

Table 8.2 **Responsibilities of Three Different Roles in the Office of the President**

Chairman of the board	Supervision of the board of directors in its monitoring role
Chief executive officer	Strategy formulation
Chief operating officer	Strategy implementation

Although divisional staff managers usually have a less formal relationship with their division general managers, in practice division general managers can have an important influence on the activities of divisional staff. After all, divisional staff managers may formally report to corporate staff managers, but they spend most of their time interacting with their division general managers and with the other functional managers who report to their division general managers. These divided loyalties can sometimes affect the timelines and accuracy of the information transmitted from divisional staff managers to corporate staff managers and thus affect the timeliness and accuracy of the information the senior executive uses for strategy formulation and implementation.

Nowhere are these divided loyalties potentially more problematic than in accounting staff functions. Obviously, it is vitally important for the senior executive in an M-form organization to receive timely and accurate information about divisional performance. If the timeliness and accuracy of that information are inappropriately affected by division general managers, the effectiveness of senior management can be adversely affected. Moreover, in some situations division general managers can have very strong incentives to affect the timeliness and accuracy of divisional performance information, especially if a division general manager's compensation depends on this information or if the capital allocated to a division depends on this information.

Efficient monitoring by the senior executive requires that corporate staff, and especially the accounting corporate staff function, remain organizationally independent of division general managers—thus the importance of the solid-line relationship between divisional staff managers and corporate staff managers. Nevertheless, the ability of corporate staff to obtain accurate performance information from divisions also depends on close cooperative working relationships between corporate staff, divisional staff, and division general managers—hence the importance of the dotted-line relationship between divisional staff managers and division general managers. How one maintains the balance between, on the one hand, the distance and objectivity needed to evaluate a division's performance and, on the other hand, the cooperation and teamwork needed to gain access to the information required to evaluate a division's performance distinguishes excellent from mediocre corporate staff managers.

Overinvolvement in Managing Division Operations

Over and above the failure to maintain a balance between objectivity and cooperation in evaluating divisional performance, the one sure way that corporate staff can fail in a multidivisional firm is to become too involved in the day-to-day operations of divisions. In an M-form structure, the management of such day-to-day operations is delegated to division general managers and to functional managers who report to division general managers. Corporate staff managers collect and transmit information; they do not manage divisional operations.

One way to ensure that corporate staff does not become too involved in managing the day-to-day operations of divisions is to keep corporate staff small. This is certainly true for some of the best-managed diversified firms in the world. For example, just 1.5 percent of Johnson & Johnson's 82,700 employees work at the firm's headquarters, and only some of those individuals are members of the corporate staff. Hanson Industries has in its U.S. headquarters 120 people who help manage a diversified firm with $8 billion in revenues. Clayton, Dubilier, and Rice, a management buyout firm, has only 11 headquarters staff members overseeing eight businesses with collective sales of over $6 billion.[8]

Division General Manager

Division general managers in an M-form organization have primary responsibility for managing a firm's businesses from day to day. Division general managers have full profit-and-loss responsibility and typically have multiple functional managers reporting to them. As general managers, they have both strategy formulation and strategy implementation responsibilities. On the strategy formulation side, division general managers choose strategies for their divisions, within the broader strategic context established by the senior executive of the firm. Many of the analytical tools described in Parts 1 and 2 of this book can be used by division general managers to make these strategy formulation decisions.

The strategy implementation responsibilities of division general managers in an M-form organization parallel the strategy implementation responsibilities of senior executives in U-form organizations. In particular, division general managers must be able to coordinate the activities of often-conflicting functional managers in order to implement a division's strategies.

In addition to their responsibilities as a U-form senior executive, division general managers in an M-form organization have two additional responsibilities: to compete for corporate capital and to cooperate with other divisions to exploit corporate economies of scope. Division general managers compete for corporate capital by promising high rates of return on capital invested by the corporation in their business. In most firms, divisions that have demonstrated the ability to generate high rates of return on earlier capital investments gain access to more capital or to lower-cost capital, compared to divisions that have not demonstrated a history of such performance.

Division general managers cooperate to exploit economies of scope by working with shared activity managers, corporate staff managers, and the senior executive in the firm to isolate, understand, and use the economies of scope around which the diversified firm was originally organized. Division general managers can even become involved in discovering new economies of scope that were not anticipated when the firm's diversification strategy was originally implemented but nevertheless may be both valuable and costly for outside investors to create on their own.

Of course, a careful reader will recognize a fundamental conflict between the last two responsibilities of division general managers in an M-form organization. These managers are required to compete for corporate capital and to cooperate to exploit economies of scope at the same time. Competition is important, because it leads division general managers to focus on generating high levels of economic performance from their divisions. If each division is generating high levels of economic performance, then the diversified firm as a whole is likely to do well also. However, cooperation is important to exploit economies of scope that are the economic justification for implementing a diversification strategy in the first place. If divisions do not cooperate in exploiting these economies, there are few, if any, justifications for implementing a corporate diversification strategy, and the diversified firm should be split into multiple independent entities. The need to simultaneously compete and cooperate puts significant managerial burdens on division general managers. It is likely that this ability is both rare and costly to imitate across most diversified firms.[9]

Shared Activity Managers

One of the potential economies of scope identified in Chapter 7 was shared activities. Divisions in an M-form organization exploit this economy of scope when one or more of the stages in their value chains are managed in common. Typical examples of activities shared across two or more divisions in a multidivisional firm include common sales forces, common distribution systems, common manufacturing facilities, and common research and development efforts (also see Table 7.2). The primary responsibility of the individuals who manage shared activities is to support the operations of the divisions that share the activity.

The way in which M-form structure is often depicted in company annual reports (as in Figure 8.1) tends to obscure the operational role of shared activities. In this version of the M-form organizational chart, no distinction is made between corporate staff functions and shared activity functions. Moreover, it appears that managers of shared activities report directly to a firm's senior executive, just like corporate staff. These ambiguities are resolved by redrawing the M-form organizational chart to emphasize the roles and responsibilities of different units within the M-form (as in Figure 8.2). In this more accurate representation of how an M-form actually functions, corporate staff groups are separated from shared activity managers, and each is shown reporting to its primary internal "customer." That "internal customer" is the senior executive for corporate staff groups and two or more division general managers for shared activity managers.

Shared Activities as Cost Centers

Shared activities are often managed as cost centers in an M-form structure. That is, rather than having profit-and-loss responsibility, **cost centers** are assigned a budget and manage their operations to that budget. When this is the case, shared activity managers do not attempt to create profits when they provide services to the divisions they support. Rather, these services are priced to internal customers in such a way that the shared activity just covers its cost of operating.

Because cost center shared activities do not have to generate profits from their operations, the cost of the services they provide to divisions can be less than the cost of similar services provided either by a division itself or by outside suppliers. If a shared activity is managed as a cost center, and the cost of services from this shared activity is *greater than* the cost of similar services provided by alternative sources, then either this shared activity is not being well managed or it was not a real economy of scope in the first place. However, when the cost of services from a shared activity is *less than* the cost of comparable services provided by a division itself or by an outside supplier, then division general managers have a strong incentive to use the services of shared activities, thereby exploiting an economy of scope that may have been one of the original reasons why a firm implemented a corporate diversification strategy.

Shared Activities as Profit Centers

Some diversified firms are beginning to manage shared activities as profit centers, rather than as cost centers. Moreover, rather than requiring divisions to use the services of shared activities, divisions retain the right to purchase services from internal shared activities or from outside suppliers or to provide services for themselves. In this setting, managers of shared activities are required to compete for their internal customers on the basis of the price and quality of the services they provide.[10]

One firm that has taken this profit-center approach to managing shared activities is ABB, Inc., a Swiss engineering firm. ABB eliminated almost all its corporate staff and reorganized its remaining staff functions into shared activities. Shared activities in ABB compete to provide services to ABB divisions. Not only do some traditional shared activities—such as research and development and sales—compete for internal customers, but many traditional corporate staff functions—such as human resources, marketing, and finance—do as well. ABB's approach to managing shared activities has resulted in a relatively small corporate staff and in increasingly specialized and customized shared activities.[11]

Of course, the greatest risk associated with treating shared activities as profit centers and letting them compete for divisional customers is that divisions may choose to obtain no services or support from shared activities. Although this course of action may be in the self-interest of each division, it may not be in the best interest of the corporation as a whole if, in fact, shared activities are an important economy of scope around which the diversified firm is organized.

In the end, the task facing the managers of shared activities is the same: to provide such highly customized and high-quality services to divisional customers at a reasonable cost that those internal customers will not want to seek alternative suppliers outside the firm or provide those services themselves. In an M-form organization, the best way to ensure that shared activity economies of scope are realized is for shared activity managers to satisfy their internal customers.

Management Controls and Implementing Corporate Diversification

The M-form structure presented in Figures 8.1 and 8.2 is complex and multifaceted. However, no organizational structure by itself is able to fully implement a corporate diversification strategy. The M-form structure must be supplemented with a variety of management controls. Three of the most important management controls in an M-form structure—systems for evaluating divisional performance, for allocating capital across divisions, and for transferring intermediate products between divisions—are discussed in this section.[12]

Evaluating Divisional Performance

Because divisions in an M-form structure are profit-and-loss centers, evaluating divisional performance should, in principle, be straightforward: Divisions that are very profitable should be evaluated more positively than divisions that are less profitable. In practice, this seemingly simple task is surprisingly complex. Two problems typically arise: (1) How should division profitability be measured? and (2) How should economy-of-scope linkages between divisions be factored into divisional performance measures?

Measuring Divisional Performance

Divisional performance can be measured in at least two ways. The first focuses on a division's accounting performance, the second on a division's economic performance.

Accounting Measures of Divisional Performance.   Both accounting and economic measures of performance can be used in measuring the performance of divisions within a diversified firm. Common accounting measures of divisional performance include the return on the assets controlled by a division, the return on a division's sales, and a division's sales growth. These accounting measures of divisional performance are then compared with some standard to see if a division's performance exceeds or falls short of that standard. Diversified firms use three different standards of comparison when evaluating the performance of a division: (1) a hurdle rate that is common across all the different business units in a firm, (2) a division's budgeted level of performance (which may vary by division), and (3) the average level of profitability of firms in a division's industry.

Each of these standards of comparison has its strengths and weaknesses. For example, if a corporation has a single hurdle rate of profitability that all divisions must meet or exceed, there is little ambiguity about the performance objectives of divisions. However, a single standard ignores important differences in performance that might exist across divisions.

Comparing a division's actual performance to its budgeted performance allows the performance expectations of different divisions to vary, but the budgeting process is time-consuming and fraught with political intrigue. One study showed that corporate managers routinely discount the sales projections and capital requests of division managers on the assumption that division managers are trying to "game" the budgeting system.[13] Moreover, division budgets are usually based on a single set of assumptions about how the economy is going to evolve, how competition in a division's industry is going to evolve, and what actions that division is going to take in its industry. When these assumptions no longer hold, budgets are redone—a costly and time-consuming process that has little to do with generating value in a firm.

Finally, although comparing a division's performance with the average level of profitability of firms in a division's industry also allows performance expectations to vary across divisions within a diversified firm, this approach lets other firms determine what is and is not excellent performance for a division within a diversified firm. This approach can also be manipulated: By choosing just the "right" firms with which to compare a division's performance, almost any division can be made to look like it's performing better than its industry average.[14]

No matter what standard of comparison is used to evaluate a division's accounting performance, most accounting measures of divisional performance have a common limitation. All these measures have a short-term bias. This short-term bias reflects the fact that all these measures treat investments in resources and capabilities that have the potential for generating value in the long run as costs during a particular year. In order to reduce costs in a given year, division managers may sometimes forgo investing in these resources and capabilities, even if they could be a source of sustained competitive advantage for a division in the long run.

Economic Measures of Divisional Performance.   Given the limitations of accounting measures of divisional performance, several firms have begun adopting economic methods of evaluating this performance. Economic methods build on accounting methods but adjust those methods to incorporate short-term investments that may generate long-term benefits. Economic methods also compare a division's performance with a firm's cost of capital (see Chapter 1). This avoids some of the gaming that can characterize the use of other standards of comparison in applying accounting measures of divisional performance.

Perhaps the most popular of these economically oriented measures of division performance is known as **economic value added**, or **EVA**.[15] EVA is calculated by subtracting the cost of capital employed in a division from that division's earnings in the following manner:

$$EVA = \text{adjusted accounting earnings}$$
$$\text{(weighted average cost of capital} \times \text{total capital employed by a division)}$$

Several of the terms in the EVA formula require some discussion. For example, the calculation of economic value added begins with a division's "adjusted" accounting earnings. These are a division's traditional accounting earnings, adjusted so that they approximate a division's economic earnings. Several adjustments to a division's accounting statements have been described in the literature. For example, traditional accounting practices require R&D spending to be deducted each year from a division's earnings. This can lead division general managers to underinvest in longer-term R&D efforts. In the EVA measure of divisional performance, R&D spending is added back into a division's performance, and R&D is then treated as an asset and depreciated over some period of time.

One consulting firm (Stern Stewart) that specializes in implementing EVA-based divisional evaluation systems in multidivisional firms makes up to 40 "adjustments" to a division's standard accounting earnings so that they more closely approximate economic earnings. Many of these adjustments are proprietary to this consulting firm. However, the most important adjustments—such as how R&D should be treated—are broadly known.

The terms in parentheses in the EVA equation reflect the cost of investing in a division. Rather than using some alternative standard of comparison, EVA applies financial theory and multiplies the amount of money invested in a division by a firm's weighted average cost of capital. A firm's weighted average cost of capital is the amount of money a firm could earn if it invested in any of its other divisions. In this sense, a firm's weighted average cost of capital can be thought of as the opportunity cost of investing in a particular division, as opposed to investing in any other division in the firm.

By adjusting a division's earnings and accounting for the cost of investing in a division, EVA is a much more accurate estimate of a division's economic performance than are traditional accounting measures of performance. The number of diversified firms evaluating their divisions with EVA-based measures of divisional performance is impressive and growing. These firms include AT&T, Coca-Cola, Quaker Oats, CSX, Briggs and Stratton, and Allied Signal. At Allied Signal, divisions that do not earn their cost of capital are awarded the infamous "leaky bucket" award. If this performance is not improved, division general managers are replaced. The use of EVA has been touted as the key to creating economic wealth in a diversified corporation.[16]

Economies of Scope and the Ambiguity of Divisional Performance

Whether a firm uses accounting measures to evaluate the performance of a division or uses economic measures of performance such as EVA, divisional performance in a well-managed diversified firm can never be evaluated unambiguously. Consider a simple example.

Suppose that in a particular multidivisional firm there are only two divisions (Division A and Division B) and one shared activity (R&D). Also, suppose that the two divisions are managed as profit-and-loss centers and that the R&D shared activity is managed as a cost center. To support this R&D effort, each division pays $10 million per year and has been doing so for 10 years. Finally, suppose that after 10 years of effort (and investment) the R&D group develops a valuable new technology that perfectly addresses Division A's business needs.

Obviously, no matter how divisional performance is measured it is likely to be the case that Division A's performance will rise relative to Division B's performance. In this situation, what percentage of Division A's improved performance should be allocated to Division A, what percentage should be allocated to the R&D group, and what percentage should be allocated to Division B?

The managers in each part of this diversified firm can make compelling arguments in their favor. Division general manager A can reasonably argue that without Division A's efforts to exploit the new technology, the full value of the technology would never have been realized. The R&D manager can reasonably argue that without the R&D effort, there would not have been a technology to exploit in the first place. Finally, division general manager B can reasonably argue that without the dedicated long-term investment of Division B in R&D, there would have been no new technology and no performance increase for Division A.

That all three of these arguments can be made suggests that, to the extent that a firm exploits real economies of scope in implementing a diversification strategy, it will not be possible to unambiguously evaluate the performance of individual divisions in that firm. The fact that there are economies of scope in a diversified firm means that all of the businesses a firm operates in are more valuable bundled together than they would be if kept separate from one another. Efforts to evaluate the performance of these businesses as if they were separate from one another are futile.

One solution to this problem is to force businesses in a diversified firm to operate independently of each other. If each business operates independently, then it will be possible to unambiguously evaluate its performance. Of course, to the extent that this independence is enforced, the diversified firm is unlikely to be able to realize the very economies of scope that were the justification for the diversification strategy in the first place.

Divisional performance ambiguity is bad enough when shared activities are the primary economy of scope that a diversified firm is trying to exploit. This ambiguity increases dramatically when the economy of scope is based on intangible core competencies. In this situation, it is shared learning and experience that justify a firm's diversification efforts. The intangible nature of these economies of scope multiplies the difficulty of the divisional evaluation task.

Even firms that apply rigorous EVA measures of divisional performance are unable to fully resolve these performance ambiguity difficulties. For example, the Coca-Cola division of the Coca-Cola Company has made enormous investments in the Coke brand name over the years, and the Diet Coke division has exploited some of that brand name capital in its own marketing efforts. Of course, it is not clear that all of Diet Coke's success can be attributed to the Coke brand name. After all, Diet Coke has developed its own creative advertising, its own loyal group of customers, and so forth. How much of Diet Coke's success—as measured through that division's economic value added—should be allocated to the Coke brand name (an investment made long before Diet Coke was even conceived) and how much should be allocated to the Diet Coke division's efforts? EVA measures of divisional performance do not resolve ambiguities created when economies of scope exist across divisions.[17]

In the end, the quantitative evaluation of divisional performance—with either accounting or economic measures—must be supplemented by the experience and judgment of senior executives in a diversified firm. Only by evaluating a division's performance numbers in the context of a broader, more subjective evaluation of the division's performance can a true picture of divisional performance be developed.

Allocating Corporate Capital

Another potentially valuable economy of scope outlined in Chapter 7 (besides shared activities and core competencies) is internal capital allocation. In that discussion, it was suggested that for internal capital allocation to be a justification for diversification the information made available to senior executives allocating capital in a diversified firm must be superior, in both amount and quality, to the information available to external sources of capital in the external capital market. Both the quality and the quantity of the information available in an internal capital market depend on the organization of the diversified firm.

One of the primary limitations of internal capital markets is that division general managers have a strong incentive to overstate their division's prospects and understate its problems in order to gain access to more capital at lower costs. Having an independent corporate accounting function in a diversified firm can help address this problem. However, given the ambiguities inherent in evaluating divisional performance in a well-managed diversified firm, independent corporate accountants do not resolve all these informational problems.

In the face of these challenges, some firms use a process called **zero-based budgeting** to help allocate capital. In zero-based budgeting, corporate executives create a list of all capital allocation requests from divisions in a firm, rank them from "most important" to "least important," and then fund all the projects a firm can afford, given the amount of capital it has available. In principle, no project will receive funding for the future simply because it received funding in the past. Rather, each project has to stand on its own merits each year by being included among the important projects the firm can afford to fund.

Although zero-based budgeting has some attractive features, it has some important limitations as well. For example, evaluating and ranking all projects in a diversified firm from "most important" to "least important" is a very difficult task. It requires corporate executives to have a very complete understanding of the strategic role of each of the projects being proposed by a division, as well as an understanding of how these projects will affect the short-term performance of divisions.

In the end, no matter what process firms use to allocate capital, allocating capital inside a firm in a way that is more efficient than what could be done by external capital markets requires the use of information that is not available to those external markets. Typically, that information will be intangible, tacit, and complex. Corporate managers looking to realize this economy of scope must find a way to use this kind of information effectively.[18] The difficulty of managing this process effectively may be one of the reasons why internal capital allocation often fails to qualify as a valuable economy of scope in diversified firms.[19]

Transferring Intermediate Products

The existence of economies of scope across multiple divisions in a diversified firm often means that products or services produced in one division are used as inputs for products or services produced by a second division. Such products or services are called **intermediate products or services**. Intermediate products or services can be transferred between any of the units in an M-form organization. This transfer is perhaps most important and problematic when it occurs between profit center divisions.

The transfer of intermediate products or services among divisions is usually managed through a **transfer-pricing system**: One division "sells" its product or service to a second division for a transfer price. Unlike a market price, which is typically determined by market forces of supply and demand, transfer prices are set by a firm's corporate management to accomplish corporate objectives.

Setting Optimal Transfer Prices

From an economic point of view, the rule for establishing the optimal transfer price in a diversified firm is quite simple: The transfer price should be the value of the opportunities forgone when one division's product or service is transferred to another division. Consider the following example. Division A's marginal cost of production is $5 per unit, but Division A can sell all of its output to outside customers for $6 per unit. If Division A can sell all of its output to outside customers for $6 per unit, the value of the opportunity forgone of transferring a unit of production from Division A to Division B is $6—the amount of money that Division A forgoes by transferring its production to Division B instead of selling it to the market.

However, if Division A is selling all the units it can to external customers for $6 per unit but still has some excess manufacturing capacity, the value of the opportunity forgone in transferring the product from Division A to Division B is only $5 per unit—Division A's marginal cost of production. Because the external market cannot absorb any more of Division A's product at $6 per unit, the value of the opportunity forgone when Division A transfers units of production to Division B is not $6 per unit (Division A can't get that price), but only $5 per unit.[20]

When transfer prices are set equal to opportunity costs, selling divisions will produce output up to the point that the marginal cost of the last unit produced equals the transfer price. Moreover, buying divisions will buy units from other divisions in the firm as long as the net revenues from doing so just cover the transfer price. These transfer prices will lead profit-maximizing divisions to optimize the diversified firm's profits.

Difficulties in Setting Optimal Transfer Prices

Setting transfer prices equal to opportunity costs sounds simple enough, but it is very difficult to do in real diversified firms. Establishing optimal transfer prices requires information about the value of the opportunities forgone by the "selling" division. This, in turn, requires information about this division's marginal costs, its manufacturing capacity, external demand for its products, and so forth. Much of this information is difficult to obtain. Moreover, it is rarely stable. As market conditions change, demand for a division's products can change, marginal costs can change, and the value of opportunities forgone can change. Also, to the extent that a selling division customizes the products or services it transfers to other divisions in a diversified firm, the value of the opportunities forgone by this selling division become even more difficult to calculate.

Even if this information could be obtained and updated rapidly, division general managers in selling divisions have strong incentives to manipulate the information in ways that increase the perceived value of the opportunities forgone by their division. These division general managers can thus increase the transfer price for the products or services they sell to internal customers and thereby appropriate for their division profits that should have been allocated to buying divisions.

Setting Transfer Prices in Practice

Because it is rarely possible for firms to establish an optimal transfer-pricing scheme, most diversified firms must adopt some form of transfer pricing that attempts to approximate optimal prices. Several of these transfer-pricing schemes are described

Table 8.3   **Alternative Transfer Pricing Schemes**

Exchange autonomy	■ Buying and selling division general managers are free to negotiate transfer price without corporate involvement.
	■ Transfer price is set equal to the selling division's price to external customers.
Mandated full cost	■ Transfer price is set equal to the selling division's actual cost of production.
	■ Transfer price is set equal to the selling division's standard cost (i.e., the cost of production if the selling division were operating at maximum efficiency).
Mandated market based	■ Transfer price is set equal to the market price in the selling division's market.
Dual pricing	■ Transfer price for the buying division is set equal to the selling division's actual or standard costs.
	■ Transfer price for the selling division is set equal to the price to external customers or to the market price in the selling division's market.

Source: Eccles R. (1985). *The Transfer Pricing Problem: A Theory for Practice.* Lexington Books: Lexington, MA. Used with permission of Rowman and Littlefield Publishing Group.

in Table 8.3. However, no matter what particular scheme a firm uses, the transfer prices it generates will, at times, create inefficiencies and conflicts in a diversified firm. Some of these inefficiencies and conflicts are described in Table 8.4.[21]

The inefficiencies and conflicts created by transfer-pricing schemes that only approximate optimal transfer prices mean that few diversified firms are ever fully satisfied with how they set transfer prices. Indeed, one study found that as the

Table 8.4   **Weaknesses of Alternative Transfer-Pricing Schemes**

1. Buying and selling divisions negotiate transfer price.
   - ■ What about the negotiating and haggling costs?
   - ■ The corporation risks not exploiting economies of scope if the right transferprice cannot be negotiated.
2. Transfer price is set equal to the selling division's price to external customers.
   - ■ Which customers? Different selling division customers may get different prices.
   - ■ Shouldn't the volume created by the buying division for a selling division be reflected in a lower transfer price?
   - ■ The selling division doesn't have marketing expenses when selling to another division. Shouldn't that be reflected in a lower transfer price?
3. Transfer price is set equal to the selling division's actual costs.
   - ■ What are those actual costs, and who gets to determine them?
   - ■ *All* the selling division's costs, or only the costs relevant to the products being purchased by the buying division?
4. Transfer price is set equal to the selling division's standard costs.
   - ■ Standard costs are the costs the selling division would incur if it were running at maximum efficiency. This hypothetical capacity subsidizes the buying division.
5. Transfer price is set equal to the market price.
   - ■ If the product in question is highly differentiated, there is no simple "market price."
   - ■ Shouldn't the volume created by the buying division for a selling division be reflected in a lower transfer price?
   - ■ The selling division doesn't have marketing expenses when selling to a buying division. Shouldn't that be reflected in a lower transfer price?
6. Transfer price is set equal to actual costs for the selling division and to market price for the buying division.
   - ■ This combination of schemes simply combines other problems of setting transfer prices.

level of resource sharing in a diversified firm increases (thereby increasing the importance of transfer-pricing mechanisms) the level of job satisfaction for division general managers decreases.[22]

It is not unusual for a diversified firm to change its transfer-pricing mechanisms every few years in an attempt to find the "right" transfer-pricing mechanism. Economic theory tells us what the "right" transfer-pricing mechanism is: Transfer prices should equal opportunity cost. However, this "correct" transfer-pricing mechanism cannot be implemented in most firms. Firms that continually change their transfer-pricing mechanisms generally find that all these systems have some weaknesses. In deciding which system to use, a firm should be less concerned about finding the right transfer-pricing mechanism and more concerned about choosing a transfer-pricing policy that creates the fewest management problems—or at least the kinds of problems that the firm can manage effectively. Indeed, some scholars have suggested that the search for optimal transfer pricing should be abandoned in favor of treating transfer pricing as a conflict-resolution process. Viewed in this way, transfer pricing highlights differences between divisions, and thus makes it possible to begin to resolve those differences in a mutually beneficial way.[23]

Overall, the three management control processes described here—measuring divisional performance, allocating corporate capital, and transferring intermediate products—suggest that the implementation of a corporate diversification strategy requires a great deal of management skill and experience. They also suggest that sometimes diversified firms may find themselves operating businesses that no longer fit with the firm's overall corporate strategy. What happens when a division no longer fits with a firm's corporate strategy is described in the Strategy in the Emerging Enterprise feature.

Compensation Policies and Implementing Corporate Diversification

A firm's compensation policies constitute a final set of tools for implementing diversification. Traditionally, the compensation of corporate managers in a diversified firm has been only loosely connected to the firm's economic performance. One important study examined the relationship between executive compensation and firm performance and found that differences in CEO cash compensation (salary plus cash bonus) are not very responsive to differences in firm performance.[24] In particular, this study showed that a CEO of a firm whose equity holders lost, collectively, $400 million in a year earned average cash compensation worth $800,000, while a CEO of a firm whose equity holders gained, collectively, $400 million in a year earned average cash compensation worth $1,040,000. Thus, an $800 million difference in the performance of a firm only had, on average, a $204,000 impact on the size of a CEO's salary and cash bonus. Put differently, for every million dollars of improved firm performance, CEOs, on average, get paid an additional $255. After taxes, increasing a firm's performance by a million dollars is roughly equal in value to a good dinner at a nice restaurant.

However, this same study was able to show that if a substantial percentage of a CEO's compensation came in the form of stock and stock options in the firm, changes in compensation would be closely linked with changes in the firm performance. In particular, the $800 million difference in firm performance just described would be associated with a $1.2 million difference in the value of CEO compensation if CEO compensation included stock and stock options in addition

Strategy in the Emerging Enterprise

A **corporate spin-off** exists when a large, typically diversified firm divests itself of a business in which it has historically been operating and the divested business operates as an independent entity. Thus, corporate spin-offs are different from asset divestitures, where a firm sells some of its assets, including perhaps a particular business, to another firm. Spin-offs are a way that new firms can enter into the economy.

Spin-offs can occur in numerous ways. For example, a business might be sold to its managers and employees who then manage and work in this independently operating firm. Alternatively, a business unit within a diversified firm may be sold to the public through an **initial public offering**, or **IPO**. Sometimes, the corporation spinning a business unit off will retain some ownership stake in the spin-off; other times, this corporation will sever all financial links with the spun-off firm.

In general, large diversified firms might spin off businesses they own for three reasons. First, the efficient management of these businesses may require very specific skills that are not available in a diversified firm. For example, suppose a diversified manufacturing firm finds itself operating in an R&D-intensive industry. The management skills required to manage manufacturing efficiently can be very different from the management skills required to manage R&D. If a diversified firm's skills do not match the skills required in a particular business, that business might be spun off.

Second, anticipated economies of scope between a business and the rest of a diversified firm may turn out to not be valuable. For example, PepsiCo acquired Kentucky Fried Chicken, Pizza Hut, and Taco Bell,

Transforming Big Business into Entrepreneurship

anticipating important marketing synergies between these fast-food restaurants and PepsiCo's soft drink business. Despite numerous efforts to realize these synergies, they were not forthcoming. Indeed, several of these fast-food restaurants began losing market share because they were forced to sell Pepsi rather than Coca-Cola products. After a few years, PepsiCo spun off its restaurants into a separate business.

Finally, it may be necessary to spin a business off in order to fund a firm's other businesses. Large diversified firms may face capital constraints due to, among other things, their high level of debt. In this setting, firms may need to spin off a business in order to raise capital to invest in other parts of the firm. Moreover, spinning off a part of the business that is particularly costly in terms of the capital it consumes may not only be a source of funds for other parts of this firm's business, it

can also reduce the demand for that capital within a firm.

Research in corporate finance suggests that corporations are most likely to spin off businesses that are unrelated to a firm's corporate diversification strategy; those that are poorly performing compared to other businesses a firm operates in; and relatively small businesses. Also, the amount of merger and acquisition activity in a particular industry will determine which businesses are spun off. The greater the level of this activity in an industry, the more likely that a business owned by a corporation in such an industry will be spun off. This is because the level of merger and acquisition activity in an industry is an indicator of the number of people and firms that might be interested in purchasing a spun-off business. However, when there is not much merger and acquisition activity in an industry, businesses in that industry are less likely to be spun off, even if they are unrelated to a firm's corporate diversification strategy, are poorly performing, or small. In such settings, large firms are not likely to obtain the full value associated with spinning off a business and thus are reluctant to do so.

Whatever the conditions that lead a large diversified firm to spin off one of its businesses, this process is important for creating new firms in the economy.

Sources: F. Schlingemann, R. Stulz, and R. Walkling (2002). "Divestitures and the liquidity of the market for corporate assets." *Journal of Financial Economics,* 64, pp. 117–144; G. Hite, J. Owens, and R. Rogers (1987). "The market for inter-firm asset sales: Partial sell-offs and total liquidations." *Journal of Financial Economics,* 18, pp. 229–252; P. Berger and E. Ofek (1999). "Causes and consequences of corporate focusing programs." *Review of Financial Studies,* 12, pp. 311–345.

to cash compensation. In this setting, an additional million dollars of firm performance increases a CEO's salary by $667.

These and similar findings reported elsewhere have led more and more diversified firms to include stock and stock options as part of the compensation package for the CEO. As important, many firms now extend this noncash compensation to other senior managers in a diversified firm, including division general managers. For example, the top 1,300 managers at General Dynamics receive stock and stock options as part of their compensation package. Moreover, the cash bonuses of these managers also depend on General Dynamics' stock market performance. At Johnson & Johnson, all division general managers receive a five-component compensation package. The level of only one of those components, salary, does not vary with the economic profitability of the business over which a division general manager presides. The level of the other four components—a cash bonus, stock grants, stock options, and a deferred income package—varies with the economic performance of a particular division. Moreover, the value of some of these variable components of compensation also depends on Johnson & Johnson's long-term economic performance.[25]

To the extent that compensation in diversified firms gives managers incentives to make decisions consistent with stockholders' interests, they can be an important part of the process of implementing corporate diversification. However, the sheer size of the compensation paid to some CEOs raises ethical issues for some. These ethical issues are discussed in the Ethics and Strategy feature on page 269.

Organizing to Implement Corporate Diversification in an International Context

Because international strategies are really just a special case of corporate diversification strategies, it follows that many of the issues firms face in implementing corporate diversification strategies also exist for firms implementing international strategies. It also follows that many of the organizational tools used to implement corporate diversification strategies can be used to implement international strategies.

Despite these similarities, there are some differences between how corporate diversification within a country and corporate diversification across multiple countries is implemented. Differences in organizational structure, management controls, and compensation policies will all be briefly discussed.

Firms pursuing an international strategy have four basic organizational structural alternatives, which are listed in Table 8.5 and discussed later. Although each of these structures has some special features, they are all special cases of the M-form structure.

Table 8.5 **Structural Options for Firms Pursuing International Strategies**

Decentralized federation	Strategic and operational decisions are delegated to divisions or country companies.
Coordinated federation	Operational decisions are delegated to divisions or country companies; strategic decisions are retained at corporate headquarters.
Centralized hub	Strategic and operational decisions are retained at corporate headquarters.
Transnational structure	Strategic and operational decisions are delegated to those operational entities that maximize responsiveness to local conditions and international integration.

Sources: C. A. Bartlett and S. Ghoshal (1989). *Managing across borders: The transnational solution.* Cambridge, MA: Harvard Business School Press.

Ethics and Strategy

The tag line "What do you have in your wallet?" is from a well-known Capital One advertising campaign. The ad was designed to draw consumer attention to the low interest rates and other benefits of owning a Capital One credit card.

So, who is Richard Fairbank? Richard Fairbank is the CEO of Capital One—and the reason he may be "in your wallet" is that he was the highest paid CEO in the United States in 2005.

At first, this is hard to understand, because Fairbank received zero dollars in salary or bonus in 2005. So how can someone who receives no salary or bonus end up being the highest paid CEO in the country? Stock options, of course. In 2005, Richard Fairbank cashed in stock and stock options valued at $249.42 million. From 2000 to 2005, Faibank's total compensation as CEO at Capital One has been $448.58 million, mostly coming from stock and stock options. That is an average of $89.72 million per year. Assuming that Fairbank worked 50 hours a week and took two weeks of vacation a year, he earned just less than $36,000 per hour over this five-year period. In 2005, Fairbank earned just under $100,000 per hour.

But Fairbank did not have the highest level of compensation from 2000 to 2005. That honor goes to Lawrence J. Ellison, CEO of Oracle. Ellison's total compensation over this five-year period was $868.93 million—an average of $173.79 million per year, or just under $70,000 per hour over a five-year period.

Indeed, the average compensation over the years 2000 to 2005 of the 25 highest paid executives in the

What Do You Have in Your Wallet? Maybe It's Richard Fairbank

United States was $215.84 million, or $43.17 million per year. This is the equivalent of just over $17,000 per hour. To put this in context, in 2005 the median income for U.S. households was around $45,000. This means that these CEOs have to work about 2 hours and 15 minutes to earn as much as the median family in the United States.

These compensation levels would seem more reasonable if CEO compensation was closely tied to firm performance. But this is not always the case. Some of the best-performing CEOs are among the lowest paid. John Bucksbaum, CEO of General Growth Properties, earned only $600,000 per year over the last six years, while his firm generated an average return to investors of 35 percent. Brett Harvey, CEO of Consol Energy, earned only $3.1 million per year over the last six years, while his firm generated an average return to

investors of 42 percent. And Michael McCallister, CEO of Humana, earned only $2.7 million per year over the last six years, while his firm generated an average return to investors of 36 percent.

Some of the worst-performing CEOs are among the best paid. Alain Belda, CEO of Alcoa, averaged $8.5 million in compensation over the last six years, even though his firm averaged only a .3 percent annual return to investors. Paul Curlander, CEO of Lexmark International, averaged $8.9 million in compensation over the last six years, even though his firm averaged only a 15 percent annual return to investors. And Steve Appleton, CEO of Micron, averaged $7.8 million in compensation over the last six years, even though his firm has averaged only 5 percent annual return to investors during his tenure.

Apologists for these high levels of CEO compensation suggest that they simply reflect market forces in the labor market for CEOs. An alternative explanation is that high CEO compensation, especially when it is unrelated to a firm's performance, may reflect more of a CEO's power and influence over a firm's board of directors than any competitive market process. If the latter is true, such levels of CEO compensation may not be consistent with the interests of a firm's equity holders.

Moreover, all of this begs the simple moral question: Is anyone really worth $70,000 per hour?

Sources: www.forbes.com/lists/2006/12; S. Finkelstein and D. C. Hambrick (1996). "Chief executive compensation: A study of the intersection of markets and political processes." *Strategic Management Journal,* 10, pp. 121–134.

Some firms organize their international operations as a **decentralized federation**. In this organizational structure, each country in which a firm operates is organized as a full profit-and-loss division headed by a division general manager who is typically the president of the company in that particular country. In a decentralized federation, there are very few shared activities or other economies of scope among different divisions or country companies; corporate headquarters plays a limited strategic role. Corporate staff functions are generally limited to the collection of accounting and other performance information from divisions or country companies and to reporting this aggregate information to appropriate government officials and to financial markets. Most employees within the divisions or country companies in a decentralized federation may not even be aware that they are part of a larger, internationally diversified firm. Both strategic and operational decision making are delegated to division general managers or country company presidents. There are relatively few examples of pure decentralized federations in today's world economy, but firms such as Nestlé, CIBA-Geigy, and Electrolux have many of the attributes of this type of structure.

A second structural option for international firms is the **coordinated federation**. In a coordinated federation, each country operation is organized as a full profit-and-loss center, and division general managers can be presidents of country companies. However, unlike decentralized federations, strategic and operational decisions are not fully delegated to division general managers. Operational decisions are delegated to division general managers or country presidents, but broader strategic decisions are made at corporate headquarters. Moreover, coordinated federations attempt to exploit various shared activities and other economies of scope among their divisions or country companies. It is not uncommon for coordinated federations to have corporately sponsored central research and development laboratories, corporately sponsored manufacturing and technology development initiatives, and corporately sponsored management training and development operations. There are numerous examples of coordinated federations in today's world economy, including General Electric, General Motors, IBM, and Coca-Cola.

A third structural option for international firms is the **centralized hub**. In centralized hubs, operations in different companies may be organized into profit-and-loss centers, and division general managers may be country company presidents. However, most of the strategic and operational decision making in these firms takes place at the corporate center. The role of divisions or country companies in centralized hubs is simply to implement the strategies, tactics, and policies that have been chosen at headquarters. Of course, divisions or country companies are also a source of information for headquarters staff when these decisions are being made. However, strategic and operational decision rights are retained at the corporate center. Many Japanese and Korean firms, including Toyota, Mitsubishi, and NEC (in Japan) and Goldstar, Daewoo, and Hyundai (in South Korea), are managed as centralized hubs.

A fourth structural option for international firms is the **transnational structure**. This structure is most appropriate for implementing the transnational strategy described in previous chapters. In many ways, the transnational structure is similar to the coordinated federation. In both, strategic decision-making responsibility is largely retained at the corporate center, and operational decision making is largely delegated to division general managers or country presidents. However, important differences also exist.

In a coordinated federation structure, shared activities and other cross-divisional or cross-country economies of scope are managed by the corporate center. Thus, for many of these firms, if research and development is seen as a potentially valuable economy of scope, a central research and development laboratory is created and managed by the corporate center. In the transnational structure, these centers of corporate economies of scope may be managed by the corporate center. However, they are more likely to be managed by specific divisions or country companies within the corporation. Thus, for example, if one division or country company develops valuable, rare, and costly-to-imitate research and development capabilities in its ongoing business activities in a particular country, that division or country company could become the center of research and development activity for the entire corporation. If one division or country company develops valuable, rare, and costly-to-imitate manufacturing technology development skills in its ongoing business activities in a particular country, that division or country company could become the center for manufacturing technology development for the entire corporation.

The role of corporate headquarters in a transnational structure is to constantly scan business operations across different countries for resources and capabilities that might be a source of competitive advantage for other divisions or country companies in the firm. Once these special skills are located, corporate staff must then determine the best way to exploit these economies of scope—whether they should be developed within a single division or country company (to gain economies of scale) and then transferred to other divisions or country companies, or developed through an alliance between two or more divisions or country companies (to gain economies of scale) and then transferred to other divisions or country companies, or redeveloped for the entire firm at corporate headquarters. These options are not available to decentralized federations (which always allow individual divisions or country companies to develop their own competencies), coordinated federations, or centralized hubs (which always develop corporate-wide economies of scope at the corporate level). Firms that have been successful in adopting this transnational structure include Ford (Ford Europe has become a leader for automobile design in all of the Ford Motor Company) and Ericsson (Ericsson's Australian subsidiary developed this Swedish company's first electronic telecommunication switch, and corporate headquarters was able to help transfer this technology to other Ericsson subsidiaries).

It should be clear that the choice among these four approaches to managing international strategies depends on the trade-offs that firms are willing to make between local responsiveness and international integration (see Figure 8.3). Firms that seek to maximize their local responsiveness will tend to choose a decentralized federation structure. Firms that seek to maximize international integration in their

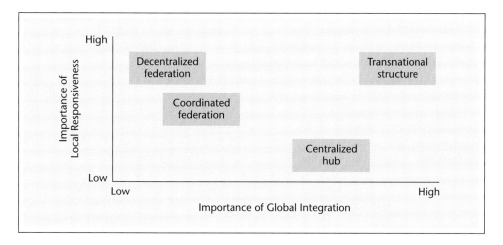

Figure 8.3 Local Responsiveness, International Integration, and Organizational Structure

Sources: From R. Grant, *Contemporary Strategy Analysis,* (1991). Cambridge, MA: Basil Blackwell. Used with permission of Blackwell Publishing.

operations will typically opt for centralized hub structures. Firms that seek to balance the need for local responsiveness and international integration will typically choose centralized federations. Firms that attempt to optimize both local responsiveness and international integration will choose a transnational organizational structure.

Of course, none of the organizational structures described in Table 8.5 can stand alone without the support of a variety of management control systems and management compensation policies. All the management control processes discussed previously, including evaluating the performance of divisions, allocating capital, and managing the exchange of intermediate products among divisions, are also important for firms organizing to implement an international strategy. Moreover, the same management compensation challenges and opportunities discussed previously apply in the organization of international strategies as well.

However, as is often the case when organizing processes originally developed to manage diversification within a domestic market are extended to the management of international diversification, many of the management challenges highlighted earlier in this chapter are exacerbated in an international context. This puts an even greater burden on senior managers in an internationally diversified firm to choose control systems and compensation policies that create incentives for division general managers or country presidents to appropriately cooperate to realize the economies of scope that originally motivated the implementation of an international strategy.

SUMMARY

To be valuable, diversification strategies must exploit valuable economies of scope that cannot be duplicated by outside investors at low cost. However, to realize the value of these economies of scope, firms must organize themselves appropriately. A firm's organizational structure, its management control processes, and its compensation policies are all relevant in implementing a corporate diversification strategy.

The best organizational structure for implementing a diversification leveraging strategy is the multidivisional, or M-form, structure. The M-form structure has several critical components, including the board of directors, institutional investors, the senior executive, corporate staff, division general managers, and shared activity managers.

This organizational structure is supported by a variety of management control processes. Three critical management control processes for firms implementing diversification strategies are (1) evaluating the performance of divisions, (2) allocating capital across divisions, and (3) transferring intermediate products between divisions. The existence of economies of scope in firms implementing corporate diversification strategies significantly complicates the management of these processes.

Finally, a firm's compensation policies are also important for firms implementing a diversification strategy. Historically, management compensation has been only loosely connected to a firm's economic performance, but the last few years have seen the increased popularity of using stock and stock options to help compensate managers. Such compensation schemes help reduce conflicts between managers and outside investors, but the absolute level of CEO compensation is still very high, at least in the United States.

These same implementation issues exist for firms looking to diversify their operations internationally. In this international context, firms can choose between a decentralized federation, a coordinated federation, a centralized hub, and a transnational organizational structure. The effectiveness of these different approaches depends on the relative importance of local responsiveness and global integration.

CHALLENGE QUESTIONS

1. Agency theory has been criticized for assuming that managers, left on their own, will behave in ways that reduce the wealth of outside equity holders when, in fact, most managers are highly responsible stewards of the assets they control. This alternative view of managers has been called *stewardship theory.* Do you agree with this criticism of agency theory? Why or why not?

2. Suppose that the concept of the stewardship theory is correct and that most managers, most of the time, behave responsibly and make decisions that maximize the present value of the assets they control. What implications, if any, would this supposition have on organizing to implement diversification strategies?

3. The M-form structure enables firms to pursue complex corporate diversification strategies by delegating different management responsibilities to different individuals and groups within a firm. Will there come a time when a firm becomes too large and too complex to be managed even through an M-form structure? In other words, is there a natural limit to the efficient size of a diversified firm?

4. Most observers agree that centrally planned economies fail because it is impossible for bureaucrats in large government hierarchies to coordinate different sectors of an economy as efficiently as market mechanisms do. Many diversified firms, however, are as large as some economies and use private sector hierarchies to coordinate diverse business activities in a firm. Are these large, private sector hierarchies somehow different from the government hierarchies of centrally planned economies? If yes, in what way? If no, why do these large, private sector hierarchies continue to exist?

5. Suppose that the optimal transfer price between one business and all other business activities in a firm is the market price. What does this condition say about whether this firm should own this business?

6. Suppose a firm pursuing an international diversification strategy requires neither local responsiveness nor global integration to realize valuable economies of scope that cannot be duplicated by outside equity holders at low cost. What type of organizational structure should this firm pursue?

PROBLEM SET

1. Which elements of the M-form structure (the board of directors, the office of the CEO, corporate staff, division general managers, shared activity managers) should be involved in the following business activities? If more than one of these groups should be involved, indicate their relative level of involvement (e.g., 20% office of the CEO, 10% shared activity manager, 70% division general manager). Justify your answers.

(a) Determining the compensation of the CEO
(b) Determining the compensation of the Corporate Vice President of Human Resources
(c) Determining the compensation of a Vice President of Human Resources in a particular business division
(d) Deciding to sell a business division
(e) Deciding to buy a relatively small firm whose activities are closely related to the activities of one of the firm's current divisions
(f) Deciding to buy a larger firm that is not closely related to the activities of any of a firm's current divisions
(g) Evaluating the performance of the Vice President of Sales, a manager whose sales staff sells the products of three divisions in the firm
(h) Evaluating the performance of the Vice President of Sales, a manager whose sales staff sells the products of only one division in the firm
(i) Determining how much money to invest in a corporate R&D function
(j) Deciding how much money to invest in an R&D function that supports the operations of two divisions within the firm
(k) Deciding whether to fire an R&D scientist

(l) Deciding whether to fire the Vice President of Accounting in a particular division

(m) Deciding whether to fire the corporation's Vice President of Accounting

(n) Deciding whether to take a firm public by selling stock in the firm to the general public for the first time

2. Consider the following facts. Division A in a firm has generated $847,000 of profits on $24 million worth of sales, using $32 million worth of dedicated assets. The cost of capital for this firm is 9 percent, and the firm has invested $7.3 million in this division.

(a) Calculate the ROS and ROA of Division A. If the hurdle rates for ROS and ROA in this firm are, respectively, .06 and .04, has this division performed well?

(b) Calculate the EVA of Division A (assuming that the reported profits have already been adjusted). Based on this EVA, has this division performed well?

(c) Suppose you were CEO of this firm, how would you choose between ROS/ROA and EVA for evaluating this division?

3. Suppose that Division A sells an intermediate product to Division B. Choose one of the ways of determining transfer prices described in this chapter (not setting transfer prices equal to the selling firm's opportunity costs) and show how Division Manager A can use this mechanism to justify a higher transfer price while Division Manager B can use this mechanism to justify a lower transfer price. Repeat this exercise with another approach to setting transfer prices described in the chapter.

END NOTES

1. The structure and function of the multidimensional firm was first described by Chandler, A. (1962). *Strategy and structure: Chapters in the history of the industrial enterprise.* Cambridge, MA: MIT Press; The economic logic underlying the multidimensional firm was first described by Williamson, O. E. (1975). *Markets and hierarchies: Analysis and antitrust implications.* New York: Free Press; Empirical examinations of the impact of the M-form or firm performance include Armour, H. O., and D. J. Teece (1980). "Vertical integration and technological innovation." *Review of Economics and Statistics,* 60, pp. 470–474; There continues to be some debate about the efficiency of the M-form structure. See Freeland, R. F. (1966). "The myth of the M-form? Governance, consent, and organizational change." *American Journal of Sociology,* 102(2), pp. 483–626; and Shanley, M. (1996). "Straw men and M-form myths: Comment on Freeland." *American Journal of Sociology,* 102(2), pp. 527–536.

2. See Finkelstein, S., and R. D'Aveni (1994). "CEO duality as a double-edged sword: How boards of directors balance entrenchment avoidance and unity of command." *Academy of Management Journal,* 37, pp. 1079–1108.

3. Kesner, I. F. (1988). "Director's characteristics and committee membership: An investigation of type, occupation, tenure and gender." *Academy of Management Journal,* 31, pp. 66–84; Zahra, S. A., and J. A. Pearce II (1989). "Boards of directors and corporate financial performance: A review and integrative model." *Journal of Management,* 15, pp. 291–334.

4. *Investor Relations Business* (2000). "Reversal of fortune: Institutional ownership is declining," May 1, pp. 8–9; Federal Reserve Board (2006). "Flow of funds report." www.corpgov.net.

5. See Hansen, G. S., and C. W. L. Hill (1991). "Are institutional investors myopic? A time-series study of four technology-driven industries." *Strategic Management Journal,* 12, pp. 1–16.

6. See Bergh, D. (1995). "Size and relatedness of units sold: An agency theory and resource-based perspective." *Strategic Management Journal,* 16, pp. 221–239; and Bethel, J., and J. Liebeskind (1993). "The effects of ownership structure on corporate restructuring." *Strategic Management Journal,* 14, pp. 15–31.

7. Burdens that are well described by Westley, F., and H. Mintzberg (1989). "Visionary leadership and strategic management." *Strategic Management Journal,* 10, pp. 17–32.

8. See Dumaine, B. (1992). "Is big still good?" *Fortune,* April 20, pp. 50–60.

9. See Golden, B. (1992). "SBU strategy and performance: The moderating effects of the corporate–SBU relationship." *Strategic Management Journal,* 13, pp. 145–158; Berger, P., and E. Ofek (1995). "Diversification effect on firm value." *Journal of Financial Economics,* 37, pp. 36–65; Lang, H. P., and R. Stulz (1994). "Tobin's *q,* corporate diversification, and firm performance." *Journal of Political Economy,* 102, pp. 1248–1280; Rumelt, R. (1991). "How much does industry matter?" *Strategic Management Journal,* 12, pp. 167–185.

10. See Halal, W. (1994). "From hierarchy to enterprise: Internal markets are the new foundation of management." *The Academy of Management Executive,* 8(4), pp. 69–83.

11. Bartlett, C., and S. Ghoshal (1993). "Beyond the M-form: Toward a managerial theory of the firm." *Strategic Management Journal,* 14, pp. 23–46.

12. See Simons, R. (1994). "How new top managers use control systems as levers of strategic renewal." *Strategic Management Journal,* 15, pp. 169–189.

13. Bethel, J. E. (1990). "The capital allocation process and managerial mobility: A theoretical and empirical investigation." Unpublished doctoral dissertation, UCLA.

14. Some of these are described in Duffy, M. (1989). "ZBB, MBO, PPB, and their effectiveness within the planning/marketing process." *Strategic Management Journal,* 12, pp. 155–160.

15. See Stern, J., B. Stewart, and D. Chew (1995). "The EVA financial management system." *Journal of Applied Corporate Finance,* 8, pp. 32–46; and Tully, S. (1993). "The real key to creating wealth." *Fortune,* September 20, pp. 38–50.

16. Applications of EVA are described in Tully, S. (1993). "The real key to creating wealth." *Fortune,* September 20, pp. 38–50; Tully, S. (1995). "So, Mr. Bossidy, we know you can cut. Now show us how to grow." *Fortune,* August 21, pp. 70–80; Tully, S. (1995). "Can EVA deliver profits to the post office?" *Fortune,* July 10, p. 22.

17. A special issue of the *Journal of Applied Corporate Finance* in 1994 addressed many of these issues.

18. See Priem, R. (1990). "Top management team group factors, consensus, and firm performance." *Strategic Management Journal,* 11, pp. 469–478; and Wooldridge, B., and S. Floyd (1990). "The strategy process, middle

management involvement, and organizational performance." *Strategic Management Journal*, 11, pp. 231–241.

19. A point made by Westley, F. (1900). "Middle managers and strategy: Microdynamics of inclusion." *Strategic Management Journal*, 11, pp. 337–351; Lamont, O. (1997). "Cash flow and investment: Evidence from internal capital markets." *The Journal of Finance*. 52(1), pp. 83–109; Shin, H. H., and R. M. Stulz (1998). "Are internal capital markets efficient?" *Quarterly Journal of Economics*, May, pp. 531–552; and Stein, J. C. (1997). "Internal capital markets and the competition for corporate resources." *The Journal of Finance*, 52(1), pp. 111–133.

20. See Brickley, J., C. Smith, and J. Zimmerman (1996). *Organizational architecture and managerial economics approach*. Homewood, IL: Irwin; and Eccles, R. (1985). *The transfer pricing problem: A theory for practice*. Lexington, MA: Lexington Books.

21. See Cyert, R., and J. G. March (1963). *A behavioral theory of the firm*. Upper Saddle River, NJ: Prentice Hall; Swieringa, R. J., and J. H. Waterhouse (1982). "Organizational views of transfer pricing."

Accounting, Organizations & Society, 7(2), pp. 149–165; and Eccles, R. (1985). *The transfer pricing problem: A theory for practice*. Lexington, MA: Lexington Books.

22. Gupta, A. K., and V. Govindarajan (1986). "Resource sharing among SBUs: Strategic antecedents and administrative implications." *Academy of Management Journal*, 29, pp. 695–714.

23. A point made by Swieringa, R. J., and J. H. Waterhouse (1982). "Organizational views of transfer pricing." *Accounting, Organizations and Society*, 7(2), pp. 149–165.

24. Jensen, M. C., and K. J. Murphy (1990). "Performance pay and top management incentives." *Journal of Political Economy*, 98, pp. 225–264.

25. See Dial, J., and K. J. Murphy (1995). "Incentive, downsizing, and value creation at General Dynamics." *Journal of Financial Economics*, 37, pp. 261–314, on General Dynamics' compensation scheme, and Aguilar, F. J., and A. Bhambri (1983). "Johnson & Johnson (A)." Harvard Business School Case No. 9-384-053, on Johnson & Johnson's compensation scheme.

Strategic Alliances

LEARNING OBJECTIVES

After reading this chapter, you should be able to:

1. Define a strategic alliance and give three specific examples of strategic alliances.

2. Describe nine different ways that alliances can create value for firms and how these nine sources of value can be grouped into three large categories.

3. Describe how adverse selection, moral hazard, and hold-up can threaten the ability of alliances to generate value.

4. Describe the conditions under which a strategic alliance can be rare and costly to duplicate.

5. Describe the conditions under which "going it alone" and acquisitions are not likely to be substitutes for alliances.

6. Describe how contracts, equity investments, firm reputations, joint ventures, and trust can all reduce the threat of cheating in strategic alliances.

7. Describe the role of strategic alliances in an international context.

A 40-Year-Old Skater?

He was born in Carlsbad, California. He started skateboarding at age 9, entered his first competition at 11, turned pro at 14, and won the world vertical skateboarding championship at 15. He was ranked number one in the world in vertical skating for 12 years in a row. Although he pioneered several tricks, he is best known for being the first to land a 900 (two and a half complete revolutions in the air off a steeply banked ramp called a "half pipe"). His name is Tony Hawk, and he is still is among the most popular skateboarders in the world. An editor for a teen-oriented movie recently said of him, "Anyone who doesn't know Tony Hawk lives in a cave."

And he will be turning 40 shortly (he was born in 1968).

So, how does a man in his forties with three children continue to appeal to teenage skateboarders? As important, how does he continue to appeal to these kids parents, who, after all, shell out most of the money to buy their kids Tony Hawk stuff?

The key, according to Pat Hawk, Tony's sister and chief operating officer of Tony Hawk, Inc., is to form alliances with companies and products that reinforce his image as a top skater without appearing to sell out to big corporate interests. So far, this balancing act has been working; Hawk's endorsements have been generating between $5 million and $7 million per year.

Hawk's first alliance was with Activision, to endorse, and help improve, the first skateboarding video game, *Tony Hawk's Pro Skater*, originally published in 1999. By 2000, this video game was outselling traditional video game bestsellers such as *Madden* and *Mario*. Tony worked closely with Activision to improve the feel and play of the video game, ensuring that it came as close as possible to duplicating the experience of the sport. This is ironic, because over 75 percent of those who play Hawk's video game don't even own a skateboard.

Since 2000, Tony has lent his name and legend to several other projects, all of which reinforce his image as a great skateboarder—for the kids—and a good guy—for their parents. In addition to working with Activision to bring out new editions of his video games (Hawk recently extended his contract with Activision to 2015), Hawk has partnered with Sirius on a weekly radio show, with Six Flags, Inc. on Tony Hawk attractions in many of this firm's theme parks, with a mobile phone company to provide Tony Hawk–inspired ring tones, and with independent movie producers to release a direct-to-DVD movie titled *Boom Boom Sabotage*. He has also cooperated with other skaters and bikers to produce a traveling skateboarding and biking extravaganza called *Boom Boom Huckjam*, a show that features skateboarders, inline skaters, bikers, and motorcyclists flying through the air off huge ramps, flipping, twirling, and spinning, all accompanied by a heavy back beat of loud rock music. Very cool!

All the while, Tony has been able to resist endorsement relations that might put his image at risk. For example, Tony has yet to sign with Nike or any other big shoe company. A natural endorsement, Tony apparently feels that such an alliance would be too corporate for his teenage following, too much of a sellout.

However, a couple of Tony's alliances seem to put some of his coolness at risk. For example, Tony Hawk, Inc. recently signed an agreement with Kohl's—a family-oriented clothing store—to distribute Tony Hawk clothing. Kohl's? Tony's fans don't shop at Kohl's; their mothers do. Also, it is now possible to buy the Tony Hawk birthday collection—paper cups and plates with pictures of Tony Hawk doing various skateboarding tricks. Just how cool is that?

Despite the few examples to the contrary, Tony Hawk has been able to develop alliances with products and companies that reinforce his personal brand both with his teenage following and their parents. Not bad for a guy who is old enough to be these kids' father.

Sources: M. Hyman (2006). "How Tony Hawk stays aloft." *BusinessWeek*, November 13, pp. 84–87; www.tonyhawk.com.

Tony Hawk's work with other companies to build and exploit his image in skateboarding is an example of using strategic alliance to implement a corporate strategy. The use of strategic alliances to manage economic exchanges has grown substantially over the last several years. In the early 1990s, strategic alliances were relatively uncommon, except in a few industries—including the entertainment industry. However, by the late 1990s they had become much more common in a wide variety of industries. Indeed, over 20,000 alliances were created worldwide in 2000 and 2001. In the computer-technology–based industries, over 2,200 alliances were created between 2001 and 2005. And in 2006, both General Motors and Ford were considering alliances as a way to help solve their economic problems.[1]

What Is a Strategic Alliance?

A **strategic alliance** exists whenever two or more independent organizations cooperate in the development, manufacture, or sale of products or services. As shown in Figure 9.1, strategic alliances can be grouped into three broad categories: nonequity alliances, equity alliances, and joint ventures.

In a **nonequity alliance**, cooperating firms agree to work together to develop, manufacture, or sell products or services, but they do not take equity positions in each other or form an independent organizational unit to manage their cooperative efforts. Rather, these cooperative relations are managed through the use of various contracts. **Licensing agreements** (where one firm allows others to use its brand name to sell products), **supply agreements** (where one firm agrees to supply others), and **distribution agreements** (where one firm agrees to distribute the products of others) are examples of nonequity strategic alliances. Most of the alliances between Tony Hawk and his partners take the form of nonequity licensing agreements.

In an **equity alliance**, cooperating firms supplement contracts with equity holdings in alliance partners. For example, when General Motors began importing

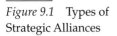

Figure 9.1 Types of Strategic Alliances

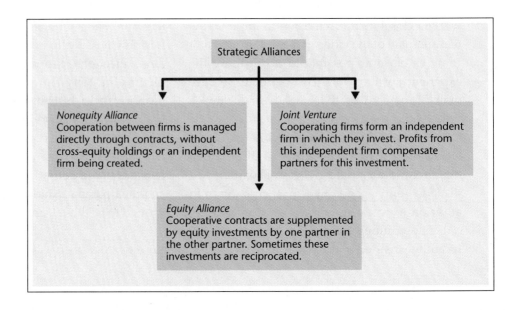

Strategic Alliances

Nonequity Alliance
Cooperation between firms is managed directly through contracts, without cross-equity holdings or an independent firm being created.

Joint Venture
Cooperating firms form an independent firm in which they invest. Profits from this independent firm compensate partners for this investment.

Equity Alliance
Cooperative contracts are supplemented by equity investments by one partner in the other partner. Sometimes these investments are reciprocated.

small cars manufactured by Isuzu, not only did these partners have supply contracts in place, but GM purchased 34.2 percent of Isuzu's stock. Ford had a similar relationship with Mazda, and DaimlerChrysler had a similar relationship with Mitsubishi.[2] Equity alliances are also very common in the biotechnology industry. Large pharmaceutical firms such as Pfizer and Merck own equity positions in several start-up biotechnology companies.

In a **joint venture**, cooperating firms create a legally independent firm in which they invest and from which they share any profits that are created. Some of these joint ventures can be very large. For example, Dow and Corning's joint venture, Dow-Corning, is a Fortune 500 company on its own. AT&T and BellSouth are co-owners of the joint venture Cingular, one of the largest wireless phone companies in the United States—AT&T owns 60 percent of this joint venture; BellSouth owns 40 percent. And CFM—a joint venture between General Electric and SNECMA (a French Aerospace firm)—is one of the world's leading manufacturers of jet engines for commercial aircraft. If you have ever flown on a Boeing 737, then you have placed your life in the hands of this joint venture, because it manufactures the engines for virtually all of these aircraft.

How Do Strategic Alliances Create Value?

V R I O

Like all the strategies discussed in this book, strategic alliances create value by exploiting opportunities and neutralizing threats facing a firm. Some of the most important opportunities that can be exploited by strategic alliances are listed in Table 9.1. Threats to strategic alliances are discussed later in this chapter.

Strategic Alliance Opportunities

Opportunities associated with strategic alliances fall into three large categories. First, these alliances can be used by a firm to improve the performance of its current operations. Second, alliances can be used to create a competitive environment favorable to superior firm performance. Finally, they can be used to facilitate a firm's entry into or exit from new markets or industries.

Table 9.1 **Ways Strategic Alliances Can Create Economic Value**

Helping firms improve the performance of their current operations
1. Exploiting economies of scale
2. Learning from competitors
3. Managing risk and sharing costs

Creating a competitive environment favorable to superior performance
4. Facilitating the development of technology standards
5. Facilitating tacit collusion

Facilitating entry and exit
6. Low-cost entry into new industries and new industry segments
7. Low-cost exit from industries and industry segments
8. Managing uncertainty
9. Low-cost entry into new markets

Improving Current Operations

One way that firms can use strategic alliances to improve their current operations is to use alliances to realize economies of scale. The concept of economies of scale was first introduced in Chapter 2. **Economies of scale** exist when the per-unit cost of production falls as the volume of production increases. Thus, for example, although the per-unit cost of producing one Bic pen is very high, the per-unit costs of producing 50 million Bic pens is very low.

To realize economies of scale, firms have to have a large volume of production, or at least a volume of production large enough so that the cost advantages associated with scale can be realized. Sometimes—as was described in Chapters 2 and 4—a firm can realize these economies of scale by itself; other times, it cannot. When a firm cannot realize the cost savings from economies of scale all by itself, it may join in a strategic alliance with other firms. Jointly, these firms may have sufficient volume to be able to gain the cost advantages of economies of scale.

But, why wouldn't a firm be able to realize these economies all by itself? A firm may have to turn to alliance partners to help realize economies of scale for a number of reasons. For example, if the volume of production required to realize these economies is very large, a single firm might have to dominate an entire industry in order to obtain these advantages. It is often very difficult for a single firm to obtain such a dominant position in an industry. And even if it does so, it may be subject to anti-monopoly regulation by the government. Also, although a particular part or technology may be very important to several firms, no one firm may generate sufficient demand for this part or technology to realize economies of scale in its development and production. In this setting as well, independent firms may join together to form an alliance to realize economies of scale in the development and production of the part or technology.

Firms can also use alliances to improve their current operations by learning from their competitors. As suggested in Chapter 3, different firms in an industry may have different resources and capabilities. These resources can give some firms competitive advantages over others. Firms that are at a competitive disadvantage may want to form alliances with the firms that have an advantage in order to learn about their resources and capabilities.

General Motors formed this kind of alliance with Toyota. In the early 1990s, GM and Toyota jointly invested in a previously closed General Motors plant in Fremont, California. This joint venture—called NUMI—was to build compact cars to be distributed through GM's distribution network. But why did GM decide to build these cars in an alliance with Toyota? Obviously, it could have built them in any of its own plants. However, GM was very interested in learning about how Toyota was able to manufacture high-quality small cars at a profit. Indeed, in the NUMI plant, Toyota agreed to take total responsibility for the manufacturing process, using former General Motors employees to install and operate the "lean manufacturing" system that had enabled Toyota to become the quality leader in the small-car segment of the automobile industry. However, Toyota also agreed to let GM managers work in the plant and directly observe how Toyota managed this production process. Since its inception, GM has rotated thousands of its managers from other GM plants through the NUMI plant so that they can be exposed to Toyota's lean manufacturing methods.

It is clear why GM would want this alliance with Toyota. But why would Toyota want this alliance with GM? Certainly, Toyota was not looking to learn about lean manufacturing, per se. However, because Toyota was contemplating entering the United States by building its own manufacturing facilities, it did need to learn how to implement lean manufacturing in the United States with U.S. employees. Thus, Toyota also had something to learn from this alliance.

When both parties to an alliance are seeking to learn something from that alliance, an interesting dynamic called a *learning race* can evolve. This dynamic is described in more detail in the Strategy in Depth feature.

Finally, firms can use alliances to improve their current operations through sharing costs and risks. For example, HBO produces most of its original programs in alliances with independent producers. Most of these alliances are created to share costs and risks. Producing new television shows can be costly. Development and production costs can run into the hundreds of millions of dollars, especially for long and complicated series like HBO's *Deadwood, Entourage, and The Sopranos*. And, despite audience testing and careful market analyses, the production of these new shows is also very risky. Even bankable stars like Dustin Hoffman and Warren Beatty and Ben Affleck and Jennifer Lopez—remember *Gigli*?—cannot guarantee success.

In this context, it is not surprising that HBO decides to not "go it alone" in its production efforts. If HBO was to be the sole producer of its original programming, not only would it have to absorb all the production costs, but it would also bear all the risk if a production turned out not to be successful. Of course, by getting other firms involved in its production efforts, HBO also has to share whatever profits a particular production generates. Apparently, HBO has concluded that sharing this upside potential is more than compensated for by sharing the costs and risks of these productions.

Creating a Favorable Competitive Environment

Firms can also use strategic alliances to create a competitive environment that is more conducive to superior performance. This can be done in at least two ways. First, firms can use alliances to help set technology standards in an industry. With these standards in place, technology-based products can be developed and consumers can be confident that the products they buy will be useful for some time to come.

Such technologic standards are particularly important in what are called **network industries**. Such industries are characterized by **increasing returns to scale**. Consider, for example, fax machines. How valuable is one fax machine, all by itself? Obviously, not very valuable. Two fax machines that can talk to each other are a little more valuable, three that can talk to each other are still more valuable, and so forth. The value of each individual fax machine depends on the total number of fax machines that can talk to each other that are in operation. This is what is meant by increasing returns to scale—the value (or returns) on each product increases as the number of these products (or scale) increases.

If there are 100 million fax machines in operation but none of these machines can talk to each other, none of these machines has any value whatsoever—except as a large paper weight. For their full value to be realized, they must be able to talk to each other. And to talk to each other, they must all adopt the same—or at least compatible—communication standards. This is why setting technology standards is so important in network industries.

Standards can be set in two ways. First, different firms can introduce different standards, and consumers can decide which they prefer. This is how the standard for home videotapes was set. Sony sold one type of videotape machine—the Betamax—and Matsushita sold a second type of videotape machine—VHS. These

Strategy in Depth

A **learning race** exists in a strategic alliance when both parties to that alliance seek to learn from each other but the rate at which these two firms learn varies. In this setting, the first firm to learn what it wants to learn from an alliance has the option to begin to underinvest in, and perhaps even withdraw from, an alliance. In this way, the firm that learns the fastest is able to prevent the slow-learning firm from learning all it wanted from an alliance. If, outside of this alliance, these firms are competitors, winning a learning race can create a sustained competitive advantage for the fast-learning firm over the slow-learning firm.

Firms in an alliance may vary in the rate they learn from each other for a variety of reasons. First, they may be looking to learn different things, some of which are easier to learn than others. For example, in the GM–Toyota example, GM wanted to learn about how to use "lean manufacturing" to build high-quality small cars profitably. Toyota wanted to learn how to apply the "lean manufacturing" skills it already possessed in the United States. Which of these is easier to learn— "lean manufacturing" or how to apply "lean manufacturing" in the United States?

An argument can be made that GM's learning task was much more complicated than Toyota's. At the very least, in order for GM to apply knowledge about "lean manufacturing" gleaned from Toyota it would have to transfer that knowledge to several of its currently operating plants. Using this knowledge would require these plants to change their current operations—a difficult and time-consuming process. Toyota, however, only had to

Winning Learning Races

transfer its knowledge of how to operate a "lean manufacturing" operation in the United States to its other U.S. plants—plants that at the time this alliance was first created had yet to be built. Because GM's learning task was more complicated than Toyota's, it is very likely that Toyota's rate of learning was greater than GM's.

Second, firms may differ in terms of their ability to learn. This ability has been called a firm's **absorptive capacity**. Firms with high levels of absorptive capacity will learn at faster rates than firms with low levels of absorptive capacity, even if these two firms are trying to learn exactly the same things in an alliance. Absorptive capacity has been shown to be an important organizational capability in a wide variety of settings.

Third, firms can engage in activities to try to slow the rate of learning of their alliance partners. For example, although a firm might make its technology available to an alliance partner—thereby fulfilling the alliance agreement—it may not provide all the

know-how necessary to exploit this technology. This can slow a partner's learning. Also, a firm might withhold critical employees from an alliance, thereby slowing the learning of an alliance partner. All these actions, to the extent that they slow the rate of a partner's learning without also slowing the rate at which the firm engaging in these activities learns, can help this firm win a learning race.

Although learning race dynamics have been described in a wide variety of settings, they are particularly common in relations between entrepreneurial and large firms. In these alliances, entrepreneurial firms are often looking to learn about all the managerial functions required to bring a product to market, including manufacturing, sales, distribution, and so forth. This is a difficult learning task. Large firms in these alliances often are only looking to learn about the entrepreneurial firm's technology. This is a less difficult learning task. Because the learning task facing entrepreneurial firms is more challenging than that facing their large-firm partners, larger firms in these alliances typically win the learning race. Once these large firms learn what they want from their alliance partners, they often underinvest or even withdraw from these alliances. This is why, in one study, almost 80 percent of the managers in entrepreneurial firms felt unfairly exploited by their large-firm alliance partners.

Sources: S. A. Alvarez and J. B. Barney (2001). "How entrepreneurial firms can benefit from alliances with large partners." *Academy of Management Executive*, 15, pp. 139–148; G. Hamel (1991). "Competition for competence and inter-partner learning within international alliances." *Strategic Management Journal*, 12, pp. 83–103; W. Cohen and D. Levinthal (1990). "Absorptive capacity: A new perspective on learning and innovation." *Administrative Science Quarterly*, 35, pp. 128–152.

two technologies were incompatible. Some consumers preferred Beta and purchased Sony's technology. Others preferred VHS and bought Matsushita's technology. However, because Matsushita licensed its VHS technology to numerous other firms, whereas Sony refused to do so, more and more consumers started buying VHS machines, until VHS became the de facto standard. This was the case even though most observers agreed that Beta was superior to VHS on several dimensions.

Of course, the biggest problem with letting customers and competition set technology standards is that customers may end up purchasing technologies that are incompatible with the standard that is ultimately set in the industry. What about all those consumers who purchased Beta products? For this reason, customers may be unwilling to invest in a new technology until the standards of that technology are established.

This is where strategic alliances come in. Sometimes, firms form strategic alliances with the sole purpose of evaluating and then choosing a technology standard. With such a standard in place, technologies can be turned into products that customers are likely to be more willing to purchase, because they know that they will be compatible with industry standards for at least some period of time. Thus, in this setting strategic alliances can be used to create a more favorable competitive environment.

Such alliances have been important in setting standards in a wide variety of industries, including the mobile telephone industry. The history of standard-setting in this industry, and how it has affected competition in the mobile phone industry around the world, is described in the Global Perspectives feature.

Another incentive for cooperating in strategic alliances is that such activities may facilitate the development of tacit collusion. As explained in Chapter 3, **collusion** exists when two or more firms in an industry coordinate their strategic choices to reduce competition in an industry. This reduction in competition usually makes it easier for colluding firms to earn high levels of performance. A common example of collusion is when firms cooperate to reduce the quantity of products being produced in an industry in order to drive prices up. **Explicit collusion** exists when firms directly communicate with each other to coordinate their levels of production, their prices, and so forth. Explicit collusion is illegal in most countries.

Because managers that engage in explicit collusion can end up in jail, most collusion must be tacit in character. **Tacit collusion** exists when firms coordinate their production and pricing decisions, not by directly communicating with each other, but by exchanging signals with other firms about their intent to cooperate. Examples of such signals might include public announcements about price increases, public announcements about reductions in a firm's productive output, public announcements about decisions not to pursue a new technology, and so forth.

Sometimes, signals of intent to collude are very ambiguous. For example, when firms in an industry do not reduce their prices in response to a decrease in demand, they may be sending a signal that they want to collude, or they may be attempting to exploit their product differentiation to maintain high margins. When firms do not reduce their prices in response to reduced supply costs, they may be sending a signal that they want to collude, or they may be individually maximizing their economic performance. In both these cases, a firm's intent to collude or not, as implied by its activities, is ambiguous at best.

Global Perspectives

The mobile telephone industry is a classic example of a network industry—that is, an industry with increasing returns to scale where standards are important. The more people who own mobile phones that can talk to each other, the more valuable those mobile phones are. Because of the role that standards play in realizing these increasing returns to scale, standard-setting has been an important determinant of competition in the mobile phone industry around the world.

However, this standard-setting process has been anything but smooth; nor has there been agreement about what the technological standard in the industry should be. Although alliances can facilitate the creation of standards, sometimes sets of competing alliances can make it more difficult, not less difficult, to create a standard for an entire industry. This has been the case in the worldwide mobile telecommunications industry.

The first round of technical standards in mobile telephones was developed in the early 1980s. In the United States, the federal government adopted Ameritech's AMPS standard and required all mobile phone operators to use this analogue system. In Europe, two analogue standards emerged: NMT-450, developed by an alliance between Ericsson and Nokia, dominant in the Scandinavian countries and much of continental Europe, and TACS, developed by an alliance between Vodaphone and Cellnet for operations in the United Kingdom and Italy. Many mobile phones operating in the United Kingdom still use

Can You Hear Me Now?

the TACS standard. And in Japan, two additional analogue standards were created—NTT, created by Nippon Telephone and Telegraph, and JTACS, created by an alliance that involved Toyota Motor Corporation. None of these standards were compatible with each other. For example, a person with a phone that operated on the NMT-450 standard could not talk to a person with a phone operating on the AMPS standard.

The emergence of digital technology in the late 1980s led to a new round of standard-setting. In the United States, several potential standards were allowed to compete. The two dominant competing digital standards in the United States were TDMA and CDMA. In Europe, an alliance among all the major mobile phone companies, with government support, developed a single pan-European standard known as

GSM—Global System for Mobile Communication. In Japan, two competing digital standards emerged: PDC, supported by an alliance that included Nissan Motors, and PHS, a system that relies on a dense network of antennas, each with a very restricted range, to provide mobile telephone services. Countries around the world have generally adopted one or more of these standard technologies. As was the case with analog standards, none of these digital standards are compatible.

This cacophony of standards has led to a search for a third-generation standard that would be applicable around the world. This standard—known as 3G—would have to be backward compatible (i.e., previous standards would have to be able to operate in conjunction with the new standard) and facilitate the full range of digital communications technology around the world. Two standards are currently competing for the right to become the worldwide 3G standard: UMTS, a standard supported by an alliance of European and Japanese mobile telecommunications companies, and CDMA-2000, a standard supported by most American mobile telecommunications companies. How this standards competition will unfold is still not entirely known.

Sources: www.cellular-news.com/history_of_telecoms/; C. Arnst, S. Jackson, and M. Shari (1995). "The last frontier: Telecommunications in developing countries." *BusinessWeek,* September 18, pp. 98 +; T. Rapport (1996). *Wireless communications: principles and practices.* Upper Saddle River, NJ: Prentice Hall.

In this context, strategic alliances can facilitate tacit collusion. Separate firms, even if they are in the same industry, can form strategic alliances. Although communication between these firms cannot legally include sharing information about prices and costs for products or services that are produced outside the alliance, such interaction does help create the social setting within which tacit collusion may develop.[3] As suggested in the Research Made Relevant feature, most early research on strategic alliances focused on their implications for tacit collusion. More recently, research suggests that alliances do not usually facilitate tacit collusion.

Facilitating Entry and Exit

A final way that strategic alliances can be used to create value is by facilitating a firm's entry into a new market or industry or its exit from a market or industry. Strategic alliances are particularly valuable in this context when the value of market entry or exit is uncertain. Entry into an industry can require skills, abilities, and products that a potential entrant does not possess. Strategic alliances can help a firm enter a new industry by avoiding the high costs of creating these skills, abilities, and products.

For example, recently DuPont wanted to enter into the electronics industry. However, building the skills and abilities needed to develop competitive products in this industry can be very difficult and costly. Rather than absorb these costs, DuPont developed a strategic alliance (DuPont/Philips Optical) with an established electronics firm, Philips, to distribute some of Philips's products in the United States. In this way, DuPont was able to enter into a new industry (electronics) without having to absorb all the costs of creating electronics resources and abilities from the ground up.

Of course, for this joint venture to succeed, Philips must have had an incentive to cooperate with DuPont. Whereas DuPont was looking to reduce its cost of entry into a new industry, Philips was looking to reduce its cost of continued entry into a new market—the United States. Philips used its alliance with DuPont to sell in the United States the compact discs it already was selling in Europe.[4] The role of alliances in facilitating entry into new geographic markets will be discussed in more detail later in this chapter.

Alliances to facilitate entry into new industries can be valuable even when the skills needed in these industries are not as complex and difficult to learn as skills in the electronics industry. For example, rather than develop their own frozen novelty foods, Welch Foods, Inc., and Leaf, Inc. (maker of Heath candy bars) asked Eskimo Pie to formulate products for this industry. Eskimo Pie developed Welch's frozen grape juice bar and the Heath toffee ice cream bar. These firms then split the profits derived from these products.[5] As long as the cost of using an alliance to enter a new industry is less than the cost of learning new skills and capabilities, an alliance can be a valuable strategic opportunity.

Some firms use strategic alliances as a mechanism to withdraw from industries or industry segments in a low-cost way. Firms are motivated to withdraw from an industry or industry segment when their level of performance in that business is less than what was expected and when there are few prospects of it improving. When a firm desires to exit an industry or industry segment, often

Research Made Relevant

Several authors have concluded that joint ventures, as a form of alliance, do increase the probability of tacit collusion in an industry. As reviewed in books by Scherer and Barney, one study found that joint ventures created two industrial groups, besides U.S. Steel, in the U.S. iron and steel industry in the early 1900s. In this sense, joint ventures in the steel industry were a substitute for U.S. Steel's vertical integration and had the effect of creating an oligopoly in what (without joint ventures) would have been a more competitive market. Other studies found that over 50 percent of joint venture parents belong to the same industry. After examining 885 joint venture bids for oil and gas leases, yet another study found only 16 instances where joint venture partners competed with one another on another tract in the same sale. These results suggest that joint ventures might encourage subsequent tacit collusion among firms in the same industry.

In a particularly influential study, Pfeffer and Nowak found that joint ventures were most likely in industries of moderate concentration. These authors argued that in highly concentrated industries—where there were only a

Do Strategic Alliances Facilitate Tacit Collusion?

small number of competing firms—joint ventures were not necessary to create conditions conducive to collusion. In highly fragmented industries, the high levels of industry concentration conducive to tacit collusion could not be created by joint ventures. Only when joint venture activity could effectively create concentrated industries—that is, only when industries were moderately concentrated—were joint ventures likely.

Scherer and Barney also review more recent work that disputes these

findings. Joint ventures between firms in the same industry may be valuable for a variety of reasons that have little or nothing to do with collusion. Moreover, by using a lower level of aggregation, several authors have disputed the finding that joint ventures are most likely in moderately concentrated industries. The original study defined industries using very broad industry categories—"the electronics industry," "the automobile industry," and so forth. By defining industries less broadly—"consumer electronics" and "automobile part manufacturers"—subsequent work found that 73 percent of the joint ventures had parent firms coming from different industries. Although joint ventures between firms in the same industry (defined at this lower level of aggregation) may have collusive implications, subsequent work has shown that these kinds of joint ventures are relatively rare.

Sources: F. M. Scherer (1980). *Industrial market structure and economic performance.* Boston: Houghton Mifflin; J. B. Barney (2006). *Gaining and sustaining competitive advantage,* 3rd ed. Upper Saddle River, NJ: Prentice Hall; J. Pfeffer and P. Nowak (1976). "Patterns of joint venture activity: Implications for anti-trust research." *Antitrust Bulletin,* 21, pp. 315–339.

it will need to dispose of the assets it has developed to compete in that industry or industry segment. These assets often include tangible resources and capabilities, such as factories, distribution centers, and product technologies, and intangible resources and capabilities, such as brand name, relationships with suppliers and customers, a loyal and committed workforce, and so forth.

Firms will often have difficulty in obtaining the full economic value of these tangible and intangible assets as they exit an industry or industry segment. This reflects an important information asymmetry that exists between the firms that currently own these assets and firms that may want to purchase these assets. By forming an alliance with a firm that may want to purchase its assets, a firm is giving its partner an opportunity to directly observe how valuable those assets are. If those assets are actually valuable, then this "sneak preview" can lead the assets to be more appropriately priced and thereby facilitate the exit of the firm that is look-ing to sell its assets. These issues will be discussed in more detail in Chapter 10's discussion of mergers and acquisitions.

One firm that has used strategic alliances to facilitate its exit from an indus-try or industry segment is Corning. In the late 1980s, Corning entered the medical diagnostics industry. After several years, however, Corning concluded that its resources and capabilities could be more productively used in other businesses. For this reason, it began to extract itself from the medical diagnostics business. However, to ensure that it received the full value of the assets it had created in the medical diagnostics business upon exiting, it formed a strategic alliance with the Swiss specialty chemical company Ciba-Geigy. Ciba-Geigy paid $75 million to purchase half of Corning's medical diagnostics business. A couple of years later, Corning finished exiting from the medical diagnostics business by selling its remaining assets in this industry to Ciba-Geigy. However, whereas Ciba-Geigy had paid $75 million for the first half of Corning's assets, it paid $150 million for the second half. Corning's alliance with Ciba-Geigy had made it possible for Ciba-Geigy to fully value Corning's medical diagnostics capabilities. Any information asymmetry that might have existed was reduced, and Corning was able to get more of the full value of its assets upon exiting this industry.[6]

Finally, firms may use strategic alliances to manage **uncertainty**. Under con-ditions of high uncertainty, firms may not be able to tell at a particular point in time which of several different strategies they should pursue. Firms in this setting have an incentive to retain the flexibility to move quickly into a particular market or industry once the full value of that strategy is revealed. In this sense, strategic alliances enable a firm to maintain a point of entry into a market or industry, with-out incurring the costs associated with full-scale entry.

Based on this logic, strategic alliances have been analyzed as **real options**.[7] In this sense, a joint venture is an option that a firm buys, under conditions of uncertainty, to retain the ability to move quickly into a market or industry if valu-able opportunities present themselves. One way in which firms can move quickly into a market is simply to buy out their partner(s) in the joint venture. Moreover, by investing in a joint venture a firm may gain access to the information it needs to evaluate full-scale entry into a market. In this approach to analyzing strategic alliances, firms that invest in alliances as options will acquire their alliance part-ners only after the market signals an unexpected increase in value of the venture; that is, only after uncertainty is reduced and the true, positive value of entering into a market is known. Empirical findings are consistent with these expectations.[8]

Given these observations, it is not surprising to see firms in new and uncer-tain environments develop numerous strategic alliances. This is one of the reasons that strategic alliances are so common in the biotechnology industry. Although there is relatively little uncertainty that at least some drugs created through biotechnology will ultimately prove to be very valuable, which specific drugs will turn out to be the most valuable is very uncertain. Rather than investing in a small number of biotechnology drugs on their own, pharmaceutical companies have invested in numerous strategic alliances with small biotechnology firms. Each of these smaller firms represents a particular "bet" about the value of biotechnology in a particular class of drugs. If one of these "bets" turns out to be valuable, then the large pharmaceutical firm that has invested in that firm has the right, but not the obligation, to purchase the rest of this company. In this sense, from the point of view of the pharmaceutical firms, alliances between large pharmaceutical firms and small biotechnology firms can be thought of as real options.

Alliance Threats: Incentives to Cheat on Strategic Alliances

Just as there are incentives to cooperate in strategic alliances, there are also incentives to cheat on these cooperative agreements. Indeed, research shows that as many as one-third of all strategic alliances do not meet the expectations of at least one alliance partner.[9] Although some of these alliance "failures" may be due to firms forming alliances that do not have the potential for creating value, some are also due to parties to an alliance cheating—that is, not cooperating in a way that maximizes the value of the alliance. Cheating can occur in at least the three different ways presented in Table 9.2: adverse selection, moral hazard, and holdup.[10]

Adverse Selection

Potential cooperative partners can misrepresent the skills, abilities, and other resources that they will bring to an alliance. This form of cheating, called **adverse selection**, exists when an alliance partner promises to bring to an alliance certain resources that it either does not control or cannot acquire. For example, a local firm engages in adverse selection when it promises to make available to alliance partners a local distribution network that does not currently exist. Firms that engage in adverse selection are not competent alliance partners.

Adverse selection in a strategic alliance is likely only when it is difficult or costly to observe the resources or capabilities that a partner brings to an alliance. If potential partners can easily see that a firm is misrepresenting the resources and capabilities it possesses, they will not create a strategic alliance with that firm. Armed with such understanding, they will seek a different alliance partner, develop the needed skills and resources internally, or perhaps forgo this particular business opportunity.

However, evaluating the veracity of the claims of potential alliance partners is often not easy. The ability to evaluate these claims depends on information that a firm may not possess. To fully evaluate claims about a potential partner's political contacts, for example, a firm needs its own political contacts; to fully evaluate claims about potential partners' market knowledge, a firm needs significant market knowledge. A firm that can completely, and at low cost, evaluate the resources and capabilities of potential alliance partners probably does not really need these partners in a strategic alliance. The fact that a firm is seeking an alliance partner is in some sense an indication that the firm has limited abilities to evaluate potential partners.

In general, the less tangible the resources and capabilities that are to be brought to a strategic alliance, the more costly it will be to estimate their value before an alliance is created, and the more likely it is that adverse selection will

Table 9.2 **Ways to Cheat in Strategic Alliances**

- *Adverse selection*: Potential partners misrepresent the value of the skills and abilities they bring to the alliance.
- *Moral hazard*: Partners provide to the alliance skills and abilities of lower quality than they promised.
- *Holdup*: Partners exploit the transaction-specific investments made by others in the alliance.

occur. Firms considering alliances with partners that bring intangible resources such as "knowledge of local conditions" or "contacts with key political figures" will need to guard against this form of cheating.

Moral Hazard

Partners in an alliance may possess high-quality resources and capabilities of significant value in an alliance but fail to make those resources and capabilities available to alliance partners. This form of cheating is called **moral hazard**. For example, a partner in an engineering strategic alliance may agree to send only its most talented and best-trained engineers to work in the alliance but then actually sends less talented, poorly trained engineers. These less qualified engineers may not be able to contribute substantially to making the alliance successful, but they may be able to learn a great deal from the highly qualified engineers provided by other alliance partners. In this way, the less qualified engineers effectively transfer wealth from other alliance partners to their own firm.[11]

Often both parties in a failed alliance accuse each other of moral hazard. This was the case in the abandoned alliance between Disney and Pixar, described in the Strategy in the Emerging Enterprise feature.

The existence of moral hazard in a strategic alliance does not necessarily mean that any of the parties to that alliance are malicious or dishonest. Rather, what often happens is that market conditions change after an alliance is formed, requiring one or more partners to an alliance to change their strategies.

For example, in the early days of the personal computer industry Compaq Computer Corporation relied on a network of independent distributors to sell its computers. However, as competition in the personal computer industry increased, Internet, mail order, and so-called computer superstores became much more valuable distribution networks, and alliances between Compaq and its traditional distributors became strained. Over time, Compaq's traditional distributors were unable to obtain the inventory they wanted in a timely manner. Indeed, to satisfy the needs of large accounts, some traditional distributors actually purchased Compaq computers from local computer superstores and then shipped them to their customers. Compaq's shift from independent dealers to alternative distributors looked like moral hazard—at least from the point of view of the independent dealers. However, from Compaq's perspective, this change simply reflected economic realities in the personal computer industry.[12]

Holdup

Even if alliance partners do not engage in either adverse selection or moral hazard, another form of cheating may evolve. Once a strategic alliance has been created, partner firms may make investments that have value only in the context of that alliance and in no other economic exchanges. These are the transaction-specific investments mentioned in Chapter 6. For example, managers from one alliance partner may have to develop close, trusting relationships with managers from other alliance partners. These close relationships are very valuable in the context of the alliance, but they have limited economic value in other economic exchanges. Also, one partner may have to customize its manufacturing equipment, distribution network, and key organizational policies to cooperate with other partners. These modifications have significant value in the context of the alliance, but they do not help the firm, and may even hurt it, in economic exchanges outside the alliance. As was the case in Chapter 6, whenever an investment's value in its

Strategy in the Emerging Enterprise

*I*n 1994, Pixar was a struggling start-up company in northern California that was trying to compete in an industry that really didn't yet exist—the computer graphics animated motion picture industry. Headed by the former founder of Apple Computer, Steven Jobs, Pixar was desperately looking for a partner that could help finance and distribute its new brand of animated movies. Who better, Pixar thought, than the world's leader in animated feature length films: Disney. And thus, a strategic alliance between Pixar and Disney was formed.

In the alliance, Disney agreed to help finance and distribute Pixar's films. In return, they would share in any profits these films generated. Also, Disney would retain the right to produce any sequels to Pixar's films—after first offering Pixar the right to make these sequels. This agreement gave Disney a great deal of control of any characters that Pixar created in movies distributed through Pixar's alliance with Disney. Of course, at the time the alliance was originally formed there were no such characters. Indeed, Pixar had yet to produce any movies. So, because Pixar was a weak alliance partner, Disney was able to gain control of any characters Pixar developed in the future. Disney, after all, had the track record of success.

A funny thing happened over the next 10 years. Pixar produced blockbuster animated features such as *Toy Story* (total revenues of $419.9 million); *A Bug's Life* (total revenues of $358); *Toy Story 2* (total revenues of $629.9 million); *Monsters, Inc.* (total revenues of $903.1 million); *Finding*

Disney and Pixar Have a Falling Out

Nemo (total revenues of $1,281.4 million); *The Incredibles* (total revenues of $946.6 million); and *Cars* (projected total revenues of $331.9 million). And these revenue numbers do not include sales of merchandise associated with these films. During this same time period, Disney's traditional animated fare performed much more poorly—*Treasure Planet* generated only $112 million in revenues, *The Emperor's New Groove* only $169 million, and *Brother Bear* only $126 million. Disney's "big hit" during this time period was *Lilo & Stitch*, with revenues of $269 million—less than any of the movies produced by Pixar.

Oops! The firm with the "proven track record" of producing hit animated features—Disney—stumbled badly, and the upstart company with no track record—Pixar—had all the success. Because Disney did not have many of its own characters upon

which to base sequels, it began to eye Pixar's characters.

Fast forward to 2004. It's time to renew this alliance. But now Pixar has the upper hand, because it has the track record. Disney comes knocking and asks Pixar to redo the alliance. What does Pixar say, "Okay, but . . . we want control of our characters, we want Disney to act just as a distributor"—in other words, "We want Disney out of our business!" Disney balks at these demands, and Pixar—well, Pixar just cancelled the alliance.

But Pixar still needed a distribution partner. Pixar simply does not produce enough films to justify the expense of building its own distribution system. After a several-month search, Pixar found what it considered to be its best distribution partner. The only problem was—it was Disney.

Reestablishing the alliance between Pixar and Disney seemed out of the question. After all, such an alliance would have all the challenges as the previous alliance.

Instead, Disney decided to buy Pixar. On January 25, 2006, Disney announced that it was buying Pixar in a deal worth $7.4 billion. Steve Jobs became Disney's single largest investor and became a member of Disney's board of directors. John Lasseter—the creative force behind Pixar's success—became Chief Creative Officer at Disney.

Sources: S. Levy and D. Jefferson (2004). "Hey Mickey, buzz off!" *BusinessWeek*, February 9, pp. 4; T. Lowry et al. (2004). "Megamedia mergers: How dangerous?" *BusinessWeek*, February 23, pp. 34 +; http://money.cnn.com/2006/01/24/newscompanies/disney_pixar_deal.

first-best use (in this case, within the alliance) is much greater than its value in its second-best use (in this case, outside the alliance), that investment is said to be **transaction specific**.[13]

When one firm makes more transaction-specific investments in a strategic alliance than partner firms make, that firm may be subject to the form of cheating called **holdup**. Holdup occurs when a firm that has not made significant transaction-specific investments demands returns from an alliance that are higher than what the partners agreed to when they created the alliance.

For example, suppose two alliance partners agree to a 50–50 split of the costs and profits associated with an alliance. To make the alliance work, Firm A has to customize its production process. Firm B, however, does not have to modify itself to cooperate with Firm A. The value to Firm A of this customized production process, if it is used in the strategic alliance, is $5,000. However, outside the alliance, this customized process is only worth $200 (as scrap).

Obviously, Firm A has made a transaction-specific investment in this alliance and Firm B has not. Consequently, Firm A may be subject to holdup by Firm B. In particular, Firm B may threaten to leave the alliance unless Firm A agrees to give Firm B part of the $5,000 value that Firm A obtains by using the modified production process in the alliance. Rather than lose all the value that could be generated by its investment, Firm A may be willing to give up some of its $5,000 to avoid gaining only $200. Indeed, if Firm B extracts up to the value of Firm A's production process in its next-best use (here, only $200), Firm A will still be better off continuing in this relationship rather than dissolving it. Thus, even though Firm A and Firm B initially agreed on a 50–50 split from this strategic alliance, the agreement may be modified if one party to the alliance makes significant transaction-specific investments. Research on international joint ventures suggests that the existence of transaction-specific investments in these relationships often leads to holdup problems.[14]

Although holdup is a form of cheating in strategic alliances, the threat of holdup can also be a motivation for creating an alliance. Bauxite-smelting companies often join in joint ventures with mining companies in order to exploit economies of scale in mining. However, these firms have another option: They could choose to operate large and efficient mines by themselves and then sell the excess bauxite (over and above their needs for their own smelters) on the open market. Unfortunately, bauxite is not a homogeneous commodity. Moreover, different kinds of bauxite require different smelting technologies. In order for one firm to sell its excess bauxite on the market, other smelting firms would have to make enormous investments, the sole purpose of which would be to refine that particular firm's bauxite. These investments would be transaction specific and subject these other smelters to holdup problems.

In this context, a strategic alliance can be thought of as a way of reducing the threat of holdup by creating an explicit management framework for resolving holdup problems. In other words, although holdup problems might still exist in these strategic alliances, the alliance framework may still be a better way in which to manage these problems than attempting to manage them in arm's-length market relationships. Some of the ethical dimensions of adverse selection, moral hazard, and holdup are discussed in the Ethics and Strategy feature.

Strategic Alliances and Sustained Competitive Advantage

The ability of strategic alliances to be sources of sustained competitive advantage, like all the other strategies discussed in this book, can be analyzed with the VRIO framework developed in Chapter 3. An alliance is economically valuable when it exploits any of the opportunities listed in Table 9.1 but avoids the threats in Table 9.2. In addition, for a strategic alliance to be a source of sustained competitive advantage it must be rare and costly to imitate.

The Rarity of Strategic Alliances

The rarity of strategic alliances does not only depend on the number of competing firms that have already implemented an alliance. It also depends on whether the benefits that firms obtain from their alliances are common across firms competing in an industry.

Consider, for example, the U.S. automobile industry. Over the last several years, strategic alliances have become very common in this industry, especially with Japanese auto firms. GM developed an alliance with Toyota that has already been described; Ford developed an alliance with Mazda before it purchased this Japanese firm outright; and DaimlerChrysler developed an alliance with Mitsubishi. Given the frequency with which alliances have developed in this industry, it is tempting to conclude that strategic alliances are not rare and thus not a source of competitive advantage.

Closer examination, however, suggests that these alliances may have been created for different reasons. For example, until recently, GM and Toyota have cooperated only in building a single line of cars, the Chevrolet Nova. GM has been less interested in learning design skills from Toyota and has been more interested in learning about manufacturing high-quality small cars profitably. Ford and Mazda, in contrast, have worked closely together in designing new cars and have joint manufacturing operations. Indeed, Ford and Mazda have worked so closely together that Ford finally purchased Mazda. Mitsubishi has acted primarily as a supplier to DaimlerChrysler, and (until recently) there has been relatively little joint development or manufacturing. Thus, although all three U.S. firms have strategic alliances, the alliances serve different purposes, and therefore each may be rare.[15]

One of the reasons why the benefits that accrue from a particular strategic alliance may be rare is that relatively few firms may have the complementary resources and abilities needed to form an alliance. This is particularly likely when an alliance is formed to enter into a new market, especially a new foreign market. In many less developed economies, only one local firm or very few local firms may exist with the local knowledge, contacts, and distribution network needed to facilitate entry into that market. Moreover, sometimes the government acts to limit the number of these local firms. Although several firms may seek entry into this market, only a very small number will be able to form a strategic alliance with the local entity and therefore the benefits that accrue to the allied firms will likely be rare.

The Imitability of Strategic Alliances

As discussed in Chapter 3, the resources and capabilities that enable firms to conceive and implement valuable strategies may be imitated in two ways: direct duplication and substitution. Both duplication and substitution are important considerations in analyzing the imitability of strategic alliances.

Ethics and Strategy

Firms in strategic alliances can cheat on their alliance partners by engaging in adverse selection, moral hazard, or holdup. These three activities all have at least one thing in common—they all involve one alliance partner lying to another. And these lies can often pay off big in the form of the lying firm appropriating more than its "fair share" of the value created in an alliance. Are alliances one place in the economy where the adage "cheaters never prosper" does not hold?

There is little doubt that, in the short run, firms that cheat on their alliance partners can gain some advantages. But research suggests that cheating does not pay in the long run, because firms that cheat on their alliance partners will find it difficult to form alliances with new partners and thus have many valuable exchange opportunities foreclosed to them.

One study that examined the long-term return to "cheaters" in strategic alliances analyzed alliances using a simple game called the "Prisoner's Dilemma." In a "Prisoner's Dilemma" game, firms have two options: to continue cooperating in a strategic alliance or to "cheat" on that alliance through adverse selection, moral hazard, or holdup. The payoffs

When It Comes to Alliances, Do "Cheaters Never Prosper"?

to firms in this game depend on the decisions made by both firms. As shown in Table 9.3, if both firms decide to cooperate, they each get a good size payoff from the alliance ($3,000 in Table 9.3); if they both decide to cheat on the alliance, they each get a very small payoff ($1,000 in Table 9.3); and if one decides to cheat while the other decides to cooperate, then the cheating firm gets a very big payoff ($5,000 in Table 9.3) while the cooperating firm gets a very small payoff ($0 in Table 9.3).

If Firm 1 and Firm 2 in this game are going to engage in only one strategic alliance, then they have a very strong incentive to "cheat." The worst that could happen if they cheat is that they earn a $1,000 payoff, but there is a possibility of a $5,000 payoff. However, research has shown that if a firm is contemplating engaging in multiple strategic alliances over time, then the optimal strategy is to cooperate in all its alliances. This is true even if all these alliances are not with the same partner firm.

The specific "winning" strategy in repeated "Prisoner Dilemma" games is called a "tit-for-tat" strategy. "Tit-for-tat" means that Firm 1 will cooperate in an alliance as long as Firm 2 cooperates. However, as soon as Firm 2 cheats on an alliance, Firm 1 cheats as well. "Tit-for-tat" works well in this setting because adopting a cooperative posture in an alliance ensures that, most of the time, the alliance will generate a high payoff (of $3,000 in Table 9.3). However, by immediately responding to cheaters by cheating, the firm implementing a "tit-for-tat" strategy also minimizes the times when it will earn the lowest payoff in the table ($0). So, "tit-for-tat" maximizes the upside potential of an alliance while minimizing its downside.

All this analysis suggests that although cheating on an alliance can give a firm competitive advantages in the short to medium term, in the long run, "cheaters never prosper."

Sources: R. M. Axelrod (1984). *The evolution of cooperation.* New York: Basic Books; D. Ernst and J. Bleeke (1993). *Collaborating to compete.* New York: Wiley.

Table 9.3 **Returns from Cooperating and Cheating in a "Prisoner's Dilemma"**

		Strategic Alliance	
Firm 1			
		Cooperates	Cheats
	Cooperates	1: $3,000 2: $3,000	1: $5,000 2: $0
Firm 2			
	Cheats	1: $0 2: $5,000	1: $1,000 2: $1,000

Direct Duplication of Strategic Alliances

Recent research suggests that successful strategic alliances are often based on socially complex relations among alliance partners.[16] In this sense, successful strategic alliances often go well beyond simple legal contracts and are characterized by socially complex phenomena such as a trusting relationship between alliance partners, friendship, and even (perhaps) a willingness to suspend narrow self-interest for the longer-term good of the relationship.

Some research has shown that the development of trusting relationships between alliance partners is both difficult and essential to the success of strategic alliances. In one study, the most common reason that alliances failed to meet the expectations of partner firms was the partners' inability to trust one another. Interpersonal communication, tolerance for cultural differences, patience, and willingness to sacrifice short-term profits for longer-term success were all important determinants of the level of trust among alliance partners.[17]

Of course, not all firms in an industry are likely to have the organizational and relationship-building skills required for successful alliance building. If these skills and abilities are rare among a set of competing firms and costly to develop, then firms that are able to exploit these abilities by creating alliances may gain competitive advantages. Examples of firms that have developed these specialized skills include Corning and Cisco, with several hundred strategic alliances each.[18]

Substitutes for Strategic Alliances

Even if the purpose and objectives of a strategic alliance are valuable and rare, and even if the relationships on which an alliance is created are socially complex and costly to imitate, that alliance will still not generate a sustained competitive advantage if low-cost substitutes are available. At least two possible substitutes for strategic alliances exist: "going it alone" and acquisitions.[19]

"Going It Alone." Firms "go it alone" when they attempt to develop all the resources and capabilities they need to exploit market opportunities and neutralize market threats by themselves. Sometimes "going it alone" can create the same—or even more—value than using alliances to exploit opportunities and neutralize threats. In these settings, "going it alone" is a substitute for a strategic alliance. However, in other settings using an alliance can create substantially more value than "going it alone." In these settings, "going it alone" is not a substitute for a strategic alliance.

So, when will firms prefer an alliance over "going it alone"? Not surprisingly, the three explanations of vertical integration, discussed in Chapter 6, are relevant here as well. These three explanations focused on the threat of opportunism, the impact of firm resources and capabilities, and the role of uncertainty. If you need to review these three explanations, they are described in detail in Chapter 6. They are relevant here because "going it alone"—as a potential substitute for a strategic alliance—is an example of vertical integration. The implications of these three explanations for when strategic alliances will be preferred over "going it alone" are summarized in Table 9.4. If any of the conditions listed in Table 9.4 exist, then "going it alone" will not be a substitute for strategic alliances.

Recall from Chapter 6 that opportunism-based explanations of vertical integration suggest that firms will want to vertically integrate an economic exchange when they have made high levels of transaction-specific investment in that exchange. That is, using language developed in this chapter, firms will want to vertically integrate an economic exchange when using an alliance to manage that exchange could subject them to holdup. Extending this logic to strategic

Table 9.4   **When Alliances Will Be Preferred Over "Going It Alone"**

Alliances will be preferred over "going it alone" when:

1. The level of transaction-specific investment required to complete an exchange is moderate.
2. An exchange partner possesses valuable, rare, and costly-to-imitate resources and capabilities.
3. There is great uncertainty about the future value of an exchange.

alliances suggests that strategic alliances will be preferred over "going it alone" and other alternatives when the level of transaction-specific investment required to complete an exchange is moderate. If the level of this specific investment is low, then market forms of exchange will be preferred; if the level of this specific investment is high, then "going it alone" in a vertically integrated way will be preferred; if the level of this specific investment is moderate, then some sort of strategic alliance will be preferred. Thus, when the level of specific exchange in a transaction is moderate, then "going it alone" is not a substitute for a strategic alliance.

Capabilities-based explanations suggest that an alliance will be preferred over "going it alone" when an exchange partner possesses valuable, rare, and costly-to-imitate resources and capabilities. A firm without these capabilities may find them to be too costly to develop on its own. If a firm must have access to capabilities it cannot develop on its own, it must use an alliance to gain access to those capabilities. In this setting, "going it alone" is not a substitute for a strategic alliance.[20]

Finally, it has already been suggested that, under conditions of high uncertainty, firms may be unwilling to commit to a particular course of action by engaging in an exchange within a firm. In such settings, firms may choose the strategic flexibility associated with alliances. As suggested earlier in this chapter, alliances can be thought of as real options that give a firm the right, but not the obligation, to invest further in an exchange—perhaps by bringing it within the boundaries of a firm—if that exchange turns out to be valuable sometime in the future. Thus, under conditions of high uncertainty, "going it alone" is not a substitute for strategic alliances.

Acquisitions.   The acquisition of other firms can also be a substitute for alliances. In this case, rather than developing a strategic alliance or attempting to develop and exploit the relevant resources by "going it alone," a firm seeking to exploit the opportunities listed in Table 9.1 may simply acquire another firm that already possesses the relevant resources and capabilities. However, such acquisitions have four characteristics that often limit the extent to which they can act as substitutes for strategic alliances. These are summarized in Table 9.5.[21]

First, there may be legal constraints on acquisitions. These are especially likely if firms are seeking advantages by combining with other firms in their own industry. Thus, for example, using acquisitions as a substitute for strategic alliances in the aluminum industry would lead to a very concentrated industry and subject some of these firms to serious antitrust liabilities. These firms have acquisitions foreclosed to them and must look elsewhere to gain advantages from cooperating with their competition.

Table 9.5   **Reasons Why Strategic Alliances May Be More Attractive Than Acquisitions to Realize Exchange Opportunities**

Alliances will be preferred to acquisitions when:
1. There are legal constraints on acquisitions.
2. Acquisitions limit a firm's flexibility under conditions of high uncertainty.
3. There is substantial unwanted organizational "baggage" in an acquired firm.
4. The value of a firm's resources and capabilities depends on its independence.

Second, as has already been suggested, strategic alliances enable a firm to retain its flexibility either to enter or not to enter into a new business. Acquisitions limit that flexibility, because they represent a strong commitment to engage in a certain business activity. Consequently, under conditions of high uncertainty firms may choose strategic alliances over acquisitions as a way to exploit opportunities while maintaining the flexibility that alliances create.

Third, firms may choose strategic alliances over acquisitions because of the unwanted organizational baggage that often comes with an acquisition. Sometimes, the value created by combining firms depends on combining particular functions, divisions, or other assets in the firms. A strategic alliance can focus on exploiting the value of combining just those parts of firms that create the most value. Acquisitions, in contrast, generally include the entire organization, both the parts of a firm where value is likely to be created and parts of a firm where value is not likely to be created.

From the point of view of the acquiring firm, parts of a firm that do not create value are essentially unwanted baggage. These parts of the firm may be sold off subsequent to an acquisition. However, this sell-off may be costly and time-consuming. If enough baggage exists, firms may determine that an acquisition is not a viable option, even though important economic value could be created between a firm and a potential acquisition target. To gain this value, an alternative approach—a strategic alliance—may be preferred. These issues will be explored in more detail in Chapter 10.

Finally, sometimes a firm's resources and capabilities are valuable because that firm is independent. In this setting, the act of acquiring a firm can actually reduce the value of a firm. When this is the case, any value between two firms is best realized through an alliance, not an acquisition. For example, the international growth of numerous marketing-oriented companies in the 1980s led to strong pressures for advertising agencies to develop global marketing capabilities. During the 1990s, many domestic-only advertising firms acquired nondomestic agencies to form a few large international advertising agencies. However, one firm that was reluctant to be acquired in order to be part of an international advertising network was the French advertising company Publicis. Over and above the personal interests of its owners to retain control of the company, Publicis wanted to remain an independent French agency in order to retain its stable of French and French-speaking clients—including Renault and Nestlé. These firms had indicated that they preferred working with a French advertising agency and that they would look for alternative suppliers if Publicis were acquired by a foreign firm. Because much of the value that Publicis created in a potential acquisition depended on obtaining access to its stable of clients, the act of acquiring Publicis would have had the effect of destroying the very thing that made the acquisition attractive. For this reason, rather than allowing itself to be acquired by foreign advertising agencies, Publicis developed a complex equity strategic alliance and joint venture with a U.S. advertising firm, Foote, Coyne, and Belding. Although, ultimately, this alliance was not successful in providing an international network for either of these two partner firms, an acquisition of Publicis by Foote, Coyne, and Belding would almost certainly have destroyed some of the economic value that Publicis enjoyed as a stand-alone company.

Organizing to Implement Strategic Alliances

VRIO

One of the most important determinants of the success of strategic alliances is their organization. The primary purpose of organizing a strategic alliance is to enable partners in the alliance to gain all the benefits associated with cooperation while minimizing the probability that cooperating firms will cheat on their cooperative agreements. The organizing skills required in managing alliances are, in many ways, unique. It often takes some time for firms to learn these skills and realize the full potential of their alliances. This is why some firms are able to gain competitive advantages from managing alliances more effectively than their competitors. Indeed, sometimes firms may have to choose alternatives to alliances—including "going it alone" and acquisitions—even when those alternatives are not preferred, simply because they do not have the skills required to organize and manage alliances.

A variety of tools and mechanisms can be used to help realize the value of alliances and minimize the threat of cheating. These include contracts, equity investments, firm reputations, joint ventures, and trust.

Explicit Contracts and Legal Sanctions

One way to avoid cheating in strategic alliances is for the parties to an alliance to anticipate the ways in which cheating may occur (including adverse selection, moral hazard, and holdup) and to write explicit contracts that define legal liability if cheating does occur. Writing these contracts, together with the close monitoring of contractual compliance and the threat of legal sanctions, can reduce the probability of cheating. Earlier in this chapter, such strategic alliances were called *nonequity alliances.*

However, contracts sometimes fail to anticipate all forms of cheating that might occur in a relationship—and firms may cheat on cooperative agreements in subtle ways that are difficult to evaluate in terms of contractual requirements. Thus, for example, a contract may require parties in a strategic alliance to make available to the alliance certain proprietary technologies or processes. However, it may be very difficult to communicate the subtleties of these technologies or processes to alliance partners. Does this failure in communication represent a clear violation of contractual requirements, or does it represent a good-faith effort by alliance partners? Moreover, how can one partner tell whether it is obtaining all the necessary information about a technology or process when it is unaware of all the information that exists in another firm? Hence, although contracts are an

Table 9.6   **Common Clauses in Contracts Used to Govern Strategic Alliances**

Establishment Issues

Shareholdings
> If an equity alliance or joint venture is to be formed, what percentage of equity is to be purchased by each firm involved in the alliance.

Voting rights
> The number of votes assigned to each partner in an alliance. May or may not be equal to shareholding percentages.

Dividend percentage
> How the profits from an alliance will be allocated among cooperating firms. May or may not be equal to shareholding percentages.

Minority protection
> Description of the kinds of decisions that can be vetoed by firms with a minority interest in an alliance.

Board of directors
> Initial board of directors, plus mechanisms for dismissing and appointing board members.

Articles of association
> Procedures for passing resolutions, share issuance, share disposal, etc.

Place of incorporation
> If a joint venture, geographic location of incorporation.

Advisors
> Lawyers, accountants, and other consultants to the alliance.

Identification of parties
> Legal entities directly involved in an alliance.

Operating Issues

Performance clauses
> Duties and obligations of alliance partners, including warranties and minimum performance levels expected.

Noncompete clauses
> Partners are restricted from entering the primary business of the alliance.

Nonsolicitation clauses
> Partners are restricted from recruiting employees from each other.

Confidentiality clauses
> Proprietary information from partners or from the alliance cannot be shared outside the alliance.

important component of most strategic alliances, they do not resolve all the problems associated with cheating.

Although most contracts associated with strategic alliances are highly customized, these different contracts do have some common features. These common features are described in detail in Table 9.6. In general, firms contemplating a strategic alliance that will be at least partially governed by a contract will have to include clauses that address the issues presented in Table 9.6.

Licensing intellectual property rights
  Who owns the intellectual property created by an alliance and how this property is licensed to other firms.

Liability
  Liability of the alliance and liability of cooperating partners.

Changes to the contract
  Process by which the contract can be amended.

Dispute resolution
  Process by which disputes among partners will be resolved.

Termination Issues

Preemption rights
  If one partner wishes to sell its shares, it must first offer them to the other partner.

Variations on preemption rights
  Partners are forbidden to ever discuss the sale of their shares to an outsider without first informing their partner of their intention to do so.

Call options
  When one partner can force the other partner to sell its shares to it. Includes discussion on how these shares will be valued and the circumstances under which a call option can be exercised.

Put options
  A partner has the right to force another partner to buy its alliance shares.

Drag-along rights
  One partner can arrange a sale to an outside firm and force the other partner to sell shares as well.

Tag-along rights
  A partner can prevent the sale of the second partner's shares to an outside firm unless that outside firm also buys the first partner's shares.

Initial public offering (IPO)
  Circumstances under which an IPO will be pursued.

Termination
  Conditions under which contract can be terminated and consequences of termination for partners.

Source: Adapted from E. Campbell and J. Reuer (2001). "Note on the legal negotiation of strategic alliance agreements." *Business Horizons* 44(1), pp. 19–26.

Equity Investments

The effectiveness of contracts can be enhanced by having partners in an alliance make equity investments in each other. When Firm A buys a substantial equity position in its alliance partner, Firm B, the market value of Firm A now depends, to some extent, on the economic performance of that partner. The incentive of Firm A to cheat Firm B falls, for to do so would be to reduce the economic performance of Firm B and thus the value of Firm A's investment in its partner. These kinds of strategic alliances are called *equity alliances*.

Many firms use cross-equity investments to help manage their strategic alliances. These arrangements are particularly common in Japan, where a firm's largest equity holders often include several of its key suppliers, including its main banks. These equity investments, because they reduce the threat of cheating in alliances with suppliers, can reduce these firms' supply costs. In turn, not only do firms have equity positions in their suppliers, but suppliers often have substantial equity positions in the firms to which they sell.[22]

Firm Reputations

A third constraint on incentives to cheat in strategic alliances exists in the effect that a reputation for cheating has on a firm's future opportunities. Although it is often difficult to anticipate all the different ways in which an alliance partner may cheat, it is often easier to describe after the fact how an alliance partner has cheated. Information about an alliance partner that has cheated is likely to become widely known. A firm with a reputation as a cheater is not likely to be able to develop strategic alliances with other partners in the future, despite any special resources or capabilities that it might be able to bring to an alliance. In this way, cheating in a current alliance may foreclose opportunities for developing other valuable alliances. For this reason, firms may decide not to cheat in their current alliances.[23]

Substantial evidence suggests that the effect of reputation on future business opportunities is important. Firms go to great lengths to make sure that they do not develop a negative reputation. Nevertheless, this reputational control of cheating in strategic alliances does have several limitations.[24]

First, subtle cheating in a strategic alliance may not become public, and if it does become public the responsibility for the failure of the strategic alliance may be very ambiguous. In one equity joint venture attempting to perfect the design of a new turbine for power generation, financial troubles made one partner considerably more anxious than the other partner to complete product development. The financially healthy, and thus patient, partner believed that if the alliance required an additional infusion of capital, the financially troubled partner would have to abandon the alliance and would have to sell its part of the alliance at a relatively low price. The patient partner thus encouraged alliance engineers to work slowly and carefully in the guise of developing the technology to reach its full potential. The financially troubled, and thus impatient, partner encouraged alliance engineers to work quickly, perhaps sacrificing some quality to develop the technology sooner. Eventually, the impatient partner ran out of money, sold its share of the alliance to the patient partner at a reduced price, and accused the patient partner of not acting in good faith to facilitate the rapid development of the new technology. The patient partner accused the other firm of pushing the technology too quickly, thereby sacrificing quality and, perhaps, worker safety. In some sense, both firms were cheating on their agreement to develop the new technology cooperatively. However, this cheating was subtle and difficult to spot and had relatively little impact on the reputation of either firm or on the ability of either firm to establish alliances in the future. It is likely that most observers would simply conclude that the patient partner obtained a windfall because of the impatient partner's bad luck.[25]

Second, although one partner to an alliance may be unambiguously cheating on the relationship, one or both of the firms may not be sufficiently connected into a network with other firms to make this information public. When information about cheating remains private, public reputations are not tarnished and future opportunities are not forgone. This is especially likely to happen if one or both alliance partners operate in less developed economies where information about partner behavior may not be rapidly diffused to other firms or to other countries.

Finally, the effect of a tarnished reputation, as long as cheating in an alliance is unambiguous and publicly known, may foreclose future opportunities for a firm, but it does little to address the current losses experienced by the firm that was cheated. Moreover, any of the forms of cheating discussed earlier—adverse selection, moral hazard, or holdup—can result in substantial losses for a firm currently in an alliance. Indeed, the wealth created by cheating in a current alliance may be large enough to make a firm willing to forgo future alliances. In this case, a tarnished reputation may be of minor consequence to a cheating firm.[26]

Joint Ventures

A fourth way to reduce the threat of cheating is for partners in a strategic alliance to invest in a joint venture. Creating a separate legal entity, in which alliance partners invest and from whose profits they earn returns on their investments, reduces some of the risks of cheating in strategic alliances. When a joint venture is created, the ability of partners to earn returns on their investments depends on the economic success of the joint venture. Partners in joint ventures have limited interests in behaving in ways that hurt the performance of the joint venture, because such behaviors end up hurting both partners. Moreover, unlike reputational consequences of cheating, cheating in a joint venture does not just foreclose future alliance opportunities; it can hurt the cheating firm in the current period as well.

Given the advantages of joint ventures in controlling cheating, it is not surprising that when the probability of cheating in a cooperative relationship is greatest, a joint venture is usually the preferred form of cooperation. For example, bauxite mining has some clear economies of scale. However, transaction-specific investments would lead to significant holdup problems in selling excess bauxite in the open market, and legal constraints prevent the acquisition of other smelter companies to create an intraorganizational demand for excess bauxite. Holdup problems would continue to exist in any mining strategic alliances that might be created. Nonequity alliances, equity alliances, and reputational effects are not likely to restrain cheating in this situation, because the returns on holdup, once transaction-specific investments are in place, can be very large. Thus, most of the strategic alliances created to mine bauxite take the form of joint ventures. Only this form of strategic alliance is likely to create incentives strong enough to significantly reduce the probability of cheating.[27]

Despite these strengths, joint ventures are not able to reduce all cheating in an alliance without cost. Sometimes the value of cheating in a joint venture is sufficiently large that a firm cheats even though doing so hurts the joint venture and forecloses future opportunities. For example, a particular firm may gain access to a technology through a joint venture that would be valuable if used in another of its lines of business. This firm may be tempted to transfer this technology to this other line of business even if it has agreed not to do so and even if doing so would limit the performance of its joint venture. Because the profits earned in this other line of business may have a greater value than the returns that could have been earned in the joint venture and the returns that could have been earned in the future with other strategic alliances, cheating may occur.

Trust

It is sometimes the case that alliance partners rely only on legalistic and narrowly economic approaches to manage their alliance. However, recent work seems to suggest that although successful alliance partners do not ignore legal and economic disincentives to cheating, they strongly support these narrower linkages with a rich set of interpersonal relations and trust. Trust, in combination with contracts, can help reduce the threat of cheating. More important, trust may enable partners to explore exchange opportunities that they could not explore if only legal and economic organizing mechanisms were in place.[28]

At first glance, this argument may seem far-fetched. However, some research offers support for this approach to managing strategic alliances, suggesting that successful alliance partners typically do not specify all the terms and conditions in their relationship in a legal contract and do not specify all possible forms of cheating and their consequences. Moreover, when joint ventures are formed, partners do not always insist on simple 50–50 splits of equity ownership and profit sharing. Rather, successful alliances involve trust, a willingness to be flexible, a willingness to learn, and a willingness to let the alliance develop in ways that the partners could not have anticipated.[29]

Commitment, coordination, and trust are all important determinants of alliance success. Put another way, a strategic alliance is a relationship that evolves over time. Allowing the lawyers and economists to too-rigorously define, a priori, the boundaries of that relationship may limit it and stunt its development.[30]

This "trust" approach also has implications for the extent to which strategic alliances may be sources of sustained competitive advantage for firms. The ability to move into strategic alliances in this trusting way may be very valuable over the long run. There is strong reason to believe that this ability is not uniformly distributed across all firms that might have an interest in forming strategic alliances and that this ability may be history-dependent and socially complex and thus costly to imitate. Firms with these skills may be able to gain sustained competitive advantages from their alliance relationships. The observation that just a few firms, including Corning and Cisco, are well known for their strategic alliance successes is consistent with the observation that these alliance management skills may be valuable, rare, and costly to imitate.

Strategic Alliances in an International Context

As suggested in Table 9.1 strategic alliances are especially important for firms looking to enter into new foreign markets. In this context, one partner typically brings products or services (as resources) to the alliance, and the other partner brings local knowledge, local distribution networks, and local political influence (as resources) to the relationship. The development of local distribution networks can be a costly and difficult process. Such actions generally require a great deal of knowledge about local conditions. Local alliance partners may already possess this knowledge. They may even already have a local distribution network in place. By cooperating with local partners, firms can substantially reduce the cost of entry into these markets.

Of course, some governments require new entrants to have local alliance partners. Governments see such relationships not only as a way to facilitate entry of foreign firms into their market place, but also as a way that domestic firms can learn from foreign firms. This has been the case with General Electric's entry into the Chinese electricity production market. The Chinese government has required GE, if it wants to sell its generators in China, to form joint ventures with local Chinese companies. This has enabled GE to sell over $900 million worth of generators in the Chinese market.

However, recently, China began to require GE to provide its Chinese joint venture partners information about its generator technology and information about how to manufacture that technology. GE has spent over $500 million developing its new line of generators and obviously does not want to share this knowledge with firms that might some day become its competitors. But the Chinese government is now saying: "If you want to sell in China, you need to share your technology." Several other firms, besides GE, have had to share technology with their Chinese alliance partners to continue doing business in China as well, including Motorola, Microsoft, Seimens, and Nokia.[31] These actions by the Chinese government have the effect of increasing the cost of entry into the Chinese market.

All the potential threats that exist in alliances—from adverse selection to moral hazard, from holdup to learning races—can exist in an international context. Indeed, although it is often the case that there will be important information asymmetries between firms in an alliance, these asymmetries are likely to be much greater when alliance partners come from different countries, operate in different cultures, and speak different languages.

Ironically, it is precisely these kinds of threats that often motivate firms to engage in alliances in exploiting international opportunities. These same kinds of threats exist if a firm vertically integrates into its international operations—either on its own or by acquiring another firm. However, once a firm has vertically integrated, it can be relatively costly for it to extract itself from this investment if it turns out that it has been unfairly taken advantage of in deciding to begin operations in a country. However, it is much less costly for a firm to withdraw from an international alliance. For these reasons, it is not unusual to observe firms, as they begin to explore international opportunities, to do so first by engaging in market-based forms of exchange (simple importing or exporting), followed by nonequity alliances (including licensing agreements). Only after a firm has developed trust and confidence in its international partners will it be willing to engage in equity alliances and, perhaps, joint ventures. In the end, if it makes economic sense to do so, a firm may even decide to vertically integrate into its international operations; however, this is often the last step in exploiting international opportunities, not the first.

Thus, although all the threats associated with alliances exist in an international context, so do all the tools that can be used to reduce these threats. Over time, firms can even develop very strong and trusting relationships with their international alliance partners—relationships that create all the economic value of vertical integration, but at much lower cost.

SUMMARY

Strategic alliances exist whenever two or more organizations cooperate in the development, manufacture, or sale of products or services. Strategic alliances can be grouped into three large categories: nonequity alliances, equity alliances, and joint ventures.

Firms join in strategic alliances for three broad reasons: to improve the performance of their current operations, to improve the competitive environment within which they are operating, and to facilitate entry into or exit from markets and industries. Just as there are incentives to cooperate in strategic alliances, there are also incentives to cheat. Cheating generally takes one or a combination of three forms: adverse selection, moral hazard, or holdup.

Strategic alliances can be a source of sustained competitive advantage. The rarity of alliances depends not only on the number of competing firms that have developed an alliance, but also on the benefits that firms gain through their alliances.

Imitation through direct duplication of an alliance may be costly because of the socially complex relations that underlie an alliance; however, imitation through substitution is more likely. Two substitutes for alliances may be "going it alone," where firms develop and exploit the relevant sets of resources and capabilities on their own, and acquisitions. Opportunism, capabilities, and uncertainty all have an impact on when "going it alone" will be a substitute for a strategic alliance. Acquisitions may be a substitute for strategic alliances when there are no legal constraints, strategic flexibility is not an important consideration, when the acquired firm has relatively little unwanted "organizational baggage," and when the value of a firm's resources and capabilities does not depend on its remaining independent. However, when these conditions do not exist, acquisitions are not a substitute for alliances.

The key issue facing firms in organizing their alliances is to facilitate cooperation while avoiding the threat of cheating. Contracts, equity investments, firm reputations, joint ventures, and trust can all reduce the threat of cheating in different contexts. These tools can also be used to reduce the threats to alliances in an international context.

CHALLENGE QUESTIONS

1. One reason why firms might want to pursue a strategic alliance strategy is to exploit economies of scale. Exploiting economies of scale should reduce a firm's costs. Does this mean that a firm pursuing an alliance strategy to exploit economies of scale is actually pursuing a cost leadership strategy? Why or why not?

2. Consider the joint venture between General Motors and Toyota. GM has been interested in learning how to profitably manufacture high-quality small cars from its alliance with Toyota. Toyota has been interested in gaining access to GM's U.S. distribution network and in reducing the political liability associated with local content laws. Which of these firms do you think is more likely to accomplish its objectives, and why? What implications, if any, does your answer have for a possible "learning race" in this alliance?

3. Some researchers have argued that strategic alliances are one way in which firms can help facilitate the development of a tacit collusion strategy. In your view, what are the critical differences between tacit collusion strategies and strategic alliance strategies? How can one tell whether two firms are engaging in an alliance to facilitate collusion or are engaging in an alliance for other purposes?

4. Some researchers have argued that alliances can be used to help firms evaluate the economic potential of entering into a new industry or market. Under what conditions will a firm seeking to evaluate these opportunities need to invest in an alliance to accomplish this evaluation? Why couldn't such a firm simply hire some smart managers, consultants, and industry experts to evaluate the economic potential of entering into a new industry? What, if anything, about an alliance makes this a better way to evaluate entry opportunities than alternative methods?

5. If adverse selection, moral hazard, and holdup are such significant problems for firms pursuing alliance strategies, why do firms even bother with alliances? Why don't they instead adopt a "go it alone" strategy to replace strategic alliances?

PROBLEM SET

1. Which of the following firms faces the greater threat of "cheating" in the alliances described, and why?
(a) Firm I and Firm II form a strategic alliance. As part of the alliance, Firm I agrees to build a new plant right next to Firm II's primary facility. In return, Firm II promises to buy most of the output of this new plant. Who is at risk, Firm I or Firm II?
(b) Firm A and Firm B form a strategic alliance. As part of the alliance, Firm A promises to begin selling products it already sells around the world in the home country of Firm B. In return, Firm B promises to provide Firm A with crucial contacts in its home country's government. These contacts are essential if Firm A is going to be able to sell in Firm B's home country. Who is at risk, Firm A or Firm B?
(c) Firm 1 and Firm 2 form a strategic alliance. As part of the alliance, Firm 1 promises to provide Firm 2 access to some new and untested technology that Firm 2 will use in its products. In return, Firm 2 will share some of the profits from its sales with Firm 1. Who is at risk, Firm 1 or Firm 2?

2. For each of the strategic alliances described in the above question, what actions could be taken to reduce the likelihood that partner firms will "cheat" in these alliances?

3. Examine the Web sites of the following strategic alliances and determine which of the sources of value presented in Table 9.1 are present:

(a) Dow-Corning (an alliance between Dow Chemical and Corning)
(b) CFM (an alliance between General Electric and SNECMA)
(c) Cingular (an alliance between SBC and BellSouth)
(d) NCAA (an alliance among colleges and universities in the United States)
(e) Visa (an alliance among banks in the United States)
(f) The alliance among United, Delta, Singapore Airlines, AeroMexico, Alitalia, and Korean Air

END NOTES

1. See www.pwc.com/extweb/exccps.nsf/docid; www.addme.com/issue208; J. McCracken (2006). "Ford doubles reported loss for second quarter." *The Wall Street Journal*, Thursday, August 3, pp. A3; www.msnbc.msn.com/id/13753688.
2. Badaracco, J. L., and N. Hasegawa (1988). "General Motors' Asian alliances." Harvard Business School Case No. 9-388-094.
3. See Burgers, W. P., C. W. L. Hill, and W. C. Kim (1993). "A theory of global strategic alliances: The case of the global auto industry." *Strategic Management Journal*, 14, pp. 419–432.
4. See Freeman, A., and R. Hudson (1980). "DuPont and Philips plan joint venture to make, market laser disc products." *Wall Street Journal*, December 22, p. 10.
5. Teitelbaum, R. S. (1992). "Eskimo pie." *Fortune*, June 15, p. 123.
6. Nanda, A., and C. A. Bartlett (1990). "Corning Incorporated: A network of alliances." Harvard Business School Case No. 9-391-102.
7. See Knight, F. H. (1965). *Risk, uncertainty, and profit.* New York: John Wiley & Sons, Inc., on uncertainty; Kogut, B. (1991). "Joint ventures and the option to expand and acquire." *Management Science*, 37, pp. 19–33; Burgers, W. P., C. W. L. Hill, and W. C. Kim (1993). "A theory of global strategic alliances: The case of the global auto industry." *Strategic Management Journal*, 14, pp. 419–432; Noldeke, G., and K. M. Schmidt (1998). "Sequential investments and options to own." *Rand Journal of Economics*, 29(4), pp. 633–653; and Folta, T. B. (1998). "Governance and uncertainty: The tradeoff between administrative control and commitment." *Strategic Management Journal*, 19, pp. 1007–1028.
8. See Kogut, B. (1991). "Joint ventures and the option to expand and acquire." *Management Science*, 37, pp. 19–33; and Balakrishnan, S., and M. Koza (1993). "Information asymmetry, adverse selection and joint-ventures." *Journal of Economic Behavior & Organization*, 20, pp. 99–117.
9. See, for example, Ernst, D., and J. Bleeke (1993). *Collaborating to compete: Using strategic alliances and acquisition in the global marketplace.* New York: John Wiley & Sons, Inc.
10. These terms are defined in Barney, J. B., and W. G. Ouchi (1986). *Organizational economics.* San Francisco: Jossey-Bass; and Holmstrom, B. (1979). "Moral hazard and observability." *Bell Journal of Economics*, 10(1), pp. 74–91. Problems of cheating in economic exchanges, in general, and in alliances in particular, are discussed by Gulati, R., and H. Singh (1998). "The architecture of cooperation: Managing coordination costs and appropriation concerns in strategic alliances." *Administrative Science Quarterly*, 43, pp. 781–814; Williamson, O. E. (1991). "Comparative economic organization: The analysis of discrete structural alternatives." *Administrative Science Quarterly*, 36, pp. 269–296; Osborn, R. N., and C. C. Baughn (1990). "Forms of interorganizational governance for multinational alliances." *Academy of Management Journal*, 33(3), pp. 503–519; Hagedoorn, J., and R. Narula (1996). "Choosing organizational modes of strategic technology partnering: International and sectoral differences." *Journal of International Business Studies*, second quarter, pp. 265–284; Hagedorn, J. (1996). "Trends and patterns in strategic technology partnering since the early seventies." *Review of Industrial Organization*, 11, pp. 601–616; Kent, D. H. (1991). "Joint ventures vs. non-joint ventures: An empirical investigation." *Strategic Management Journal*, 12, pp. 387–393; and Shane, S. A. (1998). "Making new franchise systems work." *Strategic Management Journal*, 19, pp. 697–707.
11. Such alliance difficulties are described in Ouchi, W. G. (1984). *The M-form society: How American teamwork can capture the competitive edge.* Reading, MA: Addison-Wesley; and Bresser, R. K. (1988). "Cooperative strategy." *Strategic Management Journal*, 9, pp. 475–492.
12. Pope, K. (1993). "Dealers accuse Compaq of jilting them." *Wall Street Journal*, February 26, pp. 8, B1 +.
13. Williamson, O. E. (1975). *Markets and hierarchies: Analysis and antitrust implications.* New York: Free Press; Klein, B., R. Crawford, and A. Alchian (1978). "Vertical integration, appropriable rents, and the competitive contracting process." *Journal of Law and Economics*, 21, pp. 297–326.
14. See, for example, Yan, A., and B. Gray (1994). "Bargaining power, management control, and performance in United States–China joint ventures: A comparative case study." *Academy of Management Journal*, 37, pp. 1478–1517.
15. See Badaracco, J. L., and N. Hasegawa (1988). "General Motors' Asian alliances." Harvard Business School Case No. 9-388-094, on GM and Toyota; Patterson, G. A. (1991). "Mazda hopes to crack Japan's top tier." *Wall Street Journal*, September 20, pp. B1 +; and Williams, M., and M. Kanabayashi (1993). "Mazda and Ford drop proposal to build cars together in Europe." *Wall Street Journal*, March 4, p. A14, on Ford and Mazda; and Ennis, P. (1991). "Mitsubishi group wary of deeper ties to Chrysler." *Tokyo Business Today*, 59, July, p. 10, on DaimlerChrysler and Mitsubishi.
16. See, for example, Ernst, D., and J. Bleeke (1993). *Collaborating to compete: Using strategic alliances and acquisition in the global marketplace.* New York: John Wiley & Sons, Inc.; and Barney, J. B., and M. H. Hansen (1994). "Trustworthiness as a source of competitive advantage." *Strategic Management Journal*, 15, winter (special issue), pp. 175–190.
17. Ernst, D., and J. Bleeke (1993). *Collaborating to compete: Using strategic alliances and acquisition in the global marketplace.* New York: John Wiley & Sons, Inc.
18. Bartlett, C., and S. Ghoshal (1993). "Beyond the M-form: Toward a managerial theory of the firm." *Strategic Management Journal*, 14, pp. 23–46.
19. See Nagarajan, A., and W. Mitchell (1998). "Evolutionary diffusion: Internal and external methods used to acquire encompassing, complementary, and incremental technological changes in the lithotripsy industry." *Strategic Management Journal*, 19, pp. 1063–1077; Hagedoorn, J., and B. Sadowski (1999). "The transition from strategic technology alliances to mergers and acquisitions: An exploratory study." *Journal of Management Studies*, 36(1), pp. 87–107; and Newburry, W., and Y. Zeira (1997). "Generic differences between equity international joint ventures (EIJVs), international acquisitions (IAs) and International Greenfield investments (IGIs): Implications for parent companies." *Journal of World Business*, 32(2), pp. 87–102, on alliance substitutes.
20. Barney, J. B. (1999). "How a firm's capabilities affect boundary decisions." *Sloan Management Review*, 40(3), pp. 137–145.
21. See Hennart, J. F. (1988). "A transaction cost theory of equity joint ventures." *Strategic Management Journal*, 9, pp. 361–374; Kogut, B. (1988). "Joint ventures: Theoretical and empirical perspectives." *Strategic Management Journal*, 9, pp. 319–332; and Barney, J. B. (1999). "How a firm's capabilities affect boundary decisions." *Sloan Management Review*, 40(3), pp. 137–145, for a discussion of these limitations.

22. See Ouchi, W. G. (1984). *The M-form society: How American teamwork can capture the competitive edge.* Reading, MA: Addison-Wesley; and Barney, J. B. (1990). "Profit sharing bonuses and the cost of debt: Business finance and compensation policy in Japanese electronics firms." *Asia Pacific Journal of Management,* 7, pp. 49–64.

23. This is an argument developed by Barney, J. B., and M. H. Hansen (1994). "Trustworthiness as a source of competitive advantage." *Strategic Management Journal,* 15, winter (special issue), pp. 175–190; Weigelt, K., and C. Camerer (1988). "Reputation and corporate strategy: A review of recent theory and applications." *Strategic Management Journal,* 9, pp. 443–454; and Granovetter, M. (1985). "Economic action and social structure: The problem of embeddedness." *American Journal of Sociology,* 3, pp. 481–510.

24. See, for example, Eichenseher, J., and D. Shields (1985). "Reputation and corporate strategy: A review of recent theory and applications." *Strategic Management Journal,* 9, pp. 443–454; Beatty, R., and R. Ritter (1986). "Investment banking, reputation, and the underpricing of initial public offerings." *Journal of Financial Economics,* 15, pp. 213–232; Kalleberg, A. L., and T. Reve (1992). "Contracts and commitment: Economic and Sociological Perspectives on Employment Relations." *Human Relations,* 45(9), pp. 1103–1132; Larson, A. (1992). "Network dyads in entrepreneurial settings: A study of the governance of exchange relationships." *Administrative Science Quarterly,* March, pp. 76–104; Stuart, T. E., H. Hoang, and R. C. Hybels (1999). "Interorganizational endorsements and the performance of entrepreneurial ventures." *Administrative Science Quarterly,* 44, pp. 315–349; Stuart, T. E. (1998). "Network positions and propensities to collaborate: An investigation of strategic alliance formation in a high-technology industry." *Administrative Science Quarterly,* 43(3), pp. 668–698; and Gulati, R. (1998). "Alliances and networks." *Strategic Management Journal,* 19, pp. 293–317.

25. Personal communication, April 8, 1986.

26. This same theoretic approach to firm reputation is discussed in Tirole, J. (1988). *The theory of industrial organization.* Cambridge, MA: MIT Press.

27. Scherer, F. M. (1980). *Industrial market structure and economic performance.* Boston: Houghton Mifflin.

28. See again, Ernst, D., and J. Bleeke (1993). *Collaborating to compete: Using strategic alliances and acquisition in the global marketplace.* New York: John Wiley & Sons, Inc.; and Barney, J. B., and M. H. Hansen (1994). "Trustworthiness as a source of competitive advantage." *Strategic Management Journal,* 15, winter (special issue), pp. 175–190. In fact, there is a great deal of literature on the role of trust in strategic alliances. Some of the most interesting of this work can be found in Holm, D. B., K. Eriksson, and J. Johanson (1999). "Creating value through mutual commitment to business network relationships." *Strategic Management Journal,* 20, pp. 467–486; Lorenzoni, G., and A. Lipparini (1999). "The leveraging of interfirm relationships as a distinctive organizational capability: A longitudinal study." *Strategic Management Journal,* 20(4), pp. 317–338; Blois, K. J. (1999). "Trust in business to business relationships: An evaluation of its status." *Journal of Management Studies,* 36(2), pp. 197–215; Chiles, T. H., and J. F. McMackin (1996). "Integrating variable risk preferences, trust, and transaction cost economics." *Academy of Management Review,* 21(1), pp. 73–99; Larzelere, R. E., and T. L. Huston (1980). "The dyadic trust scale: Toward understanding interpersonal trust in close relationships." *Journal of Marriage and the Family,* August, pp. 595–604; Butler, J. K., Jr. (1983). "Reciprocity of trust between professionals and their secretaries." *Psychological Reports,* 53, pp. 411–416; Zaheer, A., and N. Venkatraman (1995). "Relational governance as an interorganizational strategy: An empirical test of the role of trust in economic exchange." *Strategic Management Journal,* 16, pp. 373–392; Butler, J. K., Jr., and R. S. Cantrell (1984). "A behavioral decision theory approach to modeling dyadic trust in superiors and subordinates." *Psychological Reports,* 55, pp. 19–28; Carney, M. (1998). "The competitiveness of networked production: The role of trust and asset specificity." *Journal of Management Studies,* 35(4), pp. 457–479.

29. Ernst, D., and J. Bleeke (1993). *Collaborating to compete: Using strategic alliances and acquisition in the global marketplace.* New York: John Wiley & Sons, Inc.

30. See Mohr, J., and R. Spekman (1994). "Characteristics of partnership success: Partnership attributes, communication behavior, and conflict resolution techniques." *Strategic Management Journal,* 15, pp. 135–152; and Zaheer, A., and N. Venkatraman (1995). "Relational governance as an interorganizational strategy: An empirical test of the role of trust in economic exchange." *Strategic Management Journal,* 16, pp. 373–392.

31. Kranhold, K. (2004). "China's price for market entry: Give us your technology, too." *Wall Street Journal,* February 26, pp. A1 +.

Mergers and Acquisitions

LEARNING OBJECTIVES

After reading this chapter, you should be able to:

1. Describe different types of mergers and acquisitions.

2. Estimate the return to the stockholders of bidding and target firms when there is no strategic relatedness between firms.

3. Describe different sources of relatedness between bidding and target firms.

4. Estimate the return to stockholders of bidding and target firms when there is strategic relatedness between firms.

5. Describe five reasons why bidding firms might still engage in acquisitions, even if, on average, they do not create value for a bidding firm's stockholders.

6. Describe three ways that bidding firms might be able to generate high returns for their equity holders through implementing mergers or acquisitions.

7. Describe the major challenges that firms integrating acquisitions are likely to face.

8. Discuss unique challenges to merger and acquisition strategies in an international context.

The New Acquirers

Mergers and acquisitions have been an important part of the business scene for decades. Historically, acquirers have tended to fall into two categories: strategic acquirers and investment acquirers. **Strategic acquirers** use acquisitions to extend their current business, to leverage their current capabilities, or to diversify into new businesses. These are the acquirers that are the subject of most of the discussion in this chapter.

Investment acquirers have traditionally taken a different approach to acquisitions. These firms typically do not have a central business they are looking to extend or enhance. Instead, they acquire a portfolio of underperforming firms and then implement a variety of incentives and control systems to help turn these underperforming firms into high-performing firms. When the performance of these firms begins to improve, investment acquirers will either "take these firms public" by selling shares to the general public or sell them to strategic acquirers. In general, investment acquirers will hold on to a firm only long enough to turn it around, whereas strategic acquirers will operate the firms they acquire for longer periods of time.

Recently, a new type of acquirer has emerged—the **private equity firm**. Private equity firms are similar to traditional investment acquirers. For example, private equity firms try to buy underperforming firms and install incentives and management controls designed to improve a firm's performance. Once this higher level of performance is achieved, the private equity firms will sell the firms in their portfolio, either by taking them public or by selling them to strategic acquirers. However, private equity firms differ from traditional investment acquirers in one important way: Whereas traditional investment acquirers would often hold on to a firm for 7 to 10 years— to complete its turnaround—and only realize the value they created by selling a firm, private equity firms impose a variety of fees and other charges on the firms they acquire almost immediately. This means that private equity firms are able to appropriate much of the value of their

investments much sooner than was the case for traditional investor acquirers.

All of this is perfectly legal, and appropriating more of the value of its investments sooner rather than later is generally consistent with the wealth-maximizing interests of a private equity firm's owners. Recently, however, some of the short-term activities of private equity investors have been questioned. In particular, private equity firms sometimes charge the companies they acquire huge fees for the services they supposedly provide. In one case, these fees totaled over $1 billion. These firms can also charge the firms they have acquired the same fee several times. Private equity firms can also load their acquisitions with debt. This can weaken the balance sheet of these firms and has even sent some firms into bankruptcy.

Consider a few examples. In 2004, Blackstone Group charged a fee of $45 million to Celanse Corporation, a firm it had recently acquired, for the advice it had given Celanse about the acquisition. The owners of Warner Music (including Bain Capital, Thomas H. Lee, and Providence) charged a $75 million fee for giving advice to Warner about being acquired. One group of private equity firms charged Warner Chilcott—a pharmaceutical maker—a fee of $27.4 million when it went public because Warner Chilcott would no longer need its management advice. Another group of private equity firms accumulated $576 million in dividends and fees from Intelsat Global Services—a satellite operator—within one year of buying the firm for $513 million. And while this money was being collected, Intelsat lost $325 million, doubled its debt to $4.75 billion, and laid off 20 percent of its employees. Bare Escentuals Inc., a

San Francisco–based cosmetic maker, borrowed $412 million mostly to pay $309 million in dividends and transactions fees to its private equity owners, even though this firm earned only $24 million in 2005. Despite its low credit rating, in 2006 Bare Escentuals borrowed again to pay its private equity owners $342 million in dividends and fees.

None of this would matter if private equity firms were creating enough long-term value through restructuring the low-performing firms they have acquired. Historically, this has been the case. From 1980 through 2003, the value of companies sold to the public by private equity firms was greater than the value of similar companies sold to the public without the involvement of private equity firms. However, in 2006, this trend turned around. The value of private-equity–backed sales was 10 percentage points lower than the value of similar firms sold without the involvement of private equity firms. This is consistent with private equity firms using fees and dividends to squeeze cash out of the firms in their portfolio, perhaps to the detriment of the long-term performance of those firms.

Sources: E. Thornton (2006)."Gluttons at the gate." *BusinessWeek*, October 30, pp. 58 +; J. Lerner and P. Gompers (2002)."Money chasing deals? The impact of fund inflows on the valuation of private equity investments." *Journal of Financial Economics*, 55, pp. 281–325; G. Ip and H. Sender (2006)." In today's buyouts, payday for firms is never far away." *Wall Street Journal*, July 25, pp. A1 +.

Mergers and acquisitions are one very common way that a firm can accomplish its vertical integration and diversification objectives. However, although a firm may be able to accomplish its vertical integration and diversification objectives through mergers or acquisitions, it is sometimes difficult to generate real economic profit from doing so. Indeed, one of the strongest empirical findings in the fields of strategic management and finance is that, on average, the equity holders of target firms in mergers and acquisitions make money while the equity holders of bidding firms in these same mergers and acquisitions usually only "break even."

What Are Mergers and Acquisitions?

The terms *mergers* and *acquisitions* are often used interchangeably, even though they are not synonyms. A firm engages in an **acquisition** when it purchases a second firm. The form of this purchase can vary. For example, an acquiring firm can use cash it has generated from its ongoing businesses to purchase a target firm; it can go into debt to purchase a target firm; it can use its own equity to purchase a target firm; or it can use a mix of these mechanisms to purchase a target firm. Also, an acquiring firm can purchase all of a target firm's assets; it can purchase a majority of those assets (greater than 51 percent); or it can purchase a **controlling share** of those assets (i.e., enough assets so that the acquiring firm is able to make all the management and strategic decisions in the target firm).

Acquisitions also vary on several other dimensions. For example, **friendly acquisitions** occur when the management of the target firm wants the firm to be acquired. **Unfriendly acquisitions** occur when the management of the target firm does not want the firm to be acquired. Some unfriendly acquisitions are also known as **hostile takeovers**. Some acquisitions are accomplished through direct negotiations between an acquiring firm's managers and the managers of a target firm. This is especially common when a target firm is **privately held** (i.e., when it has not sold shares on the public stock market) or **closely held** (i.e., when it has not sold very many shares on the public stock market). Other acquisitions are accomplished by the acquiring firm publicly announcing that it is willing to purchase the outstanding shares of a potential target for a particular price. This price is normally greater than the current market price of the target firm's shares. The difference between the current market price of a target firm's shares and the price a potential acquirer offers to pay for those shares is known as an **acquisition premium**. This approach to purchasing a firm is called a **tender offer**. Tender offers can be made either with or without the support of the management of the target firm. Obviously, tender offers with the support of the target firm's management are typically friendly in character; those made without the support of the target firm's management are typically unfriendly.

It is usually the case that larger firms—in terms of sales or assets—acquire smaller firms. For example, this was the case both for DaimlerChrysler's acquisition of Mitsubishi and Renault's acquisition of Nissan. In contrast, when the assets of two similar-sized firms are combined, this transaction is called a **merger.** Mergers can be accomplished in many of the same ways as acquisitions, that is, using cash or stock to purchase a percentage of another firm's assets. Typically, however, mergers will not be unfriendly. In a merger, one firm purchases some percentage of a second firm's assets while the second firm simultaneously purchases some percentage of the first firm's assets. For example, DaimlerChrysler—the firm that purchased Mitsubishi—was created as a merger between Daimler-Benz (the maker of Mercedes-Benz) and Chrysler. Daimler-Benz invested some of its capital in Chrysler, and Chrysler invested some of its capital in Daimler-Benz.

Although mergers typically begin as a transaction between equals—that is, between firms of equal size and profitability—they often evolve after a merger such that one firm becomes more dominant in the management of the merged firm than the other. For example, most observers believe that Daimler (the German part of DaimlerChrysler) has become more dominant in the management of the combined firm than Chrysler (the American part). Indeed, although Daimler management may be willing to "write off" their interests in Mitsubishi as a bad investment, Chrysler management is very reluctant to do so, because they have worked with Mitsubishi to help develop platforms for many of Chrysler's best-selling cars. How long a Daimler-dominated DaimlerChrysler will put up with a "bad" investment that only helps the Chrysler part of the firm is an open question.[1] Put differently, although mergers usually start out as something different from acquisitions, they usually end up looking more like acquisitions than mergers.

The Value of Mergers and Acquisitions

That merger and acquisition strategies are an important strategic option open to firms pursuing diversification and vertical integration strategies can hardly be disputed. The number of firms that have used merger and acquisition strategies to become diversified over the last few years is staggering. Worldwide, the total value of announced merger and acquisition activities from 2003 through 2005 was $2.58 trillion. In 2005 alone, 11,013 deals were completed for a market value of $1.2 trillion.[2] These firms ranged in size from Procter & Gamble and Bank of America, two of the largest firms in the world, to Inflazyme Pharmaceuticals, a relatively small biotechnology start-up that acquired Glycodesign, Inc.

The list of firms that engaged in mergers and acquisitions in 2005 was long and varied. For example, SBC purchased its former parent AT&T in a deal valued at $16 billion and then renamed the entire firm AT&T. Procter & Gamble purchased

Gillette for $57 billion. SABMiller bought Columbian brewer Bavaria for $5.6 billion. eBay bought Skype (a firm in the voice over Internet business) for $2 billion. Adidas bought Reebok for $4 billion. Verizon bought MCI for $6.8 billion. Viacom bought DreamWorks for $1.5 billion. The list goes on and on.[3]

That mergers and acquisitions are common is clear. What is less clear is that they actually generate value for firms implementing these strategies. Two cases will be examined here: mergers and acquisitions between strategically unrelated firms and mergers and acquisitions between strategically related firms.

Mergers and Acquisitions: The Unrelated Case

Imagine the following scenario: One firm (the target) is the object of an acquisition effort, and 10 firms (the bidders) are interested in making this acquisition. Suppose the **current market value** of the target firm is $10,000—that is, the price of each of this firm's shares times the number of shares outstanding equals $10,000. Also, suppose the current market value of each of the bidding firms is $15,000.[4] Finally, suppose there is no strategic relatedness between these bidding firms and the target. This means that the value of any one of these bidding firms when combined with the target firm exactly equals the sum of the value of these firms as separate entities. In this example, because the current market value of the target is $10,000 and the current market value of the bidding firms is $15,000, the value of this target when combined with any of these bidders would be $25,000 ($10,000 + $15,000). Given this information, at what price will this target be acquired, and what are the economic performance implications for bidding and target firms at this price?

In this, and all acquisition situations, bidding firms will be willing to pay a price for a target up to the value that the target firm adds to the bidder once it is acquired. This price is simply the difference between the value of the two firms combined (in this case $25,000) and the value of the bidding firm by itself (in this case $15,000). Notice that this price does not depend on the value of the target firm acting as an independent business; rather, it depends on the value that the target firm creates when it is combined with the bidding firm. Any price for a target less than this value (i.e., less than $10,000) will be a source of economic profit for a bidding firm; any price equal to this value (i.e., equal to $10,000) will be a source of zero economic profits; and any price greater than this value (i.e., greater than $10,000) will be a source of economic losses for the bidding firm that acquires the target.

It is not hard to see that the price of this acquisition will quickly rise to $10,000, and that at this price the bidding firm that acquires the target will earn zero economic profits. The price of this acquisition will quickly rise to $10,000 because any bid less than $10,000 will generate economic profits for a successful bidder. These potential profits, in turn, will generate entry into the bidding war for a target. Because entry into the acquisition contest is very likely, the price of the acquisition will quickly rise to its value, and economic profits will not be created.

Moreover, at this $10,000 price the target firm's equity holders will also gain zero economic profits. Indeed, for them, all that has occurred is that the market value of the target firm has been capitalized in the form of a cash payment from the bidder to the target. The target was worth $10,000, and that is exactly what these equity holders will receive.

Mergers and Acquisitions: The Related Case

The conclusion that the acquisition of strategically unrelated targets will generate only zero economic profits for both the bidding and the target firms is not surprising. It is very consistent with the discussion of the economic consequences of unrelated diversification in Chapter 7. There it was argued that there is no economic justification for a corporate diversification strategy that does not build on some type of economy of scope across the businesses within which a firm operates, and therefore unrelated diversification is not an economically viable corporate strategy. So, if there is any hope that mergers and acquisitions will be a source of superior performance for bidding firms, it must be because of some sort of strategic relatedness or economy of scope between bidding and target firms.

Types of Strategic Relatedness

Of course, bidding and target firms can be strategically related in a wide variety of ways. Three particularly important lists of these potential linkages are discussed here.[5]

The FTC Categories. Because mergers and acquisitions can have the effect of increasing (or decreasing) the level of concentration in an industry, the Federal Trade Commission (FTC) is charged with the responsibility of evaluating the competitive implications of proposed mergers or acquisitions. In principle, the FTC will disallow any acquisition involving firms with headquarters in the United States that could have the potential for generating monopoly (or oligopoly) profits in an industry. To help in this regulatory effort, the FTC has developed a typology of mergers and acquisitions (see Table 10.1). Each category in this typology can be thought of as a different way in which a bidding firm and a target firm can be related in a merger or acquisition.

According to the FTC, a firm engages in a **vertical merger** when it vertically integrates, either forward or backward, through its acquisition efforts. Vertical mergers could include a firm purchasing critical suppliers of raw materials (backward vertical integration) or acquiring customers and distribution networks (forward vertical integration). eBay's acquisition of Skype is an example of a backward vertical integration as eBay tries to assemble all the resources to compete in the Internet telephone industry. Disney's acquisition of Capital Cities/ABC can be understood as an attempt by Disney to forward vertically integrate into the entertainment distribution industry, and its acquisition of ESPN can be seen as backward vertical integration into the entertainment production business.[6]

Table 10.1 **FTC Categories of Mergers and Acquisitions**

■ Vertical merger	A firm acquires former suppliers or customers.
■ Horizontal merger	A firm acquires a former competitor.
■ Product extension merger	A firm gains access to complementary products through an acquisition.
■ Market extension merger	A firm gains access to complementary markets through an acquisition.
■ Conglomerate merger	There is no strategic relatedness between a bidding and a target firm.

314   Part 3   Corporate Strategies

A firm engages in a **horizontal merger** when it acquires a former competitor; Adidas' acquisition of Reebok is an example of a horizontal merger, as the number 2 and number 3 sneaker manufacturers in the world combined their efforts. Obviously, the FTC is particularly concerned with the competitive implications of horizontal mergers because these strategies can have the most direct and obvious anticompetitive implications in an industry. For example, the FTC raised antitrust concerns in the $10 billion merger between Oracle and PeopleSoft, because these firms, collectively, dominated the enterprise software market. Similar concerns were raised in the $16.4 billion merger between ChevronTexaco and Unocal and the merger between Mobil and Exxon.

The third type of merger identified by the FTC is a **product extension merger**. In a product extension merger, firms acquire complementary products through their merger and acquisition activities. Examples include SBC's acquisition of AT&T and Verizon's acquisition of MCI.

The fourth type of merger identified by the FTC is a **market extension merger**. Here, the primary objective is to gain access to new geographic markets. Examples include SABMiller's acquisition of Bavaria Brewery Company in Columbia, South America.

The final type of merger or acquisition identified by the FTC is a **conglomerate merger**. For the FTC, conglomerate mergers are a residual category. If there are no vertical, horizontal, product extension, or market extension links between firms, the FTC defines the merger or acquisition activity between firms as a conglomerate merger. Given our earlier conclusion that mergers or acquisitions between strategically *unrelated* firms will not generate economic profits for either bidders or targets, it should not be surprising that there are currently relatively few examples of conglomerate mergers or acquisitions; however, at various times in history, they have been relatively common. In the 1960s, for example, many acquisitions took the form of conglomerate mergers. Research has shown that the fraction of single-business firms in the *Fortune* 500 dropped from 22.8 percent in 1959 to 14.8 percent in 1969, while the fraction of firms in the *Fortune* 500 pursuing unrelated diversification strategies rose from 7.3 to 18.7 percent during the same time period. These findings are consistent with an increase in the number of conglomerate mergers and acquisitions during the 1960s.[7]

Despite the popularity of conglomerate mergers in the 1960s, many mergers or acquisitions among strategically unrelated firms are divested shortly after they are completed. One study estimated that over one-third of the conglomerate mergers of the 1960s were divested by the early 1980s. Another study showed that over 50 percent of these acquisitions were subsequently divested. These results are all consistent with our earlier conclusion that mergers or acquisitions involving strategically unrelated firms are not a source of economic profits.[8]

Other Types of Strategic Relatedness.   Although the FTC categories of mergers and acquisitions provide some information about possible motives underlying these corporate strategies, they do not capture the full complexity of the links that might exist between bidding and target firms. Several authors have attempted to develop more complete lists of possible sources of relatedness between bidding and target firms. One of these lists, developed by Professor Michael Lubatkin, is summarized in Table 10.2. This list includes **technical economies** (in marketing, production, and similar forms of relatedness), **pecuniary economies** (market power), and **diversification economies** (in portfolio management and risk reduction) as possible bases of strategic relatedness between bidding and target firms.

Table 10.2 **Lubatkin's List of Potential Sources of Strategic Relatedness Between Bidding and Target Firms**

Technical economies	Scale economies that occur when the physical processes inside a firm are altered so that the same amounts of input produce a higher quantity of outputs. Sources of technical economies include marketing, production, experience, scheduling, banking, and compensation.
Pecuniary economies	Economies achieved by the ability of firms to dictate prices by exerting market power.
Diversification economies	Economies achieved by improving a firm's performance relative to its risk attributes or lowering its risk attributes relative to its performance. Sources of diversification economies include portfolio management and risk reduction.

Source: M. Lubatkin (1983). "Mergers and the performance of the Acquiring Firm." *Academy of Management Review*, 8, pp. 218–225. © 1983 by the Academy of Management. Reproduced with permission.

A second important list of possible sources of strategic relatedness between bidding and target firms was developed by Michael Jensen and Richard Ruback after a comprehensive review of empirical research on the economic returns to mergers and acquisitions. This list is summarized in Table 10.3 and includes the following factors as possible sources of economic gains in mergers and acquisitions: potential reductions in production or distribution costs (from economies of

Table 10.3 **Jensen and Ruback's List of Reasons Why Bidding Firms Might Want to Engage in Merger and Acquisition Strategies**

To reduce production or distribution costs:

1. Through economies of scale.
2. Through vertical integration.
3. Through the adoption of more efficient production or organizational technology.
4. Through the increased utilization of the bidder's management team.
5. Through a reduction of agency costs by bringing organization-specific assets under common ownership.

Financial motivations:

1. To gain access to underutilized tax shields.
2. To avoid bankruptcy costs.
3. To increase leverage opportunities.
4. To gain other tax advantages.
5. To gain market power in product markets.
6. To eliminate inefficient target management.

Source: Reprinted from "The Market for Corporate Control: The Scientific Evidence." *Journal of Financial Economics*, 11, pp. 5–50. Vol. II, Jensen M. C. and R. S. Ruback. Copyright © 1983, with permission from Elsevier.

scale, vertical integration, reduction in agency costs, and so forth); the realization of financial opportunities (such as gaining access to underutilized tax shields, avoiding bankruptcy costs); the creation of market power; and the ability to eliminate inefficient management in the target firm.

To be economically valuable, links between bidding and target firms must meet the same criteria as diversification strategies (see Chapter 7). First, these links must build on real economies of scope between bidding and target firms. These economies of scope can reflect either cost savings or revenue enhancements that are created by combining firms. Second, not only must this economy of scope exist, but it must be less costly for the merged firm to realize than for outside equity holders to realize on their own. As is the case with corporate diversification strategies, by investing in a diversified portfolio of stocks, outside equity investors can gain many of the economies associated with a merger or acquisition on their own. Moreover, investors can realize some of these economies of scope at almost zero cost. In this situation, it makes little sense for investors to "hire" managers in firms to realize these economies of scope for them through a merger or acquisition. Rather, firms should pursue merger and acquisition strategies only to obtain valuable economies of scope that outside investors find too costly to create on their own.

Economic Profits in Related Acquisitions

If bidding and target firms are strategically related, then the economic value of these two firms combined is greater than their economic value as separate entities. To see how this changes returns to merger and acquisition strategies, consider the following scenario: As before, there is one target firm and 10 bidding firms. The market value of the target firm as a stand-alone entity is $10,000, and the market value of the bidding firms as stand-alone entities is $15,000. However, unlike the earlier scenario in this chapter, the bidding and target firms are strategically related. Any of the types of relatedness identified in Table 10.1, Table 10.2, or Table 10.3 could be the source of these economies of scope. They imply that when any of the bidding firms and the target are combined, the market value of this combined entity will be $32,000—note that $32,000 is greater than the sum of $15,000 and $10,000. At what price will this target firm be acquired, and what are the economic profit implications for bidding and target firms at this price?

As before, bidding firms will be willing to pay a price for a target up to the value that a target firm adds once it is acquired. Thus, the maximum price bidding firms are willing to pay is still the difference between the value of the combined entity (here, $32,000) and the value of a bidding firm on its own (here, $15,000), or $17,000.

As was the case for the strategically unrelated acquisition, it is not hard to see that the price for actually acquiring the target firm in this scenario will rapidly rise to $17,000, because any bid less than $17,000 has the potential for generating profits for a bidding firm. Suppose that one bidding firm offers $13,000 for the target. For this $13,000, the bidding firm gains access to a target that will generate $17,000 of value once it is acquired. Thus, to this bidding firm, the target is worth $17,000, and a bid of $13,000 will generate $4,000 economic profit. Of course, these potential profits will motivate entry into the competitive bidding process. Entry will continue until the price of this target equals $17,000. Any price greater than $17,000 would mean that a bidding firm is actually losing money on its acquisition.[9]

At this $17,000 price, the successful bidding firm earns zero economic profits. After all, this firm has acquired an asset that will generate $17,000 of value and has paid $17,000 to do so. However, the owners of the target firm will earn an economic profit worth $7,000. As a stand-alone firm, the target is worth $10,000; when combined with a bidding firm, it is worth $17,000. The difference between the value of the target as a stand-alone entity and its value in combination with a bidding firm is the value of the economic profit that can be appropriated by the owners of the target firm.

Thus, the existence of strategic relatedness between bidding and target firms is not a sufficient condition for the equity holders of bidding firms to earn economic profits from their acquisition strategies. If the economic potential of acquiring a particular target firm is widely known and if several potential bidding firms can all obtain this value by acquiring a target, the equity holders of bidding firms will, at best, earn only zero economic profits from implementing an acquisition strategy. In this setting, a "strategically related" merger or acquisition will create economic value, but this value will be distributed in the form of economic profits to the equity holders of acquired target firms.

Because so much of the value created in a merger or acquisition is appropriated by the stockholders of the target firm, it is not surprising that many small and entrepreneurial firms look to be acquired as one way to compensate their owners for taking the risks associated with founding these firms. This phenomenon is discussed in more detail in the Strategy in the Emerging Enterprise feature.

What Does Research Say About Returns to Mergers and Acquisitions?

The empirical implications of this discussion of returns to bidding and target firms in strategically related and strategically unrelated mergers and acquisitions have been examined in a variety of academic literatures. One study reviewed over 40 empirical merger and acquisition studies in the finance literature. This study concluded that acquisitions, on average, increased the market value of target firms by about 25 percent and left the market value of bidding firms unchanged. The authors of this report concluded that "corporate takeovers generate positive gains, . . . target firm equity holders benefit, and . . . bidding firm equity holders do not lose."[10] The way these studies evaluate the return to acquisition strategies is discussed in the Strategy in Depth feature.

Strategy researchers have also attempted to examine in more detail the sources of value creation in mergers and acquisitions and the question of whether these sources of value creation affect whether bidders or targets appropriate this value. For example, two well-known studies examined the impact of the type and degree of strategic relatedness (defined using the FTC typology summarized in Table 10.1) between bidding and target firms on the economic consequences of mergers and acquisitions.[11] These studies found that the more strategically related bidding and target firms are, the more economic value mergers and acquisitions create. However, like the finance studies, this work found that this economic value was appropriated by the owners of the target firm, regardless of the type or degree of relatedness between the bidding and target firms. Bidding firms—even when they attempt to acquire strategically related targets—earn, on average, zero economic profits from their merger and acquisition strategies.

Strategy in the Emerging Enterprise

*I*magine you are an entrepreneur. You have mortgaged your home, taken out loans, run up your credit cards, and put all you own on the line in order to help grow a small company. And finally, after years of effort, things start going well. Your product or service starts to sell, customers start to appreciate your unique value proposition, and you actually begin to pay yourself a reasonable salary. What do you do next to help grow your company?

Some entrepreneurs in this situation decide that maintaining control of the firm is very important. These entrepreneurs may compensate certain critical employees with equity in the firm, but typically limit the number of outsiders who make equity investments in their firm. To grow these closely held firms, these entrepreneurs must rely on capital generated from their ongoing operations (called **retained earnings**) and debt capital provided by banks, customers, and suppliers. Entrepreneurs who decide to maintain control of their companies are compensated for taking the risks associated with starting a firm through the salary they pay themselves.

Other entrepreneurs get more outside equity investors involved in providing the capital a firm needs to grow. These outside investors might include wealthy individuals—called **business angels**—looking to invest in entrepreneurial ventures or **venture capital firms.** Venture capital firms typically raise money from numerous smaller investors that they then invest

Cashing Out

in a portfolio of entrepreneurial firms. Over time, many of these firms decide to "go public" by engaging in what is called an **initial public offering**, or **IPO**. In an IPO, a firm, typically working with an investment banker, sells its equity to the public at large. Entrepreneurs who decide to sell equity in their firm are compensated for taking the risks associated with starting a firm through the sale of their equity on the public markets through an IPO. An entrepreneur who receives compensation for risk-taking in this manner is said to be **cashing out**.

Finally, still other entrepreneurs may decide to not use an IPO to cash out, but rather to have their firm acquired by another, typically larger, firm. In this scenario, entrepreneurs are compensated by the acquiring firm for taking the risks associated with

starting a firm. Indeed, because the demand for IPOs has been volatile since the technology-bubble burst of 2000, more and more small and entrepreneurial firms are looking to be acquired as a way for their founders to cash out. Moreover, because the stockholders of target firms typically appropriate a large percentage of the total value created by an acquisition, and because the founders of these entrepreneurial firms are also often large stockholders, being acquired is often a source of great wealth for an entrepreneurial firm's founders.

The choice between keeping a firm private, going public, or being acquired is a difficult and multidimensional one. Issues such as the personal preferences of a firm's founders, demand for IPOs, how much capital a firm will need in order to continue to grow its business, and what other resources—besides capital—the firm will need to create additional value all play a role. In general, firms that do not need a great deal of money or other resources to grow will choose to remain private. Those that need only money to grow will choose IPOs, whereas those that need managerial or technical resources controlled by another firm to grow will typically be acquired. Of course, this changes if the entrepreneurs decide to maintain control of their firms because they want to.

Sources: R. Hennessey (2004). "Underwriters cut prices on IPOs as market softens." *Wall Street Journal*, May 27, p. C4; F. Vogelstein (2003). "Can Google grow up?" *Fortune*, December 8, pp. 102 +.

Why Are There So Many Mergers and Acquisitions?

Given the overwhelming empirical evidence that most of the economic value created in mergers and acquisitions is appropriated by the owners of the target firm most of the time, an important question becomes: "Why do managers of bidding

Table 10.4 **Possible Motivations to Engage in Mergers and Acquisitions Even Though They Usually Do Not Generate Profits for Bidding Firms**

1. To ensure survival
2. Free cash flow
3. Agency problems
4. Managerial hubris
5. The potential for above-normal profits

firms continue to engage in merger and acquisition strategies?" Some possible explanations are summarized in Table 10.4 and discussed in this section.

To Ensure Survival

Even if mergers and acquisitions, on average, generate only zero economic profits for bidding firms, it may be necessary for bidding firms to engage in these activities to ensure their survival. In particular, if all of a bidding firm's competitors have been able to improve their efficiency and effectiveness through a particular type of acquisition, then failing to make such an acquisition may put a firm at a competitive disadvantage. Here, the purpose of a merger or acquisition is not to gain competitive advantages, but rather to gain competitive parity.

Many recent mergers among banks in the United States seem to have competitive parity and normal economic profits as an objective. Most bank managers recognize that changing bank regulations, increased competition from nonbanking financial institutions, and soft demand are likely to lead to a consolidation of the U.S. banking industry. To survive in this consolidated industry, many U.S. banks will have to merge. As the number of banks engaging in mergers and acquisitions goes up, the ability to earn superior profits from those strategies goes down. These lower returns from acquisitions have already reduced the economic value of some of the most aggressive acquiring banks. Despite these lower returns, acquisitions are likely to continue for the foreseeable future, as banks seek survival opportunities in a consolidated industry.[12]

Free Cash Flow

Another reason why firms may continue to invest in merger and acquisition strategies is that these strategies, on average, can be expected to generate at least competitive parity for bidding firms. This zero economic profit may be a more attractive investment for some firms than alternative strategic investments. This is particularly the case for firms that generate free cash flow.[13]

Free cash flow is simply the amount of cash a firm has to invest after all positive net present-value investments in its ongoing businesses have been funded. Free cash flow is created when a firm's ongoing business operations are very profitable but offer few opportunities for additional investment. One firm that seems to have generated a great deal of free cash flow over the last several years is Philip Morris. Philip Morris's retail tobacco operations are extremely profitable. However, regulatory constraints, health concerns, and slowing growth in demand limit investment opportunities in the tobacco industry. Thus, the amount of cash generated by Philip Morris's ongoing tobacco business has probably been larger than the sum of its positive net present-value investments in that business. This difference is free cash flow for Philip Morris.[14]

Strategy in Depth

*B*y far, the most popular way to evaluate the performance effects of acquisitions for bidding firms is called **event study analysis**. Rooted in the field of financial economics, event study analysis compares the actual performance of a stock after an acquisition has been announced to the expected performance of that stock, if no acquisition had been announced. Any performance greater (or less) than what was expected in a short period of time around when an acquisition is announced is attributed to that acquisition. This **cumulative abnormal return**, or **CAR** can be positive or negative, depending on whether the stock in question performs better or worse than what was expected without an acquisition.

The CAR created by an acquisition is calculated in several stages. First, the expected performance of a stock, without an acquisition, is estimated with the following regression equation:

$$E(R_{j, t}) = a_j + b_j R_{m, t} + e_{j, t}$$

where $E(R_{j, t})$ is the expected return of stock j during time t; a_j is a constant (approximately equal to the rate of return on risk-free equities); b_j is an empirical estimate of the financial parameter β (equal to the covariance between the returns of a particular firm's stock and the average return of all stocks in the market, over time); $R_{m, t}$ is the actual average rate of return of all stocks in the market over time; and $e_{j, t}$ is an error term. The form of this equation is derived from the capital asset pricing model in finance. In this model, $E(R_{j, t})$ is simply the expected performance of a stock, given the historical relationship between that stock

Evaluating the Performance Effects of Acquisitions

and the overall performance of the stock market.

To calculate the unexpected performance of a stock, this expected level of performance is simply subtracted from the actual level of performance for a stock. This is done in the following equation:

$$XR_{j, t} = R_{j, t} - (a_j + b_j R_{m, t})$$

where $R_{j, t}$ is the actual performance of stock j during time t, and $XR_{j, t}$ is the unexpected performance of stock j during time t.

In calculating the CAR for a particular acquisition, it is necessary to sum the unexpected returns ($XR_{j, t}$) for a stock across the t periods when the stock market is responding to news about this acquisition. Most analyses of acquisitions examine the market's reaction one day before an acquisition is formally announced to three days after it is announced. The sum of these unexpected returns over this time period is the CAR attributable to this acquisition.

This methodology has been applied to literally thousands of acquisition episodes. For example, when Manulife Financial purchased John Hancock Financial, Manulife's CAR was –10 percent, whereas John Hancock's CAR was 6 percent; when Anthem acquired Wellpoint, Anthem's CAR was –10 percent, and Wellpoint's was 7 percent; when Bank of America acquired FleetBoston Financial, Bank of America's CAR was –9 percent, and FleetBoston's was 24 percent; and when UnitedHealth acquired Mid Atlantic Medical, UnitedHealth's CAR was –4 percent, and Mid Atlantic Medical's was 11 percent.

Although the event study method has been used widely, it does have some important limitations. First, it is based entirely on the capital asset pricing model, and there is some reason to believe that this model is not a particularly good predictor of a firm's expected stock price. Second, it assumes that a firm's equity holders can anticipate all the benefits associated with making an acquisition at the time that acquisition is made. Some scholars have argued that value creation continues long after an acquisition is announced as parties in this exchange discover value-creating opportunities that could not have been anticipated.

Sources: A. Arikan (2004). "Long-term returns to acquisitions: The case of purchasing tangible and intangible assets." Unpublished, Fisher College of Business, Ohio State University; S. J. Brown and J. B. Warner (1985). "Using daily stock returns: The case of event studies." *Journal of Financial Economics*, 14, pp. 3–31; D. Henry, M. Der Hovanseian, and D. Foust (2003). "M&A deals: Show me." *BusinessWeek*, November 10, pp. 38 +.

A firm that generates a great deal of free cash flow must decide what to do with this money. One obvious alternative would be to give it to stockholders in the form of dividends or stock buybacks. However, in some situations (e.g., when stockholders face high marginal tax rates), stockholders may prefer a firm to retain this cash flow and invest it for them. When this is the case, how should a firm invest its free cash flow?

Because (by definition) no positive net present-value investment opportunities in a firm's ongoing business operations are available, firms have only two investment options: to invest their free cash flow in strategies that generate competitive parity or in strategies that generate competitive disadvantages. In this context, merger and acquisition strategies are a viable option, because bidding firms, on average, can expect to generate at least competitive parity. Put differently, although mergers and acquisitions may not be a source of superior profits, there are worse things you could do with your free cash flow.

Agency Problems

Another reason why firms might continue to engage in mergers and acquisitions, despite earning only competitive parity from doing so, is that mergers and acquisitions benefit managers directly, independent of any value they may or may not create for a bidding firm's stockholders. As suggested in Chapter 8, these conflicts of interest are a manifestation of agency problems between a firm's managers and its stockholders.

Merger and acquisition strategies can benefit managers—even if they do not directly benefit a bidding firm's equity holders—in at least two ways. First, managers can use mergers and acquisitions to help diversify their human capital investments in their firm. As discussed in Chapter 7, managers have difficulty diversifying their firm-specific human capital investments when a firm operates in a narrow range of businesses. By acquiring firms with cash flows that are not perfectly correlated with the cash flows of a firm's current businesses, managers can reduce the probability of bankruptcy for their firm and thus partially diversify their human capital investments in their firm.

Second, managers can use mergers and acquisitions to quickly increase firm size, measured in either sales or assets. If management compensation is closely linked to firm size, managers who increase firm size are able to increase their compensation. Of all the ways to increase the size of a firm quickly, growth through mergers and acquisitions is perhaps the easiest. Even if there are no economies of scope between a bidding and a target firm, an acquisition ensures that the bidding firm will grow by the size of the target (measured in either sales or assets). If there are economies of scope between a bidding and a target firm, the size of the bidding firm can grow at an even faster rate, as can the value of management's compensation, even though, on average, acquisitions do not generate wealth for the owners of the bidding firm.

Managerial Hubris

Another reason why managers may choose to continue to invest in mergers and acquisitions, despite the fact that, on average, they gain no profits from doing so, is the existence of what has been called **managerial hubris**.[15] This is the unrealistic belief held by managers in bidding firms that they can manage the assets of a target firm more efficiently than the target firm's current management. This notion can lead bidding firms to engage in acquisition strategies even though there may not be positive economic profits from doing so.

The existence of managerial hubris suggests that the economic value of bidding firms will fall once they announce a merger or acquisition strategy. Although managers in bidding firms might truly believe that they can manage a target firm's assets more efficiently than the target firm's managers, investors in the capital markets are much less likely to be caught up in this hubris. In this context, a commitment to a merger or acquisition strategy is a strong signal that a bidding firm's management has deluded itself about its abilities to manage a target firm's assets. Such delusions will certainly adversely affect the economic value of the bidding firm.

Of course, empirical work on mergers and acquisitions discussed earlier in this chapter has concluded that although bidding firms do not obtain profits from their merger and acquisition strategies, they also do not, on average, reduce their economic value from implementing these strategies. This is inconsistent with the "hubris hypothesis." However, the fact that, on average, bidding firms do not lose economic value does not mean that some bidding firms do not lose economic value. Thus, although it is unlikely that all merger and acquisition strategies are motivated by managerial hubris, it is likely that at least some of them are.[16]

The Potential for Economic Profits

A final reason why managers might continue to pursue merger and acquisition strategies is the potential that these strategies offer for generating profits for at least some bidding firms. The empirical research on returns to bidding firms in mergers and acquisitions is very strong. On average, bidding firms do not gain profits from their merger and acquisition strategies. However, the fact that bidding firms, *on average*, do not earn profits on these strategies does not mean that *all* bidding firms will *always* fail to earn profits. In some situations bidding firms may be able to gain competitive advantages from merger and acquisition activities. These situations are discussed in the following section.

Mergers and Acquisitions and Sustained Competitive Advantage

We have already seen that the economies of scope that motivate mergers and acquisitions between strategically related bidding and target firms can be valuable. However, the ability of these economies to generate profits and competitive advantages for bidding firms depends not only on their economic value, but also on the competitiveness of the market for corporate control through which these valuable economies are realized. The **market for corporate control** is the market that is created when multiple firms actively seek to acquire one or several firms. Only when the market for corporate control is imperfectly competitive might it be possible for bidding firms to earn profits from implementing a merger or acquisition strategy. To see how the competitiveness of the market for corporate control can affect returns to merger and acquisition strategies, we will consider three scenarios involving bidding and target firms and examine their implications for the managers of these firms.[17]

VRIO

Valuable, Rare, and Private Economies of Scope

An imperfectly competitive market for corporate control can exist when a target is worth more to one bidder than it is to any other bidders and when no other firms—including bidders and targets—are aware of this additional value. In this setting, the price of a target will rise to reflect public expectations about the value of the target. Once the target is acquired, however, the performance of the special bidder that acquires the target will be greater than generally expected, and this level of performance will generate profits for the equity holders of the bidding firm.

Consider a simple case. Suppose the market value of bidder Firm A combined with target firms is $12,000, whereas the market value of all other bidders combined with targets is $10,000. No other firms (bidders or targets) are aware of Firm A's unique relationship with these targets, but they are aware of the value of all other bidders combined with targets (i.e., $10,000). Suppose also that the market value of all bidding firms, as stand-alone entities, is $7,000. In this setting, Firm A will be willing to pay up to $5,000 to acquire a target ($12,000 – $7,000), and all other bidders will only be willing to pay up to $3,000 to acquire a target ($10,000 – $7,000).

Because publicly available information suggests that acquiring a target is worth $3,000 more than the target's stand-alone price, the price of targets will rapidly rise to this level, ensuring that if bidding firms, apart from Firm A, acquire a target, they will obtain no profits. If there is only one target in this market for corporate control, then Firm A will be able to bid slightly more than $3,000 (perhaps $3,001) for this target. No other firms will bid higher than Firm A, because, from their point of view, the acquisition is simply not worth more than $3,000. At this $3,001 price, Firm A will earn a profit of $1,999—Firm A had to spend only $3,001 for a firm that brings $5,000 in value above its stand-alone market price. Alternatively, if there are multiple targets, then several bidding firms, including Firm A, will pay $3,000 for their targets. At this price, these bidding firms will all earn zero economic profits, except for Firm A, which will earn an economic profit equal to $2,000. That is, only Firm A will gain a competitive advantage from acquiring a target in this market.

In order for Firm A to obtain this profit, the value of Firm A's economy of scope with target firms must be greater than the value of any other bidding firms with that target. This special value will generally reflect unusual resources and capabilities possessed by Firm A—resources and capabilities that are more valuable in combination with target firms than are the resources and capabilities that other bidding firms possess. Put differently, to be a source of economic profits and competitive advantage, Firm A's link with targets must be based on resources and capabilities that are rare among those firms competing in this market for corporate control.

However, not only does Firm A have to possess valuable and rare links with bidding firms to gain economic profits and competitive advantages from its acquisition strategies, but information about these special economies of scope must not be known by other firms. If other bidding firms know about the additional value associated with acquiring a target, they are likely to try to duplicate this value for themselves. Typically, they would accomplish this by imitating the type of relatedness that exists between Firm A and its targets by developing the resources and capabilities that enabled Firm A to have its valuable economies of scope with targets. Once other bidders developed the resources and capabilities necessary to obtain this more valuable economy of scope, they would be able to enter into bidding, thereby increasing the likelihood that the equity holders of successful bidding firms would earn no economic profits.

Target firms must also be unaware of Firm A's special resources and capabilities if Firm A is to obtain competitive advantages from an acquisition. If target firms were aware of this extra value available to Firm A, along with the sources of this value, they could inform other bidding firms. These bidding firms could then adjust their bids to reflect this higher value, and competitive bidding would reduce profits to bidders. Target firms are likely to inform bidding firms in this way because increasing the number of bidders with more valuable economies of scope increases the likelihood that target firms will extract all the economic value created in a merger or acquisition.[18]

Valuable, Rare, and Costly-to-Imitate Economies of Scope

V R I O

The existence of firms that have valuable, rare, and private economies of scope with targets is not the only way that the market for corporate control can be imperfectly competitive. If other bidders cannot imitate one bidder's valuable and rare economies with targets, then competition in this market for corporate control will be imperfect, and the equity holders of this special bidding firm will earn economic profits. In this case, the existence of valuable and rare economies does not need to be private, because other bidding firms cannot imitate these economies, and therefore bids that substantially reduce the profits for the equity holders of the special bidding firm are not forthcoming.

Typically, bidding firms will be unable to imitate one bidder's valuable and rare economies of scope with targets when the strategic relatedness between the special bidder and the targets stems from some rare and costly-to-imitate resources or capabilities controlled by the special bidding firm. Any of the costly-to-imitate resources and capabilities discussed in Chapter 3 could create costly-to-imitate economies of scope between a firm and a target. If, in addition, these economies are valuable and rare, they can be a source of profits to the equity holders of the special bidding firm. This can happen even if all firms in this market for corporate control are aware of the more valuable economies of scope available to this firm and its sources. Although information about this special economy of scope is publicly available, equity holders of special bidding firms will earn a profit when acquisition occurs. The equity holders of target firms will not obtain all of this profit, because competitive bidding dynamics cannot unfold when the sources of a more valuable economy of scope are costly to imitate.

Of course, it may be possible for a valuable, rare, and costly-to-imitate economy of scope between a bidding and a target firm to also be private. Indeed, it is often the case that those attributes of a firm that are costly to imitate are also difficult to describe and thus can be held as proprietary information. In that case, the analysis of profits associated with valuable, rare, and private economies of scope presented earlier applies.

Unexpected Valuable Economies of Scope Between Bidding and Target Firms

Thus far, this discussion has adopted, for convenience, the strong assumption that the present value of the strategic relatedness between bidders and targets is known with certainty by individual bidders. This is, in principle, possible, but certainly not likely. Most modern acquisitions and mergers are massively complex, involving numerous unknown and complicated relationships between firms. In these settings, unexpected events after an acquisition has been completed may make an acquisition or merger more valuable than bidders and targets anticipated it would be. The price that bidding firms will pay to acquire a target will equal the expected value of the target only when the target is combined with the bidder. The difference between the unexpected value of an acquisition actually obtained by a bidder and the price the bidder paid for the acquisition is a profit for the equity holders of the bidding firm.

Of course, by definition, bidding firms cannot expect to obtain unexpected value from an acquisition. Unexpected value, in this context, is a surprise, a manifestation of a bidding firm's good luck, not its skill in acquiring targets. For example, when the British advertising firm WPP acquired J. Walter Thompson for $550 million, it discovered some property owned by J. Walter Thomson in Tokyo. No one knew of this property when the firm was acquired. It turned out to be worth over $100 million after taxes, a financial windfall that helped offset the high cost of this acquisition. When asked, Martin Sorrel, president of WPP and the architect of this acquisition, admitted that this $100 million windfall was simply good luck.[19]

Implications for Bidding Firm Managers

The existence of valuable, rare, and private economies of scope between bidding and target firms and of valuable, rare, and costly-to-imitate economies of scope between bidding and target firms suggests that although, on average, most bidding firms do not generate competitive advantages from their acquisition strategies, in some special circumstances it may be possible for them to do so. Thus, the task facing managers in firms contemplating merger and acquisition strategies is to choose strategies that have the greatest likelihood of being able to generate profits for their equity holders. Several important managerial prescriptions can be derived from this discussion. These "rules" for bidding firm managers are summarized in Table 10.5.

Search for Rare Economies of Scope

One of the main reasons why bidding firms do not obtain competitive advantages from acquiring strategically related target firms is that several other bidding firms value the target firm in the same way. When multiple bidders all value a target in the same way, competitive bidding is likely. Competitive bidding, in turn, drives out the potential for superior performance. To avoid this problem, bidding firms should seek to acquire targets with which they enjoy valuable and rare linkages.

Operationally, the search for rare economies of scope suggests that managers in bidding firms need to consider not only the value of a target firm when combined with their own company, but also the value of a target firm when combined with other potential bidders. This is important, because it is the difference between the value of a particular bidding firm's relationship with a target and the value of other bidding firms' relationships with that target that defines the size of the potential economic profits from an acquisition.

Table 10.5 **Rules for Bidding Firm Managers**

1. Search for valuable and rare economies of scope.
2. Keep information away from other bidders.
3. Keep information away from targets.
4. Avoid winning bidding wars.
5. Close the deal quickly.
6. Operate in "thinly traded" acquisition markets.

326 Part 3 Corporate Strategies

In practice, the search for valuable and rare economies of scope is likely to become a search for valuable and rare resources already controlled by a firm that are synergistically related to a target. For example, if a bidding firm has a unique reputation in its product market, and if the target firm's products could benefit by association with that reputation, then the target firm may be more valuable to this particular bidder than to other bidders (firms that do not possess this special reputation). Also, if a particular bidder possesses the largest market share in its industry, the best distribution system, or restricted access to certain key raw materials, and if the target firm would benefit from being associated with these valuable and rare resources, then the acquisition of this target may be a source of economic profits.

The search for valuable and rare economies of scope as a basis of mergers and acquisitions tends to rule out certain interfirm linkages as sources of economic profits. For example, most acquisitions can lead to a reduction in overhead costs, because much of the corporate overhead associated with the target firm can be eliminated subsequent to acquisition. However, the ability to eliminate these overhead costs is not unique to any one bidder, and thus the value created by these reduced costs will usually be captured by the equity holders of the target firm.

Keep Information Away from Other Bidders

One of the keys to earning superior performance in an acquisition strategy is to avoid multiple bidders for a single target. One way to accomplish this is to keep information about the bidding process, and about the sources of economies of scope between a bidder and target that underlie this bidding process, as private as possible. In order for other firms to become involved in bidding for a target, they must be aware of the value of the economies of scope between themselves and that target. If only one bidding firm knows this information, and if this bidding firm can close the deal before the full value of the target is known, then it may gain a competitive advantage from completing this acquisition.

Of course, in many circumstances, keeping all this information private is difficult. Often, it is illegal. For example, when seeking to acquire a publicly traded firm, potential bidders must meet disclosure requirements that effectively reduce the amount of private information a bidder can retain. In these circumstances, unless a bidding firm has some valuable, rare, and costly-to-imitate economy of scope with a target firm, the possibility of economic profits coming from an acquisition is very low. It is not surprising that the research conducted on mergers and acquisitions of firms traded on public stock exchanges governed by the U.S. Securities and Exchange Commission (SEC) disclosure rules suggests that, most of the time, bidding firms do not earn economic profits from implementing their acquisition strategies.

However, not all potential targets are publicly traded. Privately held firms may be acquired in an information environment that can create opportunities for above-normal performance for bidding firms. Moreover, even when acquiring a publicly traded firm, a bidder does not have to release all the information it has about the potential value of that target in combination with itself. Indeed, if some of this value reflects a bidding firm's taken-for-granted "invisible" assets, it may not be possible to communicate this information. In this case, as well, there may be opportunities for competitive advantages for bidding firms.

Keep Information Away from Targets

Not only should bidding firms keep information about the value of their economy of scope with a target away from other bidders; they should also keep this information away from target firms. Suppose that the value of a target firm to a bidding firm is $8,000, but the bidding firm, in an attempt to earn economic profits, has bid only $5,000 for the target. If the target knows that it is actually worth $8,000, it is very likely to hold out for a higher bid. In fact, the target may contact other potential bidding firms and tell them of the opportunity created by the $5,000 bid. As the number of bidders goes up, the possibility of superior economic performance for bidders goes down. Therefore, to keep the possibility of these profits alive, bidding firms must not fully reveal the value of their economies of scope with a target firm. Again, in some circumstances, it is very difficult, or even illegal, to attempt to limit the flow of information to target firms. In these settings, superior economic performance for bidding firms is very unlikely.

Limiting the amount of information that flows to the target firm may have some other consequences as well. For example, it has been shown that a complete sharing of information, insights, and perspectives before an acquisition is completed increases the probability that economies of scope will actually be realized once it is completed.[20] By limiting the flow of information between itself and a target, a bidding firm may actually be increasing the cost of integrating the target into its ongoing business, thereby jeopardizing at least some of the superior economic performance that limiting information flow is designed to create. Bidding firms will need to carefully balance the economic benefits of limiting the information they share with the target firm against the costs that limiting information flow may create.

Avoid Winning Bidding Wars

It should be reasonably clear that if a number of firms bid for the same target, the probability that the firm that successfully acquires the target will gain competitive advantages is very low. Indeed, to ensure that competitive bidding occurs, target firms can actively encourage other bidding firms to enter into the bidding process. The implications of these arguments are clear: Bidding firms should generally avoid winning a bidding war. To "win" a bidding war, a bidding firm will often have to pay a price at least equal to the full value of the target. Many times, given the emotions of an intense bidding contest, the winning bid may actually be larger than the true value of the target. Completing this type of acquisition will certainly reduce the economic performance of the bidding firm.

The only time it might make sense to "win" a bidding war is when the winning firm possesses a rare and private or a rare and costly-to-imitate economy of scope with a target that is more valuable than the strategic relatedness that exists between any other bidders and that target. In this setting, the winning firm may be able to earn a profit if it is able to fully realize the value of its relationship with the target.

Close the Deal Quickly

Another rule of thumb for obtaining superior performance from implementing merger and acquisition strategies is to close the deal quickly. All the economic processes that make it difficult for bidding firms to earn economic profits from acquiring a strategically related target take time to unfold. It takes time for other bidders to become aware of the economic value associated with acquiring a target; it takes time for the target to recruit other bidders; information leakage becomes more of a problem over time; and so forth. A bidding firm that begins and ends the bidding process quickly may forestall some of these processes and thereby retain some superior performance for itself.

The admonition to close the deal quickly should not be taken to mean that bidding firms need to make their acquisition decisions quickly. Indeed, the search for valuable and rare economies of scope should be undertaken with great care. There should be little rush in isolating and evaluating acquisition candidates. However, once a target firm has been located and valued, bidding firms have a strong incentive to reduce the period of time between the first bid and the completion of the deal. The longer this period of negotiation, the less likely it is that the bidding firm will earn economic profits from the acquisition.

Complete Acquisitions in "Thinly Traded" Markets

Finally, an acquisition strategy can be a source of economic profits to bidding firms if these firms implement this corporate strategy in what could be described as "thinly traded markets." In general, a **thinly traded market** is a market where there are only a small number of buyers and sellers, where information about opportunities in this market is not widely known, and where interests besides purely maximizing the value of a firm can be important. In the context of mergers and acquisitions, thinly traded markets are markets where only a few (often only one) firms are implementing acquisition strategies. These unique firms may be the only firms that understand the full value of the acquisition opportunities in this market. Even target firm managers may not fully understand the value of the economic opportunities in these markets, and, if they do, they may have other interests besides maximizing the value of their firm if it becomes the object of a takeover.

In general, thinly traded merger and acquisition markets are highly fragmented. Competition in these markets occurs at the local level, as one small local firm competes with other small local firms for a common group of geographically defined customers. Most of these small firms are privately held. Many are sole proprietorships. Examples of these thinly traded markets have included, at various points in history, the printing industry, the fast-food industry, the used car industry, the dry cleaning industry, and the barber shop/hair salon industry.

As was suggested in Chapter 2, the major opportunity in all highly fragmented industries is consolidation. In the context of mergers and acquisitions, consolidation can occur by one firm (or a small number of firms) buying numerous independent firms to realize economies of scope in these industries. Often, these economies of scope reflect economies of scale in these industries— economies of scale that were not realized in a highly fragmented setting. As long as the number of firms implementing this consolidation strategy is small, then the market for corporate control in these markets will probably be less than perfectly competitive, and opportunities for profits from implementing an acquisition strategy may be possible.

More generally, if a merger or acquisition contest is played out through full-page ads in the *Wall Street Journal*, the ability of bidding firms to gain competitive advantages from their acquisitions is limited. Such highly public acquisitions are likely to lead to very competitive markets for corporate control. Competitive markets for corporate control, in turn, assure that the equity holders of the target firm will appropriate any value that could be created by an acquisition. However, if these contests occur in obscure, out-of-the-way industries, it is more likely that bidding firms will be able to earn profits from their acquisitions.

Service Corporation International: An Example

Empirical research on mergers and acquisitions suggests that it is not easy for bidding firms to earn economic profits from these strategies. However, it may be possible for some bidding firms, some of the time, to do so. One firm that has been successful in gaining competitive advantages from its merger and acquisition strategies is Service Corporation International (SCI). SCI is in the funeral home and cemetery business. It grew from a collection of five funeral homes in 1967 to being the largest owner of cemeteries and funeral homes in the United States today. It has done this through an aggressive and what was until recently a highly profitable acquisitions program in this historically fragmented industry.

The valuable and rare economy of scope that SCI brought to the funeral home industry is the application of traditional business practices in a highly fragmented and not often professionally managed industry. SCI-owned funeral homes operate with gross margins approaching 30 percent, nearly three times the gross margins of independently owned funeral homes. Among other things, higher margins reflected savings from centralized purchasing services, centralized embalming and professional services, and the sharing of underutilized resources (including hearses) among funeral homes within geographic regions. SCI's scale advantages made a particular funeral home more valuable to SCI than to one of SCI's smaller competitors, and more valuable than if a particular funeral home was left as a stand-alone business.

Moreover, the funeral homes that SCI targeted for acquisition were, typically, family owned and lacked heirs to continue the business. Many of the owners or operators of these funeral homes were not fully aware of the value of their operations to SCI (they are morticians more than business managers), nor were they just interested in maximizing the sale price of their funeral homes. Rather, they were often looking to maintain continuity of service in a community, secure employment for their loyal employees, and ensure a comfortable (if not lavish) retirement for themselves. Being acquired by SCI was likely to be the only alternative to closing the funeral home once an owner or operator retired. Extracting less than the full value of the funeral home when selling to SCI often seemed preferable to other alternatives.

Because SCI's acquisition of funeral homes exploited real and valuable economies of scope, this strategy had the potential for generating superior economic performance. Because SCI was, for many years, the only firm implementing this strategy in the funeral home industry, because the funeral homes that SCI acquired were generally not publicly traded, and because the owner or operators of these funeral homes often had interests besides simply maximizing the price of their operation when they sold it, it seems likely that SCI's acquisition strategy generated superior economic performance for many years. However, in the last several years, information about SCI's acquisition strategy has become widely known. This has led other funeral homes to begin bidding to acquire formerly independent funeral homes. Moreover, independent funeral home owners have become more aware of their full value to SCI. Although SCI's economy of scope with independent funeral homes is still valuable, it is no longer rare, and thus it is no longer a source of economic profits to SCI. Put differently, the imperfectly competitive market for corporate control that SCI was able to exploit for almost 10

Global Perspectives

*I*n the late 1980s, managers at Ford Motor Company faced a problem. While Ford had been able to get its quality on par with the best manufacturers—through its "Quality Is Job One" program—worldwide competition in small and medium-sized cars had reduced the profit margin on Ford's small-car lines to almost nothing. The only cars that continued to deliver high profit margins to Ford were its luxury cars—the Lincoln and related cars. Unfortunately, Lincoln was an aging brand. It was being rapidly displaced in the highly profitable luxury car market by Mercedes Benz and BMW—German automobiles that had more attraction among younger car buyers than Lincoln. Moreover, Nissan (through its Infiniti division), Honda (through its Acura division), and Toyota (through its Lexus division) were beginning to invest in the luxury car market.

At the same time, managers at Jaguar also faced a problem. They were about to go out of business. Despite having a well-known brand and beautifully designed cars, Jaguar's quality problems had just about driven this firm out of business; its poor quality was legendary. The joke was that

Ford's Acquisition of Jaguar

you had to buy two brand-new Jaguars—one to drive and one for parts. To give its customers some sense of security, Jaguar introduced a free towing service for new-car buyers. The service would tow your broken-down Jaguar to a Jaguar dealer free. The usage rate of this free towing service among Jaguar owners was 118 percent—essentially every Jaguar owner had to have his or her new car towed in for repairs, and some more than once. In the J. D. Power ratings of initial quality, Jaguar in the early 1990s

was ranked ahead of only one other firm: Yugo. Yugo manufactured very low-quality cheap cars for sale in Europe and import into the United States. Jaguar was manufacturing very low-quality cars for sale around the world, but they were not cheap! What a deal—a luxury car price with Yugo quality!

The match between Ford and Jaguar seemed perfect. Ford needed a new luxury brand to compete with Mercedes, BMW, Lexus, and so forth; Jaguar had such a brand. Jaguar desperately needed to learn how to manufacture quality automobiles; Ford now knew how to do that. Assuming Ford could use its manufacturing skills with Jaguar without destroying the value of Jaguar's brand name, it seemed likely that a Ford acquisition of Jaguar would create real economic value.

But who would appropriate that value—Ford's stockholders or Jaguar's stockholders? To answer this question, it is necessary to understand if any other firms would profit from acquiring Jaguar in about the same way as Ford. What about General Motors? GM faced the same profit squeeze in small cars as Ford. It also had its own aging luxury line of cars, the Cadillac.

years has become more perfectly competitive. Future acquisitions by SCI are not likely to be a source of sustained competitive advantage and economic profit. For these reasons, SCI is currently reevaluating its corporate strategy, attempting to discover a new way that it might be able to generate superior profits.[21]

This same form of analysis can be applied to virtually any merger and acquisition strategy. Consider, for example, the acquisition discussed in the Global Perspectives feature.

Implications for Target Firm Managers

Although bidding firm managers can do several things to attempt to maximize the probability of earning economic profits from their merger and acquisition strategies, target firm managers can attempt to counter these efforts, to ensure

And GM had also recently begun improving its manufacturing quality dramatically. Would GM be interested in purchasing Jaguar?

It turns out that although GM never made a formal offer for Jaguar, it did hold discussions about a possible acquisition. The bid that Ford made to take over Jaguar had to anticipate the possibility that GM was also interested. Initially, Ford paid $2.5 billion for Jaguar; since the acquisition, Ford has invested another $3.5 billion. Together, the almost $6 billion invested in Jaguar is almost $2.5 billion more than Jaguar's market price when it was a stand-alone company. This means that in order for this acquisition to pay off for Ford's stockholders, Ford must create more than $2.5 billion of extra value from its acquisition of Jaguar.

What has Ford done with Jaguar? First and foremost, it helped Jaguar improve its quality problems. Indeed, Jaguar went from having the second-worst initial quality of any car manufacturer ranked by J. D. Powers in 1992 to having the best initial quality in 1999. Since 1999, Jaguar's rankings have dropped some, but it is still among the world's elite in initial quality rankings. However, it is reasonable to expect that much of the value created through this quality effort was anticipated in the price for Jaguar. That is, the value created here is part of the $2.5 billion premium paid for Jaguar. For it to be a source of profits for Ford's stockholders, Ford must create value in excess of this $2.5 billion.

Ford also helped Jaguar develop new models, including the mid-size "S-Type" and the smaller "X-Type" Jaguars. Although these vehicles have dramatically increased Jaguar's volume of production, some observers worry that these automobile lines blur the distinction between the Ford and Jaguar brands. This is especially a problem for the "X-Type," or "baby Jag"—a car that looks disturbingly like a Hyundai Sonata. Although it seems reasonable to assume that the premium paid for Jaguar anticipated Ford's ability to help Jaguar introduce some new models, the specific details of these models and their ultimate success would have been difficult to anticipate at the time Jaguar was acquired. If these models turn out to be successful, they may be a source of superior profits for Ford's shareholders.

More recently, Ford has used additional acquisitions to round out its line of luxury cars—including its recent acquisition of Volvo and Range Rover. Ford is currently experimenting with the creation of single dealerships that sell Jaguars, Volvos, and Range Rovers. In this way, Ford's customers can gain access to a full line of luxury cars in a single location. It is also likely that these additional acquisitions were not anticipated at the time Ford acquired Jaguar. If this "one-stop-shop" approach to luxury car shopping ends up creating value, this value is also likely to be a source of superior performance to Ford's shareholders.

Of course, all this discussion begs a more fundamental question: Did Ford have to acquire Jaguar to obtain all the value described here? Couldn't Ford have created its own new luxury brand, the same way that Nissan, Honda, and Toyota did? And, which would have been cheaper, Ford paying a $2.5 billion premium for Jaguar or developing its own new luxury brand?

Sources: T. Luehrman (1991). "Jaguar plc, 1989." Harvard Business School Case No. 9-291-034; J. D. Powers (1999). "Jaguar is top make in initial quality." *Special Power Report;* J. Flint (2004). "Tarnished jewels." www.forbes.com, January 27, 2004; D. Kiley (2001). "$29,950 soon can buy you a 'baby' Jag," *USA Today,* February 14, p. 1.

that the owners of target firms appropriate whatever value is created by a merger or acquisition. These "rules" for target firm managers are summarized in Table 10.6.

Seek Information from Bidders

One way a bidder can attempt to obtain superior performance from implementing an acquisition strategy is to keep information about the source and value of the strategic relatedness that exists between the bidder and target private. If that relationship is actually worth $12,000, but targets believe it is only worth $8,000, then a target might be willing to settle for a bid of $8,000 and thereby forgo the extra $4,000 it could have extracted from the bidder. Once the target knows that its true value to the bidder is $12,000, it is in a much better position to obtain this full

Table 10.6 **Rules for Target Firm Managers**

1. Seek information from bidders.
2. Invite other bidders to join the bidding competition.
3. Delay but do not stop the acquisition.

value when the acquisition is completed. Therefore, not only should a bidding firm inform itself about the value of a target, target firms must inform themselves about their value to potential bidders. In this way, they can help obtain the full value of their assets.

Invite Other Bidders to Join the Bidding Competition

Once a target firm is fully aware of the nature and value of the economies of scope that exist between it and current bidding firms, it can exploit this information by seeking other firms that may have the same relationship with it and then informing these firms of a potential acquisition opportunity. By inviting other firms into the bidding process, the target firm increases the competitiveness of the market for corporate control, thereby increasing the probability that the value created by an acquisition will be fully captured by the target firm.

Delay, but Do Not Stop, the Acquisition

As suggested earlier, bidding firms have a strong incentive to expedite the acquisition process in order to prevent other bidders from becoming involved in an acquisition. Of course, the target firm wants other bidding firms to enter the process. To increase the probability of receiving more than one bid, target firms have a strong incentive to delay an acquisition.

The objective, however, should be to delay an acquisition to create a more competitive market for corporate control, not to stop an acquisition. If a valuable economy of scope exists between a bidding firm and a target firm, the merger of these two firms will create economic value. If the market for corporate control within which this merger occurs is competitive, then the equity holders of the target firm will appropriate the full value of this economy of scope. Preventing an acquisition in this setting can be very costly to the equity holders of the target firm.

Target firm managers can engage in a wide variety of activities to delay the completion of an acquisition. Some common responses of target firm management to takeover efforts, along with their economic implications for the equity holders of target firms, are discussed in the Research Made Relevant feature.

V R I O   ## Organizing to Implement a Merger or Acquisition

To realize the full value of any strategic relatedness that exists between a bidding firm and a target firm, the merged organizations must be organized appropriately. The realization of each of the types of strategic relatedness discussed earlier in this chapter requires at least some coordination and integration between the bidding and target firms after an acquisition has occurred. For example, to realize economies of scale from an acquisition, bidding and target firms must coordinate

Research Made Relevant

*M*anagers in potential target firms can respond to takeover attempts in a variety of ways. As suggested in Table 10.7, some of these responses increase the wealth of target firm shareholders, some have no impact on target firm shareholders, and others decrease the wealth of target firm shareholders.

Management responses that have the effect of reducing the value of target firms include greenmail, standstill agreements, and "poison pills." Each of these is an anti-takeover action that target firm managers can take reduces the wealth of target firm equity holders. **Greenmail** is a maneuver in which a target firm's management purchases any of the target firm's stock owned by a bidder and does so for a price that is greater than the current market value of that stock. Greenmail effectively ends a bidding firm's effort to acquire a particular target and does so in a way that can

The Wealth Effects of Management Responses to Takeover Attempts

greatly reduce the wealth of a target firm's equity holders. Not only do these equity holders not appropriate any economic value that could have been created if an acquisition had been

completed, but they have to bear the cost of the premium price that management pays to buy its stock back from the bidding firm.

Not surprisingly, target firms that resort to greenmail substantially reduce the economic wealth of their equity holders. One study found that the value of target firms that pay greenmail drops, on average, 1.76 percent. Another study reported a 2.85 percent drop in the value of such firms. These reductions in value are greater if greenmail leads to the cancellation of a takeover effort. Indeed, this second study found that such episodes led to a 5.50 percent reduction in the value of target firms. These reductions in value as a response to greenmail activities stand in marked contrast to the generally positive market response to efforts by a firm to repurchase its own shares in non-greenmail situations.

Standstill agreements are often negotiated in conjunction with greenmail. A standstill agreement is a contract between a target and a bidding firm wherein the bidding firm agrees not to attempt to take over the target for some period of time. When a target firm negotiates a standstill agreement, it prevents the current acquisition effort from being completed, and it reduces the number of bidders that might become involved in future acquisition efforts. Thus, the equity holders of this target firm forgo any value that could have been created if the current acquisition had occurred, and they also lose some of the value that they could have appropriated in future acquisition episodes by the target's inviting multiple bidders into a market for corporate control.

Table 10.7 **The Wealth Effects of Target Firm Management Responses to Acquisition Efforts**

1. Responses that reduce the wealth of target firm equity holders:
   - Greenmail
   - Standstill agreements
   - Poison pills

2. Responses that do not affect the wealth of target firm equity holders:
   - Shark repellents
   - Pac Man defense
   - Crown jewel sale
   - Lawsuits

3. Responses that increase the wealth of target firm equity holders:
   - Search for white knights
   - Creation of bidding auctions
   - Golden parachutes

Standstill agreements, either alone or in conjunction with greenmail, reduce the economic value of a target firm. One study found that standstill agreements that were unaccompanied by stock repurchase agreements reduced the value of a target firm by 4.05 percent. Such agreements, in combination with stock repurchases, reduced the value of a target firm by 4.52 percent.

So-called **poison pills** include any of a variety of actions that target firm managers can take to make the acquisition of the target prohibitively expensive. In one common poison-pill maneuver, a target firm issues rights to its current stockholders indicating that if the firm is acquired in an unfriendly takeover, it will distribute a special cash dividend to stockholders. This cash dividend effectively increases the cost of acquiring the target and can discourage otherwise interested bidding firms from attempting to acquire this target. Another poison-pill tactic substitutes the distribution of additional shares of a target firm's stock, at very low prices, for the special cash dividend. Issuing this low-price stock to current stockholders effectively undermines the value of a bidding firm's equity investment in a target and thus increases the cost of the acquisition. Other poison pills involve granting current stockholders other rights—rights that effectively increase the cost of an unfriendly takeover.

Although poison pills are creative devices that target firms can use to prevent an acquisition, they generally have not been very effective. If a bidding firm and a target firm are strategically related, the value that can be created in an acquisition can be substantial, and most of this value will be appropriated by the stockholders of the target firm. Thus, target firm stockholders have a strong incentive to see that the target firm is acquired, and they are amenable to direct offers made by a bidding firm to them as individual investors; these are called **tender offers.** However, to the extent that poison pills actually do prevent mergers and acquisitions, they are usually bad for the equity holders of target firms.

Target firm management can also engage in a wide variety of actions that have little or no impact on the wealth of a target firm's equity holders. One class of these responses is known as shark repellents. **Shark repellents** include a variety of relatively minor corporate governance changes that, in principle, are supposed to make it somewhat more difficult to acquire a target firm. Common examples of shark repellents include **supermajority voting rules** (which specify that more than 50 percent of the target firm's board of directors must approve a takeover) and state incorporation laws (in some states, incorporation laws make it difficult to acquire a firm incorporated in that state). However, if the value created by an acquisition is sufficiently large, these shark repellents will neither slow an acquisition attempt significantly nor prevent it from being completed.

Another response that does not affect the wealth of target firm equity holders is known as the **Pac Man defense**. Targets using this tactic fend off an acquisition by taking over the firm or firms bidding for them. Just as in the old video game, the hunted becomes the hunter; the target turns the tables on current and potential bidders. It should not be too surprising that the Pac Man defense does not, on average, either hurt or help the stockholders of target firms. In this defense, targets become bidders, and we know from empirical literature that, on average, bidding firms earn only zero economic profits from their acquisition efforts. Thus, one would expect that, on average, the Pac Man defense would generate only zero economic profits for the stockholders of target firms implementing it.

Another ineffective and inconsequential response is called a **crown jewel sale**. The idea behind a crown jewel sale is that sometimes a bidding firm is interested in just a few of the businesses currently being operated by the target firm. These businesses are the target firm's "crown jewels." To prevent an acquisition, the target firm can sell off these crown jewels, either directly to the bidding firm or by setting up a separate company to own and operate these businesses. In this way, the bidding firm is likely to be less interested in acquiring the target.

A final, relatively ineffective defense that most target firm managers pursue is filing lawsuits against bidding firms. Indeed, at least in the United States, the filing of a lawsuit has been almost automatic as soon as an acquisition effort is announced. These suits, however, usually do not delay or stop an acquisition or merger.

Finally, as suggested in Table 10.7, some of the actions that the management of target firms can take to delay (but not stop) an acquisition actually benefit target firm equity holders. The first of these is the search for a **white knight**—another bidding firm that agrees to acquire a particular target in the place of the original bidding firm. Target firm management may prefer to be acquired by some bidding firms more than by others. For example, it may be that some bidding firms possess much more valuable economies of scope with a target firm than other bidding firms. It may also be that some bidding firms will take a longer-term view in managing a target firm's assets than other bidding firms. In both cases, target firm managers are likely to prefer some bidding firms over others.

Whatever motivation a target firm's management has, inviting a white knight to bid on a target firm has the effect of increasing the number of firms bidding for a target by at least one. If there is currently only one bidder, inviting a white knight into the bidding competition doubles the number of firms bidding for a target. As the number of bidders increases, the competitiveness of the market for corporate control and the likelihood that the equity holders of the target firm will appropriate all the value created by an acquisition also increase. On average, the entrance of a white knight into a competitive bidding contest for a target firm increases the wealth of target firm equity holders by 17 percent.

If adding one firm into the competitive bidding process increases the wealth of target firm equity holders

some, then adding more firms to the process is likely to increase this wealth even more. Target firms can accomplish this outcome by creating an **auction** among bidding firms. On average, the creation of an auction among multiple bidders increases the wealth of target firm equity holders by 20 percent.

A third action that the managers of a target firm can take to increase the wealth of their equity holders from an acquisition effort is the institution of **golden parachutes**. A golden parachute is a compensation arrangement between a firm and its senior management team that promises these individuals a substantial cash payment if their firm is acquired and they lose their jobs in the process. These cash payments can appear to be very large, but they are actually quite small in comparison to the total value that can be created if a merger or acquisition is completed. In this sense, golden parachutes are a small price to pay to give a potential target firm's top managers incentives not to stand in the way of completing a takeover of their firm. Put differently, golden parachutes reduce agency problems for the equity holders of a potential target firm by aligning the interests of top managers with the interests of that firm's stockholders. On average, when a firm announces golden parachute compensation packages for its top management team, the value of this potential target firm's equity increases by 7 percent.

Overall, substantial evidence suggests that delaying an acquisition long enough to ensure that a competitive market for corporate control

emerges can significantly benefit the equity holders of target firms. One study found that when target firms did not delay the completion of an acquisition, their equity holders experienced, on average, a 36 percent increase in the value of their stock once the acquisition was complete. If, however, target firms did delay the completion of the acquisition, this average increase in value jumped to 65 percent.

Of course, target firm managers can delay too long. Delaying too long can create opportunity costs for their firm's equity holders, because these individuals do not actually realize the gain from an acquisition until it has been completed. Also, long delays can jeopardize the completion of an acquisition, in which case the equity holders of the target firm do not realize any gains from the acquisition.

Sources: R. Walkling and M. Long (1984). "Agency theory, managerial welfare, and takeover bid resistance." *Rand Journal of Economics*, 15(1), pp. 54–68; R. D. Kosnik (1987). "Greenmail: A study of board performance in corporate governance." *Administrative Science Quarterly*, 32, pp. 163–185; J. Walsh (1989). "Doing a deal: Merger and acquisition negotiations and their impact upon target company top management turnover." *Strategic Management Journal*, 10, pp. 307–322; L. Y. Dann and H. DeAngelo (1983). Standstill agreements, privately negotiated stock repurchases, and the market for corporate control." *Journal of Financial Economics*, 11, pp. 275–300; M. Bradey and L. Wakeman (1983). "The wealth effects of targeted share repurchases." *Journal of Financial Economics*, 11, pp. 301–328; H. Singh and F. Haricento (1989). "Top management tenure, corporate ownership and the magnitude of golden parachutes." *Strategic Management Journal*, 10, pp. 143–156; T. A. Turk (1987). "The determinants of management responses to inter-firm tender offers and their effect on shareholder wealth." Unpublished doctoral dissertation, Graduate School of Management, University of California at Irvine.

in the combined firm the functions that are sensitive to economies of scale. To realize the value of any technology that a bidding firm acquires from a target firm, the combined firm must use this technology in developing, manufacturing, or selling its products. To exploit underutilized leverage capacity in the target firm, the balance sheets of the bidding and target firms must be merged, and the resulting firm must then seek additional debt funding. To realize the opportunity of replacing the target firm's inefficient management with more efficient management from the bidding firm, these management changes must actually take place.

Post-acquisition coordination and integration is essential if bidding and target firms are to realize the full potential of the strategic relatedness that drove the acquisition in the first place. If a bidding firm decides not to coordinate or integrate any of its business activities with the activities of a target firm, then why was this target firm acquired? Just as corporate diversification requires the active management of linkages among different parts of a firm, mergers and acquisitions (as one way in which corporate diversification strategies can be created) require the active management of linkages between a bidding and a target firm.

Post-Merger Integration and Implementing a Diversification Strategy

Given that most merger and acquisition strategies are used to create corporate diversification strategies, the organizational approaches previously described for implementing diversification are relevant for implementing merger and acquisition strategies as well. Thus, mergers and acquisitions designed to create diversification strategies should be managed through the M-form structure. The management control systems and compensation policies associated with implementing diversification strategies should also be applied in organizing to implement merger and acquisition strategies. In contrast, mergers and acquisitions designed to create vertical integration strategies should be managed through the U-form structure and have management controls and compensation policies consistent with this strategy.

Special Challenges in Post-Merger Integration

Although, in general, organizing to implement merger and acquisition strategies can be seen as a special case of organizing to implement corporate diversification strategies or vertical integration strategies, implementing merger and acquisition strategies can create special problems. Most of these problems reflect the fact that operational, functional, strategic, and cultural differences between bidding and target firms involved in a merger or acquisition are likely to be much greater than these same differences between the different parts of a diversified or vertically integrated business that was not created through acquisition. The reason for this difference is that the firms involved in a merger or acquisition have had a separate existence, separate histories, separate management philosophies, and separate strategies.

Differences between bidding and target firms can manifest themselves in a wide variety of ways. For example, they may own and operate different computer systems, different telephone systems, and other conflicting technologies. These firms might have very different human resource policies and practices. One firm might have a very generous retirement and health care program; the other, a less generous program. One firm's compensation system might focus on high salaries; the other firm's compensation system might focus on large cash bonuses and stock options. Also, these firms might have very different relationships with customers. At one firm, customers might be thought of as business partners; in another, the relationship with customers might be more arm's-length in character. Integrating bidding and target firms may require the resolution of numerous differences.

Perhaps the most significant challenge in integrating bidding and target firms has to do with cultural differences.[22] In Chapter 3, it was suggested that it can often be difficult to change a firm's organizational culture. The fact that a firm has been acquired does not mean that the culture in that firm will rapidly change to become more like the culture of the bidding firm; cultural conflicts can last for very long periods of time. Indeed, the difference between the relative success of Renault's acquisition of Nissan and DaimlerChrysler's acquisition of Mitsubishi has largely been attributed to the inability of Mitsubishi to modify its traditional management culture.

Cultural differences were apparently an important part of the post-merger integration challenges in the merger between Bank One and First Chicago Bank. Bank One had many operations and offices in small and medium-sized cities in the Midwest. First Chicago was a more urban bank. Different kinds of employees may have been attracted to these different firms, leading to significant cultural clashes as these two firms sought to rationalize their combined operations.[23] Most reports suggest that First Chicago employees have come to dominate this "merger." Unlike the merger between Bank One and First Chicago, JP Morgan Chase clearly acquired Bank One in 2004.

Operational, functional, strategic, and cultural differences between bidding and target firms can all be compounded by the merger and acquisition process—especially if that process was unfriendly. Unfriendly takeovers can generate anger and animosity among the target firm management that is directed toward the management of the bidding firm. Research has shown that top management turnover is much higher in firms that have been taken over compared to firms not subject to takeovers, reflecting one approach to resolving these management conflicts.[24]

The difficulties often associated with organizing to implement a merger and acquisition strategy can be thought of as an additional cost of the acquisition process. Bidding firms, in addition to estimating the value of the strategic relatedness between themselves and a target firm, also need to estimate the cost of organizing to implement an acquisition. The value that a target firm brings to a bidding firm through an acquisition should be discounted by the cost of organizing to implement this strategy. In some circumstances, it may be the case that the cost of organizing to realize the value of strategic relatedness between a bidding firm and a target may be greater than the value of that strategic relatedness, in which case the acquisition should not occur. For this reason, many observers argue that potential economies of scope between bidding and target firms are often not fully realized. For example, despite the numerous multimedia mergers in the 1990s (Time Warner, Turner Broadcasting, and AOL; The Walt Disney Company, Capital Cities/ABC, and ESPN; GE and NBC; Westinghouse and CBS), few seem to have been able to realize any important economies of scope.[25]

Although organizing to implement mergers and acquisitions can be a source of significant cost, it can also be a source of value and opportunity. Some scholars have suggested that value creation can continue to occur in a merger or acquisition long after the formal acquisition is complete.[26] As bidding and target firms continue to coordinate and integrate their operations, unanticipated opportunities for value creation can be discovered. These sources of value could not have been anticipated at the time a firm was originally acquired (and thus are, at least partially, a manifestation of a bidding firm's good luck), but bidding firms can influence the probability of discovering these unanticipated sources of value by learning to cooperate effectively with target firms while organizing to implement a merger or acquisition strategy.

Mergers and Acquisitions in an International Context

All the issues associated with mergers and acquisitions described thus far also apply to those that occur in an international setting. For example, firms exploring international merger and acquisition opportunities will need to follow the guidelines in Table 10.5 if they hope to gain competitive advantages from these strategies; international targets need to follow the guidelines in Table 10.6 if they are to extract as much of the value created by an acquisition as possible. However, one additional aspect of international mergers and acquisitions requires additional discussion: Challenges created for post-merger integration caused by cultural differences between countries.

We have already seen that post-merger integration usually involves resolving conflicts between the cultures of merged or acquired firms. However, when these organizational cultures reflect deep-seated country cultures, post-merger integration can be even more difficult. Thus, the integration of merged firms in an international context is often confounded by the need to discover how different country cultures can work together.

The most influential study of cultures around the world, by Geert Hofstede, suggests that cultures can be described as varying along the five dimensions presented in Figure 10.1.[27] Differences along each of these dimensions create potential challenges when integrating acquisitions conducted across country and cultural borders. These differences are rarely easy to resolve.

For example, a firm that operates in an individualistic culture may have a compensation scheme that celebrates individual achievement. If this firm acquires a company that operates in a collectivist culture, imposing an individualistic compensation policy can lead to misunderstanding and disagreement. Senior managers in a firm that operates in a culture that respects power may assume that their orders to employees in a firm that operates in a culture that only tolerates power will be carried out, but these employees will not do anything until they hear the boss's justification of those orders. A firm used to innovation and risk-seeking may be very frustrated if it acquires a company that operates in a culture that avoids rather than celebrates uncertainty. Employees that work in a firm that operates in a culture that values material possessions and hard work to obtain those possessions may be shocked to see employees in an acquired firm that operates in a culture that values the quality of life over material possessions go home at 5:00 P.M.—even if the work for the day is not done. Finally, employees that work in a firm that operates in a culture that values looking to the future may find it very difficult to work with employees in a firm that operates in a culture that values looking to the past.

Figure 10.1 Dimension of Culture and Their Implications for Integration in International Acquisition

Source: Hofstede G. (1980). *Culture's consequences: International differences in work-related values.* Copyright © 1980 Sage Publications. (Thousand Oaks, CA: Sage Publications).

Of course, acquiring firms can engage in specific activities to modify some aspects of the culture of the firms they acquire. However, to the extent that the organizational cultures of these acquired firms reflect differences in national cultures, there are few things that can be done to modify them. In such settings, acquiring firms must look to sources of value creation in an acquisition that do not depend on the integration of the organizational cultures of the bidding and target firms.

SUMMARY

Firms can use mergers and acquisitions to create corporate diversification and vertical integration strategies. Mergers or acquisitions between strategically unrelated firms can be expected to generate only competitive parity for both bidders and targets. Thus, firms contemplating merger and acquisition strategies must search for strategically related targets.

Several sources of strategic relatedness have been discussed in literature. On average, the acquisition of strategically related targets does create economic value, but most of that value is captured by the equity holders of target firms. The equity holders of bidding firms generally gain competitive parity even when bidding firms acquire strategically related targets. Empirical research on mergers and acquisitions is consistent with these expectations. On average, acquisitions do create value, but that value is captured by target firms, and acquisitions do not hurt bidding firms.

Given that most mergers and acquisitions generate only zero economic profits for bidding firms, an important question becomes: "Why are there so many mergers and acquisitions?" Explanations include (1) the desire to ensure firm survival, (2) the existence of free cash flow, (3) agency problems between bidding firm managers and equity holders, (4) managerial hubris, and (5) the possibility that some bidding firms might earn economic profits from implementing merger and acquisition strategies.

To gain competitive advantages and economic profits from mergers or acquisitions, these strategies must be either valuable, rare, and private or valuable, rare, and costly to imitate. In addition, a bidding firm may exploit unanticipated sources of strategic relatedness with a target. These unanticipated sources of relatedness can also be a source of economic profits for a bidding firm. These observations have several implications for the managers of bidding and target firms.

Organizing to implement a merger or acquisition strategy can be seen as a special case of organizing to implement a corporate diversification or vertical integration strategy. However, historical differences between bidding and target firms may make the integration of different parts of a firm created through acquisitions more difficult than if a firm is not created through acquisitions. Cultural differences between bidding and target firms are particularly problematic. Bidding firms need to estimate the cost of organizing to implement a merger or acquisition strategy and discount the value of a target by that cost. However, organizing to implement a merger or acquisition can also be a way that bidding and target firms can discover unanticipated economies of scope.

Post-merger integration challenges are likely to be particularly important for mergers and acquisitions in an international context. Important differences between the country cultures of different firms can raise the cost of post-merger integration. In these settings, it may be necessary for acquiring firms to find economies of scope to exploit that do not require the integration of cultures.

CHALLENGE QUESTIONS

1. Consider the following scenario: A firm acquires a strategically related target after successfully fending off four other bidding firms. Under what conditions, if any, can the firm that acquired this target expect to earn an economic profit from doing so?

2. Consider this scenario: A firm acquires a strategically related target; there were no other bidding firms. Is this acquisition situation necessarily different from the situation described in question 1? Under what conditions, if any, can the firm that acquired this target expect to earn an economic profit from doing so?

3. Some researchers have argued that the existence of free cash flow can lead managers in a firm to make inap-propriate acquisition decisions. To avoid these problems, these authors have argued that firms should increase their debt-to-equity ratio and "soak up" free cash flow through interest and principal payments. Is free cash flow a significant problem for many firms? What are the strengths and weaknesses of increased leverage as a response to free cash flow problems in a firm?

4. The hubris hypothesis suggests that managers continue to engage in acquisitions, even though, on average, they do not generate economic profits, because of the unrealistic belief on the part of these managers that they can manage a target firm's assets more efficiently than that firm's current management. This type of systematic nonrationality usually does not last too long in competitive market conditions: Firms led by managers with these unrealistic beliefs change, are acquired, or go bankrupt in the long run. Are there any attributes of the market for corporate control that suggest that managerial hubris could exist in this market, despite its performance-reducing implications for bidding firms? If yes, what are these attributes? If no, can the hubris hypothesis be a legitimate explanation for continuing acquisition activity?

5. It has been shown that so-called poison pills rarely prevent a takeover from occurring. In fact, sometimes when a firm announces that it is instituting a poison pill, its stock price goes up. Why?

PROBLEM SET

1. For each of the following scenarios, estimate how much value an acquisition will create, how much of that value will be appropriated by each of the bidding firms, and how much of that value will be appropriated by each of the target firms. In each of these scenarios, assume that firms do not face significant capital constraints.

(a) A bidding firm, A, is worth $27,000 as a stand-alone entity. A target firm, B, is worth $12,000 as a stand-alone entity, but $18,000 if it is acquired and integrated with Firm A. Several other firms are interested in acquiring Firm B, and Firm B is also worth $18,000 if it is acquired by these other firms. If Firm A acquired Firm B, would this acquisition create value? If yes, how much? How much of this value would the equity holders of Firm A receive? How much would the equity holders of Firm B receive?

(b) The same scenario as above except that the value of Firm B, if it is acquired by the other firms interested in it, is only $12,000.

(c) The same scenario in part a, except that the value of Firm B, if it is acquired by the other firms interested in it, is $16,000.

(d) The same scenario as in part b, except that Firm B contacts several other firms and explains to them how they can create the same value with Firm B that Firm A does.

(e) The same scenario as in part b, except that Firm B sues Firm A. After suing Firm A, Firm B installs a "supermajority" rule in how its board of directors operates. After putting this new rule in place, Firm B offers to buy back any stock purchased by Firm A for 20 percent above the current market price.

END NOTES

1. See Welch, D., and G. Edmondson (2004). "A shaky automotive *ménage à trois*." *BusinessWeek,* May 10, pp. 40–41.
2. See www.mergerstat.com/new/free_reports_m_and_a_activity.asp.
3. A list of larger acquisitions is available at www.oligopolywatch.com/2006/01/04.html.
4. Here, and throughout this chapter, it is assumed that capital markets are semi-strong efficient, that is, all publicly available information about the value of a firm's assets is reflected in the market price of those assets. One implication of semi-strong efficiency is that firms will be able to gain access to the capital they need to pursue any strategy that generates positive present value. See Fama, E. F. (1970). "Efficient capital markets: A review of theory and empirical work." *Journal of Finance,* 25, pp. 383–417.
5. See Trautwein, I. (1990). "Merger motives and merger prescriptions." *Strategic Management Journal,* 11, pp. 283–295; and Walter, G., and J. B. Barney (1990). "Management objectives in mergers and acquisitions." *Strategic Management Journal,* 11, pp. 79–86. The three lists of potential links between bidding and target firms were developed by the Federal Trade Commission; Lubatkin, M. (1983). "Mergers and the performance of the acquiring firm." *Academy of Management Review,* 8, pp. 218–225; and Jensen, M. C., and R. S. Ruback (1983). "The market for corporate control: The scientific evidence." *Journal of Financial Economics,* 11, pp. 5–50.
6. See Huey, J. (1995). "Eisner explains everything." *Fortune,* April 17, pp. 44–68; and Lefton, T. (1996). "Fitting ABC and ESPN into Disney: Hands in glove." *Brandweek,* 37(18), April 29, pp. 30–40.
7. See Rumelt, R. (1974). *Strategy, structure, and economic performance.* Cambridge, MA: Harvard University Press.
8. The first study was by Ravenscraft, D. J., and F. M. Scherer (1987). *Mergers, sell-offs, and economic efficiency.* Washington, DC: Brookings Institution. The second study was by Porter, M. E. (1987). "From competitive advantage to corporate strategy." *Harvard Business Review,* 3, pp. 43–59.
9. This is because if the combined firm is worth $32,000 the bidder firm is worth $15,000 on its own. If a bidder pays, say, $20,000 for this target, it will be paying $20,000 for a firm that can only add $17,000 in value. So, a $20,000 bid would lead to a $3,000 economic loss.
10. This is Jensen, M. C., and R. S. Ruback (1983). "The market for corporate control: The scientific evidence." *Journal of Financial Economics,* 11, pp. 5–50.
11. See Lubatkin, M. (1987). "Merger strategies and stockholder value." *Strategic Management Journal,* 8, pp. 39–53; and Singh, H., and C. A. Montgomery (1987). "Corporate acquisition strategies and economic performance." *Strategic Management Journal,* 8, pp. 377–386.
12. See Grant, L. (1995). "Here comes Hugh." *Fortune,* August 21, pp. 43–52; Serwer, A. E. (1995). "Why bank mergers are good for your savings account." *Fortune,* October 2, p. 32; and Deogun, N. (2000). "Europe catches merger fever as global volume sets record." *Wall Street Journal,* January 3, p. R8.
13. The concept of free cash flow has been emphasized in Jensen, M. C. (1986). "Agency costs of free cash flow, corporate finance, and takeovers." *American Economic Review,* 76, pp. 323–329; and Jensen, M.
14. (1988). "Takeovers: Their causes and consequences." *Journal of Economic Perspectives,* 2, pp. 21–48.
14. See Miles, R. H., and K. S. Cameron (1982). *Coffin nails and corporate strategies.* Upper Saddle River, NJ: Prentice Hall.
15. Roll, R. (1986). "The hubris hypothesis of corporate takeovers." *Journal of Business,* 59, pp. 205–216.
16. See Dodd, P. (1980). "Merger proposals, managerial discretion and stockholder wealth." *Journal of Financial Economics,* 8, pp. 105–138; Eger, C. E. (1983). "An empirical test of the redistribution effect in pure exchange mergers." *Journal of Financial and Quantitative Analysis,* 18, pp. 547–572; Firth, M. (1980). "Takeovers, shareholder returns, and the theory of the firm." *Quarterly Journal of Economics,* 94, pp. 235–260; Varaiya, N. (1985). "A test of Roll's hubris hypothesis of corporate takeovers." Working paper, Southern Methodist University, School of Business; Ruback, R. S., and W. H. Mikkelson (1984). "Corporate investments in common stock." Working paper, Massachusetts Institute of Technology, Sloan School of Business; Ruback, R. S. (1982). "The Conoco takeover and stockholder returns." *Sloan Management Review,* 14, pp. 13–33.
17. This section of the chapter draws on Barney, J. B. (1988). "Returns to bidding firms in mergers and acquisitions: Reconsidering the relatedness hypothesis." *Strategic Management Journal,* 9, pp. 71–78.
18. See Turk, T. A. (1987). "The determinants of management responses to interfirm tender offers and their effect on shareholder wealth." Unpublished doctoral dissertation, Graduate School of Management, University of California at Irvine. In fact, this is an example of an antitakeover action that can increase the value of a target firm. These antitakeover actions are discussed later in this chapter.
19. See Bower, J. (1996). "WPP-integrating icons." Harvard Business School Case No. 9-396-249.
20. See Jemison, D. B., and S. B. Sitkin (1986). "Corporate acquisitions: A process perspective." *Academy of Management Review,* 11, pp. 145–163.
21. Blackwell, R. D. (1998). "Service Corporation International." Presented to The Cullman Symposium, October, Columbus, OH.
22. Cartwright, S., and C. Cooper (1993). "The role of culture compatibility in successful organizational marriage." *The Academy of Management Executive,* 7(2), pp. 57–70; Chatterjee, S., M. Lubatkin, D. Schweiger, and Y. Weber (1992). "Cultural differences and shareholder value in related mergers: Linking equity and human capital." *Strategic Management Journal,* 13, pp. 319–334.
23. See Deogun, N. (2000). "Europe catches merger fever as global volume sets record." *Wall Street Journal,* January 3, p. R8.
24. See Walsh, J., and J. Ellwood (1991). "Mergers, acquisitions, and the pruning of managerial deadwood." *Strategic Management Journal,* 12, pp. 201–217; and Walsh, J. (1988). "Top management turnover following mergers and acquisitions." *Strategic Management Journal,* 9, pp. 173–183.
25. Landro, L. (1995). "Giants talk synergy but few make it work." *Wall Street Journal,* September 25, pp. B1 +. Indeed, one of these mergers was reversed when Viacom spun off CBS as a separate firm.
26. See Haspeslagh, P., and D. Jemison (1991). *Managing acquisitions: Creating value through corporate renewal.* New York: Free Press.
27. See Hofstede, G. (1980). *Culture's consequences: International differences in work-related values.* Thousand Oaks, CA: Sage Publications.

Case 3–1: eBay*

To Drop-Off or Not?

"That's a source that didn't even exist 10 years ago. Four hundred thousand people make some money trading on eBay."

—Vice President Dick Cheney, on why official unemployment rates may be overstated, September 9, 2004

Meg Whitman spun her desk chair around to face her office window. As another busy week came to a close, the CEO of eBay gathered her thoughts as she surveyed the company's San Jose, California, campus. Watching the sun dip below the horizon, Whitman thought of the success that eBay had experienced under her leadership. However, she was concerned that a relatively small percentage of registered users were classified as active users—users who bought an item, listed an item, or bid on an item. This suggested that some people wishing to use the site balked and abandoned the system for some reason. The emergence of online auction drop-off stores was a new development poised to reverse this trend. Whitman wondered how best to position eBay to capitalize on this new industry.

Online Auction Industry

Since before the time of Socrates, Plato, and Alexander the Great, auctions have existed as a way of creating a market between buyers and sellers. Some of the earliest recorded auctions took place in ancient Babylon, where single women were auctioned to available men for marriage. The Romans advanced the concept of the auction to include agricultural products and goods produced by artisans. The rules that govern modern auctions come to us from Great Britain. With the founding of auction houses like Sotheby's and Christie's, rules such as "the winning bid is the highest bid," and "goods are sold as is" were formalized.[1]

One of the most attractive aspects of an auction is that buyers and sellers are matched and create a market where the price received for an item is the highest price that an individual buyer is willing to pay. Sellers typically allow buyers to inspect items available for sale. The logistics required to get groups of buyers and sellers together can limit the number of individuals that participate in an auction. Additionally, some items may not hold enough broad-based appeal to ever make a traditional auction attractive. Indeed, how many people can you pull together in Rhinelander, Wisconsin, to bid on a Star Wars R2-D2 action figure?

eBay History

With the rapid integration of the Internet into everyday life, this logistical limitation vanished. Suddenly, an inexpensive, relatively easy way of connecting large numbers of buyers with large numbers of sellers existed. This was the vision behind eBay when Pierre Omidyar and Jeff Skoll started the company in September 1995 as Auction Web.[2] Within a few weeks, high traffic forced Omidyar to move the site to a business account and begin charging users a listing fee for their auctions and commissions on sales. The site was renamed "eBay." eBay's founders sought to create a community of individuals who came together to communicate and trade obscure items (e.g., Pez dispensers).[3] This community gradually developed its own sense of values, which governed transactions between members of eBay. Exhibit 1 lists the values that guide eBay community members.

The founding belief that eBay was a "community" meant that community members, along with eBay management, were responsible for developing the enterprise. Member feedback was a huge driver behind changes.

---

* This case was written by Ida Abdalkhani, Austin Anderson, Neil Bansal, Ryan Furnick, Bob Hamzik, Avinash Wadhwa, and Esteban Zamora, November 16, 2004. Written under the direction of Professor Jay Barney.

Exhibit 1   People Community Values

eBay is a community that encourages open and honest communication among all its members. Our community is guided by five fundamental values:

- We believe people are basically good.
- We believe everyone has something to contribute.
- We believe that an honest, open environment can bring out the best in people.
- We recognize and respect everyone as a unique individual.
- We encourage you to treat others the way you want to be treated.

eBay is firmly committed to these principles. And we believe that community members should also honor them—whether buying, selling, or chatting with eBay friends.

Source: www.eBay.com

Exhibit 2

Category	1Q03 Global GMS
eBay Motors	$8.7B
Computers	$2.6B
Consumer Electronics	$2.5B
Books/Movies/Music	$2.4B
Clothing and Accessories	$2.2B
Sports	$2.0B
Collectibles	$1.6B
Home & Garden	$1.6B
Toys	$1.5B
Jewelry & Gemstones	$1.3B
Cameras & Photo	$1.2B
Business & Industrial	$1.1B

Source: Company reports. Note: Figures are annualized.

Omidyar was overwhelmed by e-mails asking him whether particular sellers were trustworthy. He responded by creating a voluntary, participant-driven reputation mechanism that allows community members to describe exceptional and forgettable service experiences. Buyers and sellers could leave one line of text feedback for each other about each transaction and a +1, –1, or 0 score. This mechanism helped foster a robust online community, where users discussed common interests on message boards and in chat rooms related to the auction categories. The simple one-line feedback mechanism developed over a period of time into an elaborate feedback forum, largely because a good reputation within the eBay community had become a precious resource. In addition to the feedback forum, eBay put in place the SafeHarbor™ program, which provides guidelines for trading, provides information to resolve user disputes, and responds to reports of misuse of the eBay service. eBay's trust and safety initiatives, including user identity verification, insurance, integrated escrow, authentication, and other proactive antifraud efforts, are key elements of its effort to make eBay a safe place to trade.

Developing the infrastructure to support buyers and sellers was one key component of eBay's strategy. Attracting buyers and sellers to the site was another component. However, to market the company, eBay initially spent nothing on advertising, allowing word of mouth from users to generate new traffic. eBay did cross-promote and partner with other online and offline auctioneers, Web portals, search engines, and new sites.[4] It became the exclusive consumer-to-consumer (C2C) auction site for AOL's Web sites and online service in September 1998.

The growth of the company created a gap in management capabilities and the service levels demanded by customers. Shortly before taking the company public, Omidyar brought Meg Whitman aboard to succeed him as CEO. At that time, community members were largely selling and buying collectibles and antiques. Whitman brought with her a Harvard Business School pedigree, marketing experience at Procter & Gamble and PepsiCo, and consulting experience at Bain & Co. She began to fill senior management positions with other former consultants. The ex-consultants' focus on gathering data and measuring performance meant that eBay's managers could better decide on which projects to spend money. Whitman began to segment eBay's product offerings into categories, such as collectibles, jewelry, or apparel, each with its own category manager.[5] Exhibit 2 lists the product categories and the sales per category.

eBay's Performance Since Going Public

Seven months after Whitman's arrival, the firm went public. eBay's IPO in September 1998 was a frenzied event. The offer price of $18 quickly rose above $54 in early trading. The stock closed at $47.37 at the end of first-day trading.[6] Exhibit 3 provides a graphical view of eBay's share price since September 1998, and a comparison with the S&P 500 over a similar period. eBay's revenue performance has also been impressive. Table 1 shows the company's net revenues on a quarterly basis since 2002.

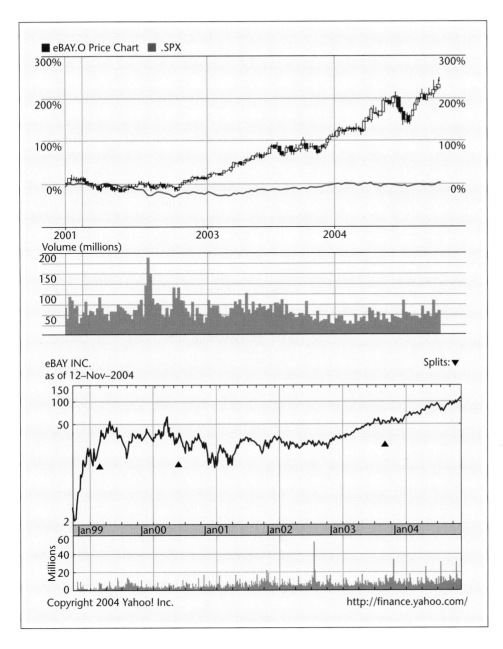

Exhibit 3   eBay Stock Price Performance

Triangles indicate a 3:1 stock split in March 1999, a 2:1 split in May 2000, and a 2:1 split in August 2003.

Table 1   **($ in thousands)**

	1Q02	2Q02	3Q02	4Q02*	1Q03	2Q03
Net Revenues	$245,106	$266,287	$288,779	$413,928	$476,492	$509,269
Change versus prior quarter	12%	9%	8%	43%	15%	7%

	3Q03	4Q03	1Q04	2Q04	3Q04	
Net Revenues	$530,942	$648,393	$756,239	$773,412	$805,876	
Change versus prior quarter	4%	22%	17%	2%	4%	

*Includes revenue from PayPal acquisition completed in October 2002.

A large portion of eBay's pre-2000 revenue came from collectibles. As eBay grew, it opened other product categories and specialty sites (e.g., motor vehicles). By 2004, its product categories spanned over 16,000 types of goods in 28 international markets. Both expansions involved partnerships and acquisitions of specialized and local auction Web sites.

To address the growing concerns of eBay users over payment speed and security, the company acquired PayPal in July 2002. PayPal is an online payment system that solves the problems associated with traditional payment methods such as money orders or personal checks. PayPal users fund their PayPal accounts using bank accounts or credit cards. When a customer pays for goods and services using PayPal's payment system, funds are transferred from his/her account to the PayPal seller's account. The PayPal seller can then withdraw these funds via bank account, debit card, or check. Alternatively, these funds can be used to make other PayPal purchases. Exhibit 4 depicts the PayPal payment process.[7]

By mid-2004, eBay reported 114 million registered users on eBay, reflecting a six-year CAGR of 126 percent. This figure includes all users who have an eBay log-in ID and password. Of these registered users, 41 million were active users—users who bid, bought, or listed over the preceding 12 months.[8] Exhibit 5 shows the growth in active users in the United States and Internationally. Analysts estimated that these users would list 1.389 billion items in fiscal 2004, and 1.807 billion in 2005.[9] eBay's growth explosion has made enforcing sanctions for site violations (e.g., fraud) more difficult. The growth of the company has also been marked by Web site attacks and outages. Disgruntled sellers in the eBay community recently filed a lawsuit for eBay's failure to remedy faulty billing.[10]

Online Auction Drop-Off

The online auction drop-off selling refers to the selling of items online for other people. There are a number of ways that this can be done, but the most common is for the seller or consignee to collect items for sale from the client or consignor. The consignee then handles the whole listing and selling process, and then pays the proceeds of the sale to the client, less an agreed-upon fee for the seller's services. If the item does not sell, it is either returned to the client or donated to charity. One great advantage of online auction drop-off selling is that the seller does not have to buy items up front—there is no risk of losing money on items that do not sell. Alternative approaches to online auction drop-off selling include:

- Offering it as a free service for friends, family, or charities
- Leaving the item with the owner and providing a listing service only
- Operating a retail store or "drop-off" location where customers leave items at the store

Exhibit 6 is a graphical depiction of the selling process completed by online auction drop-off stores. The emergence of retail brick-and-mortar storefronts to do eBay selling for customers has been a recent trend. Numerous auction drop-off stores have sprouted up all over the nation and the world. The industry is extremely fragmented, with several smaller players that compete with a number of major players. Some of the major competitors in this arena include AuctionDrop (www.auctiondrop.com), QuikDrop (www.quikdrop.com), and Trading Circuit (www.tradingcuit.com).

Each of the players has adopted a unique business format to compete in this industry. Franchising, partner-

Exhibit 4   PayPal Payment Process

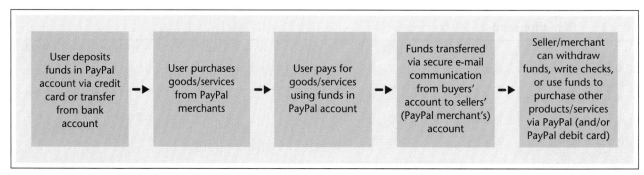

Source: Company reports and JP Morgan.

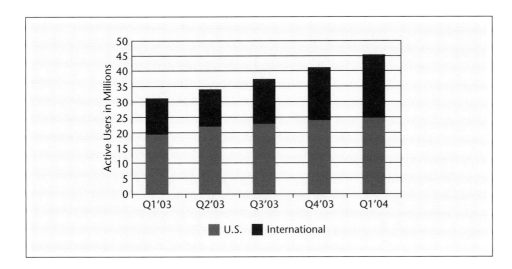

Exhibit 5   eBay Active User Growth

Source: Company reports and JP Morgan estimates.

ships, retail implanting, and opening a central warehouse with satellite stores are some major business formats deployed. Examples of fee structures that some drop-off store utilizes are outlined in Exhibit 7. The industry has two different types fee packages: basic and premium. The major difference between these two packages is that the premium package allows the seller to set a minimum opening bid price and/or reserve price (i.e., a minimum price that the seller is willing to accept) for the auction. This ensures that a drop-off store will not sell an item for less than the customer wishes to sell it for. Setting a reserve price and minimum starting price, however, decreases the probability that the item will sell. Because of this, eBay drop-off stores require a prepayment for the premium package.

Many predict that the online auction drop-off industry will become a big market. The majority of these con-signment stores utilize eBay as their auction host of choice. There are only a select few that provide Yahoo! Auctions as a choice to customers. An executive from one of the many sprouting brick-and-mortar retail stores offering eBay selling services said that eBay itself is upping its estimate of the industry size for the drop-off services. Where once the firm estimated the potential revenue at $5 to $10 billion, it now deems it more likely to grow to $20 to $25 billion, according to Auction-Drop CEO Randy Adams.[11]

Online auction drop-off stores are expanding the eBay market. The drop-off store model has the full support of eBay, which it believes will open up business from potential sellers currently unwilling or unable to sell online themselves. eBay CEO Meg Whitman said recently: "We're excited about this. Clearly they are getting an incremental customer that would never have come to eBay on their own."[12]

Exhibit 6   The Auction Drop-off Selling Process

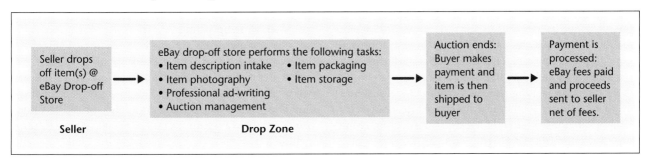

Exhibit 7   Online Auction Drop-Off Fee Structure Comparison

Name	Fee Structure
Auction Drop	Basic Service-No prepay: Premium Service-$19.99 prepay: Minimum: $19.99 38% of the first $200 30% of the next $300 ($200.01–$500) 20% of the remaining amount (over $500) Special quotes for items estimated to sell at more than $5,000.
QuikDrop	The fees are calculated from the selling price: 38% of the first $200 30% of the next $300 20% of the remaining (over $500) A $20 fee will be charged for items with a reserve price, Buy it Now, and/or high minimum bid.
Trading Circuit	Commission is 35% of the first $500 of the item's final selling price and 25% of the remaining amount over $500. There may also be other expenses associated with selling item, including eBay charges.
DropSmart	30% of the first $500 20% of the remaining balance (over $500) $10 minimum commission Rates are applied on a per-item basis. DropSmart incurs all listing fees.

Source: www.auctiondrop.com, www.quikdrop.com, www.tradingcircuit.com, www.dropsmart.com

Players in the Online Auction Drop-Off Industry

AuctionDrop

Founded in December 2002 by Bill Rollinson and Andy Jeffrey, AuctionDrop received $3.2 million in venture capital funding from Mobius Venture Capital & Draper Associates. It opened its first location in California in March of 2003. Its goal was to have 100 stores in 10 major areas by 2005; however, it stumbled onto a new approach to the drop-off store market as it conducted its business. It now runs a model that includes a central warehouse where the entire selling process is completed, and individual storefronts with mini-warehouses for temporary storage. AuctionDrop is no longer planning on opening individual storefronts but will maintain the ones it currently has open on the West Coast. It has also reached an

agreement with UPS to have "drop-off" locations at each of its 3,400 nationwide locations. As a result of this agreement, customers can bring items to any UPS store in the nation and UPS will take the item and send it to AuctionDrop's central warehouse to complete the eBay selling process. This agreement with UPS has helped AuctionDrop develop a national reach. Recently, AuctionDrop formed a partnership with Best Buy to open five pilot locations in northern California. At these locations, customers can bring unwanted items into Best Buy so that AuctionDrop can sell them on eBay. When the item sells, the customer will receive a Best Buy gift card in the amount of the item sold less any commissions to AuctionDrop.

AuctionDrop has averaged approximately 500 auctions per week since June of 2004 (see Exhibit 8). Despite having numerous drop-off locations, every store operates using a single eBay ID. This is because one central warehouse is controlling the entire listing and selling process. One advantage to having a central warehouse in control of the selling process is the ability to administer quality control and maintain a high feedback rating. AuctionDrop also averages a 90 percent sell-through rate,[13] compared to a much lower industry average. (See Exhibit 9.) A sell-through rate is a statistic that measures the success of auctions that are listed. Basically, a 90 percent sell-through rate signifies that 9 out of 10 auctions that AuctionDrop lists successfully result in sales. How do drop-off stores achieve much higher sell-through rates? AuctionDrop only accepts items for sale that meet certain criteria it has set. It uses databases such as Andale (www.andale.com) to access historical information on what sells, the amount it sells for, and the success rate for each sale. It also requires that an item have a perceived value of at least $75 in order to accept it for sale, recognizing that accepting any item lower than this value will not cover the costs or provide the required return.

QuikDrop

QuickDrop, another major player in the online auction drop-off industry, runs an individual storefront approach with each store operating as a franchise. Each individual store has its own eBay ID, since stores operate independently of each other. The cost of opening a QuikDrop varies depending on size and location. An applicant needs a minimum of $35,000 to open an average QuikDrop store. Larger stores in higher-priced locations could require a minimum of $55,000. These figures include a franchise fee of $15,000 and the QuikFlow software license fee of $1,995. QuikFlow is proprietary software developed to connect each franchise to the QuikDrop network and completely automate administrative operations such as point-of-sale transactions, managing and billing bidder accounts, and paying customers for their items. In a few simple steps, a franchisee can sign up new customers and pre-set the billing parameters. QuikDrop also charges an ongoing monthly royalty fee of $1,800. The term of its franchise agreement is 15 years and is renewable for $2,500.[14] QuikDrop has averaged 1,200 auctions per week across all of its stores nationwide since June of 2004 (refer to Exhibit 8), and has diversified its business by utilizing its individual storefronts to do more than just sell items on eBay.

QuikDrop currently has 18 storefront locations and plans to open more in the next year. To open up franchise locations, QuikDrop needs to receive authorization from the territories in which it wishes to operate. Franchise contracts are currently in place to open over 500 stores in the United States and 100 stores internationally. QuikDrop currently has authorization to do business in the following regions: California, Texas, Alabama, Virginia, South Carolina, Florida, Pennsylvania, Nevada, New York, Kentucky, Illinois, Ohio, New Jersey, North Carolina, Indiana, Georgia, Oregon, Arizona, Ontario Canada, and Australia.

Trading Circuit

An eBay drop-off store that was started by Circuit City, Trading Circuit utilizes existing excess capacity within Circuit City stores and is classified as a "retail implant." Trading Circuit started off with eight pilot locations in Georgia and Pennsylvania. Each Trading Circuit operates under different eBay user Ids. During this trial period, Trading Circuit averaged 438 auctions per week, which equated to approximately 55 auctions per storefront (refer to Exhibit 8). Trading Circuit initiated a referral program in which they offer $5 for every item brought in by the referred person.

In September of 2004, Trading Circuit shut down four of its eight pilot stores. Circuit City spokesperson Steve Mullen said Trading Circuit is a test business. It got "somewhat uneven results," he reported, and decided to close the four Atlanta centers to control costs and focus efforts on the Pittsburgh centers. "We are learning lots of lessons," Mullen said.[15] Trading Circuit currently operates six stores in Pennsylvania, Virginia, and most recently in Oklahoma. Circuit City plans on rolling out Trading Circuit in all of its retail stores throughout the United States and Canada, depending on the success of these pilot locations.

Table 2

Researching prices
Taking photographs
Cropping, resizing, and editing photographs
Writing descriptions
Listing the item
Answering questions
Corresponding with the buyer
Paying in checks
Monitoring your bank account for checks to clear
Packing the item
Shipping the item
Updating spreadsheets or accounting software

Why Would People Choose Online Consignment?

There are several steps that are needed to sell on eBay, or any other auction site, for that matter. For many sellers the process seems easy because they enjoy doing it, but even for professionals who sell many items daily, the process can be very time-consuming.

An hour or more to sell an item may seem unrealistically long, but consider every part of the selling process step by step. Table 2 lists the tasks required to sell an item using an online auction site. A seller could spend 5 to 30 minutes on each task.

It is likely that most households could easily find 10 or more items that are no longer of any use to them, and could raise upwards of several hundred dollars if they were to sell these items on eBay. However, many people are either too busy, do not enjoy working on computers, are not computer savvy, or simply cannot be bothered to sell their own property—these are the potential customers for online auction drop-off stores. Other common clients are businesses with slow-moving stock, particularly those with limited space to display their stock, such as car and antique dealers. Additional customers may also include businesses that have upgraded equipment among other things and wish to sell excess items on eBay but do not have the time or manpower to complete such an intense process.

An additional reason why customers would utilize the services of online auction drop-off stores is that these stores generally have experienced sellers who know the ins and outs of how to get maximum dollar for an auction. This involves anything from putting in key words in the subject line to attract bidders to taking professional

Exhibit 8   Weekly Auction Counts, 2004

Name	eBay Auction ID	23-Jul	2-Jul	9-Jul	16-Jul	23-Jul	30-Jul	6-Aug
AuctionDrop	auctiondrop	532	489	359	421	475	584	719
Trading Circuit	Robinson (Pitt)	NA	NA	NA	NA	NA	NA	NA
Trading Circuit	Ross Park (Pitt)	NA	NA	NA	NA	NA	NA	NA
Trading Circuit	Wilkins (Pitt)	NA	NA	NA	NA	NA	NA	NA
Trading Circuit	Century (West Mifflin)	NA	NA	NA	NA	NA	NA	NA
Trading Circuit	Ardmore, Ok	NA	NA	NA	NA	NA	NA	NA
Trading Circuit	Richmond, Virginia	NA	NA	NA	NA	NA	NA	NA
Trading Circuit Circuit City (reduced to 6 locations)	tradingcircuit1020, trading_circuit_730, trading_circuit_768, trading_circuit_770, trading_circuit_772, trading_circuit_773, trading_circuit_809, trading_circuit_781, trading_circuit_584, trading_circuit_111, quikdropvavir quikdroplv	52	291	613	539	482	470	396
QuikDrop	quikdropcaps1 quikdroptxdfw quikdropcasd	845	551	487	714	792	978	1,308
NuMarkets	numarkets	1,147	1,302	2,331	1,446	1,489	1,629	2,028
iSold it	isoldit isoldit_tx100	554	492	487	625	607	450	612
e-Powersellers	e-powersellers e-powersellers-cal	2,552	2,657	3,245	2,689	2,657	2,683	2,770
AuctionASAP	auctionasap Snappyauctions2	7	1	9	10	11	13	1
Snappy Auctions	snappyauctions snappyauctions4	206	173	157	154	120	172	128
AuctionBin	auctionbin	101	112	86	50	64	79	99
AuctionValet	myauctionvalet	61	65	105	78	97	95	86
ExpressDrop	expressdropchicago	114	147	86	114	106	130	155
eLOT	elotonline	194	192	187	199	213	183	167
AuctionWagon	auctionwagon	151	86	116	193	178	207	190
Cash it in	cashitinnow	110	79	87	91	83	75	93
NY Oasis	online_auction_service	539	867	1144	911	721	713	842
Auction it Easy	auctioniteasy	60	166	93	131	61	122	117
DropPro/Sell2All	droppro Edropshop	2	0	1	0	0	0	0
DropSmart	dropsmart	147	142	141	171	144	135	134
ez Auction Stop	ezauctionstop	38	61	58	54	80	61	58
EZBayer	ezbayertx	91	105	85	150	100	110	99
AuctionHARBOR	auctionharbort1	159	170	99	99	114	61	92
Ways Center	wayscenter	202	183	171	220	232	212	215
1stop Auctions	1stopauctions	62	58	77	35	65	66	47
DigaDeal	digadealny	0	30	73	50	51	30	56
Auction-Fest	siempre26	14	29	5	28	4	12	16
AuctionFarm	palleyd	250	180	359	369	488	274	226
Auction Shoppe	auctionshoppe	31	28	33	50	36	50	72
Auction Genie	yourauctiongenie	NA	NA	NA	NA	NA	5	6
United Auction Brokers	uabcorporate	NA	NA	NA	NA	NA	15	0
FastEZAuctions	fastezauction_san_diego	NA	NA	NA	NA	NA	NA	53
Auction Pointe	auction-pointe	61	61	21	119	20	0	NA
Drop n' Sell	dropnsell01	52	12	1	0	0	0	0

Source: eBay Historical Auction Data

13-Aug	20-Aug	27-Aug	13-Sep	22-Sep	22-Oct	29-Oct	Average Auctions per week	Average Auctions per Year
530	339	397	352	403	406	447	496	25,812
NA	NA	NA	NA	NA	114	107	111	5,746
NA	NA	NA	NA	NA	112	105	109	5,642
NA	NA	NA	NA	NA	76	135	106	5,486
NA	NA	NA	NA	NA	127	152	140	7,254
NA	NA	NA	NA	NA	0	122	61	3,172
NA	NA	NA	NA	NA	67	56	62	3,198
501	491	313	529	579	496	677	495	25,716
1,381	1,565	1,416	1,327	1,453	NA	1,645	1,205	62,669
2,201	2,330	2,026	1,711	2,991	NA	1,033	1,972	102,544
734	756	970	1,061	1,034	NA	NA	699	36,322
2,542	1,001	1,099	1,223	1,327	NA	NA	2,204	114,595
5	2	20	21	8	NA	NA	9	468
138	128	113	161	151	NA	NA	150	7,804
125	77	150	59	84	NA	NA	91	4,706
99	117	101	76	91	NA	NA	89	4,641
122	102	126	100	135	NA	NA	120	6,227
113	202	117	192	133	NA	NA	174	9,065
104	99	143	59	98	NA	NA	135	7,037
46	42	54	54	49	NA	NA	72	3,740
609	854	731	847	277	NA	NA	755	39,238
161	117	145	152	142	NA	NA	122	6,357
11	16	19	8	14	NA	NA	6	308
41	22	29	52	65	NA	NA	102	5,300
49	73	64	59	89	NA	NA	62	3,224
77	123	134	143	110	NA	NA	111	5,750
142	98	109	110	82	NA	NA	111	5,785
242	188	180	160	200	NA	NA	200	10,422
45	71	31	38	35	NA	NA	53	2,730
43	65	49	60	82	NA	NA	49	2,552
9	24	1	17	7	NA	NA	14	719
173	280	290	184	257	NA	NA	278	14,430
57	61	53	74	85	NA	NA	53	2,730
4	3	4	0	10	NA	NA	3	139
0	2	2	9	12	NA	NA	3	173
29	4	11	0	0	NA	NA	8	420
NA	NA	NA	NA	NA	NA	na	35	1,833
1	NA	NA	NA	NA	NA	NA	8	429

Exhibit 9

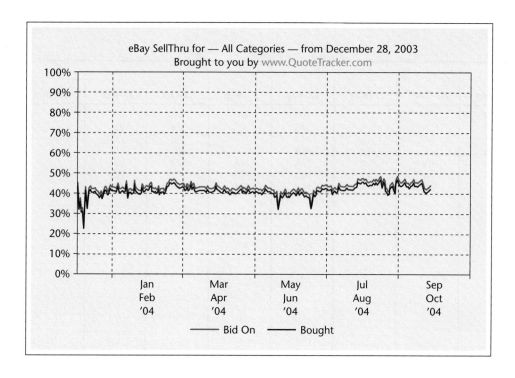

photographs to ensure that bidders know what they are getting. Higher bids also result from a high feedback rating generally associated with the online auction drop-off stores. As these stores claim to get higher values for goods they sell compared to an average online seller, the commission charged to a customer is somewhat offset by the higher sale price.

Competitors

Yahoo!

Founded in 1994 by two Stanford Ph.D. candidates, David Filo and Jerry Yang, Yahoo! was one of the largest Web portals by the time it entered online auctions in September 1998. Headquartered in Sunnyvale, California, Yahoo! has operations in North America, Europe, Asia, Latin America, and Australia. The company's number one operating philosophy is to provide the best Internet experience for its users. To this end, Yahoo! provides services across four major segments: Search & Marketplace, Information & Content, Communications & Consumer Services, and Affiliate Services. Yahoo! Auctions and many of the company's revenue generating activities fall under the area of Search & Marketplace.

Going into 2003, the company had a positive outlook on long-term growth and revenue-generation. According to Susan Decker, Chief Financial Officer of Yahoo!, the company had a clear plan:

> As we move into 2003, we continue to focus on maximizing long-term free cash flow per share. . . . Our long-term financial strategy of attracting significantly more revenue from our growing user base without commensurately increasing our expense appears to be gaining traction. In 2003, we expect strong growth in revenue, profitability and free cash flow, even as we continue to invest in areas that we expect will drive long-term growth.[16]

The company's broad offerings have enabled it to grow its user base greatly over the past year. Yahoo! has 263 million unique users worldwide, up 23 percent from 2002. Approximately 50 percent of the users are classified as active registered users (log in once per month or more), up 30 percent from 2002.[17]

The company also demonstrated phenomenal revenue growth of 71 percent over 2002. In 2003, revenues were at $1.6 billion, up from $953 million the previous year. Revenue is generated from three primary activities: marketing services, fees, and listings. Gross profits also increased to $1.3 billion, up from $790 million in 2002, and net income showed strong growth at $238 million, up from

Exhibit 10   Revenue Sources for eBay, Yahoo!, and Overstock.com

eBay Inc.

($ in millions)

	2002	2003	2004E	2005E
Gross Merchandise Sales	$14,868.0	$23,779.0	$34,154.0	$46,162.0
% change-Y-o-Y		60%	44%	35%
Payment Revenue	$159.8	$429.5	$647.2	$776.7
eBay Online Revenue	$949.2	$1,682.8	$2,479.3	$3,481.7
Total Transactions	$1,109.0	$2,112.2	$3,126.5	$4,258.4
3rd Party Advertising Revenue	$61.0	$47.1	$69.4	$80.0
End-to-end Services	$22.2	$5.7	-	-
Total Online Revenue	$1,192.3	$2,165.1	$3,195.9	$4,338.4
% change Y-o-Y		81.6%	47.6%	35.7%

Source: eBay Annual Reports; JP Morgan North America Equity Research, June 7, 2004.

Yahoo! Revenue-Mix

($ in thousands)

	2002	2003	Yr-over-Yr Growth ($)	Yr-over-Yr Growth (%)
Marketing Srvs	$651,568	$1,199,733	$548,165	84%
Fees	$207,941	$298,192	$90,251	43%
Listings	$93,558	$127,172	$33,614	36%
Total Revenues	$953,067	$1,625,097	$672,030	71%

Source: Yahoo! Annual Report 2003.

Overstock Financials

($ in thousands)

	2002	2003	Yr-over-Yr Growth ($)	Yr-over-Yr Growth (%)
Revenues (Sales)	$91,800	$238,900	$147,100	160%
Net Income (Loss)	($4,600)	($11,900)	($7300)	(158%)

Source: http://premium.hoovers.com.proxy.lib.ohio-state.edu/subscribe/co/fin/factsheet.xhtml?ID=105874.

$43 million the previous year. Much of the total revenue increase is attributed to a growth in paying users and thus, fee revenues. Fees increased over 2002 due to a rise in the number of paying users. In 2003, Yahoo! had 4.9 million paying users, up from 2.2 million in 2002; a 123 percent increase. However, average revenue per user declined to $5 per month, down from $7 per month in 2002. This decline is attributed to user growth in the lower-priced offerings. Exhibit 10 shows the growth of 43 percent in fee revenues. Paying users are currently "the fastest growing subset of users on the Yahoo! network."[18]

The current fee structure of Yahoo! Auctions generates revenues via both a list and final selling fee; buyers do not pay any fees. The listing fee starts at $0.05 and goes up to $0.75 (for items $50 and up). A final selling fee is also charged if the item sells, and ranges from 2 percent for small-value items ($25 and less) to a graduated scale of 0.5 percent (for items with a closing price over $1,000).[19]

Exhibit 11 provides further details on Yahoo! Auction's fee structure.

However, Yahoo! Auctions is still not a substantial player in the overall online auction market. The majority of online auction dollars go through eBay (64 percent). A distant second is uBid.com (14.7 percent). Yahoo! Auctions, Amazon auctions, and Egghead.com accounted for the rest of the top five online auction players, at less than 4 percent each. eBay also had the highest satisfaction and conversion rates among users.[20]

Overstock.com

Overstock.com's central organizing principle is to offer an online retail environment to provide consumers the opportunity to purchase brand-name merchandise at a discount. The merchandise itself is obtained from manufacturers holding excess production stock, or stock that is dated or

Exhibit 11 Fee Structures of Main Online
Auction Players: eBay, Yahoo!
Auctions, Overstock.com Auctions

eBay

Charges two fee types: Graduated listing fee & final selling price percentage

Final value fee is only charged if item sells:

Closing Price	Final Value Fee
$0–$25	5.25% of the closing price
$25–$1,000	5.25% of the first $25 ($1.31) plus 2.75% of the remaining closing price
$1,000 and up	5.25% of the first $25 ($1.31) plus 2.75% of the first $25–$1,000 ($26.81) plus 1.5% of the remaining closing price

Yahoo! Auctions

Charges two fee types: Graduated listing fee & final selling price percentage

Starting Price or Reserve Price	Listing Fee
$0.01–$9.99	$0.05
$10.00–$24.99	$0.15
$25.00–$49.99	$0.35
$50.00 and up	$0.75

Final value fee is only charged if item sells:

Closing Price	Final Value Fee
$0–$25	2% of the closing price
$25–$1,000	2% of the first $25 ($0.50) plus 1% of the remaining closing price
$1,000 and up	2% of the first $25 ($0.50) plus 1% of the first $25–$1,000 ($9.75) plus 0.5% of the remaining closing price

Overstock.com Auctions

Charges two fee types: Graduated listing fees & final selling percentage

Starting Price or Reserve Price	Listing Fee
$0.01–$0.99	$0.20
$1.00–$9.99	$0.23
$10.00–$24.99	$0.40
$25.00–$49.99	$0.79
$50.00–$199.99	$1.58
$200.00–$499.99	$2.38
$500.00 and up	$3.17

Final value fee is only charged if item sells:

Closing Price	Final Value Fee
$0–$25	3.25% of closing price
$25–$1,000	2.00% of closing price
$1,000 and up	1.00% of closing price

Sources: http://pages.ebay.com/help/sell/fees.html;
http://help.yahoo.com/help/auctions/afee/afee-06.html;
http://auctionbytes.com/cab/pages/sitepricing.

even of the wrong color. In essence, the company functions primarily as a liquidator for manufacturers, distributors, importers, retailers, and catalog companies, selling their excess inventory.[21]

Overstock.com has its origins in Discounts Direct, a firm formed in 1997. In 1999, Overstock.com entered the e-commerce sphere. Company president and CEO Dr. Patrick Byrne, 42, earned his Ph.D. in Philosophy from Stanford, and is the son of former GEICO Insurance CEO, Jack Byrne, and a friend of Warren Buffett.[22] The company went public in 2002, and Byrne holds 40 percent of the shares. The company has a current market capitalization of $1.1 billion.

Overstock.com has been described as a "Persian bazaar," selling anything from books and music CDs, to electronics, jewelry and even luxury cruises. While it was originally conceived to sell this broad assortment of merchandise to retail customers in their homes, the company now also sells in small blocks to small business retailers through a sister site, www.overstockb2b.com. Additionally, the company often serves as a "fulfillment partner" for other merchants, selling their merchandise—which Overstock.com never actually owns or handles—via the Overstock.com Web site.

A relatively new player in the world of online commerce, Overstock.com has grown dramatically. Sales in 2000 were $25.5 million and had grown to $91.8 million in 2002, and to $238.9 million by 2003. But, as with many nascent Internet commerce companies, the net income picture is far less rosy: Annual net income in 2000 was a negative $21.3 million. This figure improved to negative $4.6 million by 2002, and was a negative $11.9 million in 2003.[23] Byrne has been successful in growing the business and making it competitive, and in September of 2004 attempted to translate that success beyond the world of simply selling excess merchandise, to compete in the online auction market. Overstock.com offers an auction venue similar to that of eBay internally code-named "o-cean."

Overstock.com will attempt to compete against eBay on price, charging 30 percent less to list items on its auction site, and it charges graduated insertion fees for placing an item on its site for auction (refer to Exhibit 11). For example, a $50 item would have an insertion fee of $1.58, and a $250 item, $2.38. Overstock.com also realizes revenue when an item is sold, charging a graduated percentage of the sale price. Items selling for less than $1,000 produce a 2 percent fee; items closing at more than $1,000 generate 1 percent for Overstock.com.[24]

Overstock is hoping to use its customer base from its fixed-price business to drive its success in the auction market. It is unclear what proportion of current customers will actually utilize the service, however. Early figures show growth in the number of products listed, from 400 in September, to over 17,700 in October.

Byrne is convinced that there is a place for Overstock.com Auctions:

> First there was "e-Bay" and now there is "o-cean"— the internal code name for Overstock.com Auctions. I think this will work for three reasons: 1) certain dynamics within eBay's marketplace are causing eBay's Powersellers to itch for an alternative; 2) our auction tab scratches that itch; and 3) the social networking imbedded within our auction tab may turn out to be powerful.[25]

Byrne's optimism must be tempered by the fact that successful online retailing and auctioning is somewhat like that of the brick-and-mortar variety in that it depends on the customer "seeing" the product. In the online world this is measured by number of unique visits to a Web site, among other metrics. Overstock.com has witnessed dramatic increases in sales through its retail business, and hopes this will continue in its auction site. But to offer some perspective on the level of success in being "seen" by customers, one can look at industry peers and their success in being "seen." In August 2004, eBay had 15.4 million visitors weekly to its site, Yahoo! had 2.9 million, and Overstock.com had 1.6 million.[26] (See Exhibit 12.)

It's clear that Overstock.com and its burgeoning auction site have a long hill to climb. The recent auction of the historic 700th home run ball of San Francisco Giants' left-fielder Barry Bonds for $804,000 is precisely the sort of high profile event the company needs to help draw the

Exhibit 12   Overview of Web Presence

Unique Web Site Visitors (millions/week)

eBay	15.47
Yahoo Shopping	2.92
Overstock.com	1.62

Gender Differential (% Female)

eBay	48.7
Yahoo Shopping	53.2
Overstock.com	56.5

Source: http://www.internetretailer.com/dailynews.asp?id=12602.

attention of potential users and to successfully launch its auction site.[27]

Conclusion

As the sun set on San Jose, Meg Whitman felt uncertain about how to best pursue the opportunities that online auction drop-off stores presented. It was clear to her that this industry presented unforeseen opportunities and their future impact on the online auction industry could be substantial. These stores could definitely help eBay grow the number of sellers and make the site more accessible to the general population or they could simply be just another fad that would eventually dissipate. As the final glimmers of sunlight beamed through her office window, she sat back and pondered the possible options.

Notes

1. Cassady, Ralph. *Auctions and auctioneering.* Berkeley: University of California Press, 1967, URL: http://www.agorics.com/Library/Auctions/auction9.html.
2. Bjornsson, Magus. "eBay: A concise analysis." March 16, 2001; URL: http://www.cs.brandeis.edu/~magnus.
3. "Q&A with eBay's Pierre Omidyar." *Fortune,* December 13 2001, URL: http://www.businessweek.com/magazine/content/01_49/b3760605.htm.
4. "Z Auction and eBay announce strategic alliance." eBay Press Release, 10-Feb-1998.
5. Lashinsky, Adam. "Meg and the machine." *Fortune,* August 11, 2003.
6. Sullivan, Jennifer. "Investory frenzy over eBay IPO." *Wired,* September 24 1998, URL: http://www.wired.com/news/print/0,1294,15212,00.html
7. Gaither, Chris. "eBay to acquire PayPal for $1.513 stock deal, unites online auction giant, net payment service." *The Boston Globe,* July 9, 2002.
8. eBay Inc. 2Q 2004 Financial Results, Press Release, July 21, 2004; URL: http://investor.ebay.com/news/Q204/EBAY072104-139863.pdf.
9. eBay presentation at 2004 Pacific Crest Technology Forum, August 10, 2004.
10. Matt Hines, "eBay sellers file billing suit." CNET News.com,July 7, 2004.
11. "eBay drop-off stores optimistic." *Marketing Vox News,* News Archives, February 3, 2004 http://www.marketingvox.com/archives/2004/02/03/ebay_dropoff_stores_optimistic
12. "eBay drop-off stores herald $10bn sales boost." *The Retail Bulletin,* July 21, 2004; URL: http://www.theretailbulletin.com/index.php?page=5&cat=news&id=4403&size=up&PHPSESSID=9797 d0bd1ab6b9d477elf0ded843a79d.
13. Anne B. McDonald from the September 2004 issue of PC World Magazine, "Auction stores do ebay selling for you." URL: http://www.pcworld.com/news/article/0,aid,117090,pg,1,00.asp.
14. "Circuit City closes four ebay drop-off centers." AuctionBytes.com, URL: http://www.auctionbytes.com/cab/abn/y04/m10/i04/s02.
15. Ibid.
16. Matthew Clark. ENN electricnews.net, "Yahoo raises the bar for 2003." January 16, 2003; URL: http//www.enn.ie/news.html?code=8894192.
17. Yahoo! 2003 Annual Report, page #4, Terry S. Semel's letter to shareholders.
18. Ibid.
19. URL: http://help.yahoo.com/help/auctions/afee/afee-06.html.
20. "Nielsen Net Ratings: Auction sites ever more popular." July 2, 2001; URL: http://www.nua.ie/surveys/index.cgi?f=VS&art_id=905356927&rel=true.
21. Company Profile, Overstock.com; URL: http://www.shareholder.com/overstock/history.cfm?page=do.
22. James K. Glassman. "Profit-from-doom Overstock boss prophesizes e-tailing's quick demise." Tech Central Station; URL: http://www.techcentralstation.com/011501L.html.
23. From Company's 10Q and 10K filings.
24. Ibid.
25. From the company's October 21, 2004, SEC Form 8-K.
26. Internet retailer, August 6, 2004; URL: http://www.internetretailer.com/dailynews.asp?id=12602.
27. News, October 27, 2004, "Overstock.com auction closes for Barry Bonds' historic 700th home run ball." Morningstar.com; URL: http://news.morningstar.com/news/PR/M10/D27/1098907868159.html.

Case 3-2: Nucleon, Inc.*

Robert Moore, a recent graduate of a top-ranked M.B.A. program, now realized what it was like to be on the other side of a case study. It was December 1990, and Nucleon, the young biotechnology start-up at which he had recently become project manager, faced critical manufacturing choices. Moore and Jeff Hurst, the firm's CEO, had met to discuss the situation, and within the next few weeks, Hurst needed to present the company's manufacturing strategy to the board of directors. In the meantime, he asked Moore to evaluate in detail Nucleon's options and give his own recommendation.

Nucleon's first potential product, "cell regulating ein-1" (CRP-1), had been undergoing extensive experimentation and analysis in the company's R&D laboratories for several years. The next major hurdle was human clinical trials, which also typically took place over several years. However, before Nucleon could launch clinical trials, it had to decide how and where CRP-1 would be manufactured. To ensure participants' safety, the U.S. Food and Drug Administration (FDA) imposed strict guidelines; products being tested in humans had to be made in facilities certified for "clinical grade" production.[1]

Since CRP-1 was the company's first product to go into the clinic, Nucleon had no manufacturing facilities which met FDA requirements. It was faced with three options for supplying CRP-1 to the clinic: The first was to

build a new 5000 square-foot pilot plant with enough capacity to supply all the CRP-1 needed for Phases I and II of clinical trials. The second option was to contract clinical manufacturing to an outside firm. And a third option was to license the manufacturing to another biotechnology company or to a pharmaceutical firm. Under this third option, the licensee would be responsible for all manufacturing, clinical development, and eventual marketing of CRP-1.

Definite risks and rewards were attached to each option, and Moore knew that the one ultimately chosen by Hurst would have long-term consequences for Nucleon's survival in the intensively competitive and high-stakes drug industry.

Background

Nucleon was founded in 1985 by Dr. Alan Ball, an internationally respected researcher at the Children's Hospital and an Associate Professor of Clinical Medicine at the Greaves Medical Center, to develop pharmaceutical products based on a class of proteins known as cell regulating factors. From 1985 to 1988, Dr. Ball and a small group of scientists who joined Nucleon researched ways of producing CRP-1 outside the human body. Although CRP-1 was a naturally occurring protein contained in human blood plasma, the amount that could be extracted was far too small to be of any commercial use.

Scientists first isolated a small amount of naturally occurring CRP-1 and determined the gene that instructed human cells how to produce CRP-1. The gene was then cloned. While this laboratory process for producing CRP-1 was still very small scale, it generated enough material to send to academic collaborators who were exploring the potential therapeutic uses of CRP-1. Although an actual product was still several years and millions of dollars away, early research indicated that CRP-1 had potential as a treatment for burns and for kidney failure.

* Professor Gary Pisano wrote this case as the basis for class discussion rather than to illustrate either effective or ineffective handling of an administrative situation.

Data and names have been altered for purposes of confidentiality.

Reprinted by permission of Harvard School Press from Nucleon, Inc. by Professor Gary Pisano. Copyright © 1991 by the President and Fellows of Harvard College. To order copies or request permission to reproduce materials, call 1-800-545-7685, write Harvard Business School Publishing, Boston, MA 02163, or go to http://www.hbsp.harvard.edu. No part of this publication may be reproduced, stored in a retrieval system, used in a spreadsheet, or transmitted in any form or by any means—electronic, mechanical photocopying, recording, or otherwise—without the permission of Harvard Business School.

Strategy and Competition

Nucleon was one of over 200 firms founded since the mid-1970s to develop pharmaceutical technologies based on recent advances in molecular biology and immunology. This new field of R&D, commonly called "biotechnology," also attracted the attention of established companies. By 1989, most of the world's largest pharmaceutical enterprises, such as Eli Lilly, Merck, and Hoffman LaRoche, had extensive in-house biotechnology R&D programs as well as collaborative ties with many of the new entrants.

Competition was intense. Scientists at both start-up and established companies were racing to be the first to clone certain genes and establish proprietary positions for their firms in emerging areas such as cell regulating factors. Establishing a strong patent position was particularly important for small companies such as Nucleon. Moore explained: "Given the enormous costs of developing and commercializing a new drug, potential investors want to see a strong proprietary position before they commit serious capital. Just one strong patent on the right molecule can ensure survival for years by allowing you to attract capital."

Biotechnology patent law, however, was as new and uncertain as the technology itself. Indeed, the legality of patenting a genetically engineered microorganism was only established in 1980 by a landmark United States Supreme Court decision, and the ensuing decade saw many legal battles over the scope and efficacy of specific patents. In some cases, two or more companies had claims on different proprietary elements of the same molecule. For example, one company might claim ownership of the molecule itself while another of the genetic sequence used to synthesize the molecule. Further, it was extremely difficult to patent the process technology used to obtain a biologically important molecule, even though the starting material and the resulting molecule were considered original enough to be patented. Given the lack of precedent, it was always difficult to predict how the courts would rule in any given situation.

Moreover, the United States Patent Office might take several years to process an application. And while few companies could afford to wait until a patent was granted before continuing development, there were big risks in going ahead with development before the granting of a patent. A company could spend tens of millions of dollars in clinical trials and manufacturing facilities yet wind up not having a proprietary position if the patent office denied the application. Even if patents were granted, it was always possible for a competitor to challenge them in court. While Nucleon believed it had a strong patent position on the CRP-1 molecule, its rights to other necessary proprietary components (such as the genetic sequence) were less certain.

Nucleon management believed that several factors were critical to the company's survival. As Hurst commented:

> Given how small we are, it's absolutely essential that we pick the right projects. We can't hedge our bets with a big portfolio of projects, like the big pharmaceutical companies can. We've got to pick winners the first time.

Gordon Banks, Nucleon's vice president of R&D, and one of the leading scientists in the field of cell regulating factors added:

> That's why it's so important for us to be at the leading edge of scientific research. This means not only attracting the best in-house scientists, but also maintaining close contact with universities. If someone at a university clones the genes for a new cell regulating factor, we want to know about it.

Nucleon management believed that it had found an attractive niche: relatively few firms were working on cell regulating proteins. Banks believed that the company's distinctive technical capability lay in its ability to identify potentially therapeutic cell regulating factors. Although Nucleon was a leader in cell regulating factors, the company was not free from competition. Other companies were developing drugs using somewhat similar technology. Also, many companies were using alternative technologies to develop drugs for some of the same diseases for which cell regulating factors were being developed. As Hurst commented, "We're a leader, but we're not alone. It's important for us to get our products into the clinic before others do."

Biotechnology firms were using different strategies for developing and commercializing their technologies. Virtually all the biotechnology companies started, like Nucleon, as specialized R&D laboratories. Over time, some vertically integrated into production, and a few of the oldest companies, like Genentech, were even vertically integrating into marketing. Nucleon was presently contemplating its manufacturing strategy. Its marketing strategy, however, was clear. Nucleon management believed that the company could not afford to market its products on its own. Instead, it planned to link up with established pharmaceutical companies, with strong distribution capabilities, to market its products. Hurst, who once worked in marketing for a large pharmaceutical company, noted:

> Companies like Merck have hundreds of salespeople. They can reach every doctor's office in the country within one week. It would be crazy for a company like

us to go up against them in marketing. Besides, our products are likely to be targeted at a variety of therapeutic markets. We would need a few hundred salespeople to market all these products directly. We're much better off linking up with the best company in each therapeutic market.

By December 1990, the privately held company had grown to 22 employees, 18 of whom were engaged in R&D; of these about one-third had Ph.D.s from scientific disciplines such as biochemistry, molecular biology, protein chemistry, and immunology. Most of the R&D staff had been recruited from leading university research laboratories and were strongly attracted to cutting-edge, product-oriented research. Nucleon's size and entrepreneurial spirit created an academic atmosphere in R&D and tight links to the academic/scientific community.

Since its founding, Nucleon had raised approximately $6 million in venture capital and received research grants from the U.S. Department of Agriculture totaling $600,000.

Drug Development: From Research to Market

Establishing the safety and efficacy of products like CRP-1 that were based upon novel genetic engineering technology was enormously complex, time-consuming, and expensive. Nucleon's drug development process, divided into several distinct phases, is discussed below.

Research

Before launching a research project to develop a new drug, Nucleon management considered several factors in evaluating a project's profit potential. First, there had to be a chance of achieving a dominant proprietary position. Second, the market had to be large enough to justify the R&D investment. Finally, Nucleon wanted to develop drugs where no alternative treatments were available. During the research phase, Nucleon's scientists sought to identify and purify from human plasma minute quantities of cell regulating proteins that might have therapeutic value. Some critical information to pursue this research was obtained by perusing scientific literature or by consulting with leading academic researchers. Much necessary information, however, was still undiscovered and came only from in-house research and experimentation, which seldom moved in a straight-forward, logical manner but from one obstacle to the next. This could entail abandoning one strategy and starting over again.

Cloning and Purification

Products like CRP-1 and others that Nucleon intended to develop were fundamentally different from most drugs developed by pharmaceutical companies, which traditionally were synthetic chemicals. Chemical synthesis was effective for relatively small and simple molecules, but proteins like CRP-1 were simply too big and complex to be synthesized that way and instead were produced by genetic engineering.

Through genetic engineering, the scientist created a microscopic protein factory. The gene for the protein was identified, isolated, and cloned, then inserted into different strains of the bacterium *E. coli.* In theory, the genetically engineered bacteria could then produce the protein in a test tube or shake flask. However, since genetic engineering was still a relatively new scientific discipline, it was not always easy to either identify the relevant genes or to get "host" (genetically altered) bacteria to produce a specific protein. In practice, it was usually necessary to try different types of host cells to find one or more capable of producing the protein in quantities that could be scaled-up to an economically feasible process.

Only a few milligrams of protein could be produced from genetically engineered cells grown in shake flasks. Thus, an extensive amount of work then had to go into developing the processes for making each of these proteins in large quantity.

Pre-clinical Research

Before a pharmaceutical was tested in humans it underwent pre-clinical evaluation, consisting of experiments in animals to evaluate its efficacy. Over six to eight months, increasing doses were administered to animals with and without the simulated disease. Another six months might be needed to evaluate the data.

By this point, the company might have spent $6 to $10 million in R&D and preparation of regulatory documents. Only after completing all the requisite animal tests, and having a suitable production process, could the company file for permission with the FDA to commence clinical trials in humans. Though Nucleon had not begun human clinical trials, management expected to file an application with the FDA to begin human trials for CRP-1 as a burn wound treatment in 1992. The company was also doing research to determine if CRP-1 might have other therapeutic applications. There was some preliminary data suggesting that it might treat kidney failure. Moore estimated that about another two years and $3 million of work were needed before the kidney failure application could be tested in the clinic.

Human Clinical Trials

Most governments required every new pharmaceutical product to undergo extensive clinical testing before it could be marketed widely, and the FDA regulations were considered the most stringent in the world. To meet them, any new drug, or any approved drug being modified for a different therapeutic application, had to undergo three phases of clinical trials.

Phase I trials assessed basic safety. During these trials, the drug was administered to a small group of healthy volunteers and any adverse reactions (such as fevers, dizziness, or nausea) were noted.[2] This phase usually required between 6 and 12 months. As long as there were no serious side effects, the product moved to phase II trials where it was administered to a small group of patients having the disease the drug was presumed to treat. The patients were monitored to determine whether their condition improved as a result of the drug and whether they suffered any adverse side effects. It was during phase II trials that appropriate dosages were determined. This phase typically required between one to two years to complete. If Phase II trials succeeded, the product then moved to Phase III trials.

Phase III trials assessed the product's efficacy with a relatively large sample of patients on a statistically rigorous basis. Typically, these trials involved multiple hospitals and could require from two to five years to complete. Because of the large number of patients, doctors, and hospitals involved, this stage was by far the most expensive. The costs of manufacturing the drug, administering it to patients, monitoring results, analyzing data, and preparing the requisite regulatory paperwork could run between $30–$100 million. It was imperative for regulatory reasons to manufacture the product with the same process that would be used when the product was marketed commercially. Any change in manufacturing would mean repeating human clinical trials to prove that the deviation did not alter the product's safety and efficacy. This also added significantly to the costs of running Phase III clinical trials.

The CRP-1 Project: Current Applications

Since Nucleon's founding, its main development project had been CRP-1 and most of the company's R&D resources had been focused on the CRP-1 projects. While CRP-1's commercialization was still a few years away, Nucleon's scientists and investors were optimistic about its potential. Exhibit 1 depicts the expected time for FDA approval. Initial research focused on developing two major therapeutic applications—one for topical treatment of burn wounds, the other for acute kidney failure. Both the burn wound and kidney failure markets were estimated to be similar in size. Furthermore, in 1988, the company had also begun investigating two new cell regulating factors, still in the early stages of research. Dr. Banks estimated that these could be ready for clinical trials in about four years if the company spent $10 million on each one.

One of the most critical activities currently taking place on the CRP-1 project was the development of a larger scale production process, with sufficient capacity to meet all clinical trial requirements. Every step of the process had to be carefully documented and validated to ensure that it could produce identical product from batch to batch.

Exhibit 1	Approximate Time Frame for CRP-1 Project
April 1992	Begin Phase I Clinical Trials
December 1992	Begin Phase II Clinical Trials
December 1993	End Phase II Clinical Trials
June 1994	Begin Phase III Clinical Trials
December 1996	Complete Phase III Clinical Trials; File data with FDA
January 1998	Expected FDA approval and commencement of sales

Process Development and Manufacturing

CRP-1 production would require four basic process steps: 1) fermentation, 2) purification, 3) formulation, 4) filling and packaging (see Exhibit 2).

Fermentation.   Fermentation initially focused on growing the genetically engineered *E. coli* in small laboratory flasks; the process was then scaled up to successively larger vessels. Unfortunately, the process used to grow cells in a 1-liter glass bottle might not work when attempted in a 10-liter glass chamber or a 100-liter stainless steel tank (also known as a fermentor or bioreactor), given differences in heat exchange, tank aeration, and fermentor geometry. The kinds of nutrients cells were fed, bioreactor temperature, acidity level, oxygen flow rate into the bioreactor, and dozens of other process parameters, were all determined during fermentation process development.

While crude fermentation processes existed for over 6000 years, fermentation using genetically engineered cells dated to the early 1980s. Many biotechnology firms encountered major difficulties when trying to run pilot and

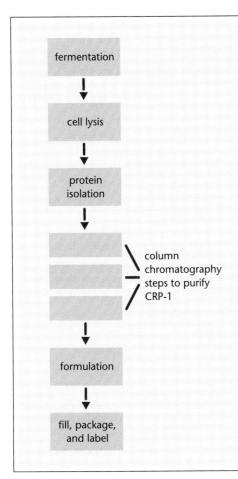

Fermentation: A process in which organisms such as bacteria or yeast are suspended in a nutrient growth medium, consisting of sugars, salts, and amino acids (protein building blocks), at an appropriate temperature and aeration level (oxygen and other gases) in order to promote these organisms' growth and metabolism. The desired products of the organisms' metabolism may be the whole organism itself, metabolic products, modified compounds, or in this case proteins.

Cell Lysis: In cases where the protein of interest is not excreted by the cell into the surrounding medium but remains inside, the cell needs to be broken open to obtain the protein. This process is know as cell lysis. Lysis can be done mechanically or chemically.

Isolation and Purification: After cells are lysed, the protein of interest must be isolated and purified from among all of the other contents of the cell. Initially, methods such as centrifugation (using centrifugal force to separate heavy and light debris) and chemical precipitation can be used to concentrate the mixture.

After a series of initial separation steps have been performed, finer, more precise separation techniques can be employed to isolate the protein of interest from other similar protein molecules. For example, chromatography isolated substances based upon their ability to separate between a liquid and a solid.

Formulation: In drug formulation, the protein of interest is put into an appropriate medium for administration as a therapeutic drug. The protein may be dissolved in purified water or another pure solvent such as ethanol for injection. In some cases, a protein must be formulated to be applied in a topical form such as a cream or put in an aerosol suspension. The challenge is to ensure the drug's safety and efficacy.

Filling: The therapeutic is then placed in an appropriate container under sterile conditions and is packaged and labeled.

Exhibit 2   Process Flow for CRP-1[1]

[1]Diagram does not include holding points where work-in-process is stored between operations. The diagram also does not include quality control steps which are conducted after every operation.

commercial scale fermentation processes for the first time, as Dr. Ann Dawson, Nucleon's director of process science, explained:

> *There are so many unknowns and so many things which can go wrong. If a virus gets into your bioreactor, you could be shut down for weeks. Incredibly tight process control is an absolute must, and even then, you may still run into troubles.*

For regulatory reasons, it was absolutely critical to run the process exactly as specified. Such strict adherence to process specifications was necessary because even minor process deviations could impact product quality. In addition, the efficiency of the process could be severely affected by changes in any one of the key process parameters.

Because such production methods were new, process development required a great deal of trial-and-error and close collaboration between research scientists and process development scientists early on in the project. Research scientists had to design a process that worked in a test tube as well as on a larger scale, and process development scientists had to be aware of and understand the details of the product and its host cell. Some genetically engineered cell lines, for example, were extremely difficult to grow large-scale. Dr. Dawson noted:

> *Ideally, we want the research scientists to work with only those cell lines which we know can be scaled-up. While I think they agree with this in principle, they really don't want to be constrained, particularly if they're having trouble getting expression with one of our "preferred" cell lines.*

While much progress had been made over the past decade, many people considered biotechnology production process very much an art. It was not unheard of for a process to work well in one facility but fail completely when transferred to another. One Nucleon researcher who had experience with such transfers explained:

> You would be surprised at all the little things that could be done differently from one organization to another. Most of these things are so minor you would not even think of writing them down. But they make the difference between a successful and unsuccessful process.

Currently, Nucleon had scaled up the process for making CRP-1 to 10 liters, enough to supply material for its own biochemical studies, academic collaborators, and potential joint venture partners who wanted to evaluate the product. Early phase clinical trials were likely to require a 100-liter process, and commercial production a much larger scale process.

As complex as it was, bacterial fermentation was considered one of the more efficient ways of producing proteins like CRP-1. In some cases, product characteristics could be enhanced if a mammalian cell (e.g., from a mouse or human) rather than a bacterial cell was used as a host. Mammalian cell processes, while desirable from the product side, were much more complex than bacterial processes, not well understood, and much more expensive to maintain. Mammalian cells had to be fed more expensive nutrients, and they grew much more slowly than bacterial cells. They required different bioreactors, and even stricter adherence to original process specifications than bacterial cells. Dr. Dawson explained, "With bacterial cells, a one degree Centigrade temperature change can slow the growth rate and increase your costs, whereas mammalian cells might just die altogether."

Although most biotechnology companies had some experience with bacterial cell processes, many fewer had mammalian cell capabilities. Fortunately, CRP-1 could be produced using bacterial cells. The company's R&D lab, however, was already working on second generation CRP-1 molecules produced in mammalian cells. And biotechnology companies overall were unsure whether existing process development technology would be viable in the future to produce biological products.[3]

Purification.   After fermentation, the cells would be broken apart and the CRP-1 protein separated from all other proteins and cell debris contained in the fermentation tank. A series of fractionation and centrifugation steps would isolate the cell protein from carbohydrates, fatty acids, and DNA. The CRP-1 containing protein mixture would then be purified in three additional steps using a filtration procedure known as column chromatography. Like fermentation, the purification process specified during process development had to be strictly followed during manufacturing. After purification, the material would be subjected to extensive quality testing to ensure that the product met the FDA's extremely high purity standards.

Formulation.   Purification process yielded nearly pure quantities of the protein of interest, for example CRP-1. At this stage, the product was made into the intended dosage form (e.g., oral, topical, injectable), and subjected to extensive quality testing. For burn treatment, CRP-1 would be formulated into a topical dosage form.

Filling and Packaging.   During the final step, bulk quantities of the formulated product were put into tubes, bottles, or other vessels required for administration to patients. The sealed vessels were then inserted into packages, which were also sealed.

The Financial Environment

A critical issue affecting Nucleon was capital availability. The situation had changed dramatically since the late 1970s and early 1980s when investors lined up to provide capital to brand new biotechnology companies. By the mid- to late-1980s, private and public equity markets grew tighter, and venture capitalists, who expected investment returns of 30 percent, became more selective. The state of the public equity markets in 1990 made "going public" virtually impossible for a company like Nucleon; furthermore, potential corporate partners, who had been disappointed by previous biotechnology relationships, were unwilling to fund early stage projects. As Hurst described it:

> In the early 1980s, a company like ours could have gotten corporate funding with just our idea. By the mid-1980s, we probably would have needed to have started some lab work and have had some preliminary experimental data. Now, it's hard to get a large pharmaceutical company to talk to you unless you've got some solid Phase I and Phase II clinical results and can demonstrate that you've got a stable manufacturing process. And even then, they'll cut some pretty tough terms with you. When it comes to raising capital today, it's a buyers' market.

Nucleon was just about to receive another $6 million infusion from its venture capitalist. This funding, combined with existing cash on-hand, revenues, interest, and grants, would give Nucleon about $6.5 million. Furthermore, if CRP-1 showed promise in pre-clinical trials, Hurst felt that

Nucleon could raise enough money to pursue Phase I and II clinical trials. Some analysts were predicting that by 1991 or 1992, Wall Street would once again find biotechnology stocks attractive and there would be opportunities for smaller companies to raise money by selling stock to the public. Others thought the capital situation would stay tight for at least several more years. The possibility that a long awaited "shake-out" was about to hit the biotechnology industry was making many investors cautious. One promising sign was that large corporations again seemed willing to fund some selected projects at very early stages of research. As Moore noted, "Today, some brand new start-ups in new fields, like antisense, are cutting some deals on projects which are still years away from the clinic."

Manufacturing Options for Phase I and Phase II CRP-1 Development

Nucleon management contemplated three options to produce clinical grade CRP-1: 1) build a new pilot facility, 2) contract CRP-1 production to a third-party, or 3) license manufacturing and marketing rights to another biotechnology company or pharmaceutical firm in exchange for up front cash payments and royalties on future product sales. Each option is described below.

The New Pilot Plant

Nucleon commissioned an engineering consulting firm to study the physical requirements and costs of a new pilot plant (Exhibit 3). The proposed 5,000 square-foot plant would be fully equipped with all the state-of-the-art processing equipment and environmental controls necessary to meet clinical production standards. Planned capacity would meet Nucleon's requirements for Phase I and Phase II clinical trials. The pilot facility, however, could not be used to produce CRP-1 for Phase III trials, because it would

not meet FDA manufacturing standards for those trials. It was beyond Nucleon's financial capability to build such a plant at this time.

The main advantage in building a pilot plant, as Moore saw it, was that it would enable the firm to develop the nucleus of a future larger-scale, in-house manufacturing capability. Because most of Nucleon's employees were Ph.D. scientists engaged in R&D, it currently lacked supervisors and technicians who could carry out the maintenance, procurement, quality assurance, technical support, logistics, and other functions to operate even a small manufacturing plant. Recruiting people with the appropriate skills and getting the manufacturing organization to work effectively would take time. Supplying clinical trials would allow manufacturing time to accumulate experience dealing with many complicated technical and regulatory issues. Moore noted:

> If Nucleon waits until Phase III trials to bring manufacturing in-house, we might find ourselves with a "green" manufacturing organization just when the stakes are highest. By starting now, we'll have the basic manufacturing skills in-house and ready to go when we are really going to need them. The second big advantage of the pilot facility is that it would keep control over process and quality procedures firmly in Nucleon's hands.

Dawson added, "Scaling up will be much easier if we have our own pilot plant to experiment in."

Of course, building a pilot plant was risky. Moore knew that despite its promise in laboratory experiments, it was uncertain at this point how well CRP-1 would work when tested in humans. Indeed, if the history of the pharmaceutical industry was any guide, most drugs that entered clinical trials never reached the market. This high risk of failure was offset somewhat by the fact that CRP-1 had several potential therapeutic applications. If clinical trials for burn wounds were not promising, it might be used in other applications. Nevertheless, Nucleon management had to consider the possibility of the pilot plant being

---

Exhibit 3 Time and Cost to Obtain Phase II Data for CRP-1 (Burn Treatment) Using a New Pilot Facility for Clinical-Grade Production of CRP-1. Midrange estimate ($000).

Pilot Facility	1991	1992	1993	Total Thru 12/93
Construction and Equipment Costs	3,100	0	0	3,100
Variable Production Expenses and Overhead	0	800	1,204	2,004
Pre-Clinical Development	250	0	0	250
Clinical Trials (Phase I/II)	0	1,040	1,000	2,040
Total	3,350	1,840	2,204	7,394

idled if CRP-1 performed poorly in the clinic. Other products under development were still years away from requiring pilot manufacturing capabilities.

Another major risk involved process uncertainty. The pilot plant would be designed to produce products using bacterial fermentation, but the company was already in the early stages of developing a version in mammalian cells, which would require vastly different process development capabilities.

Some board members believed that Nucleon should focus all of its financial, managerial, and technical resources on R&D. Manufacturing, they felt, would only distract the company from its main mission of exploiting its unique scientific capabilities in the discovery of cell regulating proteins. According to Hurst:

> Our venture capitalists are asking us where we, as a company, add the most value. As a small research-intensive company, we can be the "fastest guns on the block" when it comes to drug discovery. But that means funneling our limited resources into R&D. Some of our investors are concerned that we could get bogged down in manufacturing. On the other hand, it's getting to the point where anyone can clone a gene. I keep wondering whether we can still differentiate ourselves on R&D alone.

Contract Manufacturing

Contracting manufacturing was a second option for Phase I and Phase II CRP-1 development. The biggest advantage of this option was that it required no major capital investments on Nucleon's part. If CRP-1 failed, the contract could be easily terminated. Aside from relatively small termination penalties, the company would have little else at risk. Another advantage was that companies supplying contract manufacturing services had facilities and personnel in place.

Contract production was not inexpensive (see Exhibit 4). There were very few U.S. companies capable and willing to contract manufacture pharmaceuticals from bacteria. Nucleon management was meeting with several potential contractors. These included other biotechnology companies who had excess capacity. In recent years, many biotechnology companies had built GMP plants in anticipation of future products. When product approvals were delayed or even rejected by the FDA, these companies found themselves with tremendous excess manufacturing capacity. Because of mounting financial pressures, some of these companies were providing contract manufacturing services. Some industry experts believed that excess manufacturing capacity would continue to accumulate during the next few years.

One of contract manufacturing's biggest risks was confidential information disclosure. It was virtually impossible for any contractor to provide reliable time and cost estimates without knowing many proprietary product details. Moreover, the complexity of the products and processes made estimates of time and cost painstaking; reaching an agreement could take many months. Even after a contract was signed, technology transfer and scale-up might take another nine months. Moore noted, "It will take about as much time to negotiate an agreement and transfer and validate the process as it will for us to build a pilot plant."

Although production contracts typically were negotiated for fixed quantities (e.g., 100g of CRP-1 over 10 months), in contract negotiations, a balance needed to be struck. On one hand, it was risky to commit to large quantities of material—which might not be required if product specifications changed or the product was pulled from the clinic. On the other hand, short-term contracts usually involved a higher price to offset fixed costs of scale-up and batch set-ups.

Under either the pilot plant or the contract manufacturing option, Nucleon would retain ownership of the product rights at least until the commencement of Phase III clinical trials. At that point, the company would enter into licensing and marketing with a large corporate partner. The options for Phase III trials and beyond are discussed later.

Exhibit 4   Time and Cost to Obtain Phase II Clinical Trial Data for CRP-1 (Burn Treatment) Using Contract Production for Clinical-Grade CRP-1

	1991	1992	1993	Total thru 12/93
Contract Production and Related Expense	0	955	1,550	2,505
Pre-clinical Development	250	0	0	250
Clinical Trials (Phase I/II)	0	1,040	1,000	2,040
Total	250	1,995	2,550	4,795

Licensing the Product to Another Company

Rather than waiting until Phase III trials to enter a licensing deal, Nucleon could license the product immediately in exchange for fixed payments and future royalties. Under this option, the licensed partner, not Nucleon, would make all the requisite expenditures in clinical development, clinical manufacturing, regulatory filings, and commercial manufacturing and marketing. The partner would have the right to market CRP-1 to treat burn wounds. Nucleon would retain the right to develop CRP-1 for other therapeutic applications. Nucleon also would receive an upfront, fixed licensing fee and reimbursement for any additional development work it performed on the project. If and when CRP-1 was commercialized, Nucleon would receive royalties as a percentage of sales.

This licensing option had the chief benefit of generating cash immediately; it also spared Nucleon from making large capital investments in clinical development and manufacturing, and allowed the company to concentrate all of its financial and human resources on R&D. Of course, if the product turned out to be successful, Nucleon would receive far lower revenues than if it had made all of these investments itself. Some Nucleon employees viewed this option as "mortgaging away" the company's future.

Whether this option would mortgage the company's future depended upon the exact terms of the agreement that Nucleon could negotiate. While it was virtually impossible to know for sure what kind of deal could be struck, Nucleon management had conducted preliminary discussions with several firms. From these and consultations with the company's venture capitalists, Moore determined that Nucleon could expect to reach an agreement with the following terms:

Upon signing the contract Nucleon would get a $3 million payment. After the FDA approved CRP-1 for burn wounds, Nucleon would receive annual royalty payments from the partner equivalent to 5 percent of gross sales (see Exhibit 5).

Manufacturing Options for Phase III and Commercialization

One of the chief advantages of either in-house pilot manufacturing or contract manufacturing over immediate licensing was that it gave Nucleon more options if the project survived Phase I and Phase II trials. As noted earlier, under these two options, Nucleon intended to line up with a partner who would be responsible for conducting Phase III trials, handling regulatory filings, and marketing the product.

Exhibit 5	Estimated Gross Sales of CRP-1 (As Topical Burn Wound Treatment)

Year	Sales ($000)
1998	53,700
1999	99,500
2000	125,000
2001	130,000
2002	150,000

*After the year 2000, sales of CRP-1 as a burn wound treatment were expected to grow at approximately 5 percent per year, assuming no introduction of a substitute product.

However, under such an arrangement, Nucleon could either retain commercial manufacturing responsibilities or license these to the partner. Each of these approaches are discussed below.

Vertically Integrate into Commercial Manufacturing

Before Phase III trials began, Nucleon could invest in a full-scale commercial manufacturing facility that met the FDA guidelines for Good Manufacturing Practice (see Exhibit 6). The FDA required that Phase III trials be supplied largely by the plant that would be used to supply the commercial market. Thus it would be necessary to commence construction in mid-1993 so that the plant could be fully validated and operational by the scheduled commencement of Phase III trials.

Moore estimated that the costs of such a facility would be about $20 million, and another $1 million in development resources would be required to perform scale-up. He and Nucleon's financial advisors believed that once the project cleared Phase II trials, it would have little difficulty raising the needed funds to build the plant. The company would also have to hire at least 20 people to handle such functions as procurement, quality control, maintenance, technical support, and logistics.[4]

It was difficult to know exactly what terms could be reached. If Nucleon built a commercial plant, it would be the sole supplier of CRP-1 to its marketing partner. Judging by what other firms in the industry were receiving for similar products, Nucleon management estimated that the company could negotiate a combined supply contract and royalty agreement with the following terms: Nucleon would receive a $5 million payment upon FDA approval of CRP-1, plus royalties equal to 40 percent of the partner's gross sales of the product. Nucleon would sell CRP-1 to the partner at cost.[5]

Exhibit 6   Good Manufacturing Practices (GMPs)

The following are some of the major concepts behind "Good Manufacturing Practices" (GMPs):

- A facility must have an uncluttered fermentation area, precautions for fermentation spills, and surfaces that are easily cleaned.
- Adequate air systems to prevent cross-contamination of the product from other research products or micro-organisms in the facility. Closed system fermenters. Steps must be performed in a controlled environment. (A controlled environment is defined as being adequate to control air pressure, humidity, temperature, microorganisms, and particulate matter.) An environmental monitoring system is necessary for all manufacturing areas.
- The water used in the downstream manufacturing steps should be of high quality and, again, there should be a monitoring system in place.
- A trained Quality Assurance department is required to oversee and assure GMP manufacturing and control.
- A documentation system is required for the process or support systems.
- Uni-directional production flow is required.

- Validated processes to demonstrate removal of major contaminants are required.
- Validated cleaning procedures to demonstrate those in place are adequate for multi-use of equipment are required.
- A uni-directional flow of raw material, product, and personnel is required with product moving from less clean and controlled areas (fermentation) to very clean areas (formulation and filling). There should be positive air pressure differentials between clean and less clean areas.
- Space should be designated for raw material and final product storage. The area should be designed to allow for separate areas for quarantined, released, and rejected material and there should be adequate security.
- Space should be designated for media/reagent preparation with a controlled environment.
- There should be adequate space for glassware washing and autoclaving.
- There should be gowning areas for very clean areas (formulation/filling) and possibly the fermentation area.
- Find out now what other microorganisms are being used in the facility and keep track of any new organisms which may be used in the future.

Licensing Out Manufacturing and Marketing Rights at Phase III

A second option at the beginning of Phase III trials would be to license out both the manufacturing and marketing rights to a partner. This option would be similar to that discussed above, except, in this case, the partner would also be responsible for Phase III and commercial manufacturing. Nucleon therefore would not have to invest the $20 million in a commercial plant. Under this option, Nucleon could expect to receive a $7 million

payment if and when CRP-1 was approved by the FDA. After that, Nucleon would receive a royalty equivalent to 10 percent of the partner's gross sales of CRP-1.

Moore recognized that Hurst leaned towards manufacturing CRP-1 in-house. He had said, "I keep asking myself, 'How many times will we get to the plate?' If I thought that this were our only chance, I'd go for the home run and take the risks of manufacturing." For his part, Moore decided to review Nucleon's options another time before making a recommendation.

Notes

1. "Clinical grade" indicates the minimum conditions under which drugs must be produced for use in human clinical trials.
2. For some very serious diseases, Phase I trials were performed on afflicted patients.
3. On the horizon was a hybrid of biotechnology and synthetic chemical techniques that could alter or replace existing process technologies. These hybrid companies used molecular biology techniques to clone and produce small amounts of biologically important proteins. The protein was studied to learn the chemical and physical structure of its therapeutically active site and then, using computer-aided modeling techniques, the active site of the protein could be constructed synthetically.
4. This assumes the company already has a pilot plant with a staff of six.
5. All costs, except depreciation, would be reflected in the transfer price.

Case 3-3: British Sky Broadcasting Group PLC*[1]

British Sky Broadcasting Group plc (BSkyB) packaged television content into channels and distributed it retail via satellite within the United Kingdom and the Republic of Ireland and wholesale to other distribution platforms. Born out of the merger of two satellite TV companies in 1990, BSkyB was listed on the London and New York stock exchanges with a market capitalization of (pounds) GBP8.7 billion (as of February 1999). Exhibits 1 and 2 detail the company's financial data. Its largest shareholder, with a 40% stake, was News International, a wholly owned subsidiary of News Corporation, 30% of which was, in turn, owned by the family of Rupert Murdoch.

Sports programming and, in particular, live coverage of Premier League Football was one of the main attractions of BSkyB to its customers (Exhibit 3). Live coverage of sporting events had earned BSkyB the recognition of 15 industry awards, from such institutions as the Royal Television Society. Premier League Football was both the most regularly watched and the most popular sport among BSkyB subscribers (Exhibit 4). In 1996, BSkyB had acquired a four-year license to the exclusive broadcasting rights of all Premier League football matches for GBP670 million. The year was 1999 and, as the expiration of the Premier League license drew nearer, new strategies for the upcoming licensing round had to be formulated.

* This case was prepared by Matthias Hild, Assistant Professor of Business Administration. It was written as a basis for class discussion rather than to illustrate effective or ineffective handling of an administrative situation. Copyright © 2005 by the University of Virginia Darden School Foundation, Charlottesville, VA. All rights reserved. *To order copies, send an e-mail to sales@dardenpublishing.com. No part of this publication may be reproduced, stored in a retrieval system, used in a spreadsheet, or transmitted in any form or by any means-electronic, mechanical, photocopying, recording, or otherwise-without the permission of the Darden School Foundation.*

BSkyB

BSkyB operated both as a channel provider and as a retailer of pay-TV; it also had announced plans to begin production of its own movies to reduce its reliance on the major movie studios. In September 1998, more than six million households in the United Kingdom consumed pay-TV (Exhibit 5). Like other pay-TV services, BSkyB generated the bulk of its revenue from subscription fees and to a smaller extent from pay-per-view channels and advertising receipts (the latter amounted to 7% of total TV advertising). Pay-TV was mainly financed by subscriptions fees from viewers, with additional revenues from advertising. While pay-per-view broadcasts covered mainly movies, concerts, and boxing matches, BSkyB also started to apply the model to some football matches in the Nationwide League. In 1999, programming costs were GBP 688 million, about half of which was accounted for by the annualized cost of broadcasting rights for sporting events.

As a channel provider, SkyB bought content from program-makers and packaged it into channels, which it supplied wholesale to retailers. BSkyB packaged, for example, its Sky Sports 1 channel, retailed it directly to customers via satellite, and distributed it wholesale to the NTL cable network and to ONdigital, a digital terrestrial retailer. BSkyB's wholesale prices for premium channels were equal to 57% to 59% of retail prices, with additional discounts for acceptance of such targets as the number of subscribers and penetration rates. Failure to meet the target resulted in a penalty for the retailer.

BSkyB offered a range of programming packages to its customers (Exhibit 6), including six wholly owned, nine partially owned, and 28 third-party channels. It was typical for the industry to price subscription rates by which channels were included in a package. The basic package could be upgraded by two premium sports and two premium movie channels. Sky One had the largest number of viewers among all satellite and cable channels in the United Kingdom. Sky Box Office was a pay-per-view service with

Exhibit 1   BSkyB, Revenues
and Pre-tax Profits

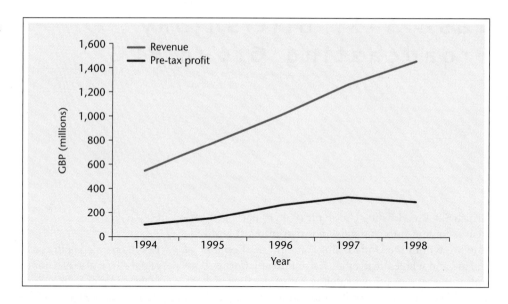

Exhibit 2   **BSkyB, Consolidated Balance Sheet (GBP millions)**

	1994	1995	1996	1997	1998
Tangible fixed assets	32	46	73	110	175
Investments	–	1	24	38	44
Stock and debtors less creditors	222	26	45	150	134
Net operating assets	254	73	142	298	353
Borrowings less cash	(1,712)	(768)	(659)	(627)	(518)
Dividend payable	–	(43)	(52)	(56)	(56)
Provisions	(28)	(30)	(39)	(37)	(79)
Deficit of shareholders' funds	(1,486)	(768)	(608)	(422)	(300)

Exhibit 3   **Sky Sports and Premier League Football as Reasons for Pay-TV Subscription**

	If Sky Sports were not offered*	If Premier League Football were not offered**
Very likely to continue subscription (+2)	36%	35%
Fairly likely to continue subscription (+1)	19%	28%
Would have to consider after a while (0)	12%	17%
Fairly unlikely to continue subscription (–1)	9%	9%
Very unlikely to continue subscription (–2)	23%	11%
Mean	0.36	.68
Sample size †	654	654

* Based on the question, "If the Sky Sports channel was not available as part of your cable/satellite package and you were not able to continue to get the sports that are shown on any other cable/satellite channel, how likely would you be to continue your subscription to cable/satellite TV?"

** Based on the question, "If live Premier League football was no longer available but you could still get other football and other sport, how likely would your household be to continue with your subscription to the Sky Sports channel?"

† Subscribers to satellite and cable TV who receive Sky Sports.

Source: NOP.

Exhibit 4   Popular Sports on Sky Sports

	Regularly watched sports on Sky Sports	Most favorite sport on Sky Sports
Football	82%	47%
Cricket	38%	7%
Boxing	33%	7%
Rugby league	25%	—
Rugby union	18%	—
Snooker	9%	—
Darts	7%	—
Motor sport	18%	7%
Golf	18%	5%
Athletics	6%	6%
Tennis	12%	12%
Skiing	6%	6%
Wrestling	10%	10%
Sample size†	654	654

† Subscribers to satellite and cable TV who receive Sky Sports.

Source: NOP.

four analog and 48 digital channels. BSkyB's movie channels featured both major recent releases and older movies.

BSky had embarked on an ambitious marketing campaign that would last for the next five years. Consequently, its expenditures on advertising and marketing rose from GBP59 million in 1997 to GBP152 million in 1998 (including a GBP49 million write-off for two previous Christmas promotions). An interactive television services company called Open, a recent joint venture of BSkyB (32.5%) with British Telecommunications Holdings (32.5%), Midland Bank (20%), and Matsushita Electric Europe (15%), aimed to expand its broadcasting activities into the provision of home shopping, banking, and travel services and interactive games. In 1998, BSkyB started MUTV, a subscription magazine channel dedicated to Manchester United, as a joint venture with Manchester United and Granada.

Free-to-air TV

The BBC was a public service broadcaster under the guidance of the Secretary of State for Culture, Media, and Sport. It was financed mainly by a license fee that all the 23 million TV-owning households in the United Kingdom had to pay. It offered two free-to-air channels (BBC1 and BBC2), three free-to-air channels distributed by cable, satellite, and digital terrestrial transmitters (BBC News 24, BBC Choice, and BBC Parliament), five national radio networks, over 30 local radio stations, and had pioneered online news services

Exhibit 5   Pay-TV Subscriptions

	1994	1995	1996	1997	1998	1998
All Subscriptions						
BSkyB	72.71%	69.04%	64.84%	61.65%	56.31%	54.14%
Cable	27.29%	30.96%	35.16%	38.35%	43.69%	45.86%
Total(million)	3.45	4.12	4.9	5.6	6.15	6.13
Premium Subscriptions						
BSkyB	78.94%	76.01%	72.19%	70.01%	69.18%	67.57%
Cable	21.06%	23.99%	27.81%	29.99%	30.82%	32.43%
Total (million)	3.05	3.59	4.24	4.67	4.47	4.36

Source: MMC calculations based on BSkyB data.

Exhibit 6 BSkyB Analog Retail Prices per Month (Including Value-added-Tax) (in GBP)

	9/1/92	9/1/93	10/1/94	11/1/95	9/1/96	9/1/97	9/10/98
Basic package	—	6.99	9.99	10.99	11.99	11.99	11.99
One Sky premium channel							
Sky Sports 1 (including Sky Sports 2 free)	5.99	11.99	14.99	15.99	17.99	—	—
Sky Sports 1 or Sky Sports 2	—	—	—	—	—	20.99	20.99
Sky MovieMax	11.99	11.99	14.99	15.99	17.99	20.99	18.99
Sky Premier	11.99	11.99	14.99	15.99	17.99	20.99	22.99
Two Sky premium channels							
Sky MovieMax or Sky Premier and Sky Sports 1 (including Sky Sports 2 free)	16.98	16.99	19.99	21.99	23.99	—	—
Sky MovieMax or Sky Premier and Sky Sports 1 or Sky Sports 2	—	—	—	—	—	24.99	22.99
Sky Sports 1 and Sky Sports 2	—	—	—	—	—	24.99	24.99
Sky Premier and Sky MovieMax	16.99	16.99	16.99	21.99	23.99	24.99	24.99
Sky Premier and Sky Sports 1 or Sky Sports 2	—	—	—	—	—	24.99	26.99
Three Sky premium channels							
Sky MovieMax, Sky Premier and Sky Sports 1 (including Sky Sports 2 free)	19.98	19.99	22.99	24.99	26.99	—	—
Sky MovieMax, Sky Sports 1 and Sky Sports 2	—	—	—	—	—	27.99	26.99
Sky MovieMax, Sky Premier and Sky Sports 1 or Sky Sports 2	—	—	—	—	—	27.99	27.99
Sky Premier, Sky Sports 1 and Sky Sports 2	—	—	—	—	—	27.99	28.99
Four Sky premium channels							
Sky MovieMax, Sky Premier and Sky Sports 1 and Sky Sports 2	—	—	—	—	—	29.99	29.99

in the United Kingdom. BBC Worldwide, a wholly owned commercial subsidiary, operated internationally and held a 50% stake in a joint venture with Flextech. A second, small public service broadcaster specialized in Welsh-language programming.

In addition to those public service broadcasters, the British government had licensed several commercial independent channels (ITV channels) that broadcast terrestrial signals under the free-to-air model. Those channels were financed mainly through advertising revenue and accumulated batches of regional licenses. The largest operators, Carlton TV Limited and Granada Group PLC, each accounted for about one-third of ITV advertising revenue and covered 38% and 47% of the U.K. population, respectively. Granada held the ITV license for the London region and was the largest program supplier to the ITV channels. The company cross-invested in ONdigital, BSkyB, GMTV, MUTV, ITN, and others and had a highly diversified range of business activities (including the rental of TV systems to hotels, businesses, and private households; travel services; and the operation of an international chain of hotels).

Other ITV channels included United News & Media plc, Channel 4, and Channel 5. Channel 4 was recognized for its independent movie productions and claimed 19% of total TV advertising revenue. In November 1998, Channel 4 launched FilmFour, a subscription channel, on all three distribution platforms (terrestrial, cable, and satellite). It had also recently outbid the BBC for the next four years of English home cricket coverage.

Exhibit 7 compares the viewing shares of the main free-to-air channels with the total viewing share of pay-TV.

Pay-TV

Flextech was the largest channel provider, catering to both cable networks and BSkyB. It owned five channels (Bravo, Trouble, Living, Challenge TV, and Screen Shop), held a majority stake in one channel (TV Travel Shop), and had assumed management responsibility of three additional channels (Discovery, Discovery Home and Leisure, and Playboy TV). A joint venture with BBC Worldwide (UKTV) packaged six more

Exhibit 7   Share of Viewing (percent)

	1993/94	1994/95	1995/96	1996/97	1997/98	1.11.98
In all TV homes						
BBC1	32.61	32.51	32.31	31.88	30.04	28.11
BBC2	10.4	10.72	11.62	11.52	11.24	11.12
ITV	39.6	38.38	36.22	33.99	32.44	32.34
C4	10.73	10.9	10.6	10.81	10.33	10.61
C5	0	0	0	0.69	3.54	4.77
Pay TV	6.67	7.5	9.24	11.1	12.42	13.04
Total	100	100	100	100	100	100
In all multichannel homes						
BBC1	24.28	24.31	23.54	22.99	21.74	20.17
BBC2	6.31	6.19	6.62	6.52	6.53	6.58
ITV	30.1	29.29	27.47	25.34	24.84	25.23
C4	6.87	7.17	6.89	6.92	6.82	6.89
C5	0	0	0	0.57	2.59	3.49
Pay TV	32.49	33.04	35.48	37.65	37.47	37.63
Total	100	100	100	100	100	100

Source: MMC calculations on BSkyB data.

channels with BBC content (UK Gold, UK Gold-Classics, Classics, UK Plays, UK Horizons, UK Style, UK Arena) to which the company was granted the right of first refusal.

Retailers of pay-TV channels were typically the operators of one of the three distribution platforms (cable, satellite, or digital terrestrial transmitters). In 1999, the cable operator with the largest customer base, Telewest Communications, was in takeover negotiations with AT&T. The second-largest provider, Cable & Wireless Communications, was a majority-owned subsidiary of Cable & Wireless (18% of which belonged to Bell Atlantic), with a strong telephony business and a new digital service. NTL, the third-largest cable operator, was partially owned by its management (22%) with a strong business in call-handling and infrastructure services (e.g., satellite uplinking and terrestrial transmission).

The main retailer of digital terrestrial programming, ONdigital, offered 22 pay-TV channels and could reach 70% of the U.K. population. It was equally owned by Carlton and Granada after the Independent Television Commission forced BSkyB to sell its stake in what had begun as a joint venture with Carlton and Granada. In March 1999, ONdigital announced that it would form a joint venture with SDN to provide pay-per-view services.

BSkyB was the only major retailer on the satellite platform, surrounded by such small niche channel as The Racing Channel, Zee TV (focused on Asian programming), Fantasy Channel, Playboy TV, and The Adult Channel.

Exhibit 8 breaks down the viewing shares of the main pay TV channels.

Premier League Football

Sports programming and, in particular, live coverage of Premier League Football was at the core of BSkyB's value proposition to its customers (Exhibits 3, 4, and Exhibit 9). BSkyB accounted for half the total viewing hours of all televised football matches (Exhibit 10). During the five largest matches between 45% and 86% of its subscribers joined the broadcast (Exhibit 11).

The exclusive broadcasting rights for the 60 live matches per season were highly contested. In 1992, BSkyB secured the rights for the first time for GBP192 million. In 1996, BSkyB had to bid GBP670 million for a four-year contract to beat both a GBP1.5 billion bid by United News & Media plc for a 10-year license and a joint bid by Carlton and the Mirror Group that offered GBP650 million and half of all profits for a five-year license. In addition, BSkyB owned exclusive rights to 60 live matches per season from the Nationwide League, 12 from the FA Cup, 10 from the Worthington Cup, 30 from the Scottish League and Cup, three from the Spanish League, a small number from other European leagues, and all England home matches (the away matches aired on Channel 5). BSkyB retailed all of those matches through its Sky Sports 1 channel and also distributed them to cable operators and ONditigal. BSkyB expected ITV channels to cover 17 live matches from the Champions' League, six from the FA Cup, and two from the Worthington Cup. It expected ONdigital to cover 32 live matches between top foreign and domestic clubs and Channel 4 to cover 30 live matches from the Italian top league.

Exhibit 8   Share of Viewing for Pay TV 1997–98 (percent)

	All U.K. TV homes	TV multi-channel homes		All U.K. TV homes	TV multi-channel homes
Sky One	1.36	4.1	Living Discovery/Homes &	0.46	1.38
Sky News*	0.39	1.18	Leisure	0.41	1.23
MovieMax	0.75	2.26	Bravo	0.29	0.88
Sky Premier	0.72	2.16	Trouble	0	0
Sky Cinema	0.27	0.82	TCC	0.07	0.2
Sky Sports 1	0.87	2.61	Challenge TV	0.21	0.64
Sky Sports 2	0.6	1.82	*Flextech*	*1.44*	*4.33*
Sky Sports 3	0.22	0.65			
Sky 2†	0.01	0.04	UK Gold	0.62	1.87
Sky Soap	0.02	0.05	UK Horizons	0.03	0.1
Sky Travel	0.01	0.02	UK Style	0.01	0.04
TV/The Computer Channel	0	0	UK Arena	0	0
Sky Scottish†	0	0.01	Animal Planet	0	0
Sky Box Office	0.01	0.02	*BBC and Flextech*	*0.67*	*2.01*
Total Sky	*5.22*	*15.75*			
			TNT*	0.14	0.41
Nickelodeon	0.68	2.05	Cartoon network*	0.84	2.54
The Paramount Comedy			*Turner*	*0.98*	*2.95*
Channel	0.13	0.4			
Granada Plus†	0.23	0.7	MTV	0.28	0.85
Breeze/Granada Good Life	0.03	0.08	VH-1	0.2	0.6
Granada Talk TV	0	0.01	*Viacom*	*0.48*	*1.45*
The History Channel	0.05	0.14			
National Geographic	0.06	0.18	Eurosport*	0.28	0.83
Total Sky joint ventures	*1.18*	*3.56*	Disney Channel	0.3	0.92
			CMT†	0.03	0.08
			Sci-fi Channel	0.14	0.41
			Bloomberg*	0.01	0.02
			Fox Kids	0.11	0.34
			Others	1.6	4.82
			Total pay TV	*12.42*	*37.47*

* Free-to-air on analog DTH.   † Stopped broadcasting.   ‡ Includes viewing figures for Granada Men & Motors.

The Premier League was a private company owned equally by its member clubs (Exhibit 12). It organized and managed the league and its annual competition, and negotiated broadcast licenses on behalf of its member clubs, which authorized contracts by a two-thirds majority. The clubs had agreed on a formula that distributed half of the broadcasting income equally among the clubs, one quarter as a variable merit pay that depended on a club's performance, and the remaining quarter as facility fees. In the 1998–99 season, each member club received a fixed share of GBP3,300,505, GBP172,619 for each rank the club held above rank 21,[2] and GBP269,551 in facility fees for each match shown by BSkyB (compared with GBP28,704 for each replay shown by the BBC; Exhibit 13). The negotiations with potential bidders would be informal and stretch over a series of meetings to discuss the terms of the contract.

Exhibit 9   Most Popular Satellite Programs, Week Ending 20 December 1998

Program	Day	Time	Viewers (millions)	Channel
Live football*	Wed	20	1.95	Sky Sports 1
Super Sunday Live*	Sun	16	1.4	Sky Sports 1
Live football post-match*	Wed	21.5	1.39	Sky Sports 1
The Simpsons	Sun	18.05	1.06	Sky One
Monday Night Football*	Mon	19	0.96	Sky Sports 1
Super Sunday post-match*	Sun	17.5	0.73	Sky Sports 1
South Park	Sun	23	0.72	Sky One
Monday Night Football post-match*	Mon	21.5	0.71	Sky Sports 1
The Simpsons	Wed	19	0.68	Sky One
Only Fools and Horses	Sun	19.5	0.66	UK Gold
Magic Secrets Revealed 4	Sun	22	0.63	Sky One
The Simpsons	Mon	19	0.61	Sky One
The Rock	Sun	21	0.57	Sky Premier
The Simpsons	Tues	19	0.56	Sky One
Stargate SG-1	Wed	20	0.55	Sky One
Sky News	Wed	23	0.54	Sky News
Fierce Creatures	Sat	20.05	0.52	Sky Premier
Friends	Mon	18.3	0.49	Sky One
The Simpsons	Fri	19	0.47	Sky One
Friends	Wed	18.3	0.45	Sky One

Source: Broadcast, 8 January 1999.

*Premier League football.

Exhibit 10   Football on TV, 1997–98 (percent)

	Total Hours	No. of Live Matches	No. of Live Hours*	No. of Nonlive Hours
Including World Cup matches				
BSkyB	58.6	49.4	58.3	58.7
BBC	5.3	6.8	5.3	5.2
ITV	7.4	10.1	9	6.7
C4	4.2	6.6	5.2	3.7
C5	1.5	4.4	4.3	0.3
Free-to-air	18.4	27.8	23.7	16
Eurosport	23	22.8	18	25.3
Total	100	100	100	100
Total (volume)	4,204	504	1,281	2,923
Excluding World Cup matches				
BSkyB	72.6	63.2	70.9	73.3
BBC	1.7	2.3	1.7	1.8
ITV	3.8	5.3	4.5	3.5
C4	5.2	8.4	6.3	4.7
C5	1.9	5.6	5.2	0.4
Free-to-air	12.5	21.6	17.7	10.2
Eurosport	14.9	15.2	11.4	16.4
Total	100	100	100	100
Total (volume)	3,395	394	1,053	2,342

Source: MMC calculations based on data provided by BSkyB.

*Estimates.

Exhibit 11 Most Popular Live Premier League Matches on BSkyB*

	Match					Difference between audience	
Season	Home team	Away team	Day	Date	Audience (millions)	Second-ranked match (millions)	Average (millions)
1997/98	Arsenal	Manchester United	Sunday	11/9/97	2.86	0.36	1.47
1996/97	Newcastle United	Manchester United	Sunday	10/20/96	2.60	0.28	1.13
1995/96	Newcastle United	Manchester United	Monday	3/4/96	2.75	0.48	1.48
1994/95	Manchester United	Blackburn Rovers	Sunday	1/22/95	2.00	0.19	1.03
1993/94	Blackburn Rovers	Manchester United	Saturday	4/2/94	1.48	0.12	0.67

Source: MMC calculations based on BSkyB data.

*Excludes viewing in pubs and clubs.

Exhibit 12 Premier League, Revenues

	1992/93 Revenue (GBP millions)*	1992/93 (%)	1996/97 Revenue (GBP millions)*	1996/97 (%)	Growth in revenue (%)
Manchester United	25,177	13.6	87,939	19.0	249.3
Newcastle United	8,743	4.7	41,134	8.9	370.5
Liverpool	17,496	9.4	39,153	8.4	123.8
Tottenham Hotspur	16,594	9.0	27,874	6.0	68.0
Arsenal	15,342	8.3	27,158	5.9	77.0
Chelsea	7,891	4.3	23,729	5.1	200.7
Middlesbrough	3,968	2.1	22,502	4.9	467.1
Aston Villa	10,175	5.5	22,079	4.8	117.0
Leeds United	13,324	7.2	21,785	4.7	63.5
Everton	7,994	4.3	18,882	4.1	136.2
Leicester City	4,775	2.6	17,320	3.7	262.7
West Ham United	6,571	3.5	15,256	3.3	132.2
Notts Forest	7,651	4.1	14,435	3.1	88.7
Sheffield Wednesday	12,806	6.9	14,335	3.1	11.9
Blackburn Rovers	6,305	3.4	14,302	3.1	126.8
Sunderland	3,806	2.1	13,415	2.9	252.5
Coventry City	4,592	2.5	12,265	2.6	167.1
Derby County	4,183	2.3	10,738	2.3	156.7
Wimbledon	3,556	1.9	10,410	2.2	192.7
Southampton	4,307	2.3	9,238	2.0	114.5
Total	185,256	100	463,949	100	150.4

Source: MMC calculations based on data in the Deloitte & Touche Annual Review of Football Finance, August 1988.

*Excludes transfer fees.

Exhibit 13   Premier League, Distribution of TV Revenues, 1997–98

	TV appearances		Merit award (GBP millions)	Facility fee (GBP millions)	Equal share (GBP millions)	Total (GBP millions)%	Club
	BSkyB	BBC					
Arsenal	12	14	3.25	3.42	3.04	9.71	7.52
Manchester United	12	13	3.09	3.4	3.04	9.52	7.38
Liverpool	10	10	2.93	2.81	3.04	8.77	6.79
Chelsea	9	9	2.76	2.53	3.04	8.33	6.45
Leeds United	7	4	2.6	1.88	3.04	7.52	5.82
Blackburn Rovers	6	9	2.44	1.77	3.04	7.25	5.61
Aston Villa	5	5	2.28	1.4	3.04	6.72	5.2
West Ham United	5	2	2.11	1.32	3.04	6.47	5.01
Derby County	5	5	1.95	1.4	3.04	6.39	4.95
Newcastle United	6	9	1.3	1.77	3.04	6.11	4.73
Coventry City	5	3	1.63	1.35	3.04	6.01	4.66
Leicester City	4	4	1.79	1.12	3.04	5.95	4.61
Tottenham Hotspur	5	14	1.14	1.66	3.04	5.83	4.52
Southampton	4	5	1.46	1.15	3.04	5.65	4.38
Everton	6	10	0.65	1.8	3.04	5.49	4.25
Wimbledon	4	5	0.98	1.15	3.04	5.17	4.00
Bolton Wanderers	5	5	0.49	1.4	3.04	4.93	3.82
Sheffield Wednesday	3	2	0.81	0.81	3.04	4.67	3.61
Crystal Palace	4	5	0.16	1.15	3.04	4.35	3.37
Barnsley	3	5	0.33	0.9	3.04	4.26	3.30
Total	120	138	34.13	34.18	60.81	129.11	100

Source: Manchester United.

Notes

1. This case is closely based on a 1999 report by the United Kingdom's Monopolies and Mergers Commission (MMC). See the report at: http://www.competition-commission.org.uk/ rep_pub/reports/1999/426Sky.htm.
2. The lowest ranking club is allocated GBP172,619, the second lowest ranking club is allocated GBP172,619 × 2 = GBP345,238, etc. up to the top receipt of GBP172,619 × 20 = GBP3,452,380.

Case 3-4: L'Oreal's Growth Strategy*

The Body Shop Acquisition

"Has L'Oreal, the world's No. 1 cosmetic group, just committed a beauty blunder? Its $1.1 billion acquisition of British-based retailer The Body Shop International, announced on Mar. 17, does look odd at first glance."[1]

"A partnership between our companies makes perfect sense. Combining L'Oreal's expertise and knowledge of international markets with The Body Shop's distinct culture and values will benefit both companies."[2]

—Lindsay Owen-Jones, Chairman & CEO, L'Oreal

Introduction

On March 17, 2006, The Body Shop International (Body Shop), a United Kingdom (UK) based retailer of natural-based cosmetics, announced that it had agreed to be taken over by the French cosmetics giant, L'Oreal, in a cash deal worth US $1.14 billion (bn). L'Oreal's interest in buying Body Shop was published by the British media a month before, on February 21, 2006. The company's offer price of US $5.25 per share of Body Shop, was a premium of more than 34% over the share price on the day before the speculation of the takeover published in the media (February 20, 2006). L'Oreal, following an inorganic strategy, had acquired many companies and brands and achieved a leadership position in the global cosmetics industry. But this was the first time it had planned to take over a retail chain. Some analysts expressed their concern about L'Oreal's integration of Body Shop, while considering the challenges faced by another French luxury products maker, LVMH Moet Hennessy Louis Vuitton,[3] after acquiring the beauty products retail chain, Sephora, in 1997.[4]

Since Body Shop's inception, it had a strong ethical stand of not testing ingredients on animals, which helped the company to build the image of a progressive and socially responsible business. On the other hand, L'Oreal had no such ethical policy and tested certain ingredients on animals. Industry experts were skeptical whether L'Oreal would be able to reconcile its divergent views on the issue of animal testing. Analysts expressed concern that, post-acquisition, Body Shop would face difficulty in maintaining its ethical standards. They questioned whether that would dilute the Body Shop brand and, in turn, result in declining market share of its products.

Company Background

L'Oreal

In 1907, Eugene Schueller (Schueller), a French chemist, developed an innovative hair-dye called 'Aureoie, which became very popular with Parisian hair-dressers. Two years later, Schueller established L'Oreal to pursue his growing hair-care product business and, in quick succession, added shampoos and soaps to its product portfolio. In 1912, Schueller began to export his products to Netherlands (Holland), Italy and Austria. During 1920s, the company expanded its export market to the United States (US), Russia and South America. After World War II, L'Oreal widened its product line by developing perfumes. In 1953, the company started distributing its products to beauty salons in the US, through a newly established subsidiary, Cosmair Inc.[5] During the 1960s and 1970s, the company diversified into pharmaceuticals and publications through two acquisitions.[6] From 1980 onwards, the company strengthened its presence in the global cosmetics industry by acquiring different companies in varied geographic locations and product segments. (Refer Exhibit 1) During this time, it also made its presence felt in generic pharmaceuticals. However, the company reduced its stake in the publication business. By 2004, L'Oreal had a presence in over 130 countries worldwide through its different businesses like cosmetics, pharmaceuticals and publications.[7]

* This case was written by Abhijit Gupta, under the direction of Supratim Majumdar, IBS Research Centre, Kolkata. It is intended to be used as the basis for class discussion rather than to illustrate either effective or ineffective handling of a management situation. The case was compiled from published sources.

© 2006, IBS Research Centre, Kolkata, The ICFAI Business School. No part of this publication may be copied, stored, transmitted, reproduced or distributed in any form or medium whatsoever without the permission of the copyright owner. Reference no 306–358–1

Exhibit 1   L'Oreal's Acquisitions

Year	Company	Country	Product Segment
1965	Lancome	France	Pharmaceutical
1973	Marie Clair*	France	Publication(Magazine)
1980s	Warner Communications' Cosmetics Operations, Helena Rubenstein, Laboratories Pharmautiques, Lanvin**		Cosmetics
1990s	Lichenstein Pharmzeutica Irex	Germany France	Generic Drug Co. (Diversification) Make up
(1995)	Maybelline	US	Cosmetics
2000	Matrix Essentials	US	Hair Care (Salon only)
	Kiehl's Shu Uemura	US Japan	Hair Care, Skin Care Make up
2001	Colorama	Brazil	Make up, Hair Care
2002	ARtee	US	Hair Care
2003	Inneov (JV with Nestle)	US	Marketing of nutritional supplements for skin & hair Skin Care
2004	Yue-Sai	China	Make up and Skin Care
2005	SkinCeuticals	US	Professional Skin Care

* L'Oreal divested 49% stake in Marie Claire in 2001   ** L'Oreal divested 100% stake in Lanvin also in 2001

Sources: Compiled by IRCK from Datamonitor Company Profile and L'Oreal's company website.

L'Oreal's cosmetics business had four product divisions, which included eighteen global brands. The four divisions were Consumer Products, Professional Products, Luxury Products and Active Cosmetics (Refer Exhibit 2). These divisions offered various brands of hair-care and skin-care products, as well as perfumes and make-up that were distributed through different channels such as mass-market outlets, departmental stores, professional hair salons etc. The company had products in different price segments to cater to various market segments, ranging from mass market to upscale market. The company, through its subsidiary Galderma Laboratories[8], was involved in making and selling dermatological products for treatment of skin diseases such as rosacea, psoriasis, eczema, acne etc. The company's pharmaceutical business was engaged in developing, manufacturing and marketing of drugs for different therapeutic segments like cardiovascular, thrombosis, central nervous system, oncology, metabolic disorders, etc.

In 2005, L'Oreal's consolidated sales increased by 6.5% to US $17.3 billion (Refer Exhibit 3). The different divisions of the company—Consumer Products Division, Professional Products, Luxury Products and Active

Cosmetics—recorded revenues worth US $ 9,073 million (mn), US $ 2,494 mn, US $4,334 mn and US $ 1,193 mn, respectively.[9] However, in 2005, the company recorded a net profit of US $2.35 bn.

The Body Shop

In 1976, Body Shop was established in the UK, by Anita Roddick.[10] Initially, it was engaged in retailing of home-made naturally inspired health and beauty products with minimal packaging. The company rapidly evolved from one small shop in Brighton[11] with 25 hand-mixed products to a worldwide network of retail outlets for cosmetics based on natural ingredients. The company created a niche market for its specialized skin and hair care products, with more than 600 products and about 400 accessories in its product portfolio, though the main emphasis was on shampoos, bath products, soaps, skin creams and conditioners. (Refer Exhibit 4) In 2005, Body Shop had sales of US $ 729 mn and a net profit of US $ 47 mn in 2005. (Refer Exhibit 5)

In 2005, Body Shop marketed its products in 52 countries worldwide through 2045 outlets. It had 429 stores in the America, 304 stores in UK & Republic of Ireland, 758 stores in

Exhibit 2   L'Oreal's Product Divisions and Select Brands

Division	Product Segment	Brands
Consumer Products Division	Offers hair care, skin care, make up and perfume products at competitive prices through mass-market retailing channels	L'Oreal Paris Garnier Maybelline New York Soft Sheen. Carson Le Club des Creatures de Beaute
Professional Products Division	Offers specific hair care products for use by professional hair-dressers and sold exclusively through hair-salons	L'Oreal Professional Kerastase Redkin Matrix Mizami
Luxury Products Division	Offers premium and high end skin care, hair care, make up and perfume products through selective retail outlets (department stores, specialty stores and brands' own boutiques) offering personalized advice	Lancôme Biotherm Helena Rubenstein Kiehl's Shu Uemura Giorgio Armani Ralph Lauren Cacharel Victor & Rolf
Active Cosmetics Division	Offers dermo-cosmetic skin care, sun care, hair care and make up products sold through pharmacies and specialist retailers with advice from pharmacists and dermatologists	Vichy La Roche Posay Inneov SkinCeuticals

L'Oreal also has dermatological and pharmaceutical activities

Sources: Compiled by IRCK from Datamonitor Company Profile and L'Oreal's company website.

Exhibit 3   L'Oreal Financial Figures

Summary	2005
Consolidated Sales (US $ m)	17,584
Operating Profit (US $ m)	2,741
Net Profit (US $ m)	1,983
Profit Per Share (US $)	3.15
Dividerid Per Share (US $)	1.21

Source: L'Oreal Annual Report, 2005, www.loreal.com
Conversion rate 1 Euro = 1.21 US$ as on March 17, 2006

Exhibit 4   Products Offered by Body Shop

Product Category	Product Name
Bath & Shower	Spa Wisdom Range
Body Care	Africa Spa, Bajic Spa, Body Butter, Cocoa Butter
Fragrances	Invent Your Scent Range
Hair care	Honey Shampoo, Brazil Nut Moisture Mask
Home Fragrances	Fragrance Oils In Aroma Jars, Room & Linen Spray
Make Up	Lipstick
Skin Care	Grapeseed, Hemp, Seaweed, Soy&Calendula, Tea Tree
Sun Protection	Self Tan, Mineral Sunscreen
Wellbeing	Aromatherapy Range Of Oils Face Scrub, Men's Perfume
Men's Grooming	Face Scrub, Men's Perfume

Sources: Compiled by IRCK from company website and Datamonitor Company Profile.

Exhibit 5   The Body Shop—Financial Figures

Summary	2005
Turnover (US $ m)	729.0
Operating Profit (US $ m)	62.6
Net Profit (US $ m)	47.0
Earnings Per share (US $)	0.22
Dividend Per share (US $)	0.10

Source: Company Annual Report, 2005
Conversion rate 1 pound = 1.74 US $ as on March 17, 2006

Europe, Middle East and Africa and 554 stores in Asia Pacific (Refer Exhibit 6). In the US, UK, France, Germany and Singapore, the company had its own outlets, while in the remaining countries it appointed independent franchisees. In 1994, the company started direct selling model in the UK, which was later extended to the US and Australia. In 1995, the company launched online selling facility through its website.

Body Shop had strongly opposed the testing of all its products on animals long before the European Union (EU)[12] introduced the ban on finished cosmetic products. The company continued to uphold its ethical banner which enhanced its corporate reputation and brand value. The company achieved a unique position as a pioneering figure in the movement for more socially and environmentally responsible business enterprises. (Refer Exhibit 7) it also campaigned against human rights abuses and raised voice in favour of animal and environmental protection. This helped the company to earn the support and respect of consumers.

L'Oreal's Growth by Acquisitions

Since its inception, L'Oreal had grown through acquisitions, which provided the company-wide geographic reach and a diversified product portfolio. The company had also ventured into other businesses like pharmaceuticals and publication, apart from its core business of cosmetics. Mainly 1980 onwards, the company aggressively followed this inorganic growth strategy.

In 1995, L'Oreal acquired the US make-up manufacturer, Maybelline,[13] which catapulted the company's market share in the $2.2 bn US cosmetic market to 28% from 11% in 1994 Further consolidating in the US market, in 2000, L'Oreal acquired Matrix Essentials[14], a manufacturer and marketer of hair care products. Matrix had 80,000 exclusive hair care salons in the US and sales of $342 mn in 2000. In the same year, Kiehl's,[15] the $40 mn US-based manufacturer of premium hair care and skin care products was taken over by L'Oreal. Since then, Kiehl's stores were expanded in the US, France and England, and its turnover reached US $70 mn in 2004. In 2000, L'Oreal entered the Japanese market with the acquisition of the Japanese make-up brand, Shu Uemura[16] which had sales of around $152 mn.

In 2001, it was Brazil's turn to become L'Oreal's new target market. The company acquired Colorama, a Brazilian brand of lip-color, conditioners and shampoo, with sales of US $34.63 mn. L'Oreal also ventured into the booming Chinese cosmetics market, with the acquisition of two Chinese skin care and make-up brands, Mininurse[17] and YueSai,[18] in 2003 and 2004, respectively. In 2005, L'Oreal acquired the US-based premium skin

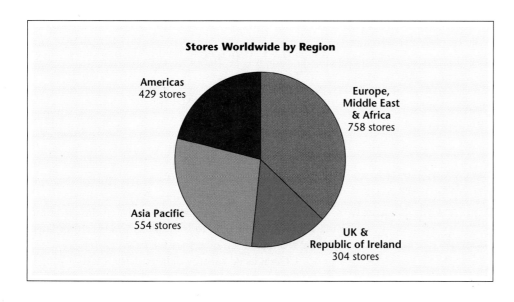

Exhibit 6 The Bodyshop Stores Worldwide (By Region)

Source: Company Annual Report, 2005

Exhibit 7   The Body Shop—Mission Statement

- To dedicate our business to the pursuit of social and environmental change.
- To creatively balance the financial and human needs of our stakeholders: employees, customers, franchisees, suppliers and shareholders.
- To courageously ensure that our business is ecologically sustainable: meeting the needs of the present without compromising the future.

- To meaningfully contribute to local, national and international communities in which we trade by adopting a code of conduct which ensure care, honesty, fairness and respect.
- To passionately campaign for the protection of the environment, human and civil rights and against animal testing within the cosmetics and toiletries industry.
- To tirelessly work to narrow the gap between principle and practice, whilst making fun, passion and care part of our daily lives.

Source: www.thebodyshopinternational.com

---

care brand, SkinCeuticals.[19] The company's products were sold to dermatologists, plastic surgeons and high-end spas. The latest in its string of acquisitions was its offer to buyout Body Shop.

Expected Synergies

Lindsay Owen-Jones,[20] Chairman and CEO of L'Oreal, said that the Body Shop acquisition would give it access to a ready basket of natural-based cosmetics and the impeccable brand image of Body Shop. Body Shop's products would complement and not compete with L'Oreal's products, as these were exclusively made from natural sources. L'Oreal would let Body Shop retain its separate identity and its stores would continue to stock only Body Shop branded items.

In the past few years, L'Oreal's sales growth was slow largely due to increasing competition and the economic slowdown of its major markets in Western Europe, which accounted for about 50% of its sales between 2001 and 2004. During this period, the global cosmetics & toiletries market grew from about US $175 mn to about US $230 mn at an average annual growth rate of 8%. While, L'Oreal's sales growth rate was much lower, except in 2001, some of its major competitors were growing at a much higher rate. (Refer Exhibit 8) Procter& Gamble (Beauty Care Division) registered sales growth rate of 10% and 12% in 2004 and

2005, respectively, whereas L'Oreal registered 3.6% and 6.5%, in the same period.

The acquisition of Body Shop would provide L'Oreal a scope to strengthen its position in the global natural beauty products market, which was expected to be worth more than US $10 bn by end 2006.[21] L'Oreal had the largest market in Western Europe, which contributed 50.9% of its revenue, followed by North America, which accounted for 27.2%. The rest of the world contributed only 21.9% to the company's revenue. Body Shop would provide the company access to new markets of Eastern Europe and South America. The acquisition would also strengthen its position in Asian markets. Asian markets exhibited a surge in consumer spending in personal care and grooming products, mainly in the urban areas. These markets had been considered as the demographically high opportunity markets due to increasing population. Moreover, L'Oreal's growth rate in Western Europe was limited to 0.1% in 2005, which probably would be revived in the post-acquisition era by integrating Body Shop's 892 stores in this region with sales of about US $ 530 million.[22] Industry experts were of the view that Body Shop acquisition would provide immense opportunity for L'Oreal's expansion as the company was in desperate need of diversification. (Refer Exhibit 9)

In terms of new distribution channels, L'Oreal expected to gain from the experience of Body Shop in direct home sales operations. The direct selling unit of Body Shop, 'The Body Shop at Home', had shown impressive growth in the UK, the US and Australia. This unit had a group of consultants who successfully reached a wider audience by demonstrating the availability of the company's products quality within the home environment. This resulted in operational efficiencies in direct selling. L'Oreal would be able to share Body Shop's expertise in direct selling in their own similar initiative.

L'Oreal faced severe public criticism for its testing of ingredients on animals and use of harmful ingredients in

---

Exhibit 8   L'Oreal's Consolidated Sales Growth Rate

2001	2002	2003	2004	2005
+ 8.4%	+ 4.0%	−1.8%	+ 3.6%	+ 6.5%

Source: www.loreal.com

Exhibit 9	Composition of Global Cosmetics & Toiletries by Region

Region	% of Market
Western Europe	31%
Asia Pacific	25%
North America	22%
Latin America	10%
Eastern Europe	6%
Africa/Middle East	4%
Australasia	1%
Other	1%

Source: wwww.in-cosmetics.com

its cosmetic products. The company was using alpha-hydroxy acids (AHA)[23] in moisturizers, toners, and cleansers that exposed consumers to the risk of skin cancer. Similarly, propylene glycol present in suntan lotions, lipsticks and other cosmetics, was found to cause liver abnormalities and kidney damage. Increased consumer awareness about harmful ingredients in cosmetics resulted in an increasing number of consumers abstaining from using chemical-based cosmetics. This caused a decline in L'Oreal's sales. Body Shop marketed natural-based products which had no health hazard in contrast to chemical-based products. Body Shop's squeaky clean image would lend the much needed credibility that had been missing in the case of L'Oreal.

L'Oreal was using polystyrene[24] for packaging its products. The price of it was increasing over the years due to escalating raw material cost, resulting in declining margins for the company. Body Shop, on the other hand, used minimal packaging for its products and thus the company had better control over packaging cost. L'Oreal would be able to incorporate Body Shop's packaging techniques and thereby control its surging packaging costs. Body Shop's acquisition would provide L'Oreal access to the growing male grooming products market. French men spent the most on grooming products followed by the Germans, Dutch and the Americans, respectively. In the US, young men were increasing usage of grooming products. L'Oreal would be benefited by Body Shop's acquisition in this high-growth male grooming products.

Road Ahead

Body Shop, unlike the earlier companies acquired by L'Oreal, was a retailer. Hence, the industry experts felt that blending of L'Oreal's manufacturing activities with retail-ing could prove to be difficult. The integration of manufacturing and retailing had turned out to be not very successful in the case of LVMH Moet Hennessey Louis Vuitton's acquisition of French upscale perfume retail chain, Sephora. After the acquisition, LVMH increased the number of retail outlets of Sephora but most of them turned to be loss making and were closed down. Analysts were skeptical whether L'Oreal would face a similar fate with Body Shop.

Moreover, the issue of ethical commitment was a crucial one between L'Oreal and Body Shop. Body Shop, with its distinct philosophy of being dedicated to betterment of social and environmental conditions and its total commitment against animal testing was not in tune with L'Oreal which tested on animals and had not been known to show any commitment to ethical issues. In fact, L'Oreal had for years been the target of campaigns against testing cosmetics on animals by animal-rights lobbyists in Europe. This conflict of business philosophy and difference in ethical standards between L'Oreal and The Body Shop could cause confusion among the consumers, according to industry experts. Industry experts and animal rights campaigners were concerned how Body Shop could maintain its reputation as an ethical organization when it would be owned by a company with opposing values. The market for ethical goods was estimated to be worth £250 billion in the UK alone and increasing by 15% per annum. UK-based Organic Monitor[25] predicted that other natural and organic personal care companies would be in a stronger position compared to Body Shop, post-acquisition. However, Anita Riddick of Body Shop was confident that after the acquisition, its values would not change as she commented, "L'Oreal has displayed visionary leadership in wanting to be an authentic advocate and supporter of our values." Even Owen-Jones of L'Oreal said that the company wouldn't be able to stop animal testing overnight, but it had the long-term plan of "joining Body Shop on the issue".

A UK-based alternative consumer organization, Ethical Consumer,[26] observed "This deal would have a seriously negative impact on the Body Shop. It has built itself up on the principle of not testing on animals, but in one fell swoop this would completely ruin its reputation".[27] A consumer survey just after the deal was made public found that Body Shop's "buzz rating" had fallen 10 points to –4, while "satisfaction" rating declined from 25 points to 14. Whether L'Oreal's deal with The Body Shop turned out to be a good match ensuring growth for L'Oreal in the long term or whether it led to a dilution of the brand value of Body Shop, and loss of its market, was something that only time would tell.

References

1. "L'Oreal Latest Leap," www.businessweek.com, March 17, 2006.
2. Kusta, Elizabeth. "Body Shop agrees to takeover by France's L'Oreal," Associated Press, March 17, 2006.
3. Armitage, Jim." L'Oreal mulls (pounds sterling) 600m Body Shop takeover," *The Evening Standard*, February 23, 2006.
4. "Body Shop takeover 'hit image'," www.news.bbc.co.uk, April 10, 2006.
5. Pitman, Simon. "L'Oreal's Body Shop acquisition meets with mixed reaction," www.cosmeticsdesign-europe.com, March 22, 2006.
6. "L'Oreal buys out Body Shop for $1.4 billion US," www.ctv.ca, March 17, 2006.
7. "L'Oreal to buy Body Shop for $1.14 bn," http://economictimes.indiatimes.com, March 17, 2006.
8. O'Loughlin, Sandra. "L'Oreal goes green with Body Shop acquisition," www.brandweek.com, March 17, 2006.
9. Bones, Chris. "Taking over an ethical business," http://news.bbc.co.uk, March 17, 2006.
10. Bidlake, Suzanne. "Body Shop brand reputation is battered by sale to L'Oreal," www.brandrepublic.com, March 29, 2006.
11. "Customer loyalty helps Body Shop," www.telegraph.co.uk, May 05, 2005.
12. "Roundup L'Oreal buys Body Shop," www.forbes.com, March 17, 2006.
13. http://search.epnet.com.
14. www.loreal.com.
15. www.thebodyshopinternational.com.

Notes

1. "L'Oreal's Latest Leap," www.businessweek.com, March 17, 2006
2. Elizabeth, Kusta. "Body Shop agrees to takeover by France's L'Oreal," Associated Press, March 17, 2006.
3. A French luxury products group and maker of the renowned Dior and Guerlian perfumes.
4. After the acquisition, LVMH Moet Hennessey Louis Vuitton had rapidly expanded Sephora's store network, but this move harmed the original selective store image of Sephora and it was not doing well in Europe.
5. It is the former name of L'Oreal USA, Inc., the US subsidiary of the French cosmetics giant L'Oreal Group.
6. In 1965, L'Oreal acquired a French pharmaceutical firm, Lancome, and then in 1973, it brought Marie Clair, a French publication house.
7. Datamonitor Company Spotlight on L'Oreal in www.in-cosmetics.com.
8. It is a US (Texas)-based pharmaceutical company, manufactures skin products. It is a joint venture between L'Oreal and Nestle.
9. Annual Report for 2005 of L'Oreal, conversion rate 1Euro=1.21US $ as of March 17, 2006.
10. She was born in the United Kingdom in 1942 to an Italian immigrant family. She was trained as a teacher, and social and environmental activist. She was married to Gordon Roddick in 1970 and six years later both started The Body Shop for producing and retailing ethical beauty products.
11. A city situated on the south coast of England.
12. EU is the intergovernmental and supranational union of 25 nations of the European continent. It was established by the Treaty on EU, in 1992. It has a common market, common currency managed by the European Central Bank. Its activities include development of public policy, economic policy, health policy, foreign affairs, and defense.
13. A popular global makeup brand, established in 1913. It is named for its founder's sister (Mabel) and mascara created by the founder for his sister using Vaseline petroleum jelly.

14. Matrix is the leading professional hair care and hair color company, based in the US. It was founded in 1980 by Arnie and Sydell Miller.
15. It was established in 1851 as an old-world apothecary in New York. It is famous for its skin and hair products through the most attentive, personalized service.
16. It was founded in 1983 by world famous Japanese make-up artist and skin care specialist, Shu Uemura. It has three segments—make-up, skin care and professional tools.
17. It was established in 1992, a mass-market brand. Before its acquisition by L'Oreal in 2003, it was one of the top three skin care brands in China with 5% market share.
18. It was established in 1992 by Chinese-American TV celebrity Yue-Sai Kan.
19. It was established in 1997 and specialized in skin care products. It is one of the first companies to provide scientific evidence to support product benefits.
20. He was born in 1946 in the UK. He studied literature at Oxford and management at INSEAD. He joined L'Oreal in 1969 as a sales representative. In 1988, he became the Chairman and CEO of the company, at the age of 42.
21. Company Spotlight - L'Oreal," www.in-cosmetics.com, 20/04/06
22. Annual Report and Accounts 2005 of The Body Shop, conversion rate 1Euro=1.21 US $ as of March 17, 2006
23. It is one of the naturally occurring carbolic acids, derived from fruit and milk sugar and used to reduce wrinkles, spots, sun-damaged skin and other signs of aging.
24. Polystyrene is a type of plastic that that can be rigid or foamed and used extensively for protective packaging, and the making of containers, lids, cups, bottles and trays.
25. It is a business research and consultancy company, founded in 2001, specializing in the global organic and related product industries.
26. A UK-based magazine published by the Ethical Consumer Research Association, a non-profit, research co-operative, since 1989. It promotes universal human rights, environmental sustainability, and animal welfare through ethical purchasing.
27. Armitage, Jim." L'Oreal mulls (pounds sterling) 600m Body Shop takeover." *The Evening Standard*, February 23, 2006.

Annexure 1   A Note on Cosmetics Industry

Cosmetics, as beauty enhancers, had been an important part of our lives since the days of our earliest civilizations. Traditionally, extracts of flowers, plants, herbs and ores were used to manufacture make-up and perfumes and there was no organized cosmetics industry as such. It was in the late 19th century that advancements in the field of organic chemical sciences were made and cosmetic products such as shampoos and perfumes could be made from synthetics. In the early decades of the 20th century the cosmetics industry became organized and various brands of cosmetics began to be mass-produced by manufacturers.

The industry came to be categorized as cosmetics & toiletries industry and included hair-care, skin-care, fragrance, color-cosmetics, deodorants, baby-care, depilatories, sun-care, oral-hygiene, men's grooming and bath & shower products. The market for cosmetics and toiletries was segmented on the basis of price and distribution channels. There were mass market products at competitive prices available through retail channels and high priced luxury or premium products sold through department stores, specialty stores and brand shops. Gradually in the 20th century the cosmetics and toiletries sales worldwide grew into billions of dollars. World cosmetics & toiletries sales stood at around US $170 billion in 1997 which grew to around US $ 230 billion in 2004. The largest market was Western Europe (31%), followed by Asia-Pacific (25%) and North America (22%). The top three manufacturers in the global cosmetics & toiletries industry in terms of market share in 2004 were L'Oreal, Procter & Gamble and Unilever.

Source: Compiled by IRCK

Annexure 2 Global Sales of Cosmetics and Toiletries 1997–2004

Source: www.in-cosmetics.com

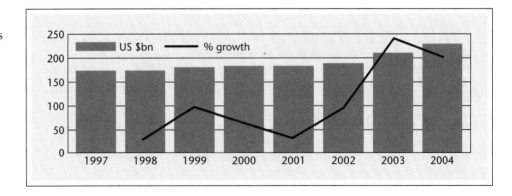

Annexure 3 Composition of Global Cosmetics & Toiletries Market by Company

Source: www.in-cosmetics.com

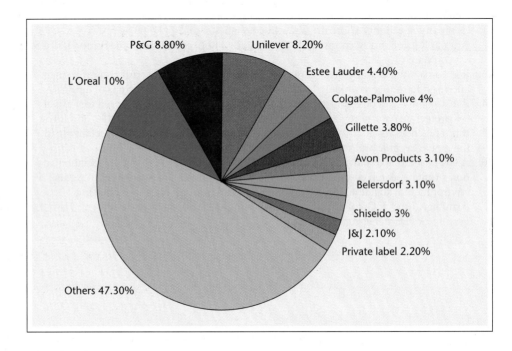

Annexure 4   The LVMH–Sephora Merger

Comparable to L'Oreal in terms of revenues, LVMH was an international group of companies active in a number of global markets including wines & spirits, fashion & leather goods, cosmetics, jewelry etc. LVMH had acquired the French retail chain Sephora in 1997. Sephora was at that time the biggest retail chain of perfumes in France with 54 shops and sales of more than $ 32 Million. Sephora had the image of being a high-end selective store offering assisted self-service. As the Sephora chain was expanded rapidly by LVMH in Europe, US and Asia in the next few years, its image of being a selective store was badly affected. In 2001 LVMH had to close Sephora operations in Germany and Japan. The operating margin remained at a low of 1% to 3%. In the US, 70 Sephora shops were established by 2002, but all of which incurred losses that were put at around 150 million euros in that year. Although the performance in the U.S had picked up since then, with 85 shops established in 2004, Sephora was still lagging in Europe and all Sephora stores in the U.K. had to be shut down in 2005. Analysts said that LVMH might eventually close down Sephora stores in some more countries.

Source: Compiled by IRCK

Case 3–5: Extending the "easy" Business Model*

What Should easyGroup Do Next?

"The only quoted conglomerate I know that works on the stock markets is General Electric. easyGroup is not about unrelated ventures, but about developing a formula for success that can be replicated across seemingly disparate businesses."

—Stelios Haji-Ioannou

easyGroup's Planned Entry into the UK Cinema Market

easyGroup was reviewing its plans to open a multiplex in May 2003, under the easyCinema banner to compete head-on against established national operators in the UK like Odeon, Warner Village and UGC Cinema. The group's CEO, serial entrepreneur Stelios Haji-Ioannou, aimed to replicate the success of easyJet, the low-cost airline that he had established in 1995 by creating a similar no-frills concept in the cinema industry. The millionaire businessman's stand was, "Nobody has tried to do this and I am told covert practices abound that prevent cinemas cutting prices. Current prices are far too high—they put people off going to the cinema."

easyGroup believed that it could create a successful cinema exhibition venture by applying the principles that had worked in the low-cost airline business. Firstly, the yield management capabilities that had served them so well in running an airline could be re-deployed in easyCinema. easyJet prices were closely linked to demand and how far in advance tickets were booked: a ticket booked three months in advance would be significantly cheaper than one booked a week before the flight. Likewise, peak-time tickets, like 6pm Friday, would cost more than at a less busy time. While incumbent cinemas in the UK typically operated at 20% capacity, they had never pursued the strategy of offering extremely cheap seats for advance bookings or at off-peak times, or of differentiating price by type or length of film.

Several cinema operators had invested in refurbishing cinemas and upgrading seats in order to attract audiences back. Stelios viewed this as analogous to the business-class on airplanes and questioned whether people would be willing to pay for bigger, more comfortable seats. He believed a cinema operator ". . . should be thinking about squeezing another 30% in there. Why are cinemas charging so much money when they're so empty? It's like what airlines once were." By maximizing both capacity and the extent to which it was utilized, easyGroup hoped to grow cinema admissions well above current rates.

Secondly, the group planned to rely on technology to automate the process of serving customers, thereby reducing labor costs. All bookings would be made through the Internet or from a machine in the foyer, with fares for advance bookings down to 20p. The average cinema had a crew of 20 people. easyGroup's plan was to reduce that number to four primarily comprising security staff and projectionists. The easyCinema concept would dispense with the box-office and ushers. Consumers would purchase tickets on the Internet and print out a unique bar code which would activate an entry turnstile at the cinema.

Thirdly, as in the airline business, the concept would be strictly no-frills with a view to maximizing the number of films screened. The cinema would not show any advertising nor would it support marketing activities or promotional events associated with films. Customers would be allowed to bring in their own food and drink. The group thought that there was no danger of destroying the magic of the cinema-going experience by removing the box-office and the traditional concession stand-on the contrary, "what we're doing is taking away a consumer rip-off. Three quid for popcorn is a rip-off."

Stelios tasked Matthew Lee, part of the six-member New Ventures team, with responsibility for assessing the potential for easyCinema and developing the concept for this new business idea. The core management team comprising Stelios, Nick Manoudakis (Chief Operating

* This case was written by Yves L. Doz, the Timken Chaired Professor of Global Technology and Innovation at INSEAD, and Anita Balchandani, Senior Consultant at Roland Berger Strategy Consultants. It is intended to be used as a basis for class discussion rather than to illustrate either effective or ineffective handling of an administrative situation.

Copyright © 2003 INSEAD, Fontainebleau, France.

Exhibit 1   Cinema Revenues and Admissions in the UK, 1997–2001

	1997	1998	1999	2000	2001
£ million, current RSP[1]	826.5	811.2	841.6	879.5	974.4
£ million, constant 1997 RSP[1]	826.5	784.5	801.9	813.6	883.7
Admissions (million)	138.9	135.2	139.1	143	155.9
Cinema revenues as % of leisure entertainment	1.8	1.7	1.7	1.7	1.8

[1] Retail Selling Price

Source: Euromonitor: Global Market Information Database - *UK Market Focus: Cinema*; Published October 2002.

Officer), Steven Hall (Chief Financial Officer) and the New Ventures Team, would meet in a week's time to discuss whether they should launch easyCinema.

The Market for Cinema in the UK

The cinema industry in the UK was experiencing a revival of sorts. Admissions in 2001 were at the highest level in decades—156 million admissions generated £974 million in ticket sales (Exhibit 1) and were expected to continue to rise at an annual rate of 4% between 2003 and 2010.

One of the factors that had contributed to the steady rise in cinema admissions in the UK since the 1980s was the emergence of the multiplex—the first one in the UK was built in Milton Keynes in 1984 and was an instant success. These venues, with up to 20 screens, comfortable seats, superior picture quality and acoustics and free parking provided a classy alternative to their precursors, the cramped and poorly-furbished one-or-two-screen High Street cinemas often described as "fleapits." Multiplexes also offered consumers a wider choice of films and enabled cinema-going to become a more spontaneous leisure activity. A study by Euromonitor stated that ". . . the majority of the people decide at the last minute to go to the cinema because there is so much choice. Multiplexes are so big that if a film is full there is either another session starting in 40 minutes, or there is something else that they really want to see." Multi-screen cinemas had transformed film-going habits and were credited with luring people out of their homes. In its early years, a multiplex was typically the monopoly supplier to its local catchment area.

However, as the number of multiplexes in the country increased (Exhibit 2), competition intensified and it became increasingly common for multiplex operators to compete directly against one another within a locality, giving consumers a wider choice of films and timings to choose from.

From an operational standpoint, multiplexes enabled better use of personnel. Staggered starting times allowed more efficient use of ushers and cleaning staff. Further, UK health and safety laws required that each cinema be manned by one employee per screen to handle emergency situations such as a fire. The multiplex environment enabled cinema operators to employ the mandatory number of employees to manage additional revenue-generating activities such as concession stands and ticket booths.

The Movie Industry

Film production, distribution and exhibition were the fundamental elements of the movie business.

Film Production.   Film production was an expensive and very risky business with profitability reliant on the success of a small number of films. In 2001, the cost of making and marketing a Hollywood movie averaged $78.7 million, according to the Motion Picture Association of America. Over $14 billion had been invested in movie productions in the US, the European Union and Japan in 2000, a 12% increase from 1998. With the increase in old and new outlets such as cinemas, DVDs and the Internet, investment was expected to increase even more, according to a media research group in London. The commercial per-

Exhibit 2   Number of Cinema Sites and Screens in the UK, 1997–2002

	1997	1998	1999	2000	2001	2002
Sites	747	761	751	754	766	780
Screens	2,383	2,638	2,825	3,017	3,248	3,400

Source: Euromonitor.

formance of films in most national markets could be best described as a heavy-tailed distribution, e.g. the top 20% of films in the UK earned approximately 85% of the revenue. The industry referred to this as "Murphy's Law" or alternatively as "the blockbuster effect".

The making of big-budget films for international distribution had long been dominated by the Hollywood studios: Warner Bros., owned by Time Warner Entertainment; Sony Pictures Entertainment; Disney Studios; Fox Filmed Entertainment, a Fox Entertainment company and VUE owned by Vivendi Universal. The production of a film would begin only when the necessary financial backing had been secured. In most cases this required an assurance that arrangements to distribute the finished product were in place. The Hollywood studios had vertically integrated into the distribution business and were usually able to finance production from their own resources. UK film companies, however, were not large integrated organizations and therefore had to pre-sell film distribution rights to a separate distribution company which contributed to the production budget either in the form of an advance against expected distribution profits or guarantees against which the production company could raise bank finance.

The Hollywood studios accounted for a high proportion of box-office receipts in the UK but there was vigorous competition between them and no one studio dominated. 2001 was a year of big-budget releases. *Harry Potter and the Philosopher's Stone, Lord of the Rings: The Fellowship of the Ring, and Spiderman,* epitomized the shift in film-making towards bigger budget productions.

Distribution.   The distribution companies operating in the UK cinema industry were of two types: studio-owned or independent. The top-five distributors—20th Century Fox, UIP, Buena Vista, Warner and Columbia Tristar—were each owned by one or more of the Hollywood studios (Exhibit 3). Their market share fluctuated widely from year to year, reflecting the success of individual films, and their main role was to distribute the films made or acquired by their parent companies. They did not have to bid or pay in advance for the UK distribution rights to those films but acted as the sales and marketing arms of their respective parent companies. Their role was to advise on which films should be released across cinemas in the UK, to develop and execute release and marketing strategies, and to sell exhibition rights to independent cinema operators. In most cases, film release costs, e.g. advertising, promotion and the manufacture of prints, were undertaken by their respective corporate parents. In return the distributors would remit rental receipts to their parents after retaining a proportion of income deemed to be acceptable to the Inland Revenue as a fair reflection of the profits of the UK-based activity.

Independent distributors, on the other hand, did not have access to an assured supply of films. They bid for distribution rights to films made by independent producers and would finance all or part of the production in exchange for the rights to exploit the film. Independent distributors typically specialized in niche, art-house films.

Distributors determined the marketing plans and release strategies on a film-by-film basis taking into account several inter-related factors: type of film; estimated size and composition of potential audience; other films likely to be released around the same time; number of cinemas available and interested in the film; budget available to support the release. Discussions between distributors

Exhibit 3   Film Distributors in the UK, 2001

Film distributors	Number of films shown	% of all films	% of box Office revenue
20th Century Fox	16	4.2	10.8
UIP	43	11.3	27.7
Buena Vista	31	8.1	21.4
Warner	23	6	6.3
Columbia Tristar	30	7.9	13.3
Total US majors	**143**	**37.4[1]**	**79.5**
Pathé	22	5.8	7.8
FilmFour	16	4.2	0.9
All other independent distributors	201	52.6	11.8
Total	382	100	100

[1] Rounding error

Source: BFI Film and Television Handbook 2002/British Video Association/Screen Finance.

and cinema exhibitors regarding films that were expected to be popular, would commence up to 12 months before the film was expected to be ready for UK theatrical release. The two parties would agree upon a release date and reserve screens on a provisional basis (a process often referred to as "penciling in"). Distributors targeted exhibitors in three waves: leading exhibitors, followed by specialist multiplex operators, and finally the independent exhibitors. This advance planning enabled distributors to finalize plans for advertising and other promotional activity, expenditure that could be as high as £1 million on the promotion of a major release. Independent distributors, however, were not in a position to plan well in advance because, unlike the integrated distributors, they were not involved with the films that they handled from the outset. Further, they found it more difficult to convince exhibitors to "pencil in" their films before they become available for viewing and consequently had difficulty obtaining the bookings that they desired.

Distribution was essential for a film's financial success, as highlighted by the company that co-produced the film *Trainspotting*. UK box-office takings were just the "shop window" for their product. Investors could recoup their cash from sales to foreign territories, TV stations and, most importantly, from video and DVD rentals. A distributor usually released a film in successive periods to these different channels, beginning with the cinema release and proceeding through to pay-TV, video/DVD rental and sale, and finally free-to-air television. Therefore consumers keen to see new releases had no alternative but to visit the cinema. While cinema represented approximately one quarter of total revenues (Exhibit 4), it remained highly important

because the success of a film in the cinema was viewed as being critical to its success in multiple other markets.

Competition between distributors heightened with the growing importance of advertising and promotional activities which played an increasing role in determining the commercial success of a new release. These included in-cinema marketing (such as "trailers," and point-of-sale promotions), television and radio advertisements, poster advertising and interviews with actors, directors and producers. Music from films was sometimes released simultaneously on CDs and cassettes. Merchandising agreements, such as those with fast-food retailers or consumer product companies, e.g. Coca-Cola's hugely successful campaign as the "drink of choice" with the movie *Bridget Jones's Diary*, and the launch of its special silver packaging at cinema venues.

Exhibition.   Cinevan, with its flagship brand, Odeon, was the leading cinema operator in the UK, both in terms of market share and number of screens. Other key operators were UCI, UGC, Warner, National Amusements and Cine-UK (Exhibit 5).

Cinevan, a private equity firm, had purchased Odeon Cinemas in February 2000. It merged the company with ABC Cinemas, which had been acquired from Virgin in 1996. The company, with approximately 3,400 employees, was re-branding its portfolio of 106 sites and 600 screens, under the Odeon banner. Odeon Cinemas had developed a strong proposition as the film-lover's brand, with its slogan "Fanatical About Film." In keeping with these values, it also launched Alternative Odeon, a sub-

---

Exhibit 4   UK Consumer Expenditure on Feature Films by Channel of Distribution (£ mil.) 1986–2000

	Box office	Video rental	Video Sales	DVD Sales	Total
1986	142	284	55	—	481
1987	169	326	110	—	605
1988	193	371	184	—	748
1989	227	416	345	—	988
1990	273	418	374	—	1,065
1991	295	407	440	—	1,142
1992	291	389	506	—	1,186
1993	319	350	643	—	1,312
1994	364	339	698	—	1,401
1995	385	351	789	—	1,525
1996	426	382	803	—	1,611
1997	506	369	858	—	1,733
1998	515	437	940	—	1,892
1999	535	408	882	68	1,893
2000	577	444	1,104	264	2,389

Source: Euromonitor.

Exhibit 5   Market Shares of Cinema Operators in the UK, 2001

Cinema operator	Market share (%)
Cinven (Odeon/ABC)	25
UCI	15
UGC Warner Bros/Village	15
Roadshow	13
Cine-UK National Amusements	10
Showcase	7
Others	15
Total	100

Source: Euromonitor: Global Market Information Database–UK Market Focus: Cinema; Published October 2002.

brand that brought niche, alternative cinema to a targeted customer base. Odeon was also considering other ideas to grow its core cinema business. These included business conference hosting services in cinemas and exhibitions of alternative film content such as Broadway musicals, rock concerts, opera and ballet. In 2002, it showed the World Cup games beamed live from Japan and South Korea. "We will sweat assets going forward," said Richard Segal, CEO of Odeon Cinemas.

In 1984, UCI, an international specialist multiplex operator, pioneered the multiplex in the UK, operating 36 sites with 365 screens. It positioned itself at the leading-edge of technology by offering digital projection and IMAX screens. During the summer of 2002, it launched a website targeted at children. UCI also aimed to capture the premium-segment with initiatives such as "The Gallery," a private balcony where film-goers had access to an exclusive bar, free refreshments and luxurious seats. Both Vivendi and Viacom-owned Paramount had significant stakes in UCI.

UGC Cinemas, owned by Vivendi in conjunction with a private French multiplex operator, had 42 cinemas and was the only exhibitor to invest in customer retention initiatives such as a loyalty card. In July 2002, it launched an initiative to dramatically increase subscriptions to its month-long Unlimited Pass by reducing the price from £19.99 to £12.99 for West End cinemas and £9.99 for all other venues. By November 2002 they had captured 100,000 subscribers.

US-owned Warner Bros and Australian cinema operators Village Roadshow's joint venture, Warner Village, had a portfolio of 36 cinemas including the largest multiplex in the UK—a 30-screen multiplex in Birmingham with six screens dedicated to showing Bollywood films. The company's website, re-launched in February 2002, also included a Bollywood section. In May 2003, Warner Bros sold this chain to SBC International Cinemas, a little-known British

exhibitor backed by venture capital investors, for £250 million. SBC intended to rebrand Warner's properties across the UK under the "Vue" banner over the next six months and planned to appeal to a wider film-going audience.

National Amusements, a subsidiary of a US company which belonged to media and entertainment giant Viacom, operated 19 cinemas under the Showcase brand. These cinemas had more screens than the average multiplex in the UK.

Backed by a consortium of venture capital firms, Cine-UK, with its portfolio of 28 Cine-World cinemas concentrated in small towns and suburban areas, had featured strongly in the Deloitte & Touche Indy 100 list of fast-growing companies and was reported to be up for sale.

Despite the growth in the market, several new cinema ventures had had to exit the market due to the high degree of competition, pressure on profitability and poor capacity utilization. "For the past 10 years there has been a seductive view that you made money by building cinemas. What I hope we are seeing now is a realization that you actually make money by filling them," said an industry expert.

Most industry participants expected consolidation in the market and felt that expansion would be more likely to result from mergers and acquisitions rather than new site development, owing to the difficulty of obtaining sites that fulfilled the space and planning-permission requirements of a multiplex. Further, the cost of building a new cinema was extremely high—a 16 to 18 screen complex could cost up to £15 million—magnified by the fact that operators would compete with each other for the best sites. The industry was at a stage where the cost of entry had "reached prohibitive levels for all but those with the deepest pockets."

The most significant operational cost incurred by a cinema exhibitor was the film rental paid to distributors. There were three main methods of calculating film rentals in the industry:

1. *Nut method,* whereby a monetary figure, the "nut," was agreed for each screen in the exhibitor's portfolio. The nut was intended to represent the screen's weekly operating costs plus an element for profit. However, in practice, the agreed figure was the result of negotiations between the exhibitor and the distributor. The rental fee was the greater of the two sums: 25% of the total box-office takings or 90% of takings above the nut.

2. *Sliding scale method.* Under this approach, the rental paid varied from a minimum of 25% to a maximum of 50% in steps of five percentage points as the takings rose above pre-determined break figures.

3. *Datum scale method.* The rental was 25% of the takings up to a break figure and 75% thereafter, subject to an overall maximum of 50%.

Other methods, such as a flat percentage, were used by a small minority of exhibitors. The exhibitor chose which method of calculation to use but the nut and break figures were agreed with distributors and these had to be negotiated for every film. Usually an exhibitor would agree figures with a leading distributor. If these were satisfactory, the exhibitor sought to persuade other distributors to align to the same method of calculation and terms. Typically, if a film ran well, distributors took the lion's share of the takings. However, if screens were virtually empty, the cinema got a bigger proportion to help it cover its costs. Rental costs varied considerably across what was referred to in the industry as "first-run", "second-run" and "third-run" films. The most expensive first-run films were those screened immediately upon release. After 10 to 14 weeks, an exhibitor could negotiate a lower rental on the film which was then classified as "second-run." Once a movie was released on video some exhibitors—typically small, independent operators—chose to run them as "third-run" releases.

Labor, facility lease expenses, utilities and maintenance were the other key cost elements (Exhibit 6). Labor costs had both a fixed and a variable component. During non-peak periods, a minimum number of staff was required to operate the facility. However, theatre staffing levels were increased to handle attendance volume increases during peak periods (Friday and Saturday evenings), as film-goers typically purchased tickets at the cinema box-office 10 to 15 minutes before the show commenced, except in the case of long-awaited blockbusters. Health and safety laws required movie houses to have a minimum of one staff member per screen to handle emer-

gency situations. Lease expenses and associated property taxes were primarily fixed costs. Recent studies suggested that intense competition between operators had increased rents by up to 30%.

The Target Audience

Two broad categories of distinction were used in the industry: mainstream (also referred to as "commercial") and art-house. Mainstream films were those aimed at a wide audience, while art-house films were more special interest in nature. The term art-house, for example, was used to refer to most foreign-language films released in the UK. Films that started out as art-house but attracted a wider audience than expected were referred to as "cross-overs." However, mainstream films generated the majority of box-office receipts and rentals.

National cinema operators historically played mainstream, populist movies, while the smaller, independent venues typically focused on art-house films aimed at the more serious cinema goer. However, over the past few years, larger cinema operators were beginning to realize the benefits of targeting their product to niche customer segments. By bringing art and cult films to appropriate audiences they were able to widen their customer base significantly.

Film-goers in the UK visited the cinema three times a year on average compared with 5.2 times for their US counterparts. 15–24 year olds were the most prolific cinemagoers (Exhibit 7), and were targeted heavily by most cinema operators with special fares, timings and films. Families were another key segment for cinemas, with weekend offers designed around making the movie-going experience more affordable and enjoyable for a family: "We acknowledge that mum and dad don't really want to see Jimmy Neutron for the third time, so why should they have to pay for it?" quoted a multiplex operator in a study by Euromonitor on the market for cinema in the UK. Most cinemas marketed heavily to children—dedicated websites with interactive features from forthcoming children's films and giveaways in cinema foyers were standard. Increasingly, cinema houses were also starting to cater to an older audience, typically couples with no kids referred to as "contented couples" by the industry. These moviegoers were willing to pay a premium for a superior experience. For instance, The Electric Cinema, one of the UK's oldest cinemas, had reopened as a cinema with a brasserie, bar and private members-only club. The newly refurbished cinema, boasting leather seating, footstools and tables for food and drink, emphasized comfort, service and quality films.

Exhibit 6	Typical Structure of the Profit & Loss Account of a Cinema Exhibitor in the UK

	%
Box office takings	73%
Concession income	22%
Screen advertising	4%
Other	1%
Total	**100%**
Film rental	27%
Staff costs	21%
Depreciation	9%
Concession cost of sales	8%
Advertising & publicity	3%
Other	19%
Operating profit	13%
Total	**100%**

Source: Industry analysts.

Exhibit 7   Frequency of Cinema Going in the UK

Percentage population	At least once a month	At least twice a year	Once a year or less	Never go to cinema
Male	25	31	24	80
Female	23	40	20	83
ABC1[1]	29	39	20	88
C2DE[1]	19	31	24	74
4–14	31	48	13	92
15–24	50	35	11	96
25–34	29	42	21	92
35+	15	31	27	73

[1] Refers to the hierarchy of socio-economic classes in the UK. This classification spans all dimensions of occupation skill. For example, A represents Professionals, while E represents Unskilled occupations.

Source: The Lifestyle Pocket Book 2002, UK.

Use of New Technology

Research showed that young, avid cinema-goers tend to be heavy users of mobile phones and the Internet. By nature, movies were amenable to content-rich advertising over the web. Most cinema houses had adopted the Internet as a means of reserving seats and purchasing tickets. Some let customers buy tickets using WAP mobile phones. Cinema houses also used mobile messaging services and e-mail to inform customers of special offers.

Pricing Strategies

There was little difference in average prices charged by the leading exhibitors but prices did vary by region. All operators used the simple strategy of varying prices by time of day, day of week, type of seating or customer segment—students, senior citizens and children obtained discounted rates.

The average ticket price in the UK during 2001 was £6.25 which compared with £5.95 in 1997. This represented a 5% increase over the 5-year period. However, prices in London—the highest in the country—were more likely to be in the range of £7 to £8.

The Film Distributors Association (FDA), the main trade association of film distributors in the UK Regulation, of which all major companies and several independent distributors were members, had established a set of Standard Conditions for the licensing and exhibition of films in cinemas in the UK. Under the Standard Conditions, the use of which was widespread in the industry, exhibitors could only charge the admission price for a film that had been agreed upon with the distributor. Consequently, distributors would sometimes refuse permission for price reductions and even take action against unauthorized promotions. Major exhibitors viewed this regulatory provision as being reasonable since a decrease in ticket prices could affect a distributor's rental revenues. The inclusion of this provision in the Standard Conditions had the effect of restricting exhibitors' ability to compete by cutting prices.

easyGroup: 1995 to Present

36-year-old Stelios Haji-Ioannou, son of a Greek shipping tycoon, joined his father's shipping company, Troodos Shipping, in 1988 after graduating in Economics from the London School of Economics and in Shipping Trade and Finance from the City University Business School. In January 1992, he founded his first venture, Stelmar Tankers, a fleet shipping company that was listed on the New York Stock Exchange in March 2001.

easyJet

In 1995, Stelios founded easyJet, Europe's first low-cost, no-frills, point-to-point airline, initially modeled on the successful US-based Southwest Airlines formula: a homogenous fleet, point-to-point services to short haul destinations, rapid turnaround times, high aircraft utilization, and no in-flight meal services. In addition to studying Southwest Airlines, Stelios and his team studied Valuejet, another US-based low-cost carrier, in order to understand why it was unsuccessful. The team regularly traveled to the US, spending time in the headquarters of both corporations to understand the reasons for success and failure in the low-cost airline business. Stelios believed that while they learnt from the low-cost carriers in the US, easyJet essentially "moved ahead of the Southwest business model" by entirely bypassing travel agents—initially reservations were taken over the telephone and subsequently customers migrated to the Internet for most transactions—deploying a more sophisticated yield management system and pursuing more flexible deployment of planes during the course of the day and from one day to another (unlike Ryanair and other low-cost competitors who dedicated individual planes to specific routes).

The airline started operations with a loan of £5 million from Stelios' father and two leased aircraft operating out of London Luton airport. easyJet's first flight, from London to Glasgow, was priced at £29 one-way. An extensive public relations campaign and compelling advertising slogan—"Fly to Scotland for the price of a pair of jeans"—supported the launch of the service. Passenger figures were encouraging and over the next five years the airline owned and/or leased 18 Boeing 737-300s and covered 27 routes in Europe.

easyJet operated a simple fare structure. All prices were quoted one-way to allow customers the flexibility to choose where and when they would like to fly. Fares were based on supply and demand. The earlier passengers booked, the cheaper the fare would be. The booking system would review bookings daily for all future flights and predict how popular each flight was likely to be. If the percentage of seats sold, i.e., the load factor, was higher than normal, then the price would go up to avoid selling out popular flights months in advance.

In order to offer low fares, easyJet worked towards engineering out costs from its operations (Exhibit 8). £14 per passenger was saved by not offering an in-flight meal, £10 worth of savings per passenger resulted from the use of Luton airport instead of Gatwick. In other countries, however, easyJet operated from major airports, e.g., Charles de Gaulle and Nice in France, while competitors such as

Ryanair focused purely on smaller airports, e.g., Beauvais (France). Overall seating capacity was maximized by not offering business-class seating. Travel agents were entirely eliminated because they added 25% to total operating costs—telephone and Internet sales were the primary distribution channels. easyJet also reduced the turnaround time of its aircraft and flew its planes more hours per day—11.5 hours vs. an industry average of 6 hours, and negotiated progressive landing charge agreements with the airports. Cost efficiencies were also captured by operating a "ticketless airline"—passengers required only a confirmation number and passport in order to check-in. Corporate overheads were also kept to a minimum—the airline was based in "easyLand," a bright orange building adjacent to the main taxiway at Luton Airport that reflected the easyJet low-cost ethos.

Despite the emphasis on cost reduction, the airline ensured that passenger safety was not compromised. The fleet comprised only brand new Boeing 737s and experienced pilots were hired who were paid prevailing market rates.

By 1999, the airline had started receiving recognition. easyJet was voted "Best Low Cost Airline" by readers of *Business Traveller* magazine. *Marketing* magazine described the launch of easyJet as "one of the 100 great marketing moments of the 20th century." Given its low-cost focus, the company relied on marketing the brand through PR and sales promotions. Stelios was a skilled PR operator who was able to establish easyJet with minimum of marketing expenditure. He pulled off several publicity stunts such as distributing free easyJet tickets on the launch flight of rival low-cost carrier, Go Airline, while dressed in a bright orange boiler-suit. The company was able to attract an impressive amount of media coverage. Stelios' tongue-in-cheek advertising, positioning easyJet as the David against

---

Exhibit 8   easyJet—Reengineering the Cost Structure in the Airline Business

Costs borne by all airlines including easyJet	Costs reduced by easyJet	Costs eliminated by easyJet
–Telesales staff	–Advertising	–In-flight catering
–Cabin crew	–Airport and landing fees	–Business class cabin crew
–Pilots	–Aircraft non-utilisation due	–Travel agent commission
–Group handling	to delays at congested airports	–Ticketing costs
–Insurance		
–Aircraft ownership cost		
–Air traffic control fees		
–Maintenance		
–Fuel		

Source: Company website.

Exhibit 9   easyJet Passenger Statistics

Year	Annual total ('000)
1995	30
1996	420
1997	1,140
1998	1,880
1999	3,670
2000	5,996
2001	7,664
2002	11,400

Source: Company website.

the airline industry's Goliaths, was highly effective. The company did not retain any advertising agencies—Stelios and his marketing team were the self-styled ad designers of easyJet's campaigns. The company also used its own aircraft as marketing tools to serve as airborne billboards sporting the Internet address, telesales numbers and marketing slogans. A similar marketing approach was to play a useful role in establishing easyJet's subsequent brands.

In 2000, easyJet seat sales over the Internet reached the one million mark (the first ticket was sold online in April 1998). That same year, easyJet went public and was formally admitted to the London Stock Exchange.

In 2002, easyJet's passenger numbers (Exhibit 9) continued to soar. It had a market value of £1.5 billion and, while most full-service airlines were making losses, it posted record profits of £71.6 million (Exhibit 10) and completed the acquisition of Go for £374 million from British Airways. The airline had a strong, stable management team led by Ray Webster, Chief Executive Officer since 1998, who had been with the company since its inception. However, following pressure from shareholders, Stelios stepped down as easyJet chairman and was replaced by Sir Colin Chandler, the former chairman of Vickers Defence Systems. At the time, Stelios said: "I intend to remain a significant shareholder of this company

for a very long time," referring to his 21.9% stake, adding, "However, as I have made clear on several occasions in the past, I have no other source of income from easyJet other than disposal of shares and as I engage in new ventures, I may need to liquidate some of my stock from time to time. "Stelios, his wealth estimated at £500 million, was keen to augment his position as Britain's 26th richest man and to expand the "easy" concept to a range of new businesses.

By 2003, against the backdrop of a weak global economy, easyJet announced its interim results (six months to March 31). Revenues were up 25%, the load factor was at 82.1%, average air fares were down to approximately £37, but losses were at £24 million. Despite this, the company was confident of its ability to succeed in the competitive low-cost carrier market. As a signal of this confidence, shareholders had ratified a move to augment the existing fleet of 65 Boeing aircraft with 102 Airbus A319s.

easyGroup

In 1998, three years after easyJet, Stelios had two assets in place—an airline and a brand. He decided to explore new ventures that would leverage the "easy" brand across new businesses, thus creating easyGroup, a "branded incubator" with a mission to "create long-term capital growth by selecting and incubating substantial, profitable and sustainable businesses that reduce the cost of living and extend the easy brand ("paint the world orange") while maintaining the core brand values."

In addition to the belief that that the "easy" brand could be "stretched," central to easyGroup's philosophy was the belief that, "the Internet and yield management techniques are here to say" in the words of Nick Manoudakis, COO. All new ventures at easyGroup would be built around these three business fundamentals.

After the public offering of easyJet, the relationship between easyGroup and the airline became that of a brand licensor-licensee. easyGroup licensed the "easy" brand to easyJet, providing the airline with a set of Brand Standards—rules regarding use of the logo, color, and professional standards that the brand was required to adhere to. In the event of a breach of these standards, easyGroup could retract its brand license.

easyInternetcafé

easyGroup's first venture was to establish a chain of Internet cafés based on the application of the same no-frills, low-cost and yield management principles that had worked so well in the airline business. The first branch opened in July 1999 in London near the busy Victoria

Exhibit 10   easyJet Revenue and Profit, Year to End September

	Revenue (£ mil.)	Profit (£ mil.)
1998	77.0	5.9
1999	139.8	1.3
2000	263.7	22.1
2001	356.9	40.1
2002	552.0	71.6

Source: Company website.

Station, with approximately 360 PCs over two floors of rented premises. The café had a clean, uncluttered layout, high quality hardware and offered attractive prices.

The business deployed the principles of yield management developed for the airlines to vary prices dynamically based on demand levels. Customers would pay between 50p and £1 for an hour of Internet surfing. To aid yield management, the business deployed a particular "pricing curve" (relationship between occupancy level and price), from a potential set of 10 options. For instance, a steep pricing curve would be used at the Oxford Street store on a day with peak summer tourist traffic. Alternatively, when demand was expected to be low, a soft pricing curve would be used, i.e. rising occupancy levels would trigger small, non-aggressive price increases (Exhibit 11). The business had a Yield Manager whose role it was to monitor store occupancy levels, seasonality and historical demand patterns in order determine the pricing curve to be deployed in each store on a daily basis.

The success of the first opening led to an initial wave of expansion within London. Each store capitalized on a different mix of users but all were in high footfall areas. Demand drivers varied across the stores. Matthew Lynwood, Property Director of the business, remarked, "Tottenham Court Road is more 'techie-land' and very close to the universities. Oxford Street is retail, pure and simple. Victoria has a more backpacking, traveling, touristy profile. Kensington High Street is more upper-class retail with some residents and offices. Then you have the Strand, which is 24-hours and our busiest store overnight."

Over time, however, the business model of the venture evolved considerably. Initially, the cafés housed a "learning zone" with uniformed advisors who would help customers find things online and support the counter from which coffee and snacks were sold. In the second-generation stores, these features were abandoned in favor of a simple, no-frills concept that offered the basic service of Internet access and could be operated with minimal staff. Following this, the group moved away from the "gargantuan" stores and successfully experimented with smaller stores with approximately 100 PCs. In the third phase of expansion, easyInternetcafé began establishing smaller Points of Presence (PoP) within existing fast food establishments-primarily McDonald's, Burger King and Subway. Staff requirements were reduced by introducing computerized vending machines that allowed customers to buy Internet time automatically. As of 2003, easyGroup intended to drive expansion through franchises. Franchisees would take care of store establishment, local marketing and store maintenance, while easyInternetcafé would run the yield management/pricing system and ensure that franchisees operated under the rules of the "easy" brand license.

The group paid significant attention to international expansion as well—21 Internet cafes were in operation in eight countries within two years. Its Internet café located in New York's Times Square was a symbol of the group's intention to expand into the US. Franchises were to be made available in 15 states across the US and in 10 other countries.

Exhibit 11 Pricing Curves Used at easyInternetcafé— Sample

Source: easyInternetcafé.

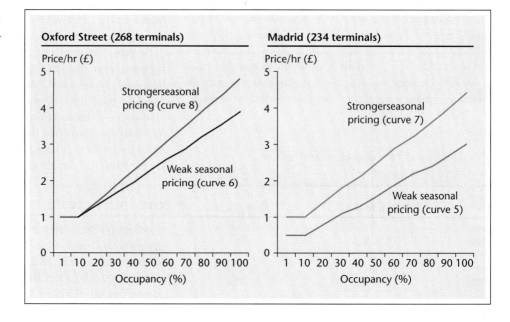

Exhibit 12   easy Internetcafé—Growth Statistics

Fiscal Year (y/e September)	1999	2000	2001	2002	2003 (to 15/4/03)
Number of PCs in use, incl. franchises	358	4,525	8,495	7,469	7,276
Total number of sites	1	11	22	23	28
Legacy stores	1	11	22	21	21
Points of Presence (PoPs)	—	—	—	—	5
Franchises	—	—	—	2	2
Number of international (non—UK) sites	—	5	14	14	16
Legacy stores	—	5	14	12	12
Points of Presence (PoPs)	—	—	—	—	2
Franchises	—	—	—	2	2
Number of customer logons, incl. franchises (mil.)	*NA*	*5.5*	*16.7*	*17.8*	*7.7*

Source: easyInternetcafé.

While easyInternetcafé grew considerably (Exhibit 12), it had been a loss-making (Exhibit 13) business since its launch. However, the efforts of the group to improve the cost structure of the business looked promising (Exhibit 14) and easyInternetcafé was expected to reach cash-flow break-even by mid-2003 and profitability by 2004.

easyCar

easyCar, a car rental service based on similar principles of dynamic pricing, yield management and online booking, was established in April 2000. The first few sites had a rental capacity of 500 cars each. Initially, easyGroup's entire fleet of cars

Exhibit 13   easyInternetcafé Limited—Profit & Loss Account

Date of Accounts	30/09/2002	30/09/2001	30/09/2000	30/09/1999
UK Turnover	3,021,000	10,543,000	6,668,000	
Export Turnover	8,993,000	11,481,000	684,000	
Turnover	**12,014,000**	**22,024,000**	**7,352,000**	**392,000**
Cost of Sales	24,158,000	72,674,000	4,421,000	316,000
Total Expenses				
Gross Profit	**−12,144,000**	**−50,650,000**	**2,931,000**	**76,000**
Depreciation	6,104,000	44,619,000	2,331,000	132,000
Other Expenses	5,817,000	13,640,000	15,696,000	2,178,000
Operating Profit		−64,290,000	−12,765,000	−2,102,000
Other Income	187,000	196,000	525,000	293,000
Interest Payable	3,977,000	3,753,000	1,230,000	17,000
Exceptional Items	9,182,000	0	0	0
Discontinued Operations	0	0	0	
Pre-Tax Profit	**−12,569,000**	**−67,847,000**	**−13,470,000**	**−1,826,000**
Tax Payable	0	0	0	55,000
Extraordinary Items	0	0	0	0
Dividends Paid	0	0	0	0
Retained Profit	**−12,569,000**	**−67,847,000**	**−13,470,000**	**−1,881,000**

Source: easyInternetcafé.

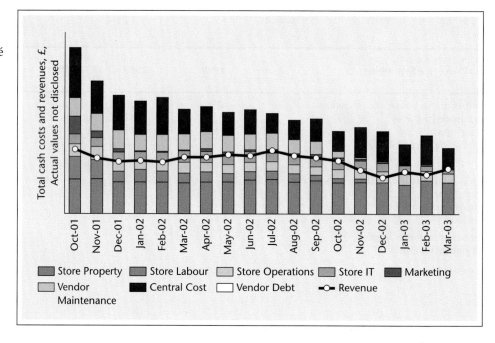

Exhibit 14 Evolution of Total Cash Costs and Revenues, easyInternetcafé

Source: easyInternetcafé.

comprised a single model—the Mercedes A-Class—that customers could rent for as little as £10 per day on low-demand days, as opposed to average daily rental charges of £30–40. Launching the business, Stelios said, "The choice of Mercedes reflects the easyGroup brand. easyCar will use brand new Mercedes cars in the same way that easyJet uses brand new Boeing aircraft. We do not compromise on the hardware, we just use innovation to substantially reduce costs. The car hire industry is where the airline industry was five years ago: a cartel feeding off the corporate client. easyCar will provide a choice for consumers who pay out of their own pockets and who will not be ripped off for traveling mid-week."

By May 2003, the car rental business operated from 50 sites across the UK, France, Spain, the Netherlands and Switzerland, with plans to expand that to 80 by the year end. Rental sites were not located directly at airports—seven sites were located close to airports while the rest were located in city centers targeting urban dwellers who would rather rent than own a car. easyGroup refined the operational model of the business in order to pursue innovative cost-saving measures. The average fleet-per-site was reduced because, as Stelios was known for saying, "The skill is never to allow utilization to fall below 90%." easyCar also departed from its policy of procuring cars from a single supplier by creating a competitive market for multiple suppliers. Economies of scale from a uniform fleet were realized only at site level. A particular site rented only one type of vehicle. Cars were no longer rented with full fuel tanks—customers were expected to fuel them—to eliminate the cost of checking and refueling them, thereby enabling

quicker re-renting. The policy that cars be returned clean to avoid a £10 cleaning charge was another successful tactic to engineer out labor costs from operations and accelerate turn-around. Customers that picked up and dropped off vehicles at off-peak times benefited from lower prices. Essentially the business had migrated to a pit-stop concept, with car pick-up points situated within a mile of a petrol station. One means to accelerate growth was the establishment of pick-up points in car parks using mobile vans staffed by a single employee. By February 2003, sites had been established in two central London locations—car park owners were guaranteed revenue for 15 to 20 spots in return for permission to operate a car rental site on their premises. The complexity of managing operations at car rental sites had been engineered out by providing a user-friendly, foolproof software that would guide the employee. No transactions were handled on-site as customers would pay at the time of reservation via the Internet.

Yield management also played a critical role in ensuring that utilization rates in the business remained at 85% to 95%. Based on historical demand patterns, seasonality and capacity, the yield manager would vary the pricing curves deployed at site level (Exhibit 15).

The car rental business missed its target of reaching profitability in 2002 (Exhibit 16). However, the group believed that initiatives to reduce labor costs and expand both the size of the fleet and the number of sites (Exhibit 17) would enable it to do so in 2003. It was expected that easyCar would be the second business to go public and the group targeted an Initial Public Offering (IPO) in 2005.

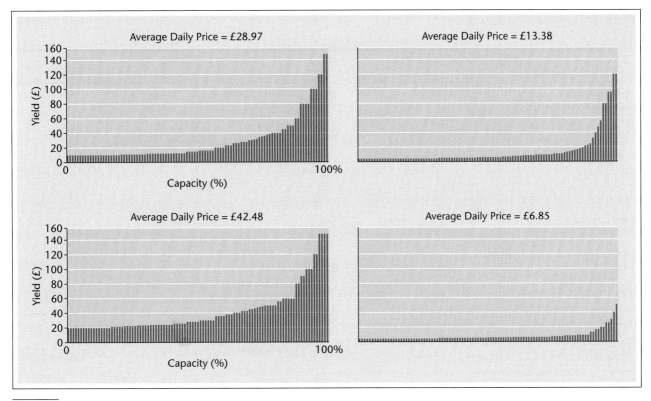

Exhibit 15   easyCar—Illustrative Pricing Curves on Four Days, Location X

Source: easyCar.

Other Ventures

In November 2000, the group launched easyValue.com, an impartial online price comparison engine, and easy.com, a free web-based e-mail service. A year later, easyMoney, an online financial services business, was launched. Its first product was a dynamically personalized credit card. It was estimated that Stelios had spent £100 million to expand his easyGroup empire. However, his non-airline businesses had lost £75 million in three years. Funding for all new ventures came from Stelios' personal wealth. In May 2003, all the businesses in operation or being planned, were financed personally by Stelios, with minimal investments from other members of the easyGroup management team.

New Venture Development

easyGroup was constantly in quest of new business opportunities—even visitors to the group website were encouraged to submit business ideas. The group had a New Ventures team comprising six employees tasked with championing and developing new ideas. At any given point in time two to three ideas were in the pipeline.

Exhibit 16 easyCar (UK) Limited-Profit & Loss Account		
Date of Accounts	**30/09/2001**	**30/09/2000**
UK Turnover	9,430,000	2,007,000
Export Turnover	8,557,000	1,337,000
Turnover	**17,987,000**	**3,344,000**
Cost of Sales	11,019,000	3,273,000
Total Expenses		
Gross Profit	**6,968,000**	**71,000**
Depreciation	3,067,000	494,000
Other Expenses	19,196,000	7,496,000
Operating Profit		–7,425,000
Other Income	181,000	110,000
Interest Payable	1,356,000	163,000
Exceptional Items	–139,000	0
Discontinued Operations	0	0
Pre-Tax Profit	**–13,542,000**	**–7,478,000**
Tax Payable	6,000	17,000
Extraordinary Items	0	0
Dividends Paid	0	0
Retained Profit	**–13,548,000**	**–7,495,000**

Source: easyCar.

Exhibit 17   easyCar—Growth Statistics

Fiscal Year (y/e September)	2000	2001	2002	2003[1]
Fleet size (Number of cars)	2,358	5,066	6,080	7,552
Total number of UK sites	4	8	10	28
Legacy sites	4	8	9	8
Pit stop	—	—	1	20
Number of international (non-UK) sites	5	7	10	22
Legacy sites	5	7	10	9
Pit stop	—	—	—	13

[1] (to 05/03)

Source: easyCar.

The company's very nature—described as being "information hungry"—led employees to surf websites and trawl through information about industries (size, growth, etc.) to identify potentially attractive opportunities. These ideas were presented and discussed informally, typically through conversation, debate and e-mail exchanges. Most business decisions were made on the basis of data available in the public domain.

Geographic expansion was also high on the group's agenda. The car rental and Internet café businesses were represented in Europe. A team of two was based in the US with a view to spearheading new opportunities in the region as well as growing the existing Internet café operations in the US.

In addition to the planned cinema venture, several new projects were being examined including budget hotels, gyms, budget cruises, bus transportation and home catering. The easyCinema project, however, was the one closest to decision point.

Criteria for New Business Selection

The criteria for new business selection had evolved over time (Exhibit 18). Having learnt from past experience, easyGroup now had a more selective approach to the choice of business that it entered, i.e., understanding *ex ante* whether capabilities such as yield management could be truly powerful in a particular industry context. "Our eureka moments," said David Rawsthorn, who was involved in conceptualizing the cinema project, "come after days, weeks of being exposed to our principles and to how they apply in an industry." The group sought to operate simple businesses and to explore how it could engineer a complex business into a much simpler one. The "easy" formula essentially required consumer-facing businesses

Exhibit 18   Criteria for Idea Selection

Industry requirements—The idea proposed must be in an industry that:

- Is consumer facing
- Is a price elastic market with the opportunity to grow the market through lower prices
- Is a perishable commodity, e.g., something that cannot be sold again like a night at a hotel room
- Has incumbents with a high unit cost base
- Has no low-cost competitors in its market

Aligned with "easy" principles—A new venture must:

- Use, fit and build the "easy" brand
- Provide good value to the customer
- Use technology to cut costs and improve quality
- Sell direct to the consumer, e.g., internet sales
- Be a simple offering
- Not play by traditional market rules
- Not be a white-label
- Not bundle products
- Be easy-to-use

Business model requirements—The business model must:

- Have unit cost-savings of the order of 50% compared with the best in the market
- Have zero or very low marginal cost
- Be possible to yield manage the price
- Have the potential to significantly increase utilization/ occupancy rates compared with the industry

Financial requirements—The business must:

- Have the potential for floatation in c.5 years, typically requiring an annual profit of £10 mil. pre-floatation and strong growth potential

Source: Company website.

that displayed significant price elasticity, required a high fixed-cost base and low marginal-cost to service additional customers—factors that would enable easyGroup to effectively yield manage. Further, the group believed that industries with strong but complacent incumbents were particularly well suited for easyGroup's approach.

Businesses That easyGroup Would Not Consider

Based on the above principles of business selection, the group had developed a common understanding of some of the businesses that they would not enter. With characteristic humor, Stelios cited the example of the funeral business as one of these as funeral spending did not represent discretionary spending and therefore could not be yield managed!

Process of Entering New Businesses

Business models for most new ventures were developed by extracting out complexity from business processes, e.g., easyCar's policy that customers return their cars clean or pay a £10 fine was a way of eliminating significant labor costs incurred in washing cars: "Most car rental companies are a euphemism for car-wash companies," said Stelios. The focus on operational simplicity was facilitated by a conscious "de-skilling" of jobs at car rental sites and by a complete elimination of personnel in the Internet cafés. The newly-launched mobile vans that served as car rental pick-up points, for instance, were one-person operations enabled by a user-friendly computerized software to ensure that all "check-out" process steps were executed at the required service level.

Another approach that easyGroup used to develop its business model was to reverse engineer business operations with the target of arriving at a cost structure that would be half that of its competitors.

The mode of scaling up the business underwent a change from the early days of Stelios' entrepreneurship—from accelerated roll-outs, as characterized by the café and car business, to a phased roll-out. The company decided that, going forward, it would focus on piloting and refining new ideas before replicating them, caution that stemmed from Stelios' "reluctance to be railroaded by expensive mistakes."

Incubation of New Businesses

easyGroup operated with clear guidelines on what the role of the central group should be during the lifetime of a business. The group's involvement over time decreased as a

particular business became increasingly self-sufficient and ultimately ready for an IPO. Until the time of an IPO, all businesses were located in the corporate office. After a business had gone public, it would be physically moved out of the corporate offices and into new facilities of its own.

The corporate office, The Rotunda, based in a converted piano factory in Camden, housed three functions:

- Brand protection, which ensured that encroachments on the "easy" brand were dealt with appropriately and that licensees were complying with brand rules.
- Incubation, which identified, screened, selected and developed new business ideas.
- Services, which supported the organization through functions such as Intellectual Property, Legal, Finance and Human Resources.

The Rotunda was a circular building and the easyGroup office was arranged in a wheel-like formation. Stelios and the core management team sat in open plan spaces in the center while the businesses and corporate functions were crammed along aisles that ran like imaginary spokes. "I like to sit in the middle of everyone else," said Stelios. "It sends a message that, first, you are more accessible, and second, you know what's happening. Luxury doesn't belong at the office, mainly because at some stage you will expect outside investors to invest in your company and these investors should not be funding your lifestyle." The Guardian newspaper described easyGroup's offices as follows: "The place looks as if it is just capable of turning out a student newspaper, but hardly the hub of an empire that now comprises a fistful of easy-branded, orange-hued, cheap 'n' cheerful businesses."

It was in the Rotunda that every evening at 5pm the company would hold a stand-up meeting in which all business units would provide a daily update on their respective Key Performance Indicators (KPI). The objective was to communicate performance figures, highlight strategic developments and address operational concerns. This meeting played an important role in reinforcing the group's ambitions for all its employees and in ensuring that each of the businesses were on track for profitability.

5-year Vision

The group planned to have two public businesses in its portfolio—easyCar and easyInternetcafé—over the next five years. The car rental business targeted an IPO in 2005. During this timeframe, it also planned to have five new start-ups in operation. Stelios aimed to build a cadre of people who would move across new ventures, sharing knowledge and competencies of the "easy" way of doing business.

The group invested in developing its managers. Some of them were about to attend conferences that addressed how franchises could be managed. COO Nick Manoudakis had just returned from the Advanced Management Program at Harvard and had shared his learnings with the entire organization.

easyGroup: Growth Choices

As easyGroup examined the opportunities of launching a no-frills cinema in 2003, another blockbuster year with big budget new releases including *The Matrix Reloaded* and part three of *The Lord of the Rings*, its management team realized that it would face resistance from powerful distributors and incumbent exhibitors who worked in sync with each other. But this would not deter them. easyGroup believed that it would legally challenge the trading practices of these powerful companies, if required, in order to revolutionize the manner in which cinemas were operated. It had successfully targeted industries with strong but "fat, complacent" incumbents in the past. This would be another such opportunity.

The easyGroup team grappled with several questions. How should they roll-out the business? What payment structure for film rentals would be the most viable? Should they build a new cinema or acquire an existing chain? Most important of all was the fundamental question—Was this the right business for easyGroup?

Case 3-6: Hallmark Cards, Inc. in 2006*

Kansas city based Hallmark Cards Inc. (Hallmark Cards) a leader in the social expression industry, had a market share of 50% in the US. Hallmark's products were distributed across the US through more than 43,000 retail outlets. Apart from its flagship brand, Hallmark marketed its products under the brand names Expressions, Ambassador, Party Express, Shoebox and Tree of Life. Hallmark's subsidiary, "Binney & Smith" marketed art products under the brand names "Crayola" and "Silly Putty".

In 1991, Hallmark ventured into the entertainment business (cable television) and introduced the *Hallmark Channel*. It attained huge success and in 2005, was rated as the No.1 channel (in terms of viewership growth) in the US. Due to the consolidation amongst other media players, lack of a prominent media company's support and poor financial performance, Hallmark thought it desirable to get out of the entertainment business, and sold its international and national operations in 2005.

In 2006, Hallmark announced that it would publish lifestyle magazines for women. Would Hallmark be able to make a mark in the magazine publishing business?

Hallmark Cards

Hallmark Cards was founded in 1910 by Joyce C Hall (J C Hall) and his brothers who sold postcards. In 1911, they named the company "Hall Brothers" and sold Valentines and Christmas cards which were made of colored tissue paper. In 1917 when the procurement of the colored tissue paper became difficult the JC Hall brothers began using modern wrapping based greeting cards.

---

* This case was written by Anandan Pillai, ICFAI Business School, Ahmedabad, under the direction of AV Vedpuriswar, ICFAI Knowledge Center. It is intended to be used as the basis for class discussion rather than to illustrate either effective or ineffective handling of a management situation. The case was compiled from published sources. Reference no 306-348-1

© 2006, ICFAI Business School, Ahmedabad.

No part of this publication may be copied, stored, transmitted, reproduced or distributed in any form or medium whatsoever without the permission of the copyright owner.

In 1928, the company adopted the name "Hallmark" for its products and started printing the name on the back of every card and also promoted it in its advertising campaigns. In 1944, it adopted the slogan "When You Care Enough to Send the Very Best," which became popular. Because of its quality and the slogan Hallmark's reputation grew as a brand. Initially, the slogan was used in radio broadcasts. The company created a niche in the minds of people with the help of its products, its network of specialty retail stores, national advertising and as a sponsor of *"Hallmark Hall of Fame,"* (Exhibit 1) television's most honored and enduring dramatic series.

In 1949, the Hallmark Cards signature and crown logo[1] was created. In 1954, the official name of the company was accepted as Hallmark Cards Inc. By 1960 (50th anniversary), Hallmark's 350 artists produced 4 million cards per day and created 15,000 new cards and product designs every year.

In 1984, Binney & Smith, a manufacturer of Crayola crayons and art products was acquired by Hallmark. In 1986, Hallmark Cards introduced Shoebox Greetings cards and a year later introduced Mahogany cards for Afro-American consumers. In 1995, it introduced Tree of Life cards for Jewish consumers and a year later launched its website Hallmark.com. In 1997, Hallmark Cards introduced the 'Expressions' brand of greeting cards.

In 2004, Hallmark Cards, with net revenues of $4.4 billion, employed 18,000 full time employees. The 800 creative personnel included artists, designers stylists, writers, editors and photographers. They generated more than 19,000 new and redesigned greeting cards per year. Hallmark licensed its designs to other manufacturers in the apparel, domestics and table top industries.

As a part of its corporate social responsibility, the company allocated funds to the Hallmark Corporate Foundation, which supported human service, education, health and arts organizations in the community.

Knowledge Resource

Hallmark Cards with the help of in-house expertise and third party information providers ensured that they identified future trends accurately and well in time. They also had a rich

---

Exhibit 1   Hallmark Hall of Fame

It was launched on Christmas Eve 1951 with a world premiere of *Amahl and the Night Visitors,* an original opera. Since then Hallmark Hal of Fame became the longest running and most honored series of dramatic specials in the history of American television. The next original production, William Shakespeare's *Hamlet,* was launched in 1953. Any program broadcasted was viewed by about 10 to 20 million households. It received high viewership, as the average number of Hallmark commercials was just 8 (against 12 in other movies) during a two hour program. The Hallmark commercials prepared for Hallmark Hall of Fame continued for 2 minutes, but highlighted an emotional story of how closely Hallmark was involved in people's lives and relationships. The series won about 56 Oscar awards and 78 Emmy awards during its presence. In 2000, it reached Australia and New Zealand and earned success there too.

Source: www.hallmark.com

---

library and subscribed to a wide variety of paper and electronic publications. Hallmarks research teams traveled widely, attended professional and creative conferences to identify trends and suggested changes to be made in the products to suit the customer tastes. Hallmark trends expert, Wesley Clough mentioned that, *"It is essential to stay close to consumers to learn what is influencing the thoughts and feelings they want to express. We look ahead so when people are comfortable expressing new ideas, attitudes and thoughts, or using new language, Hallmark already has thought of that and the right cards are on the market[2] ".*

Product Differentiation

Hallmark Cards offered e-cards, printed cards in more than 30 languages and distributed them across 100 countries. The company produced customized greeting cards for businesses and organizations through its Hallmark Business Expressions division.

Hallmark Cards introduced news cards called 'Warm Wishes' for 99 cents (for the lower end of the market). It periodically conducted research and found that consumers were in need of cards for casual situations. These cards enabled consumers to share their feelings during times such as a co-worker's birthday or neighbor's anniversary etc. The effort was supported by an advertising campaign[3] *"You Get What You Ask For"*. The campaign was successfully aired on national, as well as on local television networks, and radio. This product line increased the number of casual sending situations and was able to outpace other low priced retailers. Hallmark's market share increased by 3% as consumers thronged to their stores.

Technology

Hallmark Cards used information solutions for its retail distribution and global procurement applications. The technology was used for analyzing sales performance, retail display and customer data and determine the most profitable mix. The adaptation of information solutions and technology enabled Hallmark Cards to reduce time between product development and merchandising, in-store testing. It also helped the company in evaluation of promotional programs, planning for individual stores and improved inventory control. Hallmark planned to incorporate such technologies in the future for financial reporting, retail point-of-sale, retailer and sales productivity analysis.

Distribution Channel

Out of the 43,000 retail outlets about 1,600 were specialty stores, 4,000 Gold Crown Stores and about 30,000 were mass merchandise retailers (which included discount, food and drug stores) (Exhibit 2).

In 2005, UNICEF decided to sell greeting cards[4] for children through the nationwide Hallmark[5] Gold Crown Stores. President of the US Funds, mentioned, *"Greeting cards are one of UNICEF's greatest assets, beloved by generations of Americans. Through Hallmark's capabilities, the cards will be available nationally starting in June 2006, every day of the year, helping us to protect and enhance the lives of many more children[6] ."*

Brand Image

Hallmark Cards had three different brands of social expression products; Hallmark, Expressions from Hallmark and Ambassador (Exhibit 3). J.C Hall, without any formal educational qualification gave prime importance to the brand image and realized that consumers would like to know the source of a card before sending them to their near and dear ones. Hence he printed the name of Hallmark on the back of his cards, which gave a promise of quality.

The symbol and logo of Hallmark itself pronounced quality. 9 out of 10 consumers were aware of the Hallmark greeting cards and 4 out of 10[7] consumers could recall the crown of the Hallmark logo according a study.

Exhibit 2   Hallmark Gold Crown Stores

These stores projected the excellence in specialty sore retailing. These type of stores were preferred by the consumer who valued a warm, inviting atmosphere, expected a higher level of customer service and preferred an extensive selection of greeting cards, gifts and other social expression products. It was positioned as a premiere channel of distribution for Hallmark branded products. More than 4,000 stores were established nationwide. The advantages that consumers availed from these stores were:

- The broadest selection of Hallmark branded and other social expression products in retail marketplace.
- Convenient and unique in-store services.
- The Hallmark Gold Crown Card consumer loyalty program.
- Hallmark Gold Crown exclusive products.

The store format was:

- The floor space of around 4,000 and 6,000 square feet.
- Stores within regional shopping malls, strip centers.
- Freestanding stores in power centers anchored by-major mass merchants.
- Offered more than 18,000 products.
- Featured the Hallmark brand on 60% of products, including Hallmark Gold Crown exclusive items.
- Privately owned and operated.
- Offered in-store services such as, postage stamps, a consistent returns and exchange policy and four payment methods (cash, personal cheque, MasterCard or Visa)

Store owners had licensing agreements to sell Hallmark branded products and to display the Hallmark name.

Source: www.hallmark.com

In 1997, Hallmark Cards launched a new brand of cards called *Expressions* which was intended to leverage Hallmark's reputation for quality. They were available in 9,500 mass channel stores, including major discount stores and supermarkets.

Greeting Cards in the US

About 100,000 retail outlets in the US sold approximately 7 billion greeting cards every year[8] . Since 1993, the number of people in the US purchasing greeting cards increased by 6%. The number of greeting publishers increased from 100 in 1941 to 3,000 in 2005 in the industry which was valued at US $10.3 billion[9] (with a growth rate of 3.9% from 2002). The industry grew consistently through 1980s and 1990s, but the growth rate decreased after 9/11 incident (Box I).

Box I   Industry Revenue Growth

Year	Historical Growth	Year	Forecasted Growth
1999	0.00%	2004	8.20%
2000	4.10%	2005	5.80%
2001	−1.90%	2006	5.90%
2002	−3.50%	2007	5.20%
2003	3.40%	2008	5.20%

Source: www.forbes.com

Since competition was intense the players had to invest in research to develop innovative products for consumers. Besides Hallmark Cards, the other major player in the industry was American Greetings Corporation who held a market share of 35%. Apart from these two grants there were about 2,000 niche players in the market.

Cardsmart Retail Corp.[10] a value priced greeting card retailer sold cards and other gift products at 50% discount. It opened 44 stores in 2003, 50 stores in 2004 and about 70 to 75 stores in 2005.

According to the analysts, 64% of Americans preferred to receive greeting cards made of paper rather than email and text messaging. Analysts also mentioned that there was a significant change in the purchasing behavior of consumers. Most of them now preferred to buy greeting cards and gifts at the drugstores, supermarkets and discount stores, for convenience and one-stop shopping pleasure.

Consumer's sensitivity to price was also increasing as they were ready to pay more for the wrapping paper along with the card. They were ready to pay $5 for the card and wrapping extras easily.

Over the last 10 years sales of paper greeting cards were flat, but the Greeting Card Association did not attribute the flat sales to online cards. According to a research study 80% of adult Americans purchased greeting cards in 2004. Of which about 78% purchased about 10 greeting cards.[11]

Niche Players

The Covina, California based DaySpring Cards was founded (1971) by four Christians to spread the message of Christ through the printed word. As time passed, they offered cards for other occasions with a tag line *"When You Want to Share Your Heart and God's Love"*. For about 8 years, the company experienced good growth and response from within the Christian publishing industry. In 1979, they shifted to Arkansas and built their plant and started selling Christian books and footages. DaySpring grew fast with new employees and new buildings being added. In 1987, they formed a partnership with David C Cook Publishing Company and became a wholly owned division of Cook Communications Ministries. In 1997, they acquired Personal Expressions from Warner Press. In 1999, it was acquired by Hallmark Cards Inc. from Cook Communications. During this period DaySpring offered more than 6,000 products each year that reached about 850 million people.

In 2004, a graphic designer dissatisfied with the cards available in the market began producing greeting cards for college-aged people. The cards were written in language that had in-built humor, with messages such as "Weird Foreign Guy", "Horrorscope", "Sorry Cards" and so on.

In 2005, an entrepreneur Aki Tymes started his firm Pointe Five Group[12], hired local artists and photographers to provide the artwork and manufactured cards for prison inmates. The card illustrated a black bearded man with arms tied up, wearing a black skullcap, holding a phone to his ear and sitting behind a pane of glass. The message inside the card was, "I'll be glad when this isn't between us".

Another player Secret Lovers introduced cards for men and women (who cheated on their spouse) with the messages, *"In the precious moments that we spend together, we enjoy our love"* and *"The challenge is our time apart"*. The cards were sold through their website and had a national market.

Commenting on the emerging niche players, a spokeswoman for the Greeting Card Association in Washington mentioned, *"There's no question card companies are looking for smaller niches in the industry. And, increasingly many smaller companies are filling these roles".*

Entertainment Business

In 1991, Hallmark Cards entered the family entertainment business as a part of its overall corporate strategy. In 1994, it acquired RHI Entertainment Inc.[13] and formed Hallmark Entertainment Inc. In 1995, the company expanded its business with the formation of Crown Media Inc. and launched its first pay television channel, the Hallmark Entertainment Network, in Belgium, The Netherlands and Luxembourg.

Hallmark Channel

The Hallmark Channel was a 24 hour basic cable television network specializing in series and movies which were broadcasted in over 100 countries. It had a national audience of over 71 million subscribers. The program service was distributed through more than 5,200 cable systems and communities as well as direct-to-home satellite services across the country. The Channel was owned by Crown Media Holdings (Hallmark Entertainment held 84% share) which was earlier known as the Faith and Values Channel and broadcasted religious and secular programs. In 1998, Hallmark Entertainment purchased a majority stake and the channel was renamed in 2001, as the Hallmark Channel.[14] It broadcasted made-for-television movies and 14 miniseries under the title Hallmark Hall of Frame[15] Though Hallmark Channel featured mostly religious programs, it also included inoffensive movies and miniseries that were aimed to be viewed by the family together.

Hallmark Channel grew rapidly after its launch in 2001 and was ranked high among all cable networks within five years (Exhibit 3). David Evans, CEO Hallmark Channel mentioned that *"Since its launch just four years ago, Hallmark Channel has experienced tremendous growth in all of its key business areas, including distribution, ratings and revenues. Today, Hallmark Channel is one of the top ten rated cable channels in both total day and prime time with nearly 70 million subscribers and is well positioned for continued success[16] ".*

Hallmark Channel ended 2005, with its best ratings scorecard ever. The channel was consistently ranked among the Top 10 ad supported cable networks in both Prime Time and Total Day household services. An Executive Vice President mentioned that *"This remarkable ratings performance is the result of the channel's ongoing original programming appropriate for audiences of all ages[17] ".*

Exhibit 3	Highlights of Hallmark Channel Ratings for the Year 2005

- 0.7 Total Day HH rating ranks network No. 9 among all ad supported cable.
- Total Day HH ratings up +34%, ranking No .7 in growth.
- Total Day A18–49 delivery scared +36%, ranking No. 5 in growth.
- Total Day A25–54 delivery improved +28%, ranking No. 7 in growth.
- Prime Time HH ratings jumped +34%, ranking No. 9 in growth.
- Prime Time A18–49 delivery rose +28%, ranking No. 9 in growth.

Source: www.hallmark.com

Exiting the Entertainment Business

In 2005, Crown Media Holdings Inc. sold the Hallmark Channel's international business for $242[18] million to an investor group in the UK. The deal included the international distribution network comprising of 152 countries, 60 million subscribers, international rights to more than 580 titles in the Crown Media library and a state-of-the-art broadcast facility in Denver.

Crown Media felt that they would not be able to thrive as an independent cable network operator without the support of a major media company as other competitors were well equipped with assets of cable networks, broadcasting networks, TV and radio stations and other media. Evans, mentioned, *"After considering various factors, including the strong performance of the Hallmark Channel and the prevailing current economic realities of being a one channel business in our industry, the Board unanimously determined that now is the time to look at all alternatives."*[19]

The Channel had growing viewership due to its family-friendly and female dominated programs broadcast on it. During the third quarter of 2005, the number of viewers increased by 28%. The viewership in the age group of 18–49[20] and 25–54 increased by 38% and 28% respectively. Yet it had a poor financial record (Exhibit 4).

Entering Lifestyle Magazine

Hallmark planned to launch a lifestyle magazine by September/October, 2006 using its own publishing operations. The magazine was to be positioned in the women's lifestyle category, having a distinctive editorial point of view around home, food, decorating, entertainment, relationships and self. The magazine would be competing with some leading lifestyle magazines such as *Cosmopolitan* and others (Exhibit 5). The public relations director of Hallmark mentioned that *"We're taking all the things we learned from our test issues and trying to put together the best book possible. It's just a logical extension of the Hallmark brand. We feel that there is a need out there for a different type of women's consumer lifestyle publication."*[21]

Hallmark published three test issues (focused on subjects like relationships, home, crafts and food) in 2003 and 2004. The magazines were published in association with Time Inc. which helped Hallmark in the creation of editorial content and worked along with the creative staff of Hallmark. In the first test issue Hallmark distributed about 100,000[22] copies of magazines in May/June 2003. Hallmark planned for distribution of 380,000 copies of the magazines through retail outlets and its Hallmark Gold Crown stores.

Exhibit 4   Hallmark Channel Income Statement

	(All figures in $Millions)				
	FY End	FY End	FY End	FY End	FY End
	04-Dec	03-Dec	02-Dec	01-Dec	00-Dec
Revenue	241	208	161	107	67
Cost of Sales	378	222	275	189	91
Gross Profit	−137	−15	−114	−82	−24
Operating Expenses					
Selling, General & Administrative	102	86	109	110	68
Operating Profit Before Depreciation & Amortization	−239	−101	−223	−192	−91
Depreciation & Amortization	9	10	11	29	14
Operating Income after D & A	−248	−111	−234	−221	−106
Other Income (net)	0	−38	−54	−2	−9
Interest Expense	67	70	23	10	0
Pre-Tax Income (EBT)	−315	−219	−311	−233	−114
Net Income from Total Operations	−317	−222	−313	−230	−116
Total Net Income	**−317**	**−205**	**−313**	**−230**	**−116**
Preferred Stock Dividends	0	0	25.5	1.4	0
Net Income available for Common Shareholders	−317	−205	−339	−231	−116
Dividends Paid/Share	0	0	0	0	0

Source: www.corporate-ir.net

Exhibit 5   Leading 20 Women's Magazines in the US

Sr. No.	Name of Magazine	Brief Profile of Magazine
1	Cosmopolitan	Since its inception in 1886, it has been famous for its upbeat style, focus on the young career woman and candid discussion of contemporary male/female relationships.
2	Tear Sheet	It focused on the modeling and fashion industry and was preferred by models, photographers, designers, stylists, makeup artists, and hairdressers and those who had thrill of the industry.
3	Seventeen	It was the favorite magazine preferred by teenage girls as it focused on style, friends, guys, college, careers, the stars and love. The magazine provided hot tips on beauty, fashion, fitness, and relationships. Each issue comprised of exciting features including fiction, quizzes, music, video, trends and more.
4	Bitch	The magazine was devoted to in depth information on media. The magazine featured critiques of TV, movies, magazines, advertising, and interviews with and profiles of cool, smart women in all areas of pop culture.
5	In Style	It gave information on film celebrities, their inclination of beauty, fashion etc.
6	Shape	The magazine focused on health aspects of women's lifestyle.
7	Fitness	The magazine covered aspects of total well-being, mind, body & spirit along with the expert's advice on fitness, beauty, relationships, health, diet and nutrition.
8	People	A weekly publication that provided latest celebrity, personalities and popular culture news. It was well known for its kind credible Hollywood gossip.
9	Vanity Fair	It was addressed to the readers who were interested in contemporary society and culture. It included the news on top popular culture faces, places, issues and disgraces. With extraordinary journalism and photography, exceptional personalities were profiled by the best writers and photographers.
10	Jane	It reflected the lives and tastes of a generation that grew up on MTV and was accustomed to starting trends rather than following them. It was a magazine for new generation of confident, media-savvy women (aged 18-34) which covered topics as entertainment, fashion, beauty, fiction, food, pop culture, politics, travel, sex and computers.
11	Allure	Every issue of it consisted of celebrity tips and secrets on beauty, health and fashion. Editors picked their favorite new products and read what new styles suited to different people.
12	Honey	Honey was a preeminent magazine for the style conscious 18-to 34-year-old woman.
13	Glamour	It gave the best hair and beauty tips, fashion do's and don'ts, answered to relationship questions, with monthly horoscopes and important health and diet news.
14	Marie Claire	It explored the passions and events that shape and intrigue modern women. It updated the women on all latest developments in the arena of lifestyle.
15	A woman's view	It gave all information on beauty, health, fashion and women entrepreneurial activities carried out across the world.
16	Health	More than just magazine it reflected women's lives and addressed the issues and concerns that influenced their overall sense of well-being.
17	Prevention	It focused on healthy living, with practical tips on weight loss, nutritional exercise, prevent illness and the latest medical breakthroughs.
18	Redbook	It addressed fashion, beauty, health, and entertainment news and included an in-depth interview of a celebrity in each of its issue.
19	National Enquirer	The National Enquirer featured exclusive, in-depth coverage and photos of late breaking news and events. Each issue covered stars, famous personalities and human interest stories and medical breakthroughs.
20	Bridal Guide	Bridal Guide was a bimonthly magazine for the women who were to get married soon. It was equipped with all the information such as wedding fashions, decorating, etiquette, relationships, marriage, sex, health, travel, home design honeymoon and travel needed to ensure a beautiful, memorable wedding day.

Source: www.allyoucanread.com

The Road Ahead

After attaining the leadership position in greeting cards and a reasonable success in the entertainment businesses, Hallmark felt very confident with its new magazine venture. An analyst mentioned that *"Over the years, people have come to trust Hallmark to help them express themselves. Through Hallmark magazine, women will begin to see a new face of Hallmark but one they can continue to trust for insight into relationships, emotional connections and expressions of caring."*[23]

An experienced print and media services consultant mentioned that *"The Hallmark brand is a terrific one but that Hallmark magazine will need a unique voice to survive in the densely packed women's lifestyle category. As strong as the brand is, the editorial they seem to be pursuing doesn't sound as if its particularly new or different."*[24]

Would Hallmark Cards be able to succeed in its lifestyle new venture as it did in greeting cards or would it repeat its misadventure in the entertainment business?

References

1. www.hallmark.com.
2. "Greeting card marketers and retailers struggle," www.merchandisegroup.com, October 14, 2005.
3. "Hallmark Channel for sale," www.thestreet.com, August 18, 2005.
4. "Crown will sell Hallmark Channel's international operations," www.kansascity.bizjournals.com, February, 23, 2005.
5. Abbey Klaassen, "Hallmark bails out of branded entertainment," www.erma.org, October 5, 2005.
6. "Time publishes holiday issue of Hallmark magazine," www.kansascity.bizjournals.com, November 4, 2003.
7. "Hallmark Cards to launch magazine," www.mynameiskate.ca, February 16, 2006.
8. www.allyoucanread.com.
9. www.magazine.org.

Notes

1. The logo was created by a consultant to Hallmark and staff artists. The logo consisting of a distinctive five-point crown and Hallmark signature type. It became a registered trademark in 1950.
2. "Trends and countertrends for 2006 and beyond," www.pressroom.hallmark.com, March 2006.
3. www.fleishman.com.
4. UNICEF raised funds from the sale of greeting cards since 1949. By the end of 2005, it had sold over 4 billion cards.
5. "UNICEF announces pioneering alliance with Hallmark to market greeting cards," www.hallmark.com, 7 November, 2005.
6. www.hallmark.com
7. Research conducted by Hallmark Cards.
8. www.forbes.com.
9. "Greeting card marketers and retailers struggle," www.merchandisegroup.com, October 14, 2005.
10. The chain was owned by Rhode Island–based Paramount Cards.
11. Op cit., "Greeting Card Marketers and Retailers Struggle."
12. Alan Bastable, "Finding the perfect card for your favorite prisoner," www.jrscms.jm.columbia.edu, December 13, 2005.
13. It was an independent producer of movies-of-the-week and miniseries in the US and owned an extensive production library containing more than 1,800 hours of widely appealing programming, including Laurel & Hardy and The Little Rascals.
14. A miniseries in a serial storytelling medium is a production that tells a story in a limited number of episodes.
15. Hallmark Hall of Fame was the longest-running and most honored anthology program in the history of American television.

16. "Hallmark Channel for Sale," www.thestreet.com, August 18, 2005.
17. Annual reports.
18. "Crown will sell Hallmark Channel's international operations," www.kansascity.bizjournals.com, February 23, 2005.
19. Wayne Friedman, "Hallmark Channel no longer in the cards, Crown to greet bidders," www.publications.mediapost.com, August 19, 2005.
20. Abbey Klaassen, "Hallmark bails out of branded entertainment," www.erma.org, October 5, 2005.
21. www.hallmark.com.
22. "Time publishes holiday issue of Hallmark magazine," www.kansascity.bizjournals.com, November 4, 2003.
23. "Hallmark magazine prepares for national launch," www.pressroom.hallmark.com, March 2006.
24. "Hallmark Cards to launch magazine," www.mynameiskate.ca, February 16, 2006.

Annexure 1   Hallmark Brand Essence Statement

Enriching Lives

Hallmark is here
to help people
define and express
the very best in themselves,
to serve their spirit of kindness,
their need to comfort and to heal,
to love and be loved,
to laugh and to celebrate,
to reach out and to remember.

We are here
to offer gifts of thoughtfulness,
messages of care,
moments of beauty created to heighten
the pleasure of giving, the thrill of receiving
and the joy of sharing.

We are here
to commemorate the smallest events
and the largest milestones,
to affirm our respect for humanity,
our belief in its future
and our unwavering reverence
for the sweetness and fullness of life.

We are here
to make connections
with timely humor and timeless inspiration,
with gentle affection and genuine surprise,
with light and music and color,
with stirring images
and powerful stories
that speak to what is universal
in the human heart.

We are here
to enhance relationships,
to enrich lives,
to play our unique
and cherished role
in the always changing,
never changing seasons
of friendship and family and love.

Source: www.hallmark.com

Annexure 2 Popularity of Reading Amongst the US Population		
	1995	**2004**
Reading	28%	35%
Watching TV	25	21
Going to Movies	8	10
Computer Activities	2	7
Listening to Music	5	6

Source: www.magazine.org

Annexure 3   New Magazine Launches By Category, 2004

Metro/Regional/State	57	TV/Radio/Communications/ Electronics	11	Sex	5
Crafts/Games/ Hobbies/Models	49	Pop Culture	10	Travel	5
Automotive	25	Computers	9	Bridal	4
Sports	23	Entertainment/Performing Arts	9	Media Personalities	4
Epicurean	22	Motorcycles	9	Teen	4
Fashion/Beauty/Grooming	20	Arts/Antiques	7	Children's	3
Home Service/Home	20	Boating/Yachting	6	Comics/Comic Technique	3
Black/Ethnic	18	Dressmaking/Needlework	6	Gay/Lesbian	3
Special Interest	18	Men's	6	Science/Technology	3
Music	16	Camping/Outdoor Recreation	5	Babies	2
Business/Finance	14	Fishing/Hunting	5	Gaming	2
Fitness	14	Literary Reviews/Writing	5	Horses/Riding/Breeding	2
Women's	13	Military/Naval	5	Mystery/Science Fiction	2
Health	12	Photography	5	Dogs/Pets	1
Political/Social Topics	12	Religious/Denominational	5	Nature/Ecology	1
				TOTAL	**480**

Source: www.magazine.org

Annexure 4   Cost of Magazines, 1994–2004

Year	Average Single Copy Price	Average 1-Year Basic Subscription Price
1994	2.81	28.51
1995	2.93	29.42
1996	3.06	29.44
1997	3.22	28.60
1998	3.33	25.38
1999	3.44	24.83
2000	3.83	24.41
2001	3.88	25.30
2002	4.11	25.70
2003	4.22	26.55
2004	$4.40	$25.93

Source: www.magazine.org

Annexure 5   Sales of Magazines by Different Channels

Supermarkets	41.5%	38.3%
Mass Merchandisers	10.7	16.6
Bookstores	5.7	11.4
Drugstores	7.9	10.3
Terminals	4.9	6.0
Convenience Stores	15.3	7.4
Newsstands and Miscellaneous	14.0	10.0
TOTAL	**100%**	**100%**

Source: www.magazine.org

Annexure 6   Consumer Perception

Consumers usually trust and believe advertising in:

43%	Magazines
32%	Network TV
15%	Cable TV
10%	Internet

Source: www.magazine.org

Case 3–7: Cooper Industries' Corporate Strategy (A)*

"The business of Cooper is value-added manufacturing."

—**Cooper Industries' management philosophy**

"Manufacturing may not be glamorous, but we know a lot about it."

—**Robert Cizik, Chairman, President and CEO**

Cooper Industries, a company more than 150 years old, spent most of its history as a small but reputable maker of engines and compressors to propel natural gas through pipelines. In the 1960s, the firm's leaders decided to expand the company to lessen its dependence on the capital expenditures of the cyclical natural gas business. During the next 30 years, the company acquired more than 60 manufacturing companies that dramatically increased the size and scope of Cooper Industries (Exhibits 1 and 2). Through a process that both insiders and outsiders called "Cooperization," the company welded a group of "independent, over-the-hill companies into a highly efficient, profitable, competitive business."[1]

By 1988, the diversified industrial products company derived $4.3 billion in annual revenues from manufacturing 2 million items. Cooper's products ranged from 10¢ fuses to $3 million turbine compressor sets marketed under an array of brand names, the most famous of which was Crescent wrenches. "We decided a long time ago," said Robert Cizik, chairman, president, and CEO, "then we could do an outstanding job at the unglamorous part by making necessary products of exceptional quality, be successful indeed."[2]

In early 1989, Cooper Industries tested this philosophy when it launched a $21-a-share, $825 million tender offer for Champion Spark Plug. The Cooper bid trumped a

* Research Associate Toby Stuart prepared this case under the supervision of Professor David Collis as the basis for class discussion rather than to illustrate either effective or ineffective handling of an administrative situation.

Copyright © 1995 by the President and Fellows of Harvard College. To order copies or request permission to reproduce materials, call 1-800-545-7685 or write Harvard Business School Publishing, Boston, MA 02163. No part of this publication may be reproduced, stored in a retrieval system, used in a spreadsheet, or transmitted in any form or by any means—electronic, mechanical, photocopying, recording, or otherwise—without the permission of Harvard Business School. Reprinted by permission of Harvard School Press.

$17.50-a-share bid by Dana Corp., a $4.9 billion auto-parts manufacturer. Although Champion had a well-known brand name and worldwide manufacturing facilities, it faced a shrinking market for spark plugs as the auto industry shifted to smaller engines. In response to the declining market, Champion's aggressive attempts to diversify into other automotive product lines had failed, and 1988 profits had fallen to $24 million. At 25 times 1988 EBIT, Cooper's bid was highly risky.

Company History

In 1833, Charles and Elias Cooper built an iron foundry in Mount Vernon, Ohio. C&E Cooper evolved in stride with the Industrial Revolution, making first a steam powered Corliss Engine that generated power for manufacturing plants and then switching by 1900 to produce natural gas compressors, which pumped gas through pipeline networks to customers. By 1920, Cooper was the recognized leader in pipeline compression equipment. However, another company, Bessemer, manufactured the engines that initially extracted the gas from underground wells. The compatibility of these two companies led to a merger that Cooper initiated in 1929.

By the late 1950s, Cooper-Bessemer was still a small company with about $50 million in annual sales. However, it had developed production expertise and had built a reputation for customer service in the natural gas industry. In 1957, the company elected 38-year-old Gene Miller as president. Miller, an engineer, was also only the second president outside the strong chain of Cooper family influence to lead the company.

In 1958, Cooper suffered a cyclical downturn, during which a corporate raider acquired enough Cooper shares to elect two board members. This experience had a profound impact on Miller, convincing him of the need to diversify. Said Miller, convincing him of the need to diversify, Said Miller, "We shouldn't dare limit ourselves to

Exhibit 1   Cooper Industries' Acquisitions

Year	Business	Description
1963	Ajax Iron Works	Engines and compressors
1964	Pennsylvania Pump & Compressor Co.	Process compressors
1966	Ken-Tool Manufacturing Co.	Tire changing tools
1967	Lufkin Rule Co.	Measuring tapes and wooden rules
1968	Crescent Niagara Corp.	Wrenches, pliers and screwdrivers
1970	Weller Electric Corp.	Electric soldering tools
1970	Dallas Airmotive, Inc.	Aircraft engine overhaul and service
1971	Howard Industries' Micro Grinder line	Motor-driven hobby tools
1972	Nicholson File Co.	Hand files
1973	Southwest Airmotive Co	Aircraft engine overhaul and service
1973	Xcelite Inc.	Screwdrivers, nutdrivers and pliers
1973	Nordberg Engine & Parts Services	Engine parts and services
1975	Standard Aircraft Equipment, Inc.	Aircraft engine overhaul and service
1976	J. Wiss & Sons Co.	Scissors, shears and snips
1978	Dallas Fixed Base Operations	Aircraft engine overhaul and service
1979	*Gardner-Denver Co.	Petroleum drilling and mining equipment
1980	Pinking Shears Corp. Product Line	Pinking shears
1980	Cannon Manufacturing Corp.	Ball valves
1980	McDonough's Plumb tool line	Hammers, axes and hatchets
1981	*Crouse-Hinds	Electrical distribution products, traffic control equipment, lighting fixtures, and electronic wire and cable
1981	*Kirsch Co.	Drapery, hardware and window coverings
1981	Pfaff & Kendall, and Hilldale Co.	Light poles
1982	Sullair Mining Equipment Corp.	Mining equipment
1982	Escadril Pump Product Line	Hydraulic pumps
1982	Westinghouse's Lighting Products	Lighting fixtures
1982	G.E.'s One-Piece Terminal Board Line	Terminal boards
1984	Risdon Corporation	Specialty wire products
1984	Turner Industries, Inc.	Portable propane torches
1984	Phalo's Computer Cable Line	Electronic cable
1985	*McGraw–Edison Co.	Electrical power distribution equipment, lighting fixtures, and auto products
1985	OPI, Inc	Well service pumps
1985	The Breneman Co.	Roller shades
1987	H.K. Porter, Inc.	Bolt cutters
1987	*Joy Petroleum Equipment and Products	Pumps and compressors
1987	Underwriter's Safety Device Division	Fuseholders
1987	Joy Molded Rubber Products	Electrical connectors
1987	*Joy Industrial Compressor Group	Air and gas compressors
1988	Wiltshire File Pty. Ltd.	Hand files
1988	*Beswick Division	Power and electronic fuses
1988	B.C. Richards & Co. Pty.	Valves
1988	Macey Mining Services Pty. Ltd.	Electrical connectors
1988	*RTE Corp.	Electrical power distribution equipment
1988	Enterprise Engine Aftermarket Business	Engine repair parts

*Indicates transaction price in excess of $50 million.

being engine builders, with perhaps a few sidelines to get us over the rough spots. We had to work toward a radical change in our outlook."[3] Miller planned to guide Cooper through a phase of corporate growth that would put the company in a wider range of product markets.

Instrumental to Miller's strategy was growth and diversification through acquisitions.

To help him achieve these goals, Miller enlisted a leader with "current ideas" and expertise in finance. In 1961, Miller recruited Robert Cizik from Standard Oil, to

Exhibit 2   Cooper Industries' Divestitures

Year	Business	Description
1971	Lufkin Dial Indicators Line	Measuring instruments
1973	Atkins Saw Product Line	Hand and band saws
1974	Ken-Tool Division	Tire changing tools and equipment
1975	C-B Southern	Compressor packaging
1977	Wiss Garden Tool	Garden Tools
1978	Danco Division	Plastic tool accessories
1981	Rotor Tool Division	Portable air and electric tools
1981	Vanguard Studios	Decorative accessories
1981	Cooper Airmotive	Airmotive engine overhaul and service
1982	Svenska Kirsch AB	Window hardware distributor
1982	Belden Distribution	Electrical products distributor
1982	Arrow–Hart Dano	Electrical coils
1983	EDCON	Seismic services
1983	Traffic Control Products	Traffic lights and systems
1984	Cooper Electronics Division	Electronics production equipment
1984	Arrow–Hart PPS/PNS Switches	Micro switches
1984	Belden Bit–Driver	Data transmission equipment
1984	Worldsbest Industries, Inc.	Infant furniture
1985	Weller Mini-Shop	Motor-driven hobby tools
1985	Bussmann Process Automation Prod. Line	Automated plating systems
1985	Chain Link Fence Business	Vinyl coated link fence
1985	Alex Stuart Design	Office furniture
1985	Carlton Santee	Real estate development
1986	Onan, Inc.	Portable electric generators
1986	Boker Knives Product Line	Pocket knives
1986	Gardner–Denver Company Africa Pty. Ltd.	Mining equipment
1986	Gleason Reel Division	Cable reels
1986	Battery, Inc.	Storage batteries
1986	Clarke	Floor cleaning equipment
1987	McGraw–Edison Service/Controls	Electric motor services/control
1987	Nicholson Sawblade Product Line	Sawblades
1987	SPI Lighting Product Line	Indirect office lighting
1988	Hughes W-K-M Do Brazil	Valve service and repair

join Cooper as executive assistant for corporate development. Cizik, a Midwesterner, had earned a degree in accounting and economic from the University of Connecticut. After briefly working as an accountant, he joined the Air Force during the Korean War. He then entered the Harvard Business School and graduated as a Baker Scholar in 1958.

One of the first items on Miller's and Cizik's agenda was to free top managers and corporate board directors from the restraints of daily operations. To this end, Miller and Cizik formally redesigned Cooper's structure. Under the new system, a small, ten-member policy-making management team headed the company, with a number of operating division managers underneath. Each division manager was responsible for his division's operations and

profits and reported directly to President Miller. In the 1965 annual report, Miller called it a "relatively simple, yet highly flexible organizational structure."

To fortify the new structure, Miller and Cizik established clear lines of communication between the parent management team and the divisions, and among the divisions themselves. Cizik also established a uniform accounting system that included comprehensive planning and reporting techniques and capital investment procedures for each division.

In 1965, the company changed its name to Cooper Industries and, in 1967, moved its headquarters to Houston. Cooper was ready to make acquisitions, but would not diversify wildly under the assumption that professional managers can oversee any kind of business, regardless of products, markets, or manufacturing processes. Cizik articulated his opposition to conglomeration, "I believe that to exercise [management control], management must thoroughly understand the company's activities—its production process, products, and markets; the laws that relate to its various activities; and the cultures and customs of the areas in which it operates."[4] Therefore, Cooper's leaders would set limits on the degree of diversification and the timing of their acquisitions. Cooper decided to pursue only companies that exhibited stable earnings, or earnings countercyclical to the oil and gas transmission industry. To ensure consistent earnings, Cooper would focus on products that served basic needs and that were manufactured with mature production technologies. Furthermore, Cooper would seek acquisition candidates that possessed its own strongest assets: it would concentrate on high-quality manufacturing companies preferably with market-leading positions.

Diversification began in 1967 when Cooper acquired the Lufkin Rule Company. Founded in Cleveland, Ohio, in 1869, Lufkin manufactured measuring rules for the lumber industry. By the 1960s, Lufkin was a market leader in measuring tapes and rules and produced premium-quality products used mainly by architects, carpenters, and home "do-it-yourselfers." When Lufkin came up for sale in 1967, Cooper believed the company and its hand tool business offered exactly the right kind of diversification. Virtually everyone recognized and used hand tools; they were also simple products whose designs and technology changed very slowly in an evolutionary fashion. "Few products are lower tech than a hammer," Cizik once explained.[5] Most importantly, with few market fluctuations in their sales, hand tools would help Cooper level its cyclical revenues, which were so closely attached to the natural gas industry.

Lufkin also brought to Cooper its recently appointed president, Bill Rector, who envisioned building the world's best hand-tool manufacturing group. Rector proposed adding a "tool basket" group to Cooper, which would be comprised of selected, high-quality, brand leaders joined under modern management. The hand-tool industry was comprised of hundreds of small companies, many of them a century old and still under the influence of their founding families. Cizik described these businesses as "third generation companies . . . suffering from a lack of capital investment and effective management."[6] The companies, many of them unprofitable, reinvested minimally and their manufacturing operations were high cost. Additionally, most hand-tool producers had extended their product line beyond their original best-selling items to provide something for everybody. In many instances, a company's money-losing hand tools outnumbered the profitable ones. In 1967, Cooper signed Rector on as a corporate vice president and provided him with capital to develop the Tool Group.

With Lufkin in place, Cooper quickly acquired two more hand-tool companies. The first, Crescent Niagara Corporation, was one of the most recognized names in the industry and made the well-known Crescent wrench. In 1968, Cooper acquired the unprofitable Crescent Niagara from a small group that had recently bought the company from its family owners. Two years later, Cooper bought Weller Manufacturing Corporation from family owners hoping to retire. Weller, the world's leading manufacturer of soldering tools, operated throughout North and South America and in Europe and gave Cooper's Tool Group added marketing power.

While retaining their original brand names, the three companies, Lufkin, Crescent, and Weller, were folded into the new Tool Group, headed by Rector. The Tool Group revamped the manufacturing operations of the acquisitions, updating processes and equipment and consolidating plants. In some cases, Cooper completely shut down manufacturing sites in the North and opened new plants in the South. The advantages of moving to the South, explained Cizik, were not solely in lower wages or even in new facilities. The key was to "move into an atmosphere where you're able to train your people from scratch. You're not locked into the practices of 20 years ago. You go to South Carolina, and even with the high cost of training and scrappage and breakage that you may have to take for two or three years, you get to a stage where you have a skilled work force doing things without an eye toward history."[7] While implementing manufacturing changes, Cooper also concentrated production on the most profitable and popular hand tools. Tools selling at low rates and most left-handed items were eliminated. At Lufkin alone, Cooper scaled back 3,500 different measuring rules and tapes to 500. In the more drastic case of the Nicholson Company, a maker of saws, rasps, and files that Cooper acquired in 1972, the product count was streamlined from 30,000 to 3,000. Among the products eliminated was a rasp for scraping burned toast.

By 1970, the Tool Group had set up headquarters in Apex, North Carolina, on the same site where Lufkin had opened a new state-of-the-art manufacturing plant. C. Baker Cunningham, another Harvard Business School graduate who had started at Cooper's corporate planning department in 1970, joined the Tool Group in 1971 as director of finance and introduced a new computer system to manage inventories, sales, shipping, and billing for all tool products. Also at Apex, the Tool Group centralized sales and marketing of all the hand tools. As the Tool Group

Exhibit 3

expanded, it developed a small sales force by retaining only the best people from each acquisition and training them to promote all the products under the Cooper umbrella. After the first three companies had joined the Tool Group (Lufkin, Crescent, and Weller), the size of the combined sales force was smaller than Lufkin's original team. The consolidated force allowed international sales-people in a country where one brand name was particularly popular to use its leverage to sell other tools in the Tool Group (Exhibit 3).

Cooper's early experience with the Tool Group helped further define its diversification program. Cizik, who by 1969 was chief operating officer, felt that Cooper needed an approach to evaluate acquisitions within its manufacturing focus. Division managers would seek

"complementary" acquisitions, defined as logical extensions of Cooper's existing products or markets. The corporate staff, meanwhile, would pursue "diversification" acquisitions. Together these acquisitions would fulfill Cooper's basic corporate growth objective (an increase in pre-tax earnings per share at a compound rate of 11%) and would improve the "quality" of earnings by adding stability. At the same time, Cizik emphasized that the process of building Cooper Industries could involve subtraction as well. "People often think success is measured only by adding, adding, and more adding," said Cizik. "That's extremely important, but you have to keep examining what you have, and you can't be afraid to get rid of the things that have served their useful time."[8] Cooper divested 33 businesses between 1970 and 1988 (Exhibit 2).

Throughout the 1970s, "complementary" development continued in the Tool Group with four more acquisitions (Nicholson File in 1972, Xcelite nut runners in 1973, Wiss scissors in 1976, and Plumb hammers in 1980). The most important, Nicholson, was a file and saw maker based in Providence, Rhode Island, whose main asset was its expansive distribution system of independent hardware wholesalers and industrial distributors that reached 53,000 retail outlets in 137 countries. Additionally, at Apex, a quasi-R&D group tested new products and designs for all the group's acquired companies and introduced new hand-tool products under its existing brand names during the 1970s. By 1974, all of Cooper's acquisitions had relocated their manufacturing operations to new plants, mostly in the South. Shortly after, Cooper was recognized as the world's largest and most efficient manufacturer of non-powered hand tools. At this time, Cizik decided not to enter the electric power-tool industry in the face of Black & Decker's commanding market share.

Besides the complementary mergers in the Tool Group, Cooper's corporate staff orchestrated an important diversifying acquisition. In 1970, Cooper had quickly followed Lufkin with a second diversification, this time into the aircraft service business. Cooper purchased Dallas Airmotive, a company that repaired and leased jet engines and distributed aircraft parts and supplies. Cooper later supplemented this acquisition with four more air-service companies.

With the "tool basket" well underway and the aircraft service division established, in the early 1970s Cooper's corporate management team turned to the Energy Division and applied some of its hand-tool strategies there. Specifically, Cooper retrenched and concentrated its resources on compression equipment for oil and gas, where it was the industry leader. In 1976, Cooper purchased Superior, a maker of engines and natural gas compressors that filled the gap between Cooper-Bessemer's largest and smallest products. After the Superior deal, Cooper supplied 40% of the horsepower requirements for gas transmission in North America. Concurrently, it stopped producing compressors for petrochemical applications (ethylene, ammonia, nitrogen, oxygen markets, etc.), where Dresser Industries and Carrier dominated the market. This meant reducing the work force at the original Mount Vernon plant from 1,300 to 250. Cizik reasoned that supporting engineering, development, and service for the multiple applications cost too much. "We could probably have gone ahead and invested $100 million over four to five years for the latest technology. But competitors weren't going to be standing still. I thought we could come out of that and still be third or fourth in many of those lines."[9]

In 1975, in the midst of the oil embargo, Cooper elected Robert Cizik as CEO. Cooper's Energy Division benefitted greatly from the increased activity in the United States that persisted into the early 1980s, and its climbing energy income offset falling hand-tool sales during the simultaneous recession. According to Cizik's vision of a multimarket company, "not everything will be clicking at the same time." However, there will be "movement back and forth between businesses as you need them."[10] Correspondingly, Cooper rerouted the flow of capital expenditures to the energy division.

In 1979, Cooper made its biggest move to date, purchasing Dallas-based Gardner-Denver in what then qualified as one of the 10 largest mergers in U.S. history. A company equal in size to Cooper, Gardner-Denver manufactured machinery for petroleum exploration, mining, and general construction. Cizik described the merger, valued at $635 million, as a "complementary move," involving Cooper in natural gas and petroleum exploration for the first time, and thus filling out Cooper's existing Energy Division. By adding Gardner-Denver, Cooper now served a range of needs spanning exploration, production, transmission, distribution, and storage for the oil and natural gas industry, and doubled the number of employees, shareholders, and plants.

Gardner-Denver had grown rapidly in the 1960s and 1970s, but was notorious for its lack of planning and cost controls. For example, it had invested heavily in developing a blasthole drill for mining that turned out to be a "gold plated" white elephant. It was also known as the company that cut prices at just the wrong time, and its sales force, in the words of another industry player, was "looking for nothing but payday and five o'clock."[11]

After the merger, Cizik closed Gardner's Dallas headquarters and moved its corporate functions to Cooper's Houston headquarters. Cooper believed Gardner-Denver's management structure was too centralized and stifled effective decision making at the operational level. Cooper also thought that Gardner's centralized functions were overused. Cizik appraised the situation, "If you try to combine too much under one umbrella, such as consolidating sales into a corporate function, you end up with a lot of people who can't possibly cover such a huge, diverse marketplace, or know much about the plethora of products they're trying to sell."[12] Cooper trimmed Gardner's sales and administrative expenses from the pre-acquisition 16.6% of revenues to Cooper's 11.4% level. It also cut Gardner-Denver's working capital: Cizik was convinced that inventories and receivables were too high. In a review of Gardner-Denver's products, Cizik spoke about "reclaiming" what was useable. Cooper kept product lines capable of healthy development, eliminating others with little potential.

By the late 1970s, Cooper's acquisition guidelines had evolved to include an additional dimension, acquisition by necessity. When Colorado Fuel & Iron (CF&I), a specialty supplier to Lufkin, stopped production of its 1095 steel, Cooper could find only one other source in the world, a German company offering a much more expensive product. Instead, Cooper bought the CF&I equipment and moved the operations to a newly acquired plant, forming Cooper Steel.

In 1981, as Cooper was in the process of absorbing Gardner-Denver, the company engineered its third diversification (following its move into tools and aircraft service) by capitalizing on an unexpected opportunity to acquire Crouse-Hinds. An electrical products company, Crouse-Hinds had been on Cooper's wish list for years. Subject to a hostile takeover attempt, Crouse-Hinds welcomed Cooper as a white knight, and after a prolonged, acrimonious battle, it joined Cooper on friendly terms. Equal in size to the pre-merger Cooper or Gardner-Denver, Crouse-Hinds became the core of Cooper's new electrical and electronic business. It was a worldwide producer of electrical plugs and receptacles, fittings, and industrial lighting, and had just acquired Belden, a well-known manufacturer of electronic wire and cable and electrical cords. Together, Crouse-Hinds and Belden increased Cooper's revenues by 50% and gave the company a foothold in the "path of power"—the transmission, control, and distribution of electrical energy from the generating plant to the end user. Describing the acquisition, Cizik said, "This is a true diversification, compared with what I referred to as a complementary move with Gardner-Denver. In that respect it compares to our acquisitions of Lufkin and Dallas Airmotive, except on a much larger scale."[13]

Throughout the electrical industry, Crouse-Hinds was considered one of the best managed companies. Crouse-Hind's CEO, who had joined the company in 1965, stayed on at the helm after the Cooper acquisition until he retired two years later, and Cooper assigned an experienced, younger Crouse-Hinds executive to succeed him.

Many Wall Street analysts criticized this acquisition for reducing Cooper's exposure to the booming oil and gas business. New criticisms of Cooper's ability to service its increasing debt burden were also voiced in 1981 when Cooper acquired Kirsch, the world's largest manufacturer of drapery hardware. In a similar hostile takeover attempt/white knight situation, Cooper had been forced to move quickly to acquire Kirsch, a company it had been eyeing since the 1970s. In fact, Cooper's board gave first approval to purchase Kirsch on the same day that it had closed the Crouse-Hind's deal. Commenting on the action, one investment banker said, "If Cooper had its choice, it probably would have wanted to finish one deal and then work on the other, but the world doesn't wait for you."[14] Kirsch had a customer base similar to Cooper's and employed many of the same manufacturing processes.

Closing out the busy year of 1981, Cooper sold off its Airmotive Division. Cooper had built its airmotive group into a "decently profitable" unit that it divested at a net profit of $27 million. During the time it was part of Cooper, the unit balanced Cooper's revenue and income stream, but by 1981, Cizik concluded that continued operation of the group conflicted with Cooper's manufacturing-oriented corporate strategy.

Following this period of heavy activity, Cooper repeated its historical pattern of concentrating on digesting recent acquisitions. Said Cizik, "A growing company can outrun its capabilities if it isn't careful to bring up the supply lines. . . . We have to restructure ourselves at a time like this, before we feel comfortable moving out again."[15]

Electricity became Cooper's next target for complementary business-unit development as energy prices slid in the mid-1980s. As one initial skeptic later commented, "I don't know whether Cooper saw the downturn in energy coming, but it eventually proved to be a wise move to diversify and reduce exposure in that area."[16] In 1985, Cooper acquired McGraw-Edison, an electrical company that was put into play by Forstmann Little & Company, a New York firm specializing in leveraged buyouts. Before Forstmann's intentions of a McGraw-Edison buyout were made public, Cizik had approached McGraw's chairman to propose a friendly merger. Cizik, however, was rebuffed; the company was not interested in pursuing a combination. After the Forstmann-McGraw announcement at $59-a-share, Cooper tendered a $65-a-share offer for McGraw-Edison that was eventually accepted.

McGraw-Edison, a leading manufacturer of products for the control and transmission of electrical power, as well as lighting fixtures and fuses, put Cooper at the first stage of electrical power distribution with its transformers, power capacitors and other products. These connected directly, in the "path of power," to the many secondary electrical power distribution products Cooper had acquired through Crouse-Hinds (for example, circuit breakers, receptacles, and plugs). The "path of power" continued to a third level, the point of consumer use in the home or commercial area, where McGraw's recessed, emergency, and track lighting augmented Crouse-Hind's leading position in the indoor and outdoor lighting market.

Following the acquisition, Cooper retained most McGraw senior managers, but began streamlining and consolidating its operations and, in the process, spun off a number of incompatible divisions. Three years later, in 1988, Cooper complemented McGraw's transformer product line with the $324 million acquisition of RTE, a maker of transformers and a supplier of transformer components to Cooper.

At the time of the merger, RTE was fighting a hostile takeover by Mark IV Industries. The company was also suffering from capital constraints resulting from an unsuccessful acquisition program, and Cooper subsequently pumped over $50 million in capital expenditures into the RTE operations. Because of a culture clash with Cooper's "lean and mean" cost structure, many senior managers at RTE left within a year of the acquisition. Cooper consolidated McGraw's and RTE's R&D staffs in one facility and reduced the size of their combined sales force, while also limiting RTE's free-spending habits. In addition, Cooper consolidated computing functions so that RTE's mainframe could be shut down, and eliminated 30 to 40 financial and treasury positions. The RTE restructuring created over $10 million in annual savings for Cooper.

In late 1987, Cooper expanded its existing industrial compressor business with the $140 million purchase of Joy's industrial air and turbo compressor business. After the deal, Cooper eliminated duplicate product lines and suspended manufacture of unprofitable products. It also rationalized manufacturing operations, closing Joy's Indiana plant. Furthermore, Cooper consolidated the two companies' competing distribution channels. The total number of distributors serving the combined company was expected to fall from 160 to 120 over four to five years. However, Cooper would gain leverage with each remaining distributor because it would have a much greater sales volume and a wider product offering.

Cooper's Businesses in the Late 1980s

In 1988, Cooper was a broadly diversified manufacturer of electrical and general industrial products, and energy-related machinery and equipment. U.S.-based Cooper had 1988 revenues of $4.3 billion and over 46,000 employees worldwide, although 85% of sales were in North America. The company operated in 3 distinct business segments with 21 separate profit centers (Exhibit 4, 5, 6, and 7).

Electrical and Electronic. The E&E segment was Cooper's largest in 1988, generating one-half of corporate sales and 57% of operating profits. Cooper had entered this segment with the 1981 purchase of Crouse-Hinds. By 1988, E&E had four sub-segments, each representing quite diverse businesses (Exhibit 7), but all focused on the mature North American market that accounted for over 90% of segment sales.

Cooper competed in power transmission and distribution systems with its McGraw-Edison and RTE operations. About 85%–90% of power system sales were direct to utilities, where the transformers increased and reduced the voltage and channeled the power produced by a generator. Prior to their acquisition by Cooper, McGraw and RTE were roughly tied for third place in the U.S. transformer market, behind GE and Westinghouse. Following the acquisitions, however, Cooper gained a leading market position, despite other consolidations in the industry that reduced the number of major competitors from seven to three. At the consolidated level, the division used the "Cooper Power Systems" brand name because its competitors were so well-known, but each of the products maintained the McGraw or RTE brand name. Because these products were sold directly, offering a complete product line that met North American standards provided an important competitive advantage. Furthermore, Cooper's reputation for quality products helped garner sales because of the high costs associated with product failure in such vital systems.

Cooper's lighting division was composed of three formerly independent entities: Crouse-Hinds Lighting and McGraw-Edison's Halo and Metalux subsidiaries. In the mid-1980s, Cooper combined the three businesses and rationalized manufacturing facilities, adopting a focused-factory approach that allowed three underutilized plants to be closed. In 1988, Cooper was in the process of eliminating duplicate administrative functions among the companies and developing a unified market identity through consolidating sales representatives and marketing programs. Cooper also began constructing a showroom to display all of its lighting products and to train architects, designers, and lighting distributors in its full product line.

In the broad and highly fragmented lighting fixture market, Cooper was perhaps the most widely spread manufacturer, participating in fluorescent, high-intensity discharge, and incandescent fixtures. In this industry, the top eight firms had a combined 60% market share in 1988, but as the eighth firm represented only 2% of the total, the industry was characterized by a large fringe of small producers. Foreign competition was limited because the large size-to-weight ratio of lighting fixtures made transport costs prohibitive. Distributors and manufacturers tended to develop stable, long-term relationships, and, in 1988, Cooper was looking to the day when it could install

Exhibit 4   Cooper Industries' Financials ($000s)

	1988	1987	1986	1985	1984
SALES	4,258,275	3,585,785	3,433,296	3,067,169	2,029,915
Cost of sales	2,904,336	2,430,183	2,301,970	2,070,992	1,357,949
Depreciation and amortization	154,650	135,368	127,131	105,815	73,636
Selling and administrative	701,859	622,643	615,943	534,471	368,376
Interest	111,922	86,075	103,080	97,723	20,572
Total costs and expenses	3,872,767	3,274,269	3,148,124	2,809,001	1,820,533
Total operating income	385,508	311,516	285,172	258,168	209,382
Income taxes	161,102	137,705	137,450	123,088	102,518
NET INCOME	224,406	173,811	147,722	135,080	106,864
Long-term debt	1,170,267	884,351	863,615	1,158,310	156,765
Capital expenditures	128,249	100,889	109,497	115,794	68,509
Net plant and equipment	1,115,181	1,016,647	937,741	973,235	685,548
TOTAL ASSETS	4,383,976	3,800,363	3,400,032	3,635,873	1,953,698
SHAREHOLDERS' EQUITY	1,771,712	1,592,912	1,419,946	1,318,001	1,240,143
Number of employees	46,300	43,200	40,200	46,000	30,000
Return on year-end assets	5.1%	4.6%	4.3%	3.7%	5.5%
Return on year-end equity	12.7%	10.9%	10.4%	10.2%	8.6%
Earnings per share	2.20	1.73	1.52	1.39	1.06

[a] Includes gain on the sale of Dallas Airmotive.   [b] Restated to include Crouse–Hinds on a pooling of interest basis.
[c] Includes income from discontinued aircraft service operations.

Exhibit 5   Cooper Segment Financials ($000)

Electrical & Electronic	1988	1987	1986	1985	1984	1983	1982	1981	1980*
Revenues	2,077,522	1,736,446	1,699,708	1,425,463	798,310	768,174	798,440	872,127	825,726
Operating Income	307,644	264,657	259,973	225,633	126,166	105,913	90,774	109,397	95,368
Identifiable Assets	1,985,361	1,521,455	1,441,857	1,426,135	435,592	430,218	428,290	449,767	439,060
Group Return on Sales	14.8%	15.2%	15.3%	15.8%	15.8%	13.8%	11.4%	12.5%	11.5%
Group Return on Assets	15.5%	17.4%	18.0%	15.8%	29.0%	24.6%	21.2%	24.3%	21.7%

Commercial & Industrial	1988	1987	1986	1985	1984	1983	1982	1981	1980
Revenues	1,260,121	1,195,829	1,142,372	927,283	586,453	518,162	489,353	540,812	403,577
Operating Income	184,318	171,143	162,675	134,146	98,798	84,581	64,945	92,340	97,518
Identifiable Assets	1,006,904	985,528	990,512	1,020,648	495,310	447,310	446,977	479,986	346,318
Group Return on Sales	14.6%	14.3%	14.2%	14.5%	16.8%	16.3%	13.3%	17.1%	24.2%
Group Return on Assets	18.3%	17.4%	16.4%	13.1%	19.9%	18.9%	14.5%	19.2%	28.2%

Compression & Drilling	1988	1987	1986	1985	1984	1983	1982	1981	1980
Revenues	912,320	642,825	564,647	691,926	642,926	556,001	1,106,836	1,447,970	1,101,206
Operating Income	47,093	(4,529)	(21,865)	11,987	28,266	(4,872)	161,072	341,639	212,442
Identifiable Assets	1,177,758	1,131,090	826,675	937,831	928,850	974,111	1,071,732	1,193,762	1,045,832
Group Return on Sales	5.2%	−0.7%	−3.9%	1.7%	4.4%	−0.9%	14.6%	23.6%	19.3%
Group Return on Assets	4.0%	−0.4%	−2.6%	1.3%	3.0%	−0.5%	15.0%	28.6%	20.3%

*Restated to include Crouse-Hinds on a pooling of interest basis.

1983	1982	1981	1980[a]	1975	1970
1,850,280	2,393,989	2,866,031	2,335,923	478,066	225,651
1,250,359	1,642,279	1,864,738	1,555,022	346,291	164,037
67,909	63,816	56,598	46,282	9,571	4,280
363,101	401,878	429,207	356,749	54,848	29,477
28,460	44,202	56,712	50,320	7,439	3,924
1,709,829	2,152,175	2,407,255	2,008,373	418,149	201,718
140,451	241,814	458,776	327,550	59,917	23,933
69,282	106,679	217,506	156,120	28,783	11,553
71,169	135,135	284,545[b]	185,216	31,134	12,380
175,005	272,888	154,270	301,016	71,030	31,496
86,237	117,650	128,653	115,414	17,817	7,698
683,318	685,067	624,230	532,025	102,843	47,227
1,949,447	2,036,547	2,335,381	2,023,705	369,196	183,926
1,250,649	1,265,646	1,284,899	1,076,407	177,150	100,262
30,000	31,000	39,000	37,000	11,262	8,247
3.7%	6.6%	12.2%	9.2%	8.4%	6.7%
5.7%	10.7%	22.1%	17.2%	17.6%	12.3%
0.64	1.38	2.84	2.02	NA	NA

paperless ordering and invoicing of all Cooper lighting products. Cooper believed that its service level and premium-priced, market-leading products would attract distributors to offer its full product line exclusively or with only one other manufacturer's products.

In the distribution and control area, Cooper dominated the market with its Construction Materials Division (CMD), the crown-jewel of Crouse-Hinds. CMD manufactured protective electrical equipment for hazardous applications. CMD's reputation was so widespread that its products were often included in engineers' design specifications because of its reputation for superior quality.

Cooper's Belden division produced wire and cable used in the electronics industry. Although the cable business was fundamentally low-tech, Belden participated in the more sophisticated end of the product range. Cooper had invested heavily in upgrading Belden's manufacturing facilities. Sales through distributors comprised 75% of the division's revenues; the remainder came from the OEM market.

Commercial and Industrial. In the commercial and industrial segment Cooper participated in the non-powered handtool and window treatment businesses, and in the automotive aftermarket. In the Tool Group, consolidation of acquisitions was completed and new manufacturing facilities constructed by 1988, and the company held the preemi-

nent market position in most of its tool lines. Cooper's automotive division consisted of Belden's auto-related cable business and Wagner Lighting and Wagner Brakes, acquired with McGraw-Edison. These businesses serviced the automotive aftermarket, where operating through effective distribution networks was the key to accessing the myriad small car-repair outlets. After revamping its production equipment for quick changeovers, Wagner was positioned to take advantage of Cooper's experience in managing distribution-oriented businesses.

Compression, Drilling, and Energy Equipment. The compression and drilling segment had been Cooper's largest in 1981, generating over 50% of revenues and over 60% of operating profit. However, the collapse of the energy industry in the early and mid-1980s caused sales of oil and natural gas equipment to fall precipitously. By 1988, this segment accounted for 21% of Cooper sales and less than 10% of operating income.

The size and breadth of the collapse of the energy industry induced Cooper to take drastic actions. Employment in the compression and drilling segment was reduced by half, as eight plants were closed to control costs and pare down operations. However, Cooper took advantage of the depressed prices in the petroleum industry to make acquisitions that complemented existing product

Exhibit 6   Cooper
Industries Comparative
Stock Price Performance

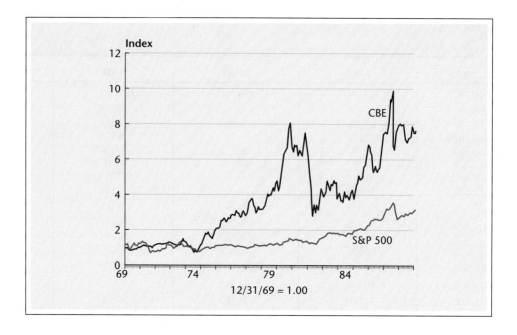

lines. The acquisition of Joy's petroleum equipment business and several smaller mergers increased Cooper's participation in flow control products. Primary competition in this area came from Cameron Iron Works and FMC, while competition for the remaining production and drilling equipment was fragmented.

In the market for natural gas compression equipment, Cooper retained its number one position with the Cooper-Bessemer, Ajax, and Superior product lines. Despite a weak market, the company was optimistic about the prospects for this equipment, as the five competitors consolidated to three.

Corporate Role

Cooper Industries held increasing shareholder value as a central corporate objective. Management had established a long-term earnings-per-share growth rate target of 5% above the rate of inflation and a return on equity objective of 12% on top of inflation, reflecting sustainable targets for a "superior" manufacturing company. Furthermore, Cooper targeted 40% as a desirable debt to total capital ratio and preferred to finance expansion with cash or convertible preferred stock. These goals were to be achieved in part through a strong corporate emphasis on cash flow; Cooper acted on the motto "cash flow is king." In particular, strong cash flow would allow Cooper to aggressively pursue its acquisition program and meet its earnings growth target. During the 1980s, internal growth generated

one-half of total corporate growth, with the other 50% arising from acquisitions. Because of Cooper's numerous acquisitions, $1.38 billion of Cooper's total $1.77 billion in stockholders' equity represented goodwill.

A number of guidelines directed Cooper's pursuit of potential acquisitions (Exhibit 8). Cooper sought companies that had stable earnings and had proven manufacturing operations using well-known technologies. Ideally, these products were mature and filled essential needs. Additionally, Cooper looked for companies that served a broad customer base. Finally, Cooper searched for firms with high-quality products that were market leaders with widely recognized brand names. Cooper reviewed about 100 potential acquisitions annually, and signed confidentiality agreements to analyze internal documents for roughly one-half of these. While in principle Cooper would divest any business at the right price, it was not transaction-driven and was unlikely to divest the cores of the company. Cooper discouraged management bids on divisional sell-offs.

In 1988, Cooper derived 16% (reaching as high as 20% during the previous decade) of its revenues from overseas operations, although almost all of its manufacturing operations were located in the United States. Each of Cooper's divisions had a global responsibility for its operations. Cizik was a strong advocate of improving manufacturing efficiency in the United States, believing that high volume, a cooperative and involved work force, and technological advantages in the U.S. were adequate to compete with overseas producers. Consequently, he believed that

Exhibit 7   Cooper Industries Segment Information

Electrical & Electronic	Primary Products	% of Revenues	Market Position	Distribution Method
Power Systems		15%		Direct Sales
RTE	Transformers		Co-Leader	
McGraw Edison	Dist Switchgear		#1	
Lighting Fixtures		12%		Distributor
Halo	Incandesent		#2 (Tied)	
Metalux	Fluorescent			
Crouse-Hinds	High Intensity			
Electronic Cables		8%		Distributor
Belden	Wire & Cable		#1	
Distribution and Control		14%		Distributor
Crouse-Hinds	Elec. Constr. Mat.		#1	
Arrow-Hart	Dist. Equip		#2	
Bussmann Beswick	Fuses	—	#1	
Subtotal		49%		
Commercial & Industrial				
Automotive Aftermarket		10%		Distributor
Wagner	Brakes		#1	
Headlights			#1 (Aftermarket)	
Tools		14%		Distributor
Campbell/Lufkin	Non-power		#1	
Nicholson/Crescent	Hand Tools			
Window Treatments		6%		Distributor
Kirsch	Drapery Hardware	—	#1	
Subtotal		30%		
Compression & Drilling				
Industrial Compressors		7%		Distributor
Gardner-Denver/Joy	Air-Compressors		#2 (Tied)	
Energy Equipment		13%		Direct Sales
Cooper Energy Services	Gas Compressors		#1	
Gardner-Denver	Drilling Equip		NA	
Demco/WKM	Valves	—	NA	
Subtotal	20%			

Source: Lovett, Mitchell, Webb & Garrison, Inc., September 20, 1989.

investing outside the U.S. was unnecessary if its sole purpose was to achieve lower manufacturing costs.

With each acquisition, Cooper tailored its structure to suit the new configuration of businesses. Management sought to weld synergistic business units under the responsibility of one individual. Therefore, when new companies were acquired, Cooper typically broke them up and combined the pieces with other Cooper divisions to minimize both product transfers between divisions as well as resources shared among business units. Breaking up newly acquired businesses also allowed Cooper to closely exam-

ine their parts. For example, when Cooper acquired Wagner Brakes with McGraw-Edison, it separated the brake operations from the automotive lighting business so that it could focus on production difficulties. Only after the problems were ameliorated through manufacturing improvements did Cooper consider reconsolidating the division.

Continuing with its original decentralized operating philosophy, Cooper exercised central control over corporate policy but delegated day-to-day operating decisions to the "semi-autonomous" operating units. Each of the three

Exhibit 8	Cooper Industries' Acquisition Guidelines for Diversification

- Seek acquisitions that exhibit stable earnings or earning patterns that are countercyclical to those we already have.
- Acquire products that serve basic and essential needs and that are derived from proven technologies, thereby contributing to the objective of operating in stable markets with predictable growth.
- Acquire manufacturing companies with products that are of high quality and that are leaders in their markets.

Cooper Industries' Guidelines for Acquired Complementary Products

- Broaden existing product lines.
- Offer opportunities for enhanced earnings through cost management.
- Enhance Cooper's strength in distribution.
- Strengthen a business unit's market position.
- Enjoy widespread brand name recognition.
- Serve a broad customer base.

Source: Cooper Industries Management Philosophy.

executive vice presidents (EVPs) were entitled to a staff of one assistant and one secretary, and division heads had no formal relationships with each other. In 1988, Cooper maintained a total corporate staff of 317 that occupied four floors of a Houston office building, and had total corporate expenses of $50 million. Politics played a negligible role at the company and decisions were made quickly. Despite Cooper's decentralized operating philosophy, however, Cizik stressed that "Cooper puts a great deal of emphasis on control—control that's achieved by working as an operating company, not a holding company. To us that means that we just don't buy and sell businesses; we're actively involved in running them. Our corporate management team participates in every policy decision made in our organization. But at the same time, day-to-day questions are answered at the operational level, and those operations are also heavily involved in determining their own future direction."[17]

Cooper's three senior vice presidents oversaw administrative, financial, and manufacturing consulting functions that were conducted at the corporate level, and they dealt directly with division managers (Exhibit 9). Each division focused primarily on operations. The CEO was removed from daily operating decisions and concentrated on developing the corporate strategy, appraising management performance, and evaluating potential acquisitions and asset dispositions.

Senior Vice President of Finance. Dewain Cross, senior VP of finance, and his department had responsibility for implementing and monitoring corporate standard accounting and control functions at all the divisions. One member of the corporate finance staff tracked each division in detail and was responsible for understanding its financial reports. Corporate finance also had an internal audit staff and a four person team of manufacturing cost systems experts who were available at the request of division management.

Following acquisitions, Cooper set up reserves to cover anticipated closing costs involved in rationalization. This ensured that division managers incurred no write-offs on their monthly profit and loss statements as they went through the rationalization process. Also, within 30 days after every acquisition, Cooper began to install its own financial and cost accounting systems on an IBM. As Cross said, "There are only two times to change a business. One is right after you buy it. The second is when it is losing a lot of money. These are the two times when there is the least resistance to change."

All divisions were required to submit Cooper's standard monthly financial report (approximately 150 line items) to corporate headquarters, but they had discretion over how to keep their internal ledgers. Cooper used direct variable cost accounting rather than a full cost absorption system. It also had a large set of internal control guidelines that each division had to follow, such as the number of people required to sign a check above a specified dollar value. Indeed, Cooper's two books of procedures were bigger than its accounting manual.

Because Cooper was extremely cash-conscious, the austerity of Cooper's financial control systems often collided with the systems in place under previous managers. This meant that incumbent managers often left following a Cooper acquisition because they were unable to adjust to the new culture. Cooper tightly controlled working capital and charged divisions interest for its use, although there were no corporate overhead charges or charges for corporate services to divisions. The finance department had central control over treasury and taxation functions so that all divisions effectively maintained a zero-dollar balance in their accounts.

Cross also set guidelines for developing the business unit strategies that each of the 21 Cooper divisions prepared every 3 years. Cooper's strategic planning approach was bottom-up: Each profit center developed its own plan under the guidance of its EVP, assisted by Cross's corporate planning and development group, comprised of a staff of seven MBAs. Headquarters was, however, actively involved in strategic planning and all plans had to be pre-

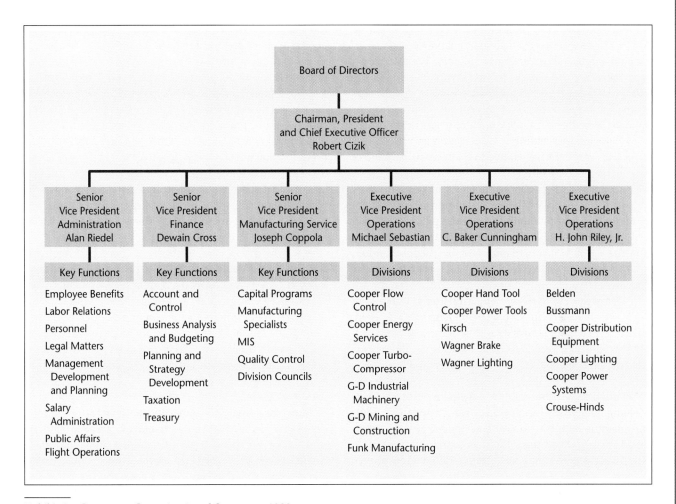

Exhibit 9   Corporate Organizational Structure, 1988.

sented to and accepted by Cizik and the corporate staff, often after many suggestions and improvements. Cooper only occasionally used outside consultants. In any given year, 7 of the 21 divisions prepared a plan, with new acquisitions formulating their first strategic plan in the year following their acquisition. These comprehensive analyses identified the market, projected market demand, presented an industry overview, and identified types of companies viewed to be desirable acquisition candidates. Separate strategies were developed for each major product line within a division. They elucidated the business unit's view of the competitive situation and outlined strategic options and reasons for the strategies chosen.

Cross, along with the appropriate EVP, also reviewed the annual budget for each division. The annual budgeting process enabled the corporate officers and division managers to agree on short-term performance objectives for each division.

Senior Vice President of Administration.   Attorney Alan Riedel, Cooper's Sr. VP of administration, was the only director inside Cooper besides Cizik. Riedel had as his foremost responsibilities managing the company's legal affairs and establishing and administering personnel policy and benefits programs. He also handled labor relations, shareholder and public relations, and environmental matters, and oversaw the management development and planning (MD&P) program. Cooper maintained a uniform pay scale based on the Hay System. Base salaries throughout the company were similar for employees of corresponding ranks in different divisions, and all were competitive with industry standards. However, bonuses often reached 20%–40% of base salaries, and were discretionary; division managers had a bonus pool determined by Corporate Administration that could be awarded largely at their and the EVP's discretion. In addition to salary and bonuses, key managers were granted stock options. With each new acquisition, Riedel's office gradually adjusted pay scales at the acquired division up or down until they reached Cooper's targeted level, with the adjustments taking three to five years. Typically, however, these adjustments were small as pay scales in the industries Cooper participated in tended to be homogeneous. Cooper also required all acquisitions to adopt its standard benefits package for medical insurance and pensions, which could lead to dissatisfaction because it was sometimes conservative relative to the benefits package of the premerger company.

Cooper handled labor relations at the corporate level. Half of Cooper's plants were non-union; the company maintained a strong union-avoidance policy. Contract renewal and National Labor Relations Board matters were handled by the labor relations staff. Riedel handled antitrust matters, an area particularly important because of Cooper's active acquisition program.

Management Development & Planning, initiated in 1970, was integral to Cooper's management system. MD&P evaluated organizational effectiveness and individual strengths and weaknesses by focusing on the performance of key managers. Under the program, about 800 division and corporate executives and managers developed qualitative professional development or project-related goals for the forthcoming year. Quantitative goals often reinforced business unit objectives that were established through the annual budgeting and strategic planning processes. At the end of the year, each employee prepared a progress review worksheet that compared achieved to targeted objectives. Additionally, employees in the program were reviewed by their supervisors. For example, as CEO, Cizik met annually with each executive vice president to review his personal progress, the managerial capabilities in his segment, and the detail of necessary future improvements. The objectives for the EVP in the upcoming year, mutually determined at that meeting, became, in Riedel's words, "the road map for action items that are to occur during the year." Similarly, each EVP conducted annual reviews of all of the managers in the division he supervised. While review results were not formally tied to incentive compensation, managers with poor reviews were unlikely to receive substantial bonuses.

Each EVP and Sr. VP fully embraced MD&P, even though it was extremely time consuming. Cizik noted that "everybody hates the MD&P because it is so much work, but when it is done everyone loves it." The program uncovered existing or potential management gaps and identified people worthy of promotion: it was the method that Cooper used to determine management succession. In addition, the program distinguished candidates for interdivisional transfers, which generally occurred at the higher echelons of the organization; 24 such transfers were made in 1988. Cooper preferred to bring in one of its own people as general manager or controller of a new division, and typically had many personnel requirements in the finance and plant manager areas following an acquisition. MD&P developed an internal pool of people in these areas that could be moved around, but a lack of a sufficient number of such people was often the constraint on further acquisitions. Internal transfers were less frequent in the marketing and sales areas where experience was believed to be business specific. Also, MD&P identified managers who would benefit from corporate-developed management training programs, with courses such as "finance for non-financial managers."

Senior Vice President of Manufacturing Services. In 1975, Robert Cizik formed a corporate-level Manufacturing Services Group, chartered to institute manufacturing improvements throughout the company's operating divisions. Cizik felt that "the problem with U.S. manufacturing [was] manufacturing itself." He promoted Joe Coppola, an operating manager with an engineering background, to lead the new manufacturing group.

In 1988, the Manufacturing Services Group consisted of 14 professionals, all with 10 to 15 years of operations experience, and had an operating budget of $1.8 million. Its staff included experts in facilities, automation, and environmental engineering, and in materials management, quality control, and management information systems. The Group had four major objectives: to promote major manufacturing improvements to reach the point of "best value delivered" for the products in each segment; to administer the $200 million 1988 capital expenditure budget; to operate interdivisional councils focused on such aspects of operations as quality control; and, with Riedel's personnel department, to run a manufacturing training program for recent engineering schools graduates. The group also published guides on manufacturing issues for the divisions.

The Manufacturing Services Group used benchmarking and cross-referencing to improve production methods and had a bifurcated strategy for introducing the manufacturing improvements. In the case of new acquisitions, the group simply stepped in and worked with EVPs and their operating managers to improve plant efficiency and to transfer Cooper's manufacturing know-how and processes to the new division. In almost every acquisition, Cooper considered the majority of the plants to require production improvements. In contrast, in keeping with Cooper's philosophy, the group maintained a strict policy of never entering an old Cooper division unless they were invited by division managers. There was, however, no charge for their services.

Once requested, the group used a three-tiered approach to implementing improvements, acting as a catalyst for change. The first stage was conceptual: the engineering department, assisted by local personnel, determined the ideal configuration for the factory. The process stage followed, designed to show current employees how the new methods would be more efficient than the old ones. This stage typically involved reconfiguring the machinery in the plant for cell rather than batch production. The process stage was heavily communicative: its primary goal was to inculcate factory workers into the new production process, convincing them of its superior efficiency, and would often take two to three years. The final step was the technological stage, during which the group introduced new machinery and technology into the factory. The group spent about 60% of its time on acquisitions and 40% on existing Cooper divisions.

At all stages of the manufacturing improvement process, the group relied heavily on the participation of local personnel, attempting to give them ownership of the project. The group generally coordinated and directed the three stages, but division employees implemented the changes. Bill Brewer, president of Cooper Power Systems, said of the group, "One of the greatest aspects of Coppola's group is that they are viewed as an extension of our organization. They are constantly called on and are available for concepts and opinions. They have a broader perspective than any one plant can have, and are therefore able to broker success and failure throughout the company."

Coppola's group administered capital expenditures. The capital budget for each division was reached after balancing division requests with available funds and was made consistent with division strategies. Cizik was often involved in the capital budgeting process, making suggestions and amendments to proposals. Corporate headquarters supported all capital and personnel needs that were required to meet division strategies, which often involved sizable investments in newly acquired companies to improve their manufacturing capabilities. Division managers could authorize expenditures up to $100,000; an EVP's approval was needed for expenditures above $100,000; Cizik's signature was required for all projects over $1 million; and the board of directors approved all investments over $5 million.

The Manufacturing Services Group also ran quality, purchasing, traffic, environmental, plant engineering, and technology councils that met four times annually. Each council typically had 12 members, each representing a different operating division, who rotated on an annual basis. For example, in 1984, Cooper established the purchasing council, which soon discovered that some divisions were purchasing steel from the same supplier at different prices.

The council then negotiated advantageous prices with various steel companies for all Cooper divisions (Cooper purchased over $100 million of steel annually). In similar instances, the councils allowed managers from different divisions to share information and insights, which helped maximize Cooper's leverage in negotiating with suppliers and vendors.

Finally, the group oversaw a manufacturing training program for entry-level engineering graduates. In 1988, Cooper recruited 16 graduates, primarily from 12 "preferred" Midwestern universities. The two-year program consisted of four intensive six-month job rotations; each participant was required to work in at least three of Cooper's four manufacturing sub-functions, as well as to hold a foreman's job. Program graduates were offered supervisory positions, or assignments leading to supervisory and managerial positions.

Executive Vice President of Operations. Each of Cooper's three EVPs headed a worldwide operating segment. Describing his job, H. John Riley, Jr., EVP of the Electrical and Electronics Division, said "Cizik invests a lot of authority in our hands. Each of us functions in a capacity similar to that of the typical chief operating officer. This is what makes the system work." Cooper's EVPs served four major functions. They handled organizational and administrative matters, including selecting key division managers, conducting personnel reviews under the MD&P program, and prioritizing tasks. They also approved all capital expenditures up to $1 million. Second, they worked with the Sr. VP of Finance and division managers to develop the three-year business unit strategic plans. Likewise, they performed strategic planning and analysis at the segment level: they set the long-term strategies for the business segment, and attempted to balance short-term performance with long-term strategic objectives. Third, EVPs located and analyzed potential acquisitions that complemented their segments. As soon as Cooper engineered a complementary acquisition, the appropriate EVP would spend a considerable amount of time on "Cooperizing" the new operating unit. Welding the acquisition with a Cooper division generally required that he make multiple visits to plants and distribution facilities, overseeing the transition while Cooper installed its management systems and culture. EVPs spent approximately 50% to 60% of their time in the field.

Finally, the EVPs regularly reviewed financial statements, annual budgets, and quarterly forecasts. They received monthly financial statements from each division, which allowed them to roughly compare actual to budgeted performance. EVPs did not focus on any single measure in evaluating a division's performance, but looked at all financial data that would indicate if the strategy was on course, such as sales, profitability, growth, cash flow, and return on assets. These financial data were supplemented with operating data, including order rates, which served as indicators of the level of product demand for the upcoming period, and first-pass line fill, or service-level data, which provided information on the number of orders that could be filled from stock. In many of Cooper's businesses, the ability to immediately fill orders was important for effective distribution, and Cooper maintained first-pass fill targets of 95% to 98% of orders.

Each EVP had a general management background and had risen through a division within his operating segment. For example, Michael Sebastian, EVP of Compression and Drilling, was a group manager at Gardner-Denver and joined Cooper when Gardner was acquired. He rose to the EVP position by 1981. Similarly, Riley joined Crouse-Hinds in 1963, became a division head of Crouse-Hinds in 1972, and then was promoted to EVP of Cooper in 1982. Cunningham rose through the Tool Group to head the Commercial and Industrial Products division.

Except during the Cooperization process, EVPs had a management-by-exception philosophy, seldom intervening in routine division management unless a division suffered prolonged, unsatisfactory performance or violated the boundaries set during the strategic planning process. However, each EVP maintained an ongoing dialogue with his division managers and encouraged them to be up front with problems. Conversations were initiated by either party. In addition to reviews of monthly financial performance, EVPs also advised division managers on resolving particularly difficult operating situations. If unsatisfactory performance continued unattended for a quarter, an EVP would probably request a meeting with division managers to question the methods they had planned to improve the situation. At all times the discussion focused on the steps necessary to comply with the strategy rather than on assigning blame for poor performance. Division managers valued the knowledge, understanding, and support of the EVPs, whom they viewed as extensions of the divisions. Only after extended poor performance would an EVP take direct corrective action.

Chairman, President, and CEO.

As chairman, president, and CEO, Robert Cizik developed Cooper's corporate strategy. Initially, his idea that Cooper adopt a manufacturing focus met some resistance. He noted, "I had to argue for five or six years about being a manufacturing

company before the others finally accepted it." In 1988, Cizik, Riedel, Cross, and Cunningham had been at Cooper for about 20 years over which time they had developed a team approach, centered on Cizik's strategic vision. At headquarters, Cizik, the three EVPs and the three Sr. VPs had offices near each other and often met informally to apply their collective talents to problems.

Cizik approved all acquisitions and took charge of investor relations. "Cooper" was used as a brand name only on Wall Street, where Cizik closely interacted with investors and analysts. Cizik was approached by many investment bankers and personally reviewed many of Cooper's acquisition candidates. In particular, he focused on diversifying acquisitions. Because Cooper had few decision makers, the company was able to act quickly on acquisitions, opportunistically undertaking purchases, such as the Kirsch and Crouse-Hinds mergers.

At Cooper, each of the three operating segments had little physical interaction with the other two: divisions in different segments rarely supplied each other, and Cooper did not have a transfer pricing policy. However, if a division in the commercial and industrial segment was building a new plant, for example, it would be expected to purchase Cooper lighting products and construction materials. If disputes developed between the divisions about these transactions, Cizik would ask the EVPs of the two operating segments to resolve the conflict.

As CEO, Cizik was not involved in day-to-day operations. His biggest regret was that he no longer had time to visit each plant annually. However, he was always available if a serious problem developed at the operational level, and a telephone conversation with a division manager would bring him up to date on the division's progress. Cizik's involvement with each division became more visionary: his role was to push the frontiers, for example, suggesting to divisions that they expand into Europe. His strategic concepts, such as maintaining "strong brand image," provided focus for divisions. Said Bill Brewer, "Cizik is a very lively participant in the strategy meetings. He makes excellent, directed comments and has a keen sense of the potential of a proposed strategy for success."

Cizik spent an average of twelve days a year on the MD&P process. His participation was essential: he reviewed each EVP and Sr. VP and their organizations and scrutinized the minutes from the divisional MD&P meetings. He also conducted probing, all-day reviews with each EVP and pushed managers to make difficult personnel decisions under MD&P.

Champion

In January, 1989, Champion agreed to a "sweetheart" sale of the company to Dana for $17.50. Dana was a $4.9 billion, Toledo-based manufacturer of power transmission equipment for the automotive original equipment market. At the time of the Dana-Champion announcement, Chinook Partners L.P., a partnership formed by descendants of Champion's founding family, held 35% of Champion's stock. The partnership objected to the proposed Dana merger, referring to it as a deal done at "the Toledo Country Club." According to *Business Week,* three weeks after the Dana bid, Cooper "crashed the party" with a $21-a-share tender offer.

At the time of the takeover battle, Champion principally manufactured spark plugs and windshield wipers and derived most of its revenues from sales to spare-parts distributors (Exhibit 10). In early 1989, it had a brand name that was recognized worldwide and was a market leader in spark plugs and wipers (35% of Champion's sales were overseas). However, motivated by declines in the spark plug market, Champion had attempted to leverage its internationally recognized brand name by expanding into other automotive product lines. In the most extreme case, the company proposed to penetrate the automotive tool business, although Snap-On, MAC, and Matco had a combined market share of 92%. In addition, Champion began licensing its brand name as well as putting it on bought-in parts. These new ventures required significant management and capital outlays, and after a short period of time, most proved unprofitable.

Champion's capital expenditures from 1975 to 1988 were 2% of sales, and its overall operating margin was 4.7% for 1988. Its U.S. division suffered an operating loss of $6.4 million in 1988, however its Asian-African and European divisions had operating margins of 13.7% and 11.6%, respectively. *Forbes* described Champion as a "bloated auto parts maker" that, according to industry sources, was manufacturing with 1950s technology. The company had swollen corporate overhead expenses that included the operation of its own fleet of jets.

At the time of the tender offer, Cooper was also considering a $700 million bid for Cameron Iron Works, which manufactured petroleum and natural gas-related equipment, including valves and technically advanced forged products. These product lines would complement Cooper's Compression and Drilling segment. However, undertaking both acquisitions was likely to send Cooper's debt to total capitalization ratio to the 55% to 60% range, and Cooper was aware of the risks of attempting both deals. Cizik realized that, in addition to the financial risks, purchasing either or both companies would have profound operational and organizational ramifications for Cooper Industries.

Notes

1. *Wall Street Transcript,* October 15, 1984, pp. 75, 590.
2. *Houston Post,* August 6, 1989, p. D1.
3. Keller, David N. *Cooper Industries 1933–1983* (Ohio University Press, 1983), p. 98.
4. Keller, David N. *Cooper Industries 1933–1983* (Ohio University Press, 1983), p. 244.
5. *Wall Street Transcript,* October 15, 1984, pp. 75, 590.
6. Fletcher, Sam. "Cooper industries builds on merits," *The Houston Post,* August 8, 1990, p. D4.
7. Flanigan, James. "Bob Cizik: He talks a good game—Plays one, too," *Forbes,* July 8, 1979, pp. 100–104.
8. Keller, David N. *Cooper Industries 1933–1983* (Ohio University Press, 1983), p. 157.
9. Flanigan, James. "Bob Cizik: He talks a good game—Plays one, too," *Forbes,* July 8, 1979, pp. 100–104.
10. Keller, David N. *Cooper Industries 1933–1983* (Ohio University Press, 1983), p. 211.
11. Flanigan, James. "Bob Cizik: He talks a good game—Plays one, too," *Forbes,* July 8, 1979, pp. 100–104.
12. Keller, David N. *Cooper Industries 1933–1983* (Ohio University Press, 1983), p. 9.
13. Keller, David N. *Cooper Industries 1933–1983* (Ohio University Press, 1983), p. 314.
14. *Wall Street Transcript,* December 13, 1981.
15. Keller, David N. *Cooper Industries 1933–1983* (Ohio University Press, 1983), p. 339.
16. *Wall Street Transcript,* March 7, 1988, pp. 88, 618.
17. *Wall Street Transcript,* May 31, 1982, pp. 65, 989.

Exhibit 10 Champion Spark Plug Financials ($000)

	Dec 88	Dec 87	Dec 86	Dec 85	Dec 84	Dec 83	Dec 82	Dec 81	Dec 80
SALES	738,000	719,900	883,800	829,400	816,500	764,400	783,700	818,600	799,800
Selling, General, & Administrative Expense	189,600	187,200	213,800	194,200	183,800	178,400	171,900	185,400	190,600
Net Income	23,600	19,100	(17,200)	15,200	27,300	27,000	26,800	30,300	36,900
Earnings Per Share	0.670	0.500	−0.450	0.400	0.710	0.700	0.700	0.790	0.960
Dividends	0.200	0.050	0.200	0.400	0.400	0.400	0.800	0.800	0.800
Total Current Assets	375,800	462,500	436,700	443,300	398,000	387,200	394,000	421,500	428,100
Net Plant, Property & Equip	185,500	177,100	194,800	177,800	163,500	163,900	173,400	178,400	181,300
TOTAL ASSETS	575,600	653,000	647,700	640,800	579,300	571,700	590,900	626,000	636,200
Total Current Liabilities	170,300	202,900	236,100	211,600	165,800	161,000	176,700	183,800	162,900
Long Term Debt	13,900	17,500	23,500	29,700	26,000	22,300	23,300	31,400	41,400
TOTAL EQUITY	349,900	387,400	351,800	368,700	359,400	359,500	361,100	384,300	405,900

Case 3–8: Ben & Jerry's—Japan*

On an autumn evening in Tokyo in 1997, Perry Odak, Angelo Pezzani, Bruce Bowman and Riv Hight gratefully accepted the hot steaming oshibori towels that their kimono-bedecked waitress quietly offered. After a full day of meetings with Masahiko Iida and his lieutenants at the Seven-Eleven Japan headquarters, the men from Ben & Jerry's welcomed the chance to refresh their hands and faces before turning to the business at hand. It had been just over nine months since Odak had committed to resolving the conundrum of whether to introduce Ben & Jerry's ice cream to the Japan market and, if so, how. The next morning would be their last chance to hammer out the details for a market entry through Seven-Eleven's 7,000 stores in Japan or to give the go-ahead to Ken Yamada, a prospective licensee who would manage the Japan market for Ben & Jerry's. Any delay in reaching a decision would mean missing the summer 1998 ice cream season, but with Japan's economy continuing to contract, perhaps passing on the Japan market would not be a bad idea.

Perry Odak was just entering his eleventh month as CEO of the famous ice cream company named for its off-beat founders. He knew that the Seven-Eleven deal could represent a sudden boost in the company's flagging sales of the past several years. He also knew that a company with the tremendous brand recognition Ben & Jerry's enjoyed needed to approach new market opportunities from a strategic, not an opportunistic, perspective. Since meeting Masahiko Iida, the president of Seven-Eleven Japan just 10 months earlier, Odak was anxious to resolve the question of whether entering the huge Japan market via Seven-Eleven was the right move or not.

---

* James M. Hagen prepared this case solely to provide material for class discussion. The author does not intend to illustrate either effective or ineffective handling of a managerial situation. The author may have disguised certain names and other identifying information to protect confidentiality.

Ivey Management Services prohibits any form of reproduction, storage or transmittal without its written permission. This material is not covered under authorization from CanCopy or any reproduction rights organization. To order copies or request permission to reproduce materials, contact Ivey Publishing, Ivey Management Services, c/o Richard Ivey School of Business, The University of Western Ontario, London, Ontario, Canada, N6A 3K7; phone (519) 661-3208; fax (519) 661-3882; e-mail cases@ivey.uwo.ca. One time permission to reproduce granted by Ivey Management Services on February 9, 2007.

Copyright © 1999, Ivey Management Services Version: (A) 2001-10-31

Ben & Jerry's Background: 1978 To 1997

1978 to 1994: Growth from Renovated Gas Station to $160 Million in Sales[1]

Brooklyn school mates Ben Cohen and Jerry Greenfield started their ice cream company in a defunct gas station in Burlington, Vermont in 1978, when both were in their mid 20s. The combination of their anti-corporate style, the high fat content of their ice cream, the addition of chunky ingredients and catchy flavor names like "Cherry Garcia" found a following. In addition to selling by the scoop, they began selling pints over the counter and the business grew. With the help of less visible team members, Jeff Furman and Fred (Chico) Lager, the founders took the company public to Vermont stockholders in 1984, later registering with the Securities and Exchange Commission (SEC) for nationwide sale of stock. The company name was Ben & Jerry's Homemade, Inc. and it began trading over the counter with the symbol, BJICA.

Stockholder meetings were outdoor festivals where standard attire included cut-offs and tie dyed T-shirts and where Cohen was liable to call the meeting to order in song. In addition to being a fun company, Cohen and Greenfield determined that it would be a socially responsible company, known for its caring capitalism. Highlighting its community roots, Ben & Jerry's would only buy its cream from Vermont dairies. In the case of one of its early nut flavors, "Rain Forest Crunch," the nuts would be sourced from tribal co-operatives in South American rain forests where nut harvesting would offer a renewable alternative to strip cutting the land for wood products, and where the co-op members would hopefully get an uncommonly large share of the proceeds. As another part of its objective of "caring capitalism," Ben & Jerry's gave 7.5 percent of pretax profits to social causes like Healing Our Mother Earth, which protected community members from local health risks, and Center for Better Living, which assisted the homeless.

The product Cohen and Greenfield were selling was exceptionally rich (at least 12 percent butterfat, compared with about six to 10 percent for most ice creams). It was also very dense, which was achieved by a low overrun (low ratio of air to ice cream in the finished product). This richness and density qualified it as a superpremium ice cream.

Häagen-Dazs (founded in New Jersey in 1961) was the only major competitor in the superpremium market. While Häagen-Dazs promoted a sophisticated image, Ben & Jerry's promoted a funky, caring image.

As Ben & Jerry's began to expand distribution throughout the Northeast, it found increasing difficulty obtaining shelf space in supermarkets. Charging Häagen-Dazs with unfairly pressuring distributors to keep Ben & Jerry's off their trucks, Greenfield drove to Minneapolis and gained national press coverage by picketing in front of the headquarters building of food giant Pillsbury which had earlier acquired Häagen-Dazs. His homemade sign read "What is the Doughboy afraid of?", a reference to Pillsbury's mascot and to the company's apparent efforts against the underdog ice cream makers from Vermont. This David versus Goliath campaign earned Ben & Jerry's national publicity and, when combined with some high powered legal action, it gave them freer access to grocery store freezer compartments.

A policy was in place that the highest paid employee would not be paid more than seven times what the lowest paid worker earned. Part of the anti-corporate culture of the company was a policy which allowed each employee to make up his or her own title. The person who might otherwise have been called the public relations manager took the title "the Info Queen." Cohen and Greenfield took turns running the company. Whether despite, or because of, these and other unusual policies, the company continued to grow (see Exhibit 1). In 1985 the company bought a second production plant, this one in nearby Springfield, Vermont. A third plant was later built in St. Albans,

Vermont. By the late 1980s, Ben & Jerry's ice cream had become available in every state of the union.

1994 to 1997: Responding to Fallen Profits

By 1994, sales exceeded $150 million, distribution had extended beyond the U.S. borders and the company had over 600 employees. The future was not encouraging, though, with 1994 actually bringing in a loss. While Ben & Jerry's unquestionably held the second largest market share (at 34 percent compared to Häagen-Dazs' 44 percent) of the American superpremium market, the company had started to lose market share. Net income had also suffered badly since reaching a high in of $7.2 million in 1993 (Exhibit 2). While Cohen was most often the company's CEO, much of the company's growth occurred while Chico Lager was either general manager or CEO between 1982 and 1990. Ben was particularly engaged in efforts to further the cause of social justice by such activities as attending meetings of similarly-minded CEOs from around the world. Board member Chuck Lacy had taken a turn at the helm, but he lacked aspirations for a career as a CEO, just as the company's namesakes did. The slowdown in growth and retreat in market share comprised a threat to the company's survival and to the continuation of its actions and contributions for social responsibility.

The company had never had a professional CEO and it had avoided commercial advertising, relying for publicity on press coverage of its founders' antics and social

Exhibit 1   Ben & Jerry's Annual Sales

Source: Ben & Jerry's Annual Reports.

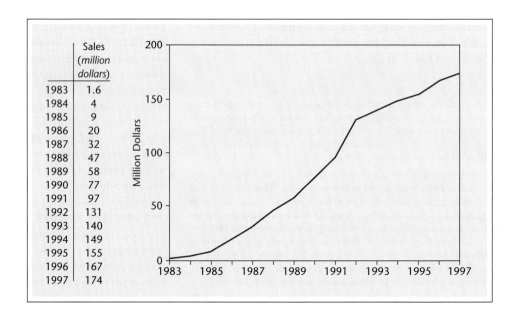

Year	Sales (million dollars)
1983	1.6
1984	4
1985	9
1986	20
1987	32
1988	47
1989	58
1990	77
1991	97
1992	131
1993	140
1994	149
1995	155
1996	167
1997	174

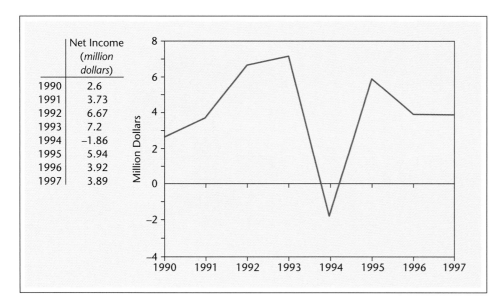

Exhibit 2   Ben & Jerry's
Net Income

Source: Ben & Jerry's Annual
Reports.

	Net Income (million dollars)
1990	2.6
1991	3.73
1992	6.67
1993	7.2
1994	–1.86
1995	5.94
1996	3.92
1997	3.89

interest causes. This approach was apparently losing its effectiveness and the company could no longer feature an underdog image in its appeals for customer support. Relaxing the rule on executive compensation, the company launched a highly publicized search for a CEO, inviting would-be CEOs to submit a 100-word essay explaining why they would like the job. In 1996, Bob Holland, a former consultant with McKinsey & Co., took the presidency, bringing a small cadre of fellow consultants with him. All of Holland's highly schooled management sensibilities were put to the test as he took over a company that had lacked effective management in recent years, commencing employment for a board of directors that was suspicious of traditional corporate culture. By this time, Cohen, Greenfield and Furman still had considerable influence over the company, controlling about 45 percent of the shares. This permitted them, as a practical matter, to elect all members of the board of directors and thereby effectively control the policies and management of the firm. Holland's relationship with the board didn't work and eighteen months later he was out, the company's decline had not been reversed and morale among the employees was at a low.

While the board was willing to pay a corporate scale salary to its CEO, it was unwilling to let go of the company's tradition of donating 7.5 percent of before tax profits to not-for-profit social causes. A spirit of socially responsible business management would need to continue, as that was still the company's stock in trade as much as the ice cream was. With this, as well as the need to survive, in mind, the board hired Perry Odak at the recommendation of one of its members at a base salary of $300,000, with a start date in January 1997.

While Odak had grown up on a dairy farm in upstate New York, it was not this dairy background that landed him the job as CEO of Ben & Jerry's. His experience at turning around troubled companies was far more important. Odak was recruited away from a consultancy assignment at U.S. Repeating Arms Company, which he had been instrumental in turning around from its decline into red ink. This followed diverse experiences ranging from senior vice president of worldwide operations of Armour-Dial, Inc. to president of Atari Consumer Products, along with numerous consultancies and entrepreneurial activities that included the start-up team and management of Jovan, a fragrance and cosmetic company. A professional manager who thrived on challenges and abhorred mere maintenance of a company, Odak had entered the business world with a degree in agricultural economics from Cornell University topped with graduate coursework in business.

The Market for Superpremium Ice Cream

Ice cream is noted as far back as the days of Alexander the Great, though it was first commercially manufactured in the United States in 1851. By 1997, almost 10 percent of U.S. milk production went into ice cream, a $3.34 billion market. The ice cream brands that dominated American supermarket freezer cases are given in Exhibit 3 and Exhibit 4. National (as opposed to regional) branding of dairy products, including ice cream, was a recent phenomenon. Dreyer's (owned in part by the Swiss food giant, Nestlé,

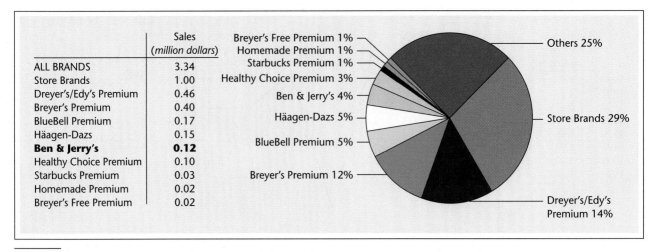

	Sales (million dollars)
ALL BRANDS	3.34
Store Brands	1.00
Dreyer's/Edy's Premium	0.46
Breyer's Premium	0.40
BlueBell Premium	0.17
Häagen-Dazs	0.15
Ben & Jerry's	**0.12**
Healthy Choice Premium	0.10
Starbucks Premium	0.03
Homemade Premium	0.02
Breyer's Free Premium	0.02

Pie chart labels: Breyer's Free Premium 1%, Homemade Premium 1%, Starbucks Premium 1%, Healthy Choice Premium 3%, Ben & Jerry's 4%, Häagen-Dazs 5%, BlueBell Premium 5%, Breyer's Premium 12%, Others 25%, Store Brands 29%, Dreyer's/Edy's Premium 14%

Exhibit 3   Top U.S. Ice Cream Brands, 1996 To 1997

Source: Ben & Jerry's.

and branded Edy's on the East Coast) was the biggest brand at 13.9 percent of the U.S. market, in terms of value. The next biggest was Breyer's, a unit of the Dutch-English firm, Unilever, at 12 percent. Blue Bell (from Texas) was fourth biggest at 5.2 percent, and Häagen-Dazs (owned by the U.K. beverage and food company then known as Grand Metropolitan) was at 4.6 percent. Ben & Jerry's came in at about 3.6 percent of the market. Healthy Choice Premium ice cream (owned by the agribusiness and consumer food firm ConAgra) was close behind with 3.2 percent. Starbucks (one of Dreyer's brands) had 1.0 percent. The biggest share of the market (some 30.2 percent) came from the retailers' private label products and a number of economy brands (with which Ben & Jerry's did not regard itself to be competing) made up the balance.

There are considerable economies of scale in ice cream production, so despite the advantages of having dispersed production in order to reduce costs of transporting the frozen finished product or the highly perishable cream, milk and egg yolks that are principle raw ingredients, each major manufacturer generally had only a few plants to serve vast markets. Market leader, Häagen-Dazs, had just two plants in the United States, while Ben & Jerry's had three. Even with relatively few plants, Ben & Jerry's was operating at only about half of plant capacity in 1997.

While the Ben & Jerry's brand had the country's fifth highest share of the ice cream market (in terms of value), it still accounted for only a small 3.6 percent of the market. Ben & Jerry's, though, measured its competitive strength not in general ice cream sales (including many store brands and economy ice creams), but rather in sales of super-premium (high fat content) ice cream. The market for this product was much less fragmented, with Häagen-Dazs getting 44 percent and Ben & Jerry's getting

Exhibit 4   Share of Superpremium Ice Cream Brands, U.S. Market

Source: Ben & Jerry's.

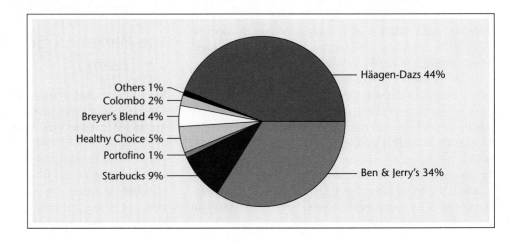

Pie chart labels: Others 1%, Colombo 2%, Breyer's Blend 4%, Healthy Choice 5%, Portofino 1%, Starbucks 9%, Häagen-Dazs 44%, Ben & Jerry's 34%

34 percent of the $361 million of supermarket (excluding convenience store and food service) sales measured and monitored by scanner data. If the two companies' frozen yogurts and sorbets were included, their market shares would be 36 percent for Ben & Jerry's and 42 percent for Häagen-Dazs. Both companies specialized in super-premium products, with additional sales being derived from sorbets, frozen yogurts and novelties. Häagen-Dazs had really pioneered the category back in 1961 when Reuben Mattus in New Jersey founded the company. The company was later acquired by the giant food company, Pillsbury, which in turn was bought in 1989 by the U.K. liquor and food giant, Grand Metropolitan.

Both Ben & Jerry's and Häagen-Dazs had achieved national distribution, primarily selling their product in supermarkets and convenience stores. Ben & Jerry's had 163 scoop shops, compared to 230 Häagen-Dazs shops. Dairy Queen (with 5,790 shops worldwide) and Baskin Robbins dominated the scoop shop business, though their products were not superpremium. Prices for Ben & Jerry's and Häagen-Dazs would range from $2.89 to $3.15 per pint, often more than twice as expensive as conventional (high overrun/lower butterfat) ice cream and premium brands. Starbucks and Portofino ice creams were other much smaller contenders in the United States with their "premium plus" products, characterized by a butterfat content slightly under that of the superpremium category.

Statistical evidence indicated that ice cream consumption increased with income and education. Starting in the mid 1990s, though, sales growth started to fall off and Ben & Jerry's experienced a decline in profits, even suffering a loss in 1994. Häagen-Dazs and Ben & Jerry's product sales were very widely available across the entire U.S. market and it was clear that future growth would have to come from new products or from new (non-U.S.) markets. More troubling was that Ben & Jerry's was beginning to lose market share in both the total ice cream market and, more importantly, the superpremium market.

Ben & Jerry's International Sales

Ben & Jerry's was intentionally slow to embrace foreign markets. Cohen was opposed to growth for growth's sake, so the company's few adventures overseas were limited to opportunistic arrangements that came along, primarily with friends of the founders. Meanwhile Häagen-Dazs had no such hesitation. By 1997, it was in 28 countries with 850 dipping shops around the world. Its non-U.S. sales were

about $700 million, compared to about $400 million of domestic sales. Ben & Jerry's, on the other hand, had foreign sales of just $6 million, with total sales of $174 million. In terms of non-U.S. superpremium ice cream sales, Häagen-Dazs and Ben & Jerry's were still the leading brands, but Häagen-Dazs was trouncing Ben & Jerry's.

Canada

Ben & Jerry's first foreign entry was in Canada in 1986, when the company gave a Canadian firm all Canadian rights for the manufacture and sale of ice cream through a licensing agreement. While about one-third of the product was exported from the United States, high Canadian tariffs (15.5 percent) and particularly quotas (only 347 tons annually) made export impractical. In 1992 Ben & Jerry's repurchased the Canadian license and as of 1997 there were just four scoop shops in Quebec. The Canadian dairy industry remained highly protective even after enactment of the North American Free Trade Agreement.

Israel

Avi Zinger, a friend of Cohen's, was given a license, including manufacturing rights, for the Israel market in 1988. His 1997 sales totaled about $5 million, but the only revenue accruing to Ben & Jerry's Homemade, Inc. would be licensing income and this amount was negligible. To assure quality coming from the plant in Yavne, Israel, Zinger and his staff received training at the Waterbury factory. As of fall 1997, there were 14 Ben & Jerry's scoop shops in Israel, with the shops selling such items as gifts, baked goods and beverages, in addition to the ice cream. Zinger also sold Ben & Jerry's products through supermarkets, hotels, delis and restaurants.

Russia

The company entered into its first foreign joint venture in 1990 by establishing the firm Iceverk in the Russian republic of Karelia, which is Vermont's sister state. This grew out of Cohen's travel to Karelia as part of a sister state delegation in 1988. A goal of the joint venture effort was to promote understanding and communication between the peoples of these two countries. The joint venture agreement specified the following division of ownership shares: Ben & Jerry's—50 percent; the Intercentre cooperative—27 percent; Petro Bank—20 percent; and Pioneer Palace (a facility similar to a YMCA, that provided the location)—three percent. Half of any profits would stay with the Iceverk and the balance would be divided among the partners. Ben & Jerry's contributed equipment and know-how to the venture, while the local partners provided the facilities for the factory and for two scoop shops. After considerable, mostly bureaucratic, delays, the shops opened in July 1992. By 1993, there were three scoop shops and about 100 employees. Iceverk opened several more scoop shops and the venture began to sell pints in supermarkets locally, as well as in Moscow. Ben & Jerry's hired James Flynn to put his University of New Hampshire marketing degree to good use by serving as marketing rep in Moscow. Sales improved as food service customers increasingly bought the product. In 1996, Ben & Jerry's terminated the joint venture, giving its equity and equipment at no cost to its joint venture partners. A retrospective view of that decision is that the company felt that the management time needed to keep the partnership going was too demanding, given the perceived potential. Iceverk no longer uses the Ben & Jerry's name, though it does continue to make ice cream in Petrozavodsk, Karelia's capital.

United Kingdom

In 1994 there was much discussion at Ben & Jerry's headquarters in Burlington about whether the company was ready to strategically (rather than just opportunistically) move into international markets. Susan Renaud recalled the consensus being that no, they were not, but just three months later the company shipped a container of product to Sainsbury, an upscale supermarket chain in the United Kingdom. Cohen had met a Sainsbury executive at a meeting of the Social Venture Network and the executive had encouraged him to ship over some product. This launch was made with no idea of what the pricing would be, nor any knowledge of what kind of packaging and ingredients were acceptable in that market. The company was shipping a 473 ml package, while the standard was 500 ml. With its foot in the door, the company thought it best to try other outlets in England, as well. It tried out one distributor, which had agreed to donate one percent of its Ben & Jerry's turnover to charity. Sales did not materialize and another distributor was tried, this time without the charity constraint. The product had a distinctive market position, with one radio commentator alleged to have said, "If Häagen-Dazs is the ice cream you have after sex, Ben & Jerry's is the ice cream you have instead of sex." By 1997, U.K. sales totalled $4 million.

France

In 1995, the company entered France with great ambivalence. CEO Holland was all for entering the French market and the company sent off a container of product to Auchan,

a major retailer Cohen was introduced to through Social Venture Network ties. As global protests grew over French nuclear testing, though, there were discussions in the company about withdrawing from the French market or vocally protesting against the French government. With this internal disagreement concerning the French market, there was no marketing plan, no promotional support and no attempt to address French labelling laws. The company hired a French public relations firm, noted for its alternative media and social mission work, and separately contracted with a sales and distribution company. But there was no plan and nobody from Ben & Jerry's to coordinate the French effort. In 1997, sales in France were just over $1 million.

Benelux

Ben & Jerry's entry into the Benelux market was also without strategic planning. In this case, a wealthy individual who had admired the company's social mission asked to open scoop shops, with partial ownership by the Human Rights Watch. By 1997, there were three scoop shops in Holland. Sales totalled a mere $287,000, but there was the prospect of using the product reputation from the scoop shops to launch supermarket and convenience store sales.

In short, Ben & Jerry's fell into several foreign markets opportunistically, but without the consensus of the board and without the necessary headquarters staff to put together any kind of comprehensive plan. As the company had never developed a conventional marketing plan in the United States, it lacked the managerial skill to put together a marketing campaign for entering the foreign markets.

As a result, by 1997, Ben & Jerry's international sales totaled just three percent of total sales. While the company had nearly caught up with Häagen-Dazs in U.S. market share, Häagen-Dazs was light years ahead in the non-U.S. markets. With declining profits and domestic market share at Ben & Jerry's, it was beginning to seem time to give serious attention to international market opportunities.

Focus on Market Opportunities in Japan

Background on the Market for Superpremium Ice Cream in Japan

In the 1994 to 1996 period when Ben & Jerry's was having its first taste of a hired professional CEO (Bob Holland), it struggled with the prospects of strategically targeting a foreign market and developing a marketing plan for its fledg-

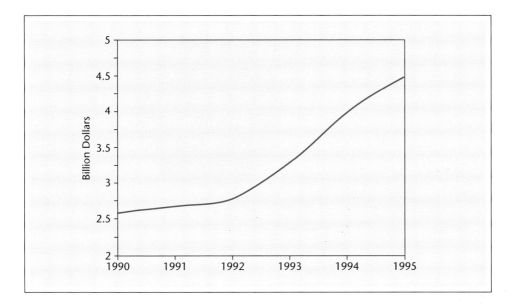

Exhibit 5 Japan Ice Cream Market Size

Source: Ben & Jerry's.

ling overseas operations. In particular, the company made inquiries about opportunities in Japan, the second largest ice cream market in the world, with annual sales of approximately $4.5 billion (Exhibit 5). While the market was big, it was also daunting. Japan was known to have a highly complex distribution system driven by manufacturers, its barriers to foreign products were high and the distance for shipping a frozen product was immense. Ben & Jerry's would be a late entrant, more than 10 years behind Häagen-Dazs in gaining a foothold in the market. In addition, there were at least six Japanese ice cream manufacturers selling a superpremium product. A major Japanese frozen desserts company, Morinaga Seika, had made proposals to Ben & Jerry's on two different occasions in 1995. In both cases the proposals were rejected. In January 1996, Morinaga actually conducted focus groups to evaluate Ben & Jerry's products. It was beginning to seem appropriate to taking a closer look at the Morinaga proposals and other options.

Despite the challenges of entering Japan, that market had several compelling features. It was arguably the most affluent country in the world, Japanese consumers were known for demanding high quality products with great varieties of styles and flavors (which practically defined Ben & Jerry's) and it seemed that the dietary shift toward more animal products was still underway. By 1994, Japan's 42 kilogram annual per capita consumption of milk was less than half that (103 kg) of the United States, and cheese consumption was about one-tenth that of the United States. Commercial dairy sales had really only taken off after World War II, when school lunch programs were initiated with milk as a regular component. Incomes in Japan increased dramatically from the 1950s to the 1980s so that animal-based food products and home refrigerators were affordable to a large number of people.

Though Häagen-Dazs' financial figures were not published by its parent, Grand Metropolitan, market intelligence suggested that the ice cream maker had Japanese sales of about $300 million, with Japan providing the highest margins of any of its markets. Häagen-Dazs had managed to capture nearly half the superpremium market in Japan. It entered the market as an imported product and later began production in Japan at a plant owned jointly by Häagen-Dazs, Sentry and Takanashi Milk Products. About 25 percent of Häagen-Dazs' sales there appeared to be from scoop shops. In addition to gaining visibility through scoop shops, Häagen-Dazs operated a fleet of ice cream parlor buses, with upper deck cafe tables, at exhibitions and other public gatherings. On the one hand, Häagen-Dazs would be a formidable competitor that would likely guard its market share. On the other hand, there would be no apparent need for Ben & Jerry's to teach the local market about superpremium ice cream. The market seemed to welcome imported ice cream and expectations of falling tariffs on dairy products suggested new opportunities for ice cream imports from abroad. Häagen-Dazs' flavors were generally the same as U.S. flavors, with some modifications, such as reduced sweetness. While prices were attractive in Japan, about $6 per pint, it was unclear how much of that would go into the pockets of the manufacturer versus various distributors.

In contemplating an entry in the Japan market, it was hard to avoid thinking about the case of Borden Japan. Borden introduced a premium ice cream to the market in 1971 through a joint venture with Meiji Milk. The product

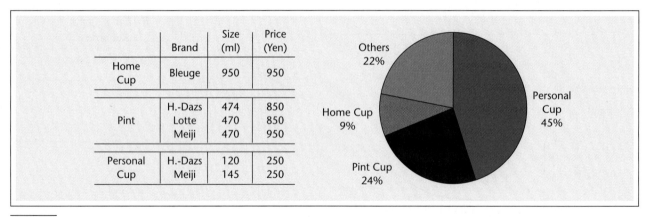

	Brand	Size (ml)	Price (Yen)
Home Cup	Bleuge	950	950
Pint	H.-Dazs	474	850
	Lotte	470	850
	Meiji	470	950
Personal Cup	H.-Dazs	120	250
	Meiji	145	250

Others 22%
Personal Cup 45%
Home Cup 9%
Pint Cup 24%

Exhibit 6   Japan Superpremium and Premium Sales by Package

Source: Fuji Keizal Co.

was highly successful and Borden was leader of the category. In 1991, the Borden-Meiji alliance came to an end and Borden had extreme difficulty gaining effective distribution. Borden did not follow industry trends toward single serving cups of ice cream and it suffered greatly when distributors started lowering the price of the product, sending the signal to consumers that Borden was an inferior product. After sales had fallen by more than two-thirds in just two years, Borden withdrew from the Japan market. Desserts were uncommon in Japan, leaving ice cream primarily for the snack market. Thus, single serving (about 120 ml) cups became popular, accounting for about 45 percent of sales (Exhibit 6) and ice cream came to be sold increasingly in convenience stores. By 1993, about a quarter of all ice cream sales were in convenience stores, compared to 29 percent in supermarkets (Exhibit 7).

One concern at Ben & Jerry's was its size. With total worldwide sales of just over $150 million, it was very small in comparison to Häagen-Dazs, which had estimated sales of $300 million in Japan alone. At least five Japanese companies already in the superpremium market were larger than Ben & Jerry's, with leaders Glico, Morinaga, Meiji and Snow Brand all having total ice cream sales three to four times that of Ben & Jerry's and, in each case, ice cream was just part of their product line.

Cohen was not very enthusiastic about the sort of financial or managerial commitment that was apparently required to enter the Japan market and he couldn't see how entering that market fit in with the company's social mission. Others on the board shared his attitude. Two immediate problems were that entering Japan would not be the result of any social mission (the concepts of social mission

Exhibit 7   Japan Ice Cream Market by Channel

Source: Ice Cream Data Book (Morinaga).

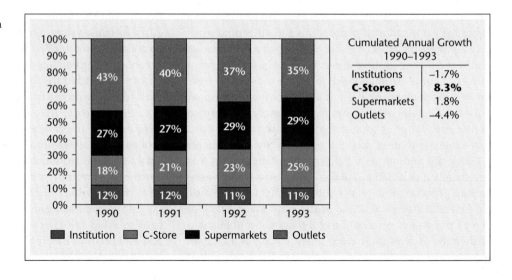

Cumulated Annual Growth
1990–1993

Institutions	–1.7%
C-Stores	**8.3%**
Supermarkets	1.8%
Outlets	–4.4%

and corporate charity being very foreign in Japan) and the company's lack of international success suggested that it may already have been spread too thin in too many countries. Jerry Greenfield, however, was interested enough to visit Japan on a market research tour in early 1996. The purpose was to see just how Ben & Jerry's might gain distribution if the company were to enter the Japanese market. Valerie Brown of Ben & Jerry's fledgling marketing department accompanied Greenfield. Contacts for the visit came primarily from Valerie's classmates at Harvard Business School, from a consulting company and from the Japan External Trade Organization.

Alternative Strategies for a Ben & Jerry's Entry into Japan

In his visit to Japan, Greenfield was willing to consider entry into Japan through such diverse distribution channels as Amway Japan, Domino's Pizza and department stores. One of his meetings was with the Japanese distributor of Dreyer's, the American company with partial ownership by the Swiss food giant Nestle. Dreyer's, not being perceived as a direct competitor, was Ben & Jerry's largest distributor in the United States. Dreyer's had licensed its trademark with a joint venture operation in Japan in 1990. Sales had since fallen and the joint venture seemed to have had difficulty with its biggest customer, Seven-Eleven Japan. The retailer's demands for just-in-time delivery required Dreyer's to maintain large inventories and the retailer demanded the right to rapidly drop flavors which did not meet sales expectations.

Another meeting was with a high level team of Seven-Eleven executives, including Masahiko Iida, the senior managing director, and Yasayuki Nakanishi, the merchandiser of the Foods Division. Iida expressed interest in selling Ben & Jerry's ice cream, suggesting that Ben & Jerry's could sell directly to Seven-Eleven, avoiding some of the distribution costs that are typical of the usual multi-layer distribution system in Japan. On the other hand, a major American beverage distributor in Japan warned that it would be the kiss of death to enter the market through some kind of exclusive arrangement with a huge convenience store chain like Seven-Eleven. The balance of power would be overwhelmingly in the retailer's favor.

Meiji Milk Products (with $447 million of ice cream sales), in combination with its importer, the giant Mitsubishi Trading Company, expressed interest in distributing Ben & Jerry's products. This team clearly had very strong distribution resources, including an exclusive supply contract for Tokyo Disneyland. One concern was that Meiji already had

a superpremium brand called Aya. Despite Meiji's strong interest, though, this option had probably become a long shot on account of earlier protests by Ben & Jerry's leadership of deforestation practices by another division of Mitsubishi.

Other marketing possibilities that had surfaced in 1996 included an arrangement with the advertising agency that had charge of Japan Airlines' in-flight entertainment, as well as a chance to open a scoop shop at a highly visible new retail development about to be built at Tokyo Disneyland. If anything, the many options, focus groups and proposals made the decision about what to do with Japan even more difficult. The fact that the Ben & Jerry's board was divided on whether the company even had any business in a Japan launch discouraged further action. By late 1996, Holland was following up discussions with a well-recommended Japanese-American who was available to oversee marketing and distribution of Ben & Jerry's products in Japan. Ken Yamada, a third generation Japanese American from Hawaii, had obtained the Domino's Pizza franchise for Japan. His compensation would be a margin on all sales in Japan. When Bob Holland's employment with Ben & Jerry's ended later in the year, he was still in discussion with Yamada, but he was still lacking the enthusiastic support of the board of directors for a possible entry into Japan.

A Fresh Look at the Japan Options

Perry Odak assumed leadership of Ben & Jerry's in January 1997, inheriting the file of reports on possible strategies for entering the Japan market. Neither the file nor institutional memory indicated much momentum leading toward any one of the Japan strategies. In being hired, however, Odak had the board's agreement that the company's sales (and especially profits) must grow and that non-U.S. markets were the most likely key to that growth.

In February 1997, Odak added a business-related detour to a scheduled trip to Thailand with his wife. He stopped by Tokyo for a courtesy call to Mr. Iida, the President of Seven-Eleven Japan, a controlling parent company of 7-Eleven U.S.[2] This was to more or less make up for Ben & Jerry's inability to send a CEO to a January "summit" meeting in Dallas at which Mr. Iida and the head of the U.S. 7-Eleven operations had wished to meet face to face with the leaders of its major suppliers. 7-Eleven U.S. was, in fact, Ben & Jerry's biggest retail outlet and Ben & Jerry's was a major supplier to Seven-Eleven.

After about 10 minutes of pleasantries at this introductory meeting at the Seven-Eleven headquarters in Tokyo, Iida asked Odak point blank: "Is there anyone at

Ben & Jerry's who can make a marketing decision? We'd like to sell your product, but don't know how to proceed or with whom." Rather taken aback at this surprisingly direct inquiry, Odak replied that he could indeed make a decision and he resolved to sort through the Japan options and get back to Iida in short order.

Back in Burlington, Odak installed Angelo Pezzani as the new international director for Ben & Jerry's Homemade. Odak had known Pezzani since 1982 when they both started work at Atari on the same day. Pezzani's position was then general consul of Atari Consumer Products Worldwide. Going over the options with Pezzani, it appeared that partnering with Yamada was still the strongest option for entering Japan, but the Seven-Eleven option had not yet been well developed for consideration. Yamada represented considerable strength with his Domino's success and with the fact that Domino's already offered ice cream cups as part of its delivery service in Japan. Possible drawbacks were his insistence on having exclusive rights to the entire Japan market, with full control of all branding and marketing efforts there.

Pezzani and Odak decided to continue negotiations with Yamada, keeping that option alive, and to simultaneously let Iida know that they wanted to explore options with Seven-Eleven. They requested an April meeting with Iida in Japan to move things along. The April meeting would include Mr. Nakanishi, the head of frozen ice desserts for Seven-Eleven Japan, and Bruce Bowman, Ben & Jerry's head of operations. To work out ground arrangements for the meeting, Odak and Pezzani needed someone on the ground in Japan and they called on Rivington Hight, an American who had learned Japanese in the U.S. intelligence service, married a Japanese woman and had been living in Japan for much of the past 30 years. No stranger to Odak or Pezzani, Hight had also worked for Atari in 1982 as president of Atari Japan. Like Odak and Pezzani, he had held a variety of management positions and consultancies in the years since.

The April meeting in Japan was basically intended to lay the framework to begin hashing out the many details that would be involved if Ben & Jerry's were to enter the Japan market through Seven-Eleven. It was a chance for the critical players in each company to get together. Perry brought Pezzani, Bowman and Hight. Arriving at the Ito-Yokado/Seven-Eleven headquarters building at the foot of Tokyo Tower, the Ben & Jerry's team walked into a lobby full of sample-laden salespeople and manufacturers nervously awaiting their chance to put their products on the shelves of some 7,000 stores. The receptionist quickly identified Odak and company and immediately put VIP pins on their dark lapels, directing them to the VIP elevator that went straight to the executive suite on the 12th floor. A hostess there immediately guided the group across the plush white carpeting to a spacious meeting room, where they were served tea while awaiting Iida and Nakanishi. Odak arrived with more questions than answers, but he was determined that any product Ben & Jerry's might sell in Japan would be manufactured in Vermont, where the company had considerable excess capacity. Also, the costs of labor and raw dairy products were higher in Japan than the United States, so the 23.3 percent tariff and cost of shipping seemed not to be prohibitive. As a result of the Uruguay Round of GATT, the tariff would be reduced to 21 percent in the year 2000. The introductory meeting went well, but they had not yet addressed any of the difficult issues except to establish that it would be possible to export the product from Vermont to Japan.

Wrestling with the Details of the Seven-Eleven Option

Odak, Pezzani and Bowman had a full plate of issues to resolve. The first question was market. Iida had said he was interested in Ben & Jerry's product because it was something new to Japan and particularly unique with its chunks. Seven-Eleven had even tried to get a Japanese company to co-pack a chunky superpremium ice cream, but the Japanese packer was unsuccessful with its production processes. Research supporting a clear market for this novel product in Japan was scant, though it seemed unlikely that Seven-Eleven would commit shelf space to a product it had any doubt about and both Iida and Nakanishi certainly knew their market. A skeptical view of Seven-Eleven's interest in bringing Ben & Jerry's to Japan was that Seven-Eleven's combined U.S. and Japan operations would become so important to Ben & Jerry's (potentially accounting for a substantial portion of its sales) that Seven-Eleven could, in some fashion, control the ice cream maker. Even if that were not part of Seven-Eleven's motivation, it could be a concern.

While Ben & Jerry's management was leaning toward an entry into Japan, it was not a foregone conclusion. The entry would require a commitment of capital and managerial attention. As the product would be exported from the United States, there would be the risk of negative exchange rate movements that could make exports to Japan no longer feasible, thus making Ben & Jerry's financial picture less predictable. Commodity risk was also a serious concern in that the price of milk could rise in the United States, hurting Ben & Jerry's relative to competitors producing ice cream in Japan.

Assuming that an entry into the Japanese market was desirable, there were a number of apparent options for gaining distribution there, making it necessary to seriously consider the pros and cons of entering by way of Seven-Eleven. The most obvious pro was immediate placement in the freezer compartments of over 7,000 convenience stores in that country. In the early 1990s, the convenience store share of the ice cream market had increased and it appeared that these stores were now accounting for at least 40 percent of superpremium ice cream sales in Japan. Equally positive was the fact that Seven-Eleven had taken advantage of its size and its state-of-the-art logistics systems by buying product directly from suppliers, avoiding the several layers of middlemen that stood between most suppliers and Japanese retailers. These cost savings could make the product more affordable and/or allow a wider margin to protect against such risks as currency fluctuation.

On the negative side, if the product was introduced to the market through a convenience store and it was just one of many brands there, would it be able to build its own brand capital in Japan like Häagen-Dazs had? Would the product essentially become a store brand? Without brand capital it could be difficult to distribute the product beyond the Seven-Eleven chain. An alternative approach of setting up well located scoop shops, along with an effective marketing or publicity campaign, could give the product cache, resulting in consumer pull that could give Ben & Jerry's a price premium, as well as a range of marketing channels. Would committing to one huge retail chain be a case of putting too many eggs in one basket? A falling out between Ben & Jerry's and Seven-Eleven Japan could leave the ice cream maker with nothing in Japan. Even during discussions with Ben & Jerry's, the retailer was known to be terminating its supply agreement with the French ice cream manufacturer Rolland due to allegedly inadequate sales. Presumably Seven-Eleven could similarly cut off Ben & Jerry's at some future date.

While weighing the pros and cons of the business arrangement, there were also production issues which Ben & Jerry's had to consider. Nakanishi insisted the ice cream be packaged only in personal cups (120 ml) and not the 473 ml (one pint) size that Ben & Jerry's currently packed. The main argument for the small cups was that ice cream is seldom consumed as a family dessert in Japan, but rather is consumed as a snack item. A secondary argument was that, for sanitation purposes, customers liked their own individual servings. Cake, for example, was generally served in restaurants with each slice individually wrapped. Nakanishi's insistence was despite the fact that Seven-Eleven stocked Häagen-Dazs and some of its local competitors in both sizes.

Bruce Bowman embraced the challenge of designing a production system that would accommodate small cups that the company had never packed before. It seemed that about $2 million of new equipment would be needed, though it could be installed in the existing buildings. The sizes of some of the chunks would have to be reduced in order for them to not overwhelm the small cups. Besides requiring these known adjustments to production operations, Seven-Eleven might be expected to request other product changes. Japanese buyers were known for being particularly demanding in their specifications.

Ben & Jerry's had long been shipping ice cream to the West Coast and to Europe in freezer containers. Shipments to Japan were feasible, though the Seven-Eleven approach to just-in-time inventory procedures would make delivery reliability especially key and, of course, costs would have to be minimized. Logistics research indicated it would likely take at least three weeks shipping time from the plant in Vermont (the St. Albans plant would be used if the Japan plan were implemented) to the warehouse in Japan. Because of the Japanese label needed in Japan, production would have to carefully meet the orders from Seven-Eleven. The product could not be shifted to another customer, nor could another customer's product be shifted to Japan.

A number of sticky points needed to be resolved. In addition to changing the package size, Seven-Eleven wanted to provide its own design for the package art and the design would definitely not include a photo of Ben and Jerry. Packaging had always been an important part of the Ben & Jerry's product. Funky lettering and the images of Ben and Jerry are part of what made the product unique. If Seven-Eleven were given control over the package art, what would that do to the benefits of developing a global branded product? Would consumers be confused about the placement of the product as they travelled? On the other hand, the carton designs had already been evolving somewhat and maybe a bit more evolution would satisfy Seven-Eleven. In fact, the earlier focus groups by Morinaga brought out the concern that it was too bad the "strange Ben & Jerry's packaging" had to detract from the good ice cream.

Ben & Jerry's sent a number of samples to consider and Nakanishi developed a short list that would be tested (if the deal went forward) in a couple dozen Seven-Eleven stores so that the top five flavors could be identified for the market entry. "Chunky Monkey" was near the top of Nakanishi's list, though the name absolutely had to change, he said. It turned out that only minor ingredient modifications would be needed to reduce the sweetness and to replace "vegetable gum" with "protein solids."

Through numerous communications and several meetings during the summer of 1997, a number of issues were discussed and resolved. For example, Seven-Eleven would acquire only a six-month exclusive right to Ben & Jerry's and even that would be only for the specific flavors being sold to Seven-Eleven. Because of its relatively small size and inability to cover a loss, Ben & Jerry's was asking for sale terms that would transfer title (and all risk) for the product at the plant gate. It also was asking for 12 weeks lead-time on any order to allow for sourcing of ingredients, as well as efficient production scheduling. It appeared that these requests would not be too burdensome for Seven-Eleven. The sensitive issue of price was intentionally left until late in the discussions. Häagen-Dazs was being sold for 250 yen per 120 ml cup and Seven-Eleven wanted to position Ben & Jerry's at a slightly lower price point. This would be problematic for Odak, who had recently increased the domestic price for Ben & Jerry's ice cream in part to support the product's position as equal or superior in quality to Häagen-Dazs.

A concern yet lurking in the boardroom in Burlington, Vermont was what would be the company's social mission in Japan. Since the early 1990s, the company had moved beyond using its profit to fund philanthropy. The new imperative was to make the workplace, community and world a better place through regular day-to-day operations. On the other hand, profits were still needed in order to even have day-to-day operations and a new market (such as Japan) could be the ticket to those profits. In the meantime, no particular social mission had emerged from the summer discussions of entering the Japan market.

The Approaching Deadline for a Summer 1998 Japan Launch

Odak and his staff had made steady progress narrowing and developing their Japan options during the summer of 1997. If they were to enter the Japan market for the summer 1998 season, though, they would have to commit to one plan or another no later than autumn 1997. Two distinct entry options had emerged.

The Yamada option was largely the same as it had been at the beginning of the year. His proposal was to have full control of marketing and sales for Ben & Jerry's in Japan. He would position the brand, devise and orchestrate the initial launch and take care of marketing and distribution well into the future. He would earn a royalty on all sales in the market. By giving Yamada full control of the Japan market, Ben & Jerry's would have instant expertise in an otherwise unfamiliar market, as well as relief from having to address the many issues involved in putting together an entry strategy and in ongoing market management. Yamada knew frozen foods and he had an entrepreneurial spirit and marketing savvy, evidenced by his success in launching and building up the Domino's pizza chain in Japan. Giving up control of a potentially major market, though, could not be taken lightly. Because Yamada would invest his time in fleshing out and executing a marketing plan only after reaching agreement with Ben & Jerry's, there was no specific plan available for consideration. Even if there were, Yamada would retain the rights to change it. For the near term, however, Yamada would expect to add selected flavors of Ben & Jerry's ice cream cups to the Domino's delivery menu, providing an opportunity to collect market data based on customer response.

The Seven-Eleven option would leave Ben & Jerry's in control of whatever market development it might want to pursue beyond supplying Seven-Eleven in Japan. While Seven-Eleven would provide an instant entry to the market, the company would not be in a position to help Ben & Jerry's develop other distribution channels in Japan. The retailer thought it could sell at least six cups per day at each store, which would be the minimum to justify continuing to stock Ben & Jerry's. Looking at the size of Seven-Eleven's ice cream freezer cases suggested that this would require approximately 10 percent of Seven-Eleven's cup ice cream sales to be Ben & Jerry's products. Ben & Jerry's was as yet unknown in Japan and it did not have the budget for a marketing campaign there. Sales would have to rely primarily on promotional efforts by Seven-Eleven, but the company was making no specific commitment for such efforts.

Another option was increasingly compelling—that of holding off on any Japan entry. Japan's economy was continuing to languish, with increasing talk that it could be years before recovery. A financial crisis that had commenced with a devaluation of Thailand's currency in July 1997, seemed to be spreading across Asia. If the pending Asia crisis hit an already weakened Japanese economy, the economics of exporting ice cream from Vermont to Japan could become infeasible.

Though the value of the yen had recently fallen to 125 yen to the dollar, Ben & Jerry's could still sell the product at the plant gate at an acceptable profit with room for both shipping expense and satisfactory margins for Seven-Eleven and its franchisees. If the rate went as high as 160 yen to the dollar, then the price in Japan would have to be raised to a level that might seriously cut into demand, especially relative to Häagen-Dazs, which had manufacturing facilities in Japan.

It would be a long evening meal as Odak, Pezzani, Bowman and Hight gave their final thoughts to the decision before them. Not only had Odak promised Iida that he could make a decision, but Yamada needed an answer to his proposal as well. In any event, Ben & Jerry's had to proceed with one plan or another if it was going to have any Japanese sales in its 1998 income statement.

Notes

1. Monetary values are in U.S. dollars unless otherwise noted.
2. A brief explanation of the relationship between the Japan Seven-Eleven organization and the U.S. 7-Eleven organization is in order. 7-Eleven convenience stores originated in Texas in 1927 as a retail concept of Southland Corporation, which had been in the ice business. Southland began using the 7-Eleven banner in the 1950s because the stores would be open from 7 A.M. to 11 P.M. The business grew through company-owned and franchised stores. Southland gave a master franchise for Japan to the Ito Yokado Company, a large supermarket operator there, which in turn established Seven-Eleven Japan to conduct the 7-Eleven business in Japan through company-owned and franchised stores. In the 1980s, Southland was in financial distress and Ito Yokado, along with its subsidiary, Seven-Eleven Japan, bailed out Southland, acquiring a controlling interest in the company. In this light, Odak's dinner with Iida in Japan constituted a sort of executive summit between Ben & Jerry's and its largest customer.

Case 3–9: Toyota's Strategy and Initiatives in Europe*

The Launch of the Aygo

"Since 2000 the output of the global [auto] industry has risen by about 3 million vehicles to some 60 million: of that increase, [more than] half came from Toyota alone. While most attention over the past four years has focused on a spectacular turnaround at Nissan, Toyota has undergone a dramatic growth spurt all round the world."

—*The Economist*, **January 29, 2005: 61**

For Toyota Motor Europe (TME), locally designed cars and the availability of diesel engines led to impressive results: 2005 was the ninth consecutive year of record sales for Toyota in Europe. Sales grew by almost 50% from 2000 to 2005. The new strategy paid off financially, too. According to *Business Week,* the operating profit increased nine-fold to $654 million in 2003. After plant openings in France, Turkey, Poland and the Czech Republic, local production was expected to reach 60% in 2006. This lowered exposure to exchange rates and import tariffs. Within Toyota, sales increases from Europe were needed to meet ambitious global sales targets.

But for the European marketing team of Toyota's Aygo minicar, the challenge continued. In a fiercely competitive market they had to find 100,000 buyers annually for the 3.41-meter Aygo. This segment was seen as a difficult market: low prices meant low margins. Mercedes-Benz's "MCC smart" recorded losses of €4 billion between 2000 and 2005.[1] Other competitors also had difficulties making money in this segment.

With the launch of the Aygo, Toyota challenged many of its traditional views: the car was specifically designed for the European market and exclusively sold there. The factory was a 50/50 joint venture with the Peugeot/Citroën Group (PSA) in the Czech Republic. But for the marketing managers of the Aygo the challenge was how to sell the 100,000 units annually they guaranteed to buy from the factory in the Czech Republic.

---

* Research Associate George Rädler prepared this case under the supervision of Professor Kazuo Ichijo as a basis for class discussion rather than to illustrate either effective or ineffective handling of a business situation.

Copyright © 2006 by **IMD** - International Institute for Management Development, Lausanne, Switzerland. Not to be used or reproduced without written permission directly from **IMD**.

Toyota Global: Becoming Number 1[2]

Toyota Motor Corporation (Toyota) maintained its record growth. Sales reached 7.97 million units, an increase of about 2.5 million since 2000 (*refer to* Table 1).

For Toyota, North America remained the most important international market and its market share was increasing rapidly. In 2005 sales hit the 2 million unit level for the first time and Toyota held 13.7% of the important US market (up from 9.3% in 2000). 60% of the American demand was satisfied by 12 plants in the NAFTA region.

For 2006 Toyota was expected to reach 9 million units in production—with luxury brand Lexus reaching the 500,000 units mark for the first time (up from 400,000 units in 2004). Between 1990 and 2005, the number of Toyota plants increased from 20 factories in 14 countries to 47 factories in 26 countries. Within Toyota, there was concern that such rapid expansion could hurt the company. Toyota president Katsuaki Watanabe explained:[3]

> Everyone should be dissatisfied with the present situation and should constantly try to improve or change things. It's important to realize that there is always something more we need to aim at. That's what needs to be recognized by every individual. When you are growing you are satisfied with the status quo, and that's no good.

A European supplier, listening to a presentation by former chairman Fujio Cho in 2004, later remembered:[4]

> Listening to them [the top management], you get the impression that Toyota is facing its biggest crisis in history.

The company was one of nine members of the "$10 billion club," indicating a net income in excess of $10 billion (2005: net income of $12.35 billion on revenues of $189 billion; revenue grew by 14%). Toyota was one of two manufacturing companies on that list, the other seven compa-

Table 1   **Vehicle Sales of Toyota Motor Corporation**

	1999	2000	2001	2002	2003	2004	2005
Global sales (million units)	5,182	5,526	5,543	6,113	6,719	7,400	7,970

Note: Toyota publishes its numbers for the financial year ending March 31.

Source: Various annual reports, press reports

Table 2   **Shares of Global Sales and Market Capitalization (2006)**

	Share of global vehicle sales	Share of global market capitalization
Toyota	11%	35.0%
Honda	5.2%	11.0%
Nissan	5.4%	8.5%
Daimler-Chrysler	7.7%	7.5%
Ford	11%	2.9%
General Motors	13%	2.2%

Note: According to this study, Asian manufacturers accounted for no more than 43% of all passenger cars sold in the world but for 73% of the worth of all car makers. GM's sales data is likely to include volume from foreign manufacturers, in which GM holds a minority stake.

Source: *Wall Street Journal Europe*, March 23, 2006: 4.

nies were in either oil/gas or financial services. In order to avoid complacency, Toyota set the ambitious goal of reaching 15% global share by 2010 (up from 11% in 2005). On the financial markets, Toyota had the reputation of delivering on its ambitious goals. As of March 2006, Toyota accounted for 35% of the total market capitalization in the global automotive industry (*refer to* Table 2).

It was expected that as early as 2006, Toyota could overtake General Motors (GM) as the world's largest car manufacturer. But Jim Farley, Toyota's VP of marketing in the US was cautious:[5] "And if we do become No. 1, we'll still act like we're No. 3 or 4, because that's the Toyota Way." A spokesperson explained: "Our goals are not directly positioned against competitors. Our goals are around customers." However, in order to reach the 15% share by 2010, continued growth in Europe was essential.

Toyota in Europe: "We Are Growing Step-by-Step"[6]

With the launch of the Yaris model in 1999, Toyota's sales took off. The initial goal of reaching a European sales volume of 800,000 units was reached two years ahead of time–in 2003 instead of 2005 (*refer to* Table 3).

Besides attractive models from the design center in Nice (France), Toyota benefited from the much better availability of diesel engines (starting in 2002), which reached penetration rates of almost 40% in 2005.

Moreover, Toyota's position in the market was different: for the first time the company was able to exploit a more emotional positioning around "green issues." The Prius hybrid model won the coveted "2005 [European] Car of the Year Award." In 2005 Toyota sold around 18,000 units of Prius in Europe (global sales: 180,000 units) and by 2010 was expecting to sell 1,000,000 units worldwide. Hybrid technology gave Toyota a good opportunity to position itself as a technology leader since the competition had only just started to sell hybrid models. The technology was also launched in the Lexus RX 400h in 2005. The hybrid version fetched a price premium of €6,200* over the gasoline-powered RX 300. In Europe, Toyota was also one of the first to offer its D-Cat diesel engines with a diesel particulate filter. Toyota's environmental initiatives were widely recognized. In a 2006 survey on "who builds the most environment-friendly car," Toyota came first in the five biggest European markets plus Poland.[7] Toyota drivers were on average around 53 years of age.[8] Customers were very loyal and Toyota usually topped customer satisfaction indexes such as JD Power. Lexus continued to secure top ratings in JD Power surveys, but its sales continued to be below expectations, with the volume fluctuating around 25,000 units–compared to over 250,000 units in the US. In Europe, Lexus models were sold with extended warranties, including a six-year warranty, three years of free services, maintenance and roadside assistance (compared with two years at most luxury car manufacturers).

Apart from Lexus, Toyota was in the passing lane in Europe. It had considerably increased its sales volumes in Europe, unlike some of the other Japanese manufacturers (*refer to* Table 4 *for annual sales in Western Europe*).

In 2005 Toyota's largest markets were: UK (138,500 units), Italy (130,507 units), Germany (130,275 units), France (92,024 units) and Spain (65,498 units). However, Toyota executives believed there was still a huge potential

*Exchange rate €1 = $1.27 (May 7, 2006)

Table 3   Key figures for Toyota in Europe (Western and Eastern Europe)

	2000	2001	2002	2003	2004	2005
Sales (thousand units)	656	666	756	835	916	964
Market share	3.56	3.58	4.4	4.7	4.9	5.1

Source: Toyota in Europe (2005): 15; Toyota website www.toyota-europe.com

Table 4   Annual Sales of Asian Brands in Western Europe (2000 vs. 2005)

Brand	Country of origin	2000		2005	
		Units sold	Market share	Units sold	Market share
Honda	Japan	181,600	1.2%	238,368	1.6%
Mazda	Japan	181,710	1.2%	226,427	1.6%
Mitsubishi	Japan	160,281	1.1%	127,351	0.9%
Nissan	Japan	393,736	2.7%	343,023	2.4%
Suzuki	Japan	131,587	0.9%	182,415	1.3%
Toyota	Japan	542,771	3.7%	762,736	5.3%
Daewoo	South Korea	202,058	1.4%	12,972	0.1%
Hyundai	South Korea	227,210	1.5%	298,389	2.1%
Kia	South Korea	68,300	0.5%	232,309	1.6%

Note: The Kia numbers are for 2001 (not 2000)

Source: ACEA

for the brand. Despite record sales in Europe, Toyota made it to the top-10 best-selling list only for Italy (*refer to* Exhibit 1 *for the top registrations in the largest four markets in Europe*).

But Toyota wanted more: It stated its sales goal of 1.2 million units annually in Europe by 2010. However, the press was already speculating on whether the goal could be reached two years earlier.[9]

Localizing Production in Europe

After the 1992 opening of Toyota's first car and engine plant in the UK, the speed of plant openings accelerated in the new millennium. A car plant in France started production in 2001; in the same year Toyota produced over 200,000 cars in Europe for the first time. Only three years later, the

Exhibit 1   Top-10 Car Registrations in Europe in 2005 in the Biggest European Market (model, units)

France		Germany		Italy		United Kingdom	
Renault Megane	188,373	VW Golf	237,990	Fiat Punto	173,502	Ford Focus	145,010
Renault Clio	132,982	Opel Astra	122,841	Fiat Panda	130,972	Opel Astra	108,161
Peugeot 206	119,907	Audi A4	100,910	Ford Fiesta	69,946	Opel Corsa	89,463
Peugeot 307	113,484	VW Passat	98,136	**Toyota Yaris**	**66,271**	Renault Megane	87,093
Citroën C3	79,259	BMW 3-series	96,311	Lancia Ypsilon	64,436	Ford Fiesta	83,803
Peugeot 407	68,130	MB A-Class	85,691	Ford Focus	63,050	VW Golf	67,749
Citroën C4	63,798	Ford Focus	78,899	VW Golf	60,004	Peugeot 206	67,450
Renault Modus	61,877	MB C-Class	77,845	Renault Megane	58,896	Ford Mondeo	57,589
Ford Focus	48,930	VW Touran	76,077	Citroë C3	58,152	Renault Clio	56,538
Renault Twingo	45,594	VW Polo	71,061	Opel Astra	54,972	BMW 3-series	44,844

Source: Auto-Motor Sport 3/2006: 12.

Table 5   **Toyota's Production in Europe**

UK	245,000 units	Avensis: 180,000 units, Corolla Hatchback
France	204,000 units	All Yaris
Turkey	134,000 units	Corolla Sedan/Wagon/Verso
Total	**583,000 units**	

company was already producing 583,000 cars per year in Europe. (*Refer to* Table 5 *for European production volumes.*)

By 2005 Toyota had produced 638,000 vehicles in Europe and this was expected to increase to over 800,000 units in 2006. Table 6 *gives an overview of the factory openings in Europe.*

By 2005, Toyota had a total of eight plants in six countries (total investment: about €6 billion since 1990). A spokesperson for the company explained the dilemma they were facing, "We really don't want to be perceived as a Japanese invader."[10] But the question was, how to get round it?

Toyota and PSA Join Forces

The automotive industry was surprised when Toyota and PSA (holding company for the Peugeot and Citroën brands) announced a 50/50 joint venture in late 2001. The factory, to be located in Kolin, Czech Republic (about 60 km to the east of Prague), was planned for an annual capacity of 300,000 units. The joint venture was limited to manufacturing, with cars being sold separately through the Toyota/Peugeot/Citroen distribution channels. Manufacturing, purchasing and R&D

accounted for around 70% of value-added in car manufacturing (*refer to* Exhibit 2 *for the business system*).

The objective was to produce a minicar with 93% common parts between the Toyota, Peugeot and Citroën cars. For Toyota, this was a completely new segment. Peugeot's aim was to produce the replacement model for the Peugeot 106. This model was on sale between 1991 and 2004 and sold a total of 2.8 million units over that period. It was also sold under the Citroën Saxo brand between 1997 and 2003. Until the Kolin factory opened in mid-2005, PSA did not have a replacement for the Peugeot 106 and the Citroën Saxo.

PSA Company Background

Paris-based PSA had been the big success story of the European automobile sector. Although the PSA name was almost unknown to the majority of end customers, the company's two brands (Peugeot and Citroën) were very popular. Sales increased from 2.8 million units in 2000 to 3.39 million units in 2005 (5.5% share globally). Non-European sales surpassed 1 million units in 2005 for the first time ever. The non-European growth averaged 17% up to 2005 (mostly from Asia and South America).

In the five years up to 2003, PSA increased its European share from 12% to 15.5%, but it fell to 14% in 2005. Nevertheless, it remained Europe's second biggest manufacturer (after the VW Group). The company was praised for its good vehicle designs, diesel engines, clever advertising and excellent cost position in manufacturing, but it was disappointed by the results of quality surveys (*refer to* Exhibit 3 *for an overview of quality ratings*).

PSA strongly pushed its platform strategy. By 2008, the three main platforms were expected to account for 3

Table 6   **Timeline for Toyota's Factory Openings in Europe**

Start of production	2001	2002	2002	2002	2005	2005
Type of factory	Car	Petrol engines	Transmissions, later also engines	Car	Diesel engines	Car (JV with PSA)
Location	Valenciennes, France	Valenciennes, France	Walbrzych, Poland	Adapazari, Turkey	Jelcz-Laskowice, Poland	Kolin, Czech Republic
Capacity	240,000 units	250,000 engines	550,000 transmissions	134,000 units	180,000 engines	300,000 units, of which Toyota will take 100,000
Total investment	€ 790 m	See 2001	€ 400 m	€ 730 m	€ 200 m	€ 1.3 billion (Toyota: 50%)

Source: Various Toyota documents

Exhibit 2   Business System in the Automotive Industry

Source: McKinsey, ATK earney

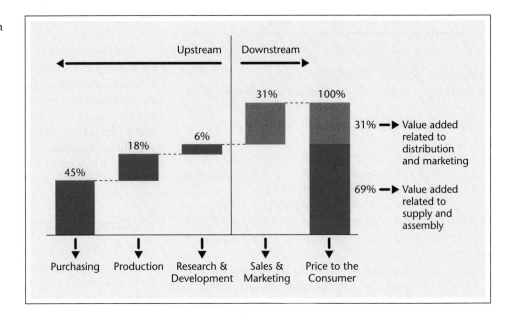

million units (up from 1.5 million in 2005). Factories were specializing in platforms and manufactured both Peugeot and Citroën models on the same line. PSA had an annual savings target of around €600 million. In the industry, PSA was known for its various joint ventures: diesel engines with Ford, gasoline engines with Renault and BMW, commercial trucks with Fiat and SUVs with Mitsubishi.

At the same time, PSA was actively involved in Eastern Europe. In addition, the company also opened a new factory in Slovakia (annual capacity: 300,000 units). It was estimated that PSA would source 15% of its total European production from Eastern Europe by 2008, up from 0% in 2004.[11] Industry sources were expecting the factory in Slovakia to grow to 500,000 units. This would make it the fifth largest car plant in Europe.

Exhibit 3   The Perception of Various Car Brands in Europe (as seen by drivers of the brands)

Source: *Auto Motor und Sport,* "Best Cars 2006," 6/2006: 139

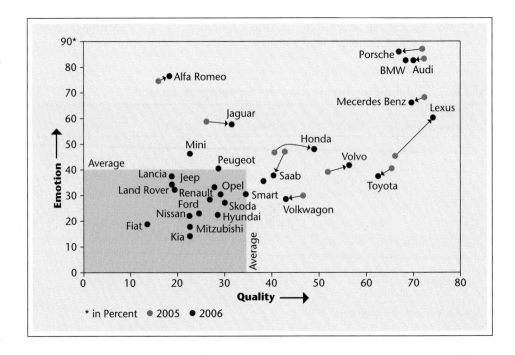

Intricacies of the Minicar Segment

The Challenge: Operating Profitably

The segment for minicars (also referred to as the A-segment in the industry) had existed for a long time, but had only became popular again in recent years. Economic uncertainty, high unemployment and increasingly high fuel prices had led to volume gains in this segment. Competitors either relied on cars from low-cost countries such as the Fiat Panda (built in Poland), VW Fox (Brazil), Hyundai Getz (South Korea). Some other competitors opted for very long product lifecycles: Renault's Twingo had sold for over a decade without major changes, as had the former model of the Nissan Micra (both models were built in Western Europe). The base price for this category was normally below €10,000, but it could increase with the addition of features.

In the case of MCC smart, the company went furthest in differentiating their offering. The car was positioned as a fashion item. Customers could have the color of the plastic exterior body panels completely changed within 90 minutes at a cost of between €825 and €1,225. However, only 0.8% of customers made use of this option–mostly after accidents or other damage. Most other innovative features around the car such as the mobility concept, for example special rates at parking garages, were either stopped or drastically reduced. Cumulated losses reached in excess of €4 billion between 2000 and 2005 and the future of the car remained uncertain.

Volkswagen Group tried entering this segment by offering the technological advanced aluminum frame for its Audi A2 model and offering a 3-liter version of its VW Lupo minicar with a fuel consumption of less than 3 liters/100 km. However, the Audi model became too expensive and the 3-liter Lupo initially lacked convenience features, such as power windows and power steering in order to keep the fuel consumption low. Neither of the models reached sales targets and both were discontinued in 2004. Soon afterwards, Volkswagen started to import the Fox model as a replacement for the Lupo. BMW's MINI model was relaunched in 2001 and stressed its rich heritage. At average transaction prices in excess of €22,000, it sold around 200,000 units in 2005 (refer to Exhibit 4 for the actual sales data).

Minicars Please Regulators

Regardless of the economics around minicars, they were helping car makers to make big improvements with regard to their voluntary target for reducing carbon dioxide by 2008. Under a 1999 agreement with the European Union, the European car industry pledged to reduce the per-car

Exhibit 4   New Vehicle Registrations in Europe in the Minicar Segment (2001–2005)

Brand, Model Name	2001	2002	2003	2004	2005
Toyota Aygo	0	0	0	0	21,224
Peugeot 107	0	0	0	0	19,552
Citroën C1	0	0	0	0	17,730
BMW Mini	24,980	144,119	176,465	184,357	200,428
Chevrolet Matiz	0	0	0	22,066	53,247
Daewoo Matiz	91,476	72,232	59,176	36,528	1,879
Citroën Saxo	243,962	164,477	71,478	1,737	19
Fiat Panda	101,924	117,959	131,677	224,055	228,106
Hyundai Atos	60,606	40,130	19,679	37,186	37,450
Kia Picanto	0	0	0	58,135	83,076
MCC smart	115,000	120,000	123,000	152,000	125,000
Mercedes A-Class	165,915	151,646	132,911	125,950	172,539
Opel/Vauxhall Agila	86,236	79,218	74,518	55,237	37,143
Peugeot 106	109,244	67,764	38,656	1,919	11
Renault Twingo	168,358	143,441	116,472	85,580	76,853
VW Fox	0	0	0	0	50,862

Note: The data covers 19 European countries.   Chevrolet took over Daewoo and is fading out the Daewoo brand.   The numbers for BMW Mini and MCC smart are world-wide sales data.

Source: Toyota, various annual reports, press releases.

carbon dioxide (CO_2) emissions to 140 grams per kilometer by the year 2008, compared to 175 grams per kilometer in 1999. Japanese and Korean manufacturers also accepted this challenge, but they were given an additional year to implement it. Car makers took this seriously, as such a voluntary agreement could easily find its way into regulations. The best way to reduce CO_2 was to reduce fuel consumption. Minicars usually had small engines and hence low-fuel consumption. Minicars usually had small engines and hence low-fuel consumption. While the popularity of diesel engines greatly helped (they consumed less fuel), the increasing consumer demand for air conditioning, more horsepower, big SUVs, as well as new regulations including better protection for pedestrians, often added additional weight to the car and new sources for electricity consumption (hence higher fuel consumption). So fuel-efficient engines became crucial for meeting the needs of this voluntary target. PSA developed a new 1.6-liter engine which consumed 10% less fuel, but this development came at a cost of €610 million.[12] PSA decided to share this cost with BMW.

Toyota Peugeot Citroën Automobile (TPCA) in the Czech Republic*

Set-up: Simple, Slim, Lean

The TPCA factory was the biggest foreign direct investment ever made in the Czech Republic at a cost of €1.3 billion. Located in Kolin, it was about 60 km from Mlada Boleslav, the home town of Skoda Auto (member of the VW Group) and many suppliers.

The factory was set up by Masatake Enomoto from Toyota. A lawyer by training, he led the negotiations that resulted in the establishment of the Kolin plant. The negotiations ended with a clear arrangement on the financial side. Jean-Martin Folz, CEO of PSA, later explained,[13] "We shared the development cost and we paid for only two-thirds of the new factory in Kolin." The pillars of the agreement included: PSA would absorb 200,000 units annually and Toyota half of that. Toyota would be responsible for running the factory (according to the Toyota Production System [TPS]) and would be responsible for the development of the three vehicles to be produced at the factory (including the Peugeot 107 and Citroën C1). This helped greatly to build in the 93% parts commonality between the different brands. In return, PSA would handle all purchasing and supplier relations including their selection. Toyota was hoping to benefit from PSA's experience with European suppliers. Each partner would also bring one engine to the venture with the right [size] specification. Toyota would produce a 3-cylinder gasoline engine (also to be used in the bigger Toyota Yaris model) and PSA would bring a 4-cylinder diesel engine (also used in the Peugeot 206, Citroën C2 and C3). Engines were among the most expensive components of a car, averaging at around 32% of total vehicle cost.[14]

Enomoto oversaw the construction and start-up. This could explain why the factory looked very much like a Toyota factory. Automotive News, an industry newspaper, reported:[15]

> In many ways, the Kolin plant is a typical Toyota factory. The principles of efficient production that Toyota has established over the years are practiced in full at TPCA, including kaizen (continuous improvement), jidoka (fixing problems right away, where they occur), and just-in-time delivery.

Much of this can be attributed to Satoshi Takae. Takae was a Toyota veteran who started in Kolin as factory manager and was promoted to president of TPCA in 2005. His goal for the factory was very clear: "To be the number one plant in Europe."

In order to realize this, he had to work together with not only his 30 expatriate colleagues from Toyota, but also with nine permanent members of staff from PSA. For Takae, this meant exposing the Toyota Way, the "mysterious" Toyota DNA to outsiders (refer to Exhibit 5 for the key concepts of the Toyota Way).

At the same time, this working arrangement implied transferring control of suppliers to PSA.

Role of PSA

With an increasing trend towards outsourcing, PSA's task to manage all purchasing functions was hugely important to the outcome. Developing the local supply infrastructure, which accounted for 80% of all parts purchased (by value and volume), was seen as a major task. TPCA was directly dealing with around 150 Tier-1 suppliers. These were the big suppliers at the top of the hierarchy and many of them were the Czech or Slovak subsidiaries of the big international suppliers.

Within the automotive industry, PSA was known for its cost focus and its various JVs. Nicolas Guibert, TPCA's executive VP and highest ranking PSA official in Kolin and previously a plant manager in one of Peugeot's French factories, explained:

*Readers of this case are strongly encouraged to have a look at the official website of TPCA for a virtual factory tour. http://www.tpca-cz.com/en/about_factory_how.php#)

Exhibit 5   The Toyota Way

Section 1: Long-Term Philosophy
Principle 1: Base your management decisions on a long-term philosophy, even at the expense of short-term financial goals

Section 2: The Right Process will Produce the Right Results
Principle 2: Create continuous process flow to bring problems to the surface
Principle 3: Use "pull" systems to avoid "overproduction"
Principle 4: Level out the workload (Heijunka)
Principle 5: Build a Culture of stopping to fix problems, to get quality right the first time
Principle 6: Standardized tasks are the foundation for continuous improvement and employee empowerment
Principle 7: Use visual control so no problems are hidden
Principle 8: Use only reliable, thoroughly tested technology that serves your people and processes

Section 3: Add Value to the Organization by Developing Your People and Partners
Principle 9: Grow leaders who thoroughly understand the work, live the philosophy, and teach it to others

Principle 10: Develop exceptional people and teams who follow your company's philosophy
Principle 11: Respect your extended network of partners and suppliers by challenging them and helping them to improve

Section 4: Continuously Solving Root Problem Drives Organizational Learning
Principle 12: Go and see for yourself to thoroughly understand the situation (Genchi Genbutsu)
Principle 13: Make decisions slowly by consensus, thoroughly considering all options; implement decisions rapidly (Nemawashi)
Principle 14: Become a learning organization through relentless reflection (hansei) and continuous improvement (Kaizen)

Source: The Toyota Way, Jeffrey K. Liker, McGraw-Hill, 2004

PSA is one of the most joint-ventured companies [in the industry]. But this JV is different from other JVs. Usually, the responsibilities are clearly shared and each company works with high autonomy for what it is in charge. PSA has two JVs with Fiat—one in Italy and one in France. In Italy, Fiat does the design, process engineering and production operation and PSA pays for each car. In France, it is the contrary. Our engine JV with Ford is structured in a similar way: PSA is in charge of some engines from design to manufacturing and Ford of others. In our engine JV with BMW, they do the design and we do the industrialization. But here it is slightly different. We also share the tasks within the production operation. In TPCA we are not only spectators but also actors.

The level of difference could be seen in Guibert's role. He was reporting to Takae. Guibert was also responsible for accounting and finance functions of the factory.

•

Supplier Selection

European suppliers were very eager to supply TPCA since this was seen as the entry point for supplying Toyota. European suppliers were struggling, as many of their traditional customers had cut their production volumes considerably in recent years. Therefore, by supplying TPCA they hoped to grow with Toyota in Europe. TPCA was quite clear

on what it would not do. The company did not outsource external surfaces and key structural parts for quality reasons.

While supplying Toyota was an excellent reference in the industry, dealing with the company was not seen to be easy. Toyota's search for simplicity and economic efficiency was still a big question mark for many suppliers. Takae explained:

We are relationship-oriented with regards to the suppliers. We were surprised to see this transaction orientation with some of the suppliers here.

Suppliers to TPCA could also qualify for PSA's factory in neighboring Slovakia, about 250 km from Kolin. PSA had big plans at this factory, too.

Running TPCA

Toyota's Production System (TPS) was running all over the world, but in each market, it needed some minor adjustments. In the case of TPCA, the rapid ramp-up worked well (reaching full production capacity in less than 12 months). The factory produced four body types (both Toyota and PSA had a 3-door and 5-door version of their respective models) on the same line. TPCA had around 3,000 employees. Extensive training took place at various European factories and in Japan for the senior positions.

The trainings sessions lasted for a anywhere between one month and six months.

The normal shift system saw employees working for four days (10 hours each) and then they were off for three days. Newspapers reported:[16]

> *Few line workers have cars. Many live far from Kolin, often staying locally during the workweek and returning home only on days off.*

Management at TPCA soon started to wonder about high absenteeism among employees. A detailed analysis showed that in some cases, employees were asked to work six days in a row. And often, they did not show up on the sixth day. TPCA's management soon changed the allocation of shifts and it lowered absenteeism. But turnover remained an issue.

Regarding talent management, the question was, what would happen once competitor Hyundai Motor started hiring for its new Czech factory? Would employees switch to the new factory or would they stay with TPCA?

Overall, the management made every effort to embed the TPS at TPCA. It was willing to make some of the displays (ANDON) showing the status of the plant operation using pictures only, with no text, unlike in Japan and the US. With regard to running TPCA, Takae explained:

> *Of course, we had to overcome cultural and language barriers. We are dealing here with three national cultures—Japanese, French and Czech—and two company cultures with very different histories and production systems. But we found an overriding principle—cost reduction. Everything would depend on cost. In order to overcome the language barriers, we visualized everything; we never had to do this before [to this extent].*

At the same time, TPCA actively tried to work around local regulations. Automotive News Europe reported:[17]

> *To keep a promise it would not bring weekend heavy-truck traffic through town to the plant, TPCA must stockpile extra parts before the weekend starts. (. . .) It's built a parking lot. (. . .) The new parking lot can hold up to 180 trailers full of parts and raw materials. Then as the assembly lines move on Saturday and Sunday, logistics workers can move the parts via forklifts and cranes into the plant. It is an indication of how flexible the joint venture between PSA and Toyota is being to accommodate public feeling in its new Czech home. Because of local political pressures, the automaker gave up its promised exemption to Czech laws that limit weekend truck traffic. These laws ban trucks of 7.5 tons and larger between midnight and 10 pm on Sundays and during the summer months from 7 am to 8 pm on Saturdays.*

It seems that this also created a lot of goodwill within the company.

Meeting Structure

Managers at TPCA had to represent the interests of both TPCA and their employers. In order to minimize miscommunication, TPCA had a systematic meeting structure:

- Daily production meeting: This meeting took place every morning at 8:30. At this meeting, most managers were present in order to discuss quality, absenteeism and announce major decisions.
- Project Leaders Meeting: Managers from both companies originally met on a monthly basis and then only once a quarter. These meetings were attended by 10 to 20 managers from PSA and around 30 to 40 from Toyota.
- Steering Committee—TPCA's highest decision-making committee: Critical decisions were discussed here. There were five members from each side including Takae and Guibert. The meetings took place either at Toyota's HQ in Tokyo or PSA's HQ in Paris. This committee met twice a year.

Kolin, the New Travel Destination

Kolin became the new travel destination for plant managers and other executives from both Toyota and PSA. The factory was of interest, as it was a place for both companies to try new things. Generally speaking, with only 100,000 square meters, this factory was seen as having very little space. Guibert commented:

> *In this project we see interesting new methodologies compared to PSA's production system. But first, the TPS is a lot more than what we see and secondly, we cannot modify deeply our system because it is coherent and it has also its strong points. While both systems have their qualities, they are above all different.*

Nevertheless, within TPCA there were a few things that were off-limits to managers from the parent companies, as they were protected by patents or seen as proprietary.

Understanding the Market Space

As the construction of the factory was progressing, marketing managers at Toyota were getting ready for the positioning of the Aygo. The marketing challenge for selling the Aygo was considerable:

- How could a car with 93% standardized parts be differentiated in the marketplace from its two siblings? Colors were one differentiator, but only to a limited extent.

There were six shared colors among the three brands and two colors were specific to each brand.

■ Toyota also launched the new Yaris in 2005. The car was a bit bigger than the Aygo, but €3,000 more expensive. Sales representatives were likely to push the more expensive Yaris, as commissions were normally based on transaction prices.

■ The plant set-up with fixed volumes of 200,000 units for PSA and 100,000 for Toyota was unusual. In comparable joint ventures, there was normally a transfer pricing agreement, so the production volumes could be determined according to the market situation.

■ The average age of Toyota's customers was relatively high (50+ years in Europe). The dealerships were not really accustomed to serving younger clients.

■ Toyota had neither a recent history of selling cars in the A-segment nor a loyal customer base in that segment.

■ The agreement with PSA prohibited the use of car pictures until the launch of the car.

For marketing managers working on the launch of the Aygo, this was a tough list to work on. For Andrea Formica, marketing manager at Toyota's European HQ in Brussels, these constraints were seen as a challenge:[18]

> We will take the car out of the traditional showroom and bring it to the customer through special events, experience centers and concept cafes.

But would younger customers select the Toyota?

Knowing Younger Customers: What Makes Generation Y different?

Roughly speaking, Generation Y were those customers born after 1976 and was expected to be bigger than Generation X (1965–1976). Market research revealed major differences for Generation Y:

1. Consumers were more individualistic. Cars were not just transportation, they were another form of fashion apparel–it's about "making it mine."

2. Young consumers were internet-savvy–generally they had done their homework online before physically inspecting the car.

3. This group was immune to traditional advertising. Members of Generation Y were not likely to sit in front of the TV. A study by McKinsey[19] found that American teenagers spent 2.4 hours per day online, about six times the average of the overall population. By contrast, teenagers spent less than half the time watching TV compared with the overall population.

Generation Y was definitely attractive size wise, but reaching them would require many changes to the existing ways of doing things.

Launching the Aygo

Given the challenge of entering a new segment, there were different approaches for launching the Aygo in Europe. As one manager put it, "It is difficult to coordinate between the different countries. And what is good for one country may not necessarily be good for another." To capture the European spirit, Toyota asked ten artists from different European countries to redo the outside of an Aygo. These cars could be seen at many European car shows. Although the European HQ provided some background marketing material, the approaches for launching were different.

In Sweden, initially it was not even possible to buy the Aygo. Until May 2006, customers could only lease it as part of a mobility package, for €190 per month, including insurance, service and repairs. This was seen as a way to make the cost of owning the car more transparent.

An Example from the German Market

Markus Schrick, managing director of Toyota in Germany, outlined the initial situation:

> With Aygo we had a historic opportunity: Targeting young people who were new to Toyota with a completely new and appealing product in a [for Toyota] new segment of the market.
> The launch was phased in several steps, of which the first ones were the most important and maybe also the most impressive ones: (1) Identifying trendsetters amongst young people, (2) getting in touch with them personally to "promote" Aygo via (3) so-called "players." These players followed the trends discovered and created by the trendsetters and brought them to a broad young mainstream audience.
> This is what "viral marketing" is all about - but we needed to remain credible with our brand and product in order not to fail or to be misunderstood.
> "Go to where the people are" was one of our central ideas - and all together it worked well. And of course the fact that we discussed our strategies prior to our actions with these respective people helped a lot in understanding their lifestyle, attitudes and dreams.

Soon, it became apparent that the 18–30 age group was going to be the target market. Michael Potthast, Toyota's product manager for the Aygo in Germany, remembered the beginning:

> In hindsight, this was the most exciting launch I have done in my career. We wanted to sell into a market that Toyota did not know but, as always, understanding the customers was important. We had to make the car attractive to young, first-time buyers. We wanted to position ourselves as young, but we had to be credible in what we do.
>
> [Generation Y] was definitely a good target group, but they were difficult to get in touch with. Our dealers were not used to them as customers, except when the parents were buying a car for their children. We had a similar reaction in focus groups. One of our main findings, which became a motto for the Aygo retail experience was the Generation Y attribute: "Don't sell to me make me buy."

For Aygo's product managers in Europe, reaching the customers would require new approaches. At the same time, they could not change everything. For example, Toyota did not want - under any circumstances—to alter its reputation of having sufficient safety equipment on board. Starting with the first Aygo models sold, the standard equipment included six airbags, ABS and power steering at price points below £9,000.

Early Promotional Activities.

For the executives around Potthast and the agencies involved, it became clear that Generation Y could not be reached through "traditional marketing" practices. They would rely on very little traditional advertising, opting instead for direct contact with potential customers at the places they frequented:

- *Phase 1 (about 9 months prior to the launch)*: Toyota started communication with potential customers very early on. They created an interactive "Aygo online community" without the Toyota name. Visitors to the website wondered: who/what is Aygo? At that point, there were no answers to that question. The goal was to get into dialogue with this market. The website included, among other things, videogames.
- *Phase 2 (a few months before the launch in July 2005)*: Aygo trendscouts arrived at discotheques and pointed visitors to the Aygo booths inside the venue. There, booths for playing videogames were set up. The highest scorers of the evening would get attractive prizes, including leather cowboy hats, which were very popular at the time. Visitors could also continue their game from home via the Aygo website. Inside another booth, pictures and video messages of visitors were taken. The pictures were posted on the website; the video message could be sent to any e-mail address. The cowboy hats and other prizes were marked, "Aygo by Toyota," with "by Toyota" in a much smaller font size. Other prizes included mints in the shape of "ecstasy" drug pills and were also marked, "Aygo by Toyota."

Toyota also became involved in sponsoring rap concerts, among others a popular rap band–Fantastischen Vier. While the rappers did not actively promote the car during the concert, an Aygo poster was hanging on the stage. By sending text messages from their mobiles, visitors could win tickets to an after-hour VIP party with the band, which was sponsored by Toyota. The band also produced four video clips and a music contest. Here the public could send in their music files and the best one would then be recorded professionally. This partnership attracted a lot of attention by the media, and eventually led to an open-air concert, which was also sponsored by MTV, a popular TV station among teenagers.

Getting closer to the Launch.

Besides the website, Toyota put great emphasis on other ways of communicating with potential customers. The goal was to launch Aygo as a lifestyle vehicle.

Besides a thorough dealer training, there were several innovative ways to reach customers:

- *Dealer Training:* As dealers did not have much experience with young customers, they were sent to an extensive dealer training. The location, an unused subway station in the center of Berlin, provided an unusual location. The subway station was remodeled into a living room. The goal was to get the dealers in the minds of the core customers in the 18–30 age group. This covered everything from how do these people live to what kind of technologies were important to them, for example MP3 players. The subway station was also used for the press launch.
- *Aygo Nights:* The launch was on a Friday night in early July 2005 and it was intended to be something special. The logic was to take the car to where the customers were. The dealers either picked their showroom or, if they felt that their location was unsuitable for the target group, various other locations where young people would go. Some organized beach parties/volleyball tournaments, disco nights and concerts.
- *Aygo Lifestyle Magazine:* On the one hand, this was a car brochure dealing with the Aygo, but on the other hand,

it was a real lifestyle magazine covering typical topics such as fashion, travel, food and sports. The lifestyle side also included commercials from Calvin Klein, Samsonite and Fossil watches. It was also used for communicating product news, such as the arrival of new colors. The magazine was initially published every quarter and subsequently twice a year. It was produced on a European basis, with some variation according to countries.

■ *Aygo City Tour:* to the biggest universities. This was a way for university students to test-drive the Aygo. But it was far from a normal test-drive. The Tour consisted of several renovated caravans from the 1970s. One caravan was for booking test-drives. Another caravan was converted into a lounge, another one was set up for sending video messages via the Internet.

■ *Mobile Services:* Potential customers could have car specifications sent to their mobile phones and register for brochures via SMS, a technology heavily used by members of Generation Y.

Features of the Aygo.   The Aygo had emission rates that were among the lowest–only 109 grams per kilometer. This was an important argument for the target market. The car came with a full warranty for three years or 100,000 km. But here the commonalities with other car manufacturers stopped. The interest rates for the cars were calculated according to the age of the driver. An 18-year old customer would pay 1.8% interest, a 30-year old customer had to pay 3.0%. The positioning of the Aygo was quite different from its siblings.

Customers could also opt for a package including insurance and service contracts; they could get better rates on the insurance if they joined a one-day driving training.

Accessories.   It was possible to select from a wide range of accessories including window covers in "crazy" colors, costing €179. Covers for the side were available at €215.

In early 2006 Aygo was doing extremely well on the forecasted resale values of the major leasing companies. This limited the risk Toyota had to take when financing the cars. The launch was widely seen as successful and Toyota won the coveted "best media strategy award" in Germany. This was the trophy everyone wanted to have, but for managers at Toyota in Europe in 2006, the question was, how to keep up the momentum?

Notes

1.   Hillebrand, Walter. "Zetsche's Schlachtplan." *Capital*, September 2006, p. 4.
2.   Parts of the global overview of Toyota were taken from IMD-case "Toyota: Repositioning the brand in Europe (D): Growing step-by-step" (Case IMD-5-0701), by George Rädler and Dominique Turpin, 2006.
3.   "10 questions for Katsuaki Watanabe." Interview in *Time* Magazine, August 22, 2005, p. 10.
4.   "Formel Toyota." *Manager Magazine,* December 2004. 72 ff.
5.   "Toyota searches for love." *Wall Street Journal Europe,* January 11, 2006, p. 28.
6.   Toyota press release January 12, 2006. Quote taken from Mr. Shinichi Sasaki, President & CEO of Toyota Motor Europe (TME).
7.   See *Auto Motor Sport*, September 2006.
8.   Krix, Pia. "Von schweinen, frauen und lifestyle." *Automobilwoche Online,* June 11, 2005.
9.   *Automotive News,* July 11, 2005.
10.   Kanter, James. "Toyota leads Asia drive in Europe." *International Herald Tribune,* July 23, 2005.
11.   Jonas, Adam and David Cramer. "PSA Peugeot Citroen—The Toyota of Europe." *Morgan Stanley Company Update,* November 18, 2005, p. 7.
12.   *Automotive News Europe,* July 25, 2005, p. 19.
13.   Eschment, Wolfgang. "PSA plant keine weiteren Kooperationen." *Automobilwoche Online,* March 12, 2005.

14. Radtke, Philipp and Eberhard Abele/Andreas E. Zielke. "Die smarte Revolution in der Automobilindustrie." *Ueberreuter* (Redline Wirtschaft), 2004, p. 133.

15. Kochan, Anna. "Toyota transfers high standards to Czech factory." *Automotive News Europe,* July 11, 2005, p. 26.

16. Frink, Lyle. "Day One at Kolin: Czech plant starts regular output of PSA." *Automotive News Europe,* March 7, 2005.

17. Frink, Lyle. "Add a shift? Build a parking lot." *Automotive News Europe,* September 19, 2005, p. 4.

18. Weernink, Wim Oude. "Toyota taps US Scion brand for Aygo Marketing." *Automotive News,* March 7, 2005, p. 18.

19. Court, David C., Jonathan W. Gordon and Jesko Perry. "Boosting returns on marketing investment." *McKinsey Quarterly* 2005, Number 2, pp. 37–47.

Case 3–10: Hewlett-Packard in 2001*[1]

"To remain static is to lose ground."[2]

—David Packard, co-founder of HP

Introduction

Carly Fiorina, president and chief executive officer of Hewlett-Packard (HP), was considering a proposed merger of HP and one of its main rivals, Compaq Computer Corporation (Compaq). The idea of a merger was developed when Fiorina, attending an industry seminar in late 2000, met Michael Capellas, chief executive officer of Compaq. HP insiders estimated that the final purchase price would be $25 billion.[3] Sensing that there was interest in collaboration from both sides, Fiorina wanted to continue her dialogue with Capellas as soon as possible.

It was early February 2001, and Fiorina believed that the combined entity would position HP well for the anticipated resurgence in industry demand. However, a merger was fraught with business risk, and there would be no promises that HP's many stakeholders would endorse the bid. Fiorina wondered whether other options, including joint ventures, division spin-offs or divestitures, could be considered. Furthermore, was Compaq the right target?

Hewlett-Packard

In early 2001, HP's 600 sales and support offices were located in more than 120 countries. HP employed 88,500

* Ken Mark and Jordan Mitchell prepared this case under the supervision of Professor Charlene Zietsma solely to provide material for class discussion. The authors do not intend to illustrate either effective or ineffective handling of a managerial situation. The authors may have disguised certain names and other identifying information to protect confidentiality.

Ivey Management Services prohibits any form of reproduction, storage, or transmittal without its written permission. This material is not covered under authorization from CanCopy or any reproduction rights organization. To order copies or request permission to reproduce materials, contact Ivey Publishing, Ivey Management Services, c/o Richard Ivey School of Business, The University of Western Ontario, London, Ontario, Canada, N6A 3K7; phone (519) 661-3208; fax (519) 661-3882; e-mail cases@ivey.uwo.ca.

Copyright © 2004, Ivey Management Services
Version: (A) 2006-09-21

people and generated profits of $3.7 billion on revenues of $48.8 billion. Sales and profit growth were slowing and negative, respectively, and HP's January 2001 stock price was trading below October 1999 levels. In January 2001, HP was valued at $71.1 billion. David Packard and Bill Hewlett founded Hewlett-Packard in 1938 with the mission of creating first-class instruments. In a speech to young engineers, Packard once stated: "You're not here to make the average instrument. You're going to make a breakthrough in the art of instrumentation—or we're not going to put it in the catalogue."

Instead of the typical office layout where executives were located on higher floors, Hewlett and Packard created open-plan seating where employees of all levels worked next to each other. In addition, employees, even the founders, were known to each other by their first names. The goal for pretax earnings was 20 percent of sales. New businesses were evaluated based on whether they could produce profits from the beginning. Once these businesses were developed and incubated by engineers, they would be handed over to managers to be run as if they were independent companies. These little differences in operations (as compared to norms in many technology firms in the 1950s) became known, collectively, as the "HP Way."

HP's first foray into computers occurred in the 1960s despite hesitancy on the part of both Hewlett and Packard. In the late 1970s, its printer division emerged as a result of a key manager breaking many of HP's rules: licensing printer technology from Canon and using HP's own distribution and sales staff to sell the products. But by the 1990s, HP seemed to be stagnating. It became known less for its products and services and more for its employee programs such as diversity and telecommuting (which gave employees the option of working from their homes). The organization developed an aversion to risk. For example, executives found it difficult to carry out bold moves without consensus from multiple stakeholders (who were reluctant to challenge the status quo).

In the late 1990s, even as the technology boom was driving up growth rates at most companies, HP missed analysts' expectations for nine consecutive quarters. Employees at HP argued that their company did not have a strategy for the Internet, and worse, did not understand it. In order to focus its energies on the computer and printing divisions, HP's instruments division was spunoff as Agilent Technologies in 1999.

With the mandate to find "an incredible leader," HP's board of directors hired Fiorina.

Carly Fiorina at Hewlett-Packard

Fiorina joined HP in July 1999 after having spent 20 years at AT&T and Lucent Technologies. At Lucent, Fiorina held several senior leadership positions and directed Lucent's initial public offering and subsequent spin-off from AT&T. She had a bachelor's degree in medieval history and philosophy from Stanford University, an MBA from the Robert H. Smith School of Business (University of Maryland at College Park, Maryland), and a master of science degree from MIT's Sloan School.

Fiorina's first year was considered by many to have been a success. She had injected new energy into the firm by reinterpreting its longstanding values, and she had set the company on track towards an Internet-centric strategy. During her first 12 months, year-over-year revenues rose by 15 percent and net income by 14 percent. However, in mid- to late-2000, the overall computing industry was experiencing the beginnings of a recession. Revenue and profit growth at HP fell. Industry observers opined that HP was not responding satisfactorily to competitive threats, notably from IBM and Sun Microsystems (Sun) in the server market, Lexmark in the printer market, and Dell in personal computers.

In late 2000, HP was unsuccessful in its attempt to take over PriceWaterhouseCoopers (PWC), a consulting partnership. The deal was aimed at increasing HP's depth in the IT services market. The fact that it failed (and that PWC was subsequently absorbed by IBM's global services division) was not entirely a negative result: Some observers strongly felt that the deal was ill-advised—the terms were expensive and integration was considered to be an issue—and, if it had succeeded, would have put Fiorina's job at risk.

In 2001, after a year and a half of service at HP, Fiorina voluntarily handed back her second-half bonus of $625,000 because HP's financial performance did not pass muster.[4] Fiorina was accustomed to pressure. A few years previously, while she was deputy president at Lucent, she became known as Lucent's informal chief executive officer (CEO), with the company turning to her to figure out how to make quarterly financial results.[5] She was certain that Wall Street's pressure on HP would not abate.

Attempting to look beyond HP's current declining performance and the general malaise in the industry, Fiorina wondered whether there existed a great opportunity, with her proposed merger with Compaq, to effect significant and lasting change.

Products and Services

HP had three principal operating areas: imaging and printing systems, computer systems, and information technology (IT) services. In addition, the company also offered financing to customers entering into HP service agreements.

Imaging and printing systems made up 41 percent of the company's revenues and 64.8 percent of its operating profits. HP divided their activities into printer hardware, imaging, printing supplies and commercial printing. The printer hardware division included black and white and color laser and inkjet printers. During 2001, HP released the lowest priced printer of its family, the LaserJet 1000, as well as printers with capabilities to print from wireless devices and from mobile devices using the Bluetooth technology. In Imaging, HP offered scanners, digital cameras, copiers, faxes and other imaging products. Printing supplies included ink and LaserJet cartridges, paper and related products. Commercial printing involved solutions in storing, managing and producing digital solutions for printing presses.

Computing Systems made up 42.2 percent of the company's revenues and 22.7 percent of the company's operating profit. The division included home and commercial PCs, workstations, Unix and PC servers, storage and software products. HP developed their PCs and laptops to complement Microsoft's latest XP operating system. HP produced the Pavilion and Vectra desktop series and OmniBook and Pavilion laptop series. Servers ranged from platforms such as Unix, HP-UX to Linux and Microsoft Windows. A major initiative in the server business was using Intel's new Itanium processor (developed in conjunction with HP). By focusing on the Itanium processor market, HP had already garnered a 12 percent share of this small-but-growing market. (Incidentally, HP also had a 12 percent share of the Unix market.) HP believed in offering multiple platforms allowing customers to choose the best solution for their environment. However, some industry observers felt that HP's real strength in servers was still based in Unix (where competitor Sun Microsystems had a 51 percent share in that segment).

IT services generated over 14.3 percent of the company's revenues and made 15 percent of the company's operating profit. The IT services division was involved the planning, implementation, support and ongoing operations of IT solutions. The company offered breadth from infrastructure, storage, supply chain management, e-services, business intelligence, CRM, portals, Internet, networking and mobile communications. HP saw its advantage was its knowledge of infrastructure and its ability to provide strong outsourcing services to clients.

See Exhibit 1 for HP's performance by division.

The Computing Industry

Global spending in the computing industry was estimated at $950 billion in 2000, and growing to $1 trillion in 2003. The computing industry could be broken out into the following categories:

- Computer hardware, including personal computers, servers and storage devices
- Printers and imaging devices
- IT consulting services
- Computer software

For a breakdown of the segments by revenues and estimated future growth, see Exhibit 2. According to industry and stock analysts, competition in each segment was intensifying because of the sudden slowdown in demand. The major players, such as HP, IBM, Compaq, Dell, Lexmark, and Sun Microsystems (to name a few who competed in the overall industry), had different product and service line-ups—no two firms had exactly the same menu to offer to their customers. Product and service overlap, between one major player and the next, ranged from high (consider Toshiba and Gateway, both of whom sold personal computers) and low (consider Dell [personal computing hardware] and IBM [business services and hardware]). As a result, any two major firms could be potential partners in one segment and fierce competitors in another. One factor contributing to this diversity in offerings was the sheer number of segments in the industry; another factor was the ongoing stream of mergers and acquisitions between firms in related segments.

Despite the differences, firms competed in similar ways across all segments, i.e. is product or service innovation and performance, perception of quality and reliability, service and support, perception of brand value, and strength of value-added reseller (VAR) relationships.

In early 2000, as a result of the current economic malaise, analysts predicted that the computing industry would experience a new wave of consolidation.

Industry Segments in More Detail

The following discussion focuses on four segments in the computing industry: personal computers, printing and imaging, servers and storage, and IT services.

The Personal Computer (PC) Segment. The total PC market was estimated at $174 billion for 2000, of which $122 billion were desktop PC sales and $52 billion were laptop sales.[6] Gross margins in the industry ranged from about 10 percent to 18 percent. Key competitors in this industry included Compaq, Dell, IBM, HP and Fujitsu Siemens. For the market shares (dollar shares) of key competitors, see Exhibit 3.

Growth in the PC segment had been high in the late 1990s, with industry revenues in 1999 rising 25 percent over the previous year. The sudden downturn in 2000, with

Exhibit 1   HP Performance by Division (in millions of dollars)

	1998	1999	2000
Printing Systems			
Net Revenue	**16,709**	**18,550**	**20,476**
% of Total	*41.3%*	*42.6%*	*41.0%*
Earnings (loss) from			
Operations	2,043	2,335	2,746
Earnings % to Revenue	12.2%	12.6%	13.4%
% of Total	*62.6%*	*63.3%*	*64.8%*
Computing Systems			
Net Revenue	**17,315**	**17,814**	**21,095**
% of Total	*42.8%*	*40.9%*	*42.2%*
Earnings (loss) from			
Operations	480	850	960
Earnings % to Revenue	2.8%	4.8%	4.6%
% of Total	*14.7%*	*23.0%*	*22.7%*
IT Services			
Net Revenue	**5,685**	**6,255**	**7,129**
% of Total	*14.0%*	*14.4%*	*14.3%*
Earnings (loss) from			
Operations	748	575	634
Earnings % to Revenue	13.2%	9.2%	8.9%
% of Total	*22.9%*	*15.6%*	*15.0%*
All Other			
Net Revenue	**773**	**886**	**1,299**
% of Total	*1.9%*	*2.0%*	*2.6%*
Earnings (loss) from			
Operations	(5)	(71)	(103)
Earnings % to Revenue	-0.6%	-8.0%	-7.9%
% of Total	*-0.2%*	*-1.9%*	*-2.4%*
TOTAL Segments			
Net Revenue	**40,482**	**43,505**	**49,999**
% of Total	*100.0%*	*100.0%*	*100.0%*
Earnings (loss) from			
Operations	3,266	3,689	4,237
Earnings % to Revenue	8.1%	8.5%	8.5%
% of Total	*100.0%*	*100.0%*	*100.0%*

Note: Total Segments do not equal overall company.

Source: "HP Annual Report," www.sec.gov. October 31, 2000, p. 57.

Exhibit 2   Selected Computing Industry Segments by Revenue and Growth Prospects

Market Size (US$ millions)	2000	Growth Prospects for Next Few Years
Personal Computers	$ 152,185	
Desktop PCs	$ 105,011	Optimistic: 5–10% per year; Pessimistic: Flat to negative growth
Notebook PCs	$ 47,174	Expected to grow significantly faster than Desktop PCs
Printing and Imaging	$ 40,000	
Inkjet Printers	$ 33,851	Low growth (under 10% per year)
Monochrome Laser Printers	$ 5,824	Low growth (under 10% per year)
Desktop Color Laser Printers	$ 325	High growth (over 15% per year)
Servers	$ 40,677	Low growth (under 10% per year)
Storage	$ 19,549	
Open Systems SAN	$ 4,793	Low growth (under 10% per year)
Unix Disk Storage Systems	$ 14,756	Low growth (under 10% per year)
IT Services	$ 395,000	About 10% per year

global PC shipments dropping 3.6 percent from the third to fourth quarter of 2000, prompted one observer to note: "This is the worst it's been in the history of the industry."[7] Looking ahead, industry growth prospects in 2001 and beyond were uncertain, with revenue growth estimates ranging from five percent to 15 percent.

PCs were generally sold through VARs and retail outlets, with the exception of Dell, which sold direct to consumers and businesses. The other major firms, including IBM, HP and Compaq, had largely failed to transition over to a direct-to-consumer model. One explanation was that they underestimated the challenges posed by the sophisticated supply chain logistics of the direct model.[8]

In 2001, competition based on price was increasing, with Dell (and its 10 percentage point cost advantage over the major firms) leading the charge. A Gartner Group analyst suggested, "We anticipate a price war in the United States in 2001, as direct vendors [like] Dell . . . endeavor to gain market share from Compaq, Hewlett-Packard and IBM."[9] Another analyst suggested,

The PC industry is at a critical juncture. Managements and investors need to recognize that the problem is not the end of the PC, but slower growth and overcapacity. It is time for bold moves. It is time to do it before it is done to you. We believe investors should stay on the sidelines until they see concrete steps toward consolidation.[10]

Printing and Imaging.   The total printing and imaging market was estimated at $40 billion in 2000. This segment experienced growth similar to that of the PC segment. Printers typically had gross margins ranging from five to 15 percent. In the last few years, many printer manufacturers had begun selling printers at cost or at a negative margin of five to 10 percent in order to benefit from future printer cartridge sales; printer cartridges generated gross margins of approximately 70 percent.[11]   The dominant players in printers and printer supplies included Hewlett-Packard, Lexmark, Canon and Seiko-Epson.

Exhibit 3   Global Market Shares by Competitor

Market Share (2000)	HP	Compaq	Dell	IBM	Lexmark	Sun
Personal Computers	13.9%	13.6%	12.8%	7.3%	0.0%	0.0%
Printing and Imaging	51.2%	5.6%	0.0%	2.5%	9.5%	0.0%
Servers	16.3%	16.6%	7.0%	15.7%	0.0%	23.9%
Storage						
Open Systems SAN	8.8%	16.1%	3.9%	8.9%	0.0%	13.6%
Unix Disk Storage Systems	11.4%	8.2%	0.0%	10.8%	0.0%	21.9%
IT Services	1.9%	1.7%	0.0%	8.4%	0.0%	0.7%

Industry observers felt that the printer market would flatten out because of the declining consumer demand for PCs. While the printer market had suffered in the downturn, sales of cartridges had remained steady and continued to grow in line with PC shipments. Like PCs, printers were generally sold through VARs and retailers, with the former relying on cartridge sales to generate repeat visits from consumers.

Significant innovation had occurred in the printer industry in the last five years, with HP leading the way by being one of the first firms to introduce a sub-$100 printer. The effects of HP's subsequent market share gain (in the inkjet market) on its competitors were mitigated by strong overall segment growth. It was not clear how competitors would react now that growth was slowing.

Servers and Storage.   The word *server* was used to denote both the physical piece of hardware such as mainframes, minicomputers or personal computers, as well as software that ran applications for a number of users. *Storage* referred to any device that was used to save information apart from an actual PC, work terminal, or server.

In 2000, the total server market was estimated at $40.7 billion. The server market had posted a growth rate of 30.9 percent in 2000. By early 2001, however, the slowdown in the rest of the industry had led to a decrease in the demand for servers. Gross margins on servers were estimated to be between 20 and 40 percent. The top five vendors of servers held 79.4 percent of market share (measured on revenues) in 2000.

Most servers were purchased by businesses and sold through VARs and by a firm's direct sales force (typically in combination with a consulting and hardware installation package).

In 2000, the total storage market was worth $29 billion and gross margins were estimated to be between 15 and 30 percent.[12] Storage was divided into either disk storage or tape storage, with such solutions like storage area networks (SANs) being common links between disk array controllers and servers. The major players in storage were EMC, Compaq and Sun.

The majority of storage devices were purchased by businesses through VARs and a firm's direct sales force. Like the rest of the computing industry, storage sales were expected to slow, with 2001 growth rates projected between 15 percent and 20 percent.

IT Services.   IT services were defined as any range of consulting, education, design, installation, implementation, ongoing support and maintenance and outsourcing services provided to other companies.[13] The size of the IT services market in 2000 was estimated at $395 billion with an average growth of nine percent over the last three years. Some industry observers predicted that IT services would continue to enjoy consistent growth rates of eight percent to 10 percent over the next three years. Gross margins on IT services ranged from 10 to 200 percent, depending on many variables including personnel cost and ability to meet standards and deadlines. Additional products and services were often sold to IT clients.

The industry for IT services was highly fragmented, with the top 10 providers accounting for roughly 30 percent of the market. The key players were IBM with Electronic Data Systems (EDS), Fujitsu, Accenture, and Computer Sciences Corporation (CSC).

Compaq

Compaq was founded in 1982 and competed in the following markets: consumer and corporate PCs, handheld devices, workstations and servers. In 1995, Compaq was the global leader in PCs with a strong position in the PC server business. In 1996, it moved into the enterprise segments of the computing market with servers and powerful workstations, placing it in direct competition with IBM and HP. In order to penetrate the enterprise segment against the strong sales and field service and support organizations of IBM and HP, Compaq developed alliances with systems integrators such as Andersen Consulting, and with SAP, the leading enterprise resource-planning software vendor.

As part of its growth strategy, Compaq had made two major acquisitions: Tandem Corporation in 1997 for $3 billion, and Digital Equipment Corporation (DEC) in 1998 for $9.6 billion. The acquisitions were aimed at strengthening their position in the enterprise market. With Tandem, Compaq acquired the Himalaya server, giving the company greater strength in high-end computing. With DEC, Compaq inherited its proprietary Unix server platform, some important storage technology and access to its NT service organization. This meant that Compaq had the largest channel structure, delivering 80 percent of its products and services through its channel partners. The merger between DEC and Compaq was viewed as being difficult and uneven as it involved combining DEC's 50,000 employees and Compaq's 33,000 employees and the company's two distinct cultures.[14] Observers noted that Compaq continued to be a company with at least three distinct cultural environments cobbled together. For example, employees from the original companies—Compaq, Tandem, and DEC—continued to identify with their previous pre-merger, organizations.

By the fall of 1999, Compaq was organized into three large business units: enterprise solutions and services,

Exhibit 4   Compaq Revenues by Division (in millions of dollars)

	1998	1999	2000
Enterprise Computing			
Revenue	10,498	12,974	14,316
% of TOTAL	33.7%	33.7%	33.8%
Operating Income	948	1,201	2,140
Operating Income %	9.0%	9.3%	14.9%
% of TOTAL	54.3%	63.8%	59.9%
Compaq Global Services			
Revenue	3,990	7,162	6,993
% of TOTAL	12.8%	18.6%	16.5%
Operating Income	776	1,148	944
Operating Income %	19.4%	16.0%	13.5%
% of TOTAL	44.4%	61.0%	26.4%
Commercial Personal Computing			
Revenue	11,846	12,185	13,136
% of TOTAL	38.0%	31.6%	31.0%
Operating Income	(46)	(448)	289
Operating Income %	–0.4%	–3.7%	2.2%
% of TOTAL	–2.6%	–23.8%	8.1%
Consumer			
Revenue	4,932	5,994	7,586
% of TOTAL	15.8%	15.6%	17.9%
Operating Income	183	262	170
Operating Income %	3.7%	4.4%	2.2%
% of TOTAL	10.5%	13.9%	4.8%
Other			
Revenue	(97)	210	352
% of TOTAL	–0.3%	0.5%	0.8%
Operating Income	(115)	(281)	27
Operating Income %	118.6%	–133.8%	7.7%
% of TOTAL	–6.6%	–14.9%	0.8%
TOTAL			
Revenue	31,169	38,525	42,383
% of TOTAL	100.0%	100.0%	100.0%
Operating Income	1,746	1,882	3,570
Operating Income %	5.6%	4.9%	8.4%
% of TOTAL	100.0%	100.0%	100.0%

Source: "Compaq Annual Report," www.sec.gov. December 31, 2000, p. 12.

commercial personal computing (small and mid-sized businesses) and consumer. A significant proportion of the revenues in the enterprise solutions and services segment came from professional and support services, an important result of the Tandem and DEC acquisitions. The business critical server business was largely a legacy of the Tandem acquisition.

Operating in over 200 countries with 94,600 employees, Compaq had increased revenues by 10 percent from 1999 to $42.4 billion in 2000. For the same period, net income had stayed flat. Refer to Exhibit 4 for Compaq's performance by division. For financial comparisons between selected competitors, see Exhibit 5. Compaq's market capitalization had suffered a major decline, falling 42.7 percent from early 2000 to $25.9 billion in early 2001.[15]

Compaq aimed to be the leading global provider of information technology products, services and solutions. Compaq sold its goods through dealers, VARs (value added resellers) and system integrators. With direct sales increasing, pressure was mounting on VAR margins, estimated to be approximately four percent to five in 2000. Its customers included large and medium-sized businesses as well as government and educational facilities. Compaq employed a direct sales force and offered its products on its Internet site and by telephone—a reaction to Dell's success with its direct model. Compaq used a variety of channels to sell its products. It sold to large and medium-sized business and government customers through dealers, value-added resellers and system integrators. Small business and home customers were reached through dealer and consumer channels. Compaq also had a direct sales force and sold its product on an Internet site and by telephone.

When Compaq attempted to bypass its 44,000 resellers by touting its direct-to-consumer sales, resellers responded by steering their customers to other brand-name manufacturers such as HP or to their own "white label" PCs. At the end of 2000, Capellas still had not resolved the channel issues, particularly in the important commercial personal computing segment. In this segment of the business, more than 85 percent of Compaq's sales were still generated by the traditional, indirect channel, and less than 10 percent of sales came from Compaq's new direct-to-consumer channel. Yet Capellas persisted with the latter option, most likely because it was the model used by Dell, Compaq's fiercest competitor.

Although Capellas had estimated Compaq revenue growth for 2001 to be between six percent and eight , Compaq cut its revenue forecasts for 2001 a few days into the fiscal year, citing the unexpectedly sharp slowdown in the desktop PC market.

In early 2001, Compaq Computer Corp.'s (Compaq) chairman and chief executive officer, Michael D. Capellas, was answering questions about his firm's future. After a confident presentation about his company's global prospects, Capellas added; "I think the fact that we have a global business protects us reasonably well, but some U.S. companies will be hammered and will have to make dramatic changes. Are we concerned about economic slowdown? Yes, these are uncertain times."

Exhibit 5   Financial Comparisons (Selected Items from the Income Statement)

Revenues (US$ millions)	1997	1998	1999	2000
Hewlett-Packard Co.	42,895	47,061	42,370	48,782
Compaq Computer Corp.	24,584	31,169	38,525	42,383
International Business Machines Corp.	78,508	81,667	87,548	88,396
Sun Microsystems Inc.	8,598	9,791	11,726	15,721
Dell Inc.	12,327	18,243	25,265	31,888
Lexmark International Inc.	2,494	3,021	3,452	3,807

Operating Margin (before depreciation)	1997	1998	1999	2000
Hewlett-Packard Co.	13.7%	12.7%	11.8%	10.3%
Compaq Computer Corp.	14.0%	5.6%	5.5%	9.1%
International Business Machines Corp.	16.7%	16.7%	18.5%	18.3%
Sun Microsystems Inc.	16.2%	17.8%	19.4%	20.2%
Dell Inc.	11.2%	11.8%	10.3%	9.4%
Lexmark International Inc.	14.1%	15.2%	16.1%	14.4%

Net Profit Margin	1997	1998	1999	2000
Hewlett-Packard Co.	7.3%	6.3%	7.3%	7.3%
Compaq Computer Corp.	7.5%	-8.8%	1.5%	1.4%
International Business Machines Corp.	7.8%	7.7%	8.8%	9.2%
Sun Microsystems Inc.	8.9%	7.8%	8.8%	11.8%
Dell Inc.	7.7%	8.0%	6.6%	7.0%
Lexmark International Inc.	6.5%	8.0%	9.2%	7.5%

Current Assets (US$ millions)	1997	1998	1999	2000
Hewlett-Packard Co.	20,947	21,584	21,642	23,244
Compaq Computer Corp.	12,017	15,167	13,849	15,111
International Business Machines Corp.	40,418	42,360	43,155	43,880
Sun Microsystems Inc.	3,728	4,148	6,116	6,877
Dell Inc.	3,912	6,339	7,681	9,491
Lexmark International Inc.	776	1,020	1,089	1,244

Total Assets	1997	1998	1999	2000
Hewlett-Packard Co.	31,749	33,673	35,297	34,009
Compaq Computer Corp.	14,631	23,051	27,277	24,856
International Business Machines Corp.	81,499	86,100	87,495	88,349
Sun Microsystems Inc.	4,697	5,711	8,420	14,152
Dell Inc.	4,268	6,877	11,471	13,435
Lexmark International Inc.	1,208	1,483	1,703	2,073

Common Equity	1997	1998	1999	2000
Hewlett-Packard Co.	16,155	16,919	18,295	14,209
Compaq Computer Corp.	9,429	11,351	14,834	12,080
International Business Machines Corp.	19,564	19,186	20,264	20,377
Sun Microsystems Inc.	2,742	3,514	4,812	7,309
Dell Inc.	1,293	2,321	5,308	5,622
Lexmark International Inc.	501	578	659	777

Free Cash Flow	1997	1998	1999	2000
Hewlett-Packard Co.	1,451	2,820	1,250	2,050
Compaq Computer Corp.	2,959	(51)	(160)	(738)
International Business Machines Corp.	1,289	1,919	3,273	2,729
Sun Microsystems Inc.	551	696	1,734	2,772
Dell Inc.	1,600	2,140	3,529	3,713
Lexmark International Inc.	205	187	180	180

Source: Compustat Database.

An accountant by training, Capellas worked in steel and oil before joining Compaq in 1998, coming from Oracle Corporation. When he arrived at Compaq, Capellas received a three-year contract that more than doubled his pay after he became chairman in September 2000. Just two weeks later, he received an $850,000 onetime bonus, base pay of $1.6 million a year and an annual bonus of twice his base pay. Capellas also had performance-based stock options and incentive awards that were targeted to a range of seven to 10 times his salary.

In addition, Capellas received options for close to one million shares of Compaq stock. About half the options vested at various dates, based on Capellas's employment through 2004. The remainder vested according to a schedule of stock-price targets or if increases in earnings per share matched or exceeded those of major rivals. As an incentive to raise the company's stock price, 250,000, or a quarter of Capellas's options, would vest if shares stayed above a stair-stepped schedule of stock-price targets for 15 days in a row.

Conclusion

Many onlookers predicted that the economic situation would worsen, inevitably hurting the entire computing industry. In addition, competitive actions were hard to predict. Dell and Lexmark could continue their aggressive pricing in PCs and printers respectively. On the other hand, there were rumors that IBM would end its involvement in the PC market in the next year. As for smaller competitors—see Exhibit 6 for a partial list—it was difficult to predict what they would do.

Exhibit 6   Other Competition

Apple
Apple had had success with innovative hardware such as the iMac and iBook, which had revived its mid-90s struggling business performance. Apple was relatively small in comparison to other PC manufacturers, with $8.0 billion in sales, but had carved a niche with innovative products and releases, such as the iPod.[1]

EMC
EMC was the world leader within the storage sector and was dedicated to automated networked storage. The company slogan, "where information lives," demonstrated EMC's commitment to storage and server resources. EMC had revenues of $8.9 billion and profits of $1.8 billion in 2000.[2] In 2001, it was expected that the company would sign a deal with Dell, allowing the resale of its storage system under a co-branded name.

Gateway
Gateway posted revenues of $9.7 billion in 2000 and was a supplier of PCs, sold mostly through the company's own distribution network and owned a chain of approximately 200 "Country Stores." In 2001, Gateway slowed retail expansion and decided to focus on the U.S. market by exiting its international business.[3] Gateway also supplied TVs and was known for its direct-to-consumer touch and warranty programs.[4]

IT Services
There were several firms that completed in IT services. Besides the leader, IBM, other major companies included EDS (Electronic Data Systems) with revenues of $21 billion, Accenture with revenues of $10 billion and Computer Sciences Corporation with revenues of $10 billion.

Japanese Competitors
NEC (marketing Packard Bell PCs) and Fujitsu Siemens had a stronghold of the Western European market with prominence in Japan. Sony was a leader in its many divisions, ranging from audio, video and communications to information technology. It had worldwide sales of $62 billion; $20 billion was accounted for by U.S. sales. Sony was leveraging its other divisions and was trying to make headway into the PC market.[5] Toshiba had U.S. sales of $5.5 billion and worldwide sales of $41 billion; it was also a major player within the laptop computer segment.[6] Seiko Epson, a Japanese-based company, began in 1942 and had experienced steady increases in sales over 10 percent in the last three years. Seiko Epson aimed to deliver cutting-edge imaging solutions on paper, screen and glass (such as mobile displays). Canon was founded in 1937, originally as a camera company, but grew as a major force within the printer market. By 2001, computer peripherals, which included printers made up nearly half of Canon's revenues; 20 percent of sales were from cameras.

PDA Manufacturers
Palm, Handspring, Research in Motion and Sony all fought against HP and Compaq for market share in the PDA market. Palm was the leader in the market and had sales of over $1 billion, in comparison to Handspring with sales of $371 million and Research in Motion with sales of $220 million.

---

[1] "Apple Company Capsule," www.hoovers.com, August 27, 2003.
[2] "EMC Company Capsule," www.hoovers.com, August 23, 2003.
[3] "Credit Suisse First Boston Equity Analyst Report," January 9, 2002, p.18.
[4] "Gateway Corporate Web site," www.gateway.com, August 20, 2003.
[5] "Sony Corporate Web site," www.sony.com, August 20, 2003.
[6] "Toshiba Corporate Web site," www.toshiba.com, August 20, 2003.

In light of all the issues facing her industry, and the scrutiny on her company, Fiorina wanted to know what she should do to position her company for the next few years. She knew that, aside from short-term pressures to meet forecasts, a more dramatic move was needed in the longer term to get HP back on track.

The Richard Ivey School of Business gratefully acknowledges the generous support of Canada Life in the development of these learning materials.

Notes

1. This case has been written on the basis of published sources only. Consequently, the interpretation and perspectives presented in this case are not necessarily those of Hewlett-Packard or any of its employees.
2. "HP fires back . . . ," ITworld.com, December 31, 2001.
3. All figures in U.S. dollars.
4. "HP chief gave back her bonus," *The Wall Street Journal*, January 9, 2001, p. C16.
5. Anders, George. "Perfect enough," *Penguin Book*, 2003.
6. "Hewlett-Packard Analyst Report," *CIBC World Markets*, July 10, 2003, p. 26.
7. "Dataquest and IDC: PC shipments," *Purchasing*, February 22, 2001.
8. Wolf, Charles. "PC Hardware: PC industry overview—perception vs. reality," *Needham Analyst Report*, January 2001, p. 5.
9. Connell, James. "Tech brief: PC price war," *International Herald Tribune*, March 27, 2001.
10. "PC industry manifesto," *Bear Stearns Analyst Report*, January 2001, p. 3.
11. "Print Prevue," *Credit Suisse First Boston Analyst Report*, March 13, 2001, p. 4.
12. "Hewlett-Packard Analyst Report," *CIBC World Markets*, July 10, 2003, p. 26.
13. "Hewlett-Packard Annual Report," www.sec.gov, October 31, 2000, p. 2.
14. "ABN-AMRO Analyst Report," *Compaq Computer*, December 19, 2001.
15. "Compaq Company Capsule," www.hoovers.com. Accessed August 10, 2004.

Case 3-11: Vodafone; E Pluribus Enum*

Abstract

In 2006, Vodafone Group PLC was the world's largest cell phone provider by revenue. Since 1999, Vodafone had invested US$270 billion (€225 bn) mostly in stock, building an empire spanning 26 countries. It controlled cell phone operations in 16 countries and had minority stakes in companies in ten other countries. This case traces the history of Vodafone's growth and its capability to transform and adapt itself to the dramatically changing market environment in the dynamic telecommunication sector. The case analyzes Vodafone's growth through acquisitions and the subsequent integration of acquired units with a key focus on how it manages to coordinate its businesses on a global scale.

Arun Sarin reclined in his seat in a first-class compartment en route to London. The CEO of Vodafone, the world's largest mobile telephone operator, began reflecting on the events of the last few days, in particular Vodafone's decision to exit the Japanese market by selling Vodafone's stake in Japan Telecom to Tokyo-based Softbank in a deal valued at $15.4bn, confirming that after the sale the company would return $10.5bn to its shareholders. Vodafone had trailed behind NTT DoCoMo and KDDI since its entry into Japan in 2001, thanks to fickle consumers, the lack of a low-end tier in the segment, and the challenge of coordinating terminals and technologies across borders. The time had come to make a hard decision, and Sarin had made it.

It was not the first time he had been faced with such a decision. Two years earlier Vodafone had made headlines in the financial press with its failed attempt to take over the US mobile operator, AT&T Wireless. After a long takeover battle, Vodafone's American rival Cingular Wireless had offered $41bn in cash for AT&T Wireless[1]. At the time, Sarin had not been sure whether to regret the failed takeover. He could have easily financed a larger sum for the bid, but major shareholders had been very explicit that anything beyond an offer of $38bn would be detrimental to their interests.[2] Vodafone's offer had forced Cingular to increase its bid from $30bn to $41bn, meaning that it might take Cingular many years to digest the merger (refer Exhibit 1 for share prices of Vodafone since 1989). There might also yet come more promising and cheaper ways for Vodafone to enhance its presence in the world's largest economy with a huge growth potential.

Sarin knew he could not afford to alienate Vodafone's shareholders by pursuing growth at all costs. However, Vodafone's current hold in the American market (the non-controlling stake in Verizon Wireless but the only one in US) was not comforting either. The relationship with the other main shareholder Verizon, was quite strained, management had refused to adopt the single Vodafone brand, and had insisted on using the outdated American CDMA network standard instead of the group-wide GSM/UMTS standard.[3]

* E Pluribus Enum means "Out of many, One" signifying the harnessing of global scale and scope synergies of One Vodafone. This case was prepared by Ashok Som, Associate Professor, Strategy and Management Area at ESSEC Business School, Paris, together with help from Johannes Banzhaf while on his double-degree ESSEC-Mannheim management program. The case was made possible by the permission of Mr. Arun Sarin, CEO and the active participation of Mr. Alan Harper, Group Strategy and Business Integration Director, for his helpful comments and support. The case was developed as a basis for class discussion rather than to illustrate either effective or ineffective handling of an administrative situation.
Reproduction or distribution of this case is strictly prohibited without the prior permission of the author. To obtain reprints of this case, ECCH Reference number 304-625-1, please contact the ECCH at http://www.ecch.com

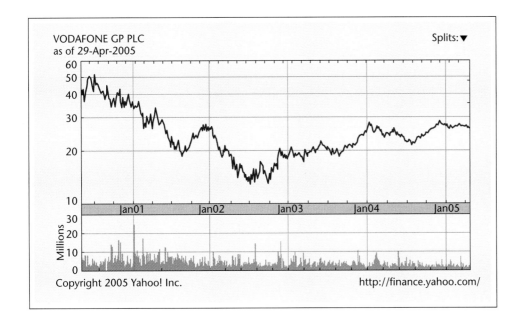

Exhibit 1   Vodafone Share Price Since 2001, in Pence

Source: http://finance.yahoo.com

Being the CEO was definitely not an easy job, with so many things to consider and the shadow of his larger-than-life predecessor Sir Chris Gent looming over him. But this was exactly the reason why he was being paid £1.2m a year as base salary.[4]

Company Overview: Vodafone Group Plc

In 2005, Vodafone was the leading mobile phone operator in the world. It had more than 150 million customers worldwide in 26 different countries.[5] Vodafone employed approximately 67,000 people around the world and had its headquarters in Newbury, England. Being listed on the stock exchanges of New York (ticker: VOD); London and Frankfurt, it boasted a market capitalization of US$ 165.7bn[6]–making it the eleventh most valuable company in the world. In FY2003 it suffered a loss of US$15.5bn (on revenues of approximately US$ 48 bn)—a figure that was the result of large write-downs on the goodwill of acquired companies and huge amortization charges related to the acquisition of other mobile operators like Mannesmann D2. These charges amounted to US$18.8bn.[7] In fact, if one excluded these extraordinary non-cash charges, Vodafone was very profitable, as indicated by its gross margins and its capacity to generate huge positive cash flows: The cash flow from operating activities (before capital expenditure and other outflows) amounted to £12.3bn (approximately US$22.7bn) in Financial Year 2004, while free cash flow

exceeded an unbelievable £8 billion (US$ 15.7 bn—refer to Exhibit 2 for an overview of Vodafone Group's financials).[9] Vodafone had been consistently paying dividends and had recently announced a £3 billion share repurchase program.[10]

History of Vodafone[11]

The company was formed as "Racal Telecom Limited" in 1984 as a subsidiary of Racal Electronics Plc., a British electronics manufacturing company. It successfully bid for a private sector UK cellular license in 1982 and hosted the first ever mobile phone call in the UK in 1985. The customer base stood at 19,000 on December 31, 1985.

In October 1988, Racal Telecom Ltd. Went public by offering approximately 20% of the company's stock to the public. Three years later, it was fully de-merged from Racal Electronics and became an independent company, with a different name Vodafone Group Plc, which was listed on the London and New York Stock Exchanges. Corporate legend wants that the "founders had the foresight to realize that people would do more than talk over their phones and so created a future-proof name that would embrace both Voice and Data mobile communication: Vodafone"[12] . Due to its early start, it managed the largest mobile network in the world by 1987.

In 1992, Vodafone pioneered again when it signed the world's first international "roaming" agreement with Telecom Finland, allowing Vodafone's customers to use

Exhibit 2 Vodafone Key Financials 1995–2004

For the financial year ended 31 March	Turnover (in £m)	Profit (loss) for the financial year (after taxation, in £m)	Net cash inflow from operating activities (in £m)	Dividends per share (pence)	Registered proportionate customers (in thousands)
1995	1,153	238	386	3.34p	2,073
1996	1,402	311	615	4.01p	3,035
1997	1,749	364	644	4.81p	4,016
1998	2,408	419	886	5.53p	5,844
1999	3,36	637	1,045	3.77p	10,445
2000	7,873	487	2,510	1.34p	39,139
2001	15,004	(9,763)	4,587	1.40p	82,997
2002	22,845	(16,155)	8,102	1.47p	101,136
2003	30,375	(9,819)	11,142	1.70p	119,709
2004	33,559	(9,015)	12,317	2.03p	133,421

Source: Company Annual Reports

Group Turnover for the Year Ended 31 March 2003, in £m, by Geographic Region

	2003	2002
Mobile telecommunications:		
Northern Europe	6,057	
Central Europe	4,775	
Southern Europe	8,051	
Americas	5	
Asia Pacific	8,364	
Middle East and Africa	290	
= Total mobile operations	**27,542**	**20,742**
Other operations:*		
Europe	854	
Asia Pacific	1,979	
= Total group turnover	**30,375**	**22,845**

* "Other operations" mainly include the results of the group's interests in fixed line telecommunications businesses in Germany (Arcor), France (Cegetel) and Japan (Japan Telecom). The turnover figure for the Americas does not include the 45% stake in Verizon Wireless (U.S.).

Source: Adapted from Company Annual Report 2003

their phone on a different network while still being billed in their home country. Four years later, Vodafone became the first operator in the UK to offer so-called "pre-paid" packages that do not require the customers to sign a long-term contract.

Christopher Gent succeeded Sir Gerald Whent at the helm of the company on January 1, 1997. Gent was responsible for shifting Vodafone's growth strategy from organic to aggressive external, orchestrating its move towards globalization. In the same year, Vodafone's 100th roaming agreement was signed.

In early 1999, Vodafone signed up its 10 millionth customer, five million of them in the UK. Vodafone's

growth reached the next level when it successfully merged with AirTouch Communications Inc. of the U.S.–a $61bn deal. Vodafone renamed itself briefly into Vodafone AirTouch and more than doubled its customer base to over 31 million customers worldwide (September 1999), having operations in 24 countries across five continents.[13] In the late nineties and the early new millenium, stock markets were steering towards a bubble, with "mobile" being the latest hype and insane sums being paid for mobile operators and the licenses to operate mobile networks. At the end of November 1999, the company had a market capitalization of approximately £90 billion. Vodafone's North American branch was integrated into a new entity branded

Verizon Wireless together with Bell Atlantic's mobile business, with Vodafone retaining a 45% stake in the new venture. Verizon Wireless was the largest mobile phone operator in 2003 in a very fragmented North American market (36 million customers, 24% market share as of September 30, 2003).[14]

In a move that sent shockwaves through corporate Germany in 1999, Vodafone launched a €100bn takeover bid for Mannesmann in order to get hold of its "D2" mobile phone business, the private market leader in Germany. A bitter struggle for Mannesmann's independence ensued, but finally the board of Mannesmann gave in and the deal was closed in 2000: €190bn paid in stocks - Germany's largest takeover ever.[15] The customer base was once again doubled and Vodafone found itself among the ten largest companies in the world in terms of market capitalization. The mobile telephony boom reached its peak and former national providers (such as Deutsche Telekom, France Télécom, Telefonica) embarked on a buying binge that brought them on the verge of bankruptcy, when the bubble finally burst (Deutsche Telekom shares fell from more than 100€ to 15€).

The year 2001 saw a consolidation and restructuring within Vodafone, which reported 82.9 million customers for the financial year ending March 31, 2001. It grew at a somewhat slower pace than in previous years, about half of it generated by internal growth and the other half by acquisitions (e.g. acquiring of Ireland's Eircell and increasing its stake in Spanish AirTel Movil to 91.7%). However, "slower growth" still meant that Vodafone had added approximately 20 million customers by the end of the year 2002. At that time, the company board announced that the Indian-born American Arun Sarin would take over the CEO position on July 30, 2003.

There were no large scale acquisitions in 2002 and 2003, but instead a host of smaller deals and partnership agreements. In February 2004, Vodafone's bid for AT&T Wireless in the U.S. failed against a higher offer by Cingular, yet clearly indicating that Vodafone had all but renounced its growth ambitions.

Growth at Vodafone

Traditionally growth at Vodafone was by acquisitions rather than organic. It had a track record in takeovers and their subsequent successful integration, For example, Germany's Mannesmann being the most prominent example. Today branded as "Vodafone Germany", Mannesmann was the group's most profitable venture (in terms of EBIT, which surpassed £2bn in 2003) and its largest subsidiary. On the mobile telephony acquisition strategy, Alan Harper, Group Strategy and Business Integration Director, commented,

> "In the past 10 years there had been a sea change in the evolution of the telecommunication industry. The rule in this industry has been 'Hunt or Be Hunted'. The strategy of the global players had been mobile-centric, multi-market strategies. Most of the companies like Hutchison, Mannesmann, Airtouch started much smaller, like a start-up, did not have any history as an operator and the parent company was usually a trading company. Vodafone acquired Mannesmann, Airtouch and the rest of the small players. FT acquired Orange. Docomo was restructured back into NTT".

Unlike many of its competitors, Vodafone used shares for its acquisitions. This might be one of the reasons why Vodafone emerged from the telecom crisis relatively early and could concentrate on growth again, while virtually all of its competitors were still occupied in trying to reduce their debt burden (Deutsche Telekom, France Télécom, MMO2, KPN etc.).[16] However, as Vodafone's shares had shown only lackluster performance in prior months, Vodafone increasingly had to use hard cash to increase its holdings in subsidiaries or for new acquisitions. As Vodafone did not want to compromise on its very good credit ratings (by industry standards) under any circumstances, it had slowed down on acquisitions and had been focusing on internal growth for the past two years (refer Exhibit 3 for Vodafone's strategic intent).

Vodafone had acquired other businesses along with the mobile phone business as in the case of Japan Telecom and Mannesmann, where it got ownership of fixed line operations, Vodafone had been always explicit in its concentration on its core business of mobile telecommunications. Usually it started looking for potential buyers for the other business. In the words of Alan Harper, Group Strategy and Business Integration Director,

> "We had been always mobile focused. In 1995, when I joined Vodafone, it was mobile focused. It has a turnover of 8 bn £, it was the 3rd largest mobile operator in UK and had 80% business in the UK. Today, in 2005, we are still mobile focused with a turnover of 100 bn £, biggest in the world and only 10% in UK".

Vodafone balanced its investment options by taking its time to ensure a good investment and disinvestments

Exhibit 3   Strategic Intent of Vodafone

The Company had maintained a strategy of focusing on global mobile telecommunications and providing network coverage to allow its customers to communicate using mobile products and services. The Company's strategy was increasingly focused on revenue growth and margin improvement from providing enhanced services to its customer base. This growth strategy had three principal components:

- to grow voice and data revenues through an increased marketing focus on our established high quality customer base;

- to extend our operational leadership of the industry through maximizing the benefits of scale and scope, through the use of partner network agreements, by increasing equity interests in businesses where the Group had existing shareholdings and by promoting the Vodafone brand; and
- to extend service differentiation, investing in delivering Vodafone branded, easy to use, customer propositions for mobile voice and data.

Where appropriate, and if circumstances allow, the Company may also make further acquisitions or disposals of businesses.[8]

Source: Company website.

option. For example, it sold Japan Telecom's fixed line operations in 2003 for ¥261.3 billion (£1.4 billion)[17] while it reinforced its long term commitment to Japan in 2005 by making a further investment of up to £2.6 billion. Arun Sarin, pointed out,

> "Our transactions in Japan will simplify the structure, confirm our commitment to the Japanese marketplace and enable us to deliver on the changes needed to improve our position."

While Arcor was not divested, and was still part of Vodafone Germany as of 2005. Arcor might even serve as a strategic weapon to cannibalize on incumbent Deutsche Telekom's profitable fixed line business.[18]

Since mid 2001, Vodafone had entered into arrangements with other network operators in countries where it did not hold any equity stake. Under the terms of so-called "Partner Network Agreements", Vodafone cooperated with its counterparts in the development and marketing of global services under dual brand logos. By 2003, Vodafone had extended its reach into eleven other countries, thus establishing a first foothold in these markets.[19] Such an agreement was a classical win-win situation: Vodafone not only gained new market insight with little risk but at the same time was able to assess the quality of the partner in order to identify possible takeover targets, while the partner benefited from Vodafone's unique marketing and technological capabilities.

Vodafone's acquisition strategy always followed a similar pattern: First, the number one or two player within a national market was identified, while it carefully avoided acquiring the incumbent mobile operator that was linked to the state-owned telecom monopoly (like

T-Mobile, which was the mobile division of Deutsche Telekom or Orange, a business unit of France Télécom). It seems that Vodafone feared a bureaucratic inertia of these organizations, and would rather focus on more flexible, entrepreneurially-minded challengers (with Mannesmann's D2 once again being a good example, or France's SFR) that would challenge the incumbents in different local markets. Referring to this strategy Alan Harper explained,

> "Our vision has been to leverage scale and scope benefits, reduce response time in market, and ensure effective delivery to customers. This we have achieved by collecting or acquiring national (operational) companies and gave them a mission of a 'challenger company' in each of the national markets. For e.g., Vodafone with SFR is a challenger to France Telecom in France, Vodafone UK is a challenger to British Telecom in UK, and Vodafone Germany a challenger to Deutsch Telekom in Germany. Together with this challenger mindset, we nurture and instil an entrepreneurial spirit inside Vodafone Group companies, and in this respect we do not behave as a traditional telephone company. Since we differ from being a traditional company, the cultural alignment of people working for Vodafone is a key issue in sustaining this challenger and entrepreneurial mindset. To focus on this cultural alignment, we give autonomy to the local entity and reiterate that the local entity did not join a global company like IBM or HP. The local entity has to work in a matrix structure and keep alive the 'challenger mindset' on fixed line telephony and other incumbents, challenge the status quo every day and evolve by being local entrepreneurs."

Branding, Identity and Pricing

After a successful bid for a takeover target, Vodafone followed a diverse strategy in terms of branding, creating its identity and its own pricing models. Alan Harper explained,

> "We play different models of creating Vodafone's identity in the market. Which way we adapt depends on a number of factors and considerations, such as the strength of the local brand, the prevalent company culture and the general fit between Vodafone's processes and the acquired business' processes. But frankly, at the end of the day, it comes down to a question of management judgment. For example, in New Zealand when we acquired Bellsouth, we changed Bellsouth almost overnight to Vodafone New Zealand. Similarly in Portugal, we undertook an overnight integration of Telecel to Vodafone Portugal. Telecel transformed into Vodafone Portugal and became challenger to the traditional PTT. Whereas in Italy, when we acquired Omnitel, it took us 2.5 years to change Omnitel to Omnitel Vodafone. Onmitel colours were Green and White and we could not change it to Vodafone Red immediately. It was because Omnitel had a strong brand image, very well known and we had to be very cautious during the transition. The market would never have accepted it. The same was the case with DT in Germany."

The management judgment of fast or slow re-branding harped on the customer and organizational response of the acquired market and acquired company. Usually the national brand was kept alive for sometime until the dust of the takeover battle had settled. Vodafone then carefully launched its phased re-branding campaign to bring the new subsidiary under the "Vodafone" umbrella. Usually, they added "Vodafone" to the original corporate brand. To better coordinate these branding efforts, Vodafone appointed David Haines, a former Coca-Cola manager, as global brand director.[20] Davin Haines explained,

> "For example "D2" became "D2 Vodafone". Within a year, Vodafone modified the logo to its typical red color and changed the order of company name, for example "D2 Vodafone" to "Vodafone D2". During the last phase, the original "national" name was eliminated completely and only the global brand and logo remained. This process could take more than two years and usually passed almost unnoticed by the customers, who got accustomed to the new logo due to the extensive branding campaigns, often in conjunction with the launch of a new global product (like Vodafone's Mobile Connect Card, enabling e-mailing and internet access via a laptop and the mobile network) or service (e.g. Vodafone live! Mobile internet portal).

> Following this pattern, Vodafone Omnitel in Italy and J-Phone Vodafone in Japan became a single brand in May 2003 and October 2003, respectively".[21]

Vodafone launched its first truly global communications campaign in the beginning of August 2001 to reinforce its brand awareness and a global brand identity. Arun Sarin re-iterated,

> "Throughout the past few years, Vodafone has done a terrific job of building brand awareness as we have moved towards a single global brand. Beyond brand awareness, we want people to understand that the Vodafone name represents great service, great value and great innovation. When our name becomes synonymous with these attributes we will achieve brand preference and expect to see our market share climb as a result".

Across all media, a homogenous corporate brand and identity was communicated including the slogan "How are you?" and introduced the inverted comma as logo. To keep in sink with Vodafone's global aspirations, the group selected two globally recognized brands, it sponsored the Manchester United Football Club and the Ferrari Formula 1 team to improve awareness and perception of the brand. In addition, it supported its brand by individual sponsorship contracts and other marketing communication programs at the local level. According to a Vodafone statement,

> "an audit of the first year of sponsorship of Scuderia Ferrari reveals that the sponsorship had outperformed all of the annual targets set internally by Vodafone and helped establish exceptional global brand awareness".[22]

Being number one or number two in most markets[23] it had entered, Vodafone never used "low prices" to attract new customers. Instead, it focused on creating and marketing new value-added services that enticed customers to sign up with Vodafone, even if it implied paying not the lowest rates available. According to Arun Sarin,

> "We have rededicated ourselves to delighting our customers because we believe this is the foundation for our continued success. We recognize that every customer interaction provides another opportunity to win loyalty and that's why we continue to raise standards on the quality of customer care in our call centers and our stores and the quality of our networks. Key to delighting our customers is our ability to deliver superior voice and data services according to differing customer needs".

Vodafone was not immune to the pricing policies of its competitors, which meant that it lowered its tariffs whenever the price differential became too great and the new subscriber market share dropped below a critical level. Given its size and healthy finances, it could usually weather price wars and simply waited until the aggressive player lost its thrust. Appendix I explores in some detail the role of fixed costs and their impact on pricing in the mobile telecommunication market.

Integrating to One Vodafone

Vodafone realized that real business integration extends far beyond having a single brand. Critics had pointed out that establishing a global brand and logo is among the easier tasks of managing a multinational corporation. Alan Harper stressed,

> "The careful re-branding policy not only targeted customers, but also tried to address the needs and concerns of the employees. The employees had to adjust to the fact that though they were 'national challengers with an instilled entrepreneurial spirit' they were also part of the family of the global Vodafone Corporation based in Newbury, England. It was perceived that most employees were proud of having contributed to the success of challenging the incumbent operator were reluctant to be incorporated into a larger corporation that they perceived as 'distant.'"

After the heady days of Chris Gent and the acquisitions by the dozen, Arun Sarin had to find innovative ways to integrate "a disparate group of national operations" into one company. Arun Sarin recognized that winning over the hearts of the employees and achieving cultural alignment was perhaps the "biggest challenge of all". An analyst of Merrill Lynch praised Arun Sarin as "smart" and "strategically as good as it gets".[24] Sarin seemed to be a good fit for this extraordinary task ahead, as he was described as "an operating man rather than a dealmaker" and "the archetypal international executive".[25] The portrait of Sarin went on like this:

> "Born and brought up in India, but now an American citizen, Mr Sarin's background was an asset. There might seem to be a certain irony in putting an Indian-American in charge of the world's biggest mobile-phone operator, each of these countries had made a mess of introducing wireless telecoms. But Vodafone was a British company that aspired to be a true multinational. It had large operations in Germany, where it bought Mannesmann in 2000, in Italy and in Japan. To put another Brit into the top job might have bred resentment. [. . .] The son of a well-to-do Indian military officer, he went to a military boarding-school, but his mother encouraged him not to follow his father's career. Instead, he took an engineering degree at the Indian Institute of Technology, the country's equivalent of MIT. From there he went to the University of California at Berkeley on a scholarship, to earn a further degree in engineering and a MBA. He had lived in America ever since. The main remnants of his origins were an Indian wife (whom he met at Berkeley), a touch of an accent and a passion for cricket, which he shares with Sir Chris [Gent, his predecessor]."[26]

Sarin, however, was not the only director on Vodafone's board with a distinct international background. As a result of Vodafone's past acquisitions and their pragmatic integration into the group, many skilled foreign (non-British) managers had been retained and had since joined the board, including two German, one Italian, one South African, one Suede etc. (see Exhibit 4(a) and (b)).

Exhibit 4a   Vodafone's Executive and Non-Executive Directors 2005

As of July 30, 2005, Vodafone had six executive directors and eight non-executive directors, including the Chairman, Lord MacLaurin.

- **Lord MacLaurin of Knebworth,** *Chairman*
- **Paul Hazen,** *Deputy Chairman and Senior Independent Director*
- **Arun Sarin,** *Chief Executive:* (**Indian-born** and raised, graduated from the Indian Institute of Technology, but now American citizen). Former Chief Executive Officer for the United States and Asia Pacific region until April 15, 2000, when he became a non-executive director. Former director of AirTouch from July 1995 and President and Chief Operating Officer from February 1997 to June 1999. Appointed Chief Executive on 30 July 2003.

- **Peter R. Bamford,** *Chief Marketing Officer*
- **Thomas Geitner,** *Chief Technology Officer*
- **Julian M. Horn-Smith,** *Group Chief Operating Officer*
- **Kenneth J. Hydon,** *Financial Director*
- **Sir John Bond**
- **Dr. Michael J. Boskin**
- **Professor Sir Alec Broers**
- **Dr. John Buchanan**
- **Penelope L. Hughes**
- **Sir David Scholey, CBE**
- **Professor Jürgen Schrempp**
- **Luc Vandevelde**

Source: Company website.

Exhibit 4b   Vodafone's Executive and Non-Executive
Directors 2006

- **Arun Sarin,** Chief Executive
- **Sir Julian Horn-Smith,** Deputy Chief Executive
- **Ken Hydon,** Financial Director
- **Peter Bamford,** Chief Marketing Officer
- **Thomas Geitner,** Chief Technology Officer
- **Jürgen von Kuczkowski,** Chief Executive Germany
- **Pietro Guindani,** Chief Executive Italy
- **Bill Morrow,** Chief Executive United Kingdom
- **Paul Donovan,** Regional Chief Executive
- **Brian Clark,** Chief Executive Asia Pacific and Group Human Resources Director Designate
- **Shiro Tsuda,** Chief Executive Japan
- **Alan Harper,** Group Strategy and Business Integration Director
- **Phil Williams,** Group Human Resources Director
- **Stephen Scott,** Group General Counsel and Company Secretary
- **Simon Lewis,** Group Corporate Affairs Director

At the annual general meeting on July 2003, Sarin emphasized the need to benefit from economies of scale and scope. In June, 2004, Arun Sarin re-defined,

"At Vodafone, everything we do furthers our desire to create mobile connections for individuals, businesses and communities. Our Vision is to be the world's mobile communications leader and we're delighted by the prospects for the future of our industry. Our commitment to this industry is underlined by our company values, which state that everything we do is driven by our passion for customers, our people, results and the world around us . . . Operating in 26 markets (together with Partner Networks in a further 14 countries (with approximately 151.8 million registered customers, and approximately 398.5 million total venture customers) puts us in an enviable position to leverage our global scale and scope. . . Another competitive advantage is our leadership position on cost and time to market. From network services to sales, and marketing to customer care and billing, we have many varied systems in use across the business. With strong cooperation between our various operating companies we can achieve further savings".

To co-ordinate restructure and integrate its varies systems across 26 countries, Vodafone launched its "One Vodafone" initiative that aimed to boost operating annual pre-tax operating profit by £2.5 bn by FY2008.[27] Alan Harper explained in details:

"We are in a period when we are integrating our company. With acquisitions all over the world, one of our challenges is to integrate seamlessly not only technol-

ogy (which by the way are more or less similar across the world) but people. And this is a key part of the Branding Evolution that we had witnessed. The challenge of this restructuring program is to balance the need of co-ordination and synergies while encouraging local initiatives. The One Vodafone *program is a business integration activity and we are in the process of 'gradual integration of our business architecture'. For example, we are running down a real-time billing system to an integrated system for 28mn customers. It is a very difficult task if one tries to understand the billing system of mobile telephones. Under the One Vodafone, there are currently 8 programs, Networks (design and supply procurement, so-ordination and consolidation initiatives), IT (design, back office, billings, ERP/HR, operations–data center processes), Service platforms, Roaming (mapping footprints), Customer (next practice services), Handset portfolio, MNC accounts, Retailing (one won't believe, we are the 8th largest retailer in the world taking together our stores that are owned or franchised). . . We are trying to integrate national operating units across footprints and trying to leverage scale and scope while trying to retain the local autonomy and responsiveness of our challenger national units".*

Alan Harper agreed that implementation of "One Vodafone" is a challenge. He explained,

"To implement One Vodafone, we have undertaken a change in organizational structure of the Group (refer Exhibit 5). We still operate in a matrix format. What One Vodafone tries to achieve is to simplify the integration issues in terms of brand strength and integrating local culture and processes. We centralize all our marketing efforts, branding and product development. Technology is standardized. Network design (switching, radio) are co-ordinated. Best-practices are benchmarked by Advance Services such as service platforms and portals (Vodafone Live!). Knowledge, is shared via the HQ, HR, strategy, and Marketing departments, through lateral processes, including our governance processes. We keep and encourage local initiatives such customer services, sales, network billing, IT systems. We are trying to incorporate the best of all the cultures to the maximum extent possible and in this way we tried to transform Vodafone UK into a new Vodafone".

One Vodafone was clearly communicated across the company via internet, intranet, different training programs as well as a monthly employee magazine called *"Vodafone life! The global magazine for all Vodafone people"*. The HR department prepared special "initiation" training programs to acquaint new employees to the Vodafone way,

Exhibit 5   Board Changes and New Organizational Structure as of January 2005

Vodafone Group Plc ("Vodafone") announces Board changes and a new organizational structure which will enable continued improvement in the delivery of the Group's strategic goals. This structure will become effective as from 1 January 2005.
The new organization is designed to:

- Focus more attention on customers in Vodafone's local markets;
- Enhance Vodafone's ability to deliver seamless services to corporations;
- Facilitate co-ordinated delivery of 3G across all markets;
- Function as an integrated company, delivering on One Vodafone; and
- Simplify decision-making, accountabilities and governance structures to speed up execution

Vodafone will simplify its existing regional structure with major countries and business areas reporting into the Chief Executive. All first line management functions in the Operating Companies will have a dual reporting line to the respective functions at Group level.
Arun Sarin, Chief Executive said: "We are creating an organization that is better positioned to respond to the high expectations of our customers. Faster execution will enable us to extend our lead within the mobile industry and deliver the benefits to our customers, our employees and our shareholders."

Main Board Appointments
Sir Julian Horn-Smith will be appointed Deputy Chief Executive with effect from 1 January 2005. Vodafone separately announces that Andy Halford has been appointed Financial Director Designate. Andy will succeed Ken Hydon when he retires on 26 July 2005.

Operating Company Structure
Vodafone's operating company structure will be streamlined to ensure effective and fast decision-making, enabling improved time to market across a number of business initiatives.

Consequently, the following operating companies and business areas will report directly into the Chief Executive:

- European Affiliates (Belgium, France, Poland, Romania and Switzerland) and Non-European Affiliates (China, Fiji, Kenya, South Africa and United States), led by Sir Julian Horn-Smith;
- Germany, led by Jürgen von Kuczkowski;
- Italy, led by Pietro Guindani;
- United Kingdom, led by Bill Morrow;
- Other EMEA Subsidiaries (Albania, Egypt, Greece, Hungary, Ireland, Malta, Netherlands, Portugal, Spain and Sweden), led by Paul Donovan;
- Asia Pacific (Australia, Japan and New Zealand), led by Brian Clark who will also be appointed Group Human Resources Director Designate

Vodafone's Group functions will be strengthened to support the delivery of seamless global propositions and Vodafone's continued integration. The following functions will also report directly into the Chief Executive:

- Marketing, led by Peter Bamford, the Chief Marketing Officer. This function will be reinforced by a newly created Multi National Corporates unit which will assume full accountability for serving Vodafone's global corporate customers. Group Marketing will also manage the global handset portfolio and procurement;
- Technology, led by Thomas Geitner, the Chief Technology Officer. In addition to standardized network design and global supply chain management, this function will introduce the concept of shared service operation for IT and service delivery;
- Business Development, a new function led by Sir Julian Horn-Smith. Sir Julian will be responsible for driving Vodafone's product and services portfolio into Vodafone's affiliates and the Partner Networks. In addition, this function will assume responsibility for expanding and consolidating Vodafone's footprint through the Partner Network programme and any Corporate Finance activities

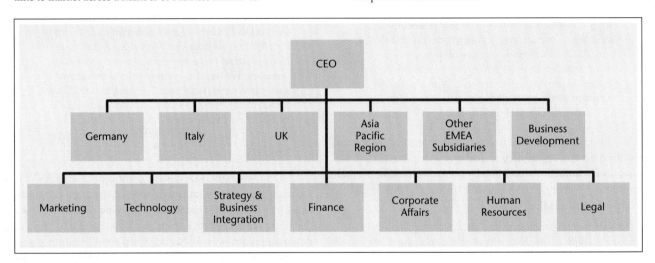

New Governance Structure

Vodafone also announces changes to its governance process. The Group will have two management committees which will oversee the execution of the Main Board's strategy and policy.

- The Executive Committee

Chaired by Arun Sarin, this committee will focus on the Group's strategy, financial structure and planning, succession planning, organizational development and Group-wide policies.

- The Integration and Operations Committee

Chaired by Arun Sarin, this committee will be responsible for setting operational plans, budgets and forecasts, product and service development, customer segmentation, managing delivery of multi-market propositions and managing shared resources.

Source: Company website.

labeled the "Vodafone footstep", which included its vision and values (see Exhibit 6) and the "Ten Business Principles".[28] On translating the vision and values along side changes in structure and systems Vodafone witnessed revamping of people processes within the organization. Commenting on employees, Arun Sarin explained.

"As the business expands and the environment around us evolves, it is crucial for us to develop, recruit and retain the people that will lead us into this new world. We are working hard to make sure our employees have the right skills and knowledge to anticipate our customers' needs. We are identifying new ways to share

Exhibit 6   Vodafone's Vision & Values

We have one vision and a set of values that underpins everything we do. Both our vision and our values were shared throughout the global organization.

Our vision

To be the world's mobile communications leader—enriching customers' lives, helping individuals, businesses and communities be more connected in a mobile world.

- Our customers use mobile communications to make their lives richer, more fulfilled, more connected. They will prefer Vodafone because the experience of using Vodafone will be the best they can find.
- We will lead in making the mobile the primary means of personal communications for every individual around the world.
- Through our leadership, our scale, our scope and our partnerships, we will bring online mobile services to the world.

Our values

Passion for customers

Our customers have chosen to trust us. In return, we must strive to anticipate and understand their needs and delight them with our service.

- We value our customers above everything else and aspire to make their lives richer, more fulfilled and more connected.
- We must always listen and respond to each of our customers.
- We will strive to delight our customers, anticipating their needs and delivering greater quality and more value, faster than anyone else.

Passion for our people

Outstanding people working together make Vodafone exceptionally successful.

- We seek to attract, develop, reward and retain outstanding individuals.
- We believe in empowerment and personal accountability.
- We enjoy what we do.
- We believe in the power of our teams.

Passion for results

We were action-oriented and driven by a desire to be the best.

- We were committed to be the best in all we do.
- We all play our part in delivering results.
- We seek speed, flexibility and efficiency in all we do.

Passion for the world around us

We will help people of the world to have fuller lives—both through the services we provide and through the impact we have on the world around us.

- We recognize the responsibilities that accompany the growth we have achieved.
- We will be a force for good in the world.
- A spirit of partnership and mutual respect was critical in all our activities.

Source: Company website.

the best of what we do on a global basis. We continue to reap the benefits of a motivated team with a strong customer service culture, which will help earn a reputation for Vodafone that is second to none."

The HR Department had set up a fast-track career path (the Global Leadership Programme, GLP) for high potential managers, rotating them across business functions and countries and equipping them with crucial multicultural skills.

Despite the integration and standardization efforts, the corporate headquarters had to ensure a certain level of independence for individual country subsidiaries to take into account differing business models and customer expectations. For example, 48% of Vodafone's customers in Germany had a contract, while this kind of long-term commitment to an operator was almost unheard of in Italy (92% were prepaid customers).[29]

To orchestrate the move towards greater coordination as well as to identify and disseminate best practices, the group had created two new central functions, Group Marketing (to drive revenue growth), and Group Technology and Business Integration (to drive cost and scale benefits).[30] Communicating Vodafone's new focus on integrating the bits and pieces resulting from past acquisitions was clearly a top management task. The "Integration and Operations Committee" was instituted, staffed with members of the Executive Board and chaired by Arun Sarin himself. This committee was responsible for "setting operational plans, budgets and forecasts, product and service development, customer segmentation, managing delivery of multi-market propositions and managing shared resources" across geographies.[31] Alan Harper, who had been heading the group strategy department at Vodafone since 2000, saw his job title changed to "Group Strategy and Business Integration Director". Simultaneously, Vodafone restructured itself at the corporate level to include the two new functions which directly reported to the group's COO, Julian Horn-Smith.

Thomas Geitner was appointed head of the new unit "Group Technology & Business Integration" as Chief Technology Officer.

"The purpose of Group Technology will be to lead the implementation of a standardized architecture for business processes, information technology and network systems. This will support the next generation of products and services and the critical role of introducing and operating 3G capacity."[32]

A key focus of the Group Technology activities were the management and control of Group wide projects in relation to the ongoing rollout of "third generation" (3G) networks, the enhancement of Vodafone live! and the development of the Group's business offerings. This work included the continued development of technical specifications, creation and management of global contracts with suppliers as well as testing of terminals.[33]

It was committed to provide underlying terminal and platform technologies on a global basis. Within the mobile phone industry, a shift of power away from handset Vodafone had increasingly succeeded in forcing the producers to offer specially designed and branded products: the thriving Vodafone live! multimedia service was launched on Sharp GX-10 handsets exclusively manufactured and branded for Vodafone.[34] If this trend persisted, Vodafone would be the first to benefit from its huge purchasing power and could even force Nokia (which had an almost 40% world market share) to cater more towards Vodafone's needs.[35] Vodafone could also use its unrivalled clout when negotiating with network equipment suppliers (such as Alcatel, Nokia, Siemens etc.) to squeeze their margins.

Peter Bamford was appointed Chief Marketing Officer and head of the Group Marketing department, which was in charge of

"Providing leadership and co-ordination across the full range of marketing and commercial activities including brand, product development, content management, partner networks and global accounts."[36]

For Vodafone, the question was how customers could derive a benefit from Vodafone's increasingly global reach, ultimately driving top-line growth. Alan Harper explains,

"We are a technology and sales & distribution group focused on local companies winning market share against incumbents is respective countries.. We do not develop technology but we are users of technology. Technology is developed by companies such as Nokia, Ericksson, Nortel. We buy their technology–and technology evolution in our sector is more or less standard, it evolves, grows without major differentiations and after a period of time it is standardized. Now the challenge is how best we can leverage using and integrating the technology across our companies . . . With the evolution and growth of our company we are today more of a company that prides itself in the differentiation of services that we bring to our customers. We are still 100% sales driven but we are much more customer centric and customer service oriented and take pride in understanding customer needs as we graduate to offering our customers the next best service and focusing on customer delight (e.g., Amazon). We now execute much better and it is because of the reason of the shift in our competencies".

Vodafone started creating service offerings and product packages directly leveraging Vodafone's network and delivering tangible value to customers. For example, it created a tariff option that enabled customers to seamlessly roam the globe, on a special per minute rate, on the same network, without having to worry about high interconnection fees or differing technical standards. A new unit within Group Marketing was created to develop and market services specifically tailored to the needs of global co-ordination, such as seamless wireless access to corporate IT systems and special rates for international calls on the network. Such a global service offering could clearly serve as a differentiating factor to competitors that could not match Vodafone's global footprint.

Woes in the U.S. and France

There were still two nagging issues for Arun Sarin: Vodafone's 45% stake in Verizon Wireless and the unresolved issues about control in France's SFR, for which Vodafone had been at loggerheads with Vivendi for several years now. Vodafone was far from happy about these minority stakes, because it did not fit with its single-brand, "One Vodafone" strategy.

In the U.S., Vodafone customers still could not use their cell phones on the Verizon Wireless network, because it operated under a different standard. It was indicated that this situation was likely to continue well into the era of 3G, because Verizon planned to adopt an incompatible standard.[37] Without a single technological platform and a uniform brand, Vodafone could extract little value from its American venture (except the cash dividend of $1 billion a year it received from it).[38] After the failed bid for AT&T Wireless, Vodafone had several options at its disposal, all of them with their own pros and cons.

Probably the most obvious option would be to take over Verizon (the parent company of Verizon Wireless) completely, including its fixed line business, in order to force them to adopt Vodafone standards. It was deemed likely that such a bid could escalate to a US$150 billion hostile takeover battle, a figure that might be too large even for juggernaut Vodafone.[39] Verizon's management clearly was not willing to cede the wireless operations to Vodafone, but dreamt of becoming the single owner of Verizon Wireless itself.

Alternatively, Vodafone could buy another operator outright. But regulatory constraints would require it to sell its stake in Verizon Wireless first, because it was prohibited to own more than a 20% stake in two competing operators at once. Under the current agreement with Verizon, Vodafone held a put option, which allowed it to sell some

of the shareholding each year at a fixed price to Verizon. If Vodafone decided to exercise this option, it had to do so until July 2006 in order to realize a maximum value of US$20 billion. Verizon could choose to pay Vodafone either in cash or stock, although Vodafone had a right on a minimum cash sum of US$7.5 billion.[40]

Some observers questioned the idea of selling Verizon and buying another operator, as Verizon Wireless was the most successful and profitable one—why swap "a minority stake in a very good operator for a controlling stake in a less good one"?[41]

In France, Vodafone was in an equally uncomfortable position. It shared ownership of Cegetel, the parent company of France's #2 mobile phone business SFR (35% market share with 13.3 million customers), with Vivendi having the majority stake in the venture. On 31 March, 2003, Vodafone's ownership interest in SFR was approximately 43.9%, comprising a direct holding of 20% in SFR and an indirect holding through its stake in Cegetel.[42] Commenting on Vodafone's struggle with Vivendi about SFR, an analyst at Global Equities SA joked: "We have a saying: small minority shareholdings for little idiots; big minority shareholdings for big idiots".[43]

While Vodafone managers had a certain say about the operations and strategy of SFR (SFR launched the co-branded multimedia services of Vodafone live!), Vivendi continued to refuse to sell SFR to Vodafone. Several talks between Sarin and Fourtou, the CEO of Vivendi, had not yielded any results, and Vivendi's true strategic intentions with SFR remained unclear.[44] The remaining 56% stake in SFR was valued at roughly £8 billion ($13 billion).[45] After Vivendi declined Vodafone's offer for SFR in 2002, Vodafone issued a statement claiming that it was "a long-term investor in Cegetel and SFR" and that it "looks forward to continuing its successful partnership with Vivendi".[46]

> "France is a very simple market for us", noted Alan Harper in April 2005. "We know the market, we know the business model and we know the management of SFR, which takes part in routine Vodafone management meetings." Pugnaciously, he added: "The natural home of SFR is Vodafone. We are a very patient company."

It remains to be seen whether Vivendi wants to keep its cash cow or if it was simply trying to push the price in this cat-and-mouse game.

Challenges Ahead

Arun Sarin knew that his job would not become uninteresting anytime soon as many challenges lay ahead! Certainly,

Vodafone was the largest player in the industry, but being active in 26 countries out of 200 in the world left a lot of room to grow. As he closed his eyes and thought of Vodafone's global footprint, instantly he was reminded that Vodafone was not present in Latin America and in many African countries. Then there was the Middle-East. Vast untapped markets lay ahead with today's mobile penetration of about 1.7 bn, of which Vodafone has abut 3.5mn, in 5 years it shall be 2.5 bn, only $1/_2$ of world's population! And there was his native country, India, where he invested US$1.5 bn to buy a 10 per cent stake in Bharti Tele-Ventures, the largest mobile operator in the country. Countries of Eastern Europe, many of which had recently entered the E.U., should definitely become Vodafone's home turf: Vodafone had just announced that it would be willing to invest up to US$18 billion on acquisitions in Russia and other Eastern European countries.[47] The 2005 acquisition of the mobile operators MobiFon (Romania) and Oskar (Czech Republic) was certainly just the first step in enlarging Vodafone's footprint.[48] Not to mention China. The sheer size of the market was awe-inspiring. Vodafone's strategic partner, China Mobile, alone had more than 150 million customers, but Vodafone only had a minuscule 3.27% stake in the company.[49] For Vodafone, this stake served as a:

> "strategic foothold in a very important market with a relatively small scale investment. China Mobile is the fasted growing mobile company in the world today, connecting about 2-3 mn customers a month. It has 70% of the Chinese market share. Vodafone clearly understands that China Mobile can never become Vodafone China. That is a reality due to investment options and the quasi-political situation of Chinese Mobile telephony market. We learn everyday from China Mobile and our intention is to have regular knowledge flow between Vodafone and China Mobile. This is because our strategy is to make the technology standardized so that the learning between us is much faster . . . Our investment in China mobile is through China Mobile HK. We have a clear exit strategy with liquid assets, if our investment does not do well in the future. If it does well, we might think of increasing our foothold but not to a sizeable extent. We are happy to have a foothold in one of the largest and fastest growing markets of the world, with our investment we have an insider position, we have a position of influence with the operator, with the Chinese government, we have seat on the board, we have regular dialogue and our interest is to make China use the same tech-

nology as ours so that we can benefit from the scale and scope" Alan Harper.

At the same, significant business risks lurked in all markets and Arun Sarin was well aware of them. In 2006, the merger of AT&T with Bellsouth Corp. had put pressure on Verizone Wireless to buy off Vodafone and force it to exit the US market. The introduction of 3G, which had a very promising start in Germany with good sales of mobile connect cards, might shift the focus of the whole industry away from networks to content. Revenue from voice traffic was flat or even declining due to competing technologies as Internet calling that was fundamentally changing the telecom industry. Sarin knew that most of the growth would have to come from new data services. Competitors had also begun to get their feet on the ground again, with rumors about a merger between MMO2's German operations (O2 Germany) and KPN's E-Plus.

Nokia had just presented its first WiFi-powered phone that did not need the traditional mobile network but a wireless LAN hotspot—if this technology should ever become popular, it would undermine Vodafone's current business model and could turn billions of fixed assets into worthless electronic scrap.[50]

Beginning of 2006, Arun Sarin took some tough decisions. He faced up to slowing growth in his core market by unveiling an impairment charge of £23bn to £28bn ($40bn to $49bn) and exited the Japanese market by selling its stake to Tokyo-based Softbank in a deal valued at $15.4 billion and confirmed that after the sale it would return $10.5 billion to its shareholders. Vodafone had trailed behind NTT DoCoMo and KDDI since its entry in 2001 in Japan, due to fickle consumers, the lack of a low-end tier in the segment, and the challenge of coordinating terminals and technologies across borders. He managed to tighten his grip on the company and put down a boardroom revolt that had questioned his leadership. He not only won a public expression of support from Lord Ian MacLaurin, the company's chairman, but he also forced out Sir Christopher Gent, the honorary life president and former chief executive.

Arun Sarin thought, Vodafone could have the best of two worlds. Now it was the time to combine Vodafone's superior skills in acquiring companies with best-of-breed business integration and operational capabilities. He could ensure Vodafone's exceptional profitability for many years to come by keeping Vodafone's a wireless company to the core and also use innovations such as broadband wireless technology known as WiMAX, to offer new services. It was now up to him to shape Vodafone's future.

APPENDIX 1   The Economics of the Mobile Phone Market: The Role of Fixed Costs

The mobile phone market was characterized by extremely high fixed costs. The setting up of a nation-wide network could require significant investments running into billions of euros.[51] Usually, an operator did not have the choice to offer network coverage limited to metropolitan areas (which would dramatically reduce the scale of initial investment required), either because of regulation prohibiting such a selective offer, or simply because national coverage was a key success factor for literally "mobile" customers.

In some countries, the licenses to operate using a certain bandwidth cost as much as £8 billion (the record price each operator in Germany paid for its UMTS license to the government), adding huge financing charges to the already existing fixed costs.[52] However, once capacity was installed, the cost of an additional customer using the network was virtually zero, while every euro of revenue adds to the companies' bottom line. An installed and running network was a foundation for reaching very high operating margins. Vodafone, for example, estimates that once the initial investments had been made, less than ten percent of revenues were needed to maintain the network.[53] Even the marketing campaigns also benefited from the economies of scale: the larger an operator's customer base, the lower its per-user cost of such advertising efforts.

Much of the costs described here were not only fixed, but also sunk, further aggravating the problem of price pressure. The investment into network could hardly be sold to anybody else (because of differing technological standards) and hence the initial cost was "sunk". Companies realize that they cannot undo their decision to invest, because the infrastructure is already there—it is rational for companies to act as if their initial investment was zero.

The existence of high fixed costs explained the periodic price wars that had driven prices down ever since mobile telecommunications started. Some operators had begun offering free calls or flat rates during the weekend (when capacity utilization was at the lowest). Usually, it was the smaller operators and the new market entrants who offered lower prices to reach as quickly as possible a critical mass. In Germany, which had one of the largest markets for mobile telephony with more than 60 million customers and a high population density, the threshold for an acceptable return on investment was estimated to be around 20% of the total market share, which had neither been attained by O2 (a subsidiary of MMO2) nor by E-Plus (KPN).

The economics of the market necessitated that there were no more than three or four operators in a country (refer Exhibit 7). In Germany, Mobilcom and Quam never reached the critical size and had to exit the market in 2003 and 2002, respectively, writing off their individual investments of £8bn each in 3G licenses.[54]

Growth for a mobile phone company had so far mainly come from increased penetration, which stood around 80% (e.g., Germany: 74%) in most mature markets. With new customers becoming increasingly rare (refer to Exhibit 8 for customers by country of Vodafone), operators were constantly searching for new sources of revenues and had introduced text messaging and other basic value-added services, such as downloadable ringtones and logos.[55] The standard measure in the industry to measure the quality of the customer base was the Average Revenue Per User (ARPU).[56]

As the new 3G networks (third generation, enabling high-speed data transmission) go online, available capacity will take another quantum leap with unpredictable consequences for pricing. There seem to be promising opportunities to concentrate on the huge market for fixed line telephony. Not surprisingly, there was a clear relation between the per minute price of a call and the average amount of cell phone usage. Conversely, there was no relation between the ARPU and the average price per minute charged, which indicated that customers substituted their fixed line minutes with cell phone minutes whenever a price drop occurs. In other words, the increased quantity usually compensated the operator for the lower revenue per minute. (refer to Exhibit 9).

Another key performance indicator that had attracted management attention in recent years was the so-called "churn rate", a percentage of the customer base being lost to competitors each year. In competitive markets with high handset subsidies, churn rates of operators could be anywhere between 19% (Germany) and 30% (UK).[57] In other words, on average after three to five years, an operator had churned its entire customer base! These churn rates carried high costs for the operators, because they had to spend heavily mainly on marketing and handset subsidies to attract new customers and to retain the old ones. Customer acquisition costs easily exceeded 100€ per new customer or make up to 12.4% of service revenue (figure for Vodafone Germany).[58] If an operator added low value customers (i.e. those with a low monthly ARPU), it could take many months until the operator could break even on a customer.

Exhibit 7   Customers by Country (in '000s), as of June 30, 2003

Country	Customers
UK	13,313
Ireland	1,765
Germany	23,261
Hungary	952
Netherlands	3,312
Sweden	1,331
Italy	15,044
Albania	364
Greece	2,373
Malta	126
Portugal	3,129
Spain	9,184
United States	15,332
Japan	10,035
Australia	2,593
New Zealand	1,349
Egypt	1,609
Others	17,614
Group Total	**122,686**

Source: Adapted from Interim Report November 2003.

Exhibit 8   Vodafone's Subsidiaries, Partners and Investments around the Globe

Country	Service name:	Ownership (%):	Subsidiary (S), Associate (A) or Partner (P):	Proportionate customers (1000s):	No. of Competitors:
		Europe			
Albania	Vodafone Albania	83.0	S	472 (31 Dec 2003)	1
Austria	A1	n/a	P	n/a	n/a
Belgium	Proximus	25.0	A	1,067 (31 Mar 2003)	2
Croatia	VIP	n/a	P	n/a	n/a
Cyprus	Cytamobile	n/a	P	n/a	n/a
Denmark	TDC Mobil	n/a	P	n/a	n/a
Estonia	Radiolinja	n/a	P	n/a	n/a
Finland	Radiolinja	n/a	P	n/a	n/a
France	SFR	43.9	A	5,931 (30 Jun 2003)	2
Germany	Vodafone Germany	100.0	S	24,668 (31 Dec 2003)	3
Greece	Vodafone Greece	98.2	S	2,373 (30 Jun 2003)	2
Hungary	Vodafone Hungary	87.9	S	1,170 (31 Dec 2003)	2
Iceland	Og Vodafone	n/a	P	n/a	n/a
Ireland	Vodafone Ireland	100	S	1,871 (31 Dec 2003)	2
Italy	Vodafone Italy	76.8	S	15,852 (31 Dec 2003)	3
Lithuania	Bite GSM	n/a	P	n/a	n/a
Luxembourg	LUXGSM	n/a	P	n/a	n/a
Malta	Vodafone Malta	100.0	S	162 (31 Dec 2003)	1
Netherlands	Vodafone Netherlands	99.8	S	3,400 (31 Dec 2003)	4
Poland	Plus GSM	19. Jun	A	949 (31 Mar 2003)	2
Portugal	Vodafone Portugal	100.0	S	3,332 (31 Dec 2003)	2
Romania	Connex	20. Jan	A	537 (31 Mar 2003)	3
Slovenia	Si.mobil	n/a	P	n/a	n/a
Spain	Vodafone Spain	100.0	S	9,685 (31 Dec 2003)	2
Sweden	Vodafone Sweden	99.1	S	1,409 (31 Dec 2003)	3
Switzerland	Swisscom Mobile	25.0	A	3,635 (31 Mar 2003)	3
United Kingdom	Vodafone Group	n/a	n/a	n/a	n/a
United Kingdom	Vodafone UK	100.0	S	13,947 (31 Dec 2003)	4
		Americas			
United States	Verizon Wireless	44.3	A	16,638 (31 Dec 2003)	Various
		Africa and Middle East			
Bahrain	MTC-Vodafone Bahrain	n/a	P	n/a	n/a
Egypt	Vodafone Egypt	67.0	S	1,838 (31 Dec 2003)	1
Kenya	Safaricom	35.0	A	303 (31 Mar 2003)	1
Kuwait	MTC-Vodafone	n/a	P	n/a	n/a
South Africa	Vodacom	35.0	A	2,756 (31 Mar 2003)	2
		Asia Pacific			
Australia	Vodafone Australia	100.0	S	2,676 (31 Dec 2003)	4
China	China Mobile (Hong Kong) Ltd	3.3	Investment	4,048 (31 Mar 2003)	2
Fiji	Vodafone Fiji	49.0	A	44 (31 Mar 2003)	None
Japan	Vodafone K.K. (Japan)	69.7	S	10,268 (31 Dec 2003)	3
New Zealand	Vodafone New Zealand	100.0	S	1,527 (31 Dec 2003)	1
Singapore	M1	n/a	P	n/a	n/a

Source: Adapted from corporate website (www.vodafone.com), accessed on March 10, 2004.

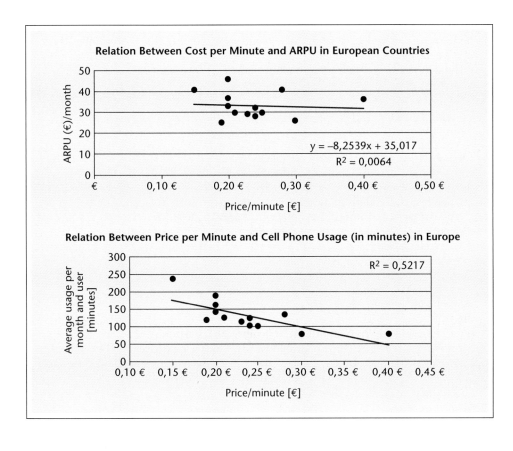

Exhibit 9   The Relationships Between per Minute Prices and ARPU in European Countries

Source: Own analysis based on data by Merrill Lynch, Diamond Cluster; published in the Frankfurter Allgemeine Zeitung, Octobre 27, 2003, p. 21

Countries included in this sample: Belgium, Germany, Netherlands, Spain, Greece, Austria, Sweden, Italy, Denmark, France, Ireland, UK, Portugal and Finland.

Notes

1.   The scenario described herein was fictional. However, all data relating to the AT&T Wireless deal was factual: *Financial Times Deutschland*, February 17, 2004, www.ftd.de.
2.   *Financial Times Deutschland*, February 12, 2004, www.ftd.de.
3.   *Financial Times Deutschland*, February 17, 2004, www.ftd.de.
4.   Equal to Christopher Gent's compensation as reported in the Company Annual Report 2003. This figure does not include stock options and performance-based pay.
5.   http://www.vodafone.com. Data current as of December 31, 2003
6.   Yahoo! Finance, http://finance.yahoo.com, March 13, 2004.
7.   Annual Report 2003 available at www.vodafone.com.
8.   Interim Results for the Six Months to 30 September 2003, published November 18, 2003; available at www.vodafone.com.
9.   Company Annual Report 2004.
10. This historic overview follows information provided at http://www.vodafone.com. Accessed on March 5, 2004.
11. www.vodafone.com.
12. Reportedly, Sir Gent closed the deal with AirTouch via his cell phone from Australia, where he was watching a game of cricket: *The Independent* (London), January 17, 1999: "Vodafone's boss realises long-held ambition with the acquisition of AirTouch."
13. *Financial Times Deutschland*, February 17, 2004, www.ftd.de.
14. A chronology of the takeover battle was provided at http://www.manager-magazin.de/unternehmen/artikel/0,2828,242161-2,00.html.
15. "A new voice at Vodafone," *The Economist*; August 2, 2003, Vol. 368

16. www.vodafone.com.
17. Interim Results for the 6 Months to September 30, 2003, published November 18, 2003; available at www.vodafone.com.
18. "Vodafone starts wireline attack, first in Germany," *Dow Jones International News*; March 10, 2005.
19. Ibid.
20. "Keeping pole position," *Total Telecom Magazine*, August 2003.
21. Ibid.
22. www.vodafone.com.
23. With Australia and Japan being notable exceptions.
24. Quoted in "Vodafone dominance tipped to keep rolling;" *Utility Week*, January 31, 2003
25. "A new voice at Vodafone," *The Economist*; August 2, 2003, Vol. 368
26. "A new voice at Vodafone," *The Economist*; August 2, 2003, Vol. 368
27. Presentation to analysts and investors on September 27, 2004, available at www.vodafone.com.
28. www.vodafone.de and www.vodafone.com.
29. Ibid, p.8.
30. Press release on June 23, 2003, available at www.vodafone.com.
31. www.vodafone.com.
32. Ibid.
33. Interim Results for the 6 Months to September 30, 2003, p. 16.
34. According to the "Key Performance Indicators" for the quarter ended December 31, 2003; released on January 28, 2004; available at www.vodafone.com, Vodafone live! Had over 4.5 million customers in 15 countries as of November 13, 2003.
35. "Keeping pole position," *Total Telecom Magazine*, August 2003.
36. Ibid.
37. "A new voice at Vodafone," *The Economist*, August 2, 2003, Vol. 368.
38. "Where does Vodafone turn now?" *Business Week Online*, February 18, 2004, "Keeping pole position," *Total Telecom Magazine*, August 2003, quotes £564 million as cash dividend in financial year 2002/2003, equivalent to 11% of Vodafone's free cash flow. This arrangement expires in April 2005.
39. "Where does Vodafone turn now?" *Business Week Online*, February 18, 2004.
40. "Keeping pole position," *Total Telecom Magazine*, August 2003.
41. Bob House of Adventis, a consultancy, quoted in "Vodafone's dilemma," *The Economist*, February 12, 2004.
42. Annual Report 2003.
43. Laurent Balcon quoted in: "Keeping pole position," *Total Telecom Magazine*, August 2003.
44. "Clear as mud: Vodafone versus Vivendi," *The Economist*, December 7, 2002.
45. Euromoney, November 2003, Vol. 34 Issue 415.
46. "Clear as mud: Vodafone versus Vivendi," *The Economist*, December 7, 2002.
47. www.Vwd.de Vereinigte Wirtschaftsdienste GmbH, February 26, 2004.
48. According to a Vodafone press release on March 15, 2005, the Group paid approximately US$3.5bn in cash for the transaction and thus could add 6.7m customers.
49. Annual Report 2004, p. 8.
50. "Nokia takes leap into Wi-Fi Phones," *Wall Street Journal Europe*, February 23, 2004
51. Vodafone for example had £24.1 bn as gross fixed assets in its balance sheet, 83% of which were accounted for by network infrastructure. Annual Report 2003, p. 90.
52. "Vodafone prescht im Rennen um UMTS-Einführung vor," *Handelsblatt*, February 13/14, 2004.
53. Annual Report 2003, p. 94.
54. "Vodafone prescht im Rennen um UMTS-Einführung vor," *Handelsblatt*, February 13/14, 2004.
55. In some instances, these new services already generate up to 20% of revenues. Ibid.

56. For example, Vodafone's ARPU in the UK was £297 and 312€ in Germany for the year, according to the "Interim Results for the Six Months Ended September 30, 2003"; available at www.vodafone.com.
57. Data for Vodafone, which can be considered as representative for the industry. Ibid.
58. Ibid.

APPENDIX

Analyzing Cases and Preparing for Class Discussions

This book, properly understood, is really about how to analyze cases. Just reading the book, however, is no more likely to fully develop one's skills as a strategist than reading a book about golf will make one a golfer. Practice in applying the concepts and tools is essential. Cases provide the opportunity for this necessary practice.

Why the Case Method?

The core of many strategic management courses is the case method of instruction. Under the case method, you will study and discuss the real-world challenges and dilemmas that face managers in firms. Cases are typically accounts of situations that a firm or manager has faced at a given point in time. By necessity, cases do not possess the same degree of complexity that a manager faces in the real world, but they do provide a concrete set of facts that suggest challenges and opportunities that real managers have faced. Very few cases have clear answers. The case method encourages you to engage problems directly and propose solutions or strategies in the face of incomplete information. To succeed at the case method, you must develop the capability to analyze and synthesize data that are sometimes ambiguous and conflicting. You must be able to prioritize issues and opportunities and make decisions in the face of ambiguous and incomplete information. Finally, you must be able to persuade others to adopt your point of view.

In an applied field like strategic management, the real test of learning is how well you can apply knowledge to real-world situations. Strategic management cases offer you the opportunity to develop judgment and wisdom in applying your conceptual knowledge. By applying the concepts you have learned to the relatively unstructured information in a case, you develop judgment in applying concepts. Alfred North Whitehead discussed the importance of application to knowledge:

> This discussion rejects the doctrine that students should first learn passively, and then, having learned, should apply knowledge. . . . For the very meaning of the things known is wrapped up in their relationship beyond themselves. This unapplied knowledge is knowledge shorn of its meaning.

Alfred North Whitehead (1947). *Essays in Science and Philosophy.* New York: Philosophical Library, Inc. pp. 218–219.

Thus, you gain knowledge as you apply concepts. With the case method, you do not passively absorb wisdom imparted from your instructor, but actively develop it as you wrestle with the real-world situations described in the cases.

How to Analyze Cases

Before discussing how to analyze a case, it may be useful to comment on how *not* to prepare a case. We see two common failings in case preparation that often go hand-in-hand. First, students often do not apply conceptual frameworks in a rigorous and systematic manner. Second, many students do not devote sufficient time to reading, analyzing, and discussing a case before class. Many students succumb to the temptation to quickly read a case and latch on to the most visible issues that present themselves. Thus, they come to class prepared to make only a few superficial observations about a case. Often, they entirely miss the deeper issues around why a firm is in the situation that it is in and how it can better its performance. Applying the frameworks systematically may take more time and effort in the beginning, but it will generally lead to deeper insights about the cases and a more profound understanding of the concepts in the chapters. As you gain experience in this systematic approach to analyzing cases, many of you will find that your preparation time will decrease. This appendix offers a framework that will assist you as you analyze cases. The framework is important, but no framework can substitute for hard work. There are no great shortcuts to analyzing cases, and there is no single right method for preparing a case. The following approach, however, may help you develop your ability to analyze cases.

1. **Skim through the case very quickly.** Pay particular attention to the exhibits. The objective in this step is to gain familiarity with the broad facts of the case. What apparent challenges or opportunities does the company face? What information is provided? You may find it especially useful to focus on the first and last few paragraphs of the case in this step.

2. **Read the case more carefully and make notes, underline, etc.** What appear to be important facts? The conceptual frameworks in the chapters will be essential in helping you identify the key facts. Throughout the course, you will want to address central questions such as the following:

   - What is the firm's performance?
   - What is the firm's mission? strategy? goals?
   - What are the resources involved in the firm's value chain? How do they compare to competitors on cost and differentiation?
   - Does the firm have a competitive advantage?
   - Are the firm's advantages and disadvantages temporary or sustainable?
   - What is the value of the firm's resources?
   - Are the firm's resources rare?
   - Are the firm's resources costly to imitate?
   - Is the firm organized sufficiently to exploit its resources?

   Depending on the case, you may also want to consider other frameworks and questions, where appropriate. Each chapter provides concepts and frameworks that you may want to consider. For example:

   - What are the five forces? How do they influence industry opportunities and threats? (Chapter 2)
   - What are the sources of cost differences in an industry? (Chapter 4)
   - What are the bases and potential bases for product differentiation in an industry? (Chapter 5)

Each chapter suggests more specific questions and concepts than those above. You will want to consider these concepts in detail. In some cases, the instructor may offer direction about which concepts to apply to a given case. In other instances, you may be left to use your judgment in choosing which concepts to focus on in analyzing a case.

3. **Define the basic issues.** This is perhaps the most important step and also the stage of analysis that requires the most wisdom and judgment. Cases are rarely like tidy problem sets where the issues or problems are explicitly stated and the tools needed to address those issues are prescribed. Generally, you need to determine what the key issues are. In doing this, it may help for you to begin by asking: What are the fundamental issues in the case? Which concepts matter most in providing insight into those issues? One trap to avoid in defining basic issues is doing what some decision-making scholars label "plunging-in," which is drawing conclusions without first thinking about the crux of the issues involved in a decision.[1] Many students have a tendency to seize the first issues that are prominently mentioned in a case. As an antidote to this trap, you may want to consider a case from the perspective of different conceptual frames.

4. **Develop and elaborate your analysis of the key issues.** As with all of the steps, there is no substitute for painstaking work in this stage. You need to take the key issues you have defined in Step 3, examine the facts that you have noted in Step 2, and assess what are the key facts. What does quantitative analysis reveal? Here it is not just ratio analysis that we are concerned with. Just as body temperature, blood pressure, and pulse rate may reveal something about a person's health but little about the causes of a sickness, ratio analysis typically tells us more about the health of a company than the causes of its performance. You should assemble facts and analysis to support your point of view. Opinions unsupported by factual evidence and analysis are generally not persuasive. This stage of the analysis involves organizing the facts in the case. You will want to develop specific hypotheses about what factors relate to success in a particular setting. Often, you will find it helpful to draw diagrams to clarify your thinking.

5. **Draw conclusions and formulate a set of recommendations.** You may be uncomfortable drawing conclusions and making recommendations because you do not have complete information. This is an eternal dilemma for managers. Managers who wait for complete information to do something, however, usually act too late. Nevertheless, you should strive to do the most complete analysis that you can under reasonable time constraints. Recommendations should also flow naturally from your analysis. Too often, students formulate their recommendations in an ad hoc way. In formulating recommendations, you should be clear about priorities and the sequence of actions that you recommend.

6. **Prepare for class discussion.** Students who diligently work through the first five steps and rigorously examine a case should be well prepared for class discussion. You may find it helpful to make some notes and bring them to class. Over the years, we have observed that many of the students who are low

---

[1] J. E. Russo and P. J. H. Schoemaker (1989). *Decision Traps: The Ten Barriers to Brilliant Decision-Making and How to Overcome Them*. New York: Fireside.

contributors to class discussions bring few or no notes to class. Once in class, a case discussion usually begins with a provocative question from the instructor. Many instructors will "cold call"—direct a question to a specific student who has not been forewarned. Students who have thoroughly analyzed and discussed the case before coming to class will be much better prepared for these surprise calls. They will also be better prepared to contribute to the analysis, argument, and persuasion that will take place in the class discussion. Discussions can move rapidly. You will hear new insights from fellow students. Preparation helps you to absorb, learn, and contribute to the insights that emerge from class discussion.

Summary

Students who embark in the case method soon learn that analyzing cases is a complex process. Having a clear conceptual approach such as the VRIO framework does not eliminate the complexity. This systematic approach, however, does allow the analyst to manage the complexity of real-world business situations. In the end, though, neither cases nor real-world businesses conclude their analyses with tidy solutions that resolve all the uncertainties and ambiguities a business faces. However, the case method coupled with a good theory such as the VRIO approach and hard work do make it more likely that you will generate valuable insights into the strategic challenges of firms and develop the strategic skills needed to lead a firm.

above average accounting performance when a firm's accounting performance is greater than the industry average

above normal economic performance when a firm earns above its cost of capital

absorptive capacity the ability of firms to learn

accounting performance a measure of a firm's competitive advantage; calculated from information in the firm's published profit-and-loss and balance sheet statements

accounting ratios numbers taken from a firm's financial statements that are manipulated in ways that describe various aspects of the firm's performance

acquisition a firm purchases another firm

acquisition premium the difference between the current market price of a target firm's shares and the price a potential acquirer offers to pay for those shares

activity ratios accounting ratios that focus on the level of activity in a firm's business

ad valorem tariffs a tariff calculated as a percentage of the market value of an import, regardless of its weight or volume

adverse selection an alliance partner promises to bring to an alliance certain resources that it either does not control or cannot acquire

agency problems parties in an agency relationship differ in their decision-making objectives

agency relationship one party to an exchange delegates decision-making authority to a second party

agent a party to whom decision-making authority is delegated

architectural competence the ability of a firm to use organizational structure and other organizing mechanisms to facilitate coordination among scientific disciplines to conduct research

auction in mergers and acquisitions, a mechanism for establishing the price of an asset when multiple firms bid for a single target firm

audit committee sub-group of the board of directors responsible for ensuring the accuracy of accounting and financial statements

average accounting performance when a firm's accounting performance is equal to the industry average

backward vertical integration a firm incorporates more stages of the value chain within its boundaries and those stages bring it closer to gaining access to raw materials

barriers to entry attributes of an industry's structure that increase the cost of entry

below average accounting performance when a firm's accounting performance is less than the industry average

below normal economic performance when a firm earns less than its cost of capital

board of directors a group of 10 to 15 individuals drawn from a firm's top management and from people outside the firm whose primary responsibilities are to monitor decisions made in the firm and to ensure that they are consistent with the interests of outside equity holders

business angels wealthy individuals who act as outside investors in a typically entrepreneurial firm

business cycle the alternating pattern of prosperity followed by recession followed by prosperity

business strategy a firm's theory of how to gain competitive advantage in a single business or industry

buyers those who purchase a firm's products or services

capabilities a subset of a firm's resources, defined as tangible and intangible assets, that enable a firm to take full advantage of other resources it controls

cashing out the compensation paid to an entrepreneur for risk-taking associated with starting a firm

causally ambiguous imitating firms do not understand the relationship between the resources and capabilities controlled by a firm and that firm's competitive advantage

centralized hub each country in which a firm operates is organized as a full profit-and-loss division headed by a division general manager; strategic and operational decisions are retained at headquarters

chairman of the board the person who presides over the board of directors may or may not be the same person as a firm's senior executive

chairman of the board (duties of) supervision of the board of directors in its ratifying and monitoring roles

chief executive officer (CEO) person to whom all functional managers report in a U-form organization; the person to whom all divisional personal and corporate staff report to in an M-form organization

chief executive officer (CEO) (duties of) strategy formulation and implementation

chief operating officer (COO) (duties of) strategy implementation

closely held firm a firm that has not sold many of its shares on the public stock market

co-brand tying the brand of a product to the brand of another firm's or division's product

collusion two or more firms in an industry coordinate their strategic choices to reduce competition in that industry

compensation policies the ways that firms pay employees

competitive advantage a firm creates more economic value than rival firms

competitive disadvantage a firm generates less economic value than rival firms

competitive dynamics how one firm responds to the strategic actions of competing firms

competitive parity a firm creates the same economic value as rival firms

competitor any firm, group, or individual trying to reduce a firm's competitive advantage

complementary resources and capabilities resources and capabilities that have limited ability to generate competitive advantage in isolation but in combination with other resources can enable a firm to realize its full potential for competitive advantage

complementor the value of a firm's products increases in the presence of another firm's products

compound tariffs a tariff based on both the market value and the weight or volume of a product

conduct strategies implemented by firms in an industry

conglomerate merger a merger or acquisition where there are no vertical, horizontal, product extension, or market extension links between the firms

consolidation strategy strategy that reduces the number of firms in an industry by exploiting economies of scale

controlling share when an acquiring firm purchases enough of a target firm's assets to be able to make all the management and strategic decisions in the target firm

coordinated federation each country in which a firm operates is organized as a full profit-and-loss division headed by a division general manager; operational decisions are delegated to these divisions or countries, but strategic decisions are retained at headquarters

core competence the collective learning in an organization, especially how to coordinate diverse production skills and integrate multiple streams of technologies

corporate spin-off exists when a large, typically diversified firm divests itself of a business in which it has historically been operating and the divested business operates as an independent entity

corporate staff provides information about a firm's external and internal environments to the firm's senior executive

corporate strategy a firm's theory of how to gain competitive advantage by operating in several businesses simultaneously

cost centers divisions are assigned a budget and manage their operations to that budget

cost leadership business strategy focuses on gaining advantages by reducing costs below those of competitors

cost of capital the rate of return that a firm promises to pay its suppliers of capital to induce them to invest in a firm

cost of debt the interest that a firm must pay its debt holders to induce them to lend money to the firm

cost of equity the rate of return a firm must promise its equity holders to induce them to invest in the firm

crown jewel sale a bidding firm is interested in just a few of the businesses being operated by the target firm, known as its *crown jewels*, and the target firm sells these businesses

culture the values, beliefs, and norms that guide behavior in a society and in a firm

cumulative abnormal return (CAR) performance that is greater (or less) than what was expected in a short period of time around when an acquisition is announced

current market value the price of each of a firm's shares multiplied by the number of shares outstanding

customer-switching costs customers make investments in order to use a firm's particular products or services that are not useful in using other firms' products

debt capital from banks and bondholders

decentralized federation each country in which a firm operates is organized as a full profit-and-loss division headed by a division general manager and strategic and operational decisions are delegated to these country managers

declining industry an industry that has experienced an absolute decline in unit sales over a sustained period of time

deep-pockets model a firm that takes advantage of its monopoly power in one business to subsidize several different businesses

demographics the distribution of individuals in a society in terms of age, sex, marital status, income, ethnicity, and other personal attributes that may determine their buying patterns

depression a severe recession that lasts for several years

direct duplication the attempt to imitate other firms by developing resources that have the same strategic effects as the resources controlled by those other firms

diseconomies of scale a firm's costs begin to rise as a function of the volume of production

distinctive competence a valuable and rare resource or capability

distribution agreements one firm agrees to distribute the products of others

diversification economies sources of relatedness in a diversified firm

divestment a firm sells a business in which it had been operating

division each business that a firm engages in, also called strategic business units (SBUs) or business group

dominant-business firms firms with between 70 percent and 95 percent of their total sales in a single product market

dominant logic when each business in a diversified firm shares a common theory of how to gain competitive advantages

economic climate the overall health of the economic systems within which a firm operates

economic measures of competitive advantage measures that compare a firm's level of return to its cost of capital instead of to the average level of return in the industry

economic value the difference between the perceived benefits gained by a customer who purchases a firm's products or services and the full economic cost of these products or services

economic value added (EVA) calculated by subtracting the cost of the capital employed in a division from that division's earnings

economies of scale the per unit cost of production falls as the volume of production increases

economies of scope the value of a firm's products or services increases as a function of the number of different businesses in which that firm operates

emerging industries newly created or newly re-created industries formed by technological innovations, change in demand, or the emergence of new customer needs

emergent strategies theories of how to gain competitive advantage in an industry that emerge over time or have been radically reshaped once they are initially implemented

environmental threat any individual, group, or organization outside a firm that seeks to reduce the level of that firm's performance

equity capital from individuals and institutions that purchase a firm's stocks

equity alliance cooperating firms supplement contracts with equity holdings in alliance partners

escalation of commitment an increased commitment by managers to an incorrect course of action, even as its limitations become manifest

event study analysis evaluates the performance effects of acquisitions for bidding firms

executive committee typically consists of the CEO and two or three functional senior managers

explicit collusion firms directly communicate with each other to coordinate levels of production, prices, and so forth (illegal in most countries)

external analysis identification and examination of the critical threats and opportunities in a firm's competitive environment

finance committee subgroup of the board of directors that maintains the relationship between the firm and external capital markets

financial resources all the money, from whatever source, that firms use to conceive and implement strategies

firm-specific human capital investments investments made by employees in a particular firm over time, including understanding the culture, policies, and procedures and knowing the people to contact to complete a task, that have limited value in other firms

firm-specific investments the value of stakeholders' investments in a particular firm is much greater than the value those same investments would be in other firms

first-mover advantages advantages that come to firms that make important strategic and technological decisions early in the development of an industry

five forces framework identifies the five most common threats faced by firms in their local competitive environments and the conditions under which these threats are more or less likely to be present; these forces are the threat of entry, of rivalry, of substitutes, of buyers, and of suppliers

flexibility how costly it is for a firm to alter its strategic and organizational decisions

formal management controls a firm's budgeting and reporting activities that keep people higher up in a firm's organizational chart informed about the actions taken by people lower down in the organizational chart

formal reporting structure a description of who in the organization reports to whom

forward vertical integration a firm incorporates more stages of the value chain within its boundaries and those stages bring it closer to interacting directly with final customers

fragmented industries industries in which a large number of small or medium-sized firms operate and no small set of firms has dominant market share or creates dominant technologies

free cash flow the amount of cash a firm has to invest after all positive net present-value investments in its ongoing businesses have been funded

friendly acquisitions the management of a target firm wants the firm to be acquired

functional manager a manager who leads a particular function within a firm, such as manufacturing, marketing, finance, accounting, or sales

functional organizational structure the structure a firm uses to implement business-level strategies it might pursue where each function in the firm reports to the CEO

general environment broad trends in the context within which a firm operates that can have an impact on a firm's strategic choices

generic business strategies another name for business-level strategies, which are cost leadership and product differentiation

geographic market diversification strategy when a firm operates in multiple geographic markets simultaneously

global opportunities opportunities for a firm to optimize production, distribution, and other business functions throughout the world in all the markets in which it operates

golden parachutes   incentive compensation paid to senior managers if the firm they manage is acquired

greenmail   a target firm's management purchases any of the target firm's stock owned by a bidder for a price that is greater than its current market value

harvest   a firm engages in a long, systematic, phased withdrawal from a declining industry, extracting as much value as possible

hedonic price   that part of the price of a product or service that is attributable to a particular characteristic of that product or service

holdup   one firm makes more transaction-specific investments in an exchange than partner firms make and the firm that has not made these investments tries to exploit the firm that has made the investments

horizontal merger   a firm acquires a former competitor

hostile takeovers   the management of a target firm does not want the firm to be acquired

human capital resources   the training, experience, judgment, intelligence, relationships, and insight of individual managers and workers in a firm

imperfectly imitable   resources and capabilities that are more costly for other firms to imitate, compared to firms that already possess them

increasing returns to scale   in network industries, the value of a product or service increases as the number of people using those products or services increases

inelastic in supply   the quantity of supply is fixed and does not respond to price increases, such as the total supply of land, which is relatively fixed and cannot be significantly increased in response to higher demand and prices

industry structure   attributes of an industry that determines its competitiveness; measured by such factors as the number of competitors in an industry, the heterogeneity of products in an industry, and the cost of entry and exit in an industry

informal management controls   include a firm's culture and the willingness of employees to monitor each others' behavior

initial public offering (IPO)   the initial sale of stock of a privately held firm or a division of a corporation to the general public

institutional owners   pension funds, corporations, and others that invest other peoples' money in firm equities

intermediate products or services   products or services produced in one division that are used as inputs for products or services produced by a second division

internal analysis   identification of a firm's organizational strengths and weaknesses and of the resources and capabilities that are likely to be sources of competitive advantage

invented competencies   illusory inventions by creative managers to justify poor diversification moves by linking intangible core competencies to completely unrelated businesses

investment acquirers   when a firm acquires other firms not seeking to realize synergies but instead implements a variety of incentives and control system to create value; once these incentives and control systems create value, these kinds of acquirers typically sell the firm they acquired

joint venture   cooperating firms create a legally independent firm in which they invest and from which they share any profits that are created

learning curve   a concept that formalizes the relationship between cumulative volumes of production and falling per unit costs

leverage ratios   accounting ratios that focus on the level of a firm's financial flexibility

licensing agreements   one firm allows others to use its brand name to sell products in return for some fee or percentage of profits

limited corporate diversification   all or most of a firm's business activities fall within a single industry and geographic market

liquidity ratios   accounting ratios that focus on the ability of a firm to meet its short-term financial obligations

management control systems   a range of formal and informal mechanisms to ensure that managers are behaving in ways consistent with a firm's strategies

managerial hubris   the unrealistic belief held by managers in bidding firms that they can manage the assets of a target firm more efficiently than the target firm's current management

managerial know-how   the often taken-for-granted knowledge and information that are needed to compete in an industry on a day-to-day basis

managerial perquisites   activities that do not add economic value to the firm but directly benefit the managers who make them

managerial risk aversion   because managers cannot diversify their firm-specific human capital investments, they may engage in less risky business decisions than what would be preferred by equity holders

market extension merger   firms make acquisitions in new geographical markets

market for corporate control   the market that is created when multiple firms actively seek to acquire one or several firms

market leader   the firm with the largest market share in an industry

matrix structures   one employee reports to two or more people

mature industries   an industry in which, over time, ways of doing business have become widely understood, technologies have diffused through competitors, and the rate of innovation in new products and technologies drops

merger   the assets of two similar-sized firms are combined

M-form an organizational structure for implementing a corporate diversification strategy whereby each business a firm engages in is managed through a separate profit-and-loss division

mission a firm's long-term purpose

mission statement written statement defining both what a firm aspires to be in the long run and what it wants to avoid in the meantime

monopolistically competitive industries industries in which there are large numbers of competing firms and low-cost entry and exit, but products are not homogeneous with respect to cost or product attributes; firms are said to enjoy a "monopoly" in that part of the market they dominate

monopolistic industries industries that consist of only a single firm

moral hazard partners in an exchange possess high-quality resources and capabilities of significant value to the exchange but fail to make them available to the other partners

multinational opportunities opportunities for a firm to operate simultaneously in several national or regional markets but the operations are independent of each other

multipoint competition two or more diversified firms simultaneously compete in the same multiple markets

mutual forbearance a form of tacit collusion whereby firms tacitly agree to not compete in one industry in order to avoid competition in a second industry

network industries industries in which a single technical standard and increasing returns to scale tend to dominate; competition in these industries tends to focus on which of several competing standards will be chosen

new entrants firms that have either recently begun operations in an industry or that threaten to begin operations in an industry soon

niche strategy when a firm reduces its scope of operations and focuses on narrow segments of a declining industry

nominating committee sub-group of the board of directors that nominates new board members

nonequity alliance cooperating firms agree to work together to develop, manufacture, or sell products or services, but they do not take equity positions in each other or form an independent organizational unit to manage the cooperative efforts

nontariff trade barriers the establishment of product performance standards that cannot be met by imports, the restriction of access to domestic distribution channels, imposition of local purchasing requirements for government purchases, or implementation of a variety of other restrictions on imports

normal economic performance a firm earns its cost of capital

objectives specific, measurable targets a firm can use to evaluate the extent to which it is realizing its mission

office of the president together, the roles of chairman of the board, CEO, and COO

oligopolies industries characterized by a small number of competing firms, by homogeneous products, and by costly entry and exit

operational economies of scope shared activities and shared core competencies in a diversified firm

operations committee typically meets monthly and usually consists of the CEO and each of the heads of the functional areas included in the firm

opportunism a firm is unfairly exploited in an exchange

organizational chart a depiction of the formal reporting structure within a firm

organizational resources a firm's formal reporting structure; its formal and informal planning, controlling, and coordinating systems; its culture and reputation; and informal relations among groups within a firm and between a firm and those in its environment

Pac Man defense fending off an acquisition by a firm acquiring the firm or firms bidding for it

path dependence events early in the evolution of a process have significant effects on subsequent events

pecuniary economies sources of relatedness in market power between bidding and target firms

perfectly competitive industry when there are large numbers of competing firms, the products being sold are homogeneous with respect to cost and product attributes, and entry and exit are very low cost

personnel and compensation committee sub-group of the board of directors that evaluates and compensates the performance of a firm's senior executive and other senior managers

physical resources all the physical technology used in a firm

poison pills a variety of actions that target firm managers can take to make the acquisition of the target prohibitively expensive

policy choices choices firms make about the kinds of products or services they will sell—choices that have an impact on relative cost and product differentiation position

policy of experimentation exists when firms are committed to engage in several related product differentiation efforts simultaneously

predatory pricing setting prices so that they are less than a business's costs

price takers where the price of the products or services a firm sells is determined by market conditions and not by the decisions of firms

principal the party who delegates the decision-making authority

private equity firm a type of investment acquirer that uses debt and equity to purchase underperforming firms; these firms generate profits through fees, dividends, and selling the firms they have purchased.

privately held   a firm that has stock that is not traded on public stock markets and that is not a division of a larger company

processes   the activities a firm engages in to design, produce, and sell its products or services

process innovation   a firm's effort to refine and improve its current processes

process manufacturing   when manufacturing is accomplished in a continuous system; examples include manufacturing in chemical, oil refining, and paper and pulp industries

product differentiation   a business strategy whereby firms attempt to gain a competitive advantage by increasing the perceived value of their products or services relative to the perceived value of other firms' products or services

product diversification strategy   a firm operates in multiple industries simultaneously

product extension merger   firms acquire complementary products through merger and acquisition activities

productive inputs   any supplies used by a firm in conducting its business activities, such as labor, capital, land, and raw materials, among others

product-market diversification strategy   a firm implements both product and geographic market diversification simultaneously

profitability ratios   accounting ratios with some measure of profit in the numerator and some measure of firm size or assets in the denominator

profit-and-loss centers   where profits and losses are calculated at the level of the division in a firm

proprietary technology   secret or patented technology that gives incumbent firms important advantages over potential entrants

question of imitability   "Do firms without a resource or capability face a cost disadvantage in obtaining or developing it compared to firms that already possess it?"

question of organization   "Is a firm organized to exploit the full competitive potential of its resources and capabilities?"

question of rarity   "How many competing firms already possess particular valuable resources and capabilities?"

question of value   "Does a resource enable a firm to exploit an external opportunity or neutralize an external threat?"

quotas   a numerical limit on the number of particular items that are allowed to be imported into a country

real options   investments in real assets that create the opportunity for additional investments in the future

recession   a period of relatively low prosperity; demand for goods and services is low and unemployment is high

related-constrained diversification   all the businesses in which a firm operates share a significant number of inputs,

product technologies, distribution channels, similar customers, and so forth

related corporate diversification   less than 70 percent of a firm's revenue comes from a single product market and its multiple lines of business are linked

related-linked   the different businesses that a single firm pursues are linked on only a couple of dimensions or different sets of businesses are linked along very different dimensions

reputation   beliefs customers hold about a firm

resource-based view (RBV)   a model of firm performance that focuses on the resources and capabilities controlled by a firm as sources of competitive advantage

resource heterogeneity   for a given business activity, some firms may be more skilled in accomplishing the activity than other firms

resource immobility   resources controlled by some firms may not diffuse to other firms

resources   the tangible and intangible assets that a firm controls, which it can use to conceive of and implement its strategies

retained earnings   capital generated from a firm's ongoing operations that is retained by a firm

rivalry   the intensity of competition among a firm's direct competitors

seemingly unrelated diversified   diversified firms that exploit core competencies as an economy of scope, but are not doing so with any shared activities

senior executive   the president or CEO of a firm

shakeout period   period during which the total supply in an industry is reduced by bankruptcies, acquisitions, and business closings

shared activities   potential sources of operational economies of scope for diversified firms

shark repellents   a variety of relatively minor corporate governance changes that, in principle, are supposed to make it somewhat more difficult to acquire a target firm

single-business firms   firms with greater than 95 percent of their total sales in a single product market

"skunk works"   temporary teams whose creative efforts are intensive and focused

socially complex   resources and capabilities that involve interpersonal, social, or cultural links among individuals

social welfare   the overall good of society

specific tariffs   a tariff that is calculated as a percentage of the weight or volume of the goods being imported, regardless of their market value

stakeholders   all groups and individuals who have an interest in how a firm performs

standstill agreements   contract between a target and a bidding firm wherein the bidding firm agrees not to attempt to take over the target for some period of time

stock grants   payments to employees in a firm's stock

stock options   employees are given the right, but not the obligation, to purchase a firm's stock at predetermined prices

strategic acquirers   when firms use acquisitions to extend their current businesses, leverage their current capabilities, or diversify into new businesses

strategic alliance   whenever two or more independent organizations cooperate in the development, manufacture, or sale of products or services

strategic management process   a sequential set of analyses that can increase the likelihood of a firm's choosing a strategy that generates competitive advantages

strategy   a firm's theory about how to gain competitive advantage

strategy implementation   occurs when a firm adopts organizational policies and practices that are consistent with its strategy

strengths   valuable resources and capabilities

structure-conduct-performance model (S-C-P)   theory that suggests that industry structure determines a firm's conduct, which in turn determines its performance

substitutes   products or services that meet approximately the same customer needs but do so in different ways

substitution   developing or acquiring strategically equivalent, but different, resources as a competing firm

supermajority voting rules   an example of a shark repellent that specifies that more than 50 percent of the target firm's board of directors must approve a takeover

suppliers   firms that make a wide variety of raw materials, labor, and other critical assets available to firms

supply agreements   one firm agrees to supply others

sustainable distinctive competencies   valuable, rare, and costly to imitate resources or capabilities

sustained competitive advantage   a competitive advantage that lasts for a long period of time; an advantage that is not competed away through strategic imitation

tacit collusion   firms coordinate their production and pricing decisions not by directly communicating with each other, but by exchanging signals with other firms about their intent to cooperate; special case of tacit cooperation

tacit cooperation   actions a firm takes that have the effect of reducing the level of rivalry in an industry and that do not require firms in an industry to directly communicate or negotiate with each other

tactics   the specific actions a firm takes to implement its strategies

tariffs   taxes levied on goods or services imported into a country

tax haven   a country that charges little or no corporate tax

technical economies   sources of relatedness in marketing, production, and similar activities between bidding and target firms

technological hardware   the machines and other hardware used by firms

technological leadership strategy   firms make early investments in particular technologies in an industry

technological software   the quality of labor–management relations, an organization's culture, and the quality of managerial controls in a firm

temporary competitive advantage   a competitive advantage that lasts for a short period of time

temporary cross-divisional and cross-functional teams   groups of individuals from different businesses and different functional areas who are brought together to cooperate on a particular new product or service

tender offer   a bidding firm offers to purchase the shares of a target firm directly by offering a higher than market price for those shares to current shareholders

thinly traded market   a market where there are only a small number of buyers and sellers, where information about opportunities in this market is not widely known, and where interests besides purely maximizing the value of a firm can be important

transaction specific investment   the value of an investment in its first-best use is much greater than its value in its second-best use; any investment in an exchange that has significantly more value in the current exchange than it does in alternative exchanges

transfer price   the price that one part of a diversified firm charges another part of the firm for intermediate products or services

transnational opportunity   firms treat their global operations as an integrated network of distributed and interdependent resources and capabilities

transnational structure   each country in which a firm operates is organized as a full profit-and-loss division headed by a division general manager and strategic and operational decisions are delegated to operational entities that maximize local responsiveness and international integration

U-form structure   organization where different functional heads report directly to CEO; used to implement business-level strategies

uncertainty   the future value of an exchange cannot be known when investments in that exchange are being made

unfriendly acquisition   the management of the target firm does not want the firm to be acquired

unrelated corporate diversification   less than 70 percent of a firm's revenues is generated in a single product market and a firm's businesses share few, if any, common attributes

value added as a percentage of sales   measures the percentage of a firm's sales that are generated by activities done within the boundaries of a firm; a measure of vertical integration

value chain   that set of activities that must be accomplished to bring a product or service from raw materials to the point that it can be sold to a final customer

venture capital firms   outside investment funds looking to invest in entrepreneurial ventures

vertical integration   the number of steps in the value chain that a firm accomplishes within its boundaries

vertical merger   when a firm vertically integrates, either forward or backward, through its acquisition efforts

visionary firms   firms whose mission is central to all they do

VRIO framework   four questions that must be asked about a resource or capability to determine its competitive potential: the questions of value, rarity, imitability, and organization.

weaknesses   resources and capabilities that are not valuable

weighted average cost of capital (WACC)   the percentage of a firm's total capital that is debt multiplied by the cost of debt plus the percentage of a firm's total capital that is equity times the cost of equity

white knight   another bidding firm that agrees to acquire a particular target in place of the original bidding firm

zero-based budgeting   corporate executives create a list of all capital allocation requests from divisions in a firm, rank them from most important to least important, and then fund all the projects the firm can afford, given the amount of capital it has available

Illustration/ Photo Credits

Illustration for part openers by P.J. Loughran
Illustration for boxed features by Gary Hovland

Part 1

Chapter 1
2   AP Wide World Photos

Chapter 2
30   Ian O'Leary/Dorling Kindersley Media Library

Chapter 3
72   Chris Stowers/Dorling Kindersley Media Library

Part 2

Chapter 4
114   Peter Frischmuth/Argus/Peter Arnold, Inc.

Chapter 5
144   Getty Images - Photodisc

Part 3

Chapter 6
178   Sherwin Crasto/CORBIS- NY

Chapter 7
206   Jennifer Pottheiser/NBAE via Getty Images/Getty Images

Chapter 8
244   APF/CORBIS/Corbis/Bettmann

Chapter 9
276   AP Wide World Photos

Chapter 10
308   Getty Images/Digital Vision

Company Index

Name Index

In the page references, the number after "n" refers to the number of the end note in which the name is cited.

A

Abrahams, J., 9
Agins, Teri, 176n30
Aguilar, F. J., 70n52; 275n25
Alchian, A., 205n2; 306n13
Alexander, R. C., 111n28
Allen, M., 70n23
Alley, J., 111n16
Alvarez, S. A., 24; 80; 282
Amit, R., 111n27; 233; 242n33
Anders, George, 110n7
Angwin, J., 157
Ansoff, H. I., 217
Applebaum, A., 29n7
Appleton, Steve, 269
Arikan, A., 320
Armour, H. O., 274n1
Armstrong, L., 176n17
Arnst, C., 284
Arthur, W. B., 111(n14, n16)
Artz, K. W., 110n1
Auletta, K., 243n40
Axelrod, R. M., 293

B

Badaracco, J. L., 306(n2, n15)
Baetz, M. C., 29n2
Bain, J. S., 69(n9, n12)
Balakrishnan, S., 306n8
Balmer, Steve, 58
Barnes, B., 69n6
Barnett, W. P., 110n1
Barney, J. B., 24; 29n8; 38; 40; 69n9; 79; 91; 110(n1, n5, n10, n13); 111(n19, n22); 143n19; 205(n4, n9); 215; 233; 242n18; 286; 306(n10, n16, n20, n21); 307(n22, n23, n28); 342(n5, n17)
Barrett, A., 253
Bart, C. K., 29n2
Bartlett, C. A., 71(n61, n62, n63); 143n28; 176n32; 268; 274n11; 306(n6, n18)
Baughn, C. C., 306n10
Baum, J. A. C., 242n24
Beane, William Lamar, 134
Beatty, R., 307n24
Becker, G. S., 110n3; 205n8
Belda, Alain, 269
Bennett, Tim, 196
Bennis, Warren G., 111n36
Berg, N. A., 143n2
Berg, P. O., 111n21
Berger, P. G., 242n21; 267; 274n9
Bergh, D., 274n6
Berner, R., 35
Bernheim, R. D., 242n24

Besanko, 29n8
Bethel, J. E., 242n19; 274(n6, n13)
Bettis, R. A., 242n15
Bezos, Jeff, 69n8
Bhambri, A., 275n25
Bhide, Amar, 80
Bigelow, L. S., 242n33
Bilefsky, D., 79
Blackman, A., 71n62
Blackwell, R. D., 342n21
Bleeke, J., 293; 306(n9, n16, n17); 307(n28, n29)
Blois, K. J., 307n28
Bond, R. S., 70n44
Bower, J. L., 70n52; 342n19
Boyd, Brian K., 251
Bradey, M., 335
Brady, D., 32; 35
Brandenburger, Adam, 29n8; 51; 53; 70n33
Brando, Marlon, 72
Branson, Richard, 222
Breen, B., 110n12; 111n15
Brennan, M., 242n23
Bresnahan, T. F., 70n40
Bresser, R. K., 306n11
Brickley, J., 275n20
Bright, A. A., 70n40
Bromiley, P., 110n1
Brown, S. J., 320
Brush, T. H., 110n1
Bryan-Low, C., 246
Bucksbaum, John, 269
Burgers, W. P., 306(n3, n7)
Burke, Jim, 7
Burrows, P., 241n4
Bush, George W., 245
Butler, J. K., Jr., 307n28
Buzzell, R. D., 123
Byrnes, N., 35

C

Camerer, C., 307n23
Cameron, K. S., 342n14
Campbell, E., 299
Cantrell, R. S., 307n28
Capell, K., 116
Carlisle, K., 125
Carnevale, M. L., 242n30
Carney, M., 307n28
Carroll, G. R., 242n33
Carroll, P., 176n4
Cartwright, S., 342n22
Cauley, L., 70n27
Celestino, M., 140

Chamberlin, Edward H., 154–155; 175
Chandler, A., 274n1
Chartier, John, 70(n24, n46, n48)
Chatterjee, S., 241n12; 342n22
Chen, M.-J., 242n24
Chew, D., 274n15
Chiles, T. H., 307n28
Choi, F., 15
Christensen, C. R., 70n54; 143n2; 165
Coase, Ronald, 181; 182; 205n1
Cockburn, I., 70n21; 110n1; 111n19; 176n9
Cohen, Ben, 8
Cohen, W., 282
Collins, Jim C., 7; 29(n5, n6, n11); 111n36
Collis, D. J., 111n37; 143n30
Comment, R., 214–215; 242n21
Conner, K. R., 110n1; 205n4
Cool, K., 70n19; 110(n1, n13, n14)
Cooper, C., 342n22
Copeland, T., 22
Cowling, K., 148
Cox, J., 242n23
Cox, M., 70n27
Coyne, W., 166
Crawford, R., 205n2; 306n13
Crockett, R., 241n6
Cubbin, J., 148
Curlander, Paul, 269
Cyert, R., 275n21

D

Dalton, D., 251
Dann, L. Y., 335
D'Aveni, R. D., 251; 274n2
Davidson, J. H., 70n44
Davis, P., 241n8
Davis, S. M., 143n22
Dawley, H., 125
de Lisser, E., 241n7
DeAngelo H., 335
DeFillippi, R. J., 111n17
DeGeorge, R., 125
Delaney, K. J., 179
Delmar, Frederic, 80
Demetrakakes, P., 70n47
Demsetz, H., 38; 229
Dent-Micallef, A., 110n1
Deogun, N., 342(n12, n23)
DePalma, A., 140
Der Hovanseian, M, 320
Deutsch, C. H., 176n17
Deutschman, A., 69n8
Devinney, T. M., 242n33
DeWitt, W., 70n30
Dial, J., 70n56; 275n25
Dichtl, E., 238; 243n39

Subject Index